The Rise and Fall of Alexander Hamilton

The Rise and Fall of Alexander Hamilton

Robert A. Hendrickson

VNR VAN NOSTRAND REINHOLD COMPANY
New York Cincinnati Toronto London Melbourne

Copyright © 1981 by Van Nostrand Reinhold Company
Library of Congress Catalog Card Number 80-24546
ISBN 0-442-26113-6

Printed in the United States of America
Designed by Karin Batten

Published by Van Nostrand Reinhold Company
135 West 50th Street, New York, NY 10020

Van Nostrand Reinhold Limited
1410 Birchmount Road, Scarborough, Ontario M1P 2E7, Canada

Van Nostrand Reinhold Australia Pty. Ltd.
17 Queen Street, Mitcham, Victoria 3132, Australia

Van Nostrand Reinhold Company Limited
Molly Millars Lane, Wokingham, Berkshire, England

16 15 14 13 12 11 10 9 8 7 6 5 4 3 2 1

Library of Congress Cataloging in Publication Data

Hendrickson, Robert A   1923–
    The rise and fall of Alexander Hamilton

    Bibliography: p.
    Includes index.
    1. Hamilton, Alexander, 1757–1804.
2. United States—Politics and government—1783–
1809. 3. United States—Politics and government—
1775–1783. 4. Statesmen—United States—Biography.
I. Title.
E302.6.H2H45   973.4'092'4 [B]   80-24546
ISBN 0-442-26113-6

CONTENTS

PART THREE   *An Angel Daubed by Wizard Painters*

. . . the great principles of the live Greeks
Are thrown down by time. I heard
A commissar in Washington in 1960 . . .
Discredit the entire classical Greek establishment,
Say the tragic flaw is a defunct idea,
There could be no tragedy in this country
Because all were equal, none could fall
From a high state to a low state because of a flaw
In character. . . .

—Richard Eberhart, *Great Principles Are Thrown Down by Time,* 1977

Credit public and private is of the greatest consequence . . . the invigorating principle. . . . Credit is an *intire thing*. Every part of it has the nicest sympathy with every other part. Wound one limb and the whole Tree shrinks and decays.

—Final Report on the Public Credit, January 16, 1795

In the twilight, in the evening, in the black and dark night:
There met him a woman with the attire of an harlot,
and subtil of heart.
So she caught him, and kissed him,
And with an impudent face said unto him,
Come, let us take our fill of love until the morning:
Let us solace ourselves with loves.
For the goodman is not at home,
He is gone a long journey:
He hath taken a bag of money with him,
And will come home at the day appointed.
With her much fair speech she caused him to yield,
With the flattering of her lips she forced him.
He goeth after her straightaway,
As an ox goeth to the slaughter,
Or as a fool to the correction of the stocks;
Till a dart strike through his liver;
As a bird hasteth to the snare,
and knoweth not that it is for his life.

—Proverbs 7:9–23.

PREFACE

The Grange and Monticello

The rather short life of Alexander Hamilton—he was 47 when Burr's bullet ended it July 12, 1804—remains mysterious, contemporary, and widely ignored. It is the story of a penniless, illegitimate orphan boy, born on Nevis, who emigrates at 16 and slips into the homogeneous ranks of established New York middle-class society, helps overthrow its royal master, yokes the former colonies into a new republic under a constitution that owes much to his efforts, and finally becomes its first (undercover) prime minister before being brought down by a sex scandal—and Burr's bullet. As an American success story Alexander Hamilton's ranks with those of Benjamin Franklin, Abraham Lincoln—and Richard Nixon. It would hardly be too much to claim for it a tragic grandeur of Shakespearean intensity and Marlovian sweep—but to do so would run against his and twentieth-century America's grain.

Some tangible Hamilton memorabilia remain.

On the U.S. ten dollar bill, in an engraving from the Jonathan Trumbull portrait, his steady gaze reproaches us as the currency which he first put on a sound basis is eroded by the inflation against which he inveighed. There is a statue in Washington on the steps of the U.S. Treasury Department, for which he first mobilized armed militiamen to collect taxes; in a glade of New York's Central Park is another statue near where he led his artillerymen north during the Battle of Manhattan; and there is a small bust on a pedestal on the New Jersey Palisades at Weehawken, above the ledge where he received his mortal wound. In Trinity Churchyard in lower Manhattan is the sarcophagus where he and his wife Elizabeth Schuyler Hamilton are interred, a short block west of 57 Wall Street, the address of their first home in New York City.

Their last home was Hamilton Grange, at 287 Convent Avenue in Harlem. It is a two-and-a-half story clapboard house set about 25 feet back from the sidewalk. The building is wedged endwise into a 50-foot wide lot and jammed flush against two bulky structures that abut and loom above it on either side: the red brick, Victorian pile of St. Luke's Episcopal Church to the south and a nondescript four-story tenement building to the north.

On a granite pedestal beside a stunted flagpole in the weedy little patch of front yard is a grimy bronze statue of Hamilton in greatcoat and knee pants. He seems to be striding purposefully west with head turned slightly southward, eyes looking across the Hudson past the duellists' ledge below Weehawken, in the direction of the continental empire beyond. His view of all this is, however, cut off by the row of brownstone tenements opposite him on Convent Avenue. On the pedestal are graven the name of the sculptor, W. Ordway Partridge; the date, 1892: HAMILTON, 1757–1804; and the following inscriptions:

> The name of Hamilton would have honored Greece in the age of Aristides.
>
> —Ames
>
> Model of eloquence and most fascinating of orators.
>
> —Story
>
> His rare powers entitled him to the fame of being the first intellectual product of America.
>
> —Stevens
>
> He smote the rock of the national resources and abundant streams of revenue gushed forth.
>
> —Webster
>
> There is not in the Constitution of the United States an element of order or force or of duration which he has not powerfully contributed to introduce and cause to predominate.
>
> —Guizot

Beside his granite pedestal the small freestanding landmark plaque emplaced by the U.S. Department of the Interior reads:

> Hamilton Grange. General Alexander Hamilton, one of the Framers of the Constitution, First Secretary of the Treasury, built this house in 1802.

Another plaque bolted to the dirty white clapboards beside the entrance door reads:

> Hamilton Grange. The Home of Alexander Hamilton, 1757, A.B., A.M., L.L.M., 1804.
>
> Statesman
> Soldier
> Administrator
> Lawyer
> Captain
> Lt. Col. Staff of General Washington
> Major General
> Member of Congress
> Member New York Legislature
> Delegate to Constitutional Convention
> First Secretary of the Treasury
> Leader of the Federalist Party
>
> He built this house in 1802.

This is a fairly impressive list of accomplishments, of course, but the list of many a long-forgotten politician would better it. Offices did not make this man.

The Grange's front door is kept locked at all times and opened by the caretaker only when a visitor rings the bell. The interior, almost bare of furnishings, is dominated by a marble portrait bust of Hamilton done from life by Giuseppe Ceracchi in 1796. The nose is long and Roman, deeply indented at the bridge. The plane of his high forehead seems to be thrust forward by the power of the mind behind it. It juts out over the recesses of his penetrating yet genial eyes. His chin is prominent; the curve of his jaw is smooth and strong; his mouth is firm and moderately large but rather thin-lipped and set in a confident line. His expression is warm and only a thought short of a smile.

But the most important monuments to Hamilton, not so tangible as Ceracchi's bust, are pervasive features of modern American life that few identify as monuments to anyone, fewer still as monuments to Hamilton. *The Federalist Papers* of Hamilton's authorship remain root authority when the gravest issues concerning the meaning of the Constitution must be resolved—as in the case of the impeachment of President Richard Nixon. The exercise of judicial supremacy by the Supreme Court of the United States remains as seldom questioned as Hamilton's invention of the doctrine remains unacknowledged.

The Bank of New York, which Hamilton helped to found, remains the first bank in the modern world's financial capital. The New York *Post,* which he founded, is the oldest surviving newspaper in the nation's communications capital; his brief in *People* v. *Croswell* remains one of the most eloquent defenses of thè freedom of the press. He planned, named, and for a while largely managed The Society for Establishing Useful Manufactures—the SUM—in a 38-acre industrial park by the falls of the Passaic at Paterson, New Jersey, thus providing America with its earliest model of a large-scale conglomerate corporation.

To partisans of Thomas Jefferson, Democrats in particular and democrats in general, Hamilton was a monarchist and an elitist. To them he will always be the insider who tolerated the unscrupulous speculation that came with the first financial measures he intended to create a sound currency; who was uncivil to George Washington in 1781; who attacked the second president in a pamphlet that would have been better left unwritten; who explained away charges of illicit speculation as Secretary of the Treasury by publicly confessing to a clandestine affair with Mrs. James Reynolds; who manifested impatience, immoderation, and inordinate ambition; and who had a tendency to glorify the military, to exalt the wealthy, and to affect an unpardonable *hubris.* Abraham Lincoln is venerated for policies of preserving the Union indivisible and emancipating the slaves, policies that are in essence and precedent Hamiltonian. But when Lincoln's name is praised, Hamilton's is not only ignored even by Republicans, it also remains all but unmentionable. Professor Clinton Rossiter has written that ''Alexander Hamilton is the least known and most misunderstood major figure in American history,'' the one about whom ''it is considered bad form to be too enthusiastic.'' Noah Webster defined Hamilton as ''the evil genius of this country.''

Noah Webster had a knack of finding pointed words that defined things. In his epithet for Hamilton—the evil genius of this country—more may be read than Jeffersonian revulsion at the idea of the free American yeoman someday becoming a vassal of the Leviathan corporate state foreshadowed by Hamilton's Report on Manufactures. There is also moral outrage at the cool insensitivity to conventional Federalist morality flaunted by Hamilton's publication of his Reynolds Pamphlet—in which he broadcast to the public that ''more frequent intercourse was pressed upon me'' by a harlot who would turn out to have been a client of Aaron Burr's. The anguished sensibilities of his loving wife Elizabeth, of his adoring sister-in-law Angelica Church, of his beloved children, of his wide circle of friends, clients, and political followers who saw him as the next and future Federalist president, all were sacrificed by Hamilton's pamphlet to his deranged idea that it would vindicate the former Secretary of the Treasury's public credit. His disenchantment with himself and his suicidal acceptance of Burr's bullet not long afterward became all but a foregone conclusion.

Five thousand people or so vist the evil genius's Grange each year. By contrast, 500,000 or so each year trail through Thomas Jefferson's lordly chateau at Monticello—with its 35 rooms, its palatial cupolas, hidden staircases, and the sprawling warrens that once quartered more than 150 slaves. Thousands more each year gape at Monticello's marble counterpart, the Jefferson Memorial on the Potomac in Washington. The slave quarters of the original have not been reproduced in the marble.

The present state of Hamilton's Grange, rotting in Harlem, and Jefferson's Monticello on its Albemarle hilltop and in its marbleization in Washington, seem to correspond to the contrasting places the two great rivals in life hold in the hearts of their countrymen two centuries later. "Monticello," said one perceptive historian, is "a chateau high above contact with man." It bears no relation to the way people live now. Hamilton's Harlem Grange, for better or worse, is in the grim thick of inner-city life. The image of Jefferson that Monticello evokes is the image of what we wish we were, but the image of Hamilton evoked by The Grange is what we are.

When Aaron Burr was Vice-President of the United States his Manhattan mansion, Richmond Hill, commanded a magnificent view from its hilltop near the corner of what is now Charlton and Varick Streets. When he fled after the duel, it was foreclosed to pay his creditors. It was lowered from its hilltop in 1811 when the city commissioners levelled the hilltop to its present flatness. It next failed as a tavern, then failed as a theater, and was finally razed. Burr's name appears, of course, on the plaque below Hamilton's bust at the little plot above the Weehawken duelling ledge. But unlike his two great rivals, Burr left no significant imprint on the past, present, or future of the United States—apart from the killing of Hamilton.

Written constitutions like the one Hamilton helped the United States to create are no guarantee of freedom under law. Some of the world's most repressive governments, like that of Soviet Russia, boast written constitutions and impressive-sounding declarations of independence that flatter their American prototypes by imitation on paper. But more is required to achieve what the United States achieved: a sound economic underpinning for free representative government, a decent standard of living for the people, a tradition of adherence to legal and administrative precedent against arbitrary exercise of power, energy in administration, a free press, and appeals to reason and argument more often than emotion and coercion to enlist the people in support of governmental policies. These are American traditions for which those who still remember Hamilton give him much public credit.

Among the major nations of the modern world, the government under which the people enjoy more political freedom than under any other remains the only one that stands unchanged in essentials since 1787: the federal union of the 50 states that grew out of the 13 former British colonies on the East Coast of North America. It is the thesis of what follows that the ideas, precepts, and actions that established the unique character of the United States at its creation, the policies that have "shaped us"—and "what has resulted therefrom" for better and for worse—owe as much to Alexander Hamilton as to any other man.

PART ONE

A
Constant
Projector

1

Restless Love in the Lesser Antilles

[She had] shown herself to be shameless rude and ungodly . . . completely forgotten her duty . . . left her husband and child . . . and given herself up to whoring with everyone.

—John Michael Lavien, petition for divorce from Alexander Hamilton's mother, Rachel Fawcett Lavien, April 18, 1759.

The spring of 1804 was the most brilliant social season Alexander Hamilton's Grange would ever see. Hamilton's wife, the former Elizabeth Schuyler, daughter of General Philip Schuyler of The Pastures, Albany, and Old Saratoga, was still giving parties there in the "true good housewife style" that began with an early breakfast, went on all day, and wound up with a ball and a dinner. But Elizabeth's beautiful sister, Angelica Schuyler Church, older by one year, had entertained and been entertained for years in the most brilliant social circles of London and Paris, and to her such parties seemed absurdly quaint. In a letter to her son Philip on June 14, 1804, Angelica joked,

> Mrs. Hamilton is extremely gracious, for her Angelica gives a breakfast, a ball and a dinner on Tuesday next, to 70 persons; and! oh direful misfortune! they sent their cards but neglected to invite an engagé Contois, and as they are without a saelev [slave?] the Breakfast hour is fixed for nine o'clock, this is in the true good housewife stile, the company must wear their nightcaps to arrive in time.

By such an entertainment as this Angelica Hamilton, Alexander and Elizabeth's 19-year-old eldest daughter—namesake of her glamorous aunt—might be roused out of the

3

unmentionable but horrifying simplemindedness that had overcome her after her 2-year older brother Philip had been killed two years ago by George Eaker, a political ally of Aaron Burr's. Philip had been shot in a duel on the same Weehawken ledge where his father would fall to Burr's bullet within the month.

In May the Hamiltons had given another dazzling party at The Grange for Jerome Bonaparte, the youngest brother of Napoleon, and the former Elizabeth Patterson of Baltimore, the beautiful bride of five months he had taken for love, heedless of dynastic considerations. At their wedding on Christmas Eve, Aaron Burr had praised her as "just the size and nearly the figure of Theodosia Burr Alston," but "perhaps not so well in the shoulders." Burr could praise no one more highly than his only legitimate child. Still, he said, she "dresses with taste and simplicity (by some thought too free)," though not by him. Jefferson's friend Margaret Bayard Smith disagreed; to her, Princess Elizabeth Bonaparte was not only "too free," but "mobs of boys have crowded about their splendid equipage to see what I hope will not often be seen in this country, an almost naked woman."

Invitations to the dinner and all details were handled by Hamilton from his downtown law office. From there he wrote Elizabeth up at The Grange, "On Sunday Bonaparte and wife with the Judges will dine with you. We shall be 16 in number if Gouverneur Morris will come. Send him the enclosed note on horseback, this Evening, that James may bring me an answer in the morning. He is promised the little horse to return."

Claret poured from the wine cooler the Washingtons had given the Hamiltons and many a toast was raised in elegant cut-glass goblets to young Bonaparte, his beautiful new American bride, Franco-American détente, and a future entente cordiale. Unfortunately, when Jerome returned to France, his brother the emperor refused to recognize the beautiful Baltimorean in the buff as his bride, remarried him for inscrutable reasons of state to Catherine of Wurtemberg, and named him the King of Westphalia.

Hastening home from presiding over the Senate in Washington to rally his lagging campaign against Judge Morgan Lewis for the governorship of New York, Vice-President Aaron Burr confided to Charles Biddle, his fellow passenger on the shuttle coach, that "He was determined to call out the first man of any respectability concerned in the infamous publications concerning him."

The worst of the "infamous publications" that now threatened to cost Burr an election he had at first been favored to win was an intercepted letter from Dr. Charles Cooper to Philip Schuyler in which Dr. Cooper reported that Hamilton, at a dinner party at Judge Tayler's in Albany, had declared that he "looked upon Mr. Burr to be a dangerous man" and "one who ought not to be trusted with the reins of government."

To make matters worse for Burr's campaign—and Hamilton's life expectancy—Dr. Cooper had added that "I could detail to you a still more despicable opinion which General Hamilton has expressed of Mr. Burr."

On June 18, 1804, the day before the Hamiltons' party for Angelica, Burr sat down in his private study, wrote Hamilton a concise, laconic, deadly letter, and handed it to their mutual friend William P. Van Ness, who brought it to a preoccupied Hamilton. Van Ness stood waiting silently beside Hamilton as he read it and turned over in his mind the limited possibilities it left him for reply.

> SIR,
>
> I send for your perusal a letter signed Charles D. Cooper, which, though apparently published some time ago, has but very recently come to my knowledge.

Mr. Van Ness, who does me the favour to deliver this, will point out to you that clause of the letter to which I particularly request your attention. You must perceive, sir, the necessity of a prompt and unqualified acknowledgement or denial of the use of any expressions which would warrant the assertions of Mr. Cooper. I have the honour to be

Your obedient servant,
A. Burr

Hamilton stared at the letter and the enclosed newspaper accounts of Dr. Cooper's correspondence. Van Ness would have no need to point out the offensive sentence. Van Ness waited with formal politeness and a solemn air while Hamilton canvassed in his mind the few possible replies to the challenge that his own words—and the mysterious interception of Dr. Cooper's correspondence—had brought upon him. Hamilton chose his words with care. The matter required careful consideration. A reply would be sent shortly. Van Ness bowed out and departed.

No one knew better than Hamilton that the first two quotations were mild compared to the things subsumed by the third—"despicable"—that he had been saying about Burr in private conversations and letters to friends for years. He had insulted Burr's family, impugned his honesty, and accused him of almost every imaginable crime, from taking bribes to cowardice in the army. Neither Hamilton nor his friends could realistically doubt that Burr's undercover intelligence network had told him many of the "despicable" things that Hamilton had been saying about him.

At about five o'clock in the morning of Wednesday, July 11, 1804, Hamilton "left town" and crossed the Hudson to the Weehawken duelling ground in a small sailboat with his law clerk, Nathaniel Pendleton, who was to act as his second, and Dr. David Hosack, the celebrated surgeon. Burr's challenge letter was a foreseeable consequence of Hamilton's rise. The July morning's baleful crossing, and recrossing, were the foreseeable consequences of Burr's challenge letter.

Afterward Hamilton's corpse was transported from the William Bayard house on Jane Street, where he had died in agony, to Angelica Church's town house on Robinson Street—where Philip Hamilton's corpse had been taken two years earlier—to await the great public funeral procession.

Elizabeth Hamilton tore open and read the two letters Hamilton had written her, one on July 4 and the other the night before the duel, to be opened only in case of his death:

July 4, 1804

This letter, my very dear Eliza, will not be delivered to you, unless I shall first have terminated my earthly career; to begin, as I humbly hope from redeeming grace and divine mercy, a happy immortality. If it had been possible for me to have avoided the interview, my love for you and my precious children would have been alone a decisive motive. But it was not possible, without sacrifices which would have rendered me unworthy of your esteem.

His anguish at the thought of death taking him from her found moving penultimate phrases:

I need not tell you of the pangs I feel, from the idea of quitting you and exposing you to the anguish I know you would feel. Nor could I dwell on the topic lest it should unman me . . . With my last idea, I shall cherish the sweet hope of meeting you in a better world. Adieu, best of wives and best of women. Embrace all my darling children for me. Ever yours

A H

In the second letter, an afterthought at the very end, he thought of his beginnings—of his cousin Ann Lytton Mitchell, who had given the poor St. Croix orphan boy some money to come to America—and of duty undone:

My beloved Eliza, Mrs. Mitchell is the person in the world to whom as a friend I am under the greatest obligations. I have not hitherto done my duty to her. . . . I intend, if it shall be in my power, to render the evening of her days comfortable.

But if it shall please God to put this out of my power . . . I entreat you to do it, and to treat her with the tenderness of a sister.

There was a sense of inevitability, of suicide perhaps, of fitness, an eloquent melancholy, a feeling of mystery, of work unfinished, like that which hovers over the lines of Vergil's first Ecologue. He had become disenchanted with himself.

. . . The scruples of a Christian have determined me to expose my own life to any extent, rather than subject myself to the guilt of taking the life of another. This much increases my hazards, and redoubles my pangs for you. But you had rather I should die innocent than live guilty. Heaven can preserve me, and I humbly hope will; but, in the contrary event, I charge you to remember that you are a Christian. God's will be done! The will of a merciful God must be good. Once more,

Adieu, my darling, darling wife.

Alexander Hamilton was born on the island of Nevis in the British West Indies, on the eleventh of January, 1757. No birth certificate, baptismal record, or other contemporaneous document has been found to corroborate this statement. It is the same simple, flat declarative sentence with which Hamilton's son John Church Hamilton begins the first biography of his father. When his son published it in 1834, 30 years after Hamilton's death, Hamilton's widow, seven of their children, and many of Hamilton's friends—and enemies—were still alive; none of them is known to have disputed the date. However, his son's statement conflicts with the evidence provided by the first undisputed contemporaneous written document in which Alexander Hamilton's name appears.

The date of this document is February 22, 1768, when according to his son's statement Hamilton would have been 11 years old. It is the record of transaction No. XXIX of the probate court of Christiansted, St. Croix, in the Danish Virgin Islands of the Lesser Antilles. It names Alexander as one of the three sons of a "Madame Rachel Lewine" who had died there that February 19. According to this court record, her eldest son was "Peter Lewine, born in the marriage of the decedent with John Michael Lewine who, later, is said for valid reasons to have obtained from the highest authorities a divorce from her (according to what the probate court has been able to ascertain)." Peter Lewine had resided "and still resides in South Carolina and according to reports is about 22 years old." The record goes on to say that her two other sons, James Hamilton and Alexander Hamilton, the one 15 and the other 13 years old, "are illegitimate children born after the decedent's separation from the aforesaid Lewine."

Alexander Hamilton here makes his bow on the stage of recorded history as an illegitimate child born to an impoverished white woman who had been the guilty party in a squalid divorce proceeding, and who had just died.

If he was 13 in 1768, as the probate court record states, then he would have to have been born in 1755; his son's statement that he was born in 1757 would have been wrong. Some of Hamilton's biographers accept the probate record as proof that Hamilton was two years older than is commonly believed, and thus two years less precocious.

In this writer's view the hearsay statement of Hamilton's son outweighs the circumstantial hearsay contained in the 1768 St. Croix probate court paper. There, Hamilton's exact age was of no significance except to show that when his mother died he was under 21 and so needed a guardian *ad litem* to appear in the proceeding for him, just as a minor would in such a proceeding today. A smalltown clerk fills in a blank on a court form with whatever age he is told that seems reasonable, and mistakes like this occasionally occur. An 11-year-old as precocious as Alexander Hamilton might easily have been taken for 13.

The dispute over Hamilton's birth date is the first of many evidentiary disputes that make most assertions of fact about the first 16 years of Hamilton's life a problem of proof that will never be completely resolved. The few undisputed facts about Hamilton's youth in the islands of Nevis, St. Kitts, and St. Croix in the Lesser Antilles are of a rather pitiful and embarrassing nature. His enemies later would revile him about his misdeeds with money and his affair with Maria Reynolds. It is therefore hardly surprising that neither Hamilton nor his son wished to say much about these early years in the Antilles, and so left this part of his story in a semimythical state.

Hamilton's mother, Rachel (or Rachael) Fawcett Lavien, was probably born on the small island of Nevis in 1729. No birth record has been found to prove it. She was the sixth of seven children of Dr. John Fawcett's marriage to Mary Uppington, his second wife. Their first child had been born two months before John and Mary had been married. All but Rachel died in infancy or childhood. After 22 years of such child births and deaths, Mary left John alleging "diverse disputes and controversies." She appealed to the Nevis chancellor ordinary and in chief "to be relieved against the said John Fawcett" of the harrowing obligation to go on procreating young corpses with him. On February 5, 1740, the court issued her a writ of supplicavit for separate maintenance. To obtain her freedom she bargained away her one-third dower rights to all of Fawcett's still apparently extensive estate in consideration for his agreement to pay her an annuity of £53 4s. Upon the granting of her writ, she is reputed to have moved briskly with her only surviving and all the more beloved child, Rachel—now about 11—to the neighboring island of St. Kitts.

Dr. John Fawcett's first wife had also been a Mary. They had had a daughter named Ann, 15 years older than Rachel, her half-sister, and Hamilton's only maternal aunt. Ann Fawcett married James Lytton about 1730, had four children, and moved from Nevis to St. Croix, where Lytton prospered and bought The Grange plantation in the Company Quarter near Christiansted in 1738.

Dr. Fawcett died in 1745, leaving real estate on St. Croix. His will left everything to Rachel and appointed her as his sole executrix. He left nothing to Hamilton's aunt Ann Lytton or any of her children, whose number had reached six by the time Dr. Fawcett died and would eventually reach eight. Of these maternal first cousins only Ann Lytton, her mother's namesake, 14 years older than Hamilton, would remain close to Hamilton for life.

To assume her executorial duties and manage her inheritance, Rachel and her mother changed islands again, this time from St. Kitts to St. Croix. There, 16-year-old Rachel married 28-year-old John Michael Lavien, who would become Hamilton's angry and unforgiving stepfather.

Lavien owned property on St. Croix at the time of his marriage to Rachel, and was involved in business dealings with her half brother-in-law James Lytton, whose affairs continued to prosper. Lavien was reputed to be rich. The most widely accepted spelling of his name is Lavien, but in island records and by Hamilton and others it was also variously spelled Levine, Lavine, Levin, Lavin, Lewine, Lawin, Lawien, Lewien, Lovien, Lovine and Lavion. His first name was often spelled Johan or Johann as well as John. Hamilton's grandson, the noted alienist Allan McLane Hamilton, wrote of Lavien, probably expressing his grandfather's belief, that "attracted by Rachel's beauty and recommended to her mother by his wealth, he received her hand against her inclination." He added that the "rich Danish Jew . . . treated her cruelly."

St. Croix records of the time generally identified Jews as such, but Lavien is not so identified. It may be that he had disavowed Judaism by the time of his marriage to Rachel. She may have cost him a fortune as well as his orthodoxy. The year they were married, he increased his debt to the Danish West India Company to 1,930 rigsdalers, two reals—twice the cost of a sugar plantation he had given up the year before. He had suffered a disastrous crop failure, so perhaps he married her hoping to bail himself out. Each may have had delusions that the other was richer than was the case, which neither did anything to dispel before the wedding day.

The son born to them the year after their marriage—Hamilton's half brother—was Peter Lavien. The first home of Rachel and John Michael Lavien and Peter, their only child, was an imposing plantation named Contentment, southwest of Christiansted. Contentment proved temporary, however, and three years later they moved to a lesser estate called Beeston Hill, which buzzed with their discord.

By now Lavien owed the Danish West India Company the large sum of 2,432 rigsdalers. From this time on, Lavien's efforts as an independent planter were marked, like his marriage, by decline and failure. To Rachel it became a "hateful marriage" and she began to consort openly with other men. In 1750 Lavien swore out a complaint, had her arrested, and thrown into jail; the old red brick fort still stands on the quay at Christiansted. A monument to Alexander Hamilton stands in front of it.

After serving her prison term, Rachel ran away from St. Croix to "an English island." Lavien sued her for divorce in absentia, alleging among other things that she had "given herself up to whoring with everyone." As a result, he charged, she had begot several whore children. One of these would be Alexander Hamilton.

Rachel's mother Mary published notice to her St. Croix creditors that she intended to leave the island. Gertrude Atherton, author of a splendid fictional biography of Hamilton, *The Conqueror,* published in 1902, says that after Rachel's release, she and Mary fled to St. Kitts, but there is no other evidence of much probative value, only tradition and Miss Atherton's powerful intuition.

Miss Atherton imagined Rachel and Mary's St. Kitts house as a "Great House, with spacious open galleries and verandahs." But wherever Rachel and her mother lived after 1750, it seems certain that "open galleries and verandahs" were not part of their outlook, for Dr. John Fawcett's decline and death had cut off Mary's annuity and dower. In 1754 a notice published in St. Croix announced that Mary Uppington Fawcett's debts to the estate of one John Roach were uncollectible "as she is not here, but in poverty has left the island."

By July 1755 Mary Uppington Fawcett was living on the Dutch island of St. Eustatius, where court writs issued in creditors' actions on a British or Danish island could not reach her. She described herself as late of the island of Nevis, but not of St. Eustatius, and a widow. Her death probably occurred shortly after her move, but the date is not known, nor is anything else of probative value about her, except that she had deeded her three slaves to her friend Archibald Hamm, directing that on her death they should pass to her daughter, Rachel. Rachel soon took possession of them. She had not made the hop to St. Eustatius with her mother because by now she was living with her lover, James Hamilton, back on Nevis, thus rounding out the circuit of islands that lack of money and restless loves had driven both mother and daughter to run.

No one knows exactly where or when Rachel Fawcett Lavien and James Hamilton met, when they began living together, or when they parted. It is little more than tradition that they met on St. Kitts or Nevis about 1750, when James was 32 or 33 and she was ten years younger, began living together on Nevis not long after that, lived together for about 15 years in all, on Nevis till about 1760, then on St. Kitts until 1765, and finally on St. Croix for a few months at the end of that year before parting forever. James returned to St. Kitts while Rachel remained in the bustling town quarter of Christiansted for three more years until she died February 19, 1768. James Hamilton retreated from St. Kitts to Tobago, and from there to St. Vincent where he died 31 years later, in 1799, only five years before his by then famous son.

Writing to Thomas Jefferson years later, John Adams would call Hamilton "the bastard brat of a Scotch pedlar." Not much more than this is known of James Hamilton, the obscure father of a famous son and the obscure son of a lordly father. He was no doubt Scotch. He was the fourth of nine sons of Alexander Hamilton, laird of The Grange in the Parish of Stevenston, Ayrshire, Scotland. The laird's wife was Elizabeth, the eldest daughter of Sir Robert Pollock. The Hamiltons of Grange belonged to the Cambuskeith branch of the notable House of Hamilton, and claimed as ancestors the dukes of Hamilton and Abercorn, the earls of Haddington, the Viscounts Boyne, the Barons Bellhaven, and most of the other Hamilton families of Scotland and Ireland.

James Hamilton's three older brothers had been born in 1712, 1715, and 1717, and James was probably born in 1718, but the exact date is not known. James's brothers remained in Scotland, and in time two of them and a nephew would succeed to lairdship of The Grange and correspond with Alexander Hamilton. Not much patrimony would be left at Ayrshire for a fourth son, so when James was 19 he had set out for the Leeward Islands to seek the fortune he would never find.

At various times in his later life, Alexander Hamilton sent sums of money totaling more than a thousand dollars back to his father and brother in the islands—when Hamilton himself was hard-pressed for money. Years later, Hamilton asked his friend Robert Troup, in case of his own death, to see that his father's drafts were paid so that they should not "return upon him and increase his distress."

During the 15 years from 1750 to 1765, when Rachel Fawcett Lavien and James Hamilton are supposed to have lived together out of wedlock, the only documentary evidence of their status is a Baptismal Record of the island of St. Eustatius that shows them as man and wife. On October 1, 1758, "James Hamilton and Rachel Hamilton his wife" stood as godfather and godmother at the christening of Alexander, the four-month-old son of "Alexander Fraser and Elizabeth Thornton his wife." Those responsible for little Alexander Fraser's religious upbringing could hardly, with propriety, be listed as living in sin.

The substantial house in Charlestown on Nevis where Rachel and James were living together when Hamilton was born is believed to have stood at the north edge of the town where the main street ends and the rough, dusty road circling the island turns inland. All that remains today are two coral block walls and a flight of steps descending from the road toward the pinkish gray white beach. The site is marked by a sign saying "Hamilton House" and a plaque which quietly suggests the serendipitous quality of the later career, as seen from Nevis:

> At this site on January 11, 1757, was born Alexander Hamilton who subsequently went to the North American colonies in search of education and who became one of the Founding Fathers of the United States of America.

Rachel and James Hamilton lived there together out of wedlock in defiance of Lavien's St. Croix divorce decree. But in the rigidly stratified world of these sugar islands they lived at the lowest social level of any of the whites. St. George's Gingerland Anglican church would certainly not have happily welcomed Rachel and James to celebrate the sacrament of baptism for their illegitimate children, so it is not surprising that no baptismal certificates for Alexander Hamilton, or his older brother James, born in 1755, have ever been found.

Two or three years after Hamilton's birth, in 1760 or thereabouts, the family moved from Nevis to St. Kitts. They remained there until about 1765 before taking their last trip together to the still larger island of St. Croix, 50 miles further to the northwest across the Saba bank. On St. Kitts not even ruined walls mark the place where Rachel and James Hamilton lived with their two children.

Two years after Alexander had been born, John Michael Lavien, still back on St. Croix, had brought suit against Rachel for absolute divorce, on February 26, 1759. Lavien summoned Rachel and three witnesses to her alleged lewdness to appear at a hearing on April 18 in Baron von Proeck's house. Rachel, of course, not being on St. Croix nor even within the jurisdiction of the Danish court's writ, did not respond to the summons.

Lavien alleged that she had already "twice been guilty of adultery." Although Lavien named no correspondent, Rachel's cohabitation with James on Lavien's former home island of Nevis may have become so open and notorious that there was no need to name anyone, nor mention James Jr. and Alexander as living proof of at least two of her adulteries. Lavien's charges covered the entire decade from when she had run away from him in 1750 to 1759, so his charge that Rachel had been whoring with "everyone" said that a wider public had enjoyed her favors than James Hamilton alone.

Lavien was suing Rachel for divorce at this late date, he alleged, because she "ought not to have" anything from his "little" estate if he should die to "give to her whore children" James and Alexander.

The court found that Lavien's case against Rachel was proved and dissolved their marriage. It declared that "said Rachel Lewin shall have no rights whatsoever as wife to either John Michael Lewin's person or means. . . . Also, Rachel Lewin's illegitimate children are denied all rights or claims to the plaintiff's possessions." Lavien was judged free to marry again, but Rachel, being the guilty party, was forbidden to remarry. She was warned that "you are to be further punished (if seized) in this country."

Lavien married again and had another son and a daughter who died in infancy, but his fortunes continued to fail. He died on February 28, 1771, leaving an estate of 172 rigsdalers, 8 reals, and a few gold buttons in pawn. He seems never to have held an office of public honor or trust. Hamilton's half-brother Peter took the pittance his father's suit had secured for him from Rachel, James Jr., and Alexander, and departed for South Carolina.

It was largely Lavien's suit that lent vivid color to later charges like John Adams's and Thomas Jefferson's that Hamilton was a "bastard brat" and a "foreign bastard." It gave rise to public speculation that some other man, not James Hamilton, was his father: Lavien; the planter Thomas Stevens of Antigua and St. Croix and father of Hamilton's lifelong friend Edward Stevens; and William Leslie Hamilton, of Olivees, the Governor General of Nevis. And George Washington, who was visiting in Barbados about the time Rachel conceived Hamilton. There is no evidence that Rachel was ever on Barbados, but that has not prevented endless speculation over the years that Hamilton was Washington's illegitimate son. Some have said that Hamilton was a Jew—his right name was Alexander Levine; others that Negro blood flowed in his veins. No evidence lends support to these possibilities. Rachel's name is shown on the St. Croix tax lists among the non-Jewish whites.

In 1765 James Hamilton's employer, a St. Kitts merchant, sent him to St. Croix as his representative to collect a large debt of £807 11s. 11d. due from the Christiansted firm of Moir & Gordon. James took Rachel and their two sons, James Jr., now ten, and Alexander, now eight, with him on the trip. He failed to collect the debt immediately but arranged for attorneys to institute suit, and returned to St. Kitts, leaving his family in Christiansted behind him. He never saw Rachel or Alexander again.

When James and Rachel and their two sons debarked in Christiansted, memories of Rachel's imprisonment there 15 years earlier, revived by Lavien's public charges of adultery against her six years earlier, would not have been forgotten. On the quay with her consort and two sons of the right ages to confirm the charges, the old scandal would take on new life. A question might exist about her legal relationship, if any, with her traveling companion, James Hamilton, but there could be no question that young James and Alexander were their sons. With his fair complexion, ruddy cheeks, deep-set violet blue eyes, finely textured light brown hair with a trace of red, and his handsome, regular well-proportioned features, Alexander in particular strongly resembled his father James. The pressures of the St. Croix scene were probably what drove James Hamilton back to the calm of St. Kitts early in 1766, without Ingram's £807 11s. 11d. or his family.

The conventional notion is that James Hamilton callously abandoned Rachel and his two sons on St. Croix. It seems at least as likely that she abandoned him. In the tonic air of the larger, bustling world of Christiansted, whose Danish colonial masters ruled with a light, absentminded hand, Rachel freed herself from free love and refused to return to St. Kitts with James Hamilton. She resumed her maiden name of Fawcett for purposes of the tax rolls, used that name or Lavien's for other dealings, and never again called herself by the name of Hamilton.

Alexander Hamilton always afterward spoke and wrote to and about his seeming failure of a father with tenderness, warmth, and kindness. He never reproached him for deserting their family, although he noted that his having left them had thrown him "upon the bounty of my mother's relatives," the Lyttons, "some of whom were then wealthy. . . ."

Alone with her two boys and no support from their father, Rachel would have a hard life unless she could find a sponsor or aegis for protection. She did. She briskly joined St. John's

Anglican (Protestant Episcopal) Church. She rented a house at No. 34 Kompagnietstrade (Company's Street) from the prominent merchant Thomas Dipnall for 12 rigsdalers a month. At various times, certainly for some months in 1767 and 1768, she lived across the street at No. 23 at the house of Captain William Egan; whether she did so for business or amorous reasons, or both, is not known. According to the poll tax lists, there were with her two white boys, her sons; the three slaves, Rebecca, Flora, and Esther that she had inherited from her mother; and four of the slaves' 12 children who were under age.

Rachel opened a small provision store in the Dipnall house and dealt in pork, beef, flour, fish, rice, apples, and other plantation staples that she bought from him as well as from the firm of David Beckman and Nicholas Cruger, recently opened by two young merchants from New York. From the age of eight or nine Alexander would help his mother and his brother and the slaves who lived with them stock the shelves, wait on customers, post the ledgers, pay or stall off consignors and dun debtors for accounts receivable. In 1767 or 1768 he also began working for the firm of Beckman and Cruger.

In February 1768 Rachel was taken ill with a terrible racking fever that Alexander soon caught too. Ann McDonnell took care of Rachel for a week before Dr. Herring was called on February 17. He bled her and gave her fever medicine. On the nineteenth Rachel was given still more fever medicine and also valerian and alcohol for her head. So was Alexander. In the afternoon she was given a decoction, whereas Alexander was bled and given an enema. Rachel died at nine in the evening. Alexander survived.

The official burial record at St. John's Church gives her age at death as 32. If this is correct, it would mean that she had given birth to her son Peter, a date also officially recorded, when she was only ten years old. In fact, she was born in 1729, and would have been 39 when she died. The entry making her seven years younger than she was is consistent with the reputation for seductive youthful beauty that remained with her until the end. It is also consistent with treatment of chronological truth in tropical towns when it comes into conflict with emotional or physiological reality.

Ann McDonnell laid out Rachel's body. The parish clerk of St. John's Anglican Church summoned Rachel's friends to the ceremony and assembled the pallbearers. Her body was taken in a hearse to James Lytton's family plot on Grange plantation and buried there on February 20. Beside the grave at the interment stood James and Ann Lytton; their son Peter; their daughter Ann and other Lytton children; and 13-year-old James and 11-year-old Alexander Hamilton.

Rachel was laid to rest at the Lytton plantation on St. Croix, which was—like James Hamilton's family seat in Ayrshire—always known as The Grange. The burial ground is now discovered only with difficulty a few hundred yards downhill from what remains of the old plantation house. One of the dozen or more brick-mounded graves in the woods is probably hers, but identifying slabs have long been carried away. Rachel's grave is lost. Broadus Mitchell wrote that "This lost spot is part of America's story. For here lies the original of Alexander Hamilton's peculiar ardor."

Hamilton's son John Church wrote that Hamilton almost never spoke of his mother to outsiders, but within his family, he "recollected her with inexpressible fondness, and often spoke of her as a woman of superior intellect, highly cultivated, of elevated and generous sentiments, and of unusual elegance of person and manner."

Under the ancient mahogany trees in a glade below the St. Croix hillock where what remains of the old Lytton Grange still stands, Gertrude Atherton erected a monument to Rachel. Her inscription says much by saying only, "She was the mother of Alexander Hamilton."

The Hamiltons now were orphans alone in the world with no father or any other known relatives except Peter and the other Lyttons. Hamilton's son John Church wrote that "indigence" had thrown his father "upon the bounty of his mother's [Lytton] relatives." His reference to the "bounty" of the Lytton relatives was apparently without irony.

Hamilton afterward expressed gratitude toward his aunt and cousin, both named Ann Lytton, but the Lytton family fortunes had reached a zenith in 1760, and by now had fallen far. There is no evidence that any of the other Lyttons gave Hamilton money.

Disasters now befell the Lyttons that would dispel any remaining misplaced hopes Hamilton might have had of "bounty" from them. His cousin Ann's husband went bankrupt. James Lytton, Jr., having stolen some slaves that had belonged to his first wife's estate, became insolvent and ran away from the island with them, also taking a second wife. James Lytton died insolvent as well. Peter Lytton became increasingly unstable and irresponsible, lost all his money, and committed suicide within the year after Rachel's death.

Two years after his mother's death the "bounty" of Hamilton's Lytton connections had meant nothing to him. He was in a despairing mood, which he poured out to his friend Edward Stevens in a letter which is the first undisputed document written by Hamilton that history has preserved. It is datelined St. Croix, November 11, 1769, when Hamilton was two months short of being 13 years old. It is an extraordinary projection of an entire life to come.

Edward "Neddy" Stevens was the son of Thomas Stevens, a successful merchant on St. Croix. Like Nicholas Cruger, the older Stevens was one of many men whose friendship to Rachel gave rise to whispers that he might be Hamilton's father. Neddy was the closest friend of Hamilton's boyhood and they would remain as close as brothers all of Hamilton's life. In 1769 when the 12-year-old Hamilton writes, Neddy has just been sent north to the continent for further studies at Kings College in New York City. The letter is stilted, funny, and touching, and a skeleton key to any life of Hamilton.

St. Croix, November 11, 1769

Dear Edward

This just serves to acknowledge receipt of yours per Cap Lowndes.

. . . The truth of Cap Lightbourn & Lowndes information is now verifyd by the Presence of your Father and Sister for whose safe arrival I Pray.

. . . As to what you say respecting your having soon the happiness of seeing us all, I wish, for an accomplishment of your hopes provided they are Concomitant with your welfare, otherwise not, tho doubt whether I shall be Present or not for to confess my weakness, Ned, my Ambition is prevalent that I contemn the grov'ling and condition of a Clerk or the like, to which my Fortune, etc. condemns me and would willingly risk my life tho' not my Character to exalt my Station. Im confident, Ned, that my Youth excludes me from any hopes of immediate Preferment nor do I desire it, but I mean to prepare the way for futurity. Im no Philosopher you see and may be jusly said to Build Castles in the Air. My Folly makes me ashamd and beg youll Conceal it, yet Neddy we have seen such Schemes successfull when the Projector is Constant I shall conclude saying I wish there was a War.

I am Dr. Edward Yours

Alex Hamilton

P.S. I this moment receivd yours by William Smith and am pleasd to see you Give such Close Application to Study.

Captain Lowndes's and Captain Lightbourn's ships always sailed at risk of seizure by Spanish *Guarda Costas*. Hence Hamilton's prayers for Stevens's father and sister.

Here is the fierce ambition that drives Hamilton all his life. Almost nowhere else in his thousands of extant writings does Hamilton so frankly admit to ambition or vanity not tied to what he conceives to be the public good. The letter's open and candid quality is characteristic of the indiscreet private manner that would win Hamilton adoring friends, mortal enemies, and scandalous notoriety the rest of his life.

A realist like Hamilton would not expect a hardheaded merchant like Cruger to promote him out of the groveling condition of a clerk in which he was proving himself to be too valuable. The rigidly stratified social and economic structure of the islands put a ceiling with no other opening upward for a poor orphan boy in Hamilton's condition of place. Ambition, preparation for futurity, constancy, willingness to "risk my life tho not my Character" might forever take him nowhere unless—"I wish there was a war." It flashes with abrasive frankness out of a thicket of platitudes. To Hamilton's apologists it is the earliest example of the searing honesty that is one of his most distinctive qualities. To critics it is the earliest indiscretion of a life of ever more egregious indiscretions. Both apologists and critics would agree that a flaw is here exposed that would be likely to lead to the tragedy that occurred. In this first letter, more than in any of the thousands that follow it, is uncovered the quintessence of all possible lives of Alexander Hamilton.

2

The Secretary of the Treasury Wept

The vigour of his genius corresponding with the importance of the prize . . . over-came the natural moderation of his temper. . . . . Animated by an enlightened sense of the value of free government, he cheerfully resolved to stake his fortune his hopes his life and his honor upon an enterprise of the danger of which he knew the whole magnitude in a cause which was worthy of the toils and the blood of heroes.

—Eulogium on General Nathanael Greene, July 4, 1789

The Electoral College provided for by the new Constitution of the United States met on February 4, 1789, less than 20 years after Alexander Hamilton's letter to Neddy Stevens. It unanimously elected George Washington first president of the United States. Alexander Hamilton, the party leader of the Federalist party that was organizing the new government, had suggested that a few Federalist electors withhold their votes from John Adams, his other candidate, thereby avoiding a tie in electoral votes, causing John Adams to be elected vice-president, and incurring his undying enmity.

Washington and Adams were inaugurated in New York City on April 30, 1789, and the new government under the Constitution got under way.

In the organization of the new Congress in the tapestried chamber of Federal Hall, Hamilton could not prevent the election of James Madison's protégé and Hamilton's enemy, John Beckley, as chief clerk of Congress. Elias Boudinot then moved the House into a committee of the whole to take up the creation of executive departments for foreign affairs, war, and finance.

First and most controversial for debate would be the Department of Finance.

Robert Morris had closed out his accounts as superintendent of finance on November 1, 1784, and turned the books over to a new Board of Treasury. A committee, of which Nathan Dane was chairman, after reviewing the board's records, reported back to Congress on September 30, 1787, that the records of Robert Morris and the board were disorderly, inconclusive, and full of shortages and imbalances, if not outright proof of wrongdoing and embezzlement. The charges against Morris led to return of the Treasury to a board, whose record had been even worse than Morris's.

Should the Treasury Department now be placed under a single head or under a board of three commissioners? It was no mere routine debate.

Elbridge Gerry of Massachusetts was for a three-man board, arguing that by putting "all this power into the hands of one great man, . . . we shall establish an office giving one person a greater influence than the President of the United States, and more than is proper for any person to have in a republican government." He doubted whether a fit person could be found in the whole country.

Hamilton's close friends in Congress knew better and insisted that a single head would be better than a board. The bill finally passed, preserving the Treasury Department, ranking with War and Foreign Affairs, under a single all-powerful secretary, as one of the three great departments.

Hamilton's name had been kept out of the debates as much as possible by his friends, but his presence just below the surface as the likely appointee brought an extra edge of sound and fury to consideration of such abstractions as that of a single head versus a board.

When Washington had asked Robert Morris for suggestions, Morris replied "There is but one man in the United States": Alexander Hamilton. Robert Troup recalled that Washington, immediately after his inauguration, "called on Hamilton, and told him it was his intention to nominate him to the charge of the financial department" as soon as it should be organized. The next day, Hamilton asked Troup to take over his law practice if he should be appointed. Willing to oblige, Troup duly pointed out the financial sacrifice it would mean. Hamilton readily admitted this, but said he could not refuse an assignment in which he "could essentially promote the welfare of the country."

Only a few weeks after Washington's inauguration, James Madison confided to Thomas Jefferson, with critical passages in cipher, that John Jay or Hamilton would be proposed for the Treasury. It became an open secret that summer that Hamilton was Washington's choice. Testimonials to an unnamed person exactly like him emerged from support by friends—and attacks by foes—in the debates that were going on in Congress.

Fisher Ames of Massachusetts, a friend in the House, noted that governmental finance "presents to the imagination a deep, dark, and dreary chaos; impossible to be reduced to order without the mind of the architect is clear and capacious, and his power commensurate to the occasion . . . . it is with an intention to let a little sunshine into the business that the present arrangement is proposed. . . ."

John Page of Virginia, a foe, feared that the duty of the secretary to "digest and report plans for the improvement and management of the revenue, and the support of the public credit," was not only "a dangerous innovation upon the constitutional privilege of this House," but might even lay "a foundation for an aristocracy or a detestable monarchy." He feared that "Members might be led, by the deference commonly paid to men of abilities . . . to support the minister's plan, even against their own judgment."

Egbert Benson, a friend, pointed out that the representatives in Congress, there for brief tenure and uninformed except by local views, would flounder with fiscal matters, whereas the secretary, with superior and comprehensive knowledge, could bring things to a focus by presenting plans that could be amended or corrected as legislative wisdom required.

The most important work of the secretary would be ''that of digesting and *reporting* plans for the improvement of the revenue, supporting public credit,'' and drawing forth the riches of the country. Such business must be ''submitted into the hands of an able individual.''

James Madison now brought winning support to his coauthor of *The Federalist Papers.* The danger of his exercising undue influence, Madison insisted, was far less than the injury from the House's bungling without his guidance. ''From a bad administration of the Goverment, more detriment will arise than from any other source,'' he pointed out.

There had been no objection to the secretary's working up a plan ''and giving it in when it was called,'' so by merely changing the word *report* to *prepare,* the House could protect itself from its own presumed weakness before a powerful secretary. Thomas FitzSimons's amendment to this effect carried the day.

The final question was whether the head of one of the great departments, whose appointment had to be with the ''advice and consent'' of the Senate, could be removed by the president at will, or only with ''advice and consent'' of the Senate once again. The Constitution and *The Federalist* left room for doubt.

In foreign affairs and war, it seemed clearer that the president should have a free hand, but with revenue powers vested in the House, Jackson of Georgia charged, ''if the President has the power of removing all officers who may be virtuous enough to oppose his measures . . . Your Treasury would fall into his hands; for nobody in that department would dare to oppose him. Having then the army and the treasury at his command, we might bid a farewell to the liberties of America forever.''

Thomas Scott of Pennsylvania made fun of these ''frightful pictures,'' ''that the Treasurer must be the mere creature of the President,'' who ''arbitrarily removes him from office, and lays his hands violently upon the money chest. . . .'' Even a virtuous Treasurer could not halt a wicked President who, supported by army and navy, ''would . . . carry away the money and the Treasurer too. . . .''

Wide suspicion that the Treasury would fall to the powerful Federalist party leader, who would work hand in glove with his ''aegis'' the Federalist president he had served as chief aide, lent fierce personal intensity to the whole abstract subject of ministerial powers. Benson finally brought both sides together by amendments that would leave the president's power of removal of the head of a department to construction of the Constitution, not to legislation by the House. The bill passed, 31–19. The president could remove cabinet ministers at will without the further advice and consent of the Senate. The Treasury Department bill took effect September 2, and Hamilton was commissioned secretary of the Treasury on September 11.

The legislative history that now lay behind the creation of the department showed that the secretary was to have the widest and most significant powers in the government, even broad jurisdiction over western lands. Debates had rejected the idea of subjecting him to control of Congress as inconsistent with the theory of separation of powers. The department was firmly within the executive branch. Yet charged with reporting to the House of Representatives on all proposals affecting finance, he would have more intimate access to the people's branch of the tripartite government than any other member of the executive branch.

Few aspects of foreign affairs or war could be imagined that would not significantly involve finances. It was, after all, a government supported largely by import duties, under constant threat from warlike Indians and great powers on northern, western, and southern borders and everywhere on the high seas. Hamilton would be the cabinet minister who in practice would hold the office most resembling that of an American prime minister.

With powers so vast, it is not particularly surprising that the secretary of the treasury shunted aside warnings of the dangers of calumny he had heard or insufficiently noted—dangers implied by specifically penal provisions of the Treasury's enabling legislation to the effect that anyone employed in the Treasury who was concerned in commerce or speculated in public funds should be held guilty of a high crime. Suspicion of his inattention to such strictures would lead to Hamilton's ultimate disgrace.

Inauguration of the new government roughly coincided with an upturn in the economy. Short grain crops in Europe created brisk demand in America. President Washington wrote Lafayette: "In the last year, the plentiful crops and great prices of grain have vastly augmented our remittances." People could afford to import more European goods so the "duties payable into the public treasury" had increased. Trade with the West Indies flourished. There was reason to hope that being secretary of the treasury would not be as disastrous for Hamilton as it had been for his predecessors and the Board of Treasury.

Even so, Hamilton's mood was more somber than usual on the Fourth of July, 1789, as he and Baron von Steuben bade farewell to Hamilton's wife Betsy and their four children and went off to join fellow members of the New York Society of the Cincinnati and friends and brethren from the other state societies. The Sons of the Cincinnati fell into irregular formation behind Colonel Sebastian Baumann's artillery regiment and marched off stiffly in cadence behind the crash and blare of a band playing a wartime tune. The Cincinnati had called upon Hamilton, their greatest orator, to deliver an eulogium this afternoon to the memory of General Nathanael Greene, the man who had recommended him to be Washington's aide. Greene had died three years earlier.

The brilliant audience assembled in the pews of St. Paul's Chapel on Vesey Street included Vice-President Adams, members of the Senate, the Speaker and members of the House of Representatives, and their ladies. Hamilton looked down on the crowded rows and spoke in a low, intense voice. His eulogium recounted at first hand major actions in which both he and Greene had played a part—Trenton, Princeton, Springfield, and Monmouth. In all perils, Greene's "calm intrepidity and unshaken presence of mind [served] to arrest the progress of the disorder and retrieve the fortune of the day." Hamilton went on to describe Greene's brilliant campaigns in the South—his strategy and tactics at places like Hick's Creek; Guilford Court House; the river crossings of the Catawba, the Yadkin, and the Dan; and the Battle of Eutaw Springs. He had forced the British to evacuate Charleston and Savannah and saved the South for the nation.

Hamilton made no mention of his own role in battles where both he and Greene had fought—he rarely spoke about himself—but in another striking passage he made the ascending arch of Greene's life story sound remarkably like the arch of Hamilton's own to date during the 20 years since he had written his letter to Neddy Stevens from the tiny "colonial dependency" of St. Croix:

> Nathanael Greene descended from reputable parents, but not placed by birth in that elevated rank, which under a monarchy is the only sure road to those employments, that give activity and scope to abilities, must in all probability have contented himself with the humble lot of a private citizen, or at most with the contracted sphere of an elective office, in a colonial and dependent government, scarcely conscious of the resources of his own mind, had not the violated rights of his country called him to act a part on a more splendid and ample theater. . . .

Removed from St. Croix's "contracted sphere" to the continent, "the resources of his own mind" had been brought to full consciousness by the part Hamilton had been called upon to act on Greene's recommendation in "a more splendid and ample theater." There was no mistaking the pride he projected on Greene for having done it all without having been placed by birth in the "elevated rank" that gives "activity and scope to abilities." Telling more about his unmentioned self than about Greene, Hamilton added:

> The vigour of his genius corresponding with the importance of the prize to be contended for, overcame the natural moderation of his temper; and though not hurried on by enthusiasm, but animated by an enlightened sense of the value of free government, he cheerfully resolved to stake his fortune his hopes his life and his honor upon an enterprise of the danger of which he knew the whole magnitude in a cause which was worthy of the toils and of the blood of heroes.

Since writing Neddy Stevens, Hamilton, like Greene, had often "willingly risk[ed] my life tho not my character to exalt my station." From then "being jusly said to Build Castles in the air," Hamilton now had risen to a civil station, largely through his army contacts, if not an army rank, more exalted than Greene's. As he spoke there from the lectern in St. Paul's Chapel, his was a station more exalted than that of any political man of his age and youth except the younger William Pitt's—in everything that mattered but personal wealth. As his distinguished audience in St. Paul's Chapel that Fourth of July looked beyond the older generation of leaders like Washington and Adams, they saw no one in view—except Hamilton's rival Aaron Burr, who came to church only on special occasions like this—more likely to be president within the next two or three decades.

So far no official concerned with the Treasury—as the disastrous experiences of Robert Morris and William Duer had shown—had been able to preserve his honor, integrity, and public credit, while remaining unsmeared by calumny and scandal. Lacking the personal wealth of his ill-fated predecessors, Hamilton remained a source of sorrow to some of his friends. Just as he was beginning to build a law practice that would soon have repaired his fortune, he was turning his best clients over to Robert Troup, as he briskly set to work to create precedental legal, economic, and administrative foundations for enduring free Constitutional government—on a salary of $3,500 a year.

As he took up his duties of office in September, Hamilton quickly became the most conspicuous figure of the new government, as much by default of others as conscious effort of his own. The federal judiciary, under John Jay, did little but wait for cases to work their way up to the highest court. But the executive department was new, had operative responsibility and a proliferation of active appointive agents, some with senatorial sanction. The War Department was anemic, the State Department seemed to deal with foreign relations remote in place and time. Hamilton's Treasury Department, by contrast, was domestic, vital, and immediate. It extracted taxes, gave out jobs, turned down worthy applicants, and was a chief target of criticism. Its activities clothed every action of the secretary with political blessing or bane.

Even before taking over the Treasury, Hamilton had been a focus of controversial public attention. In the spring of 1789, Governor Clinton, or one of his supporters, purporting to tell all under the name of *William Tell,* replied to a series of anti-Clinton broadsides— probably written by Hamilton over the initials H. G. (perhaps meaning "Hamilton of Grange"). *William Tell* charged, "Your private character is still worse than your public one, and it will yet be exposed by your own works, for [you] will not be bound by the *most* *solemn* of all obligations! *******'' In the tone and context of *William Tell's* abuse, few alert readers would have much difficulty figuring out that each of the seven asterisks stood for one letter of the more or less sacred word *wedlock.*

On the demands of the busy Wall Street law practice that generated the fees to support his growing family during the years 1786 through 1789, Hamilton had been superimposing a seemingly monomanic frenzy of payless *pro bono* activity in the cause of the union of the states. The Annapolis Convention; the Constitutional Convention; *The Federalist Papers;* Federalist party leadership in the battle for ratification at Poughkeepsie and throughout the 13 states; authorship of uncounted broadsides, bills, petitions, and polemics; reelection as a delegate to the Continental Congress on January 22, 1788, where he would be able to shepherd in the new government, all consumed his days and nights. The inference is irresistible that some secret loneliness, somewhere near the center of his soul, an unrequited passion that even his own acierating realism would not acknowledge, possessed him.

"I seldom write to a lady without fancying the relation of lover and mistress," he wrote to his sister-in-law, Angelica Church, wife of John Barker Church, his most important client, on December 6, 1787. "It has a very inspiring effect." He added, "In your case the dullest materials could not help feeding that propensity." He asks her to "Imagine, *if you are able* the pleasure" she gives him. He is thanking her for her "invaluable letter by the last packet" of October 2. She had written him, "Indeed my dear, Sir if my path was strewed with as many roses as you have filled your letter with compliments, I should not now lament my absence from America."

Instead of addressing him conventionally—"Indeed, my dear sir"—her delicate hand has rewarded his roses by omitting from the phrase the commas that would ordinarily follow the words *indeed* and *sir,* and by inserting a special, secret, improper comma after the word *dear.* She thus magically transforms a conventional salutation into an endearment of unguessable depths. At least, in the ache of his loneliness, he could read it that way.

Angelica's tiny, misplaced pen prick seemed to pierce his heart. With a characteristic mixture of scoffing and emotional outpouring, he assured her that her pen had not failed to cause his heart an exquisite pang.

"You ladies despise the pedantry of punctuation," he wrote her. "There was a most critical *comma* in your last letter. It is my interest that it should have been designed; but I presume it was accidental." If her "most critical comma" had really been accidental and she had not kept an exact copy of her letter, she would, of course, have had no idea what he was raving about. Despite his "presuming" that her comma was accidental, he really was certain that it had not been and that her lonely passion for him matched his for her. "I have a great opinion of your *discernment* and, therefore, I venture to rant," he confides, but "If you read this letter in a certain mood you will easily divine that in which I write it." All the roses he has strewn in her path "could give you but a feeble image of what I should wish to convey." At the end, he adds, "Betsy sends her love. I do not choose to say *joins in mine.* Tis old fashioned."

Hamilton closes to Angelica by matching her endearing and pointed error of punctuation with one of his own: "Adieu ma chere, Soeur. A. Hamilton."

Though this preoccupation with commas has comical overtones, it serves to draw into the tiny focus of two discreet scratches of their quills the whole range of frustrated, sublimated passion that seemed to consume Hamilton and his beautiful, brilliant, witty, sister-in-law separated from each other by an Atlantic. It had smoldered for years. When he is on her mind, her intensity of focus on him easily matches his on her, even when she is writing to his wife, her sister Betsy.

Writing from Paris, she had complained to Betsy on January 27, 1784, of not having had a separate letter from Hamilton. She resolutely gives news of others, but her thoughts keep turning back to Betsy's "lord":

> I should like Paris if it was nearer to America, for I have a very agreeable set of acquaintances. Mrs. Jay lives in a small house, about half a mile from Paris. The Americans have the pleasure to drink tea with her once a week. Mr. [Benjamin] Franklin has the gravel and desires to return to America. They talk of Papa or Col. Hamilton as his successor. How would you like to cross the Atlantic? Is your lord a Knight of the Cincinnati? It has made a wonderful noise here, but the order will probably exist in France when it will be neglected in America.

There are other things she wants from America, but most on her mind is the embrace of Betsy's lord. She says his name or a pronoun or other word that stands for his name over and over again, no fewer than 14 times in three short sentences. In the sentence before her close, he crops up no less than nine times:

> Will you send me the newspapers regularly instead of sending me fruit, for it is generally spoiled, and the trouble getting it thro. the custom house is immense. But the papers must be those that contain your husband's writings. Adieu, my dear embrace your *master* for me, and tell him that I envy you the fame of so clever a husband, one who writes so well: God bless him, and may he long continue to be the friend and brother of your affectionate

> Angelica

Her postscript reverts to her obsession:

> P.S. Tell Colonel Hamilton, if he does not write to me, I shall be very angry. A.C.

Many letters that have never been found passed between Alexander and Angelica over the years, but her spell hovers over the few that are extant like a rare perfume.

"All the graces you have been pleased to adorn me with," she writes Hamilton in October 1787, would fade before the good works of her sister. But Betsy was no rival to her in their kind of passion, any more than her husband, Church, was to Hamilton. She jeered to Hamilton that Church's "head is full politics," as if her love were blind to Hamilton's other obsession. She was confident that she had no rival for the kind of passion her sister's husband had for her, but that did not keep her from being suspicious that once there had been one. Angelica, from strength, adds a nervous postscript: "Is Kitty Livingston married?"

Amid the jumble of events of December 1787, with new numbers of *The Federalist* due at the printer's two and three and four times a week, Kitty's name in Angelica's hand must have released a flood of memories in Hamilton. They carried him all the way back to his first winter in America 15 years earlier, to Elizabethtown, where Hamilton, the 17-year-old guest of the William Livingstons, had at first worshiped their 23-year-old daughter Catharine, their Lady Kitty, as a votary might worship a chaste Diana on her pedestal. At 20, he whirled with her through the activities of the winter quarters at Morristown or sauntered beside her on summer picnics at The Pastures, keeping only a step or two ahead of the other swains who ardently pursued her. Kitty had been the darling of them all, Hamilton, Tilghman, Troup, Meade, Humphreys, Laurens—poor Laurens—and all the rest.

Hamilton had shown one of the letters she had written him to Laurens and reported to her how his dearest friend had been smitten with her too: "The liveliest emotions of approbation were pictured in his face, 'Hamilton,' cries he, 'when you write to this divine girl again, it must be in the style of adoration: none but a goddess, I am sure, could have penned so fine a letter.' "

He told Kitty he had risked Washington's wrath for "dedicating" as much precious time to Kitty then as he was now spending dawdling dreamily over memories to compose an answer to Angelica's postscript, "Is Kitty Livingston married?" He ought not to be wasting so much precious time over "so trifling and insignificant a toy as—woman." Besides, as he had told Kitty long ago, danger from the jealousy of a dear friend gave their own romance a special savor.

There was the risk "of being run through the body by saucy inamorato's who will envy me the prodigious favor, forsooth, of your correspondence." But "between the morose apathy of some and the envious sensibility of others," Kitty's love-struck young correspondent had remained unworried about being run through by any lances but Cupid's or pricks of her pen. He had proclaimed to Kitty, in capital letters, "ALL FOR LOVE is my motto."

Angelica would remember that even Gouverneur Morris's most eloquent sallies had failed to sweep Kitty off her chaste pedestal. He had even gone so far as to offer her "any part of me which you think proper."

Six years later, Hamilton had tried another tack, writing Kitty owlishly that "I know you have an invincible aversion to all flattery and extravagance" like Morris's. Hamilton was not "afraid that a Quixote, capable of uttering himself perfectly in the language of Knight-errantry, will ever be able to supplant me in the good graces of a lady of your sober understanding."

Ten years later, Kitty's father, William Livingston, still governor of New Jersey, had written in March 1787 that "my daughter, Kitty," now serving as his "principal Secretary of State," was off to New York "to kick up her heels at the balls and assemblies of a metropolis." It was hard to realize that La Kitty, the onetime darling of them all, had ripened or withered, into a spinster of 36, still kicking up her heels at balls.

On December 6, 1787, Hamilton finally got around to answering Angelica's question: "You ask if your friend Kitty Livingston is married? You recollect the proverb. She was ready, with as much eagerness as can be ascribed to the chaste wishes of a virgin heart, to sip the blissful cup, when alas! it slipped through her fingers—at least for a time, if not for ever."

Now, ten years after Hamilton had projected onto Gouverneur Morris his image of himself as a sort of Quixote, Hamilton's mind completed the quixotic metaphor it had begun then. He fills Angelica in on the sad fate of Quixote's mistress: "Her love a buxom widower of five and forty braving summer heats and wintry [blasts] exerted himself with so much zeal in the service of his Dulcinea that there is every appearance it will cost him his lungs. He is gone to the South of France, if possible, to preserve them," leaving Dulcinea waiting at the church.

Hamilton's own rueful reflections on Kitty's imperviousness to his finest knight-errantry allows him to share with Angelica the faintly malicious pleasure he knew his report would give her. He lightheartedly pleads his innocence of any such ungentlemanly pleasure: "This method of speaking of the *misfortune of your friend* proceeds from pure levity not a particle of malice. I beg your pardon for it; and I hope you will be able to tell me in your next that you have not by the least propensity to a smile verified the maxim of that scurvy defamer of human nature—.Rochefoucault."

"Not by the least propensity of her smile"—Hamilton muses as his own smile flickers briefly before a new onset of his loneliness: "Despairing of seeing you here my only hope is that the jumble of events will bring us together in Europe."

Nothing he puts in writing to his sister-in-law would slip over the edge of an impropriety to a client's wife except the private code of their eccentric punctuation. He closes: "Wherever I am believe always that there is no one can pay a more sincere or affectionate tribute to your deserts than I do—adieu ma chere, Soeur."

After taking up the tasks of his Treasury secretariat, Hamilton continued to post entries in the clients' Cash Book he had maintained since 1782 in the meticulous manner of Cruger's careful bookkeeper. He also kept a few personal ledgers in the Cash Book under such heads as "House Expenses," an account showing debits to his wife Betsy, as "Mrs. Hamilton." The ledgers for John B. Church are extensive, showing credits for dividends and other items received for his account, as well as debits for disbursements made on his behalf to others.

From late May through early November of 1789, Angelica Church was on a visit to New York—without her husband. He had just won his long-sought election from Westover to a seat in the British Parliament. So there is fascination in comparing the debit entries Hamilton posts in Church's ledger as he pays for Angelica's absence in New York—at the climax of Hamilton's life—with the entries Hamilton posts to a separate account headed "Angelica Church" (on the same page Hamilton posts another ledger for his wife as "Mrs. Elizabeth Hamilton"). From the comparison it appears that out of a total of £1705.9.3 spent for Angelica's lodging, coachman, valet de chambre, servants, coach hire, and miscellaneous, Church and Angelica have paid for only about half themselves. The other half seems to have been defrayed out of Hamilton's own flat pocket. Three of the most intriguing items paid by Hamilton for Angelica ("yourself") are for money she is to take back with her, for a mysterious unnamed "last" landlady (a lady different from the Mrs. Cuyler Church has paid), and for her "Music Master."

Angelica's ledger is untypical of Hamilton's Cash Book because it contains only debit but no credit entries. It is posted in a more disorderly manner than any of the others. It is buried amid the dreary regularity of names, notations, and figure postings. Unlike any of the more than 150 other accounts, Angelica's is subdivided into two uniquely labeled subheads which are "Monies paid to Yourself" and "For You." These leap off the page to strike an auditor's eye in much the same way the words "I love you" tucked randomly into a logarithm table would strike an arithmetician's.

Amid the kaleidoscopic "jumble of events," the secret lonely passion the exalted bookkeeper felt "For You," and she for him, seemed to go on consuming them both, year after year, whether she was in New York or an Atlantic away, in the pages of books of account or letters full of stifled passion. When Angelica took ship to return to England early in November, her poor heart was undone, as she wrote back to him from shipboard having just sailed out of his sight:

[November 5–7, 1789]

Me voila mon très cher bien en mer et le pauvre coeur bien effligé de vous avoir quitté. I have almost vowed not to stay three weeks in England. . . .

She cannot seem to wring thoughts of him out of her sentences, solicitous as she tries to be for her ailing sister Betsy:

I am not much disposed for gaiety, and yet I endeavour already to make myself tolerable to my fellow passengers, that my sweet friends advice may not be lost on me. Do my dear Brother endeavour to sooth my poor Betsey, comfort her with the assurances that I will certainly return to take care of her soon. Remember this also yourself my dearest Brother and let neither politics or ambition drive your Angelica from your affections.

. . . Adieu my dear Brother, may God bless and protect you, prays your ever affectionate Angelica ever ever yours.

Alone on the wintry passage after spring, summer, and early autumn in New York with him, she seems to unravel in an attack of despairing anxiety:

Bitter whilst in sight of my friend, thus far my dear Brother I am content with my company, and apparently they with me, but how can I be content when I leave my best and most valuable invaluable friends. Adieu my dear Hamilton, you said I was as dear to you as a sister keep your word, and let me have the consolation to believe that you will never forget the promise of friendship you have vowed. A thousand embraces to my dear Betsey, she will not have so bad a night as the last, *but poor Angelica* adieu mine plus cher

my best affectionate wishes to my Baron.

Same to Van Berckal and l'Enfant

packet, six O'Clock, all well on board.

Anything but drily matter-of-fact like his meticulous ledger entries memorializing her visit—except those posted under the subhead "For You"—was the letter Hamilton wrote Angelica that crossed hers of the same date sent *"effligé"* from her packet. His yearning is a match for hers. After seeing her up the gangplank and going home for a little while, he has walked back down to the Battery with Baron von Steuben and his son Philip to wave to her ship as it sails past the tip of the island and toward the Narrows out of sight, and wept:

New York, November 8, 1789

My dear Sister

After taking leave of you on board of the Packet, I hastened home to sooth and console your sister. I found her in bitter distress; though much recovered from the agony, in which she had been. After composing her by a flattering picture of your prospects for the voyage, and a *strong infusion* of hope, that she had not taken a last farewell of you; The Baron little Philip and myself, with her consent, walked down to the Battery; where with aching hearts and anxious eyes we saw your vessel, in full sail, swiftly bearing our loved friend from our embraces. Imagine what we felt. We gazed, we sighed, we *wept;* and casting "many a lingering longing look behind" returned home to give scope to our sorrows, and mingle without restraint our tears and our regrets. . . .

His sentences try to be as full of Betsy as Angelica's are; he and Betsy are dutifully serving out a life term of fruitful wedlock to each other. But

Betsey and myself make you the last theme of our conversation at night and the first in the morning. We talk of you; we praise you and we pray for you. We dwell with peculiar interest on the little incidents that preceded your departure. Precious and never to be forgotten scenes!

He is open in courtship, but checks his ardor:

> But let me check, My dear Sister, these effusions of regretful friendship. Why should I alloy the Happiness that courts you in the bosom of your family by images that must wound your sensibility? It shall not be. However difficult, or little natural it is to me to suppress what the fulness of my heart would utter, the sacrifice shall be made to your ease and satisfaction.

Gentlemanly understatement can hardly speak more eloquent volumes of mixed but deep emotion:

> I shall not fail to execute my commission you gave me nor neglect any of your charges . . . already have I addressed the consolation, I mentioned to you, to your Father. I have no doubt the arguments I have used with him will go far towards reconciling his mind to the unexpected step you took. I hope the inclosed letters may not be such as to give you pain. They arrived the day after you set sail.

What was the "unexpected step you took" that had so displeased her father and her mother? Why was Betsy in such distress? Hamilton's "For You" entry shows he paid for her separate lodgings the last month of her stay. Neither in his busy household nor with the Schuylers' nor at Mrs. Cuyler's were they likely to have been able to spend an hour alone together.

In separate lodgings with the "last" unnamed landlady during the last weeks of her lone visit, it may be comforting to some, perhaps shocking to others, to suppose that these two indiscreet, emotion-wracked souls lived with each other through at least a few precious hours and nights. Or perhaps his unreimbursed payment to her music master means no more than that in her separate lodgings once in a while she played her pianoforte for him and joined her voice with his singing some old wartime tunes like "The Drum" and "A Successful Campaign."

Angelica's father and mother would, no doubt, begrudge her these absent hours—hence their reproofs. Perhaps they would soften them a little in their letters he now was forwarding to her.

With his letter to Angelica, Hamilton encloses another to her from his wife. Few of Betsy's letters have survived; none of hers to her husband. But hers to Angelica joins her to both of them in a triangle of yearning hearts. All three are embraced by Betsy's closing benediction:

Enclosure
Elizabeth Hamilton to Angelica Church

New York, November 8, 1789

> My Very Dear Beloved Angelica—I have seated myself to write to you, but my heart is so saddened by your Absence that it can scarcely dictate, my Eyes so filled with tears I shall not be able to write you much but *Remember Remember,* my dear sister of the Assurances of your returning to us, and do all you can to make your Absence short. Tell Mr. Church for me of the happiness he will give me, in bringing you to me, not to me alone but to fond parents sisters friends and to my Hamilton who has for you all the Affection of a fond own Brother. I can no more
>
> Adieu Adieu.
>
> E.H.
>
> *heaven protect you.*

To their three yearning hearts may be subjoined those of young Philip Hamilton and Baron von Steuben, the gruff old lord of the Cincinnati, standing there on the Battery beside Hamilton gazing out to sea as the sails of her packet slide below the horizon, and weeping with him. It is a kind of fugue in five parts for their warm and anxious hearts—Angelica's, Alexander's, Betsy's, von Steuben's, and Philip's—hauntingly played behind the crash and blare of the band celebrating Hamilton's arrival at the most exalted station of his rise.

Heaven protect them all!

3

The Importance of
Strict College Entrance
Requirements

Don't listen to him, gentlemen; he is crazy! he is crazy!

> —President Myles Cooper of King's College as Hamilton harangues
> an angry mob storming the college entrance gates the night of May
> 10, 1775

In Christiansted today some of the old red-tile roofed plaster and stucco buildings washed white or tinted pale pastel were new when Alexander Hamilton was a clerk at the counting-house of Beckman and Cruger on Konigsstrade. Colonnaded sidewalks and interior arcades shade the midday visitor from the tropic sun and trap some of the cool early morning air. The thick stone walls still work as an eighteenth-century form of air conditioning. A Cruzan woman, her black hair bound up in a colorful kerchief, may occasionally still be seen beside a donkey cart piled high with avocados ambling past Hamilton's statue on the quay where his mother Rachel was imprisoned for whoring. The scene is not greatly changed from the way it looked from 1765 to 1773 when Hamilton was growing up there from eight to sixteen.

After Rachel's death Hamilton's older brother James became apprenticed to the carpenter Thomas McNobeny. Alexander stayed on as a full-time clerk with Beckman and Cruger. The firm carried on export of island products, especially raw sugar, and importation of plantation supplies.

Nicholas Cruger, born in New York in 1743, became Hamilton's first employer after his late mother, and would remain Hamilton's friend, patron, and sometime law client for the rest of his life. Cruger gave Hamilton his invaluable early apprenticeship, made it financially possible for him to go to the continent to seek his fortune, and steered him toward New York.

On October 16, 1771, Cruger left St. Croix for New York "By reason of a very ill state of health," leaving the 14-year-old Hamilton in full charge of the business. Hamilton dealt with ship captains, planters and merchants, customers, and suppliers and kept Cruger informed of all developments. He consulted Cruger's attorneys. Like a good proxy, he took care to save his principal unnecessary trouble and worry, although Hamilton himself just then was suffering from another spell of sickness, perhaps contracted from his employer, more likely brought on by the tension of his new responsibilities. He reported to Cruger that he had "sold about 30 bbls flour more & Collected a little more money from different people."

A month later, on November 12, 1771, he was critical. He had checked and found that

> Your Philadelphia flour is . . . of a most swarthy complexion—& withal very untractable; the Bakers complain that they cannot by any means get it to rise. . . . I have observ'd a kind of worm . . . about the surface—which is an indication of age—it could not have been very new when shipped.

It was not a total loss, however; a practical solution could be found; the market was overstocked; so he was considering accepting eight pieces of eight from any buyer of good credit who would take as many as 40 or 50 barrels. Otherwise, he might be obliged "in the end to sell it at a much greater disadvantage."

Not satisfied to rest the business decision on this sound general proposition, he proved the wisdom of the decision arithmetically; he advised Cruger that New York flour of the same weight "is gladly sold by everybody at [eight pieces of eight] at retail, and a great part of your Philadelphia weighs but little more, so that 8½ by the quantity is more than a proportionate price for the difference of weight."

Two weeks later, on November 27, Philadelphia flour remained a serious problem, because "Mr. Neall's brig is daily expected with a quantity of superfine . . . so that I must endeavor at all events to get your flour off soon, or it will be unsaleable. Every day brings in fresh complaints against it."

But just when things looked blackest, the market turned. By January 10, 1772, Neall's superfine was sold out, so Hamilton was raising the price of the wormy Philadelphia flour to the same bakers who had been complaining of it so bitterly. He added to Cruger, "Believe me, Sir, I dun as hard as is proper." He had his employer's business well in hand and was letting him know it.

Getting rid of flour was a continuing problem. Cruger's business ethics did not rule out tax evasion. A Cruger letter of May 25, 1772, in Hamilton's hand, explains one kind of deception for which a future revenue collector should be alert:

> Rye flour will sell for ps 7 a barrel here readily, but the duty is 25 ct. However, we enter it as cornmeal and give the weighter a fee, which hint you must give the Capt, if you send any down, and tell him to see me before he enters. . . .

Hamilton dispatched Captain William Newton to Tileman Cruger at Curaçao, warning him against the dangers of the Spanish revenue patrols. Privately, to Tileman, the 15-year-old Hamilton expresses disappointment that Captain Newton is not more sophisticated at the dangerous game of smuggling: "You cannot be too particular in your instructions to him. I think he lacks experience in such voyages."

No one who received an education in such a school as Cruger's Christiansted counting-house could afterward slide into financial corruption unwittingly, or truthfully plead lack of *scienter,* or guilty knowledge, if he did.

The flags of Spain, England, Holland, France, and the Knights of Malta had already flown over St. Croix before Denmark first ran up her ensign in 1733. It was a good place to study firsthand the economic and political lessons of what it meant to be a colony. The island provided a sharp intensity of focus impossible to find in the backward, spacious, sprawling, diffused colonies on the continent to the northward.

St. Croix rivalled Barbados as the leading sugar-producing island in the West Indies. Of the population of about 24,000, only 2,000 or so were white; almost 11 out of every 12 were black or mulatto slaves. Three hundred eighty-one plantation estates covered almost all of the island's 50,000 arable acres with cane fields.

On the great plantations, the aristocratic white planter minority lived amid imported mahogany furniture, silver sconces, Belgian laces, and Chinese damasks, in splendid luxury and nervous dread of slave revolts, shipwrecks, pirates, and financial panics. Whites like Rachel's sons existed on the fringes of the social order, close to the slaves but not of them, shamefacedly unequal with the ruling class of plantation-owning fellow whites.

Having lived with slaves in their quarters, never part of the life of luxurious ease that slavery made possible for the white aristocracy, Hamilton eventually became an active foe of slavery. But in his years with Cruger he gained experience with slavery as business. In 1771, "Three Hundred Prime Slaves" were advertised for sale at Cruger's yard. A letter from Nicholas Cruger to John H. Cruger of March 19, 1772, partly in Hamilton's hand, asks for "Two or three poor boys" and instructs him, charitably, to "Have them bound in the most reasonable manner you can. I fancy you cant fail of getting them by applying at the Poor-House. I want them to put on plantations."

There was not much hope for the bound boys from the poorhouse ever to get off the plantations, but at times Hamilton was bound to think that there was not much better hope for his rising above the groveling condition of one of the rich slavetrader's clerks. Unlike the vast continent to the north, there were no open frontiers in this mature colonial economy, no place to which a man could move on to make a fresh start. But the price of sea passage to the continent to make his way in the world called for more capital than anyone who was not a plantation owner could scrape together in a year.

Hamilton's son John Church Hamilton noted that Cruger had left Hamilton in charge of the business while away in New York because of his rapid advancement in Cruger's confidence and "his aptitude in conforming himself to his situation." Hamilton's son added that "Foreign as such an avocation was to his inclinations, he nevertheless gave to it all his habitual assiduity, and soon mastered its details; but the inward promptings of his mind looked far beyond it." John Church recalled that Hamilton felt that this "avocation" was of great and lasting benefit to him because it taught him "method" and "facility." In after years he often "adverted to it as the most useful part of his education."

To his son Hamilton also mentioned having "been taught to repeat the Decalogue in Hebrew, at the school of a Jewess, when so small that he was placed standing by her side on a table." This must have been on Nevis. His son adds that "the circle of his early studies was very limited, probably embracing little more than the rudiments of the English and French languages, the latter of which he subsequently wrote and spoke with the ease of a native." His knowledge of mathematics seems largely self-taught, and although his proficiency in chemistry was small, according to his son, "he often urged it as a pursuit well adapted to excite curiosity and create new combinations of thought."

John Church Hamilton insisted that "with a strong propensity to literature, he early became a lover of books." His education was deficient in the classics, said his son, but "The time which other youth employ in classical learning was by him devoted to miscellaneous reading, happily directed by the advice of Dr. Knox, a respectable Presbyterian divine."

Thirty years older than Hamilton, born in the north of Ireland of Scottish blood, learned in the classics and with a "remarkably prepossessing . . . personal appearance and manners," Dr. Hugh Knox had spent a few years teaching school and preaching in Pennsylvania and Delaware, under the patronage of the Reverend John Rodgers. He then spent a decade on the Dutch island of Saba, a 2,851-foot volcanic cone only five miles square, 16 miles northwest of St. Kitts. Knox visited St. Croix in 1771 and began preaching there regularly in 1772 as a minister of the newly established Presbyterian church. "Delighted with the unfolding" of Hamilton's mind, John Church Hamilton wrote, Hugh Knox "took a deep interest in his welfare."

Knox supplied young Alexander with books; directed his miscellaneous reading; contributed to his lifelong piety and religious feeling, his disapproval of slavery, and probably, being a Scot and a Presbyterian, to his rebellious feelings toward England. Hamilton would have received no such nudge in the direction of colonial freedom from the rector of Rachel's St. Croix Church, St. John's Anglican.

Beyond his visits with Dr. Knox, it is not known where or whether Hamilton went to school before coming to the continent in his sixteenth year. He had a lifelong fondness for Vergil's *Eclogues*, and among his other favorite authors were Pope and Plutarch. Whatever his formal schooling, he must have supplemented it by much wide-ranging miscellaneous reading of his own.

Having risen from the condition of a schoolteacher to pastorship of the large new Presbyterian church in Christiansted, Hugh Knox would open Hamilton's eyes in directions beyond the narrowly religious, particularly to the uses of journalism.

In *The Royal Danish American Gazette* of April 10, 1771, appeared a piece entitled "Rules for Statesmen." It was ostensibly from a correspondent in London, but it contained the same thoughts from the same sources that Cruger's clerk would later put to work yoking the United States of America together into a union. From "some years gleaning from Machiavelli, Puffendorff, etc.," he wrote, he would endeavor to advise "by what means a Premier may act most to the honor of his Prince, and the enlargement of his own power." He praised the British system of setting over all the departments "a Prime Minister like a Commander-in-Chief; . . . I think this wise regulation a wholesome restraint on the people, whole [whose] turbulence, at times, . . . require[s] a Dictator. . . ." A wish for a "dictator," as for "a war," was an abrasive but honest way to express an important conviction: the need for unified leadership in a crisis.

At the end of August 1772, one of the most devastating hurricanes in the history of the West Indies struck the island at dusk without warning. The following Sunday the Reverend Hugh Knox uncorked a ripsnorting sermon to a meeting of survivors that drew powerful lessons from the disaster. A week later, in Knox's most uplifting style, Hamilton addressed some powerful preachments to his ne'er-do-well father. Hamilton had not seen his father since he had drifted back to St. Kitts six years earlier.

> Honoured Sir,
>   I take up my pen just to give you an imperfect account of one of the most dreadful hurricanes that memory or any records whatever can trace, which happened here on the 31st ultimo at night.

There is a vivid description of the hurricane, then he hits his father with the moral:

> Where now, O! vile worm, is all thy boasted fortitude and resolution? What is become of thine arrogance and self-sufficiency? Why dost thou tremble and stand aghast? How humble, how helpless, how contemptible you now appear.

Hamilton was not making a belated effort to reform his father; the strict conventions of the literary form he had adopted called for an absent addressee. None of such nonsense would much trouble his father.

If James Hamilton had read further after such a reproof (which was unlikely), he would find that the accusation was directed upon the author of the letter, his son, not the addressee: It is rhetorical self-accusation in sermon form:

> Hark—ruin and confusion on every side. 'Tis thy turn next; but one short moment, even now, O Lord help, Jesus be merciful!
> Thus did I reflect, and thus at every gust of the wind did I conclude, till it pleased the Almighty to allay it. . . .

With the overtones of Dr. Knox's sermon out of the way, there followed a remarkable emotional intensity and feeling for social injustice in the contrast Hamilton drew between the rich at their ease, who had escaped harm, and the sufferings of the poor, who had lost everything. Alexander's advice to the rich was to "succour the miserable and lay up a treasure in Heaven." He admonished the white masters of the island who "revel in affluence" to "see the afflictions of humanity, and bestow your superfluity to ease them."

He was apologetic that such preaching might sound a little silly to his easygoing father, or any father: "I am afraid, Sir, you will think this description more the effort of imagination than a true picture of realities. But I can affirm with the greatest truth, that there is not a single circumstance touched upon, which I have not absolutely been an eyewitness to."

Full of admiration for religious sentiments that coincided so remarkably with those of his own post-hurricane sermon, Hugh Knox arranged to have Hamilton's letter printed, its authorship secret, a month later in *The Royal Danish American Gazette*. But the "hurricane letter" was soon traced to Hamilton. It has been said that the hurricane blew Hamilton into history, as if by divine intervention. The human assist from the Reverend Hugh Knox was not inconsiderable.

A dozen years later from St. Croix, on July 28, 1784, Dr. Knox would write Hamilton in New York, "I have always had a just & secret pride in having Advised you to go to America, & in having recommended you to Some of my old friends there," among them the Reverand John Rodgers. He had also spoken to his friends on St. Croix about young Alexander and asked them to aid him with contributions of money he would need for his education in America. A period of preparation and three years of college would cost at least £ 400.

Hamilton's cousin, Ann Lytton Venton, would help a little with remittances, hardwon advances from her late father's estate. Hamilton's other benefactors were Nicholas Cruger, who was grateful for Alexander's services and knew New York, and his partner after Beckman, Cornelius Kortright, who had observed Alexander's efficient management of the business in Cruger's absence. The firm consigned some West Indies produce to New York, "to be sold and appropriated to the support of Hamilton." Thomas Stevens, father of Alexander's young friend Neddy, may also have helped.

Hugh Knox surely, and perhaps some of these others, saw Hamilton off, possibly from the wharf by the fort in Christiansted or more likely from the deeper harbor at Frederiksted, where he set sail for the continent in the winter of 1772–1773. In his letter of a dozen years later, Hugh Knox recalled his affectionate pleasure at having recommended to friends that they help the young prodigy on his way:

> You have not only *Answered,* but even far *Exceeded,* our most Sanguine hopes & Expectations. I am glad to find that your popularity increases, & that your fine talents are coming into play, in a way that Contributes so much to your own honour & Emolument, & to the Good of the public.

A three-week winter voyage up the North Atlantic on a shallow draft vessel was not an easy pleasure cruise. Hamilton later recalled that as the vessel approached the continent, a fierce fire broke out on board and put all hands and passengers in mortal peril. All this, and his frail constitution, must have made him an unusually thankful young man of almost 16 as he walked down the gangplank on to the wharf and the firm soil of North America that late winter in 1773. Authorities dispute whether Hamilton landed first in New York or Boston, but the case for New York as his first landfall is the more convincing.

Early in 1773, when Hamilton arrived, New York's population was between 15,000 and 20,000 people, but this was enough to make it, with Boston and Philadelphia, one of the three most populous cities of the continent. It was already well known throughout a world whose cities were still small—even in England there were only a few that were larger.

Part of Hamilton's expenses had been provided by proceeds of sale of West Indian produce consigned by Nicholas Cruger to Lawrence Kortright in New York, so it is likely that Hamilton's first call was at the firm's New York store. There Hugh Mulligan, Kortright's partner, would turn Alexander over to his bachelor younger brother, Hercules Mulligan, who had a haberdashery, tailor shop, and home in Water Street "next door to Philip Rhinelander's china store, between Burling's Slip and the Fly Market." Alexander would lodge there before moving over to Elizabethtown, New Jersey, for the winter.

Hamilton had a letter of introduction from the Reverend Hugh Knox to the Reverend John Rodgers, now pastor of the Wall Street Presbyterian Church. Other letters of Knox's brought Hamilton to the Reverend John Mason, minister of the Cedar Street Church, and to Elias Boudinot and William Livingston of Elizabethtown. Hamilton's name and abilities would already be well known to Kortright through correspondence for the firm; so when he presented his letter to the head of the firm at his counting house, it would be a reunion with an old friend from the world of commerce and trade. By contrast, his first encounters with the two great divines would seem more like audiences with avenging angels out of the Old Testament.

Hamilton met his old St. Croix friend Ned Stevens and checked on current entrance requirements at King's College. His knowledge of geography, history, natural and moral philosophy, and the Decalogue in Hebrew were important qualifications for admission to King's, but he was deficient in the classical languages, Latin and Greek, and mathematics beyond the quick arithmetic of commerce and the double-entry bookkeeping he had picked up at Cruger's countinghouse. King's required more book learning for admission.

A week or so after arriving in New York, Hamilton ferried across the Hudson to New Jersey and rode through the forest to the village of Elizabethtown, now Elizabeth, to present his last two letters of introduction from Hugh Knox to two remarkably well-selected addressees: William Livingston and Elias Boudinot. During the winter and spring Alexander would live mostly in the household of William Livingston while attending Francis Barber's grammar school. As he solemnly told his son John Church Hamilton, he "was accustomed to labour until midnight" over the work he brought home. It must have mortified the son that his father did not slack off when summer came on: "In summer, it was his habit to retire at dawn to the quiet of a neighboring cemetery, where he was often seen preparing his lessons for the day." The Academy was located on the grounds of the Presbyterian church near the upper end of Burial Yard Lot. Omission of this key fact gave the tale more cautionary inspirational force.

William Livingston, his wife and their four daughters, furnished Hamilton with a more cheerful place than the cemetery to live and study and probably also helped his neighbor Elias Boudinot arrange a scholarship for Hamilton at the Academy as one of "a Number of Free Scholars in this Town." Like so many others of Hamilton's early acquaintances, both Livingston and Boudinot remained firm patrons, mentors, and followers throughout the rest of his life. Hamilton's gift for forming deep lifelong friendships with remarkable men of all ages is as striking, if less often noticed, than his gift for making unforgiving enemies.

When Alexander was racing through the course in 1773, Francis Barber's Academy was the best in the area, offering Latin and Greek, English literature and composition, elocution, mathematics, and geography. It prepared boys for any college, but especially Princeton, whose entrance requirements included the ability to translate Vergil and Cicero, to write Latin prose, and to sight-read the gospels in Greek. The first-year curriculum included Horace, Cicero, Greek testaments, Lucian, and Xenophon.

Francis Barber, born at Princeton, New Jersey, in 1750, the eldest of four children of an upwardly mobile Irish immigrant, holder of A.B. and A.M. degrees from Princeton, was another of Hamilton's early mentors who became a fast friend for his short life. If a classical curriculum more systematic than Hugh Knox's is required to qualify Barber for the honor, then he was Hamilton's first teacher.

Tuition was five pounds sterling a year, plus one pound, ten shillings for "wood and cost of house cleaning" and another pound for "Entrance light money." Most of this came through remittances from sales of his St. Croix patrons' sugar and rum through Kortright & Company. When Barber had taught in a Latin school at Hackensack, all "those of his Pupils who have been sent to the Colleges, were found well fitted for Reception."

Hamilton's son described Barber as "a man of strong sense, considerable attainments, and respectable connections." He broke up his school at the commencement of the revolution, entered the army, soon rose to the rank of colonel, "and in the course of the contest was often and much distinguished." Near the army's last headquarters at New-burgh, just as the final peace was about to be proclaimed, Barber was killed by a falling tree.

Room and board were provided Hamilton through the hospitality of the Livingstons and the Boudinots, who also supplied intangible advantages whose value was beyond any tuition fee. William Livingston and Elias Boudinot were men of parts, position, and Presbyterian patrimony that linked them to Dr. Knox and his young protégé. Both men were deliberate by training and habit and conservative by economic interest, but their Presbyterian heritage left them more open to the emotional appeal of independence than their Anglican friends.

William Livingston, a younger son of Philip Livingston, the second lord of Livingston Manor, New York, and his wife, Catherine Van Brugh, was born to the best of Scottish and Dutch patrician and patroon traditions. After graduating from Yale at the head of his class in 1741, he read law with James Alexander and married Susannah French of Albany, whose father's landholdings in New Jersey brought with them enough complications to keep his New Jersey law practice a busy one. A growing Wall Street law practice across the river in New York did not prevent him from indulging a literary bent by publishing verse and contributing regular columns to New York newspapers, advocating civil liberties, the separation of church and state, and the value of representative government.

Hamilton was as indebted to Elias Boudinot as host and patron as he was to Livingston. Like Hamilton's mother, Boudinot's father was of French extraction; the parents of both men had lived in the West Indies, and Boudinot's father had been married in Antigua. Elias and his brother, Elisha Boudinot, were "two brothers, lawyers, elegant men, tall, handsome and every way prepossessing," who "used to attend the court . . . and whenever they spoke, crowds were attracted to hear them. . . ."

Hamilton would absorb from William Livingston polemic skill, a straightforward, driving writing style, his habit of publication, and his zeal for civil liberties. Later on, Livingston would support Hamilton in condemning the weakness of the Confederation, urging adoption of the Constitution, and firmly backing Hamilton's economic program.

Boudinot would later work with Hamilton bargaining with the British over prisoner exchanges and in opposing the mutinous threat of unpaid soldiers against Congress. On all critical votes on Hamilton's most important measures in Congress, Boudinot and Livingston would unfailingly come forward to support him.

It is not as remarkable as it might seem that Livingston, 34 years older than Hamilton, and Boudinot, 15 years older, would follow as their political leader a man so much their junior. Hamilton's political views and style reflected their own because theirs were the patterns on which his were now being significantly modeled.

Susannah Livingston was as strong a Presbyterian patriot and foe of kingly rule as her husband, William, and their brilliant son Brockholst was Hamilton's schoolmate at Elizabethtown and King's. Their daughter Sarah, beautiful, sweet, and clever, was perhaps already pensively in love with young John Jay, her future husband, but Sarah's handsome and dashing sisters, Kitty, Susan, and Judith, were still heart-whole and free, and eagerly welcomed the handsome, delicate-looking orphan from the exotic tropical islands, with his fair Scottish complexion, charming Gallic manners, gay good humor, and no false humility.

Five years later, from the army's winter headquarters at Morristown, Hamilton would write to Kitty Livingston in the tone of an old and dear intimate, "I challenge you to meet me in whatever path you dare . . . in the flowery walks and roseate bowers of Cupid. You know, I am renowned for gallantry, and shall always be able to entertain you with a choice collection of the prettiest things imaginable." As if remembering their evenings together at Liberty Hall, he added, "I fancy my knowledge of you affords me a tolerably just idea of your taste." He admits that he may be mistaken—a rare admission, made only to compel belief in the rest of what he has to say. He asks what she really thinks, because if she does not tell him herself, it will not be easy for him to guess! If she will tell him her thoughts and whether she is "of a romantic, or discreet temper, as to love affairs," he will regulate his conduct toward her by it. "If you would choose to be a goddess, and to be worshipped as such," he adds, "you shall be one of the graces, or Diana, or Venus."

Kitty was a dashing 22-year-old beauty, six years older than Hamilton, and that winter she was being fervently wooed by Gouverneur Morris, but Hamilton was undaunted. If she would come down off her goddess's pedestal, he vowed, she would become "something surpassing them all." Then he would offer poems "at your Goddesship's shrine."

But if, he goes on, "conformable to your usual discernment, you are content with being a mere mortal, and require no other incense than is justly due to you, I will talk to you like one [in] his sober senses.''

He rounds off his letter to her with a slap and a tickle of self-confident laughter. ''. . . and, though it may be straining the point a little, I will even stipulate to pay you all the rational tribute applicable to a fine girl.''

History does not record whether Kitty and Alexander became lovers that winter in Elizabethtown, but it is unlikely that Kitty was the very first ''to reveal to him the fascination of her sex,'' as the novelist Gertrude Atherton put it. A handsome teen-ager growing up in the tropics, where many took him to be older than his years, would not spend every waking hour ambitiously girding for futurity and war.

When Kitty's sister Sarah married John Jay at Liberty Hall in the spring of 1774, Hamilton would be on hand. The groom's name would be allied with Hamilton's in like causes the rest of their lives. Other memorable men and women Hamilton would have met at the Livingstons or Boudinots with whom he would always be closely identified were Livingston's brother-in-law William Alexander and his wife, Catherine, also known as Kitty and as Lady Kitty. He was called Lord Stirling because of a dubious claim to a Scottish title, and he was to be Hamilton's major general in the Revolution. There was William Duer, soon to marry Lord and Lady Stirling's daughter Catherine, who was still another Lady Kitty. Duer would become Hamilton's first assistant in the Treasury. Hamilton's friendship with him would be one of the two or three most disastrous of his life.

At Elizabethtown he would also have met Jonathan Dayton, afterward Speaker of the House of Representatives; James Duane, later mayor of New York; other members of the Livingston, Morris, Schuyler, Ogden, Clinton, and Stockton families; and Dr. John Witherspoon, the president of the College of New Jersey at Princeton to which all the Presbyterian elders he met as well as his headmaster Francis Barber urged Hamilton to go instead of King's.

Hamilton's New York City friend Hercules Mulligan urged him to come back to King's College, but Hamilton insisted on applying first to Presbyterian Princeton, which was less royalist and ''more republican.'' The former young man of the world now in prep school did not think he needed as much college time as his less worldly fellow students might. When he went to see President Witherspoon in his study, a small room somber with mahogany furniture in the southwest corner of the house that is now the residence of the dean of the college, Hercules Mulligan went with him, and recalled:

> . . . I introduced Mr. Hamilton to Dr. Witherspoon and proposed to him to Examine the young gentleman which the Doctor did to his entire satisfaction. Mr. Hamilton then stated that he wished to enter either of the classes to which his attainments would entitle him but with the understanding that he should be promoted to advance from Class to Class with as much rapidity as his exertions would enable him to do. Dr. Witherspoon listened with great attention to so unusual a proposition from so young a person and replied that . . . he would submit the request to the trustees.

There was a crushing disappointment. As Mulligan relates, ''In about a fortnight after a letter was received from the President stating that the request could not be complied with because it was contrary to the usage of the College.'' President Witherspoon had been impressed, but he had not been able to prevail on the trustees to waive the usual standards. His letter went beyond the merely perfunctory. ''He was convinced that the young gentleman would do honor to any seminary at which he should be educated.''

Hamilton's second choice, King's College, accepted him for the spring of 1774 in the sophomore class, granting the privileges of flexible choice of courses and optional acceleration that Princeton had denied him.

By contrast to Princeton, established by Presbyterian dissenters who tended to lean toward the cause of independence, King's College was fostered by Anglicans firmly attached to the British Crown. The president, Myles Cooper, born in the Church of England, bred at King's College, Oxford, had become a deacon and priest in his early twenties. In accordance with King's charter, he was a member of, and "in communion with the Church of England, as by law established." Morning and evening, Cooper or his deputy intoned liturgical prayers, and the students chanted responses.

Hamilton matriculated at this New York bastion of bishops and the Book of Common Prayer late in the fall of 1773 but did not lose his Presbyterian piety there at once. His roommate, Robert Troup, marveled somewhat that Alexander "was attentive to public worship, and in the habit of praying upon his knees both night and morning." He did not confine his prayers to public observances, Troup added: "He had read many of the polemical writers on religious subjects, and he was a zealous believer in the fundamental doctrines of Christianity."

The communicative power of Hamilton's religious zeal even helped make a believer of his roommate. "I confess," Troup wrote, "that the arguments with which he was accustomed to justify his belief, have tended in no small degree to confirm my own faith in revealed religion."

The examples of Edward Stevens and Reverend Hugh Knox helped inspire Hamilton to early emulation and he "originally destined himself to the Science of Physic" and "was regular in attending the anatomical lectures, then delivered in the college by Dr. Clossey." Hamilton also studied as the private pupil of Robert Harpur, a professor of mathematics and natural philosophy, beginning in September 1774, paying four pounds, four shillings per quarter. The subject matter of the course included commercial applications in discount, partners' shares, "simple interests," and the exchange of currencies but probably did not carry into more complicated realms of mathematics like astronomical calculations, of which Harpur was a master.

Hamilton made good use of the college library. There is no complete book list, but pamphlets he published in 1774 and 1775 while at King's flash a knowledge of Grotius, Pufendorf, Locke, Montesquieu, Berlamaqui, Hobbes, Blackstone, Postlethwayt, Hume, the *lex mercatoria,* records of recent debates and acts of the British Parliament, colonial charters, acts of the General Assembly of New York, Samuel Johnson's dictionary, and an account of the wars of Charles XII and Peter the Great. Some of Hamilton's sources may also have been books and journals that he borrowed from the library of another remarkable man who would be an early patron, mentor, and lifelong friend, Alexander McDougall.

Robert Troup recalled that Hamilton, Edward Stevens, Samuel and Delancey Nicoll, Nicholas Fish, and himself were "particular associates . . . in college." They formed a club that met weekly for mutual self-improvement in writing and debating, "until we were separated by the Revolution." He remembered Hamilton's performances at the club as "displays of richness, of genius, and energy of mind." All his life Hamilton would read swiftly, remember much, learn quickly and profoundly, and speedily bring quick study to bear on a point that would lead to action. Other young men of his circle were still uncertain of themselves; he would leap at a bound from their quiet circle to the court of public opinion. Troup recalled one occasion when John Holt, who then published a Whig paper, *The New York Journal,* had "by his zeal in the American cause, drawn upon himself the invectives of all the ministerial writers,'' that is, loyalists like President Cooper. Hamilton burlesqued the king's men "in doggerel rhyme, with great wit and humour.'' As one example of his many experiments with different literary forms, Hamilton presented Troup with "a manuscript of fugitive poetry.'' To Troup this was such "strong evidence of the elasticity of his genius'' that Troup preserved it until it had been "lost with my books and papers during the war.''

Opposed political loyalties were drawing men to opposite poles of the revolutionary split that was widening, but these did not keep Hamilton from becoming a friend of President Myles Cooper. Though 20 years older, Cooper shared with Hamilton good looks, a gift for expression in many literary modes, and a sense of elegance.

Cooper was a different man from his predecessor as president of King's, Dr. Samuel Johnson, at first a Congregationalist, who had become "dubious of the lawfulness of [his] ordination,'' and was posted back to England for priest's orders. The somber Johnson confined his pen to prose, while Cooper the year he was ordained published *Poems on Several Occasions*, some of it polite love verse to Sylvia, Cynthia, and Delia, but some scornful and carnal. Alumni more gruff than Hamilton granted that Cooper's "moral character was without any serious reproach,'' but grumbled that "grave men were occasionally offended by the . . . conviviality of his social habits.''

Cooper was a member of a circle of prominent New York Tories that included the Reverend T.B. Chandler, Isaac Wilkins, and Samuel Seabury. When the time came for Hamilton to write such papers as *A Full Vindication of the Measures of Congress* and *The Farmer Refuted*, in opposition to Tory pamphleteers, he would have already heard their arguments and marshaled his replies over sherry and port and Madeira at President Cooper's table. He would then retest them by writing them out and reading them to the more intimate circle of his revolutionary student friends at the gatherings of their club.

Deep differences of political principle in no way affected Hamilton's personal friendship for President Cooper. In May of 1775 the rising revolutionary ferment in the outside world burst in upon the tranquil disputations of scholars beneath the sycamores and elms of King's. A mob tried to seize President Cooper and kill him. Hamilton and Troup saved their president's life by arranging his rescue.

A widely published letter had brought news of the electrifying events of April at Lexington and Concord, saying "the crimson fountain was opened, and God only knew when it would close.'' Another, datelined Philadelphia, April 25, 1775, addressed to Dr. Myles Cooper and four other "obnoxious gentlemen of New York,'' blamed the strong attachment of the city to the king on them. It threatened: "Fly for your lives, or anticipate your doom by becoming your own executioners,'' and was signed "Three Millions.''

On the night of May 10, 1775, a surly mob gathered to make good "Three Millions'' threat and surged toward the King's College gates. Shouts rose, calling for tarring and feathering Dr. Cooper and riding him out of town on a rail or killing him.

The mob 400 strong, excited by the flickering glare of crackling pine knot torches, in a murderous temper to wreak violence, swirled against the college gates and tried to smash them down. If such a bloody-minded mob caught Dr. Cooper, Troup and Hamilton feared that it might kill him by accident in the uproar, if not by design. Dr. Cooper feared the same. Hamilton jumped up on one of the stoops and began to harangue the mob. Violence to Cooper would bring disgrace to the cause of liberty, of which they claimed themselves to be champions, he shouted.

President Cooper, in his nightshirt, peered down from an upper window of the college on the terrifying scene: the mob, with swirling torches blazing, Hamilton on the stoop facing them down, with his stout roommate Robert Troup there by his side.

But as Cooper's frightened eyes searched the lurid night scene, he at first misunderstood what Hamilton and Troup were trying to do, remembering the arguments he and his Tory circle had had with Hamilton and Troup over port and cigars. He thought Hamilton was inciting the mob to kill him.

Dr. Cooper cried out, "Don't listen to him, gentlemen; he is crazy! he is crazy!" But they kept on listening to Hamilton anyway—long enough at least for Cooper to start putting on his clothes.

Hamilton ran into the college building, leaving Troup alone on the stoop to carry on the diversionary harangue as the mob rattled the "groaning gates" to break into the college grounds. Hamilton breathlessly reassured Cooper that he and Troup had been trying to distract the crowd from killing him, then hustled Cooper out by the back way just as the mob broke through the front gates. The leaders rushed up the stairs to force the door into his rooms while Troup continued to try to divert the crowd. Hamilton led Dr. Cooper, still only partly dressed, over the college fence and down to the bank of the Hudson. Cooper's account described how he, with "my faithful pupil by my side," had worked his way northward along the Hudson under cover of darkness until by morning they reached "The good Palemon's cot," which was apparently the house of Cooper's friend Peter Stuyvesant. The next night, Dr. Cooper boarded the British ship *Kingfisher* under command of Captain James Montague, which sailed for Bristol on May 25.

King's strict entrance requirements had sent Hamilton to Elizabethtown for a year of Presbyterian preparatory schooling with Francis Barber, the Boudinots and the Livingstons. Presbyterian Princeton's refusal to let him take a speeded-up course had thrust him back on King's.

Princeton early caught and sustained the revolutionary spirit but there, 50 miles from the metropolis, Hamilton would have missed the stirring public events in New York City, in which, as a student at King's, he would now play a spectacular part. He would have made valuable friends at Princeton, but not of the men who became his faithful corps of allies throughout his later life. After Princeton he might have settled down as a successful New Jersey lawyer, perhaps commuting to New York City like his Elizabethtown friends Livingston and Boudinot, returning home at night to a squire's slippered ease. Instead, New York City became his home for life. Another quarter-century of intense, sometimes feverish activity centered on New York City would pass before he could finally settle at The Grange as a would-be squire to imitate the Livingstons of Liberty Hall and the Boudinots of Boxwood Hall. But by then The Grange was not a visible monument to his success; it was, among other things, a sublimation of his disappointment that the presidency would forever be beyond reach of his efforts, no matter how intense and feverish they might be.

His first recorded public speaking engagement before the angry mob in the blazing torchlight, with Robert Troup at his side, kept it from breaking down the college's entrance barriers till no irreversible damage could be done to President Cooper, or to the revolutionary cause. Hamilton agreed with the revolutionary political goals of the mob whose violence he resisted, and opposed the politics of Cooper and the college he sought to protect. Not long afterward, King's quietly changed its name to Columbia and aligned its political stance to reflect more closely the politics of student revolutionaries like Troup and Hamilton.

All of which shows the vital importance of strict college entrance requirements.

4

To Free the Slaves
Held Thrall by
the ASIA'S Guns

All men have one common original . . . one common right. No reason can be assigned why one man should exercise any power or preeminence over his fellow creatures more than any other; unless they have voluntarily vested him with it.

> —A Full Vindication of the Measures of Congress by A Friend to America, 1774

To the king and his ministers in Whitehall, to the French court at Versailles, and to the other powers of Europe whose opinions counted, British domination of New York City symbolized British dominion and control over all 13 North American colonies. Occasional British setbacks on the colonial periphery at Lexington, Concord, and Bunker Hill did not change the imperial symbolism of control of New York. The sailing of the *Kingfisher* with its two refugees, President Cooper and the printer James Rivington, did not much weaken British naval domination. The huge battleship *Asia* remained at anchor just off the foot of Wall Street. Her high-riding, thick-planked hull and skyscraping masts and spars loomed above all other vessels that could be seen at the ends of the streets running down to the margins of the island. Sixty-four cannons, 32 on each side, glowered from even rows of gunports that punctuated her high sides. New Yorkers knew that their wood-framed city was fatally vulnerable to fire and that the *Asia*'s spacious ammunition lockers were well stocked with incendiary powder and shot. They were also aware almost all of their own powder and shot—a thousand pounds of gunpowder—had been dispatched to Boston in June 1775 to help rearm the revolutionary cause there after Lexington, Concord, and Bunker Hill. Another purpose of this gift was symbolic—it was an attempt to overcome suspicions that

New Yorkers lacked commitment to the revolutionary cause.

Such suspicions were well-founded. Of all the colonies, New York, as a result of geography, history, commercial ties to Europe, and exposure to the fiercest of the Indian tribes on her frontiers, was the colony where popular resistance to the idea of revolution against British rule and British protection would persist most naturally.

By 1774 in any of the other 12 colonies, a 17-year-old like Alexander Hamilton would have been too late to make a mark as a writer and speaker for the revolutionary cause. But in New York loyalists to England were numerous, and the Anglican church, and the *Asia*, remained powerful influences. The Sons of Liberty and other activist revolutionary groups, like those that would seek to break down the college gates and seize President Cooper, were still a minority. Many moderates favored the revolutionary cause, but dissociated themselves from the violent tactics of the Sons of Liberty. Another large group was undecided, but ready to swing to whichever side looked as if it would win.

Born a British subject in a crown colony, Hamilton had naturally taken the British side when he arrived, and then changed sides. His revolutionary convictions were the better articulated for his being a convert.

John Church Hamilton wrote that his father had formed and entertained "strong prejudices on the ministerial side" of the controversy, "until he became convinced by the superior force of the arguments in favor of the colonial claims." Hamilton's decision to make a public stand in New York for independence was "kindled by a visit to Boston a short time after the destruction of the tea" on December 16, 1773. The peaceful and orderly symbolic mode of expressing protest and the avoidance of ambiguous violence were what had impressed him. His son writes, "Excited by the high tone" that prevailed in Boston, Hamilton "directed his attention to the leading topics of this great controversy." On his return to New York, his son points out, Hamilton "enlisted warmly on the side of America" and gave "early and public pledge of his devotion to her cause. A short time only elapsed before he hastened to redeem it."

In his two years at King's before he shouted down the revolutionary mob, Hamilton's extracurricular activities had won him the right to the mob's hearing as one of New York's leading pamphleteers and spokesmen for their cause.

"A Defense of the Destruction of the Tea" is the way Hamilton described to his son two pieces of his published in Holt's *The New York Journal*, or *General Advertiser*, one on December 16, 1773, over the pen name of *Monitor*, and the other on February 24, 1774, under the pen name of *Americanus*. With energy, force, and wide range of allusion, his "Defense" infused reasoned argument and citation of authorities with a staccato, impassioned, emotional appeal:

"The British *Parliament* has no more right of legislation here than it has in the empire of the Great Mogul." At this time Hamilton, like most moderates, still acknowledged some sovereignty of the King: "The case as to His Majesty is widely different; . . . the very charters which confirm our liberty reserve to him a sovereign authority." But the British colonies in America are "distinct independent states," and admitted to be so by Charles II. The acts of Parliament are "an unwarrantable exercise of . . . arbitrary power unknown to the British Constitution" insofar as they are intended to bind persons "out of the realm" like the colonists.

Americanus applauded the proposal of the Virginia Burgesses to form a union of counsel for opposition. He recommended "an annual congress, as tending to greater intimacy of union." Such a congress should meet in the metropolis of the most central colony, Hamilton's own New York.

On June 17, 1774, Samuel Adams called for a meeting of all the colonies; on June 20, Pennsylvania called for a colonial congress. New York's "honest, loyal and prudent" Committee of 51 insisted that it had the exclusive right to nominate New York's delegates to the First Continental Congress in Philadelphia and that no candidates were to be put up by popular nomination. But this did not satisfy Captain Alexander McDougall and the Sons of Liberty, who claimed to be acting in concert with the "true sons" of liberty in Boston. They insisted on a much stronger stand for independence than the Committee of 51 would countenance, and demanded a voice in the nomination of delegates. The Committee of 51 voted down their slate of nominees, and called a meeting of freeholders to rubber-stamp its nominations July 7, 1774, at City Hall. Angered by this direct rebuff, Alexander McDougall called a "Great Meeting in the Fields" for July 6, the day before the public meeting of freeholders.

Robert Troup met Hamilton as the Great Meeting in the Fields was gathering. On the spur of the moment he urged Hamilton to mount the platform as a speaker. Hamilton recoiled, but began to listen more attentively. Captain Alexander McDougall, the chairman of the meeting, condemned "the dangerous tendency of the numerous vile arts used by the enemies of America to divide and distress her councils, as well as the misrepresentations of the virtuous intentions of the citizens of this metropolis." He cried, "The liberties of America are in an alarming state."

At some point McDougall looked in Hamilton's direction and beckoned the young collegian, to whom he had lent books from his library, to the rostrum to speak, a gesture that summoned Alexander Hamilton from the fringes of the crowd into the mainstream of the history of the American Revolution.

The boy who sprang to the speaker's stand was no unkempt, wild-eyed revolutionary. His slight frame, fine-featured face, reddish curling hair tied loosely with a ribbon, delicate lawn shirt, lace cuffs and broadcloth coat, and quick, supple gestures made him look even younger than his 17 years, but a most unlikely defector from the loyalist stronghold at King's.

No text of his address survives, but he no doubt made the same points he would make later that year and early in 1775 in his great pamphlets *A Full Vindication of the Measures of Congress* and *The Farmer Refuted*. He denounced the Boston Port Bill under which "our brethren" are "now suffering in the common cause of these colonies." He called for unity of all America in resisting unconstitutional parliamentary taxation. He urged an agreement "to stop all importation from, and exportation to, Great Britain" till Boston's harbor was unblocked. This "will prove the salvation of North-America and her liberties"; otherwise, "fraud, power, and the most odious oppression, will rise triumphant over right, justice, social happiness, and freedom."

The issue was, in short, freedom or slavery:

> The only distinction between freedom and slavery consists in this: in the former state, a man is governed by the laws to which he has given his consent, either in person, or by his representative; in the latter, he is governed by the will of another. In the one case his life and property are his own, in the other, they depend upon the pleasure of a master. No man in his senses can hesitate in choosing to be free, rather than a slave.

A man has no right to be master of another, any more than any man was born to be a slave, said Hamilton as the "Vindicator of Congress": "All men have one common original; they participate in one common nature, and consequently have one common right. No reason can be assigned why one man should exercise any power, or preeminence over his fellow creatures more than another; unless they have voluntarily vested him with it.''

As Hamilton saw it, this applied to the dispute with Britain: ''Since then, Americans have not by any act of theirs impowered the British Parliament to make laws for them, it follows they can have no just authority to do it.''

This elevated the dispute from a tax evasion case over three pence per pound duty on tea to a question of the fundamental rights of man. His formulation of the issue leads straight on to the opening words of the Declaration of Independence.

Having grown up at close quarters with human chattel slavery, Hamilton did not leave his condemnation of slavery at this abstract, metaphorical level. He spoke of it in human terms, the way a fervent abolitionist might have seen it three-quarters of a century later; he foresaw that it would lead to the ''hideous train of calamities'' that it did:

> Were not the disadvantage of slavery too obvious to stand in need of it, I might enumerate and describe the hideous train of calamities, inseparable from it. I might show that it is fatal to religion and morality; that it tends to debase the mind, and corrupts its noblest springs of action. I might show, that it relaxes the sinews of industry, clips the wings of commerce, and introduces misery and indigence in every shape. . . . The life of the subject is often sported with; and the fruits of his daily toil are consumed in oppressive taxes, that serve to gratify the ambition, avarice and lust of his superiors. Every court minion riots in the spoils of the honest laborer, and despises the hand by which he is fed. The page of history is replete with instances that loudly warn us to beware of slavery.

Imperial Britain, like Imperial Rome before her, ''was the nurse of freedom, celebrated for her justice and lenity; but in what manner did she govern her dependent provinces? They were made the continual scene of rapine and cruelty.'' This demonstrated ''how little confidence is due to the wisdom and equity of the most exemplary nations.''

Religious freedom went hand in hand with personal and political freedom. Hamilton denounced ''that unparalleled stride of power'' by which ''popery'' had been established in Canada as a result of the Quebec bill:

> How can any of you be sure you would have the free enjoyment of your religion long? Would you put your religion in the power of any set of men living? Remember civil and religious liberty always go together, if the foundation of the one be sapped, the other will fall. Reflect upon the situation of Canada. . . . The Romish faith is made the established religion of the land, and his majesty is placed at the head of it. The free exercise of the Protestant faith depends upon the pleasure of the governor and council.

Besides freedom of person and religion, another indispensable safeguard of true freedom was the right of trial by jury and habeas corpus, rights that were now denied in Canada: ''The subject is divested of the right of trial by jury, and an innocent man may be imprisoned his whole life, without being able to obtain any trial at all.'' And military encirclement also threatened the colonies:

> The Parliament has annexed to it the vast tracts of land that surrounded all the colonies. . . . They may as well establish popery in New York and the other

colonies as they did in Canada. They had no more right to do it there than here. Your lives, your property, your religion are all at stake.

Looking defiantly toward the *Asia* he would shake his fist and cry that the supposed

> . . . omnipotence and all sufficiency of Great Britain is altogether visionary. She is oppressed with a heavy national debt, which it requires the utmost policy and economy ever to discharge. Luxury has arrived to a great pitch; and it is a universal maxim that luxury indicates the declension of a state. Her subjects are loaded with the most enormous taxes; all circumstances agree in declaring their distress. The continual immigrations, from Great Britain and Ireland, to the continent, are a glaring symptom, that those kingdoms are a good deal impoverished.

By contrast, the colonies were strong:

> . . . these colonies, as they are now settled and peopled, have been the work of near two centuries; they are blessed with every advantage of soil, climate and situation. They have advanced with an almost incredible rapidity. . . . The total and sudden loss of so extensive and lucrative a branch, would . . . produce the most violent effects to a nation that subsists entirely among its commerce.

The colonies would be a military match for the British:

> Our numbers are very considerable; the courage of Americans has been tried and proved. Contests for liberty have ever been found the most bloody, implacable and obstinate. The disciplined troops Great Britain can send against us, would be but few, our superiority in number would overbalance our inferiority in discipline. It would be a hard, if not an impracticable task to subjugate us by force.
> We can live without trade of any kind. Food and clothing we have within ourselves.

Indeed, a war could be a blessing in disguise, which would help foster the American domestic manufacturing that Britain's mercantile policy had up to now suppressed:

> If by the necessity of the thing, manufacturers should once be established and take root among us, they will pave the way, still more, to the future grandeur and glory of America, and by lessening its need of external commerce, will render it still secure against the encroachments of tyranny.

If he wished to find a war, he would stir one up right here by the side of Captain McDougall.

There was a breathless silence; then, according to Hamilton's son's account, murmurous whispers rose from the crowd:

> It is a collegian!
> A collegian!
> It is a collegian!

Not only was he young, but he was also from Dr. Myles Cooper's bastion of loyalist sentiment at King's. There was a roar of applause. After Captain McDougall had quieted the crowd, nine resolutions going far beyond what the Committee of 51 had proposed were twice read and "being separately put . . . they were passed without one dissentient."

Next day the ruling Committee of 51 briskly voted to rebuke McDougall and the resolutions adopted at his rump meeting of the day before. It criticized "all such proceedings . . . calculated to throw an odium on this committee."

While losing the battle with the Committee of 51, Hamilton won identification as a radical champion of liberty in the most loyalist of the colonies. But he had framed the issues in broad, continent-wide, black and white terms, not limited to New York.

No one who had seen and heard Hamilton calling for freedom on the platform beside Alexander McDougall could afterward feel much but contempt for charges like those later reiterated by men like Thomas Jefferson that Hamilton was a "monarchist," an ambiguous term that slyly implied disloyalty to colonial independence.

By a one-vote margin delegates for full independence seized control of the Continental Congress in Philadelphia. England was notified that the colonies would boycott all English imports starting December 1, and forbid exports after December 10, 1775. An association was to be formed "in every county, city and town in America" to denounce publicly all who did not agree with the rebels.

Many in New York and elsewhere found much to criticize in British policy toward the colonies, but sought to limit colonial resistance to petitions and remonstrances through established channels to avoid provoking open war. A leading spokesman for these loyalists was President Myles Cooper's good friend Samuel Seabury, a missionary and physician who had settled in Westchester County as an Episcopal rector. One of his many roles was that of the rustic country bumpkin who is shrewder than city folk, a perennial American favorite. On November 16, 1774, assuming the name and style of a Westchester farmer, Seabury issued a pamphlet called *Free Thoughts on Congress,* which provided Hamilton with the occasion to spread his revolutionary views to a wider audience than he had commanded from the platform beside Alexander McDougall at the Great Meeting in the Fields.

The pamphlets he published as the self-appointed refuter of the Westchester Farmer are two early examples of Hamilton's talent for using reverses like the adverse vote of the Committee of 51, as stepping stones, forward and upward.

As A. W. Farmer from rural Westchester, Seabury craftily sought to turn the revolutionary turmoil on itself to save the status quo. The full 90-word title of his pamphet *Free Thoughts on Congress* gives the flavor of the performance and the occasion: "Free Thoughts on the Proceedings of the Continental Congress, Held at Philadelphia Sept. 5, 1774: Wherein Their Errors are exhibited, their Reasoning Confuted, and the fatal Tendency of their Non-Importation, Non-Exportation, and Non-Consumption Measures, are laid open to the plainest Understandings; and the Only means pointed out for Preserving and Securing our present Happy Constitution: In a letter to the Farmers and other inhabitants of North America in General, and to those of the Province of New York in particular. By a Farmer. Hear me, for I Will speak!" It is signed A. W. Farmer.

Seabury urged all colonists to put their trust in the magnanimity of Great Britain rather than in colonial union and attempts at economic coercion. He ridiculed the "confounded combustion" caused by a trifling tax on tea. The Continental Congress was the real enemy of farmers, he insisted, and he ridiculed the inconsistency of a Congress that, pretending to protect the liberties of the people, had sanctioned public denunciation of dissenters.

Free Thoughts on Congress became the textbook of Tory arguments. Whigs resented the clergy's devotion to the Crown and some demanded that the author and publisher of "Free

Thoughts'' be indicted for treason. In one county Seabury's pamphlet was tarred and feathered and nailed to the pillory amid shouts of rage from a mob.

Revolutionary excitement rose. Here was a target of opportunity for Hamilton. On December 15, 1774, one month after Seabury's *Free Thoughts,* Hamilton's answer appeared in Rivington's *Gazetteer.*

The full title of Hamilton's pamphlet is a pamphlet in itself: "A Full Vindication of the Measures of Congress, from the Calumnies of their Enemies: In Answer to A Letter, Under the signature of A. W. Farmer. Whereby his Sophistry is exposed, his Cavils confuted, his Artifices detected, and his Wit ridiculed; in a General Address to the Inhabitants of America, and a Particular Address to the Farmers of the Province of New York. Veritas magna est. & proevalebit. Truth is powerful and will prevail."

According to Hamilton, beneath Seabury's homespun shrewdness was the same fell purpose that underlay British policy as formulated by Lord North, the prime minister: prevent union of the colonies, divide and conquer, and continue to rule. Hamilton first summarizes his opponent's arguments in a way that discredits them. Anticipating Thomas Paine, he appeals to the "Common Sense" of his readers, and equates his opponents with slave masters.

> Whence arises that violent antipathy they seem to entertain, not only to the natural rights of mankind; but to common sense and to common modesty. That they are enemies to the natural rights of mankind is manifest, because they wish to see one part of their species enslaved by another.

Near the close of *A Full Vindication,* Hamilton puts a figurative arm around his countrymen's shoulder to speak in a folksy political style that matches A. W. Farmer's. "My good countrymen," he says disarmingly, "I am one of your number, or connected with you in interest more than with any other branch of the community. I can venture to assure you, the true writer of the pieces signed A. W. Farmer, is not in reality a Farmer. He is some ministerial emissary, that has assumed the name to deceive you."

Hamilton concludes: "Give me the steady, uniform, unshaken security of constitutional freedom; give me the right to be tried by a jury of my own neighbors, and to be taxed by my own representatives only."

Liberty under law was the keynote: "I would die to preserve the law upon a solid foundation; but take away liberty, and the foundation is destroyed." Then the "shadow may remain, but the substance will be gone."

He closes with a benediction that he may have heard from the Reverend Samuel Seabury himself at daily services at King's or President Myles Cooper's dinner table:

> May God give you wisdom to see what is your true interest, and inspire you with becoming zeal for the cause of virtue and mankind.

Signed,

A Friend to America

The Tories could not let *A Full Vindication of Congress by a Friend to America* stand unanswered; so Samuel Seabury took up the ministerial pen once again for a second pamphlet, *A View of the Controversy.* It was published by James Rivington January 5, 1775.

Hamilton, in turn, replied to Seabury for the second time on February 23, 1775, also in

Rivington's *Gazetteer*, with "The Farmer Refuted, or A More Impartial and Comprehensive View of the Dispute between Great Britain and the Colonies, intended as a further vindication of the Congress: In answer to a letter from A. W. Farmer, entitled 'A View of the Controversy' . . ."

Hamilton's second reply begins what he calls his "More Impartial and Comprehensive View of the Dispute" at a less impartial, more narrowly partisan pitch:

> Notwithstanding, I am naturally of a grave and phlegmatic disposition, your curious epistle has been the source of abundant merriment to me. The spirit that breathes throughout is so rancorous, illiberal and imperious; the argumentative part of it so puerile and fallacious; the misrepresentation of facts so palpable and flagrant; the criticism so illiterate, trifling and absurd; the conceits so low, sterile and splenetic, that I will venture to pronounce it one of the most ludicrous performances, which has been exhibited to public view, during all the present controversy.

The "Farmer" had stung Hamilton by writing of him that "If you seldom sink into meanness of diction, you never soar into that brilliancy of thought; nor, even with the help of Johnson's dictionary, into that classical elegance of expression which is absolutely necessary for the arduous attempt of ridiculing wit."

Hamilton answered, "I addressed myself to the judgment, not to the imagination. In works, where fancy is predominant, as is the case with yours, there is a better opportunity for displaying brilliancy of thought, than where reason presides and directs."

Hamilton's self-assessment, if sarcastic, is nonetheless correct. His lack of "imagination" for the kind of writing "where fancy is predominant" is the best defense he would later have against the accusation that he had fabricated some wildly extravagant love letters. They were the letters he would use to defend himself against the charges of speculating in Treasury funds while secretary of the treasury—charges which would in the end destroy him.

Hamilton attacked the Clergyman-Farmer for the heresy of denying the existence of natural law. Most eighteenth-century men like Hamilton shared a common belief in natural law, one that has vanished from most minds today. Hamilton believed that:

> Good and wise men, in all ages, have supposed, that the deity, from the relations we stand in, to himself and to each other, has constituted an eternal and immutable law, which is, indispensably, obligatory upon all mankind, prior to any human institution whatever.
>
> This is the "law of nature," which, being coeval with mankind, and dictated by God Himself, is, of course, superior in obligation to any other. It is binding all over the globe, in all countries, and at all times. No human laws are of any validity, if contrary to this; and such of them as are valid, derive all their authority, mediately or immediately, from the original.

In phases that recall Dr. Hugh Knox's Hurricane Sermon, Hamilton drives home the idea in one of his most uncharacteristically poetic passages:

> The sacred rights of mankind are not to be rummaged for, among old parchments, or musty records. They are written, as with a sunbeam, in the whole *volume* of human nature, by the hand of the divinity itself; and can never be erased or obscured by mortal power.

"Sacred rights" was the source from which Hamilton, by a linear logical process, reached the conclusion that the colonies must be free and were endowed "with an inviolable right to personal liberty and personal safety."

Furthermore, "the origin of all civil government, justly established, must be a voluntary compact, between the rulers and the ruled; and must be liable to such limitations, as are necessary for the security of the absolute rights of the latter; for what original title can any man or set of men have, to govern others, except their own consent?"

The form of government was dictated by these principles:

> The principal aim of society is to protect individuals, in the enjoyment of those absolute rights, which were vested in them by the immutable laws of nature; but which could not be preserved, in peace, without that mutual assistance, and intercourse, which is gained by the institution of friendly and social communities.

The Farmer had argued that the colonists could not claim to be liege subjects to the king of Great Britain while disavowing the authority of Parliament, because "The king of Great Britain was placed on the throne, by virtue of an act of Parliament; and he is king of America, by virtue of being king of Great Britain."

Hamilton meets this argument by hedging on the question of the degree of sovereignty of the king: He was only the grantor of a charter; he is king of America only by virtue of a compact between us and the king of Great Britain.

Hamilton then opens up the view of a glorious future for a free America: "There seems to be, already, a jealousy of our dawning splendor. It is looked upon as portentous of approaching independence . . . and though it may have chiefly originated in the calumnies of designing men, yet it does not entirely depend upon adventitious or partial causes; but is also founded in the circumstances of our country and situation."

He sees that "The boundless extent of territory we possess, the wholesome temperature of our climate, the luxuriance and fertility of our soil, the variety of our products, the rapidity of our population, the industry of our countrymen and the commodiousness of our ports, naturally lead to a suspicion of independence, and would always have an influence pernicious to us."

Hamilton foresaw, finally, a continental union much larger than the original 13 colonies. It would include Nova Scotia and Canada. "The Farmer builds too much upon the present disunion of Canada, Georgia, the Floridas, the Mississippi and Nova Scotia from other colonies. I please myself with a flattering prospect, that they will, ere long, unite in one indissoluble chain with the rest of the colonies."

He closed with the supreme paradox: "The best way to secure a permanent and happy union, between Great Britain and the colonies, is to permit the latter to be as free as they desire." He signed off as "a Sincere Friend to America."

A Full Vindication and *The Farmer Refuted* created a sensation. Some attributed the pamphlets to John Adams or to Governor William Livingston of New Jersey, but the secret that the pseudonymous Friend to America was Hamilton did not remain a secret long. He was talked of as a prodigy of colonial intellect surprisingly nurtured within the gates of the loyalist bastion at King's. Of New York's revolutionary leaders, Marinus Willett wrote, "Hamilton, after these great writings, became our oracle."

Hamilton became known throughout the other colonies as "The Vindicator" of the First Continental Congress at a time when the Second Continental Congress was preparing to convene in Philadelphia on May 5, 1775. Fiery, ardent leaders of the Sons of Liberty like

Isaac Sears and Alexander McDougall, and careful moderates like William Livingston and John Jay, could now proudly cite as their own the facts and arguments for revolution that had been marshaled so forcefully by their brilliant protégé. Hamilton had promoted himself to the unoccupied office of New York's most articulate spokesman for the continental revolutionary cause.

Hamilton contributed no new principles to the controversy. He elaborated doctrines that were being advanced in the Continental Congress and other colonies by men like John Adams, Thomas Jefferson, and others. John Locke's writings, particularly his *Two Treatises of Government*, were his political Bible, like theirs, but Hamilton did more than reduce Locke to everyday terms for the benefit of New Yorkers. He marshaled facts and figures to show that the colonies would be economically and militarily invincible in their struggle with Britain, and that America formed an economic whole in which the various sections complemented each other in such a way that a great nation—an empire—was destined to arise upon the American continent.

In their time *A Full Vindication* and *The Farmer Refuted* were not just public statements—they were great events that broke through the public's consciousness. Hamilton's pen was a mighty weapon. Writing to James Madison of the impact of some of Hamilton's later pamphlets, Thomas Jefferson would say two decades later: "Hamilton is really a colossus to the anti-Republican party. Without numbers, he is an host within himself."

Every morning during the winter and spring of 1774 and 1775 in St. George's churchyard, Hamilton, Fish, Troup, and a number of their other friends turned out to practice close-order drill under Major Edward Fleming, a disciplinarian who had been an adjutant of a British regiment, but who was now attached to the American cause. Hamilton's attendance was eager and constant and "he became exceedingly expert in the manual exercise." His company of volunteers was called The Corsicans and later The Hearts of Oak. Their short green uniform coats and the front of their leather caps bore the ominous motto, "Freedom or Death."

The shooting war actually began with the shot fired near Concord Bridge on April 17, 1775, whose report was heard 'round the world. Three weeks later, on May 10, Ethan Allen and his Green Mountain Boys and a fiery Connecticut officer named Benedict Arnold surprised and seized Fort Ticonderoga in upstate New York. In June, British generals William Howe, Sir Henry Clinton, and John Burgoyne landed in Boston with reinforcements for General Gage, assaulted Breed's Hill, and lost more than 1,000 men in the Battle of Bunker Hill. Full of over-optimistic enthusiasm, Congress launched a two-pronged military invasion of Canada under General Philip Schuyler and Arnold which sallied forth in August from Ticonderoga and Cambridge only to suffer one of the most tragic disasters of the war in January.

By August 1775 the New York Provincial Congress and the patriot Committee of Safety had taken over direction of the restless city. The royal governor, William Tryon, and his lieutenant governor, Cadwallader Colden, had retired for safety to a retreat in Flushing.

The New York Provincial Congress ordered the British cannon to be hauled away from the fort at the Battery to the Liberty Pole at the Fields. With his Hearts of Oak, Hamilton and the rest of the infantrymen of Colonel Lasher's battalion marched to the Battery at eleven the night of August 23, but drew no fire from the fort. Earlier in the summer the main British garrison that manned it had been taken aboard the *Asia* to avoid incidents. Captain Vanderput of the *Asia* received advance word that Colonel Lasher's militia intended to seize the cannons, and launched one of the *Asia*'s sloops with a full complement of armed men to remain close to shore and monitor the Americans. Hamilton, with his fellow Hearts of Oak militiamen, was in the guard detail that formed a semicircle at the fort facing the harbor while others were hauling away the cannon. Sighting the *Asia*'s sloop lying offshore, they loaded, primed, and cocked their muskets. Then they waited for the British to make the first move.

Other units of Colonel Lasher's battalion broke into the fort, made ropes fast to the gun carriages, and began dragging the cannons out of their portals, off the ramparts, out toward the Bowling Green, and up the Broad Way toward the Fields to the ironclad Liberty Pole. There were 21 naval guns in all, an assortment of 9-, 12-, and 18-pounders weighing near a ton or more apiece. Manhandling them up the Broad Way at night was hard, sweaty, noisy work. Much loud confused cursing and swearing rose in the August night.

Suddenly, shortly after midnight, from the *Asia*'s sloop offshore, a muzzle flash and musket report blazed out in the darkness. Hamilton's jittery guard detail instantly returned the fire. No one ashore could be certain whether the fire from the *Asia*'s sloop was an aimed shot, an accidental discharge, or a signal to the *Asia* to open up with all her guns. Under fire from Hamilton's company, the sloop's crew bent to their sweeps and rowed out of range, but the armed detachment aboard her continued to fire on Hamilton's guard detail. One of the militia's shots fatally wounded a British crewman aboard the sloop.

The exchange of musket fire between land and water continued as the sloop pulled away. Then, suddenly, from a thousand yards away, there was a flash, an enormous orange ball of flame, then a thunderous "boom!" The *Asia*'s main batteries had opened fire. The flash and boom of her salvo reverberating across the night sky like thunder and lightning was the most fearsome sight and sound Hamilton or any other New Yorker had ever seen or heard in their lives.

The sleeping city roused itself in panic. Alarm drums began to beat. Militiamen groped and stumbled and lurched through the darkness to find their assigned posts, blinded by the glare. Householders ran into the streets, down into cellars, fled to the countryside, or sought to find a boat for New Jersey. Some thought the British invasion had begun.

Lasher's men went on dragging the cannon out of the fort up Broad Way. As the *Asia*'s sloop pulled out of range of his men's muskets, Hamilton seized a rope from the hand of his friend Hercules Mulligan and handed Mulligan his empty musket to hold for him. He put his shoulder to the rope to help haul a cannon up the Broad Way.

Having lodged the cannon near the Liberty Pole at the Fields, he was running back down toward the Battery for another when he met Mulligan running up the street toward him. Hamilton demanded that Mulligan give him back his musket. Mulligan apologized. He had thrown it down in panic back at the Battery. Hamilton brushed past him and continued on back toward the Battery to find his musket. According to the timorous Mulligan's later account, Hamilton did so, "notwithstanding the firing continued, with as much concern as if the vessel had not been there."

At about three in the morning, the *Asia*'s guns opened up again with an assortment of 9-, 18-, and 24-pound shells in a full, 32-gun broadside on the defenseless city. The muzzle blasts of her cannon formed a sheet of white orange fire stretching all the way from the foot of Wall Street to the very ceiling of the August night sky. The blasts shook the whole city. Cannon shot crashed through walls and roofs of houses. Citizens' nostrils and lungs burned with the acrid odor of powder and smoke. No one who saw or heard or felt or smelled the broadsides the *Asia* laid on New York that night could ever forget them.

The *Asia*'s display of firepower had merely been meant as a warning. Captain Vanderput's gunners had aimed generally toward Fort George, not the city itself. They had used solid lead and iron shot, not fire bombs. But most of the shot fell short of Fort George—one struck Roger Morris's townhouse, and another fell through the roof of Fraunces Tavern. Others damaged smaller buildings in Whitehall Street. Three or four New Yorkers were wounded, but no one was killed. When the panic died down and the wreckage was surveyed by cool morning light, it was remarkable that so little actual damage could have been done.

Hamilton would always afterward be identified in the public's mind as one of the men who had been on the firing line against the enemy's guns on the first night of New York's armed resistance to the British. By surviving without too much trouble, he had demonstrated the truth of his published thesis that the royal masters were not omnipotent. The practical demonstration that the *Asia*'s guns were not as fearsome as they looked and sounded weakened the hitherto awesome ultimate symbol of British imperial control. The night of August 23, 1775, marked the night when de facto control of New York city and state passed from the British Crown and the loyalist-dominated Provincial Assembly to the revolutionary Provincial Congress.

In November, Captain Isaac Sears, the radical leader of the Sons of Liberty, gathered a gang in New Haven to march on New York and root out loyalist rot. On their march westward, they captured Samuel Seabury, the Westchester Farmer himself, and packed him off back to New Haven, where he was jailed for five weeks. Riding on in triumph, Sears's gang clattered into New York City at noon on November 23 and drew up in close order with fixed bayonets in front of James Rivington's bookstore and print shop in Hanover Square. Rivington had fled; along with Dr. Cooper, whose pamphlets he had published, he had slipped away from the mobs of May to safety aboard the *Kingfisher*. The gang broke in and wrecked his establishment, filled sacks with his precious imported type and threw it away, spilled his files and smashed his presses. A crowd of spectators stood and watched from a wooden platform nearby called Coffee House Bridge. Hamilton's son reports that Hamilton appeared here "as the advocate of order, and relying on his former success, renewed his appeals to the discretion of the citizens." Besides, he was "indignant at the encroachment of unlicensed troops from another colony" coming in and destroying the publisher of his own pamphlets, just because he had published Seabury as well. Hamilton "offered to join in opposition to the intruders and check their progress." But Hamilton's son admits that "His exhortation was unsuccessful. The outrage was perpetrated."

The day after the Sons of Liberty destroyed Rivington's press, Hamilton, without mentioning his own role but writing with all the authority of a disapproving eyewitness, sent a long letter to John Jay, then sitting in the Second Continental Congress in Philadelphia. He entreated Jay to use his influence to send some continental troops to New York to help keep a check on patriotic mob violence. A more important reason for sending troops was to meet the British invasion and the loyalist counterinsurrection that he foresaw coming soon. Hamilton's analysis looked several ways:

> If your body gently interposes a check for the future, Rivington will be intimidated & the Tories will be convinced that the other colonies will not tamely see the general cause betrayed by the Yorkers. A favorable idea will be impressed of your justice & impartiality in discouraging the encroachments of any one province on another.

Here is the plan:

> Let [Congress] station in different parts of the province most tainted with the ministerial infection, a few regiments of troops, raised in Philadelphia, the Jerseys

or any other province except New England. These will suffice to strengthen and support the Whigs, who are still, I flatter myself, a large majority, and to suppress the efforts of the Tories. . . .

"In times of such commotion as the present," he lectured Jay, "there is greater danger of fatal extremes." He went on:

> The same state of the passions which fits the multitude, who have not a sufficient stock of reason and knowledge to guide them, for opposition to tyranny and oppression, very naturally leads them to a contempt and disregard of all authority. . . . When the minds of these are loosened from their attachment to ancient establishments and courses, they seem to grow giddy and are apt, more or less, to run into anarchy.
>   In such tempestuous times, it requires the greatest skill in the political pilots to keep men steady and within proper bounds.

Hamilton then sounds the great theme that colors all his—and Jay's—political thought. "I am always more or less alarmed at everything which is done of mere will and pleasure without any proper authority."

Hamilton was acting in a complex situation calling for high standards of order, rectitude, moderation, and political acumen that Jay could not fail to notice seemed to match his own. Hamilton's son concluded that his father's failure to save his publisher's press "elevated him still more in the estimation of the patriots, who saw in his love of order and respect for the authority of the laws assurances of those high qualities which, rising above the wild uproar of the times, disdained to win popularity from popular delusion."

5

Covering the Beaten Retreat of an Essential Aegis to Be

After escaping the grasp of a disciplined and victorious enemy, this little band of patriots were seen skillfully avoiding an engagement until they could contend with advantage, and then by the masterly enterprises of Trenton and Princeton, cutting them up in detachments, rallying the scattered energies of the country, infusing terror into the breasts of their invaders, and changing the whole tide and fortune of the war.

—"Eulogium on General Nathanael Greene," July 4, 1789

Alexander McDougall, since summoning Hamilton from the fringes of the crowd to the platform at the Great Meeting in the Fields, had been appointed colonel of the First New York Regiment, the highest ranking military man in the city. He would soon be promoted again to Continental brigadier and in 1777 to major general.

On February 23, 1776, a week after Hamilton had helped Col. Alexander McDougall's successful campaign for the Provincial assembly, it was recorded in the journals of the New York Provincial Congress that "Col. McDougall recommended Mr. Alexander Hamilton for captain of a company of artillery." At McDougall's prodding, Jay pushed approval through the Provincial Congress, so on March 14, 1776, two months after his 19th birthday, the Provincial Congress "Ordered that Alexander Hamilton be, and he is hereby appointed captain of the Provincial company of artillery of this Colony."

It was a volunteer army, and officers had to recruit their own men. Hamilton's commission was conditioned on his raising at least 30. He first had to find them, then inspire them to join him as volunteers, and then persuade the province to pay them.

Hamilton's Provincial company was subject to the same regulations as the Continental

52

artillery, but the pay scale for Continental troops was higher. According to Hamilton, "this makes it difficult for me to get a single recruit" and caused "many marks of discontent" among his men. He appealed to the Provincial Congress: "Men will naturally go to men who pay them best." To pay for the uniforms and equip and arm his men before his fund requisitions were approved by the Provincial Congress, Hamilton advanced the second and last of the remittances he had received from St. Croix to help pay for his education at King's.

Mulligan and others often spoke of the zeal with which Hamilton trained his men: "he proceeded with indefatigable pains, to perfect [his company] in every branch and duty; and it was not long before it was esteemed the most beautiful model . . . in the whole army."

The 40-gun frigate *Phoenix* joined the *Asia* in the river, lying a little to the north of her, about where Brooklyn Bridge now spans the East River. Sir Henry Clinton arrived from Boston aboard the 24-gun frigate *Mercury,* accompanied by a transport ship with five or six hundred armed troops. By April of 1776 there was no doubt that still more British were on their way in force.

General Charles Lee marched down from Boston under orders from General Washington and began deploying Continental troops for defense of the island. This touched off a "convulsion" in the city. Fearful residents tried to flee in a panic that matched the uproar created by the *Asia*'s broadsides of the previous August.

The Provincial Congress resolved to move all the colony's official records out of danger up the Hudson to Kingston. They had been under the guard of New York City's First Regiment of Infantry, but the Provincial Congress ordered this guard duty undertaken by Hamilton's spruce artillery company, manifesting its awareness that Hamilton's company had attained a high level of readiness for spit-and-polish guard duty.

Hamilton's Provincial company helped John Lasher's City Battalion of Independents construct a heptagonal fort on Bayard's Hill, located at what is now the intersection of Canal and Mulberry Streets. From high ground there, overlooking the city of about 4,000 houses and 25,000 people to the south, Hamilton's guns could command the lower end of Manhattan Island below what is now Chambers Street. Seeing this fort's 12 six-pound cannons and its garrison of two commissioned officers, four noncommissioned officers, and 20 privates, Nicholas Fish with ill-founded optimism called the Bayard's Hill fort "a fortification superior in strength to any my imagination could ever have conceived." It was a key strong point in the chain of earthworks that stretched across lower Manhattan from the Jersey Battery on the Hudson side to Horn's Hook on the East River.

The Continental Congress concentrated its strongest defenses around New York, the strategic hub and finest harbor of all the colonies. By the spring of 1776 the Continental Army in New York had grown to about 9,000 strong. Congress fitted out privateers to prey on British commerce, sought to disarm loyalists and loyalist sympathizers in the colonies, declared American ports to be open to the trade of all countries not subject to the British Crown, and established independent governmental relations directly with France. By the spring of 1776, from Montreal and Quebec on the north to Charleston in the Carolinas far to the south, American regulars and Provincial militia units had already been seeing action against the enemy in tangential engagements. Hamilton however was still drilling his men, sprucing up his Provincial Artillery Company, throwing up earthworks, firing futilely at British ships in the harbor out of cannons that backfired on their matrosses, preparing for the main event.

Washington arrived from Boston in mid-April. Brushing aside General Charles Lee's doubts that New York City could be defended, he insisted that it be held. It was a political decision. He charged William Alexander, Lord Stirling, who had taken over command at

New York from General Lee early in March, that "It is the place that we must use every endeavor to keep from them. For should they get that town, and the command of the North River, they can stop the intercourse between the Northern and Southern colonies, upon which depends the safety of America."

All speculation ended on June 29. The first waves of the greatest seaborne expeditionary force that any nation had sent abroad since the disastrous Athenian expedition to Syracuse hove into view sailing up the Narrows. From his Staten Island window with a view of the Narrows, Daniel McCurtin gasped at what he saw as he peered out at sunrise: "I . . . spied as I peeped out . . . something resembling a wood of pine trees trimmed . . . the whole Bay was full of shipping as ever it could be. I . . . thought all London was afloat." The enemy fleet of more than one hundred sail had dropped anchor in the Lower Bay.

The British expeditionary force to take New York would grow to about 34,000 in all, including 25,000 regulars, against whom Washington could field about 10,000 Continental regulars and 12,000 militia, including Hamilton's Provincial Artillery Company.

As Hamilton kept his cannons primed to aim and fire while the enemy buildup in the harbor continued, he heard with growing excitement the news coming back from Philadelphia. On July 4 the Continental Congress had formally adopted a Declaration of Independence. It echoed many of the things he had shouted in his speech in The Fields and published in *A Full Vindication* and *The Farmer Refuted*.

The Liberty Bell pealed in Philadelphia. A courier rushed the text to New York. George Washington came down from his headquarters house at Richmond Hill to hear the Declaration formally read at a July meeting in The Fields.

On August 8, 1776, Washington warned of impending British attack in a portentous general order:

> The movements of the enemy, and intelligence by deserters, give the utmost reason to believe that the great struggle, in which we are contending for everything dear to us, and our posterity is near at hand.

Admiral Lord Richard Howe and his brother, General Sir William Howe, made an amphibious landing on the Long Island periphery of the defense system that would win them an immediate victory, and set a pattern for the tactics that would lose them the eight-year war. After the landing they attacked westward toward Brooklyn Heights.

General Nathanael Greene had fallen sick, leaving General John Sullivan as a replacement who was not his equal. Colonel Rufus Putnam, still less able, then replaced Sullivan. The American sectors of command were not clearly marked and the British made the most of the weaknesses of the unblooded American command.

Washington notified the New York Provincial Congress that he had troops enough to hold the fortifications on Brooklyn Heights, but a council of general officers on Long Island late on August 29 concluded that "under all circumstances it is . . . eligible to leave Long Island . . . and remove to New York. . . ."

Hamilton's son claims, in a rather vague way, that Hamilton was with Washington on Long Island and, like Washington, one of the last to escape: "In the retreat, Captain Hamilton brought up the rear, having lost his baggage and a field piece." Washington's evacuation of all positions on Long Island resulted in about 1,000 American casualties with 200 killed. British casualties were fewer than 400. A British historian called the evacuation "a master stroke by which Washington saved his army and his country." It was a master stroke that saved the survivors for many a disaster to come.

Washington then felt it prudent to ask Congress on September 2, "If we should be obliged to abandon the town, ought it to stand as a winter quarters for the enemy? Or should it be razed to the ground? . . . If Congress should resolve upon destruction of it, the resolution should be kept a profound secret." Save the city, Congress ordered.

On the morning of September 15, British warships opened up a cannonade "to scour the ground and cover the landing of the troops" on Manhattan, then called York Island. The Howes struck at the green and panicky American militia cowering in carelessly dug earthworks at the weakest sector of York Island's defenses—in the middle, at Kip's Bay, near what is now East 30th Street—overran them with ease, and fanned out through the woods and meadows of what is now midtown Manhattan. An observer reported, "On the appearance of the enemy, not more than 60 or 70 in number," the militiamen "ran away in the greatest confusion without firing a single shot."

According to Hercules Mulligan, Hamilton and his Provincial artillery held fast at Bayard's Hill fort in lower Manhattan, ready to defend it to the last man. Suddenly Colonel Henry Knox, the army's artillery commander, came running in to take cover, mistakenly supposing that all roads of escape to the North had been cut off. He and Hamilton aimed their cannons northward for a last ditch defense of a besieged bastion cut off behind enemy lines. General Putnam, who had joined his other brigades in flight to the north, sent his aide Major Aaron Burr back to Bayard's Hill fort "to call off the pickets and guards" and bring them up with the main body. Burr passed the order along to Colonel Knox and Captain Hamilton, pointed out to them that the road north, up the west side of the island, was still open, and offered to lead the way.

Some say that this rescue of Hamilton by Aaron Burr was the first time the two men had ever met. Both had been prominent young army officers in New York, and Hamilton knew the way to Harlem Heights as well as Burr. Whether or not it was the first meeting of the two men, in drama it would be surpassed only by their last—and one other encounter in between.

Dragging their cannons and ammunition, Hamilton and his New York Provincial artillery took till after nightfall to rout-march the nine miles to Harlem Heights, where the main force of the army already encamped there opened ranks to let them pass through. They finally halted near what is now about 147th Street and Broadway, close to where Hamilton would later build his Grange.

Before flinging themselves down for some exhausted sleep, they dug emplacements, threw up earthworks around their guns in defilade positions formed by Harlem ridge, and set up a watch for the night.

Earlier that day at Kip's Bay, General Washington had furiously tried to rally his beaten militia from astride his horse, laying his riding crop smartly across the men's backs to check their flight and lash them into a stand, with no success. The contrast between those fleeing militiamen and the discipline of Hamilton's artillerymen caught the commander's eye. According to Hamilton's son Washington inspected "the works which he was engaged in throwing up, entered into conversation with him, and formed a high estimate of his military capacity." So began Hamilton's relationship with the man he would describe as "an aegis very essential to me."

Washington's orders for the following day called for the courteous, elegant, affable Lieutenant Colonel Thomas Knowlton to lead a counterattack on the British pursuers with his 100 Connecticut Rangers. Knowlton's men ran into British light infantry moving north up the slope of the ridge, formed a skirmish line, held firm, and exchanged fire with the enemy. A sudden skirl of bagpipes signaled that the Black Watch were moving up to reinforce the light infantry. Knowlton's Rangers broke off in good order and beat a disciplined retreat.

The British then launched a general attack on the ridge. Washington ordered larger American forces to counterattack, committing to action the reorganized militiamen who had so cravenly fled Kip's Bay in panic the day before. Now he saw them stand and fight against the same British regulars who had chased them off Long Island and smashed through them at Kip's Bay. From well dug-in emplacements on the Heights, Hamilton's cannoneers kept up a steady morale-stiffening blanket of covering fire on the enemy line.

Here was a remarkable achievement. Troops from different provinces thrown into the battle for New York had finally demonstrated that when it came to courage, there was little to choose between them. Washington's army had been transformed from the beaten mob of Kip's Bay the day before into a fighting army. On Harlem Heights that day every man knew it. Among the 130 American casualties was Colonel Knowlton.

On October 9, British frigates broke through underwater obstructions in the Hudson River channel and sailed up the river, flanking Washington's position on the west. Three days later Howe's troops landed in force on Throg's Neck and Pell's Point, flanking him to the east. The Americans on the ridge at Harlem Heights were in a cul-de-sac, cut off from the rest of the colonies.

By October 16, evacuation was decided upon, with one foolish politically motivated reservation: Even though all supply and communication from the Jersey shore would be interdicted by British cruisers in the Hudson, a toehold at Fort Washington, on the rocky ledge near what is now West 180th Street, was to be held by a large garrison of 2,800.

The army's main force withdrew north to White Plains. General Howe followed in pursuit, and on October 28 his army attacked an outpost of Washington's army at Chatterton's Hill, a detached ridge lying to the southwest of the main American lines. In 15 minutes, the British and Hessians were in possession of the field. The Americans "moved off the hill in a . . . body," one apologist said, "neither running nor observing the best order."

Hamilton's son and others ascribed to his father a valiant role at the Battle of White Plains, but no records have been found to show exactly what he did or where his cannons were that day.

Sir William Howe moved to invade New Jersey, and sent a force south to storm isolated Fort Washington which, like Fort Lee on the New Jersey Palisades nearly opposite, was useless.

The American forces surrendered Fort Washington unconditionally on November 16. Timely evacuation would have saved 2,800 troops, many cannons, and arms and supplies. The calamity was blamed on Washington's hesitation to give positive orders for evacuation until, standing on the ground, he saw that he had delayed too long. Its fall was the final event of the war on Manhattan Island until the commander in chief would enter the city in triumph seven years later.

Hamilton's son reported that "The fall of that fortress which sealed the fate of the city of New York, and cut off so large a portion of the army, awakened all the soldier's spirit in his [father's] breast; and, after a careful observation of the post, he volunteered to General Washington to storm it, saying that if he would confide to him an adequate number of men, one-half under the command of Major Ebenezer Stevens, the residue of himself, he would promise him success."

Nothing would have warmed Washington's heart more at this dark hour than to recapture the fort bearing his name. It would mean at least symbolically that he had not entirely lost the city. The more foolhardiness the commander in chief saw in the proposal, the more he would admire the courage and zeal of its young maker.

Hamilton's company retreated from White Plains with Lord Stirling's brigade, crossed the Hudson to Haverstraw on November 9, 1776, and then hurried south to Hackensack through the gap in the Palisades known as the Clove, just ahead of Washington and the main army.

By the time Washington reached Hackensack, he had with him "not above 3,000 men and they much broken and dispirited." On November 19, Cornwallis landed 3,000 troops at Alpine, New Jersey, opposite Yonkers, and next morning they clambered up the Palisades and captured Fort Lee. General Nathanael Greene pulled out in such haste that his men abandoned all weapons and stores and when they joined Washington at Hackensack, Greene's demoralized regiments brought his total to about 5,400 poorly supplied troops.

Hamilton's company kept marching, deployed and redeployed its guns to provide cover for Stirling's brigade of 1,200 when it crossed the Passaic, and moved on down to Newark. Washington followed behind with the main body of the men. Enemy columns pursued them to Hackensack, and an American rear guard had to destroy the bridge to delay their pursuit. Still in the van with Lord Stirling, Captain Hamilton's company marched 20 miles westward, dragging their guns and ammunition to the Raritan River and across the wooden bridge there into New Brunswick, while Washington rested five more days at Newark with what he called "the wretched remains of a broken army."

At New Brunswick, Hamilton sited his cannons high on the west bank of the Raritan, on what is now the main campus of Rutgers University, to cover the army's river crossing, as Washington and the remnants of his retreating army straggled across the wooden bridge with Cornwallis pressing his pursuit close behind. As the last of the rear guard made it across the wooden bridge ahead of the pursuers, Hamilton's guns laid down and returned a "smart cannonade." Washington wrote Congress: "The enemy appeared in several parties on the heights opposite Brunswick and were advancing in a large body towards the crossing place. We had a smart cannonade while we were parading our men, but without any or but little loss on either side." Washington was in despair, but still indomitable. "It being impossible to oppose them with our present force . . . we shall retreat to the west side of Delaware." That meant somewhere far to the south, near Philadelphia or still further west.

As Hamilton and his artillerymen covered the epic retreat of Washington, a veteran artillery officer observing Hamilton wrote that he "noticed a youth, a mere stripling, small, slender, almost delicate in frame, marching . . . with a cocked hat pulled down over his eyes, apparently lost in thought, with his hand resting on a cannon, and every now and then patting it, as if it were a favorite horse or a pet plaything." He watched Hamilton march into the college town: "The day Hamilton's company marched into Princeton, it was a model of discipline. At their head was a boy, and I wondered at his youth; but what was my surprise when . . . he was pointed out to me as that Hamilton of whom we had already heard so much."

To make Washington's peril worse, his only reserves, the army under General Charles Lee at North Castle, ignored Washington's orders until every excuse was exhausted and then moved southwest at a leisurely pace—so leisurely, in fact, that Lee was captured by the British after being routed out of a prostitute's blankets in a tavern at Baskenridge, New Jersey. The name of the place was changed to Basking Ridge.

Death and desertion dogged the ranks of the stumbling Continentals. A British officer was shocked to see that "many of the Rebels who were killed . . . were without shoes or Stockings, & Several were observed to have only linen drawers . . . without any proper shirt or Waistcoat . . . also in great want of blankets . . . they must suffer extremely.''

Washington appealed through Governor Livingston for help from the people of New Jersey, but many could see for themselves that things were going badly for the Americans; instead of rallying to aid the desperate remnants of the patriot army, they signed oaths of allegiance to the British. Still Washington remained indomitable. He asked Adjutant General Joseph Reed of Philadelphia whether, if he were driven to retreat ''to the back parts of Pennsylvania,'' the inhabitants there would support him. If the enemy overran the eastern counties, and they gave up, Reed said, ''the back counties will do the same.'' In that case, Washington retorted, he would take refuge in mountainous Western Virginia. If the British pushed him from there too, he would move further west across the Alleghenies and fight on from there, at the head of whatever band of revolutionaries might remain with him then.

At this desperate hour nothing really remained of the American Revolution but the courage and resolve of George Washington and the little band of officers and men like Hamilton and his company who remained faithful through the long bitter marches of the retreat. Cornwallis and his army could cover 20 miles in a single day, and in pursuit the miles are shorter than in retreat. When the Americans flung themselves down to rest at night after fleeing the same distance, they were twice as weary and spent.

A few days before Christmas, Adjutant General Joseph Reed wrote a plea to Washington to make some kind of an attack on Cornwallis. If nothing else, it would be good for the morale of the colonies: ''We are all of opinion that something must be attempted to revive the aspiring credit, give our cause some degree of reputation and prevent total depreciation of the continental money . . . even a failure cannot be more fatal than to remain in our present situation.''

Reed called for a bold move: ''In short, some enterprise must be undertaken . . . or we must give up the cause. Will it not be possible . . . to make a diversion or something more at or about Trenton. . . . Our affairs are hastening fast to ruin if we do not retrieve them by some happy event.''

On the night of December 25, Hamilton's and other New Yorkers, New Hampshiremen, Virginians, and Pennsylvanians—men from all the provinces—bending forward against the gale-driven sleet, slogged toward the Delaware River and the waiting Durham boats. Their paths through the snow were ''tinged here and there with blood from the feet of men who wore broken shoes''—or no shoes. ''It will be a terrible night for the soldiers,'' wrote one officer, ''but I have not heard a man complain.''

Hamilton's boat and the others shoved out into the ice-choked flood, low in the water with the weight of guns, horses, and shivering men in remnants of blue and buff uniforms. If river-soaked muskets should become useless, Washington ordered, ''Tell General Sullivan to use the bayonet. I am resolved to take Trenton.''

The crossing was so slow that it was not until four in the morning that Hamilton and his company assembled on the Jersey shore to begin the nine-mile march to Trenton. A snowstorm, which from time to time turned to driving sleet, slowed their march still further, but kept them well hidden from Colonel Johann Gottlieb Rall's patrol and pickets as dawn broke.

Hamilton positioned his company's cannons at the edge of the town to fire into it from the head of King Street. The assault of the American infantry caught the Hessian garrison completely by surprise and badly hung over from their Christmas revelries of the night before. Hessian Lieutenant Andreas Wiederhold saw movement, heard shouts, then raised the alarm. *''Der Feind! Der Feind!''* he screamed. *''Heraus! Heraus!''* (The enemy! The enemy! All out! All out!)

It was too late. Hamilton's fieldpieces thumped out their cannonballs to cover the advancing infantry. Mercer's men charged in attacking columns with bayonets fixed. Washington sent Lord Stirling's brigade into action, spearheaded by George Weedon's Third Virginia Regiment. More Americans under Captain William Washington and Lieutenant James Monroe (later to assume higher rank) shot down and bayoneted the gunners and loaders who manned two Hessian artillery pieces.

Arthur St. Clair's brigade joined the charge. Leading its right wing, John Stark "dealt death wherever he found resistance and broke down all opposition before him." General Sullivan wheeled his whole command up from the river to meet St. Clair's moving down from the north.

In a snow-covered apple orchard, after a battle of less than three-quarters of an hour, the beaten remains of the British garrison of Trenton stacked their arms and surrendered.

Washington counted 918 enemy prisoners, including 30 officers, as many muskets as men, six brass cannons, and four of the prized Hessian battle standards. Thirty Hessians had been killed and three times as many wounded. No American had been killed and only four slightly wounded.

The snowstorm was getting worse. Weary from battle after the long night's march, the Americans retraced the nine miles to McKonkey's Ferry, and Glover's Durham boats and were back in their bivouacs 48 hours after the Trenton Christmas present for America had begun.

A home leave General Cornwallis had scheduled was abruptly canceled. He rushed 8,000 men from Princeton toward Trenton to take reprisal against the exhausted American force of only 5,000, now isolated on Cornwallis's side of the river. As he advanced, the Americans retreated back to the south of Assunpink Creek, near Trenton. Interdicting artillery fire from Hamilton's company held off Cornwallis for a few critical hours while Washington put their planned escape into action.

A rear guard flung on more logs to build up blazing campfires and kept up a noisy clatter with entrenching tools to deceive the British pickets. Washington's main army, with Captain Hamilton in the "great train of artillery," hitched up their horses and wrapped the wheels of the gun carriages with sacking to silence them on the frozen road. Hamilton's cannoneers held the trace chains with gloved hands to silence the slightest clank. They marched northward out of the trap toward Princeton.

British regimentals, moving unconcernedly out of Princeton by the old road toward what is now Lawrenceville, saw American General Hugh Mercer's column advancing on them in broad daylight. "Follow me!" cried Mercer, urging his men forward in a bloody charge toward British Colonel Charles Mawhood's line. A hail of British grapeshot and musket balls hit them. At the line, thrusting British bayonets slashed American bodies. Mercer's men, along with Cadwalader's, who had come up to support them, fled in disorderly retreat. An eyewitness reported that "Hamilton's two pieces of artillery stood their ground and were served with great skill and bravery." Panicky American troops swirled around Hamilton's exposed artillery position to provide what protection they could. Washington moved up with a relief column, rallied what remained of Mercer's and Cadwalader's brigades, and drove back toward the British line and through it, routed them from the field, and drove on into the college town, waving Knox's and Hamilton's artillerymen forward with the van. Units of the British South Lancashire Regiment rallied to form a new line of defense around the college buildings, but fell back again and finally took refuge in Nassau Hall.

Washington pressed the attack. Hamilton deployed and laid his gun sights on Nassau Hall. A well-aimed round crashed through a window and smashed through a portrait of

King George II. So goes the soldier's tale, hallowed by countless retellings. In any event, Hamilton was there.

Cornwallis marched his army back from Trenton at double time to bring its full weight to bear on Washington at Princeton. With his commander, Henry Knox, Hamilton could chuckle over the arrival of Cornwallis and his men at Princeton "in a most infernal sweat—running, puffing and blowing and swearing at being so outwitted," too late to catch Washington who had moved on.

Washington wheeled his columns north, passed them by route-march through Kingston, Rocky Hill, Somerset Court House, and Pluckemin to winter quarters on the Morristown plateau below Thimble Mountain. Twenty-five miles due west of New York City, almost equally distant from the main British strongholds at New York, Amboy, Newark, and New Brunswick, Morristown was protected on its easterly approaches from attack by any large body of enemy by heavy forests and inaccessible heights. Defiles to the west, leading to fertile and sympathetically peopled countryside, provided secure avenues for last-ditch retreat to the rear.

Captain Hamilton's New York Provincial Artillery Company, on arrival at Morristown winter quarters, positioned their guns to cover the easterly approaches with flat fields of grazing fire, dug gun emplacements, threw up earthworks, camouflaged them with branches, set out sentries in a perimeter defense, and pitched their tents. Those not on the roster of the first watch fell to the ground for some exhausted sleep until the time would come for them to be shaken awake by their comrades to stand the second watch.

Crude six-pound cannons like Hamilton's had to be positioned close behind the front line infantry. They fired their shot and ball on a flat trajectory aimed over open sights at enemy troops cannoneers could see. Artillerymen had to stay with their guns until their positions were overrun. The climactic moment of a losing battle usually meant bloody slaughter for the gun crews.

For the cannoneer and the company grade combat officer battle is an experience of random terror. Comrades fell or survived, were quickly killed or agonizingly wounded to die later, or escaped unscathed as part of a process of arbitrary selection decreed as much by luck as by skill, bravery, or cowardice. For one who survives it, a single day of battle in the line may contain more moments of fright, cowardice, despair, pain, gallantry, terror, luck, irony, heroism, and grandeur than all the other days of a long lifetime. In 1776, at places with such deceptively peaceful sounding names as Brooklyn, Long Island, Manhattan, Harlem, White Plains, Hackensack, New Brunswick, Trenton, and Princeton, Hamilton spent four months of such days.

Few generals but Washington, with his early years in the French and Indian War, could overmatch Hamilton's record of combat experience with a line company. It is not surprising that he and Washington would see so much else alike. The combat service of Hamilton with his company is of no historical importance in itself. But the imprint it left on Hamilton and all who knew him for the rest of his life is all-important for an understanding of him and of them.

While busy fleeing and retreating and deploying and covering, Hamilton kept meticulous records of his men's pay and other important matters of company management. He jotted down in his Pay Book some maxims for the management of men that in the years that followed he would use in the management of the nation. One such jotting was the following extract from Demosthenes' *First Philippic:*

As a general marches at the head of his troops, so ought wise politicians, if I dare use the expression, to march at the head of affairs; insomuch that they ought not to wait *the event,* to know what measures to take, but the measures which they have taken ought to produce the *event.*

War was a terrible thing, of course, as conventional wisdom held. But there was an important further point about it that Demosthenes had noted in the *First Philippic,* as recorded in Hamilton's Pay Book:

> Where attack him it will be said? Ah, Athenians, war, war itself will discover to you his weak sides, if you seek them.

To Demosthenes' observation, Hamilton wrote his marginal assent: "Sublimely simple."

Being Hamilton, not content with his own untested assent to Demosthenes' proposition, he tested it to see whether other wise men agreed. Racking his recollection, he recalled another scholar who agreed with the thesis, so he added the following citation to the entry in his Pay Book: "Vide Long: Ch. 16."

This meant that the passage he admired so much in Demosthenes was also cited in Dionysius Longinus' tract *On the Sublime.* Scholars since have pounced upon the fact that Hamilton's Pay Book citation of Longinus quoting the admired passage from Demosthenes is in error because it is not in Chapter XVI, as Hamilton recalled, but in Chapter XVIII.

It is somewhat reassuring to an ordinary reader that Hamilton, as a combat artilleryman on the march, recalling and jotting down classical cross-references in his company's pay book—shepardizing them mentally, as a lawyer might say—was sufficiently human to make this mistake.

Diversionary sniping by scholars from their armchairs does not obscure the point made by Demosthenes, Dionysius Longinus, and Hamilton about a man at war: "War itself will discover to you his weak sides, if you seek them." Discovering no weak sides in Hamilton at war, many a comrade in arms who had outranked him would later unhesitatingly follow him wherever he led in peacetime. No weak sides that peace might discover could matter at all, after a shared wartime experience of such intensity.

Or so they mistakenly thought.

6

The Idol of America Governed by One of His Aides

Prompt obedience to the orders conveyed by Hamilton, on the parts of Gates and Putnam, would have cut off the communication between the British army and fleet, and fulfilling Washington's prophecy, Howe would have been reduced to the situation of Burgoyne, thus probably terminating the war in the second year of our independence.

—John Church Hamilton, 1834

On January 20, 1777, Washington wrote Robert Hanson Harrison, one of his senior aides, asking that Harrison "forward the enclosed to Captain Hamilton." It was Washington's personal invitation to Hamilton to join his staff as an aide-de-camp.

Washington set high standards of excellence for his aides: "Aides de camp are persons in whom entire confidence must be placed." He added that "it requires men of abilities to execute the duties with propriety and dispatch." Most of all, perhaps, it requires the capacity "to comprehend at one view the diversity of matter, which comes before me, so as to afford the ready assistance which every man in my situation must stand more or less in need of." He added plaintively: "I give in to no kind of amusement myself, and consequently those about me can have none, but are confined from morning to eve, hearing and answering the applications and letters."

Hamilton's formal appointment as Washington's aide came March 1, 1777; the same day he was promoted to the rank of lieutenant colonel. He had just turned 20. Skipping the rank of major, he thus skipped majority of rank almost a year before attaining majority of status.

When Martha Washington arrived at the Morristown winter camp, it was the signal for the wives of the other ranking officers to join their husbands, and some of them brought their daughters. While the British were led by Sir William Howe, war could be a seasonal business. When there were reviews and parades for visiting diplomats, Hamilton, his friends John Laurens and Tench Tilghman and the other young aides turned out in their best dress uniforms of blue and buff with yellow lining and piping, flat double gilt buttons, corded dimity waistcoats and breeches, gold epaulets, and white gloves, with their hair powdered and kept in place with pomatum and a comb, and silver spurs on their boots.

Brother officers were invited to join Washington's table, and Hamilton became friendly with many of them. Alexander Graydon wrote of Hamilton during this first winter at Morristown: "He presided at the General's table, where we dined, and in a large company in which there were several ladies, among whom I recollect one or two of the Miss Livingstons and a Miss Brown, he acquitted him with an ease, propriety, and vivacity which gave me the most favorable impression of his talents and accomplishments. . . ."

When spring came on, Martha Dangerfield (Mrs. Theodorick) Bland wrote to her sister-in-law from Morristown, "We often make parties on horseback, the general, his lady, Miss Livingston & his aide de camps . . . at which time General Washington throws off the Hero and takes on the chatty agreeable companion—he can be downright impudent sometimes. . . ." Colonel Hamilton who is in "our riding party generally" is a "sensible, genteel, polite young fellow, a West Indian." She recalled the "pretty, airy look" of the surrounding villages: "They present us with just such scenes as the poets paint Arcadia: purling rills, mossy beds, etc., but not crying swains or lovely nymphs."

The lack of swains and nymphs was surprising to Mrs. Bland because "there are some exceeding pretty girls." The problem was that "they appear to have souls formed for the distaff rather than the tender passions."

Cantering on ahead of the other aides, alone with the adorable Kitty Livingston, Hamilton would dissent from Mrs. Bland's bleak conclusion, testing out for himself whether Kitty's soul was not formed for warmer playthings than her distaff. Spring was very much in the air, and his mind far from the serious business of the war, when he wrote her on April 11:

"Amidst my amorous transports, let me not forget that I am also to perform the part of a politician and intelligencer. I challenge you to meet me in whatever path you dare." He added dreamily: "We will even sometimes make excursions in the flowery walks, and roseate bowers of Cupid. You know, I am renowned for gallantry."

General Philip Schuyler, the father of another pretty visitor to Morristown, Elizabeth Schuyler, looked over all of Washington's aides and concluded that the young man who had earlier manhandled heavy guns across the state of New Jersey outshone them all. Not knowing then that the young man he described would become his closest confidant, political ally, dearest friend, and son-in-law besides, General Schuyler appraised the aides-de-camp and "discovered in all, an attention to the duties of their station; in some, a considerable degree of ability, but [in Hamilton] only I found those qualifications so essentially necessary to the man who is to aid and counsel a commanding general, environed with difficulties of every kind, and . . . whose correspondence must . . . be . . . frequently so delicate as to require much judgment and address."

Lieutenant Colonel Hamilton, with leonine vigor restored after his illness of the fall campaign—he would suffer recurrences of illness often through his lifetime—quickly assumed first place among his peers of equal rank and more seniority. G. W. P. Custis recorded that in 1777 and 1778, "the habit at . . . headquarters was for the General to dismiss his officers at a very late hour of the night to catch a little repose, while he, . . . drawing his cloak around him, and trimming his lamp, would throw himself upon a hard couch, not to sleep, but to think." Close by, in a blanket but "all accoutred," snored the short but active Billy, his body servant. If an express arrived, the "dispatches being . . . read, there would be heard in the calm deep tones of that voice, so well remembered . . . , the command of the chief to his now watchful attendant, 'Call Colonel Hamilton.' "

Washington complained of being bogged down in paper work: "At present my time is so taken up at my desk, that I am obliged to neglect many other essential parts of my duties; it is absolutely necessary . . . for me to have persons that can think for me, as well as execute orders." He carefully explained that his letters from his headquarters were "first drawn by his secretary and . . . aide de camp."

Of Hamilton's contribution, Adjutant General Timothy Pickering wrote, "I have every reason to believe that not only the composition, the clothing of the ideas, but the ideas themselves, originated generally with the writers. . . . Hamilton and Harrison in particular, were scarcely in any degree his amanuenses."

In the course of the war, Washington had 32 aides in all, but only five or six were with him at any one time. Among all the aides Hamilton's closest friend was the one who displayed the greatest personal devotion to Washington: John Laurens. When General Charles Lee spoke disparagingly of Washington's generalship after the Battle of Monmouth and Laurens challenged Lee to a duel to vindicate Washington's honor, Hamilton served as Laurens's second.

Aaron Burr had served for a few weeks as an aide before Hamilton arrived, but soon departed after a dispute with Washington. Washington always evinced suspicions of Burr which he never explained; when Burr's name would come up, Washington was content to misprize him by calling him an "intriguer."

Washington's headquarters was a political as well as a military headquarters. The whole ideological point of the war was representation of the American people through Congress in their struggle to throw off the yoke of a dictatorial king and parliament in which they were unrepresented. Every question had to be dealt with in the context of the Continental Congress's executive as well as legislative power over the associated colonies in rebellion at war. Washington could not prosecute the war as a chief executive himself, but only as the servant and agent of an often refractory and divided Congress. Money was short; inflation was rampant; terms of troop enlistment were continually expiring. Each state treated its own provincial or state forces as its own so continental generals could not deploy them without weighing the geographical and political effect that such deployments, and the resulting casualties and costs, would have on the states from which they came. From time to time troops mutinied because their pay was in arrears. All the while the British, with more and better-trained troops and naval control of the entire seaboard, held the principal city at the central notch of the colonies. Hamilton would spend most of the next four years in Washington's company at the political as well as military center of these not yet united, often disunited states.

As the only chief executive America possessed during these critical years, Washington had to rely on aides to produce documents for him so that he could carry on the many other kinds of state business he was called upon to perform. His ability to draw from his aides a huge volume of useful, necessary, elegantly styled documentary material that brought the authority of his signature, pen, and office effectively to bear on so many areas of military and executive leadership is further proof, if any were needed, of his greatness.

As general and aide, Washington and Hamilton worked together as a team in as many different ways as the situations and people they were dealing with required. Sometimes Washington dictated a memorandum of what was to be said and Hamilton then transcribed it. Other times, Washington stated the general idea and let his aide-de-camp compose the text and send it out over the aide's signature. Sometimes Washington signed what Hamilton had written. At other times Washington copied in his own hand without change what Hamilton had written out, and sent it as his own. There were thousands of documentary collaborations between the general and his aide. In these it is impossible to be certain, or even fairly sure, how much content, form, and style are Washington's and how much are Hamilton's, or even which of the two men originated the idea of creating the document in the first place.

It was an age of style, when style in writing counted for as much, or almost as much, as style in fighting. Hamilton's schoolmate and lifelong friend Robert Troup neatly straddled the profound question of which man was primarily responsible for the conspicuous elegance of Washington's and Hamilton's joint products. Troup wrote, "The pen for our army was held by Hamilton; and for dignity of manner, pith of matter, and elegancy of style, General Washington's letters are unrivalled in military annals."

Like all such valued aides, Hamilton did not boast about the largeness of his own contribution to such collaborations. In later years, all those who had worked closely with both of them tended to credit without question advice and orders from Hamilton as if they came from Washington. None doubted that both men's thoughts were grooved to run along the same lines.

Hamilton had a genius for friendships, and kept them in good repair by writing friends often, even during the rush of the army's business. Still suffering from his postcampaign illness, he wrote Hugh Knox a letter on February 14 that his old mentor in St. Croix found "very circumstancial and satisfactory." In March, he wrote another which Knox described as "the fine, impartial, laconic and highly descriptive account you favour'd me with of your last year's campaign."

In April 1777 Knox wrote:

> We rejoice in your *Good Character and Advancement* which is indeed only the just reward of merit. . . . May you still live . . . to justify the choice and merit the approbation of the Great and Good General Washington, a name which will Shine with distinguished Lustre in the Annals of History—A name dear to the friends of the Liberties of mankind!

Hugh Knox urged the headquarters intelligencer to write the inside story of the war:

> You must be the Annalist & Biographer, as well as the Aid de Camp, of General Washington, & the Historiographer of the American War! . . . take Minutes & Keep a Journal! . . . If you Survive the present troubles, I Aver few men Will be as well qualified to Write the History of the present Glorious Struggle. . . .

The year 1777 opened propitiously. Prisoner exchanges brought missing comrades back to the Morristown plateau. But beyond the horizons around the plateau, events were conspiring to destroy illusions that victory would come any time soon.

To encompass the military grand strategy of 1777, the situation maps kept by Hamilton as headquarters intelligencer at Morristown army headquarters took in the whole eastern half of the continent of North America, from Montreal and Quebec to Charleston and south, and from the British forts on the upper Mississippi and the Great Lakes to the British fleets prowling the ports of the Atlantic coast, holding sway over the trackless reaches of the continental shelf and all seven seas beyond.

Fort Ticonderoga was the supposedly invincible bastion guarding the northern corridor from Canada to New York, but it always seemed to be falling to one side or the other. On July 6, 1777, not knowing of the latest disaster that was breaking there that day, Hamilton wrote Gouverneur Morris a cool appraisal of British grand strategy: "I am loth to risk a conjecture about Mr. Howe. . . . If he acted like a man of sense, he would wait quietly on Staten Island, and there concenter all his forces. He would draw around all the men that could be spared from Canada and all that are now at Rhode Island."

But instead of doing what Hamilton expected of a sensible enemy commander, Sir William Howe had just embarked thousands of the best British and Hessian troops from New York and headed out into the Atlantic hazes with a great flotilla that could have had any number of important objectives. Hamilton confided in a letter to Hugh Knox on July 5 that "Appearances lead us to suppose that Howe is fool enough to meditate a southern expedition." Scouting the conventional strategy that would call for Washington holding the principal cities, Hamilton would willingly write off the capital, Philadelphia, if this would serve the larger purposes of the war. Should Howe "be satisfied with the splendour of his acquisition, and shut himself up in Philadelphia, we can ruin him by confinement."

Despite Hamilton's scorn of it, Howe's plan for an attack on Philadelphia had much to recommend to strategists back in Whitehall. With New York secure, Howe could dominate the middle colonies from Philadelphia, the largest city in America and the capital and seat of the Continental Congress. Worsening inflation would contribute to destroying the fragile continental economy; unpaid soldiers would desert. Then, to save his capital of troops and money, Washington would "have to risk a battle." Thereafter the fall of Charleston would open the door to the South. The fate of the colonies would be sealed.

The patriots of New York, chafing under enemy occupation, demanded army action, and criticized Washington for seeming to do nothing but malinger out in the hills at Morristown.

The New York Provincial Convention had appointed the Committee of Correspondence to report all developments in Washington's camp and named Gouverneur Morris to be chief correspondent. Hamilton had taken over from Tench Tilghman, responding to Morris:

> With cheerfulness, I embrace the proposal of corresponding with your convention, through you, and shall from time to time as far as my leisure will permit, and my duty warrant, communicate such transactions as shall happen, such pieces of intelligence as shall be received and such comments upon them as shall appear necessary to convey a true idea of what is going on in the military line.

Hamilton went out of his way to dispel any idea the committee might have that he spoke for the general or was improperly disclosing official secrets: "whatever opinions I shall give, in the course of our correspondence, are to be considered merely as my private sentiment and are never to be interpreted as an echo of those of the *General*. . . ." He was being ostentatiously discreet, protecting both himself and his commander in a situation where the temptation was great for a young man on the rise to inflate both his own self-importance and the authority of his views by issuing them with nothing more than this general disclaimer.

On March 22, 1777, Hamilton again protested that ''Wherever I give opinions, they are merely my own and will probably, so far from being a transcript of those of the General, differ widely from them in many respects.'' He was not only keeping his fences mended in his home state, but he was also quietly building himself a political base among the leaders there entirely independent of his dependent status as Washington's first aide.

When New York proclaimed a new state constitution on April 20, 1777, Hamilton voiced concern to Gouverneur Morris about a requirement that senators have a freehold worth £100 and members of the lower house £20. It was too restrictive a property qualification.

''The evil I mean is,'' he argued, ''that in time, your Senate, from the very name and from the mere circumstance of its being a separate member of the legislature, will be liable to degenerate into a body purely aristocratical.'' A simple, single-house legislature might be preferable. The danger of an abuse of power would not be great, he thought, ''in a government where the equality and fullness of popular representation is so wisely provided for as in yours.''

Whether there were two houses or one, the main thing was a broad base of popular representation in the legislature. Hamilton distinguished sharply between what he considered true representative government, on the one hand, and mob rule on the other.

> When the deliberative or judicial powers are vested wholly or partly in the collective body of the people, you must expect error, confusion and instability. But a representative democracy, where the right of election is well secured and regulated and the exercise of the legislative, executive and judicial authorities, is vested in select persons, chosen *really* and not *nominally* by the people, will in my opinion be most likely to be happy, regular and durable.

He recognized that ''unstable democracy, is an epithet frequently in the mouths of politicians,'' but criticism on this count was unjustified.

Robert R. Livingston, of the New York Committee of Correspondence and scion of the great old Livingston dynasty, urged that the army make feints toward New York with two or three thousand men at a time on bold commando-style sorties. If nothing else, this would have a good effect on wavering Tories.

The practical politics of the situation mandated army action even though grand strategy did not, so Hamilton wrote up what was really a near-debacle to sound like a victory for the benefit of Livingston and New York. Hamilton grasped the complex interrelationship of politics, local tactics, and grand strategy that were basic ingredients of ultimate success for Washington's command:

> I know the comments that some people will make on our Fabian conduct. It will be imputed either to cowardice or to weakness; but the more discerning, I trust, will not find it difficult to conceive that it proceeds from the truest policy, and is an argument neither of the one nor the other.

The 20-year-old added in organ tones: ''The liberties of America are an infinite stake. We should not play a desperate game for it or put it upon the issue of a single cast of the die.''

From secret correspondence as headquarters intelligencer, Hamilton knew as well as any man that ''We are continually strengthening our political springs in Europe, and may every day look for more effectual aid than we have yet received. . . . Their affairs will be growing worse—ours better;—so that delay will ruin them. . . . Our business then is to avoid a general engagement and waste the enemy away by constantly goading their sides, in a desultory teasing way.''

In another letter Hamilton reminded Gouverneur Morris that Wasbington's Fabian tactics had been working pretty well so far: ''Their flourishes in the Jerseys, I believe, cannot have cost them less than six or seven hundred men. We have not lost above a hundred. This is the best way to ruin them, without risking anything.''

Washington moved his army down off the heights of Morristown westward into Bucks County, Pennsylvania. There the Marquis de Lafayette, his petition for a command granted by Congress, joined the army as an unsalaried major general at the camp near Neshaminy Ridge.

News of Washington moving west made nervous New Yorkers and New Englanders feel all the more defenseless. ''Gentleman Johnny'' Burgoyne was now moving south from Canada toward Fort Ticonderoga. From the northwest, British Colonel Barry St. Leger and his bloodthirsty Indian allies were driving east from Oswego along the Mohawk Valley toward Oriskany. Sir Henry Clinton with some of the forces that Howe had left behind was threatening to move north up the Hudson from New York City. The lines of march of all three British expeditionary forces converged on Albany.

If Burgoyne from the north, St. Leger from the west, and Sir Henry Clinton from the south should link up at Albany, while Howe kept Washington's main army drawn off by what might turn out to be only a feint at Philadelphia, the Empire State would be dismembered north to south and east to west all the way north to Quebec and west to Lake Ontario. The dream of a contiguous continental nation of 13 states would be untenable. On General Philip Schuyler, based at Albany, with the northern outpost of his command under Arthur St. Clair at Fort Ticonderoga, rested the awesome responsibility for thwarting Britain's grand strategy in the northern theater.

General Schuyler would have 5,000 Continentals to stop the invaders; New England, roused to the danger, would, he hoped, supply up to twice as many militia. Two regiments from Peekskill and Daniel Morgan's picked corps of sharpshooters were also marching north to reinforce Schuyler. They were ''well-used to rifles and to woodfights'' and would help dissipate the people's ''panic dread'' of Burgoyne's Indians. Hamilton's confidence in their bold expertness was borne out in the event at Saratoga. The rest of his hopeful forecast turned out disastrously wrong.

Early in July, John Burgoyne's second in command, Major General William Phillips, secretly hauled up to the undefended summit of Mount Defiance and emplaced there a hidden battery of artillery with muzzles aimed to fire pointblank down into the inner works of Fort Ticonderoga. Looking up, discovering the guns, and realizing that the artillery on the mountain crest placed the defenders under a hopeless checkmate, General Arthur St. Clair evacuated the fort and its entire garrison and fled southward. Burgoyne's men and their Indian cohorts fell upon the panicked and fleeing Americans. The Americans tried to make a stand at Hubbardton, and were overrun; they were overrun again at Bemis Heights; Burgoyne moved on. He seized General Schulyer's own country house at Old Saratoga and turned it into his headquarters for what he planned as the final victorious push to Albany, only about 40 miles downriver.

A shocked and angry Robert R. Livingston wrote Hamilton in alarm. Hamilton wrote back, trying to mollify him a little by reluctantly concurring in Livingston's scathing criticism of General Philip Schuyler, his future father-in-law:

> I have been always a very partial Judge of General Schuylers Conduct, and

Vindicated it frequently from the Charges brought against it, but I am at last forced to suppose him inadequate to the Important Command with which he has been intrusted. There seems to be a want of firmness in all his Actions, and this last Instance in my Opinion is too unequivocal to be doubted. The Reason assigned for his last retreat is the panic among the army, which he seems to say is beyond anything that was ever known.

Out of his own combat experience with panicky troops, Hamilton drew an important distinction for Livingston's benefit. "Soldiers Commonly look up to those that Command them & take their Complection from their Armies. Under the best, Leaders may be seized with a sudden panic that may precipitate them into the most cowardly behaviour for the Moment, but a settled durable panic is generally a Reflection upon the Leader." St. Clair, not Schuyler, had been the leader responsible. The panic had been momentary, not "a settled durable panic." The army had fought its retreat; it was still in being.

Political pressure forced Washington to recall Schuyler and St. Clair to his headquarters command and put General Horatio Gates in overall command of the North. Of Schuyler, Hamilton wrote Livingston, "I wish among other things he had not rendered himself odious to your state . . . but his appointment to this command could not be avoided."

The mystery of what had happened to Howe and his flotilla continued to keep Washington's army headquarters and Congress off balance. Out of the cloud of rumors about where Howe's flotilla had gone finally emerged hard news on August 22. John Adams wrote his wife, Abigail, "It is now no longer a secret where Mr. Howe's fleet is . . . it is arrived at the head of Chesapeake Bay. . . . His march by land to Philadelphia may be about sixty or seventy miles."

On August 29, Hamilton wrote to Gates for Washington that "his intentions against Philadelphia" were now "reduced to a certainty."

But Howe's month-long voyage had given Washington ample time to move the American army from Morristown through Philadelphia to the heights of Wilmington and position itself once again, as it had been before, between the British and the City of Brotherly Love.

Hamilton wrote to Gouverneur Morris from Washington's headquarters on September 1, "The enemy will have Philadelphia if they dare make a bold push for it, unless we fight them a pretty general action. I opine we ought to do it, and that we shall beat them soundly if we do. The militia seem pretty generally stirring; our army is in high health & spirits." Howe had 15,000 men to Washington's 11,000, yet Hamilton boasted, "We shall I hope have twice the enemy's numbers." This miscalculation led to a serious misjudgment. "I would not only fight them, but I would attack them; for I hold it an established maxim, that there is three to one in favor of the party attacking." With so much in its favor, the American army would be extremely inept to lose. It was and did.

It fell to the lot of Washington and his aides on the Brandywine to help spread the "complection" of courage among the fleeing troops that day to keep the contagion of panic to the dimensions of a "sudden panic," and not allow it to swell into "a settled durable panic."

Little by little order was regained. The army, beaten but still in being, trailed over the bridge at Chester Creek and beyond the village of Chester. Washington was too fatigued to write the bad news to Congress himself, Harrison was too "distressed," so Timothy Pickering wrote the bitter communiqué from the once more defeated commander in chief: "I am sorry to inform you that in this day's engagement we have been obliged to leave the enemy masters of the field." He put the best face he could on the casualties and concluded,

"Notwithstanding the misfortune of the day, I am happy to find the troops in good spirits."
He added, "I hope another time we shall compensate for the losses now sustained."

Washington sent Dr. Benjamin Rush, the Philadelphia physician-politician, through the
lines to treat wounded American prisoners that the losers had abandoned to the British on the
field. When Dr. Rush returned, he compared the beaten, dispirited patriot army to the
disciplined British regulars he had just been with; the contrast he drew necessarily "gave
offense" to his American countrymen. In his notebook he jotted down his diagnosis of what
was wrong with the army just as he might have done for any of his other wounded, sick,
disturbed, or distressed patients:

> The state and disorders of the American Army:
> 1. The Commander in Chief, at this time the idol of America, governed by
> General Greene, General Knox, and Colonel Hamilton, one of his aides, a young
> man of twenty-one years of age.
> 2. Four major generals, Greene, Sullivan, Stirling and Stevens [sic]. The first a
> sycophant to the General, speculative, without enterprise. The second weak, vain,
> without dignity, fond of scribbling, in the field a madman. The third a proud, vain,
> lazy, ignorant drunkard. The fourth a sordid, boasting cowardly sot. The troops
> undisciplined and ragged, guns fired a hundred a day, pickets left five days and
> sentries twenty-four hours without relief; bad bread, no order, universal disgust.

The only nongeneral and by far the youngest member of Dr. Rush's "enemies list" of
officers who "governed" Washington, Hamilton is the only one who emerges unscathed
from his critique, the only one whose influence on the "idol of America" is not in Rush's
words prima facie a malignant one. Insofar as Washington was not under his generals'
malignant influences, the idol of America was governed by this one of his aides.

Howe, as usual, failed to follow up his victory by pursuing Washington's army, and
instead plodded on toward Philadelphia, where Congress sat nervously watching his
unimpeded progress toward the capital, wondering why Washington's army did nothing to
stop him and save it.

A delicate message had to be written.

From Yellow Springs on September 17, Hamilton wrote Washington's dispatch warning
Congress of danger, but Congress did not act.

Hamilton wrote a second warning to John Hancock in Congress. The main body of the
enemy was only four miles from Swedes' Ford, he pointed out, at a point on the Schuylkill
on the site of what is now Norristown, and they could use flat-bottomed boats to ferry 50
men at a time, "in a few hours perhaps sufficient to overmatch the militia who may be
between them and the city. This renders the situation of Congress extremely precarious. . . . My apprehensions for them are great. . . ."

Congress took alarm. An entry for September 18, 1777, in the Journals of the Continental
Congress 1774–1779, cited Hamilton's letter as the authority for "the necessity of Congress
removing immediately from Philadelphia" to Lancaster.

Howe reached and crossed the Schuylkill, and one of his foraging parties blundered into a
little-known spot called Valley Forge, where guards were not posted, and seized a depot.
Not far away the usually alert Anthony Wayne likewise failed to post a proper watch.
Trapped in their bivouacs near Paoli, his men were overrun by a British force that swept
down on their camp in total silence, using only bayonets, and killed the Americans by
stabbing them as they aroused themselves from sleep in disorganized horror. Survivors fled
the field screaming cries of "Massacre!"

On September 26, Lord Cornwallis triumphantly led the British and Hessian grenadiers into Philadelphia "amidst the acclamations of some thousands of inhabitants." The rest of the victorious Anglo-German force took up forward posts at Germantown.

Thanks to Hamilton, the Continental Congress had escaped capture by eight days with much of its dignity intact. Moving on west from Lancaster, Congress sequestered itself still more safely in the little town of York, which now became the new capital of the United States. Like Washington's beaten army encamped between it and the enemy at Penny-packer's Mill on Perkiomen Creek, Congress remained in existence after a summer of dashed hopes to keep the flame of independence alive through another winter.

Washington had now demonstrated to Congress that he could not defend New York, the most strategic city, or Philadelphia, the capital, or Congress itself, the only national executive and legislative body. Was he really the right man to continue in command of the army? In York there were serious doubts. Men close to Washington began to doubt him. Adjutant General Timothy Pickering said to General Nathanael Greene, "Before I came to the army, I entertained an exalted opinion of General Washington's military talents, but I have since seen nothing to enhance it." General Greene, who had urged Washington to hold Fort Washington, seen it fall, and then abandoned Fort Lee with all its supplies intact, agreed. "Why," he said, "the General does want decision."

No such doubts were heard from Hamilton, who was helping Washington plan a full-scale attack that would redeem his reputation. On October 3, Hamilton wrote out the General Orders to the Army for the attack on Germantown, translating Washington's order to Count Casimir Pulaski and his cavalrymen into French. The text called for four columns to attack the heart of the British advance position at dawn after a long night march of more than 20 miles.

Seven P.M., October 3, 1777, saw Washington's four columns on the march toward the village of small houses and stone mansions strung along the main highway leading to Philadelphia. By 3:00 A.M. Washington and Hamilton, with Sullivan's column, were inside the British picket lines. As dawn approached, an autumn mist rose with the sun, wrapping the whole sloping countryside in a thick, ghostly fog. Other columns followed roads on the extreme right and left and delayed and strayed and failed to reach the scene of the main battle at all. Seeing the American advance guard, British sentries at Mr. Airy put up a noisy resistance that alerted the main British force a mile to the rear. The American columns charged past the outposts. Inside Benjamin Chew's stone mansion, Colonel Musgrave and his men barricaded the doors and fired down on the attacking Americans from second-floor windows.

Hamilton and Timothy Pickering urged Washington and Sullivan to drive on ahead, bypassing the Chew house, to keep up the momentum of the attack. Washington should leave behind only enough troops to surround it and keep Colonel Musgrave's men bottled up there.

But Henry Knox opposed Hamilton's advice. According to Pickering, the former Boston bookseller rummaged through his well-read mind and came up with a perfectly proper military maxim that was fatally wrong for this situation: Knox opined, "It would be unmilitary to leave a castle in our rear."

Hamilton and Pickering pleaded that the time it would take to reduce the house would sacrifice the momentum of the advance toward the main force battle ahead. If the whole attack focused on the Chew mansion, a call for surrender might be ignored by Musgrave's men or mistaken in the fog of the battle. Any American who advanced with the flag might be killed. But the final decision of "the idol of America" on this occasion was not governed by his aide. Knox's military aphorism won the battle of words on the battlefield.

Brigadier Knox brought up all his six-pounders and blasted away at the stone fortress with no more effect than to leave some cannonball scars on it that are visible on the old stones to this day. Worse still, General Adam Stephen, hearing Knox's cannonade through the mist and thinking that the sound marked the scene of the main battle, turned his own column aside from its assigned route to the front and added his artillery to the useless clatter of Knox's on the stones of the Chew house.

Timothy Pickering's aide, Lieutenant William Smith, volunteered to advance toward the house with a summons for the enemy to surrender, did so, and was mortally wounded. Lieutenant Colonel John Laurens, leading a patrol with a young French engineer, the Chevalier de Mauduit du Plessis, circled around to the stable behind the house to set fires and scorch the British out, and was shot through the shoulder.

American ammunition ran low. Militia fired on each other in the persistent fog, and each then turned and fled blindly from the other. Self-activated panic spread to other units. Some commands fell back to draw more ammunition, found irresistible charm in movement to the rear, and began to break and run out of impulse and old habit.

With the main American column wasting more than an hour battering at the Chew house, the British were handed a chance to rally their troops.

Greene's columns, spent by their long march into action, fighting blind in smoke and mist, counterattacked by fresh British troops, lost some guns and then fell back in reasonably good order. Hamilton, shouting commands in French, rallied Count Casimir Pulaski's cavalrymen to cover Greene's retreat.

Off to the west, John Sullivan's command was pulling back from the field they had come so close to winning. "The enemy kept a civil distance behind, sending now and then a shot after us and receiving the same from us," soldier-pamphleteer Thomas Paine drily wrote later.

Anthony Wayne wrote in angry frustration that when "the Enemy were broke, Dispersed & flying on all Quarters . . . a *Wind Mill* attack was made on a House into which Six Light Companies had thrown themselves to Avoid our Bayonets—this gave time to the Enemy to Rally. Our Troops . . . fell back to Assist in what they deemed a Serious matter—" Defeat was snatched from the jaws of victory, "the Enemy finding themselves no further pursued and believing it to be a Retreat followed—Confusion ensued, and we ran away from the Arms of Victory ready Open to receive us."

Washington and Hamilton and other aides sought to rally the fleeing men once again, but their complexion of courage was not enough to stem the "settled durable panic" of the day. The rout did not end until sheer exhaustion set in back at Perkiomen, 24 miles north of Germantown.

Hamilton wearily drafted Washington's report to Congress, which attributed retreat "at the instant when Victory was declaring herself in our favor" to "the extreme haziness of the weather." Another crushing defeat, with American casualties of about 1,000, in the same hazy weather in which the British won! The ominous tide of criticism of Washington's generalship rose in the Continental Congress at York and spread throughout the country.

As Washington's star with Congress sank low into the Delaware and Hamilton's with it, that of Major General Horatio Gates, up on the Hudson at Saratoga, as rapidly rose. Of medium build, shortsighted and bespectacled, with thin graying hair, Gates looked more like a chief clerk than a commander in chief. Even without overtly joining a cabal or adding his voice to the rising rumble of dissatisfaction with Washington's performance as commander in chief, Gates's existence as an alternative to Washington called for no action on his part to rise as a formidable threat. Soon he would win credit for the decisive victory of the war.

General Charles Lee, who was now intriguing widely against Washington, did not let his and Horatio Gates's supporters in Congress forget Washington's deficiencies as a military leader. To Horatio Gates himself, Lee wrote, *"Entre nous,* a certain great man is most damnably deficient.''

Below Philadelphia the Americans still held Fort Mifflin on the Pennsylvania bank of the Delaware and Fort Mercer on the New Jersey bank opposite it. In the channel between the two forts was strung a chevaux-de-frise—a protective barrier of timbers and projecting spikes—stretching across the river, which was covered by American gunboats as well as by the guns of the two forts. This prevented British ships from bringing supplies upriver to Howe's troops in Philadelphia. When Howe bypassed these two forts, Benjamin Franklin commented shrewdly that he could not tell whether Howe had taken Philadelphia, or Philadelphia had taken Howe. Howe's army had fought its way into a trap in Philadelphia, unless it could free itself by taking the two forts and removing the chevaux-de-frise between them.

To save the forts and close the noose on Howe would redeem for Washington the reputation he had lost in the debacles of Germantown, Paoli, the evacuation of Philadelphia, and on the Brandywine.

Hamilton wrote a letter for Washington's signature October 15, 1777, to Colonel Christopher Greene, whose First Rhode Island Regiment was helping defend the two forts; it provides a good example of the trust Washington now placed in his aide's military and tactical judgment: "The British attempt will probably be sudden and violent as they are hardly in a situation to delay a matter so essential to them as that of removing the river obstructions.'' He went on, ''It is of infinite importance . . . their keeping or evacuating Philadelphia materially depends'' on their taking Forts Mercer and Mifflin. ''Keep fully in mind the prodigious importance of not suffering the enemy to get entire possession of the Delaware . . . spare no pains or activity to frustrate their efforts''

The draft of this letter is in the third person, for Hamilton's signature, while the original, the receiver's copy, is written in the first person for Washington's signature. The receiver's copy contains the following postscript: ''The above letter was written by his Excellency's orders; but as he went to bed before it was finished, it will be handed you without his signature.'' Hamilton had written it and been so certain that Washington approved he had not bothered to awaken the general to sign it.

Following this urgent advice, Colonel Greene, ably seconded at Fort Mercer by the Chevalier de Mauduit du Plessis, turned back a powerful Hessian attack. Over in flimsy Fort Mifflin, Colonel Samuel Smith and Major Simeon Thayer of Rhode Island and their men held out under heavy British bombardment from ship and shore. But if fresh troops could not soon be found to raise the siege, still another disaster loomed close to home for Congress to chew over in York and blame on their perennial loser of a commander in chief—governed, some would say, by one of his easily panicked young aides.

After seizing Fort Ticonderoga in July, Burgoyne's advance had become slow and painful. St. Leger's eastward invasion along the Mohawk was beaten back by Marinus Willett at Fort Stanwix and by Nicholas Herkimer's Tryon County men at Oriskany. But gambler that he was, Burgoyne pressed on southward toward Saratoga, where Philip Schuyler's own lands and large country house stood directly in his path. Schuyler, who knew the terrain better than anyone else, combed the Hudson Valley for woodsmen, found tools for them, and sent them North to fell trees across trails, build up existing deadfalls, dam up brooks, and create viscous swamps where sure footing had been. He carefully laid out fortified positions for a final line of defense beside the Hudson at Old Saratoga.

To New Englanders, Schuyler's sins included the failure of ill-fated expeditions to Canada, and rejection of the claims of the Green Mountain Boys to the New Hampshire Grants, which would later become Vermont. He was a patroonish holder of spreading lands in the Dutch tradition and influential with the Indians who supplied the rich fur trade, which made him an object of jealous suspicion by the small yeomen farmers east of the Hudson. He was the friend of Washington, who had withdrawn from Boston, which he held, for New York, which he lost. He had an aristocratic way of not turning the other cheek, and he had just lost Fort Ticonderoga.

In the name of all New England, congressional delegates like Samuel Adams demanded that Horatio Gates replace him. Washington demurred, reminding Congress that as they had taken separate responsibility for the northern department, the portentous choice of a substitute general should be theirs. They had promptly appointed Gates.

Well dug into the fortifications Schuyler had laid out blocking the route down the Hudson, the northern army, now under Gates, brought Burgoyne to a halt at Saratoga. In September and again in early October, Burgoyne's men attacked in vain to break through. Sir Henry Clinton in New York City, concerned at the possibility of disaster northward, moved some columns up the Hudson and by the middle of October had reached Esopus, now Kingston, leaving a gap of only 80 miles between him and Burgoyne's army. On October 16, Clinton set fire to the town. More important, the next day at Saratoga, Burgoyne surrendered to Gates with all 5,700 men he had left in his army.

Saratoga, one of the ten decisive battles of world history, was saluted around the world as a sensational defeat for British arms and a notable victory for Americans. James Lovell, a Massachusetts member of Congress, depicted a hapless Washington powerless to halt an enemy rampaging unopposed around Philadelphia on the Delaware. "Your army & the eastern militia are now strongly contrasted with those in the Middle State(s). . . . It is said Howe would not have passed more than 70 Miles, from the Ships which landed him, in his whole Skin in Y neighbourhood, or among Yankee Stone walls. . . . Our hope springs all from the Northward, and about all our Confidence."

Leaders of Washington's own army hustled to congratulate Gates effusively on a success that so spectacularly highlighted Washington's failures. Joseph Reed, one of Washington's former aides, saluted Gates, regretting that "this Army,. . . notwithstanding the Labours . . . of our amiable Chief[,] has yet gathered no Laurels." Brigadier General Thomas Conway would send Gates a plan for instruction of the whole army. To his letter he added a slur on Washington's command that would soon cause a sensation: "Heaven has determined to save your Country, or a weak General and Bad Councillors would have ruined it." To Conway, the worst of the "Bad Councillors" around the "weak general" was Hamilton.

Congress thanked Gates in the name of the 13 United States for defeating an army of 10,000 men and securing the surrender of 5,700. It voted to strike a gold medal, and presented it to him. It called on the people for a day of thanksgiving that God "hath been pleased . . . to crown our arms with most signal success."

Washington theoretically was in overall command, even in the northern theater, but when

Gates officially announced his victory to Congress he bypassed his commander in chief, and sent the news direct by his adjutant, Colonel James Wilkinson. Far from rebuking Gates for the slight to Washington, Congress complied with a request of Gates's by promoting his messenger, Wilkinson, the bearer of glad tidings, from colonel to brigadier general.

On October 29, 1777, ten days after receiving the officially glorious but inwardly galling news of Burgoyne's surrender to Gates, Washington called five major generals and ten brigadiers to a council of war at his temporary camp at Whitpain. He assigned Hamilton, his loyal aide with the ready pen, to keep the minutes, as well as to see and be seen by the innermost circle of his generals. Howe had 10,000 men; Washington, 11,000. But expiration of enlistments would soon reduce Washington's number to 9,000. The generals agreed that 20 regiments must be drawn down from the northern theater to the main army, in addition to Daniel Morgan's riflemen, who were already on their way. To pry the reinforcements loose from Gates's command, Washington must dispatch one of his aides northward.

From Washington's point of view this was one of the most delicate missions of the war—and of his own career. His position as the commander in chief, the continental effort in the most critical theater of the war, and the safety of the Continental Congress itself were all at stake. For this critical mission Washington chose the youngest of his aides, writing Hamilton October 30, 1777, from his headquarters at Philadelphia:

> Dear sir—It having been judged expedient by the members of a Council of War held yesterday, that one of the Gentlemen of my family should be sent to General Gates in order to lay before him the state of this army; I thought it proper to appoint you that duty, and desire that you will immediately set out for Albany, at which place you will find General Gates.

The problem was to persuade Gates to release some of his troops voluntarily without bringing the matter to a test of wills or a test vote in Congress. There New England's backing of Gates and the Middle States' and Southern disillusionment with Washington might well result in a fatal split in colonial unity, and Washington's own replacement by Gates. Because Congress, at Washington's insistence, had replaced Schuyler with Gates in the northern command, Gates was "more peculiarly under . . . direction of Congress." So Hamilton's mission was one of diplomacy and persuasion, not just to deliver an order. There was no certainty that Washington any longer even had the authority to give an order to Gates or that Gates would obey it. Or that Congress would back Washington if Gates should defy it.

Washington explained to Hamilton, "What you are chiefly to attend to, is to point out in the clearest and fullest manner to General Gates the absolute necessity that there is for his detaching a very considerable part of the army at present under his command to the reinforcement of this."

With additional troops from Gates, Washington hoped "in all probability" to "reduce General Howe to the same situation in which General Burgoyne now is, should he attempt to remain in Philadelphia without being able to remove the obstructions in Delaware, and opening a free communication with his shipping."

Washington wrote a separate letter to Gates, congratulating him coolly on his victory, but in reproof regretting that Gates had bypassed him sending back news of it. His letter revealed full understanding of the hostility Hamilton could expect to meet when he arrived at Gates's headquarters.

The key passage of Washington's instructions to Hamilton entrusted to him complete discretion in final judgment: "If . . . you should find that [General Gates] intends, in consequence of his Success, to employ the troops under his command upon some expeditions, by the prosecution of which the common cause will be more benefited than by their being sent down to reinforce this army, it is not my wish to give interruption to the plan."

This left Hamilton with the broadest possible discretion—and responsibility for the forts and Washington's survival. Hamilton was to decide, in the light of Gates's plans, whether the war was to be prosecuted during the next months in the North, for example, by Gates against Sir Henry Clinton, who was still burning down houses and mills around Kingston, or by Washington around Philadelphia against Sir William Howe.

Albany was 254 miles by road from Washington's camp. Reinforcements were on the way to Howe from New York City by ship to be used in reducing the two forts. If reinforcements reached Washington overland in time he might still raise the siege before Howe overran them. Every day, every hour saved by Hamilton was vital if the forts were to be saved.

On October 30 as bidden Hamilton saddled up and with Captain Caleb Gibbs cantered up the high road for Albany. They covered 60 to 75 miles a day. As they passed Daniel Morgan's riflemen moving south, Hamilton stopped long enough to hurry them on their way and send a report back to Washington. Hamilton and Gibbs reached New Windsor, at a distance of 150 miles, late on November 1, and spent some time at Fishkill on November 2. From there Hamilton wrote Washington of some extra help he had found and rushed on its way: "I have directed General Putnam, in your name, to send forward with all dispatch to join you, the two continental brigades and Warner's militia brigade[,] . . ." even though their enlistments were expiring at the end of the month. "Your instructions did not comprehend any militia, but . . . I concluded you would not disapprove of a measure calculated to strengthen you, though but for a small time." Hamilton followed up on earlier detachments: "Neither Lee's or Jackson's regiments, nor the detachments belonging to General McDougall's division, have yet marched. I have pressed their being sent, and an order has been dispatched for their instantly proceeding."

Deferentially, but unmistakably, he pointed out certain faulty troop dispositions, and added an aggressive postscript: "So strongly am I impressed with the importance of endeavoring to crush Mr. Howe, that I am apt to think it would be advisable to draw off all the regulars—'the Continental troops.' Had this been determined on, General Warner's 1600 militia might have been left here."

Hamilton arrived in Albany around noon November 5, weary and probably half sick as well. There he "waited upon General Gates immediately on the business of my mission." Gates received Hamilton in the company of several of his subordinate officers. To all the other reasons for hostility that Hamilton and Washington had foreseen was no doubt added the chagrin that the touchy Gates must have felt at first sight of the extreme youth of the emissary Washington had sent.

According to the reports Hamilton wrote to Gates and Washington, their tense confrontation went more or less as follows, omitting eighteenth-century amenities:

HAMILTON: The commander in chief requests you to send three brigades from here to White Marsh to join him, to raise the siege of the Delaware forts and bottle up Howe in Philadelphia; otherwise, they will fall to Howe.

GATES: I have received no such order from Congress. Besides I cannot spare more troops from this command.

HAMILTON: You promised Washington that when you disposed of Burgoyne's threat, you would send him reinforcements.

GATES: I have already sent on Learned's and Poor's and Warner's brigades.

HAMILTON: He is already counting on those, but they are under-strength and not enough. Washington must have more troops soon.

GATES: Are the forts really so important?

HAMILTON: Of course. They command the Delaware and keep reinforcements and supplies from New York from reaching Howe before winter.

GATES: I am inflexible in the opinion that two brigades at least of Continental troops should remain in and near this place.

HAMILTON: When you needed reinforcements last summer, you were quick enough to send for them to Artemas Ward, to Benedict Arnold, and to Benjamin Lincoln. Why can't you comply with Washington's urgent request for troops now?

GATES: Only last month Sir Henry Clinton took forts Montgomery and Clinton on the Hudson, and we had to destroy Fort Constitution ourselves. The enemy is still to the south of us and threatening.

HAMILTON: How do you know?

GATES: We unscrewed a hollow bullet swallowed by a spy we captured and found an enemy message inside.

HAMILTON: I do not think Sir Henry Clinton still intends coming on this way.

GATES: The intelligence of Sir Henry Clinton's having given up the idea of joining Burgoyne is not sufficiently authenticated to put it out of doubt.

HAMILTON: Captain Caleb Gibbs, my aide, and I have just ridden up the other side of the river from where Clinton's men are supposed to be. We saw very little trace of an enemy. Besides, your troops can bring the contents of the arsenal south with them.

GATES: It would be impossible to remove the artillery and stores for a considerable time. The roads are too difficult.

HAMILTON: Not so. We have just ridden over them to reach here.

GATES: Besides, the New England states would be left open to the ravages of the enemy.

HAMILTON: You do not need to leave more than one brigade here to assure the safety of the New England states.

GATES: Leaving only one brigade here would put it out of my power to enterprise anything against Fort Ticonderoga.

HAMILTON: You do not really mean you intend to attack it?

GATES: I think it might be done in winter.

HAMILTON: There would be surprise, certainly, at the folly of it.

GATES: I think it would be important to undertake it.

HAMILTON: The British more likely will evacuate it without an attack.

Gates remained unyielding to Hamilton's strongest arguments. He would promise only one brigade to Washington, and that would not be Nixon's or Glover's, it would be Paterson's, the weakest. Judging from Hamilton's later angry reaction, he was induced to acquiesce in this half a loaf or, really, third of a loaf by representations of Gates that

Hamilton later considered to have been false.

Robert Troup, Hamilton's King's College roommate, was now serving in Albany as an aide-de-camp to Gates. After Hamilton's long, lonely ride with Captain Caleb Gibbs and the hostile, inflexible reception by Gates, his mission seemed to be a failure. That night Hamilton was happy to find a trusted old friend with whom to share his fatigue and his sense of futility and from whom to seek useful inside information. Somehow Hamilton found out, perhaps from Troup, that Gates had grossly understated the number of men still under his command, and that Paterson's brigade was much less than even a third of a loaf.

Hamilton could find in Gates's trick a personal grievance to add still more force to his official demands. Furious, he followed up his interview with a peremptory letter to Gates: "Sir, by inquiry I have learned that General Paterson's brigade, which is the one you proposed to send, is, by far, the weakest of the three now here and does not consist of more than about 600 rank and file fit for duty. . . ." Now he did not consider himself bound by his earlier acceptance of Paterson's brigade only: "I cannot consider it either as compatible with the good of the service or my instructions from his Excellency General Washington, to consent, that [Paterson's] brigade be selected from the three, but . . . I am under the necessity of requiring, by virtue of my orders from him, that one of the others be substituted . . . and that you will be pleased to give immediate orders for its embarkation."

Hamilton admitted that he had accepted Gates's first offer too easily, but did not forbear to brandish new arguments based on the highest command judgments: "I am not myself sensible of the expediency of keeping more than one here . . . my ideas coincide with those gentlemen, whom I have consulted on the occasion. . . . Their opinion is, that one brigade with the regiments before mentioned would amply answer the purposes of this post."

Hamilton refused to quit after his initial mistake. He went back to Gates: "Knowing that General Washington wished me to pay great deference to your judgment, I ventured too far to deviate, from the instructions he gave me, as to consent, in compliance with your opinion that two brigades should remain here instead of one."

Unknown to Hamilton, the night of November 8, his last in Albany, was the very night that Washington at White Marsh would be reading the report of a mysterious letter that had been intercepted; the letter was from Brigadier General Thomas Conway to Gates, in which Conway had written the slur: "Heaven has been determined to save your country, or a weak General and Bad Councillors would have ruined it."

The day after his first meeting with Gates, crushed by the sense that his mission had been a failure, Hamilton wrote Washington no excuses. He found the pros and cons of whether to put more pressure on Gates in delicate balance.

> I found myself infinitely embarrassed, and was at a loss how to act. I felt the importance of strengthening you as much as possible, but . . . I found insuperable inconveniences in acting diametrically opposite to the opinion of a gentleman whose successes have raised him to the highest importance. General Gates has won the entire confidence of the Eastern States; if disposed to do it, by addressing himself to the prejudices of the people he would find no difficulty to render a measure odious which it might be said was calculated to expose them to unnecessary danger.

Then Hamilton gave a hint of a secret cabal of which it would be too dangerous to write more; Troup or perhaps Philip Schuyler had warned him of the strength of the Conway Cabal in Gates's inner circle: "Gates has influence in Congress to discredit the measure. It appears dangerous to insist. These considerations and others which I shall be more explicit in when I have the pleasure of seeing you determined me not to insist upon sending either of the other brigades remaining here.''

Hamilton could not know that by the time Washington received this letter, he would understand exactly what his young aide meant.

After his talks with Robert Troup, Hamilton followed up his November 5 letter to Gates with more pressure. Surprisingly, or not so, he won a reversal on appeal. After repeating all the reasons why he disagreed with the idea of doing so, Gates reluctantly agreed to send Washington two brigades instead of one, and added Glover's brigade to Paterson's.

In the first draft of Gates's letter to Washington giving this reluctant consent, he showed how much he resented the personal pressure Hamilton had brought to bear on him. ''Although it is Customery & even Absolutely necessary to direct Implicit Obedience to be paid to the Verbal Orders of Aids de Camp in Action, or while upon the Spot—yet I believe it is never practiced to Delegate that Dictatorial power, to One Aid de Camp sent to an Army 300 Miles distant.''

Gates's second draft omitted this passage and stated only his formal compliance: ''Upon mature Consideration of all Circumstances, I have, nevertheless, ordered General Glover's Brigade to be added to General Paterson's, in Reinforcement to your Army, and they will march, immediately. . . .''

Gates added cryptically, ''Col. Hamilton . . . will report everything that I wish to have you acquainted with, as well with Respect to the present State, as the future Operations this Way.''

Gates's subsequent actions showed that the ostensible reasons he had advanced against sending troops to Washington were a bluff, if not a part of the larger design of Conway's cabal. He forthwith wrote to Congress that a splendid aftereffect of his great victory was that Clinton had ''evacuated every position this side.'' The British would probably evacuate Fort Ticonderoga within the month, and they must surely have done so had Washington left him with more troops to threaten it.

Two weeks later, Gates was able to tell Congress proudly that the enemy had indeed evacuated Ticonderoga, and the mountain that looked down into it as well, and had retired all the way north to St. John's and Ile aux Noix. Southward, Sir Henry Clinton had abandoned the Hudson River posts all the way back to Kingsbridge at the north end of Manhattan. Gates's freeing of the entire Hudson Valley from the enemy would stand in proud contrast to Washington's imminent loss of the Delaware forts to Howe.

To make sure Gates's brigades actually got on their way—and by transport that was hard to turn back—Hamilton sent the troops by water. ''I procured all the vessels that could be had at Albany fit for the purpose; but could not get more than sufficient to take in Paterson's brigade. . . .'' It was the less reliable one, with more militia whose enlistments were expiring, and if left on land they could more easily wander off toward home.

He marched off Glover's brigade, with more regulars, down the east side of the river, and kept an eye on their progress. On the way, he checked to see whether the orders he had left with General Putnam had been carried out, found they had not been, and that there was a big new problem with Putnam: ''Everything has been neglected and deranged;'' Poor's and Learned's brigades had not moved, no attention had been paid to his earlier order for 1,000 men from the troops there, and ''Everything is sacrificed to [General Putnam's] whim of taking New York,'' Putnam's ''hobby horse'' that excused him from releasing troops.

Ridiculous, Hamilton said:

Tis only wasting time and misapplying men, to employ them in a farcical parade against New York; . . . New York is no object if it could be taken; and to take it would require more men than could be spared for more substantial purposes.

He then brandished command authority to the limit of its force with Putnam, something he had refrained from doing with Gates: "I now sir, in the most explicit terms, by his Excellency's authority, give it as a positive order from him, that all the Continental troops under your command may be immediately marched to Kings Ferry, there to cross the river and hasten to reinforce the army under him."

Poor's and Learned's brigades mutinied, and refused to move for lack of food and money. Hamilton reported that "several of the regiments having received no pay for six or eight months passed. . . . A captain killed a man and was shot himself by his comrade." These were only some of the "difficulties for want of proper management" that "stopped the troops from proceeding." Hamilton went on to say, "Governor Clinton has been the only man, who has done anything toward removing the difficulties, but he failed 'for want of General Putnam's cooperation.' "

Hamilton adds briskly, "On coming here, I immediately sent for Colonel Bailey who now commands Learned's brigade, and have gotten him to engage for carrying the brigade on to headquarters, as fast as possible . . . by means of five or six thousand dollars which Governor Clinton was kind enough to borrow for me. The money, Colonel Bailey thinks, will keep the men in good humor till they join you." Hamilton waited and saw that "They marched this morning toward Goshen."

Hamilton now fell into one of the acute illnesses that were to recur throughout his life. On November 12, 1777, he wrote plaintively to Washington from New Windsor: "Dear sir, I have been detained here these two days by a fever and violent rheumatic pains throughout my body. This has prevented my being active in person . . . but I have taken every other method in my power, in which Governor Clinton has obligingly given me all the aid he could." He had pressed the troops to march immediately, but they were also unwell: "I was told they were under an operation for the itch, which made it impossible to proceed till the effects of it were over." Hamilton got up before he was well, anxious to be "attending to the march of the troops." He left New Windsor and crossed by the ferry to Fishkill "in order to fall in with General Glover's brigade, which was on its march from Poughkeepsie." But at Dennis Kennedy's house near Peekskill, he had a relapse and could march no further. After about ten days, during which he several times "seemed to be drawing nigh his last," Hamilton's fever abated, and he was pronounced to be on the mend.

Colonel Hugh Hughes, a partisan of Gates, remarked that "Colonel Hamilton, who has been very ill of a nervous disorder, at Peekskill, is out of danger, unless it be from his own sweet temper." Observers of Hamilton's frequent illnesses, including Hamilton himself, often equated them with a "nervous disorder."

Apparently recovered once again, Hamilton kept harrying the reluctant troops southward on their wintry march. "They will be pushed forward as fast as I can have any influence to make them go," he wrote Washington, "I am sorry to say, the disposition for marching in the officers and men in general . . . does not keep pace with my wishes or the exigency of the occasion." He admitted to Washington that, "I am very unwell; but I shall not spare myself to get things immediately in a proper train, and for that purpose intend, unless I receive other orders from you, to continue with the troops in the progress of their march."

Washington was pleased with Hamilton's reports. From headquarters at White Marsh, Pennsylvania, November 15, 1777, Washington wrote, by Tench Tilghman's hand, "Dear sir, I have duly received your several favors from the time you left me to that of the 12 inst. I approve entirely of all the steps you have taken, and have only to wish that the exertions of those you have had to deal with had kept pace with your zeal and good intentions.''

Lacking timely reinforcement, Fort Mifflin fell November 15; and Fort Mercer, on the twentieth. As Hamilton and his son John Church saw it, if only Gates and Putnam had promptly obeyed Hamilton's orders, the forts could have been saved, the British army would have been cut off from the navy, and Sir Henry Clinton's reinforcements and all logistical support would have been cut off from the hostile countryside. Washington's prophecy to Hamilton of October 30 would have been fulfilled: "Howe would have been reduced to the situation of Burgoyne, thus probably terminating the war in the second year of our independence.''

But the bitter reality was that on November 22 British naval vessels sailed unchecked into Philadelphia harbor, bringing supplies and ammunition for Howe's army, demonstrating by their presence that Howe's lines of communication and reinforcement were now secure and that Washington had lost everything possible he could have lost, except his army command.

Congress called Gates down from the northern theater and appointed him president of the newly created Board of War, an office something like a cabinet secretary of war. None of the five members of the Board of War was a member of Congress, and Gates could keep his military rank and return to field command any time he chose. The president of Congress wrote Gates November 28 of its high regard for his fitness to fill the office on which "the safety and interest of the United States eminently depend.''

In full uniform and rank, yet also with semicivilian status as president of the Continental Congress's own Board of War, Gates was now in more than titular control of all military operations. Although Hamilton had helped pry troops away from Gates's command for Washington's, Congress in its confusing way had leapfrogged Gates back over both his own and Washington's old commands. Nothing could have been more of a threat, or an insult, to Washington's status as commander in chief.

Washington's enemies like Gates, Thomas Conway, Charles Lee, and Thomas Mifflin saw that the safest and surest way to rid him of his command would not be to oust him, but to force him to resign in anger or discouragement. Under the leadership of Mifflin, Gates's new Board of War created the office of inspector general with broad powers to reorganize the army and report directly to it without going through Washington. To it they appointed Thomas Conway, the man who had written Gates that "Heaven has determined to save your country, or a weak General and Bad Councillors would have ruined it,'' and Conway promoted him to major general at the same time. Such promotion of the man he hated most in the army was "extraordinary'' to a furious Washington and would outrage all the brigadiers in the army. The pressure on Washington to resign was becoming all but irresistible.

With Hamilton abed at New Windsor and Fishkill with recurring "violent rheumatic pains,'' near-fatal chills, and nervous disorders, Washington lacked the foreknowledge of this unfolding of the secret plot to depose him of which Hamilton had learned in Albany but had dared not put in his letter.

On November 9, Washington had reacted angrily to Conway's insulting intercepted letter to Gates, which, among other things, also charged that the Battle of Germantown would have been an American victory if Washington had kept his head. The charges were bad enough, but the fact of the letter itself, demonstrating as it seemed to the close confidential and conspiratorial relationship between Conway and Gates to bring down Washington, angered him still more.

His short note to Conway of November 9 instilled two sentences with unspoken rage:

Sir: A letter which I received last night contained the following paragraph.

In a letter from General Conway to General Gates he says: "Heaven has been determined to save your country; or a weak general and bad councillors would have ruined it."

I am, sir, your humble servant, George Washington.

For all Conway would know when he received Washington's letter, Washington had a spy network as extensive and effective as Gates's—or a headquarters intelligencer—able to supply him with the innermost secrets of the cabal that he, Lee, Gates, and Mifflin were hatching. Nowhere did Washington's bullet of a letter disclose from whom he had learned the contents of Conway's letter to Gates. Hamilton had just left Gates. Conway would easily jump to the mistaken conclusion that Hamilton was the spy who had stolen his letter.

Within a day or two of Washington's note to Conway, Gates learned from Thomas Mifflin that Conway's letter to him had been leaked to Washington. Mifflin told Gates that it was his aide Wilkinson, now newly promoted to brigadier general, who had blabbed, and that Gates was in trouble, thanks to his adjutant's loose tongue.

Gates realized that a storm was about to break, but he studiedly ignored Mifflin's warning that it was his precious adjutant Wilkinson who had been the "leak." Gates wrote to Conway in panic at what Mifflin had just told him: "I intreat you . . . to let me know which of the letters was copied off. It is of the greatest importance, that I should detect the person who has been guilty of that act of infidelity: I cannot trace him out, unless I have your assistance." Without the text Gates would have trouble constructing a holeproof cover story to protect Wilkinson and pin blame for the leak on someone in Washington's camp.

That was it! Hamilton, Washington's aide, not his own aide Wilkinson was responsible. When Hamilton had been at the interview with him in Albany, he had stolen Conway's letter to him out of a closet in his room and copied it!

According to Wilkinson (who had a lifelong record of extreme unreliability as a reporter), the very moment he returned to Albany, Gates called him in and announced angrily, "I have had a spy in my camp since you left me!"

"I do not comprehend your allusion," Wilkinson replied cautiously, somewhat relieved but still nervous. Gates put the whole blame on Hamilton: "Colonel Hamilton had been sent up by General Washington; and would you believe it, he purloined the copy of a letter out of that closet." Gates pointed an accusing finger at the closet door.

"I conceive that impossible," Wilkinson claims he said.

"I insist," Gates retorted. "When the family was called out on business . . . Colonel Hamilton was left alone an hour in this room. During that time, he took Conway's letter out of that closet and copied it, and furnished the copy to Washington."

Here was a good chance for Wilkinson to spatter suspicion on a rival aide of Gates. Wilkinson argued that Gates's aide Robert Troup was a close friend of Hamilton's and that he must have been the one who told Hamilton what was in Conway's letter; they had seen each other when Hamilton was at Albany.

Gates insisted that Hamilton was the leak, and Hamilton alone.

Wilkinson feared that if Gates pursued this line, it would lead to Hamilton's denial, and turn back to some drunken maunderings of his own at the Reading tavern and thence to Washington. He explained to Gates obliquely that he himself had not really considered Conway's letter confidential because Gates had read it *publicly* in Wilkinson's presence. Wilkinson had taken it merely "as a matter of information from the grand army." He turned blame gently back to Gates, "so therefore I did not dream of the foul imputations it was destined to draw upon me."

What had really happened, as Wilkinson later shamefacedly admitted, was that during a drunken carouse with William McWilliams and others of Lord Stirling's staff at a tavern in Reading, the conversation "became general, unreserved and copious." That "drunken sot" Stirling himself had also hoisted a few, and he and others became so drunk that they did not know what they were saying. Wilkinson could not recall details, but would "acknowledge it possible in the warmth of social intercourse, when the mind is relaxed and the tongue is unguarded, that observations may have elapsed which have not since occurred to us." They were all so drunk that, as Wilkinson put it, "the nature of our situation made it confidential."

This was all evasive double-talk. Wilkinson himself had been carrying the letter from Conway to Gates. He had read some of its choicest passages to his no doubt raucously laughing listeners at the Reading tavern. Earthy officers like that "sot" Stirling could easily join in drunken laughter at the lofty Washington's expense and then loyally pass the message on to Washington.

Gates insisted on bringing his accusation against Hamilton to Hamilton's chief. He wrote Washington:

> . . . I conjure your Excellency, to give me all the assistance you can, in tracing out the author of the infidelity which put extracts from General Conway's letters to me into your hands. Those letters have been *stealingly copied*. . . . It is . . . *in your* . . . *power* to do me and the United States a very important service, by detecting a wretch who may betray me, and capitally injure the *very operations under your immediate direction*.

Gates added that he was sending a copy of this letter to the president of Congress. Perhaps they could come up with some clues.

Hamilton had an airtight alibi. He had been on the road and had refused to write Washington what he knew. Washington demolished Gates's elaborate falsification with crushing candor. He ignored Gates's charge against Hamilton. Stirling "from motives of friendship" had passed on the story Wilkinson had blurted out at the Reading tavern. Washington closed with a stinging rebuke to Gates's efforts to prove that Hamilton was a "wretch who may betray me." Washington wrote that until now he supposed Gates had meant to forewarn him against that "dangerous incendiary," General Conway. But he added, "in this, as in other matters of late, I have found myself mistaken."

Now at the pinnacle of his power as president of the Board of War, Gates backed away from his charge and took a new tack. Yes, he said now, it was Wilkinson, not Hamilton, who was the guilty culprit and ought to be punished.

In the same letter to Washington, Gates took another entirely inconsistent tack. The paragraph that Stirling had quoted to Washington was "spurious . . . a wicked forgery." Conway's genuine letter had mentioned neither a "weak general" nor "bad councillors."

Hamilton, after his return to Valley Forge in February 1778, drafted Washington's reply. He acidly pointed out the inconsistency of Gates's first accepting the authenticity of the charge by blaming Hamilton, or Wilkinson, for disclosing it, and then denying the letter was authentic. If Conway's genuine letters did not contain the charge, why had Gates not produced them? By his silence under Washington's indictment, Gates tacitly admitted genuiness of the intercepted letter. By taking Gates's disclaimers at face value, Washington was willing to bury the correspondence in silence "and as far as future events will permit, oblivion."

Henry Laurens, president of Congress and father of Hamilton's dearest friend and fellow aide, John Laurens, said of the congressmen who lent themselves to Conway's cabal that there were men involved who respected Washington, but lacked "the honor to defend" him publicly. The majority would go whichever way a few active and powerful ringleaders pushed them: "in all such juntas there are prompters, and actors, accommodators, candle snuffers, shifters of scenes, and mutes."

Washington and others closest to him were certain that the conspiracy to replace him had been real. Hamilton at first had only thought that there was an opposing faction or party, not a real cabal or conspiracy, but changed his mind. He wrote George Clinton February 13, 1778, that he had "discovered such convincing traits of the monster that I cannot doubt its reality in the most extensive sense." Only Wilkinson's premature blabbing at the Reading tavern had forestalled its success. "I believe it unmasked its batteries too soon," the young old artilleryman wrote, "but will only change the storm to a sap." That is, instead of an open attack on Washington, the cabal would go underground and try to destroy him with a "sap," a hidden explosive charge placed against the base of his power. Hamilton cautioned Clinton that "all the true and sensible friends to their country, and of course to a certain great man, ought to be on the watch to counterplot the secret machinations of his enemies," just as they should be on guard against "Tories and other enemies of the state."

With Hamilton's return to camp at Valley Forge on January 20, 1778, and Gates's embarrassment by the rumpus over his false charges against Hamilton, Washington seemed to recover some of his old political sway over Congress. When Gates attempted to patch up the quarrel by protesting that he had had no thought of displacing Washington, he was rebuffed in a way that showed Washington's suspicions had not been laid to rest. Gates soon stepped down as president of the Board of War and was assigned to defend Fort Ticonderoga, a reward that had been a disastrous dead end for every commander so honored.

Hamilton came close to identifying loyalty to his commander in chief with loyalty to the Revolution itself. So did his commander in chief.

In the end Congress came to agree with Hamilton. Some of its members now switched so far as to say that anyone who displeased the commander in chief should forthwith be removed from the army. Of all the ways there are to weave a bond between a chief executive and an aide, none creates a stronger and longer lasting one than for the junior of the two to be seen as the enemy of the enemies of the chief. Viewed in this light, the failure of Hamilton's mission to Gates and the fall of Forts Mifflin and Mercer were probably more important events in Hamilton's rise than success could possibly have been.

Long afterward, during John Adams's administration, a dying Washington was the figurehead commander in chief of a provisional army being raised for the expected war with France, and Hamilton was his handpicked second in command. Washington could have been thinking of no one but Hamilton when in 1798 he wrote:

> The variegated, and important, duties of the aides of a commander-in-chief, or, the commander of a separate army require experienced officers, men of judgment, and men of business, ready pens to execute them properly, and with dispatch. A great deal more is required of them than attending him at a parade, or delivering verbal orders here and there; or copying a written one. They ought, if I may be allowed to use the expression, to possess the soul of the general; and from a single idea given to them, to convey his meaning in the clearest and fullest manner.

In youth they had both been combat commanders in the line of battle.

This, young men unacquainted with the service and diffident, would not do; be their abilities what they may.

No matter what other abilities an aide might display, in the end only a man not "diffident," and with "military knowledge" like Hamilton's, could bring enough steel to the style of his person and pen "to possess the soul of the general."

7

Misbehavior
at Monmouth

Q: *(To Colonel Hamilton):* **Did you conceive General Washington's orders, or the spirit of them, to General Lee, were to attack the enemy at all events?**

A: **I do not. I can't conceive that General Washington could mean to give orders so extremely positive, but that circumstances, which had been unforseen, might arise, to leave the officer, who had the execution of them, liberty to deviate.**

—Cross-examination of Alexander Hamilton by Major General Charles Lee, at Lee's Court-martial, July 4, 1778.

Back with the army at Valley Forge on about January 20, Hamilton reported to Washington all he had learned in Albany about the Conway cabal but had not been able to write. He then briskly submitted a padded expense account for himself and Captain Caleb Gibbs from October 30, 1777, through January 20, 1778. The expense account shows their expenses at each stop along the way, but the four-day period they were at Albany is a gap which tends to show that they were guests of Troup or of General Philip Schuyler at the Pastures.

Washington from Valley Forge was imploring Congress to redress the army's grievances lest they "starve, dissolve, or disperse." Hamilton wrote to Governor George Clinton February 13 that individual members of Congress were able, but "Folly, caprice, a want of foresight, comprehension and dignity" described the body as a whole. Valley Forge showed him that Congress's conduct "with respect to the army . . . is feeble, indecisive, and improvident—insomuch that we are reduced to a more terrible situation than you can conceive. . . . At this very day," Hamilton told Clinton, "there are complaints from the whole line of having been three or four days without provisions.''

The committee of congressional oversight of the army, critical of Washington's leadership, had elevated General Horatio Gates to presidency of the Board of War and Brigadier General Thomas Conway of the Conway Cabal as inspector general of the army; it had rejected Washington's and Hamilton's plans for reorganizing the army, and approved Conway's instead.

That winter Hamilton and Washington would have welcomed with open arms any reasonably well-qualified candidate for the position of inspector general whose name was not Thomas Conway. Baron Friederich Wilhelm Ludolf Gerhard Augustin von Steuben, late of the armies of Frederick the Great of Prussia, brought more than a different name to the job—although his credentials were more bogus than Conway's.

Knowing very little English, von Steuben could read only with difficulty the extravagant letters of praise that Benjamin Franklin had put in his dossier, but his ''fondness for . . . importance,'' as Hamilton put it later to his friend William Duer, prompted the baron's complicity in the amiable deception that he had formerly been ''a lieutenant general in foreign service.'' In fact, he had been only a half-pay captain, out of work for 14 years, when Benjamin Franklin met him in Paris, helped him assemble his dossier, and packed him off to America. His title of baron had been honestly conferred by the prince of Hohenzollern-Hechingen; he was a knight of the Order of Fidelity by the intercession of Princess Frederica of Wurttemberg; and on his chest he always wore the jeweled star of her order. He arrived at Valley Forge at the end of February 1778, and from the time of his first meeting with Hamilton, an affectionate, lifelong friendship grew up between the two men, Hamilton 21; von Steuben 48.

Casualties, desertions, illness, and furloughs and no new recruits coming to Valley Forge had reduced the army to impotence. Von Steuben complained that ''. . . the officers who had coats, had them of every color and make'' and as for ''military discipline, I may safely say no such thing existed.'' Washington appointed a hundred picked men to his guard to form a model corps, ''to be instructed in the maneuvers necessary to be introduced in the Army. . . .'' Von Steuben had trained it to parade with stunning effect throughout the camp. He progressed from squad to platoon to company to regiment, and then on to whole brigades and divisions, until the largest units could maneuver smoothly and in unison upon command.

With Hamilton's help, von Steuben prepared written instructions for the troops that later evolved into the standard army training manual, *Rules for the Order and Discipline of the Troops*. Congress approved, and the *Blue Book,* as it was familiarly called from its cover, remained the official army manual until the War of 1812; in transmuted form, it remains in effect to this day.

For the rest of the war when line officers, including Hamilton, would cry out, ''Follow me,'' the enlisted men were more likely to follow than before von Steuben's arrival. American soldiers' habits of panicky flight were by no means a thing of the past, but future soldiers might be counted on to respond better to the commands of a good officer than they had in the past.

Prisoner exchanges were an endlessly vexing problem for Washington and Hamilton. Major General Charles Lee, ignominiously captured in bed at Basking Ridge, and Ethan Allen, captured trying to take Montreal almost single-handed in 1775, remained in British hands. Most other American prisoners were untrained militiamen, easy to replace and not easy to find use for. On the other hand, the captive British in American hands were mostly well-trained regulars whom the British would find hard to replace at a distance of 3,000 miles.

The congressional committee appointed to watch over the army and Washington was slyly opposed to the idea of a general exchange of prisoners because they thought it would work to the disadvantage of the States. The committee suggested that the American commission be merely a pretense; when the negotiations broke down, blame for the breakdown could be placed on the British.

Hamilton castigated this congressional humbug, rejected Congress's plan, and arranged to bring back more Americans, even though it also meant bringing back Major General Charles Lee, that "sap" which Conway's cabal might still make use of to undermine Washington.

As the highest-ranking American officer in British captivity, General Lee had been quite comfortable in confinement. He may have been unpleasantly surprised, if not altogether discomfited, to find himself back on the duty roster in Washington's camp. While a prisoner, Lee had sent a proposal to Congress that they send commissioners to Sir William Howe to sue for peace, but Congress had rejected this surrender plan. It was not at all clear whether Lee was more dangerous in British or in American hands. In the American camp, at least, Washington and Hamilton could keep an eye on him, but his high rank would nonetheless make it possible for him to do their cause extraordinary harm.

At the end of February 1778, Congress received a message from Benjamin Franklin at the secret negotiations in Paris that "the most Christian King [of France] agrees to make a common cause with the United States . . . [and] guarantees their liberty, sovereignty, and independence, absolute and unlimited." Washington in April wrote Congress that "no event was ever received with more heartfelt joy." On May 5, 1778, General Orders at camp reflected official ratification of the treaty: "It having pleased the Almighty Ruler of the Universe propitiously to defend the cause of the United States of America finally by raising us up a powerful friend among the Princes of the Earth . . ." Washington would have the wholehearted cooperation of the French army and navy. The momentous news touched off a joyous celebration.

Nathanael Greene, the quartermaster general, asked Washington if military preparations could be relaxed with such powerful outside help in sight. "No," said Hamilton for Washington, for a wider audience than the quartermaster general. The favor of France could not "justify the least relaxation in . . . the provisions you . . . are making in your department. . . ." These must "be continued in their fullest vigor and extent." The letter examined all contingencies and showed how each demanded "a powerful army, well furnished with every apparatus of war." Britain, confronted by a fresh enemy, could muster further resources. Besides, the enemy army was formidable. It would not be withdrawn without a further push, "if . . . only to make the way for a negotiation." Our failure to prepare against British victories "might be fatal" to home sentiment and growing friendships abroad. We might need to take the offensive, which would call for our amplest strength at all points. In any event, salvation lay only in unremitting effort.

A congressional resolution of February 3, 1778, had required all officers of the army to swear before the commander in chief or any major general or brigadier general an oath of allegiance to the United States of America. Things had been moving in this direction since July 4, 1776, and before, but the date of the congressional resolution of February 3, 1778, may be said to be the operative date when the United States finally and officially severed the last link to the Crown and became totally independent of Great Britain.

Hamilton finally got around to complying with the resolution on May 12 before William Alexander, Lord Stirling. By it he acknowledged "the United States of America, to be free, independent, and sovereign states," declared that "the people thereof owe no allegiance or obedience to George III, King of Great Britain," and renounced, refused, and abjured any allegiance or obedience to him, swore that he would "to the utmost of my power, support, maintain and defend the United States, against the said King George III, his heirs and successors and his or their abettors, assistants and adherents." He also swore to "serve the United States in the office of aide de camp which I now hold, with fidelity according to the best of my skill and understanding."

All the rest of his life and afterward in history, charges that he was a "monarchist" or a "monocrat" and secretly subservient to the British Crown would be brought against Hamilton. In evaluating such charges and the motives of the makers, it is useful to note the specificity of the text of the congressional oath; to mark the date when Hamilton swore it, May 12, 1778; and to recall that the venue where he and the army had spent most of that winter and spring was Valley Forge. As a rule, Hamilton did not set much store by loyalty oaths, but in the case of this one, the name of the place and the date affirm more than the jurat itself.

With Thomas Conway, Thomas Mifflin, and Horatio Gates gone, the only high-ranking officers left at Valley Forge who might threaten the commander in chief were Major Generals Benedict Arnold and Charles Lee.

Arnold was the greatest hero of a fighting battlefield general the American army could boast, but he was a semi-invalid from both physical and psychic wounds—a leg badly wounded at Quebec, and reinjured fighting Burgoyne at Saratoga, and a spirit rankling with ire at the arm. failure to accord him the glory he considered his due for heroics at Quebec, Bemis Heights, and Freeman's Saratoga Farm. With the troops at Valley Forge starving, his lavish appropriations of army stores had drawn Washington's terse rebuke. Washington would soon get rid of him by sending him into Philadelphia when it was evacuated with just enough men to occupy it, but not enough to provide the setting for a hero's triumphant liberation celebration. It would be sufficient to help Arnold win himself the beauteous, extravagant young Peggy Shippen as his bride—and coconspirator in the treason plot.

Gaunt, hard-favored Major General Charles Lee remained a more serious threat than Arnold to replace Washington as commander in chief if things should continue to go badly. He disparaged everything he saw at camp, made light of von Steuben's winter troop training, and produced a set of his own plans for "the Formation of the American Army." "I understand it better than almost any man living," he claimed. He ought to stand "well with General Washington" because "I am persuaded . . . that he cannot do without me." On top of this he broached the theory that American troops could never defeat British troops, no matter what the circumstances. He confided to Elias Boudinot that Washington was not fit to command a sergeant's guard.

At three in the morning of June 18, 1778, Clinton and his army began moving out of Philadelphia across the Delaware to New Jersey for the long march overland to Sandy Hook, where they would board British vessels that would carry them the last miles back to New York City. Clinton's columns exposed long vulnerable flanks to any American attack that might sweep down from the northwest to cut them off from their ships. The von

Steuben-trained American army now outnumbered Clinton's, and Hamilton was itching to test it in battle, cut up Clinton's columns, and bring a quick end to the war.

Soon after sunrise on June 19, Hamilton galloped out of Valley Forge with Washington on the pursuit march. At Hopewell Township, about 25 miles northwest of Howe's column, Washington asked his generals if he should risk a full-scale attack on the British grand army. If so, what should the tactics be?

General Charles Lee, full of inhibitions, delivered his opinions with his usual air of authority. Let Clinton cross New Jersey unhampered; the French alliance was America's promise of victory; equal numbers of Americans could not battle successfully with trained European soldiers. Others wanted to compromise and send forward a skirmishing party. Still others wanted to attack in force—Lafayette, Wayne, and Greene. Lee's assurance carried a four to three vote of the generals in favor of his timid tactic.

Hamilton wrote out the final compromise decision, which was signed by all but Wayne. The plan was to advance 1,500 men to worry the enemy's left flank and rear, while the main body remained close behind to be governed by events. This result of the council, "unluckily called," said Hamilton, "would have done honor to the most honorable society of midwives, and to them only."

Hamilton's son John Church Hamilton reported that after the council of war broke up, Hamilton urged Greene to go with him to beg Washington to give battle. As they approached him, Washington drew himself up to his full, towering height and said, "Gentlemen, I anticipate the object of your visit—you wish me to fight." Hamilton and Greene repeated all the good reasons for the full-scale attack that the aggressive minority had advanced in the council: "The enemy was dispirited by desertion, broken by fatigue, retiring through woods, defiles, morasses . . . in the face of an army superior in numbers, elated by pursuit, and ardent to signalize their courage." He and Greene "left nothing unessayed . . . to frustrate so degrading a resolution."

Under their influence, Washington overruled the older generals. Hamilton delivered an order to Brigadier General Charles Scott to advance with 1,500 good troops to cooperate with smaller detachments "to gall the enemys left flank and rear." Morgan was to gain the right flank, and small bands of foot under General Cadwalader and of horse under Colonel White were also to press forward.

Hamilton described Lee's farcical indecision to Elias Boudinot: "General Lee's conduct . . . was truly childish. According to the incorrect notions of our army, his seniority . . . entitled him to the command of the advanced corps; but he in the first instance declined it in favor of the Marquis de Lafayette." Besides, there was a new rival: "Lord Stirling interposed his claim. So then General Lee . . . inconsistently reasserted his pretensions."

Hamilton continued: "Washington accommodated him [Lee] a second time. Then General Lee and Lord Stirling again agreed to let the marquis command. General Lee, a little time after, recanted again and became very importunate. The general [Washington], who had all along observed the greatest candor in the matter, grew tired of such fickle behavior, and ordered the marquis to proceed.

"This was still not the end of the farce. When Lee saw that a third of the army was to be turned over to the Frenchman, he reversed himself once more and demanded the honor, his third or fourth chance at the command."

The indecisive Lee was confidently playing on the indecision that he knew was also Washington's failing. Washington finally put Lee, with additional brigades, in command of the whole forward body, but with the reservation that Lee was to aid any plan of attack that Lafayette adopted, a practical but absurd compromise, that dangerously split command responsibility. Washington then sent Hamilton off into the night to give specific orders to unit commanders to keep the attack going.

When Hamilton rode into Cranbury on the night of June 25, he found Lafayette's advance detachment in disarray because it had lost contact with the British and also with Lafayette. He issued crisp orders to the scout detachments to send out new patrols at once to keep in constant contact with the enemy. He dashed off a note to Washington; he was still in favor of a swift, hard blow at the retreating foe.

Hamilton dashed off another order to Brigadier General Charles Scott: ''This part of the troops marches instantly—if you can find Morgan. Keep close to the enemy and attack when we attack.—We are to join in the Monmouth road one mile this side of Taylor's tavern.''

Hamilton issued still another order, this one to Major General Charles Lee, and handed it to a waiting horseman who galloped off with it and delivered it to Lee shortly after one in the morning of June 28. Hamilton testified that the order he gave to Lee was that ''The moment he received intelligence of the enemy's march to pursue them and to attack their rear.''

But no copy of Hamilton's order to Lee has ever been found.

Everything now depended on Hamilton's order to Lee and Lee's carrying it out. Lee's brigades deployed to form a main battle line facing the British rear, stretching northeastward from Monmouth Court House, with Lafayette on the right flank nearest the Court House, Wayne northward to his left, and Scott on the extreme left flank to the northeast of Wayne.

Lee ordered Wayne to take 600 Pennsylvanians and two fieldpieces and strike the British rear. It was the last coherent command anyone heard from Lee that day. Anthony Wayne drove ahead, smashed through some British outposts, hit unexpected strength, wisely took up a holding position at the edge of a long, swampy ravine, and called on Lee to send up support.

Behind Wayne, other regiments and brigades under Lee's command marched and countermarched aimlessly, undirected. Lafayette, cheerfully in action though having again lost touch with his troops, cried out for a general advance all along the line. But Lee hung back, saying, ''Sir, you do not know British soldiers. We cannot stand against them.''

Seeing Lee's troops in confusion back of Monmouth Court House, Hamilton ordered Lee and Lafayette to attack the British, then galloped back to Washington to report. Washington, advancing at the head of the main army, had reached Tennent Church, about three miles west of where the American and British front lines were strung out northeastward from the court house. Lee would soon engage the British, Hamilton told Washington. Hamilton recommended, for reasons ''which were thought good,'' that the right wing, under Greene, should be thrown to the south ''and . . . follow with the left wing [under Stirling] directly in General Lee's rear to support him.''

Washington ratified orders to carry out these troop dispositions and aides galloped off to deliver them. A farmer rode up with a fifer in uniform behind him. ''Our people are retreating,'' the farmer cried, pointing to the fifer. ''That man told me so.''

Robert H. Harrison recalled the awful moment. ''. . .We met a fifer, who appeared to be a good deal frightened. The General asked him whether he was a soldier belonging to the army. He answered that he was a soldier, and that the Continental troops who had been advancing were retreating.''

Washington was thunderstruck. He ''threatened the man, if he mentioned a thing of this sort, he would have him whipped. He then moved on a few paces. . . . We met two or three persons more on that road.'' One was a soldier who gave news ''that all the troops that had been advanced, the whole of them, were retreating.'' Washington still couldn't believe the report. He had not heard any firing "except a few cannon a considerable time before.''

Up front, out at the swampy ravine, Wayne's men, now backed by Scott's Virginians, fought on doggedly, waiting for the reinforcements Wayne had called on Lee to send up.

But no supporting infantry on Wayne's right or left or behind was coming up. Lee apparently, incoherently, had ordered a general retreat, leaving Wayne and Scott and the others at the spearhead of the attack isolated and cut off. Wayne, too, had to join the American retreat, and broke contact. Clinton's troops reformed and returned to the attack, while Wayne and Lafayette fell back to the west, where Stirling's and Greene's reserves had dug in in defensive positions.

At Washington's command post, an officer told William Grayson that streams of men were retreating, but he did not know why they retreated, because "they had lost but one man.'' Colonel Ogden swore, "By God! They are flying from a shadow.'' Two Continental regiments were fleeing in disorder. The men were so hot and fatigued that "They could hardly stand.'' Hamilton heard Washington exclaim that he was "exceedingly alarmed'' to find the advanced corps falling back on the main body. Lee's entire force was in disorderly retreat.

An aide galloped up and shouted to Washington, "The enemy is upon you.'' Just then, from the direction of the front lines, there came a familiar, scarecrowlike figure cantering toward Washington's command party, his pack of pet hounds capering around his horse's hooves, shouting unintelligibly. Washington spurred his huge horse forward, reined up, confronted Lee, and shouted, "What's the meaning of this?'' Lee looked up in confusion and cried, "Sir? Sir?''

Washington thundered, "What is all this confusion? Why this retreat?''

From this point reports of what was said conflict sharply. By most credible accounts, Washington erupted like a volcano and cursed out Lee with a string of sulfurous oaths.

At his court-martial Lee testified, "I confess I was disconcerted, astonished and confounded by the words and the manner in which His Excellency accosted me . . . ,'' a manner "So novel and unexpected from a man whose discretion, humanity and decorum'' he had always admired. Lee claimed to be especially "disconcerted'' by the fact that he had been "flattering myself'' that he would receive "congratulations and applause'' for rescuing the army by his timely withdrawal from terrible danger.

The cream of King George III's army—chasseurs, grenadiers, light infantry—was pounding down on them all. The fate of both grand armies was poised in delicate balance. The scales were now unbalancing in favor of the British side.

Lee's advance corps was fleeing past them where they stood. Their "settled durable panic'' might well spread to the other half of the army, past whom they rushed in headlong, *sauve qui peut* flight. Washington and his command group, Hamilton and the other aides, stood firm like an island amid the torrent of troops streaming westward around them.

Hamilton described the moment that June morning when Washington reversed Lee's retreat:

> . . . The General rode forward and found the troops retiring in the greatest disorder and the enemy pressing upon their rear. I never saw the general to so much advantage. His coolness and firmness were admirable. He instantly took measures for checking the enemy's advance, and giving time for the army, which was very near, to form and make a proper disposition.

Wayne's men fell back westward, and Wayne joined Washington's command party.

After the last of the retreaters had straggled past, some throwing away their muskets, Washington and Wayne adjudged the ground where they stood—behind a ravine southeast of Freehold Meetinghouse—"appeared to be an advantageous spot to give the enemy the first check." To the panicky troops, the giant in his sweat-stained blue and buff uniform on the huge white horse loomed up out of the dusty haze untouched by panic. Lafayette never forgot the sight: "Washington's presence stopped the retreat . . . his calm courage . . . gave him the air best calculated to excite enthusiasm." He rode "all along the lines amid the shouts of the soldiers, cheering them by his voice and example."

Hamilton, too, was spellbound by Washington's performance.

> The sequel is, we beat the enemy and killed and wounded at least a thousand of their best troops. America owes a great deal to General Washington for this day's work; a general rout, dismay, and disgrace would have attended the whole army in any other hands but his. By his own good sense and fortitude he turned the fate of the day. Other officers have great merit in performing their parts well, but he directed the whole with the skill of a Master workman . . . he brought order out of confusion animated his troops and led them to success.

If Washington had not saved that day, Congress's anger might have exploded to displace him with General Charles Lee or Horatio Gates. The attempt of Gates's friends to remove Washington from command had already been much weakened, said Lafayette, "but from that day [Monmouth] it totally vanished away."

Hamilton's exploits at the Battle of Monmouth brought him wide acclaim as a military hero—in which Major General Lee did not join.

Washington's personal assumption of front-line command had converted an impending debacle into a technical victory. The British withdrew at nightfall, leaving the Americans in possession of the battlefield. But the British army was still intact and still safely on its way to New York. As Washington and Hamilton saw it, their last best chance to smash the British army and end the war at Monmouth had been lost by Major General Charles Lee's unnecessary and disorderly retreat in disobedience of Hamilton's order to advance.

Still it might have been much worse. If Washington and Hamilton had not been at the right places at the right times on the battlefield, Lee's sudden panicky retreat might have infected all the troops with "settled durable panic." As it was, of the British army there were 294 killed, wounded, or dead of heat and 64 missing; of the American, only 62 killed, 161 wounded, and 132 missing.

Lee smoldered under the lash of Washington's battlefield reprimand for what he considered his masterful retreat. According to Lee, Washington had "sent me out of the field when victory was assured," leaving Washington "scarcely anymore to do in it than to strip the dead." Lee, not Washington, had saved the whole army, he claimed, and it was to him that "the success of the day was entirely owing." He wrote a letter to Washington claiming as much and demanding "reparation" for the "very singular expression" Washington had used on him at the critical moment. He blamed Hamilton: Surely Washington's curses had been "instigated by some of those dirty earwigs who will forever insinuate themselves near persons in high office." In a second letter, Lee hoped that the "temporary power" and "tinsel dignity" of Washington's office would not objurgate the truth. He was sure he would be vindicated by a court-martial.

Washington briskly accepted his challenge by sending Colonel Scammell to arrest him.

The statement of charges Scammell handed Lee were three: (1) disobedience of orders in not attacking the enemy pursuant to repeated instructions, (2) misbehavior before the enemy "by making an unnecessary, disorderly and shameful retreat," and (3) disrespect to the commander in chief in two letters written after the battle.

With Lord Stirling as presiding judge, the court-martial convened July 4, 1778—the second anniversary of Independence Day—at Ross Hall on the Raritan at New Brunswick, where less than two years earlier Hamilton's New York Provincial artillery company had smartly covered his aegis's retreat across the wooden bridge with Cornwallis's crack troops in very hot pursuit.

According to the transcript of the court-martial, Lieutenant Colonel Alexander Hamilton being sworn, the judge advocate general led off the questioning:

Q: Did you deliver General Lee any orders from General Washington the 27th or 28th of June, respecting his attacking the enemy?
A: (by Lieutenant Colonel Hamilton):   I wrote out an order, and delivered it to Lee by a light horseman.
Q: Do you have a copy of the order?
A: No, I do not.
Q: When did you write this order?
A: I wrote General Lee a letter the evening of the 27th of June, by General Washington's order.

Hamilton had written out the crucial order for the whole battle, but Washington had never seen it. No copy of it has ever been discovered; yet it remains the pivot on which turns the whole mystery of the glorious victory, as most contemporary Americans saw it, or the miserable lost opportunity, as many later historians saw it, or the more or less disappointingly drawn battle that it was. Surprisingly enough, at General Lee's court-martial, no one, not even Lee himself, discredited the text of the written order as Hamilton recollected it and recited it orally from the witness stand. No one questioned that when Hamilton wrote out an order and put Washington's name to it, it was Washington's order though Washington had never seen it.

Q: What was the occasion of this order?
A: It was occasioned by an apprehension (as declared to me by General Washington) that the enemy might move off either at night or very early in the morning, and get out of our reach, so that the purpose of an attack might be frustrated.
Q: What were the contents of the order?
A: The order was conceived in the spirit, as I understood, of former orders that had been given by Washington to General Lee.

Hamilton's evasive answer was unacceptable.

Q: State what the order said, if you recall.
A: The order directed that General Lee detach a party of six or eight hundred men to lie very near the enemy, as a party of observation, in case of their moving off, to give the earliest intelligence of it, and to skirmish with them so as to produce some delay, and give time for the rest of the troops to come up.
Q: Was there anything else?

A: Yes, the order also directed Lee to order Colonel Morgan to make an attack on them.

Q: How was that attack to be conducted?

A: It was to be in such a manner as might also tend to produce delay, and yet not so as to endanger a general rout of his party, and disqualify them from acting in concert with the other troops, when a serious attack should be made.

Q: Was there to be a "serious attack" at all?

A: Yes, there was.

Q: How do you know?

A: This, I understood from General Washington, was in pursuance of his intention to have the enemy attacked, and conformable to the spirit of previous orders he had given General Lee for that purpose.

Major General Charles Lee now grimly took over cross-examination. General Lee's question: What hour was the letter sent off to me?

A: It was rather late in the evening. I went to bed soon after.

Captain John Francis Mercer of Virginia, General Lee's aide, was sworn.

Q: What hour was the letter received from Colonel Hamilton by General Lee?

A: To the best of my recollection, it was past one o'clock in the morning of the 28th of June.

Captain Evan Edwards, another of Lee's aides, being sworn, added:

Q: What hour was the letter received from Colonel Hamilton by General Lee?

A: When the express came I got up and looked at the watch, and think it was near two o'clock by the watch.

Q: What did you do then?

A: I then immediately wrote to Colonel Morgan, General Dickinson, and Colonel Grayson, to comply with the contents of the letter that General Lee received from Colonel Hamilton, and sent off the light-horsemen to them.

Lee's cross-examination of Hamilton brought out that the order to attack was by no means as clear and positive as Hamilton's testimony on direct questioning made it seem.

Q: (to Colonel Hamilton): Did you conceive General Washington's orders, or the spirit of them, to General Lee, were to attack the enemy at all events?

A: I do not. I can't conceive that General Washington could mean to give orders so extremely positive, but that circumstances, which had been unforseen, might arise, to leave the officer, who had the execution of them, liberty to deviate.

So there had been no firm order to Lee to attack! "Unforseen circumstances" could mean anything, including a British force to the front that might make it seem wise to "deviate." This was broad enough to encompass a "retreat" like Lee's instead of an attack.

It all boiled down to how Hamilton, not Washington, had appraised the situation on the spot.

Hamilton's answer could not have entirely pleased Washington because it seemed to knock out the first charge against Lee: If Lee had "liberty to deviate" from the attack, then he had not necessarily been disobedient to the order. The question now became much more difficult for the prosecution to prove: whether Lee had exercised good or bad judgment, or acted in good or bad faith, taking his "liberty to deviate" by a tactical retreat.

Q: (Lee to Hamilton):   Would you explain what it means to give the officer "liberty to deviate" Sir?

A: From everything I knew of the affair, General Washington's intention was fully to have the enemy attacked on their march, and that the circumstances must be very extraordinary and unforseen, which, consistent with his wish, could justify the not doing it.

But still, were there no circumstances of any kind when a retreat such as Lee's would be encompassed within the scope of "liberty to deviate"?

Lee pressed his advantage with skill:

Q: Did you either by letter to me, or in conversation with me, communicate this idea of General Washington's intention as fully and clearly as you have done it to the Court?

Hamilton gave ground.

A: I do not recollect that I ever did.

Lee pressed his advantage with skill:

Q: Was your idea of General Washington's intention that I should attack the enemy, had I found them in the situation which General Dickinson's intelligence assured me they were; that is, the whole arranged in order of battle, at or near (the) Courthouse?

To Lee's well-framed leading question Hamilton gave still more ground:

A: I knew nothing of General Dickinson's intelligence. But if the enemy's whole army were drawn up in order of battle near the Courthouse, I do not conceive it was General Washington's intention to have them attacked by your detachment.

"No more questions," Lee could well have said to that.

The last answer of the prosecution's chief witness, Hamilton, had all but discredited the prosecution's own case on the first count.

Much as he disliked Lee; much as he would like to have served Washington by bringing down the "sap" of the Conway cabal who constantly disparaged him; embarrassing to himself as it was to back off from his own earlier testimony that he had given a clear order to attack, Hamilton did not shade his testimony as to the content and meaning of the order the relatively slight amount which would have been necessary to permit the first of the three charges against Lee to stand.

The court-martial adjourned, and Hamilton was excused until the court reconvened nine days later.

The day after his first testimony, Hamilton wrote of General Lee to his old friend Elias Boudinot: "This man is either a driveler in the business of soldiership or something much worse.'' He realized his own testimony had been weak. ''Whatever a court martial may decide, I shall continue to believe and say his conduct was monstrous and unpardonable.'' Hamilton suspected Lee of ''something much worse,'' something that went deeper than being the ''sap'' of a cabal, but he could not prove the charge of treason, and he would not give even slightly altered testimony that would contribute to a questionable verdict.

The second charge was that Lee's retreat had been ''unnecessary,'' ''shameful,'' and ''disorderly.'' Whether it had been ''unnecessary'' and ''shameful'' were subjective questions, matters of Lee's judgment. There was at least a ''scintilla of evidence'' that Lee's retreat had not been ''shameful'' or ''unnecessary.'' But ''disorderly'' was different, an objective matter. Hamilton and many other witnesses could testify to what they had seen, Lee's own misbehavior before the enemy and his troops' retreat were indeed ''disorderly,'' and worse.

The court-martial moved with the army to Paramus and reconvened July 13. On the issue of whether Lee's retreat had been ''disorderly,'' Hamilton resumed his testimony. On direct examination, all went smoothly. He averred that he ''saw nothing like a general plan or combined disposition for a retreat . . .''

Q: Were the troops, when you fell in with them the second time retreating in order or disorder, and in what particular manner?

A: The corps that I saw were in themselves in tolerable good order, but seemed to be marching without system or design, as chance should direct. . . . I saw nothing like a general plan, or combined disposition for a retreat.

Q: Was there any body drawn up in their rear to cover their retreat that you saw?

A: I saw no such thing.

Q: Were the orders that you heard General Lee give that day, given distinct and clear?

A: I recollect to have heard General Lee give two orders, at both times he seemed to be under a hurry of mind.

Q: Did General Lee to your knowledge advise General Washington of his retreat?

A: He did not to my knowledge.

On cross-examination, Lee sought to rebut Hamilton's testimony with a thrust at the aide's own excited, extravagant behavior at the critical moment. Hamilton's own valor should have been under much better control when he delivered his battlefield order to Lee. In the hushed courtroom, Lee charged his chief accuser with a ''frenzy of valor:'' ''. . . Colonel Hamilton flourishing his sword, immediately exclaimed: That's right, my dear General, and I will stay, and we will all die here on this spot.'' Lee added, ''I could but be surprised at his expression, but observing him much flustered and in a sort of frenzy of valor, I calmly requested him to observe me well and to tell me if I did not appear tranquil and master of my faculties; his answer was, that he must own that I was entirely possessed of myself; well, then (said I), you must allow me to be a proper judge of what I ought to do.''

Only then had Lee ordered the retreat.

The day after giving his testimony, Hamilton found it necessary to write to Lord Stirling to explain why he had thus approved of Lee's demeanor on the field.

Yes, it was true that Lee had asked him, ''Do I appear to you to have lost my senses, do I not possess myself?'' Yes, Hamilton's ''answer to these questions was a favourable one.'' But ''So singular and unexpected a question was not a little embarrassing'' on the battlefield. ''I may have replied in terms of less reserve and caution, than I should have done at a moment of greater tranquility and cooler reflection.'' Yes, Lee's answers to what was said to him "were pertinent." Yeṣ, "his behaviour had not the least appearance of concern on the score of personal security. He could not be said to have lost his senses," Hamilton conceded.

"But," Hamilton went on, drawing a fine distinction, "he certainly did not appear to me to be in that collected state of mind or to have that kind of self-possession, which is an essential requisite of *the General,* and which alone can enable him, in critical emergencies, to take his measures with the promptitude and decision they require. A certain indecision, improvidence and hurry of spirits were apparent." Lee's had not been a complexion that radiated courage to his men. Their "settled durable panic" was the reflection of his poor generalship.

John Laurens and Richard Kidder Meade were much better witnesses for the prosecution than Hamilton. Laurens swore that Lee gave no orders to attack, except a direction to General David Forman to cut off some of the enemy who were retreating. He had brought Lee a message from Washington that the commander in chief was ready to support Lee with his whole army and asked for Lee's reply. Lee "answered that he really did not know what to say." When part of Lee's detachment fell back and the enemy, 150 or 200 at most, pursued, Lee "ordered the whole of our troops to retreat." Lee's directions were given indistinctly. Laurens attributed Lee's embarrassment "to want of presence of mind." This stung Lee into anger that led him to ask Laurens one question too many.

Lee: "Were you ever in the action before?"

John Laurens, the South Carolina aristocrat, having been shot through the shoulder trying to set fire to the Chew house at Germantown, veteran of many another fierce engagement, drawled a crushing reply: "I have been in several actions; I did not call that an action, as there was no action previous to the retreat."

So the officer-judges found Lee guilty on all three charges, except that the word "shameful" was deleted from the second charge. His "misbehaviour" in ordering the retreat, though not necessarily shameful, remained "unnecessary" and "disorderly." He was sentenced to be suspended from command in the armies of the United States for the term of twelve months. There had been no proof of treason, and most of the evidence for the prosecution—except for Laurens's, and including Hamilton's—had been equivocal.

While Congress carefully reviewed the correctness of the verdict against its former favorite, Lee reacted in a way that confirmed Hamilton's judgment that his "hurry of mind" made him unfit for command, even of his own case. Lee published a "vindication" of his generalship which attacked the court-martial as an "inquisition," accused Washington of being a military incompetent jealous of men around him like Lee and Thomas Conway who had real skill, and imputed cowardice to von Steuben, who had testified against him at the trial, by writing that von Steuben had been only a "very distant spectator" at the battle. Lee discredited Hamilton, John Laurens, and the other "earwigs" around Washington, as nothing but "an idolatrous set of Toad Eaters who gave perjured testimony." Lee went to Congress himself, as one observer wrote, "damning Washington . . . and the Congress, and threatening to resign, *aye, God damn them, that he would,* and frowning and dancing like a Caledonian stung by a Tarantula."

Von Steuben's Prussian rage exploded at being called a "very distant spectator." His aide, Captain Benjamin Walker, brought Lee the irate baron's challenge to a duel. Lee backed down, saying he had not questioned von Steuben's courage, but only his "forwardness" in testifying for the prosecution. He would make this statement publicly, but "If you found that I have not dealt honestly, I am ready to satisfy you in the manner you desire." Von Steuben accepted this explanation and withdrew the challenge.

Laurens heard "that General Lee had spoken of General Washington in the grossest and most opprobrious terms of personal abuse." He, too, challenged Lee to a duel, choosing Hamilton for his second.

Lee accepted: "I will do myself the Honour of meeting you attended by a Friend with a brace of pistols tomorrow (Dec. 22, 1778) ½ past 3 P.M." If they should be unsuccessful killing each other with pistols, Lee would bring along swords for a backup, to make sure something would produce a fatality, but his legs and gout were a problem: "I would willingly bring a small sword at the same time, but from the effects of my fall and the quantity of Physick I have taken to baffle a fit of the Gout . . . I do not think myself sufficiently strong on my legs."

The next morning, the combatants, brandishing two pistols apiece, advanced toward each other, firing when they chose. At five or six paces they blazed away almost simultaneously. As Laurens was cocking his second pistol for another try, Lee cried out that he had been wounded. Laurens and the two seconds rushed to help him. He protested that his wound was a trifling one. He, too, wanted another shot at his opponent. Hamilton and Lee's second, Major Evan Edwards, insisted that all requirements of honor had been fully satisfied and that the encounter must end without more ado. Laurens insisted that he was not satisfied. Lee admitted that he had given an opinion of Washington's military character to his close friends, and might do so again, but that the things he had said were not as bad as some claimed. He esteemed him as a man. This was apology enough for Laurens.

Hamilton and Edwards as seconds published the usual report, pronouncing that after the two gentlemen met, "their conduct was strongly marked by all the politeness, generosity, coolness, and firmness, that ought to characterize a transaction of this nature." Lee is reported to have said later of Laurens, "I could have hugged the noble boy, he pleased me so."

Major Samuel Shaw commented acidly to John Laurens's father, Henry Laurens, that his son's challenge in defense of Washington's honor had been issued in accordance with the ancient knightly custom of *pro vidua,* by which "monks, old women (like Washington?) and widows" were allowed a champion like Henry Laurens's son John. John had written his father privately of suspicions of Lee's treachery that he shared with Hamilton: "Mr. Clinton's whole flying army would have fallen into our hands" but for Lee's "defect of good will." Henry Laurens gave voice to his son John's and Hamilton's suspicions of treason on the floor of Congress; a supporter of Lee challenged Henry Laurens to a duel; they exchanged shots; but both men missed.

Of the father's duel, Shaw observed that in Philadelphia, "duels are now exceedingly in vogue, though fortunately seldom attended with fatal consequences."

The farcical record of nonfatal fallout from the court-martial of Major General Charles Lee shows that an eighteenth-century gentleman like Hamilton could live easily with the deadly etiquette of the duello. There were innumerable ways that a challenge to a duel could be finessed or a duel once begun be broken off, without fatality yet with honor intact, if either of the parties to the challenge had a desire to avoid a fatal issue.

Five months after the court-martial's verdict, Congress finally confirmed it in December by a somewhat equivocal vote of eight states to two.

Many years later, there came to light the plan to betray the colonies to the British that Lee had drawn up for Sir William Howe while a prisoner, before Hamilton had helped arrange for his exchange. According to Lee's most sympathetic biographer, "Had this plan fallen into American hands when he could be brought before a military court, it is not unlikely that he would have been found guilty of treachery and sentenced to death." The finding confirmed the suspicions of treason that Hamilton had voiced to Boudinot, and Laurens to his father, to account for Lee's weird behavior at the Battle of Monmouth.

Lee was dismissed from the army in 1780 and died in disgrace in 1782. The only one who had a good word to say about him was Sir Henry Clinton. He complimented Lee by pointing out that Lee's retreat was excellent generalship because "the quality of all my corps far exceeded anything he had to oppose them." To Hamilton and Laurens this clinched their suspicions of Lee's guilt of something much worse than "misbehaviour at Monmouth." To them it would be no surprise that Clinton would thus help the traitor cover up his tracks. It was no more surprising that their sworn testimony at courts-martial and pistols on the duelling ground should help their own essential aegis confirm his own version of this mooted episode of American history.

8

Elizabeth Schuyler Comes to Morristown

Believe me, I am lover in earnest, though I do not speak of the perfections of my mistress in the enthusiasm of chivalry.

—To John Laurens, June 30, 1780

Making no attempt to give chase as Sir Henry Clinton's army returned to their old positions on Staten Island, Manhattan, and Long Island, Washington gave his men two days at the battlefield in which "to breath themselves," care for the wounded, and bury their dead. Congratulations from the country and Congress poured in for the technical "victory": After the battle they still occupied the battlefield. It was a definitional victory, made possible only because the British objective had been to go elsewhere anyway.

In a leisurely way, still in theory keeping Sir Henry Clinton's army covered, Washington's army marched northward to New Brunswick, where Hamilton testified at Lee's trial, on to Paramus opposite Fort Washington, where Hamilton continued his testimony, and on up the Hudson to Peekskill and Haverstraw below West Point. There the great fortesss intended to block the Hudson River valley from future invasions like Burgoyne's was under hasty construction.

War was too important a matter for Lieutenant Colonel Hamilton to leave to the generals, and he saw Congress, equally, as a battlefield on which the national interest seemed to be constantly in a retreat as disorderly as General Lee's. Two and a half months after Monmouth, Hamilton under the pseudonym of *Publius* continued the battle by political means in Holt's *New York Journal and General Advertiser*, now published in Poughkeep-

101

sie. Beginning October 16, 1778, three broadsides singled out Samuel Chase, a member of Congress from Maryland, as the target.

Publius' protest had been touched off by the good news of the arrival of the French fleet, 12 ships of the line, including six frigates and two xebecs, sailing up Delaware Bay July 8, 1778, under the command of Vice Admiral Charles Henri Hector, the Comte d'Estaing. Congress secretly planned to purchase grain for the French in the open market, and Congressman Samuel Chase had the early inside information. Thus assured of a future shortage, he sent out agents to buy up all available grain while at the same time he delayed congressional action that would have kept the price down. By the time Congress was able to act, Chase had doubled his money.

Hamilton as Publius struck out at Chase by saying that any member of Congress who turns ''the knowledge or secrets, to which his office gave him access, to the purposes of private profit . . . ought to feel the utmost rigor of public resentment, and be detested as a traitor of the worst and most dangerous kind.''

Chase merely personified the attitude of complacency and greed that was widely represented in Congress. ''There are abuses in the state, which demand an immediate remedy,'' Publius announced. ''When avarice takes the lead in a state, it is commonly the forerunner of its fall. How shocking it is to discover among ourselves, even at this early period, the strongest symptoms of this fatal disease?''

Hamilton rarely allowed himself to reveal how he saw himself inwardly: his choice of pseudonym seems more revealing than any self-serving self-revelations.

One of several prominent figures of classical times of the same name was Publius, or Publilius, Syrus, a Latin writer of the first century B.C., a native of remote Syria. Brought as a slave to Rome, his wit and talent won the favor of his master, who educated and then freed him. He enjoyed great success as a writer of mimes and still greater success as an improvisatore, an actor who composed poems and mimes extemporaneously as he performed them. In one contest Publius had vanquished all his competitors, including the celebrated Decimus Laberius, and won the prize from the hand of Caesar himself.

Hamilton's choice of *Publius* for these public performances may manifest his inward sense of wonder that a penniless illegitimate orphan boy from a remote dependency could now be at the headquarters of the effort to free the slaves from the overseas empire. There he improvises mimes as he goes along, in competition for an unannounced grand prize to be awarded at some unspecified future date—never suspecting the prize might be a bullet in his liver.

Hamilton as Publius was now reaching out beyond Washington's headquarters to make himself a political force in the country separate from his dependent status as Washington's headquarters intelligencer.

Like Hamilton, John Laurens—and von Steuben too—was becoming restless in the servitude of aideship to a sluggish Fabius Cunctator. Seeking a command of troops in the line, at the end of 1778, Laurens returned to his native South Carolina to find action in what would soon become the war's most active theater of combat.

But Washington would not hear of giving Hamilton a line command. Instead, he sent Hamilton off to hector Comte d'Estaing and his French fleet into quick action against the British, now that they had been so expensively reprovisioned by Samuel Chase and Congress.

Hamilton galloped down from Haverstraw on July 18 to meet d'Estaing at a rendezvous at Black Point on the New Jersey coast. D'Estaing's fleet outweighed the British fleet in numbers of ships and guns, but his concern for the delicacy of his ships' bottoms in New

York's harbor was profound; he made no mention of fear of British shore batteries.

Hamilton reported back to Washington on the twentieth that d'Estaing "has had the River sounded and finds he cannot enter." Realism dictated the decision to make an amphibious assault on Newport instead. Hamilton ordered the French fleet on its way, having made arrangements for d'Estaing to coordinate his and General John Sullivan's land-sea assault on Newport.

The result of Hamilton's decision on whether d'Estaing should attack New York or Newport that summer could possibly have ended the war either way for either side. For a third time, Washington had entrusted him with a battle plan that left the ultimate decision between opposite strategic alternatives to Hamilton's judgment depending on how he appraised the situation.

The operation turned out to be a disaster. As the French fleet closed in on Newport General Sullivan, who had everything a good general needed except good luck, marched a large command of more than 10,000 men bolstered by additional Continental regiments and New England militia south out of Providence to the Tiverton Ferry and the Sakonnet Passage.

A reinforced British fleet under Admiral Richard Howe hove into view up the sound before D'Estaing had disembarked his troops. Unready for action, D'Estaing reloaded his troops on their transports and put out to sea. A storm of hurricane proportions struck both fleets, and d'Estaing sailed north to Boston to refit, abandoning Sullivan's army. John Glover's Marbleheaders shuttled expertly handled craft of all sorts across the water to rescue another beaten American command. Sullivan slunk back to the beaches of Sakonnet.

"Should the expedition fail, thru' the abandonment of the French fleet," Washington wrote in Hamilton's prescient words, "the officers . . . will be apt to complain loudly. But prudence dictates that we should put the best face upon the matter and, to the world, attribute the removal to Boston to necessity" caused by the storm, not French timorousness. It was politic to avoid an open rupture with the great ally.

Sullivan's general orders, with fine Irish fury, blasted the French: "the event will prove America able to procure by her own arms, which her allies refuse her in obtaining."

D'Estaing sailed for the West Indies. Recriminations poured in on Washington, who asked Hamilton to help patch things up by writing a delicately worded reproof to Sullivan:

> The disagreement between the army under your command and the fleet has given me . . . singular uneasiness. The continent at large is concerned in our cordiality. . . . In our conduct towards [the French] we should remember that they are a people old in war, very strict military etiquette and apt to take fire where others scarcely seem warmed. Permit me to recommend in the most particular manner, the cultivation of harmony and good agreement.

Hamilton helped Washington write a similar soothing letter to d'Estaing.

Hamilton then wrote a semipublic letter to Boudinot in Congress on September 8, 1778, giving his own reading of the problem. He condemned Sullivan's tactless criticism of the French as "the summit of folly" and an "absurdity without parallel." He praised the courage of a particular French major, Louis Tousard, who had lost an arm in a charge against a British fieldpiece. Because this letter issued from American headquarters but was not signed by the commander in chief, it diplomatically helped to calm the French, "a people old in war" and etiquette. As Hamilton knew, Congress, if left its own head, would applaud Sullivan's skill at retreat, blame all on the French, and sympathize with his complaints. Hamilton's letter to Boudinot and his fulsome praise of the unfortunate Tousard resulted in Congress's avoiding all negatives. It officially thanked Sullivan and his army and at the same time declared the French admiral and his officers "fully entitled to the regards of the friends of America."

October 7, 1779, Washington entrusted to Hamilton a fourth ultimate command decision: how to deploy d'Estaing's fleet in another joint amphibious attack—this time on New York.

Washington left discretionary authority entirely to Hamilton. He and Brigadier General Louis Le Beque du Portail, Commandant of Engineers, were to work out all of the tactics and troop dispositions and the thousand and one logistical details of what was to be the biggest joint allied operation of the war. Hamilton's authority would permit him to divert the amphibious assault to Newport if he should wish to do so.

Concluding the letter which Hamilton was bringing to d'Estaing, the man who could not tell a lie told a whopper: Washington might be bringing as many as 25,000 effective men into the battle! He had never had more than about 10,000 effective troops directly under his command in the field, and Congress was showing no signs of adding more. A simpler explanation for the overstatement than calling it a lie is that Washington often did not read important papers that Hamilton wrote out for him to sign, and that Hamilton was improving the occasion.

Hamilton and du Portail set out in October to flag down d'Estaing's fleet. But after a defeat at Savannah, d'Estaing had reembarked his ground troops and given orders to his scurvy-racked helmsmen and crews to set a southerly course to sunny Martinique before another hurricane season could rack them up at sea. Hamilton and du Portail wandered along the Jersey coast looking for d'Estaing's sails in vain.

Despite d'Estaing's temporary disappearance, the whole episode may have been Washington's most masterful feint, because at the end of 1779 the British evacuated Newport and moved their entire garrison back to New York to consolidate forces—against Washington's well-advertised attack by 25,000 rebels!

After Albany, Monmouth, and each of the two unsuccessful summer sorties to activate combined operations with the French, Hamilton had suffered mysterious spells of sickness. He apologized to Washington for being out of action which "no more than a moderate attention to my frail constitution may make not improper." His friend, James McHenry, who had given up his medical practice to join Washington's staff, wrote Hamilton a prescription. He discouraged the drinking of milk, and encouraged the drinking of water as "the most general solvent" and the kindliest dilutent, and advised moderation in the drinking of wine.

McHenry nonetheless gave his sick army friend some hangover pills: "In case you should fall into a debauch, you must next day have recourse to the pills. I hope however that you will not have recourse to them often. The great Paracelsus trusted to his pill to destroy the effects of intemperance, but he died (if I forget not) about the age of 30 notwithstanding his pill." On the other hand, Luigi Coronaro, the Venetian nobleman who ate only one egg a day after forty "was wiser. He trusted to an egg, and I think he lived to above 90."

The troop levies of the Southern states were exhausted. There were hardly any white enlisted men left in the South to be commanded. John Laurens, Hamilton's closest friend, had the novel notion of raising battalions of black slaves to lead against the British. No troops would be better trained to do as ordered by their commanders in the cause of freedom than freed Negro slaves, who would be promised their freedom if they survived their soldiering in freedom's cause.

Another young Southerner who wanted to see more action was the studious, gawky James Monroe, who had just resigned his commission as an aide. On May 22, 1779, Hamilton furnished Monroe with a humorous introduction to Laurens. "Monroe . . . seems to be as much of a knight errant as your worship; but as he is an honest fellow, I shall be glad he may find some employment, that will enable him to get knocked in the head in an honorable way. . . . He will relish your black scheme . . . You know him to be a man of honor a sensible man and a soldier."

Fifteen years later, "dishonorable," "dishonest," and "insensible" would be the words Hamilton would substitute for this warm endorsement; the young Senator from Virginia would lead the congressional investigation into the secretary of the treasury's alleged insider speculations with Treasury funds—and wring out of him the self-destructive confession of his secret love affair with Maria Reynolds.

Unlucky General John Sullivan's expedition against the Indians in western New York State during the summer of 1779 was a failure; New Jersey troops unified in protest against being massacred in what would be another essentially cosmetic attack to bolster public opinion. Hamilton wrote a politic letter to the New Jersey officers for Washington, chiding the mutiny as a "hasty and imprudent step." To Congress he wrote that his rebuke of the officers "had to be mild, when our situation is considered. The causes of discontent are too great and too general and the ties that bind the officers to the service too feeble to admit of rigor." Of these events of 1779, Hamilton poured out his deepest feelings in affectionate letters to John Laurens.

On September 9 he wrote: "I think your black scheme would be the best resource the situation of your country will admit. I wish its success, but my hopes are very feeble."

Like Hamilton, Laurens despised the selfish arguments with which the institution of chattel slavery was supported by the rich planters they knew in Virginia, South Carolina, and the West Indies. ". . . We have sunk the African[s] and their descendants below the standard of humanity," he lamented to his father Henry Laurens, "and almost render'd them incapable of that blessing which equal Heaven bestow'd upon us all." He conceded that slaves probably should be brought to freedom gradually, by "shades and degrees." Enrollment in the revolutionary army, with the promise of liberty to those who survived, would be a long step toward emancipation.

Hamilton's discouragement in September arose partly out of having labored earlier to bring Laurens's plan to fruition without success. In March he had written John Jay, then the president of Congress, seeking the formal sanction of Congress for Laurens's plan and money to back it up: take two, three, or four battalions of slaves into Continental pay. As a poor white boy growing up in the same room with slaves in an aristocratic, white, slave-owning society, Hamilton knew the unpopular truth about black slavery firsthand.

To Jay he had written on March 14, 1779:

> I have not the least doubt that the negroes will make very excellent soldiers, with proper management. . . . I mention this because I have frequently heard it objected to the scheme of embodying negroes, that they are too stupid to make soldiers. This is so far from appearing to me a valid objection, that I think their want of cultivation (for their natural faculties are as good as ours), joined to that habit of subordination which they acquire from a life of servitude, will enable them sooner to become soldiers than our white inhabitants. Let officers be men of sense and sentiment; and the nearer the soldiers approach to machines, perhaps the better.

Hamilton's good offices with Jay helped produce a congressional recommendation that

South Carolina and Georgia raise 3,000 Negro troops under white officers. The Continental Congress would recompense the masters for slaves thus serving and freed at the end of the war.

But most "moneyed men," even men of good will like Washington, Jefferson, and Laurens's own father, opposed the plan and it died. "Prejudice and private interest will be antagonists too powerful for public spirit and public good," Hamilton wrote Laurens gloomily. He concluded that the institution of black chattel slavery enslaved slaves and masters alike by a golden chain of greed:

> Every hope of this kind my friend is an idle dream; every reflection will convince you that there is no virtue [in] America. That commerce which presided over the birth and education of these states has fitted their inhabitants for the chain, and that the only condition they sincerely desire is that it may be a golden one.

The self-interest of the masters that Hamilton had foretold also killed his and Laurens's plan in the South Carolina legislature. Their lily-white army remained too weak to keep the British from occupying the whole state in 1780, but Southern whites would not place army muskets in the hands of blacks even to save their state. Laurens gave up his visionary plan and rejoined the all-white ranks of the Southern army. Too weak to defend their countrymen against the British, the moneyed men remained strong enough to defend themselves against emancipation from the golden chain of chattel slavery, from which Hamilton and Laurens tried to free them 85 years before Lincoln.

In late summer of 1778, Washington's command headquarters moved from White Plains up the Hudson to Fishkill, then to Fredericksburg and Haverstraw, then, as autumn came on, southeastward to Middlebrook and Elizabethtown, New Jersey. Finally, in time for Christmas and New New Year's, it arrived in Philadelphia for a month or more of appearances, both official and unofficial, before Congress and the committee on the army. There Washington and Hamilton pressed familiar-sounding appeals for everything that the defense establishment absolutely had to have and, of course, more—to allow Congress the usual political leeway to slash the usual "fat" from the defense budget and leave only the usual "muscle."

Washington and Hamilton and the other members of the general's staff were swept into a round of lavish entertainments. Robert Morris with his wife and Peggy Shippen with Benedict Arnold led the revels. The beautiful Peggy Shippen was one suspect Tory who had remained behind when Clinton had departed and now she reigned over colonial and congressional society much as she had over the British the winter before. Her new partner on the social rounds was the commanding general of the new occupying army, Major General Benedict Arnold, still stumping about on the left leg shortened by wounds at Quebec in 1775 and again at Bemis Heights at Saratoga in 1777.

At her urging Arnold was secretly sending letters signed "Gustavus" and other false names from Philadelphia through the lines to Major John André, adjutant to Sir Henry Clinton in New York. They hinted strongly that a highly placed but unnamed American officer might offer "his services to the commander in chief of the British forces in any way that would most effectively restore the former government and destroy the then usurped authority of Congress, either by immediately joining the British army or cooperating on some concealed plan with Sir Henry Clinton."

The 38-year-old Arnold recopied a love letter he had sent without success to another young beauty five months earlier and re-sent it to 18-year-old Peggy: her "heavenly image is too deeply impressed ever to be effaced." Let her "heavenly bosom . . . expand with a sensation more soft, more tender than friendship." This time it worked better, and Peggy Shippen and Benedict Arnold were married April 8, 1779. They began to entertain ever more lavishly, seeming to favor mostly wealthy Tories as intimates.

Still, Hamilton thought Arnold had been unfairly dealt with by Congress, and at the court-martial that Arnold demanded for vindication of the charges of misappropriating army supplies, Hamilton testified as one of the witnesses to his good character and valuable services as a fighting general.

Washington's plans for 1779 and 1780 called for keeping up a show of military activity but not exposing the cause to the risk of a crushing defeat by Clinton's main British army. To keep the colonies from being split in two, it remained important above all else to keep the citadel at West Point secure; it remained the most strategic position of all. When the British seized the fort south of West Point on the same side of the Hudson, at Stony Point, and also the fort at Verplanck's on the east side of the river opposite Stony Point, Hamilton wrote for Washington to Anthony Wayne, "the importance of Verplanck's and Stony Points to the enemy is too obvious to need explanation." An assault should be made "by . . . surprise in the night." "Mad Anthony" Wayne stormed and seized Stony Point and its garrison the night of July 15–16, 1779, in an exploit of derring-do that Hamilton envied and would like to have commanded himself. Hamilton also prepared general orders for the parallel attack on Verplanck's Point, which failed.

Washington would soon abandon Stony Point, but in the meantime Congress and the public were furnished the thrill of the tale of "Mad Anthony" Wayne's brilliant stroke of American arms. The public impact outweighed the military importance. The public's impression that important victories were being won made the real, underlying Fabian policy of doing nothing politically possible.

At the 1779–1780 winter encampment in Morristown besides Martha Washington, a remarkable *omnium-gatherum* of other ladies and gentlemen found their way to the headquarters in the Jacob Ford house—wives, daughters, sisters, journalists, French travelers, tourists, curiosity seekers, and prostitutes.

Being called the general's "earwig" by Lee had enraged him, but Hamilton was known by all to have Washington's ear. Applicants plagued Hamilton with all manner of appeals. He turned few down flatly, usually managed to produce some kind of practical help, and sometimes infused his letters with a touch of humorous bawdry or flippant cynicism, or note of compassionate understanding. A letter he wrote on behalf of an elderly parson to General "Mad Anthony" Wayne was typical:

> Doctor W. Mendy is one of those characters that for its honesty, simplicity, and helplessness interests my humanity.
> He is exceedingly anxious to be in the Service, and, I believe, has been forced out of it not altogether by fair play. He is just what I should like for a military parson, except that he does not whore or drink. He will fight, and he will not insist upon your going to heaven whether you will or not. He tells me there is a vacancy in your Brigade. I should be really happy if, through your influence, he can fill it.

Hamilton asked, "Pray take care of this good old man."

Catherine "Lady Kitty" Livingston's younger sister Susannah, or Suki, daughter of the

William Livingstons of Elizabethtown with whom Hamilton had spent the winter six years earlier, wanted passes for cousins in New York to go back and forth through the lines to visit Suki's family in New Jersey, where her father was the governor. A year or so older than Hamilton, Suki had grown up to be another beauty like her older sister and played on their old friendship:

> Sir—The fond desire we all feel to be indulged with a sight of those who are dear to us, after a long detachment from them, has led my cousins Miss Van Horne Miss Clarkson, and Miss Browne to sollicit an interview with their Friends in Jersey. . . . But your own humanity will tell you that the anxious solicitude of sisters to see their brothers after a tedious absence who have passed through various perils in our service, is of itself a sufficient [reason].

On March 18, 1779, with flippant warmth, sister Suki's old friend Hamilton told her "No."

> I can hardly forgive an application to my *humanity,* to induce me to exert my influence in an affair, in which ladies are concerned; and especially when you are of the party. Had you appealed to my friendship or to my gallantry, it would have been irresistible. I should have thought myself bound to have set prudence and policy at defiance, and even to have attacked *windmills* in Ladyship's service. I am not sure, but my imagination would have gone so far, as to have fancied New York an *inchanted castle*—the three ladies, so many fair damsels, ravished from their friends and held in captivity, by the *spells* of some wicked magician—General Clinton a huge giant placed as keeper of the gates, and myself a valorous knight, destined to be their champion and deliverer.
>
>   But when instead of availing yourself of so much better titles, you appealed to the cold general principle of humanity . . . ,

. . . he had prudently checked with Washington:

> . . . I resolved to show you, that all the eloquence of your fine pen could not tempt for Fabius to do wrong. . . . I put your letter into his hands and let it speak for itself. I knew indeed, this would expose his resolution to a severer trial than it could experience, in any other way. . . .

Washington had told Hamilton to tell her no. But politely.

There was no rule against her cousins' coming out to New Jersey and staying, instead of passing back through the lines, Hamilton said, because "they will be an acquisition," provided that "the ladies on our side" are not made jealous and also providing, because New York City was infamous as a hotbed of Toryism, that Susannah's darling cousins "are not found guilty of treason."

Hamilton's reputation as a gallant spread beyond the confines of camp. A Tory newspaper wove his amatory repute and the proposed new American flag into a single snicker.

"Mrs. Washington," it reported, "has a mottled tom-cat (which she calls, in a complimentary way, 'Hamilton') with thirteen yellow rings around its tail," and "His flaunting his tail suggested to the Congress the adoption of the same number of stripes for the rebel flag."

Smythe's Journal charged Hamilton with doing what his old friend Hugh Knox's letters had taxed him with failing to do: writing a history of the American Revolution. "It is said little Hamilton, the poet and composer to the Lord Protector Mr. Washington, is engaged upon a literary work which is intended to give posterity a true estimate of the present rebellion and its supporters.''

Contemptuous of a nonexistent work in progress by the frivolous pipsqueak, Martha's ringtailed tomcat, the Tory journal held that an author of love letters and amorous pastorals would hardly be equal to setting down such a work—as he was in the process of writing.

The army's second winter encampment at Morristown in 1779–1780, amid the snows and sleets of the worst New Jersey winter of the eighteenth century, was worse than Valley Forge. Von Steuben said the men "exhibited the most shocking picture of misery I have ever seen, scarce a man having wherewithal to cover his nakedness, and a great number very bad with the itch.'' Nathanael Greene, the quartermaster general, declared, "there never was a darker hour in American prospects than this. . . . Our treasury is dry and magazines empty; how are we to support the war is beyond my conception.'' Washington warned a neglectful Congress that the army was on the point of breaking up, unburdening himself by Hamilton's hand on May 31, 1780, to President Joseph Reed of Pennsylvania: "All our . . . operations are at a stand and unless a system very different . . . be immediately adopted throughout the states our affairs must soon become desperate beyond the possibility of recover. . . . Indeed I have almost ceased to hope.''

For the headquarters officers billeted in the Jacob Ford mansion or in nearby houses, life was nothing like as rugged as it was for the enlisted men in their self-constructed huts. Young ladies busied themselves about the camp, dutifully doing good deeds daily for sick enlisted men; in off-duty hours they brightened the lives of perfectly healthy young officers who loved gazing into the lively eyes of these young angels of mercy. The horrors of war gave way to tender gallantries, witty badinage, sleigh rides, formal dinners, reels and rigadoons and agreeable balls.

In April, Hamilton had professed platonic love for Laurens, now absent in South Carolina: "Cold in my profession, warm in my friendships, I wish, my dear Laurens, it might be in my power, by action rather than words, to convince you that I love you.'' He had enclosed a letter smuggled out of New York from the mother of Martha Manning, the young bride Laurens had left in England with their infant daughter. Laurens would never see either of them again. Hamilton's own thoughts concenter on other matters matrimonial.

> And now my Dear, as we are upon the subject of wife, "I empower and command you to get me one in Carolina. Such a wife as I want will, I know, be difficult to be found, but if you succeed, it will be the stronger proof of your zeal and dexterity. Take her description—she must be young, handsome (I lay most stress upon a good shape), sensible (a little learning will do), well-bred (but she must have an aversion to the word *ton*), chaste, and tender (I am an enthusiast in my notions of fidelity and fondness), of some good nature, a great deal of generosity (she must neither love money nor scolding, for I dislike equally a termagant and an economist). In politics I am indifferent what side she may be of. I think I have arguments that will easily convert her to mine. As to religion a moderate stock will satisfy me. She must believe in God and hate a saint.

Hamilton's critics charge that he married the second daughter of General Philip Schuyler and Catharine van Rensselaer Schuyler without loving her but only to gain money, status, and power through the Schuyler connection. Their case begins with the following two sentences with which Hamilton humorously polished off the above paragraph to his dearest friend: ''But as to fortune, the larger stock of that the better. You know my temper and circumstances and will, therefore, pay special attention to this article in the treaty.''

It is not easy to think of a Founding Father or Framer who married a woman who did not bring him a respectable fortune of her own: Martha Custis Washington, Martha Wayles Jefferson, and Sarah Livingston Jay are ready examples. For the upstart immigrant to match his native-born peers by his conquest seems to be what makes it so unforgivable to his critics.

Laurens should not leave Hamilton's assignment simply dangling in the air, he must follow through with practical steps:

> If you should not readily meet with a lady that you think answers my description you can only advertise in the public papers and doubtless you will hear of many competitors for most of the qualifications required, who will be glad to become candidates for such a prize as I am. To excite their emulation, it will be necessary for you to give an account of the lover—his *size,* make [i.e., ''shape''], quality of mind and *body,* achievements, expectations, fortune, &c.

Hamilton breaks off the word picture of himself at a point just beyond the length of his nose. ''In drawing my picture, you will no doubt be civil to your friend; mind you do justice to the length of my nose and don't forget, that I (————).''

Leaving what is broken off unsaid catches Hamilton as close as he is ever found to talking ''off the top of his head.'' His stream of consciousness ripples across the features of the all but inexhaustible subject of wife:

> After reviewing what I have written, I am ready to ask myself what could have put it into my head to hazard this Jeu *de follie.* Do I want a wife? No—I have plagues enough without desiring to add to the number that *greatest of all;* and if I were silly enough to do it, I should take care how I employ a proxy. Did I mean to show my wit? If I did, I am sure I have missed my aim. Did I only intend to [frisk]? In this I have succeeded, but I have done more. I have gratified my feelings, by lengthening out the only kind of intercourse now in my power with my friend. Adieu.

>   Yours.

> A. Hamilton

By and large, she met his specifications. Except that in some eyes she might not have been quite as beautiful as he had specified, and her piety was deeper than he required. But so far as anyone knows, it was not so deep as ever to cause her to be a nuisance or fail to hate a saint.

The second daughter of Philip and Catharine van Rensselaer Schuyler, Elizabeth was born on August 9, 1757. She was therefore only seven months younger than Hamilton, a Lioness well starred for his Capricorn. Not as much of a belle as her sister Angelica, one year older, or her sister Margarita, one year younger, she nonetheless had a decided charming luster of her own.

To Hamilton she brought with her things he had not even thought of asking of the ideal wife requisitioned from Laurens. Politically, socially, militarily, and financially, there was no better family than hers to be found in the state of New York, and only three others might lay claim to equal distinction—the Livingstons, the Van Cortlandts, and the Van Rens-salaers, of whom Elizabeth's mother was one.

Her father, General Philip Schuyler, was of the fourth generation of Dutch patroons with vast holdings along the Mohawk River and in the region surrounding Albany, where he dwelt like a feudal baron. His word was the law; his will was supreme; from his fertile valleys came flax; and from his forests, prime lumber. He built his own ships and floated them down the Hudson for trade with England and the West Indies.

Unlike most men of his class and status, with the coming of the Revolution he chose the side of the colonies and rose rapidly to the rank of major general. He was one of Washington's closest friends—a comrade-in-arms from French and Indian War days. His proud air and aristocratic style, not to mention the military reverses he had suffered in Canada and at Fort Ticonderoga, had made him many enemies, particularly among the small holders of New England. They were quick to accuse him of incompetence and even treason, and urge that he be replaced by General Gates, his natural enemy. In court-martial proceedings brought against him for the loss of Ticonderoga, he had been acquitted, but not left without scars.

The time and place where Elizabeth Schuyler and Alexander Hamilton first met remain, like the dates of his other rites of passage—his birth, arrival in New York, and his first meeting with Washington—subjects of intense disagreement among authorities of various qualifications.

They may have first met at Elizabethtown, when she was visiting the William Livingstons with her parents, and when Hamilton would probably have had eyes only for her cousins Kitty Livingston and sister Suki.

But it is more likely that Hamilton first met Elizabeth in early November of 1777 on his mission from Washington to General Gates. It would have been surprising if Hamilton had not improved his trip by a secret visit to the house of the man in Albany closest to Washington who also most hated Gates. In any event, those nights are the only four with no out-of-pocket expenses listed for night lodgings on the expense voucher he and Captain Caleb Gibbs turned in after their trip.

Even if reasons of state had not brought Hamilton to The Pastures, his friend Robert Troup would know where to take his old college roommate to find not one, but three of the most beautiful girls in Albany. Neither Schuyler nor Troup would trouble their mother with a dangerous secret like knowledge of the rendezvous of two of Gates's most notable enemies.

Of the Schuyler's 11 children, five daughters and three sons survived infancy. The youngest of the five beauteous sisters, Catharine van Renssaelaer Schuyler, was 21 years younger than Elizabeth. In her book *A God-Child of Washington*—she was the godchild— she recalls as fact that in the afternoon of a pleasant fall day "shortly after the surrender of Burgoyne a young officer wearing the uniform of a member of Washington's military family, accompanied by an orderly, left the ferryboat," mounted their horses, and rode westward toward the Schuyler mansion, The Pastures. His bearing "exhibited a natural, yet unassuming superiority; his features gave evidence of thought, intellectual strength and a determined mind." His "high expansive forehead, a nose of the Grecian mold, a dark bright eye, and the line of a mouth expressing decision and courage completed the contour of a face never to be forgotten."

The Pastures was a foursquare, rose-red brick structure with two chimneys. A white wooden balustrade surrounded the white shuttered dormer windows on the top floor. It had a center hall design typical of important Hudson Valley houses of the 1760s. Hamilton dismounted, gave his horse's reins to his orderly and his card to a Schuyler servant who appeared at the door. "In a few moments [he] was welcomed by the General himself, to a mansion destined ever after to be linked with his future destiny.'' Gertrude Atherton, who studied the facts of Hamilton's life as carefully as anyone else, agreed with Washington's godchild that Elizabeth and Hamilton first met that day at The Pastures three years before Elizabeth Schuyler came to Morristown. In these opinions this writer joins the ladies.

Had they not first met on the occasion of such a dramatic secret visit, it seems likely that one or the other of them would have mentioned the date and circumstances of their first meeting at some later time in their romance. Their meeting in Albany three years earlier would help account for the quick intimacy they reached at Morristown later.

Having won acquittal at his trial for the loss of Fort Ticonderoga, Philip Schuyler had been elected to the Continental Congress and progressed to Philadelphia with his wife and daughters. From Philadelphia, Elizabeth came up to Morristown to visit her aunt, Mrs. John Cochran, the wife of the surgeon general of the Middle Department. Elizabeth and her sister Angelica helped out with volunteer work among the sick enlisted men in the wards near the encampment at Jockey Hollow. When the Schuylers came up from Philadelphia, they stayed at the Cochrans' too.

Elizabeth referred discreetly to ''Mr. Hamilton'' as being Washington's secretary at the time. She said nothing about this first visit to his headquarters being her first meeting with him.

Early in his courtship of Betsy, in February 1780, Hamilton writes to her sister Margarita, or Peggy, as she is called, ''I venture to tell you in confidence,'' confident that she would tell her sister instantly,

> that by some odd contrivance or other your sister has found out the secret of interesting me in everything that concerns her; and though I have not the happiness of a personal acquaintance with you, I have had the good fortune to see several very pretty pictures of your person and mind which have inspired me with a more than common partiality for both. Among others, your sister carries a beautiful copy constantly about her drawn by herself, of which she has two or three times favored me with a sight.

For the most part, Hamilton's letter is the familiar one of a man in love burning to tell someone else of his love who will tell his love of his love. But there is an overtone that seems to go beyond merely ingratiating himself with a future sister-in-law.

The pictures of Margarita that Betsy had drawn for him, of her person in pencil and of her mind in words, excited Hamilton's interest in her too, thus testifying to Margarita's beauty; Betsy's ability to sketch vividly with both pencil and language; and Hamilton's sensitivity to art and beauty, women in general, and Schuyler daughters in particular.

To Margarita he continued, ''I have already confessed the influence your sister has over me—yet notwithstanding this, I have some things of a very very serious and heinous nature to lay to her charge.—She is most unmercifully handsome''—She thus satisfies one of his stipulations to Laurens—''And so perverse that she has none of those pretty affectations which are the prerogatives of beauty.'' He goes on:

> Her good sense is destitute of that happy mixture of vanity and ostentation which would make it conspicuous to the whole tribe of fools and foplings as well as to men of understanding so that as the matter now stands it is little known beyond the circle of these. She has good nature, affability and vivacity unembellished with that charming frivolousness which is justly deemed one of the principal accomplishments of a *belle*. . . .

Peggy's own reputation as belle full of the charming frivolousness that Betsy lacks is not lost on Hamilton.

"In short she is so strange a creature," he writes,

> that she possesses all the beauties, virtues and graces of her sex without any of these amiable defects, which from their general prevalence are esteemed by connoisseurs necessary shades in the character of a fine woman. The most determined adversaries of Hymen can find in her no pretext for their hostility, and there are several of my friends, philosophers who railed at love as a weakness, men of the world who laughed at it as a phantasie whom she has presumptuously and daringly compelled to acknowledge its power and surrender at discretion. I can the better assert the truth of this, as I am myself of the number.

Hamilton has tried to resist, but it is no use.

> She has had the address to overset all the wise resolutions I had been framing for more than four years past, and from a rational sort of being and a professed condemner of Cupid has in a trice metamorphosed me into the veriest inamorato . . .

The scoffing benedict has fallen in love with her!

> I should never have done, were I to attempt to give you a catalogue of the whole—of all the hearts she has vanquished—of all the heads she has turned—of all the philosophers she has unmade, or of all the standards she has fixed to the great prejudice of the general service of the female world.

Notwithstanding his fixation on her sister, Hamilton is also opening wide his arms to welcome a frivolous belle like Peggy.

> It is essential to the safety of the state, and to the tranquility of the army—that one of two things take place, either that she be immediately removed from our neighborhood, or that some other nymph qualified to maintain an equal sway come into it. By dividing her empire it will be weakened and she will be much less dangerous when she has a rival equal in charms to dispute the prize with her. I solicit your aid.

Peggy must come to Morristown too.

Nothing in his letter rules out, and much invites, an affair with a belle like Peggy whenever she might arrive. It is only a question of time before he falls under the still more powerful spell of the third variation on the Schuyler sister theme, their sister Angelica.

One wintry evening Hamilton was not sure whether it would be he or Tench Tilghman who would be called on to work late into the night with Washington, planning a summer campaign. Hamilton had received an invitation to bring both Elizabeth Schuyler and Kitty Livingston to a ball. He wrote both of them a joint, simultaneous declination and acceptance, offered them Tench Tilghman as a consolation prize, a gallant classical allusion that would flatter their brains, and kept all possible options open for himself, in the following masterpiece of amorous ambiguity that he sent to them in January 1780:

> Col. Hamilton's compliments to Miss Livingston and Miss Schuyler. He is sorry to inform them that his zeal for their service makes him forget that he is so bad a

Charioteer as hardly to dare to trust himself with so precious a charge; though if he were only to consult his own wishes like Phaeton he would assemble the chariot of the sun, if he were sure of experiencing the same fate. Col. Tilghman offers himself a volunteer. Col. Hamilton is unwilling to lose the pleasure of the party; but one or the other will have the honor to attend the ladies.

Hamilton's addresses to Betsy and her parents vary greatly in their nature—some are ardent and full of extravagant language and graceful romantic conceits characteristic of the late eighteenth century; others tell her of the momentous historical events of the times as they swirl past his eyes at the side of his chief at command headquarters. He does not write her as if he thinks of her as a self-centered doll incapable of joining him in his excitement at seeing these great events unfold, even though they divert him a good deal from thinking of her.

Early in March 1780, in Perth Amboy on one of the endless prisoner exchange missions, Hamilton found that the proceedings still depended more on the quantity of wine downed than the merits of the case. The three Schuyler sisters, Betsy, Angelica, and Peggy, as he wrote Betsy on Thursday afternoon, March 17, were "the daily toasts at our table, and for this *honor* you are chiefly indebted to the British gentlemen; though, as I am always thinking of you, this naturally brings Peggy to my mind, who is generally my toast."

Hamilton is not impressed with the personal qualities of his British counterparts:

> Our interview is attended with a good deal of sociability and good humor, but I begin, notwithstanding, to be tired of our British friends. They do their best to be agreeable and are particularly civil to me, but, after all, they are a compound of grimace and jargon and, out of a certain fashionable routine, are as dull and empty as any gentlemen need to be.

Absent from Eliza with only the "grimace and jargon" of his British friends for solace spurs Hamilton's ardor.

> I should regret the time already lost in inactivity if it did not bring us nearer to that sweet reunion for which we so ardently wish. I never look forward to that period without sensations I cannot describe.
>
> I love you more and more every hour. The sweet softness and delicacy of your mind and manners, the elevation of your sentiments, the real goodness of your heart—its tenderness to me—the beauties of your face and person—your unpretending good sense and that innocent simplicity and frankness which pervade your actions, all these appear to be with increasing amiableness, and place you in my estimation above all the rest of your sex.

He proposed formally to her, was accepted, and sought an interview with General Schuyler.

A generation apart in ages, Hamilton and Schuyler had a similar cast of mind as well as common enemies like Gates. Both favored a strong, forceful government and the maintenance of Washington's command against the machinations of the Gates faction in Congress; both shared a general disapproval of the slackness of the times. Both were military men, veterans of warfare in the line, and knew how to manhandle bug guns across rough country; and both had known staff responsibilities as well. In Congress, Schuyler was one of the best-informed members on fiscal matters, the author of a 1779 pamphlet entitled

Causes of Depreciation of the Continental Currency. He read and discussed with pleasure the fiscal and economic proposals for the United States that Hamilton would soon make in his masterful letter to Robert Morris over the pseudonym of James Montague, Esq.

An alliance with Schuyler through ties of marriage would be of inestimable benefit to an ambitious young man; a patrician patroon like Schuyler would easily sniff out an arriviste adventurer when he saw one. But the proud, aristocratic father raised no objections to his beloved daughter's marriage to a moneyless Creole bastard from somewhere down in the Lesser Antilles, and extended him his warmest paternal blessings. But when the ardent swain asked for an immediate wedding the general put down his gouty foot. Mrs. Schuyler had returned to Albany, and he must write to her for her approval.

On April 8 General Schuyler reported to Hamilton that "yesterday I had the pleasure to receive a line from Mrs. Schuyler in answer to mine on the subject of the one you delivered me at Morristown. She consents to comply with your and her daughter's wishes." But this related only to their engagement. As for Hamilton's insistence on an immediate marriage, "you will see the Impropriety of taking the *dèrnier pas* where you are. Mrs. Schuyler did not see her Eldest daughter married. That also gave me pain, and we wish not to Experience it a second time."

Angelica, the eldest, most brilliant and beautiful of the Schuyler daughters, had just eloped with an unknown Englishman who had suddenly appeared in the colonies under the name of John Carter, reportedly fleeing from a scandal in England caused by killing a man in a duel.

John Carter was, in fact, John Barker Church, and after the war when word arrived that the man he had supposedly killed in the duel remained alive and well, he resumed his own name. With the charming, nay irresistible Angelica as his wife, and Schuyler's belated blessing, he would become commissary supplier to Admiral Rochambeau and General Jeremiah Wadsworth, profiteer in American war supplies and other profitable enterprises, and accumulate a large fortune. On his later return to England, accompanied by Angelica, he would win election to the British Parliament, freeing Angelica to return to America in 1789 to visit Hamilton at the flood tide of his career.

In April Catharine Schuyler finally consented to their marriage; Hamilton agreed to postpone the wedding until December, when it could be solemnized with suitable ceremony at The Pastures.

As the long year of their engagement wore on, Hamilton wrote Betsy on July 6, 1780, from Colonel Dey's house in Bergen County, New Jersey: "Here we are in a house of great hospitality—in a county of plenty." There is "a buxom girl under the same roof—pleasing expectations of a successful campaign—and everything to make a soldier happy, who is not in love and absent from his mistress."

A rich coquette who insists on waiting until after the solemn rites before becoming her fiancé's lover is not likely to receive letters like this from him before the wedding.

Hamilton's sufferings through Betsy's absence are not of the most serious order: "I cannot be happy; but it is a maxim of my life to enjoy the present good with the highest relish. . . ."

With that buxom girl still under the same roof? "Besides I alleviate the pain of absence by looking forward to that delightful period which gives us to each other forever, and my imagination serves up such a feast of pleasure as almost makes me forget the deprivation I now experience."

He continues: ". . . Assure yourself my love that you are seldom a moment absent from my mind, that I think of you constantly."

Being apart from her now is the more painful because when they were together, he had become her "lover in earnest." He writes:

> I have told you, and I told you truly, that I love you too much. You engross my thoughts too entirely to allow me to think of anything else. You not only employ my mind all day, but you intrude on my sleep. I meet you in every dream, and when I wake I cannot close my eyes for ruminating on your sweetness.

With their lovemaking the "nut-brown maid" has worn down the hardy soldier to a "puny lover":

> 'Tis a pretty story indeed that I am to be thus monopolized by a little *nut-brown maid* like you, and from a soldier metamorphosed into a puny lover. I believe in my soul you are an enchantress. I have tried in vain, if not to break, at least to weaken the charm, but you maintain your empire. In spite of all my efforts, my heart clings to you with increased attachment. To drop figures, my lovely girl, you become dearer to me every moment. I am more and more unhappy and impatient under the hard necessity that keeps me from you.

The love affair of the 23-year-olds is full of warmth, humor, and trust; it is confiding and passionate. It has begun nearer the beginning than the end of their long year's engagement.

At the end of a letter to John Laurens written from Ramapo, New Jersey, on June 30, 1780, following long paragraphs commenting upon the surrender of Charleston to the British, at which Laurens had been captured; on an enemy "incursion" into the Jerseys and excursion out of it; on countrymen who "have all the folly of the ass and all the passiveness of sheep in their compositions," Hamilton offhandedly lets drop the sensational news: he has managed to find for himself the wife he had a year earlier requisitioned from Laurens. With soldierly bluffness, just before the close, Hamilton drops the bombshell:

> Have you not heard that I am in the point of becoming a benedict? I confess my sins. I am guilty. Next fall completes my doom. I give up my liberty to Miss Schuyler. She is a goodhearted girl who I am sure will never play the termagent; though not a genius she has good sense enough to be agreeable, and though not a beauty she has fine black eyes—is rather handsome and has every other requisite of the exterior to make a lover happy.

Here to Laurens he has revised his earlier chivalrous raptures to Peggy: Not a genius, but good sense, fine eyes, and handsome, yes, and a popular belle, too, but not a "beauty" in the more conventional sense that her sisters are. These are merely her "requisites of the exterior" to "make a lover happy." As for her interior, it is hardly necessary to tell his friend that "believe me, I am lover in earnest, though I do not speak of the perfections of my Mistress in the enthusiasm of chivalry."

After Hamilton and Betsy's marriage at The Pastures the following winter, Schuyler hastened to congratulate his new son-in-law: "You cannot my Dear Sir be more happy at the connection you have made with my family than I am. Until a child has made a judicious choice the heart of a parent is continually in anxiety, but this anxiety vanished in the moment I discovered where you and she had placed your affections."

It was known that Hamilton had come from the West Indies while still a boy; but very little else of his antecedents was known. Hamilton must have disclosed the bar sinister to

General Schuyler before soliciting his final consent: "I am pleased with every instance of delicacy in those who are dear to me," Schuyler wrote Hamilton after the ceremony. "And I think I read your soul on that occasion you mention." Hamilton found no need to explain to Betsy why his late brother, Peter Lavien, had a different surname from his own.

No letters from Betsy to Hamilton are extant, although there are many tantalizing acknowledgments in his letters of those she sent to him. She destroyed all copies. Although she did not outshine her husband or her sisters Angelica and Peggy in society, she left an indelible impression of being a woman of grace, charm, and beauty with all who met her as the years went by.

In the barely 25 years she and Hamilton had left, she wore herself out carrying, bearing, nursing, weaning, and rearing their eight children, and entertaining their many friends and clients at parties in the old Dutch housewife style, like the ones for Angelica and Jerome and Elizabeth Bonaparte. Unfaithful to her though he was, no record is extant of any reproach from her to him.

When Elizabeth Schuyler Hamilton died in 1854 at the age of 97, having survived by half a century the death of both her husband and firstborn son in duels, there was found in a tiny bag that hung from around her neck, which she had evidently worn there all her adult life, a piece of frayed and yellowed paper, the torn fragments of which at some time or other she had sewn together with a piece of ordinary thread. Sometime during the spring of the first year of their love of 75 years earlier, Alexander Hamilton, recalling a lyric of Sir John Suckling, had written out for her in that neat hand of his, which would elsewhere indite a federal empire, the following little love poem:

Answers to the Inquiry Why I Sighed

Before no mortal ever knew
A love like mine so tender—true—
Completely wretched—you away—
And but half blessed e'en while you stay.

If present love [illegible] face
Deny you to my fond embrace
No joy unmissed my bosom warms
But when my angel's in my arms.

9

Reconciled to His Being Shot, but Not to His Being Hanged

My remedies were good. . . . . You can hardly conceive in how dreadful a situation we are. . . . The worst of evils seems to be coming upon us . . . a loss of our virtue.

—To John Laurens, September 12, 1780

The authorized maxims and practices of war are the satires of human nature.

—To John Laurens, October 11, 1780

The war had dwindled into a war of attrition, the commander in chief of the army had eschewed the role of chief executive, and Hamilton had no doubt of his own ability to take over this role. During the spring and summer of 1780 he continued to construct a power base of his own, independent of and unknown to Washington, by circulating two wide-ranging position papers among the "moneyed men" of the country.

He did not sign his own name to the first of these, but if Robert Morris or any other addressee wanted further explanations or a personal conference, "a letter directed to James Montague Esqr. lodged in the Post Office at Morristown will be a safe channel of any communication . . . and an immediate answer will be given." This soon stirred up an inquiry from James Duane, a New York deputy to the Continental Congress, to whom Hamilton eagerly responded with more advice on September 3, 1780. With no false modesty, he assured Duane, "Apply it and the country can be saved."

The opening sentence of Hamilton's letter to Duane drove straight to the heart of the national malaise: "The fundamental defect is a want of power in Congress." The want of power in Congress was largely due to the timidity of Congress itself. To those who said

118

Congress had no authority to act because the Articles of Confederation granted no definite powers to it, that it could only recommend but not command, "Nonsense," replied Hamilton. "They have done many of the highest acts of sovereignty . . . the declaration of independence, the declaration of war, the levying an army, creating a navy, emitting money, making alliances with foreign powers, appointing a dictator, etc., etc."

A bold Congress, Hamilton explained, would have assumed the necessary powers: "The public good required that they should have considered themselves as vested with full power to preserve the republic from harm." Here was the seed of the great constitutional doctrine of implied powers.

Let Congress assert those powers that were inherent in its original appointment. If the delegates were too timid to do so, then let it call a convention of all the states with full authority to form a general confederation. This confederation should grant Congress complete and unhampered sovereignty over war and peace, foreign affairs, trade, finance, coinage, banks, and treaties. To the states should be left only matters relating "to the rights of property and life among individuals." Here is the earliest call for a constitutional convention.

Such a Congress should appoint a series of executives. Each would be responsible for the administration of a great department: "A secretary for foreign affairs—a President of war—a President of marine—a Financier—a President of trade." Or instead of this last, "a Board of Trade may be preferable as the regulations of trade are slow and gradual and require prudence and experience (more than other qualities), for which boards are very well adapted."

Congress could be no substitute for a single executive. "Congress," he declared, "have kept the power too much in their own hands, and have meddled too much with details of every sort. Congress is, properly, a deliberative corps, and it forgets itself when it attempts to play the executive." Here was the earliest call for a single national chief executive.

Let the war be fought with a regular army enlisted for at least three years or for the duration, Hamilton advised. State militia were all but worthless. If an army could not be raised by voluntary enlistment, introduce conscription according to the Swedish plan. Then pay and supply the army from funds raised by Congress. Where would the money come from? Borrow from France, raise taxes, and, above all, create a national bank. "Free countries have ever paid the heaviest taxes," Hamilton pointed out. "The obedience of a free people to general laws however hard they bear is ever more perfect than that of slaves to the arbitrary will of a prince."

Congress was not entirely to blame: "The Confederation itself is defective, and requires to be altered. It is neither fit for war nor peace." As long as each state had complete sovereignty in internal affairs, there could be no proper union. What was the essential precondition for a strong and vigorous nation? Centralized power with independent control of its own funds: "Without certain revenue, a government can have no power. That power which holds the purse-strings absolutely, must rule."

Let perpetual sources of revenue be placed at the sole disposition of Congress. For this Hamilton recommended a poll tax, a general tax on land, and imposts on commerce.

A national bank was the centerpiece of Hamilton's program. Paper credit was of no value unless founded "on a joint basis of public and private credit." New emissions of paper money were depreciating as rapidly as the old. Why? Because—and here Hamilton hammered home another of his fundamental theses—"The moneyed men have not an immediate interest to uphold its credit. They may even, in many ways, find it in their interest to undermine it."

Hamilton wasted no time on politically easy but practically useless criticism of "moneyed men." Greed was no more a part of the human nature of moneyed men than it was of small farmers, but no less.

To establish permanent paper credit, a bank was needed in which "moneyed men" would be granted pro rata shares and control plus "the whole or a part of the profits." Such shares had to be made a sound investment, or money would not find its way into them. It would, of course, find its way elsewhere; perhaps to England or France.

Hamilton drew analogies to the bankers of Venice and the Bank of England: "The Bank of England underwrites public authority and faith with private credit; and hence we see what a vast fabric of paper credit is raised on *a visionary basis*. Had it not been for this, England would never have found sufficient funds to carry on her wars." He drove home the point: "with the help of this she has done, and is doing wonders."

The "moneyed men" in America "are not very rich, but this would not prevent their instituting a bank."

They "are governed by opinion," he concluded; "This opinion is as much influenced by appearances as by realities. If a government appears to be confident of its own powers, it is the surest way to inspire the same confidence in others." He admitted: "The only plan that can preserve the currency is one that will make it the *immediate* interest of the moneyed men to cooperate with government in its support."

Hamilton's strategy, he claimed, "stands on the firm footing of public and private faith. . . . it links the interest of the State in an intimate connection with those of the rich individuals belonging to it. . . . it turns the wealth and influence of both into a commercial channel, for mutual benefit, which must afford advantages not to be estimated."

This was the first time that a bank with governmental assistance and, in part, for governmental purposes had been proposed in America though the idea itself, not original with Hamilton, was modeled on the existing Bank of England. Though he was, at present, busily prosecuting a war against the country where his model flourished, he made no secret of his admiration for the practical model of governmental institutions for free men that he saw working there.

Hamilton's basic economic ideas were fully developed by the time he was 22, as these two papers of 1780 show. In 1790 and in 1800, his basic philosophy would remain consistent with the points he made in 1780. The national bank he put into effect as secretary of the treasury bore a marked resemblance to the one he had outlined in these letters to Robert Morris and James Duane. Nowhere had the theory of private capitalism in America been put with more concision, practicality, and realism.

But by the late summer of 1780, it seemed that time was running out for the United States. In the South, things were even worse than in the North. French fleets had been beaten off by strong British squadrons. Almost all of South Carolina was in enemy hands. General Horatio Gates, the hero of Saratoga, dispatched south to stem the tide, had met Cornwallis at Camden, South Carolina, on August 16, 1780, and suffered one of the most crushing American defeats of the war. At the first onslaught the militia had fled in yet another "settled, durable panic." Gates had outrun even his own militia. A thousand Americans were killed or wounded; another thousand taken prisoner; the brave Baron de Kalb was dead in a vain attempt to rally panic-stricken troops; Gates was found safe at Hillsborough, 180 miles away!

As an immediate result of Gates's rout, all four Southern states—Georgia, the Carolinas, and Virginia—now lay defenseless before Lord Cornwallis and his seasoned regulars, secure in a string of recent victories at Savannah, Charleston, and Camden, pressing north to Virginia.

Congress could still save the situation said Hamilton. His solution consisted of only two words. It was contained in a masterful letter analyzing the military situation written to Duane only three days after the letter containing his masterful analysis of the political and economic situation. The two word solution was, "Send Greene." Hamilton recommended, Duane passed the idea on to Congress, Congress decreed, and Washington acted. On October 14, 1780, he was pleased to appoint Major General Nathanael Greene to replace Gates as commander of what was left of the broken Southern army.

Confiding his thoughts about Gates's debacle to Betsy, Hamilton wrote that "this misfortune affects me less than others . . . because I think our safety depends on a total change of system, and this change of system will only be produced by misfortune."

Out of this black mood, he speculated about flight in strange phrases: "Pardon me my love for talking politics to you. What have we to do with anything but love? Go the world as it will, in each other's arms we cannot but be happy. . ." But mixed up with his love for her was a weird sense of personal responsibility for the fate of America.

> If America were lost we should be happy in some other clime more favourable to human rights. What think you of Geneva as a retreat? 'Tis a charming place; where nature and society are in their greatest perfection. I was once determined to let my existence and American liberty end together. My Betsy has given me a motive to outlive my pride, I had almost said my honor; but America must not be witness to my disgrace.

In this odd love letter Hamilton is not saying anything as simple as give me liberty or give me death. He is saying that if America does not turn out to be a country as "favourable to human rights" as he thinks it should be, he would consider suicide. Flight with Betsy to Geneva would permit him to outlive his "pride," but not even Betsy could make him "outlive my honor." This identification of his sense of personal honor with the cause of American liberty regardless of all other consequences—his sense of public responsibility, of public credit—is the essence of Hamilton, up to the last moment of his life after the last duel.

Here was one of the earliest of the moods of black depression that would recur throughout his life: "As it is always well to be prepared for the worst, I talk to you in this strain; not that I think it probable we shall fail in the contest. . . . I think the chances are without comparison in our favour."

He closed with classic fatalism: If the worst does not happen, "my Aquileia and I will plant our turnips in her native land."

Writing Laurens on September 12, Hamilton was still in the same black mood:

> My remedies were good, but you were afraid would not go down at the time. I tell you necessity must force them down; and if they are not speedily taken the patient will die. . . . You can hardly conceive in how dreadful a situation we are. The army, in the course of the present month, has received only four or five days' rations of meal.

His pathological depression brought with it uncanny foresight. In two weeks tragedy and treason would explode at West Point: "The officers are out of humour, and the *worst* of evils seems to be coming upon us—*a loss of our virtue.*"

Hamilton went on angrily: "I am losing character, my friend, because I am not over-complaisant to the spirit of clamour—so that I am in a fair way to be out with everybody. With one set I am considered as a friend to military pretensions however exorbitant, with another as a man, who secured by my situation from sharing the distress of the army, am inclined to treat it lightly." The groveling condition of an aide grated on the former line commander.

His mind seemed all but unbalanced by the burden of his and the nation's troubles: "The truth is I am an unlucky honest man, that speak my sentiments to all and with emphasis."

The moment of sudden self-insight failed to break his terrible anxiety: "I hate Congress—I hate the army—I hate the world—I hate myself. The whole is a mass of fools and knaves." At the end, he pulled back from the brink: "I could almost except you and Meade. Adieu." And as a postscript: "My ravings are for your own bosom. The General and family send you their love."

Things were not as bad as Hamilton said; they were really much worse. On the secure defense of the looming citadel at West Point hinged all American grand strategy, north and south. The newly appointed commander in chief of West Point was Major General Benedict Arnold, who had long considered himself unjustly treated by Congress. He was in debt from the extravagances and demands of his captivating young wife, the former Peggy Shippen. He shared the spreading conviction that the states were losing the war and could never win.

When Hamilton wrote angrily to Laurens of "officers out of humour," the "worst of evils," and "a loss of our virtue," there is no evidence that he or Washington had received intelligence that Arnold had accepted a secret British offer to pay him and Peggy good hard British silver and gold in escalating sums: the more American troops and positions he was able to betray, the larger the bribe he would receive. Another kind of American was in thrall to another kind of golden chain.

The French allies were stationary in Newport, vainly awaiting the arrival of a second division, which the British kept blockaded in Brest. Admiral de Guichen's fleet was far away somewhere at sea in the West Indies. British Admiral George Rodney had arrived at Sandy Hook with a dozen ships of the line and four frigates to add to British naval superiority. In the Carolinas, where Cornwallis was now the master of Gates's beaten army, the British were poised to move north to invest Virginia.

With General Nathanael Greene no longer quartermaster general, transport had broken down. Local farmers refused to accept worthless Continental currency in payment for food. The terms of enlistment for a large part of the army would run out, as usual, in December. Washington had to turn away new recruits he could not feed.

Hamilton wrote out for Washington another set of plans for an attack on New York City, but West Point must be held secure at all events: "When the garrison of West Point will permit, another corps may come to this side." The attack on New York was to be coordinated with a French feint at Charleston to draw Rodney's British fleet back to the south. If the New York plan failed, Hamilton proposed another winter expedition into Canada.

Hamilton carried these plans with him when he took horse on September 17 from army headquarters at New Bridge, New Jersey, with the small headquarters party—Washington, Knox, Lafayette, McHenry, and a few others. They were to meet at Hartford with Comte Jean B. D. de Rochambeau, commander of the French expeditionary forces, and Charles

Louis d'Arsac, the Chevalier de Ternay, commander of the French naval squadron, to plan joint strategy for salvaging something creditable from 1780's military activities before winter froze another lost year to a standstill. On the return trip they would pause for an inspection of the defenses at West Point.

On the night of September 17, Washington and Hamilton and the rest of the party lodged at Haverstraw in the house of Joshua Hett Smith, the brother of Sir Henry Clinton's Tory friend, William Smith, the royal chief justice. General Benedict Arnold was one of the guests at Smith's for dinner that night, and he boldly sought to ensnare Washington in his cover story for the first stage of his plot.

As Arnold slyly explained it to Washington, he had just received a letter from Colonel Beverly Robinson, a well-known Tory, written from on board the British sloop of war *Vulture*, anchored offshore in the river; Robinson had enclosed a letter addressed to General Israel Putnam asking to interview Putnam on a private matter, adding that if Arnold could not reach Putnam, Arnold should come to see Robinson aboard the *Vulture* himself. Arnold assumed that Washington would make no objection to a routine communication between officers and gentlemen from opposite sides under the cover of a "flag" of truce.

But Washington turned down Arnold's request.

Hamilton later wrote Laurens that Washington's decision ". . . fortunately deranged the plan and was the first link in the chain of events that led to the detection. The interview could no longer take place in the form of a flag, but was obliged to be managed in a secret manner."

The next day, Washington and Hamilton rode on to Hartford for their meeting with the French commanders. With Washington's party gone for a few days, the *Vulture* moved in a little closer to Joshua Hett Smith's treason house to hover in wait for its prey.

On the night of September 21, Smith, at the direction of Benedict Arnold, was rowed out to the *Vulture* by the Cahoon (or Colquhoun) brothers with a letter and picked up a man who was not Robinson. It was Major John André, adjutant general of the British army of occupation in New York City. When Smith's boat grated onto shore just below Haverstraw, the hooded man clambered up the bank and there was met by a shadowy figure who emerged from among the trees: General Benedict Arnold himself. The two men talked for awhile, and then all three went back through sentry lines to Smith's own house. There Arnold gave André a packet containing a plan of the fortifications of West Point, an engineer's report on methods of attack and defense of the citadel, and a duty return of the garrison, ordnance, and stores showing the numbers of men manning the mazy ramparts and the level of their supplies. There was a copy of the minutes of a council of war held by Washington three weeks before. And a pass for one "John Anderson," written out in Arnold's hand.

The next morning, a second lucky event occurred to derange the plot. An alert artillery-man, Colonel James Livingston, the commanding officer at King's Ferry across from Stony Point, with no orders from Arnold, moved a couple of cannon to a point opposite where the *Vulture* lay, fired on her, and "obliged her to take a more remote station" about 10 miles down the river near Ossining.

The *Vulture*'s move downriver and the extra rowing distance caused Smith's oarsmen to refuse to row André, alias John Anderson, back to the *Vulture* after his nocturnal rendez-vous with Arnold. Also, the *Vulture*'s move "disconcerted Arnold so much," Hamilton wrote, "that . . . he insisted on André's exchanging his uniform for a disguise." Though "André remonstrated warmly against this new and dangerous expedient," his protests were unavailing. A high-ranking British officer, if captured wearing his uniform under his cloak, could expect to be treated as a military prisoner, not as a spy. "But Arnold persisting in declaring it impossible for [André] to return as he came, he at length reluctantly yielded to his direction." So instead of being able to row back to the safety of the *Vulture* in uniform as he had come ashore, André was obliged to make his uncertain way south toward New York City by land, wearing the disguise of a merchant. His way led through Westchester, a no-man's land in which roving bands waged guerrilla war, to the nearest British outpost at White Plains.

Meanwhile, Washington and Hamilton, journeying back from Hartford by easy stages toward West Point, had arrived at Fishkill, where the Chevalier de la Luzerne invited them to spend the night at his lodgings before proceeding on to the Robinson house.

Next morning majors Samuel Shaw and James McHenry rode on ahead to the Robinson house, and notified Arnold that the general would breakfast with him before making the tour of inspection. Fifteen minutes earlier that same morning a messenger had brought Arnold a letter from Lieutenant Colonel John Jameson telling of André's capture near Tarrytown. Arnold rushed upstairs to his wife as another messenger arrived, announcing that Washington and his party were at hand. Arnold's aide, Major David Franks, went up to Peggy's room behind Arnold to inform him that the commanding general had arrived.

According to Franks, Arnold "came down in great confusion, and, ordering a horse to be saddled, mounted him and told me to inform His Excellency that he was gone over to West Point . . ." McHenry, who had already arrived at the Robinson house, "observed an embarrassment [in Arnold] which I could not at that time account for."

At the front door of the Robinson house, Washington and Hamilton were met by Arnold's aides, Franks and Lieutenant Colonel Richard Varick, who told them that Arnold had been called across the river to the fortress and would return within the hour. Peggy remained in seclusion in her bedroom upstairs.

Washington and Hamilton and the other members of the party took a leisurely breakfast, still unsuspecting, as Arnold meanwhile was fleeing in his barge down the river toward the *Vulture*. After breakfast Washington left with his command party for his inspection of the fortifications with the still-absent commander. Hamilton was left behind to receive dispatches.

Suddenly Peggy's cries "called us all to her assistance," Hamilton later wrote Elizabeth. "I paid her a visit and endeavoured to soothe her by every method in my power. . . ."

Pretending to a composure she did not feel, Peggy first inquired after Varick's health. Then she burst into "hysterics and utter frenzy." She was "raving distracted" and screamed of hot irons on her head. Varick had ordered her baby to be murdered. She rolled out of her bed on to her knees to entreat him to spare the child's life. He sought to assure her that all were her friends and that Arnold would soon return, but she cried, "General Arnold will never return. He is gone. He is gone forever, *there, there, there*: the spirits have carried him up there." She pointed at the ceiling. "They have put hot irons in his head."

According to Varick, her hair was "disheveled and flowing about her neck." She was clad only in "her morning gown with few other clothes remaining on her—too few to be seen even by a gentleman of the family." Hamilton's emotions too were profoundly affected by feminine beauty in such distress. It is not known how far his eager efforts to console her had carried him toward her arms by the time Washington returned to the Robinson house from West Point that afternoon.

In Washington's absence, Captain Jeronimus Hoogland, a courier from Jameson, delivered to Hamilton a packet addressed to Washington. Hamilton by now had many reasons to suspect Arnold of treason: his unaccountable absence at Washington's arrival, reports of

Arnold's barge being seen going down river, and "of a spy . . . being detected nigh our lines." Peggy's ravings confirmed Arnold's guilt.

Washington dismounted and strode to the door, enraged. He had not found Arnold; West Point's defenses were in disarray. Hamilton met him and handed him the packet from Jameson. There was also a letter from André to Washington, which had been enclosed with Jameson's. Washington quickly scanned Jameson's letter, leafed through the papers taken from André, and read André's letter. In it André identified himself as adjutant general of the British army, ashore from the *Vulture* seeking military intelligence. He had been forced against his will, he said, to come within American lines and put on civilian clothing as a disguise. By his letter he wanted to rescue himself "from an imputation of having asserted a mean character for treacherous purposes . . . " He was not a spy, he insisted. He did not name Arnold as the person with whom he had negotiated, but the pass in Arnold's handwriting, Arnold's inexplicable absence, and the other contents of Jameson's letter left little doubt in Washington's mind by now that Arnold had betrayed him.

Hamilton called out to Lafayette to come instantly. Lafayette rushed down the hall to Washington's room. Washington pulled shut the door behind Lafayette and Hamilton. Holding the dispatches in a trembling hand, his voice choked with rage, Washington said to his two closest confidants, "Arnold has betrayed us. Whom can we trust now?"

Washington then ordered Hamilton to summon McHenry and ride to Verplanck's Point, some eight miles downriver, where there was an American post from which Arnold might be intercepted if he had not already reached the *Vulture*. The two aides leaped to their saddles and galloped south as fast as their horses could carry them. But when they looked out from the shore of Verplanck's Point, they saw no barge. The *Vulture* was under sail, and moving swiftly down the tide toward New York City with Arnold aboard.

Hamilton scribbled a note back to Washington: Arnold had outrun their pursuit. Hamilton was taking command steps on his own responsibility to meet the emergency. They might prove to be unnecessary, but grave risk remained. "I shall write to General Greene, advising him, without making a bustle, to be in readiness to march, and even to detach a brigade this way; for, though I do not believe the project will go on, yet it is possible Arnold has made such dispositions with the garrison as may tempt the enemy, in its present weakness, *to make the stroke this night*, and it seems prudent to be providing against it."

With speed and force, Hamilton issued commands for the emergency deployments: "I shall endeavor to find Meigs, and request him to march to the garrison, and shall make some arrangements here. I hope your Excellency will approve these steps, as there may be no time to be lost. The *Vulture* is gone down to New York."

Hamilton's letter to General Greene (who had not yet departed for the south to take over Gates's command) reported the terrible story to him and warned that the British might yet strike; he concluded, "I advise your putting the army under marching orders, and detaching a brigade immediately this way."

The Americans received one more lucky break. After Hamilton wrote Greene, the wind shifted from fair to foul for Clinton. His sloops would make but slow headway tacking upstream against it. Clinton's chance to move up in force and bag the entire American high command was gone.

Hamilton galloped back to Robinson's to find Peggy Arnold had gone into another fit of hysterics. Hamilton was deeply touched. Here was beauty in distress, a lovely woman deserted by a traitor husband and crying out in anguish. Of her innocence he had no doubt at all.

That night he wrote Eliza about her pathetic condition:

> An amiable woman, frantic with distress for the loss of a husband she tenderly loved; a traitor to his country and to his fame. . . . It was the most affecting scene I ever was witness to. She, for a considerable time, entirely lost herself. One moment she raved, another she melted into tears. . . . All the sweetness of beauty, all the loveliness of innocence, all the tenderness of a wife, and all the fondness of a mother showed themselves in her appearance and conduct.

Hamilton seemed to betray disquieting passion for Peggy in her disheveled distress:

> This morning she is more composed. I paid her a visit and endeavoured to soothe her by every method in my power, though you may imagine she is not easily to be consoled . . . her sufferings were so eloquent that I wished myself her brother, to have a right to become her defender. As it is, I have entreated her to enable me to give her proof of my friendship.

Elizabeth Schuyler's love for Alexander Hamilton must have been constant indeed, and he supremely confident of it, if she could keep on reading his insistent effusions about pretty Peggy without annoyance—and he not expect her to be annoyed.

Much later, when Sir Henry Clinton's private papers came to light, they revealed that Peggy had been the inspiration and accomplice, if not the instigator, of Arnold's treason. Part of Arnold's correspondence with the British had passed through her hands. Hamilton was completely taken in.

Washington had Joshua Hett Smith arrested, protesting furiously, and brought to Robinson's house under guard.

In the presence of Knox, Lafayette, Harrison, and Hamilton, Washington himself, still in high temper, conducted the preliminary questioning. Smith was wary, perhaps on the advice of his brother William, the royal chief justice. He had only been an innocent go-between, he claimed. Arnold had deceived him like everyone else by telling him that the hooded man in the red coat who had been the uninvited guest at his house was one "John Anderson," an American spy. Smith said he had believed him.

No stenographic transcript of Washington's angry early morning interrogation of Smith was kept. Later testimony conflicted sharply about what had actually been said. But after the questioning, Washington was more certain than ever that Smith "had a considerable share in this business," had even "confessed facts sufficient to establish his guilt." But others, less emotionally committed to a guilty verdict than Washington, denied that Smith's testimony had implicated him.

Four days later, Smith was brought to trial before a general court-martial in Tappan, New York, about 25 miles downriver from West Point. The charges: going aboard the enemy ship *Vulture*; hiding André in his house, furnishing him with civilian clothes, and passing him through the sentry posts at Stony Point and Verplanck's in disguise, under a false name, and carrying secret intelligence to the enemy; conspiring with Arnold and the enemy to "take, kill and seize . . . loyal citizens and soldiers . . . in garrison at West Point and its dependencies"; and for acting as a spy. The chief witness for the prosecution: Hamilton.

On October 26, the court-martial acquitted Smith for lack of proof that he had known that Robinson and Arnold had been up to treason. This did not mean he had not known in fact, nor convince Washington or Hamilton that he was innocent. It meant only that guilt of a high crime that turned on guilty knowledge, or scienter, had failed of proof beyond a reasonable doubt. Smith was handed over to New York civil authorities for a new trial, escaped from a Goshen jail, and fled to safety behind the British lines, thus corroborating all of Washington's and Hamilton's suspicions but leaving them helpless to do anyting about them.

Washington's disappointment at Smith's acquittal was less keen than it would have been if the public's clamor for a scapegoat, aroused by Arnold's treason, had not been largely satisfied by the bigger and better scapegoat who by now had already been hanged.

As Hamilton explained it crisply to John Laurens October 11, 1780:

> André was without loss of time conducted to the Head Quarters of the army, where he was immediately brought before a board of General Officers, to prevent all possibility of misrepresentation or cavil on the part of the army. The Board reported, that he ought to be considered as a spy and according to the laws and usage of nations to suffer death; which was executed two days after.

Major André's trial at a closed hearing before a board of generals two days after his capture produced an unappealable verdict of "guilty," and a sentence of death by hanging.

There had been no military campaigns in 1780 to produce anything that might be called a victory, only crushing defeats at Camden and everywhere else, so the lucky deliverance from disaster—the preservation of West Point and the narrow escape of Washington and Rochambeau and others of the top command from Clinton's bag—was received by the public with as much emotional release as if a major victory had been won. The hanging of a redcoat scapegoat like André would add mightily to the momentary elation of popular opinion. Hamilton eloquently urged objections to the hanging on Washington, but the general could not allow Hamilton's scruples to stand against a cyclone of popular feeling. It would help revive flagging support for the Army's cause by gratifying popular clamor.

An acquaintance of less than a week consisting of meetings in André's prison cell between the time of his capture and his death brought André and Hamilton into a friendship of the most intense and instantaneous kind.

Describing him in a long letter to John Laurens, Hamilton expresses his own idea of the masculine beau ideal that includes proficiencies Hamilton himself never displayed—skill in poetry and painting, for example. Hamilton writes:

> There was something singularly interesting in the character and fortunes of André. To an excellent understanding, well improved by education and travel, he united a peculiar elegance of mind and manners, and the advantage of a pleasing person. 'Tis said he possessed a pretty taste for the fine arts, and had himself attained some proficiency in poetry, music and painting.

He also had a peculiar modesty of style that appealed to Hamilton, suggesting emulation:

> His knowledge appeared without ostentation, and embellished by a diffidence that rarely accompanies so many talents and accomplishments; which left you to suppose more than appeared. His sentiments were elevated, and inspired esteem: they had a softness that conciliated affection. His elocution was handsome; his address easy, polite, and insinuating.

To Hamilton, André's inadvertent self-entrapment in Peggy and Benedict Arnold's get-rich-quick scheme contained elements of high tragedy:

By his merit he had acquired the unlimited confidence of his general, and was making a rapid progress in military rank and reputation. But in the height of his career, flushed with new hopes from the execution of a project, the most beneficial to his party that could be devised, he was at once precipitated from the summit of prosperity, and saw all the expectations of his ambition blasted, and himself ruined.

The remarkable thing was that André did not seem concerned about himself, but only that his death might cause Sir Henry Clinton some self-reproach. André

begged me to be the bearer of a request to the General, for permission to send an open letter to Sir Henry Clinton. "I forsee my fate," said he, "and though I pretend not to play the hero, or to be indifferent about life, yet I am reconciled to whatever may happen, conscious that misfortune, not guilt, has brought it upon me. [Sir Henry Clinton] has been too good to me; he has been lavish of his kindness. I am bound to him by too many obligations, and love him too well, to bear the thought that he should reproach himself, or that others should reproach him, on the supposition of my having conceived myself obliged, by his instructions, to run the risk I did. I would not for the world leave a string in his mind that should embitter his future days.

[André added,] "I wish to be permitted to assure him I did not act under this impression, but submitted to a necessity imposed upon me, as contrary to my own inclination as to his orders."

Deeply touched by such selfless sentiments of a kind he could not feel for Washington, Hamilton assured Laurens that he had complied with André's next-to-last wish.

When the sentence of the general court-martial was announced to André, he had remarked that he would be happy, if possible, to be indulged with a professional death as a soldier before a firing squad, not by hanging like a spy. He made a second application by letter in concise but persuasive terms. With memories of Nathan Hale's famous martyrdom and his own characteristic preoccupation with niceties in the manner of dying in mind, Hamilton urged André's wishes on Washington. But Washington insisted that André be hanged like a spy instead of being shot like a soldier, and that André not be told of his decision.

On October 2, the day of André's hanging, Hamilton wrote Betsy:

I urged a compliance with André's request to be shot and I do not think it would have had an ill effect; but some people are only sensible to motives of policy, and sometimes from a narrow disposition mistake it. When André's tale comes to be told, and present resentment is over, the refusing him the privilege of choosing [the] manner of his own death will be branded with too much obduracy.

On this rock of obduracy Hamilton and Washington would soon break.

A spy like André was a better scapegoat than a go-between like Smith, but a traitor like Arnold would be a better scapegoat than an accidental spy like André. All sympathy was on André's side; yet the rules of war made the exchange of a mere spy like him for a traitor like Arnold unthinkable. Such an exchange was contrary to international law and military honor, but from the American side it had an irresistible popular appeal. Washington came down on the popular side; Hamilton, on the unpopular side.

Washington gave orders that would have had the practical effect of making the exchange possible, and took steps to have his proposal made known to Sir Henry Clinton. Because André was such a favorite, the British commander might be willing to waive the niceties of honor to retrieve him. Washington, no doubt, understood as well as Hamilton the legal and moral difficulties involved in hanging André as a spy, but he did not want his own name and person to be associated with a proposal that he knew Hamilton and a like-minded minority would find dishonorable. Yet he did not scruple to lend the talents of his aide to it.

Hamilton confided his side of this strange episode to Elizabeth: ''It was proposed to me to suggest to him [André] the idea of an exchange for Arnold.'' Such a proposal could have come from no one but Washington. Hamilton turned down his chief: ''I knew I should have forfeited André's esteem by doing it, and therefore declined to do it. As a man of honor he could not but reject it and I would not for the world have proposed to him such a thing, which must have placed me in the unamiable light of supposing him capable of a meanness, or of not feeling myself the impropriety of the measure.''

From Washington's headquarters quickly came a second attempt to play upon Clinton's vulnerable personal affection for André, whose sexual identity seemed ambiguously defined.

The key document in this second approach is a mysterious letter in a disguised hand dated September 30, 1780, addressed to Sir Henry Clinton. Signed AB (or AH) and found among Clinton's papers; some historians have attributed it to Hamilton's authorship. Others, perhaps misguidedly zealous to defend him, have denied he had a hand in it. Still others claim that it was *by* his hand though not *in* his hand.

According to Lieutenant Colonel John Graves Simcoe, commander of the Queen's Rangers, ''amongst some letters which American Captain Aaron Ogden passed [from American to British headquarters] a paper was slid in without signature, but in the handwriting of Hamilton, Washington's secretary, saying that the only way to save André was to give up Arnold.''

The text of the ''AH'' letter in the disguised handwriting read:

> Major André . . . was captured in such a way as will according to the laws of war justly affect his life. Though an enemy, his virtues and his accomplishments are much admired. Perhaps he might be released for General Arnold, delivered up without restriction or condition. . . . Arnold appears to have been the guilty author of the mischief, and ought more properly to be the victim, as there is great reason to believe he meditated a double treachery, and had arranged the interview in such manner, that if discovered in the first instance, he might have it in his power to sacrifice Major André to his own safety. . . .
>
> I have the honor to be etc.
> AH
>
> No time is to be lost.

How did this document find its way to Clinton? On the morning of September 30, 1780, Washington met Captain Aaron Ogden all alone at the door of his headquarters in the old DeWint house at Tappan and, giving him a packet of letters addressed to Clinton, ordered Ogden to take it, with a powerful escort of 25 dragoons, to Lafayette for special instructions. Thereafter the packet should be delivered under a flag of truce to the enemy post at Paulus Hook (Jersey City). The ''AH'' letter was later found ''slid in'' among the letters in this packet. Ogden's ''special instructions'' from Lafayette were to arrive so late in the evening that it would be necessary to spend the night. Lafayette also told Ogden that he should let it come out to Clinton that if he would allow Arnold somehow to get within Washington's power (for example, by allowing Arnold to be "accidentally" captured by Ogden's dragoons), André would at once be released.

When Ogden arrived at Paulus Hook, he told the British post commander that he had an important message for Clinton and gave him the packet. The post commander returned from British headquarters with the curt message "that a deserter was never given up" and that Captain Ogden's horse would be ready in the morning. The message that the post commander passed back to Ogden seemed to come from the highest authority—Clinton himself. It responded directly to the oral message Ogden had delivered. But it did not respond directly to the letter signed "AH." Perhaps Clinton had not yet noticed it—or perhaps the "AH" letter had not yet been "slid in" to the packet of letters from Washington that Ogden delivered.

The next day, Clinton posted three commissioners aboard the *Greyhound* to sail up the river to Dobbs Ferry to make a plea to Washington to rescind André's death sentence. When the vessel anchored at Dobbs Ferry, the British commissioners were informed that General Nathanael Greene would receive only Lieutenant General James Robertson and his aide, but that the other British commissioners, Chief Justice William Smith, Joshua's brother, and Lieutenant Governor Andrew Elliot, should not even land.

To Greene, Robertson stated Clinton's argument that André was not a spy. In his response, Greene echoed Hamilton, saying that "The time, manner, object of the interview, change of dress, and other circumstances" all pointed to spying. But there was one way André could be saved. Greene managed to convey Washington's proposal for an exchange to Robertson as a mere suggestion, without appearing to do so on Washington's responsibility or even on Washington's initiative—and perhaps it was Greene who delivered the "AH" note.

Upon returning to the *Greyhound*, General Robertson wrote Clinton, "He [Greene] said that there was no treaty about spies. I said no military Casuist in Europe would call André a spy, and I would suffer death itself if Monsieur Rochambeau or General Knyphausen would call him by that name." Greene replied coolly that "the army must be satisfied by seeing spies executed—but there was one thing that would satisfy them—they expected if André was set free, Arnold should be given up."

Robertson professed to be appalled and shocked at Greene's proposal, seeming as it did to come from Washington, as it had. Not fooled by Greene's offhand manner, Robertson wrote, "This I answered with a look only, which threw Greene into confusion."

Perhaps recalling the campfires Washington had left burning in Brooklyn Heights and at Trenton while his troops escaped traps in the darkness, Robertson thought Washington was bluffing again and that Clinton would think so too. He wrote Clinton: "I am persuaded André will not be hurt."

His misreading of Washington's intentions sealed André's fate.

André was hanged the next day as a spy.

At some unknown time after the hanging, the "AH" letter in the disguised handwriting "slid in" to Clinton's packet from Washington was endorsed by Clinton in a sketchy fashion: "Hamilton was [or possibly "W's," meaning Washington's] aide-de-camp received after A's [André's] death."

The "AH" letter differs from Hamilton's usual handwriting in being written in a backhand slant. Some capitals are structurally different from his, the bottom lines run uphill, but the same thing is often true of Hamilton's own manuscripts. The initials "AB" might just as easily be read "AH." There is no reason to suppose that Simcoe or Clinton would have known Hamilton's regular handwriting well enough to recognize the disguised hand as his unless Hamilton had passed word to them through Aaron Ogden or Robertson's aide Murray at the parley the previous day to be on the lookout for his important note. Hamilton's note, coupled with the wide knowledge that he was the aide closer to Washington than any other, would show Clinton that Greene's seemingly casual suggestion to the outraged Robertson was backed up by written evidence of the authority of the American commander in chief himself.

This writer's conclusion is that the penmanship was Hamilton's, but the proposal was Washington's alone. Hamilton put down on paper against his own will and over the objections of his conscience words dictated by his chief. Hamilton's crude dissembling of his handwriting and signature was his only way of protesting. The use to which he was being put writing it was a painful reminder of his groveling condition as an aide.

The argument against Hamilton's having written the note rests on the same clear record of Hamilton's disapproval of the exchange proposal. The "Gentleman" (for which read *Washington*) had suggested that André propose such an exchange to Clinton, and André had declined to do so, to Hamilton's intense satisfaction. When asked to suggest the exchange proposal to André, Hamilton had refused to offend André's honor or stain his own with "the impropriety of the measure." Much against his will, scruples, and principles of honor, at Washington's command, Hamilton wrote the letter and made sure it was "slid in" to Ogden's packet, probably at the time when Ogden received his orders from Lafayette. Next day at the parley, Hamilton through Greene had passed along word to Murray that Clinton should look for it there and note from whom it came.

There was no logical reason for Clinton to append to the "AH" letter the curious footnote he did ("received after A's death") unless he had, in fact, received it before André's death. Then it would be a necessary, if self-serving, exoneration of himself to history and the memory of André. But it could never exonerate Clinton's conscience from the inward shame of having failed to act when a response to Hamilton's letter might have saved his beloved aide's neck from the noose.

On October 2, André's execution day, Hamilton wrote Betsy, "Poor André suffers to-day. Everything that is amiable in virtue, in fortitude, in delicate sentiment, and accomplished manners, pleads for him; but hard hearted policy calls for a sacrifice. He must die. . . ."

The macabre procession from cell to gallows passed close by Washington's head-quarters. Closed windows did not shut out the sound of the muffled drums of the death march from the ears of the commander in chief. After reaching the place for the hanging there would be the awful moment when handsome young André's eyes swung round, expecting to see a firing squad, and fell instead on the empty noose dangling from the gibbet. Would granting the condemned man's dying wish have been too serious a deviation from principle and accepted procedure? Was popular clamor so insistent on this? In deep gloom Washington sat alone in his room. The hanging of Clinton's favorite, his adjutant general, a charming young man so like one of his own beloved aides, had already reduced many in camp to tears. Washington ordered that none of his own aides be witness to the hanging itself.

In a letter to Laurens afterwards, Hamilton described André's last moments with economy and not without emotion.

"In going to the place of execution, he bowed familiarly as he went along, to all those with whom he had been acquainted in his confinement. A smile of complacency expressed the serene fortitude of mind. Arrived at the fatal spot, he asked with some emotion, 'Must I die in this manner?' '' He was astonished to be told so late of the denial of his request to be shot, not hanged. All, including Hamilton, had kept from him this last awful secret. Hanging was unavoidable, he was told. "I am reconciled to my fate," said he, "but not to the mode." Soon, however, recollecting himself, he added: "It will be but a momentary pang." Springing upon the cart, he performed the last offices to himself, with a composure that excited the admiration and melted the hearts of the beholders. Upon being told that the final moment was at hand and asked if he had anything to say, he answered: "Nothing but to request you will witness to the world that I die like a brave man." Hamilton gave a benediction: "Among the extraordinary circumstances that attended him, in the midst of his enemies, he died universally esteemed and universally regretted." Hamilton's account of the affair was published in many newspapers, and the public's opinion of what had happened was to a large extent formed by what Hamilton wrote.

Of Arnold, Hamilton wrote, "This man is in every sense, despicable. Added to the scene of knavery and prostitution during his command in Philadelphia, which the late seizure of his papers has unfolded, the history of his command at West Point is a history of little, as well as great villainies. He practised every dirty act of peculation, and even stooped to connections with the sutlers of the garrison to defraud the public."

André had attempted to bribe the three good patriot guerrillas who had arrested him, Isaac Van Wart, John Paulding, and David Williams, with offers of his watch, his horse, and any sum of money they should name. Hamilton's account of the exemplary conduct of André's captors formed a striking contrast to Arnold's dirty acts of peculation. These heroes of the common people "rejected his offers with indignation, and the gold that could seduce a man high in the esteem and confidence of his country, who had the remembrance of past exploits, the motives of present reputation and future glory, to prop his integrity, had no charms for three simple peasants, leaning only on their virtue and an honest sense of their duty." Out of the whole tragic episode, wrote Hamilton, the real heroes were these Westchester members of the silent majority. "While Arnold is handed down with execration to future times, posterity will repeat with reverence the names of Van Wart, Paulding, and Williams."

Though the names of Van Wart, Paulding, and Williams never managed to become household words in the pantheon of American heroes, Hamilton's moving account convinced the public that the plot against West Point had been the work of only one man, that the plot had been skillfully thwarted by Washington and his aides, and that there would be no widespread repercussions during the autumn when American fortunes lay so low. It brought a feeling of relief, even exultation, that Washington and the other leaders had safely escaped the traitor's bag.

As a result of the upswing in popular gratitude for Washington's deliverance, Joseph Reed and the Pennsylvania radicals gave up their efforts to tar Washington, Schuyler, and Hamilton with guilt-by-association with Arnold's treason. They contented themselves with banishing Peggy from her father's house in Philadelphia and forcing her to join her connubial conspirator behind the British lines in New York.

For public consumption, Hamilton would pass off an event that had moved him so deeply in private by saying rather neatly, "Never . . . did a man suffer death with more justice, or deserve it less." More complex and revealing of the inward Hamilton was his private opinion as a 23-year-old man of the world. Far from welling up out of undifferentiated sentiment, kindliness or benevolence toward André, his view was based on reasoning from a peculiarly Hamiltonian premise, which he carefully and consciously identified with honor. He wrote Laurens:

> I speak not of André's conduct in this affair as a philosopher, but as a man of the world. The authorized maxims and practices of war are the satires of human nature. They countenance almost every species of seduction as well as violence; and the general that can make most traitors in the army of his adversary is frequently most applauded.
>
> On this scale we acquit André; while we could not but condemn him, if we were to examine his conduct by the sober rules of philosophy and moral rectitude. It is, however, a blemish on his fame, that he once intended to prostitute a flag; about this, a man of nice honor ought to have had a scruple; but the temptation was great: let his misfortunes cast a veil over his error.

Thus, like André himself, Hamilton had reconciled himself to what Washington had insisted be done, "but not to the mode."

To a chief executive, the perfect aide is one whose loyalty to his chief is such that the aide's personal views are never pressed where they differ from the chief's. For all his energy, experience, skill, discretion, and power of statement, by such standards, Hamilton in André's case had proved himself to be something less than the perfect model of a Washingtonian aide.

And something more.

10

I Am No Longer
a Member of the
General's Family

—To Philip Schuyler from Headquarters, New Windsor, New York, February 18, 1781

The double promotion to lieutenant colonel Hamilton had won on becoming Washington's chief aide was almost four years behind him. Others with less time in grade had gone on to higher rank. As 1780 drew to a close, Hamilton grew more and more restless in the groveling condition of an aide.

This same length of service in the same rank and staff position was what now made him irreplaceable to Washington. He shared with Washington a unique fund of experience and knowledge gained both as a headquarters intelligencer and a former line commander. To Washington and the states, Hamilton was infinitely more valuable continuing as he was than he could possibly be doing anything else.

Much of Hamilton's frustration came from his own perception of the inescapable logic of Washington's position. If there were to be any change, it would have to come from action of the aide.

The aborted exchange of André for Arnold and the hanging of André had added personal resentment against Washington himself.

Hamilton most wanted a transfer to a line regiment. A second possibility was the diplomatic service, for which Washington's consent would not be necessary: the post of secretary to the Ministry to France was open.

The most pressing purpose of the Ministry to France was to obtain a loan. Hamilton had urged such a loan upon Congress as one of the most important steps America could take to stabilize her finances. He had studied the subject thoroughly, he knew the arguments that

134

would appeal to the French mind, he had many French connections through his intimacy with French comrades-in-arms, and he spoke their language with a West Indies flavor that even Parisians found beguiling.

On December 11 a vote was taken in Congress to decide between Hamilton and his friend John Laurens. On the first ballot, Hamilton and Laurens tied, but on succeeding ballots some votes shifted to Laurens, whereas Hamilton received no additional support. Laurens was elected unanimously.

Laurens, who had not even known he was being considered for the mission, felt that the vote was really a vote for his father, Henry Laurens, the former president of Congress. Besides, he did not wish to block his own best friend, Hamilton. When he received the news, he promptly declined and suggested Hamilton in his place as being much better qualified.

Congress ignored his suggestion and on December 17 nominated James Lovell, who also declined in favor of Hamilton. The mission was offered again to Laurens, who now saw no alternative but to accept.

Congress's true reasons for voting against Hamilton cannot be gleaned from the dry husks of the proceedings recorded in the *Secret Journals,* but the suspicion is that Washington had good reasons for seeing that Congress did not take his aide away, and the influence to translate the reasons into enough votes for Laurens.

Hamilton did all he could to prosper Laurens's mission to France, including a letter for Washington's signature for Laurens to take with him that was a plea to the French Ministry for all possible aid.

Hamilton next proposed to Washington that he be given a battalion command in Lafayette's expedition against the British on Staten Island. Washington refused. Line unit commanders were constantly being lost in such actions.

On November 22, he made another request by letter, though he saw Washington in person every day:

> Some time last fall, when I spoke to your Excellency about going to the south-ward, I explained to you candidly my feelings with respect to military reputation, and how much it was my object to act a conspicuous part in some enterprise that might perhaps raise my character as a soldier above mediocrity. You were so good as to say you would be glad to furnish me with an occasion.

Yet Washington had turned him down. Now there was talk of an attack on Bayard's Hill on Manhattan, where Hamilton had seen his first combat of the Revolution. With a corps of 200 men, Hamilton said, he would storm and capture the hill. Appalled by his recklessness, Washington turned him down again.

Between commander and aide there was no longer much personal warmth or trust. It was as if Washington were keeping Hamilton a prisoner on his staff.

Colonel Alexander Scammell, the former adjutant general, had just been promoted to the rank of brigadier general; his old post was vacant; and Hamilton set to work on two of his warmest friends in the army, the Marquis de Lafayette and General Nathanael Greene, to obtain the vacant post.

Lafayette wrote to Washington:

> If . . . you were to cast your eye on a man, who, I think, would suit better than any other in the world, Hamilton is, I confess, the officer whom I should like to see

in that station. . . . His knowledge of your opinions and intentions on military arrangements, his love of discipline, the superiority he would have over all the others, principally when both armies shall operate together, and his uncommon abilities, are calculated to render him perfectly agreeable to you. . . . On every public or private account, my dear general, I would advise you to take him.

Lafayette's strongest argument was that promotion would not really take Hamilton away from Washington: "An adjutant general ought always to be with the commander in chief. Hamilton should, therefore, remain in your family."

Greene wrote a similarly strong endorsement.

Requests from Lafayette and Greene could not be brushed aside by Washington as easily as requests from the aide himself. Nonetheless, Washington had replied stiffly to Greene: "Without knowing that Colo. Hamilton ever had an Eye to the office of Adj. General, I did . . . recommend Genl. Hand for reasons which may occur to you."

He told Lafayette that it was too late because he had already dispatched his recommendation of Hand to Congress by messenger on horseback. Lafayette offered to send an express to intercept Washington's messenger; Washington retorted that to do so would be highly irregular.

Breaking the bad news to Hamilton gently, Lafayette assured him:

I know the General's friendship and gratitude for you [are] greater than you perhaps imagine. I am sure that he needs only to be told that something will suit you, and when he thinks he can do it he certainly will. Before this campaign, I was your . . . very intimate friend. . . . Since my second voyage, my sentiment has increased to such a point the world knows nothing about.

The British had recently been making threatening forays down Lake Champlain toward Fort Ticonderoga and raided to within five miles of The Pastures. But these customary perils of a northern outpost did not prevent family, friends, and relations from responding to Catherine van Rensselaer and Philip Schuyler's request for the pleasure of their company at the great reception to be held in the family mansion on December 14, 1780.

With a cloak thrown over his uniform against the upstate chill, surrounded by his galaxy of army friends, Hamilton easily slipped through high patroon class lines. In the wide upper hall of The Pastures, decorated with holly and lighted by dozens of wax candles, the young people danced until early hours of the morning for three nights before the ceremony itself. The bride wore white, which provided a striking contrast to her nut-brown complexion and sparkling dark eyes. Her shining black hair was hidden beneath a towering white wig, from which hung a lace veil that had belonged to her grandmother, Angelica Livingston Van Rensselaer. At the ceremony itself, Colonel Hamilton did not wear his uniform. Instead he wore a black velvet coat, white satin knee breeches, white silk stockings, and the rhinestone shoe buckles he had received as a wedding present from Lafayette. In accordance with the dictates of current fashion, a white wig with a long queue behind covered his own reddish-blond hair.

"As they have given and pledged their troth, each to the other," Dominie Westerlo of the First Reformed Church of Albany intoned solemnly, "I pronounce that they are man and wife." He raised his hand and gave the benediction. Afterward, in front of the carved mantel in the blue drawing room opening off the great hall, Alexander and Betsy Hamilton received their guests. A long line moved slowly past to wish the young couple happiness. A finer-looking pair had not often been seen in those parts. The groom of 23, rosy and fair as a

Scot, exuded self-assurance and energy. The bride, three inches shorter, seven months younger, known best as a spirited tomboy, on the day of her wedding at least was not much outshone by her brilliant, blonde younger sister Margarita, or Peggy.

Nor, on that day at least, was Betsy much outshone by her older sister Angelica Carter Church. And no guest present could fail to be dazzled by Angelica. Her powdered and bejewled hair was piled high in a tower that stood taller than that of any other woman in the hall. Her swelling bosom was drawn tightly down by the curve of a seductive corset into the smallest waist of any woman there. Angelica Church was acknowledged, not only in Albany, not only in Philadelphia and New York, but also in London and Paris as well, as one of the most beautiful women and greatest belles of the age.

The ardent attention of the groom to the bride did not keep him too preoccupied to fail to ply his comely sisters-in-law with smiling gallantries.

Hamilton's close friend, groomsman and physician, James McHenry, wrote a 72-line Epithalamium in celebration of Alexander and Betsy's wedding night. McHenry had noticed his friend Ham taking long, hard looks at Peggy, and still longer and harder looks at Angelica, and included a possible forecast of future infidelity in his verse:

> when love his choicest giffs has giv'n
> He flies to make another heav'n.

The first of the year found Hamilton back with Washington at the New Windsor encampment. Betsy immediately established herself as one of the most popular of the circle of official wives. Martha Washington welcomed her with kindness and came to know her well. Betsy, quick to note the coldness between her husband and his aegis, reported that Washington "expressed himself as not having been treated, for some time, with proper respect."

Congress voted to replace the inept Committee on Finances with a single "Financier," and General John Sullivan inquired of Washington about Hamilton. Washington could not exactly tell a lie:

> How far Colo. Hamilton, of whom you ask my opinion as a financier, has turned his thoughts to that particular study, I am unable to ansr., because I never entered upon a discussion of this point with him. But this I can venture to advance, from a thorough knowledge of him, that there are few men to be found, of his age, who have a more general knowledge than he possesses; and none, whose soul is more firmly engaged in the cause, or who exceed him in probity and sterling virtue.

The kind letter was of a sort quickly recognized by politicians as one calculated to guarantee the job seeker's not getting the job.

As 1781 began, troops of the Pennsylvania line mutinied on January 1; troops of the New Jersey line mutinied at Pompton, New Jersey, on January 20; troops in Albany were also threatening to mutiny unless they were better paid and supplied. Washington sent Major General Robert Howe to suppress the New Jersey mutiny and he hanged two of the mutineers. On February 4, Hamilton wrote John Laurens in despair about the "deplorable" situation of the southern army "destitute of everything," with Cornwallis about to recommence his offensive northward. "Part of the Jersey troops having [emulated] the Pennsylvanians by mutinying," Hamilton added, "we uncivilly compelled them to an unconditional surrender and hanged their most incendiary leaders." Hamilton's anger was unmistakably directed against Washington's early slackness and late overreaction.

Benedict Arnold's legion of Americans loyal to the British had just triumphantly sacked Richmond, put to flight Virginia's unready governor, Thomas Jefferson, and left the most important state defenseless in the path of Cornwallis, who was now marching north.

On the night of February 15, Washington and Hamilton worked by smoky candlelight until "very early in the morning," writing dispatches to Rochambeau in Newport planning a joint land and sea venture to capture the traitor. After a night of such work, giving "the most positive directions concerning expedition," tempers were short the following day.

Hamilton was hurrying down the narrow stairs in the headquarters house with an order that had to be delivered immediately to the commissary department. Halfway down, he met Washington coming up.

The general paused. "I would like to speak to you, Colonel Hamilton," he said.

Hamilton nodded. "I will wait upon you immediately, sir." Then he continued down, as Washington continued up. On the lower floor Hamilton found Tench Tilghman and handed him the order. It was "of a pressing and interesting nature." He gave instructions for its delivery. He started back up the stairs to attend on Washington, but Lafayette stopped him. They spoke together briefly on a matter of business; then Hamilton excused himself rather abruptly and hastened on up the stairs.

Washington was waiting for Hamilton on the top landing, his hand clenched on the balustrade and his face grim. Washington accosted him "in a very angry tone."

"Colonel Hamilton," Washington said, "you have kept me waiting at the head of the stairs these ten minutes. I must tell you, sir, you treat me with disrespect."

"I am not conscious of it, sir," Hamilton replied, "but since you have thought it necessary to tell me so, we part."

According to Hamilton, his reply was "without petulancy, but with decision."

Washington stared at him. "Very well, sir," he said, "if it be your choice."

They separated. In anger, general and aide departed each for his own room.

The only eyewitness account of the incident is Hamilton's, contained in the letter he wrote explaining it two days later to Philip Schuyler, his father-in-law of two months. "I sincerely believe my absence which gave so much umbrage did not last two minutes." He and Lafayette had conversed only about half a minute, and "he can testify how anxious I was to get back, and that I left him in a manner which but for our intimacy would have been more than abrupt."

Within the hour Washington sent Tilghman to Hamilton, "assuring me of his great confidence in my abilities, integrity, usefulness, etc., and of his desire, in a candid conversation, to heal a difference which could not have happened but in a moment of passion."

Hamilton gave Tilghman a message to take back to Washington that was obviously the product of much careful thought, not something dashed off in a few minutes of pique and dispatched without rereading: it was in five well-planned parts. Hamilton's decision would not be revoked. He begged to be excused from a face-to-face interview that would be mutually disagreeable. Out of the family, he would conduct himself toward the general just as he had while in it. He would not embarrass Washington's business by quitting him until absent aides returned. Meanwhile, he proposed that they behave toward each other as if nothing had happened. Washington agreed to all points. He "consented to decline the conversation and thanked me for my offer of continuing my aid, in the manner I had mentioned."

Lafayette, distressed that it was Hamilton's half minute or so with him that had caused the breach, "explained the delay" and "privately expressed to each of them his own feelings. . . .'' But, with a logical Gallic shrug at the neatness and balance of the thing, he "found each disposed to believe that the other was not sorry for the separation."

It was uncharacteristic of Hamilton to do much rewriting, but he rewrote his first draft of his letter to Philip Schuyler extensively. The rewriting masks the indiscreet slips he had first put down in heat with more careful, less revealing second thoughts.

"I am no longer a member of the General's family," he begins. He then tersely relates the trivial encounter on the stairway and its aftermath.

"I always disliked the relation of an Aide de Camp to his general as having in it a kind of personal dependence.'' Then he changed *relation* to *office* and crossed out the phrase "to his general.'' This made the sentence less personal, more guarded: "I always disliked the office of an Aide de Camp, as having in it a kind of personal dependence."

He had refused invitations to serve two other generals, but "an idea of the General's character which experience taught me to be false overcame my scruples . . . and induced me to accept his invitation to enter into his family." Rewriting, he softens the harsh *false* to *unfounded*. His private opinion of Washington would shock a public that idolized him: "It was not long before I discovered he was neither remarkable for delicacy nor good temper, which revived my former aversion to the station . . . and it has been increasing ever since."

Here was an astonishing secret: "The place I held in the General's confidence and councils . . . will make it the more extraordinary to you to learn that for three years past I have felt no friendship for him and professed none. The truth is our own dispositions are the opposites of each other, and the pride of my temper . . . could not suffer me to profess what I did not feel."

Washington had an intense desire for affection from Hamilton and sought admission to Hamilton's circle of friendships with Laurens, Lafayette, and McHenry. "When advances of this kind have been made to me by the General,'' Hamilton went on, "they were received in a manner that showed at least I had no inclination to court them, and that I wished to stand rather upon a footing of military confidence than of private attachment." Such brusque rebuffs from the junior would cruelly hurt the senior.

Secret dislike for Washington's curious "disposition" does not prevent Hamilton from working with him successfully: "The General is a very honest man. His competitors have slender abilities, and less integrity. His popularity has often been essential to the safety of America, and is still of great importance to it. . . . I think it is necessary he should be supported."

Many a secret about a childless chief that is hidden from his wife, friends—and, of course, biographers—is known to an aide of four years. Writing his shocked father-in-law, the aide is shrewd enough to add: "You are too good a judge of human nature not to be sensible how this conduct in me must have operated on the self love of a man to whom all the world is offering incense." Hamilton then crossed out the phrase "the self love of" and added, "I give you this as a key to the rest." Then he struck out the entire sentence and rewrote it to read "with this key you will easily unlock the present mystery. At the end of the war I may say many things to you concerning which I shall impose upon myself 'till then an inviolable silence."

Later relationships between the two men that were fruitful for the new nation would have been less so, or impossible, if Hamilton had been content to acquiesce in Washington's insistence on keeping him on as an aide. Once Hamilton had won his release, he and Washington were free to form a new relationship that would render better service to their mutual client. The old relationship of master to servant or principal to agent changed to that of senior to junior partner, but partners nevertheless in public service to the nation in war and peace. Afterward Hamilton would always acknowledge that Washington was not a friend, not a mentor, but "an aegis very essential to me."

Hamilton's divorce from Washington's family to enter Schuyler's was "unalterable," but his decree did not immediately become final. Tilghman was "just recovering from a fit of illness the consequence of too close application to business," as Hamilton wryly wrote McHenry, and Humphrey and Harrison were away. Between the break on February 16 and his formal resignation on April 30, 1781, Hamilton continued for ten weeks to perform diligent services as Washington's aide, to all outward appearances as if nothing had happened.

On April 30, Hamilton said good-bye, quit the headquarters at New Windsor, and went home to face a bleak spell of unemployment—just when his pregnant bride would be plumpening with their first child—with no better job offer in his pocket.

Hearing the news of the break with Washington, Hamilton's friend, the Marquis de Fleury, making ready to move south from French headquarters at Newport, wrote, "I have very Little time left, but enough to inquire after your happiness. Are you come back from Albany, with your sweet-heart; are you already, out of the general's family? What are you doing? What are you thinking? Let me know everything, which may be interesting to you; you know it is so to me."

Lafayette, marching south toward Virginia, now a major general leading his first independent command, wrote from Head of Elk (present day Elkton), Maryland, on April 10, 1781, that "had the French fleet come in [,] Arnold was ours," but the archtraitor had escaped. Lafayette continued, "Owing to the tender sentiments of my friendship . . . public and private nature conspire in making me wish your woe be not accomplished . . . ."

Fleury blamed the alarming news from Virginia on the debilitating effect of southerly climes on the character of the people: "I pity much our virginia friends. They want Constance and patriotics virtues which I believe, are scarce in those southern countrys."

In his charming Franglais, the Marquis de Fleury was referring to the panicky flight of Governor Thomas Jefferson from the capital, and the disappearance of all semblance of civil government there at the time of the incursions and invasions of Benedict Arnold, Cornwallis, and Banastre "Bloody" Tarleton.

Sent to Virginia to train militia to fight, Hamilton's friend Baron von Steuben criticized Jefferson's unreadiness and defection. So did a resolution later introduced into the state legislature.

Civil government in Virginia had completely broken down and disappeared, a thing that had not happened in Massachusetts, New York, Pennsylvania, or South Carolina when the British seized those states' capitals. When Tarleton's brigade, the "scourge of the South," occupied Monticello itself, Jefferson was outraged that the British freed some of his slaves there.

Lafayette, with a force of about 1,200 New Englanders and New Jerseymen, pushed on south as far as Richmond before realizing the strength of the enemy forces massing against him.

In late May 1781 Lafayette wrote Washington, "Were I to fight a battle, I should be cut to pieces, the militia dispersed and the arms lost. Were I to decline fighting, the country would think itself given up. I am therefore determined to skirmish, but not to engage too far. . . ." He was one degree worse off than Greene who had said, "Were I always equal to the enemy, I should be extremely happy in my present command, but I am not strong enough even to get beaten.''

Hamilton's last public business at New Windsor headquarters after his break with Washington that spring of 1781 was the most important headquarters business of all: planning the summer and fall campaigns, and coordinating them with the French allies.

Hamilton and Elizabeth moved out of the headquarters about the middle of April 1781 to the east side of the Hudson at de Peyster's Point near King's Bridge, but there Hamilton remained near enough headquarters to keep in touch and in the way of any new opportunity for a command in the line that might open up.

Philip Schuyler, on the other hand, felt that Hamilton would be safer in the moribund Congress; combat infantrymen are not immortal. On May 30 he wrote from Albany that he was down with the quinsy, ''but I propose to attend the [New York] Legislature the latter end of next week, when I shall have the pleasure of seeing you at Fishkill [where the Legislature met] on the Sunday following. I believe you may prepare yourself to go to Philadelphia, as there is little doubt but you will be appointed [to Congress].''

Hamilton turned down Schuyler's well-meant offer, though the rumor of his impending election as delegate to Congress had already reached his friend John Laurens, who wrote:

> I would not wish to have you, for a moment, withdraw from the public service: at the same time, my friendship for you, and the knowledge of your value to the United States, makes me most ardently desire, that you should fill only the first offices of the Republic. . . .
>   . . . I must confess to you, that, at the present stage of the war, I should prefer your going into Congress, and from thence becoming a minister plenipotentiary for peace, to your remaining in the army, where the dull system of seniority, and the tableau, would prevent you from having the important commands to which you are entitled.

From Richmond, Lafayette wrote his friend on May 23, ''Come here, my dear friend, and command our artillery in Virginia. I want your advice and your exertions.''

But Washington remained silent, so Hamilton remained in wait across the river, silent, too, except for his pen; he was now writing a series of great state papers that would soon begin appearing in the press under the overall title of ''The Continentalist.''

In desperation, Hamilton appealed directly to Washington: ''It has become necessary to me to apply to your Excellency to know in what manner you foresee you will be able to employ me in the ensuing campaign. I am ready to enter into activity whenever you think proper, though I am not anxious to do it till the army takes the field, as before that period I perceive no object.''

Washington gave the excuse that regular officers of the line were resentful at being pushed aside to make room for newcomers fresh from the staff, whose previous experience consisted only of chairborne pen-pushing.

Washington laboriously explained that he never deviated from the rules. Hamilton's appointment would, ''I am certain, involve me in a difficulty of a very disagreeable and delicate nature, and might perhaps lead to consequences more serious than it is easy to imagine.'' Hamilton should not think his refusal had been caused by their personal breach: ''My principal concern arises from an apprehension, that you will impute my refusal of your request to other motives than those I have expressed.'' Hamilton did, of course.

Meanwhile, Sir Henry Clinton had depleted the northern forces in New York that Washington's army had been covering, to send 1,500 men south to support Cornwallis's army. Washington again proposed to the French his scheme for a joint assault by land and sea on New York City.

Hamilton cared little whether the battle was north or south as long as he held a command. Hearing of the proposed operation, he sent Betsy to Albany and went south to Dobbs Ferry on July 8 to press Washington once again for a field command. Once again Washington brushed him off. Finding that "nothing was said on the subject of a command," Hamilton wrote a letter to Washington, resigning from the army, enclosing his prized lieutenant colonel's commission. All his hopes of again finding the war that had lost him were staked on a last desperate, dramatic gesture.

Out of one of his blackest moods, on July 13 Hamilton wrote Betsy from Dobbs Ferry. He has "no object of sufficient importance to occupy my attention." His "dissipations are a very imperfect suspension of my uneasiness." He is absorbed in thoughts of her, but things are bad: "Indeed Betsey, I am intirely changed—changed for the worse I confess—lost to all the public and splendid passions and absorbed in you." Not his usual gallant style, this put-down of her: "Amiable woman! nature has given you a right to be esteemed, to be cherished, to be beloved; but she has given you no right to monopolize a man, whom, to you I may say, she has endowed with qualities to be extensively useful to society."

His idleness, dissipation, and strange black thoughts raise terrible questions: "Yes my Betsey, I will encourage my reason to dispute your empire and restrain it within proper bounds, to restore me to myself and to the community. Assist me in this; reproach me for an unmanly surrender of that to love and teach me that your esteem will be the price of my acting well my part as a member of society." He closes, "love me and let your happiness always consist in loving." He promises to send her some money, not right away but soon. He also, curiously, directs her to deliver two separate letters he is enclosing to her sisters, one to Angelica and one to Margarita. He does not give her permission to read them. "Your sisters will show them to you." Would they?

It was Washington who yielded. He sent Tench Tilghman to Hamilton on another peace mission.

> He pressed me to retain my commission, with an assurance that he would endeavor, by all means, to give me a command, nearly such as I could have desired in the present circumstances of the army. Though I know my Betsy would be happy to hear had I rejected this proposal, it is a pleasure my reputation would not permit me to afford her. I consented to retain my commission and accept my command.

General orders of July 31, 1781, announced that the light companies of the First and Second New York Regiments, with two newly raised companies, "will form a battalion under command of Lieutenant Colonel Hamilton and Major Fish," Hamilton's old King's College classmate. When formed, Lieutenant Colonel Hamilton's battalion would join the advanced corps under Colonel Alexander Scammell.

Hamilton set to work taking care of the needs of the men of his new command with his usual zeal, just as he had done for his artillerymen five years before. No fear of wasting a favor from the highly placed would keep him from going straight to the top for supplies without going through usual channels.

Conventional history is that until late July 1781 Washington was undecided whether to launch the main American attack on New York City or in Virginia. Early signs had pointed to an attack on New York. Washington had written to Lafayette and Greene that from every point of view an attack on New York was preferable to a southern operation "as we had not command of the water." Sent out by regular post, this plausible plan was intercepted, not very surprisingly, by the British on June 3. But when Washington learned that Sir Henry Clinton had found out these secret plans, he made light of it, telling Rochambeau that "The enemy can gain no material information from my letters." This led Clinton to suspect a ruse. At headquarters, Hamilton allowed a double agent in British pay to see a map marked for a land and naval attack on New York. The spy asked Hamilton the destination of the army. Hamilton replied, "We are going to Virginia."

Whether Washington's indecision was real or feigned and whether Hamilton was wittingly or unwittingly being used by Washington as part of the ruse, all such conflicting disclosures served splendidly to confuse Clinton, who astutely deduced that New York was indeed Washington's real objective.

Washington eventually admitted that the French had conceived and planned the Yorktown campaign, whereas he had pressed for an attack on New York; he never publicly admitted that he had unwillingly gone along with the "southern strategy." Rochambeau, in his *Memoirs*, depicted Washington as a military primitive so obsessed with attacking New York that he could see no other alternative. No wonder Sir Henry Clinton had once again misread a Washington "bluff."

Americans and French would march south overland to join Lafayette and "Mad Anthony" Wayne in Virginia. There the French Admiral, Comte Francois Joseph Paul de Grasse, would land three West Indies regiments. There were three disturbing "ifs." If de Grasse failed to keep control of the waters about Chesapeake Bay, Cornwallis could be reinforced or whisked out of reach by the Royal Navy. If the allied troops failed to reach Virginia in time, the whole effort would abort because de Grasse would not stay in North American waters after October 15, 1781. And because there was no money in the Continental Treasury for such a large-scale expedition, and no time to wait for Congress to appropriate some, the expedition would fail unless funds could be raised from other sources. It arrived by way of a loan from France arranged through Rochambeau.

Hamilton wrote Betsy in Albany on August 22, trusting his beloved to keep the secret: "A part of the army, my dear girl, is going to Virginia, and I must, of necessity, be separated at a much greater distance from my beloved wife." He does his best to sound unhappy, but the more he tries to convince her of his unhappiness about marching off to the war he had always sought, the more he fails: "I cannot announce the fatal necessity, without feeling every thing that a fond husband can feel." So far so good. But his further protestations are laughable:

> I am unhappy my Betsy. I am unhappy beyond expression. I am unhappy because I am to be so remote from you; because I am to hear from you less frequently than I am accustomed to do. I am miserable because I know you will be so. I am wretched at the idea of flying so far from you, without a single hour's interview to tell you all my pains and all my love. . . .
>
> But I cannot ask permission to visit you. It might be thought improper to leave my corps at such a time and upon such an occasion. I must go without seeing you—I must go without embracing you;—Alas! I must go.

The French expeditionary force in Newport passed in review one last time. Then they marched off the parade ground—and kept on marching—onto ferry boats that carried them west across Narragansett Bay, off again, and up to the high road near Westerly. Five thousand well-drilled regulars of the king of France were on the march to help the states fling off the yoke of the king of England. They marched on through southern New England with lances and sabers glittering in the August sun, varicolored pompoms slanting up from little cocked hats, gaitered legs swinging in long, easy strides. Through little Connecticut villages like Plainfield and Windham and Farmington, with the clank and rumble of d'Abouville's seemingly endless imperial artillery trains, they rattled all the windows along the rutted high roads.

Rolling over all resistance, marching on through Westchester, at Dobbs Ferry they caught a glimpse of America's supreme monument, General George Washington. General Cromot du Bourg reported that Washington was "a very fine looking man," with a "bearing noble in the highest degree. . . ." His "dignified address . . . won every heart." At King's Ferry the French fell into columns behind Alexander Hamilton's Connecticut and New York light infantry and John Laurens's mixed brigade of Massachusetts, Connecticut, and New Hampshire men. The brilliantly caparisoned French were struck by the lack of regulation uniforms and the great number of fringed hunting shirts among their allies. Americans, traveling light, carried "not over forty pounds of baggage." They shambled and slouched along, arms unslung or trailed behind, at an easy gait that could carry them far in a day's march. When passing through a town, they hardly bothered to form their columns or bring their muskets to shoulder arms, although sometimes they struck up a popular marching song like Hamilton's favorite, "The Drum."

They marched through Philadelphia in choking dust on September 1, the Americans in their nondescript outfits of every ragtag kind, followed by the French "in complete uniform of white broadcloth, faced with green."

From Head of Elk, Maryland, on September 6, Hamilton wrote Betsy, five months pregnant with their first child, "Tomorrow we embark for Yorktown." And words of affection: "I would give the world to be able to tell you all I feel and wish, but consult your own heart and you will know mine . . . you, who have the most female of female hearts."

His thoughts reverted to military matters: "Circumstances that have just come to my knowledge assure me that our operations will be expeditious, as well as our success certain."

Then he impulsively added, "Every day confirms me in the intention of renouncing public life and devoting myself wholly to you. Let others waste their time and their tranquility in a vain pursuit of power and glory; be it my object to be happy in a quiet retreat with my better angel." To this kind of thing for home consumption in Albany, Hamilton could bring a quality of conviction that would compel belief only in someone who knew him less well than his wife.

The "circumstances" that Hamilton felt would make "success certain" were, no doubt, the sighting of de Grasse's 28 ships and four frigates within the Virginia capes, carrying 3,000 more ground troops to be debarked immediately at Jamestown to join the Americas under Lafayette already bivouacked there.

Just at this time Hamilton received an unsettling letter from Philip Schuyler. His pregnant Betsy had been about to have a miscarriage, but now the danger had passed: "My dear daughter is in good health but was so sensibly affected by your removal to the southward that I apprehended consequences; she is now at ease."

From Annapolis about September 15, Hamilton dashed off a reassurance to Betsy that was anything but reassuring. "How chequered is human life!" he philosophized. "How precarious is happiness! How easily do we often part with it for a shadow! These are the reflections that frequently intrude themselves upon me, with a painful application. I am going to do my duty. Our operations will be so conducted, as to economize the lives of men. Exert your fortitude and rely upon heaven.'' Would he ''economize'' with his own, she might well ask.

From Annapolis, Hamilton's light infantry sailed down Chesapeake Bay and up the James River and waded ashore at College Landing, then called Archers Hope, on the south side of the peninsula a mile from Williamsburg and only ten miles from Yorktown itself.

Now with the Americans and French astride the peninsula of which Yorktown formed the tip Cornwallis found himself in a trap about to snap shut. Out at sea De Grasse fought off the covering British fleet, under admirals Thomas Graves and Samuel Hood, leaving the British remnants fleeing toward New York and Cornwallis at Yorktown to fend for themselves. With Hamilton's light infantry battalion and other reinforcements from the North now on the peninsula, the numbers of French and American forces under Lafayette and Wayne grew from 11,000 to 14,000 and finally to a peak of 16,500, the largest force ever assembled under Washington's command. Cornwallis's army was about half that size, but it was dug in behind a maze of fortifications well covered by heavy artillery.

On September 28, 1781, at five in the morning, Hamilton's light infantry marched down from Williamsburg to join the rest of the army deployed in a semicircle facing Cornwallis in his Yorktown defenses. Other British forces held Gloucester Point across the water to the north, but the French fleet, instead of Cornwallis's, was now in command of the straits between. The French held the left sector of the semicricle around Yorktown, and the Americas the right, with Hamilton's battalion in advance on the far right under the overall command of Lafayette.

The well-disciplined French infantry regiments, artillery batteries, and cavalry troops were about 7,200 strong, under the overall command of Rochambeau, who reported to Washington. Particular friends of Hamilton among the French officers were Marquis Francois Louis de Fleury and the Vicomte Louis Marie de Noailles, a brother-in-law of Lafayette. Angelica's husband John B. Church was also with the French at Yorktown on profitable business in his capacity as their commissary contractor.

Hamilton made ready for a long siege. His men dug trenches and threw up earthworks in the sandy soil, then reinforced the protective mounds with gabions, saucissons, and fascines, which served to protect the men against sudden assault from the British redoubts in the same way later armies used barbed wire to entangle charging infantrymen.

Hamilton's battalion took cannon fire from the British redoubts opposite; one British cannon shot off the leg of one of Hamilton's men.

The infantry pushed advance trenches and earthworks closer and closer toward British lines. Artillery and small arms fire from the allied lines covered the advance.Without enough troops to man them all, Cornwallis was forced to abandon some of his outer works.

On the night of September 29, an allied patrol probed the British defensive works, and Colonel Alexander Scammell, Hamilton's immediate superior, was shot, wounded, and captured. After a few days he died, reportedly of his wounds. Lafayette now proposed to Washington that, with Scammell gone, Hamilton's battalion should be enlarged to the size of Huntington's and that he should ''put the eldest of the two lieutenant colonels [Hamilton] upon the right [that is, the leading position] of the brigade.'' Washington approved.

Cornwallis had collected many small boats just offshore of the town of Yorktown, keeping open the possibility of escaping by night across the water to Gloucester Point, even under the guns of the French fleet. He had received word from Clinton that a large rescue fleet and 5,000 men would be sailing from New York October 5 to reinforce him, and it was usually no more than an eight-day voyage. In the face of such a formidable British naval threat, only about two weeks' time remained for de Grasse to keep his blocking fleet in position at the mouth of the Chesapeake. There would not be time to starve out Cornwallis.

If it were to be taken at all, Yorktown had to be taken quickly and by storm, without necessarily trying to economize on infantrymen's lives.

On October 3 de Choisy pushed the French lines forward, closer to the British works on the left. A sudden charge by Lauzun's brightly uniformed troopers badly mauled Banastre Tarleton and one of his columns and nearly killed Tarleton himself.

In front of Hamilton's sector, extending outward from the town of Yorktown, were two advance British redoubts from which deadly flanking cross fire could be poured upon any frontal attack on the town itself. To economize on the lives of charging American infantrymen, these two redoubts would have to be destroyed before the main assault on Yorktown could succeed.

Under fire of the British cannon, Hamilton and his men and the other American troops began laboriously digging siege approach trenches toward the fortified redoubts. By October 6 they had dug a "parallel" trench three and a half feet deep and seven feet wide, extending for more than a mile across the exposed flat level ground in front of the British fortifications.

Next morning, after a clamorous French diversionary night attack, the left, or French, end of the first parallel trench was 600 yards from the British center; and the right, where Hamilton's troops were, was about 800 yards from the two advanced British redoubts, known as numbers 9 and 10.

The allies' softening-up bombardment began at three in the afternoon of October 9, with the heaviest barrage ever laid down in the western hemisphere up to that time.

The heaviest British artillery were only 18-pounders; the defenders of the fortified town were outgunned by the American 24-pounders. As time went on, the allied barrage and allied marksmanship silenced the lighter British guns one by one.

An uncle of Governor Thomas Nelson was sent out from Yorktown under a flag of truce to report to Washington that the fortifications had been damaged and that the defenders were killing horses they could not feed. But Cornwallis would not surrender because he expected Clinton's fleet to arrive with relief within a week. The allied pounding resumed.

Well-aimed shells from the French cannoneers on the allied left set fire to the British warship *Charon*, lying just offshore. The blaze spread to Cornwallis's smaller getaway vessels moored offshore. This emboldened de Grasse to dispatch some of his ships past the guns of the town to cut off Cornwallis's line of retreat to Gloucester Point across the water.

Under the bombardment, Hamilton's troops kept pushing their siege trenches closer to British redoubts 9 and 10 until by October 11, working into close-range fire from the redoubts, they had extended a second parallel trench to a point only about 350 yards away from them.

Redoubts 9 and 10 had earthen walls rising some 20 feet from deep ditches to the top. Sharpened stakes driven in at a menancing angle bristled from the walls. In front was a 25-yard-wide barricade of felled trees also bristling with tangled and sharpened sticks and branches. Veteran British troops, 120 strong, garrisoned redoubt number 9; about 45 defended redoubt number 10.

Sunday afternoon, October 14, Rochambeau assigned his chasseurs and grenadiers under Baron de Viomenil to assault redoubt number 9 while American light infantry of Lafayette's division would make the final assault on redoubt number 10. Lafayette chose his former aide, Lieutenant Colonel John Joseph Gimat, to command the American forces in the van.

According to the initial order of battle, Gimat's battalion would lead, Hamilton's would follow, Laurens's would come up on the flank, and Colonel Francis Barber's would follow as a supporting column.

Hamilton was bitterly disappointed that his chance to lead the charge seemed to have slipped away. He had not schemed, marched, ridden, sailed, dug and burrowed for a year to take a secondary place in the final assault on the last redoubt at Yorktown. He went to Lafayette and demanded that he be put in overall command. Lafayette pointed out that Gimat's battalion had been with Lafayette much longer and had wearily fought, pursued, and fled from Cornwallis all summer, whereas Hamilton's had "just come from the Northward." Hamilton was senior to Gimat, it was true. After his line duties as an artilleryman, his long service as an aide had left him "over age" in grade. Besides, for what it was worth, that particular Sunday happened to fall on Hamilton's regular turn as "officer of the day." Lafayette took Hamilton's demand directly to Washington; Hamilton came along to help argue his case on this technicality. Soon he burst out of Washington's tent. He embraced Major Nicholas Fish. He cried, "We have it, we have it!"

Hamilton was to have command of the entire American assault team, with Gimat in charge of the right column, reinforced by a detachment of sappers and miners under John Gililand to remove obstructions. Laurens's column on the left would circle the redoubt "to take the enemy in reverse, and intercept their retreat." Major Fish, now commanding Hamilton's old battalion, was to bear to the left to enter the redoubt from that side. All troops would advance under cover of darkness, as silently as possible, with rifles and muskets unloaded, bayonets fixed and at the ready. They would rely on surprise and terror to repeat the success that similar tactics learned from the enemy at Paoli had won for "Mad Anthony" Wayne at Stony Point.

Just before dark, Washington paid brief visits to both the French and American assault teams. The whole army was expecting "something grand to be done by our infantry."

Soon after darkness, the general cannonade fell silent. Then six quick aerial shellbursts from a French battery signaled the beginning of the attack. On the far left flank, Saint-Simon's forces staged a noisy diversionary demonstration. Over across the water from Gloucester Point, de Choisy's troops began to fire, raising fears inside Yorktown of an attack from the water side. In the darkness over on the left, Hamilton could hear the muffled shuffle of boots and the clank of bayonets being snapped on to muskets. French light infantry were massing behind Comte Guillaume de Deux-Ponts in the trench at the line of departure; Hamilton's New York and Connecticut Continental Light infantry assembled in the trench behind him.

Now was the time. The shuffle and clank fell silent. Shell bursts and muzzle flashes from the diversionary demonstrations and British counterfire in the distance glinted fitfully on the bayonet blades jutting from the rifles and muskets of his men crouching in the trenches at port arms, pointing toward Yorktown. Suddenly, Hamilton stood erect in the trench facing redoubt number 10, his upper body outlined against the night sky by the muzzle flashes of the firing opposite. He extended his right arm straight up above his head, pointing his sword toward the sky.

"Fix bayonets!" he whispered loudly. He paused as his men tested the fit of bayonet collar and flange in the slot one last time. Keeping his sword, wrist, and elbow straight and stiff, as if all were a guidon's lance, he swung his arm downward in an arc until it and his sword paralleled the ground and pointed ahead. As he did so he called back over his shoulder in a low voice, "Follow me!" He lunged forward, bending low, running ahead of the infantrymen of Mansfield's vanguard strung out behind him. He moved swiftly and silently through the first parallel trench to the end and on into the second to the end of it, and then up over the lip of the trench onto the exposed flat sandy plain, pitted with shell holes and treacherous puddles of water from the weeks of artillery cannonading. With another thrust of his sword, Hamilton waved his men on toward the last redoubts. There remained a 300-yard run across the flat, muddy, shell-pocked, open field sporadically illuminated by signal flares and muzzle flashes from enemy guns in the darkness. It seemed like three miles.

Over on the left flank, toward where the French were moving in on redoubt number 9, a Hessian guard gruffly challenged an advancing Gatinois of Colonel L'Estrade's battalion, *"Wer da?"*

The Gatinois returned no countersign or password. There was a moment's stillness. Then Hessian musket fire flashed and roared point-blank into the faces of the French attackers. The defenders' volley scorched and deafened Hamilton and his men. But they pushed on into the sharpened ends of the branches of the first prickly abatis, mounted it, and skidded down the sloping wall of the counterscarp into the ditch, then up palisades of stakes beyond. The firing of the aroused defenders now flashed out at terrified attackers all along the line. Hamilton at first could not climb over the heavy stakes of the palisade, but now under fire, there was no time to pause for engineers and sappers to clear an opening. Hamilton ordered one of his men coming up behind him to kneel, climbed upon his shoulders, vaulted over the palings onto the scarp and scrambled up the parapet wall. More enemy muskets blazed along the line, but Hamilton's men still held their fire. Now on the top of the parapet wall, he thrust his sword forward once again, looked back toward his men, and again brought his arm down to the horizontal, softly calling, "Follow me!" He leaped down into the inner works of the redoubt.

The men behind him clambered and fell and picked themselves up and slashed and scrambled on through the barrier, across the ditch, and up the bristling embankments of the redoubt. Gasping for breath, they clambered up it, slipping between the stakes. Some pulled themselves up on the outthrust, sharpened ends.

Musket blasts banged at point-blank ranges, blinding eyes, deafening ears, and filling up lungs with the acrid smell of burned powder and smoke. As shot hit flesh, startled, plaintive cries broke out. Sharp bayonet blades sliced and slashed through to blood. Screams erupted. Steel scraped on bone. The first American over the top and inside the works was Hamilton. Men of Gimat's battalion clambered down close behind him, their bayonets quivering at the ready, with some already dripping blood or raggedly fringed with bloody flesh. Laurens's men crashed into the open rear of the redoubt. Major Patrick Campbell, the commander of the little fortress now overwhelmed by sudden superior force brought to bear with shock effect on all sides of it, surrendered his person to Laurens. At the same moment, Fish, leading Hamilton's old battalion, swarmed in from the left flank.

Colonel Gimat had been struck in the foot by a defender's musket ball. Captains Thomas Hunt and Stephen Betts of Laurens's company suffered bayonet wounds, and Lieutenant Captain Kilpatrick of the sappers and miners lay wounded in the ditch. One sergeant and eight privates were killed, and 25 privates were wounded. The British garrison of the redoubt, Hamilton later acknowledged, were "intitled to the acknowledgement of an honorable defence." Eight were killed or wounded by the Americans' bayonets. Major Campbell, a captain, an ensign, and 17 others were taken prisoner. The rest escaped in the darkness back to the inner defenses of Yorktown. It was all over in less than ten minutes.

De Viomenil's French had a harder fight for redoubt number 9, and it took them longer to invest it at a much higher cost—15 killed and 77 wounded.

The British defenders lost 18, and 50 were taken prisoner.

The French had borne the brunt and suffered the most. Hamilton had been more successful in economizing lives of his infantrymen. The same day, October 15, Hamilton wrote a report of the attack to Lafayette, mentioning the gallantry of everyone but himself.

Anyone who has ever led troops in taking an enemy redoubt knows that the personal side of the experience is too intense for any but the kind of matter-of-fact, dry, impersonal words he used: "The rapidity and immediate success of the assault are the best comment on the behaviour of the troops," Hamilton wrote. "As it would have been attended with delay and loss to wait for the removal of the abatis and palisades the ardor of the troops was indulged in passing over them." Good planning had produced effective coordination of movement: "The redoubt was in the same moment envelloped and carried on every part."

Lafayette forwarded Hamilton's report to Washington, filling the gap that the intensity of Hamilton's own personal involvement had left in it, writing:

> I beg leave to refer Your excellency to the report I have received from Colonel Hamilton, whose well known talents and gallantry were on this occasion most conspicuous and serviceable. Our obligation to him, to Colonel Gimat, to Colonel Laurens, and to each and all the officers and men, are above all expression.

Washington's praise must have given Hamilton special satisfaction: "The bravery . . . was emulous. . . . Few cases have exhibited stronger proofs of Intrepidity, coolness and firmness than were shown upon this occasion." The success in capturing the redoubts on the enemy's left flank, Washington wrote to Greene, "will prove of almost infinite importance in our Approaches. . . ."

The allied forces at once extended their second set of parallel trenches to take in the two captured redoubts. They hauled Knox's cannon forward and emplaced them to fire out of the open backs of the redoubts directly down upon Cornwallis's inner works in the town only about 200 yards away.

The capture of the two redoubts broke effective British resistance. On the sixteenth, the British made a desperate predawn sortie, entered the Americans' second parallel trench, and spiked six of Knox's cannon before being driven off, leaving casualties on both sides.

After this sortie, the allied bombardment rose to a crescendo; return fire from enemy guns diminished. On the night of the sixteenth, Cornwallis attempted to ferry his main force across the river to Gloucester Point, but the overloaded little fleet of 16 boats was dispersed by a violent rainstorm and returned to Yorktown.

With all going well against the British, Comte de Grasse suddenly announced that his fleet had to depart within 48 hours. Washington remonstrated that he would be compelled to raise the siege on the brink of victory. De Grasse refused to change his mind.

Washington once again used a trusted subordinate for a secret strategem of a kind that no commander could countenance in his own name and could readily disavow. Elias Boudinot later revealed the curious episode. Hamilton and some other officers moved toward the British lines under a flag of truce. During a brief conversation with some of the British— their amicable sortie was supposedly a private venture—they made it known to the British that an American assault in force was, in fact, in the making; that everyone was "so exasperated at the Conduct of the British to the Southward, that they could not answer for the Consequences, as they did not think they could be restrained by authority and Discipline."

However, Hamilton added, they knew Washington's "humane Temper." If the British would surrender now, before the final all-out attack got under way, heavy casualties would be spared; Washington would certainly grant more favorable surrender terms. There is little corroboration for this Hamilton story of Boudinot's, but it serves to explain the otherwise inexplicable promptness of Cornwallis's surrender.

On the morning of the seventeenth, a red-coated drummer mounted the parapet of the nearest British fortification and "beat a parley." An officer waved a white handkerchief. Washington ordered his guns silenced. Out of the ruined British fortifications a messenger brought to him one of the most momentous documents of American history. It read:

> Sir, I propose a cessation of hostilities for twenty-four hours, and that two officers may be appointed by each side, to meet at Mr. Moore's house, to settle the terms for the surrender of the posts at York and Gloucester.
>
> I have the honor to be, etc.
> Cornwallis.

Well aware that reinforcements from Clinton might arrive at any moment, or that de Grasse might sail away, Washington agreed to suspend the artillery barrage for two hours, but not 24. Lieutenant Colonel John Laurens and Vicomte Louis Marie de Noailles from the allies met with Lieutenant Colonel Alexander Dundas and Major Alexander Ross from the British army to negotiate the detailed surrender terms.

Washington had ordered that American deserters caught with the British army be, as usual, hanged. Formal surrender terms would not permit them to be exchanged as prisoners of war. For Cornwallis to have included them in the surrender by sending them back to the American lines would have been to consign them to Washington's gibbets. So it was agreed that Cornwallis would be permitted to send the armed sloop *Bonetta* back to New York with dispatches for Sir Henry Clinton "without examination," which would permit Cornwallis to ship out some 250 deserters. Washington's liking for stern measures being known, it was also provided that captured British officers would not be subjected to retaliatory hangings.

In the same redoubt Hamilton had stormed, Washington, Rochambeau, and Barras put their signatures to the surrender document.

Hamilton's turn as officer of the day came round again on October 19, four days after his assault on redoubt number 10, thereby putting him center stage for the ceremony as well as the charge. It took place on the Yorktown siege ground at one in the afternoon f October 19, 1781. Lord Cornwallis did not appear, pleading sickness. In his place he sent Brigadier General Charles O'Hara, his second in command, who marched up to Rochambeau, mistaking him for Washington, and presented his credentials. Rochambeau corrected him. O'Hara then marched up to where Washington stood with Hamilton at his side. Washington ignored him. A deputy should treat with a deputy, not the chief, Hamilton told him, sending O'Hara on down the line to General Benjamin Lincoln, Washington's second in command.

Eighteenth-century warfare set great store by the right of the vanquished to salute the victor by playing one of the victor's tunes. This was to show that even in surrender, the vanquished had not given over their pride. But at Charleston, where John Laurens had been captured, the British winners had not allowed the American losers to play a British tune. So as part of the Yorktown surrender ceremony, Laurens stipulated that the British must play one of their own tunes, not an American tune.

British commissioned color bearers objected to handing over their regimental colors to American sergeants—noncommissioned officers—in accordance with the original plans.

Hamilton interceded. He directed that an ensign, the youngest commissioned officer in the American army, but an officer nevertheless, accept the colors from the British guidons and then turn them over to a sergeant. Then after Hamilton's display of American generosity, the British and Hessian troops, with their unit colors cased, marched through the ranks of American and French troops drawn up in parade formation while British army bands played the British air, "The World Turned Upside Down."

Hamilton had finally found the elusive war he had wished for. It had released him from the groveling condition of clerk, aide, and earwig. He had helped show the states he thought of as a nation how to win an offensive battle (partly) on its own. He had won a hero's image in the minds of his countrymen for the rest of his life. More important, he had relieved himself of a self-doubt of his own. He had passed a self-sought test that would exculpate his troubled conscience from his weak side—the "hurry of mind" that he had exposed to Major General Charles Lee that hot summer's day at Monmouth. Ever since then his own ideal of public credit had insisted that his inward doubts somehow or other be scraped away—on something like the parapet of the last redoubt at Yorktown.

11

A Few Months More in Public Life

You may render America and the world no less a service than the establishment of American independence! 'Tis by introducing order into our finances—by restoring public credit—not by gaining battles, that we are finally to gain our object.

—To Robert Morris, April 30, 1781

Two days before storming redoubt number 10, on October 12, 1781, Hamilton had written Betsy: "Five days more the enemy must capitulate or abandon their present position . . . and then I fly to you. Prepare to receive me in your bosom . . . receive me decked in all your beauty, fondness and goodness. Adieu my darling wife, my beloved angel adieu."

His successful storm was the night of the fifteenth, the informal surrender the seventeenth, the white flag on the eighteenth, and the formal surrender ceremony the 19th. His forecast had turned out to be precisely correct: five days.

On October 16 he had written her again: "Two nights ago, my Eliza, my duty and my honor obliged me to take a step in which your happiness was too much risked." But he had risked it anyway: "I commanded an attack on one of the enemy's redoubts; we carried it in an instant and with little loss. You will see the particulars in the Philadelphia papers. . . ."

In Philadelphia, there had been rave reviews. "There will be, certainly, nothing more of this kind. . . . If there should be another occasion, it will not fall to my turn to execute it."

He concluded his last letter from Yorktown:

> My uneasiness at not hearing from you is abated by the sweet prospect of soon taking you in my arms. . . . In two days after I shall . . . set out for Albany, and I hope to embrace you in three weeks from this time. . . . Conceive my love from your own

152

feelings, how delightful this prospect is to me. Only in your heart and in my own can any image be found of my happiness. . . . Adieu my charming beloved wife, I kiss you a thousand times, adieu, my love.

A. Hamilton

With more than 500 miles to ride from Yorktown to The Pastures at Albany, Hamilton anxiously spurred his horse northward over the newly rutted roads as fast as its shanks and lungs could keep him a-going.

". . . he thought of nothing but reaching [his wife] the soonest possible," Philip Schuyler later reported from Albany, "and Indeed he tyred his horses to accomplish it, and was obliged to hire others to come on from Red Hook."

Having restored the public credit called into self-doubt at Monmouth on the parapet of the last redoubt at Yorktown, Hamilton now withdrew from active service in the army with Washington's tacit consent. He agreed to forego army pay ("the difficulties I experienced in the last campaign in obtaining a command will not suffer me to make any further applications on that head"). But "I shall accordingly retain my rank" because "I am unwilling to put it out of my power to renew my exertions in the common cause, in the line."

In May of 1777, four and a half years earlier, Hamilton had written Catharine Livingston:

I do not wonder at your antipathy to [war]. Every finer feeling of a delicate mind revolts from the idea of shedding human blood and multiplying the common evils of life by the artificial methods incident to that state. Were it not for the evident necessity; and in defence of all that is valuable in society, I could never be reconciled to a military character; and shall rejoice when the restoration of peace on the basis of freedom and independence shall put it [in] my power to renounce it.

The costs of the Battle of Yorktown, and the war, were enormous. There was very little hard coin in circulation; the paper money issued by Congress had depreciated over 40 to one. The national government was still dependent on requisitions from the states for its own support and for support of the war. But the states, jealous of each other, reluctant to burden their own citizens complaining that their particular allotments were unfair through their delegates in Congress, had failed to supply the sums that were requisitioned. The appeal to France that Hamilton had written for Washington and John Laurens had taken with him to France as envoy had helped secure a loan of 10 million livres, 4 million to be appropriated to cover bills drawn by Congress on Franklin; 6 million for military supplies. Without French troops, the French naval blockade, and the French loans, the victory at Yorktown would not have been possible. The war would have long since gone bankrupt.

After Yorktown, Robert Morris had said, "What remains of the war is only a war of finance." Hamilton had been saying much the same thing in many different ways—but less succinctly—for years. On April 30, 1781, the day his resignation as Washington's aide had become final, Hamilton had sealed and placed in the mail a long essay addressed to Morris, setting forth another comprehensive plan for putting the disordered finances of the country on a sound and durable basis. The third such plan he had written within a year and a half, it contained much of the best from the earlier letters he had written for Morris and James Duane.

Morris, the leading Philadelphia merchant banker, was financier of the Office of the Finance, the highest-ranking fiscal officer of the Confederation. Hamilton's friend Gouverneur Morris was Robert Morris's assistant. Both Morrises' readiness to pledge their growing wealth to Congress and to make loans out of their own private capital stood in sharp contrast to many others, nearly as wealthy, who were fearful of taking the same risks—what if the revolution should fail?

In his letter Hamilton had projected on Robert Morris his own idea of how to win the "war of finance."

"In the frankness of truth I believe, Sir," Hamilton wrote, that "You may render America and the world no less a service than the establishment of American independence!"

What must he do?

" 'Tis by introducing order into our finances—by restoring public credit—not by gaining battles, that we are finally to gain our object."

What was the obstacle?

"While Congress holds the reins of administration in their own hands, the Court of France will never give half the succours to this country that they would grant if these were intrusted to individuals of established reputation and conspicuous for probity, abilities and fortune."

What was Hamilton's solution?

"An administration by single men is essential to the proper management of the affairs of this country . . . an executive ministry of the department of finance"—with Morris in charge, or someone like him.

To Morris, Hamilton wasted no ink wringing his hands over the alleged lack of patriotism of moneyed men. He acidly observed that "They can employ their money to greater advantage in traffic rather than by merely lending it on interest," and more safely.

The timidity of capital was part of the natural order of things. Only a national or central bank could bring it out of hiding by the prospect of attractive profits. Such a bank would

> erect a mass of credit that will supply the defect of moneyed capital, and answer all the purposes of cash; a plan which will offer adventurers immediate advantages, analogous to those they receive by employing their money in trade, and eventually greater advantages

This, in turn, "will not only advance their own interest and secure the independence of their country, but, in its progress, have the most beneficial influence upon its future commerce, and be a source of national wealth and strength."

On a national scale the sum of all of these separate efforts would add up to Adam Smith's "invisible hand" guiding all men and women in the general direction of the common good. Management was to be placed in a directorate of 12—eight chosen by the private stockholders and four by Congress.

Hamilton's idea that the new government should burden itself with a large debt seemed improvident to many, but Hamilton saw a national debt as a positive good in itself. "A national debt," he asserted, "if it is not excessive, will be to us a national blessing. It will be a powerful cement of our Union. It will also create a necessity for keeping up taxation to a degree, which, without being oppressive, will be a spur to industry."

Hamilton turned to his second lifelong theme—the need for a strong, central government with sovereignty independent of, and superior to, that of the several states. The Articles of Confederation were worse than useless, and unless immediately revised, must lead to dissolution. "It has ever been my opinion," he told Morris, "that Congress ought to have complete sovereignty in all but the mere municipal law of each state; I wish to see a convention of all the States, with full power to alter and amend, finally and irrevocably, the present futile and senseless Confederation.''

This sentence pointed to Hamilton's call at Annapolis for the Constitutional Convention, to the Convention of 1787, to *The Federalist Papers*, and to the adoption of the Constitution.

Hamilton had previously expressed many of the same basic ideas he now did again at 24, and although he would continue to elaborate and refine them, he would not change them in essentials for the rest of his life.

A few days after receiving Hamilton's letter, Morris submitted a plan for a bank to Congress but it was on a more modest scale than Hamilton's. Congress approved his scheme, and The Bank of North America was duly incorporated as a quasi-public bank, for which the government provided most of the capital and kept the right of supervision.

Hamilton had described his existence between the time of his resigning as Washington's chief aide in April, 1781, and his departure for Yorktown in August as being wasted in idleness and ''dissipation.'' One product of this period was his masterful letter to Robert Morris. Another was the series of essays which he called ''The Continentalist.'' He had sent the first of the series off to Samuel Loudon, editor of the *New York Packet* and *American Advertiser,* published at Fishkill, on July 12, 1781, with an introductory note which boldly proclaimed, ''I send you the first number of a series of papers which I intend to publish on matters of the greatest importance to these States.'' They should be ''read with as much candour and attention as the object of them deserve.'' ''No conclusions will be drawn till these are fully developed,'' he added.

While Hamilton had been marching south to Yorktown with his infantrymen, publication of the first four numbers of this series, on July 12, 19, and August 9 and 30, 1781, had been making a powerful impact on the minds of thinking men and women throughout the states.

''The Continentalist'' hammered away at a single theme: Continental nationalism. It proposed a single solution: more power to Congress!

The fatal defect in the Articles of Confederation, he insisted, was a ''want of power in Congress.''

Justifiably fearful of asserting implied powers, Congress should have an express grant of powers: it should be ceded the right to regulate trade and impose import duties, to appoint its own officers, to levy land and poll taxes, and to become the custodian of the Western territories.

''The Continentalist'' examined in detail regulation of trade by Congress. He had read and digested Adam Smith, but he steered a cautious middle course between the old mercantilism and the heady new spirit of free enterprise: ''to preserve the balance of trade in its favor ought to be the leading aim of a nation's policy.'' New opportunities for trade beyond the resources of private capital ''may require no small assistance, as well from the revenue, as from the authority of the state.'' Yet, he added quickly, he was utterly opposed to any governmental interference with prices or to any restrictions on private enterprise.

Hamilton's remarkable linking of what seemed to be opposites laid the foundations of that combination of laissez-faire and benevolent assistance to business that has been a familiar feature of the American scene and the platforms of both political parties.

In the two last articles of the series, to be published on April 18 and July 4, 1782, he argued that both the landed interests and ''the laboring poor'' ought to favor federal control of external commerce. Otherwise, each state, fearful of imposing import duties lest commerce be diverted to others and to freer ports, would be compelled to rely on heavy land taxes for revenue. This, in turn, would raise the prices of food and other necessities, and the poor would suffer both from the higher cost of living and from unemployment because of foreign competition.

Federal regulation should not look primarily to the interests of the trading and mercantile classes, but should insure that ''the laboring poor'' would not be thrown out of work and that labor that remained employed would not command too high a price. ''To reduce which, and not increase it, ought to be a capital object of our policy,'' he maintained. His peroration to the sixth and final paper of ''The Continentalist'' series, published on the sixth anniversary of the Declaration of Independence, would offer a stirring vision and a characteristic warning:

> There is something noble and magnificent in the prospect of a great Federal Republic, closely linked in the pursuit of a common interest, tranquil and prosperous at home; respectable abroad; but there is something proportionably diminutive and contemptible in the prospect of a number of petty states, with the appearance only of union, jarring, jealous, and perverse, without any determined direction, fluctuating and unhappy at home, weak and insignificant by their dissensions in the eyes of other nations.

The formerly obscure young lieutenant colonel who dismounted warily at The Pastures late in November had become a famous public figure while away. He was no longer just the handsome young man who had been a shrewd, articulate aide. The public image of ''The Continentalist'' was that of a political leader in command of the most sophisticated economic and political ideas of his age, a scholar with a seemingly inexhaustible stock of knowledge, a prose stylist who could thrust to the heart of public issues like an Addison, or dissolve an opponent with the acidulousness of a Junius. The report of his heroic sword-waving night charge leading New York and Connecticut light infantry with fixed bayonets over the ramparts of the last Yorktown redoubt had been reprinted in newspapers all over the United States. He was General Philip Schuyler's son-in-law. He was the most famous young man in the country with the brightest future. With the possible exception of Aaron Burr.

That January, Betsy had written her sister Peggy, ''I am the happiest of woman; my dear Hamilton is fonder of me every day; get married, I charge you.''

But after only a month and a half of marriage to Betsy, Hamilton had written Peggy in a slightly different vein. He was, he whispered, a ''fanatic in love,'' or else, ''a good dissembler.'' This left him room for an affair with Peggy:

> Because your sister has the talent of growing more amiable every day, or because I am a fanatic in love, or both—or *if you prefer another interpretation, because I have address enough to be a good dissembler*, she fancies herself the happiest woman in the world, and would need persuade all her friends to embark with her in the matrimonial voyage.

Hamilton explained to Peggy: ''Do not let her advice make you matrimony-mad.'' With a little dissembling, an extramarital love affair could be managed nicely: ''Tis a very good thing when their stars unite two people who are fit for each other, who have souls capable of relishing the sweets of friendship and sensibilities.'' He seemed about to propose one, but checked himself add wrote instead, ''The conclusion of the sentence would carry me too far; I trust the rest to your fancy.'' His son (or another later editor) thought he had already gone too far and struck out the offending words ''would carry me too far'' and ''the rest,'' so that the passage read lamely, "The conclusion of the sentence I trust to your fancy." Hamilton concludes with the practical message that

> it's a dog of life when two dissonant tempers meet, and 'tis ten to one but this is the case. I join her in advising you to marry, but I add the cautions in the choice. Get a man of sense, not ugly enough to be pointed at—with some good-nature—a few grains of feeling—a little taste—a little imagination—and above all a good deal of decision to keep you in order; for that I foresee will be no easy task. If you can find one with all these qualities, willing to marry you, marry him as soon as you please.

There is no question of Hamilton's deep affection for Betsy, only whether his extra-marital passion for one of her sisters would take him "too far." He closed discreetly, "I must tell you in confidence that I think I have been very fortunate," whichever sister he meant. He probably meant both of them, and Angelica too.

Betsy's labor pains came again. The family doctor, Dr. Samuel Bard, was summoned.

While in camp before Yorktown on October 12, Hamilton had written Betsy that he had no doubt the unborn child would be a boy: "You shall engage shortly to present me with *a boy*. You will ask me if a girl will not answer the purpose. By no means. I fear, with all the mothers charms, she may inherit the caprices of her father and then she will enslave, tantalize and plague one half [the] sex." Of Angelica, who had just been delivered of her Phil, "Tell Mrs. Carter I partake in the joy she has made a present of to the world." He hoped his and Betsy's boy "may have as many good qualities" as Angelica's Phil; "but I protest against his being too much a rival."

On January 22, 1782, Betsy gave birth to the first of their eight children born alive. The requisite boy was named Philip for his grandfather, just as Angelica's had been.

After his 500-mile ride from Yorktown and his hero's homecoming—and the ordeal of being an expectant father—Hamilton collapsed in another serious spell of illness. He was "in and out of bed" past the end of December. So he did not set to work to become a lawyer until January of 1782. A three-year clerkship before admission was the new rule, even for holders of an A.B. degree from Columbia, but in January the three-year rule was suspended for "young gentlemen who had directed their studies to the profession of the law, but upon the breaking out of the present war had entered into the defense of their country." This veteran's exception could be availed of only until the end of the April term of court, leaving Hamilton less than five months to prepare for bar exams that formerly would have called for as much as five years of preparation.

Alexander and Betsy and their little Philip moved out of The Pastures into a small, shabby house of their own on the Albany waterfront. In April, Robert Troup, Hamilton's old King's College friend who was already working as a lawyer, moved in to help Hamilton with his bar review course.

In the 18th-century state of the law in America, Blackstone's *Commentaries* was a sufficient text for most purposes. Hamilton had read Blackstone, Coke's *Reports*, Beawe's *Lex Mercatoria*, and works on principles of feudal tenures; his political pamphlets showed that somewhere or other he had picked up the law of nations from the treatises of Berlamaqui, Grotius, Locke, Vattel, Montesquieu, and Pufendorf. But he knew almost nothing of New York practice and procedure, the bread and butter of most lawyers' work.

Matters of practice and procedure were not generally committed to writing, but persisted as usage among judges, clerks, and the more experienced members of the bar, a "memory jurisprudence." So as a way to cram for his bar examination Hamilton wrote a 177–page practice manual known as *Practical Proceedings in the Supreme Court of the State of New York*. Written at a time when New York's first state constitution was but five years old and the British army still occupied New York City, it was the earliest treatise on practice and procedure in the courts of the independent state of New York. It remained in use among members of the profession until 1794, when large portions of it were incorporated in Wyche's *Practice Manual*. This handbook of practice rules is the direct ancestor of all the innumerable volumes of *New York Civil Practice Acts, Laws,* and *Rules* that have been published since then.

Hamilton made much use of the library at The Pastures, where he would often meet another young veteran who was also cramming for the bar exams, Aaron Burr.

Burr, after dropping out of the army, had begun studying law a year earlier with Judge William Paterson in New Jersey, where a three-year requirement was still in effect. But when he heard that New York had waived the requirement for veterans, he hastened to Albany armed with a letter of introduction to General Schuyler from Hamilton's early backer, General Alexander McDougall.

Only a year older than Hamilton, and almost as handsome but in a darker way, Burr may have found the Schuyler sisters a beguiling distraction. But there is no evidence that any of them were among the almost innumerable casual romantic conquests with which he punctuated his life. Hamilton would have more than enough other differences with Burr without a clandestine affair of Burr's with a precious Schuyler sister being among them.

Burr had, after all, dropped out of service almost three years earlier. Mr. Chief Justice Morris objected to granting Burr the veteran's waiver but Burr with Chesterfieldian *suaviter in modo* argued, "surely, no rule could be intended . . . to injure one whose only misfortune is having sacrificed his time, his constitution and his fortune to his country." Burr passed the examination and was admitted three months before Hamilton.

When Hamilton's April term deadline for admission to the bar as a veteran came round, the Supreme Court of Judicature granted him an extension to October that it apparently had granted no one else. The extension was more time than he needed. He was "admitted as attorney" in July 1782 and was able to be admitted to the "degree of counsellor" by October 26.

Not too much need be made of the rigor of the bar examinations, which were as much tests of whom one knew as what one knew. Levi Beardsley, a prominent upstate attorney, related how he had won his admission from Chancellor James Kent.

> "What books on chancery had I read? Kent asked.
> "Not any, but I have today bought your new rules and am going to read them."
> "Well," ruled the Chancellor, "I knew your brother Sam. . . . Your father and I were born in the same neighborhood. . . . I will admit you."

By joining the legal profession, Hamilton and Troup and Burr joined a new American aristocracy, which was nothing like the nobles, the princes, and the landed and moneyed rich of European aristocracy. Lawyer aristocrats, enjoying no tenure based on birth, wealth, or the arbitrary favor of a prince, prospered only as they performed useful service for people. They could be hired and fired by clients in much the same way as household servants, or elected and defeated by constituents.

In this sense, Hamilton, though an aristocrat of the bar, became, as de Tocqueville put it, a servant of the people "whom the people can choose."

Hamilton's most immediate "practical proceeding" was to earn legal fees to support his family.

He explained to Colonel Richard Kidder Meade that he was determined to shun public affairs. "You cannot imagine how entirely domestic I am growing," he wrote in March 1782. "I lose all taste for the pursuits of ambition. I sigh for nothing but the company of my wife and my baby. The ties of duty alone, or imagined duty, keep me from renouncing public life altogether. It is, however, probable I may not any longer be engaged in it."

Hamilton found his and Betsy's Philip at the age of seven months to be remarkably different from the rather undifferentiated puddings that other seven-month-olds are. He wrote Meade:

> He is truly a very fine young gentleman, the most agreeable in his conversation and manners of any I ever knew—nor less remarkable for his intelligence and sweetness of temper. It is agreed on all hands that he is handsome, his features are good; his eye is not only sprightly and expressive but it is full of benignity.
>
> His attitude, in sitting, is, by connoisseurs, esteemed graceful; and he has a method of waving his hand that announces the future orator. He stands however rather awkwardly and his legs have not all the delicate slimness of his father's. It is feared he may never excel as much in dancing, which is probably the only accomplishment in which he will not be a model. If he has any fault in manners, he laughs too much.

Little Phil had been less than two months old when Hamilton wrote Meade in March that "Betsy proposes to form a match between his Boy & your girl provided you will engage to make the latter as amiable as her mother."

Before little Phil could dance attendance on the Meade's daughter, his future powers as an orator, inherited from his father, would entangle him at 19 in the duel with an enemy of his father in which he would be shot to death.

In the cloud of national euphoria that followed Yorktown, the army's soldiers remained short of supplies and food. Congress asked the states to cede to the general government the right to raise funds by collecting a tax of 5 percent on foreign commodities imported into the United States, known as the "impost." To make the "impost" mandatory, an amendment of the Articles of Confederation was necessary, which required unanimous consent of all 13 states.

In the fifth and sixth papers of "The Continentalist," Hamilton joined Morris's campaign to urge the states to vote Congress the power to collect the "impost." Without import duties, Hamilton argued, taxes on land would be too burdensome, would make labor dear, would raise costs of necessaries of life, and would induce migration from old settlements to new frontiers. He repudiated the physiocratic contention that because all taxes ultimately rested on land, they were most economically collected at the source, on land itself. Agriculture and commerce were mutually dependent; if one were penalized, the other would suffer too.

In the meantime, Congress had set New York's quota of Continental taxes at $375,598. On May 2 Robert Morris, the superintendent of finance, offered law student Hamilton the job of receiver of Continental taxes for New York. As compensation, Hamilton would be entitled to keep "one fourth of the monies you receive."

On May 18, Hamilton told Morris he was immersed in his legal studies, the position was politically unpopular, the pay was small compared with the labor required, he was under the pressure of the imminent expiration of the veterans' bar admission waiver. But there was a deeper problem: the job was not big enough for him. "Time is so precious to me," he said, "that I could not put myself in the way of any interruptions unless for an object of consequence to the public or myself. The present is not of this nature."

Morris was insistent. A man with Hamilton's talent could easily handle the job as a part-time affair, he explained. He increased the pay. Hamilton's salary would be based on New York's full quota, whether or not he actually succeeded in collecting all of it, and would come to about $940 a year. Hamilton accepted.

Morris was passing over another man with better formal qualifications for the job, who had been strongly recommended by Governor George Clinton: Abraham Yates, Jr., of Schenectady, who was already the Continental loan officer of the state. Yates demanded that the New York Congressional Committee of Oversight institute an investigation. Hamilton passed along to Morris his private opinion of Yates: "The people have been a long time in the habit of choosing him in different offices," because he was "preacher to their taste." Yates "assures them, they are too poor to pay taxes."

Governor George Clinton was stubborn, provincial in character, agrarian in outlook, a wealthy landowner who posed as the Populist champion of small farmers against large landed proprietors and seaboard merchants. He was suspicious of congressional encroachment on the sovereign powers of his or any state, and he fought the drive toward centralization of Continental government that Hamilton symbolized. During the war, he had staked Hamilton to money and medical aid on Hamilton's mission to Gates, but from now on the partisan lines that would make them bitter political enemies were drawn for life.

The state legislature, under the skillful leadership of Philip Schuyler and other like-minded men in the state senate, passed a bill granting Congress the import duties at the port of New York, to be levied and collected "under such penalties and regulations, and by such officers, as Congress should from time to time make, order and appoint." With Sir Henry Clinton and 13,000 British troops still occupying the city, this cost no votes and raised no money, but it would serve Hamilton as a precedent for the future. Other states refused to grant similar powers; New York was the only state that could pass such a law secure in the knowledge that British occupation would keep it a dead letter.

Hamilton lobbied the legislature to pass the bill and was proud to report: "Both Houses have unanimously passed a set of resolutions, to be transmitted to Congress and the several States, proposing a convention of the States, to enlarge the powers of Congress and vest them with funds."

Although Hamilton did not say so, it is probable that he had ghostwritten these 1782 resolutions for Philip Schuyler. As the first official resolutions issued by any state for a convention to alter the Articles of Confederation, they pointed the way to 1787 and the Constitutional Convention and marked the beginning of the movement that culminated in the Constitution.

Hamilton argued that the call for a constitutional convention did not bind New York to any particular course of action at the convention; once there, it might either favor or oppose. The proposed powers to Congress were left unspecified; in any event, there was small likelihood that any other state would follow suit. The very fact that most of his tax plan had been voted down was the key to successful passage of this resolution. From Clinton's point of view, adoption of the resolution would be a gesture that showed New York's good will and harmed no one.

Under Hamilton's spell, the legislature the same day passed two other significant measures, of which Hamilton mentioned only one to Morris: "The Legislature have also appointed, at my instance, a committee to devise, in its recess, a more effectual system of taxation, and to communicate with me on this subject." The other action was not so agreeable to Morris: The legislature had elected Hamilton as a delegate to the Continental Congress, requiring his resignation as New York's Continental receiver of taxes only four months after taking office.

Hamilton was a rather surprising choice for Congress in view of Yates's and Clinton's control of the assembly. His election was most likely the result of the legislature's wish to rid itself of a nuisance who sought more power for Congress and more tax collection. Sending him to Congress without voting it more taxing powers was their perverse way of giving Hamilton his wish: "more power to Congress."

Hamilton notified Morris of his resignation, effective on October 30, and of his election to a one-year term in Congress beginning in November. Morris conceded that Hamilton might do more in Congress than in New York to help solve the problems and wrote: "Your description of the mode of collecting taxes, contains an epitome of the follies which prevail from one end of the continent to the other . . . God grant you success in your views to amend it."

There was the question of Hamilton's successor. Yates continued to have strong political qualifications and Clinton's backing.

Solving this problem for Morris, Hamilton presented the opportunity to Yates in a way that would force him to reject it.

Yates wrote:

> About a month or better ago, [Hamilton] said that the People Blamed him supposing that he had got this office upon his own Solicitation. I told him I Never Blamed him; that the world was open to him. Indeed I thought [it] hard that he should Possess an office by way of Sine Cure with Immediate pay Torn as it [were] from the Loan Office while I had served as Loan Officer Near three years and had R[eceive]d Nothing.

Staying with Yates on the tangential issue, Hamilton assured Yates that he had not solicited the office. Yates said:

> In this Conversation, and from letters he showed me it appears that so far from being the Solicitor that he [Hamilton] had Reluctantly taken the office upon him. He then told me he intended to resign the office and would have no pay for what he had Done.

Hamilton went on to tell Yates, a leader of the states' rights party,

> that it was Necessary the Receiver of Taxes should be able to Look Continentally. He should have Continental Eyes, should not be under governmental Regulation &c That the Loan Officer was in some Measure a Provincial officer, was under [state] governmental Influence and Regulations &c.

Having thus obtained Yates's assent to propositions he knew would make the job offer he was about to make unthinkable for a states' rights democrat, Hamilton proceeded to offer Yates the job. He had not misread his man. Yates blew up. As Yates put it, "I got a little out of Temper.'' Consistency ruled him. "I told him I was an Honest Man and Acted agreable to the Dictates of my Conscience." He turned down the job he had sought.

The appointment of Dr. Thomas Tillotson, whom both Hamilton and Morris preferred to Yates, smoothly ensued without political static.

Hamilton's dearest friend, John Laurens, hailed Hamilton's decision to "put on the *toga*" and enter Congress. "I would not wish to have you for a moment withdrawn from the public service. . . . Knowledge of your value to the United States, makes me most ardently desire, that you should fill only the first offices of the Republic."

Laurens was making some headway in the South Carolina Legislature with his plan to grant slaves their freedom if they would enlist. He railed at landed slaveowners, who still opposed him. Laurens reproached Hamilton for not telling him sooner of his election to Congress and entreated him not to withdraw "the *consolation* of your letters. You know the unalterable sentiments of your affectionate Laurens." In Congress Hamilton would be able to help push along his friend's plan for granting slaves their freedom.

Hamilton's son John C. Hamilton would write that Laurens had "all the endearing and social affections, all the attractions of a noble nature, all the graces of a refined and cultivated intellect, and an address which possessed an irresistible, endless charm." He had also a certain weakness that inspired friendship of the stronger: "his intrepid spirit was coupled with a self-distrust, a confiding weakness of temper, which awakened in his friends surprise and love."

Hamilton was free, confiding, and open with Laurens in a way that he was with no one else, except Angelica Church. It was a unique friendship. That Laurens was the closest friend Hamilton would ever have and Hamilton the closest friend Laurens would ever have tells much about both men. Hamilton's son said of Laurens that "while the world saw him graced with every virtue, he was still aspiring to some higher excellence—an ideal perfection, which is denied to our nature, and exists only in the warm conceptions of a mind deeply tinged with romance." Of Laurens's gentle reproach to Hamilton for not telling him at once of his election to Congress, Hamilton's son wrote that "nothing can more fully express this inward struggle for superior excellence, than his letter to Hamilton, and the latter's elegant rebuke: 'he refined on the refinements of sensibility.' ''

With classical models like Damon and Pythias at the forefront of their minds, elegant criticism was a necessary incident of an affair between two young 18th-century men. As Hamilton's son pointed out, Hamilton's and Laurens's intercourse approached "the tenderness of feminine attachment.''

Hamilton had written to Laurens in April of 1779: "Cold in my professions, warm in [my] friendships, I wish, my Dear Laurens, it might be in my power, by action rather than words, [to] convince you that I love you. I shall only tell you that 'till you bade us Adieu, I hardly knew the value you had taught my heart to set upon you."

Now on his way to Congress, writing his dearest friend on August 15, 1782, Hamilton was full of open, expansive enthusiasms that he knew Laurens would share:

> This State has pretty unanimously elected me to Congress. . . . Peace made. . . . a new scene opens. The object then will be to make our independence a blessing. To do this we must secure our Union on solid foundations—a herculean task,—and to effect which, mountains of prejudice must be levelled! It requires all the virtues and all the abilities of the country. Quit your sword . . .; put on the toga. Come to

Congress. We know each other's sentiments; our views are the same. We have fought side by side to make America free; let us hand in hand struggle to make her happy.

It is probable that Laurens never received his dearest friend's letter.

To his less special friend Richard Kidder Meade, Hamilton broke the news of his election in a bluff, soldierly, offhand way. At the very end of the long letter of August 27, otherwise devoted to the future graces of seven-month-old little Phil, Hamilton tossed in, "I had almost forgotten to tell you, that I have been pretty unanimously elected by the legislature of this State, a member of Congress . . . I do not hope to reform the state although I shall do all the good I can."

From the perspective of his flourishing medical practice in Balitmore, James McHenry wrote Hamilton August 11, "I hear you are chosen a delegate to Congress . . . I would rather have heard you had not been chosen." The author of the knowing "Epithalamium" for Hamilton's and Betsy's wedding night at The Pastures warned:

Hamilton, there are two lawyers of this town, one of which has served the public in the General Assembly for three years with reputation, and to the neglect of his practice. The other has done nothing but attend to his profession, by which he has acquired a handsome competency. Now the people have taken it into their heads to displace the lawyer who has served them till he is become poor, in order to put in his stead the lawyer who has served himself and become rich.

For the Continental economic expert, here was a telling parable of personal economics:

To be dependent on a father is irksome . . . the good things of this world are all to be purchased with money, and the man who has money may be whatever he pleases . . . The moment you cease to be a candidate for public places, the people will lament your loss and wait with impatience till they can persuade a man of your abilities to serve them. In the mean time, you will be doing justice to your family.

Taking last fond looks at little Phil and scenes of happy domesticity, Hamilton readied himself to leave for Philadelphia. On November 3, he wrote Lafayette, who had returned to France soon after the victory at Yorktown, "I have been employed for the last ten months in rocking the cradle and studying the art of *fleecing* my neighbors. I am now a grave counsellor-at-law, and shall soon be a grave member of Congress. . . ."

He wound up his affairs as receiver of taxes, collected his license as a counselor-at-law, and concluded his letter to Lafayette, "I am going to throw away a few months more in public life, and then retire a simple citizen and good *pater familias*. I set out for Philadelphia in a few days. You see the disposition I am in. You are condemned to run the race of ambition all your life. I am already tired of the career, and dare to leave it."

Lafayette's decline and imprisonment at the hands of succeeding regimes in France during the next two decades, set against Hamilton's rise to the peak of power in America, would mock Hamilton's assertion. Hamilton was projecting onto his friend the unconscious realization that he, not Lafayette, was "condemned to run the race of ambition" all his life, not just throwing away "a few months more in public life."

But much of Hamilton's joy at the "new scene" opening for him and Laurens, the joy of putting on the toga with him "to secure our union on solid foundations," suddenly drained away in anguish. He read the letter from General Nathanael Greene: "Poor Laurens has fallen in a paltry little skirmish."

On a plantation near the Combahee River in South Carolina, Laurens had been out late dancing and late to bed. An hour or two after he had fallen asleep there came an alarm and word of a British foraging party in the neighborhood. Laurens had roused himself, taken horse, gone to search it out and destroy it. With the war all but over, he had been shot down in a meaningless skirmish.

Hamilton was heartbroken.

"That sensible, gallant elegant fellow," the South Carolina idealist who planned to free the slaves, the aide Hamilton had seconded on the dueling ground to defend Washington's honor against Charles Lee; the brave leader of Americans in battles at Savannah, Charleston, Rhode Island, Monmouth, Germantown, Brandywine, everywhere; the hero who had burst into the rear of the last redoubt at Yorktown moments after Hamilton had stormed the parapet at the front—John Laurens was dead. Only 12 days after Hamilton had called on him to "Quit your sword . . . put on the toga," he had been killed in a meaningless fire fight.

"You knew his temper," Hamilton replied to Greene. "I predicted his fate. The love of military glory made him seek it upon occasions unworthy of his rank. This state will feel his loss."

Hamilton grieved:

> I feel the deepest affliction at the news we have just received of the loss of our dear and [inesti]mable friend Laurens. His career of virtue is at an end. How strangely are human affairs conducted, that so many excellent qualities could not ensure a more happy fate? The world will feel the loss of a man who has left few like him behind, and America of a citizen whose heart realized that patriotism of which others only talk.

Hamilton mourned, "I feel the loss of a friend I truly and most tenderly loved, and one of a very small number." No evidence exists of Hamilton's having shared deeper intimacy with any man. There would never be anyone else to whom he could say, "We have fought side by side to make America free; let us hand in hand struggle to make her happy."

12

Forfending Mutineers

I will not conceal from your Excellency a truth which it is necessary you should know. . . . in the army [your] delicacy carried to an extreme prevents your espousing its interests with sufficient warmth. . . . the difficulty will be to keep a complaining and suffering army within the bounds of moderation.

—To George Washington, February 13, 1783

When Hamilton took his seat in the meeting room in the State House in Philadelphia, James Madison had already been a member of Congress for two years and was now by far the best-informed man in the hall. Of a slighter physique than Hamilton and without Hamilton's erect military bearing, he dressed habitually in black. A graduate of the College of New Jersey at Princeton, where the president "had never known him to do or say an improper thing," he was on his way to outgrowing a priggish youth. He would eventually marry Dolley Todd, who, like Angelica Church, was one of the most glamorous women of the age, an age of philosophers, in which such women paid their deepest homage to such men. Madison's skill in the thrust and parry of debate and his engaging and ingratiating manners made him Hamilton's match as a political man, but unlike Hamilton, he aroused neither hatreds nor hero worship. It was said of Madison that he united "The profound politician with the scholar." In Congress the Virginian and the New Yorker were quickly drawn to each other by an affinity of abilities, interests, and outlook. For the next five years both would work together in friendly harness for all measures that would "tend to cement the union."

Hamilton never abandoned this standard, but after those five years of fruitful collabora-

165

tion with Hamilton in its service, Madison would fall under the influence of his rising fellow Virginian, Thomas Jefferson, make an about-face, and march off with those who championed the rights of states and policies designed to uncement the union.

Of New York's five delegates—Hamilton, James Duane, William Floyd, Ezra L'Hommedieu, and John Morin Scott—all but Hamilton were holdovers from the previous session. On Hamilton's arrival, most left for home, leaving the state's delegation often short of the quorum of three that was necessary for casting the state's one vote.

Among other state delegates, for longer or shorter stays, were a few other men of conspicuous talents—Oliver Ellsworth of Connecticut, James Wilson of Pennsylvania, John Rutledge of South Carolina, and Elias Boudinot, Hamilton's old friend of Elizabethtown days, who was president of Congress during the term Hamilton was a member. Others could be described as "high in the second order of ability." Attendance on any given day was rarely more than 20 delegates, and the same few men took the major roles in debate and committee work.

Hamilton quickly became one of the leading figures, producing streams of motions and resolutions directed toward two purposes that were intertwined: sound finances and centralized national power. He was on innumerable committees, in many instances as chairman.

His quick pen was constantly drafting reports, memorials, and bills. Most members acted as if they considered themselves envoys from their own state governments, engaging in diplomatic negotiations and seeking a state and local advantage from every national measure. Hamilton and Madison were almost alone in their willingness to oppose state legislatures and governors when their policies and actions ran counter to the best interests of the country as a whole.

With each state regulating its own money, exchange rates differed much as they did between different sovereign nations. The day after Hamilton arrived in Philadelphia, according to James Madison's notes, Congress called on the states to redeem the Continental currency, which had been devalued to one-fortieth of face value, and leave it to the states to "level the money" or fix exchange rates by means of negotiations among themselves. This leveling of the money "was Mr. Hamilton's idea," because "it would multiply the advocates for federal funds for discharging the public debts, and tend to cement the union."

Writing for a congressional committee to the governor of Rhode Island, Hamilton adopted a peremptory tone strikingly different from the usual deferential tone of communications from Congress to the chief executives of states. "The unceasing discontents of the army, the loud clamours of the public creditors, and the extreme disproportion between the current supplies and the demands of the public revenues were so many invincible arguments for the fund recommended by Congress." Insisting that Congress had implied powers, he asked that congressional requisitions be considered compulsory. If Rhode Island continued to reject the impost, Hamilton foresaw "calamities of a most menacing nature." Tom Paine, often a critic, joined Hamilton in an argument directed toward Rhode Island for "a more compact union." Paine was denounced in the state along with Hamilton as a subversive agent of Congress.

The impost failed, Hamilton lost, but he gained nationwide attention by his fight for it. He also gained the favor of the merchants, the hard-money men, the creditors, and the nationalists who turned to him now as their spokesman and champion—even though one of his most telling arguments for the impost had been that it would tend to "soak the rich."

Unlike Hamilton, his brother-in-law John Barker Church had come to Philadelphia with his wife, Angelica, to look out for no one else's finances but his own. As Hamilton grew poorer, Church was growing richer. Formerly a commissary supplier for Rochambeau, he was now, in association with Jeremiah Wadsworth, a supplier of the Continental army. How he could do so well for himself by doing so poorly by the army is a question lacking a satisfactory answer. Hamilton, having left Betsy back in Albany as an economy measure, would often relax from the frustrations of Congress Hall in Angelica and John Church's elegant drawing room, frequently with Angelica's sister Peggy present as well.

Hamilton's friend James McHenry wrote:

> I must tell you something of your relations. Mr. Church is the mere man of business; and, I am informed, has riches enough to make the longest life very comfortable. Mrs. Church is a fine woman. She charms in all companies. No one has seen her, of either sex, who has not been pleased with her.
>
> [But] Peggy, though perhaps a finer woman, is not generally thought so. Her own sex are apprehensive that she considers them poor things, as Swift's Vanessa did, and they, in return, do not scruple to be displeased. In short, Peggy, to be admired as she ought, has only to please the men less and the ladies more. Tell her so.

One night the following summer, in July 1783, Peggy climbed out of an upstairs window of The Pastures and down a ladder propped against the sill just as Angelica had done, and eloped with Stephen Van Rensselaer III, the boy patroon from next door. Till now Hamilton's gallantries when in Philadelphia had been divided evenhandedly between Angelica and Peggy; from now on they focused only on Angelica—and with twice the tumid intensity.

George Washington had written Secretary of War Benjamin Lincoln that "The patience and long sufferance of his army are almost exhausted. There never was so great a spirit of discontent as at this instant." Many officers had become almost as dissatisfied as the men. In December, Washington transmitted to Congress a petition presenting the officers' minimum demands: an advance of part of the pay due, security for the rest, and commutation of the previously promised half pay for life into either a lump sum or full pay for a number of years. It was couched in "very respectful terms," but General Alexander McDougall and other high-ranking officers who brought it to Philadelphia did not agree with Washington's "respectful terms." When they met with Hamilton and other congressmen on the evening of January 13, 1783, McDougall described the officers' grievances "in very high colored expressions." The army was "verging on a state which will make a wise man mad," he cried. The fiery Colonel John Brooks threatened that "the temper of the army was such that a disappointment might throw them blindly into extremities." Hamilton was used to hearing this kind of tough talk from fellow officers in camp; it made a deeper impression on congressional civilians like Madison—potentially to useful purpose, Hamilton thought.

The committee told Hamilton that Washington was becoming too remote and distant from lower-ranking officers and the troops; he was too immersed in problems of his plantation at Mount Vernon, disheartened by the death of his cousin Jack Custis, too concerned with his position of chief executive, too preoccupied with "crownmanship" to push the army's cause with Congress as forcefully as his top circle of officers thought he should. As he settled into the role of uncrowned de facto chief executive of the Confederation, Washington's stiff inflexibility was destroying his effectiveness in his de jure role as commander in chief of the army.

No man in the country but Hamilton had ever dared provoke a breach with Washington and later returned to his good graces on his own terms. On February 13, in the firm, almost paternal tone of a fond but worried Dutch uncle, Hamilton let Washington have some hard truths:

> I will not conceal from Your Excellency a truth which it is necessary you should know. An idea is propagated in the army that delicacy carried to an extreme prevents your espousing its interests with sufficient warmth. The falsehood of this opinion no one can be better acquainted with than myself; but it is not less mischievous for being false.

Hamilton was better informed about the true state of opinion among Washington's own officers than Washington himself was: "It appears to be a prevailing opinion in the army that the disposition to recompence their services will cease with the necessity for them, and that if they once lay down their arms, they will part with the means of securing their rights." Hamilton in Philadelphia knew better than Washington at Newburgh that "It is to be lamented that appearances afford too much ground for their distrust."

What should Washington do about the situation? Money, of course, was a problem. The state "of our finances was perhaps never more critical." But Congress is a body "not governed by reason [or] foresight but by circumstances." Hamilton shrugged that "It is probable we shall not take the proper measures." Washington must face up to this ugly fact.

Washington must remember always that his first duty was to remain effective as commander in chief of the army:

> The claims of the army urged with moderation, but with firmness may operate on those weak minds which are governed by their apprehensions more than their judgments, so as to produce a concurrence in the measures which the exigencies of affairs demand. . . . So far a useful turn may be given to them. But the difficulty will be to keep a complaining and suffering army within bounds of moderation.

Washington must convince his officers he was working for them. A vigorous campaign would keep the "weak minds" of the more unstable under officers of the army with him and under his control: "This Your Excellency's influence must effect. In order to [do] it will be advisable not to discountenance their endeavours to procure redress, but rather by the intervention of confidential and prudent persons, to take direction to them."

On the other hand, Washington should remain sufficiently aloof so as to hold the confidence of both the army and the country to "enable you in case of extremity to guide the torrent, and bring order perhaps even good out of confusion."

Hamilton's "Dutch uncle" letter came to Washington as a rude awakening, and another occasion for gratitude toward Hamilton. Washington replied on March 4, admitting that he had been out of touch. "So far was I from conceiving that our finances were in so deplorable a state *at this time* that I had imbibed ideas from some source or another that, with a loan from Holland we should be able to rub along." As for the army, he wrote back on March 14, "I shall pursue the same steady line of conduct, which has governed me hitherto," but he would be more visible to his officers in urging the claims of the army: "The just claims of the army ought, and it is hoped will have their weight with every sensible legislature in the United States, if Congress point to their demands."

Washington's problems with army pay at Newburgh converged with debates in Congress on the provision of a uniform system of collecting revenue throughout the states for which Hamilton was fighting on the floor.

On January 27, 1783, James Wilson of Pennsylvania introduced a resolution calling for the establishment of general funds to be collected solely by Congress, and Hamilton leaped to his feet to speak in its favor. Wilson's bill called for a system to raise permanent revenue, universal and uniform, throughout the United States, with Congress-appointed tax collectors in charge to replace the existing system of separate funds drawn at the will of each state from whatever sources it wished through its own collectors. Wilson's method, Hamilton argued, was simple, direct, and invariable and required only a few officials, while the other was complicated, uncertain, and peculiarly vicious in that the popularly elected state collectors, men like Abraham Yates, were interested in maintaining their vote-collecting popularity by not collecting collectible revenues.

As Hamilton framed the issue, he was saying that it was the Continental one: which method would best serve the federal government in "pervading and uniting the States."

Madison, who usually agreed with Hamilton on the need for Continental measures, nevertheless thought he had been indiscreet. He wrote: "All the members of Congress who concurred, in any degree with the States in this jealously smiled at the disclosure. . . . Mr. Hamilton had let out the secret," that congressional collectors would "pervade" the states.

Beyond the walls of Congress's meeting room in the State House, the situation in the nation was swiftly changing for the worse. In Februrary, Robert Morris threatened to resign as superintendent of finance unless Congress should immediately appropriate Continental funds to pay the army. This would not only have brought down the public credit, but Morris's own private credit as well.

One of General Horatio Gates's aides, Major John Armstrong, and others including Colonel Walter Stewart, another friend of Gates, began to circulate inflammatory rumors in the Newburgh camp, known as the "Newburgh Addresses." These said "that it was universally expected the army would not disband until they had obtained justice; that the public creditors looked up to them for redress of their own grievances; would afford them every aid, and even join them in the field, if necessary." Hamilton was tarred with the charge that "some members of Congress wished the measure might take effect, in order to compel the public, particularly the delinquent states, to do justice. . . ." There was even talk of a coup d'etat to establish a monarchy and to give Washington the crown.

Washington said he viewed all such talk from Gates and his cohorts "with abhorrence" and reprehended it "with severity." He claimed that there was "something very mysterious in this business" because the reports in Philadelphia of mutiny in the army came "at a time when there was not a syllable of the kind of agitation in camp."

Washington told Hamilton that the agitation—of which, supposedly, "there was not a syllable" in camp—arose out of well-founded suspicion in camp that Congress intended using the army "as mere puppets to establish continental funds, and that rather than not succeed in this measure, or weaken their ground, they would make a sacrifice of the army and all its interests."

Hamilton knew that such a strained and artificial hypothesis could not be the proximate cause or even a significant factor in bringing on a mutiny of properly led officers. He thought Washington was merely seeking to unshoulder some of the blame for allowing the situation to arise by asserting that "the scheme was not only planned but also digested and matured in Philadelphia . . . with great art." Still claiming that no agitation existed in camp, Washington nevertheless found it necessary to issue a general order "to arrest the [mutinous] officers on the spot.'' Arrest would ''prevent the officers from being taken by surprise while the passions were all inflamed, and to rescue them from plunging themselves into a gulph of Civil Horror.''

Washington beseeched Hamilton to urge Congress to do something for the army without delay to avert a bloodbath. ''If any disastrous consequences should follow, by reason of [the delegates'] delinquency . . . they must be answerable to God and their country for the ineffable horrors which may be occasioned thereby.''

It has been charged by some that Hamilton was trying to use Gates as a threat to frighten the states into granting plenary powers to Congress and funds for the benefit of the public creditors. Others charge the opposite, namely, that he was hatching a plan for the army to overthrow Congress and set up a military monarchy with Washington as its head.

The record shows that both charges are nonsense.

Hamilton coolly replied to Washington on March 14: ''I do not wonder at the suspicions that have been infused; nor should I be surprised to hear, that I have been pointed out as one of the persons concerned in playing the game described.'' Among his colleagues in Congress ''there are dangerous prejudices in the particular states opposed to those measures which alone can give stability and prosperity to the union. There is a fatal opposition to Continental views. Necessity alone can work a reform.''

He went on:

> I have myself urged in Congress the propriety of uniting the influence of the public creditors, and the army as part of them, to prevail upon the states to enter into their views. I have expressed the same sentiments out-of-doors. Several other members of Congress have done the same.

This meant simply that

> Congress should adopt such a plan as would embrace the relief of all public creditors, including the army, in order that the personal influence of some, the connections of others, and a sense of justice to the army, as well as the apprehension of ill consequences, might form a mass of influence in each State in favor of the measures of Congress.

Hamilton was well aware of the danger of threats of force or mutiny from any direction. Any such threat would work against the army's interests in Congress: ''Any combination of FORCE would only be productive of the horrors of a civil war, might end in the ruin of the Country & would certainly end in the ruin of the army.''

Anonymous pamphlets appeared in the Newburgh encampment calling for a great meeting of all officers on March 11 to demand forceful action. They alleged that the army's deputation in Philadelphia had ''solicited in vain.'' A surly throng of disgruntled officers and men turned out in an angry mood. Alerted to the danger by Hamilton, Washington acted with unusual force. He addressed the meeting with a speech that owed much, including its moderate tone, to the letters Hamilton had written to him to dispel his delusions about the situation in Congress and his own personal standing with his officers.

Washington began with a moving plea for patience and trust in the good faith of Congress and the states. But the mutinous officers continued to mutter in sullen silence, unmoved, until Washington came to his concluding words. He said, haltingly:

> You will, by the dignity of your conduct, afford occasion for posterity to say,

when speaking of the glorious example you have exhibited to mankind, had this day been wanting, the world had never seen the last stage of perfection to which human nature is capable of attaining.

Washington paused and reached into his pocket for a letter he had brought with him from Joseph Jones, a member of Congress from Virginia, who had written of the "mountains" of prejudice (Hamilton had used the same word to Laurens) that delegates like Hamilton there had been trying to overcome in their efforts to help the army. When he looked down to try to read Jones's handwriting, Washington misread the words. He reached into his pocket again and pulled out and unfolded a new pair of spectacles. "Gentlemen," he said, fumbling with Jones's letter in one hand and his spectacles in the other, "You must pardon me. I have grown gray in your service, and now find myself growing blind."

One of the officers who was present wrote, "This little address, with the mode . . . of delivering it, drew tears from [many] of the officers."

Washington's spontaneous, humble self-reproach summoned up in the mutinous officers' memories seven years of service in the common cause and suddenly bridged the gulf that had opened up between the chief executive and his command. Recalling the ripple of quiet laughter, the tears, and the solemn hush that had fallen as Washington finished his little speech and the mass meeting dispersed in silence, Samuel Shaw remembered, "What he says of the army may with equal justice be applied to his own character. 'Had this day been wanting, the world had never seen the last stage of perfection to which human nature is capable of attaining.'"

Congress, stirred by news of the dangerous imbroglio at Newburgh, hastily adopted a resolution introduced by Hamilton that praised Washington for "his prudence and attachment to the welfare of the community" and praised the officers as well, not excluding the rebellious among them, for their patriotism. It voted to grant the officers five years' full pay in the form of interest-bearing securities.

The uprising suppressed at Newburgh blazed up among troops of "Mad Anthony" Wayne's command in central Pennsylvania.

On June 7 Washington sent Congress a letter enclosing an angry complaint from officers who were to be turned out unpaid. Then, in mid-June, sergeants in command of new recruits in a barracks in Philadelphia—on Congress's doorstep—remonstrated against accepting their discharges until they were paid. Congress took no notice of this "mutinous memorial from the sergeants," as Madison described it.

On Tuesday, June 17, 80 armed soldiers broke out of control of their officers in Lancaster and rampaged off to Philadelphia "to co-operate with those now in the city . . . to procure their pay (or perhaps to possess themselves of money at any rate)." They might "rob the bank, the treasury, & c. & c."

The Executive Council of Pennsylvania convened at the State House on June 19 and "immediately transmitted" a warning of the troop uprising to Congress, which met in a room directly across the hall. Congress named a committee—Hamilton, Oliver Ellsworth, and Richard Peters—to forfend it from a real, not a hypothetical army mutiny.

Hamilton and his committee hurried back across the hall to President John Dickinson's Executive Council. "Send out militia at once," they ordered. "Intercept the mutineers before they join forces with the rebellious sergeants in Philadelphia." The council turned down their request, unwilling to act unless the mutinous troops actually committed some outrage—on the scale of physical violence to congressmens' persons.

The mutineers reached the city Friday morning, June 20, their ranks swelled by several companies of veterans from Charleston barracks and 500 troops from the city barracks. Friday afternoon Congress adjourned for a weekend recess until Monday morning.

Hamilton, meanwhile, arranged with his friend Robert Morris, still superintendent of finance, for money to pay the unwelcome arrivals as promptly as possible, but only on condition that they turn around and march back to Lancaster to collect it there. Boudinot summoned Congress into special session for one o'clock Saturday afternoon. By the time members convened, the mutineers had posted sentinels at the State House doors, and surrounded the building with 300 or more soldiers. Armed with guns and ammunition looted from the arsenals, the rebellious and disorderly troops now menaced all councilmen and congressmen alike with fixed bayonets. Some drunkenly threatened further outrages.

President John Dickinson of the Executive Council rushed from the meeting room into Congress's chamber. He announced that the troops had demanded that the council immediately grant "authority to appoint commissioned officers to command us and redress our grievances. . . ." Otherwise, the troops "shall instantly let in those injured soldiers upon you, and abide by the consequences. You have only twenty minutes to deliberate on this important matter."

Congress ordered General St. Clair to make an attempt to regain command of his Charleston regulars, and dispatched a call to General Washington in Newburgh for a detachment of his troops to help. After sitting surrounded for nearly three hours, the members rose, put on brave faces, and walked through the cordon without being physically attacked. Though some of the mutineers were drunk and shouted imprecations, they did not break discipline, make good their loud threats to break into the State House, or attack individual congressmen.

Congress met again in the evening. The authority of the United States had been insulted, the peace of the city was endangered, and effectual countermeasures must be taken at once. Congress directed Hamilton's committee to meet with the Executive Council, and if satisfactory assurances of protection were not obtained, to decide whether Congress should flee Philadelphia and hold its next session at either Trenton or Princeton the following Thursday, June 26.

Hamilton and Ellsworth took the resolutions to Dickinson immediately, read them to him and the council, and demanded action. The militia must be called out! Congress would hold no more sessions in Philadelphia until it could be sure its members would receive protection. The Pennsylvania Executive Council continued to stall.

Furious that Dickinson hugged the sovereignty of Pennsylvania with "an unbecoming stateliness" and "overwhelming nicety" in this crisis, Hamilton insisted that the safety and dignity of the national sovereignty symbolized by Congress was paramount to any state's rights. "Reserve" on the part of a state was "uncandid" and contrary to a working federal system. He reported back that the Executive Council regretted the insult to Congress, but he scouted the sentiment because, he said, the members of the council "themselves had a principal share in it." Pennsylvania delegates in Congress rebuked Hamilton for this, offering a watered-down resolution not blaming the Executive Council, merely noting that it had shared in suffering insult from the mutineers.

The following day the mutineers were more bellicose and threatening than ever. Hamilton's committee recommended on Tuesday, June 24, that Congress meet two days later at Princeton. President Boudinot, welcoming the prestige and prosperity that having the national capital would bring to his state, immediately issued a proclamation citing the peril and officially ratifying removal.

Aroused at last by the departure of Congress and finding the soldiers still "in a very tumultous disposition,'' the Executive Council bestirred itself to adopt the strong measures Hamilton had urged on it from the outset. Hamilton's measures worked. The mutineers, learning that a detachment from Washington's northern army was marching south, deserted by two of the officers who had been their instigators, put down their arms and capitulated. The Lancaster contingent marched home. The remaining four officers of the rebels' committee were arrested. Too late to prevent discredit, the Pennsylvania authorities bowed in ''dutyfull submission to the offended Majesty of the United States.''

Abashed Philadelphia newspapers sought to minimize the danger, exculpate city and state authorities, and unshoulder blame on Congress and Hamilton as having been too alarmist. They soon began to beg Congress to return and to heap blame on Hamilton for having been so quick to order it out of the city of brotherly love, as he had once before in 1777, and none too soon.

To Hamilton, Congress's flight or its savaging by a mutinous army, with no citizens coming forward to defend the country's most important, indeed only republican institution, would have had disastrous consequences: ''I viewed the departure of Congress as a delicate measure,'' Hamilton said, with ''consequences important to the national character abroad, and critical with respect to the State of Pennsylvania, and . . . the city of Philadelphia.'' Worse still, to Hamilton, was the effect on public credit: ''the triumph of a handful of mutinous soldiers, permitted in a place which is . . . the capital of America, to . . . imprison Congress, without the least effort on the part of the citizens to uphold their . . . authority, so as to oblige them to remove . . . would . . . be viewed at a distance as a general dissatisfaction of the citizens to the Federal Government.'' Such an unedifying spectacle would ''discredit its negotiations [for peace], and affect the national interests. . . .''

Hamilton and Mercer's motion to move Congress back to Philadelphia was overwhelmingly defeated by angry resolutions of Massachusetts and South Carolina congressmen condemning Pennsylvania for failure to provide protection. Congress moved to Annapolis in November 1783, to Trenton a year later, and thence to New York City. It would not return to Philadelphia until seven years after the troop mutinies from which Hamilton had done so much to help forfend it, and then only as the end game of some still more intricate moves of Hamilton toward fulfillment of his plans for establishment of public credit.

Hamilton always tended to make use of Philadelphia in its relationship with Congress in somewhat the same way a chess master uses his rook in the procedure known as ''castling''—he sacrifices the rook's best interests to secure a better position for his king. Philadelphia seemed to retaliate against Hamilton for such treatment by eventually becoming a dangerous and unlucky city for him. It was all right for a visit, it had its uses and he would make the most of them. But as a place for a prolonged stay, it was not for him—and it was especially dangerous for him when he was there without his wife.

13

Judicial Supremacy

**It is a rule of law that where there are two laws, one not repealing the other expressly
or virtually, the judges must construe them so as to make them stand together. . . .
When two or more laws clash that which relates to the most important concerns ought
to prevail.**

—Brief No. 6. *Rutgers* v. *Waddington* (June 1784)

In his opening speech to the third session of the Fifteenth Parliament on December 5,
1782, King George III had said, "I have pointed all my views and measures, as well in
Europe as in North America, to an entire and cordial reconciliation with those colonies."
But he had conditioned final settlement with the colonies on a settlement with France.

When word of this reached North America, Hamilton had congratulated George Clinton
February 14, 1783, "on the strong prospect of peace which the speech of the British King
affords."

The provisional peace treaty had been signed on November 30, 1782. Captain Joshua
Barney arrived with the text in March 1783, Congress professed to be shocked at one of its
terms: a secret clause setting a more generous boundary for West Florida if it should fall to
Britain than if it should fall to Spain.

Some members of Congress denounced the commissioners for a breach of faith with
France and Spain; others defended them. Hamilton rose to placate passions and take a
middle position. He had opposed the congressional resolution directing the commissioners
to seek French advice before negotiating with the British from the beginning. But because
the resolution had been passed, however unwisely, Benjamin Franklin and his associates

must be censured for signing the preliminary peace articles without first having disclosed them to France. He denounced the special secret clause setting the West Florida boundary. He criticized Britain for her "watching every occasion and trying every project for dissolving the honorable ties which bind the United States to her ally, France."

But congressional criticism of the secret article should not be made public, Hamilton advised. If it were, both internal and external dissensions would follow; in fact, the commissioners should be publicly commended, but the terms of the secret clause should immediately be communicated to the French. Hamilton's moderate position carried Congress.

A British agent in New York reported to his superiors that although Americans generally acknowledged that the peace terms "were much more liberal than they had any right to expect, at the same time they rediculed [sic] that Article [V] which says that Congress should recommend to the different Assemblys the restoration of ye property of the Loyalists, well knowing that no attention would be paid to it by the Assembly's." Though Hamilton was foremost in stressing protection of loyalists' rights, he admitted that Clause V was probably a dead letter.

Articles IV, V, and VI of the Treaty of Paris provided that no legal obstacles be placed in the way of collection of prewar debts that Americans owed to British merchants and that all further confiscations of loyalist property be prohibited. In addition, Article V provided that Congress was to recommend to the states that any British or loyalist holdings that had already been confiscated should be restored to their former owners. This was only a recommendation. It remained optional for the states to observe it or not. But so strong was sentiment against restoring loyalists' property that Virginia ordered her delegates in Congress "neither to agree to any restitution of property confiscated by the State, nor submit that the laws made by any independent State of this union be subjected to the adjudication of any power or powers on earth." Virginia was insisting that her state law was superior to, and overrode, the terms of any treaty of peace. The question of whether the treaty terms were binding on the states was to remain a blight on British-American relations for many years to come, and to be partially settled only by Jay's (and Hamilton's) Treaty of 1794.

On May 14 Hamilton notified Governor Clinton: "I wish two other gentlemen of the delegation may appear as soon as possible, for it would be very injurious for me to remain much longer here. Having no future views in public life, I owe it to myself without delay to enter upon the care of my private concerns in earnest."

On July 16 James Duane finally arrived, and after bringing him up to date, Hamilton immediately set out for Albany, finished with the Continental Congress. At the time of his leaving Congress, only six of the 13 states had any delegates present at all; and of these six, not one was fully represented.

As a sort of swan song to Congress, before moving on with Betsy to the joyous new life awaiting them in liberated New York, Hamilton informally introduced his favorite resolution of all: this was the one that, after reciting all the defects of the Articles of Confederation, called upon the states to appoint delegates to a convention "with full powers to revise the Confederation, and to adopt and propose such alterations as to them shall appear necessary; to be finally approved or rejected by the States respectively."

Hamilton included among the "essential points" in which the Confederation was "defective" his demand for broader implied powers for the national government; for separation of legislative, executive, and judicial powers into three separate and distinct branches of government; for vesting the national government with the powers of general taxation, borrowing, and lending; for providing interior and exterior defense by national land and naval forces; and for vesting the United States with "a general superintendence of trade." The national government should also be vested with all powers relating to treaties and intercourse with foreign governments. He called for a convention of all the states to overhaul the Confederation to repair these defects. In his manuscript he left blanks to be filled in that would state the time, place, and dates of the great national convention that he knew, in 1783, would someday have to be called—as it finally was in 1787.

This early call of his for a constitutional convention, with its dozen "essential points" that form a sketch of a federal constitution, is endorsed by his hand on the manuscript: "Resolution intended to be submitted to Congress at Princeton in 1783; but abandoned for want of support."

News of the mutinous army and other troubles against which Hamilton had taken up civilian arms in Congress had weakened Jay's hand in concluding the final peace treaty, as Hamilton had foreseen they would. Jay wrote to Hamilton on September 28, 1783:

> American news papers for some months past contain advices which do us Harm. . . . The Complaints of the army—The Jealousies respecting Congress— the Circumstances which induced their leaving Philadelphia—and the too little appearance of a national Spirit pervading uniting and invigorating the Confederacy, are considered as omens which portend the Diminution of our Respectability, Power and Felicity.

Foolish financial policies disturbed Jay too: "Our reputation also suffers from the apparent Reluctance to [taxes] and the Ease with which we incur Debts without providing for their Payment."

Worst of all was the lack of good faith shown by the dishonorable reprisals being taken against Tories in violation of Articles IV, V, and VI of the peace treaty: "Violences and associations against the Tories pay an ill compliment to Government and impeach our good Faith in the opinions of some, and our magnanimity in the opinion of many." Not only was harsh treatment of Tories a breach of good faith and the treaty, but it also eroded America's public credit abroad:

> The Tories are almost as much pitied in these Countries, as they are execrated in our's. An undue Degree of Severity towards them would therefore be impolitic as well as unjustifiable: They who incline to involve that whole Class of Men in indiscriminate Punishment and Ruin, certainly carry the Matter too far—it would be an Instance of unnecessary Rigour and unmanly Revenge without a parallel except in the annals of religious Rage in Times of Bigotry and Blindness.

All through the war, New York City had stood as the strategic bastion from which the British held sway over the Middle Atlantic and New England states. The state had been the principal battleground of the war and had suffered the most damage from both British and Continental armies marching and countermarching and raiding and foraging and looting. Proximity to the occupying forces had helped produce more Tory sympathizers in New York than anywhere else; the same causes had produced more fervent Tory haters in New York than anywhere else.

According to the report of the British Commissary General, some 29,000 loyalist refugees sailed out of New York in 1783, more than the entire population of the city itself before 1789. This pitiful mass exodus of innocent people because of the imputed guilt of holding unpopular political opinions was a mass tragedy more typical of twentieth-century than eighteenth-century wars.

With so many loyalists fleeing populist mobs, rentals with good New York addresses were plentiful and cheap. In November 1783, Hamilton brought Elizabeth and little Philip down from Albany, rented a house at 57 Wall Street for their home and space for an office next door at 56. Loyalists with money who remained, desperately trying to salvage their property from populist persecutions and confiscation, were only too happy to become paying clients for such legal protection as a bona fide, cockade-wearing young patriot veteran like Alexander Hamilton could supply.

As he set up his new establishment on Wall Street, Hamilton received word from Congress and a friendly note from George Washington on November 6 of his promotion to colonel by brevet, after almost seven years at the rank of lieutenant colonel. This automatic promotion of one grade granted upon leaving service to officers who, like Hamilton, had been stuck in the same grade for years was in itself the least of all possible promotions. But it would serve 15 years later as the steppingstone from which he would vault over the heads of all other generals in the army to the rank of senior major general and inspector general of the army—second in rank only to George Washington himself.

The cheering throng of happy patriots who welcomed George Washington and Governor George Clinton on their triumphant entry into the city on November 25, 1783, betrayed not a single loyalist scowl.

"Straight as a ramrod and noble as he could be," appeared the Conqueror to one viewer. He rode his magnificent gray horse at the head of the triumphal procession, followed by Governor Clinton on a fine bay gelding, and Colonel Alexander Hamilton, and a retinue of aides and civil and military officials, all escorted by the smartly caparisoned Westchester Light Dragoons. Most were wearing union cockades on their left breast and a sprig of laurel on their hats. The procession drew rein under the swinging sign of Cape's Tavern, and a committee of leading citizens presented Washington with a speech of welcome, to which he replied:

> May the tranquility of your city be perpetual—may the ruins soon be repaired, commerce flourish, science be fostered, and all civil and social virtues be cherished. . . . May every species of felicity attend you, Gentlemen, and your worthy fellow citizens.

His benediction took note of the devastation left by 2,000 days of British occupation. Two great fires had leveled 800 houses. As many Tories emigrated to safer havens—Canada, Bermuda, and England—others who remained behind saw their houses sacked and persons violated by patriot mobs; some were tarred, feathered, and driven from the city to roam the countryside like homeless curs.

After nine days of tributes and eulogies from all manner of patriot and civic organizations, church congregations, and merchants' and trade associations, the time came for Washington's final farewell to the men who had been the officers of his army. On December 4, forty or so officers of the rank of lieutenant colonel and above gathered in Fraunces Tavern, corner of Broad and Pearl Streets in lower Manhattan. Not among those present was former Colonel Aaron Burr.

Washington filled his glass with wine and passed the decanter round. Each of the officers filled his own glass. A few tentatively sampled the wine, and fell silent. Washington spoke:

> With a heart full of love and gratitude, I now take leave of you. I most devoutly wish that your later days may be as prosperous and happy as your former ones have been glorious and honorable.

Nothing could be said more eloquent than the hush that fell. After a silence, Washington's words were answered by "warm expressions and fervent wishes from the gentlemen of the army whose truly pathetic feelings" it was beyond the power of one old soldier to convey.

In a spirit more like that of a communion than of an American Legion convention, the old soldiers raised their glasses and drained them to the lees. Washington's emotions had risen so high that tears began to blind his eyes. He did not fumble for his spectacles now. "I cannot come to each of you," he said in a faltering voice, "but shall feel obliged if each of you will come and take me by the hand."

Henry Knox stepped forward silently and held out his hand. Washington extended his own. But the occasion called for more than a handshake. As he looked into Knox's eyes, Washington remembered what Knox had meant to him through their seven years together—since hauling the Ticonderoga cannons over the ice to surprise the British in Boston from the heights of Dorchester. He flung his arms around his stout chief of artillery and, weeping, kissed him. Once done with Knox, the same embrace had to be done with all, starting with the grizzled von Steuben, continuing with Hamilton, and ending with the youngest of the officers. With streaming eyes, each moved up toward Washington, exchanged an affectionate hug with him, and moved on past in silence. None found it fit to utter even a word of admiration or thanks.

When the last of the sobbing officers had let go his embrace, Washington walked across the room, raised his arm in an all-inclusive, silent farewell to all, turned on his heel, and passed through the door, out of the tavern, between the open ranks of the waiting guard of honor, along the street to Whitehall, toward the waterside. Hamilton and the other officers filed out after him, remaining at a distance. At the crowded wharf was a barge made ready for instant departure for Mount Vernon. Mothers held little children up over the heads of the throng to catch a glimpse of the tall man whose firmly set mouth, taut face muscles, and iron composure betrayed no trace of the earlier tears. Without a word he boarded the barge. As the barge shoved off and moved down the harbor, Washington once again swung wide his arms from the sides of his erect, immobile frame at the stern. An all-embracing gesture of farewell, it was wide enough to have encompassed once again the ample circumambience of even General Henry Knox.

Down in the lower habor on the *Ceres,* the last of the British transports now bearing away Sir Guy Carleton and his attendants, the boatswains happily piped "All hands" aloft to make sail; below decks the crew weighed anchor. The *Ceres* caught the breeze in her topsails and rode down through the Narrows and out past Sandy Hook on the evening's ebbing tide for England and home.

Hamilton was one of 35 lawyers listed in David Frank's *New York Directory* for 1786. Among the others, who were sometimes opposing counsel in one case and on the same side with him in the next, were Robert Troup at 67 Wall Street, Brockholst Livingston at No. 12, and John Laurence at No. 15. Aaron Burr was at No. 10, Little Queen [Cedar] Street and Edward Livingston at No. 51. Richard Varick was at 46 Dock Street and Morgan Lewis at 59 Maiden Lane.

The range of their practice was as broad as the law itself. Hamilton, like his legal brethren of those days, was a specialist in all fields: he gave advice in his office, and prepared deeds, mortgages, wills, contracts, and business charters; he gave opinions on insurance coverages and title deeds to property that created or denied legal rights; he handled civil suits in trial courts and argued appeals. He appeared in the mayor's court, traveled on circuit, drew memorials to the New York legislature and to Congress, and handled business affairs for John Barker Church and other European clients.

His fees at the beginning were small, usually one pound as a retainer; five pounds a day plus expenses for trying a case on circuit, with additional contingent fees sometimes based on results obtained for his client. He rejected some cases that seemed to go against his professional principles and some fees that he thought were excessive. Relatives often figured in his practice, and so did friends—Robert Morris, John Jay, Timothy Pickering, John Holt, Benjamin Walker, Lewis Pintard, and many others. The Bank of New York, of which he was a founder, would also send along new business. Only Robert Lansing, Burr, and one or two others who had been practicing longer, had more cases. In Hamilton's frequent enforced absences, as at Philadelphia, Annapolis, and Poughkeepsie and in Congress, Hamilton's old friends, like Troup, Laurence, and Balthasar de Haert, filled in and substituted for him. He reciprocated for them in their absences.

Chancellor James Kent spoke with expert knowledge not only of the New York bar but also of all American law. Describing for young lawyers of another generation the legal personalities and character of law practice during the years after the Revolution, he wrote that the field was left to "a number of ambitious and high spirited young men" most of them fresh from service in the army. Burr was acute, terse; Brockholst Livingston, copious, fluent; Troup, sensible and thorough; Richard Harison, scholarly and lucid; Samuel Jones was a master of older precept and practice. "But among all his brethren, Colonel Hamilton was indisputably pre-eminent," promptly earning recognition for his grasp and frankness. He benefited by the "most active business" in "the claims of real property," which opened with the peace and at the same time helped inform American jurisprudence with reliable English precedents.

Kent also noted that Hamilton "never made any argument in court without displaying his habits of thinking, and resorting at once to some well-founded principle of law, drawing his deductions logically from his premises. Law was always treated by him as a science founded on established principles."

Robert Troup, Hamilton's closest lawyer friend, put his finger on the secret of Hamilton's success as a winning lawyer: his ability to expand or contract the legal frame of reference to the size that would encompass the winning argument and elevate earnest advocacy into art: "Never failing to be busied . . . in politics, he had only time to read elementary books. Hence he was well grounded in first principles," which he applied "with wonderful facility, to every question he argued."

Many thought that Hamilton's only peer among the lawyers at the postwar New York bar was Aaron Burr. Becoming a member of the New York Assembly, which sat in the city, Burr also took up a lifelong career of speculating in stocks and real estate as well. One contemporary described him as "acute, quick, terse, polished, sententious, and sometimes sarcastic in his forensic discussions." Burr loved the joy of legal combat and reveled in sly courtroom tactics, reconnaissances, strategems, ambuscades, and flanking movements. He liked to raise eyebrows and hackles by smilingly defining law as "whatever is boldly asserted and plausibly maintained." He was a Lord Chesterfield transplanted to New York, full of precise epigrams that struck to the heart of a jury—or a mistress. He carried all five feet six inches of himself erect with a thrusting stride. From under a dark head of hair, a bulging brow rose above a face that sloped down to a chin "rather retreating and voluptuous." His nose jutted strongly forward, slightly bent to his right, giving his demeanor the effect of a hawk about to pounce. His dark eyes "glow[ed] with all the ardor of venereal fire."

A distinctive specialty that set Hamilton apart from Burr and most other New York lawyers was the series of cases he was handling for former British sympathizers. Beginning in 1779 with the Confiscation Act, under which "attainted" loyalists were made to forfeit their property, the state legislature had passed a series of harsh laws aimed at Tories. Under the Trespass Act of 1783, New Yorkers who had fled their property when the British came could bring suits for damages against those who had stayed behind and occupied it. Hamilton handled at least 45 cases in all under the Trespass Act and 20 more under other antiloyalist laws.

Seriously as he opposed Tory-baiting, Hamilton saw the paradox of advocating on principle a policy from which he stood to profit. With his friend Gouverneur Morris, he joked, "legislative folly has afforded so plentiful a harvest to us lawyers that we have scarcely a moment to spare from the substantial business of reaping."

In the spring of 1784, when the Mayor's Court of New York City took up the case of *Rutgers* v. *Waddington*, today's constitutional principle that a valid treaty is the law of the land had never been heard of.

A more momentous constitutional doctrine has rarely been invented by a less momentous tribunal than Mayor James Duane's, whose jurisdiction was on the judicial ground level where magistrate's courts are found today.

Elizabeth Rutgers, a widow in her seventies, was one of thousands of patriots who had fled New York City when the army had abandoned it to the British in 1776, leaving behind her a brewery and malt house on Maiden Lane, which the British Commissary General quickly commandeered "for the use of the Army."

By the time the British Commissary General signed it over to Benjamin Waddington and Evelyn Pierrepont two years later in 1778, it was so "stripped of everything of any value" that before they could begin brewing beer again, they had to spend about £700 on extensive repairs and build a storehouse, a stable, and an enclosure for firewood. Waddington and Pierrepont occupied the brewery without paying rent to anyone until May 1, 1780, when the British commander in chief ordered them to pay rent of £150 per year to John Smythe, the British agent, who, in turn, gave the money to the vestry for the poor. On June 20, 1783, anticipating the British evacuation of New York, General Birch, the British commandant, ordered Waddington to start paying the rent to Mrs. Rutgers's son Anthony Rutgers, who was acting as her agent, retroactive to May 1, 1783. But Rutgers demanded that Waddington pay the back rent for all seven years of occupation, not just the past two months; and refused to accept the 1783 payments tendered in settlement. Waddington argued that all the improvements he had paid for were a full offset to the back rent and offered to settle with Rutgers on that basis. Rutgers refused.

On November 23, 1783, just two days before the British had evacuated the city, the fire that destroyed much of the rest of New York had reduced the brewery "to ashes," causing a loss Waddington estimated at upward of £4,000. In December, Waddington and Pierrepont handed over the storehouse and stable keys to Rutgers and sought to settle accounts with him. Rutgers again refused. In February 1784 he brought suit in the Mayor's Court of the city of New York against Waddington and Pierrepont for £8,000 of back rent under the infamous Trespass Act, which provided that a refugee from the enemy, like Mrs. Rutgers, might "bring an Action of Trespass against any Person or Persons who may have occupied, injured, or destroyed his . . . Estate . . . within the Power of the Enemy. . . ." This Waddington and Pierrepont had allegedly done. A plaintiff's success in such an action was all but guaranteed by the additional provision that the "Defendant would not be allowed to plead in Justification" any military order or command whatever, of the enemy, for such occupancy, injury, destruction, purchase, or receipt. The act also provided that a suit like Mrs. Rutgers's might be brought in "any inferior court within this state"—the Mayor's Court was such an "inferior" court—and local magistrates were most likely to be sympathetic to aggrieved patriots.

All of this was contrary to the spirit, if not the letter, of Article V of the peace treaty, which provided that Congress should "earnestly recommend" to the states that they restore the rights and possessions of loyalists who had not borne arms against their countrymen.

When the attorney general of New York State, Egbert Benson, agreed to take the aged patriot widow Rutgers's side of the case, in association with John Laurence, William Wilcox, and Hamilton's old friend Robert Troup, it took on aspects of a political morality play. When Alexander Hamilton, Brockholst Livingston, and Morgan Lewis agreed to enter the lists as defense counsel for Waddington, the case became a battle of the emerging new legal titans as well. Hamilton's co-counsel, Brockholst Livingston, would one day sit on the Supreme Court of the United States, and Morgan Lewis, having married the sister of Chancellor Robert R. Livingston, would have a notable career as a member of the State Assembly, attorney general, justice of the Supreme Court, and chief justice. By defeating Aaron Burr in the hotly contested gubernatorial election of the unhappy spring of 1804, which Burr had been favored to win, he would inflame Burr's compulsion to challenge Hamilton to the duel.

Rutgers would be the test case for the new antiloyalist laws. Recovery by hundreds of other New York patriots rode with Mrs. Rutgers and her son. For them, the able attorney general would defend a perfectly explicit state law, which had the enthusiastic approval of most citizens and politicians. Merely taking Waddington's case exposed Hamilton as his champion to social and political odium. If by any chance the verdict should go Hamilton's way, the public's sense of outrage would run deep.

Tension ran high in the city when the case came on for argument on June 29, 1784, before Mayor Duane, who presided with a sharp "surveying eye," flanked by recorder Richard Varick, and associate judges Alderman Benjamin Blagge, William W. Gilbert, William Neilson, Thomas Randall, and Thomas Ivers.

The basic facts were not in dispute; so the result would turn on the eloquence and ingenuity of the lawyers in fashioning arguments based on the applicable law alone. That was the real question—as it usually is in great cases: what was the meaning of the applicable law, and how did it fit the facts of this case?

Laurence, followed by Wilcox, opened for the plaintiff and stood on the statute, which was clear and explicit. Elizabeth Rutgers had been an inhabitant of New York City, left it when the British came, and never came back; Waddington occupied her property. She suffered loss and sustained damage. Given the facts, and the law of the Trespass Act, they argued, judgment for plaintiff Elizabeth Rutgers had to follow as the night the day.

Hamilton's defense plea was what lawyers call a demurrer, which simply admitted all the facts of the trespass, but said, in effect, that the law that applied to the facts was different from what the plaintiff claimed or had a different effect and that, accordingly, Mrs. Rutgers was not entitled to recover.

Hamilton argued that New York's Trespass Act was in violation of the law of nations and, therefore, void. New York, by its state constitution, had received and adopted the common law of England as the law of the land in New York; the common law of England included the law of nations, which, in turn, included the laws of war. According to the laws of war, the captors had the right to use real property while that property was under military control. So Waddington had thus derived the right of the captor to use Elizabeth Rutgers's brewhouse. To subject Waddington to liability to Mrs. Rutgers would violate the law of nations, the English common law, and hence the law of New York. No state legislature had the right to alter, or the power to violate, the law of nations. That power must necessarily reside only in Congress, to which each of the states had delegated the exclusive management of its foreign affairs. So, Hamilton concluded with a flourish, the state's Trespass Act, being in violation of the law of nations, was void.

Second, the states had delegated to Congress the exclusive power to conclude treaties of peace, including the treaty of peace with England, and thus Congress necessarily possessed the "implied power" to include all reasonable conditions in the treaty. Because the treaty provided that the two countries released each other from all claims for injury or damage to individuals that one or the other might have done to the other—"in consequence of or in any-wise relating to the war"—and because Waddington was a British subject and merchant, "under the protection of the Army and of the said King," this plea argued that Mrs. Rutgers's claim against Waddington had been released or abrogated by the treaty.

Besides, Hamilton went on to argue, the law of nations implies in every final treaty of peace a general amnesty for all public and private injuries arising from the war; therefore, Congress, in approving the treaty, must have consented to a general amnesty. Observance of the treaty was obligatory on the states both by virtue of Congress's implied power and by its specific resolution on the matter. Therefore, no state legislature had the power to violate the treaty and the resolution, and any state law that did so was void.

Hamilton's third argument, interweaving the first two, was that if the Trespass Act was void, either because it was a state law in violation of the law of nations or because it was a state law in violation of the treaty, a state court, even an "inferior" court like the Mayor's Court, had the power and the obligation to declare the statute void and refuse to give it effect. When laws from two different sources came into conflict, a court must apply the law that "relates to" the higher authority in derogation of the law that relates to the lesser authority.

Hamilton shrewdly coupled this lofty third argument, which rested on the broadest possible grounds, with a narrow fourth argument that was more appropriate to a trial court of first impression with no power of review. The Trespass Act simply did not apply to the facts of this case because it failed to say in so many words that it was intended to overrule the peace treaty and the law of nations.

This shrewdly showed the court a narrow way to decide the case in favor of his client without having to strike down the Trespass Act directly.

"Forget the Trespass Act!" Robert Troup brought things back down to earth with a jolt. Even if Hamilton were right, and the Trespass Act had given Mrs. Rutgers no right to recover damages, Troup argued, she should still recover from Waddington in the old common law action of trespass *quare clausum fregit*. Under the common law, a man's house is his castle; every man has the right to exclusive possession and use of his property, and every breach or entry of this enclosure, as Waddington had entered Mrs. Rutgers's, carried along with it some damage, if for nothing else than "the treading down and bruising of his herbage." Thus Mrs. Rutgers might win on either of two grounds, Troup argued—the Trespass Act or the action of common law trespass. Troup granted with a chuckle that under the common law, some trespasses were justified, such as, for example, the pursuit of "ravenous beasts of prey as badgers and foxes" onto another man's land. But unfortunately for Hamilton's client, there were no "ravenous beasts of prey" prowling around downtown on Maiden Lane that would justify Waddington's trespass.

Hamilton was now about to be laughed out of court.

To find a justification for Waddington's trespass more plausible than a "ravenous badger" in Maiden Lane, Hamilton had to dig back again into first principles. According to the law of nations, he argued, the use of abandoned property was justifiable in time of war when authorized by the military commander in charge of occupation forces. Such a justification was also a part of the law of New York, Hamilton urged, because (as he had said before) the law of nations was deemed to be a part of the common law, which had been received as New York state law by the state constitution of 1777. Since the Trespass Act of 1783 expressly prohibited pleading military orders and authorizations by way of justification, that act was in direct conflict with the law of nations as incorporated into New York law by New York's own state constitution. The state constitution being a higher authority than an ordinary law like the Trespass Act, it overrode the act, if the act purported to cut off the defense of "justifiable" trespass.

Chancellor Kent, then only a clerk in the office of Attorney General Egbert Benson, recorded that "Colonel Hamilton, by means of his fine melodious voice and dignified deportment, his reasoning powers and persuasive address, soared far above all competition. His pre-eminence was at once universally conceded."

Hamilton rested, the defense rested, the court took the case *sub judice,* and Duane and his fellow judges pondered their verdict for more than two months.

While the public and the bar waited anxiously and the judges wrestled with their doubts, other war cases were held up because all recognized that *Rutgers* v. *Waddington* was the great test case, with international repercussions. There were indications that the British would not relinquish their Western posts at Niagara, at Oswego, on the St. Lawrence, Lake Champlain, and elsewhere in other Western territories until persecutions of loyalists in violation of Articles IV, V, and VI of the treaty were stopped. Upstate Populist patriots split with downstate merchants, businessmen, and small holders who sympathized with the loyalists. They feared that British reprisals against trade would be costly to them. For Hamilton, the case was a forge on which he hammered out and refined many of the important ideas on constitutional national government for which he would fight the rest of his life—and for which he would always be charged with "monarchical" and pro-British leanings.

On Friday, August 27, 1784, Duane delivered the opinion of the court, which he appeared to have written largely himself. He acknowledged the case to be one "of high importance; from the value of the property; from involving in it questions, which must affect the national character:—questions whose decision will record the spirit of our courts to posterity! Questions which embrace the whole law of nations!"

He saw humor in the fact that a lowly magistrate's court like his should decide a case of such lofty moment.

He drily complimented all the attorneys for filling in the judges on the "great and intricate question," noting that the "arguments on both sides were elaborate, and the authorities numerous."

As to the period between 1778 and 1780, when Waddington had paid no rent to anyone, while the brewery had been commandeered by the British commissary general, purportedly "for the use of the Army," Waddington owed rent to Mrs. Rutgers because the Commissary General was really a civilian official, not directly under orders of the British military occupation forces. But as to the period from May 1, 1780, through March 1783, Hamilton's plea was "good and sufficient in the law" because during this period, when Waddington had paid rent to the British agent, John Smythe, for the vestry poor box, he had no liability to pay a second time to Mrs. Rutgers. The treaty would protect Waddington because he had been under direct authority from the British commander in chief. An order from a civilian official would be invalid in any event; so the question of whether the Trespass Act forbade pleading it was not reached; on the other hand, an order from the commander in chief was valid under the law of nations; so the Trespass Act did not apply to it, either, Duane reasoned.

Beneath such metaphysical hairsplitting, Duane's actual decision of the rent dispute represented an equitable result that simply excused Waddington from having to pay the same rent twice. On balance, Hamilton's client had won, but the result and Duane's reasoning were sufficiently murky for all sides to take some satisfaction from it.

What did the decision really mean? It straddled Mrs. Rutgers's argument that the authority of the state legislature was supreme; it also straddled Hamilton's argument that the law of nations and the treaty were supreme and that the state legislature was not. It was almost studiously ambiguous, complex, and scholarly. It entirely pleased neither plaintiff nor defendant, patriot nor loyalist. It hinted at things more far-reaching than anything it actually decided.

On the separate question of damages, the jury of twelve citizens awarded a verdict of £791 13s. 4d. damages and sixpence costs to Mrs. Rutgers, and this amount was adopted as the judgment of the court. It fell far short of the £8,000 she had sued for; so she appealed to the state supreme court. But in July 1785, while her appeal was still pending, "a voluntary compromise between the parties took place, which superseded its prosecution to a final decision." Waddington paid something additional to her, but it is likely that his final payment was much nearer the £791 verdict than the £8,000 she had sued for. Hamilton's fee for defending the case and securing the settlement? £9 11s. 3d. It seems absurdly small, even for those days.

The assembly attacked the decision as "subversive of all law and good order." If a court could "dispense with, and act in direct violation of a plain and known law of the state," it would "end all our dear bought rights and privileges, and legislatures become useless." A committee published an open letter charging that "the mayor's court have assumed and exercised the power to set aside an act of the state" and attacked the decision as "an assumption of power in that court, which is inconsistent with the nature and genius of our government, and threatening to the liberties of the people."

A motion to impeach Duane called for his ouster and for a new mayor and recorder who "will govern themselves by the known laws of the land." It lost 31 to 9.

For the next decade and beyond, echoes of *Rutgers* v. *Waddington* would reverberate and rumble through much American foreign and domestic policy.

In 1787 Hamilton successfully argued in New York for repeal of the Trespass Act,

Citation Act, and Confiscation Act on the same grounds he had first urged in *Rutgers* v. *Waddington*. Hamilton's *Federalist Papers* of 1788, particularly number 78, amplified and refined the policy and theory of judicial supremacy that he had introduced in his argument to the Mayor's Court.

In 1792, when the British minister, George Hammond, claimed that the decision tended to repudiate the peace treaty, Secretary of State Thomas Jefferson, a lawyer himself, asked Hamilton to write to him and explain what the case really meant.

Hamilton's summary, written May 5, 1792, explained that the force of the treaty to overrule the provision of the Trespass Act against pleading a military order "was admitted by the decision, which allowed in fact the validity of such an order, when proceeding from the Commander in Chief." On the basis of Hamilton's opinion, Jefferson rebutted Hammond's claim, pointing out that this was "an unequivocal decision of the superior authority of the Treaty over the law." In fact, although Duane's reasoning had left the whole question hanging in midair, Hamilton's analysis as quoted above is correct whereas Jefferson's encapsulation is an overstatement.

So, from this rent case in a New York City magistrate's court, for a fee of £9 11s. 3d., through force of argument for an unpopular client's unpopular cause, Hamilton sent on its way to his great disciple John Marshall, wearing the robes of chief justice of the Supreme Court of the United States, writing in *Marbury* v. *Madison,* a unique precedent for doctrines that remain a central bulwark of freedom under law in the American constitutional system today.

In the aftermath of Jay's Treaty and with the passage of time, the persecution of loyalists died down, the British evacuated the Western posts, the facts of the case were forgotten, and the immediate passions that gave rise to *Rutgers* v. *Waddington* subsided. All that remained was the imprint of the case preserved in the United States Constitution as the law of the land: the supremacy of treaties over local law; the supremacy of national laws in their sphere over state law; and the power of courts to review acts of Congress and legislatures, test them against the law of the Constitution or other higher law, and decide which law prevails.

Now when swiftly shifting tides of mass popular opinion push Congress, legislatures, and executives into ill-considered but popular measures that threaten the liberties of a minority, or an unpopular individual, the doctrine of judicial review and judicial supremacy have time and again made it possible for the courts to serve as the last bastion of individual liberties. As Hamilton had insisted on behalf of his unpopular client, a citizen is truly free only in a country whose courts are free, if they choose, to find at his behest that a popular law is unconstitutional and set it aside because his unpopular view is right.

Writing to his friend Gouverneur Morris in the spring of 1784, Hamilton railed against the "Discrimination bills, partial taxes, schemes to engross public property in the hands of those who have present power, to banish the real wealth of the State, and to substitute paper bubbles . . ." Hamilton's nonchalant friend Gouverneur often rallied him for his impatience. So Hamilton abruptly switched his tone to one of Olympian resignation, an uncharacteristic mode that he knew would amuse his friend:

"Let us . . . erect a temple to time only regretting that we shall not command a longer portion of it to see what will be the event of the American drama."

In the temple of time his rent case would have more influence on "the event of the American drama" than any other tithe he would bring to it.

14

Annapolis Apostrophe: the Exigencies of the Union

The power of regulating trade is of such comprehensive extent . . . that to give it efficacy . . . may require correspondent adjustment of other parts of the Federal system . . . [by] commissioners, to meet at Philadelphia on the second Monday in May . . . to devise such further provisions as shall appear to them necessary to render the constitution of the Federal Government adequate to the exigencies of the "Union."

—Address of the Annapolis Convention, September 14, 1786

When he left Princeton, Hamilton had abandoned his constitutional resolution "for want of support in Congress." But returning to private life he continued to seek support for his platform, plank by plank. His stand for judicial supremacy and the sanctity of foreign treaties in *Rutgers* v. *Waddington* had been one such plank.

Another gaping hole in the Articles of Confederation to which Hamilton had pointed was the fourth clause of the sixth article, which seemed to mean that in time of peace, land and sea defense was each state's own responsibility. It "would preclude the United States from raising a single regiment or building a single ship, before a declaration of war, or an actual commencement of hostilities." Lack of effective powers of regulation of trade, taxation, and tax collection left the Confederation without resources to prevent "whole states and large parts of others" from being "overrun and ravaged by small bodies of the enemies' forces." Yet states were destitute of means to pay the army. As a result, troops had been rendered ineffective for military operations and "exposed to sufferings, which nothing but unparalleled practice, perseverance and patriotism could have endured."

While Hamilton was desperately trying to rally the states to find money to pay the

186

soldiers, Washington, meeting with the officers at Newburgh and seeking to regain a measure of their confidence, had appointed a committee, headed by General Henry Knox, to draw up a resolution to assure Congress of the "good sense and steady patriotism of the gentlemen of the army."

General Knox's committee reported that the citizens "who have had so conspicuous an agency in the American Revolution as those who composed the Society of the Cincinnati, should pledge themselves, in a voluntary association, to support by all means consistent with the laws, that noble fabric of united independence, which at so much hazard, and with so many sacrifices they have contributed to erect." He proposed "a society to be formed by the American officers" before they separated from the service, "To promote and cherish between the respective states that union and national honor so essentially necessary, to their happiness and the future dignity of the American empire." The society's original constitution, rather hastily thrown together at the encampment, provided that the members would be "a society of friends, to endure as long as they shall endure, or any of their eldest male posterity, and in failure thereof, the collateral branches, who may be judged worthy of becoming its supporters and members."

The Society of the Cincinnati immediately drew fire from civilians who had not served in the war. Thomas Jefferson, whose disgraceful war record as governor was the tragic embarassment of a distinguished career, talked earnestly with Washington about the problem long into the night. Jefferson fretted that the society was contrary to the spirit of American political institutions and "the natural equality of man." He agonized about the Cincinnati with an "anguish of mind" he said he had never felt before. He prayed that Washington would avoid compromising himself by refusing membership. The rights of man simply did not include the right to join such a veterans' organization.

John Adams, whose war record as a civilian contained a less tragic, more comical episode of flight (from Philadelphia) than Jefferson's, privately condemned the society and Washington's part in it. So did the popular satirist Hugh H. Brackenridge. So did the egalitarian pamphleteer Mirabeau.

Washington, who had, after all, been instrumental in creating the society and had seen its camaraderie help dispel mutinous talk at Newburgh in 1783, was rather annoyed by all the fuss and silly charges like Jefferson's and Adams's when he wrote to Hamilton on December 1, 1785.

"The Jealousies of, and prejudices against this Society were carried to an unwarrantable length . . .," he fumed. "It is a matter of little moment whether the alarm which seized the public mind was the result of foresight—envy & jealousy—or a disordered imagination; . . . I should, on that occasion, as far as my voice would have gone have endeavoured to convince the narrow minded part of our Country men that the Amor Patrie[ae] was much stronger in our breasts than theirs. . . ."

At the society's first general meeting, 15 amendments were offered to the original charter, including one urged by Washington, Hamilton, and others, abolishing the hereditary membership feature. The constitution of the general society thus altered and amended was then circulated to the state organizations for action.

In the same letter to Hamilton in which Washington fumed at Jefferson's insinuations against the Cincinnati, he agreed to help with the latest of Hamilton's many pleas and do a little lobbying in Congress to get something more for poor old Baron von Steuben. It would not do for the presiding general of the New York Society to go on living forever on handouts from junior officers like Hamilton—as he now was doing.

New York's leading "Knight of the Cincinnati," as Angelica Church liked to call Baron von Steuben, had become a more or less permanent member of the Alexander Hamilton household at 57 Wall Street. Although the Baron was 27 years older than Hamilton and had been a major general in the war when Hamilton was only a lieutenant colonel, peace brought a reversal of roles. The young protégé became guardian, protector, counselor, conservator, and host to the old general, who, once out of uniform, seemed as helpless as a child. Like the Hamiltons, Angelica welcomed von Steuben into the charmed circle of her affection. She wrote to her sister Betsy from London: "I envy you the trio of agreeable men you talk of, my father and my baron and your Hamilton, what pleasant evenings, what agreeable chit-chat, whilst my vivacity must be confined to dull, gloomy Englishmen."

A jovial, permanent houseguest, a Falstaffian resident jester and butt, von Steuben's extravagant ways kept him—and Hamilton—embarrassed for money. Hamilton would lend him large sums which Hamilton sorely needed on promissory notes, which he never repaid.

When the house they were living in was offered him to buy for £2,100, in 1785, and Hamilton did not have the money to pay for it, he instructed Betsy, whose acumen he trusted, to bargain for him while he was out of town: "If you cannot do better you may engage that the whole be paid in three months; but I could wish to pay half in a short time and the other half in a year. Adieu my angel."

Alexander's and Betsy's second child, born on September 25, 1784, was a girl, whom they named Angelica in honor of her glamorous aunt. As six more children followed at fairly regular intervals—Alexander, May 16, 1786; James Alexander, April 14, 1788; John Church, August 22, 1792; William Stephen, August 4, 1797; and Eliza, November 20, 1799, the Hamiltons' household budget stretched ever tighter. On June 2, 1802, there would be a second Philip, named after the firstborn Philip, who had been tragically killed in a duel at 19, six months before the birth of his replacement.

To his wife, Betsy, and the children as they came along, Hamilton was a tender, affectionate, loving husband and father. He gave them as much of his time, warmth, and charm as could be spared by any practicing lawyer at the beck and call of many clients. When the children were growing up, he would spend an hour or two with them in the nursery, romping with the youngest, or take a ramble in the woods with the older boys. Standing beside slim, sensitive, dark-eyed little Angelica as she accompanied him on the pianoforte that her Aunt Angelica had sent to her all the way from London, Hamilton would often sing to them old songs like "The Drum" from wartime days when he had been courting their mother.

The Hamilton family's tight household budget was stretched still tighter by generous responses to all sorts of outside appeals. In 1785 Hamilton answered a demand from his brother, James Hamilton, by agreeing to "cheerfully pay your draft upon me for fifty pounds sterling" but he was sorry he could not afford to send him more at the moment. Brother James, like their father, remained in the Antilles, shiftless and poor. Hamilton asked him:

> What has become of our dear father? It is an age since I have heard from him, or of him, though I have written him several letters. My heart bleeds at the recollection of his misfortunes. Sometimes I flatter myself his brothers have extended their support to him, and that he is now enjoying tranquillity and ease; at other times, I fear he is suffering. . . .

Both brother and father kept in touch with Hamilton by repeatedly begging him for money, which they never repaid. He never seemed to mind and helped them out with what he had as best he could. Hamilton wrote his brother that if he came to the United States, he would settle him on a farm. He invited his father to come and make his home with von Steuben and all the rest of them on Wall Street. But his brother died the following year, his father never traveled out of the islands, and he never saw either of them again.

From time to time Hamilton also sent small sums of money to his cousin Ann Lytton Venton Mitchell, who had also fallen upon hard times. At about the time he had left St. Croix, Hamilton had receipted for advances to Ann by James Lytton's executors, which indicate that she had endorsed them to him to help him out with money for his passage and earliest days in America. Concerned that he had never done all he should have for her, he made further provision for her in his will. When his half brother, Peter Lavien, died in 1782, Hamilton heard that he had been given a small legacy, but there is no evidence that he received anything from his half brother's estate.

Still another who joined the Hamilton household was the daughter of Colonel Edward Antil, of the army's Canadian Corps, who had retired penniless from the service, lost his wife, solicited aid from the Society of the Cincinnati, "and there sank under the weight of his sorrows" and died, according to a thumbnail sketch of him by Hamilton's son John Church.

Amid the laughter and scurry and bustle of all the accessions to his household and the pressures of his practice, Hamilton seemed to grow ever more lonely. While her namesake Angelica was growing up to be the closest and dearest to him of all his children, thoughts of the exquisite original Angelica were never further from the front of Hamilton's mind than thoughts of him seemed to be from hers.

John and Angelica Church had made a short visit to America in June 1785 and then returned to England. By August 3 she and Hamilton had already exchanged a number of letters, none of which has been found. On that day he sat down and wrote her yet another, which has. In it, his feelings of love and longing for her come through not less memorably for being understated, yet he never slips over the indistinct line that would mark the margin of verbal impropriety:

> You have been much better to me My Dear friend since you left America, than I have deserved, for you have written to me oftener than I have written to you. . . . I am sure you will attribute it to anything else rather than a defect of pleasure in writing to you.
> Now my Dear Sister You have I fear taken a final leave of America and of those that love you here. I saw you depart from Philadelphia with peculiar uneasiness, as if foreboding you were not to return. My apprehensions are confirmed and unless I see you in Europe I expect not to see you again.

Not to see her again—

> This is the impression we all have; judge the bitterness it gives to those who love you with the love of nature and to me who feel an attachment for you not less lively.

Hamilton's love for her is not the "love of nature"; it is a deeper, more exotic, unnatural passion "not less lively."

> I confess for my own part I see one great source of happiness snatched away . . . an ocean is now to separate us.
> You will not indeed want friends wherever you are—You will have no need of

them [besides] You have both too many qualities to engage friendship. But go where you will you will find no such friends as those you have left behind.

His love for her is different from Betsy's, which is only that of a sister:

Your Good and affectionate sister Betsy feels more than I can say on this subject. She sends you all a sisters love: I remain as ever Your Affectionate friend & Brother.

When they could afford it, the Hamiltons kept a hired servant girl or two around the house—one was named Gussie—to help Betsy cope as best she could with all she had to do. Her father may have given or loaned her an indentured servant or slave.

Slavery was still legal in New York and closely regulated by law, but only the wealthier families could afford to maintain slaves. Less affluent families preferred to hire and pay indentured servants for service as needed. On February 4, 1785, Hamilton was one of the 32 organizers of the Society for Manumission of Slaves. John Jay, its first president, appointed Hamilton chairman of a committee to devise ways and means to free the slaves by way of practicing what the society preached. Hamilton forthwith proposed a resolution that the members of the society begin by freeing their own slaves. The resolution was quashed.

He remained an active member and counsellor of the Society for the Manumission of Slaves until his death. On March 13, 1786, Hamilton and others signed a petition to the New York legislature urging the end of the slave trade as "a commerce repugnant to humanity, and inconsistent with the liberality and justice which should distinguish a free and enlightened people."

In Philadelphia, where Hamilton's old friend Gouverneur Morris had just returned, the Pennsylvania Assembly's response to news that the definitive treaty of peace with England had finally been ratified on January 14, 1784, was a call for a "public demonstration of joy."

The fireworks for peace had touched off a new excitation: "The present influence is the Bank-o-mania," said Morris. He was referring to newspaper announcements of the formation of a new bank, the Bank of Pennsylvania "or, as some call it, the Coalition Bank."

The reason for the "bankomania" was that the Bank of North America, the first and at the time only bank in Philadelphia, had been making so much money that the coalition bank—backed by men whom Morris described as extremist scoundrels of both factions—had been seized with the urge to share the wealth by going into competition with the Bank of North America. Hamilton's brother-in-law John Barker Church was a significant shareholder in the older bank too. The new one could be a serious threat to its profitable monopoly, even to its solvency. This was a simple, obvious point to a businessman like Church, but one that Hamilton at first missed completely: he saw no harm in a second bank. Replying to Morris on February 21, 1784, he disagreed with him about the threat: "A new bank in Philadelphia does not appear an evil to the community. . . . Competition will cause business to be done on easier and better terms in each to the advancement of trade in general. . . ."

As a disinterested citizen loftily considering the marketplace as a whole, Hamilton was happy to permit Adam Smith's "invisible hand" in the form of competition to cut into the Bank of North America's profitable monopoly, all for the general good. Not Morris and Church.

Neither New York nor Boston yet had a bank, and now that the Bank of North America was to have competition in its hometown, Church saw that New York offered a better prospect for a new and more profitable money monopoly. Hamilton could hardly fail to agree that New York was a better place for his brother-in-law's investments, his own law practice—and his sister-in-law Angelica as well.

Church cared not at all from which country he made his money, and everything he touched seemed to turn to gold. Now that the war was over, Church's cold eye turned more and more to America as a profitable field of operations. The prospect of owning a specie bank in prosperous New York had great appeal.

From Paris, on February 7, he wrote Hamilton about the idea and his own plans for the future: "We are taken [*sic*] measures to vest our Property in America by exporting from here and England a large quantity of ready money Articles and I hope we shall be at New York June or July." The New York bank would be controlled by Church and his business partner, Jeremiah Wadsworth.

Such a bank as Church—and Hamilton—envisaged would be one based on "established principles." That is, it would be a bank that would do business with merchants and substantial businessmen, with a capital made up of money, bonds, and commercial paper, not mortgages or other interests in land. Its initial capital would be $500,000 in specie— gold or silver—a thousand shares of $500 each. It would receive all payments in gold or silver coin on bank notes only and must never engage in trade.

The problem in New York was that Chancellor Robert R. Livingston, a large upstate landowner, had just petitioned the legislature to grant a charter for another public bank based on wholly different principles. A land bank, it would accept mortgages on land as collateral for subscriptions to its stock, and would deal largely with loans based on land as security instead of bills of lading and commercial paper and promissory notes. Its clientele would, therefore, be drawn more from the agrarian and debtor classes.

In Hamilton's view, Livingston's land bank would interfere with his and Church's specie bank, as well as "the commercial interests of the State"; so Hamilton started up "an opposition to this scheme." He urged the land bank's "absurdity and inconvenience" on the merchants, who presently began to take measures to defeat the Livingston land bank plan. This marked the beginning of the Hamilton-Livingston rivalry that would soon raise up a host of political troubles for Hamilton and Schuyler in New York State politics.

Still another group of New York merchants had the same idea as Church and Hamilton for a New York money bank. On February 23, 1784, the following announcement appeared in *The New York Packet* and *The American Advertiser*: "BANK. It appearing to be the disposition of the Gentlemen in this City, to establish a BANK on liberal principles, the stock to consist of specie only; they are therefore hereby invited to meet To-Morrow evening at Six O'Clock at the merchants' Coffee House; where a plan will be submitted to their consideration." Hamilton's old friend General Alexander McDougall was named chairman, plans for the bank were approved, and Hamilton was named a director. As counsel, he drew up a constitution and an outline for the bank's charter, which was adopted at the organizational meeting on March 15, 1784. It became New York's first bank, The Bank of New York.

Hamilton managed to persuade the other subscribers to amend the charter to give Church and Wadsworth a share interest as well as seats on the board of directors. Hamilton then introduced and sought to push the constitution and application for a charter through the legislature. Although he remained a director of the Bank of New York until 1788, Hamilton himself owned only a single qualifying share.

Hamilton's petition to the legislature for The Bank of New York's charter in the autumn of 1784 leaned against the same strong populist hostility toward all banks that had prevailed in Pennsylvania. He argued that the usefulness of banks in commercial countries had long been demonstrated; in Europe they were "regarded as one of the surest foundations of public and private Credit," which "forms a presumption in their favour, not easily to be outweighed by arguments that rest on speculation and Theory."

Hamilton went on to enumerate the benefits of such a bank. He saw a public bank not as Church did—merely another profitmaking business—but as an institution that would advance the progress of state and nation.

Returning prosperity, the usefulness of the bank, not to mention the elevation of Hamilton to secretary of the treasury, would all help beat down opposition. Hamilton's bank bill finally passed on March 21, 1791, a final victory for Hamilton, but scored only after six long years of defeats.

Hamilton knew much about the theory and principle of banking, but little about how banks carried on day-to-day business in practice, so in 1784 he dispatched Cashier William Seton of The Bank of New York to Philadelphia "to procure materials and information in the forms of business," from The Bank of North America. He inquired of Gouverneur Morris for "the best mode of receiving and paying out gold."

Hamilton admitted he could think of no substitute for gold in "a coinage"—coins that would be worth their weight in gold or silver, so that if melted down, their intrinsic value in metal would be equivalent to the denomination stamped on their faces. Nongold-backed paper currencies increasingly deteriorate in value from lack of credibility, so Hamilton's inability to think of a substitute for a specie-backed currency has contemporary resonance. Gouverneur Morris had the last word on the elusive subject of gold when he replied jokingly to Hamilton's request on June 30, "I meant to have written fully on the Subject of Gold. . . . I would say a great Deal on this subject but it would be very useless."

The Bank of North America turned away Seton and his troublesome questions without answers. The coalition bank was threatening to break its monopoly, and there were other troubles besides. In the emergency, Gouverneur Morris suggested making The Bank of New York a branch of The Bank of North America, possibly to help bail out the latter. Finally, The Bank of North America adopted a suggestion of Hamilton's that would draw the coalition men back into the fold and restore the banking monopoly that had prevailed in the good old days before competition: Writing to his bachelor friend Morris of The Bank of North America's proposal to absorb the coalition bank, Hamilton preferred an intrigue to a marriage:

> Let the [new bank] be the wife or, still to pursue your propensity, the mistress of the former. As a mistress (or you'll say a wife) it is to be expected she will every now and then be capricious and inconstant; but in the main it will [be to] the interest of both husband and wife that they should live well together and manage their affairs with good humour and concert.

To Hamilton, the success of the public banks meant more than simply service to an important client or a lawyer's sideline or attention to another moneymaking scheme of his client Church. He saw a central bank as central to the social, political, and economic well-being of the United States he was working to consolidate. State legislative hostility to public banks and trade unions were symptoms of deeper public malaise that gripped all the states from New Hampshire to Georgia. Foreign trade was at a standstill, so was agriculture.

Farmers could not pay their debts to city merchants and bankers, interest on public loans was in default, hard money was almost wholly out of circulation, and each state was printing paper money as "legal tender" as fast as presses could run it off. "Stay" laws were passed, declaring a moratorium on the collection of debts. James Madison pointed out to Thomas Jefferson "the present anarchy of our commerces"; he thought "most of our political evils may be traced up to our commercial ones. . . ." States without good harbors "were subject to be taxed by their neighbors, thro' whose parts, their commerce was carried on." New Jersey, lying between Philadelphia and New York, was like a cask tapped at both ends; and North Carolina, between Virginia and South Carolina, was like a patient bleeding at both arms. New York required that every wood boat and shallop from New Jersey of more than 12 tons be regularly entered and cleared out at the custom house, in the same manner as if it had arrived from any foreign port. This ate into the already small profits of Jersey boatmen; so Jersey retaliated by laying a stiff tax of £30 per month on the Sandy Hook Lighthouse and the plot around it, which belonged to the corporation of New York City. Connecticut laid heavier duties on imports from Massachusetts than those from Great Britain.

Like his friend Hamilton in New York, Madison in Virginia had been pressing for a national solution, but in the summer of 1784 a resolution for a constitutional convention was defeated in the Virginia legislature. On Christmas Day of that year, Madison told Richard Henry Lee that union was necessary to escape foreign danger and internal dissension, and he drafted some resolutions dealing with interstate navigation and state jurisdiction over the Potomac basin. Maryland and Virginia commissioners were soon joined by others from Pennsylvania and Delaware in a plan to smooth the commercial relations of all four states.

Since 1781, as in his 1783 resolutions calling for a constitutional convention, Hamilton had been demanding that Congress be given power to regulate trade by imposing duties, granting bounties, and laying embargoes. Finally in 1784, Congress had formally asked the states to invest it with some narrow control over commerce by permitting it to lay prohibitions upon the entry of ships and goods from countries that did not have commercial treaties with the United States. Eventually, 11 states agreed to this delegation, but New York and Rhode Island stood on the Articles of Confederation. The rule requiring unanimous consent left all as badly off as if none had approved. By 1786 even Rhode Island had approved, leaving Hamilton's New York as the only state that had refused to approve the impost.

Governor Clinton and his party were well pleased that the only visible symbol of a national government was the impotent Congress they scornfully called "King Cong." The debt-ridden rural and frontier districts that provided the backbone of Clinton's support saw in a stronger national government more hegemony of the mercantile classes, to whom they were already in debt, heavy taxes, strict enforcement of the repayment of debts, abolition of easy paper money, and an effective ban on confiscations of Tory property. They controlled the state assembly.

The same factors made the merchants and bankers of the seaboard and the landowners of the interior support strengthening the national government. They controlled the state senate—voting for which depended on a heavy property qualification. The result was a deadlock, no action on the impost, and the same practical effect as if the other 12 states had not acted at all. Here was an issue now brought into sharp focus: more votes in the New York State Assembly by Hamilton's nationalists could break the deadlock.

Let the merchants, bankers, and similar "Gentlemen of property" in the city combine and elect Robert Troup, William Duer, and Colonel William Malcolm, all loyal followers of Hamilton, to the assembly. The plan worked, and the three won election. Hamilton remained busy offstage with law practice and master strategy.

Thus, when on March 16, 1786, Governor Clinton submitted to the legislature a letter from the governor of Virginia enclosing a resolution appointing commissioners to meet with the commissioners of other states "for the purpose of framing such regulations of trade as may be necessary to promote the general interest," Hamilton had the necessary votes to make an affirmative response in the assembly. Hamilton's men proposed that recalcitrant New York send commissioners to attend and carried the assembly with them. Their attendance was subject to the express reservation that the convention be limited to commercial objects only and that the commissioners take no final action there but merely report back to the legislature. Hamilton's nationalists then managed, with an assist from Schuyler in the senate, to name all of the commissioners, including Robert Cambridge Livingston, the fourth son of the third lord of Livingston manor, James Duane, Egbert Benson, and, of course, Hamilton himself.

This limited success of Hamilton's men in the legislature was overshadowed by still another defeat for the impost. There was one last step Hamilton could take: stand for election to the assembly himself. His oratorical powers and quickness in debate might be just enough to tip the balance against the wily old governor. After a hard fight, on the list of nine elected, Hamilton received only the fourth highest number of votes. Even with the support stirred up by his election, Hamilton lost the fight to force Clinton to call a special session of the legislature to reconsider the impost.

On September 1, 1786, Hamilton broke an engagement with Richard Varick because "Mrs. Hamilton insists on my dining with her today as this is the day of departure and you (who are not a prophane bachelor like Benson) will know that in such a case implicit obedience on my part is proper."

The same day, from Newark, to his "prophane bachelor" friend Egbert Benson, Hamilton wrote that in "obedience to the appointment of the legislature respecting the proposed commercial arrangements, . . . [we] set out this afternoon on a journey to Annapolis." Their journey to Annapolis for insignificant-sounding talks on trade would lead straight on to the Constitutional Convention of 1787, *The Federalist Papers,* and Hamilton's triumphant return to New York as its greatest hero. It did not seem important enough for the other commissioners appointed by New York to take the trouble to make the trip.

Four states, including Maryland, had not even troubled to appoint commissioners. The dozen who finally appeared represented only five states—New York, New Jersey, Pennsylvania, Delaware, and Virginia. They seemed all but lost in the old senate chamber of the Annapolis State House. Few citizens took notice of the meeting, and there was nothing about it in the press except that on September 14, the last day, as the commissioners adjourned for home, the *Maryland Gazette* reported, "Several Gentlemen, members of the proposed commercial convention, are arrived in this city."

Proponents of state sovereignty criticized the men who had initiated the call. Hamilton and Duane of New York, Robert Morris of Pennsylvania, and Madison of Virginia were men who, they believed, had purposes in mind that ranged far beyond a mere conference on trade.

Hamilton pointed out to his fellow delegates that the commissioners appointed by New Hampshire, Massachusetts, Rhode Island, and North Carolina had not even bothered to show up, and that Connecticut, Maryland, South Carolina, and Georgia had not even appointed any. Yet the appointments of the commissioners present had been conditioned by their states on meeting with counterparts from all the others, not just the handful present. So without a quorum, the obvious thing to do was pack up, check out, and go home. Hamilton seized the moment. Because for lack of a quorum they could not do the obvious job of talking about trade that they had been sent to do, why not take on a less obvious job? Men like Stephen Higginson and James Monroe had charged them with secretly harboring larger designs. They already bore the onus, so why not earn it? Why not report back to their respective states that, it being impossible to proceed without better attendance, they had been obliged to issue a call for all the states to meet in another convention?

Hamilton dusted off his congressional resolutions of 1783 and produced a new draft of a call for a convention. Vigorous, forthright, broad, and sweeping, it provided "That . . . the Matters, intended for the consideration of this Convention, would essentially affect the whole System of Federal Government, and the exigencies of the United States," including "all such measures as may appear necessary to cement the Union of the States, and promote the permanent Tranquility, Security, and Happiness."

Governor Edmund Randolph of Virginia and other delegates protested against words like "cement the union," arguing that New York, Pennsylvania, and Virginia had given only narrow authority to their commissioners "to take into consideration the trade and Commerce of the United States, and to report to the several states" and nothing more.

Hamilton, a lifelong diviner of implied powers, scanned the wording of each state's authorizations carefully. He retorted triumphantly that, unlike the three states Randolph had cited, New Jersey had enlarged the authority of her commissioners, empowering them to consider *"other important matters as well."* Another memorable phrase in New Jersey's resolution authorized her commissioners to report out an act that "would enable the United States in Congress assembled, to provide for *the exigencies of the Union.*"

Randolph insisted that New Jersey was only a minority of one. Hamilton replied coolly that its wording had merit and that, as a matter of fact, the same words could even be read into the authorizations given by the other three states. Their delegates had similar "implied powers." He argued that commerce and trade and economic matters in general undergirded all parts of the federal system, including the political superstructure: "The Idea of extending the powers . . . to other objects than those of Commerce, adopted by New Jersey, was an improvement on the original plan, and will deserve to be incorporated into that of a future convention." An economic foundation underlay all political and social measures: "The power of regulating trade is of such comprehensive extent," he said, "and will enter so far into the general system of the Federal government, that to give it efficacy, and to obviate questions and doubts concerning its precise value and limits, may require a correspondent adjustment of other parts of the Foederal system."

Randolph balked. The moment cried out for moderation. Before Hamilton could drive Randolph into an uncompromising refusal, Madison took Hamilton aside to caution him, saying that: "You had better yield to this man, for otherwise all Virginia will be against you."

Without Virginia, the call to other states would lack authority. But with her in favor, even Governor Clinton could not brush it aside. Hamilton yielded. He rewrote the draft call, making its statement of the purposes of the convention less pointed, and adding an uncharacteristic deeply humble and deferential tone.

Trade, commerce, and economics underlay politics and all of Hamilton's policies. Regulation of trade became the root reason for the calling of the Constitutional Convention: "the power of regulating trade is of such comprehensive extent, and will enter so far into the general system of the foederal government, that to give it efficacy, and to obviate questions and doubts concerning its precise nature and limits, may require correspondent adjustment of other parts of the Foederal System.''

A date was set; the blanks in Hamilton's 1783 draft were filled in. The commissioners were ''to meet at Philadelphia on the second Monday in May next, to take into consideration the situation of the United States . . . to devise such further provisions as shall appear to them necessary to render the Constitution of the Federal Government adequate to the exigencies of the Union.''

The call drafted by Hamilton went forth from Annapolis on September 14, 1786. Years of effort to push a bank charter through his own state legislature had been futile. While awaiting fruition of these, Hamilton might as well push through a charter for a nation—which might then issue the charter to his bank his state withheld.

When citizens read the call that had issued from the runaway rump convention at Annapolis, the cries of outrage were drowned out by cries of alarm. Farmers in western Massachusetts rose under the leadership of Daniel Shays, a veteran of the Revolution, and took arms against the landed gentry, charging that Eastern politicians discriminated against them in levying taxes, distrained their cattle, and, through subservient courts, foreclosed their farms and packed them off to debtors jails when they defaulted on payments of debts and taxes. Great armed bands of Shays's men ranged angrily across the western counties, closing the courts, burning the records, opening jails, forcibly seizing foreclosed property, and disrupting foreclosure sales. They marched on Boston to confront the merchant-controlled legislature.

At the root of this social and political uprising were conditions of trade and economics. Interest rates charged farmers ran as high as 40 percent a year. More people were in jail for debt than for all other offenses combined. No wonder the rhetoric of the Shaysites had a frightening pre-Marxist ring: ''The property of the United States has been protected from confiscation of Britain by the joint exertions of *all,* and ought to be the *common property* of all.''

Fearful Massachusetts officials called out the militia under the command of General Benjamin Lincoln, but there was no money for pay in the state treasury, and none forthcoming from Congress. Rich merchants had to take up private subscriptions among themselves to pay for suppressing the uprising. Shays's rebellion was crushed, but fears of similar outbreaks that winter strengthened the hands of all like Hamilton who favored a strong national government with a powerful standing army that could deal effectively with such terrifying menaces to peace and order.

For Hamilton's national purposes Daniel Shays's rebellion could not have erupted at a better time, coming as it did on the heels of his Annapolis call for the Constitutional Convention to be held the following May. For the landowning, mercantile middle classes, of which he was becoming a national spokesman, it seemed to clinch Hamilton's argument that without fundamental political reform, the states were faced with a lawless and bloody social revolution.

On October 16, 1786, Virginia voted favorably to send delegates to the Philadelphia convention, but Governor Clinton had been unimpressed; he liked no part of what he had heard from Annapolis and ''expressed a strong dislike'' to the object of the address, ''declaring that . . . no such reform . . . was necessary; that the confederation as it stood was equal to the purposes of the Union. . . .'' So in New York nothing at all was being done about appointing delegates to go to Philadelphia. By shrewd political tactics that would bring self-defeats on the issue of the impost, Hamilton would win favorable action on what appeared to his opponents to be the lesser issue of the Constitutional Convention.

In his opening message to the legislature in January 1787, Clinton had finally laid Congress's request for the impost before it without comment, a committee had been appointed to draft a reply, and Hamilton had managed to wangle an appointment to the committee. Clintonians resolved the assembly into a committee of the whole to consider the message and a Clintonian was on his feet at once, proposing "approbation of your Excellency's conduct in not convening the Legislature at an earlier period." This was a slap at Congress and at Hamilton, who had demanded a special session to act on the impost the previous autumn and lost. A large docile majority duly voted approbation to Governor Clinton.

Now, on February 15, 1787, Hamilton again pressed the impost issue. The vote on it would also serve as a test of strength on the question of sending delegates to the convention. A bill to grant Congress the duties received on specific items of importation passed: Clintonians did not fight the impost itself—the battle remained over the question of who was to appoint the collectors and who was to control them.

Hamilton, staking out a position on the opposition's ground, proposed, first, that Congress both appoint and control the collectors; second, that if this were not acceptable, Congress should have the control of the collectors even if the state should have the right of appointment. With the impost now approved by all the other states and with everything turning on what the New York Assembly would do, the eyes of the nation focused on Hamilton in New York's City Hall. A large audience of visitors in the gallery was noisily sympathetic to him as he made his impassioned speech for the impost. He repeated all the arguments for national revenues he had ever made before and added new ones. New York and Pennsylvania, he pointed out, were the only states making any real contributions to the national treasury, and Pennsylvania was about to quit. Connecticut and New Jersey had already formally refused to make further payments. Did New York then want to shoulder the whole national burden itself or, likewise refusing, see the whole fabric of the nation, which had cost so much blood and tears to raise, perish now because of its own selfishness? Other states had been willing to make an unrestricted grant, but only if all the other states likewise assented; so everything now depended on New York's action. It could make or break the struggling nation. It was not enough to pass the impost. Without congressional control of collectors, the impost itself meant little. Hadn't he, Hamilton, himself been a receiver of taxes under the existing system and seen how futile it was? His own poor performance reinforced his argument now. Congress had rightly refused New York's empty gesture of approving the impost with state collectors like Yates. Now it was all or nothing.

The gallery applauded loudly. The voice of the people, as heard from the gallery, could not fail to shake the Populist Clintonians. No one from their ranks rose to refute him; it seemed that Hamilton alone was speaking in the *vox populi, vox Dei.* When the measure came up for the vote, the galleries bent forward in silence to hear the result.

The vote was announced; party lines held firm; Hamilton's resolutions had lost; his eloquence had not changed a single vote. Spectators cried out in shocked disapproval. They filed out muttering imprecations against Clinton, the absent political boss whose puppets had voted obediently without attempting to argue the merits of the issue with Hamilton. It was a typical state legislative performance. Clinton had won a great victory.

But by losing to such a bold demonstration of bossism after none of Clinton's men had stood up to argue against Hamilton, Hamilton and Schuyler built up much sympathy among members of Clinton's majority. Some Clintonians had agreed, listened in silence, and voted against only by Clinton's order. Hamilton's speech and the indignation of the gallery had made some ashamed of what they had done. According to Schuyler, they "wished an opportunity to make some atonement."

Hamilton and Schuyler gave the Clintonians their opportunity. They introduced bills simultaneously in the senate and assembly to instruct the New York delegates in Congress to recommend to the other states a convention like that which had been called for at Annapolis, but only "for the purpose of revising the Articles of Confederation." Clinton and some of his men still fought the measures, but some of his more independent followers, who had been seen privately by Hamilton and Schuyler, seemed willing to "yield an empire," or, at least, the Empire State, to Hamilton's "wild command" by way of atonement for their earlier opposition. Their votes, now called for publicly, were enough to carry the measure in favor of the Annapolis call for the Constitutional Convention.

Congress had dawdled in confirming the call, but now wasted no time. It quickly adopted the Massachusetts form of approval. The call was rushed back to the states, and Hamilton and Schuyler speedily moved the New York legislature for its approval and appointment of delegates. Their swift tactic caught Clintonian opponents off-balance. Those who had reacted to their boss by committing themselves on the first recommendation now found that "it was too late to retract, and they acquiesced with chagrin in a resolution for the appointment of delegates to the convention."

The governor's men in their turn now demanded that the delegates be appointed by both houses, voting together. With the senate almost evenly divided and the assembly heavily antinationalist, this would mean the election of antinationalist delegates. Schuyler quickly prevailed upon the senate to reject this procedure which the assembly, of course, favored. With a stalemate between the two houses, the opposing factions compromised on two antinationalists, Robert Yates and John Lansing, Jr., and a third—who was a nationalist—Alexander Hamilton.

One nationalist did not much trouble Clinton and his followers because at the convention voting would, of course, be by unit rule. The antinationalist votes of Yates and Lansing could be counted on to nullify Hamilton's and keep New York's single vote safely loyal to Clinton. Obscured by the battle over selection of delegates and Clinton's satisfaction at retaining two-to-one control of New York's convention vote was the fact that New York was now formally committed to being represented at the convention. To Hamilton, that was the climactic business of the legislative session, and it had gone his way.

On March 21 the Continental Congress had resolved that the states should repeal all acts repugnant to the treaty of peace. When the bill to make Congress's resolution effective in New York came up for debate in the assembly on April 17, Hamilton took the floor to make what the New York *Daily Advertiser* described as "a very animated and powerful speech." In broad, general terms, he urged repeal of all the anti-Tory laws. No attempt should be made to itemize specifically just what laws were to be repealed: leave that to the courts and the judges, he said. Treaties were the laws of the land, he insisted, and the bill before the house would confirm this. Now he cited Cicero as authority for the proposition he had urged as his own in *Rutgers* v. *Waddington:* "that when two laws clash, that which relates to the most important matters ought to be preferred."

Next day, still under the spell of Hamilton's eloquence, the assembly passed the bill, sweeping aside all the anti-Tory laws. The senate failed to approve it, and it died. But the assembly's vote, as the legislature adjourned for new elections, gave Hamilton the satisfaction for almost the first time of breaking through Clinton's iron control of the majority's votes in the lower house of the New York legislature.

The 1786 and 1787 sessions of the New York legislature had met in New York City, in the old City Hall building one block west on Wall Street from Hamilton's home and office. As the session adjourned, Hamilton introduced a bill on April 16 that would please his Schuyler and van Rensselaer relatives in Albany and fit his own travel plans: in future, the legislature should hold alternate sessions in New York City and Albany. Clintonians saw one last chance to rid themselves of this freshman assemblyman who had become the chief threat to their monolithic control. They knew that Hamilton and his family divided their time between their house on Wall Street and the Schuylers' at Albany and that Hamilton had many clients in the Albany area. Poughkeepsie, roughly halfway between, was Governor Clinton's bailiwick. John Church Hamilton drily explained the defeat of his father's bill: "It being known that his professional engagements would not permit him to sojourn at Poughkeepsie, that place was selected for the meeting of the next legislature." Hamilton's influence was coming to seem a threat to Clinton's sway over the state legislature, so Clintonians would have to move it out of his way. Of all political animals, a freshman assemblyman of the minority party is normally considered one of the most insignificant. He could have won no greater tribute to his forensic powers.

Having achieved this pinnacle in his first term Hamilton, observing his name being placed in nomination for a second term, wryly informed "such of [his] fellow citizens as might be inclined to honor him with their choice" in the upcoming election that the decision to meet at Poughkeepsie "renders it impracticable" for him to serve. Instead he packed his bags for a Philadelphia trip twice as far as to Poughkeepsie.

There was satisfaction in answering a summons he had composed and served on himself. He could smile at the irony that his hostile legislature, partly to rid itself of the threat he seemed to pose to its sovereignty of the state, had appointed him a delegate to the convention that he had engineered to take its sovereignty away and yoke New York once and for all into a union of states.

He gathered up and stuffed into his saddle bags his copies of a decade's harvest of unadopted, unsupported, and rejected planks for a constitution, all designed "to render the federal government adequate to the exigencies of the Union." He was probably beginning to feel in his bones that of all the great state papers he would ever write, the draft of his Annapolis apostrophe to convene in Philadelphia the following May would be the single most important of his life.

15

An Invisible Hand Guided All Toward the General Good

We are now to decide forever the fate of Republican government. If we do not give to that form due stability and wisdom, it will be disgraced . . . and lost to mankind forever. . . . I am as zealous an advocate for liberty as any man, and would cheerfully become a martyr to it. But real liberty is neither found in despotism or the extremes of democracy, but in moderate governments.

—Speech from the floor of the Constitutional Convention, June 26, 1787

Human mind fond of compromise.

—Private note on a speech of James Madison, June 6, 1787

When Thomas Jefferson, serving comfortably as American minister in Paris, first read the list of names of delegates to the Constitutional Convention of 1787, he wrote his friend John Adams, then serving uncomfortably as minister in London: ''It really is an assembly of demigods.''

Among the 55 were some of the finest political minds of the nation. Virginia had sent a notable delegation: Washington, Madison, Edmund Randolph, George Mason, and George Wythe. Pennsylvania was equally well represented by Franklin, Robert Morris, Gouverneur Morris, and James Wilson. South Carolina sent the two Pinckneys, Charles and Charles Cotesworth, and John Rutledge. Connecticut was represented by Roger Sherman and William S. Johnson; Delaware, by the former Pennsylvanian John Dickinson. Louis Guillaume Otto, French chargé d'affaires to the Comte de Montmorin wrote, with patronizing amazement, on April 10, 1787: "If all the delegates named for this Convention at Philadelphia are present, we will never have seen, even in Europe, an assembly more respectable for the talents, knowledge, disinterestedness, and patriotism of those who compose it."

Remarkable as the Framers present were, they did not represent the whole nation, nor all of its best minds: Thomas Jefferson, John Adams, Samuel Adams, John Hancock, and Patrick Henry, prime movers in the Revolution, were absent as were such good friends of Hamilton as Oliver Wolcott, Jeremiah Wadsworth, General Philip Schuyler, John Jay, James Duane, R. R. Livingston, Elias Boudinot, and Timothy Pickering. Nor were there present any representatives of poor farmers and debtors like Daniel Shays. Hamilton had probably seen as much hardship, poverty, and slavery from the underside of society as any other man present. None of the others had a mother who had served a term in prison for whoring. Aside from bibulous Luther Martin of Maryland and Clinton's men Robert Yates and John Lansing, Jr., from New York, there were no self-proclaimed champions of Populist persuasion. By and large the 55 represented the propertied people of the country.

Few were as rich in lands and slaves as Thomas Jefferson. Most had made their own way in the world as small independent free enterprisers—farmers, merchants, lawyers, bankers, and businessmen—few enjoyed inherited fortune or the tenured insulation of payrollers. From wide experience of life, they had a visceral understanding of the complex economic forces that undergird political theories—experience often missing from the lives of payrollers and inheritors.

Each delegate had been chosen by his state legislature in the same manner prescribed for electing its delegates to Congress. Although property qualifications and certain other limitations on voting make those legislatures seem undemocratic by present-day standards, they were by far the most democratic legislatures then existing anywhere in the world. The delegates rightly called themselves "representatives of the people of the United States," and they felt no sense of alienation from the mass of the people of their states.

Hamilton reached town with his fellow delegate Robert Yates on May 18. After checking in at the Indian Queen Tavern on Fourth Street, between Market and Chestnut, the first thing he did was file his credentials and instructions from President General von Steuben as a delegate from the New York State Society of the Cincinnati to the General Meeting of the Society, which was also convening a convention in Philadelphia that week. The president general of the national society, George Washington, had arrived four days earlier and was lodged at Robert Morris's three-story brick mansion, Lemon Hill, the grandest house in Philadelphia, obviously the only suitable headquarters for a national president general.

Madison had asked George Washington to come to the Constitutional Convention as head of the Virginia delegation "to give this subject a very solemn dress," as if he were about to place a mute clothes horse in a show window. Washington had responded civilly but tartly that "Influence is no government," but agreed to come.

The Cincinnati mustered their quorum of state delegates before the quorum of state delegates could be mustered for the Constitutional Convention. The Cincinnati unanimously reelected Washington president general, retold their war stories, and adjourned; the Constitutional Convention stayed.

On May 25, the delegates assembled in the chamber at the State House, now known as Independence Hall, in the same already historic room where the Declaration of Independence had been hammered out 11 years earlier. Only four years earlier, Hamilton had sat in the same room as a delegate to the Continental Congress, demanded protection for Congress from the recalcitrant Pennsylvania Executive Council, and faced down army mutineers.

In Benjamin Franklin's absence, Robert Morris, "on behalf of the deputation from Pennsylvania," rose and nominated his houseguest as president of the convention, John Rutledge of South Carolina seconded, and Washington's election was made unanimous. Morris and Rutledge than conducted Washington to the presiding officer's seat on the low dais, the same seat that had been occupied during the Revolution by Washington's titular civilian commander, the president of Congress. President General Washington called the quorum of states to order.

James Wilson of Pennsylvania moved that a permanent secretary be appointed and nominated the absent Benjamin Franklin's grandson, Mr. William Temple Franklin, for the honor. George Mason and the powerful Virginia delegation opposed him. They favored John Beckley of Virginia, who had come to Philadelphia in the company of Edmund Randolph confident of being elected with Virginia's support.

Hamilton quickly offered a third name, that of Major William Jackson of Philadelphia, who had served as assistant secretary of war under the Articles of Confederation and had quietly lobbied for the post of secretary. After a brief struggle Jackson was elected by the convention over Franklin and Beckley. In an instant, at the outset, this quick, surprising victory of Hamilton's nominee, old friend, and fellow Cincinnatian made the 30-year-old New Yorker in the eyes of his fellow delegates seem to be one of the dominant forces of the Convention. But the same tactical victory of his nominee, Jackson, made of the loser, John Beckley, the most dangerous enemy among men of the second rank that Hamilton would have for the rest of his life. Beckley became Jefferson's and Madison's most energetic anti-Hamilton informer and agent provocateur.

Hamilton, along with the venerable Chancellor George Wythe of Virginia and Charles Pinckney of South Carolina, was named by Washington to the Committee on Standing Rules and Orders, the first or second most important committee of the convention.

The job of Hamilton's man Jackson was to keep a simple orderly record of motions and votes, but Madison, knowing that posterity would want much more than the bare bones of journal minutes, appointed himself the amanuensis of the proceedings. The following account of the convention is based primarily on his notes. Madison chose a seat in front of the dais, with the other members on his right and left, and from there, he said,

> I noted . . . what was read from the chair or spoken by the members; and losing not a moment unnecessarily between the adjournment and reassembling of the Convention, I was enabled to write out my daily notes during the session or within a few finishing days after its close. . . . In the labor and correctness of this I was not a little aided by practice, and by a familiarity with the style and the train of observation and reasoning which characterized the principal speakers.

Anyone who has been involved in the inner workings of an important political convention knows that nearly everything that happens on the floor is but the staged sum of an infinite number of backstage maneuvers conceived and rehearsed by small groups off the floor at places like the hall of the Indian Queen. The Constitutional Convention was no exception. Positions forcefully stated on the floor, to which adamant objections are interposed, are but the visible "tip of the iceberg" of the offstage secret life of such conventions. An invisible convention takes place on the periphery of the floor—over tankards at taverns; in smoke-filled rooms, or the hall of the Indian Queen; at gatherings of Cincinnatians, over a quiet dinner, or under cover of a noisy brothel. Accomplishment on the floor of a collective end result that no one could have foreseen at the beginning becomes the sum of the interaction of recorded or remembered happenings on the floor with innumerable, mostly unrecorded, happenings off the floor that may be no less well remembered. Such happenings include tentative suggestions, angry rejections, delicate modifications, grudging accommodations, purposeful misunderstandings, crocodile tears, grave forebodings, feelings-out, hurt feelings, abraded egos, gratified greeds, flattering misattributions, intercepted secrets, overheard remarks, and lucky random thoughts: the list is endless. Such events also include ultimate designs and purposeful steps to carry them out.

Hamilton compressed the core strategy that underlay all his tactics into the five words he jotted down privately while listening to a speech of Madison on the floor on June 6. The words were: "Human mind fond of compromise."

Hamilton's mind did not grasp at compromise except at the last extremity. Like Phocion, progenitor of one of his pamphleteering pen names, he fought with uncompromising, immoderate tenacity for policy that he saw as "moderate." From the floor on June 26, he cried, "real liberty is neither found in despotism or the extremes of democracy, but in moderate governments." To end up with a constitution that provided "moderate government" it followed that, given the fondness of human minds for compromise, someone would have to stake out polar positions from which such minds could gratefully recede toward a moderate mean. Because Hamilton was a nationalist-minded minority of one in the most strongly Populist and antinationalist delegation any state had sent, it was obvious to all that he would not be able to cast his state's vote where his voice was and that his position was bound to be anomalous and frustrating.

Hamilton's Committee on Standing Rules and Orders had much to do with the ultimate success of the convention. Chancellor George Wythe of Virginia reported for the committee on May 28, and the report became the basis of most of the procedures of the convention. For the most part, the rules followed those of Congress, but special note should be taken of four.

First, as in Congress, voting was by states, with each state, no matter how large or small, having one vote. Virginia, with a population of 454,983 and 292,627 slaves; Pennsylvania, with 430,636 and 3,737 slaves; Massachusetts, with 387,787; and New York, with 318,796 and 21,324 slaves would have the same single vote as Delaware, with 50,209 and 8,887 slaves.

Although Hamilton and Madison and other nationalist delegates from the large states were determined to do away forever with the confederation principle of one-state, one-vote voting, they recognized that they would have to accomplish this political miracle at a meeting organized on that very principle.

Second, a decorum befitting a gathering of gentlemen was to be maintained. Members were politely forbidden to whisper, read, or pass notes while one of their colleagues was speaking. He could be "called to order by any other member as well as by the President."

Third, the proceedings were to be informal, by calls for "yeas and nays" without recording of formal or record votes or roll calls. This made it easier for delegates to grope their way toward solutions they could not immediately anticipate.

Finally, the convention voted, on the prompting of Pierce Butler of South Carolina, to guard "against licentious publications of their proceedings."

George Mason found this "secrecy rule" a "necessary precaution to prevent misrepresentations or mistakes"; Madison later insisted that "no Constitution would ever have been adopted by the convention if the debates had been public.'' The secrecy rule stirred the imaginations and loosened the tongues of delegates on the floor, permitted them to take advanced positions and then to withdraw gracefully under fire, guarded them against careless or willful misinterpretations of their gropings for compromises, allowed one consensus after another to form out of a jumble of half-formed opinions and half-baked prejudices, encouraged them to express honest doubts about such sacred cows as the sovereignty of the states and the glories of the militia, and spared orators like Randolph or Charles Pinckney from the temptation of playing to any gallery but that of posterity. This rule probably had more significance for Hamilton than for any other delegate. His was the reputation that would suffer most by a breach of it, and without it, the features of the Constitution that we now think of as characteristically Hamiltonian would have been politically impossible.

Although newspapers told their readers that the convention had elected to carry on in ''the greatest secrecy,'' no one thought it proper until the end of the summer to say openly, as Jefferson wrote privately to Adams, that the ''precedent'' of ''tying up the tongues'' of the delegates was ''abominable.'' As a member of Congress, Hamilton had urged that the doors be flung open and the public be allowed in to hear debates. But more was at stake here than scoring debating points with the populace outside the hall. It is a fact of huge consequence for history that the spirit and customs of the age encouraged the men of 1787 to produce ''an open covenant, secretly arrived at.''

The call from Annapolis had been framed in terms of exigencies that had to be dealt with in the areas of trade, commerce, and economics. On the face of it, the political overlay was to be adjusted only to the extent that economic exigencies dictated such adjustments. From London Angelica Church had sent her adored brother-in-law a copy of Adam Smith's *The Wealth of Nations* not long after its first publication in 1776. No one at the convention had learned Adam Smith's lessons better than Hamilton. An invisible hand guided all toward the general good.

On May 29 Edmund Randolph rose and presented to the convention 15 resolutions constituting the draft of a constitution, which came to be known as the Virginia plan. It provided for a bicameral legislature and a national executive to be appointed by that body. The national legislature would be vested with the right to veto any state law contravening the federal Articles and the power to employ force against a recalcitrant state. The executive, in conjunction with a national judiciary, would have a power of veto over both state and federal enactments. Such veto might be overriden by the legislature. Randolph's Virginia plan called not for ''one man, one vote,'' for all offices, but drastically limited the right of suffrage to ''the quotas of contribution'' or to ''the number of free inhabitants, as one or the other rule may seem best in different cases.''

Randolph moved adoption of the Virginia plan. The question on the floor was whether the United States ''were susceptible of one government,'' that is, whether to frame a new national government or merely to amend the Articles.

The Virginia plan as a whole went far beyond mere tinkering with the Articles of Confederation. So before debate on its provisions could even get under way, the shackles placed on the scope of the convention had to be removed. By the terms of Hamilton's call from Annapolis, as well as the enabling resolutions of Congress and the state legislatures, most delegates had been sent to the convention only for the purpose of amending the Articles of Confederation, not to introduce a whole new form of government.

In the New York delegation, Yates voted ''Nay,'' and Hamilton ''Aye.'' The third delegate, Lansing, had not yet arrived.

New York's vote being split, it was not counted either way.

This first and most fundamental resolution passed by a vote of 6 to 1: that a *national* government should be established, consisting of a supreme legislature, executive, and judiciary. In favor were Massachusetts, Pennsylvania, Delaware, Virginia, North and South Carolina, with only Connecticut opposed. But the winning majority, even with Delaware voting with the large states, represented fewer than half the 13. Only Hamilton's "aye" and Lansing's absence had prevented New York from being counted with the "nays." A few days later, after the rest of the small state delegations had arrived, the vote would have been much closer. Here at the outset, when many a delegate was barely catching his breath, the convention seemed to have decided, in effect, to scrap the Articles of Confederation and to form a new government that, as Gouverneur Morris and George Mason noted portentously, would have "a *compulsive* operation," directly "on individuals."

The following day, May 30, the delegates, having resolved to debate the Virginia plan as "a committee of the whole house," took up the first and most important of its 15 propositions—that dealing with the rights of suffrage in the national legislature.

Legally, slaves were property, chattels like cattle or any other kind of tangible personal property. Representation proportioned to "quotas of contribution" would mean that as property, nonvoting slaves would give added weight to white voters from slave states because only "free inhabitants" could actually vote. There was, of course, no obligation that the white representative vote in the interest of slaves or any other form of property. More than anything else, the extra voting power given to "free inhabitants" by Randolph's Virginia plan gave them strong incentive to keep the status quo, including the slavery that produced their great edge in voting power over states whose "free inhabitants" owned fewer slaves.

From his opening remarks to the last day of the convention, Washington presided from the dais without entering the debate. He recognized and refused to recognize speakers and kept order with a firm hand, but only once, on the last day, did he enter into the debate itself.

Hamilton, often pilloried as the champion of propertied interests, moved to alter Randolph's resolution so as to read "that the rights of *suffrage* in the national legislature ought to be proportioned to the number of free inhabitants." This struck out representation according to numbers of slaves and other property owned. Hamilton's resolution, seconded by Richard D. Spaight of North Carolina, meant that the "quotas of contribution," or propertied wealth, should have no special weight and should not be equated with the voice of the people of a state. Only people, not property, counted in voting. But consideration of the Hamilton-Spaight resolution was postponed.

On June 11 James Wilson and Hamilton moved that "the right of suffrage in the second branch [Senate] ought to be according to the same rule as in the first branch." This meant popular representation—one man, one vote, not one state, one vote, in both houses. This carried.

On June 4, again with Wilson, Hamilton proposed "to give the executive an absolute negative" on all laws, both state and federal," remarking that there was no danger of such a power being too much exercised. (The king of England had not exercised his negative since the Revolution.) All delegates except the two proponents and a Hamilton convert, Rufus King, voted down such sweeping veto power.

Wilson and Madison immediately moved, as a compromise measure, that a convenient number of judges act with the executive in vetoing acts of the national legislature. Hamilton objected to such dilution of the separation of powers. On June 2 he seconded Benjamin

Franklin's motion that the chief executive receive an expense allowance, but "no salary, stipend fee or reward whatsoever." This was postponed without debate. On June 5 he proposed that the executive nominate judges and that the Senate have the right of approving or rejecting them.

Small state delegates continued to arrive in Philadelphia. It became apparent to Hamilton that voting strength on the floor was shifting. The Virginia plan was in trouble. The question was becoming not whether the Virginia plan could be improved upon, but the much more serious one of whether any plan that went as far as the Virginia plan could survive. While this threat grew, the Virginia plan was becoming stronger and more national—and more objectionable to the smaller states.

When the committee of the whole rose at the end of the day on Wednesday, June 13, it reported out a set of 19 resolutions that were both a confirmation and an elaboration of the original Virginia plan. The authority to use force against recalcitrant states had been dropped; otherwise, the resolutions were a projection of most of the hopes Hamilton had entertained for a government "truly national." Details added in the give-and-take of debate included a three-year term for the lower house and a seven-year term for the upper; payment for members of both houses "out of the national treasury" (a solid blow for nationalism); election of members of the upper house by the state legislatures, not, as Hamilton had proposed, by the people; a single executive with a seven-year term (to be chosen by the legislature and ineligible for reelection), who could be removed "on impeachment and conviction of malpractices or neglect of duty"; and a power of veto in the executive, which could be overridden only by a two-thirds majority in both houses. There would also be the "supreme tribunal" which Hamilton had urged for so long, whose judges would be chosen by the upper house. Smooth progress thus far had been deceptive: it had built up powerful opposing forces.

By June 15 the small-state delegates had arrayed their forces for battle against the Virginia plan. William Paterson of New Jersey "laid before the Convention" a set of nine resolutions, a series of amendments to the Articles of Confederation, as "substitutes" for the Virginia plan, which came to be known as the New Jersey plan.

This plan would protect rights of the smaller states against domination by the larger ones. It kept as much as possible of the Articles of Confederation. It provided for a single national legislature, like the old Continental Congress, in which representation was by states, each with a single, equal vote. Powers of Congress would be increased somewhat by grants of imposts and some other revenues, by a grant of the right of regulation of foreign and interstate commerce, and by the significant right to enforce its laws over the objections of the states. It was much closer than Randolph's plan to what most of the state legislatures had had in mind when they sent off their delegates to Philadelphia.

By comparison with the Virginia plan, New Jersey's represented merely a tinkering with the old Articles of Confederation, leaving the states clearly sovereign; the Virginia plan looked in the direction of a strong, central, national government, and now needed rescuing.

Delaware switched to the smaller-state group, leaving only five large states of the plurality of six that had originally voted for the Virginia plan. Lansing had arrived on June 2; so now, instead of Yates's vote being canceled out by Hamilton's, the two-to-one majority against him would swing New York into the "small" state column. That meant the possibility of a seven or eight to five vote against the Virginia plan.

The most intense subject of dispute was whether representation in Congress would be based on population in both the upper and lower houses or only in the lower house.

Generally, members from large states and Hamilton, of course, favored representation based on population in both houses, but the smaller states would accept representation based on population only in the lower house. In the upper house, they insisted that all states have an equal vote.

Madison and Wilson refused to concede an inch to the small-state nationalists. A choice had to be made between the two plans as they stood. This meant that the Virginia plan, with all its other national features, might be voted down *in toto,* in favor of the New Jersey plan. The convention might break up. The whole effort to create a national government might simply be abandoned. As the crucial vote approached, it looked as though all of Hamilton's efforts might come to nothing.

Voting was scheduled to take place on Tuesday, June 19; there would, of course, be a day of adjournment for rest and prayer on Sunday, June 17.

As debates grew more heated, Hamilton kept rough notes on the proceedings. His versions of the remarks made by various delegates do not always match those reported by the other principal notetakers—Madison, John Lansing, Robert Yates, and Rufus King. It is not always possible to determine from Hamilton's notes whether a statement is one expressed by the speaker or simply Hamilton's own reaction to the speaker's remarks.

On June 6, when Madison was arguing that both branches of the legislature should be elected by the people, Hamilton's record of Madison's ideas bouncing off his own mind is as follows:

PRINCIPLES

I—Human mind fond of compromise—Madison's Theory—Two principles upon which republics ought to be constructed—

I—that they have such extent as to render Combinations on the ground of Interest difficult—

II—By a process of election calculated to refine the representation of the People—Answer—There is truth in both these principles but they do not conclude so strongly as he supposes. The Assembly when chosen will meet in one room if they are drawn from half the globe—& will be liable to all the passions of popular assemblies.

Hamilton here is not as insistent as Madison that no compromise is possible with the smaller states on the issue of voting in one house by states. Regardless of how the delegates are selected, he notes, once they meet together "in one room," they throw off the shackles of the constituency that has appointed them, whether a single state or a numerically determined constituency. They vote independently, subject to "all the passions of popular assemblies." Delegates assembled in the State House had only to consider how far beyond the limits imposed by their legislatures back home their votes for the Virginia plan had already carried them.

As Hamilton jotted down his notes and reflections, Madison went on with his argument on the floor. He referred to Roger Sherman's admission that in a very small state, faction and oppression would prevail and that it was to be inferred from this that wherever these feelings prevailed, the state was too small.

Factions had also prevailed in the largest states, he admitted, but less than in the smallest, so that we were "admonished to enlarge the sphere as far as the value of the Government would admit." This was the only defense against the inconveniences of democracy, Madison reasoned, that was consistent with the democratic form of government.

Hamilton recorded this and his reaction, as follows:

Observ. large districts less liable to be influenced by factious demagogues than small.
Note—This is in some degree true but not so generally as may be supposed. Frequently small portions of the large districts carry elections.

Hamilton jotted this down: "An influential demagogue will give an impulse to the whole." Such an evil man could spring from Madison's own social class: "Demagogues are not always *inconsiderable* persons. Patricians were frequently demagogues."

Hamilton also foresaw the danger of people developing a distaste for all politicians, plebeian and patrician alike:

I—One great defect of our Governments are that they do not present objects sufficiently interesting to the human mind.
II—A reason for leaving little or nothing to the state legislature will be that as their objects are diminished they will be worse composed. Proper men will be less inclined to participate in them.

Jotted down for his own eyes only in rough impressionistic form, these notes show Hamilton's basic agreement with Madison on the problems created by "factions" and demagogues. Patricians could as easily be demagogues as other men.

When the president general adjourned the delegates for Sunday recess, on Saturday, June 16, the question in many minds was who should be recognized by the chair as the speaker on Monday, June 18, the last day of debate before the climactic vote of Tuesday the nineteenth?

At this supreme moment in American history, perhaps the most unlikely choice for such an honor would be the man who was a minority of one in his own delegation, the largest of the states which had swung over to the small-state side.

Monday, June 18, was one of the hottest and most humid days of the Philadelphia year.

The delegates, as usual, convened at around eleven prepared to sit till about four without a break or any form of air conditioning except speakers' rhetoric. A hush fell. Washington cast his eye over the room, paused as his glance fell on the New York delegation to his right and at the rear, and nodded recognition to Alexander Hamilton.

Hamilton rose briskly, without apparent surprise, a sheaf of papers in his hands.

To many delegates, Hamilton was the most peculiar possible choice of speaker. But the overwhelming prestige of the president general frowned down any possibility that a zealous small-state delegate eager to speak would challenge him with a call of "point of order." Others, nationalists mostly, settled back in their chairs, also without much surprise.

For five hours Hamilton spoke to a silent convention, referring only occasionally to the notes he held in his long fingers. He rarely raised his voice above conversational pitch. He embroidered the severe logic of his argument with sudden flights of fancy. He paused at intervals for dramatic emphasis as if probing for the very roots of the argument.

According to James Madison's notes on the speech,

Hamilton began disarmingly by saying that he had been hitherto silent on the business before the convention, partly from respect to others whose superior abilities, age, and experience rendered him unwilling to bring forward ideas dissimilar to theirs, and partly from his delicate situation with respect to his own state, to whose sentiments, as expressed by his colleagues, he could by no means accede.

But the question was too important; the crisis too serious "to permit any scruples whatever to prevail over the duty imposed on every man to contribute his efforts for the public safety and happiness . . . ."

Hamilton artfully posed the question so that the narrow issue of state representation in the national legislature became lost within the huge frame he placed around it.

"The great question," Hamilton said, "is what provision shall we make for the happiness of our Country?"

He then carefully set the stage for a "compromise": "He declared himself unfriendly to both plans."

Neither the Virginia nor the New Jersey plan completely satisfied him; neither established a strong, centralized government that would make the United States an irresistible unity of people instead of a mere alliance among semi-independent states.

But it was the New Jersey plan whose substance he attacked: "He was particularly opposed to [it], being fully convinced, that no amendment of the Confederation leaving the states in possession of their Sovereignty could possibly answer the purpose."

"He had no criticism of the Virginia plan on its own merits," but he managed some criticism of it nonetheless: "Too much had already been claimed for it; too much was expected of it." According to Madison, Hamilton "was much discouraged by the amazing extent of the Country in expecting the desired blessings from any general sovereignty that could be substituted."

Then he launched a blistering attack on state sovereignty. This contrasted sharply with his moderation in the private notes he had jotted down a few days earlier while listening to Madison, when he had reflected that it would not be an absolute evil to give equal representation to each state, large or small, in one house.

"I have well considered the subject," he insisted loudly, "and am convinced that no amendment of the Confederation can answer the purpose of a good government, so long as the state sovereignties do, in any shape, exist."

Who else would have dreamed of saying such a shocking thing?

But it remained a foregone conclusion that the president general, who was listening intently to his former aide, would abruptly rule any hostile attempt to cut Hamilton short "out of order."

What good were the states? Hamilton went on. They gathered to themselves loyalties that should belong to the nation; they constantly pursued internal interests adverse to the interest of the whole; they were not necessary for commerce, revenue, or agriculture; they added vast and useless expenses to the cost of government. In short, if they were reduced to mere local corporations or counties or even altogether extinguished, the nation would be far the better for it.

Hamilton now claimed to be for complete sovereignty in the general government. This, of course, went much further toward reducing the power of the states than anything in the Virginia plan—further than anything Hamilton had ever proposed before or would urge afterward. Not only would these views startle and shock William Paterson and the small-state nationalists—as well as Hamilton's fellow New York delegates Yates and Lansing—they went too far for all backers of the Virginia plan. Hamilton stood alone, and then moved still further apart from all the rest:

> All the passions . . . of avarice, ambition, interest which govern most individuals, and all public bodies, fall into the current of the States, and do not flow in the stream of the General Government. The former, therefore, will generally be an

overmatch for the General Government and render any confederacy, in its very nature, precarious.

He tossed off historical examples of confederacies that had deluded themselves into believing that they had adequate central powers, including ''the power of fining and using force against delinquent members.'' He cited the Amphictionic League, the German Confederacy, and the Swiss Cantons. But ''What was the consequence? Their decrees were signals of war.''

He was, of course, exaggerating his aversion to leaving a shred of sovereignty in the state governments, in order to set the stage for voting the next day by a room full of ''human minds fond of compromise.'' Yet ridiculous as Hamilton's rhetoric might sound in the immediate context, his fear that the decrees of sovereign states of a confederacy ''were signals of war'' forecast what would happen to the ''United'' States in 1860, as a result of this convention's ultimate ''compromise'' of the issue.

Much state governmental apparatus was a waste of money; money could be saved if the states ''were extinguished.'' The only problem would be drawing representatives from the extremes to the center at the capital. Good men would not want to travel too far, and the pay would be bait only to little demagogues. Three dollars or thereabout, he supposed, would be the salary, and the Senate, he feared, would be filled only by seekers of jobs who could find nothing better.

According to Madison's notes of Hamilton's speech, such things ''almost led him to despair that a republican government could be established over so great an extent.'' But ''He was sensible at the same time that it would be unwise to propose one of any other form.''

Then followed a passage that Hamilton's enemies would use against him for the rest of his life.

He had reviewed various forms of government—those of the Germanic Empire, Sparta, Athens, Thebes, Rome, Carthage, Venice, the Hanseatic League, France under Louis XIV, and Austria under the Bourbons. He came at last to England under William and Anne and their successors as a constitutional monarchy beginning to emerge. He stressed the importance of strong governments to help avoid wars caused by squabbling of petty states. In this context he said, according to his own notes, ''The general government must, in this case, not only have a strong soul, but *strong organs* by which that soul is to operate.'' Then he cited the British example. According to his notes:

> Here I shall give my sentiments of the best form of government—not as a thing attainable by us, but as a model which we ought to approach as near as possible: British constitution best form.

It was once thought that the power of Congress was amply sufficient to link the states, he noted, but the error of that view was now seen by everyone. ''The time would come when others as well as himself would join in the praise bestowed by Mr. Neckar on the British constitution, when he said that it is the only government in the world 'which unites public strength with individual security.' ''

Therefore, in the real world of 1787, British experience provided a better working model for a government of free people than any other. The reason: its form provided a strong chief executive. No such figure existed under the Confederation or in the New Jersey plan.

As one who had fought as long and hard against King George III and his armies as anyone in the room except the silent president general on the dais, Hamilton could make this argument with more force and less fear of false imputation of disloyalty than any other man there.

Why was such a chief executive necessary?

Here is Hamilton's argument from his notes:

> Society naturally divides itself into two political divisions—the *few* and the *many*, who have distinct interests.
>
> If government in the hands of the *few*, they will tyrannize over the many.
>
> If [in] the hands of the many, they will tyrannize over the few. It ought to be in the hands of both; and they should be separated.
>
> This separation must be permanent.
>
> Representation alone will not do.

Without such an executive,

> Demagogues will generally prevail.
>
> And if separated, they will need a mutual check.

There must be checks and balances in the system:

> This check is a monarch.
>
> Each principle ought to exist in full force, or it will not answer its end.
>
> The democracy must be derived immediately from the people.
>
> 'Tis essential there should be a permanent will in a community.
>
> Vox populi, vox Dei. . . .
>
> There ought to be a principle in government capable of resisting the popular current.
>
> There must be a permanent will.
>
> A democratic assembly is to be checked by a democratic senate, and both these by a democratic chief magistrate.
>
> What is to be done?
>
> Answer. Balance inconveniences and dangers, and choose that which seems to have the fewest objections.

Hamilton was saying, as Winston Churchill would later, that "Democracy is the worst possible form of government conceived by man, except for all the others."

What, in the context of his notes, did Hamilton mean by the word *monarch*?

"*Monarch* is an indefinite term," he said. "It marks not either the degree or duration of power."

Robert Yates's notes picked up an important point that Madison failed to put down: Hamilton had given as his opinion that an executive in office for life was less "dangerous to the liberties of the people" than one who was in office for seven years. But whether the "monarch's" term was for seven years or for life, "the circumstance of being elective was applicable to both."

Both Yates and John Lansing picked up still another important point that Madison had missed: Hamilton said that "By making the executive subject to impeachment, the term monarchy cannot apply." What, then, did Hamilton actually propose? "Let electors be appointed in each of the states to elect the executive."

What Hamilton actually proposed was not a hereditary king, like Britain's, who could not be removed from office, but an executive elected by electors from each state—the general method provided under the Constitution ever since (until the Twenty-Fifth Amendment)—subject to removal from office without bloody revolution by the impeachment process. A "monarch" in other words, exactly like the American president as his office was created and has evolved under the Constitution.

Madison's notes of Hamilton's remarks subtly seem to transform Hamilton's role into that of a zealot: Madison reported, "In his private opinion he had no scruple in declaring, supported as he was by the opinions of so many of the wise and good, that the British Government was the best in the world; and that he doubted much whether anything short of it would do in America."

But according to Hamilton's own notes and those of Yates, Lansing, and Rufus King, Hamilton was merely citing the British form as a working model for a government with a strong executive whose powers were limited by the legislature. Madison's private misunderstanding became the seed of misleading public charges that Hamilton was a "monarchist"—a charge with which Hamilton's foes would assail him the rest of his life and history.

Having made these observations, Hamilton read the sketch of a plan that he preferred to either the New Jersey or Virginia plan. His plan shrewdly blunted some of the objections that the small states had raised to the Virginia plan.

Hamilton vested "the supreme legislative power of the United States of America" in two houses: the lower house to be elected by the people for a three-year term; the Senate to be elected by electors chosen by the people to serve during good behavior.

Tactically, this was a master stroke because it bypassed the divisive question of whether there would be one-state, one-vote representation in the Senate, as the small states insisted, or one-man, one-vote representation, as the larger states demanded. Besides, some of the small-state delegates in the room could also see themselves in the near future as the very senators who would be chosen to sit in the capital "during good behaviour."

His chief executive, to be elected by electors chosen by the people, was to serve during good behavior and to have an absolute veto. If no absolute majority emerged from the balloting, these "first electors" were to choose" "second electors" to complete the job.

Supreme judicial authority was to be vested in 12 federal judges, also to hold office during good behavior. All government officials were liable to impeachment before a special court consisting of the chief judges of the highest court of each state. All laws of the particular states contrary to the Constitution or laws of the United States would be void. Exclusive authority over the military and naval forces was to be vested in the federal government. Supreme Court judges would sit on the court of impeachment along with the chief judges of the state courts. In the English model, according to Hamilton, the hereditary interest of the king was so interwoven with that of the nation, and his personal emolument was so great that he was placed above the danger of corruption from abroad, and, at the same time, he was both sufficiently independent and sufficiently controlled to answer the purpose of the institution at home.

There was much to be said for a chief executive elected to serve during good behavior, rather than for a short fixed term. One of the weak sides of republics was their being liable to foreign influence and corruption. Men of little character, acquiring great power, become easily the tools of intermeddling neighbors and subvert the national interest to schemes by which to insure reelection. If the executive were not elected for life, perhaps a term of seven years would induce the sacrifice of his private affairs, which an acceptance of public trust would require, so as to ensure the services of the best citizens in the office.

When Hamilton sat down, after more than five hours of speaking in the intense heat of the State House chamber, the leaves of his plan of government still rustling in his hands, he did not meet with general approbation or applause. There was no occasion to turn to his friends and ask, like Phocion, "Have I inadvertently said something foolish?" No one rose to agree with or confute him; no one offered those additional remarks that were normal in the confidential give-and-take of the convention. Delegates were stunned. After a while, someone broke the silence with a remark on a wholly different topic, debate resumed, and the session soon adjourned for the momentous vote next day.

Hamilton's was the longest speech anyone was allowed to make at the convention. He was given the floor and the delegates' undivided attention on its most critical day. The members present heard him out in respectful silence, and many took elaborate notes on what he had said. His speech had the greatest intellectual and historical reach and thrust of any speech made at the convention. Strictly speaking, much of it was not germane to the issue before the delegates.

Hamilton's filibuster made the Virginia plan appear as but a reasonable middle ground between two extreme positions: his own extreme nationalist position and the New Jersey plan's extreme state-sovereignty position.

Hamilton's remarks about abolishing the states had been too provocative. On the day of the vote, Hamilton offered some conciliatory remarks. "He had not been understood yesterday"; he had not really intended "a total extinguishment of state governments" as some had thought; they could continue as local and police subdivisions. But the "authority of the national government must be indefinite and unlimited, without any hindrance from the states."

But his conciliatory tone created still more constitutional history in favor of strong national government. "A national government ought to be able to support itself without the aid or interference of the state governments. It is necessary to have full sovereignty. Even with corporate rights the states will be dangerous to the national government, and ought to be extinguished, modified, or reduced to a smaller scale. . . ."

James Wilson spoke more to the point:

> The declaration of independence preceded the state constitutions. What does this declare? In the name of the people of these states, we are declared to be free and independent. The power of war, peace, alliances and trade are declared to be vested in Congress.

Hamilton rose once more:

> I agree to Mr. Wilson's remark. Establish a weak government and you must at times overleap the bounds. Rome was obliged to create dictators. Cannot you make propositions to the people because we before confederated on other principles? The people can yield to them, if they will. The three great objects of government, agriculture, commerce, and revenue, can only be secured by a general government.

Hamilton concluded: "The more close the union of the states, and the more complete the authority of the whole, the less opportunity will be allowed [to] the stronger states to injure the weaker."

The vote could not have been closer: six ayes (Massachusetts, Pennsylvania, Virginia, the Carolinas, and Georgia) to five nays (Connecticut, New York, New Jersey, Delaware, and Maryland). Hamilton was outvoted in his own delegation. But the Virginia plan prevailed. The New Jersey plan lost. The "Hamilton" plan lost. The convention did not break up. The delegates' minds favored "compromise." They now buckled down to working out the details of the constitution of national union that was veiled but implicit in the Virginia plan.

In the following days all Hamilton's actions and votes tended toward strengthening the power of the people to control the national government, and to oppose any idea of unfettered kingly power or hereditary monarchs. They tended to reinforce the view that the extreme positions he had set up on Monday had been intended for voting down on Tuesday. On June 21, Charles Cotesworth Pinckney moved that the House of Representatives be elected by state legislatures instead of by the people. Hamilton, in opposition, argued that transfer of voting rights from the people to state legislatures "would essentially vitiate the plan. It would increase the state influence which could not be too watchfully guarded against." In Yates's account, Hamilton asserted that election "directly by the people" is "essential to the democratic rights of the community."

On June 22 Hamilton urged that members of the national legislature be paid "fixed stipends paid out of the National Treasury," so as not to be "dependent on the legislative rewards of the states" because "Those who pay are the masters of those who are paid." "The feelings and views of the people," he urged, "are different from the governments of the states," and not necessarily "unfriendly to the General Government." They would be freer "from personal interests and official inducements."

He argued against express provision making members of the House ineligible to other offices during their term and for one year thereafter: "We must take man as we find him, and if we expect him to serve the public must interest his passions in doing so. A reliance on pure patriotism has been the source of many of our errors."

He added, "I am against all exclusions and refinements, except only in this case; that when a member takes his seat, he should vacate every other office."

On June 26 Nathaniel Gorham moved for six-year terms for senators, one third to be elected every second year; George Read moved to amend, to make the terms nine years, one third going out triennially. Madison, favoring longer terms for senators, noted with alarm the rise of a "leveling spirit." Longer terms were one way of guarding against such a spirit "on republican principles." Roger Sherman of Connecticut argued for shorter terms and more frequent elections.

Hamilton, taking the long view, citing first principles, generally supporting Madison, said, "We are now to decide forever the fate of Republican Government. If we do not give to that form due stability and wisdom, it will be disgraced and lost among ourselves, and disgraced and lost to mankind forever." His paean to liberty and moderation contrasted sharply with the didactic impression made by his speech of the week before.

He added, "I am as zealous an advocate for liberty as any man, and would cheerfully become a martyr to it. But real liberty is neither found in despotism or the extremes of democracy, but in moderate governments." Weakness in the government, he pointed out, is what gives rise to the danger of despotic monarchy: "As long as offices are open to all men, and no constitutional rank is established, it is pure republicanism. But if we incline too much to democracy, we shall soon shoot into a monarchy."

He read America's future from Rome's past and saw that, for better or worse, it would hold inequality of property: "The differences in wealth are already great among us, nothing like equality of property exists. Inequality will exist as long as liberty exists, and it unavoidably results from that very liberty itself."

But too great inequality is a threat to moderate governments:

> In the ordinary progress of things we must look to a period as not very remote when distinctions arising from property will be greater. In Rome, the power of the tribunes had levelled the distinction between the patricians and plebeians. The plebeians instituted the power of the tribunes as a guard against the patricians. But it was not a sufficient check. The distinction between rich and poor was substituted, and this created a greater distinction between the classes than there had ever been before.

As debate on the one state, one vote versus one man, one vote issue rumbled on, Hamilton on June 29, his last day on the floor for some time to come, rose and attacked the position of Luther Martin of Maryland with new eloquence: "This position cannot be correct: Facts plainly contradict it," he urged. "States are a collection of individual men," he went on. "Which ought we to respect most? The rights of the people composing them, or of the artificial beings resulting from the composition? Nothing could be more absurd than to sacrifice the former to the latter."

He pressed his argument: "It has been said that if the smaller states renounce their *equality*, they renounce at the same time their *liberty*. The truth is, it is a contest for power, not for liberty. Men are naturally equal, and societies or states, when fully independent, are also equal."

The simple question: what is the general interest?

> It is as reasonable that states should form leagues or compacts, and lesson or part with their national equality, as that men should form the social compact and, in doing so, lessen or surrender the natural equality of men. This is done in every society, and the grant to the society affects persons and property.

So, said Hamilton, "Let the people be represented according to numbers, the people will be free: every office will be equally open to all, and the majority of the people are to make the laws."

"Yet it is said," he pointed out, "that the states will be destroyed and the people will be slaves—This is not so. The people are free, at the expense of an artificial and ideal equality of the states."

His closing speech to the convention on June 29 declared, "This is a critical moment of American liberty—We are still too weak to exist without union. We must devise a system on the spot— It ought to be strong and nervous, hoping that the good sense, and principally the necessity of our affairs will reconcile the people to it."

In Hamilton's eighteenth-century usage, *nervous* meant sinewy, muscular, vigorous, strong, full of energy and courage, and as free from weakness as his tactics and the tactics of his fellow Cincinnatian on the dais could help him to make it.

Hamilton had placed seminal ideas before the convention. The "compromise" that rejected them had made the Virginia plan the basis of union. If it were not as strong a Union or as "high toned" as his plan, it was his horrific "stalking horse" that had made it tolerable—by a one-vote margin. It would provide the basis for a workable union.

On June 28, with debate growing even more bitter, Franklin urged that a clergyman be invited to offer prayers at the beginning of each session. According to Madison, Hamilton objected. He was confident that the convention could transact its business without "the necessity of calling in foreign aid."

He left Philadelphia the following day for mysterious personal reasons.

16

We the People of the United States

I am a friend to vigorous government but I hold it essential that the popular branch of it should be on a broad foundation.

—On the floor of the Constitutional Convention, September 8, 1787

Hamilton left behind him in Philadelphia an able new recruit to hold the floor for the nationalist cause in his absence: Rufus King, a delegate from Massachusetts, whom Major William Pierce described as "five feet ten, well formed, handsome, with a sweet, high toned voice."

Hamilton's fellow New York delegates, Yates and Lansing, quit the convention on July 5, never to return, for reasons that were the opposite of Hamilton's. As they explained to Governor Clinton, they had been appointed to revise the Articles of Confederation, not to draw up a wholly new constitution. But ever since Hamilton's speech and the approval of the Virginia plan the following day, the proceedings proved to them that the latter was the true purpose of the convention; so they withdrew. They justified their absence by arguing that with Hamilton also away, there was no need for them to stay to outvote him. The fact of their presence and voting, even voting against union, might imply Clinton's assent to any contrary outcome of the convention.

But if Hamilton's absence was what brought Yates and Lansing home, it made a significant contribution to progress by other large states toward his goal of union by removing New York's opposition vote. There were four or five other possible reasons for the timing of such a mysterious absence by a leading member of the convention, but the real one can only be guessed at.

In his absence came a showdown vote on the second great issue of the convention: the Connecticut plan, or Great Compromise. On July 16 on the question of equal representation by states in the upper house and by population in the lower, the small states carried the day, five in favor (Connecticut, New Jersey, Delaware, Maryland, and North Carolina) with four against (Pennsylvania, Virginia, South Carolina, and Georgia). Massachusetts was divided; New York, Rhode Island, and New Hampshire were recorded as not voting. Hamilton's private notes had foreshadowed this compromise. The small states won by a one-vote margin without needing New York's support.

Meanwhile, the focus of political significance followed Hamilton, Lansing, and Yates back to New York. Major William Pierce of Georgia had been valuable to Hamilton in helping swing Georgia's key small-state vote to back the Virginia plan. So when John Auldjo, a sometime client of Hamilton's, asked Hamilton to be his second in a duel with Pierce, Hamilton told him, "I can never take up the character of a second in a duel . . . till I have in vain tried to be a mediator. Be content with *enough* for more ought not to be expected." After much delicate negotiating, the ultimate interview was avoided. Honor—and the possible casualty of a hard-won vote from Georgia for union—were spared.

Late in August Hamilton was back in New York again for mysterious and inscrutable reasons that must have come up quite suddenly: there is no other way to account for his rushing back to Philadelphia and forth to New York again late in August for only a week or so of not very consequential floor appearances at the convention.

Though the content of the speeches and debates in the State House chamber were supposed to be closely guarded secrets, outside the chamber nothing could prevent chance remarks from slipping out or being slyly muttered or bibulously blurted over tankards at the Indian Queen—or purposefully leaked. On June 19, the very day after Madison had rather misleadingly recorded Hamilton's lecture on comparative government as an emotional commitment to British government for America including a kinglike, nonimpeachable "monarch," an anonymous person in Philadelphia supposedly wrote a deadpan letter to a person in Portsmouth, New Hampshire, saying that the members of the Constitutional Convention wished to invite the second son of King George III "to become King of the United States." Such a young man existed; he was Frederick, duke of York, the secular bishop of Osnaburg, a town in the Prussian province of Hanover. According to the alleged letter, the plan to make him king, which is "so agreeable to the people of America, and so manifestly for their interest," not surprisingly "meets with a favorable reception from the British Court." The members of the convention "have the subject in their deliberations, and are harmonious in their opinions; the means only of accomplishing so great an event, appears principally to occupy their counsels."

Hamilton had mentioned as a possibility in private conjectures that if the constitution failed, reunion with Britain might occur, with the duke of York installed as king. Copious extracts from the supposedly private letter were gleefully published in *The Fairfield* [Connecticut] *Gazette* on July 25, in the *Pennsylvania Gazette* on August 15, in the *Pennsylvania Journal* on August 25, and elsewhere. Concerned readers, trying to piece together what had been going on in the secret sessions in Philadelphia from the fragments of such stories, were horrified. This fantastic scheme to install Frederick as king of the United States was associated with Hamilton's remarkable speech of June 18 and the vote in favor of the Virginia plan the following day. It seemed to follow logically from Madison's account of what Hamilton had urged.

Publication of the story in Philadelphia on August 15 broke it around Hamilton's head. An alarmed Connecticut reader, Hezekiah Wetmore of Stratford, had supposedly sent a copy of *The Fairfield Gazette*'s story of July 25 to one James Reynolds of New York City, who, in turn, had passed it on to Hamilton. It may have been what sent him rushing back to New York: to run the canard to its source by tracking down the earlier publication in Connecticut.

James Reynolds was the man who had a complex and mysterious personal relationship with Hamilton that ostensibly began four years later in 1791. Hamilton's relationship with Reynolds and his wife was the root cause of Hamilton's ultimate ruin as a public man. His first known mention of Reynolds's name occurs in a letter of August 20, 1787, to his friend and client, Jeremiah Wadsworth, who was also the partner of Hamilton's brother-in-law John Barker Church. Hamilton wrote Wadsworth that an extract from the purported letter from Philadelphia to the person in Portsmouth "was sent by one *Whitmore* of Stratford . . . to a James Reynold [*sic*] of this City." Hamilton does not further identify "James Reynold" to Wadsworth. This leaves many questions open: how and why did Reynolds come to Hamilton with the story if Hamilton's name was not mentioned in it? Convention debates were secret, and Hamilton was supposed to be away in Philadelphia at the time in any event. Did Hamilton come to Reynolds then? If so, why? Why did Hamilton, in writing to Wadsworth, use the article for "a" James Reynold when he mentioned his name? Was it because Reynolds claimed to know Wadsworth but Hamilton doubted that Wadsworth would admit knowing such a man? Were Beckley and Reynolds friends or coadjutors? Who "fabricated" the Philadelphia letter? John Beckley, Reynolds, or someone else? Is the "fabrication" based on the leak of a truth? Plausible hypotheses give affirmative answers to these questions, but the truth is veiled in mystery that only deepens as the tragic events of Hamilton's later career unfold.

Wadsworth promptly replied that the purpose of the letter was "to scare the anti-federal party" into opposition to the Constitution; the author can hardly be Hezekiah Wetmore, whom he knows to be a patriot.

A curious fact is that although Jeremiah Wadsworth admits knowing Wetmore, he passes over James Reynolds's name in silence, though it seems certain he knows Reynolds well. Reynolds's father, David, had served under Wadsworth during the war in the commissary department, sometimes aided by son James. David had afterward spent time in jail for various shady business dealings. But Wadsworth's reply volunteers no comment whatsoever about Hamilton's informant, James Reynolds. The information he received from Reynolds led Hamilton's investigation to a dead end on a false trail.

James Reynolds was not a person of consequence or fame or a client of Hamilton, but he was a sometime client of Aaron Burr. He spent some time in jail and, after a flash of notoriety, finally disappeared entirely from sight. History offers no explanation of why he would be passing a purported extract from a letter from someone in Philadelphia to someone in New Hampshire to Hamilton in New York during the summer of 1787 unless he or possibly his handsome wife, Maria Reynolds, or both were then already rather well known in some way to Hamilton—or to an enemy like Beckley who had reason to hate him, or to Burr.

All that Hamilton's history later recorded was his notorious affair with Maria in 1791 and 1792. It tended to wax most intense during the summer months while Elizabeth and the children were upstate with the Schuylers. The Reynoldses' literary style later became well known and was closely analyzed, but it did not encompass the subtlety and literary quality that the bishop of Osnaburg letter displays. Hamilton may have been trying, through Wadsworth, to trace the letter back to John Beckley in Philadelphia. The latter's presence at its source, political convictions, ready access to secret information about the debates, capacity for intrigue, literary skill, and a motive for reprisal against Hamilton would all qualify him as a chief object of Hamilton's suspicions.

British-born, but not, as he sometimes claimed, the son of a knight, Beckley had come to Virginia in 1769 as a precocious 11-year-old. He served as the indentured scribe of John Clayton, the famous Virginia botanist, and attended Jefferson's alma mater, the College of William and Mary. He became mayor of Richmond; and in 1789, at 31, he would be elected first clerk of the national House of Representatives, the first member of the staff to be chosen by the new constitutional Congress. Jefferson called him the "best clerk in the United States."

The same day Hamilton had sought Wadsworth's help in tracking down his Philadelphia traducer, he asked King when he thought the convention would finish its work, because he wanted to be present before the end "for certain reasons" that he failed to enumerate. He had also heard whispers "that some late changes in your scheme have taken place which give it a higher tone. Is this the case?"

There had indeed been such changes. On September 6 debate centered on the manner of electing the president, by ballot by the national legislature, or by electors in such manner as the legislature in each state should direct. If the electors gave no candidate a majority of votes, the choice was to devolve on the Senate. To Hamilton, both plans created too powerful a presidency, too much like a hereditary monarch, too far from the people. He argued that under the first plan "the President was a monster elected for seven years, and ineligible afterwards having great powers . . . and continually tempted by this constitutional disqualification to abuse them in order to subvert the government. Some other mode of election should be devised." As for the second plan, "Considering the different views of different states, northern, middle and southern, the states' votes probably will not be concentrated, and appointment would devolve upon the senate. This will perpetuate the President, and aggrandize both him and the senate too much."

What was the remedy?

Let the highest number of ballots of the electors, whether a majority or not, appoint the president without involving the Senate in the process.

What was the objection to this? Merely that too small a number might appoint.

As the plan stood the Senate might take the candidate having the smallest number of votes and make him president against the will of the people expressed through their electors.

Hamilton's pressure to keep election of the president as close as possible to the people and out of the Senate reinforced the concept of separation of powers in a practical way. The report was amended to give final choice in case of a tie in electoral votes, not to the Senate, but to the House of Representatives, the popularly elected chamber, with each state there having a single vote on the question.

On September 8 Hamilton made still another push for giving more power to the people, supporting with "earnestness and anxiety" the motion of Hugh Williamson "to increase the number of members of the House." Acknowledging that "I am a friend to a vigorous Government," he declared at the same time, "I hold it essential that the popular branch of it should be on a broad foundation."

Williamson's motion was voted down. The sting of yet another defeat was partly removed the same day by Hamilton's appointment to the Committee of Style, which, in light of history, was probably the most important of all convention committees. Charged with molding and arranging the wording of all the drafts and resolutions into final form, Hamilton's fellow members, elegant stylists all, were Gouverneur Morris, James Madison, William Samuel Johnson, and Rufus King. Of all the delegates these five men probably had closer personal ties with Hamilton and Washington than any others.

As Hamilton knew, the symmetry, phraseology, form, and style of a document like the Constitution of 1787 in time become its very essence. Innumerable decisions of courts and Congresses and legislatures in the years since the committee met have turned on individual words—their position in each phrase, clause, and sentence—and even on points of punctuation.

Now, in these final weeks, Hamilton plied all he knew of the arts of accommodation and in his work with the Committee of Style. He had unforgettably established his preeminence as a student of all forms of government and his position on these matters remained more truly national than that of any other delegate, so Hamilton now enjoyed a distinct practical advantage. He could forcefully urge compromises and adjustments between proposals that differed less from each other than they fell short of the high tone of his well-publicized ideal. When he pointed out where middle ground lay or avowed that he would not object, his view in itself became a strong recommendation for acceptance by others who were more ready to settle for less than he claimed as ideal.

On September 10 Hamilton pointed out that Congress, not the states alone, should be able to call a convention to amend the Constitution. He proposed that Congress be empowered to call a convention whenever two-thirds of each branch should concur. He then seconded and pleaded for Madison's motion, which led directly to Article V, providing that by a two-thirds vote of both houses or on the application of two-thirds of the legislatures of the several states, Congress should propose amendments to the Constitution, which would be valid when ratified by three-fourths of the state legislatures or by conventions in three-fourths of the states. Hamilton was fighting for the maximum possible flexibility and amendability and against rigidity. "An easy mode should be established for supplying defects which will probably appear in the New System," he said.

In later debate the same day, delegates came down to the mechanics of ratifying the Constitution itself. Hamilton argued that it would be wrong for any nine states, by ratifying, to jam it down the throats of the remaining four. This would be "to institute a new Government on the ruins of the existing one." The plan should be approved by the Continental Congress first, this being "a necessary ingredient in the transaction." Hamilton's motion was defeated, leaving the Constitution to provide only that ratification by nine states, without any action by Congress, would be sufficient.

But if ratification by the states meant ratification by the state legislatures, too many entrenched, vested local interests would remain in control, he warned, remembering well Clinton's monolithic control in his own assembly. Special conventions would at least open up the possibility of new faces, fresh ideas, and more representation of the current wishes of the people at large. Hamilton moved to take the question away from the entrenched interests and to require the legislatures to refer it to a "Convention of Deputies in each state to be chosen by the people thereof." If the people's conventions approved, then "such approbation shall be binding and conclusive upon the state."

The Committee of Style recommended that a vote of three-fourths of each house of Congress be required to override a presidential veto. Advocate of the strong executive though he was, Hamilton thought this was going too far. Two-thirds was all that should be required to override a veto, he urged; and, for a change, he won. So the rule has remained to this day in Section 7 of Article I of the Constitution.

The Committee of Style, that inner circle of five within the 55 demigods, produced a masterpiece of draftsmanship. Their most important single contribution came at the beginning. The first version had started off with the words "We the people of the States of New

Hampshire, Massachusetts—'' and so on, listing each of the 13 by name, "do ordain, declare and establish the following constitution—''. As reported out by the Committee of Style, there was a world of difference: The name of each separate state was omitted. All the names were replaced by the words "United States." Now it read:

> We the people of the United States, in order to form a more perfect Union, establish justice, insure domestic tranquility, provide for the common defense, promote the general welfare, and secure the blessings of liberty to ourselves and our posterity, do ordain and establish this Constitution for the United States of America.

None of the delegates objected immediately to this polished statement of the purposes of the Constitution drawn up by Morris, Hamilton, and the others. But later in the Virginia ratifying convention, Patrick Henry with a bellow balked at the deletion of the names of the sovereign states. On narrow grounds, the deletion had been made necessary by the decision of August 31 that the new government should go into operation upon ratification by nine states. Because no one could tell for certain which states would ratify and which would stall or flatly refuse to join, the practical course was to leave out any mention at all of Rhode Island or New Hampshire or their sisters. Thus, perhaps fortuitously or perhaps through Hamilton's urgings in committee that the states be abolished or both, ''We the people of the United States,'' not the separate states, were acknowledged to be, and became, the nominal as well as real sovereign and source of the Constitution.

This opening acknowledgment of the people's direct relation to the national government was balanced by an almost equally important specific restraint on state interference with people's property rights. Rufus King, having failed to persuade his colleagues on the floor in late August of the usefulness of restraints on the power of the states to ''interfere in private contracts,'' now persuaded the committee to reinsert just such a clause. On September 14 the convention reconsidered this and accepted it without a murmur, pausing only to tighten it slightly. No state, the Constitution now made clear, was to pass any ''law impairing the obligation of contracts.''

Just before adjournment, the delegates debated enlargements of the powers of the general government. Hamilton's later policies and theories of the powers of the executive owe much to such last-minute enlargements. The delegates agreed to Rutledge's motion to deprive Congress of the power to ''appoint a Treasurer,'' who would be the chief financial officer of the new government. The future secretary of the treasury would be an officer of the executive branch, not an agent of Congress; yet there remained vestiges of a closer relationship between Congress and the secretary of the treasury than existed between Congress and other cabinet officers.

The last alteration proposed and accepted on September 15 was an echo of the struggle between the larger states on one side for power, justice, and ''one man, one vote'' and the smaller, on the other, for power, survival, and ''one state, one vote.'' Gouverneur Morris proposed ''to annex a further proviso'' to the amending clause, which ordained ''that no state, without its consent, shall be deprived of its equal suffrage in the Senate.'' The proviso carried. The small-staters could now relax and look forward to the ridiculously dispropor-tionate voting power they have enjoyed over the large ever since from their one-state, two-vote equal voice in the Senate.

The finished document came remarkably close, in terms of general strength and struc-ture, if not in all details of operation, to what Hamilton had urged. No one would have predicted in May that a Constitution with such powerful national institutions as a bicameral

Congress, an executive with magisterial power, and a Supreme Court whose writ would be the supreme law of the land would come out of the State House by September. It is a lonely position, but the thesis of this book is that Hamilton's public commitment to a system that was national, centralized, and consolidated and gave less autonomy to the states than any other delegate advocated, had more to do with the high tone and nervous strength of the final result than the efforts of any other delegate, except, of course, George Washington's.

Most historians, even those most sympathetic to Hamilton, like Clinton Rossiter, are fond of saying that Hamilton played a disappointing minor role at the convention largely because his unpopular views gained no converts. Most measures he backed went down to defeat. Rossiter partly excuses him by wondering "if there were not personal reasons for his lackluster showing that have never been revealed?" Auldjo? Beckley? James Reynolds? Maria?

On the other side, it may be argued that it was because he had no concern for personal popularity, but had larger purposes in mind, and because his specific views gained few converts for themselves, they won converts for the kind of constitution that satisfied him. Because he cared nothing to draw popularity to himself, he gained much for the document that emerged. His role made possible some of the Constitution's most remarkable features as well as the elevation and elegance of tone and style that is its most notable quality.

At every opportunity, at the critical moments, not perversely, not petulantly, not proudly, sometimes taking the stance of a powerful advocate, sometimes of a disinterested judge, Hamilton had ostentatiously called attention to how much his views differed from those of the majority of the delegates. But when, with a flourish, he signed the finished product on the final day, he was the most active of all in urging every other member to sign. "A few characters of consequence, by opposing or even refusing to sign the Constitution," he said, "might do infinite mischief by kindling the latent sparks which lurk under an enthusiasm . . . which may soon subside." He pointed with a touch of pride to the defeats he had regularly suffered in the convention, in the larger interest now of pressing most forcefully for its unanimous approval.

Hamilton did not join bitter-enders like Blount, Mason, Gerry, and Randolph by voicing unalterable objection to the document and refusing to sign.

The president, George Washington, stood to put the two final questions of the day:

On the proposition of Edmund Randolph, that there be a second convention, all the states voted "Nay."

On the question to adopt the Constitution as amended, all the states voted "Aye."

The Constitution was then ordered to be engrossed, and the house adjourned at 6:00 P.M. for a Sunday recess for prayer and rest.

When the convention assembled for the last time on Monday morning, September 17, 41 of the Framers were in their seats, but for New York, only Hamilton was present, his fellow delegates Yates and Lansing having long since gone home. Randolph, Gerry, and Mason, proud of their perfect attendance records, anxious to see the end with their own eyes, were unworried by the prospect of being recusants at a communion. The sick, exhausted Dickinson had gone home over the weekend after asking Read to sign his name.

Someone, probably Major William Jackson, read the engrossed Constitution to men who by now knew its every word almost by heart, whereupon Dr. Franklin "rose with a speech in his hand." Unable to remain for long on his feet, he handed it to Wilson to read and then to Madison to copy into his notes. McHenry described the speech as "plain, insinuating, and persuasive." It would create a benign climate for the signing, prevent other dissenters from defecting, and perhaps lure Blount and Randolph, at least, back into the fold.

It was vintage Benjamin Franklin—wise, gentle, disarming, and politically realistic. As all listened that morning to the patriarch of the demigods, his words must have cast a spell:

> Mr. President: I confess that there are several parts of this constitution which I do not approve, but I am not sure I shall never approve them: For having lived long, I have experienced many instances of being obliged by better information, or fuller consideration, to change opinions even on important subjects, which I once thought right, but found to be otherwise. It is, therefore, that the older I grow, the more apt I am to doubt my own judgment, and to pay more respect to the judgment of others. . . . Though many private persons think almost as highly of their own infallibility as of that of their sect, few express it so naturally as a certain French lady, who in a dispute with her sister, said "I don't know how it happens, Sister, but I meet with no body my myself, that's always in the right—*Il ny' a que moi qui a toujours raison.*"
>
> On the whole, Sir, I cannot help expressing a wish that every member of the Convention who may still have objections to it, would with me, on this occasion, doubt a little of his own infallibility, and to make manifest our unanimity, put his name to the instrument.

The old fox then offered a motion conceived by a young fox, Gouverneur Morris, which sought to "gain the dissenting members" by inviting all delegates to sign as witnesses to the fact of "the unanimous consent of the states" on the floor. This would create at least an illusion of complete concord.

While the benevolent mood created by Franklin's speech still held the delegates in thrall, one last parliamentary moment remained to give the people more voting power in the lower house. Nine days earlier, Hamilton had spoken with great earnestness and anxiety in favor of a motion to broaden direct representation of the people by population in the House, holding that it was "essential that the popular branch should be on a broad foundation" to prevent any "connection between the President and Senate" that "would tend to perpetuate him, *by corrupt influence.*" Then Hamilton's motion had been defeated.

Nathaniel Gorham now moved that the 1:40,000 voting ratio planned for the House be changed to 1:30,000, thus creating more representatives in the House, each representing a smaller number of people, with each more responsive to popular views.

After King and Carroll had seconded the motion, Washington rose to put the question. Then, to the astonishment of all, after having maintained silence on all debatable issues since the day John Rutledge and Robert Morris had escorted him to the chair on the dais, Washington made his first and only speech of the entire convention.

> Although my situation has hitherto restrained me from offering sentiments on questions depending in the House, and it might be thought, ought now to impose silence on me; yet I cannot forbear expressing my wish that the alteration proposed might take place. . . . The smallness of the proportion of Representatives has been considered by many members of the Convention an insufficient security for the rights and interests of the people. I acknowledge that it always appeared to me among the exceptionable parts of the plan; and late as the present moment is for admitting amendments, I think this of so much consequence that it would give me much satisfaction to see it adopted.

Now, at this supreme moment in world history for the cause of free popular government, the president general, whose iron decorum had never been breached, saw fit to breach it one single time in order to support the motion that Hamilton had first urged.

Many would now no longer be in any doubt of the careful prior planning of this and many earlier parliamentary moves that had been worked out by the two men over the tankards at the Indian Queen or at Robert Morris's. This last motion drove home the fact that purposeful planning had had more to do with the success of this and earlier motions than all the speeches exchanged in all the floor debates.

The delegates adopted the amendment unanimously. What else could they do? They then approved the engrossed Constitution and made ready to sign. Blount of North Carolina was still opposed to signing. Of Gerry, one delegate wrote, "he was fond of objecting to everything he did not propose!" Randolph once again rose to explain that by refusing to sign "he meant only to keep himself free to be governed by his duty as it should be prescribed by his future judgment." This was too much for Hamilton, Gouverneur Morris, and Williamson. All resounded Franklin's theme, one that would become familiar in the fight over ratification. "The present plan," Morris said, was "the best that was to be attained," and since "general anarchy" was the "alternative," he would "take it with all its faults." "For himself," Williamson added, "he did not think a better plan was to be expected."

Now came the moment for which Hamilton's speech of June 18, his plan for a government, his draft of a Constitution, even his attack on Clinton, had laid the foundation.

"No man's ideas are more remote from the plan than mine are known to be," he averred, "but is it possible to deliberate between anarchy and convulsion on one side, and the chance of good to be expected from the plan on the other."

That no man's ideas were less remote from the strength and tone of the plan that had emerged might have been said by Hamilton with equal truth and more self-satisfaction. But for him to have done so would not have furthered the purpose that saying the opposite— which came with unique force from him—did. After Hamilton sat down, Blount changed his mind and agreed to sign the document.

Franklin's motion on the question of adoption passed ten to zero.

The delegates then came forward to place their signatures on the documents. As each came forward, Hamilton, like a good lawyer helping a lay client, wrote in the name of the state before the place each signer was to sign. His handwriting and the strokes of his pen outlining each state's name add the most intimate possible physical flourish any hand was capable of adding to all else he had contributed to the cause of human liberty in a constitutional republic under law. Technically, because of the absence of Yates and Lansing, the state of New York could not be counted as one of the "states present and voting." In the final resolution laying the Constitution before Congress and the states, 11 states are listed plus one individual, "Mr. Hamilton from New York."

Nothing Hamilton did or supposedly failed to do at the convention caused any of his great colleagues or collaborators there or later in his life to minimize the importance of his role or to concur in the modern conventional assessment that his performance was a disappointment, and they were no mean judges of other men. On the contrary, they saw him named to two of the most important committees; never forgot his speech of June 18; and always spoke, wrote, and acted as if, in matters of political philosophy and constitution building, Hamilton was not only their peer, but also their mentor.

There is nothing especially unique about a written constitution. In itself it is nothing more than a skeletal outline of old ideas. Since 1787 innumerable fine-sounding constitutions have been composed; Soviet Russia has one. When the Constitutional Convention adjourned that September 17, 1787, there was a Holy Roman Emperor; Venice was a republic;

France was ruled by a king; China, by an emperor; Japan, by a shogun; Russia, by a czar. Great Britain was a monarchy tempered by the barest beginnings of democracy, in which less than 2 percent of the population enjoyed voting representation. All those proud regimes—and scores of others—have passed into history. Among the leading nations of the world, the only government that stands essentially unchanged is the Federal Union put together in 1787 by 13 states on the East Coast of North America. It has survived foreign wars, a civil war, panics, depressions and recessions, Teapot Dome, Bobby Baker, Watergate, impeachments, and pardons.

Flesh, blood, passion, desire, intellect, experience, force, honor, and moral commitment must come together to bring reality to well-worn skeletal outlines, stay with them, and create institutions that operate according to the words and keep them alive with reverent adherence for years, decades, and centuries to make a constitution worth more than the paper it is written on.

This writer's thesis is that for the reasons given, and still to come, the unique strength, character, and freedom of the nation that has lived under this elegant Constitution owes more to Hamilton for what it is, as we see it plain after almost 200 years, than it does to any other man, of his own time or since, notwithstanding his occasional unexplained absences in New York that summer from the floor of the State House—and the hall of the Indian Queen.

17

The Federalist Papers and Other Persuaders

It seems to have been reserved to the people of this country, by their conduct and example, to decide the important question, whether societies of men are really capable or not, of establishing good government from reflection and choice, or whether they are forever destined to depend for their political constitutions, on accident and force.

—The Federalist, No. 1, October 27, 1787

The terms of the covenant "secretly arrived at" during the summer in Philadelphia were now made known to the people of all the states. Early in the morning of September 18, Major William Jackson set out by stage for New York "in order to lay the great result . . . before the United States in Congress" there.

Many of the Framers were also members of Congress. They now followed Major Jackson back to New York, changed hats, took their seats in the New York City Hall, and made ready to welcome warmly the charter they had sent up to themselves from Philadelphia. What the Framers present had wanted from Congress was a strong recommendation to the states that the Constitution be ratified; what Congress voted was much less: a noncommittal declaration providing only that it be transmitted to the states.

The resolution transmitting the Constitution to the states for ratification launched Hamilton on another consuming political contest. It was a contest that could easily have gone either way that consisted of a series of 13 separate battles for ratification waged up and down the map of the 13 states. In New York, as at Philadelphia, Hamilton was the visible champion, strategist, tactician, and polemicist for the cause; elsewhere, with Madison's collaboration, Hamilton's views would make themselves felt through correspondence and *The Federalist Papers*.

Chief support came from merchants and businessmen, small shopkeepers and tradesmen and their followers in the towns along the eastern seaboard. People whose living depended on trade and commerce by and large favored it. But in the hinterlands, among farmers and landed proprietors, debtors and frontiersmen, opposition was intense. Favorable or unfavorable economic impact was never far below the surface of what people believed was politically, socially, and morally right. Foreseeing that its chances in state legislatures were slim, the Constitutional Convention at Hamilton's urging had called instead for state ratifying conventions, popularly elected, to pass on its handiwork. There was also the revolutionary proviso that the consents of only nine of the 13 states, not unanimity, would be sufficient to start the new nation off as a going concern.

Governor Clinton of New York showed no disposition even to call the legislature into session to devise machinery for the election of a ratifying convention. In court corridors during recesses of trials, at luncheons, with groups of friends and rivals at Fraunces or Cape's Tavern, or over coffee or tankards of ale in the late afternoon at the Tontine, Hamilton's smile flickered over the irony of his own position. Over and over again he explained with quicksilver charm that "no man's ideas were more remote from the plan" than his. Even so, he now ardently urged all to support it. In private conversations with small groups of men no one could be a more powerful persuader. Private dinners were part of the tactics too, and the Hamiltons entertained frequently.

Few wives could have been better fitted than Elizabeth Hamilton for the part she now was called upon to play. She had, after all, been accustomed to helping her mother as hostess of distinguished people from everywhere in her father's houses at Albany and Old Saratoga. She now presided over a growing household at 57 Wall Street.

Late at night, by candlelight, after the guests had gone, Betsy would lend her hand to Hamilton's by making neat copies of his drafts of *The Federalist,* as her husband scribbled on. Sometimes, very late, she would grow faint, for she was now pregnant with the child of one of Hamilton's trips home from Philadelphia. When he was born April 14, 1788, their third son would be christened James Alexander.

As Hamilton's plan for *The Federalist Papers* unfolded, it became obvious that the work was too vast for any one man to carry out, even a writer as facile as Hamilton. John Jay agreed to help write some, but he was a slow, methodical writer with a somewhat tedious style. Besides, he soon fell ill.

James Madison had been one of the chief architects of the Constitition and agreed with Hamilton's arguments for a strong union. Now in New York as a Virginia delegate to Congress preparing for the fight over ratification there, Madison agreed to collaborate with Hamilton on *The Federalist.*

Gouverneur Morris later said that Hamilton had pressed him to help, too. Another good friend of Hamilton's, William Duer, helped out with three essays in defense of the Constitution, which he signed "Philo-Publius," but they were not incorporated in *The Federalist* itself and Duer dropped out of the faster intellectual company.

Speed was essential. Pennsylvania, New Jersey, and Delaware had already made provision for holding their conventions; other states were preparing to follow suit. If *The Federalist Papers* were to influence decisions of the delegates, they must appear in swift, consecutive order.

The purpose of Federalists, as the men who had fought hardest for the new, national Constitution came to be called—somewhat paradoxically—was much the same in every state: to push ratification of the Constitution through promptly and unconditionally. Delay in state ratifications had drained all vitality from the Articles of Confederation before they had gone into force. Thin margins of victory over bitter men would not be enough. If the Constitution were to last, even those who opposed it most vigorously would have to concede its legitimacy. Ratifications by nine small states would not be good enough to bring the Constitution to life. The geographical and political position of any one of the four largest states—New York, Virginia, Pennsylvania, or Massachusetts—was such that the Constitution would be a dead letter if it should vote to stay out.

In every state, Anti-Federalists made forceful cause against the Constitution in speeches, letters, pamphlets, and newspaper broadsides, repeating endlessly that the Federalists were trying to stampede the country into an untested new system by painting a picture of troubles that did not exist and horrors that might not arise.

Anti-Federalists charged that the Framers had acted contrary to both the law and spirit of the Articles of Confederation. They had done this—a damning and symbolic piece of evidence—as a "Dark Conclave" under a "thick veil of secrecy." The Constitution, they felt, was a long step toward monarchy and aristocracy—a repudiation of the Revolution of 1776. Four features drew fire in every state, even from men who wished it well: the failure to include a bill of rights ("Should not such a thing have preceded the model?" Adams asked Jefferson); the creation of a powerful and virtually irresponsible executive ("A bad edition of a Polish king," Jefferson warned Adams); the provision for "one state, two votes" in the upper house ("this host of influence and power," George Clinton described it); and the narrow scale of representation in the House of Representatives (which would make it simply an "assistant aristocratical branch," wrote one outraged Bostonian).

In Patrick Henry's angry words, the Constitution doomed the states to obsolescence by creating "one national government." The taxation clause, George Mason warned softly, "clearly discovers that it is a national government, and no longer a confederation." The supremacy clause, Robert Whitehill of Pennsylvania echoed angrily, "eradicates every vestige of state government—and was intended so—it was deliberated." Thomas Wait of Maine held that the "vast continent of America" could not be ruled on principles of freedom if "consolidated into one government." He wrote a friend, "You might as well attempt to rule Hell by prayer."

So Hamilton was taking on a mighty task of advocacy when he grasped his quill to write *The Federalist, No. 1*. When he had finished he signed it with the name of "Publius."

The pen name of the mime was the one he had used in 1778 as an army officer to attack venal congressmen like Samuel Chase. It may still have seemed appropriate to conceal the identity of three men who were writing as one—a prizewinning mime could quickly switch identity from one character to another during a single performance. Besides, as a proper name, *Publius* called to mind the common noun *publisher* and its Latin root in *publicare*, "to proclaim," "to bring before the public." At any rate, the signature *Publius* for the whole series of 85 papers served to keep the attention of readers focused firmly on the points being made rather than on the personalities or peccadillos of individual authors.

The *Federalist No. 1*, datelined New York, addressed to "The People of the State of New York," appeared in *The* [New York] *Independent Journal: or The General Advertiser* on October 27, 1787, and reappeared in both *The New York Packet* and *The* [New York] *Daily Advertiser* on October 30. Readers of these newspapers were immediately aware that here was no ordinary polemicist.

"The subject speaks its own importance," Publius announced. "Nothing less than the existence of the UNION, the safety and welfare of the parts of which it is composed, the fate of an empire, in many respects the most interesting in the world."

He was speaking not for himself nor for a faction or a party, but for all mankind for all time:

> It has been frequently remarked that it seems to have been reserved to the people of this country, by their conduct and example, to decide the important question, whether societies of men are really capable or not, of establishing good government from reflection and choice, or whether they are forever destined to depend for their political constitutions, on accident and force.

Mankind was now at a political continental divide:

> If there be any truth in the remark, the crisis at which we are arrived may with propriety be regarded as the era in which that decision is to be made; and a wrong election of the part we shall act may, in this view, deserve to be considered as the general misfortune of mankind.

Although it was true that much of the opposition to the new Constitution came from men like Clinton whose obvious interest it was to resist any diminution in the power they wielded under the present state governments, Publius would refuse to dwell on critical "observations of this nature." With a fairness that would strike a new high note in American pamphleteering, a pitch to which he would too seldom rise, Hamilton agreed that much of the opposition was honest, if wrongheaded, in intent. To this honest opposition he addressed himself. "We are not always sure," he admitted, "that those who advocate the truth are influenced by purer principles than their antagonists."

He warned his fellow citizens to be on their guard against attempts to influence their judgment "by any impressions other than those which may result from the evidence of truth." He frankly avowed that he was in favor of the new Constitution while "my motives must remain in the depository of my own breast. My arguments will be open to all, and may be judged of by all. They shall at least be offered in a spirit which will not disgrace the cause of truth."

He called attention to universal truths of human nature: "Jealousy is the usual concomitant of violent love, and the noble enthusiasm of liberty is too apt to be infected with a spirit of narrow and illiberal distrust."

He sounded a lifelong theme:

> A dangerous ambition more often lurks behind the specious mask of zeal for the rights of the people, than under the forbidding appearance of zeal for the firmness and efficiency of government . . . of those men who have overturned the liberties of republics the greatest number have begun their career, by paying an obsequious court to the people, commencing Demagogues and ending Tyrants.

He concluded with a survey of the points that Publius intended to discuss in future papers: the utility of the Union to political prosperity, the necessity of an "energetic" government, "the conformity of the proposed constitution to the true principles of republican government," and "the additional security which its adoption will afford to [republican] government, to liberty and to property."

At its most immediate level, *The Federalist* was a series of papers defending the proposed Constitution and urging its adoption by the people of New York. But as the series unfolded, it became something larger and more philosophical. From its methodical analysis of the clauses and sections of the Constitution, there emerged a coherent essay on the purposes and nature of all government, a universal political philosophy adapted to the American scene. That such a plan of composition was plainly visible to Madison or Jay at the beginning is unlikely; yet as the work proceeded, the whole took on an organic form that transmuted its immediate purpose of serving as a brief in favor of the Constitution into a great essay on the subject of free government.

Had they brooded over *The Federalist* for years before carefully putting the first word on paper, the three busy men who were Publius could hardly have created a more unified architectonic structure.

In accordance with Hamilton's overall plan, John Jay, the former secretary for foreign affairs of the Confederation, next took up pen and wrote Nos. 2 through 5, dealing with relations with foreign powers. The same thread of argument runs through all—the indispensable necessity of a firmly united nation to defend against foreign aggression and prevent a breakup into rival confederacies. With these four papers, Jay's contribution halted until he wrote No. 64, a defense of the Senate's role in the treaty-making process. Hamilton and Madison shared the rest of the labor, with Hamilton writing in all more than 50 of the 85. Madison's papers made up in substance however much they lacked in number.

New essays appeared two, three, and sometimes four times a week, rotating among the New York papers. Hamilton wrote in haste, snatching scraps of composition time from between interviewing clients and trying law suits.

In four vigorous numbers, 6 through 9, Hamilton called attention to the perils of disunion that would ensue if the Constitution were not ratified; signs and portents of civil war were already visible: "Let the point of extreme depression to which our national dignity and credibility have sunk, let the inconveniences felt everywhere from a lax and ill administration of government, let the revolt of a part of the State of North Carolina, the late menacing disturbances in Pennsylvania, and the actual insurrections and rebellions in Massachusetts, declare—!" the need for union. Hamilton employed such references with telling effect to argue for strong authority that could deal with uprisings promptly and forcefully.

In No. 10, the first of the series written by Madison, and one of the most famous of all, Madison anticipated a major thesis of Karl Marx. With plain speaking untempered by moral judgments echoing some points Hamilton had made at the convention, Madison argued that "A well-constructed union" is necessary "to break and control the violence of faction, the most common and durable source of which is the various and unequal distribution of property. Those who hold and those who are without property are always separate and distinct interests in society." Nothing Hamilton ever wrote sounded more typically Hamiltonian than Madison's first essay as Publius.

In the philosophy of John Locke, which was the then prevailing philosophical mode for thinking about governmental systems, protection of property emerged as the principal purpose of government. This was a consequence of natural law, a mandate of municipal law, and had an ethical foundation. Property was derived from labor, and each person had a different value because his ability and industry differed from that of every other person. Madison put it this way: It is "The diversity in the faculties of men, from which the rights of property originate. . . . The protection of these faculties is the first object of government. From the protection of different and unequal faculties of acquiring property, the possession of different degrees and kinds of property immediately results. . . ."

Nowhere in his own writings did Hamilton lock people and property into any such rigidly doctrinaire and simplistic equation as Madison insisted on here.

Madison added that a majority in a small area, governing directly under a "pure democracy," could and would ride roughshod over the interests and liberties of a minority. He insisted that "Neither moral nor religious motives can be relied on as an adequate control." Hence a republic, such as the Constitution envisaged, was the best form to protect minority rights. The delegation of authority to a small group of citizens chosen for wisdom, patriotism, and love of justice might avoid such madnesses as "a rage for paper money, for abolition of debts, for an equal division of property, or for any other improper or wicked project."

Hamilton at the Constitutional Convention had summed up the idea that the government must assure liberty and order by mediating between warring classes: "Give all power to the many, they will oppress the few. Give all power to the few; they will oppress the many. Both therefore, ought to have power, that each may defend itself against the other."

In later papers of *The Federalist,* Hamilton followed up Madison's economic arguments by emphasizing the commercial importance of a union that could meet European nations on an equal footing and enforce respect for its trade and commerce by a powerful army and navy. The prosperity of commerce was the "most useful as well as the most productive source of national wealth."

Hamilton's views closely followed those of Thomas Hobbes in *The Leviathan:* the national state should not be limited in its functions to police powers or to keeping of the peace, but should help promote general prosperity by positive means. Hobbes believed that "a general Providence" must overcome poverty. The weak, the poor, the handicapped, those unable to work, "ought not to be left to the Charity of private persons; but to be provided for . . . by the Lawes of the Common-wealth." Those with strong bodies should work "and to avoyd the excuse of not finding employment, there ought to be such Lawes, as may encourage all manner of Arts; as Navigation, Agriculture, Fishing, and all manner of Manufacture that requires labour." Because ". . . the Passions of men, are commonly more potent than their Reason," as Hobbes observed, "it follows, that where the publique and private interest are most closely united, there is the publique most advanced." Hamilton's sentiments exactly.

Liberty was in law; only a powerful state could enforce the law; due process was the means to private and public happiness.

In 1787 and 1788, while Madison was filling in the outlines of *Federalist Papers* suggested to him by Hamilton, most of his writing reads like vintage Hamilton. But two years later, having fallen under the aegis of his fellow Virginian Jefferson, Madison swung around to an almost opposite set of views; Hamilton hewed for the rest of his life to those Madison had earlier shared with him. It is doubtful that, without Hamilton for his aegis in 1787 and 1788, Madison would have contributed as much as he did to a national Constitution and to seeking its ratification by his contributions to *The Federalist* and by his work at the Virginia ratifying convention.

Much ink has been spilled by scholars on the question of which of the two wrote which of the disputed papers. Madison was meticulous in claiming credit for all of his own authorship, but once the job had been done and the result accomplished, Hamilton was characteristically casual about claiming personal credit for his—until the day before his duel with Burr. Then, perhaps full of a presentiment of death, Hamilton walked into the office of his old friend Judge Egbert Benson, where he learned from the judge's nephew, Robert Benson, that the judge and Rufus King had gone to Massachusetts for a few days. While the two spoke quietly, Hamilton took down a volume of Pliny's letters from one of the bookshelves in the office and held it in his hand. A few days later, after Hamilton was dead, Robert

Benson remembered his visit, looked in the Pliny, and found a scrap of paper, unsigned but in Hamilton's hand, listing the *Federalist Papers* that he had written. Judge Benson pasted the list inside the cover of his own copy of *The Federalist* and deposited it with the New York Society Library for safekeeping. From there the original was stolen in 1818 and never recovered.

The episode, which only adds to the confusion over authorship, somehow serves to symbolize the often partial, qualified, and grudging thanks that has been accorded Hamilton by the United States and other free peoples of the world and those aspiring to be free for his priceless, nonroyalty-paying, nontax-deductible gift of *The Federalist Papers* to all of them.

The great series rolled on in the newspapers, continuing through No. 77, published on April 2, 1788. The last eight numbers, ending with 85, were first printed in the second volume of J. and A. McLean's edition of *The Federalist* of May 28, 1788. Then beginning on June 14, the papers were reprinted at invervals of several days, first in *The Independent Journal* and then in *The New York Packet*.

When Hamilton had first contracted with Archibald McLean, the printer, for printing and binding *The Federalist,* he had planned only 20 or at most 25 essays. McLean estimated the cost would be £30. With the beginning of the busy term of the New York Supreme Court, Hamilton had to take a vacation from Publius to get back to his law practice and his duties as a member of the Continental Congress, to which he had just been elected again. After writing Nos. 1 and 6 through 9, 11 through 13, 15 through 17, 21 through 36, and coauthoring 18 through 20 with Madison, he took a break through the end of February, and Madison wrote Nos. 37 through 48 and 53. There is a scholarly dispute over which of the two, or both, wrote Nos. 49 through 58, 62 and 63, although Madison's claim to authorship of them is the stronger. With Madison's departure for Virginia at the end of February, it fell to Hamilton alone to complete the important papers that remained, including the detailed exposition of the meaning of particular sections of the Constitution in all the remaining papers through No. 85. As a result, it is to Hamilton that lawyers and courts, as well as historians and philosophers, have chiefly looked since 1787 for the roots of precedental authority on the meaning of the most important parts of the Constitution.

The Federalist Papers demonstrate the precision and prescience of Hamilton's answers to the knottiest problems the nation has faced for two centuries. For example, the drama of abuse of presidential power, of impeachment and pardon, as Hamilton discussed it in No. 67, has been played out before Americans within very recent history. Hamilton as Publius also explained with similar perspicacity the constitutional provisions for regulating elections (Nos. 59–61), for qualification and representation of senators (No. 62 with Madison), the general powers of the president (No. 67), the president's appointive power (Nos. 68 and 76), the importance of "energy in the executive" (No. 70), the reasons for and against a four-year term for presidents and unlimited eligibility for reelection (Nos. 71 and 72), the president's veto power (No. 73), the role of president and Senate in the treaty-making process (No. 75), and the doctrine of judicial supremacy and judicial review by extension of the doctrine of *Rutgers* v. *Waddington*.

This was perhaps Hamilton's greatest contribution of all. It was in *The Federalist No. 78* that the American people—and even some who had been delegates to the Constitutional Convention—first received the news that the Constitution had incorporated the thesis of Hamilton's brief No. 6 to the Mayor's Court. Neither the Constitution itself nor Hamilton had baldly stated that "we are under a Constitution, but the Constitution is what the judges say it is." But as a member of the Committee of Style of the Constitution, he had helped see to it that the power of interpreting the Constitution would fall logically on the Supreme Court. From this felicity of style, it was but a short step to *The Federalist No. 78*. Hamilton wrote that judicial review "only supposes that the power of the people is superior to both" judicial power and legislative power; it follows that "where the will of the legislature, declared in the statutes, stands in opposition to that of the people, declared in the Constitution, the judges ought to be governed by the latter rather than by the former." Largely on the strength of these words, constitutionalism became "one of the most persistent and pervasive characteristics of American democracy."

The concluding series of papers discuss further reaches of the judicial power, the powers of the Supreme Court and of the inferior federal courts, the relations between federal and state courts, trial by jury as the "palladium of free governments" (Nos. 79–83), and the question of the need for a Bill of Rights (No. 84).

There were important things that Publius failed to foresee. In No. 84, Hamilton said that a bill of rights was unnecessary because such protections were sufficiently provided in the Constitution as drawn and that further specification might lead to unforeseen invasions of freedom at the margins of the rights that were specifically guaranteed. Publius did not envisage the two-party system, nominating conventions, and boss rule. But Publius' fears of insufficient strength in the federal government were well founded, as Jefferson's Kentucky and Virginia Resolutions of ten years later, threats of New England secession 15 years later, the Hartford Convention, South Carolina nullification, Southern secession, and the Civil War were all to demonstrate.

Hamilton closed the great brief for his ailing client with a dose of "better than nothing" for "human minds fond of compromise": "I never expect to see a perfect work from imperfect man. . . . The compacts which are to embrace thirteen distinct States in a common bond of amity and union, must as necessarily be a compromise of as many dissimilar interests and inclinations. How can perfection spring from such materials?"

The Federalist appeared in five or six editions during Hamilton's lifetime and has been republished innumerable times since. It is the basic commentary on the fundamental law of the United States. Constant citation by the courts from that day to this has made it Constitutional authority second only to the Constitution itself. Young James Kent, later chancellor of New York, wrote in December 1787, "I think 'Publius' is a most admirable writer and wields the sword of party dispute with justice, energy and inconceivable dexterity. The author must be Alexander Hamilton who . . . in genius and political research, is not inferior to Gibbon, Hume and Montesquieu."

Washington wrote to Hamilton:

> As the perusal of the political papers under the signature of Publius has afforded me great satisfaction, I shall certainly consider them as claiming a most distinguished place in my library.—I have read every performance which has been printed on one side and the other of the great question lately agitated . . . and, without an unmeaning compliment, I will say that I have seen no other so well calculated [in my judgment] to produce conviction in an unbiased mind, as the Production of your Triumvirate.

Guizot, the French foreign minister, wrote, "In the application of elementary principles of government to practical administration, it was the greatest work known" to him. And Charles A. Beard, that great Populist among historians, acknowledged that "In my opinion it is the most instructive work on political science ever written in the United States; and owing to its practical character, it ranks first in the world's literature of that subject."

In all 13 states, in every town and village, on farm and plantation, the political controversy over ratification of the Constitution raged with a fury unexampled in previous American experience.

The pivotal states of Massachusetts, South Carolina, Virginia, New Hampshire, and New York had ample time to read and digest much of *The Federalist* before coming to final decisions. Proponents of ratification found it an inexhaustible arsenal of arguments for use in debate.

Delaware, Pennsylvania, and New Jersey ratified in state conventions before the end of 1787. Georgia and Connecticut followed early in 1788. These five had been expected; the real opposition was in the great states of Massachusetts, South Carolina, Virginia, and New York. Hamilton led the Federalist forces in New York; his collaborator Madison was the party whip in Virginia; Hamilton's disciple Rufus King worked for the cause in Massachusetts; his good friends the Pinckneys were active in South Carolina. Federalist leaders wrote to each other continually, advising, exhorting, planning, keeping one another in immediate touch with the ebb and flow of Federalist fortunes in each of their states.

The opposition was just as well organized. Using tactics that had served well during the Revolution, the Anti-Federalists spread a network of committees of correspondence out from New York to rally all forces against the Constitution. John Lamb, the collector of customs, was chairman of the New York Republican Committee, and his expresses went out to Richard Henry Lee, Patrick Henry, and George Mason of Virginia; to Aedanus Burke of South Carolina; to other cohorts in Massachusetts and Maryland. Lee's pamphlets known as "Letters of the Federal Farmer" contained some of the most cogent arguments against ratification. As in revolutionary days, letters were sent clandestinely and under false names and covers.

In New York, Governor Clinton showed no disposition even to call for an election of delegates to a ratifying convention. As 1788 began, he still had made no move. Hamilton determined to force his hand. On January 31, 1788, he arranged for a resolution to be introduced in the assembly to call a convention; on February first, a similar resolution came before the senate. They squeaked by in both houses, 27 to 25 in the assembly; 11 to 8 in the senate.

The election for delegates to the convention was held on April 3 and for five days thereafter. Both sides had agreed on universal adult male suffrage for the election, thereby insuring that the New York convention would be the most democratically chosen of any in the 13 states. The Anti-Federalists believed that such broad suffrage was in their interest, feeling certain that the poor and unpropertied yeomanry would vote overwhelmingly against the Constitution.

Most Federalists feared they were right. But unlike many other Federalists, Hamilton urged the broadest possible base for suffrage so that the legitimacy of constitutional government would come directly from the people. Since the convention had finally been called only after Federalists' urging, Hamilton's party deserved major credit for fostering the broadest possible base for suffrage in the convention.

In the voting, Clinton and the Anti-Federalists won an overwhelming victory, 46 delegates to the Federalists' 19. Clintonians swept the entire state except the four lower counties, New York, Kings, Richmond, and Westchester. Even Queens went Anti-Federal. But in New York City, within Hamilton's ambience, the Federal majority was immense. Of a total of 2,836 ballots cast, the nine Federal candidates received a minimum of 2,651 votes and a maximum of 2,735 to 134 for the chief Anti-Federalist candidate, Governor Clinton. This extraordinary show of power by Hamilton's local machine led some, out of derisory respect, to dub the city Hamiltonopolis.

From the debacle Hamilton had saved what he had to save—a power base in his home county and adjacent counties—but little else. The Anti-Federalist majority was four-sevenths of the state at large, and two-thirds in the convention. There was even talk that New York City should secede from New York State.

The city Federalists who had been elected included some of the ablest men in the state, Hamilton, John Jay, Richard Morris, John Sloss Hobart, Robert R. Livingston, Isaac Roosevelt, James Duane, Richard Harrison, and Nicholas Low. The Clintonians had Clinton himself, John Lansing, Melancton Smith, Robert Yates, and 42 others.

Far from being overawed by Clinton's majority, Hamilton briskly set about making up for his lack of votes by energy and eloquence.

Thinking continentally, Hamilton turned his repudiation by New York to good use in other states by writing friends there to point out that if they wished to avoid civil war, and so forth, they must speed through ratification in their own conventions. On February 16, Massachusetts joined the procession; on April 26, Maryland ratified; on May 23, South Carolina finally approved. With these eight states already decided, only one more was required to put the new union on a going basis. But Rhode Island was hopeless, North Carolina seemingly as bad, and New York firmly oppposed. Thus either New Hampshire or Virginia must come in or Hamilton's constitutional labors would be for nothing. Without Virginia, remote New Hampshire would mean little.

So the battle for the Constitution came down to battles for the two great states, Virginia and New York. A nine-state union without these two would be but a paper union, no union at all, a geographical monstrosity of two separated confederacies. Anti-Federalists like George Mason, Richard Henry Lee, James Monroe, William Grayson, Theodorick Bland, and Patrick Henry seemed to be winning the war of words in Virginia, and they came into the June convention at Richmond with at least half of the 170 delegates. James Madison led the Federalist side there, with the backing of George Wythe, John Marshall, Henry Lee, Edmund Pendleton, and Governor Edmund Randolph, who had at last made up his inconstant mind.

Hamilton wrote to Madison in Virginia, "It will be of vast importance that an exact communication should be kept up between us while the two conventions are in session. The moment any decisive question is taken, if favorable, I request you to dispatch an express to me, with pointed orders to make all possible diligence, by changing horses, etc. All expense shall be thankfully and liberally paid."

To John Sullivan of New Hampshire, Hamilton wrote in similar vein, and Rufus King in Boston told John Langdon in New Hampshire to send him any good news too, so that he could forward it to Hamilton by a relay of horses.

When Hamilton and his little band of Federalists—John Jay, James Duane, Robert R. Livingston among them—arrived in Poughkeepsie, they found Main Street, which was the local interruption of the post road, and East Street, which was the terminus of the Dutchess turnpike, gaily decorated with flags and sprigs of greenery. Pavements and windows of houses were crowded with people whose faces reflected the nervous excitement with which the whole country throbbed.

James Kent later recorded with his usual gusto that the New York convention "formed the most splendid constellation of the sages and patriots of the Revolution which I had ever witnessed, and the intense interest with which the meeting . . . was anticipated and regarded can now scarcely be conceived. . . .''

General Knox told Rufus King that ''the majority of the antis is so great at Poughkeepsie, that I ask no questions.'' To Madison, things looked black in Virginia too: ''I fear that overwhelming torrent Patrick Henry.''

Hamilton exuded brisk cheer, circulating widely among the leaders of the other side, and using every contact he could make to persuade all of the inevitability of ratification elsewhere. One Anti-Federalist wrote a friend in New York that Hamilton's ''manners and mode of address would probably do much mischief, were the members not as firm as they are.''

When the convention opened on June 17, Hamilton and his men enthusiastically joined in supporting the election of George Clinton as presiding officer. The perennial governor of New York State, a brigadier general of New York militia with a long record of fighting popular battles and losing them, the tall, erect 49-year-old Clinton was a well-liked, energetic Populist who would be a formidable adversary in any political battle. If the Federalists could not elect one of their own to preside, they could at least neutralize the opposition's most forceful leader by imposing on him the silence, or at least restraint, that parliamentary decorum requires of a chairman. The Anti-Federalists showed unexpected moderation, or overconfidence, by giving the Hamiltonians two out of five appointments to the important Committee on Rules.

Near the central table from which Clinton looked down his long martinet's nose sat his 45 henchmen. Melancton Smith, the Clinton floor leader, one of the most astute and brilliant debaters of the time, was well to the front. Farther away, nearer the open windows, sat Hamilton and General Schuyler, Jay, Duane, and Robert R. Livingston and their small coterie, knowing that if through the windows they heard horses' hooves below, bringing good news from Virginia or New Hampshire, it would probably be more important for their cause than any of the noisy speeches made in debate.

Beyond the railing, invited guests crowded, many of them women, as elegantly dressed as they might later have been for a summer race meeting at Saratoga.

Hamilton's tactics would necessarily be based on what happened in Virginia and New Hampshire. Any quick ballot would mean a crushing defeat for the Constitution. So would an adjournment. Hamilton had to prevent both these outcomes by holding the convention in session, marking time with debates and speeches, avoiding a defeat until word of an improvement in the situation came in from elsewhere.

In the ordinary course of procedure at such a convention, there would be debate on the pros and cons of the Constitution, the chairman would put the simple question—for or against ratification, aye or nay—the two-thirds majority of Clintonians would carry the question for the ''nays,'' the Constitution would be dead, and the convention would adjourn.

Hamilton would have to arrange moves to take events out of such an ordinary course. So he and Robert R. Livingston drafted and arranged to introduce a resolution to the effect that no vote be taken on the Constitution itself until each of its provisions had been considered by the convention, sitting as a committee of the whole, clause by clause. Thus, the issue on which each delegate would first be called upon to vote would not be the question of whether he was for or against the Constitution itself, but whether he was for or against free speech and discussion or for cutting off of discussion. If self-proclaimed Populists were called to vote for or against free speech, there was only one way they could go. As Hamilton noted to Madison, ''I imagine the minor partisans have their scruples, and an air of moderation is now assumed.''

Besides, to Melancton Smith and other moderates, Hamilton's resolution would seem but a minor point of procedure; to have voted down his request summarily would have made the Populist majority appear to be too monolithic, inflexible and boss-controlled.

Hamilton's procedural motion carried. He quietly understated his satisfaction when he wrote to Madison that "Tomorrow we go into a committee of the whole . . . a full discussion will take place, which will keep us together at least a fortnight. So far the thing is not to be despaired of."

Chancellor Livingston led off for the Federalists with a general discussion of the advantages of a well-ordered government. Hamilton, keeping notes of the various speeches, wrote of Livingston's effort: "Bravo! As far as it went one of the most excellent energetic speeches ever heard." *Energy* was his favorite word and highest form of praise.

Melancton Smith rose for the opposition. Kent called him "the most prominent and . . . responsible speaker on the Anti-Federal side. . . . The style . . . of Smith's speaking was dry, plain and syllogistic, and it behooved his adversary to examine well the ground on which they started . . . or he would find it . . . embarrassing to extricate himself from a subtle web. . . ." Smith refuted the general reasoning of Chancellor Livingston, who, he thought, had overdrawn the perils of the Confederation: "If a war with our neighbors was to be the result of not acceding, there was no use in debating here; we had better receive their dictates, if we were unable to resist them. The defects of the old Confederation needed as little proof as the necessity of an Union: But there was no proof in all this that the proposed Constitution was a good one." With sarcasm, he was pleased to hear Livingston candidly admit that the Constitution was no confederacy, but a consolidated government.

Smith considered the rule of apportionment unjust because it embraced three-fifths of the slaves, who could have no part in government. Like Hamilton, he thought the number of representatives in the House ought to be still higher—say, one for every 20,000 inhabitants.

The next day, June 21, Hamilton rose to answer Smith, and the delegates and spectators settled back in their chairs to listen to Publius in person.

"Although I am persuaded this convention will be resolved to adopt nothing that is bad," Hamilton began smoothly, "yet I think every prudent man will consider the merits of the plan in connection with the circumstances of our country; and that a rejection of the Constitution may involve most fatal consequences." He proceeded to consider, point by point, the objections to particular provisions.

He explained that compromises at Philadelphia had been necessary to accommodate clashing interests and defended the apportionment of representatives as reasonable and sound. His treatment of the last question was a model of persuasion: New York had 65 members in the state assembly—the same number that would form the first national House of Representatives; so he challenged the opposition to give a better rule than that provided by the New York example.

Melancton Smith rose to rebut him. He wanted representation in Congress to be large enough to embrace principally "men in the middling class" rather than members of the "natural aristocracy" of "birth, education, talents and wealth." Otherwise, "This will be a government of oppression."

Not at all, Hamilton argued. "I rely more on the interests and opinions of men, than on any speculative parchment provisions whatever." Despotic governments, too, depend in a great degree on opinion, but "In free republics . . . the will of the people makes the essential principle of the government; and the laws which control the community receive their tone and spirit from the public wishes."

He spoke with earnestness and energy and much gesture day after day, repeating arguments straight from *The Federalist* or employing classical and historical examples to prove the necessity of strong government. His long-windedness and his repetitions and recitations from *The Federalist* were an early filibuster, marking time, preventing the convention from voting until hoped-for news arrived from New Hampshire or Virginia. There was not much thought that all the oratory by itself would change many votes. He shaped his tactics to counter Governor Clinton's strategy and Melancton Smith's "vanity."

The mails from Virginia and New Hampshire to New York had been full of daily accounts of progress in the conventions there. Now, at last through the open windows were heard the sounds of an express rider galloping into town, lashing the last weary horse of the relay of horses he had worn out on the long journey to Poughkeepsie from New Hampshire. The tired messenger thrust an envelope from John Sullivan, president of the New Hampshire convention, into Hamilton's hands. He ripped it open and read the enclosures with joy. On June 21, New Hampshire had ratified the Constitution! That made nine. The United States of America as a nation and not a mere aggregation of states had just been born.

Hamilton surely smiled broadly as he announced the news to the convention, and Clinton surely scowled. The Federalists in New York City set church bells happily ringing. But remote New Hampshire was not enough. Without mighty Virginia there could only be a paper union, and Madison's expresses to Hamilton from there were increasingly gloomy. His opponents were demanding amendments in the form of a Bill of Rights as a condition precedent to ratification. There was talk of adjournment or even secession without it. Madison was fighting for ratification first and a "recommendation" of amendments to be submitted afterward.

Hamilton sent an express to Madison, passing on the good news from New Hampshire and adding, "There are some slight symptoms of relaxation in some of the leaders, which authorizes a gleam of hope, if you do well, but certainly I think not otherwise." Clinton asserted in a private letter that "the News from New Hampshire has not had the least Effect on our Friends at this Place."

Hamilton, nevertheless, had a powerful new argument to press on them.

"The local interests of a state ought, in every case, to give way to the interests of the Union," he cried. The Constitution made the states "essential, components parts of the union; and therefore the idea of sacrificing the former to the latter is totally inadmissible."

Debate took a crucial turn when John Williams, of remote Washington and Clinton counties, objected that the authority of Congress "to provide for the common defence, and general welfare" gave it too great power in the laying of taxes. He proposed a crippling amendment, a variant of Mason's in the Virginia convention, that would forbid an excise on any article of growth or manufacture of the United States, except when proceeds of the impost and excise on foreign goods were insufficient.

Tempers grew short. John Lansing recalled that Hamilton, now saying that the states must be preserved as repositories of the people's liberties, had said the opposite at Philadelphia; Lansing had kept notes on Hamilton's argument there "with much decision and . . . plausibility, that the state governments ought to be subverted. . . ." Hamilton jumped to his feet to deny such duplicity. "A warm personal altercation" between the two occupied the remainder of that day and much of the next, the reporter notes. In the uproar, Smith threatened to call for a vote on the crippling tax amendment, still confident of his overwhelming majority.

Hamilton and his friends remembered and shrewdly called upon the secretary to read from an old speech of Governor Clinton's to the legislature of 1780–1782, lamenting the feebleness of Congress and the burdens this threw on a state that voluntarily met its revenue obligations. Clinton and Smith were furious. Clinton was forced to declare himself "a friend to a strong and efficient government." Hamilton waded in. No, Clinton was an obstructionist; else why did he say he approved a strong federal government, but opposed the Constitution, insisting on substitute provisions? Why did he say he had favored granting Congress' power during the war to lay an import duty, when he had in fact disapproved the only practicable mode of collection? Clinton's system was "rotten, and ought forever to be banished from our government." Now the more moderate Clintonians were shocked and repelled by Hamilton's rough tactics and the violence of his language. Passions rose high between the two parties.

Clinton saw an opening, changed his tactics, and moved to take command of the moderates' middle ground.

He would be willing to accept the Constitution, he declared, provided it was revised. To that end he offered a series of no fewer than 55 amendments, arranged under three categories: explanatory, recommendatory, and conditional.

He had hit upon a formula on which he could reasonably go the people of the state; reserved rights, he insisted, were vital. He was willing to enter the union, but he wished to reserve the right to withdraw if the amendments failed of later passage. Hamilton and Jay would soon exploit this reasonable-sounding "compromise" to unravel the Clintonians' whole logical position, but first Hamilton had to make a tactical retreat and an ostentatious personal admission of error. He apologized if he had hurt the feelings of any opponent. He confessed that he had a vehement nature, which condemned "those indifferent mortals, who either never form opinions, or never make them known."

Just after noon on July 2, as Clinton was launching into a speech on the power of Congress to contract loans, the silent respect accorded the governor and president suddenly erupted into "such a bug through the House, that little of His Excellency's speech was heard." Through the open windows delegates could hear and see the uproar down below. From a horse whose muzzle was flecked with foam, a rider dismounted. He delivered a dispatch to Barclay, the courthouse doorkeeper, for Hamilton's eyes only. It was a letter from Madison, with an official certification by Edmund Pendleton, announcing that on June 25 Virginia had ratified the Constitution. Outside, jubilant Federalists crowded around and then, as a fife and drum struck up, marched in a happy throng around the convention house.

The good news of Madison's letter contained some cautionary words to the effect that Virginia's ratification carried some "highly objectionable" recommendations for amendments. Patrick Henry had announced "he should wait with impatience for the favorable moment of regaining in a constitutional way, the lost liberties of his country."

Hamilton spread word of Madison's letter to the delegates. Clinton stood speechless. James Kent noted that "a visible change took place in the disposition of the House." The problem of how to keep out of the union and still keep their power, prosperity, and New York City, now had to be faced by all Clintonians.

On July 8 Hamilton wrote Madison to ask how the crippling amendments had been dealt with in Virginia, saying that at Poughkeepsie he would yield to "constructive declarations" as far as possible, without invalidating the act, and would "concur in rational recommendations." He was regaining the middle ground he had almost lost, while leaving all "the rest for our opponents." But he was standing firm on the point that a "conditional" ratification would have no effect.

Clinton was now pressing for an immediate vote, fearing a further swing of moderate opinion against him. Hamilton pleaded with him not to call the question, "but retire and consider." Hamilton was ready, he said, to go as far as he thought safe in "recommendatory and explanatory Amendments.'' He pledged his party ''to endeavor for their adoption,'' but he begged the Clintonians not to listen to ''Jealousy'' or put ''Liberty to the hazard'' by insisting that ratification be ''upon conditions.'' The story went round that Hamilton had sent a message to the city, ''Tell them that the convention shall never rise until the Constitution is adopted!''

During the following days, news came to Poughkeepsie from New York City of the ringing of church bells and of rallies favoring the Constitution, lending credibility to threats like Jay's that the city intended to secede and join the Union however the convention might vote. Then there came word of a huge parade of all the tradesmen, merchants, and businessmen of the city, with a float honoring Hamilton as the centerpiece planned for Wednesday, July 23.

The Federalist parade planned for the twenty-third was to be the greatest anyone could recall since Evacuation Day. Carpenters would build a replica of a 32-gun frigate, 27 feet long, with a ten-foot beam. She would be full rigged as if for sea and drawn by ten white horses; she would fire her cannons as she rolled along. There would be 30 seamen arrayed on her deck under the authentic command of Commodore James Nicholson. Her figurehead would be a carved statute of Hamilton, and *Hamilton* was her name.

Not to be outdone, the sailmakers were building a four-horse stage on which another ship, the *New Constitution,* would sail along proudly bearing the figure of Hamilton holding the ''Constitution'' in his right hand and the ''Confederation'' in his left. Fame with a trumpet would hold a crown of laurel to press upon his amiable brow.

After weeks of noisy preparation and mounting excitement, reports of all of which were duly relayed to the tense delegates at Poughkeepsie, the ten sections of the parade, each honoring one of ten ratifying states, began forming in The Fields early on the morning of the twenty-third, where only a dozen years before Hamilton had made his first public speech. At ten o'clock, a 13-gun salute was fired from the cannons of the good ship *Hamilton,* and the grand march began to roll down the wide Broad Way.

The coopers' float was led by 13 apprentice boys, each 13 years old. On the rear of their float was a barrel whose ill-joined staves stood for the old Confederation. Turning their backs on the wreckage, diligent workmen on the float fashioned a snug new constitutional cask as the procession got under way.

The float of the ''artificial florists'' featured a gorgeous garland from which disconsolately drooped three broken blossoms, representing the states that had not ratified the Constitution. The block and pump makers finished a pump and made 13 blocks, sheaved and pruned complete, on their stage during the march. Then came the crash and blare of a marching band.

As the good ship *Hamilton* rode the artificial waves toward Wall Street, she made ''a fine appearance, sailing with flowing sheets and full sails, the canvas waves dashing against her sides.'' Glum Anti-Federalists in the throng looked ''as sour as the devil.'' Naturally, Betsy and von Steuben and Philip and Angelica and little Alexander and the Antil orphan cheered wildly as the *Hamilton* sailed past.

A slight accident, it is true, probably caused by some disgruntled Anti, marred the sailmakers' float: the right arm of the figure ''Hamilton'' had been broken off—the arm that had held the symbolic ''Constitution.'' Few noticed because next came the tailors, holding aloft an oversized banner on which Adam and Eve sat naked except for figleaf aprons, illustrating the motto ''And they sew'd fig leaves together.'' The furriers displayed an Indian delivering pelts. The draymen dragged a 300-gallon cask of ale with a living Bacchus on top—a handsome boy sewn from chin to toe into flesh-colored silk, wearing a cap adorned with hop vines and barley and drinking daintily from a silver goblet in his hand. His attendant Silenus sat beside him on a hogshead of porter soberly labeled, "Ale, proper drink for Americans." On other floats, printers at their presses were actually striking off and then distributing copes of an ode. Blacksmiths hammered out a symbolic constitutional anchor. Marching along behind came hatters, peruke makers, and shipwrights, nailers, paper stainers, and upholsterers, as well as representatives of all the other urban crafts of the great city. Nicholas Cruger, Esq., guided a plow drawn by six oxen. As he looked up ahead at the *Hamilton's* rigging riffling in the breeze, Cruger probably thought back in some wonder to the morning 16 years ago when he had seen his former clerk sail off from St. Croix to the continent. A quick, diligent boy, yes, with good training in the counting house. He was far along now on his way to transmuting New York City into the national as well as the commercial capital of a new empire. Yes, young Alexander had well repaid Cruger's contribution to the expense of an ocean passage to the mainland.

The parade moved amid cheering and surging throngs down the Broad Way, through Great Dock Street, into Hanover Square, and up Queen Street, where its members halted and disbanded until the evening.

Brissot de Warville, the urbane French traveler, after standing beside the line of march, described that night's huge outdoor feast in The Fields. At ten long tables members of Congress were served bullock and mutton roasted whole. "Magnificent," or possibly "Magnifique," he called it. Five or six thousand lesser citizens joined the celebration and watched the fireworks. A popular toast was to "The whole gradation of Heroes and Benefactors of mankind, from the first of the human race to the immortal Washington, and all the sons of wisdom, from Solon to the invincible Hamilton."

Some of the cartmen and sailors who had served as the *Hamilton's* ship's crew were still proudly carrying the standards bearing the legend "The Federal Ship *Hamilton*." When they turned the standards around, in the glare of the blazing torches and occasional rocket bursts, on the reverse side could be read:

> Behold the federal ship of fame;
> The *Hamilton* we call her name;
> To every craft she gives employ;
> Sure cartmen have their share of joy.

For psychological impact on Clinton's delegates upriver at Poughkeepsie the great parade and celebration could not have been better timed. On the same Wednesday, July 23, Melancton Smith wavered and switched. Instead of continuing to insist on ratification "upon conditions," Smith moved for ratification "in confidence" that the recital of the bill of rights and other amendments "will receive an early consideration." The moderates in Clinton's forces swung with Smith. His motion carried, 40 to 19. Among the "antis" voting with Smith and all the jubilant Federalists were Clinton, Lansing, and Yates.

To explain his switch Melancton Smith declared that until Virginia came in, he had hoped amendments could be made previous to the operation of the government, but now "he was satisfied they could not, and it was equally the dictate of reason and duty to quit his first ground, and advance so far as that they might be received into the Union." Now he argued that the best way to serve "the great end of opposition" that he had led was to vote against any proposition that would not be received as a ratification of the Constitution. Otherwise, his own party, too weak to amend the Constitution, would "be dispersed like sheep on a mountain."

Next day, Thursday, July 24, Lansing, still groping toward contingent ratification, moved to add that the state reserved the right to withdraw from the Union if after a fixed number of years the amendments had not "been submitted to a convention in the mode prescribed in the fifth article of the Constitution."

Hamilton and Jay, rebutting Lansing, argued that adoption, subject to the right to withdraw, implied a distrust of the other states. Hamilton read from Madison's reply of July 20 that "a conditioned ratification does not make New York a member of the new Union." Conditional ratification was voted down, 31 to 28. In six weeks an overwhelming majority of two to one against ratification had been transformed into a majority of three in favor of unconditional ratification. A thankful Federalist wrote, "The Constitution has . . . undergone an ordeal torture, and been preserved, as by fire."

The rest was formal. The body resolved itself from a Committee of the Whole back into convention, and on Saturday, July 26, the engrossed ratification, with a proposed Bill of Rights and added amendments only recommended, was approved, 30 to 27, and signed by the president and two secretaries. Jay's circular letter pressing for conventions for changes was given unanimous approval, and the convention adjourned *sine die*.

When all was done Clinton, from the chair, offered a qualified benediction. Until a convention should be called to consider amendments, "The probability was, that the body of the people who are opposed to the constitution, would not be satisfied"; he would, however, "endeavour to keep up peace and good order among them. . . ." After this generous statement of Clinton's it was reported that upon the countenances of delegates and spectators alike "more than a common pleasantness appeared."

The union was an accomplished fact. Though North Carolina and Rhode Island still refused to ratify, they could not remain out indefinitely. North Carolina ratified on November 21, 1789, and pugnacious, perverse Rhode Island finally came in on May 29, 1790.

It was common talk that Hamilton, more than anyone else, had been the man who somehow reversed what had seemed to be insurmountable odds. "Col. H——," said the *New York Journal* in a story July 4, 1788, "stands the political porcupine, armed at all points and brandishes a shaft to every opposer: a shaft powerful to repel and keen to wound." It was said that his arguments had brought about Melancton Smith's eleventh-hour conversion.

What actually caused the sudden break in the ranks of the Clintonians has never been fully explained. Several factors weighed heavily. Once Virgina ratified, New York had lost a powerful state to stand with it outside the union. The threat—and it was, in fact, no idle one—that lower New York would break away and leave the upper state without the city that made the state rich and powerful worried the moderates. The parade featuring the good ship *Hamilton* made visible the threat. Clinton's offer to ratify with reservations exposed a weakness in his earlier all-or-nothing position. Once he admitted that the document might be ratified, Madison's letter, which Hamilton read to the delegates, cut what remained of that position from under him. With that lost, he had nothing to do but surrender. Even with all these points in his favor, Hamilton's great victory was not exactly a landslide—just three votes.

The New York City convention delegates reached home the following Monday, two days after adjournment. Hamilton brought with him New York's signed and engrossed ratification of the Constitution, which he forthwith proudly presented to the expiring Continental

Congress. Resting at home for a few hours after the rough ride down from Poughkeepsie, before bathing and dressing to walk up Wall Street to City Hall to make the official presentation, Hamilton with elaborate offhandedness would let Betsy and von Steuben and young Phil and wide-eyed Angelica and little Alexander and the Antil orphan crowd around and examine the impressive document. Hamilton's offhand manner could not hide from his children the glint of proprietary pride that flickered in his eyes.

They would vie to regale him with stories of the great parade of the Wednesday just past and the banqueting and fireworks the same night and allow no detail of it all to be dimmed in the telling. No words were left to convey the magnificence of the good ship *Hamilton* as she rolled by the crowds to the blare of the bands and the excitement of their shouts and applause. When they quieted down a little, one of them, Angelica perhaps, would recite for her doting father the verses she had memorized from the waving standards held aloft by the *Hamilton*'s crew!

Behold the Federal ship of fame,
The *Hamilton* we call her name!

The greatest parade New York had ever seen since Evacuation Day had been in her sweet father's honor. It made her a little sad that he had been so busy he had missed it except in the presence of his name on the ship. It would be almost 16 years before New York City saw another parade as great again. That too would be in Hamilton's honor, with him also absent in all but name, inside the flag-draped coffin in the train of his funeral cortège.

PART TWO

A Host Within Himself

18

Suspicion
Is Ever Eagle-Eyed

For Heaven's sake, use *for once* **your influence to defer this.**

—From William Duer, March 12, 1792

In the fifteen months between that first great parade and the afternoon Angelica Church sailed for England, a jumble of momentous events would see Hamilton to the summit of his rise.

On November 5, 1789, at about five o'clock in the afternoon, Hamilton stood in the twilight on the ramparts of the Battery at the southern tip of Manhattan Island watching the vessel carrying Angelica back to her husband in England from the late summer and early fall visit she had made to New York without him. With Hamilton there on the Battery his eldest son, Philip, age seven, and Baron Friedrich von Steuben, the family's more or less permanent houseguest "with aching hearts and anxious eyes" had watched "your vessel, in full sail, swiftly bearing our loved friend from our embraces. Imagine what we felt. We gazed, we sighed, *we wept*; and casting 'many a lingering longing look behind' returned home to give scope to our sorrows, and mingle without restraint our tears and our regrets. . . ." The line from *The Aeneid* was the best way Hamilton knew to tell her that "*some* of us are and must continue inconsolable for your absence." In the separate lodgings he had rented for her, Angelica's New York stay had been full of "precious and never to be forgotten scenes" with him. But writing her later, he dared not go beyond one furtive glance back on them:

> But let me check, My dear Sister, these effusions of regretful friendship. Why should I alloy the Happiness that courts you in the bosom of your family by images that must wound your sensibility? It shall not be.

247

It would not be.

Looking back from her ship at the three of them standing there on the Battery gazing toward her as she sailed out of sight, Angelica had felt her heart overflowing with the same sense of inconsolable loss as Hamilton's. She had responded to his Vergil in her own unique quicksilver French:

> Me voilà mon très cher bien en mer et le pauvre coeur bien effligé de vous avoir quitté. . . . Remember this also my dearest Brother and let neither politics or ambition drive your Angelica from your affections. . . . adieu my dear Brother, may God bless and protect you, prays your ever affectionate Angelica ever ever yours. . . . Adieu my dear Hamilton, you said I was as dear to you as a sister keep your word, and let me have the consolation to believe that you will never forget the promise of friendship you have vowed. . . . A thousand embraces to my dear Betsey, she will not have so bad a night as the last, *but poor Angelica* adieu mine plus cher.

Home from her wintry sea passage Angelica's ardor for Hamilton had lost none of its edge. "I sometimes think you have now forgot me and that having seen me is like a dream which you can scarcely believe. Adieu I will not write this idea of being lost in the tumult of business does not enliven my spirits—*adieu soyez heureux au-dessus de tout le monde.*"

If autumn in New York is sometimes shadowed by private fears, for the public at large the fall of 1789 would be the most exciting of New York's history. It was the first year of operation of the constitutional union at "Hamiltonopolis," the nation's first capital.

Three weeks after New York had ratified the Constitution, Hamilton sent Washington "a set of papers under the signature of Publius—I presume you have understood that the writers of these papers are chiefly Mr. Madison and myself with some aid from Mr. Jay."

But the point of his letter was that Washington must agree to be the first president:

> I take it for granted, sir, you have concluded to comply with what no doubt will be the general call of your country in relation to the new government. It is indispensable you should lend yourself to its first operations—It is to little purpose to have *introduced* a system, if the weightiest influence is not given to its firm *establishment* at the outset.

Washington replied that his election "may never happen," but that in any event "It is my great and sole desire to live and die, in peace and retirement, on my own farm."

Thirty-one-year-old Hamilton took a peremptory tone with 56-year-old Washington. "I should be deeply pained my dear sir," he replied, "if your scruples in regard to a certain station should be matured into a resolution to decline it."

Hamilton talked to Washington almost as if to a backward child:

> The caution you observe in deferring an ultimate determination is prudent. I have however reflected maturely on the subject and have come to a conclusion that every public and personal consideration will demand from you an acquiescence in what will *certainly* be the unanimous wish of your country. . . . a regard to your own reputation as well as to the public good, calls upon you in the strongest manner to run that risk.

Hamilton assumed Washington would obey him. Without waiting for his reply he briskly moved on to the next point: who should be the vice-president?

The Anti-Federalists were set on putting up Clinton of New York. In Massachusetts the Federalists had split on whether to choose presidential electors by the legislature, in which case John Adams would probably win, or by popular vote, in which case John Hancock would probably win.

Hamilton told Theodore Sedgwick, a Massachusetts leader, on October 9, 1788: "I believe Mr. Adams will have the votes of this state." But, he added, "the only hesitation in my mind has arisen from a suggestion that he is unfriendly in his sentiments to General Washington." Sedgwick replied that Adams had improved: he had "corrected those jealousies" that once had governed him. Madison, recalling Adams's "cabal during the war against General Washington," had confided to Jefferson that Washington's attitude toward Adams as his "second" would hardly be "cordial." But as Hamilton saw it, Adams was "the only certain way to prevent the election of an Anti-Federalist," so Washington would simply have to take him.

On the other hand, for the good of the nation as a whole, there would be no harm done if Adams, once nominated, lost the election to the vice-presidency. A leading representative of Federalist and Anti-Federalist factions in the two highest offices of the first national government would be powerful cement for the new union. Besides, Hamilton personally would be just as happy as Washington to see Adams lose.

What embarrassed Hamilton most was the defect of draftsmanship in the Constitution—now exposed! The Framers had failed to make a distinction between ballots cast for president and vice-president. Because the voting was for two men, an obvious vice-presidential choice like a Clinton or an Adams might, through the action of one elector withholding his vote for president, defeat an obvious presidential choice like Washington, and allow the obvious vice-presidential choice to slip in to the first office. Then, too, there was always the possibility of a tie, which would throw the decision into the House of Representatives. If the worst could happen, it might happen—and did happen in 1800.

Hamilton passed the word around that some of the Federalist electors should withhold their votes from Adams. This would do Adams no harm unless he had indeed secretly hoped to snatch the first place away from Washington. Adams never forgot and never forgave Hamilton for this, even though Hamilton had not rated any man higher than Adams—for second place.

The Electoral College met on February 4, 1789, in New York and unanimously elected Washington president—and Adams vice-president by a few withheld votes. A sense of political parties was now beginning to emerge, and the man emerging as leader of the one that had put forward the winning national ticket was Hamilton.

Unfortunately, Anti-Federalists led by his old nemesis, George Clinton, pushed through a full slate of five Anti-Federalist delegates to the last moribund Continental Congress of 1789, thereby ousting Hamilton from the seat he had held in Congress the year before.

For the new Congress under the Constitution, Hamilton's candidate, John Laurence, won election to the House. Federalists won control of both houses of the New York legislature for the first time, so that it would now be possible for them to elect two Federalists to the United States Senate. After much maneuvering, the assembly nominated Philip Schuyler and James Duane. The state senate nominated Schuyler and Ezra L'Hommedieu. But Hamilton insisted that Schuyler and his friend Rufus King be chosen.

Here Aaron Burr rose, as a Federalist, and announced that the Federalists of both houses had agreed upon Schuyler and Duane. Hamilton rose to challenge Burr to a test of strength.

Duane had married a Livingston daughter. The Livingstons would accept Hamilton's father-in-law Schuyler for one Senate seat as long as he allowed one of *their* in-laws, Duane, to have the other. Besides, Rufus King was only a recent arrival in New York from Massachusetts, not, like the Livingstons, descended from three and four generations of Hudson River lords of the manor aristocracy. But Hamilton's power was now so great that he overbore the alliance of Duane, all the Livingstons, and Burr. The senate accepted Rufus King and rejected Duane—and a legion of powerful former friends of Hamilton switched to the ranks of the enemies already arrayed against him.

Hamilton's overreaching here at the pinnacle of his power had "led him into a fatal error as a politician." It also gave Burr a foothold on the first rung of his political rise. One of Clinton's first moves upon reelection to his fourth term was to appoint Burr to the office of attorney general. This would bring disaffected Federalists into the Antis' fold and solidify the defections from Hamilton's momentarily all-powerful Federalist camp.

On April 30, 1789, crowds filled up Broad and Wall Streets in front of the old City Hall, now rebuilt by Pierre L'Enfant and renamed Federal Hall.

From the second floor balcony there, George Washington looked down on the throng, solemnly held up his right hand, and swore to the Speaker of the House of Representatives, Frederick A. C. Muhlenberg, the presidential oath that is part of Section I of Article II of the Constitution: "I do solemnly swear that I will faithfully execute the Office of President of the United States, and will to the best of my ability, preserve, protect and defend the Constitution of the United States." Washington kept as much distance between himself and the short, fat figure of John Adams as the proprieties of the situation on the cramped balcony would permit. Adams, in his turn, swore to execute faithfully the duties of vice-president—although neither the Constitution, *The Federalist,* nor anybody else could tell him what they were beyond presiding over the Senate.

Resuming his closeness to Washington of the war years, Hamilton again became "the principal and most confidential aid of the Commander in Chief." Their relationship was easy and natural, though Hamilton, knowing his chief as he did, always treated his older friend in public and private with deference and reserve. In the presence of a large group, out of Washington's hearing, Hamilton once remarked that Washington "was reserved and aristocratic even to his intimate friends, and allowed no one to be familiar with him."

The most serious weakness of the old Articles of Confederation—the one that had proved fatal—was economic debility. The Continental Congress had been powerless to enforce tax levies and other economic measures against the sovereign states. During the summer just past, much of the time of the new House and Senate that convened in separate chambers in Federal Hall had been taken up with the subject of the vast powers over the economic system of the Union that were to be exercised by the secretary of the treasury. Knowledgeable New Yorkers knew Hamilton was the man whom President Washington was most likely to appoint to the post; so the harshest debates that summer had been debates about Hamilton in power.

Even when they were not at home in Mount Vernon, George Washington and his Martha seemed as remote as ever, more the same old revered symbol of, or substitute for, monarchical authority than an active new republican executive presence. Squat, rotund Vice-President John Adams seemed to be only a stiff, choleric, splenetic, humorless Yankee. To the elegant, witty New Yorkers of the Hamiltons' circle, Adams' discomfiture at the insignificance of his walk-on role was comically highlighted by the sword and scabbard he belted on when he posed for his portrait.

Thomas Jefferson remained sequestered out of touch with the common man in his chateau at Monticello. He would not arrive to take up his duties as secretary of state for months to come. Stout old Henry Knox, the secretary of war, and his stouter wife seemed no more than a typical, tippling old army couple and not to be sought out socially by New Yorkers except when his official position as a department head made their mammoth ubiety unavoidable.

Yet after Hamilton's appointment as secretary of the treasury became official on September 11, 1789, there had been no sense of a power vacuum or lack of energy in the executive branch of the government. The conduct of the Union's military affairs and foreign affairs, like its Congress, its presidency, and its judiciary, all needed funds for day-to-day operations; and Hamilton was the man to whom all looked for funding. With a firm belief in the implied powers in the Constitution and few precedents except his own from *The Federalist Papers* to constrict his sphere, it is not surprising that Hamilton as secretary of the treasury spread his influence into all branches and offices of the new government.

Hamilton thus immediately became the functional equivalent of prime minister, partly on the strength of the trust his chief reposed in him, partly by default of rivals, partly by superior knowledge of how the system was supposed to work, and partly by seizing the opportunity. In one important way, his power in the tripartite constitutional system exceeded that of a parliamentary prime minister: he was not subject to overthrow by the legislative branch. His home and office were just down Wall Street from the capital.

His commanding presence in any company was more often noted than the fact that in appearance he seemed even younger than 32. He was only about five feet seven inches in height and quite thin. His eyes were a bluish violet that would turn steely gray in anger. His complexion was exceedingly fair with a rosiness in his cheeks that gave it an almost feminine aspect. He carried himself with remarkable erectness and dignity. In the portrait of him painted by Robert Edge Pine about 1786, the noted colorist catches the deep-set eyes, the thick arching brows, the strong and slightly Roman nose, firmly set mouth, long jawbone, high forehead, and reddish brown hair turned back and powdered white, of a mature man who might be any age from 30 to 60 or more. Hamilton's face has a rather severe and thoughtful expression in the Pine portrait, but many a friend remarked on how, when he was engaged in social conversation, his face could quickly take on a warm and genial glow. He was a man whose portrait would be painted often; all make it appear that Hamilton's was an uncommonly handsome face. It was one well formed to fit the still surprisingly young man who was already perceived by many of his peers as the greatest political success story of the age.

On the 4th of July, 1789, 16 years after his arrival in New York City, it was Hamilton who had been chosen to deliver the annual Fourth of July address to his fellow members of the Society of the Cincinnati in St. Paul's Chapel at the corner of Broadway and Vesey Streets, on the 13th anniversary of the nation's first Independence Day of 1776.

Now Hamilton stood behind the lectern looking down on what was probably the most distinguished audience ever assembled under one roof in America—or anywhere in the world, for that matter—since the Constitutional Convention of 1787 had adjourned. The Clinton family was in the Governor's box. In the pews down the nave sat Vice-President and Abigail Adams, members of the Senate and House, Chief Justice John Jay and the former Sarah Livingston, his wife, and the other justices and their ladies, all dressed in their finest holiday array waiting expectantly to hear Hamilton deliver his Eulogium to the late General Nathanael Greene. It was Greene who, in first recommending him to Washington, had placed the first important rung of the ladder of Hamilton's rise beneath his instep. Down to

Hamilton's right in the President's box was only Martha Washington—after the morning's collation of the Society of the Cincinnati George, the President of the sodality, as well as of the country, had become tearful, as was his wont, and staggered home to bed with an alcoholic indisposition. Even without him it was the most distinguished audience ever gathered in New York to listen to one man's rhetoric.

What Hamilton admired most about Greene's rise were some of the most striking features of his own:

> Nathanael Greene descended from reputable parents, but not placed by birth in that elevated rank, which under a monarchy is the only sure road to those employments, that give activity and scope to abilities, must in all probability have contented himself with the humble lot of a private citizen . . . scarcely conscious of the resources of his own mind, had not the violated rights of his country called him to act a part on a more splendid and ample theater.

Happily for America, he hesitated not to obey the call!

Before Yorktown, when Hamilton's friend Baron Von Steuben had been charged with trying to mobilize troops in Virginia, Thomas Jefferson, the governor, had fled Richmond and disappeared at Cornwallis's approach. All civil government had dissolved just when stability was needed most to support the troops of Hamilton, Lafayette, and Rochambeau, all marching down to Yorktown. No such panicky flight and dissolution of state government had occurred in Massachusetts when the British had occupied Boston, nor in Pennsylvania when Howe took Philadelphia, nor in South Carolina when Charleston was lost, nor in New York State, when New York City was overrun.

Hamilton's hatred of slavery—and his opinion of Jefferson's cowardice and preoccupation with private projects—come through in his curiously irrelevant rhetorical reference to poor "Virginia deficient in order, debilitated by the dissipation of its revenues and forces in domestic projects encumbered by a numerous body of slaves bound by all the laws of injured humanity to hate their masters—deficient in order and vigor in its administration."

By contrast to the crepuscular Jefferson:

> The vigor of [Greene's] genius corresponding with the importance of the prize to be contended for, animated by an enlightened sense of the value of free government, he cheerfully resolved to stake his fortune, his hopes, his life and his honor upon an enterprise the dangers of which he knew the whole magnitude in a cause which was worthy of the toil and the blood of heroes.

Most of the audience in their pews that hot July day were self-made men themselves or the children of self-made men. Had they known the whole of Hamilton's story, most would have agreed that the distance and speed of his escalade to the summit of a significant political society were without precedent in the history of the world.

No American's rise except Washington's, and possibly Benjamin Franklin's, could come close to matching his. In all history and literature, as far as they were aware, there were only a few such successes—Julius Caesar, Shakespeare's Othello, the Joseph of Genesis, Alexander of Macedon, and a handful of Plutarch's avatars—that equaled Hamilton's to date. What they did not know, or had heard only vaguely rumored, was how much lower down the ladder the penniless, illegitimate orphan boy who had arrived on the continent at 16 from St. Croix had begun than any of these others.

As the distinguished gathering in St. Paul's Chapel that 4th of July looked toward the future, beyond the older leaders like Washington and Adams, there was no one who looked more like a future president in the next two or three decades than the eulogist before them.

Why then did he fail to fulfill his promise?

A sentence in Hamilton's Eulogium to Greene reads like a premonition of his own end 15 years and one week later:

> The sudden termination of his life cut him off from those scenes, which the progress of a new immense and unsettled empire could not fail to open to the complete exertion of that universal and pervading genius, which qualified him not less for the senate, than for the field.

Thomas Jefferson once called Aaron Burr "a crooked gun whose aim you never could be sure of." Did Burr destroy Hamilton in the duel at Weehawken by serving there as Jefferson's own crooked gun?

On December 17, 1792, three and one half years after Hamilton had delivered his Eulogium to Greene, Jefferson jotted down in his *Anas* the following entry in code. The word *anas*—as in Jeffersoniana—connotes a collection of trivia, but this entry was anything but trivial for Hamilton, or for the later history of the United States:

> Dec. 17 the affair of Reynolds and his wife—Clingman Muhlen's clerk testifies to F. A. Muhl. Monroe Venable—also Wolcott at [and?] Wadsworth. Known to James Madison, Edmund Randolph, John Beckley and Bernard Webb.
>
> Reynolds was speculating agent on the speculations of government arrearages. He was furnished by Duer with a list of claims of arrearages due to the Virginia and Carolina line and bought them up, against which the resolutions of Congress of June 4, 1790 were leveled. Hamilton advised the President to give his negative to those resolutions.

At some unknown time, probably many years later, Jefferson scored out the last three sentences; he came down particularly heavily on Hamilton's name. The scored-out portion does not even appear in Sawvel's official edition of Jefferson's *Anas*. Only an examination of the original manuscript uncovers the secret of Jefferson's first entry, and his later deletion—the gap in the tape. Jefferson called this touching-up process his "calm revisal." A later president might say that Jefferson had later made his earlier entry "inoperative."

Hamilton's closest friends like Robert Troup and James McHenry had warned him against accepting the Treasury appointment. Robert Morris and William Duer, his friends who had managed fiscal affairs at the old Board of Treasury under the Confederation, had been besmirched and all but ruined by scandal. All during the summer of 1789 the fiercest Congressional debates had centered on the dangers of corruption in the Treasury. Hamilton was fully forewarned that no Treasury Department head had been able to remain immune from calumny or preserve his own integrity in the office. Accepting the post, Hamilton cheerfully, indeed eagerly, brushed such warnings aside and resolved, like Greene, to stake his fortune, his hopes, his life, and his honor on the cause—and risk the loss of all.

Out of gratitude for Greene's liberating generalship, at the end of the war the state of South Carolina had granted Greene, who made his home in New York, lands and a homestead to induce him to settle there. Greene and his wife, the former Catherine Littlefield, whose family came from Rhode Island, accepted and moved South. Sorry to see such close and dear friends leave the city, Hamilton missed them.

Greene having died, leaving his widow in financial distress, and their friend Hamilton having delivered such a moving eulogium to his memory, nothing would seem more natural, after Hamilton had been secretary of the treasury for some months, than for Catherine Littlefield Greene to turn her "powerful influence" on him. "Surely it is not a crime" to seek a favor, she wrote him on May 30, 1790.

Her disclaimer showed she sensed that it should have been a crime if it was not. "Surely it is not wrong," she added, "to solicit a favor of one, who is as eminent for the goodness of his heart, as he is celebrated for his abilities."

She wanted him to give a job as a collector of customs to her "beloved and only brother," William Littlefield, who had been a captain in the Second Rhode Island Regiment. In addition, for herself, she would like some especially sensitive inside information that she and her agents could quickly turn to a speculative profit: "Permit me also to ask if there are any funds in France to pay the interest of The National Debt."

She was rather ashamed to be asking such things, she confessed. "Why do I palputate [sic]—why blush and condemn myself?" But she asked anyway. Because of his old affection for her, she was sure there could be no harm in his telling her, she said. "I am justified by my reason," she adds, "and prompted by my affection to commit it. Could you know my feelings I am sure you would pardon me. I will suppose you do and therefore proceed."

If Hamilton was too discreet to give her the inside information she wanted by letter, she would let him tell it to her in person, in confidence: "Will you permit me to beg the favor of an hour's conversation with you some time betwixt this and Wednesday? God bless you my dear friend and believe me most sincerely and affectionately yours."

She had already enlisted the aid of New York lawyer Royal Flint and one Peter W. J. L. Glaubeck, who went by the bogus title of Baron de Glaubeck, as her agents to help her obtain Treasury funds, and on March 1, 1790 "to make good some deficiencies in the former appropriation by Congress—and for other purposes," the large sum of 3,029 livres was paid out to them.

This payment was only one of the many that would bring charges of corruption in office and congressional investigations on Hamilton for the rest of his life. The general tenor of all was that he had abused his post at the Treasury to enrich himself and old friends and cronies—and certain ladies not his wife who held high place in his warm affections.

Hamilton's old wartime comrade in arms Henry Lee wrote from Virginia on November 16, 1789, that "from your situation you must be able to form with some certainty an opinion concerning the domestic debt." He had three questions: (1) "Will it speedily rise," (2) "Will the interest accruing command specie or anything nearly as valuable," and (3) "What will become of the indents already issued?"

These were the three big questions fhat every speculator, businessman, and financier in the country was asking everyone he knew. If he were a friend, crony, or acquaintance of Hamilton, he was probably asking Hamilton, too. Few dared commit the obvious impropriety of writing him a letter to ask the answers, like Catherine Greene and Lee.

Lee said, "These queries are asked for my private information," as if that would make answering them all right, instead of worse. He wondered if "perhaps they may be improper," as if it was not obvious that they were. Rolling his eyes heavenward, Lee piously asserted, "I do not think so, or I would not propound them," but "of this, you will decide, and act accordingly. Nothing can induce me to be instrumental in submitting my friend to an impropriety.''

To Lee's pious cant, Hamilton's reaction was dangerously soft. On December 1, 1789, he replied to Lee, ''I am sure you are sincere when you say, you would not subject me to an impropriety. Nor do I know that there would be any in my answering your queries.''

Hamilton followed this weak answer with a passage that is often cited to illustrate his high personal standards of propriety in the conduct of public office: ''You remember the saying with regard to Caesar's wife. I think the spirit of it applicable to every man concerned in the administration of the finances of a country. With respect to the conduct of such men, *suspicion* is ever eagle-eyed. And the most innocent things may be misinterpreted.'' He added, ''Be assured of the affection and friendship of your A. Hamilton.''

Hamilton was giving a soft answer to a friend, comrade-in-arms, and old crony, believing that Lee would not make improper speculative use of any inside information Hamilton might give him. In Lee's place, Hamilton would not have done so. Therefore, there would be nothing improper in Hamilton's giving it to him. The information was merely conversational. Hamilton's own motives were pure. ''Nor do I know there would be any [impropriety] in my answering your queries.'' If this premise of Hamilton's were correct, it was easy enough for him to take the next fatal step that he did.

All his life Hamilton professed to put public good ahead of his own private financial welfare. James McHenry and Robert Troup were constantly urging him to pay more attention to his own personal financial security, but he ignored them. Tempting opportunities for improper self-enrichment pressed in on him from every side. There is no evidence (beyond a few mysterious scraps of paper produced by Maria and James Reynolds) that he ever made an improper personal profit out of any of the innumerable opportunities he had to do so in the course of his Treasury Department operations. That he was forced to borrow small sums from friends from time to time; that he never seemed to have personal funds available beyond what could reasonably be accounted for by government salary, legal fees, and occasional help from Betsy's family; and that his estate was insolvent when he died are convincing evidence of his personal financial probity. He was content with his comfortable financial subsistence. He showed little or no drive to enrich himself past that level. He made a mistake in projecting this highly unusual, if not quixotic, personal attitude of his onto others. Most old cronies did not share his genuine regard for the public good and disregard for personal enrichment.

When it came to appreciating the greed and depravity of mankind in general in the mass and in mobs, Hamilton was a supreme realist. But his intense attachments to old friends and old cronies blinded him to the fact that they often acted from venal, speculative, and peculative motives that seemed to be missing from his own makeup. This projection of his own priorities on his cronies gave Hamilton a reversed image of many of them. The reality was that in such cronies, as in much of mankind, private enrichment took priority over the public good.

The most striking evidence of this blind spot was Hamilton's appointment, a day or two after his own appointment was confirmed on September 11, of William Duer to be his assistant secretary of the treasury.

Duer had served as secretary of the old Board of Treasury, the wretched malfeasances of which should have served as instant disqualification. Instead, his service on it recommended him to Hamilton on grounds of experience that Hamilton himself lacked. Eight years older than Hamilton, of English origin, he had come to America, like Hamilton, from the West Indies. George and Martha Washington had been guests at Duer's marriage to

Catharine Alexander Stirling, the daughter of General William Alexander, an American who went by the name of Lord Stirling, claiming to be an earl on the strength or color of a cloudy title to some Nova Scotia land grants. In 1776, Lord Stirling had been brigade commander of Hamilton's New York Provincial Artillery Company. In 1778, at Valley Forge, he had witnessed Hamilton's oath of allegiance to America. Duer's wife, called Lady Kitty like her mother, Catharine Livingston Stirling, was a cousin and childhood friend of Hamilton's own wife, Betsy. Duer had introduced John Barker Church to his Angelica.

But by the time of his appointment by Hamilton, Duer was the most notorious speculator in New York. He had gotten an early start by entering upon large-scale contracts to supply meat to the Revolutionary army which became more famous for being ill-fed than well fought. True, Duer had published three essays in support of the Constitution under the name of Philo-Publius, but Hamilton had not deemed them worthy of being incorporated in *The Federalist*. Duer had been a law client of Hamilton's. A still more particular disqualification was that at the time of appointing him, Hamilton held Duer's unpaid promissory demand note for two thousand specie dollars—Duer owed it immediately to Hamilton in gold.

The men Hamilton appointed to lesser Treasury posts had all been his comrades-in-arms in the Revolution, and two had served with him in the Continental Congress. They were well-known men of the world, but public-spirited amateurs in the art of governmental administration. Some, like Duer, were the kind of men whose experience of the world had taught them to be tolerant of a little nest feathering by men of good will in the private sector as long as their operations did not arouse the public by unseemly or notorious examples of cupidity.

On June 24, 1788, Duer had bought public securities with a par or redemption value of $10,000 for $1,851 and sold them within two months for $2,500. The French investors in Duer's syndicate were represented by another old wartime friend of Duer and Hamilton, Jean Pierre Brissot de Warville, who wrote Duer gleefully from Paris to congratulate him on his appointment and to introduce to him Theophile Cazenove of Amsterdam, who "is to settle himself in America, & I believe to make some speculations in your funds. I am sure, knowing your obliging temper you'll give him good informations about his speculations: & I'll be much obliged to you to do it." Duer would oblige.

Two days after Hamilton's own appointment had become official and after sending congratulations to his other appointees, Hamilton sent Assistant Secretary Duer to Philadelphia on his first official mission, to Thomas Willing, president of the Bank of North America, to obtain a loan of $50,000. Duer was given broad authority to settle all details. Indeed, Hamilton gave Duer more authority than absolutely necessary for the assignment. To Willing, he added with curious superfluity that "whatever arrangements he may concert with your bank shall be strictly observed on my part." There is no evidence that the side arrangements included Willing's arranging a loan to Duer so that he could pay off in full his $2,000 specie note to Hamilton, which was now due. Many a banker would have welcomed such a golden opportunity to be helpful.

Nothing could have been more confused and chaotic than the state of American public finance that fall of 1789. Congressmen sought private answers to the same questions Henry Lee and Catherine Greene had asked Hamilton. Being congressmen, they demanded them publicly, by congressional resolutions of September 21, duly recorded by the clerk, John Beckley, and compared for accuracy by William Duer. Mindful that "an adequate provision for the support of the public credit" was "a matter of high importance to the national honor and prosperity," the House "directed" the secretary to "prepare a plan for that purpose, and to report the same to this house at its next meeting," the first Monday in January 1790.

So with a three months' deadline to meet, Hamilton began formulating his monumental first *Report Relative to a Provision for the Support of Public Credit,* to be submitted to the House.

He began by collecting a mass of fact and opinion from many sources.

To William Bingham of Philadelphia Hamilton wrote that "there is a species of information highly requisite for the government in adjusting the policies of its treaties and laws respecting navigation for obtaining which with proper accuracy and detail no regular plan was ever yet been perused in this country."

To Hamilton, a sound economic order was of even more importance than the political order created by the Constitution because the political order had its foundations in the economic and rested on it.

He enclosed a list of searching questions, requesting Bingham to send him "any thoughts that may occur to you concerning the finances and debts of the United States. It is my earnest wish to obtain all the light I can on these subjects in order that I may be the better able to discharge the trust reposed in me."

Hamilton sent out similar inquiries to collectors of customs at important ports and to enough influential men throughout the 13 states to gain something very close to a cross-section of informed American opinion.

"May I ask of your friendship," Hamilton wrote James Madison on October 12, 1789, "to put on paper and send me your thoughts on such subjects as may have occurred to you for an addition to our revenue; and also as to any modifications of the public debt, which could be made consistent with good faith—the interest of the public and of the creditors." He added, "The Question is very much what further taxes will be *least* unpopular."

While waiting for answers, he busied himself tightening up administration in his department. With import duties the chief source of federal revenue, his first duty was to maintain the flow of collections. He ordered that regulations not be too harsh, or they would be mocked by breaches that had long been indulged. He informed himself of state and local requirements and urged collectors to suggest all improvements that could be made in federal rules. He issued warnings against traders' tricks he had learned from his boyhood experience as Cruger's clerk on St. Croix.

Hamilton authorized collectors "to employ boats for the Security of the Revenue against contraband." These were the beginnings of the United States Coast Guard as one of many long arms of the Treasury Department. "I feel a strong conviction that a certain number of cruising vessels will be found equally beneficial to the fair trader and to the revenue."

Hamilton said that "unless an Eagle eyed comptroller" made constant checks, "one half of your customs House officers will turn rascals within a year." He cracked down hard by constant writing, checking, and nagging. The James River testified that Hamilton's incessant hectoring was worse than his sufferings during the war. John Marshall of Virginia commented that Hamilton "united a patient industry, not always the companion of genius, which fitted him, in a peculiar manner, for subduing the difficulties to be encountered by the man . . . placed at the head of the American finances."

Hamilton also carried out international economic diplomacy as if he, not Jefferson, were secretary of state. He wrote his old comrade-in-arms the Marquis de Lafeyette on October 6, 1789, that, as part of the subject of foreign and domestic debt, "the debt due to France will be among the first objects" of Congress's and his own attention. He was discreet enough to add, ''I am not in a situation to address anything officially to your administration.'' He was indiscreet enough to go on to say that he planned to offer ''a speedy payment of the *arears of interest* now due, and effectual provision for the punctual payment of future interest as it arises.'' As quid pro quo, France must suspend its demands for repayment of the principal of the debt for a few years.

Replies to Hamilton's letters of inquiry trickled in as the three-month deadline for his first ''Report on Public Credit'' to Congress approached. The second most important of these was the long thoughtful letter from William Bingham of November 25, which contained much that Hamilton would refine and include in the final version of the report. Bingham, a founder and director of the Bank of North America was reputedly the wealthiest man in the United States, his fortune being based on successful privateering operations and wartime speculations in the West Indies and elsewhere. He and his beautiful wife, the former Anne Willing, daughter of the bank president, had often entertained the Hamiltons at their Philadelphia mansion when Bingham and Hamilton had been fellow members of the Continental Congress.

Citing recent British experience at a time of similar financial distress, Bingham reminded Hamilton that ''when Mr. Pitt came into administration [as first treasury lord and Chancellor of the Exchequer in 1783] he saw the deranged state of the National affairs and the necessity of restoring public credit.'' By raising taxes, he had obtained a considerable surplus. He had established a sinking fund, providing a trust under the control of commissioners for the purpose of accumulating funds to be invariably applied to the gradual extinction of the national debt. Bingham noted that ''this stroke of finance operated like a charm.'' The result was that as soon as the resources of Great Britain were discovered to be so far beyond the actual demands for interest as to admit of paying off a portion of the principal of the debt, ''public credit revived, and all the train of advantages that result from it, accompanied it.'' Then ''money flowed into the country and every channel of industry was supplied.'' Hamilton in submitting his report on public credit would be assuming the role as well as many of the policies of Pitt. ''Taxes, when used for this stimulating purpose, do not impoverish the society by diminishing the common mass of property,'' Bingham went on. They only ''interrupt the circulation to the extent of the sum drawn from the people, combined with the time that elapses, before it returns to the common mass.''

Obviously, Bingham went on, to propose taxes is ''an arduous and invidious task as it is impossible to select those, that are free from solid & manifest objection, considering the various interests of the different states.'' But a zeal for the national credit will impel a nation to raise taxes, to create a gradual diminution of the national debt, and hold out hope of future relaxation of taxes to ''place the country in a situation to support that rank of power & grandeur, which she is entitled to enjoy.''

James Madison of Virginia had stood with Hamilton at Philadelphia for a strong constitution. He had served as Hamilton's associate in writing *The Federalist*. He had been his full partner in the crucial interrelated battles for ratification in Virginia and New York. The pair had stood shoulder to shoulder at the Annapolis Convention and as members of the Confederation Congress back in 1783, where they had faced up to similar intractable questions of public finance. Now Madison was the floor leader of the House of Representatives and chief spokesman for the most populous and influential state. The most important reply to Hamilton's request letters was Madison's, not for the economic ideas it contained but as a political document, with fatefully negative implications for Hamilton's future. Madison's statements themselves contained no surprises for Hamilton, but his evasive and distant tone, so uncharacteristic of Madison's style, came as a shock.

Madison's reply of November 19 called for taxes on home distilleries, an increase in duties on imported liquor, a national land tax (before the states should start to levy a real estate tax) and a stamp tax on federal court proceedings. On the subject of public credit, Madison was equivocal but not specifically opposed to anything in Hamilton's program. It was "a subject on which I ought perhaps to be silent having not enough revolved it to form any precise ideas," he said. He approved settling the foreign part of the debt "on the most satisfactory footing," perhaps at a reduced rate of interest. This would mean a settlement less favorable to France than the generous terms Hamilton had proposed privately to Lafayette.

The domestic part of the debt was more controversial, Madison felt. It "is well known to be viewed in different lights by different classes of people. It might be a soothing circumstance to those least favorably disposed, if by some operation the debt could be lessened by purchases made on public account." But there was no question in Madison's mind that it was "very desirable that the provision to be made should be such as will put the debt in a manifest course of extinguishment."

The debt must be kept small, and what there was must be paid off quickly, he felt, for reasons peculiar to the situation of the United States. Heavier taxes would be "more acceptable than lighter" taxes if they would accomplish this. Why? Because as soon as a definite provision was made for paying off past and future interest, as soon as "the permanent views of the government" are ascertained, a very bad thing would happen. The debt would "slide into the hands of foreigners," Madison feared. "As they have more money than the Americans, and less productive ways of laying it out, they can and will pretty generally buy out the Americans." Madison admitted that he might be mistaking "local for general sentiments" on this, but was sending them to Hamilton anyway because of "unwillingness to disobey your commands."

There was not a word in Madison's letter calling for a discrimination between first and subsequent holders of public debt or opposing federal assumption of state debts, the two most critical issues in Hamilton's program. Madison had spoken out forcefully in favor of nondiscrimination between holders and for federal assumption when he was in Congress with Hamilton as far back as 1783. Nothing in Madison's letter hinted at the precise, knowing, detailed, deadly and effective opposition to Hamilton's 1790 program that Madison would begin in Congress less than three months after Hamilton introduced it.

Public suspense, as well as speculation, mounted as the date for submission of Hamilton's report to Congress approached. Hamilton wrote his friend Thomas FitzSimmons on November 27 that he feared inviting public discussion of his report in advance: "I have several times had an inclination to feeling the public pulse about the debt; but this has given way to the reflection, that bringing on a discussion might be as likely to fix prejudice as to produce good."

Speculation in the public debt of any country is, of course, not wrong in itself. The debts, or promises to pay, of the Continental Congress and the several states during and after the Revolution had depreciated greatly in value. Many of the original holders—some poor, some wealthy—had sold them at discounts. Others, as late as June 1788, when final ratification of the Constitution was still in doubt, had been able to buy up large quantities sometimes at discounts of over 80 percent of face value. From this point, of course, such debt might either become worthless—or increase in value.

Impropriety or illegality in "speculation," or "investment," arises out of inside information wrongly obtained from officials who have a duty to deal fairly with all members of the public and treat them alike. The morals of the free marketplace do not condemn private use of information once it has become publicly available, even if not all potential investors have bestirred themselves to pay attention to it.

Back on October 2, 1789, William Constable had written Robert Morris that it was more or less common knowledge that Duer in his first two months in the Treasury had been "working with John Hopkins at buying up the soldiers' pay. . . . He may not only incur censure but be turned out."

Duer's ouster would destroy his usefulness to Morris and Constable, but Constable knew that what Duer was doing was wrong.

Noah Webster, the journalist and dictionarian, was able to deduce from "the outdoor talk of Col. Duer, the Vice-Secretary," that the debt would be funded and a national bank established. So Webster, whose journal often tartly scolded public officials, including Hamilton, for peccadilloes, quickly wrote to a friend to pass on what Duer had said and to advise him that "this will be the time for your speculations."

The year and the decade turned. Hamilton's mind, through which so many complex economic concepts and tabulations of figures were flowing into the first of his great public reports, was lonely and apprehensive when he wrote Angelica Church on January 7, 1790, misdating it 1789 for the old year:

> Tomorrow I open the budget and you may imagine that today I am very busy and not a little anxious. I could not however let the Packet sail without giving you a proof, that no degree of occupation can make me forget you.
>
> We hope to hear shortly that you are safe arrived and that everything is to your wish . . . that your sons promise all to be great men, and your daughters to be like yourself.

On January 4, Hamilton advised the House of Representatives that, pursuant to its resolution of September 21, 1789, he had prepared his plan for support of the public credit. He was ready to deliver it in person and suggested January 14 for the date. This seemingly innocuous proposal touched off a hot debate. Elbridge Gerry of Massachusetts was on his feet immediately with an amendment to the motion: "That it [the report] should be made in writing."

But Hamilton's political and personal ally Elias Boudinot rose to protest. The secretary should be allowed to make his report in person. "It is a justifiable surmise," he maintained, "that gentlemen will not be able clearly to comprehend so intricate a subject without oral illustration."

But Congress overwhelmingly voted down Boudinot—and the threat of a personal appearance by Hamilton—fearful that it would be too easily swayed by his eloquence.

Hamilton thereafter laid his reports before Congress in the form of a series of massive written documents, of which the first, "The Report on Public Credit," as it came to be called, dated January 9, 1790, was submitted on January 14, without his oral commentary. It and his subsequent reports are major economic documents in the structure of American government.

"The Report on Public Credit," with proposed implementing legislation, statistical tables, and so on, runs to more than 120 pages in the Hamilton Papers. Parts of the report are tortuous and all but impossible to follow, so "intricate and so complicated it appears to require some time and attention to understand," complained Joseph Jones of Virginia. But because so much of Hamilton's and America's significant history flows out of this report, it rewards the pain of concentration on its five main points, three of which would arouse a storm of opposition led by his former ally James Madison.

First, the national debt should be "funded," more or less for the reasons and in the manner that William Bingham had recommended, drawing, for example, on the success of William Pitt in Great Britain; that is, a permanent fund of money should be collected and put in trust for paying off the whole national debt.

The debt existed in various different forms, and it was the differences in the various forms that caused most trouble. The foreign debt of $11.7 million included $1.6 million of defaulted interest. The $42 million domestic debt included overdue interest of $13 million. The great bulk of the domestic debt consisted of 6 percent certificates that had been issued to settle back pay owed to soldiers and on farmers' and contractors' claims for wartime services and supplies. Other debt certificates outstanding represented wartime loans by citizens and Continental currency redeemed after the 40 to 1 devaluation of 1780. Hamilton placed a value of only $2 million on almost $80 million worth of old Continental currency still outstanding, and it was later redeemed at 100 for 1.

Hamilton proposed that the various existing forms of the debt (but not Continental currency)—loan office certificates, army certificates, and all the rest of such government IOU's—should be consolidated into an orderly series of new interest-bearing government securities. A sinking fund drawn from "the net product of the post office" not exceeding a million dollars, would be applied by trustees "to the discharge of the existing public debt, either by purchase" of government obligations in the market, "or by payments on account of the principal, as shall appear to them most advisable . . .; to continue so vested, until the whole of the debt shall be discharged."

This would serve the triple purpose of reducing the debt, bolstering the market price of the remaining outstanding debt, and increasing public confidence in the system. Hamilton suggested that the trustees be the vice-president, John Adams, the chief justice, John Jay, the secretary of the treasury, and the attorney general, Edmund Randolph. The cardinal point of the whole system was that Hamilton "ardently wishes to see it incorporated, as a fundamental maxim, in the system of public credit of the United States, that the creation of debt should always be accompanied with the means of extinguishment."

Second, he dealt with the claims of the various classes of public creditors. There was no real dispute about the foreign debt, mostly to the governments of France and Holland or to private bankers in those countries. It "ought to be provided for according to the precise terms of the contracts relating to it," subject only to extensions of payment of principal, which might be wangled by backstage negotiations like those Hamilton had suggested to Lafayette. Precise compliance with terms would avoid even the suggestion that the United States was attempting to renege on promises to pay when due.

Third was the question of "discrimination." As to the domestic debt or "that which has been contracted at home," Hamilton understated the case when he observed, "It is to be regretted that there is no such unanimity of sentiment" about domestic "discrimination" as there was with respect to the foreign debt. "It involves this question," Hamilton explained, "whether a discrimination ought to be made between original holders of the public securities, and present possessors by purchase." The practical problem was that the original evidences of debt had been issued during the Revolution and afterward to soldiers as pay and to merchants for supplies. But many of the poorer holders, especially the soldiers, had been compelled to sell them off for cash money at discounts to speculators with ready capital like William Duer. Speculators' agents had been able to buy up such debt certificates from old soldiers at discounts as low as 12 cents on the dollar. Was it fair now to pay off present speculative holders in full while the poor old soldiers, the deserving first holders, who had sold for what they could get, would receive nothing more? Or should some discrimination be made by somehow making present holders share their profits with the first holders? Those who favored discrimination, Hamilton said, "are for making a full provision" for paying the original holders at face value, whereas the subsequent holders should receive no more than what they had paid and the interest.

Hamilton opposed this: "After the most mature reflection on the force of this argument," Hamilton found that the doctrine is "equally unjust and impolitic; as highly injurious, even to the original holders of public securities, as ruinous to public credit." Furthermore, "it is inconsistent with justice because in the first place it is a breach of contract; in violation of the rights of a fair purchaser." As a member of the Committee on Style, which had seen Article VI inserted in the Constitution at the last moment, he knew well that "all Debts contracted and Engagements entered into, before the adoption of this Constitution, shall be valid against the United States under this Constitution as under the Confederation." Failure to pay debts contracted had been the most conspicuous cause of the failure of the old government. He admitted the hard case of the needy sellers, but declared that their complaint, if any, was against the government itself and not against "the persons who relieved their necessities, by giving them the current price of their property." Their hard cases, like most hard cases, would make bad general law.

The practical problem seemed insoluble. Most certificates had passed through several hands, and each passage had been at a different price. How could any Treasury unravel the tangled skein of many transactions and restore each holder in the series to his original position? Would not such a precedent also in effect establish the rule that government securities were not freely and validly assignable? If so, what would happen to public credit? What about original holders who had hastened to sell, not because of financial needs, but because of a lack of faith in the new American state? Should they be rewarded for their lack of faith, and those who had purchased from them be penalized for their faith?

"The difficulties," Hamilton averred, "would be found immense, insurmountable . . . absurd . . . inequitable" and would "disgust even the proposers of the measure."

Fourth was the "assumption" of state debts. States, as well as the national government, had issued their own paper to cover wartime obligations. He estimated the total at $25 million. It would be wrong, he reasoned, to distinguish between local and national defense. After more "mature reflection," he had come to a "full conviction, that an assumption of the debts of the particular states by the union, and a like provision for them as for those of union, will be a measure of sound policy and substantial justice." The national government would substitute its own obligation to creditors of the states for the states' separate obligations. Such "assumption," like "discrimination," would rouse up a political uproar.

The fifth point dealt with the practical means of consolidating all the old debt into a single national debt, embodied in a new issue of government securities, and raising the money to cover interest service charges for carrying the debts to be assumed. "The debt should," he recommended, "with the consent of the creditors, be remoulded into such a shape as will bring the expenditures of the nation to a level with its income." Creditors would be entitled to prompt payment of current interest, but the government would not be required to redeem the principal of the old domestic debt at any set time. Hamilton outlined a plan by which existing public creditors could exchange their obligations for various forms of new bonds, public lands, or annuities. This adopted some of the ideas Madison's letter had suggested. Hamilton estimated government expenses, interest, and other annual obligations that would have to be covered down to the last penny: $2,839,163.09. This was to be raised by existing duties and also by increasing duties on imports that were luxuries, particularly liquor. "The consumption of ardent spirits particularly, no doubt very much on account of their cheapness," he said, "is carried to an extreme, which is truly to be regretted, as well in regard to the health and morals, as to the economy of the community."

The whole point of the report was in its title, he concluded: public credit. It was a delicate, precious thing, like private credit. It could be maintained only "by good faith," by a punctual performance of contracts. States, like individuals, who observe their engagements are respected and trusted, whereas the reverse is the fate of those who pursue the opposite course.

The true question, according to Hamilton, was not whether the new government should refuse to pay any part of the debt, nor whether it could, by devious methods, pay a part instead of the whole. The real question was how to fund, recast, and deal with the debt for the future in such a fashion that all creditors would gain confidence in the sanctity of government debt and henceforth consider it as a valuable asset, as credit, not debt.

Hamilton declared that "it is a well known fact, that, in countries in which the national debt is properly funded, and an object of established confidence, it answers most of the purposes of money." When public credit is thus created, gold and silver, specie money, is no longer necessary in quantity. As William Bingham had pointed out, gold and silver can then be taken "imperceptibly" out of circulation, and paper substituted. Hamilton agreed with him that "it costs the country a vast sum of productive labor" to produce the necessary quantity of these inert metals. There simply was not enough of them to serve as money. But with public credit once established, transfers of public debt would be equivalent to payments in specie, and cumbersome specie itself could be removed from circulation. After two centuries, the United States Treasury and many economists are still urging this very point on a world crawling with goldbugs who maintain that national central banks have moved too far in the opposite direction—printing too much paper money without maintaining public credit.

Hamilton's critics, omitting his contextual qualifications that the debt be no larger than the sum to be set aside for payment of interest, funding, and "extinguishment," belabored him for allegedly exalting the virtues of a permanent national debt of unlimited amount by quoting his words that "a national debt is a national blessing." What he actually wrote meant the opposite. "The proper funding of the present debt will render it a national blessing." The blessing was in the funding, not the debt itself. He wished "to see it incorporated as a fundamental maxim in the system of public credit of the United States, that the creation of debt should always be accompanied with the means of extinguishment." This he regarded as the "true secret for rendering public credit immortal."

This first of Hamilton's great public reports, taken together with his major and minor reports that followed it, and his drafts of implementing legislation intended to carry out their recommendations, constituted the seven-point legislative program of President George Washington's first administration. The seven points were (1) the restoration of public credit, (2) a sound system of taxation, (3) a national bank, (4) a sound currency, (5) the promotion of commerce, (6) a liberal immigration policy, and (7) the encouragement of manufactures.

In a paper entitled "Defence of the Funding System," Hamilton would later write, "The effect of energy and system is to vulgar and feeble minds a kind of magic which they do not comprehend." The program that Hamilton had begun to introduce to Congress, report by great report, as Washington's new administration got under way, was one of the most, if not the most comprehensive and far-reaching programs that any new president's administration has ever launched.

To Catherine Greene's single question, Hamilton had now given a public answer, "Yes"; and to Henry Lee's three, "Yes," "Yes," and "They will be honored."

Public debts would be paid—but only if the administration's program passed Congress.

Assistant Secretary of the Treasury William Duer was in large measure responsible for turning what in history would be one of Hamilton's greatest public achievements into a personal and private disaster. Duer had privately, and earlier, been giving the same kinds of inside information to his partners in speculation as Hamilton had held back from Catherine Greene and Henry Lee.

To successful speculators, timing is everything. After Hamilton's "Report on Public Credit" became public, it would be too late to make maximum profits. On December 23, two weeks before it was due, William Constable, the money man, and William Duer, the inside information man, who had learned that federal assumption of state debts would be a part of Hamilton's program, signed a contract "to enter into a speculation in the funds generally . . . to purchase on time as many continental securities as can be obtained, the money arising therefrom to be immediately invested in the debts of North and South Carolina, to the extent of sixteen thousand specie dollars." The Carolina debt was widely scattered among many small holders, and Duer had already had agents in the field there for months, operating under cover of the vague story that they were interested in "purchasing rights to lands." In fact, they were locating holders and buying up their debt claims at discounts. The residue would be used to buy up "indents of interest or such other paper as may be determined on." The Duer-Constable account for such speculations, leveraged and pyramided by further borrowing through Dutch bankers against what they had bought, would turn over rapidly and eventually reach a level of over $170,000.

On their side of the water, the Dutch bankers could issue 5 percent notes in small denominations to thousands of Dutch public "investors," secured by the Carolina certificates held at 80 percent of the $1 million par.

Thus it is not surprising that only four days after Hamilton's "Report on Public Credit" was placed before Congress, Senator William Maclay fumed to his journal that "an extraordinary rise of certificates has been remarked for some time past. This could not be accounted for, neither in Philadelphia nor elsewhere." But the report from the Treasury now explained it all. Hamilton had recommended indiscriminate funding, and "in the style of a British minister, has sent down his bill. 'Tis said a committee of speculators in certificates could not have formed it more for their advantage."

According to Maclay, Thomas Willing openly avowed that he had seen Hamilton's report in manuscript before it had been laid before Congress. Robert Morris, Maclay's fellow senator from Pennsylvania, was also in on the speculations, as was Pennsylvania Representative Thomas FitzSimmons; and Maclay was certain that both had been tipped off by Hamilton or someone working under him in the Treasury.

Although there is no evidence that Hamilton speculated in purchase and sale of the public debt for his own account, he acted as agent for John Barker Church, absent with Angelica in England, in negotiations with Thomas Willing for purchase and sale of public debt. Hamilton's father-in-law, Philip Schuyler, was also active in the market, though not in as great volume as Church. In 1791 the New York loan office registered securities on Schuyler's account totaling $67,509.53.

Long afterward Hamilton's son, James A. Hamilton, found it necessary to state flatly that Hamilton had requested Schuyler to keep Schuyler's son, Van Rensselaer, from speculating in the public securities to avoid suspicious inferences. Van Rensselaer had complained, but complied, and stayed out of the roaring bull market.

When a majority of the House voted to delay taking up Hamilton's report, Maclay thought it was deliberate so as to give majority members time to buy up securities in remote parts of the Carolinas and elsewhere—before news of Hamilton's report reached the holders. A man coming up from North Carolina told Maclay that he had "passed two expresses with very large sums of money on their way to North Carolina for purposes of speculating in certificates." Maclay heard that Congressman Jermiah Wadsworth of Connecticut had sent agents on two small, fast vessels to the South. "I really fear that members of Congress are deeper in this business than any others," Maclay concluded mournfully. "Nobody doubts but all the commotion originated from the Treasury; the fault is laid on Duer but respondeat superior [sic]." With grim fatalism he added, "The business of yesterday will, I think, in all probability, damn the character of Hamilton as a minister forever."

Madison, too, noted that "the avidity for stock" had raised the price from a few shillings in the pound, to eight or ten even before the report was laid before Congress. As late as January 24, he said, "emissaries are still exploring the interior & distant parts of the Union in order to take advantage of the ignorance of holders."

Hamilton was seen by Maclay as he walked through the galleries of Federal Hall barred from the session, trying to rally wavering congressmen. On February 1, Maclay acidly observed that "Mr. Hamilton is very uneasy, as far as I can learn, about his funding system. He was here early to wait on the Speaker, and I believe spent most of his time in running from place to place among the members."

Thomas FitzSimmons, a speculator himself, lacking the position of ultimate control over the value of certificates that Duer enjoyed as assistant secretary, launched a congressional investigation. Duer, he reported, had "carried his speculations to such extent, as to prevent any Claimant scarcely getting an account passed against the United States."

FitzSimmons told Hamilton that Duer must be dismissed or the committee would be obliged to issue a damning report. Duer submitted his resignation. There is no evidence that it was volunteered by Duer, or demanded by Hamilton, until after FitzSimmons and his congressional committee had forced Hamilton's hand.

Hamilton's letter to his departing assistant William Duer contains no thanks for, or even reference to, any useful services Duer performed for the public during his six months in public office:

New York April 4–7, 1790

While I truly regret, my dear friend, that the necessity of your situation compels you to relinquish a station in which public and personal considerations combine to induce me to wish your continuance, I cannot but be sensible of the force of the motives by which you are determined. . . . I confess, too, that *upon reflection* I cannot help thinking you have decided rightly.

I count with confidence on your future friendship, as you may on mine.

Adieu—God bless you, and give you the success for which you will always have the warmest wishes of

Your affectionate, A. Hamilton

Duer's partner, William Constable, had told Robert Morris that "Duer talks a good deal of going to Europe next fall, at any rate he will not continue in office longer than that period.'' Constable summed up Duer thus: ''making schemes every hour and abandoning them simultaneously. . . . I have always known him better at maring [*sic*] a plot than furthering any project.''

Hamilton's appointment of Duer and toleration of him in office for more than six months was an inexcusable blunder. Washington would never have let himself be the victim of any such warmhearted mistake. Loyalty to a warm friendship of long standing made it a flagrant example of cronyism, but no excuse.

Hamilton had only just begun to feel the force of all the suspicions that would plague him as a result of his appointment of Duer. During the next two years Duer plunged into ever-deepening speculations. He gambled in bank stock and in the Scioto Land Company, and by March 8, 1792, his outstanding notes and other obligations came to $456,183.37 by his own reckoning, and many thousands of them were overdue. The speculative orgy collapsed in a sudden, sharp financial panic. On March 12, 1792, Oliver Wolcott, Jr., comptroller of the Treasury, announced that the Treasury Department intended to bring suit against Duer to recover a $200,000 deficiency in his accounts with the United States, still unresolved from the days of his stewardship of the old Board of Treasury.

The same day, in desperation, Duer wrote Hamilton that ''if a suit should be brought on the part of the public, under my present direst circumstances, my ruin is complete.'' He swore: ''I pledge my honor'' that ''my public transactions are not blended with my private affairs. Every farthing will be immediately accounted for.'' He pleaded with Hamilton, ''For heaven's sake, use for once your influence to defer this.''

Surveying the economic wreckage caused by the panic, an alarmed Hamilton asked William Seton, cashier of the Bank of New York on March 25, 1792, in the course of frantic efforts to halt the panic, support the funds by discreet government purchases, and ''relieve the distressed'': ''Does Duer's failure affect the solidity of the government?''

That same day James Madison wrote Edmund Pendleton: ''The gambling system which has been pushed to such an excess is beginning to exhibit its explosions. Duer of New York, the prince of the tribe of speculators, has just become a victim to his enterprises, and involves an unknown number to an unknown amount in his fate.'' Some said his operations extended to ''several millions of dollars.'' He was kept afloat only by ''usurious loans from three to six percent per month.'' According to Madison, ''every description and gradation of person, from the church to the stews, are among the dupes of his dexterity and the partners of his distress.''

Duer was thrown into debtors' prison. Its thick walls saved him from a quick death by violence at the hands of mobs of creditors he had bilked, who rioted angrily outside the walls.

The greatest of the dupes of Duer's dexterity and partner of his distress was Hamilton. Was he also a silent partner in Duer's speculations? In 1792, with Duer in prison, Hamilton's affair with James Reynolds's beauteous wife Maria had been going on for about a year, and Hamilton was complaining of her that still ''more frequent intercourse was pressed upon me.'' Thomas Jefferson had no doubt that Hamilton was Duer's partner in speculations when he jotted in his *Anas* that Maria's husband ''Reynolds was speculating agent on the speculations of government arrearages. He was furnished by Duer with a list of claims of arrearages due . . . and bought them up.'' Hamilton, said Jefferson, ''advised the President to give his negative'' to the resolutions of Jefferson's friend Theodorick Bland of June 4, 1790, that would have put a stop to the kind of frauds Duer and Reynolds were carrying on. Would Hamilton help save Duer?

To Duer's frantic appeal of March 12, 1792, Hamilton replied on March 14 that he was "affected beyond measure" by his letter. But it was "too late to have any effect" upon Wolcott's lawsuit (which Hamilton had instructed Wolcott to institute the day before receiving Duer's letter).

Hamilton counseled Duer to "act with *fortitude* and *honor*. If you cannot reasonably hope for a favorable extrication do not plunge deeper. Have courage to make a full stop."

He showed delicate consideration for Duer's feelings and did not reproach him for all the calumny he had by this time brought down on Hamilton's own head: "God bless you and take care of your family. I will not now pain you with any wise remarks, though if you recover from the present stroke, I shall take great liberties with you. Assure yourself in good and bad fortune of my sincere friendship and affection."

By only one graceful sentence did Hamilton for a revealing moment bare the suffering that loyalty to Duer had cost him: "I have experienced all the bitterness of soul, on your account, which a warm attachment can inspire."

Such anguished "bitterness of soul" on Hamilton's part, unmitigated by having received a secret partner's share of Duer's and Reynolds's speculative profits, is a significant bit of evidence for the defense of Hamilton against Jefferson's shocking charge. A second such bit of evidence is Duer's use, in his last desperate appeal to Hamilton to save him from ruin, of the two little words "for once," in the sentence "for heaven's sake, use *for once* your influence to defer this."

Beseeching his influential friend Hamilton to use his influence in his favor "for once," Duer's two little words of intended reproach to Hamilton for not heretofore using his influence improperly is as convincing as anything else that can be said in Hamilton's favor to show that "the saying with regard to Caesar's wife" was to Hamilton not mere cant. When Hamilton had written that with respect to the conduct of "every man concerned in the administration of the finances of a country, *suspicion* is ever eagle-eyed," he had meant it. As he had added, "the most innocent things"—an affair with a speculator's wife, for example—"may be misinterpreted."

No one needed to tell Thomas Jefferson that—he knew how to misread Hamilton better than anyone else.

19

A Deal by Candlelight at Thomas Jefferson's

A stranger to the ground . . . as yet unaware of the object, I took no concern in [the prospect of assumption]. . . . To this I was most innocently and ignorantly made to hold the candle.

—Thomas Jefferson to his *Anas*, 1815?

During the summer of 1789 Hamilton's friends had urged him to run for the United States Senate, or against George Clinton for the governorship of New York, or to accept appointment as Chief Justice of the United States—or anything but the vulnerable post of secretary of the treasury—but all of these flattering proposals he had "steadily rejected in the most explicit manner." Washington had sent his name along to the Senate. He was quickly confirmed. "In undertaking the task," Hamilton said in October, "I hazarded much, but I thought it an occasion that called upon me to hazard." Hamilton's had been the first appointment to Washington's cabinet. The second, that of General Henry Knox to be secretary of war, took effect the day after Hamilton's. From then on, Washington referred appointments of other men to Hamilton and John Jay for review.

On September 26 Edmund Randolph accepted the office of attorney general, then only a part-time job. Thomas Jefferson, then American minister to France, had planned a temporary sojourn at home before returning to Paris but was held up at Cowes by contrary winds and was unable to sail for America until near the end of October 1789. He was at sea when his friends in Europe heard that Washington would offer him the secretaryship of state.

By the time Jefferson was officially installed in his office on March 22, 1790, Hamilton had already been in office more than six months, and actively dealing with foreign as well as domestic affairs. Various personal matters and a monthlong migraine headache during May 1790 kept Jefferson from taking up official duties in earnest until mid-June, when he would arrange a fateful candlelight dinner at his new house on Maiden Lane for those two old friends and new opponents in the debates on "assumption" and "funding," Madison and Hamilton.

Washington spoke of his cabinet as he had spoken of his wartime aides—as his "family." Hamilton, the first member to join it, seemed to be returning to a family he had left after only a temporary absence. Neither then nor now did Washington draw sharp lines of distinction between functions of one aide or his department and another. When faced with preparing his December 1790 message to Congress, Washington asked Hamilton to "revolve in [your] mind such matters as may be proper for me to lay before congress not only in your own department, but such others of a general nature, as may happen to occur to you."

To Hamilton, "most of the important measures of every government are connected with the treasury," as he would write Edward Carrington May 26, 1792. This, of course, included foreign economic policy, because Jay's early stewardship of the Department of State had been "more nominal than real."

Hamilton always thought and acted internationally and continentally. The West Indies of his boyhood on Nevis, St. Kitts, St. Croix, and St. Eustatius had "figured grandly in the world's affairs." As Washington's wartime aide, he had dealt on many missions with leading British, French, German, and Polish officers, diplomats, and travelers. As a 20-year-old, he had warned Robert R. Livingston in June 1777 of the complex maneuverings and intrigues of European power politics. Writing to Duane in 1780, he had urged that Congress appoint a full-time secretary for foreign affairs. He had served with Madison and Richard Peters in 1783 on the congressional committee to study and report on whether the Treaty of Paris with Britain ending the Revolution should be ratified; he and Madison had offered plans to get the British out of Northwest frontier posts they had hung onto after the war. In 1784 he had formed a warm friendship with the soldier of fortune Francisco de Miranda, the "flaming son of liberty" and Venezuelan apostle of Spanish American independence. At the 1788 term of Congress, Hamilton had been chairman of the committee that had demanded "a clear and absolute right" to free navigation of the Mississippi.

Within a week after Washington's inauguration, the States General had met at Versailles. By July 1789, as the United States was ushering in its new Constitutional government, the French revolution had exploded. The Northwest frontier posts that Britain still held on the Canadian borders earned Britain large profits from the fur trade and kept the Indian tribes in thrall as a constant threat to American settlers moving West. Spain controlled the Floridas and New Orleans and maintained a strong influence in the Southwest through Indians, explorers, and missionaries. America's Treaty of Paris with France remained officially in effect, but moribund. Debts due to France, Spain, and the Netherlands remained unpaid. The British Parliament had adopted restrictive trade measures to keep American merchants and commerce out of the West Indies by requiring goods to be transported in British ships, shipment from or through designated ports, and other crippling measures. France, though a nominal ally, granted only limited trading privileges there. She claimed the right, under Article XXXII of the Treaty of 1778, to "regulate" all American West Indies trade. In *The Federalist,* Nos. 24 and 25, Hamilton had warned that "The territories of Britain, Spain and the Indian nations . . . encircle our union from Maine to Georgia."

Partly because of the American alliance with France, a coldly aloof Britain had refused to send an officially accredited minister to the United States. Now Hamilton advised Washington to open regular diplomatic channels with Britain to improve commercial relations. He recommended his friend Gouverneur Morris, then in France on private business, to Washington as an emissary to sound out the British on an exchange of ministers and to find out whether Britain would be interested in a treaty of commerce. Washington consulted John Jay, who approved Hamilton's suggestion. Madison opposed it, preferring, as he told Washington, to wait until Jefferson returned to take charge of foreign affairs. Washington followed Hamilton's and Jay's advice and gave instructions to Morris to act as an unofficial emissary. The British responded warmly, but seemed interested only in a treaty of commerce, not an exchange of ministers, and not evacuating the forts on the Northwestern frontiers.

As Washington moved Morris from Paris to London to act as unofficial American emissary to Britain, Sir Guy Carleton, the first Baron Dorchester, and also British governor general of Quebec, moved George Beckwith like a pawn from Canada to New York as unofficial British emissary to the United States. During the Revolution, Beckwith in the British army secret service had used the alias of G[eorge] B[eckwith] Ring, derived from the fact that when arranging treason plans with Benedict Arnold, Beckwith had used one ring and Arnold another to authenticate secret messages that passed between them through the lines. When in London, Beckwith was a gossipy confidant of Angelica Church.

From there on April 25, 1788, Angelica had written her sister Elizabeth, with high hopes of returning soon to New York, "How many happy evenings have I already past! from dwelling on my future happiness!"—happiness that awaited her on her visit to Hamilton in New York the following summer without her husband. Angelica went on to say that "Colonel Beckwith tells me that our dear Hamilton writes too much, takes no exercise, and grows too fat. I hate both the word and the thing." But nothing that Beckwith could cattily whisper in her ear could disenthrall her from Hamilton's spell. She went on:

> I desire you will take care of his health and his good looks. Why I shall find him on my return a dull heavy fellow! He will be as unable to flirt as Robert Morris; pray, Betsy, make him walk, ride and be amused. You will see by some of Church's letters, which have caused me to shed the most delicious tears of joy, that it will not be long before we return to America. Embrace dear Hamilton for me, it is impossible to know him, and not to wish him health and pleasure. I am so proud of his merit and abilities, that even you, Eliza, might *envy my feelings*.

Angelica's summer and autumn with Hamilton in New York the following year, and her tears and his at their parting would show Angelica that her fears that her "petit fripon," Hamilton, had become a "dull heavy fellow" were foolish. It would also show her that George Beckwith, however amusing his whispers might be in her ear, was a vivid but not always reliable reporter on Hamilton. Just before Angelica had sailed home, Beckwith reported back to Carleton a conversation he had had with Hamilton in New York in October 1789 that was more candid, open, and pointed, if not indiscreet, than diplomatic exchanges are supposed to be.

To protect Hamilton's confidentiality, Beckwith substituted the secret code number "7," or "seventh" for Hamilton's name, just as he used "2" or "second" in his dispatches to denote Philip Schuyler. According to Beckwith, Hamilton had said, "we have lately established a government upon principles, that in my opinion render it safe for any nation to enter into treaties with us, either commercial or political, which has not hitherto been the case; I have always preferred a connexion with you, to that of any other country, *We think in English,* and have a similarity of prejudices and of predilections."

No doubt what Hamilton was saying was intended for diplomatic impact, but it was revealing of Hamilton's own convictions as well. ". . . we are a young and growing empire, with much enterprize and vigour, but undoubtedly are, and must be for years, rather an agricultural than a manufacturing people."

His comments about France, to her chief rival's unaccredited minister, were careful, not unfriendly to France, and realistic. For the United States, Britain was by far the more important tading partner. As he said, "I am free to say that although France has been indulgent to us, in certain points, yet, what she can furnish is by no means so essential or so suited to us as your productions, nor do our raw materials suit her so well as they do you."

Hamilton wished to "form a commercial treaty with you to every extent to which you may think it for your interest to go" because it would lead to expansion of peaceful trade. No one would know better than Hamilton that "it would be better for Great Britain to grant us admission into her [West Indian] islands . . . than by a rigid adherence to your present plan to produce a system of warfare in commercial matters." Such warfare, Hamilton observed prophetically, was "encouraged by France in this country . . . to promote coldness and animosity" between the United States and Britain. This Hamilton "viewed with much regret" as "being directly opposed to that system, which upon mature reflection, I have thought it most eligible for us to pursue."

Critics without apparently much personal experience of how one public man makes another open up and say more about large matters than he really intends to say have fretted about the typically frank, but relatively harmless, personal comments about Madison, that Hamilton let drop just as the congressional battle over discrimination, assumption, and funding was about to break. During the previous House session, Beckwith had noticed that Madison manifested a severe anti-British bias in pressing for discriminatory trade legislation. Hamilton, a fellow sufferer from Madison's tergiversations too, told Beckwith he was surprised that "the only opposition to General Washington" came from Madison's side. "The truth is," Hamilton added, "that although the gentleman [Madison] is a clever man, he is very little acquainted with the world. That he is uncorrupted and incorruptible I have not a doubt; he has the same end in view that I have, and so have those gentlemen who act with him, but their mode of attaining it is very different."

Gouverneur Morris and Hamilton would always be close friends. Morris would deliver the "Eulogium" over Hamilton's corpse at his funeral. Each was secure enough in his own self-esteem and had enough wit and respect for the other's judgment to recognize ruefully that whatever the other might say of him might with equal justice have been said by himself about himself.

Beckwith reported that in conversations in late September 1790 Hamilton had said, "I do not question this gentleman's [Morris's] sincerity in following up those objects committed to his charge, but to deal frankly with you, I have some doubts of his prudence. This is the point on which he is deficient, for in other respect he is a man of great genius, liable however to be occasionally influenced by his fancy, which sometimes outruns his discretion."

Beckwith turned Hamilton's disarming personal confidences into vivid reportage, while Hamilton laundered all gossipy doubts of Morris's "prudence" from the same conversation when he reported it to Washington on September 30, 1790. Hamilton tried to explain away his old friend's "imprudence" by telling their chief of Morris's earlier close friendships with Luzerne and Fox and their "similarity of dispositions and characters." Morris and Fox were "both brilliant men, men of wit and genius; both fond of the pleasures of society." Hamilton had assured both Beckwith and Washington that "it is impossible that there can be anything wrong.'' These were all Hamilton's kind of men—more like each other than any of them was like Madison or Jefferson—projecting their favorite vices, and virtues, on each other.

Catharine Church, the third child and eldest daughter of Angelica and John, named for Angelica's and Elizabeth Hamilton's mother, came to be called Lady Kitty as she was growing up, just as her cousins Catharine Duer and Catharine Livingston were. It was Angelica's Lady Kitty and her younger sister, Elizabeth, who were on Hamilton's mind when Angelica's ''affectionate friend and brother'' wrote her January 7, 1790 (anxious about ''opening the budget'') and fondly wishing all Angelica's sons ''to be great men, and your daughters like yourself.''

When Angelica had brought her Lady Kitty to Paris in December 1787, they and their escort, the painter John Trumbull, were warmly welcomed to town by the American minister to France, Thomas Jefferson, and into ''our charming coterie in Paris,'' as he liked to describe it. Jefferson's headquarters at the Hôtel de Langeac was a great Paris house built for one of the mistresses of Louis XV by the same architect who would later design the Arc de Triomphe. He reigned serenely over a court of philosophers and attractive women like a prince of the *ancien régime*.

Although Jefferson sometimes scolded his countrymen about the dangers of ''female intrigue,'' his coterie that Angelica and her little Lady Kitty joined there already included the 27-year-old Maria Hadfield Cosway, with her pretty head of golden curls, and the delicate, cozily domestic Madame de Corny, at whose house in the Rue Chausée d'Antin, not far from the Opéra, Angelica and Kitty lodged.

During their visit to Paris, Trumbull painted the likeness of his host, Jefferson, from life for the original of his panoramic *Declaration of Independence*. When the artist and Angelica brought a copy back to London with them, Maria Cosway, visiting Angelica, liked it so well that she asked Jefferson for another copy for herself. So Trumbull dashed off two more replicas of his little painting—one for Maria and the other for Angelica. At this point, Maria was calling Angelica her ''dearest sister,'' but Angelica was calling Maria merely ''sister.'' Jefferson wrote to Angelica, ''The memorial of me which you have from Trumbull is the most worthless part of me.'' He added, ''Could he paint my friendship to you, it would be something out of the common line.''

It seemed that no man or woman could fail to be smitten with Angelica. ''You are capable of feeling the value of this lovely woman,'' Maria Cosway nervously wrote Jefferson. But Angelica really had no wish to trouble his nice little lady friend by encouraging Jefferson's randy thoughts to stray toward herself. So she tactfully gave the 44-year-old widower a polite but firm push back up on to the pedestal of avuncular sage, where he seemed to be most at home: writing him from Down Place, where she and Maria were enjoying the quiet of the country, Angelica coolly said that they often wished Mr. Jefferson were there, ''supposing that he would be indulgent to the exertions of two little women to please him, who are extremely vain of the pleasure of being permitted to write him, and very happy to have some share of his favorable opinion.''

Jefferson wrote to Angelica, who was sending Adam Smith's *The Wealth of Nations* along to Hamilton about the same time, that ''the tender breasts of ladies were not formed for political convulsions.'' What Jefferson liked about Angelica and Maria was that they were so feminine, not at all the ''complex, intricate and enigmatical beings'' that the 20-year-old Hamilton had told Kitty Livingston he thought all women were.

At Versailles, aristocratic French ladies and gentlemen played as shepherds and shepherdesses of pastorals. Some came to think of America as an Arcadia for all—many on the authority of Jefferson's interesting conversations and his much admired *Notes on Virginia*. Jefferson told Anne Willing Bingham, the wife of William Bingham, Hamilton's friend, adviser, and confidant, that the simple domestic pleasures of America were much to be preferred to the superficial society of Europe. He tended not to worry much about rumbles of distant revolutions that troubled other capitalists closer to the upheavals. When Daniel Shays had taken up arms in western Massachusetts in 1787 to halt the dispossession of farmers by creditors in the courts, Jefferson wrote James Madison calmly that "a little rebellion now and then is a good thing." To Abigail Adams's son-in-law, William Stephens Smith, Jefferson made the dramatic declaration that "the tree of liberty must be refreshed from time to time with the blood of patriots and tyrants. It is its natural manure"—at least when spilled 3,000 miles from Paris.

The "beautiful revolution," as Jefferson called it, had begun with the storming of the Bastille. When he sailed away from France that golden autumn in 1789, he said he was going only for a short holiday to inspect his estates and slave holdings, try to untangle his confused personal finances, and put off paying his debts a little longer, before returning to rejoin his charming coterie in Paris. To Jefferson, as to most citizens of the United States of his day, his state, Virginia, not America, was "my country," to which he was going home. He sailed from Le Havre on the *Clermont,* a vessel of 230 tons, which he had chartered to transport his party alone, sparing them any personal contact with ordinary people not of his own little coterie. He was bringing home only part of his possessions, but they added up to a whole shipload.

Besides his two daughters, 17-year-old Martha, called Patsy, and 11-year-old Maria, called Polly, Jefferson's party included two slaves, Sally Hemings, a pretty 16-year-old octoroon, who had come to France as Polly's attendant two years before, and Sally's brother, Jim, who had now been well schooled in the arts of cordon bleu French cuisine. As the great Virginian's biographer Dumas Malone wrote, the diplomat came home to America with "slaves, bitch and baggage." Tenaciously held slave tradition has it that beauteous young yellow-skinned Sally Hemings was pregnant, too, by her owner.

Back at Monticello, on its high Albemarle hilltop surrounded by gullied, eroded, and heavily mortgaged fields, in the great house with its graceful dome, quaint cupolas, 35 rooms, hidden stairways, and many ingenious gadgets for the convenience of its owner, Jefferson would be in a "château high above contact with man."

Jefferson's daughter Martha reported that her father came home two days before Christmas, 1789, to a tumultuous greeting from all his slaves. Although they had not seen him for five years, they were ecstatically happy in their bondage (which he sometimes said he deplored), to have back the absentee owner who had been living so happily off them in Paris. Jefferson's homecoming scene became a part of enduring Southern slave plantation legend. Jefferson would later throw his weight behind expansion of slavery and bequeath to the South the tradition Hamilton's antislavery views as a Federalist mask for economic exploitation.

The vast lands he had inherited from his dead wife had been added by Jefferson to those he had inherited from his father, but debts and mortgage obligations to Dutch and British creditors went with them and grew larger and more pressing under inattentive absentee management. He fitfully busied himself, trying to arrange extensions and moratoriums to avoid having to meet payments on debts he had owed for years. Even with about 10,000 acres and almost 200 slaves, hard money and public credit were scarcer than lands or blacks in Virginia.

British creditors brought constant pressing demands for payment against many large Southern land and slave owners like Jefferson, who were delinquent in debt repayment. National policies that weakened British influence in the country would weaken pro tanto the ability of Britishers or of Americans who were alleged to be former loyalists to collect debts that had been owed to them for years.

Senator William Maclay, the doughty democrat from backcountry Pennsylvania, wrote in his diary that Jefferson "had been long enough abroad to catch the tone of European folly." In Philadelphia, where Jefferson stopped off on his way North to his new establishment, the rich Quakeress Deborah Logan reported that he wore "a suit of silk, ruffles, and an elegant topaz ring." Others noted admiringly that the returned diplomat gentleman farmer was "conspicuous in red waistcoat and red breeches, the fashion of Versailles."

When Jefferson arrived in New York City, he would find a state department employing only two clerks. His whole staff was five men, including one part-time translator, and Jefferson did little to increase its size.

Hamilton, by contrast, had by far the largest departmental staff with 39 on the payroll in his central office at the end of 1789 and 70 by the end of the following year. The field service of the Treasury, under the collectors at the ports, grew by leaps and bounds. Nevertheless, as Jefferson understood the situation, Hamilton's department, supposed to deal only with the single object of revenue, was much more limited and less important than his own, which, as he saw it, was the one "embracing nearly all the objects of administration."

The total annual budget of Jefferson's department, including his own salary of $3,500 (he himself used no dollar sign), was about $8,000. His "staff" did little but copying, and he would try to do many important things that could be done himself or else pass them over to Hamilton or someone else for action.

The department heads were expected to speak in President Washington's name and act only with his approval, in much the same way his wartime aides had done. Usually, each cabinet officer would make up a packet of important correspondence, with drafts of his own proposed reply letters, and send it to the president for review. Washington would return these promptly, generally signifying his approval by saying nothing. Sometimes he made comments or queries, and sometimes he would hold letters back until he could have a conference with the writer. At first, he would confer with his aides singly, sometimes asking for written opinions from each of them on the same matter and making the final decision himself only after seeing all opinions. As a result, the policies of his administration were not typically group decisions nor the result of group conferences or of what later came to be called cabinet meetings, but Washington's own decisions, based on his own review of one or another "option" suggested by one or another aide. Lines of responsibility were as clear as they had been in the army. As Jefferson put it, he "formed a central point for the different branches" and "preserved a unity of object and action among them" through his own person. He was not the captain of a team; he was the general of a command to which the departmental heads reported like staff officers.

The status of Hamilton as secretary of the treasury was different from that of his three colleagues, Jefferson, Knox, and Randolph, because he was expected to be much closer to Congress than they were. Unlike the enabling legislation creating the other departments, the act creating the Treasury provided that he give "reports"—the key word—to the legislative branch on its request. He was required to digest and prepare plans respecting the revenue and the support of the public credit and report them to Congress periodically, as he had the "First Report on Public Credit." Hamilton quickly turned the burden of his special access to the legislature into an element of power.

Washington continued to rely heavily on Hamilton and entrust him with important missions just as he had during the war. Washington well knew the importance of foreign economic aid: it had made it possible for him to lose most of the battles but still win the Revolution. So Washington tended to let Hamilton operate the Treasury under a much looser rein than he gave to his secretary of war or his secretary of state. Although it was necessary for Hamilton to gain Washington's approval of the legislative proposals of his program, under the procedure followed in the early months of Washington's administration, at least, it was not necessary for him to win his cabinet colleagues to them. Maintenance of the "unity of object and action" of his administration depended on the president alone. Internal administration of his Treasury Department, formulation of the administration's legislative program, pushing it through Congress, creating policy as a member of Washington's cabinet, helping plan and carry out foreign policy, particularly foreign economic policy, at a level of detail and consistency that seemed beyond the characteristic style of Secretary of State Thomas Jefferson—all of these things did not distract Hamilton's mind from Angelica Church for long. By February 4, 1790, she had already received three recent letters from him. Even at such a time he vowed, "no degree of occupation can make me forget you."

Unexpected opposition to his first report arose, and his mounting anxiety seemed to wireless to her across the ocean, causing her to have an anxiety attack of her own in sympathy with his:

> London february the 4, 1790
>
> You are happy my dear friend to find consolation in words and thoughts. I cannot be so easily satisfied. I regret America, I regret the separation from my friends and I lament the loss of your society. I am so unreasonable as to prefer our charming family parties to all the gaieties of London. I cannot now relish the gay world, an irresistible apathy has taken possession of my mind, and banished those innocent sallies of lively Imagination that once afforded pleasure to myself and friends— but do not let me pain your affectionate heart, all will be well and perhaps I may return to America.

She would now make Hamilton's anxieties her own, ridiculous as she might seem to herself pretending to be amused by the dreary subject of public finance.

> I shall send by the first ships every well written book that I can procure on the subject of finance. I cannot help being diverted at the avidity I express to whatever relates to this subject. It is a new source of amusement or rather of *interest*.

To prove it, she sent him a copy of Adam Smith's *The Wealth of Nations*.

But with all this said and done, Oh, how her heart still ached for her amiable absent friend.

> Adieu my dear Brother, remember me affectionately to Eliza. I have this moment received her letter, and have received three from you. I accept this attention on your part, as *I ought,* and if in return I cannot give you agreeable information, I can at

least give you the History of my Mind, which is at present very much occupied by a very great, and very amiable personage. Adieu my dear *friend*.

When the House finally began debate on Hamilton's "Report on the Public Credit" on January 28, the surge of speculation had alienated many members Hamilton counted on to support no discrimination as between original holders and later speculative transferees. James Jackson of Georgia opened the long-awaited debate to crowded galleries, rising to address the House. He had formerly agreed with Hamilton's views, he avowed, "but circumstances have occurred, to make me almost a convert to the other. A spirit of havoc, speculation, and ruin, has arisen, and been cherished by people who had an access to the information the report contained."

His angry passion rose:

> Three vessels, sir, have sailed within a fortnight from this port, freighted for speculation; they are intended to purchase up the State and other securities in the hands of the uninformed, though honest citizens of North Carolina, South Carolina and Georgia. My soul rises indignant at the avaricious and immoral turpitude which so vile a conduct displays.

Jackson's mind was "almost made up in favor of some discrimination," he cried, "by reason of the speculation, which has been carried on." On the subject of the "assumption" of the state debts, he wanted to hear first from the states themselves before he committed himself. Therefore, he proposed a long adjournment.

Hamilton's supporters, Elias Boudinot of New Jersey and Fisher Ames of Massachusetts, rose in turn. They cited the sacredness of contract, appealed to legal principles, and made passing references to "honor, justice and policy." "Shall it be said that this Government," demanded Ames, "evidently established for the purpose of securing property, that in its first act, it divested its citizens of seventy millions of money, which is justly due to the individuals who have contracted with Government!"

James Madison had not yet declared himself openly. His earlier letter to Hamilton had seemed to approve, or least not oppose, Hamilton's plans. So far he had given no hint of opposition, but now he sat silent, when his help was most needed.

Madison's views would carry great weight and authority. He had helped draft the Constitution and explain what it meant by his contributions to *The Federalist*. His learning was considered profound; his logic, severe. On the floor he was the leader of the powerful bloc from Virginia and was known to have Washington's ear. He was also close to Thomas Jefferson, the tall, broad-browed, brooding omnipresence to whom most of the Virginians looked for counsel.

No wonder all eyes in the House focused intently on Madison when he finally rose to speak on February 11.

Madison admitted that the domestic debt was valid. But to whom was the government indebted? He divided domestic creditors into four classes: (1) original creditors who still held their securities, (2) original creditors who had alienated them, (3) present holders of alienated securities, and (4) intermediate holders who had bought and sold and were no longer in possession. As to the first class, there was no dispute. They must be paid in full. As to the last class, they could be dismissed, for "their pretensions, if they have any, will lead us into a labyrinth, for which it is impossible to find a clue." With these two out of the way, he concentrated on the second and third groups as presenting the main subject for debate.

The second group, the poor old veterans, he felt, had never really been paid. They had been compelled by hard necessity to sell at a fraction of face value. For them, human sympathy reinforced justice. The third group—the present holders by alienation—also had valid claims, it was true. He presented the arguments in their behalf fully and fairly. But it would be paying double to pay both what good faith in the first instance, and legality in the second, demanded. It was equally unfair to reject wholly either group. Therefore, he suggested a compromise and so formally moved as follows: ''let it [the compromise] be a liberal one,'' he said, ''in favor of the present holders, let them have the highest price which has prevailed in the market; and let the residue belong to the original sufferers.''

But the recent speculators would be deprived of their hoped-for profit: the difference between what they had paid when they bought at a discount and par, or face value.

Madison's ''compromise'' proposal angered both sides. Hamiltonians accused Madison of having suddenly switched after misleading their leader into believing he would back the report. Senator William Maclay thought Madison's scheme was even more dangerous than Hamilton's, for it would require as heavy or heavier taxes to fund it. What was even worse was Madison's vote-catching appeal to ''the people'' by his moving but specious plea in favor of ''the little people'' who were the original holders. Though he was in basic agreement, Maclay was angry at Madison for appropriating his own Populist, vote-getting techniques.

Senator Maclay besought his colleague in the lower house to accept amendments. But Maclay's arguments only rigidified Madison in pride of his new opinion. Maclay acutely observed, ''It hurt his *littleness.* '' Madison seemed ''absorbed in his own ideas. His pride seems of that kind which repels all communication.''

The test of strength on Madison's motion came on February 22; his plan was defeated by the decisive vote of 13 to 36. Hamilton's supporters now pressed for swift action, and the first part of Hamilton's plan, the one that called for nondiscrimination, funding, and assumption of national debts, as distinguished from state debts, passed all tests and won.

But the most intractable issue of all still remained: federal assumption of state debts.

Why should the states oppose instead of favoring a plan that would relieve them of a heavy burden of debt? The question was well outlined in a report by the Grand Committee on the National Debt issued back in April of 1784, written in Thomas Jefferson's handwriting: All states complained of inequitable quotas, of having to carry burdens rightly belonging to other states, because ''almost every state thinks itself in advance'' on its quotas to the United States. Thomas Jefferson had been intimately involved with the issue of assumption for years and understood it well in all its arcane refinements.

Hamilton argued that if the national government took over the states' war debts, the states would have a continuing interest in the success of the Union that had agreed to pay them off. Creditors would support the federal government out of similar gratitude. The obvious need to fund the debts thus assumed would also give the Union its most powerful argument for a uniform and universal system of taxation.

The states viewed the matter from various points of self-interest. The New England states, especially Massachusetts, with the heaviest war debts of all, warmly embraced the theory of assumption. On the other hand, states like Georgia, whose war effort had not involved large borrowings, were opposed, fearing that national taxes on their citizens to pay off the heavier debts of other states like Massachusetts would be unfair to them. But Massachusetts felt it deserved more help, having contributed more to the war effort than Georgia. States that had already paid portions of their war debts in varying degrees feared that they would not receive due credit from the national government. Madison again listened in silence as the debate on assumption rumbled on. Among Southerners it was a matter of bitter comment that local holders of much state debt had already sold out at large discounts to Northern speculators like James Reynolds and William Duer. Assumption would thus mean taxing poor Southerners to pay off rich Northerners, so Virginia and most of the Southern states remained opposed.

House votes were closer all the time. On White's motion calling for a further report from Hamilton, there was a tie, 25 to 25. The Speaker of the House, Frederick A. C. Muhlenberg, broke the tie by voting for White's motion, thus laying a new draft of work on Hamilton. Maclay in the Senate was recording in his journal that Hamilton was causing constituents to put heavy pressure on their congressmen to push assumption through—on clergy, government officials, "the Order of the Cincinnati—and God knows who else!"

On April 1, Jeremiah Wadsworth confessed, "I almost begin to despair of the assumption of the State debts, and with that I shall despair of the National Government." The constitutional union was threatening to founder on the same kinds of fiscal shoals that had sunk the old Confederation.

On April 12 assumption finally came to a vote in the House and lost by 29 ro 31. It was a stunning blow.

According to Senator Maclay, who had walked over from the Senate chamber to watch the momentous vote in the House, "Some confusion ensued; Sedgwick took his hat and went out. When he returned, his visage, to me, bore the visible marks of weeping." Maclay was etching unforgettably in acid sketches of men he believed had lost much more than a vote on a bill—they were speculators who had bought up the debt at discounts and now were hit hard in the purse:

> Fitz Simons reddened like scarlet; his eyes were brimful. Clymer's color, always pale, now verged to a deadly white; his lips quivered, and his nether jaw shook with convulsive motions. . . . Ames's aspect was truly Hippocratic—a total change of face and features; he sat torpid, as if his faculties had been benumbed. Gerry delivered himself of a declaration that the delegates of Massachusetts would proceed no further, but send to their State for instructions. Wadsworth hid his grief under the rim of a round hat. Boudinot's wrinkles rose in ridges and the angles of his mouth were depressed and assumed a curve resembling a horse's shoe.

In the Senate: "King looked like a boy that had been whipped, and General Schuyler's hair stood on end as if the Indians had fired at him."

Then, as prospects for salvaging assumption arose, Maclay depicted the drama, as the tableau of despair coming back to life: the prospect of further successful "Speculation wiped the tear from either eye."

By April 14, two days after the debacle in the House, Hamilton had rallied his supporters. One after another, they rose to make motions designed to reintroduce the defeated portions of the bill in the guise of amendments that restored assumption transplant by transplant. Somehow the subject gradually became inextricably tangled up with the logically unrelated question of where to put the permanent national capital.

In the expiring Confederation Congress of 1788, Hamilton had done more than any other man to keep New York from losing the capital for the time being. He knew all the arguments for the placement of the capital, which were as simple as a glance at a map. Southerners demanded, nay, insisted, that the capital rightfully belonged nearer the South. New

Englanders demanded that it be placed at least equidistant between the two sections of the country. Pennsylvanians pointed as usual to Philadelphia. New York thus remained the capital provisionally.

Most of the votes against assumption came from the southward. Hamilton's successful efforts of 1788 to keep the capital in New York had given him a brightly colored poker chip to push before Southerners' eyes to win the larger issue he was pushing for the nation.

On May 31 the House voted to hold the next session of Congress in Philadelphia. Ames suspected that Madison had made a secret bargain with the Pennsylvanians to gain votes from them against assumption as a quid pro quo for letting the capital go to Philadelphia at least temporarily, pending its later displacement southward to the Potomac.

Robert Morris wrote a note to Hamilton saying "that I would be walking early in the morning on the Battery, and if Colonel Hamilton had anything to propose to him [Morris] he might meet him there, as if by accident." Morris duly went there next morning "and found him *on the sod before me*." As they strolled by the ramparts and gun ports of the old fort, Hamilton told Morris that "he wanted one vote in the Senate and five in the House" for assumption. In exchange, he "would agree to place the permanent residence of Congress at Germantown or the Falls of Delaware," both near Philadelphia, if "Morris would procure him these votes."

Morris and FitzSimmons worked over Senator Read of Delaware, and Read produced the one additional vote in the Senate that Hamilton needed. Next day Hamilton sent Morris a note that Morris took to mean that Hamilton now had the votes he needed to keep Congress in New York and carry assumption as well, although an opposite meaning could also be read into the secretary's ambiguous note. Hamilton privately realized that though he now could be sure of the Senate, the vote in the House would be so close that he would somehow have to win some more votes from Virginia and Maryland, as well as from Pennsylvania. Winning Virginia meant winning over the acquiescence of Madison, its leader, from his recent switch to implacable opposition. Hamilton knew that the place he had once held as mentor to Madison, when Madison had supported him in Congress and dutifully expanded his outlines for the numbers of *The Federalist* assigned to him, had now been taken over by Thomas Jefferson.

Although Jefferson had finally accepted appointment as secretary of state on February 14, Hamilton had seen little of him at cabinet meetings since. Jefferson had been attending to the marriage of his daughter Martha to Thomas Mann Randolph in February, then was detained in Virginia during the first three weeks of March, then had been disabled by one of his migraine headaches for all of May, which lasted on into early June. He appeared to have an open, but not vacant mind on the much vexed subject of assumption, and to be full of vague general feelings of good will. Jefferson was well aware of all the complexities involved, but "in general," he generalized, "I think it necessary to give as well as take in a government like ours."

According to Jefferson, he had met Hamilton completely by chance one mid-June day on the street in front of the McComb house, where the George Washingtons lived, on lower Broadway near the Battery, only a day or two after Hamilton had walked and talked "on the sod" there with Robert Morris to secure another Senate vote for assumption.

As Jefferson described the meeting three years later, the usually immaculate, spruce, and elegant secretary of the treasury was wearing one of his Publius' poverty masks—if Jefferson's account is to be believed. Outside the door of the president's house, according to Jefferson, Hamilton's look was "sombre, haggard & dejected beyond description, even his dress uncouth & neglected, he asked to speak with me, we stood in the street near the door, he opened the subject of the assumption of the state debts, the necessity of it in the general fiscal arrangement & its indispensable necessity towards a preservation of the union.'' If Hamilton did not have enough influence to put through assumption, he said, ''he . . . was determined to resign.'' However, before he gave up, he would remind Jefferson that ''the Administration & its success was a common concern, and . . . we should make common cause in supporting one another.'' Jefferson agreed: ''I thought the first step towards some conciliation of views would be to bring Mr. Madison & Colonel Hamilton to a friendly discussion of the subject. I immediately wrote to each to . . . dine with me the next day. . . .''

The next evening at Jefferson's newly remodeled establishment on Maiden Lane, the three statesmen sat down by candlelight to a dinner cooked to a gourmet's taste. The newly imported French wines and brandies and liqueurs passed round by soft-footed slaves were of the very best vintages.

As the host later described the evening, he had known of the breach between the two former friends who were his guests, but he gave them no opportunity to close it by preliminary amenities or social small talk. With no civilities he plunged them into the subject.

> They came, I opened the subject to them, acknowledged that my situation had not permitted me to understand it sufficiently, but encouraged them to consider the thing together. They did so, it ended in Mr. Madison's acquiescence in a proposition that the question should be again brought before the House . . . that tho' he would not vote for it, nor entirely withdraw his opposition, yet he should . . .leave it to its fate. It was observed, I forget by which of them, that as the pill would be a bitter one to the Southern states, something should be done to soothe them, that the removal of the seat of government to the Potomac was a just measure.

If Jefferson flagged, Hamilton may have remembered from Madison's letter of November 19 Madison's fear that American public debt might slide into foreign hands. Duer and Constable and their ilk might buy up debts from smallholders in the Carolinas at large discounts and pledge these to Dutch bankers abroad at near face value. Unfortunately, on the security of this American state debt, pledged abroad, the Dutch bankers would issue debt certificates to smallholders there, based on the face value of the Carolina state debts.

Because all agreed that foreign-held national debt would be honored according to its terms and because that assurance itself would give value to such debt abroad, to say now that state debt would not be honored at face value in the same way would create a hopelessly misleading situation abroad. To tell the Dutch smallholders who had bought for face value American state securities that they were now to be paid off only at a much lower market value would have a devastating effect on American public credit abroad. In so voting, Congress would make a mockery of assurances already given and further impair American public credit abroad.

It would not be surprising if on that particular June evening with his early and late mentors, poor Madison hardly got a word in edgewise.

Remembering that same evening a quarter-century later, Jefferson would put into his own mouth a surprising Hamiltonian argument he had not remembered making 24 years closer to the event: he had arranged the deal to help preserve the Union. Other interesting new facts were also embroidered into his rerembrance.

He was not attempting to pass on the propriety of assumption in and of itself, Jefferson claimed. He had exhorted Madison, as Hamilton had, that for ''preservation of the union

. . . the vote of rejection should be rescinded, to effect which, some members should change their votes.''

To give the Southern members ''an anodyne,'' a soothing pill to calm ''the ferment'' excited by assumption, Jefferson thought ''Giving [the seat of government] to Philadelphia for ten years, and to Georgetown afterwards . . . might, as an anodyne, calm . . . the ferment which might be excited by the other measure alone.''

This ''anodyne'' was much the same pill Hamilton had previously offered Pennsylvania, except that now the capital was to be placed permanently in Maryland at Georgetown. Jefferson did not say so, but it is logical to believe that Hamilton at the dinner proposed the ten-year ''pill'' for Pennsylvania. Her votes were essential now to carry the question. In any event, it was finally agreed that the capital would be placed for ten years in Philadelphia and, after that, transferred permanently to Georgetown. ''So,'' continued Jefferson, ''two of the Potomac members [Alexander] White and [Richard Bland] Lee . . . agreed to change their votes [on assumption] & Hamilton undertook to carry the other point.''

At the time Jefferson continued to pull the laboring oar for Hamilton where it drew most water. After working over both George Mason and Madison, Jefferson next went to work on Senator James Monroe, another hostile Virginian. He wrote June 20: ''Unless they can be reconciled by some . . . compromise . . . our credit will burst and vanish, and the states separate to take care everyone of itself.'' On July 11 Jefferson wrote to Monroe again: ''This measure will secure to us the credit we now hold at Amsterdam. . . . Our business is to have great credit and use it little. Whatever enables us to go to war secures our peace . . . it is essential to let both Spain and England see that we are in a condition for war. . . . Our object is to feed and theirs to fight.''

Hamilton himself could hardly have put the case for assumption more forcefully or belligerently than the new secretary of state.

Monroe, a lifelong bender to the moods of his mentor, Jefferson, could not mistake this carefully formulated opinion for uninformed naïveté. Jefferson insisted to Monroe that ''I see the necessity of yielding for this time to the cries of the creditors in certain parts of the union for the sake of union, and to save us from the greatest of all calamities, the total extinction of our credit in Europe.'' Jefferson had caught and passed on to Monroe the drift of Hamilton's clinching argument to Madison.

On July 1 the Senate voted 14 to 12 to open the next session of Congress in Philadelphia, to remain there for ten years, and then move the permanent capital to the Potomac, somewhere near Georgetown. The House adopted the same proposal July 9 by the close vote of 32 to 29. Suddenly, surprisingly, assumption passed the Senate on July 21 by the same 14-to-12 vote—as an amendment to a House-passed bill that had scuttled it.

Previously so forceful in argument, Madison now fell strangely mute. Perfunctorily, he voted against assumption, but he did not speak against it from the floor. The bill passed both houses on July 29, 1790 and became law on August 4. Thanks to a deal by candlelight at Thomas Jefferson's, Hamilton had hatched a famous victory out of an oft defeated bill.

''And so,'' Jefferson concluded his reremembrance of the event 25 years later, ''the assumption was passed.'' Hamilton, said Jefferson, had ''effected his side of the engagement'' and produced the votes to ratify the changes in the location of the capital to Philadelphia for ten years and then to the Potomac.

Forcing Madison and Monroe to switch, Jefferson had made possible Hamilton's victory.

Madison's double switch on assumption did nothing to restore him to Hamilton's friendship. Madison's only justification for his switch against had been that ''the very considerable alienation of the debt'' between the time of his conversation with Hamilton and his switch had "changed the state of the question." In fact, Madison's conscience was so full of shame for it that he found it necessary to write out a memorandum on a scrap of paper and attach it to his private notes. He referred to himself in the third person: "This explains the apparent change in Mr. Madison's opinion from his previous one opposed to discrimination. At that time the debts were due to the original holders."

Writing to his friend Edward Carrington on May 26, 1972, Hamilton said that "the change of opinion he had avowed on the point of discrimination diminished my respect for the force of Mr. Madison's mind and the soundness of his judgment." Yet Hamilton generously added that "my previous impressions of the fairness of Mr. Madison's character and my reliance on his good will towards me disposed me to believe that his suggestions were sincere."

About a year after the famous deal, Jefferson told Washington that he had been tricked by Hamilton. "I was duped into it by the Secretary of the Treasury and made a tool for forwarding his schemes, not then sufficiently understood by me; and of all the errors of my political life, this has occasioned me the deepest regret," he said.

For one of the acknowledged intellectual giants of American history to have confessed to serving as Hamilton's "dupe" and "tool" tends to exalt Hamilton to a position of mastery for which he hardly deserves credit.

As for Hamilton, there is no record of his ever saying anything afterward at any time about making a deal by candlelight at Thomas Jefferson's. He had won assumption and let the permanent capital go to the Potomac where it was was bound to have gone anyway.

Hamilton's "Report on Public Credit"—and the passage of his program with Jefferson's and Madison's help and acquiescence—constitutes a watershed in American history. It marks the end of an era of American bankruptcy and repudiation of debt and the beginning of a long era during which the public credit of the United States would be as sound as that of any other nation. At the same time, the tense debates on discrimination and assumption opened a wide gulf in opinion between Hamiltonian nationalists on one side and the proponents of states' rights, now championed by Madison, on the other. The cleavage would shortly lead to the formation of the Federal Republican or Federalist and the Anti-Federalist or Democratic Republican parties.

Was assumption really a windfall to the speculators? A heartless repudiation of the nation's obligations to its old soldiers, their widows, and their children? In his 1791 paper, "Vindication of the Funding System, No. 2," Hamilton ruefully commented that "it is a curious phenomenon in political history (not easy to be paralleled), that a measure which has elevated the credit of the country from a state of absolute prostration to a state of exalted preeminence, should bring upon the authors of it reprobation and censure."

As Hamilton explained to Washington on August 18, 1792, when Madison and "other distinguished characters of the South started in opposition to the assumption, the inhabitants of the Southern states sustained a considerable loss," because "the high opinion entertained of them made it be taken for granted in that quarter that the opposition would be successful . . . certificate holders were eager to part with them at their current prices, calculating on a loss to the purchasers from their future fall." Madison's switch had caused losses to many Southerners.

Yet sellers were spared a loss later: "A great part of the debt has been purchased by

Northern and Southern citizens at higher prices—beyond the true value. In the late delirium of speculation large sums were purchased at twenty-five per cent above par and upward."

Most important of all, much of the speculation occurred after Hamilton had publicly promulgated the assumption plan in his report to the House. "After that," he pointed out, "purchasers and sellers were upon equal ground. . . . If purchasers speculated upon the sellers, in many instances the sellers speculated upon the purchasers. Each made his calculation of chances. . . . It has turned out generally that the buyer had the best of the bargain, but the seller got the value of his commodity according to his estimate of it, and probably in a great number of instances more."

Passage of assumption provoked immediate repercussions in Virginia. Patrick Henry introduced a fiery resolution to the legislature denouncing it as "repugnant to the Constitution of the United States, as it goes to the exercise of a power not expressly granted to the general government."

An intransigent Protest and Remonstrance from Virginia followed. This declared that all powers not expressly given in the Constitution were reserved to the states and that assumption was an effort "to erect and concentrate and perpetuate a large monied interest in opposition to the landed interests." This would prostrate "agriculture at the feet of commerce" or result in a "change in the present form of Federal Government, fatal to the existence of American liberty."

Here was rebellious action that posed a new threat to Hamilton's Union and Constitution. He sent copies of the resolutions to John Jay on November 13, 1790, with a grim note: "This is the first symptom of a spirit which must either be killed, or it will kill the Constitution of the United States." Hamilton's own "sudden and indigested thought," as he put it, was that the "collective weight of the different parts of the Government [ought] to be employed in exploding the principles they contain."

Hamilton's old intimate and mentor of more than 15 years replied on November 28 from Boston like the smooth statesman that he was. Hamilton should not treat the resolutions as more important than they were. The pieces then being published in the press by the Hartford wits could do justice to the subject better by making light of it. "The assumption will do its own work—it will justify itself and not want advocates," Jay wisely counseled.

Jay's long view was right—for the short run: the Virginia resolutions had no immediate effect. But as Hamilton had foreseen in his "sudden and indigested thought," the long-range consequences of Jefferson's and Madison's great state saying that an important national law passed by Congress was unconstitutional would be devastating. Here was the doctrine of "strict construction" of the Constitution which Jefferson and Madison were to wield with telling effect in future debates. Here was the first respectable precedent for nullification and secession, which would break up the Union in the defense of slavery. In an angry flash of foresight, Hamilton had rightly identified to Jay the "spirit which must either be killed or will kill the Constitution of the United States."

Jay's reply to his mortal friend was also right. The task of binding up the wounds to which defection of mighty Virginia would lead would have to wait another 70 years for another American, who also favored freeing the slaves and preserving the Union.

20

The First Clashes in the Cabinet

"Every constitution, then, and every law, naturally expires at the end of 19 years. If it be enforced longer, it is an act of force and not of right."

—Thomas Jefferson to James Madison, September 6, 1789 [mailed January 9, 1790]

As Jefferson and Hamilton got to know each other better at cabinet meetings, they liked each other less. They were men quite unlike each other, not each other's kind of man at all. Before becoming members of Washington's cabinet, neither would have known much about the other except by report, although Hamilton would have known more about Jefferson than Jefferson would have known about him. About Jefferson there was so much that could be told that one lost sight of how much remained obscure. Born August 13, 1743, at Shadwell, Albemarle County, in western Virginia to parents who, unlike Hamilton's, were married to each other—Peter and Jane Randolph Jefferson—he was 14 years older than Hamilton. In 1776 the 33-year-old Jefferson had been helping draft the Declaration of Independence while the 19-year-old Hamilton had been training his New York Provincial Company of Artillery in preparation for imminent amphibious invasion of New York City by the British expeditionary force mobilizing out in the harbor.

Jefferson had been wartime governor of Virginia until his panicky flight into hiding from Richmond before Cornwallis's advance. This occurred shortly before Hamilton would lead the American assault on the last Yorktown redoubt and help arrange for Cornwallis's surrender there.

At ease in Paris at the Hôtel de Langeac during the hectic years from 1784 through 1789, which had seen Hamilton through the Annapolis Convention, the Constitutional Convention, *The Federalist Papers,* and the state ratifying conventions, Jefferson would have had scant occasion to hear Hamilton's name. Hamilton's powerful support of a strong and auspicious central government during this period would have come through to Jefferson as little more than an echo of the same views his correspondent Madison had espoused in the years before Jefferson's return.

Now in cabinet meetings the man who in 1776 stood for the idea of throwing off strong government rule sat opposite the man who in 1787 stood for the idea that enduring freedom and liberty were possible only under a strong, popularly elected national government. In 1790 and 1791, Jefferson unlike Hamilton was pressing no comprehensive and specific legislative program to further such general views.

Jefferson recognized the change that had taken place in the country while he had been away. On January 8, 1789, he had written an Englishman, Dr. Richard Price, that "I did not at first believe that eleven states out of thirteen would have consented to a plan consolidating themselves so much into one. A change in their dispositions, which had taken place since I left them, had rendered this consolidation necessary, that is to say, had called for a federal government which could walk upon its own legs, without leaning for support on state legislatures." But Jefferson went back and forth, depending on his audience. He had written Francis Hopkinson on March 13, 1789, that "I am not of the party of the federalists. But I am much farther from the party of the anti federalists." Nor was he yet "a trimmer between parties," he claimed. But if he were neither a Federalist nor an Anti-Federalist nor "a trimmer between," his assertions all canceled each other out. On specific hard questions of public finance like those raised by Hamilton's program of nondiscrimination, assumption, funding, the national bank, and an increase in the public debt, with provisions for paying it off by increased taxes and repurchases for the sinking fund, Jefferson took a firm stand, at least after his candlelight dinner had helped make it all possible: he was against it in principle. As he struggled ineptly with his own private burden of old private debts, Jefferson explained to Madison that no present generation had any right to incur debt that would bind future generations. He had written Madison on September 6, 1789, that "Every constitution, then, and every law, naturally expires at the end of 19 years. If it be enforced longer, it is an act of force and not of right." He added, "the earth belongs to the living." To Jefferson, this meant something deep to do with economics, something more complicated than a truism.

Jefferson's creditors compelled his hostility to Hamilton's view that a public debt, if properly funded by a proper provision for scheduled repayment at the time incurred through repurchases by a sinking fund, could be a public blessing. Jefferson had written Madison that "no nation can make a declaration against long contracted debts so disinterestedly as we, since we do not owe a shilling which may not be paid with ease, principal and interest, within the time of our own lives." When the assumption bill had suffered defeat on one of the early votes in the House, Oliver Wolcott, Jr., shocked at Madison's sudden switch to opposition, had written his father in Connecticut a comment that applied with equal force to Jefferson's quaint ideas on economics. On April 12, 1790, Wolcott wrote, "The Southern states seemed unprepared for the operation of systematic measures." He added that "very many respectable characters entertain political opinions which would be with us thought very whimsical."

A vote on a proposed amendment to the assumption bill led to the very first direct clash in the cabinet between Hamilton and Jefferson. A man named James Reynolds from New York had been moving about in rural areas of Virginia and North Carolina, buying up rights to collect arrearages of pay the Treasury owed to old soldiers. This man was the same James Reynolds Hamilton had known of at least three years earlier, in 1787. That August, Reynolds had called Hamilton's attention to scare stories in the press to the effect that, behind the closed doors of secret sessions of the Constitutional Convention, plans were afoot to install Frederick, the bishop of Osnaburg, son of King George III, as the monarch of America. Whether Hamilton ever found out for certain the source of the leak so devastating to his future reputation is not known. Nothing that happened later would dispel a strong suspicion that John Beckley was the fabricator of the canard with which James Reynolds had come to him.

In March and April of 1790, Gustavus B. Wallace, a former officer of a Virginia regiment and member of the state legislature—an unimpeachable reporter—sent James Madison two angry eyewitness accounts describing how James Reynolds carried on his fraudulent operations. They provided Madison with vivid proof not only of his thesis that Hamilton's policy of nondiscrimination permitted crooked speculators to prey on poor widows and old soldiers, but also that Hamilton's Treasury was directly involved in the frauds. According to Wallace, either Reynolds or his partner in the temporary capital, William J. Vredenbergh, of 40 Dock Street, New York City, had obtained lists of the names of the old soldiers and widows and the amounts owing to them. Where had they obtained these lists? From someone in Hamilton's Treasury Department. Who would not suspect a leading speculator on temporary duty there like William Duer?

This was shocking enough, but "What makes the speculation worse," Wallace explained to Madison, is that Reynolds would show the soldier a list "with a smaller sum than is actually due him." Then he "gets a power of attorney for the whole that is due him without mentioning the sum." This was, of course, out-and-out fraud and a very different thing from mere speculative purchases of soldiers' claims. Madison passed this information on to Jefferson, as well as to the governor of Virginia, Beverly Randolph, for prosecution in the law courts.

Theodorick Bland of Virginia sought to prevent such crude frauds by introducing resolutions into Congress on May 21, 1790, that would require payment of the arrearages to the old soldiers in person. If payment were to be made to someone else who had acquired his claim by assignment and purchase, the purchaser would have to produce a power of attorney that expressly stated the full amount of the claim and was witnessed by two justices of the peace. This would mean that claims that had been bought up before the resolutions were adopted could not be collected afterward unless reauthenticated in the prescribed manner.

Oliver Ellsworth of Connecticut, Rufus King, and others of Hamilton's supporters moved for a compromise amendment that would validate powers of attorney that had been drawn up previously, though not in accord with the required form, provided that no evidence of forgery or fraud, such as Reynolds's, had been adduced within a specified limitation period. There was a tie vote on these compromise amendments. Vice-President John Adams broke the tie by voting against them. This tie-breaking vote marked the first open clash on a public issue between John Adams and Hamilton. It would open a breach between the two men whose consequences would be as far-reaching as the breach the same vote opened between Hamilton and Jefferson.

Bland's resolutions directed Hamilton as secretary of the treasury to have transmitted to the state governors, for publication, complete lists of the amounts due each officer and soldier, as Gustavus B. Wallace's letter to Madison had suggested. Having received in many instances a good specie value for their claims, although less than face value, the veterans would now be free to collect the whole again from the Treasury, if no one else did so, thus recovering more than once on the same claim. Reynolds and Vredenbergh, as well as other less dishonest speculators who had paid hard money, if less than face value, for the assigned claims that these resolutions would invalidate, were outraged. Because the Senate vote had been so close, Hamilton thought that Washington, by making known his disapproval, might change Adams's or some senator's vote and defeat the resolutions on a new vote. Hamilton urged Washington to make his objections known. The total of all such claims, be estimated, involved only about $50,000. Retrospective invalidation of claims that had already been sold would involve incalculably greater damage to all public credit.

Those who had actually been defrauded by the likes of Reynolds could sue and recover in the courts. But few could afford the legal fees. By Hamilton's legal aid plan an attorney or agent would institute a class action on behalf of all of the original holders against allegedly fraudulent assignees: "The attorney general should be directed either to prosecute or defend for the original claimants, as should appear to him most likely to insure justice."

Washington asked Jefferson for his opinion. Jefferson disagreed with Hamilton. As a matter of local law in Virginia the original assignments were void in any event. The Bland Resolutions would only tend to confirm this. Congress should prefer to pay the assignor rather than the assignee. This would put the burden of proof on the latter and give "the advantage to the party who has suffered wrong rather than to him who has committed it." This assumed, ipso facto, that every speculator who had paid good money for claims was as guilty of fraud as Reynolds had been. Bland's Resolutions stood. On a matter of Treasury Department policy at the heart of the area of Hamilton's presumed expertness, Jefferson had won the first of many contests between them.

After an important conversation with George Beckwith on July 8, 1790, Hamilton reported to Washington the alarming intelligence that Beckwith's travel plans had been changed because of "the prospect of a war between Great Britain and Spain." Also, the British cabinet "entertained a disposition not only towards a friendly intercourse but towards an alliance with the United States." Beckwith had presumed that it would be in the interest of the United States "to take part with Great Britain rather than with Spain." The background of this new threat of war was that on May 6, Lord Grenville, Pitt's Home Secretary, had told Lord Dorchester, Beckwith's immediate superior, that Spain's seizure of three British ships in Nootka Sound off the western coast of Vancouver Island constituted a hostile act that might lead to war between the two. Grenville feared that such a war would provide the United States a pretext for seizing the posts on the Northwest frontier that the British had held since the Revolution.

Washington now requested Jefferson, Hamilton, Jay, Adams, and Knox "to revolve this matter in their minds that they may be better prepared to give me their opinions thereon in the course of two or three days." Jay was to come to the capital to confer even though his father-in-law, Governor William Livingston, was ill and soon to die—because Washington had expressed a "strong wish" that he do so. After talking with Hamilton and Jay, but not Jefferson, Washington directed Hamilton to continue his conversations with Beckwith "very civilly." Hamilton was to make use of the British agent who was making use of him: "to intimate, delicately," that Beckwith's remarks carried no official weight and that his references to an alliance were too vague to indicate what the British cabinet really thought. "In a word," Washington explained, Hamilton was to "extract as much as he could from

Major Beckwith and report to me, without committing by any assurances whatever, the Government of the United States, leaving it entirely free to pursue, unreproached, such a line of conduct in the dispute as her interest (and honour) shall dictate.''

Proceeding to extract all he could, Hamilton acquired from Beckwith the intelligence that the British were actively preparing to go to war with Spain and were drawing up plans for a naval attack on New Orleans, for an overland attack against Mexico, and even an expedition ''to seize the heart of North America for herself and erect the remainder of America into a client state.''

Washington, alarmed by the threat of ''so formidable and enterprising a people as the British on both our flanks and rear, with their navy in front,'' asked Hamilton on August 27 what the government's response should be in case Lord Dorchester ''should apply for permission to march troops through the territory of said states from Detroit to the Mississippi.'' Second, ''What notice ought to be taken of the measure, if it should be undertaken without leave, which is the most probable proceeding of the two?'' Washington asked Jay, Jefferson, and Knox for their answers to the same questions.

Jefferson's opinion was offhandedly but shrewdly elliptical, covering only a few of the several possibilities. Hamilton took more time, and his reply of September 15, 1790, covered more possibilities. Jefferson preferred to ''avoid giving any answer'' to Dorchester, should he make the request. ''They will proceed notwithstanding,'' Jefferson went on, ''but to do this under our silence, will admit of palliation, and produce apologies, from military necessity; and will leave us free to pass it over without dishonor, or to make it a handle of quarrel hereafter, if we should have use for it as such.'' Jefferson shrank from coming to a decision on such a difficult question. ''If we are obliged to give an answer,'' he continued, ''I think the occasion not such as should induce us to hazard that answer which might commit us to the war at so early a stage of it; and therefore that the passage should be permitted.''

This was a step back from the instructions Jefferson had given to the American chargé d'affaires at Madrid, William Carmichael, on August 2 to demand that Spain immediately open the Mississippi to American navigation. He told William Short, United States minister in Paris, to advise France that the United States would be hostile to Spain ''if she does not yield our right to the common use of the Mississippi.'' He instructed Gouverneur Morris in London to tell the British government that the United States would remain neutral provided the British would abide by the Treaty of Paris—that is, surrender the Northwest posts—and stay away from the Spanish possessions north of the Gulf of Mexico.

Here were surprisingly undiplomatic, veiled threats of war against the world's three strongest powers, made without at the same time having prepared American public opinion for war or even making any military preparedness efforts. Notwithstanding the provocative threat he ordered Carmichael to deliver to Spain, Jefferson told him privately that it was ''not our interest to cross the Mississippi for ages, and will never be our interest to remain united with those who do.'' It added up to undiplomatic, quixotic, blustery, and dangerous backing and filling on the part of the secretary of state. Hamilton by contrast made his reply to Washington the occasion for a careful review of all American foreign policy, as if he, not Jefferson, were the secretary of state. Hamilton thought Washington should call a special session of Congress to make preparations for war, if it should come, and in the meanwhile open negotiations to determine what concessions could be obtained by an agreement that the United States would remain neutral in the impending war. The United States had ''much to dread from war; much to expect from peace.''

Economic considerations were important. The nation should cultivate "commercial . . . intercourse with all the world in the broadest basis of reciprocal privilege." Its "true policy," therefore, was to "cultivate neutrality." Any "permanent interest" or "particular connection" with any foreign power should be avoided. Hamilton believed that the United States must eventually annex the Northwest into its territory and take possession of the Mississippi Valley, its outlet at New Orleans, and the Floridas as well.

As for the passage of British troops, because it would be by water "and almost wholly through an uninhabited part of the country, if it were unaccompanied with any violence to our citizens or posts, it would seem sufficient to be content with remonstrating against it, but with a tone that would not commit us to the necessity of going to war." But if they should force the American post on the Wabash River by arms, "there seems to be no alternative but to go to war with them, unwelcome as it may be."

France failed to come to Spain's support. Spain gave in to Britain's demands. The Nootka Sound crisis died down as suddenly as it had blown up. But it had provided Washington with a set of examination papers by which he could rate the performances of the three men he looked on as his ministers for foreign affairs, Jay, Hamilton, and Jefferson. In the second clash between Jefferson and Hamilton, this time over foreign affairs, Hamilton received highest marks from their mentor.

From Hamilton's point of view, the new law of July 16, 1790, which provided that "prior to the first Monday in December next, all offices attached to the seat of the government of the United States, shall be moved to Philadelphia," was a personal inconvenience to be cheerfully endured for the sake of the mid-June deal by candlelight at Thomas Jefferson's. On August 5, Hamilton asked his old friend Colonel Walter Stewart to find him a new house in his least favorite town. "My next wish," he wrote, "would be to have a house as near my destined office as possible. . . . As to the rent the lower the better consistently with the acquisition of a proper house."

Three weeks later he wrote Stewart that he had engaged a house for an office at the corner of Chestnut and Third Streets and asked Stewart to find a residence as close as possible to this. When he finally found one close enough—at the corner of Walnut and Third in the so-called "court end of town"—Betsy and the four children moved down to join him.

Writing from London, Angelica moved with them in spirit, but with unhappy foreboding. She wrote Betsy that "my inclinations lead me to prefer New York," but "If you remain at Philadelphia, I must be there." With a characteristically expressive rush of elision and sly setoff, of endearments with commas, she added, "My affections where you reside, but not altogether for my love to you Eliza, my dear, Hamilton has his share in this determination."

Congress Hall in Philadelphia was at Sixth and Chestnut Streets next to the State House, now Independence Hall. There a visitor who found his way into the gallery and looked down upon the House chamber, 100 by 60 feet, with semicircular rows of seats facing the Speaker's rostrum—"a kind of pulpit near the center"—could see an Ames busy at his circular writing desk, a Madison on his feet in debate, or a Sedgwick in conference with a lobbyist. The precincts of the Senate were on the floor above, but their sessions were closed to public view. John Beckley, the clerk of the House, and the other clerks had offices on the upper floor at the top of the stairs, just off the hall leading to the Senate chamber.

Jefferson's State Department office was a two-story brick building at Third and Chestnut.

Hamilton's Treasury office was next door in the old Pemberton mansion. A short distance away was George Washington's residence in the Robert Morris town house, where Washington lived as the paying guest of Morris.

Private houses opened their doors to members of Congress and boardinghouses had their famous romances. Senator Aaron Burr took James Madison to pay a call upon the winsome daughter of his landlady, and history was made for the dry little bachelor in Dolley Todd's candlelit parlor.

Hamilton, like many a successful lawyer, saved little from the income of his law practice. The move from New York was costly, and prices were much higher in Philadelphia, but, as a prominent member of Washington's cabinet, Hamilton was not a man to try to live below the standards expected of his station. While he worked on his "Further Report on the Public Credit," his "Report on a National Bank," his "Report on the Mint," and his "Report on Manufactures," and continually made arrangements for new foreign loans of as much as $14 million and more, he was often in debt to his friends for small sums of money.

Betsy paid bills out of her own money, or contrived to postpone them. She stretched the family income miraculously and for her skillful financial management acquired some public credit of her own.

On December 13, 1790, Hamilton laid before the House of Representatives two more of his great reports. One was his report on the "further provision" necessary for establishing public credit, and the other, which had been promised in the first report he had submitted back in January, was the "Report on a National Bank."

The first of the two was a proposal for paying the interest on the state debts that the Union had now assumed. Such interest would begin to accrue after 1791, and the amount necessary to pay it, Hamilton calculated, would be $826,624.73. His means of raising it? A further tax on foreign and domestic distilled whiskey.

Of greater importance was the second of the two: his "Report on a National Bank." Its opening sentence announced that "a national bank is an institution of primary importance to the prosperous administration of the finances, and would be of the greatest utility in the operations connected with the support of public credit."

Hamilton had, accordingly, devised a plan for one upon a scale that would entitle it to public confidence and "render it equal to the exigencies of the public." Of the three existing banks, the Bank of North America in Philadelphia, the Bank of New York, and the Bank of Massachusetts in Boston, only the first had ever had a direct relation to the government. But the new state charter imposed on it by Pennsylvania was now so "materially variant from the original one" and "so narrows the foundation of the institution, as to render it an incompetent basis for the extensive purposes of a national bank."

Hamilton's politically unacknowledgeable model was the Bank of England. The similarities included partial limitation of liability of shareholders, prohibitions against trade in commodities, prohibition of financial aid to the state without legislative approval, and strict limits on any branch banks. In order "to attach full confidence to an institution of this nature, it appears to be an essential ingredient in its structure that it shall be under a *private* not a *public* Direction, under the guidance of *individual interest,* not of public policy; which would be supposed to be . . . liable to being too much influenced by public necessity." He added vividly that "public necessity" would "most probably be a canker, that would continually corrode the vitals of the credit of the bank."

By contrast, the bank would prosper under "the keen steady, and, as it were magnetic sense, of their own interest, as proprietors, in the Directors of a bank, pointing invariably to its true pole, the prosperity of the institution.'' This is ''the only security, that can always be relied upon, for a careful and prudent administration.''

Back in 1779, as a youth of 22, Hamilton had written a famous letter to Robert Morris, advocating a national bank; and during the 11 years since, he had never let the subject drop.

Now that he was secretary of the treasury, his was an idea whose time and office had come. Pressing forward on the momentum of his just-won battle for assumption, using his first ''Report on the Public Credit'' as a springboard, he now put forth in his ''Second Report on the Further Provision Necessary for Establishing Public Credit,'' known as the ''Report on a National Bank,'' a plan somewhat narrower in conception than his earlier plans. It provided that the government might acquire one-fifth of the shares and could name five out of the 25 directors. It was a bank more clearly under private control than in his earlier proposals, really a private bank with semipublic functions, just as the Bank of England was.

The organizational details, not important now, included a capital stock of $10 million divided into 25,000 shares, of which the United States might subscribe to 5,000, the balance being open to private subscription; shares were payable one-fourth in gold or silver, and three-fourths in the 6 percent public debt.

Its charter was to run for 20 years; it was to be a unique monopoly during its existence. Branch banks might be established, but only for convenience of discount and deposit. With its large capital, the national bank would, in effect, be able to create money on the basis of public debt. The fact that three-fourths of the capital could be paid in certificates of the public debt, instead of gold or silver, would greatly increase the available supply of money. ''The chief object of this is to enable the creation of a capital sufficiently large to be the basis of an extensive circulation, and an adequate security for it. . . .'' This would reduce dependence on gold and silver, for ''. . . to collect such a sum in this country, in gold and silver, into one depository, may without hesitation, be pronounced impractical.''

Hamilton further explained: ''This part of the fund will always be ready to come in aid of the specie. It will more and more command a ready sale; and can therefore be expeditiously be turned into coin if an exigency of the bank should at any time require it.'' Hamilton shrewdly omitted from his report any discussion of the inflationary effects of the bank's power to create new money based on public debt, without specie backing. He knew that this had been an important issue in the debates over the rechartering of the Bank of North America that had helped to destroy its usefulness as a national bank.

The economic purposes of the bank were sound. It was an important institution; in many ways it was the forerunner of the national central bank, the Federal Reserve System. Its insulation from governmental politics, the ''canker'' that would ''corrode the vitals'' of the money, was an idea that the experience of recent years suggests was not only far ahead of its time, but timeless. Important as they were, the economic consequences of the bank were less remarkable than the political consequences of Hamilton's report and the legislation he introduced to carry it out.

In the political sense, the most important thing in the report was the legal point that the great constitutional lawyer had left out of it: It made no mention of the question of whether Congress had the power under the Constitution to charter a national bank.

Hamilton's dryly detailed plan turned out to be even more controversial and explosive than assumption had been. Out of his ''Report on the National Bank'' grew the unending debate on the theory and capabilities of the Constitution of the United States that has continued to the present day, with only a little loss of original heat. Out of it grew the great decisions of Chief Justice John Marshall and the doctrine of "implied powers," without which the Constitution as a living instrument of government would probably soon have become unworkable. With it, the aged instrument has continued strong and flexible through the changing stresses of 200 years.

The immediate impact of the report on the public was also prodigious, but in a different way. Fisher Ames sent a copy of it to a friend, with the comment: "The late surprising rise of public stock is supposed to be owing in part to this report, because it affords an opportunity to subscribe three fourths paper and one fourth silver into the bank stock." Sir John Temple, British minister in Philadelphia in charge of British financial interests, advised his government that "some of the Public Securities of these States have risen 16, & 17/ the pound! and are still rising! The Dutch have been great Purchasers into these funds, and if nothing should happen to alter present appearances, they will have made great profit indeed by their purchases, two & three for one!" Just as the speculative excitement produced by funding and assumption were wearing off, Hamilton's proposal for a national bank gave the worldwide markets in the public securities of the United States another upward boost.

Senator Maclay read the report, considered it "an aristocratic engine," doubted its constitutionality, yet feared the bank would pass. It vexed him to despair. He was grieved that Washington seemed oblivious to all the trickery his Treasury secretary was up to.

As Maclay had feared, the Senate acted first and passed the bank bill. Maclay's amendment to give the government the right to subscribe on equal terms with individuals failed.

The House was the arena where the battle over the report on the bank reached its climax, but its members were slow to pick up another of Hamilton's bristly porcupines. Finally, after three leisurely readings, on February 1, 1791, Jackson of Georgia opened debate. By now a determined foe of every Hamilton measure, he charged that the plan was "calculated to benefit a small part of the United States, the mercantile interest only; the farmers, the yeomanry, will derive no advantage from it." Then he struck at the fundamental weakness. "This bank," he cried, "is unconstitutional! We have no power to grant a charter to any private corporation!" With a triumphant smile, he quoted passages from *The Federalist Papers*—written by Hamilton, Madison, and Jay—to prove his point.

This set the stage once more for the entrance of the first man of the House, James Madison. When he spoke on a subject like *The Federalist* or the meaning of the Constitution, no one on the floor could gainsay him; off the floor there was no one but Hamilton. Now he rose to speak against the bank.

He well recollected, he said, "that a power to grant charters of incorporation had been proposed in the General Convention and rejected." His constitutional argument was careful, dispassionate, legalistic, powerful, and basically quite simple: you must adhere strictly to the letter of the document. It did not specifically permit incorporation of a bank. The simplistic symmetry of Madison's argument was unanswerable, if there were no such thing as an implied power. Madison's argument became the basis of all future arguments for "strict construction." In his later opinion to Washington opposing the bank, Jefferson took over Madison's arguments almost word for word.

Fisher Ames replied the following day. The ablest of Hamilton's supporters in the House, he did not attempt to meet Madison on his own ground. Instead, he invoked Hamilton's ground—the doctrine of "implied powers." "If Congress may not make laws conformably to the powers plainly implied, though not expressed in the frame of government," he asserted, "it is rather late in the day to adopt it as a principle of conduct. A great part of our two years' labor is lost, and worse than lost to the public, for we have scarcely made a law in which we have not exercised our discretion with regard to the true intent of the Constitution.'' Of what use was the power to borrow, as expressly provided for in the Constitution, if its most efficient instrument, a bank, were not implied in that power?

These two powerful statements of the issue drew a significant demarcation line between the political philosophies of the two emerging parties—Federalist and Republican—but not the only such line. Another significant line—a geographical line—seemed to divide the continent laterally on such issues. William Giles of Virginia was specific—and filled with foreboding: ''I have observed with regret a radical difference of opinion between gentlemen from the Eastern and Southern States, upon great Governmental questions, and have been led to conclude, that the operation of that cause alone might cast ominous conjecture on the promised success of this much valued Government.''

By this time, no simple solution of the issue at a candlelight dinner of the three men at Thomas Jefferson's was possible. The relationships of the three had changed, primarily because of Jefferson's bitterness at allegedly having been tricked by Hamilton into holding a candle to poor Madison. But none was necessary. By February 8, 1791, the opponents of the bank had played out all possible variations on their one-note argument for strict construction. Hamilton's bill passed by an overwhelming margin of 39 to 20.

Although both houses of Congress had passed the bank bill, the loud cries that it was unconstitutional troubled Washington, and he declined to sign it. He asked Randolph, the attorney general, for his opinion. Randolph declared it unconstitutional. He next asked Jefferson who also returned a written opinion: the bank was unconstitutional.

Southern speculators who had bought up public debt, hoping it would rise further with passage of the bank bill listened in panic as word spread among insiders that their powerful leaders Madison, Randolph, and Jefferson were telling their fellow Virginian Washington to veto the bill, and unloading. With the opinions of three self-proclaimed men of the people opposing the vote of the people's branch of the government in hand, Washington turned to Hamilton.

Hamilton's opinion to Washington of February 23, 1791, is a major state paper of American history. His argument was not narrowly limited to the question of banks or corporations generally, but went to the fundamental meaning of the constitution itself. He struck at the opposition's argument in terms that Washington and the people could easily follow. Narrow, legalistic ''principles of construction like those espoused by the Secretary of State and the Attorney General would be fatal to the just and indispensable authority of the United States,'' he wrote.

Furthermore, Jefferson's and Randolph's objections ''are founded on a general denial of the authority of the United States to erect corporations.''

They were wrong, Hamilton said, because

> This *general principle is inherent* in the very *definition of government,* and *essential* to every step of the progress to be made by that of the United States; namely—That every power vested in a government is in its nature *sovereign,* and includes, by *force* of the *term,* a right to employ all the *means* requisite and fairly *applicable* to the attainment of the *ends* of such power; and which are not precluded by restrictions and exceptions specified in the Constitution; or not immoral, or not contrary to the essential ends of political society.

He insisted ''that there are *implied,* as well as *express* powers, and that the former are as effectually delegated as the latter.''

Therefore, it followed, "that as a power of erecting a corporation may as well be *implied* as any other thing; it may as well be employed as an *instrument* or *mean* of carrying into execution any of the specified powers. . . ."

Incorporation, Hamilton argued, was only a means to an end. If the end were a "necessary and proper" object of the government created by the Constitution, incorporation of a bank would be "necessary and proper." Jefferson had misread the word *necessary,* reading it too strictly.

As Hamilton saw it, "neither the grammatical, nor popular sense of the term requires strict construction." Ordinary people's understanding should prevail over Jefferson's narrow technicality: "*Necessary* often means no more than needful, requisite, incidental, useful, or conducive to."

Hamilton recognized that "it is a common mode of expression to say, that it is *necessary* for a government or person to do this or that thing, when nothing more is intended or understood, than that the interests of the government or person require, or will be promoted by, the doing of this or that thing." This is the true meaning, he said, "in which it is used in the constitution. The whole turn of the clause containing it [so] indicates. It was the intent of the convention, by that clause to give a liberal latitude to the exercise of the specified powers."

Therefore, because the bank bill did not abridge a preexisting right of any state or individual, a strong presumption existed in favor of its constitutionality.

Hamilton rested his case.

Hamilton sent his monumental "Opinion on the Constitutionality of an Act to Establish a Bank" (70 pages in the Hamilton Papers) to Washington within a week of his request. It plugged the large gap he seemed to have purposely left in his original report.

Washington was not noted for his ability to weigh abstruse arguments and calculations set down in long-hand and issue quick decisions. Yet he signed the bank bill, and it became law on February 25, 1791, two days after he had received Hamilton's opinion. Only if Washington had been fully familiar with and convinced of the rightness of Hamilton's opinion long before he asked for it in writing would the time sequence of these events be otherwise than unbelievable.

On Hamilton's opinion are based all later arguments and opinions upholding the Constitution as a flexible instrument of modern government. When in 1819 Chief Justice Marshall affirmed the constitutionality of the bank in the case of *McCullough* v. *Maryland,* Hamilton's opinion on the Bank was the foundation of the Supreme Court's reasoning. On Hamilton's doctrine of implied powers, which has prevailed most of the time since, over Madison's and Jefferson's doctrine of strict construction, rests the case for calling Hamilton, not Madison or anyone else, the father of the living Constitution.

Hamilton swiftly pressed on with his winning streak. When his "further provision" for an increase of import duties and internal excise taxes came before Congress, there was little trouble about the import duties, but internal excise taxes touched off another of the furious debates that were becoming the usual reaction to Hamilton's reports. The unwillingness of people to pay taxes "even very moderate in their amount" engaged Hamilton's ready sympathy. It is a disarming theme running through all of his writings on the subject, but such words did not disarm Congress. In general, and predictably, the popular branch of government was loath to levy any type of internal taxes. The states maintained that such taxes were their sole province. Besides, the farmers and artisans of the representatives' constituencies felt that they bore on themselves with unequal hardship.

The particular tax that Hamilton pressed, a tax on whiskey, aroused extreme opposition at the fringes of the country. The settlers on the Western frontiers could market their grain in the East for cash only in the form of easily transportable liquor. Four years later the same opposition would explode into armed rebellion. Even so, Congress, under the lash of Hamilton's dynamic party, laid duties on domestic spirits of 9 to 25 cents a gallon, among other taxes, and passed his proposed "further provision" for funding of state debts in the Act of March 3, 1791.

The Pennsylvania frontiersmen, like those of North Carolina and Western Virginia, were hard hit by these measures. Their spokesman, Senator Maclay, grew more discouraged and bitter, but more vocal than ever before. Of the Excise Bill he wrote: "War and bloodshed are the most likely consequences of all this. Congress may go home. Mr. Hamilton is all-powerful, and fails in nothing he attempts."

Hamilton pressed on with his newly won power. In response to an order of the House to him of April 15, 1790, he laid before Congress his "Report on the Establishment of a Mint," of January 28, 1791, which runs to 145 pages, including editorial apparatus, in the Hamilton Papers. A mint was not just molding machines and printing presses and plates for churning out money, he pointed out. Its operations, like a national bank's, extended into the furthest recesses of national money management. A mint involved "considerations intricate, nice and important." He added:

> [It] must not only contemplate the principles of a coinage of the United States, but must extend to the coins of all other countries which shall have been introduced into them. All the revenues of the country; the general state of debtor and creditor; all the relations and consequences of *price*; the essential interests of trade and industry; the value of all property, the whole income both of the state and of individuals are liable to be sensibly influenced, beneficially or otherwise, by the judicious or injudicious regulation of this interesting object.

Those who perjorate Hamilton as a "conservative" ignore his record of these incessant calls for reform. The "question naturally arises," he noted, "whether it may not be most advisable to leave things, in this respect, in the state in which they are. Why, since they have so long proceeded in a train, which has caused no general sensation of inconvenience, should alterations be attempted, the precise effect of which cannot be calculated?" He had a quick answer. He knew, if his opposition could not see, "the immense disorder, which actually reigns in so delicate and important a concern" as national monetary policy. And so, "The still greater disorder, which is every moment possible, calls loudly for a reform."

The dollar had depreciated in value. This depreciated the value of property dependent on past contracts. Fluctuations in value of foreign money under regulation of foreign sovereigns affected domestic values. Moreover, "Unequal values were allowed in different parts of the Union to coins of the same intrinsic worth, and counterfeits, defective species of them, embarrass the circulation of some of the states." At the time, the pound was the money of account in all the states; there were also many standard coins, including the dollar, but it had never had a fixed value in terms of gold or the pound or any other certain standard. Gold specie had greater stability as a standard of value than silver.

But after weighing all arguments for either gold or silver as the monetary reserve unit, Hamilton decided in favor of both, with silver and gold as legal tender at a ratio of 15 to 1. Despite "the prejudices of mankind," there was no intrinsic, or inherent difference between the two metals, except that gold's greater scarcity as a commodity tended to make it more stable in value. Bank circulation as an expandable *auxiliary* to, but not as a complete substitute for the two precious metals was what was most important. Use of both gold and silver as a reserve was necessary, he wrote, because "to annul the use of either of the metals as money, is to abridge the quantity of circulating medium, and is liable to all the objections which arise from a comparison of the benefits of a full, with the evils of a scanty circulation."

He deplored persons who acted from "a fanciful predilection to Gold" and pointed out the error of thinking that gold or silver coins in circulation "are to be considered as bullion, or in other words, as a raw material." What happened was that "the adoption of them, as money, has caused them to become the fabric." That is, as coins, regardless of the metal content, they have "a sanction and efficacy equivalent to the stamp of the sovereign." He was troubled by the twin problems of inflation and deflation: "There is scarcely any point, in the economy of national affairs of greater moment, than the preservation of the intrinsic value of the money unit. On this the security and steady value of property depend."

He discussed the effects of favorable and adverse trade balances on the money of the country and also the effects caused by adjustments of exchange rates and transfers of gold from one country to another to balance out imbalances between nations. The situation of France, as an example of a self-sufficient country able to surmount easily any mistakes in her government's economic management, called forth singular admiration, when compared to the situation of Britain.

Hamilton specified a series of coinages, including their weights, sizes, alloy composition, and nomenclature, classified according to a decimal system. It included a copper piece, a cent (to be one-hundredth part of a dollar), a half-cent piece, a silver piece to be one-tenth of a dollar, a silver dollar, and gold dollar pieces and also a ten-dollar gold piece to be known as an eagle "not a very expressive or apt appellation for the largest gold piece, but nothing better occurs." He called for setting up a mint at Philadelphia and gave a table of organization for the personnel and also methods for periodically spot-checking the assay of the alloy composition of the coinage.

Hamilton's program rolled on. The plan embodied in his "Report on the Mint" was favorably received and became law in the Mint Act of April 2, 1792.

William Maclay's reaction was predictable: "The resolution on the Mint was foully smuggled through." Privately, Hamilton had much sympathy with Maclay's concerns and his remote constitutents. Hamilton's and Maclay's argument was really over means. His reform measures relegated Maclay, Madison, and others to the do-nothing position of seeking to block the positive programs of Hamilton, the progressive reformer.

Obviously, if Hamilton had introduced the various programs set forth in his separate reports in one omnibus report, political opposition to one or another or their features would have been able to unite to kill the whole. Later, after most of them had passed, Hamilton would give greater emphasis to the interrelationships among the various basic aspects of all. Each of his separate and politically discrete reports basically had to do with an aspect of national and central bank management of national economic policy. It was not until the emergency that would arise out of the so-called Quasi War with France of the years 1797 to 1800 that Hamilton would find it politically safe to sketch out his unified view of national central bank economic policy. In a letter to his protégé and successor as secretary of the treasury, Oliver Wolcott, Jr., he would write on August 22, 1798:

> No one knows better than yourself how difficult and oppressive is the collection even of taxes, if there be a defective circulation. This is our case in the interior parts of the country.

Individual capitalists, and consequently the facility of direct loans, are not very extensive in the United States. The banks can only go a certain length, and must not be forced. Yet government will stand in need of large anticipations.

I have come to a conclusion that our Treasury ought to raise up a circulation of its own. I mean by the issuing of Treasury-notes payable, some on demands, others at different periods. . . .

This [is] necessary to keep the circulation full and to facilitate the anticipations which government will certainly need.

Even as 1791 began, Hamilton and Jefferson still had a fairly effective, practical working relationship. Louis G. Otto, the French chargé d'affaires, complained to Jefferson that the tonnage tax on French shipping was a violation of Article V of the Franco-American treaty of commerce of 1778. Jefferson wrote Hamilton on January 1, 1791, that "I think it is essential to cook up some favour which may ensure the continuance of the good dispositions they have towards us." They buy staple products from us, and we take hard money from them, which we "pour into the coffers of their enemies" in Britain. "I would thank you sincerely to suggest any thing better than what I had thought of."

Hamilton had a better idea than to "cook up" a unilateral trade concession to France. On January 11 he wrote back, "Though there be a collateral consideration, there is a want of reciprocity in the thing itself." Jefferson's scheme would "place French vessels upon an equal footing with our own, *in our ports,* while our vessels in the *ports of France* may be subject to all the duties which are there laid on the mass of foreign Vessels." Besides, Hamilton reminded Jefferson, the funds from the tonnage tax had, in effect, been mortgaged by his funding plan to pay off the public debt. Therefore, said Hamilton, "the same act which should destroy this source of revenue should provide an equivalent. This I consider as a rule which ought to be sacred, as it affects the public Credit." A round for Hamilton.

Hamilton wrote to Jefferson again on January 13, still rejecting ex parte trade concessions in exchange for vague "good dispositions." He offered Jefferson a better idea: "endeavor, by a new treaty of commerce with France, to extend reciprocal advantages, and fix them on a permanent basis. This would be more solid, and less likely to beget discontents elsewhere." It would give "a free course to trade," and be "cultivating good humor with all the world." Jefferson did not follow through on Hamilton's idea on improving relations with France. This round must be rated a draw.

In England, Edmund Burke, in opposition to English praise of the French Revolution, had published his essay, *Reflections on the Revolution in France*, in 1790. Soon thereafter Thomas Paine had answered Burke in England with his pamphlet, *The Rights of Man*. This linked the French Revolution to the American, praised both, and attacked the British constitution. In England, Paine was charged with treason and fled to France. Arrangements for having *The Rights of Man* reprinted in America by the printer John (or Jonathan) Bayard Smith were made by John Beckley, the clerk of the House of Representatives, a Virginian who served Jefferson and Madison as messenger, agent, agent provocateur, and protégé. Beckley had lost the post of Secretary of the Constitutional Convention to Hamilton's protégé William Jackson, and naturally felt no good will toward Hamilton. Beckley had no means to finance publication of *The Rights of Man* himself; the story Jefferson and Madison later told was that before giving *The Rights of Man* to Smith, the printer, for publication, Beckley had loaned it to Madison; Madison had passed it on to Jefferson with the request that, after reading it, he give it to Smith. When Jefferson passed the book on to Smith, he accompanied it by the following transmittal letter:

Th. Jefferson presents his compliments to Mr. Jonathan B. Smith. . . . he is extremely pleased to find that it will be reprinted here, and that something is at length to be publicly said against the political heresies which have sprung up amongst us. He has no doubt our citizens will rally a second time round the standard of *Common Sense*. He begs leave to engage three or four copies of the republication.

Smith published Jefferson's blurb in the preface to the Philadelphia edition, introduced with a fulsome political advertisement for Jefferson: Jefferson's views, he averred, reflected honor on the secretary of state by "directing the mind to a contemplation of that Republican firmness and Democratic simplicity which endear their possessor to every friend of *The Rights of Man*."

Jefferson's blurb was republished in newspapers all over the country. Washington was aghast at the offense his own secretary of state's endorsement of the fugitive from British justice would give to the threatening world power on the frontiers. Jefferson told Washington that publication of his blurb was only "the indiscretion of a printer," that "committed me with my friend, Mr. Adams." He was, he said, "an utter stranger to J.B. Smith, both by sight and character." But he would not, however, withdraw, repudiate, or remove his endorsement of Paine's *The Rights of Man*.

Adams's son John Quincy Adams assailed Jefferson in the press over the signature of *Publicola*. Attacks on Jefferson and Madison spread throughout the country, but only in the Federalist press. George Beckwith, the unofficial British minister, remonstrated in pained surprise to Tobias Lear, Washington's secretary, at publication of treasonable sentiments against the British government by a fugitive from its justice carrying the secretary of state's personal endorsement.

Jefferson rather smugly noted that Hamilton and Major Beckwith were "open-mouthed" against him. Hamilton's protest on grounds of damage to national interests was drowned out by a roar of domestic political approval from republican papers. Jefferson, the aristocratic patrician, was suddenly acclaimed as the leader of those who wanted no aristocratical ideas in the government of their country. Wherever copies of Paine's best seller carried his enthusiastic self-advertisement, the domestic political stock of the secretary for foreign affairs soared high, even as his standing dropped to zero with Washington, Adams, and Hamilton.

The genius of the secretary of state's endorsement of Paine's indirect attack on the British constitution by fulsome praise of the French and American Revolutions was that it hit not one, but three high-flying Federalist birds with one semiofficial stone.

It was no longer important for Jefferson to win or lose clashes in Washington's cabinet: he was advertising himself to a political constituency of his own. It would perceive him as independent of—indeed in opposition to—the executive government of which he was an important member, but not quite as important as he thought he ought to be, or as his rival Hamilton had become.

21

Jefferson, Madison, Beckley, and Burr Hunt Down the Hessian Fly

We are going headlong into the bitterest opposition to the genl. government—I pity you—*Delenda est Carthago* is the maxim applied to your administration.

—from Robert Troup, January 19, 1791

There was a passionate courtship between the chancellor [Robert R. Livingston], Burr, Jefferson and Madison when the two latter were in town. *Delenda est Carthago* is the maxim adopted with respect to you. . . .

—from Robert Troup, June 15, 1791

The Livingston clan of Livingston Manor on the Hudson had supported the Constitution, backed Hamilton's early policies, earned the right to expect reciprocity of consideration when Hamilton became a power on the national stage, and had once been Hamilton's most powerful supporters. But Livingstons were passed over when Hamilton made his intimate, Rufus King, a senator instead of one of them. Robert R. Livingston lost out to Hamilton's even closer friend John Jay as chief justice of the Supreme Court. Livingstons were passed over for local appointments after Schuyler had defeated Duane, a Livingston in-law, to win the other Senate seat. After his narrow victory for reelection, perennial governor George Clinton had sought to divide his opposition by appointing moderate Federalist Aaron Burr as his attorney general.

Explaining the Byzantine New York State politics of the time in one sentence, James Parton said, in his life of Aaron Burr, ''The Clintons had the power, the Livingstons had the numbers, and the Schuylers had Hamilton.''

Philip Schuyler, to whom by lot the short Senate term had fallen, was up for election

299

again in January of 1791. With Federalists safely in control of the state legislature, which elected the senators, Schuyler's reelection seemed to be as certain as anything in New York politics could ever be.

But the Livingstons of Livingston Manor were a touchy old family, unused to slights from a Washington, a Jay, or a Schuyler, not to speak of an upstart bastard brat from the West Indies. Aaron Burr was a moderate, not closely identified either with Clinton and extreme Anti-Federalism or with Hamilton and Schuyler. He had served with dignity and avoided disgrace as the state's attorney general. Burr let it be known that if the Livingstons would support him to upset Schuyler in the race for Schuyler's seat, Governor Clinton would appoint Robert R. Livingston's brother-in-law, Morgan Lewis, to succeed Burr as attorney general. Clinton did nothing to discourage such talk. He too relished the idea of giving a comeuppance to Schuyler and Hamilton.

James Livingston of Montgomery, an obscure distant relation of the colonial lords of Livingston Manor, was artfully selected by Schuyler's supporters to place his name in nomination in the state assembly, but this failed to paper over the breach with the Livingstons who counted. John Smith of Orange County moved as an amendment that the name of Burr be inserted in place of Schuyler's. James Livingston's motion lost, 32 to 27; and Smith's nomination of Burr then carried, 32 to 27. Most of the votes for Burr, who was from the city, came from upstate, whereas most of Schuyler's, who was from Albany, came from New York City and Westchester. The state senate concurred, 14 to 4, and Schuyler had been unceremoniously ousted from his seemingly secure seat in the United States Senate by Aaron Burr. Most of the blame was ascribed to Hamilton and his dynamic but controversial federal programs.

Burr had Hamilton in his eye when he gloated, with mock restraint, "I have reason to believe that my election will be unpleasing to several Persons now in Philada."

Fresh from the shock of the upset, Hamilton's oldest friend, Robert Troup, wrote him, on January 19, 1791, "About an hour ago the election of Senator was brought in the assembly. Burr succeeded by a decided majority . . ." Troup was also one of Aaron Burr's old and intimate friends, so he knew more confidences than he could honorably disclose to his old friend Hamilton.

"The twistings, combinations and maneuvers to accomplish this are incredible," wrote Troup, adding, "We are going headlong into the bitterest opposition to the Genl. Government—I pity you Most sincerely—for I know that you have not a wish but what is combined with the solid honor & interests of America."

Troup feared that there was no limit or proportion, short of complete annihilation, to the lengths to which the opposition in its hatred of Hamilton and his system would go. They aimed to destroy both, said Troup: "*Delenda est Carthago* is the maxim applied to your administration."

Making an effort to put a mild face on the degrading upset he had caused her father, Hamilton wrote Angelica on January 31 that "our republican ideas stand much in the way of accumulating offices in one family." He would try to use all his influence in Philadelphia to get Schuyler a ministerial appointment abroad, although by now the secretary of state was bound to block the way. This would be the least of what he would do for her, Hamilton promised, because "there is no proof of my affection which I would not willingly give you."

Wistfully, he added, "I look forward to a period, not *very* distant, when the establishment of order in our Finances will enable me to execute a favorite wish. I must endeavor to see Europe one day; and you may imagine how happy I shall be to meet you, and Mr. Church there.''

By his small but significant comma setting her name off from her husband's, which her eyes alone would know how to read, he punctuated his love for her alone. He closed: ''God bless you, A.H.''

William Duer, whose imprisonment was still a year in the future, had acted as the floor leader in Schuyler's defeat and characteristically assigned generous blame for the debacle to everyone, except himself, including Hamilton.

The election of Burr, Duer wrote Hamilton on January 19, 1791, ''is the fruit of the Chancelor's [sic] Coalition with the Governor.'' Duer had wanted the voting postponed to give time to rally support, but had been ''unfortunately overuled'' [sic] by Hamilton's friends in the House. He was sure ''that the measures which were taken to bring over several who had United with the Anti-Federalists would have proved successful.''

Duer's own private business ventures were in disarray. Only wildly successful future speculations could bail him out. Despite his implied reproaches, he professed ardent loyalty to Hamilton and the future success of Hamilton's economic program. ''I can not Express how much I feel on the present Occasion! To see the Fabrick you have been rearing, for Ensuring the Happiness of Millions, undermined by the most profligate Part of the Community, and its most faithful Servants treated with the blackest Ingratitude. . . . The greatness of the Evil, requires however the Exertion of all our Fortitude. God knows, that my own private Concerns require all that I can Summon.'' Hamilton had been ''undermined'' and betrayed by everyone but Duer: ''Rest assured however, that whatever Defections you may Experience, in others, that in me you will Ever find that warm, and Unabated Friendship, which you have a Right to Claim. Point out what is to be done, to rally a broken Party, and trust to my Exertions to carry your Views into Execution.''

With friends like Duer, Hamilton hardly needed enemies. Later in January, James Tillary, another of Hamilton's loyal supporters in New York City, assessed the somber political situation less emotionally, but in a way that confirmed the menacing danger to Hamilton of Troup's and Duer's warnings:

> A coalition of Interests from different principles produced his [Burr's] Election—He is avowedly your Enemy, & stands pledged to his party for a reign of Vindictive declamation against your Measures. The Chancellor [R. R. Livingston] hates, & would destroy you—Nay so incautious was he at a public Masonic Dinner last St. John's Day that he declared himself to me without any Stipulation of Secrecy, that he was not only opposed to your Funding System, but that R. Morris & several other well informed Influential Characters, viewed it as a system of public injustice. . . . We want a Head, to repress & keep down the machinations of our restless Demagogue [Clinton], but alas where is he to be found?

Badly as a leader was needed, Tillary had no use for Duer: ''Duer never can prop the *good old cause* here. He is unfit as a leader & unpopular as a man.'' Furthermore, Duer was in unwitting cahoots with crooks: ''He is duped by some characters without ever suspecting it.''

Schuyler's humilation did not cause him to evince resentment toward his favotite son-in-law for his role, but Hamilton's own conscience would not exonerate him of a heavy portion of the blame. All through 1791, he repeatedly urged Schuyler to take some kind of reprisal against Burr, until on January 29, 1792, Schuyler finally had to caution Hamilton,

"As no good can possibly result from evincing any resentment to Mr. Burr for the part he took last winter, I have on every occasion behaved towards him as if he had never been the principal in the business."

Troup had closed the ominous and mysterious letter he had written to Hamilton half an hour after the news of the voting: "I shall withdraw from politics for the present. I am disgusted to my heart. God bless you."

Time passing could not erase Hamilton's sense of shame or permit him, like Troup, to resign an exposed office before it was too late.

Newspapers of the 1790s did not preen themselves on "objectivity" in political reporting, nor run self-serving statements issued by party officials as news items like matters of observable fact, like fires. Instead, they ran them as polemical broadsides by anonymous partisans who used assumed names. Often the names had a classical resonance that reinforced the subject matter.

Jefferson had been smoldering with resentment at what he considered to be the one-sided treatment of news about governmental doings in the local press for a long time before he placed the advertisement for himself in *The Rights of Man*. The *United States Gazette,* which John Fenno had started in New York in 1789, purported to be a semiofficial newspaper, devoted almost entirely to governmental affairs. Since the 34-year-old secretary of the treasury had been the most active and visible member of the government launched in his hometown, Fenno's *United States Gazette* had come to seem to Jefferson as if it were Hamilton's own personal house organ. When the seat of government moved to Philadelphia, Fenno and his newspaper followed, but to Jefferson their pro-Hamilton and progovernment bias seemed unchanged.

Hamilton's cash books show that he made a loan of $100 to Fenno on October 19, 1790, and another loan of $100 on January 8, 1791. It seems likely that Fenno needed help from Hamilton and others to cover extra expenses made necessary by the move from New York to Philadelphia, over and above the regular payments he was receiving from the Treasury Department itself and the Senate for printing official government notices.

Jefferson now denounced Fenno's *United States Gazette* as "a paper of pure Toryism, disseminating the doctrines of monarchy, aristocracy and the exclusion of the influence of the people."

Although Philip Freneau had had no previous experience as a translator or in running a newspaper, he was a Princeton man like Madison and Aaron Burr. He had done some writing for Francis Childs's *Daily Advertiser* in New York, but he was best known as a poet of republican persuasions. On February 28, 1791, Jefferson wrote to him in New York offering him the post of translating clerk in the State Department. The State Department job paid only $250 a year, but, as the secretary pointed out, its limited duties would "not interfere with any other calling" its occupant might choose. "Another calling" would be the use of Freneau's sharp, satirical pen in anti-Hamilton journalism.

Jefferson's gifts and loans to amenable journalists were small by Jefferson's lavish standards, but large by the standards of newspapermen, or of anything that Hamilton could afford to lend them. Freneau turned down this first of Jefferson's offers. The secretary of state tried to persuade the equally Republican Benjamin Franklin Bache to make a national paper out of his *Philadelphia General Advertiser,* which would later become famous as the *Aurora*. Bache shared many of Jefferson's enthusiasms, but not that of putting a newspaper on the payroll of the State Department.

Jefferson turned back to Freneau and sought Madison's help in changing Freneau's mind. From New York, Madison wrote Jefferson on May 1 that he thought he might have brought Freneau around. When there was no follow-up, Jefferson wrote Madison unhappily on May 9 that Freneau must have turned them down once more: "I suppose therefore he has changed his mind back again, for which I am really sorry."

Jefferson himself would go to New York and make another bid to Freneau. As Jefferson wrote Madison July 21, 1791, in addition to the $250 State Department salary, he would give Freneau and his paper "perusal of all my letters of foreign intelligence." He would subsidize him with "the publication of all proclamations and other public notices within my department and the printing of the laws." Freneau changed his mind, came to Philadelphia, and started his own newspaper called the *National Gazette*. It began publishing on October 31 with a series of attacks on Hamilton and his policies. Soon it became recognized as Jefferson's and Madison's news organ.

When Hamilton later angrily charged that Jefferson was using a government job in the State Department to subsidize a newspaper that continually attacked the government, Jefferson replied that Freneau had first applied to him for a job long before, in New York, but that there had been no State Department vacancy then.

Washington took Freneau's attacks as personal attacks on himself and demanded an explanation. Jefferson's answer of September 9, 1792, has the ring of that of a witness unprepared for the questions of a skeptical congressional investigating committee. Jefferson could not recollect at what point in time he learned of Freneau's running the *National Gazette,* but there were good reasons related to foreign policy for the State Department's hiring him anyway. "I cannot recollect," Jefferson testified, "whether it was at the same time, or afterwards, that I was told he had thought of setting up a newspaper there." Jefferson could not remember, but he also had a cover story. "But whether then, or afterwards, I considered it as a circumstance of some value, as it might enable me to do, what I had long wished to have done, that is, to have the material parts of the Leyden gazette brought under your eye & that of the public, in order to possess yourself and them of a juster view of the affairs of Europe. . . ."

He had not attempted "any kind of influence" to get Freneau to Philadelphia. Washington would not know of all the contrary facts that lay behind Jefferson's stammering denial, but a prosecuting attorney who did would have paused before putting the final question to discredit the witness. He would introduce as an exhibit Jefferson's May 15, 1791, letter to Thomas Mann Randolph, pause again, and allow the witness to read the exhibit. He would then refute Jefferson's denial by asking him what he had meant by writing, "We have been trying to get another *weekly* or *half weekly* paper set up . . . so that it might go through the states; & furnish a whig vehicle of intelligence. We hoped at one time to have persuaded Freneau to set up here, but failed."

As Hamilton's great reports came before Congress in majestic progression and became law statute by statute over Madison's opposition, Jefferson's frustration and anger at the irresistible advance of the Hamilton program tended to prick his interest in Aaron Burr: the newly elected senator from New York was the only man in the country who had so far shown himself able to interpose a check to the surge of success that the secretary of the treasury was riding in the spring of 1791.

Jefferson's warm curiosity was heightened by an unsolicited letter he received shortly after Burr's election from Henrietta Maria Colden, a beautiful widow who lived in New York, knew Elizabeth and Alexander Hamilton, and was a frequent guest of the Burrs at Richmond Hill. The rumors that both Burr and Hamilton had enjoyed affairs with Henrietta

Colden did nothing to dispel Jefferson's curiosity. Madison was lingering in New York from April through August, and the prim little man was taking a warm interest in this peacock lady, too. Henrietta was said by some to have "inspired in Jefferson a momentary flash." By reputation arising largely from the shaky assumption that her politics were inseparable from those of her late departed husband, Cadwallader Colden, Henrietta was reputed to be a Federalist. Hence it was especially remarkable that she should now write to Jefferson to call attention to the man who had suddenly risen from political obscurity into the best possible position to do Federalists harm:

> The attention of the good folks of this city was lately engrossed by the choice of a new Senator to Congress. The gentleman brought in by Governor Clinton's party, "Not to oppose, but to keep a sharp look out on the measures of the Government" is a man of too considerable abilities, for the side he has taken. If he moves on antifederal ground, he may do *harm*.

Nothing would have better served Burr's interests at the moment as an entrancing way to break the political ice with Jefferson than to inspire Henrietta to write him thus.

Another subject on which the House on January 15, 1790, had requested Hamilton to report to it was a plan for the encouragement of manufactures that would make the United States independent of other nations, particularly in the matter of military supplies. From the earliest years of the Confederation, Hamilton had taken a strong stand in favor of enlarging the powers of the federal government to regulate trade. This had been the immediate reason for the calling of the Annapolis Convention and for its call, in turn, of the Constitutional Convention of the following year. Hamilton favored a broad interpretation of the commerce clause of the Constitution. He did not agree with more rigid disciples of Adam Smith who felt that trade should not be subject to federal regulation. Although he believed in free markets as a general rule, he also believed that there must be "a common directing power" in the government.

As far back as April 18, 1782, in No. 5 of *The Continentalist,* Hamilton had written:

> Commerce, like other things, has its fixed principles, according to which it must be regulated. If these are understood and observed, it will be promoted by the attention of government; if unknown, or violated, it will be injured—but it is the same with every other part of administration.

He would put the same thought more concisely in the "Report on Manufactures," following Vattel: Moderate commercial restrictions do not constitute violations of natural law.

Of all Hamilton's great state papers, his "Report on the Subject of Manufactures" would be by far his most original, best informed, farsighted, far-reaching, and generally remarkable. It would have been in preparation almost two years by the time he finally laid it before Congress on December 5, 1791. One reason it took him so long was the thoroughness with which he sought out the factual background material he poured into it. In his bold, angular hand he wrote letters seeking facts and opinions to people all over the United States and all over the world. He read, filed, and digested replies that came back from such distant parts as Canton, China; London, Liverpool, and Glasgow; from France, Connecticut, and Massachusetts, to tell him what the reality of ordinary people's workaday lives was really like all over the world. The "Report on Manufactures" and background correspondence fills almost two closely printed 500-page volumes of the Hamilton Papers.

The mosaic of responses to Hamilton's inquiries presents a vivid, unforgettable picture of the way working people lived in the United States and around the real world in 1790 and 1791. Often quaintly worded and badly misspelled, they revealed America as a new, industrially backward country groping out of an agrarian economy toward an industrial revolution. The replies from his correspondents told Hamilton over and over again, "We have no capital. We have limited knowledge of business practices. We have no skilled workmen. We cannot compete with English goods." As George Cabot put it, "Our artisans have been learning their trades at our expense." With such costs added in, how could their employers compete?

Hamilton knew businessmen well enough to know that most of them greatly exaggerated their own difficulties—no doubt partly for self-serving purposes. As the responses to his inquiries poured in and he put the facts together, he came to understand better than any other man in the country what the real problems were and how to surmount them. He came to the dubious conclusion that a new manufacturing enterprise set up on a larger scale than anyone had ever dreamed possible in America would have a better chance of success than anything previously attempted or envisioned.

He did not stop with putting his thoughts into another report to be filed and forgotten, like a typical bureaucrat. Instead he put them into practice by fostering the founding of the largest and most ambitious industrial corporation conceived in the United States up to that time. With his evil genius William Duer now out of the Treasury and back in private life, Hamilton formulated elaborate plans over the summer of 1791 for the Society for Establishing Useful Manufactures. It was to be capitalized at one million dollars—more than the total assets of all the joint stock companies then in existence in the United States. Hamilton and Philip Schuyler selected the site: beside the Great Falls of the Passaic River, which Hamilton had first seen with Washington as they were moving north with the army after the Battle of Monmouth. They had picnicked there one July day in 1778 on the craggy rocks beside the misty gorge. The factories and mills at the site would be powered by a roaring wall of water 77 feet high, the second highest waterfall in the eastern part of the continent.

The prospectus Hamilton wrote and began circulating in August 1791 boldly challenged the fears of his businessmen correspondents: "What is to hinder the profitable prosecution of manufactures in this Country, when it is notorious, that . . . provisions and various raw materials are even cheaper here than in the Country from which our principal supplies come?"

His answer: "The dearness of capital and the want of capital are the two great objections to the success of manufactures in the United States."

What could be done to eliminate these objections?

"Improvements in the construction and application of machines" to decrease manual labor, employment of women and children as "auxiliary to undertakings of this nature; bringing in immigrants from countries where labor is cheap" would all contribute to overcoming these objections.

To remedy the lack of capital, the Society for Establishing Useful Manufactures would make a public offering of its stock; it must be carried on by the investors in corporate form, so that their personal liability would be limited to loss of the money they had invested; otherwise, no one would dare to invest.

According to its prospectus, it expected to manufacture paper, sail cloth, stockings, blankets, carpets, shoes, and cotton and linen goods. It would even operate a brewery. It was a free-form conglomerate with a memorable acronym for a name—the SUM. It would be located in its own industrial park in the exurbs of New York City. It lacked little more than Harvard Business School graduates in its executive suite and the word *synergy* in its lexicon—and SEC-mandated warnings of speculative risks in its prospectus—to be indistinguishable from a present-day paradigm of the genus conglomerate.

But the optimistic projections of future profits in its prospectus would have earned stern reproof from a present-day SEC. Hamilton's prospectus, like its millions of descendants, made the strongest permissible appeal to the profit motive of potential investors. It hinted that "the pecuniary aid even of Government, though not to be counted upon ought not wholly to be despaired of."

The New Jersey legislature was amenable to the influence of Hamilton's friends like Duer, the Boudinots, Jonathan Dayton, and others who were also promoters and directors. It did no harm to rename the site Paterson, after the governor, William Paterson.

The corporate charter drafted by the secretary of the treasury—one of his several dubious extracurricular activities of 1791—was comprehensive and peculiar. Subscriptions from state and national governments, as well as individuals, were welcome. All subscribers would have the right to investigate the proceedings of the society. It would enjoy exemption from all taxation of its goods and chattels forever and of its land and buildings for ten years, much as corporations in developing areas like Puerto Rico, for example, do today. Artificers and workers in its employ would be exempt from personal taxes and all military duty, except in case of actual invasion. It would have the right to build canals and roads, to operate lotteries, to charge tolls, and to exercise the power of eminent domain. The society's board of 13 directors and a "governor" would govern throughout an area of 36 square miles, to be called "the Corporation of the Town of Patterson," much as Disney World operates its fiefdom in Florida today.

Hamilton and others lobbied the legislature and it chartered the Society for Establishing Useful Manufactures on November 22, 1791. It was another ill-starred beginning for Hamilton that his former assistant in the Treasury, William Duer, was chosen its governor. Nehemiah Hubbard of Connecticut was offered the position of superintendent-general. Major Pierre Charles L'Enfant, the French engineer who in 1791 was also drawing plans for the great Columbian federal city at Washington, drew an architect's typically overambitious set of magnificent plans for an entire industrial park of factories surrounding the Great Falls and the township of Patterson. Land was purchased; machinery ordered. As the prospectus said, early prospects were glowing.

Hamilton personally interviewed and hired workmen and superintendents, among them William Hall and Thomas Marshall, who had learned cotton spinning under Richard Arkwright in England. The SUM appropriated $20,000 for luring skilled hands to America, specifying in their minutes "that the whole Business of procuring such Hands be committed to the direction and management of the Governor of this Society, subject to the advice of the Secretary of the Treasury."

Owners of large plantations worked by cheap slave labor used their free time for politics. They gained political strength by claiming to represent, under the agrarian banner, both slaves and free men—who worked their own small farms by their own labor. Exemplars like Thomas Jefferson, James Madison, and John Taylor of Virginia objected to any government patronage of manufacturing industry that would take laborers off the farms "from a more to a less beneficial channel." To leave industry to private, unaided interests, they said, is "the soundest as well as the simplest policy." Agricultural labor would not be lured away from farms and would remain cheap.

Hamilton opened his "Report on Manufactures" by anticipating their opposition. "The expediency of encouraging manufactures in the United States," Hamilton began, "which was not long since deemed very questionable, appears at this time to be pretty generally admitted." Yet there were still many who argued that "agriculture is the most beneficial and productive object of human industry" and that capital and labor should be employed in converting the existing wilderness into farms so as thus to "contribute to the population, strength, and real riches of the country."

Hamilton reasoned that agriculture's real interest was advanced, not injured, by encouraging manufactures. He pleaded for division of labor and for diversification of the resources of the country. The greater the number of industrial hands, the greater the number of mouths to consume the surplus that agriculture produced from the land. He did not swerve in his argument to stress the grim social consequences of child labor that were obvious to a later age.

Other nations exported manufactured goods to America, but set up import barriers against American goods. Only by becoming independent and competitive could America force free, unimpeded, and equal exchange. European nations aided their manufactures by bounties and tariffs; in order to attract capital into home industries, the United States should do the same.

He denied that protection gave "a monopoly of advantages to particular classes, at the expense of the rest of the community" or that his plan would favor the North and middle states, as against the South. "The internal competition which takes place soon does away with every thing like monopoly, and by degrees reduces the price of the article to the minimum of a reasonable profit on the capital employed," he argued. The interests of the North and South were interrelated; the "aggregate prosperity of manufactures and the aggregate prosperity of agriculture are intimately connected."

Government could aid manufactures by protective duties, which had the added merit of producing revenue. He urged prohibition of rival imports or prohibitive duties on them; prohibition of export of raw materials peculiar to this country; pecuniary bounties—Hamilton was particularly insistent on these; exemption from import duties of raw materials essential to home manufactures; drawbacks and rebates; encouragement of inventions brought in to the country from abroad; governmental inspection of manufactured commodities to prevent frauds, cheats, and inferior quality from being imposed on the consumer; and facilitation of cash remittances from one part of the country to another. He urged the building of a national highway system and a national system of canals for swift, economical, and nondiscriminatory transport of goods from one region to another.

But such generalities were only the prelude to specific recommendations for specific actions, each of which would rouse cries of anguish from one or another powerful sector of special interest.

The "Report on Manufactures" called attention to the private SUM, saying that "it may be announced that a society is forming, with a capital which is expected to be extended to at least half a million dollars, on behalf of which measures are already in train for prosecuting, on a large scale, the making and printing of cotton goods."

Thomas Jefferson recoiled in horror from Hamilton's vision of the future. The sound of whirring looms, the clang of machinery stitching shoes faster than the human hand could follow, were anathema to him and everything dear to him. Assembling workers in congested factories would draw them to cities away from farms and plantations and transform them into robots, in messy, disorderly, inhuman crowds. To him, people who were industrial workers seemed vicious, morally reprehensible, and enemies to the liberties of free government. In his *Notes on Virginia*, he wrote: "I consider the class of artificers as the panders of vice, and the instruments by which the liberties of a country are generally overturned." He added, "The mobs of great cities add just so much to the support of pure government, as sores do to the strength of the human body."

Hamilton valued agriculture in a more practical way than Jefferson. He would write into a speech of Washington's to Congress of December 7, 1796, that "agriculture, considered with reference either to individual or national welfare, is the best basis of the prosperity of every other object of labor and industry." Accordingly, through Washington, it was he who proposed the establishment and funding of the Board of Agriculture, which later became the cabinet department of agriculture, a vast bureaucratic empire, and a nightmare for an Adam Smithian economist.

Hamilton's "Report on Manufactures," despite its title, acknowledged that agriculture fostered "a state most favorable to the freedom and independence of the human mind." But its main thrust was that the interdependence of agriculture and manufacturing, of farmer and artificer, would benefit both. He understood Jefferson's point at its deepest political level and disagreed with it:

> It ought readily be conceded that the cultivation of the earth, as the primary and most certain source of national supply, as the immediate and chief source of subsistence to a man, as the principal source of those materials which constitute the nutriment of other kinds of labor, as including a state most favorable to the freedom and independence of the human mind—one, perhaps, most conducive to the multiplication of the human species, has intrinsically a strong claim to preeminence over every other kind of industry.
>
> But, that it has a title to any thing like an exclusive predilection, in any country, ought to be admitted with great caution; that it is even more productive than every other branch of industry, requires more evidence than has yet been given in support of the position. That its real interests, precious and important as they truly are, will be advanced, rather than injured, by the due encouragement of manufactures, may, it is believed, be satisfactorily demonstrated.

Hamilton then patiently explained, as if to a backward child, "that the labor of the artificer is as positively productive as that of the farmer, and as positively augments the revenue of the society."

Jefferson and the Jeffersonians remained unconvinced.

Hamilton went on to enumerate seven elementary points of national economics. These held that "manufacturing establishments not only occasion a positive augmentation of the Produce and Revenue of the Society, but that they contribute essentially to rendering them greater than they could possibly be without such establishments." These points are:

1. The division of labor.
2. An extension of the use of machinery.
3. Additional employment to classes of the community not ordinarily engaged in the business.
4. The promoting of emigration from foreign countries.
5. The furnishing of greater scope for the diversity of talents and dispositions that discriminate men from each other.

6. Affording a more ample and various field for enterprise or "the spirit of enterprise."
7. The creating of and securing for all "a more certain demand for the surplus produce of the soil."

Hamilton's point 5 was "that minds of the strongest and most active powers for their proper objects, fall below mediocrity, and labor without effect, if confined to uncongenial pursuits."
Hamilton's remedy?

> The results of human exertion may be immensely increased by diversifying its objects. When all the different kinds of industry obtain in a community, each individual can find his proper element, and can call into activity the whole vigor of his nature. And the community is benefited by the services of its respective members, in the manner in which each can serve it with most effect.

Hamilton had not missed the oft-noted aptitude that Americans had for working with mechanical things. "If," he added tellingly, "there is, in the genius of the people of this country, a peculiar aptitude for mechanic improvements," the propagation of manufactures "would operate as a forcible reason for giving opportunities to the exercise of that species of talent."

But more important even than increase of material production was the enhancement of human capabilities. Here is one of Hamilton's greatest and most characteristic themes: "To cherish and stimulate the activity of the human mind, by multiplying the objects of enterprise, is not among the least considerable of the expedients by which the wealth of a nation may be promoted. Even things in themselves not positively advantageous sometimes become so, by their tendency to provoke exertion." Here Hamilton couples two of the watchwords of his life, *energy* and *effort,* in the same clause: "Every new scene which is opened to the busy nature of man to rouse and exert itself, is the addition of a new energy to the general stock of effort."

Hamilton's point 7, the "creating" and "securing" for all "a more certain demand for the surplus" was far ahead of its time. It was not until the 1960s that the originality of it received wide recognition when it surfaced as a principal theme explored by John Kenneth Galbraith's best seller, *The Affluent Society.*
As Hamilton put it,

> the multiplication of manufactories not only furnishes a market for those articles which have been accustomed to be produced in abundance in a country, but it likewise creates a demand for such as were either unknown or produced in inconsiderable quantities. The bowels as well as the surface of the earth are ransacked for articles which were before neglected. Animals, plants, and minerals acquire a utility and a value which were before unexplored.

Hamilton recognized the solution for a problem common to all underdeveloped countries: the precarious reliance on foreign demand.
The solution? Development of "an extensive domestic market."
Thomas Jefferson really should not worry about agricultural workers being drawn off the land, for the outcome might indeed help, not harm, men like him, Hamilton explained:

If the effect of manufactories should be to detach a portion of the hands which would otherwise be engaged in tillage, and a smaller quantity of lands to be under cultivation; by their tendency to procure a more certain demand for the surplus produce of the soil they would, at the same time, cause the lands which were in cultivation to be better improved and more productive. The condition of each individual farmer would be meliorated, and the total mass of agricultural production would probably be increased.

Hamilton even foretold a little of what would later come to be called by such names as *The Greening of America*. After a time, an immigrant brought in to be an artificer might return to the land: "Many, whom manufacturing views would induce to emigrate, would, afterwards, yield to the temptations which the particular situation of this country holds out to agricultural pursuits." But there was no blinking away the problem that there would not be enough jobs on the farm or in handicrafts to support all former artificers who might wish to return to the simple life on the farm and there eke out a living: "While agriculture would, in other respects, derive many signal and unmingled advantages from the growth of manufactures, it is a problem whether it would gain or lose, as to the article of the number of persons employed in carrying it on."

Hamilton's "Report on Manufactures" was an eagle-eyed vision of *The Affluent Society* within *The New Industrial State*. It was strikingly modern in basic concept and essentials, lacking only the overlay of such developments as advertising, blue jeans, hard rock, acid, and grass. It contained the seed of modern America. But it was too far ahead of its time to receive serious consideration from Congress.

The House pigeonholed his report and did not take it up again. But it remained a source of ready reference and a mother lode of ideas for all who came after him who would urge government programs to aid and encourage American industry, agricultural technology, transportation, manufactures, mining, interstate highways, canals, and capital formation. It gave eloquent expression to the idea of economics that came to be known as "the harmony of interests" principle: that government-supported industry would strengthen rather than weaken agriculture, make more jobs for workers, attract immigrants, and open up new opportunities for enterprise and investment.

The press of departmental and legislative business, the affairs of SUM, and an extramarital affair that kept the secretary of the treasury engaged at the capital did not detain the secretary of state from junketing afar. On May 17, Jefferson set out from Philadelphia on a trip of 920 miles that would keep him out of touch with his office for more than a month. It was elaborately given out that the junket was for scientific purposes, including the collection of data on the Hessian fly, but Jefferson's itinerary included New York City, where Aaron Burr and Freneau could also be found; the Hudson River Valley, where Governor George Clinton and Chancellor Robert R. Livingston could be found; and Lake George, Lake Champlain, Bennington (Vermont), Pittsfield (Massachusetts), the Connecticut River Valley, and Long Island, where, among other things, the Hessian fly could probably be found.

Arriving in New York, Jefferson stayed at Mrs. Ellsworth's boardinghouse, where Madison and Freneau were lodged awaiting him. He joined Madison in urging Freneau to come to Philadelphia. John Beckley, too, was in New York. While the two middle-aged politicians from the South would proceed on their junket up the Hudson, Beckley would split off and proceed by way of the New England coast to Boston.

Hamilton's confidant George Beckwith wrote home that Jefferson's and Madison's trip was designed to promote anti-British policies. Beckwith had tried to counter them by making a more or less parallel trip of his own. In Boston John Beckley found that John Adams was still enraged at Jefferson for misrepresenting his *Discourses on Davila,* "And overwhelming me with floods and whirlwinds of tempestuous abuse, unexampled in the history of this country," Adams snorted. Beckley's report that in the debate aroused by Jefferson's self-advertisement sentiment around Boston was pro-Jefferson and anti-Adams pleased his mentor.

Years later Jefferson denied that he had conferred with Burr on this trip, or that he had even met Burr at any time before or during it. Reclusive as Jefferson was, he and Burr had both been among the most prominent of New York City's 30,000 or so citizens (of whom only about 13,000 were freeholders) during 1789 when the government had been in the city.

"I had never seen Colonel Burr," Jefferson felt compelled to say to his *Anas* years later, "until he came [to Philadelphia] . . . as a member of the Senate." Jefferson claimed to have distrusted from the first the man Hamilton's followers alleged he had journeyed so far to seek to enlist as his political ally. Jefferson added to his *Anas* that Burr's "conduct very soon inspired me with distrust. I habitually cautioned Madison against trusting him too much."

Hamilton's son and biographer, John C. Hamilton, had no doubt that Jefferson was untruthful. He wrote that "after frequent interviews with Chancellor Livingston and Burr," Jefferson and Madison "made a visit to Clinton under the pretext of a botanical excursion to Albany, thence extended their journey to Vermont; and, having sown a few tares in Connecticut, returned to the seat of government." John Quincy Adams similarly attributed to Jefferson a "double dealing" character. Charles Francis Adams, grandson of John Adams and the editor of his collected works, agreed with Hamilton's and Adams's sons:

"More ardent in his imagination than his affections, he did not always speak exactly as he felt towards either friends or enemies," Adams wrote; "as a consequence, he had left hanging over part of his public life a vapor of duplicity, or, to say the least, of indirection, the presence of which is generally felt more than it is seen."

Writing Hamilton from New York on June 15, 1791, Troup repeated with still more ominous anxiety the same words of warning he had sent in January when Burr had ambushed Schuyler to win his seat: "There was every appearance of a passionate courtship between the Chancellor [Robert R. Livingston], Burr, Jefferson and Madison when the two latter when in town. *Delenda est Carthago* is the maxim adopted with respect to you. . . . if they succeed they will tumble the fabric of the government in ruins to the ground." To the quarry selected for the coming implacable manhunt, Troup gamely tried to provide some cheer: "I cannot say I have the slightest uneasiness." But it was the tone of a man whistling in black darkness: "You are too well seated in the hearts of the citizens of the Northern and Middle States to be hunted down by them."

In February, as one of the three vice-presidents of the American Philosophical Society, Jefferson had let pass the name of Alexander Hamilton for admission to this select group, established "for promoting useful knowledge . . . advancing the Interest of the Society by associating to themselves Men of distinguished Eminence, and of conferring Marks of their Esteem upon Persons of literary Merit . . . Rights of Fellowship, with all Liberties and Privileges thereunto belonging."

While protests and applause continued to mount in the country that spring over Jefferson's blurb for Tom Paine's *The Rights of Man,* Jefferson called a committee meeting of the society. He solemnly charged it with the task of hunting down information about the

Hessian fly. Whatever else Hamilton and Adams and their circles might say about Jefferson, none would deny him credit for skill as a political operator, a game of which duplicity is sometimes the name. The choice of Hessian fly for the name of the quarry of their foray into New York had about it a touch of political genius: *Hessian* carried connotations of British monarchs and monarchists, foreign invaders, and cruel atrocities. The fly was a foreign threat to the wheat, barley, rye, and straw crops of all good and usually anti-Federalist small agrarians. To hunt down an enemy like the Hessian fly would never lose a shrewd political operator a single vote. It would win applause from all who feared insect pests, British monarchs, or overseas creditors. It was as safe a subject for fearless political attack as the rattlesnake. Only a member of the American Philosophical Society of a more scientific bent than Jefferson would quibble that the Hessian fly might more properly be called the gall midge, or that other cecidomyiids without such politically suggestive popular names were of as much or more interest to science.

From his and Madison's "passionate courtship" of Burr while ostensibly hunting down the Hessian fly, Jefferson brought back to his daughter Maria some notes he had scribbled on birchbark while sailing on Lake George. He had also shot three squirrels and, indeed, killed two rattlesnakes "of a sutty dark color and obscurely chequered." But for the scientific purposes of the American Philosophical Society's committee, Jefferson's notes on the Hessian fly were undecipherable and worthless. No matter. No more perfect code name than Operation Hessian Fly could have been conceived as a cover, and a cry to the pack as well, for hunting down a Hamilton to a kill. *Delenda est Paterson!*

"A man is indeed a city," wrote William Carlos Williams of the *Paterson* of SUM, "and for the poet there are no ideas but in things." The grayish yellow, polluted spume that rises from the mud and thickets where the Great Falls of the Passaic "comes pouring in above the city and crashes from the edge of the gorge, seasonally vociferous," is "associated with many of the ideas upon which our fiscal colonial policy shaped us through Alexander Hamilton." He and it "interested me profoundly," said Williams in his epic of industrial America, "and what has resulted therefrom."

> Oh married man!
> He is the city of cheap hotels and private
> entrances . . . of taxis at the door, the car
> standing in the rain hour after hour by
> the roadhouse entrance . . .
> You knew the Falls and read Greek fluently
> It did not stop the bullet that killed you
> You wanted to organize the country so that
> We should all stick together and make a little money.

When Williams wrote the South had long since come round to Hamilton's vision with a vengeance that falls on the ghosts of both antagonists. Old established manufactories like the textile mills that once rose in the SUM's industrial park moved away to brand-new state subsidized sites, cheap labor, and cheap government-generated power in once (but no longer) rural areas of newly industrial states of the Southern sun belt. All over northeastern America, as at Paterson, stand abandoned red brick mills with no future but forlorn oblivion crumbling into brick dust behind bronze Historical Preservation Society plaques in polluted spume like that below the Falls—where Hamilton and Washington had once picnicked beside a rainbow sparkling in white mist as they journeyed north with their winning army after the Battle of Monmouth.

Delenda est Carthago, Hamilton, and Paterson, and the SUM!

22

More Frequent Intercourse Was Pressed Upon Me

He will write Mrs. Hamilton. . . . Come here soon do not send or leave anything in his power.

—from Maria Reynolds, December 15, 1791

Shortly after Thomas Jefferson returned from his northward junket to his house at Eighth and Market in Philadelphia, Hamilton received a surprise visit at his own house from a rather well-connected woman who had also just recently journeyed down from New York, or so she said.

The best source of information about the first of her many visits to Hamilton's house in Philadelphia is the account Hamilton wrote for the American public and published in the newspapers in August of 1797, after having succeeded in keeping it a secret for more than six years from all but a widening circle of insiders like Jefferson.

The autograph draft of this account is reproduced in Volume XXI of the Hamilton Papers along with the final printed version. The differences between the draft and the printed version are slight but significant and tell a small story of their own. What follows is based on the draft, with notes added to show how Hamilton revised his story for the later printed version. It is well to keep in mind that this account is written by a man of 40 who is looking back on an illicit love affair that he had begun at 34, or earlier, and telling the newspaper reading public how it all began.

Some time in the summer of the year 1791, a woman called at my house in the city of Philadelphia, and asked to speak with me in private. She was shown into the parlour where I went to her.

314

In the printed version Hamilton changed the second sentence to read, ''I attended her into a room apart from the family.'' The first draft implies that Betsy and the children were away at the time (would a strange woman otherwise pay a call there without a prior invitation from Betsy?) and that Hamilton and Maria Reynolds were there alone, except for the servant who showed her into the parlor. The printed version changes the story to affirm that Hamilton and Maria Reynolds were not alone in the house and that ''the family''—Betsy and the children—were at home at the time, but ''apart.'' Both versions confirm that Maria Reynolds was not a social friend or acquaintance of his and Betsy's; otherwise, Betsy would not have remained apart during Maria's unannounced call. Hamilton's family being at home, instead of away at Albany for the summer, seems to fix the time of Maria Reynolds's first visit to their home at an earlier date in 1791 than would have been the case if she had come when the family was away—unless her first visit to him had been a year or years earlier. Hamilton's draft continues:

> With a seeming air of distress she informed me that she was a daughter of a Mr. Lewis, sister to a Mrs. G. Livingston of the State of New York, and wife to a Mr. Reynolds, whose father was in the Commissary or Quarter Master Department during the war with Great Britain—that her husband who for a long time had treated her very cruelly, had lately left her to live with another woman, and so destitute that though desirous of returning to her friends, she had not the means—that knowing I was a citizen of the same state of New York, she had taken the liberty to address herself to my humanity for relief.

His first draft goes on: ''There was something odd in the application and the story yet there was a [genuineness] simplicity and modesty in the manner of relating it which gave an impression of its truth.''

The words *something odd*—an admission that her mysterious visit aroused his suspicions instantly—are omitted from the later printed version.

More or less as usual, the secretary of the treasury was short of ready cash. With customary gallantry, he made amends:

> I replied, that her situation was an interesting one and that I was disposed to afford her as much aid as might be [necessary] sufficient to convey her to her friends, but that at the instant it was not convenient to me (which was truly the case) . . . I would send or bring it to her in the course of the day.

His own house did not seem quite the right place for making such a payment, particularly if his family had not yet gone north.

''She gave me the street and the number of the house where she lodged,'' continued Hamilton.

Hamilton's telegraphic account of their meeting omits the Reynoldses' Philadelphia address. The later account of Richard Folwell, who had also known the Reynoldses over a number of years, supplies it. It was not a humble rooming house. Folwell wrote that they ''lived in stile in a large house in Vine Street next to the corner of Fifth.'' Folwell had gone there to visit them, he said, ''to see if possible how people supported grandeur, without apparently friends, money, or industry.'' She was not an itinerant visitor from New York at all; they lived in a Philadelphia town house. How could Hamilton not have known of them?

One way to support such grandeur would be money from men like Hamilton or preferably men much richer. But it would be surprising if seeing the "stile" and "grandeur" of her "large house in Vine Street" did not confirm Hamilton's suspicions that her sad tale of being a transient, impoverished New Yorker longing to be home from Philadelphia was a pack of lies—if he had ever believed it in the first place.

Hamilton continued, "In the evening I put a thirty dollar bill in my pocket and went to the house. I inquired for Mrs. Reynolds and was shewn up stairs, at the head of which she met me and conducted me into a bedroom."

At this dramatic high point in his draft occurs an extraordinary, indeed, ludicrous slip of his pen. He first wrote, "I took the bill out of my pocket and delivered it to him." Then he struck out the pronoun *him* and rewrote *her*. In the printed version he rewrote the whole sentence to change the word *delivered* to say that he "gave" it to her. The earlier impression that he was "delivering" a previously agreed upon quid pro quo, as to a pimp collecting for her, was changed into the later impression that he was "giving" spontaneous charity to a poor woman in distress, without thought of quid pro quo of any kind. Thereafter, "some conversation ensued which made it quickly apparent that other than pecuniary consolation would not be unacceptable." He added that "it required a harder heart than mine to refuse it to a pretty woman in distress." Then he struck out the words *pretty woman* and promoted her to a "beauty" instead. In the printed version he struck out the whole sentence.

Peter A. Grotjean, a Philadelphia merchant, who a few years later became a friend of one Mrs. Maria Clement, a widow whom he discovered to be the former Maria Reynolds, described her as a person of intelligence, sensibility, and gentleness of manner. Aaron Burr is known to have found her agreeable; and she, him. Nathan Schachner, in his *Alexander Hamilton,* describes her as a "bold, florid, handsome woman" with "coarsely handsome features." Hamilton's old friend Jeremiah Wadsworth and others of their circle knew her and also found her attractive. Hamilton said she had a highly emotional temperament and was much given to weeping. All accounts agree that she was a woman whose generous exudations of sex appeal would have instantly shown any visitor like Richard Folwell the means by which she contrived to support "grandeur, without apparently friends, money or industry."

After these first two meetings, Hamilton went on to say that "I had frequent meetings with her—most of them at my own house. Mrs. Hamilton being absent on a visit to her father with her children," adding starkly that "the intercourse with Mrs. Reynolds, in the meantime continued." It would continue for at least the next year and a half. "Her conduct made it very difficult to disentangle myself," he explained.

Nothing in Hamilton's account tells of anything personal to her or to himself, or any flaw in their relationship that would have been a reason for his breaking off their affair when he did, except Hamilton's concern for her husband's threats. But if it had ever been true that James Reynolds had "treated her very cruelly and left her to live with another woman," as she had at first told Hamilton to arouse his sympathy, Reynolds was not long in returning to become a troublesome figure on the domestic scene.

"Various reflections (among these the knowledge I had acquired of Reynolds' speculating character and pursuits and certain symptoms of contrivance and plot between her husband and her) induced me to wish to drop it," Hamilton explained in the draft. But in the printed version Hamilton removed the pointed references to Reynolds's "speculating" character and softened his own word *knowledge* of the "plot" between them to mere vague "suspicion" of "some concert" between them.

Because he was writing six years after these events, it may have slipped Hamilton's mind that a written record existed that showed that he had had some acquaintance with Reynolds in New York at least four years earlier: Reynolds had brought him the false and damaging reports originating from the Constitutional Convention in Philadelphia that charged Hamilton with advocating that the bishop of Osnaburg, the son of King George III, be installed as the monarch of America. Originally from Connecticut and a former member of Jeremiah Wadsworth's Commissary Department, Reynolds had needed no introduction to a prominent New York businessman like Wadsworth when Hamilton had mentioned Reynolds's name in a letter. Wadsworth was John Barker Church's former partner, a representative from Connecticut and always a staunch friend and supporter of Hamilton. James Madison, too, had heard all about Reynolds, of course, and of how he was getting rich enough to have a Philadelphia town house, and a wife like Maria. The letters Madison had received in the spring of 1790 from Gustavus B. Wallace describing Reynolds's frauds on poor old Virginia and North Carolina soldiers—made possible by the use of lists obtained by Reynolds and his New York partner William J. Vredenbergh of 40 Dock Street, from a clerk in Hamilton's Treasury Department—had helped shock Madison into switching to the strongest kind of opposition to Hamilton's economic program. Hamilton probably did not know all that Madison knew about Reynolds. Reynolds's frauds had also helped shock Jefferson into the unwavering support of Bland's resolutions that had led to his first, but not last, clash in the cabinet with Hamilton.

Madison's friends had reproached him for lingering too long in New York after Jefferson had returned southward the summer of 1791, suspecting him of overfondness for Jefferson's correspondent Henrietta Maria Colden. Jefferson, however, did not reproach him. One thing that may have waylaid Madison—other than Henrietta—was the task of obtaining evidence linking James Reynolds and William J. Vredenbergh to the clerk in Hamilton's Treasury Department who had leaked out the lists of old soldiers' names and amounts due to them. Circumstantial evidence of such links between Reynolds and Wadsworth and William Duer, Hamilton's former assistant and old crony, was strong. John Beckley, the clerk of the House, and Tench Coxe, employed at the Treasury but resentful at Hamilton's failure to promote him, would be only too happy to help Madison dig up solid evidence of Hamilton's illicit speculations at 40 Dock Street, at the Duers, at Henrietta Colden's, at Aaron and Theodosia Burr's at Richmond Hill, and at many another anti-Hamilton Anti-Federalist house.

Describing his intercourse with Maria Reynolds as it continued through the busy, hot Philadelphia summer of 1791, Hamilton's first draft describes Maria as doing no more than "play acting" the "appearances of a violent attachment." She seemed merely to simulate "extreme distress at the idea of an interruption of the connection"—as a good, experienced, professional prostitute might when servicing a philandering man of the world. But Hamilton's later printed version transmutes this earlier, worldlier reading into the idea that she felt a believable, lustful, yet romantic passion for him that was genuine and that he, naïvely, returned it.

She performed with "an infinite art, aided by the more genuine effects of an ardent temperament and a quick sensibility," he said. So much so that "though I was not completely the dupe of the illusion—yet I was made to doubt of the real state of things." He made himself seem genuinely uncertain. "My vanity perhaps admitting too easily the *possibility* of a [sincere] real fondness on the part of Mrs. Reynolds, I adopted the plan of a gradual discontinuance rather than a sudden cessation of the intercourse as likely to occasion least pain."

In most men's lives, if no real affection is felt in such an affair, a sudden breaking off is the customary and, once the first shock of coitus interruptus is past, the less painful method of ending it. Hamilton's announced plan of "gradual discontinuance" proved its own absurdity; their affair would continue for at least a year and a half. The abrupt and terrifying manner by which it would finally be broken off was nowhere within the ken of any such unlikely plan of "gradual discontinuance." While the plan remained on the agenda, currents of intense passion—or at least the convincing semblance of it—flowed between the two of them.

So there can be few cat's cradles of emotion and suspicion more tangled and complex than the one in which Hamilton found himself trapped that summer of 1791. His very first impression of it was that his affair with Maria Reynolds had grown out of some sort of a plot against him. Why had she come to his house unannounced? Why had she thrust herself on him with the flimsiest of hard luck stories when the last shred of believability would vanish the same day, when he saw her luxurious town house and found her willing to accept "other than pecuniary consolation" from him? But why should she seek money from him? There were many richer men in Philadelphia than he. She seemed to need his money less, really, than he would need hers. Philadelphia gentlemen richer than he had more leisure to devote to caressing her and fewer preoccupations to distract them. He would know, or should have known, that at his and her mature ages, only his leisurely cultivation of the art of making love to her whole body and soul would excite in her any real fondness for him. No woman of Maria's beauty and experience could be expected to feel more than a quickly passing flash of excitement for a harried, married, impecunious, overworked government employee like Hamilton.

Hamilton had been a realist about women, as about most else, since 20 or earlier when he had called Kitty Livingston an enigmatical being, yet wrote to her as if she were someone through whose head coursed thoughts not much different from his own. Maria Reynolds was acting out a role in a plot. But what plot? Whose plot? Why should Reynolds, as Maria had first alleged, have left her to live with another woman and then quickly rejoined her in a "plot and contrivance between them"? Did their joint "plot and contrivance" blot out for Hamilton the subplot that was really the main plot that had just sent her to his Philadelphia home?

Badger baiting, a game well known to sports-minded 18th-century gentlemen, was the cruel sport of setting on dogs to draw a badger from its hole. By humorous association it also meant to be overextended, to overdraw one's bank account, as in the expression "he had overdrawn his badger." To badger of course also meant "to subject (one who cannot escape from it) to persistent worry or persecution." It was the strongest possible term for irritating, persecuting, and injuring a man in every way; it lacked the gentler modern shades of meaning merely to pester or to tease.

Aaron Burr was a humorous 18th-century gentleman who had enjoyed innumerable extramarital affairs. Few schemes could have seemed to him more innocuous, yet full of humor and other hopeful possibilities, than setting up Hamilton in a badger game by the use of a beautiful New Yorker like Maria Reynolds, a woman of good family and excellent connections in Philadelphia. She and her husband might well have been already acquainted with Hamilton: She would provide amorous pleasure for the displaced summer bachelor there who would otherwise be too overworked and financially overextended to woo and keep satisfied such a desirable mistress without outside help from a "friend." On nights when the press of business would detain the secretary of the treasury at his office, Maria Reynolds could also provide the newly elected senator some New York style consolation for the absence of his own Theodosia when he would take his seat in Philadelphia for the session beginning in October.

All Burr would have had to do was write one letter of recommendation to Maria and one to Hamilton, warmly commending each displaced and lonely New Yorker to the other. He might have gained much credit and thanks from both, at least at the beginning. In any event, her call provided its own cover. There is no direct evidence that Burr, after the meetings in New York reported by Troup while Jefferson, Madison, and Beckley were there, used the Reynoldses as his badger dogs to hound Hamilton from home and family, and harry him at last to a kill. In the circumstantial evidence and psychological inferences suggested above some may find things that are rather persuasive.

On June 15, 1791, about the day of Maria's first visit, Hamilton was embarrassed to have to ask his friend Robert Troup for a loan of $200. Troup, who had just warned Hamilton that *"Delenda est Carthago,"* obliged. He told Hamilton he could take his time repaying.

Learning that Washington had returned home to Mount Vernon after a tour of the South while Jefferson, Madison, and Beckley had toured in New York and eastward while he alone remained at the capital, Hamilton wrote Washington on June 19, 1791.

> There is nothing which can be said to be new here worth communicating, except generally that all my accounts from *Europe,* both private and official, concur in proving that the impressions now entertained of our government and its affairs (I may say) *throughout* that quarter of the Globe are of a nature the most flattering and pleasing.

It was the calm before the storm.

On August 17 Hamilton wrote Duer a pointed warning—and a market tip:

> The conversation here was, Bank Script is getting so high as to become a bubble in one breath—in another "tis a South sea dream," in a third "There is a combination of knowing ones in New York to raise it as high as possible by fictitious purchases in order to take in the credulous and ignorant"—in another "Duer, [William] Constable and some others are mounting the balloon as fast as possible—If it don't soon burst, thousands will rue it" etc. etc.

Hamilton politely assured his friend that he could not harbor "the most distant thought" that Duer could "wander from the path either of public good or private integrity"; nonetheless, "I had serious fears for you—for your *purse* and for your *reputation.* My friendship for you and my concern for the public cause were both alarmed."

Hamilton's inside tip that "stocks are all too high" raced around the financial districts. His friend Senator Rufus King was critical. When Hamilton had "perceived the extreme to which Bank Script and with it other stock was tending," Hamilton explained, "I thought it advisable to speak out, for a bubble connected with my operations is of all the enemies I have to fear, in my judgment, the most formidable. . . . To counteract delusions, appears to me to be the only secure foundation on which to stand." He had, therefore, thought it "expedient to risk something to dissolve the charm." It was a figure of speech gracefully turned for a mistress's bedroom. But as a finance minister's public defense of official jawboning of the securities markets, it had strangely naked nuances.

This revealing metaphor—"something to dissolve the charm"—seemed more properly at home when Hamilton tried to explain away Angelica Church's suspicion that his old passion for her had gone suddenly slack. Angelica seems to have sensed—more than a year earlier than Hamilton would admit that Maria had first come to call—that Maria or someone like her would one day come along. That was when, as Hamilton was nervously preparing to introduce his budget, Angelica seemed to be suffering an anxiety attack and had written forlornly "that having seen me is a dream which you can scarcely believe. This idea of being lost in the tumult of business and ambition does not enliven my spirits."

Still, as recently as January of 1791, Hamilton's longing for Angelica had remained a matter of first person singular intensity: "There is no proof of my affection that I would not willingly give you." But by October 2, Maria's advent had dissolved it to a noncommittal double entendre that brought his wife prominently into the foreground: Betsy consents "that I should love you as well as herself and this you are too reasonable to expect."

By November, Hamilton had receded to "kindly" feelings toward Angelica, lumping himself with Betsy under first person plural pronouns and coupling their joint "affection" to a stiff, dry, lawyerish verb: "We have been so long without a line from you. Does your affection for us abate?"

It was necessary now to insist to her that nothing had changed because, of course, everything had changed. Under the spell of Maria Reynolds, all his singular hunger for Angelica had been sated or blotted out: "I think as kindly as ever of my Dear Sister in Law and Betsy has lately given me stronger proof than she ever did before of her attachment to you."

Naturally, Betsy's attachment for Angelica could hardly help growing stronger as Angelica ceased to be her rival for her husband.

While Maria Reynolds continued her visits to their house in Philadelphia that summer, Hamilton wrote Betsy in Albany on August 9 not urging her to return, willing to sacrifice her presence for her health. His own health was good, he said. "I cannot be happy without you. Yet I must not advise you to urge your return. The confirmation of your health is so essential to our happiness that I am willing to make as long a sacrifice as the season and your patience will permit."

He awaited "with all the patience I can the time for your return." "But," he added, perhaps hearing Maria's exigent rapping on the door, "you must not precipitate it."

In a later letter, he learns that Betsy's health was suffering from anxiety attacks.

> . . . My Betsy, your health had suffered by your anxiety and you were not so well as when you left me! . . . For Heaven's sake, do not yield too much to the little adverse circumstances that must attend us in this pilgrimage. Exert your fortitude. Keep up your spirits. Never forget for a moment the delight you will give me by returning to my bosom in good health. Dear Betsy—beloved Betsy—Take care of yourself—Be attentive to yourself—Use every mean that promises you benefit. . . .
>
> I am myself in good health & only want you with me, & in health also, to be as happy as it is reasonable to wish to be.

Still, she should not hurry back: "I charge you (unless you are so anxious as to injure you, or unless you find your health declining more) not to precipitate your return. I cannot help hoping that your native air if taken long enough will be of service to you."

She wrote him in August that she most certainly would be coming back about the first of September. Still, he replied that his "extreme anxiety" for her health would "reconcile me to you staying longer." In any event, she must not arrive by surprise in Philadelphia. She "must inform me beforehand when you set out" for home. He closed his letter of August 21 to her with "Think of me—dream of me—and Love me my Betsey as I do you. Yours for ever."

In a remarkably suggestive piece urging neutrality that Hamilton would write for Fenno's *Gazette of the United States* in March or April of 1793, just after his affair with Maria Reynolds had broken off, he personified three nations, Britain, France, and America, as a man, his wife, and the man's mistress. The point he was trying to make about neutrality gets lost as these three stock characters from commedia dell'arte spring into vivid life out of the jumble of the passions of his plot:

> A . . . virtuous Citizen . . . will regard his own country as a wife, to whom he is bound to be exclusively faithful and affectionate, and he will watch with a jealous attention every propensity of his heart to wander towards a foreign country, which he will regard as a mistress that may pervert his fidelity, and mar his happiness.

Far off the subject of neutrality into something obviously more intense and personal, Hamilton added,

> There are persons among us who appear to have a passion for a foreign mistress; as violent as it is irregular; and who, in the paroxysms of their love, seem perhaps without being themselves sensible of it, too ready to sacrifice the real welfare of the . . . family, to their partiality for the object of their tenderness.

The real-life foreign mistress who had for so many years "perverted" Hamilton's fidelity to his wife was nonetheless a member of her family; so Angelica had not really perverted his fidelity, at least by Hamilton's close, if twisted, reasoning. But now the violent and "irregular" passion he had once projected on his sister-in-law had reprojected back with the same intense focus and scarcely a flicker of interruption on the domestic mistress who had pushed the foreign one out of its beam and into limbo. In paroxysms of love for the new mistress, who now came so often to his home, Hamilton had been "all too ready to sacrifice the welfare" of his family to the object of his tenderness. He seemed hardly "sensible" at the time of what he was doing to them or to himself.

Betsy and the children finally returned from Albany, and it was not long before she was pregnant again. On November 26 she and Hamilton took their precious firstborn son, Philip, almost ten, to Trenton and entered him in the boarding school there run by William Frazer, rector of St. Michael's Episcopal Church.

Hamilton had promised to send for Philip the following Saturday to come home for one weekend in December, but the Christmas break was so near that Hamilton felt it would be better to put off the trip till the holidays. However, if Philip really wanted to be picked up for the weekend, Hamilton would do as he had promised: "A promise must never be broken; and I will never make you one, which I will not fulfill as far as I am able."

A marriage vow to Betsy was a promise that he fulfilled only "as far as I am able"—with exceptions for Angelica and Maria Reynolds.

Such exceptions did not mean that once they were things of the past, Hamilton's affection for his wife and family would not flow on again with as much or more intensity and depth as before. Except that, in the case of Angelica, love might become less exigent with age, and more familial, but would always remain. In 1793 he had passed off the consequences to "a virtuous citizen" of perverted, irregular, and violent passions in extramarital "paroxysms of love" as no more than something that "may . . . mar his happiness." But by 1797 and four more years of living with the secret, Hamilton's love for his family and his sense of honor had branded his heart with a far different perception of what he had done to them and to himself, something unforgettable, unforgivable, and shattering. "I can never cease to forgive myself," he would write in his public confession, "for the pang which it may inflict in a bosom eminently entitled to all my gratitude, fidelity, and love."

Senator Aaron Burr arrived in Philadelphia in October and took lodgings in a boarding-house at 130 South Second Street. He wrote back to Theodosia in New York, "I am at length settled in winter quarters" with "many invitations to dine etc. All of which I have declined, and have not eaten a meal except at my own quarters." This was a reassuring fib for home consumption of a terminally ill wife who remained in seclusion. Their lavish parties at Richmond Hill were now a thing of the past.

Of that Philadelphia winter of 1791 and 1792, when the government unfurled itself, Rufus W. Griswold, in *The Republican Court; or, American Society in the Days of Washington*, wrote, "You have never seen anything like the frenzy which has seized upon the inhabitants here. They have been half mad ever since this city became the seat of government."

At the center around whom all social orbits wheeled were the world's most revered hero and his comfortable wife, Martha. One of her most intimate friends from as far back as wartime days at Morristown and Newburgh was Hamilton's devout and steadfast wife, Betsy. Next to the Washingtons at the center of the social nebulae were Hamilton's good friends Mr. and Mrs. William Bingham. Bingham, reputedly the richest man in the United States, had made a great fortune during the Revolution as a government purchasing agent in the West Indies, where Hamilton had grown up. He had furnished Hamilton with many of the ideas for public finance, assumption, funding, and the National Bank that were now emerging as the law of the land from Hamilton's great reports. Bingham's wife, the former Anne Willing, married when she was 16, was the daughter of Thomas Willing, Robert Morris's senior partner and president of the Bank of North America. She was one of the greatest belles of American history.

A new political star in town like Aaron Burr would receive as many invitations to dine at the Binghams' as an older friend of theirs like Hamilton. The social life of the great houses provided a setting in which charismatic newcomers like Hamilton and Burr would be much in demand and at their best.

The grandson of Jonathan Edwards, son of a president of Princeton College, as precoci-ously keen-minded as Hamilton, Aaron Burr had graduated from Princeton at 16. When the Revolution broke out, he had gone off with Benedict Arnold on the expedition to seize Quebec and returned with a citation for valor and a reputation for heroic insubordination. He had served briefly on Washington's staff in New York City and as an aide to General Putnam until, in 1777, he was appointed lieutenant colonel of Malcolm's Regiment, the youngest officer in the army to hold so high a rank. His aggressiveness won applause and citations, but four times in his military career Burr had disobeyed the orders of his superiors—Arnold's at Quebec, Washington's at Manhattan, and General Israel Putnam's in Orange County, to go chasing after Governor Tryon. The fourth time, at Monmouth, had led to calamity and well-earned self-reproach by Burr for the loss of many lives and the risk to which he had put the rest of the army. For all practical purposes, Burr had dropped out of the war after Monmouth. He had written Washington, with whom he shared a mutual lack of regard, in September of 1778:

> I have consulted several physicians; they all assure me that a few month's retirement and attention to my health are the only possible means to restore it. . . . a delicacy,

perhaps censurable, might otherwise hurry me unnecessarily into service to the prejudice of my health and without advantage to the public.

Washington had curtly replied, "You, in my opinion, carry your ideas of delicacy too far."

This crushing reply kept Burr nominally in the army on meaningless duties until March 1779, when Burr dropped out again, this time for good, without mentioning to Washington the name or loyalist connections of the lady on whom he had finally focused his heretofore notoriously random affections. She seemed to be the real reason for his military disaffections, although to Washington, Burr continued to plead reasons of health: "The reasons I did myself the honour to mention to your excellency in a letter of September last still exist and determine me to resign my rank and command in the army." This time Washington briskly accepted his resignation.

The lady's name was no secret to Burr's friends. William Paterson wrote him: "I congratulate you on your return to civil life, for which (I cannot forbear the thought) we must thank a certain lady not far from Paramus."

On leaving the army, Burr had gone to Albany, like Hamilton, to study for quick admission to the New York bar as a veteran of the service. Hamilton's friend Alexander McDougall gave Burr letters of introduction to the Schuylers, and Burr and Hamilton probably often studied side by side in the quiet of the Schuyler library at The Pastures. Since leading his men into a British trap at Monmouth, instead of protecting the army's left flank as he had been ordered to do, Aaron Burr had been steeping himself in melancholia not unlike a young Werther, but a more worldly one.

While he crammed for his bar exams, he suffered from a headache. He wrote Theodosia Prevost, "I took the fine Indian cure . . . made a light breakfast of tea, stretched myself on a blanket before the fire, fasted till evening, then tea again." He missed her desperately: "I thought through the whole day that if you could sit by me and stroke my head with your little hand, all would be well."

Their relations by correspondence ranged beyond health and gallantry. "Write me facts and ideas," he demanded, "and don't torment me with compliments or yourself with sentiments." He was going to try to pull himself together.

Burr's thought processes, less linear and intense than Hamilton's, more speculative and diversified, would lead him into worlds of print further beyond the classics, law, and the arts than Hamilton's usually probed. In the iconoclasms of Voltaire, Rousseau, and Lord Chesterfield he would find worldly mottoes for success and submit them to Theodosia by letter for her approval.

"The maxim of a man whom neither of us esteem very highly is excellent on this occasion," he wrote, "—'Suaviter in modo, fortiter in re.' See, my dear Theodosia, what you bring upon yourself by having piddled in Latin. The maxim, however, will bear sheets of comment and weeks of reflection."

He added another, "Les grandes âmes se soucient peu des petits moraux." These two would guide his life: to be "suave in manner, strong in deed" and to believe that "great souls have small use for petty bourgeois morality."

Burr's mother, Esther Burr herself, could not have replied with warnings more maternal than those Theodosia shot back:

Such lessons from so able a pen are dangerous to a young mind and ought never to be read till the judgment and the heart are established in virtue. . . . . Les faiblesses de

l'humanité is an easy apology; or rather a license to practise intemperance. . . .
Virtue, like religion, degenerates to nothing because it is convenient to neglect her
precepts. You have, undoubtedly, a mind superior to the contagion.

Theodosia's husband, a British officer, had conveniently died in 1779, about the time
Burr was quitting the army for good. Her home, The Hermitage, near Paramus, became a
center of entertainment for the American officers who manned the outposts around occupied
New York City. Major James Monroe, Jefferson's protégé, and Lieutenant Colonel Alexander Hamilton had sometimes dined there, as did General Washington.

A thoughtful, mature widow ten years older than Burr, Theodosia did not on the face of
her seem to be the lodestone to draw an amorous young spark like Burr from the pursuit of
glory and glamour. The names of Jacatacqua, Catherine, Margaret, Betsy, Hannah,
Pamela—these and the many "Miss ———s" are the fair names (and blanks) that spill out
of Aaron Burr's amorous correspondence. "His intrigues were without number," his friend
and official biographer, Matthew L. Davis, wrote, and "his conduct most licentious."

At no other period of his life is it probable that a man like Burr would have looked twice at
a woman like Theodosia. His friends could not understand Burr's clinging affection for her
and her protective devotion to him. At first, they thought his attentions focused on her
younger and much prettier sister, Catherine de Visme, and Theodosia took note of their
gossip: "Our being the subject of much inquiry, conjecture, and calumny is no more than
we ought to expect. . . ." She did not mind, for "your esteem more than compensated me
for the worst they could say."

Burr promised Theodosia that he would study assiduously and settle down and earn a
fortune if she would marry him. He needed her to coax his weakness into strength, to deny
his dependence on her, and to prod his pride. She wrote him:

> When I am sensible I can make you and myself happy, I will readily join you. . . .
> But till I am confident of this I cannot think of our union. . . . I wish you to study
> for your own sake; to insure yourself respect and independence. . . . I shall never
> look forward with confidence till your pride extends to that.

Burr replied to Theodosia that she was the first woman to prove to him that a woman
could have a soul, as well as an instinct for coquetry. Burr saved letters written to him by
dozens of other females too. "They were cast into one common receptable," according to
Davis, "the profligate and corrupt, by the side of the thoughtless and betrayed victim. All
were held as trophies of victory—all esteemed alike valuable."

Admitted to the bar, married, and moved to New York City, Burr would be cocounsel
with, or opposed to, Hamilton in many causes, but he had many enthusiasms besides the
law. There were politics and land speculations; dabblings in fireside science; and the
reading of innumerable works of fiction, philosophy, and economics. Burr became a patron
of the arts, gave many banquets, attended many others, and found time enough left over to
be the companion and tutor of his wife, Theodosia; stepfather to her five children; and
devoted father to their only child, Theodosia, and an adopted daughter Theodosia's age. He
would also eventually sire at least three children out of wedlock and still remain in the good
graces of an uncountable covey of mistresses, including Maria Reynolds.

Matthew Davis wrote of his partner Burr, "The sacred bonds of friendship were
unhesitatingly violated when they operated as barriers to the indulgence of his passions."
By March 19, 1792, Robert Troup told Hamilton he had discovered a secret "with regard to

Burr's election . . . which I cannot communicate till I see you. I have reason to suspect we have both been abused." But Troup was afraid to entrust Burr's guilty secret to the post. Newly seated as senator from New York, Burr took no partisan position toward Hamilton's pending economic measures. He had not yet had a chance "to read with proper attention the proposed establishment. I am therefore wholly incompetent to give an opinion of its merit. . . . It certainly deserves deliberate consideration—a Charter granted cannot be revoked. This appears to me to be one of those cases in which Delay can be productive of no Evil." His suave habitual manner made him many quick, casual friendships, few deep ones, the dislike of Hamilton and Washington, and soon the enmity of Jefferson. But few political opponents could lay a partisan hand on Senator Burr, who on all issues always hovered somewhere near the middle.

Having won election to the Senate by upsetting the strongly Federalist and Hamiltonian Schuyler, Burr was now letting it be known that he might be available to run with moderate Federalist backing against Clinton for governor of New York in the election to be held in June 1792. Because Burr would draw support from moderate and disaffected Clintonians as well as Federalists, he would make a strong candidate. Isaac Ledyard would soon write Hamilton that "to oppose Mr. B. with success, your friends will be necessitated to promote the interest of the Old Incumbent," Clinton. There was no one Hamilton would less rather support than Clinton, except Burr. Hamilton urged Federalists to support Robert Yates as a lesser evil who posed no threat to Hamilton's leadership, even though as a fellow delegate of Hamilton to the 1787 Constitutional Convention, Yates had strongly supported Clinton and opposed the Constitution. Now chief justice of the New York Court of Appeals, Yates seemed receptive to a Federalist bid to oppose Clinton, but was reluctant to run for various reasons, one being that he feared that he could not afford to. For lieutenant governor, Hamilton and Philip Schuyler were pushing Stephen Van Rensselaer, husband of Margarita Schuyler and patroon of the Van Rensselaer estates.

As Burr's candidacy for governor threatened to wrest control of Hamilton's own party from his grasp, Burr continued to profess to friends of Hamilton like Isaac Ledyard "an entire confidence in the wisdom and integrity of [Hamilton's] designs & a real personal friendship." As Ledyard wrote Hamilton, Burr "does not seem to suppose you doubt of his real personal friendship" or "ever will unless it may arise from meddling interveners."

That early winter of 1791, Anne and William Bingham were seeing less of Hamilton at the Mansion House; and Maria Reynolds, more of him at Fifth and Vine. Hamilton's and Maria's affair was becoming more exigent. But suddenly Maria's husband, James, demanded a reconciliation with her. At this, Maria "pretended to ask my advice," Hamilton recalled. He "advised her to the accommodation; which she shortly afterwards told me had taken place." Notwithstanding the reconciliation, "Mrs. Reynolds, on the other hand, employed every effort to keep up my attention and visits. Her pen was freely employed, and her letters were filled with those tender and pathetic effusions which would have been natural to a woman truly fond and neglected. . . . The variety of shapes which this woman could assume was endless."

Hamilton's and Maria's bedroom conversations rambled over many matters. She "informed me that her husband had been engaged in some speculation in claims upon the Treasury and she believed could give me information respecting the conduct of [some] persons in the department which would be useful to me. I desired an interview with him and he came to me accordingly."

The above passage from the draft of Hamilton's 1797 public confession implies that he asked Maria to have her husband come see him; in the printed version, Hamilton creates the impression that he sent for Reynolds in a peremptory and prosecutorial manner: ''I sent for Reynolds who came to me accordingly.''

At their interview, Reynolds ''confessed that he had obtained a list of claims from a person in my department which he had made use of in his speculations. I invited him, by the expectation of my friendship and good offices, to disclose the person.''

As Hamilton tells the story, at the time of this interview, Reynolds had no knowledge of Hamilton's ongoing intercourse with his wife. Thus there was no reason for Reynolds to be suspicious of Hamilton's ''friendship and good offices.''

Hamilton quizzed Reynolds: ''After some affectation of scruple, he pretended to yield, and ascribed the infidelity to Mr. Duer, from whom he said he had obtained the list in New York, while he [Duer] was in the department.'' So, Hamilton goes on, ''as Mr. Duer had resigned his office some time before the seat of government was removed to Philadelphia, this discovery, if it had been true, was not very important.''

Hamilton here is saying, rather shockingly, that as far as the public was concerned, the leak of secret lists from the Treasury only a year earlier was hardly more serious than a third-rate burglary. Only the lapse of six years and an overwhelmingly self-serving sentiment can account for such a misjudgment. But talking to Reynolds, Hamilton pretended that he thought Reynolds' information about the leak was more important than he later claimed he believed it to be. Hamilton explained, ''Yet it was the interest of my passions to appear to set value upon it, and to continue the expectation of friendship and good offices.''

At this point in Hamilton's 1797 account of events that supposedly occurred in the summer, fall, and winter of 1791, Hamilton throws in mention of an apparently innocuous circumstantial fact that almost certainly dates from March or April of 1790, not the fall of 1791:

> Mr. Reynolds told me he was going to Virginia, and on his return would point out something in which I could serve him. I do not know but he said something about employment in a public office.

In 1797, Hamilton still would not know of Gustavus B. Wallace's letters to Madison that placed Reynolds in Virginia with leaked lists in his hands and frauds on old soldiers on his mind in March and April of 1790, not 1791. By 1791, Bland's resolutions had made the kinds of frauds and profits that were possible for Reynolds in 1790 all but impossible in late 1791. It seems far more likely than not that Hamilton in 1797 was slipping back in recollection to a conversation he had had with Maria or James Reynolds early in 1790—in New York. This was more than a year and a half earlier than the first of their meetings to which he was confessing in his public statement: the 1791 interview in Philadelphia.

When and where did Hamilton first meet James and Maria Reynolds? When did his affair with her really begin? Circumstantial evidence places their first meeting well before her 1791 summer visitation to his house to which Hamilton confessed. Nowhere in his public statement did Hamilton explicitly assert that the beauteous New Yorker's summer visit to him immediately after Jefferson's and Madison's ''passionate courtship'' of Aaron Burr in New York was the first meeting he had ever had with her or her husband. Hamilton admitted that he was the victim of a plot, but he seemed, or pretended, not to grasp the shape and depth of the real plot hidden beneath the surface conventions of a wronged husband's scheme to blackmail Hamilton for seducing his wife.

In any event, when Reynolds returned from his trip, whether it was in early 1790 or late 1791, he applied to Hamilton for a job in the same Treasury whose leaked secret lists he had been using so successfully for his frauds in Virginia. By 1797, Hamilton knew he should have rejected Reynolds's request, but that is not what he did in 1791.

"The knowledge I had acquired of him was decisive against such a request," Hamilton wrote decisively. But his answer to Reynolds fell well short of being "decisive": "I parried it by telling him, what was true, that there was no vacancy in my immediate office, and that the appointment of clerks in the other branches of the department was left to the chiefs of the respective branches."

Nowhere did Hamilton flatly state that Reynolds did not receive an appointment as a clerk in another branch of the department. Hamilton limited his rejection of Reynolds's employment to his own immediate office, while seeming to suggest to Reynolds that an appointment elsewhere in the Treasury would not be out of the question by action of the chief of the branch (who, of course, would report to Hamilton).

Oddly enough, Reynolds became angry. He complained that Hamilton "had promised him *employment* and had *disappointed* him." Hamilton confessed that his replies to Reynolds had been equivocal: "The situation with the wife would naturally incline me to conciliate this man. It is possible I may have used vague expressions which raised expectation; but the more I learned of the person, the more inadmissible his employment in a public office became. . . ."

Hamilton argued that this equivocal refusal proved that he could not have had a connection with Reynolds in speculations because, if he had, he would not have "hazarded his resentment by a persevering refusal."

The odd thing is that Treasury Department records show that a clerk named Reynolds, who, like James Reynolds, hailed from Connecticut, was hired in the register's office of the Treasury Department in January of 1791 or perhaps earlier. The first name used for the Reynolds who was actually hired was Simeon. Another odd thing was that about the time Hamilton, according to his 1797 public account, was turning James down for employment in the Treasury, Simeon was discharged from the register's office in unexplained circumstances. Did Hamilton so far attempt to mollify James that he arranged indirectly through the head of a separate branch, the register, for the short engagement of James's kinsman Simeon? Or was "Simeon" really only an alias for James himself?

Hamilton's affair with Maria grew more exigent in other ways than James's demands for employment in the Treasury. At Anne and William Bingham's Mansion House, the approach of Christmas would bring with it the glittering crescendo of the social season, but less would be seen of Hamilton. Swept aside by "paroxisms of love," Hamilton's earlier plan for a "gradual discontinuance" with Maria failed. Her sexual appetite for him seemed to become insatiable. A more intimate kind of party became his habitat.

"A more frequent intercourse continued to be pressed upon me on the pretext of its being essential to the party," he later wrote. "The appearances of a violent attachment were played of and of a genuine extreme distress at the idea of an interruption of the connection. . . ."

He now realized that the only way to end the affair would be to break it off abruptly. "My suspicions of some [foul p] sinister contrivance at the same time increasing," he wrote, "I resolved to put an end to the affair and to see Mrs. Reynolds no more." He would stride out of her trap once and for all and celebrate his liberation at the Binghams. Such a public occasion of glittering good cheer would also be politically useful for probing inquiries and thrusts in diplomacy, economics, and politics. A carefully dropped word there could change

the course of the history of relations with France or Britain or the state of New York with a
minimum of risk. He would erase Maria Reynolds from his life.

Home from her European travels, Anne Bingham had introduced to America the custom
of having servants announce each arriving guest, calling his name as he entered the door and
shouting his full honorific title, if any, ahead of him into the ballroom. Such imported
extravagances were really the only fault anyone, even other women with sharp tongues,
could find with Anne Bingham.

Above medium height and well-formed, she had sprightliness, dignity, elegance, and
distinction in her carriage. She sparkled with wit, bubbled with vivacity, and had the knack
of convincing the most hopeless yokel, introduced into her drawing room by nothing more
than high political rank, that she found his personality peculiarly appealing. Daring at the
card table, graceful in the dance, witty in conversation, adept with all devices of Congreve
dialogue, fond of all the dissipations prescribed by fashion, and tactful in the seating of her
guests at table, she well earned the scepter she waved so authoritatively over all of
Philadelphia society. If Martha Washington had to be acknowledged as the queen mother,
Anne Bingham reigned as the crown princess of her Republican court.

"Senator James Monroe!" called the doorman.

The senator from Virginia recoiled nervously in surprise and caught his arm in the sleeve
of his coat as he tried to remove it.

"Coming" called the senator, but no one came.

"Senator James Monroe" echoed a footman down the hall; still no one came. Monroe
swore a string of oaths as he wrestled frantically with the lining of his sleeve.

At such a spectacle no flicker of amusement would cross Anne Bingham's beautiful face
to add a wince to a newly elected senator's gauche embarrassment.

Hamilton seemed born for the court over which Anne Bingham reigned. Having made his
own way upward in life from the bottom, he felt no need to playact the part of a man of the
people, or pretend to be anything other than he was. Being no Puritan and no self-anointed
democrat herself, Anne found the spruce, handsome secretary politically and personally
congenial. When she pursed her pretty lips in wicked oaths, it was said that she swore as
daintily as the duchess of Devonshire. If she relished anecdotes too spicy for the official
puritanic tone set by George and Martha, it was because she was doing her beautiful best to
dispel their austere chill. Hamilton was only too glad to help.

Of course, within the few square blocks of the government quarter of federal Philadelphia, the recent comings and goings of the most conspicuous figure in the government at the
large house at Fifth and Vine would hardly remain unremarked in Anne's repartee. Others at
her levees might profess to be shocked by her earthy vocabularly and risqué jibes, but
Hamilton would respond in kind to her wit and join her laughter. No guest appeared so much
the confident, sophisticated man of the world as he.

The Binghams provided not only social leadership, but also the perfect setting for the
compactly built reddish-haired financial genius of the government. Having laid his monumental "Report on Manufactures" before Congress on December 5, 1791, he was now at
the ascendancy of his fame, the kind of fame that meant the most to moneyed men like
William Bingham and his Anne. It would be to Anne's husband, William Bingham, not to a
closer friend like Robert Troup, that a crestfallen, self-discredited Hamilton would later
entrust his entire file of documentary evidence of the Reynolds affair for safekeeping.

With Hamilton sometimes, but not always, would be his wife, Elizabeth, an appealing
kind of woman, popular with other women, especially with Martha Washington.

Elizabeth's delicate face was set off by her "fine eyes which are very dark, and hold the life and energy" of her restrained countenance. She was gentle and retiring, but in small groups she was gay and full of humor. She often would be missing from such parties or leave early because for her, in these years, life seemed to be one pregnancy, accouchement, childbirth, and weaning after another. Her healthy pregnancies were occasionally interrupted by a miscarriage. Her husband spent many nights out on the town without her.

"Monsieur Jean Baptiste de Ternant, minister plenipotentiary of King Louis XVI of France!"

As the footmen's voices unfurled his titles of nobility like a plume, all eyes would turn to the new French minister, who had arrived in August 1791. The king had been deposed, and Ternant was only a holdover from the deposed king's regime, but the old titles introduced a touch of glory to Philadelphia; besides, no one knew how the new republican regime's man was supposed to be announced. Ternant was still the minister plenipotentiary from the most dynamic and dangerous nation in the world.

Before Ternant had arrived in America, Jefferson had protested against the action of the French Assembly in imposing heavier charges on tobacco carried in American ships than in French ships. Hamilton suggested to Ternant when he came that all disputed questions might be settled in the new treaty of commerce that he himself strongly favored. He sought to draw Ternant out to make him reveal what his instructions from his own government were, much as he had drawn out Beckwith earlier on the subject of his authority.

Jefferson's already smoldering anger at Hamilton and his policies burned more corrosively as the realization reached him of Hamilton's searching and intimate conversations with both Beckwith and Ternant about matters that Jefferson felt should be the secretary of state's alone to discuss with them, but only if he saw fit to do so.

While doubt might linger that the minister from deposed King Louis XVI was still properly accredited to Philadelphia, if not to Anne Bingham's, there could be no like doubts about the status of George Hammond, the officially accredited British minister, whom local government and society alike had been breathlessly awaiting as the replacement for the vexatiously unofficial George Beckwith. As the young British lion stepped down from his carriage, Anne Bingham's footmen made the sills and rafters ring for the newest and most important member of the resident diplomatic corps: "The minister plenipotentiary of His Majesty King George III, George Hammond." Such style and title would recall for some the excitements of the now unmentionable winter of British occupation 13 years earlier.

After bowing deeply to Anne Bingham, lifting the back of her hand gently to his lips, bestowing a kiss upon it, and paying his respects to her husband, among the first of the others he would greet would be Secretary of the Treasury Hamilton. If Jefferson had made one of his rare appearances at such a party, it is likely that he would have turned on his heel and walked away in disgust because he insisted on none but official contacts with foreign diplomats. Hammond would report to his chief, Lord Grenville, in the Foreign Office in London, that he preferred to have most of his communications with Hamilton and to have no relations with Jefferson that were not absolutely necessary.

The gaiety and warmth of the setting at levees and balls at the William Binghams' and other great Philadelphia houses helped keep important diplomatic moves and countermoves friendly, constructive, and useful, without the risks attendant upon formal moves through official channels. There were the usual countervailing risks of misunderstandings and misquotations, although to sophisticated diplomats, even purposeful misunderstandings have always had important diplomatic uses. The same could hardly be said of the suspicious, fretful peevishness and ire with which the absent Jefferson regarded Hamilton's friendly, informal, private conversations with Beckwith, Ternant, and Hammond.

Some said that George Washington, standing alone, had the look of an uncrowned king, but standing so tall beside short, squat, comfortable Martha he was only half of a faintly comic pair. The most regal-looking couple at the Binghams' would be those dazzling ornaments of American society and diplomacy, Chief Justice John Jay and his wife, Sarah Livingston Jay. Abigail Adams's daughter—and, no doubt, many another of the ladies at the Binghams'—would sigh over Jay's "benevolence stamped in every feature." He stood tall, if slightly stooped; his coal-black, deep-set eyes were the most striking feature of his pallid countenance. He wore his hair a little down over his forehead, tied behind, and moderately powdered; he was always kindly, gracious, and courtly in society and sternly uncompromising in matters of honor. He looked with abhorrence on the excesses of the French Revolution.

Seeing the chief justice of the United States at the Binghams' with so few cases yet on his docket would remind Hamilton that his old friend and colleague would make a splendid candidate for governor of New York—infinitely preferable to Yates, Burr, or Clinton. Hamilton's memories of Sarah Livingston Jay, Lady Kitty Livingston's younger sister, went all the way back to his own first winter on the continent in 1773. Gouverneur Morris had an eye for Sally as she was then, a belle of 17 with little time to waste on their 16-year-old boarder, raw and fresh from the West Indies, probably seeing snow for the first time in his life.

Morris had written her 22-year-old sister, "What do you think, Kitty? I have adopted Sally for my daughter. Never was a little creature so admired." There were "gentle Strephons who hang about her, bending forward . . . rolling [their eyes] sighing most piteously . . . in the midst of all this sits Miss with seeming unconsciousness of the whole. . . ."

Now at Anne and William Binghams', standing beside the tall, permanent Strephon she had chosen, Sally was a statuesque and beauteous 35. Many another slightly aging Strephon like Hamilton and Hammond and Ternant still swarmed admiringly about her, "bending forward" and exchanging compliments.

Jefferson, as he told his *Anas* later, was ill at ease in circles like the Binghams.' All the aristocratic talk and monarchical decadence and corruption which he saw on display there would come to dominate American life, he feared.

One reason for Jefferson's uneasiness with Anne's gossipy ways may have been the stories going the rounds that some years before, beginning in 1768, Jefferson had made a number of attempts to seduce Elizabeth Walker, the wife of his best friend from college days, John Walker. Walker had been annoyed enough to complain of the matter to several people. More or less as a consequence, poor Walker had just been dumped from his safe seat in the Senate by Jefferson's hatchet man, James Monroe, as unceremoniously as Burr had ousted Schuyler from his. Years later, in 1805, Jefferson would tell his presidential secretary, William Burwell, that Hamilton "had once threatened him with a public disclosure" of his affair with Elizabeth Walker. At the same time, Jefferson pretended to minimize the threat by saying that his affair "had been long known." In Hamilton's history there is no other record of this threat to calumniate Jefferson. At Anne Bingham's, any such gossipy, usually bantering indiscretions were supposed to be privileged as they are in all the best houses. But Jefferson had a way of jotting down as *Anas* all manner of such scraps, many of them third- and fourth-hand hearsay, relayed or invented by the likes of his creature

John Beckley. Things that might have been said as a joke in society, delivered with a smile and a twinkle to denote a meaning intended as the ironic opposite of the literal meaning of the words, when relayed literally from Beckley to the absent Jefferson and jotted down for posterity, would cause Jefferson to brood and smolder and dream of reprisals.

Ten days after laying before Congress his dream of modern industrial America, "The Report on Manufactures," a few days after resolving to make an abrupt break with Maria Reynolds and perhaps secretly celebrating it publicly at the Binghams' pre-Christmas ball, Hamilton received a nightmarish letter. Since he had vowed to break off with Maria Reynolds, Hamilton said, she had "persisted in persecuting me with letters filled with the strongest professions of tenderness and [distress] grief—to which I made no reply." But now her husband had either "discovered the connection" or "my resolution to end it having now become unequivocal, the time was arrived for a [demon] the catastrophe of the plot."

On arriving home from the Binghams' ball, a letter from Maria Reynolds was at his house awaiting him. It was as follows:

Col. Hamilton,

Dear Sir:—I have not time to tell you the cause of my present troubles only that Mr. has rote you this morning and I know not wether you have got the letter or not and he has swore that If you do not answer It or If he dose not se or hear from you to day he will write Mrs. Hamilton he has just Gone out and I am a Lone I think you had better come here one moment that you May know the Cause then you will the better know how to act Oh my God I feel more for you than myself and wish I had never been born to give you so mutch unhappiness do not rite to him no not a Line but come here soon do not send or leav any thing in his power

Maria

Unlike the "Report on Manufactures," there was no way Maria's letter could be ignored, tabled, or pigeonholed. James Reynolds had gone into the kind of dangerous angry action always to be feared from a cuckolded husband. Hamilton must now come to her at once; he must leave nothing in James's power. An invitation to more frequent intercourse at Anne Bingham's would have pleased him more.

23

A Tissue of Machinations

I will not suffer my retirement to be clouded by the slanders of a man whose history, from the moment at which history can stoop to notice him, is a tissue of machinations against the liberty of the country which has not only received him and given him bread, but heaped its honors on his head.

—Jefferson to Washington, September 9, 1792

James Reynolds followed up Maria's summons to Hamilton with a summons of his own. He was now claiming, after all these months, that he had just found out that his angel of a wife had betrayed him with Hamilton.

> Sir
>
> I am very sorry to find out that I have been so cruelly treated by a person that I took to be my best friend instead of that my greatest Enimy. You have deprived me of everything thats near and dear to me, I discovered whenever I came into the house. There I found Mrs. Reynolds weeping I ask'd her the Cause of being so unhappy. She always told me that she had bin Reding, and she could not help Crying when she Red any thing that was Afecting. But seeing her Repeatedly in that Setevation gave me some suspicion to think that was not the Cause, as fortain would have it. before matters was carred to two great a length.

She had confessed all:

> I discovered a letter directed to you which I copied of . . . without being discovered by her . . . the evening after I see [her] give a letter to a Black man in the

332

> Market Street. which I followed him to your door . . . I broached the matter to her and Red the Copy to her which she fell upon her knees and asked forgiveness and discovered every thing to me Respecting the matter.

She had told Reynolds how "she called on you for the lone of some money. which you toald her you would call on her the Next Evening. which accordingly you did. and there Sir you took the advantage a poor Broken harted woman."
Now she had fallen in love with Hamilton and cared for no one but him.

> Instead of being a friend, you have acted the part of the most Cruelist man in existence, you have made a whole family miserable. She ses there is no other man that she Care for in this world. now Sir you have bin the Cause of Cooling her affections for me. She was a woman. I should as soon sespect an angiel from heven. and one where all my happiness was depending. and I would Sacrefise almost my life to make her Happy.

Reynolds demanded satisfaction for alienation of her affections:

> it shant be onely one family thats miserable. for I am Robbed of all happiness in this world I am determined to leve her. and take my daughter with me that Shant see her poor mother Lot. . . . call and see me. for there is no person that Knowes any thing as yet. put it to your own case and Reflect one moment. that you should know shush a thing of your wife. would not you have satisfaction yes. and so will I before one day passes me more.

> I am yours
> James Reynolds

"On answer to this" impassioned threat, Hamilton later explained coolly, "I sent him a note, or message, desiring him to call upon me at my office, which I think he did the same day." This letter of Hamilton's has not been found. They met. Hamilton's confession went on:

> He in substance repeated the topics contained in his letter, and that he was resolved to have satisfaction. I replied that he knew best what evidence he had of the alleged connection between me and his wife, that I neither admitted nor denied it; that if he knew of any injury I had done him, entitling him to satisfaction, it lay with him to name it.

Reynolds was evasive. According to Hamilton:

> He concluded with the same vague claim of satisfaction, but without specifying the kind which would content him. I resolved to gratify him. But willing to manage his delicacy, if he had any, I reminded him that I had, at our first interview, made him a promise of service, that I was disposed to do it as far as might be proper, and in my power, and requested him to consider in what manner I could do it, and to write to me. He withdrew with a promise of compliance.

Oddly enough Reynolds does not seem to have demanded that Hamilton break off the affair with Maria, nor did Hamilton offer to do so. Reynolds replied by a long, inconclusive letter asking Hamilton to meet him at the Sign of the George, a public tavern, on Tuesday morning at eight o'clock.

"On receipt of this letter," Hamilton said, "I called upon Reynolds." But before going to that rendezvous, Hamilton said he wrote a mysterious letter to an unnamed correspondent, describing his strong suspicion that he was the victim of a plot. He may have intended the addressee to be Oliver Wolcott, Jr., his assistant secretary of the treasury, or he may never have sent it, or, as some would charge, he may have written it in 1797 as a self-serving confirmation of his whole story, and backdated it to the time of his eight o'clock rendezvous with Reynolds at the Sign of the George in 1791.

Hamilton wrote, "I am at this moment going to a rendezvous which I suspect may involve a most serious plot against me." It was risky to meet Reynolds in such a public place, but he would go anyway. "Various reasons, and among others a desire to ascertain the truth induce me to hazard the consequence," Hamilton added. The last sentence suggests that the letter was addressed to a public larger than Wolcott alone: "As any disastrous event might interest my fame; I drop you this line, that from my impressions may be inferred the truth of the matter."

Hamilton dated this mysterious letter "Sunday, December 17th, 1791," but Sunday that year was in fact the eighteenth, making the following Tuesday the twentieth. At the turn of a year, Hamilton had once or twice earlier given the new year the number of the old, but he almost never wrote the wrong date for a day of the week anywhere else in his correspondence. In either case, the rendezvous to which he actually went was not "at this moment," but two or three days later.

At his rendezvous with Reynolds at the Sign of the George, Hamilton claimed he had been peremptory: "Assuming a decisive tone, [I] told him that I was tired of his indecision, and insisted upon his declaring to me explicitly what it was he aimed at. He again promised to explain by letter."

Hamilton went on, "On the 19th, I received the promised letter."

Philadelphia, 19th December, 1791.

Sir.

I have this preposial to make to you. give me the Sum of thousand dollars and I will leve the town and take my daughter with me and go where my Friend Shant here from me and leve her to Yourself to do for her as you thing proper. . . .

yours
James Reynolds

Mr. Alexr. Hamilton.

The secretary of the treasury was, as usual, short of personal funds. He did not have $1,000 to his name; so he had to pay the heart balm, or hush money, in two separate installments, one of $600 and the other $400. Hamilton wrote that "I determined to give it to him and did so in two payments, as per receipts." His receipts from Reynolds are dated the twenty-second of December and the third of January. Later denying that these documents were evidence of his collaboration with Reynolds in illegal speculations, Hamilton ruefully wrote, "It is a little remarkable that an avaricious speculating Secretary of the Treasury should have been so straitened for money as to be obliged to satisfy an engagement of this sort by two different payments!"

The businesslike secretary of the treasury kept the signed receipts from Reynolds for years.

Hamilton's fresh resolve to end the affair lasted for about two weeks. It was Reynolds, not Maria, who asked Hamilton to come back again. In Hamilton's words: "On the 17th of January, I received the letter by which Reynolds writes me to renew my visits to his wife. He had before requested that I would see her no more."

Here is Reynolds's ludicrous explanation for his quick switch: "She would onely wish to see you as a friend."

Philadelphia 17th January, 1792

Sir

    I suppose you will be surprised in my writing to you . . . its Mrs. R. wish to See you. and for My own happiness and hers. I have not the Least Objections to your Calling. as a friend to Boath of us. and must rely intirely on your and her honnor . . . I am pritty well Convinsed, She would onely wish to See you as a friend. and sence I am Reconciled to live with her, I would wish to do every thing for her happiness and my own.

Hamilton did not at once accept Reynolds's astonishing invitation to resume seeing Maria as a platonic friend. Nor was a platonic friendship exactly what Maria had in mind.

"If I recollect rightly, I did not immediately accept the invitation," Hamilton said, "nor till after I had received several very importuante letters from Mrs. Reynolds."

As for Maria, she would never ask to see him again. Or else she would commit suicide if he refused to see her again:

Monday Night, Eight C., L

Sir,

    . . . Yes Sir Rest assurred I will never ask you to Call on me again I have kept my Bed those two dayes and now rise from My pillow wich your Neglect has filled with the shorpest thorns . . . [My] heart is ready Burst with Greef I can neither eat or sleep I have Been on the point of doing the moast horrid acts as I shudder to think where I might been what will become of me. . . .

She did not want to see him, but she insisted on seeing him.

    . . . all the wish I have is to se you once more that I may my doubts Cleared up for God sake be not so voed of all humanity as to deni me this Last request Call some time this night I no its late but any time between this and twelve A Clock I shall be up if you wont Come to send me a line oh my head I can rite no more do something to Ease My heart Or Els I no not what I shall do for so I cannot live Commit this to the care of my maid be not offended I beg.

Two days later she was still suffering the pangs of his withdrawal from her service:

Wednesday Morning ten of Clock

Dear Sir

    . . . I shal be misarable till I se you and if my dear freend has the Least Esteeme for the unhappy Maria whos greateest fault is Loveing him he will come as soon as he shall get this and till that time My breast will be the seate of pain and woe

adieu

Col. Hamilton.

P.S. If you cannot come thie Evening to stay just come for only one moment as I shal
be Lone Mr. is going to sup with a friend from New York.

Few things would seem more difficult for Hamilton's kind of writer to invent than the
unqualified passion of her effusions or the absurdity of her quick self-contradictions. She
was still at it a week later.

My dear Col Hamilton on my kneese Let me Intreatee you to reade my Letter . . .
you need not be the least affraid let me not die with fear have pity on me my freend
for I deserve it . . . My heart Is ready to burst and my tears wich once could flow
with Ease are now denied me Could I only weep I would thank heaven and bless the
hand that _____

Her letter breaks off at the point where tears that can no longer flow are about to burst her
heart.
Hamilton resumed the affair.

By October 1791 bank stock of a par value of $400 had risen to $500, and most other
stocks were higher too, and by the end of January they were moving higher still. Hamilton's
intervention in the money markets not only kept the market steady, but was largely
responsible for a resumption of the rise.

The Bank of the United States had opened branches in New York and elsewhere, and its
New York branch competed with the Bank of New York not only in normal business of
discounts, but also as a depository for government funds. When Seton wrote to complain of
this competition, Hamilton replied on November 25 that the branches had been established
without consulting him and against his judgment. "Ultimately it will be incumbent on me to
place the public funds in the keeping of the branch," he acknowledged, "but it may be
depended upon that I shall precipitate nothing, but shall so conduct the transfer as not to
embarrass or distress your institution." He was, after all, a founder of the Bank of New
York.

As a result of Hamilton's handling of American foreign economic policy and the success
of Hamilton's legislative program in reviving the domestic economy, the securities of the
new country gradually earned the highest credit ratings in all world securities markets. The
interest rate and extra financing charges that the new country had to pay bankers fell below
the rates that bankers demanded of Russia, Austria, and most other foreign countries. Under
Hamilton American public credit at home and abroad came to rank with the best in the
world.

It was very clear to New York bankers and businessmen like Seton and Duer that they had
an understanding friend at Washington's court in Philadelphia. A group of them, including
Roger Alden, Brockholst Livingston, Gulian Verplanck, the president of The Bank of New
York, and Joshua Waddington, who had been Hamilton's client in the famous case of
Rutgers v. *Waddington,* raised a subscription to commission John Trumbull to execute a
portrait of Hamilton, to be hung in a place of honor in a public building in New York City.
The subscribers particularly requested that the portrait "exhibit such part of your political
life as may be most agreeable to yourself." Hamilton at first declined, replying on January
15 that his portrait ought to appear "unconnected with any incident of my political life," but
the project went forward.

Upon unveiling, the full-length Trumbull portrait that was hung in the Assembly Room of the New York State Chamber of Commerce and Industry building in New York City shows Hamilton erect and in fuller flesh than he appears in later portraits. He stands confidently beside his writing desk with the arch of a classical temple looming in the background. The in-turned fingers of his right hand rest gracefully on the top page of what appears to be an important state paper—the Report on Manufactures?—awaiting his immediate attention after the necessary interruption for the purpose of striking a confident pose for the benefit of Trumbull and all his grateful friends now riding the boom in the market. Not by a drooping eyelash does his ruddy facade in 1792 betray a flicker of worry about his feverish, secret, on-again, off-again affair in Philadelphia with Maria Reynolds, or the hush money he was borrowing from friends like Troup to pay her husband James to keep quiet about it.

The whole "superstructure of credit" that Hamilton had jawboned safely through 1791 collapsed at the end of February 1792. William Duer had mismanaged his official accounts as assistant secretary of the treasury to such an extent that his successor, Oliver Wolcott, Jr., remained unable to straighten them out. In one transaction Duer had taken official Treasury warrants and pledged them as security for his own private loans; on his default the warrants had been offered for sale and purchased by one Andrew G. Fraunces, an employee of the Treasury, who sought to collect on them. Fraunces had been a coadjutor of Duer inside the Treasury, and probably also of James Reynolds as well. The Philadelphia loan office duly honored Duer's warrants on presentation and returned them to the Treasury for payment, but there Hamilton discovered Duer's fraud and refused to clear the payments. Hamilton made no public mention of the transaction and accepted Duer's assurances that he would make good the loss, but Duer failed to pay, and the default of the former assistant secretary remained an open item.

The private manipulations of Duer and his partners, Alexander McComb and Royal Flint, Catherine Greene's lawyer, became matters of public notoriety. On March 12, 1792, Oliver Wolcott, Jr., wrote to Richard Harison, the United States attorney in New York, demanding that Duer settle his accounts as secretary of the old Board of Treasury or give security for a shortage of $200,000. In the event of noncompliance, Harison should commence suit for the money. Rumors that Duer and McComb were on the verge of bankruptcy caused securities markets to fall sharply. Hamilton had sought to prevent too high a rise in 1791; now he had to support the market to prevent a crash. Duer had written Hamilton on March 12, demanding that he hold off Wolcott's suit, else "my ruin is complete," but Hamilton refused to interfere. By the nineteenth, Troup was telling Hamilton of Duer, "this poor man is in a state of almost complete insanity; and his situation is a source of inexpressible grief to all his friends." But nothing could be done. "Duer's notes unpaid amounted to about half a million dollars and Duer has not a farthing of money or a particle of stock to pay them with." "Widows, orphans, merchants and mechanics" were all unpaid. Troup warned that Duer's total bankruptcy would bring Hamilton's funding system into "odium."

Wolcott followed up the prosecution.

On March 25, Hamilton sent $50,000 to William Seton at The Bank of New York, with instruction to support the six-percents at par if they should sink below that figure. Seton was not to declare specifically on whose account he was buying, because formal authority to buy for the sinking fund was lacking—"the thing is not formally arranged and this is Sunday," Hamilton wrote. Besides, there was an advantage in acting without formal authority from the trustees because "it will very probably be conjectured that you appear for the public."

Freneau's *National Gazette* picked this moment of crisis in public confidence and threats of odium for Hamilton's funding system to declare war on the Treasury. On April 2, James Madison, writing as *Brutus,* assailed men who "pampered the spirit of speculation." *Brutus* was no more alarmed than was Hamilton himself, who wrote Philip Livingston the same day, "'Tis time there should be a line of Separation between honest Men & knaves, between respectable Stockholders and dealers in the funds, and mere unprincipled Gamblers. Public infamy must restrain what the laws cannot." Probably one reason for Hamilton's harsh language to Philip Livingston was that a number of Livingstons "were actively speculating on the 'bear' side of the market and were due to *deliver* most of the New York bank stock Duer was to *receive* in *May.*"

At a meeting of the closely divided commissioners of the sinking fund on April 3, Jefferson argued that the prices at which it was buying were all unrealistically high and would favor the speculators. Hamilton knew or sensed that more bankruptcies of his friends were on the way. He advised William Seton on April 4: "You may apply another $50,000 to purchases at such time as you judge it can be rendered most useful," but it might be best to "wait the happening of the crisis which I fear is inevitable . . . a pretty extensive explosion is to take place . . . then it may be more important than now to enter the market in force."

Hamilton was right. Alexander McComb's failure on April 12 fueled more fears and panic. "This misfortune has a long tail to it," Hamilton wrote Seton and sent on $100,000. Seton went into the market with it and explained to Hamilton on April 16, 1792, that "the applications were so numerous & so vastly beyond my expectations, I found it necessary to declare I could take but very small sums from each. . . . I averaged the whole "that no one would be left without some relief—so that the investment of the $100,000 goes to upwards of 80 persons."

Seton complimented Hamilton on his astute market strategy, but he added that such "great and universal distress prevails" that "it would be utterly impossible to make purchases equal to the relief." As an experienced Wall Streeter, Seton knew that what goes down must also go up; every well has a bottom.

Before things could turn up, however, news of Duer's failure spread. Other creditors pressed him. Duer had also lost large sums that the SUM had entrusted to his keeping. He had left its books of account rigged and indecipherable. One of Duer's and Hamilton's associates in the SUM, John Dewhurst, fled his New York creditors and declared bankruptcy in Philadelphia. Duer was clapped into jail. His angriest creditors howled for hauling him out and lynching him. Many, recalling his position at the Treasury, implicated Hamilton in Duer's fall.

Hamilton struggled to stave off the bankruptcy of the SUM, writing a careful letter to its board of directors on April 14. He sketched a businesslike salvage operation, suggesting that "the Society confine themselves at first to the cotton branch. The printing business to commence as early as possible." Unprofitable subsidiaries should be spun off. "Means should be taken to procure in Europe a *few essential* workmen." If the directors desired, he would arrange a loan. Through William Seton he managed to arrange a $10,000 loan at interest of only 5 percent—a prime rate that was as favorable as the United States itself could obtain. But all his efforts failed.

Hamilton and his friends lost all they had ever invested in the SUM when the Treasury Department's suit sent Duer to prison.

Then the market turned up again. By June 10, 1792, Fisher Ames was able to write Hamilton from Boston that "all goes well in the state. The people really prosper, and, what is more, they know it, and give credit to the general government for the change they have witnessed." Seton likewise was able to report that all was well between The Bank of New

York and the New York branch of the Bank of the United States, thanks to Hamilton: "With respect to ourselves & the Branch we go in perfect Harmony, & there does not appear any disposition on their part to do otherwise."

Later on, Seton thanked Hamilton for ordering the collector of New York to deposit his receipts in The Bank of New York, for, as he put it in confidence, he felt that the branch was trying to drain him of specie: "If I find they persist in the draining us, I must implore the aid of your all powerfull hand to convince them we are not destitute of aid in the hour of need."

To an instinct for the political jugular, Jefferson joined a deadly ability to hit two or three targets with a single well-aimed missile. Not long after Jefferson's return from his and Madison's "passionate courtship" of Aaron Burr, George Clinton, Robert R. Livingston, and Philip Freneau in New York, a series of public letters signed *Publicola* implying criticism of Jefferson had appeared in the newspapers. Jefferson denounced Vice-President John Adams for their authorship, and it did not unduly trouble him that the true author was Adams's son, John Quincy Adams. Hamilton tried to soothe the secretary of state, but only supplied Jefferson with an additional target of opportunity in himself.

On August 13, 1791, Jefferson jotted down the following notes on some private remarks of Hamilton's:

"A. H. condemning Mr. A's writing . . . as having a tendency to weaken the present govmt declared in substance as follows:

"I own it is my own opinion tho' I do not publish it in Dan and Bersheba, that the present govnmt is not that which will answer the ends of society, by giving stability & protection to its rights, and that it will probably be found expedient to go into the British form. However, since we have undertaken the experiment, I am for giving it a fair course, whatever my expectns. The success indeed so far, is greater than I had expected . . . & therefore at present success seems more possible than it had done heretofore."

Later, referring to Jay and Hamilton, Jefferson wrote on July 28, 1791, to William Short, claiming that "both are dangerous. They pant after union with England as the power which is to support their projects, and are most determined Anti-gallicans. It is prognosticated that our republic is to end with the President's life. But I believe they will find themselves all head and no body."

During the Revolution, of course, Great Britain had been the enemy and France the ally, but in the decade since there had been vast change. The French Revolution had spilled over in French threats to the rest of Europe and seemed to threaten the New World as well. Hamilton at first was favorably disposed toward the French Revolution, but, as the convulsion widened and turned more violent, and rabbles gave way to tyrants with bloodbaths at each transfer of power, it had revealed itself as a social, religious, and economic, as well as political, upheaval. It aroused his liberal, religious, and conservative instincts and enhanced his admiration for ordered stability under law on the British pattern. Jefferson, on the other hand, was a passionate admirer of the French slogan of *Liberté, Égalité, Fraternité,* regardless of the facts, or at least he professed to be. He seemed obsessed with a hatred for Britain, his fellow countrymen who did not share it, and all he dubbed as "monarchists" and "monocrats," the most pejorative epithets Jefferson could find for political adversaries. Jefferson imputed to monocrats all the worst excesses of the old royal regime in France, and ignored the virtues of limited constitutional republican monarchy in the form that closer students of world affairs saw emerging in Britain.

At the Constitutional Convention, in *The Federalist Papers,* and in many letters and state papers, Hamilton made penetrating analyses of the evolution of the British monarchy to extract such lessons as it might offer America on the subject of an executive with sufficient but limited powers. Hamilton always insisted that monarchy was not right for America, but it served Jefferson's political purposes to ignore the truth of the matter and to belabor Hamilton instead as chief examplar of the hatred monarchist tribe.

In his contributions to *The Federalist Papers*, James Madison, like Hamilton, had argued eloquently for a strong executive and against divisive political factions. Now Jefferson and Madison were speaking and writing of a "republican interest" and a "republican party," posing as the only protectors of American liberties against an allegedly subversive "monarchical party." No such party existed, but by their shrewd exploitation of and interchangeable use of scare words like *monarchical* and *monocrat*, Jefferson and Madison rallied to their faction many whose grievances were against any strong executive government like Washington's, as administered most conspicuously by Hamilton.

To Jefferson's basic charge that the Hamiltonians were a monarchical party that sought the destruction of the federal form and all state governments, Hamilton replied, "To this there is no other Answer than a flat denial, except this: that the project, from its absurdity, refutes itself."

In his extraordinary private confession to his old army friend Edward Carrington by his letter of May 26, 1792, Hamilton delivered a moving, rather touching affirmation of personal innocence of the charge of being a monarchist: "As to my own political creed, I give it to you with the utmost sincerity. I am affectionately attached to the republican theory." His commitment was broad, deep, and specific: "I desire above all things to see the equality of political rights, exclusive of all hereditary distinction, firmly established by a practical demonstration of its being consistent with the order and happiness of society." He added, "On the whole, the only enemy which Republicanism has to fear in this country is in the spirit of faction and anarchy."

Perhaps drawing a lesson from Jefferson's ability to hit multiple targets with a single broadside, Hamilton, retorting to Jefferson and Madison, also hit the "man on horseback," Senator Aaron Burr.

The "man on horseback" who had upset Schuyler was one of "those, then, who resist a confirmation of public order." They "are the true artificers of monarchy." "This is [not] the intention of the generality of them," like Jefferson and Madison, Hamilton acknowledged. But he could "lay the finger upon some of their party who may justly be suspected." To Hamilton, Burr was such a man: "unprincipled in private life, desperate in his fortune, bold in his temper, possessed of considerable talents, having the advantage of military habits, despotic in his ordinary demeanor, known to have scoffed in private at the principles of liberty." He had recently been seen "to mount the hobby-horse of popularity, to join in the cry of danger to liberty, to take every opportunity of embarrassing the general government and bringing it under suspicion, to flatter and fall in with all the nonsense of the zealots of the day." His object "is to throw things into confusion, that he may 'ride the whirlwind and direct the storm.' "

By early 1792 Senator Burr's political star had risen so high that he stood a good chance of winning the nomination to run for governor of New York as the candidate of either the Federalist party or the Anti-Federalist party. He was personally on good terms with a majority of the lesser Federalist leaders and with many of the major leaders as well. A founder of Tammany Hall, Burr received much well-organized support from artisans, mechanics, and laborers in New York City. Large holders upstate like the Livingstons and many a small farmer were also favorably disposed toward him, as much because he seemed to be an antidote to Hamilton and Schuyler as for any other reason. Even Robert Yates, Hamilton's and Schuyler's early choice to oppose George Clinton for the governorship, seemed favorably disposed toward Burr. Twice before, Chief Justice John Jay had refused to run for elective office; so Hamilton and Schuyler must have been remarkably persuasive with him or with his wife, or with both, to obtain his consent to make the race now. Even so, Jay stipulated that he would not campaign actively and would not "make any efforts to obtain suffrages." He would stand entirely on his reputation for ability and integrity.

A mass meeting of Federalists on February 9, 1792, followed Hamilton's lead and nominated Jay for governor and Stephen Van Rensselaer for lieutenant governor. Judge Yates was persuaded to appear and back the ticket. Hamilton thought he had put down the threat from Burr.

The Anti-Federalists, or Republicans, as they were beginning to call themselves, felt that Senator Burr had a better chance of defeating the formidable Chief Justice Jay than five-term Governor Clinton. After producing the maximum show of support from both sides, Burr announced that he was not a candidate, and Clinton rammed through his own renomination. The remarkable fact that Senator Burr might have won the nomination of either party was not lost on any astute political leader in the country.

The election was close and Hamilton's policies, rather than the merits of two already well-known candidates, became the central issue. Knowing that he and his policies could only cost his own candidates wavering votes from voters in the middle of the political spectrum, Hamilton avowed that he, like Jay, "scrupulously refrained from interference in elections." The nationwide newspaper war between Hamilton and Jefferson had begun. Even the politics of the French Revolution came to be an issue in the New York State election.

After the close of voting on April 13, there were disputed ballots in Otsego, Clinton, and Tioga counties which, if counted, would have resulted in a majority for Jay. A majority of the canvassers, all Clinton supporters, reported that Clinton had been elected by a majority of 108 votes. Philip Schuyler wrote Hamilton on May 9 that if the votes for Jay were fairly canvassed, Jay would prevail, "but I apprehend foul play in the returning officers at least." The canvassers, a joint committee of the senate and assembly, divided along predictable party lines, seven for Clinton to four for Jay. They invited the two senators from New York, Rufus King and Aaron Burr, to furnish them with legal opinions on the result. An opinion that the votes from the three counties could be counted would mean Jay's election. Robert Troup and a group of leading members of the New York bar joined Rufus King, giving it as their legal opinion that the majority of the canvassers were wrong in throwing out the three counties' ballots. Jay had indeed been elected.

Burr took the opposite side, and in a long and legalistic explanation backed Clinton, whom a Republican-dominated board of electors forthwith pronounced to be the new governor. Hamilton's friend Robert Troup said:

"The quibbles of chicanery he made are characteristic of the man . . . and will damn his reputation as a lawyer. . . . We all consider Burr's opinion as such a shameful prostitution of his talents, and so decisive a proof of the real infamy of his character, that we are determined to rip him up."

With this crucial assist from Aaron Burr, to whom he had given his first boost up the political ladder, George Clinton seized the governor's chair for a sixth term.

The more fiery Federalists urged calling a convention to override the decision. There was even loose talk of forcible resistance. But Hamilton set his face firmly against extralegal action by his friends. He advised King on July 25, 1792: "I do not feel it right or expedient to attempt to reverse the decision by any means not known to the Constitution or laws. The precedent may suit us to-day; but to-morrow we may see its abuse.''

And to Jay's wife Sarah's excited and perhaps ambitiously hopeful reports of the rioting in New York in his support, Jay replied that "a few years more will put us all in the dust; and it will then be of more importance to me to have governed *myself* than to have governed the *State*.''

No Founding Father's tombstone boasts a nobler epitaph.

With his old friend John Jay, instead of his perennial foe, George Clinton, secure in the governor's chair for the new term, Hamilton's New York political base would for once have been secure behind him. As the successful state leader, Hamilton would have been in full control of his national party's reins for the national elections of 1792 and after. If only Otsego County's ballots had not been handled by a deputy sheriff, if only they had not been burned, if only Burr's opinion had coincided with Rufus King's, thus assuring Jay's election, a logical series of events would have thrust Hamilton's name to the fore as a candidate for vice-president among the many Federalists who, like Washington himself, were more and more unhappy with Vice-President Adams. As Washington's vice-president in 1792, Hamilton would have stepped into the direct line of succession to the presidency whenever Washington should decide to retire. Only Burr's opinion had blocked the way to his smooth *cursus honorum*.

After King George's minister George Hammond had finally presented his credentials to the secretary of state on November 11, 1791, Jefferson in a stiff and formalistic manner presented Hammond with a list of alleged violations of the peace treaty, listing as principal grievances the continued British retention of the posts on the frontiers, the disputed U.S.-Canada boundary in the area of the St. Croix River, and the British carrying off of American slaves at the end of the war without payment to their owners. During the war thousands of slaves in Virginia and other states had fled to the British, including 22 of Jefferson's. Cornwallis had "carried off" another 30. Of those who fled from Jefferson, 12 had died, and only six had returned to their old master after the war.

The British objected to the continuing harassment of American loyalists and the laws that many states had passed that prevented British merchants and creditors from collecting prewar debts owing to them, debts such as Jefferson owed. As for the freed slaves, Hammond's reasoning was that the peace treaty did not apply to slaves like Jefferson's who had escaped from their masters to freedom by joining the British army. These had "acquired indefeasible rights of personal liberty, of which the British government was not competent to deprive them, by reducing them again to a state of slavery, and to the domination of their ancient masters.'' The treaty called for reparations to slave masters only for slaves that remained "actual property" of their owners at the end of the war. As to slaves "taken" by Cornwallis, there was a question of fact for arbitration. Those that had died would not count. Hammond reported to his superior, Lord Grenville, that in friendly private conversations with Hammond early in January 1792, Hamilton "with respect to the negroes" had "seemed partly to acquiesce in my reasoning upon this point.''

Hamilton had pointedly told Hammond that "this matter did not strike him as an object of such importance as it had appeared to other members of this government.'' Hamilton added that "the surrender of the posts was the only one which could produce any lengthy or difficult investigation.''

No point on which a large slave owner like Jefferson would more violently disagree with

Hamilton, who favored manumission, can be imagined. Hamilton not only threatened his political ambitions, but also to cost him money.

Hamilton was by no means Hammond's only confidant—Senators also leaked him tidbits of confidential information—but Jefferson blamed all on Hamilton. When the Senate held a secret session to ratify ministerial appointments to Great Britain and France, Hammond sent the results along to Grenville. "In the whole course of this discussion," he reported blandly on January 9, 1792, "I have been regularly informed of the proceedings of the Senate, and have received every mark of personal and unreserved confidence."

Jefferson fumed to Washington about Hamilton's secret diplomacy with Hammond and Ternant, but Washington refused to cancel his instructions to Hamilton to continue them.

By May of 1792, Jefferson had finally prepared a harsh and devastating reply to Hammond's list of British grievances that stretched his argument beyond his evidence. He submitted the letter to Madison, Edmund Randolph, and Hamilton for review. Hamilton replied that it went too far, supplying Jefferson with detailed reasons why. For one thing, Jefferson's reply made basic assumptions about American right and British wrong in the dispute. Hamilton pointed out that "the rule in constructing treaties" should be "to suppose both parties in the right, for want of a *common judge.*" Jefferson had tried to vindicate American repudiation of debts to British creditors, ignoring the treaty provision that seemed to protect such creditors. Hamilton advised him that *"Extenuation* rather than *Vindication* would seem to be the desirable course."* Jefferson accepted some of Hamilton's revisions, but insisted on full vindication of all American actions, including repudiation of debts. Ten years later, in April 1802, Hamilton would write that Jefferson's handling of these negotiations with the British seemed designed "to widen, not to heal, the breach between the two countries."

Hammond dispatched Jefferson's letter to his chief, Lord Grenville, accompanied by shocked comments on its "great quantity of irrelevant matter," the "positive denial of many facts," its "unjustifiable insinuations" as to the conduct of His Majesty's ministers subsequent to the peace, "and the general acrimonious stile and manner" of "this extraordinary performance."

In private, Hamilton sought to pour oil on troubled international waters. "After lamenting the intemperate violence of his colleague," reported Hammond to Grenville on June 8, 1792, "Mr. Hamilton assured me that this letter was very far from meeting his approbation, or from containing a faithful exposition of the sentiments of this Government," Hamilton absolved Washington from Jefferson's breach of diplomatic good manners by telling Hammond that Washington had not been aware of Hamilton's reservations, having just returned from Virginia, and "had relied upon Mr. Jefferson's assurance, that it was conformable to the opinions of the other members of the executive government" when he knew it had not been conformable to Hamilton's.

Hamilton's unofficial diplomatic relations, first with Major Beckwith and later with George Hammond, had their counterpart in Jefferson's contacts, through his instrument and go-between, John Beckley, with the British consul in Philadelphia, Sir John Temple. Julian Boyd, the editor of the Jefferson Papers, describes Temple as "vain, garrulous, indiscreet and lavish with exclamation points." He was also rich and, like Jefferson, resentful of the informal contacts between other agents of his own government, Beckwith and Hammond, with Hamilton. On the basis of secondhand reports received from Beckley, Jefferson described His Majesty's consul as a "strong Republican." By way of Beckley, Jefferson received and duly recorded in his *Anas* an amazing report about Hamilton taken from a letter supposedly received by Temple from the highest levels of the British government. It was, Jefferson wrote,

> of the following purport: that the government was well apprised of the predominancy of the British interest in the United States; that they considered Colonel Hamilton, Mr. King and Mr. W. [William Loughton] Smith of South Carolina, as the main supports of that interest; that particularly they considered Colonel Hamilton, and not Mr. Hammond, as the effective minister here; that if the anti-Federal interest [that was his term], at the head of which they considered Jefferson to be, should prevail, these gentlemen *had secured* an asylum to themselves in England.

So, Jefferson wrote—no longer quoting his creature Beckley quoting the local consul—Hamilton, King, and Smith knew they could continue unworried their machinations to change the government because "if they should be overset and choose to withdraw," they could count on the same sort of protection and pension Benedict Arnold had received from Britain.

Polishing up the self-image for posterity that he was creating in his *Anas,* Jefferson at some later time, probably long after Hamilton was dead, added a note: "Impossible as to Hamilton; he was far above that." Jefferson made no such marginal exceptions for the names of Senator Rufus King or Congressman William Loughton Smith of South Carolina, one of Hamilton's supporters in the House who occasionally belabored Jefferson in the press with broadsides over the name of *Scourge*.

Another source of Jefferson's ire was the success Hamilton's economic program was enjoying in Congress. The special relationship by which Congress called directly on the secretary of the treasury for reports permitted Hamilton, unlike other department heads, to introduce legislation and act almost independently of Washington. At Jefferson's behest, Madison introduced a resolution in Congress whereby it would request the president to direct the secretary of the treasury to provide it with information concerning the mode of raising supplies for troops on the Western frontiers; this would create a precedent for putting the president between Hamilton and Congress, like the other department heads. He would then be forced to deal only through Washington. Madison's motion was a call by Hamilton's enemies for a vote of no confidence in him. Madison had even enlisted support from some of Hamilton's habitual followers from motives of their "vanity, self-importance," and so on. Madison's and Jefferson's resolution failed by only four votes.

Such hard-won public victories, like the private agonies Hamilton was now suffering to keep the Reynolds affair secret, had a high personal cost. To his old Virginia friend Carrington, whom he had first known in 1780 when they had served with Arthur St. Clair as American commissioners for prisoner exchanges, Hamilton unburdened himself of a rare flash of inward self-revelation and anguish. When Madison had aimed Jefferson's resolution at him, both of them "well knew that if he had prevailed a certain consequence was my resignation; that I would not be fool enough to make pecuniary sacrifices and endure a life of extreme drudgery, without opportunity to do material good or to acquire reputation." Only the margin of four votes in the House had spared Hamilton the shame of resignation under fire.

In Madison Hamilton now saw:

> a more uniform & persevering opposition than I had been able to resolve into a sincere difference of opinion. Mr. Madison and I, whose politics had formerly so much the same point of departure . . . now diverge widely in our opinions of the

measures which are proper to be pursued. The opinion I once entertained of the candour and simplicity and fairness of Mr. Madisons character has, I acknowledge, given way to a decided opinion that it is one of a peculiarly artificial and complicated kind. . . .

Jefferson was the reason behind Madison's switch: ''Mr. Jefferson manifests his dislike of the funding system generally, calling in question the expediency of funding a debt at all.''

''In various conversations with foreigners as well as citizens,'' Jefferson ''has thrown censure of my principles of government and on my measures of administration. He has predicted that the people would not long tolerate my proceedings & that I should not long maintain my ground.''

Jefferson had delivered his opinion against constitutionality of the bank ''in a stile and manner which I felt as partaking of asperity and ill humour towards me. As one of the trustees of the sinking fund, I have experienced in almost every leading question opposition from him.'' Still worse, Jefferson spread abroad suspicious tales of Hamilton's private life: ''Some of those, whom he immediately and notoriously moves, have even whispered suspicions of the rectitude of my motives and conduct.''

Indeed, Hamilton felt that ''when any turn of things in the community has threatened either odium or embarrassment to me,'' Jefferson ''has not been able to suppress the satisfaction which it gave him. . . .''

Madison's switch had been accounted for not merely by his high regard for Jefferson, but because he was ''seduced'' by the ''expectation of popularity'' and ''advantage to Virginia.''

To Hamilton, the conclusion was inescapable ''that Mr. Madison cooperating with Mr. Jefferson is at the head of a faction decidedly hostile to me and my administration.'' To Hamilton it came naturally enough to refer to ''my administration'' in frank speaking. Jefferson and Madison were ''actuated by views in my judgment subversive of the principles of good government and dangerous to the union, peace and happiness of the country.'' Indeed, if left to their own course, Hamilton thought, ''there would be in less than six months open war between the U. States and Great Britain.''

A principal reason for this danger was that Madison's and Jefferson's ''womanish attachment to France and womanish resentment against Great Britain'' would ''draw us into the closest embrace of France'' and ''involve us in all the consequences of her politics.''

Why such a seemingly unaccountable course of action? As Hamilton saw it, ''Tis evident beyond a question, from every movement, that Mr. Jefferson aims with ardent desire at the Presidential Chair. . . . My influence, therefore, with the community becomes a thing, on ambitions & personal grounds, to be resisted & destroyed.''

Philip Freneau was Jefferson's kept journalist, although Hamilton and his friends, at first, were content to call him nothing worse than a poetaster. The first number of his *National Gazette* had appeared on October 31, 1791, the week after the opening of Congress, shortly after Jefferson and Madison had moved him from New York to Philadelphia, and Jefferson had put him on the State Department payroll under the cover story that he was a translator. Many historians have marked the date of Freneau's first issue as the beginning of party opposition to Washington's administration or, as Hamilton sometimes said, ''my administration.''

By 1792, Freneau's *National Gazette* was making the secretary of the treasury a conspicuous target of opportunity, and guilt by association tarred anyone connected with him. William Duer was blamed for originating the president's monarchical levees, but a deeper sin was his being the "councillor . . . of the S—of the T—." The Society for Establishing Useful Manufactures was fraudulent and worse because it furthered Hamilton's ambition to encourage industry instead of small farmers.

Aside from foreign news, mainly translations from Dutch and French papers, and reports of debates in Congress, Freneau filled his columns with jibes at Federalists, often in the form of reprints from other papers and letters to the editor, some fabricated. Phrases and words like "monarchical party," "monied aristocracy," and "monocrats" appeared so regularly they might have been kept in standing type. Hamilton's funding system came in for regular drubbings that echoed Jefferson's woolly wrongheadedness: "An irredeemable debt . . . is hereditary monarchy in another shape. It creates an influence in the executive part of the government, which will soon render it an overmatch for the legislative. It is the worst species of *King's evil*."

Fenno's *Gazette of the United States* had always been an independent newspaper, although, like most newspapers, it received payments from government departments for space bought for the publication of official notices. It published a wider and better balanced spectrum of political material than Freneau did.

On July 25, 1792, a letter to Fenno's *Gazette* signed *Q* scolded Fenno for reprinting so often "the anti-Federal sentiments with which the *National Gazette* is stuffed." *Q* commented that if Fenno were being paid for advertising the opposition, it was understandable, but that if Fenno were printing material from kept journalists as the other side's views, he would injure the reputation of his own paper.

Hamilton followed up Q's letter over the anonymous initials *T. L:*

> The editor of the *National Gazette* receives a salary from government.
> Quaere.—Whether this salary is paid him for translations or for publications, the design of which is to vilify those to whom the voice of the people has committed the administration of our public affairs. . . . In common life it is thought ungrateful for a man to bite the hand that puts bread in his mouth; but if the man is hired to do it, the case is altered.

Three days later an anonymous Hamilton supporter writing over the name of *Detector* followed up *T. L.* by charging that Freneau's *National Gazette* "is only the tool of a faction,. . . the prostituted vehicle of party spleen and opposition to the . . . principles of order, virtue and religion." The object of Freneau's paper was "to villify and depreciate the government of the United States, to . . . traduce the administration of it" (except for the Department of State).

Was not the editor in pay of a department of the very government he opposed?

Freneau obtained and published an affidavit sworn to before Mayor Matthew Clarkson, saying that he was "at no time urged, advised or influenced [by Jefferson to set up his paper in Philadelphia] but that it was his own voluntary act. . . ." Jefferson's and Madison's private correspondence, of course, shows this affidavit to be false.

Behind the scenes, Jefferson on May 23 had submitted to Washington 21 objections to Hamilton's funding system, which Washington, in no hurry had passed on to Hamilton for reply on July 29, accompanied by a reassuring and sympathetic note saying that "known friends to the government agree that the country is prosperous and happy" but some were "alarmed at that system of policy, and those interpretations of the Constitution" which have taken place in Congress.

Hamilton replied with a long document entitled "Objections and Answers Respecting the

Administration of the Government,'' transmitted to Washington with a short personal note dated August 18. Hamilton's answers by and large repeated all his old rebuttals to all the old charges that had been made for years, threw in some counterthrusts at his opponents for good measure, and gave Washington, like Carrington, a disavowal of any monarchical designs and a further glimpse of troubled inward feelings.

The necessity for a lengthy self-defense to Washington behind the scenes produced some irritation that erupted publicly from Hamilton in the columns of Fenno's *Gazette*. Three public letters, signed *An American,* attacked not only Freneau and the circumstances of his employment, but Jefferson, his employer, as well. Certain letters of Jefferson allegedly showed that he had opposed the Constitution in the beginning and had since opposed every important act of the government of which he pretended to be a part. Jefferson had imported the art of political intrigue learned amid the intrigues of a European court. ''If he disapproves of the government itself, and thinks it deserving of his opposition, can he reconcile it to his own personal dignity, and the principles of probity, to hold an office under it, and employ the means of official influence in that opposition?'' Hamilton asked. Hamilton condemned as transiently expedient, not durably right, Jefferson's 1789 recommendation that the American debt to France be assumed by private individuals in Holland, with American approval, so that if there should be an American default, the loss would fall upon small private holders in Holland, instead of the French court, whose good will seemed more important to Jefferson than the losses of small holders.

A defender of Jefferson, who was probably one or another of Edmund Randolph, Madison, or James Monroe, rushed into print under the name of *Aristides* to answer and counterattack Hamilton, charging that the accusations against Jefferson were ''founded in the basest calumny and falsehood.'' As *Amicus,* Hamilton answered, speaking of himself in the third person. How could it be asserted that he had opposed the Constitution as too republican when, in fact, he was the only delegate from New York who had signed it?

Monroe and Madison weighed in with a series on the *Vindication of Thomas Jefferson.* Hamilton wrote as a man of many parts: *Catullus, Amicus, Metellus, Civis,* and *A Plain Honest Man.* Jefferson remained on the sidelines, shrinking, as always, from public polemics, and let Madison, Randolph, and Monroe as *Aristides* and Freneau as *Mercator* and others scribble polemics for him.

One of Hamilton's greatest weaknesses as a politician was in not allowing supporters like Fenno and *Q* to do battle for him or else ignore attacks; Jefferson's ability to get others to do hatchet jobs for him while professing complete innocence was one of his greatest strengths as a politician.

Hamilton, as *Catullus,* in a peculiarly Roman mode, probably thinking of Jefferson's concubine Sally Hemings or his seduction of John Walker's wife, wrote that the true character of Jefferson would only be revealed ''when the visor of Stoicism is plucked from the brow of the epicurean; when the plain garb of Quaker simplicity is stripped from the concealed voluptuary; when Caesar coyly refusing the proferred diadem, is seen to be Caesar rejecting the trappings by grasping the substance of imperial domination. . . .'' William Loughton Smith of South Carolina, Hamilton's staunchest ally in the House, echoed him as *Scourge*. Jefferson's pretenses had ''long ago excited the derision of many, who know that under the assumed cloak of humility lurks the most ambitious spirit, the most overweening pride and hauteur . . . the *externals* of pure democracy afford but a flimsy veil to the *internal* evidences of aristocratic splendor, sensuality and epicureanism.''

Smith was not above recalling Jefferson's headlong flight before Tarleton's raiders, deserting his post as governor of Virginia, and his pseudoscientific observations that proved the inferiority of blacks:

> Had an inquisitive mind sought for evidence of his Abilities as a Statesman, he would have been referred . . . to certain theoretical principles fit only for Utopia: As a Warrior, to his Exploits at *Monticello;* as a Philosopher, to his discovery of the inferiority of Blacks to Whites, because they are more unsavory and secrete more by the kidnies; as a Mathematician, to his whirligig Chair.

George Washington's own political leanings were strongly Federalist and Hamiltonian, and when Freneau and others attacked Hamilton's measures, which constituted almost the whole legislative program of his executive government, he keenly felt that he himself was under siege. But he was appalled at the public airings of the private differences between members of his cabinet. He had long been aware of them, but he had hoped to keep them private, perhaps even to reconcile them. With all the weight of his character, office, and history, he tried to bring about a truce, sending cautiously phrased appeals to both antagonists. To Hamilton he wrote on August 26:

> Differences in political opinions are as unavoidable, as, to a certain point, they may perhaps be necessary; but it is exceedingly to be regretted, that subjects cannot be discussed with temper on the one hand, or decisions submitted to without having the motives, which led to them, improperly implicated on the other; and this regret borders on chagrin, when we find that men of abilities, zealous patriots, having the same general objects in view, and the same upright intentions to prosecute them, will not exercise more charity in deciding on the opinions and actions of one another.

Hamilton replied on September 9 with due respect and a frank admission of responsibility for some of the milder counterattacks on Jefferson, but declared that he could not recede "for the present." He went into the history of the quarrel and hinted at willingness to resign for the good of the administration, if Jefferson would resign too. "I pledge my honor to you, sir," he added, "that if you shall hereafter form a plan to reunite the members of your administration upon some steady principle of cooperation, I will faithfully concur in executing it during my continuance in office; and I will not directly or indirectly say or do anything that shall endanger a feud." The feud between the two men flourished; nothing would "endanger" its continued existence. Perhaps Hamilton in agitation had really meant to write *engender.*

Jefferson answered Washington on September 9, 1792, with a defense of all his actions, starting off with the old complaint that he had been duped into support of assumption "by the Secretary of Treasury and made a tool for forwarding his schemes, not then sufficiently understood by me." From that low ground he went on to attack all of Hamilton's measures, singling out especially the "Report on Manufactures" as a scheme for corrupting members of Congress so as to have a "corps under the command of the Secretary of Treasury for the purpose of subverting step by step the principles of the constitution. . . ." He complained of Hamilton's interference in his department by discussions of foreign affairs with ministers from abroad. He criticized the attacks on him in Fenno's *Gazette.* He attempted to defend his hiring of Freneau by the incredible statement that he "could not recollect" having urged him to come to Philadelphia. As one member of the Virginia elite to another, he closed with a slash at his young arriviste rival's cloudy pedigree that bespoke bottomless depths of snobbish malevolence:

> I will not suffer my retirement to be clouded by the slanders of a man whose history, from the moment at which history can stoop to notice him, is a tissue of machinations against the liberty of the country which has not only received him and given him bread, but heaped its honors on his head.

Both men had indicated willingness to resign, but each seemed to fear the loss of his own place unless the other lost place, too. Washington induced both to remain. But their feuding sorely tried his temper.

By 1792 Americans were beginning to discover the deep political, economic, and social fissure that Hamilton and other Federalists had tried to paper over for them, but which have divided them ever since. Washington did his best to stand above the partisan fray, insisting that the two avatars of these profound tendencies toward polarization remain in office under him, safely bottled up in his cabinet like two poisonous spiders.

But out in the country, finding themselves on one or the other slope of their continental divide, but still within close range of the opposing lines, Federalists and Anti-Federalists, the latter now often calling themselves Republicans, formed up as skirmishers and laid down an intensifying cross fire of anonymous squibs, cheap shots, slung mud, blind libels, and polemical broadsides. The first big quadrennial state and federal election year—1792—was at hand, setting a familiar pattern for all to follow.

The split was real; the line was drawn. For a while the president and the two antagonists might try to screen it from the public by pseudonyms and surrogates. But a continental rift ran between Hamilton's and Jefferson's followers that would divide them and their successors down to the present day.

John Fiske observed that:

> All American history has since run along the lines marked out by the antagonism of Jefferson and Hamilton. Our history is sometimes charged with a lack of picturesqueness because it does not deal with the belted knight and the moated grange, but to one who considers the moral impact of events, it is hard to see how anything can be more picturesque than the spectacle of these two giant antagonists contending for political measures which were so profoundly to affect the lives of millions of human beings yet unborn.

24

His Power
to Hang
Colonel Hamilton

This is a charge of so serious a nature that it is incumbent on Colo. Hamilton to clear it up.

—George Washington to David Stuart, October 21, 1792

All this naturally gave some uneasiness.

—The Reynolds Pamphlet, August 25, 1797

The prospect of another four years as president filled the 60-year-old Washington with gloom. His health was poor, and his hearing was failing. His factious cabinet seemed about to explode. He was weary of mediating the endless disputes between Hamilton, usually backed by Knox on the one side, and Jefferson, usually seconded by Randolph, on the other. The prospect of slippered ease in retirement at Mount Vernon to bask in the honors heaped upon the nation's great "monocrat" by grateful countrymen beckoned invitingly.

Washington could not delude himself into failing to realize that Hamilton to a significant extent was serving as a lightning rod to draw off on himself mounting Republican criticism of his administration. Much of the polemical abuse of their broadsides against "monocrats" was more applicable to Washington than to Hamilton. Long service with Washington had taught Hamilton never to act without authority from his chief except in the most exigent of circumstances. When he left Philadelphia for Mount Vernon in mid-July 1792, Washington was still undecided on a second term.

In private conversations, Hamilton had urged him to run again. He followed up his urgings by a letter of July 30, 1792, in which his tone to his chief went beyond mere urging. It was as proprietary as his casual references elsewhere to "my administration": "The impression is uniform—that your declining would be deplored as the greatest evil, that could befall the country at the present juncture, and as critically hazardous to your own reputation.'' There was ''evident necessity'' for Washington's continuance because ''the affairs of the national government are not firmly established.'' Furthermore, ''its enemies, generally speaking, are as inveterate as ever. If you quit,''—who but Hamilton would dare accuse Washington of being a quitter—?''much is to be dreaded . . . on patriotic and prudential considerations, the clear path to be pursued by you will be again to obey the voice of your country.''

This was as close to a direct order as anyone ever issued to the father of his country. Washington obeyed. He agreed to run again for president. There would be no question of a rival candidate for the first office.

But the question of the making—or unmaking—of the vice-president in 1792 divided the cabinet. John Adams, the incumbent, was, of course, the Federalists' likeliest candidate. Although Hamilton had reservations about the peppery, crusty old patriot from Massachusetts, he realized that the vigorous Republican opposition springing to life in every state meant that all Federalist energies must be directed toward returning the incumbent to office.

The Republicans recognized that Washington, from the consistent backing he gave to Hamilton's system, his legislative program, and his opinions and from the whole general tenor of his policies, far from being above party, as he sought to appear, was really a Hamiltonian Federalist at heart. Jefferson, the Republican leader, posing as an outsider inside the cabinet and as an insider outside the cabinet, knew this better than anyone else. But he was not disposed to squander growing Republican strength in direct attacks on the aging national hero who would not be in his way forever. Republicans would concentrate on unseating the equally aging Adams, a less conspicuous and more vulnerable target. If they should lose, it would matter little in either the short or long run. For Jefferson's own presidential ambitions, if Jefferson himself could not displace Adams, it would probably be better for Adams to remain in office than for a younger Republican or Federalist to replace him and thus threaten Jefferson's own place in the line of succession behind him.

The first to announce for Adams's place was the perennial candidate, Governor George Clinton of New York, who had just squeaked through to a sixth term by his disputed victory over Jay on the strength of Aaron Burr's legal opinion.

By September 9, Hamilton was becoming alarmed at Adams's overconfident absence from Philadelphia and his apparent inattention to the threat to him and the Federalists posed by Clinton's candidacy. He warned, ''I learnt with pain that you may not probably be here till late in the session. . . . it best suits the firmness and elevation of your character to meet all events, whether auspicious or otherwise, on the ground where station & duty call you.''

To the tone of respectful command with which Hamilton had bidden Washington to obey his duty, Hamilton added a touch of asperity in his summons to Adams to bestir himself: ''One would not give the ill disposed the triumph of supposing that an anticipation of want of success had kept you from your post. . . . it is the universal wish of your friends you should be as soon as possible at Philadelphia.''

News of a second, more formidable opposition candidate than Clinton soon darkened Hamilton's impatience with Adams to anger. On September 17, Rufus King wrote Hamilton the news that Aaron Burr's hat was also in the ring and that he stood a good chance of winning. ''Burr is industrious in his canvass, and his object is well understood by our Antis. Should Jefferson and his friends unite in the project, the votes of Mr. A. may be so reduced, that though more numerous than those of any other person, he may decline the office.''

Clinton was an old, stubborn, well-known, but self-limiting quantity; but Burr was another matter. He was young—only a year older than Hamilton—brilliant, able, vigorous, and with a good war record, at least in his public image. Hamilton wrote back to King on September 23, "Even now I am to be convinced that the movement is anything more than a diversion in favor of Mr. Clinton. Yet on my part it will not be neglected. . . . A good use will be made of it in this state."

Hamilton's "good" partisan use of King's news consisted of a series of letters to friends around the country in which he attacked Burr not merely as a politician, but as a private man. He attacked his probity, his honor, his honesty, and his personal life, calling him by names that might well have brought on a challenge to a duel some 12 years before the actual event. Mr. Clinton, Hamilton wrote to one correspondent, was

> a man of property, and in private life, as far as I know, of probity, . . . [but] . . . Mr. Burr's integrity as an individual is not unimpeached. As a public man, he is one of the worst sort—a friend to nothing but as it suits his interest and ambition. Determined to climb *per fas aut nefas* to the highest honors of the State, and as much higher as circumstances may permit; he cares for nothing about the means of affecting his purpose. . . . In a word, if we have an embryo-Caesar in the United States, 'tis Burr.

To another he wrote that Burr "is unprincipled, both as a public and a private man. . . . Embarrassed, as I understand, in his circumstances, with an extravagant family, bold, enterprising, and intriguing, I am mistaken if it be not his object to play a game of confusion." Hamilton added, "I pledge my character for discernment, that it is incumbent upon every good man to resist the present design." He concluded: "I feel it to be a religious duty to oppose his career."

Burr professed friendship for Hamilton; Jefferson and others were openly opponents. Yet toward none of the latter did Hamilton's language convey the same apprehensive enmity as the language he used about a Burr. The language carries undertones of danger and even fear, but none of contempt. Hamilton must have known despicable things about Burr that almost no one else knew. What could conjure up in Hamilton toward Burr but toward no one else "a religious duty to oppose his career"?

To men of affairs like himself who were only formally religious, Hamilton's emotional overreaction in these letters would be largely counterproductive of the political effect they were intended to induce. They are uncharacteristic of the usual urbane, matter-of-fact epistolary style Hamilton used when writing political allies who were not intimate friends. They are difficult to account for except by speculating that by now Hamilton had heard whispers, perhaps from Maria or James Reynolds, that Burr had contrived or abetted the plot in which he was now so deeply entangled.

Hamilton knew that he would be a "fool to make pecuniary sacrifices and endure a life of extreme drudgery, without opportunity to do material good or acquire reputation." The money Reynolds was extracting from him, the extreme emotional and physical anxieties the affair was costing him, and the possibility of its public exposure at any time constantly threatened to make of him just such a fool. Resignation from office could not save him. If Burr were indeed the trigger of the plot—there is no direct evidence that he was—Burr and the Reynoldses now held hostage all the things in life that mattered most to Hamilton. If so, it is easy to understand the shockingly apocalyptic tone of Hamilton's statements about Burr that is so difficult to account for in any other way.

Hamilton continued to receive weird letters from Maria and James Reynolds on and on through 1792, repeating with incredible variations the same basic cycle of her professions of love for Hamilton and James's sullen, but complaisant, cuckoldry. There were a total of 22 by Hamilton's numbering, the last being dated August 30, 1792. In it, James, still professing outrage, was still demanding from Hamilton small sums of hush money. Hamilton wrote some notes replying to one or the other of the Reynoldses, and these became the most damaging part of the case the prosecution would bring against him. But Hamilton's impassioned epistolary campaign against Burr had less to do with the outcome of the 1792 election than other agencies that were at work.

Down in Virginia a protégé of Jefferson with ambitions of his own also had misgivings about Burr's sudden ascendancy. James Monroe wrote Madison on September 18, "He is too young, if not in point of age, yet upon the public theatre, to admit the possibility of a union in his favor."

To head off Burr's candidacy, Monroe suggested that he be given soothing assurances of esteem and confidence and that opposition to his nomination be placed "solely on his youth and late arrival on the national scene." Adams was 64; Clinton, 53; Jefferson, 49; Madison, 42; Burr, 36; and Monroe and Hamilton, 35. Time would take care of Adams and Clinton as competitors of the Virginia junto for the presidency; but if Burr were allowed into the direct line of presidential succession, such a formidable adversary would block Old Dominion ambition for years to come. They would stick with Clinton.

Jefferson had also been mentioned as a vice-presidential possibility, but with Washington as the unanimous choice for president, two Virginians on the ticket would be one too many for electors from the other 12 states to swallow. Jefferson, who loved to tinker with mechanisms, years later confided to his *Anas* that he considered Burr "as a crooked gun, or other perverted machine, whose aim or shot you could never be sure of." Such a gun would be useful enough—at short range—to hit a Hamilton, but for little else. It might have been a coincidence, although more likely it was a cover, that Jefferson's very close, newly converted Republican friend, Dr. Benjamin Rush, chose just this time of feverish political excitement to put into the record a direct call for aid to Aaron Burr—by way of Jefferson's usual instrument for intrigue, John Beckley.

"This letter will be handed to you by Mr. Beckley," Dr. Rush wrote to Burr from Philadelphia on September 24, 1792. "He possesses a fund of information about men and things." Dr. Rush enjoined Burr warmly: "Your friends everywhere look to you to take an active part in removing the monarchical rubbish of our government. It is time to speak out, or we are undone."

Jefferson could hardly have found a better go-between to introduce John Beckley to Aaron Burr than Dr. Rush. Theodosia Burr's failing health was increasingly on Burr's mind. In New York she had the attention of Dr. Samuel Bard, whom Washington had consulted as his physician there, but when in Philadelphia, Burr constantly got second opinions from Dr. Rush.

Nothing seems less likely than that after Burr had spent a year in Philadelphia as a senator, an elaborate letter of introduction from Dr. Rush would have been necessary to introduce Beckley to him unless a need was felt for a cover.

Few conversations of the period could have been more fateful for Hamilton's future than the one which ensued in New York between Beckley and Burr concerning the "active part" Jefferson and Dr. Rush wanted Burr to take "in removing the monarchical rubbish of our government."

On September 27, 1792, Jefferson left Monticello for Philadelphia and stopped on the way at Mount Vernon for a long morning's conversation with Washington, only a day or two after Washington had received King's and Hamilton's warnings about Burr's presidential candidacy. Each Virginian as usual expatiated on his preference for his plantation to public office. Washington spoke of his concern about the differences between Jefferson and Hamilton. He dismissed as nonsense Jefferson's fears of a monarchy. There were not, he scoffed, "ten men in the United States whose opinions were worth anything, who entertained such a thought." No, Jefferson argued, there were many more than he imagined, mentioning specifically the names of Hamilton and Schuyler. Weary old Washington ended the dispute with "another exhortation" that Jefferson not decide too positively on early retirement. Jefferson returned the compliment. By the time Jefferson reached Philadelphia on October 5, the backstage maneuvering was reaching a feverish pitch. A new political party was being organized in a tangible way by the process of selecting its first candidate for national office and putting off another by a deal promising future support.

Many important Republicans—who did not look upon Burr as a threat to their own ambitions—pressed his candidacy over Clinton's now. But the power struggle between them was resolved at a key Republican caucus held in Philadelphia the night of October 16 that no one later mentioned except John Beckley, who reported it to Madison the following day:

> A meeting which was had last evening between Melancthon Smith on the part of the republican interest of N.Y. (specially deputed) and on the principal movers of the same interest here (Pennsylvania), to conclude *finally and definitely* as to the choice of a V.P.—the result of which was, unanimously, to exert every endeavor for Mr. Clinton, and to drop all thought of Mr. Burr.

Beckley added that Colonel Burr had assured him "that he would cheerfully support the measure of removing Mr. A[dams] & lend every aid in his power to C[linton]'s election.

Obviously, Beckley had helped arrange a deal with Burr whereby Burr would release his powerful New York and Pennsylvania support to join in support of Clinton—for a high political price. After the presidential election of 1796, Burr claimed that his price had been the promise of support by the Virginians in 1796 and that the Virginians had reneged on the deal. Burr stood by his side of the deal in 1792. Washington was unanimously reelected on December 5. Adams was reelected, but rebuked with only 77 votes out of a possible 132. The Republican alliance between New York and Virginia held firm, contributing its full share of 50 votes to Clinton. Jefferson got four votes, and Burr received only one, from a friend in South Carolina.

To no one's real surprise, except possibly Rufus King's, the humiliation of having so many votes withheld did not cause John Adams to refuse to serve again as vice-president. Instead of being downcast at his own amazingly small total of a single vote, Aaron Burr, when he returned for the new term, exuded all the serene confidence of a man who held a large political due bill still uncashed—as well as an unsuspected trump card yet unplayed.

The Federalists' genuine preelection alarm over Burr's candidacy and the powerful support he received from moneyed Republicans of New York and Pennsylvania made the total defection of Northern votes from his candidacy in the final tally and the reality of the deal behind it embarrassingly obvious. Hamilton did not credit his own impassioned private epistolary attacks on Burr with more than a minor part in this remarkable result. By some letters written suggesting that Adams be rebuked for monarchical views by the withholding of some votes from him, but not enough to defeat him, Jefferson kept his own political flanks well covered.

John Beckley was in his element in smoke-filled rooms full of political intrigue out of which came such curious results.

With the immediate threat from Burr put down, Hamilton remained the chief target of Anti-Federalist opportunity. John Beckley knew that nothing would make his masters happier than some publishable scandal about the fountainhead of all "monarchical rubbish." Beckley wrote Madison that William Heth, a disgruntled collector of customs on the James River who knew Hamilton, had told him that Hamilton considered Madison to be "his *personal & political* enemy."

Beckley dug up and trotted to Jefferson another tidbit about Hamilton that to Jefferson was damning enough to record in his *Anas*. On November 19, 1792, "Beckley brings me the pamphlet written by Hamilton, before the war, in answer to Common Sense. It is entitled 'Plain Truth.' "

To Jefferson, Hamilton's differences with Tom Paine meant he was guilty of less than wholehearted support of the Revolution. Only malevolent hostility would grasp at such a farfetched imputation in the face of Hamilton's known pamphlets like *The Farmer Refuted*, defending the patriot cause, his defense of Rivington, his war record, and the fact that Beckley's proffered tidbit was more than 15 years stale.

Writing Madison on October 17, 1792, Beckley curried favor by crying down Hamilton in a way that paid unwitting tribute to Hamilton as only an enemy could. With more precision and eloquence than any Federal eulogist had yet brought to Hamilton's achievement, Beckley wrote,

> It would be wise to "be watchful," [because] there is no inferior degree of sagacity in the combinations of this *extraordinary* man. With a comprehensive eye, a subtle and contriving mind, and a soul devoted to his object, all his measures are promptly and aptly designed, and like the links of a chain, dependent on each other, acquire additional strength by their union & concert.

In August the Jacobins had seized control of the French government, suspended King Louis XVI, and imprisoned the royal family; in September the national convention of the people had abolished all monarchs and royalty; in October the people's national assembly of the French Republic bestowed on Hamilton the title of honorary citizen of France.

Other revolutionary friends of the common man that the French people found to be worthy of honor were Joseph Priestley, Thomas Paine, Jeremy Bentham, William Wilberforce, N. Pestalozzi, Thaddeus Kosciuszko, George Washington, and "N. Maddisson [*sic*]." Jefferson, who had lived in royal luxury at the Hôtel de Langeac, was no such friend.

The citation, addressed to Hamilton as "M. Jean Hamilton," recited that Hamilton had consecrated his arms and waking hours to defend the cause of the people against the despotism of kings, to banish prejudice from the earth, to push back the limitations on human attainments, and done three more fulsome paragraphs of other right-minded revolutionary things. Now officially certified by the godless revolutionists as one of only three American champions of the rights of man, Hamilton jokingly jotted on the back of the elaborate certificate, underscoring the word *Christian*, "Letter from Government of French Republic transmitting me a Diploma of citizenship mistaking the *Christian* name."

It might have been a good joke on Jefferson to send him a copy.

On second thought, Hamilton would discard the idea of any such joke. An attempt to josh Jefferson out of his favorite libel by showing him such a testimonial from the people's revolution would probably jar his malevolent ire more than his sense of irony.

Harvard College, an institution that had been rating performances a century and a half longer than the French National Assembly, awarded the honorary degree of Doctor of Laws to Hamilton—and to two other popular revolutionaries—John Hancock and Samuel Adams.

On September 10, Hamilton's old friend and inquiring correspondent Henry Lee reminded him that he had already paid Lee ten guineas he owed him of "which perhaps you may have forgot," for the purchase of a horse, and returned ten guineas Hamilton had absentmindedly sent him. Just now Hamilton needed a ten guinea increment to his private credit more than the two parchment increment to his public.

John Beckley went back to Jacob Clingman looking for more anti-Hamilton gossip to bring to his master Jefferson and this time struck gold—or at least a paper money scandal. Clingman had just been named as one of the three defendants in a law suit brought on November 16, 1792 by Oliver Wolcott, Jr., as comptroller and auditor of the Treasury, for suborning perjury to defraud the government of more than $400. Clingman had been released on bail the same day he was arrested, but his codefendants, one John Delabar—and one James Reynolds—remained in the Philadelphia jail. Languishing there, Reynolds was snarling to Clingman, and anyone else who would listen, that "he had it in his power to hang Col. Hamilton." He intended to retain a tough New York lawyer to help him out.

Four hundred dollars was not a huge sum of money, even in those days, but Wolcott, who was for all practical purposes Hamilton's first assistant and alter ego in the Treasury, had a keen sense of public office as a public trust, and was rigorous in prosecuting alleged frauds against the Treasury—his prosecution of Duer to recover the $200,000 shortage in Duer's accounts as secretary of the old Board of Treasury had led to Duer's crash and the widespread financial panic of that spring. When Wolcott reported to Hamilton that Reynolds in jail was threatening "to make disclosures injurious to the character of some head of a department," Hamilton angrily instructed Wolcott to "take no step toward a liberation of Reynolds, while such a report existed and remained unexplained." This would bring on Hamilton an explanation from Reynolds's lawyer soon enough.

With the trial date only about three weeks away, Clingman decided to tell all to his employer, Frederick A.C. Muhlenberg, the Speaker of the House; a former clergyman; a moderate Federalist; a man generally respected for his honesty, impartiality, and good judgment.

Jacob Clingman was a prepossessing young man but he had collaborated with James Reynolds in at least one earlier scheme that had made fraudulent use of lists wrongfully leaked from the Treasury Department. Clingman had seen Hamilton at the Reynoldses' house on several occasions, had joined in conversation with him there, and would succeed him as one of Maria's lovers. He would soon become the star witness for the Congressional investigating committee headed by Muhlenberg that would construct the case for the impeachment of Hamilton. Muhlenberg agreed to help him out.

As Speaker of the House, Muhlenberg was Clerk John Beckley's immediate superior. Now Clingman's story would have backing in the highest political circles without any extra nudges from Beckley or Dr. Rush. Although Muhlenberg was acquainted with Reynolds, and Clingman had appealed to him both "on behalf of himself and Reynolds," Muhlenberg rather pointedly avoided involvement with Reynolds, saying "not being particularly acquainted with Reynolds [I] in a great measure declined so far as respected him." Muhlenberg did take one small measure in behalf of Reynolds that had great significance: he "waited on Col. Hamilton" to discuss the matter "in company with Col. Burr." When

Muhlenberg's and Burr's presence in his waiting room was announced, Hamilton, guessing at their mission, must have been horrified.

Muhlenberg set down a contemporaneous written statement, dated December 13, 1792, recording these events. His statement marks Burr's first recorded appearance in the Reynolds case, whatever may have been his unrecorded role earlier. Muhlenberg does not say who requested Burr to accompany him—whether Muhlenberg or Clingman or Reynolds, or whether Burr invited himself. Nor does Muhlenberg say why Burr accompanied him or in what capacity; Muhlenberg's statement is elliptically casual and matter-of-fact and says nothing more of Burr's role. Muhlenberg makes it clear that his own good offices extended only to Clingman, "who had hitherto sustained a good character." As to Reynolds, Muhlenberg said he had information that confirmed his decision that "I could not undertake to recommend Reynolds; as I verily believed him to be a rascal." But to Burr, Reynolds would be a New Yorker in a jam, with money, a beauteous wife, and an interesting tale to tell about the man who had been writing their mutual friends that he had a "religious duty" to oppose Burr's career.

Clingman had asked Maria Reynolds for any letters she had from Hamilton because "he might probably use them to obtain her husband's liberty." She had told him Hamilton had asked her to burn all letters that were signed and in his hand, and she had done so. But Clingman had pressed her for some scrap of written evidence. She searched about and found and gave Clingman "two or three" unsigned notes, which she identified as being from Hamilton. A brilliant trial lawyer like Burr would know how to make devastating use of them. Confronted by them during Muhlenberg's and Burr's surprise visit to his office, a brilliant trial lawyer like Hamilton would not have smooth impromptu explanations.

One note said merely, "Tomorrow what is requested will be done. 'T will hardly be possible to-day." This was an answer to a note of Reynolds asking for a loan "today," Hamilton explained. "A scarcity of cash which was not very uncommon," said Hamilton, had "modelled the reply."

A letter from Reynolds of June 1792 had solicited from Hamilton "a *loan* of three hundred dollars towards a subscription to the *Lancaster Turnpike*." Here seemed to be prima facie evidence of Hamilton's speculation in securities through the agency of Reynolds. Reynolds had told Burr and Clingman that Hamilton refused the $300 loan by the following note, which Burr showed Hamilton: "It is utterly out of my power, I assure you 'pon my honor, to comply with your request. Your note is returned."

Hamilton angrily pointed out that his letter "demonstrates, that here was no concern in speculation on my part—that the money is asked as a *favor* and as *loan,* to be reimbursed simply and without profit in *less than a fortnight*. My answer shows that even the loan was refused."

Reynolds had boasted to Clingman that if he wanted money, Hamilton was "obliged to let him have it," because "he had it in his power to hang Col. Hamilton." Clingman had occasionally lent money to Reynolds himself and did not worry about repayment because Reynolds claimed "that he could always get it from Col. Hamilton to repay it." On one occasion, Clingman lent Reynolds $200, which Reynolds promised to repay him "through the means of Col. Hamilton." One day Clingman went with Reynolds and saw him go in to Hamilton's house, and after Reynolds came out, he paid Clingman $100. This, Reynolds said, was part of the sum he had got from Hamilton. When Reynolds paid Clingman the balance a few days later, he again told Clingman that it came from Colonel Hamilton "after his return from Jersey, having made a visit to the manufacturing society there."

Hamilton would admit making two payments of $100 each, explaining that Reynolds had demanded the money from him for ''furnishing a small boardinghouse, which Reynolds and his wife were, or pretended to be, about to set up.''

One of Hamilton's other notes to Reynolds said merely, ''My dear sir, I expected to have heard the day after I had the pleasure of seeing you.'' To Hamilton, ''this fragment, if truly a part of a letter to Reynolds, denotes nothing more than a disposition to be civil to a man whom, as I said before, it was the interest of my passions to conciliate. But I verily believe it was no part of a letter to him, because I do not believe that I ever addressed him in such a style.''

More likely, Hamilton thought, Reynolds had stolen from his office a letter he had started to write to someone else and then thrown away. Reynolds had procured it ''by means of which I am ignorant, or it may have been the beginning of an intended letter, torn off, thrown into the chimney in my office, which was a common practice, and there, or after it had been swept out, picked up by Reynolds, *or some coadjutor of his.*''

But if ''some coadjutor'' of Reynolds were still employed in the Treasury Department at the time Hamilton wrote these notes, then Hamilton had slipped into a self-damaging admission. He went on to admit that *''there appears to have been more than one clerk in the department somehow connected with him.''* Apparently, there was more than one ''coadjutor'' of Reynolds still in the department. One of these suspected coadjutors may have been the ''Simeon'' Reynolds of Connecticut, who was a clerk in the register's office, or Andrew Fraunces. Writing his public account in 1797, Hamilton failed to follow up or explain away this cold trail of other crooked coadjutors. Instead, he turned to the task of discrediting the last of the fragments of correspondence in his own hand with which his accusers confronted him.

The sixth fragment was, ''The person Mr. Reynolds inquired for on Friday waited for him all evening at his house, from a little after seven. Mr. R. may see him at any time to-day or to-morrow, between the hours of two and three.''

Hamilton explained this away too with almost too much subtlety: ''Mrs. Reynolds more than once communicated to me that Reynolds would occasionally relapse into discontent at his situation, would treat her very ill, hint at the assassination of me, and more openly threaten, by way of revenge, to inform Mrs. Hamilton.'' Hamilton expressed his reaction to this in a majestic—or laughable—understatement: ''All this naturally gave some uneasiness.''

Five years later, Hamilton professed to be confused. Was it ''artifice or reality''? ''In the workings of human inconsistency it was very possible that the same man might be corrupt enough to compound for his wife's chastity, and yet have sensibility enough to be restless in the situation and to hate the cause of it.''

The series of notes between the Reynoldses and himself explained the entire matter of his payments to Reynolds, Hamilton avowed. He was the victim of someone's plot against him. ''The endeavor . . . to induce me to render my visits to Mrs. Reynolds more public, and the great care with which my [six] little notes were preserved, justify the belief that at a period before it was attempted, the idea of implicating me in some accusation, with a view to the advantage of the accusers, was entertained. Hence the motive to pick up and preserve any fragment which might favor the idea of friendly or confidential correspondence.'' But Maria had said she burned all of Hamilton's letters, except these six fragments!

Muhlenberg commended Clingman to Hamilton for the good character he had had, at least until falling in with Reynolds. The record is silent as to what Burr said to Hamilton about Reynolds—or whether the senator's cold eye betrayed even a glint of amusement at his old rival's embarrassment. *Les grandes âmes se soucient peu des petits moraux.*

What lay behind Burr's little-noticed visit with Muhlenberg to Hamilton's office? The obvious explanation is that Reynolds, immediately upon being arrested by Wolcott, retained Burr as his counsel. Reynolds would know Burr from New York, and that he was reputed to be the wiliest lawyer at the bar for delicate causes, enjoyed beautiful women like Maria and, while affably professing friendship for Hamilton, did not seem to be in the prosecution's camp. For Muhlenberg, there was no way to make it clearer that his intercession was limited to Clingman only than to bring Burr along as counsel for Reynolds. Only if Burr were present as Reynolds's counsel would his presence on this tense occasion not require more extended explanations by Muhlenberg, Clingman, Burr, or Hamilton. The obvious explanation would also serve nicely to cover Burr's presence at this critical juncture of the underplot hatched in New York the summer before last during the hunting down of the Hessian fly.

Whether Hamilton confessed anything more—or anything at all—to Muhlenberg and Burr concerning his payments to the Reynoldses is not known. It would be surprising if Clingman and Reynolds had failed to prime their high-priced counsel with all they knew to alert them to telltale clues in Hamilton's responses. Hamilton would say as little as possible to avoid saying too much. For Hamilton it must have been the second most horrifying confrontation with Burr of his life. It is easy to speculate that something that passed between them at this meeting in his office was the "despicable" something that would lead to their last confrontation 12 years later.

Showing Muhlenberg and Burr to the door, Hamilton would smoothly suggest that they discuss the matter further with Wolcott who had initiated the prosecutions. He would return to the chair behind his desk and bury his head in his hands for a moment, then briskly send for Wolcott to come at once, without seeing any callers first, no matter how important. "All this naturally gave some uneasiness."

25

A Concatenation of Cover-ups

We left him under an impression our suspicions were removed.

—Senator James Monroe, Sunday, December 16, 1792

Wolcott's suit against Reynolds, Clingman, and John Delabar for the $400 alleged that Reynolds would obtain from the Treasury Department a list of the names and amounts the government owed to living individuals. He or Clingman would find someone like Delabar, who would falsely swear to the register, or probate clerk, that the living individual was dead and that Clingman was the dead man's next of kin or assignee of the next of kin. Clingman would collect the money, pay part of it to Delabar for his false swearing and another part to Reynolds for the use of his list, and pocket the balance.

Wolcott's suit charged that Reynolds, Clingman, and Delabar had obtained letters of administration in this manner on the estate of one Ephraim Goodanough, who was very much alive.

Maria Reynolds later told Richard Folwell in her own inimitable way how Clingman and Reynolds had bungled the fraud, been caught, and been brought to justice. After safely pocketing the money collected from the government, they had turned the administration bond over to the real heir to permit him to commit a second fraud by collecting from the bondsman a second time. The real heir got cold feet and turned them in for fraud. As Maria described it, they "*incautiously* and *imprudently* having given the Heir-Apparent an indemnifying Bond, when the Soldier came to life, the Administration delivered the indemnifying Bond up to the real Heir, [and] was detected." To Maria, the moral was that the small-time crooks should not have tried to collect twice for the same trick. As Maria told

360

the story to Folwell, the hilarious moment when "the soldier came to life" conveys a little of the flavor of the earthy charm by which she entrapped Hamilton and so many others.

Just as Maria finished telling Folwell the sad tale, Jacob Clingman had walked into her parlor, and Maria introduced him to Folwell. As Folwell recalled, "She referred to [Clingman] for a more correct Narrative." But he was so ashamed of himself that "his Conversation seemed to me as if he wished to darken instead of throwing Light on this Information."

Then Clingman asked Maria "what Luck she had in her applications for Reynolds's Liberation" from jail. According to Folwell, Maria replied that she had "called on the Governor, Mr. Mifflin, and that he felt for her." He had "referred her to Mr. Dallas and that he felt also." She had then "called on Mr. Hamilton, and several other Gentlemen; and that they had all felt."

Tactile sympathy as well comes through in Maria's telling of the coincidence of so many gentlemenly feelings for her. It seemed no coincidence to Folwell that "In a few Days after Reynolds was liberated." Folwell owlishly explains that this was "possibly in consequence of the Coincidence of Sympathy these Gentlemen had in Feeling."

With this brief glimpse, Folwell closes the only extant first-hand account of domestic doings at the Reynoldses besides Hamilton's with the line, "Here the curtain dropt from my view."

Muhlenberg next paid a call on Wolcott, probably without Burr, because he told Wolcott, "I verily believe [Reynolds] to be a rascal." But it was not lost on Wolcott that the notes in Hamilton's hand which corroborated Clingman's story were the basis for a damning case against Hamilton—especially in the hands of a clever trial lawyer like Aaron Burr, or a newspaper reporter like Freneau.

When they came to Hamilton's explanation for the note that said merely, "My dear sir, I expected to have heard the day after I had the pleasure of seeing you,"—that Reynolds had forged, fabricated, or stolen the note *and had a collaborator in the department*—Wolcott would be aghast all over again.

Another clerk in the department connected with Reynolds leaking him letters and lists? This would be an indiscreet slip of Hamilton's tongue likely to hang him. Why had not such another "coadjutor" of Reynolds been rooted out of the department? It was just as well for Wolcott to go over the whole defense story carefully with Hamilton at once. Even so, the fateful slip about Reynolds's "coadjutor" slipped into the story Hamilton wrote out for the public in 1797.

Hamilton's explanation conflicted sharply with Clingman's. Far from saving all the many letters Hamilton had written her, Maria had burned all but these few fragments. Far from preserving them and thrusting them upon Clingman to corroborate a preconceived plot to blackmail Hamilton, she believed she had burned them all. She had found only these fragments for Clingman when he demanded that she scour the house for them. This kind of contradiction could hardly stand exposure to public airing at a trial.

Clingman was telling Muhlenberg that he had urged Reynolds to seek Hamilton's aid, that Reynolds had done so, and that Hamilton had advised Reynolds to "keep out of the way, a few days, and the matter would be settled."

After being taken into custody, Reynolds had also applied to Andrew G. Fraunces, the clerk and ubiquitous marplot who had replied to Reynolds that Hamilton had threatened him with discharge if he made any effort to help Reynolds out of jail.

Clingman had then urged Maria Reynolds to appeal to Hamilton, and she told him she had already done so. Besides, she said, she had even received some more hush money from Hamilton after her husband's imprisonment. She also told him that Hamilton had advised her to go see Wolcott, but not to mention Hamilton's name. She had done so, but had nevertheless disclosed Hamilton's name—thereby, she said, surprising Wolcott. Wolcott had promised her he would consult Hamilton.

Wolcott must have been appalled at what he had done. Upon charges that he had brought, a public trial of Reynolds and Clingman was now set down for the third Monday in December. If defense counsel for Reynolds should call Reynolds or Maria or Clingman to the stand and question them about leaked Treasury lists, and then bring in evidence of Hamilton's payments to Reynolds or Maria, his prosecution could backfire on Hamilton himself.

Newspapers enjoyed a limited privilege to report testimony given at a trial, even if false, without fear of libel suits. Anti-Hamilton papers like Freneau's *National Gazette* would have a field day telling the sordid tale of Hamilton's affair in the convincing form of a deadpan report of the trial. But without a trial to report, no newspaper would dare print a word about the scandal. It would remain a secret kept from the general public by the strict laws of libel. Obviously a public trial of Wolcott's charges was unthinkable. Hamilton's public credit would have to be saved by a plea bargain.

At a second meeting with Muhlenberg, Wolcott stipulated that (1) if "a certain List of Money due to individuals which Reynolds and Clingman were said to have in their Possession" should be delivered up and (2) if Clingman should name the person in the public offices from whom it was obtained, his request for release "might perhaps be granted with greater Propriety." Plugging the leak, recovering the leaked information, and discovering the source of the leak had been the larger purpose behind Wolcott's prosecution. The jailing of two or three clumsy small-time crooks had been his means to accomplish this, but not an end in itself. The list and the name of the faithless insider were the two key pieces of evidence.

Clingman testified that Reynolds "had books containing the amount of cash due the Virginia Line, at his own house at New York, with liberty to copy, [that] were obtained through Mr. Duer." But Duer had left the Treasury in 1790 before the move to Philadelphia. Lists obtained through Duer would by now be more than two and a half years old, dangerously out of date for purposes of fraud, made so partly by the notarization requirements and other formalities imposed by way of Bland's resolutions.

Wolcott thought Reynolds and Clingman were lying in placing all guilt on Duer, a gentleman who would hardly stoop to such small-scale skulduggery. Wolcott strongly suspected that Duer's name was only a red herring or a cover for someone who was still on the Treasury payroll—as Hamilton's slip had suggested. Did Hamilton already know what Wolcott now only suspected—that Reynolds's coadjutor was still employed at the Treasury?

Muhlenberg passed word back to Clingman that Wolcott was making no promises, but that he would regard his case in a much more favorable light if he would give up the list and also the real name of the person from whom he had obtained it.

Maria Reynolds passed on to Clingman a slightly different method of obtaining his release that she had heard from Hamilton. Clingman "should write a letter to Mr. Wolcott, and a duplicate of the same to himself, promising to give up the list and refund the money." The significant difference between Hamilton's stipulation and Wolcott's was that Wolcott had demanded to know the name of the man who was the leak, whereas Hamilton did not demand the name. If Hamilton already knew the guilty man's name, it would, of course, be unnecessary for Clingman to tell him.

Clingman agreed to the bargain. He would repay the money, give up the lists, and "disclose the name of the person *in the utmost confidence.*" He hoped this would cause Wolcott to drop the prosecution. Clingman's plea bargain made no mention of Reynolds, but it was understood that Clingman also spoke for his accomplice, who was still in jail. Muhlenberg was informed that Clingman had agreed to the deal, that the actions against both men would be dropped, and that Reynolds would be released. This ended Muhlenberg's role as sponsor for his clerk, but not his curiosity about Hamilton's true role.

Wolcott, on his part, informed the attorney general of Pennsylvania that an important discovery had been made, and a plea bargain had been struck "by which it could be rendered useful to the public in preventing future frauds." The Commonwealth dismissed the prosecutions. Wolcott explained why he had agreed to the deal to free both men and drop the case:

> The infidelity was committed by a clerk in the office of the Register—Mr. Duer resigned his office in March, 1790 . . . the clerk who furnished the lists was first employed in Philadelphia in January 1791. The Accounts from which the lists were taken, were all settled at the Treasury subsequent to the time last mentioned; on the discovery . . . the Clerk was dismissed, and has not since been employed in the public offices. The name of the Clerk . . . has not been publicly mentioned for a reason which appears in Clingman's letter but if the disclosure is found necessary to the vindication of an innocent character, it shall be made.

The only reason "which appears in Clingman's letter" is that Clingman insisted he had disclosed the name of the clerk to Wolcott "in the utmost confidence." What did Clingman care about such secrecy? How could he impose such a secrecy requirement on his prosecutors? Why would not Wolcott and Hamilton gain great public credit for rigor and make a useful example by announcing publicly that a vigilant Treasury Department had stumbled upon corruption within its ranks, and rooted it out? Why all the secrecy?

Treasury Department records indicate that on Monday, December 17, 1792, the date scheduled for the trial, the same date Jefferson jotted down his note in his *Anas*, the employment of one "Simeon" Reynolds as a clerk in the register's office of the Treasury Department ceased. He had first been employed in January 1791. Hamilton's affair with Maria Reynolds had commenced a little later that same year, according to Hamilton. The first appearance of the name Simeon Reynolds on Treasury rolls is on March 31, 1791, at a quarterly salary of $125, his last on December 17, 1792. James Reynolds had sought a job in the Treasury after returning from a trip South in 1790, and Hamilton had half promised him one. If Jefferson could hire a Freneau in his department, could not Hamilton hire whom he wished in his?

Specialists speculate that Simeon Reynolds might have been the son of Gamaliel Reynolds of Norwich, Connecticut; James Reynolds hailed from upstate Connecticut, too.

This remarkable series of interlocking coincidences of names, places, and dates raise a a cloud of questions that history does not answer. Was Simeon Reynolds a close kin of James, a friend, a coconspirator, or no connection whatever—or the same James Reynolds listed under a different Christian name for payroll purposes? Did Hamilton hire Simeon in compliance with a blackmail demand of James? Was Simeon really the clerk who leaked the lists or only a handy cover scapegoat for someone else? Did Hamilton know the names of James's coadjutors still within the Treasury?

Hamilton fully agreed with Wolcott in placing all guilt on the unidentified clerk and justifying the dismissal of the prosecutions on the ground that a greater public interest was being served by the plea bargain. "It was certainly of more consequence to the public," Hamilton declared, "to detect and expel from the bosom of the Treasury Department an unfaithful clerk to prevent future extensive mischief, than to disgrace and punish two worthless individuals." He appealed to men of candor to draw proofs of his own innocence and delicacy "from the reflection that, under circumstances so peculiar, the culprits were compelled to give a real and substantial equivalent for the relief which they obtained from a department, over which I presided."

Far from trying to cover up a scandal or a fraud in his department, Hamilton was claiming all possible credit, short of revealing the name of Simeon Reynolds, for prosecuting the ostensible offenders. When his prosecution had brought him to the "leak" in his own department, he had fired the guilty man. But the name of "Simeon" Reynolds, the clerk upon whom both Wolcott and Hamilton finally placed all the blame, was concealed from all their contemporaries. Duer's name was the guilty name that Jefferson jotted down. James Thomson Callender, who analyzed the evidence more searchingly than any other investigator of the time, suspected that the real culprit was Andrew G. Fraunces. This was a plausible surmise because Fraunces was a clerk in the Treasury, at the Board of Treasury before that, and close to Duer. Clingman testified that Reynolds had sought help from Fraunces, that Hamilton had told Fraunces to stay out of it, or he would fire him. Fraunces was, in fact, soon out of the department, spouting bitter imprecations against Hamilton.

Why was the public made to believe that only Duer was the guilty man instead of "Simeon" Reynolds? Why did Hamilton and Wolcott keep Simeon Reynolds's name so secret, under the cover of Duer's, risking censure for a slow cleanup of a stale scandal instead of inviting applause for the prompt rooting out of newly uncovered corruption?

One answer in Hamilton's defense begins with another question. Could Hamilton possibly hope to escape being pilloried in Freneau's press for guilt by association if, on the same day that he was discharging one Reynolds from the Treasury in disgrace for leaking the lists, he was allowing the other (or the same?) Reynolds, who had admitted no more than making fraudulent but profitable use of them, to walk out of jail scot free? What alert journalist could resist the temptation to banner a sensational scandal by blurring the nice distinction between Simeon and James? To Hamilton and Wolcott, this much of a relatively innocent cover-up would have been justified as a political necessity. It was also a small kindness that would serve to spare a small-time loser like Simeon the consequences of confusion with the rascally James and his long criminal record.

All of which shows the vital importance of the culprit's having any other name in the world but Reynolds.

Muhlenberg kept hearing that "Reynolds had it in his power very materially to injure the Secretary of the Treasury and . . . knew several very improper Transactions of his," echoing other sinister rumors Muhlenberg had been hearing about the leader of his party, now seemingly corroborated by the six scraps of Hamilton's notes. Muhlenberg consulted others in Congress, especially because Reynolds was now about to be released from jail.

On Wednesday, December 12, a week after Clingman had agreed to Wolcott's stipulations, Muhlenberg spoke to Senator James Monroe and Representative Abraham B. Venable, both from Virginia; showed them Hamilton's notes to Reynolds; told them what Clingman had said; and suggested that Reynolds could tell them a great deal more.

Clingman's lead now seemed to inculpate the author of the system their leader Jefferson hated, so Monroe and Venable hastened to visit Reynolds in the Walnut Street jail the same day they heard from Muhlenberg. They did not identify themselves to him by name, but only as members of Congress, and said they had been told that Reynolds was from Richmond (their cover story) and was accused of committing frauds on their constitutents. Madison may have heard Clingman's story from Burr or someone else, remembered Reynolds's name from Gustavus B. Wallace's letters to him in 1790, and coached the congressmen in their oblique approach. Being told that Reynolds was not a Virginian, they questioned him about "the other particulars" of which Clingman had spoken. Reynolds could indeed reveal "the misconduct . . . of a Person high in Office." But he was afraid to do so until after his release, which he had been assured would take place that evening. Reynolds's visitors had no doubt that he meant Hamilton: he had said that Wolcott was in the same department and under him. Boasting that the high official was in his power, Reynolds declared, at the same time, that the official had initiated the prosecution to oppress and drive him away, had found a merchant to offer bail so as to decoy him into custody, had promised to give him employment without having done so, and yet now was pressing Wolcott to have him released. Reynolds was probably acting on advice of counsel, Burr, in not telling all he knew for fear he would not be discharged. He promised to tell them the whole story next morning at ten o'clock outside of jail.

But the congressional committee would never see him again.

Overnight he would disappear from history except (according to Clingman's later testimony) for two clandestine, early morning meetings, next day on the thirteenth and again on the fifteenth, with Hamilton.

After leaving Reynolds's jail cell the evening of the twelfth, Monroe left Venable and picked up Muhlenberg and walked to the Reynoldses' house, where they found Maria alone. At first, she refused to talk. They showed her the notes "from Secretary Hamilton Esqr." that she had turned over to Clingman, told her that Clingman had talked, and soon she began to talk, too. The unsigned notes were indeed from Hamilton. She had indeed destroyed other notes and letters from Hamilton, adding that when James had gone, at Hamilton's request, she had "burned a considerable number of letters from him to her husband . . . touching business between them, to prevent their being made public." She said Reynolds "could tell something, that would make some of the Heads of departments tremble." She told them that Hamilton had advised her to go stay with friends, that he had offered to assist her, and—again confirming Clingman's report—that Hamilton had urged her husband to "leave the parts, not to be seen here again . . . in which case, he would give something clever." This offer, wide-eyed Maria told the congressmen, "did not proceed from friendship to him, but on account of his threat." She also revealed that their speculating congressional colleague Jeremiah Wadsworth had already been active to obtain Reynolds's release, at first at her request and then, she thought, with the knowledge and prompting of Hamilton.

This much merely corroborated Clingman's story. But now came a new disclosure. The visit of the congressmen to Reynolds's jail cell earlier that day had not gone unnoticed. Learning of it, Wadsworth had come to Maria before the congressmen arrived to ask her what they had been seeing Reynolds about. Wadsworth had told her that "Mr. Hamilton had enemies who would try to prove some speculations on him, but . . . he would be found immaculate." To this, so Maria told Muhlenberg and Monroe, she had replied "she rather doubted it."

She then showed them two more notes, one from Hamilton dated December 6, two days after Clingman's agreement to the plea bargain, and one from Wadsworth written the eleventh, the day before their visit to her, "both expressing a desire to relieve her." This was how the congressmen carefully described the purport of these apparent new offers to pay her hush money. But she denied any other "recent" communications with Mr. Hamilton, "or that she had received any money from him lately."

Their suspicions strengthened, the two congressmen set down an account of their interview immediately afterward and the next day signed the clerk's fair copy of it.

At the appointed hour next morning at the jail, when Monroe and Venable were told that Reynolds "had absconded or concealed himself," they were furious. The mysterious disappearance of the key witness tended to confirm their darkest suspicions of a cover-up by Hamilton.

Having been accompanied only by Venable at one interview and only by Muhlenberg at the other, only Monroe now held all the strands of the story within his grasp. Only he knew where all gaps and conflicts lay. From now on, Jefferson's protégé took the leading role in the congressional investigation.

The senator and the two representatives would now confront Hamilton with their evidence. After hearing his defense and giving him prior notice of what they proposed to do, they would lay the whole matter directly before the president. They drafted a letter to Washington, dated the fourteenth, the day after Reynolds's mysterious disappearance. The letter transmitted to Washington "some documents respecting the conduct of Colo. Hamilton, in the office of Secretary of the Treasury," to wit, Muhlenberg's statement of his role in behalf of Clingman, Monroe's and Venable's account of their interview with Reynolds in jail, Monroe's and Muhlenberg's interview with Maria Reynolds the night of the twelfth, and a separate affidavit from Clingman that they would obtain from him the next day. They would permit Hamilton either to exculpate himself or force his resignation.

Their letter to Washington shows that they gave credence to Clingman's and Maria's accusations against Hamilton. Monroe wrote out the letter for all three to sign.

The next day, the thirteenth of December, Jacob Clingman testified to the congressmen with convincing particularity about Hamilton's long intimacy with Maria and James Reynolds. Of more immediate interest was his account of what had happened the previous night after Monroe and Muhlenberg had left Maria's house. Neither Hamilton's nor any other testimony in the record contradicts Clingman on the following particulars, although Hamilton and others would draw sharply conflicting inferences as to the meaning of the facts. Hamilton would only aver generally that Clingman's and the Reynoldses' statements concerning his participation in speculations were untrue and not worthy of belief, because of their disreputable characters.

Clingman had first met James Reynolds in September 1791 and soon became intimate with him. He had met Hamilton at the Reynoldses' house in January 1792 and often thereafter. On one occasion, Hamilton gave Mrs. Reynolds a paper, which Hamilton said he "was ordered to give Mr. Reynolds."

"Ordered" to give?

"Who," Clingman asked Maria, could "order" the secretary of the treasury of the United States to "give" something to Reynolds. She replied "he did not want to be known," having seen someone else with her. "This happened in the night," Clingman said. Reynolds had told Clingman "in confidence that if Duer had held up three days longer, he should have made fifteen hundred pounds, by the assistance of Col. Hamilton . . . that Col. Hamilton had made thirty thousand dollars by speculation; that Col. Hamilton supplied him with money to speculate . . ." and that "Col. Hamilton said, he knew Reynolds and his father; that his father was a good whig in the late war; that was all he could say."

Clingman went on to testify that, after Reynolds had been arrested and thrown in jail,

Maria had gone to see Jeremiah Wadsworth because Reynolds's father had served under him in the commissary department. He had agreed to give her his assistance, saying " 'now you have made me your friend, you must apply to no person else.' " Clingman himself had heard Wadsworth at Maria's on Sunday, December 9 promise to do what he could for both Clingman and Reynolds's family, but his name must not be mentioned. Clingman "should not speak to him if he should meet him in the street" and if his name were mentioned, he would do nothing. On Wednesday the twelfth, when Wadsworth had called on Maria again, Clingman saw him leave her the note that she had shown to Monroe and Muhlenberg. Delivering it, Wadsworth had assured her that "he had seen every body and done every thing."

That same Wednesday evening of Wadsworth's and the congressmen's visits, at about eight or nine o'clock, Reynolds had been discharged from jail. At about midnight he had "sent a letter to Col. Hamilton by a girl; Reynolds followed the girl," and Clingman followed Reynolds through the dark, cobbled streets down to Hamilton's house near Treasury Row. Clingman saw the girl go into Hamilton's and then joined Reynolds. They "walked back and forward in the street" for a while in front of Hamilton's until the girl emerged with a message from Hamilton. It told Reynolds "that he need not go out of town that night," but should "call on him early in the morning." Clingman must have risen early after a late night because he testified that "in the morning between seven and eight o'clock" in the wintry dawn of the thirteenth he had seen "Reynolds go to Hamilton's house and go in." He had not seen him since, Clingman testified on the thirteenth, and supposed he had left the state. At no time afterward would Hamilton deny Clingman's testimony that he had received a letter from Reynolds the night of the twelfth and another visit from him early the next morning.

The confrontation between the congressmen and Hamilton was set for December 15. During the interval between Thursday the thirteenth and Saturday the fifteenth, Clingman brought the congressmen important new evidence. Reynolds, he reported, had secretly returned home Thursday night, bringing Clingman a letter written earlier that day. At his house, in front of Clingman, Reynolds tore out part of the letter, threw the fragment into the fireplace, and handed the mutilated remnant to him. What was left of the note seemed to accuse the secretary of the treasury—more serious than a cover-up—with obstruction of justice and subornation of perjury, among other crimes. It read:

> My dear Mr. Clingman . . . I am convinced [. . .] to have satisfaction from HIM at all events, and you onely I trust too. I will see you this evening. He has offered to furnish me and Mrs. Reynolds with money to carry us off. If I will go, he will see that Mrs. Reynolds has money to follow me, and as for Mr. Francis [Fraunces] he says he will make him swear back what he has said, and will turn him out of office. This is all I can say till I see you.—I am, dear Clingman, believe me, forever your sincere friend, James Reynolds.

Clingman turned this new scrap of evidence over to the congressmen. The torn-off portion must have puzzled them—Hamilton's name perhaps? It corroborated Clingman's previous testimony that Hamilton had wanted to get Reynolds and his wife out of the way, and explained Reynolds's mysterious disappearance.

Clingman had still more important evidence, supported by another document. This was a note from the comptroller of the Treasury, which read: "Mr. Wolcott will be glad to see Mr. Clingman tomorrow, at half after nine o'clock. Thursday." At the appointed time, but on Friday the fourteenth instead of Thursday, Clingman reported, he had been grilled by

Wolcott in the presence of Hamilton. He "was strictly examined by both respecting the Persons who were inquiring into the Matter and their Object." Clingman had not revealed the congressmen's names. Wolcott said he "should not consider himself bound" by the plea bargain, unless Clingman disclosed to Wolcott and Hamilton the congressmen's names. But Clingman professed not to know the identity of Monroe and Venable, hard as this story might be for Wolcott to swallow from an employee of Muhlenberg. Hamilton had even "desired him to go into the Gallery where he would see them and enquire their names of the Bystanders."

Clingman further reported that, under intense pressure, he claimed, he had admitted giving Hamilton's scraps of notes to the congressmen. Hamilton angrily told him "he had done very wrong." He had also told Hamilton about Reynolds's letter of the thirteenth. Of Reynolds's statement that Hamilton would cause Fraunces to "swear what he had said," Hamilton said he had meant only that "he would make Fraunces unsay any Falsity he had declared." Hamilton had added that Reynolds was "a villain or rascal and he supposed would swear to any Thing." In this interrogation, Hamilton had admitted, according to Clingman, that "he had had some Transaction with Reynolds, which he had before mentioned . . . to Mr. Wolcott, and need not go into Detail with Wolcott present." Clingman now recalled that Reynolds had said to him that "when he was about to set out to Virginia, on his last trip to buy up cash-claims of the Virginia line, he told Mr. Hamilton that [John] Hopkins [commissioner of loans for Virginia] would not pay upon these powers of attorney . . . to which he [Mr. Hamilton] replied, he would write Hopkins on the subject."

To elicit statements from Clingman so damaging to Hamilton, the congressmen must have been cross-examining Clingman sharply, well-prepared for the interrogation. Gustavus B. Wallace's 1790 letters to Madison about Reynolds's and Vredenbergh's buying up the Virginia soldiers' claims must have served as one basis for their questioning. It was a cold trail and a rather misleading one because it seemed to end at the name of Duer. From Hamilton's point of view it was fortunate that it did, because at least it led the congressional investigators away from the secret name of Simeon Reynolds, whose employment at the Treasury would not be terminated until the following Monday. Clingman's new evidence would lay the foundation for new questions, with which the well-briefed congressmen would surprise Hamilton at two confrontations the next day.

Very early that same Saturday morning, as Clingman testified later the same day to Monroe, Muhlenberg, and Venable (in a statement recorded by John Beckley's assistant, Bernard Webb), Reynolds had come back to see Hamilton one last time. At this meeting, Hamilton had been "extremely agitated, walking backward and forward, striking, alternately, his forehead and his thigh; observing to him, that he had enemies at work, but was willing to meet them, on fair ground, and requested him not to stay long, lest it might be noticed." Reynolds had left Hamilton at sunrise. Hamilton later would admit that he had met Reynolds on the thirteenth, but he never admitted to the meeting at sunrise on the fifteenth (to which Reynolds was allegedly shadowed secretly by Clingman).

From his and Wolcott's intense grilling of Clingman in Wolcott's office of the day before, Hamilton was painfully aware that his scraps of notes, partly written in a disguised hand—the most damaging evidence against him—were in the hands of the congressional committee and might be revealed to Washington or the public at any moment. Both Maria and Clingman had said that the last two meetings between Hamilton and Reynolds had been for the purpose of concocting an explanation.

Here follows Hamilton's account in his own words of his two Saturday confrontations with the three congressmen:

On the morning of 15th of December, 1792, the above-mentioned gentlemen [Monroe, Muhlenberg, and Venable] presented themselves at my office. Mr. Muhlenberg was then speaker. He introduced the subject by observing to me that they had discovered a very improper connection between me and a Mr. Reynolds.

Hamilton was outraged: "Extremely hurt by this mode of introduction, I arrested the progress of the disclosure by giving way to very strong expressions of indignation."

His accusers backed off a little from their opening charge:

The gentlemen explained, telling me in substance that I had misapprehended them; that they did not take the fact for established; that, unsought by them, information had been given them of an improper pecuniary connection between Mr. Reynolds and myself. They had thought it their duty to pursue it, and had become possessed of some documents of a suspicious complexion.

Hamilton held his temper; there was worse still to come: "They had contemplated laying the matter before the President, but before they did this they thought it right to apprise me of the affair and to afford an opportunity of explanation."

They next proceeded to lay before him the six incriminating scraps in his own disguised handwriting. Too hastily, perhaps, but goaded on by fury, "without a moment's hesitation I acknowledged [them] to be mine."

Hamilton went on, saying that he had told them, "The affair [is] now put upon a different footing—I always [stand] ready to meet fair inquiry with frank communication—it happens, in the present instance, to be in my power by written documents to remove all doubts as to the real nature of the business, and fully to convince that nothing of the kind imputed to me [does] in fact exist."

Hamilton's accusers demanded to see his "written documents."

Hamilton needed time. He agreed to meet them at his house that same evening for the fuller explanation he had promised them. They left.

"I immediately after saw Mr. Wolcott," Hamilton went on, "and for the first time informed him of the affair and of the interview just had." If, as this artfully worded statement of Hamilton seems intended to imply, Wolcott was not aware of "the affair" nor of the congressmen's knowledge of it till that morning, it sharply conflicts with Clingman's account of the grilling he had been given the day before in Wolcott's office. Only if the reference of the word *affair* in Hamilton's statement is limited to Hamilton's admission to Wolcott of his sexual liaison with Maria, can it be read as not in conflict with Clingman's.

Hamilton said he turned all his letters from the Reynoldses over to Wolcott and asked him to be at his home that night for the second confrontation.

That night at Hamilton's, as Wolcott would later certify, the interrogation was begun by Monroe. He read out Hamilton's notes and "a Narrative of conversations which had been held with the said Reynolds and Clingman." He stated fully "the grounds upon which the suspicions rested."

Hamilton took a deep breath and "entered into an explanation." As Hamilton recalled, "I stated in explanation, the circumstances of my affair with Mrs. Reynolds and the consequence of it." In corroboration, he produced the letters that Maria and James Reynolds had written to him, giving an explanatory commentary for each.

"I insisted on going through the whole," Hamilton said, "and did so." His interrogators soon wearied of the painful exercise. "One or more of the gentlemen," according to

Hamilton, "were struck with so much conviction, before I had gotten through the communication, that they delicately urged me to discontinue it as unnecessary."

Wolcott said that Mr. Venable "requested Mr. Hamilton to desist from exhibiting further proofs." Hamilton thought Muhlenberg had felt the same way. Wolcott said the explanation and the "written documents, which were read, fully evinced, that there was nothing in the transactions to which Reynolds and Clingman had referred, which had any connection with, or relation to speculations in the Funds, claims upon the United States, or any public or official transactions or duties whatever. This was rendered . . . completely evident. . . . As however an explanation had been desired by the Gentlemen before named, Mr. Hamilton insisted upon being allowed to read such documents as he possessed, for the purpose of obviating every shadow of doubt respecting the propriety of his Official conduct."

Hamilton at no point during the confrontation or afterward "entreated a suspension of the communication to the President, or from the beginning to the end of the inquiry asked any favor or indulgence whatever." He always denied "that [he] discovered any symptom different from that of a proud consciousness of innocence."

Wolcott, of course, was satisfied with the extraordinary explanation, and so, it seemed at first, were Monroe, Muhlenberg, and Venable. Wolcott wrote that "after Mr. Hamilton's explanation terminated Messrs. Monroe, Muhlenberg and Venable, severally acknowledged their entire satisfaction, that the affair had no relation to official duties, and that it ought not to affect or impair confidence in Mr. Hamilton's character;—at the same time, they expressed their regrets at the trouble which the explanation had occasioned."

As gentlemen, they were even a little apologetic about their role in such an embarrassing matter. "One of the gentlemen, I think," said Hamilton, "expressed a hope that I also was satisfied with their conduct in conducting the inquiry. I answered that they knew I had been hurt at the opening of the affair; that, this excepted, I was satisfied with their conduct, and considered myself as having been treated with candor or with fairness and liberality."

Neither Hamilton's nor Wolcott's accounts of these famous confrontations were contemporaneous with them. They were written in July 1797, four and a half years after the night of December 15, 1792. Next day, Monroe set down what was later represented to be the only contemporaneous account on Bernard Webb's [the clerk's] copy of Clingman's statement of December 13. Monroe's account more or less agreed with Hamilton's—up to a point:

> [Sunday] 16th [December 1792]. Last night we waited on Colo. H. when he informed us of a particular connection with Mrs. R. the period of its commencement and circumstances attending it—his visiting her at Inscheps [Inskeep was the proprietor of The George, an inn at the southwest corner of Second and Mulberry— later Arch—streets]

The reference to Inskeep's is puzzling because the Reynoldses' letters say that their meetings occurred at her or Hamilton's house. James Thomson Callender later thought this was a significant discrepancy because Inskeep's The George "was never a house of that sort."

Monroe went on to say that Hamilton had confirmed Clingman's testimony about receiving Reynolds's note on the night of the twelfth; that he had met with him the next morning, the thirteenth; and that he had never seen him before he came to Philadelphia. Apparently no questions were asked or answers given about Hamilton's last secret meeting with Reynolds at dawn the day of the confrontation. Monroe further noted that Hamilton had told the congressmen that the prosecution against Reynolds and Clingman had been dismissed because Reynolds had surrendered the leaked list and that the culprit "had it not in his power now to injure the department, intimating he meant Mr. Duer." The name of Simeon Reynolds never came up.

Hamilton went on to tell of

> the frequent supplies of money to her and her husband and on that account—his duress by them from the fear of a disclosure and his anxiety to be relieved from it and them. To support this he shewed a great number of Letters from Reynolds and herself, commencing early in 1791.—He acknowledged all the letters in a disguised hand, in our possession, to be his [these latter were the six brief notes or fragments].

Monroe's statement concluded with a sentence of sinister ambiguity: "We left him under the impression our suspicions were removed."

An expert wordsmith like Hamilton could read into an ambiguity like this one of Monroe his total belief, or disbelief, in his innocence of a speculating connection with Reynolds. It also left the door open for Monroe later to change his mind about Hamilton's innocence without going back on his word or being guilty of earlier duplicity.

Monroe concluded that Hamilton "acknowledged our conduct toward him had been fair and liberal—he could not complain of it. We took back all the papers even his own notes, nor did he ask their destruction.'

A day or two after the confrontation, Hamilton wrote letters to each of the three congressmen, requesting copies of the notes of his that they had shown him, the mutilated letter from Reynolds to Clingman, and the Clingman statement they had shown him at the confrontation. He also requested that the originals "be detained from the parties of whom they were had, to put it out of their power to repeat the abuse of them in situations which may deprive me of the advantage of explanation." This seemed fair and reasonable to Monroe, Muhlenberg, and Venable at the time, judging from their eagerness to comply.

Muhlenberg replied December 18, 1792, that Monroe "has all the papers . . . in his possession" and that "your very reasonable request will be speedily complied with."

Monroe sent back copies of all papers on December 20, just as Hamilton had asked, writing,

> Sir:
>
> I have the honor to enclose you copies of the papers requested in yours a few days past. That of the notes you will retain; the others you will be pleased, after transcribing, to return to me.
>
> With due respect, I have the honor to be,
> Your very humble servant,
> Jas. Monroe.

In a postscript, Monroe, like Muhlenberg, seemed to go out of his way to reassure Hamilton that all suspicions were at rest and that his secret would be kept: "Everything you desire in the letter above mentioned shall be most strictly complied with." Nothing in this warned Hamilton of the change that would soon come in Monroe's contemporaneous assessment of Hamilton's role. So, to Hamilton's vast relief, the matter seemed to rest. Simeon Reynolds was gone from the Treasury, his name still a secret. Duer in prison was blamed for an old scandal. James Reynolds was well out of the way in hiding. The story of Hamilton's affair was blocked from press and public by the word of gentlemen of honor.

So it seemed, but Hamilton failed to reckon with men on the fringes not bound by the same code as gentlemen of honor. No such code forbade men like Clingman; Beckley; and his clerk, Bernard Webb, from keeping the affair very much alive in their private whispers or Jefferson from jotting down his note about it in his *Anas*:

> *Dec. 17. The affair of Reynolds and his wife.—Clingman Muhlen's clerk, testifies to F. A. Muhl. Monroe Venable.—also Wolcott at [and?] Wadsworth. Known to J[ames] M[adison]. E[dmund] R[andolph]. [John] Beckley and [Bernard] Webb.*
>
> *Reynolds was speculating agent on the speculations of Govt. Arrearages. He was furnished by Duer with a list of the claims of arrearages due to the Virga. and Carola. lines and bought them up, against which the Resolutions of Congress of June 4, 1790. were levelled. Hamilton advised the President to give his negative to those resolutions.*

At some later time Jefferson scored out the paragraph italicized above. A later statement of Maria's old friend and family confessor, Richard Folwell, was helpful to Hamilton. In 1795 or 1796, he recalled, Maria "wrote me a Letter to call on her at a very reputable and genteel Lodging House in Arch Street, No.—. When he called at her lodgings," she "apprized him of her marriage with Mr. Clingman." She told him that she now lived in East Nottingham, Cecil County, Maryland, and had "lived there happily with Mr. Clingman, at the House of a Distant Relation of mine." The reason she had now sent for the faithful Folwell was that one careless day "she had mentioned knowing of our Family in Philadelphia." This had been a terrible gaffe on her part. A cousin of Folwell had exclaimed in a state of shock that "she must be the same Person who had left with her an infamous Character by the name of Mrs. Reynolds." What Maria now wanted Folwell to do was "clear up her Character." The ever faithful Folwell fussed and fumed at this challenging assignment. "I expostulated on the Inconsistency of this," he said. He told her "that as it was bad before she had certainly increased it." He was censorious. Here she was now living in Maryland with Jacob Clingman, her make-believe husband, while her real husband, James Reynolds, was still alive and well and living in New York. How could he clear up her character "in that situation"? Folwell had a point there, Maria conceded. But it was not a serious problem. "She said she had a Divorce." Folwell was relieved. But there was a catch, Maria went on to say. Folwell was unrelieved. There was "only one Fault she had incurred in her Change,—that she got married to Clingman one half hour before she obtained the divorce."

A new love had not cost Maria one whit of her raffish charm.

What lawyer would make a mistake like that?

The lawyer who had arranged Maria's late divorce from James Reynolds, she said, had been their old family counselor, Aaron Burr. "Les grandes âmes," etc.

In high dudgeon, Richard Folwell stalked out of Maria's genteel lodgings in Arch Street. When she appealed to him soon again, Folwell mislaid her invitation. "Since then," he said, "I have heard nothing from her," except "Only that she wrote me a very pathetic Letter—" again "begging as she was to return, that I would clear up her Character. This I have mislaid—." Though it had been mislaid, Folwell said, he would not forget her.

Hamilton would have remembered how he felt. What she had written him, Folwell said, "would move anyone almost to serve her, that was not fully acquainted with her character, confirmed by actual observation."

Reynolds and Clingman, Folwell and Wadsworth and Hamilton, and Aaron Burr. She could indeed move anyone almost to serve her.

Two weeks after the confrontation, January 3, 1793, Clingman called on Monroe, who now had custody of all the papers, and informed him "that he had been apprized of Mr. Hamilton's vindication by *Mr. Wolcott* a day or two" after the confrontation. Clingman said "that he communicated the same to Mrs. Reynolds, who appeared much shocked at it and wept immoderately." Maria denied that she had had any affair with Hamilton at all: "It had been a fabrication of Colo. Hamilton." Reynolds had joined in it, she said, and he had given Hamilton receipts for money and written letters "so as to give the countenance to the pretence." Clingman insisted to Monroe that Maria "was innocent and that the defense was an imposition." Monroe recorded this new testimony of the star witness in his own hand below his earlier account of the December 15 confrontation.

If this new tale of Clingman and Maria could now be believed, Hamilton's defense had been nothing but a pack of lies. But one point in Clingman's new tale seemed to be a lie that cast doubt on the credibility of all the rest.

Oliver Wolcott's probity, sense of official decorum, and loyalty to Hamilton were beyond question. A talebearer like Clingman, whom Wolcott had just prosecuted for fraud and released on a plea bargain, was the last man in the world, or next to last, to whom Wolcott would have spoken "at this point in time" on any subject, let alone a subject as sensitive as the nature of Hamilton's defense. Clingman could, of course, easily have learned its nature from his fellow clerk, Beckley, or Bernard Webb. Whoever told him to give the name of Wolcott as his source was creating a false trail leading away from the true source, but it was a self-discrediting cover.

Besides, Clingman's and Maria's new claim that Maria had never had an affair with Hamilton at all conflicted sharply with their earlier stories, which no one doubted confirmed that she and Hamilton had indeed had an affair. It also conflicted with Hamilton's defense, which all who heard it had believed.

A better explanation for their new claims was that, James Reynolds having vanished and Maria having become Clingman's wife (locally) and sought to "clear up her character," she had suddenly turned chaste, retroactively. As Hamilton would remember ruefully, years later, Maria could assume an endless variety of shapes and guises.

26

Impeachment

Should your prosecutors not come forward at the next session with an impeachment . . . you should explicitly call for one. . . . Resign . . . and you fail irretrievably.

—from Edward Carrington, July 2, 1793

As you have written—the throat of your political reputation is to be cut, in *whispers*.

—from William Willcocks, September 5, 1793

The first letter Hamilton would write to any close friend after the night of December 15, 1792, is the letter of a man close to the breaking point.

On December 18 he wrote John Jay ''ashamed'' that earlier letters from Jay had gone so long unanswered—as a result of his own ''delinquencies.'' ''Tis not the load of official business that alone engrosses me,'' he confessed, ''though this would be enough to occupy any man. Tis not the extra attentions I am obliged to pay to the course of legislative mannoevres that alone add to my burthen and perplexity.'' No, he groaned, ''tis the malicious intrigues to stab me in the dark, against which I am too often obliged to guard myself, that distract and harass me to a point, which rendering my situation scarcely tolerable interferes with objects to which friendship and inclination would prompt me.''

After this cry of anguish, Hamilton dealt with the business Jay's earlier letters had raised. He then reverted to his obsession with his enemies. Adams's reelection was a source of some satisfaction; Clinton's election would have been a source of ''mortification and pain.'' Hamilton would willingly ''relinquish my share of the command, to the Antifoederalists if I thought they were to be trusted—but I have so many proofs to the contrary as to make me dread the experience of their preponderancy.''

On the face of it, Hamilton was writing about the retention in office of an incumbent vice-president of his own party, a subject on which reasonable men could differ, but hardly one about which they got very excited, let alone discussed in apocalyptic accents of "dread," "malicious intrigues to stab me in the dark," and "mortification and pain." Hamilton's unbalanced reaction to and obsession with enemies contrasted sharply with the judiciousness and moderation of his own political comments of earlier years.

The same note of overreaction and obsession with enemies crept into the polemical attacks on Jefferson and all his followers and works that Hamilton had been writing for the press that summer and fall under such names as *T.L.*, *Metellus*, and *Catullus*. *Catullus* No. VI, which had been scheduled to appear in Fenno's *Gazette* on December 15, but had missed the deadline, also missed the next deadline for the issue of December 19, before finally appearing on December 22.

The authors of the *Vindication of Thomas Jefferson*, probably Monroe and Edmund Randolph, using some material furnished by Madison, had charged that Hamilton's broadsides were "in gratification of private revenge," a "pernicious example of gross violation . . . of . . . a public trust, and a glaring outrage."

With a sort of weary desperation, saying little that was new, but in dour phrases that seemed to approach the borders of hysteria, Hamilton hit back in *Catullus* No. VI. The old charges against him were "hypocritical rant" and "pathetic wailings." Their authors were "political pharisees" of "hollow and ostentatious pretensions." If *Catullus'* judgment had not been seriously skewed by the pressures of the night of December 15, he would have known that such stuff was better left missing Fenno's deadlines indefinitely.

In his reply of December 29, Jay reached out to Hamilton with compassionate understanding so far beyond his usual reserved style that it is obvious he had heard the whispers that explained the terrible personal anxieties behind Hamilton's "dread" of "intrigues to stab me in the dark."

Jay wrote:

> The thorns they strew in your way, will (if you please) hereafter blossom and furnish garlands to decorate your administration. Resolve not to be driven from your station. . . . Your difficulties from *persons* and *parties* will by time be carried out of sight, unless you prevent it.

Incidental observations in Jay's letter would fan the fears of any man obsessed by "dread" that his enemies would stop at nothing to stab him in the dark. Jay told Hamilton he suspected that Hamilton's letter "had been opened. The wafer looked very much like it. Such letters should be sealed with wax, impressed with your seal." Jay predicted grimly, "Your situation is unpleasant; your enemies will endeavour to render it still more so."

Jay was right. On December 31, Congress demanded from Hamilton lists of all Treasury Department employees and their salaries, as well as lists of all employees of the other departments. Simeon Reynolds's name was absent from the Treasury's list, but Andrew G. Fraunces's was still there.

Of much more seriousness was another set of resolutions that Thomas Jefferson was drafting. They charged Hamilton with specific violation of two acts of Congress, dated August 4 and 12, 1790, respectively, in applying portions of appropriated funds to purposes not authorized by law, with deliberately deviating from the president's instructions in handling the transfer of money raised by loans in Europe to the United States, with failing to provide Congress with official information of his actions in connection with these funds, with mishandling the sinking fund, and disregard of the public interest in negotiating a loan with the Bank of the United States at 5 percent interest at a time when ample public funds were lying idle there and in other banks. They further charged him with being "guilty of an indecorum to this House" by attempting to judge of its motives in requesting information from him on these and kindred matters and with withholding essential information in complying with their request.

The two concluding counts in Jefferson's indictment went further. One discredited Hamilton with Washington by charging "that the Secretary . . . has violated the instructions of the President . . . for the benefit of speculators and to increase the profits of [the bank]." The last demanded Hamilton's discharge from office in disgrace: "That the secretary of the treasury has been guilty of maladministration of the duties of his office, and should, in the opinion of Congress, be removed from his office by the President of the United States."

The word *impeachment* did not appear in Jefferson's statement of the charges, but no one would know better than Hamilton that impeachment was what Jefferson intended: Hamilton in *The Federalist,* No. 65, had defined impeachment for all constitutional time as "those offences which proceed from the misconduct of public men, or, in other words, from the abuse or violation of some public trust." They may, Hamilton explained, "with peculiar propriety be denominated POLITICAL, as they relate chiefly to injuries done immediately to the society itself." Impeachment proceedings would "agitate the passions of the whole community" and "divide it into parties more or less friendly or inimical to the accused," Hamilton explained. They would also connect "with the preexisting factions, and will enlist all their animosities, partialities, influence and interest on one side or on the other." In such cases, as Hamilton had foreseen, "there will always be the greatest danger that the decision will be regulated more by the comparative strength of parties, than by the real demonstrations of innocence or guilt."

Jefferson's resolutions were drawn to make Hamilton the victim of his own foresight of five years earlier. Hamilton would be saved or fall, not so much by any real demonstration of innocence or guilt, but on the basis of opinions and suspicions nowhere in the formal record, by the comparative strength of the factions that stood for and against him in Congress. One thing he had fought against more than any other man as "the greatest danger" to government was the spirit of faction, or parties. His own party now was all that stood between his public credit and public disgrace.

Republicans in the House began laying the groundwork for Jefferson's impeachment resolutions by introducing preliminary resolutions on December 24 and 27, calling on Hamilton for detailed information on government loans, in particular the two loans that Congress had authorized August 4 and 12, 1790. One of these was a $12 million borrowing, with the proceeds to be used to pay interest and amortize principal of the *foreign* debt; the other was a $2 million borrowing, with the proceeds to be used to purchase and retire *domestic* debt. The money had been duly borrowed in Amsterdam and Antwerp, but for a variety of reasons that had seemed sufficient to Hamilton at the time, the $12 million and $2 million had not been used separately to retire foreign and domestic debt, respectively. Instead, as Hamilton had advised Washington on August 26, 1790, he had used two-thirds of the $12 million and one-third of the $2 million to make a payment on the debt to France, which France was urging, plus a payment of a half year's interest on the debt to Holland plus arrears of interest on the debt to Spain. This would still leave "a sum of consequence to the operation . . . towards the reduction of our Debt and supporting our funds in conformity to the intention" of the $2 million loan to pay off domestic debt.

Hamilton quickly responded to Congress with his "Report on Foreign Loans" of January

3, 1793. It reproduced many pages of complex ledger entries showing the details of all receipts and disbursements of the proceeds of these loans. An explanatory remark referred to "reasons of weight, respecting the interests and credit of the United States" for one loan taken without previous authority. Such reasons included relative rates of interest and exchange between dollars, florins, livres, guilders, and francs at various times and places. Few subjects are worse-suited to be topics of freewheeling congressional debate or defense.

The House made clear it was not satisfied. But his prompt responses to House demands tended to deflate his enemies' hopes that enough would be found to back up wide-ranging, general charges of impeachable offenses, at least without further explorations. On January 23, William Branch Giles, a Virginia friend of Jefferson who often served as his spokesman in the House, introduced five resolutions that in form were a demand for a bill of particulars: they did not specifically charge wrongful conduct, but they demanded particulars on which later charges in the form of impeachments like those Jefferson was drafting could be based. These five "demand" resolutions called on Hamilton for copies of specific written authority for his use of the proceeds of the two loans; lists of the persons to whom payments had been made in France, Holland, and Spain; statements of transactions between the Treasury and the Bank of the United States and its branches; statements of balances in the sinking fund; and all unapplied balances. Similar resolutions were introduced into the Senate, and adopted by both houses.

The timing was significant. Congress was scheduled to adjourn at the beginning of March and would not reconvene until late in the fall. In the short space of little more than a month left before adjournment, it seemed impossible that any human being could compile the voluminous and incredibly complicated data that Giles's resolutions called on Hamilton to produce. During the long months of adjournment, suspicions generated by the unanswered questions would fester throughout the country. Later on, even if all Hamilton's books should turn out to be in perfect order, Giles and his partisans could make political capital of Hamilton's failure to submit his report earlier, before adjournment. All manner of dark suspicions could be conjured up out of nothing more than alleged delay.

Grinding away day and night with his Treasury staff, Hamilton assembled figures, ran off sums, reproduced ledgers, arranged explanations, and appended footnotes. His reports contain thousands of entries. In effect, they were financial accountings for the life of an entire nation prepared in the space of less than a month. Between February 4 and 19, he delivered to Congress the following reports in compliance with the House and Senate resolutions, and a mere listing of their shortened names serves to suggest how wearisome a work it was: "Report on the Balance of all Unapplied Revenues," a "Report Exhibiting the Amount of All Public Funds, and What Remains," three separate reports on foreign loans, a "Report on Revenue Appropriations and Expenditures," another on the "State of the Treasury at the Commencement of Each Quarter" in 1791 and 1792," and still another on the "State of the Stock Market and Stock Prices" in the same two years.

With his submission, Hamilton humbly inquired of his tormentors:

> Is it not truly matter of regret that so formal an explanation, on such a point, should have been made requisite? Could no personal inquiry, of either of the officers concerned, have superseded the necessity of publicly calling the attention of the House of Representatives to an appearance, in truth, so little significant?

All but ready to drop from exhaustion, Hamilton failed to resist an opportunity to overreact by adding a further thrust at his persecutors. His rhetorical question implied criticism of a Congress extremely touchy about its prerogatives and sensitive about its inability to detect an error in the mass of figures he had unloaded on it. "Was it seriously supposable," he asked, "that there could be any real difficulty in explaining that appearance, when the very disclosure of it proceeded from a voluntary act of the head of this Department?"

By such a challenge he had dramatically raised the stakes; one or the other, Congress or the secretary, now had to be guilty before the bar of public opinion.

The stage was set. On February 27, 1792, Giles introduced Jefferson's "charge" resolutions against Hamilton. Giles omitted from Jefferson's draft only the passages that charged Hamilton with benefiting speculators, demanded separation of the treasurer's office from the Treasury, and the impeachment article that charged Hamilton with "maladministration" and demanded his removal from office. Evidence of such studied malevolence would embarrass its author out on the floor, but even without these paragraphs, if the other charges should be sustained, they would leave only impeachment or resignation under fire as the next logical steps for Hamilton.

On February 28, Giles moved to have his resolutions considered by the House sitting as a committee of the whole. With adjournment now only a few days away, this would achieve the kind of delay through the summer that Giles had earlier failed to obtain. Hamilton's supporters objected. "Why delay?" demanded Hamilton's friend, William Loughton Smith of South Carolina. Let us proceed at once to a consideration of these charges: "The question was, had the Secretary violated a law? If so, let it be shown; every member was competent to decide so plain a question."

Hamiltonians failed to prevent commitment to the committee of the whole, but their protests against delay were so vigorous and their attitude so determined that they forced immediate debate of Giles's resolutions on the very day Congress had earlier scheduled for adjournment. On March 1, Giles led off with an all-out attack written for him by Madison. He called on Congress to help the president get rid of the guilty secretary. Robert Barnwell, a Southern Federalist, scoffed. He had heard no complaint from the president. Why did the House need to rush to his aid unasked?

Smith, although regretting that the charges against Hamilton had been brought on at the tag end of the session, was happy, nevertheless, that "the vague charges of mismanagement, with which the public had long been alarmed, were at length cast into a shape susceptible to investigation and decision." He then proceeded to analyze the criticisms of the secretary implicit in Giles's resolutions, compared the specific facts and figures that the secretary had so promptly supplied with the vague, argumentative charges of misconduct, showed that the secretary's handling had been proper, stripped away all factual basis for the charges, and left of them only a husk of personal animus empty of a kernel of evidence.

Smith's analysis of the chapter and verse of all of Hamilton's voluminous reports in the context of Giles's charges showed such minute familiarity with every detail of Hamilton's intricate financial operations there that there can be no doubt that Hamilton himself prepared the speech that Smith so eloquently delivered for him.

What Giles's hot air boiled down to, as Barnwell had put it, was not "the foul stain of peculation," but the possibly "illegal exercise of discretion, and a want of politeness in the Secretary."

Madison delivered a cautious, moderate, legalistic speech intended to show that Hamilton had violated the law. Boudinot and Ames defended Hamilton. The House moved into a night session. Hamiltonians blocked all efforts to adjourn with the question unresolved. The hour grew late. Candles guttered and smoked. The opposition tired. The chairman called the question. One after another, Giles's resolutions went down to overwhelming defeat. In the end, only five die-hard Republicans, including Giles and Madison, voted for all six. Giles's best effort was 15 to 33 on the fifth resolution. On the others, the vote ranged from 12 to 40, to 7 to 34. Congress adjourned.

Hamilton had won not merely vindication, but, by means of his risky, overreactive challenge to Congress, he had constructed a smashing personal victory.

Jefferson sought to minimize Giles's and Madison's crushing defeat. Writing to his son-in-law, Thomas Mann Randolph, on March 3, 1793, Jefferson explained it away by accusing the House of being one-third "bank directors and stock jobbers," who "would be voting on the case of their chief," and another third persons "blindly devoted to that party" or "persons not comprehending the papers" or "too indulgent to pass a vote of censure." The "people's" self-appointed champion wrote substantially the same criticism of the people's branch into his *Anas* on March 2. Not long after, on March 23, he made up a list of what he called "paper men" in Congress, a kind of "enemies list," saying that he got it from his creature, John Beckley. Writing to Washington early in the month, he had referred to the men named on his enemies list as "a corrupt squadron of voters in Congress at the command of the Treasury." It was true that of the 35 finding that the prosecution's burden of fixing blame on Hamilton had not been met, 21 were stockholders in the funds, and three were bank directors.

A week after Hamilton's vindication by the House, a set of resolutions similar to Giles's, castigating Hamilton and his "fiscal corps"—the men named on Jefferson's enemies list—was introduced into the Senate. But these resolutions withered in the face of the details in Hamilton's massive reports and died with Congress' adjournment.

All during the summer recess Hamilton's enemies would charge that his impressive vindication had been rushed through too swiftly: only a whitewash, it could not possibly be considered final or complete. It was not lost on Jefferson and his followers, nor on Hamilton and his, that if Giles's resolutions had been cast in a different form, calling for approbation of Hamilton instead of censure, fence sitters need not have let him have their votes, and he would now be discredited, instead of still riding high.

At Hamilton's request, Edward Carrington saw to it that his vindication was prominently reported in the Philadelphia newspapers of March 1793. But Carrington cautioned Hamilton that many of those who had supported him might weaken. They "were carried away by the storm" and "are much ashamed of their conduct." Nor was Jefferson's Virginia junto inclined to let Hamilton rest. Nor had they forgotten the night of December 15, 1792. Somewhere in all the massive reports he had submitted, he must have inadvertently allowed to slip in an entry that would corroborate the charges of a speculating involvement with James Reynolds or Andrew G. Fraunces or William Duer or someone else. John Beckley, for one, had heard a story from Jacob Clingman that Hamilton had paid Fraunces a bribe to give him back some papers that would implicate Hamilton in a scandal with Duer. Beckley urged Clingman to obtain corroboration. William Willcocks wrote Hamilton in August 1793 that "your enemeis are at work upon one Francis. . . . They give out that he is to make some affidavits criminating you in the highest degree, as to some money matters. As you have written—the throat of your political reputation is to be cut, *in whispers.*"

Nathanael Greene's widow, Catherine Greene, had importuned Hamilton May 30, 1790, for a favor as "a friend whom she loves and admires"; writing from Mulberry Grove, Georgia, January 26, 1791, she importuned him for another—would "my dear good friend" "Lose no time in bringing my affair before Congress." She importuned him a third

time—June 26, 1792—as his "sincerely affectionate" friend to help her out by paying off
Baron de Glaubeck's certificate obtained for her through Royal Flint and Thomas Bazen at
face value.

To provide supplies for his beleaguered Southern army, Greene had given a personal
guarantee to the Charleston firm of Hunter, Banks and Company, his commissary suppliers;
and when they defaulted, he became bound to pay their creditors "upwards of thirty
thousand pounds sterling." Greene's and Hamilton's opponents in Congress charged that
Greene had in reality been a secret silent partner in the Hunter, Banks firm, and stood to
profiteer on commissary supplies. Hamilton had prepared Catherine Greene's petition to
Congress for reimbursement, with exhibits from A to Z, consisting of letters and statements
from Edward Carrington, Nathaniel Pendleton, Anthony Wayne, Charles Cotesworth
Pinckney, William Washington, Clement Biddle, and others, which runs to 62 pages in
Volume X of the Hamilton Papers. Hamilton concluded that Greene's failure to give notice
was a valid technical obstacle to allowing the claim. He added that "motives of national
gratitude" for Greene's "very signal and very important services . . . must serve to give a
keener sting to the regret, which ought ever to attend the necessity of a strict adherence to
maxims of public policy." He mournfully apologized to Catherine Greene on March 8,
1791: "I love you too well not to be very candid with you. I am afraid my report will not
promote your interest," yet "it is impossible that I can have stronger motives than I have to
view the matter in conformity with your interests."

On the Baron de Glaubeck claim Hamilton had better news for her, but at the same time
he had given his enemies an opening, which they were quick to exploit. Hamilton used
Andrew G. Fraunces, the Treasury clerk, to arrange an assignment of de Glaubeck's
Treasury certificate (or warrant, an order directing a bank or other agency to pay the sum)
for back pay, first to one Thomas Bazen at a deep discount (for $273) and then a
reassignment to Royal Flint and Catherine Greene, who eventually was able to collect the
face value, plus interest, totaling $909.59, less attorney fees to Flint. Hamilton paid
Fraunces $50 for helping to arrange the deal. The interposition of Thomas Bazen as a
"straw man" in the chain of assignments was probably necessary to make it possible for
Catherine Greene and her attorney of record, Flint, to collect the full sum due, instead of
having to share it pro rata with other creditors of de Glaubeck. The success of this somewhat
dubious exploitation of the "holder-in-due-course" doctrine, which did not cause loss to
the Treasury, only to de Glaubeck's other creditors, would supply Jefferson with the basis
for another charge of "unclean hands" with which to discredit Hamilton.

"In whispers" would aptly characterize Jefferson's indistinct manner of speaking, or
mumbling, in private, when plotting with John Beckley to cut the throat of Hamilton's
political reputation. As is customary in such matters at the highest political levels of
command, no direct orders would be given, but John Beckley would understand perfectly
what he was expected to do. On June 12, 1793, after such a conversation with Beckley,
Jefferson jotted down in his *Anas* another note that presaged almost as much grief for
Hamilton as Jefferson's Reynolds jottings of five and a half months earlier:

> Beckley tells me that Klingham has been with him today, and relates to him the
> following fact [*sic*]. A certificate of the old Congress had been offered at the
> Treasury and refused payment, and so endorsed in red ink as usual. This certificate
> came to the hands of Francis (the quondam clerk of the treasury, who, on account of

his being dipped in the infamous case of the Baron Glaubeck, Hamilton had been obliged to dismiss, to save appearances, but with assurances of all future services, and he accordingly got him established in New York). Francis wrote to Hamilton that such a ticket was offered him, but he could not buy it unless he would inform and give him his certificate it was good. . . .

Jefferson went on to note down that "Hamilton wrote him a most friendly letter" and that Fraunces "bought the paper, came on here, got it recognized, whereby he made twenty five hundred dollars." Did Beckley really know this for a "fact"? No, but Beckley had it from Jacob Clingman, who "saw both the letter and the certificate."

Beckley pushed the plot along for Jefferson by writing a letter on June 22, which he did not finish until July 2, to an unnamed addressee in New York who was probably Governor George Clinton. Beckley told him that Fraunces had told Clingman that "he could, if he pleased, hang Hamilton," an all too familiar threat, and that Fraunces was "privy" to Hamilton's whole connection with Duer and his agent for supplying Duer with money. Beckley also reported that Clingman had told him that "Mrs. Reynolds has obtained a divorce from her husband, in consequence of his [sic] intrigue with Hamilton to her prejudice, and that Colonel Burr obtained it for her; she is thoroughly disposed to attest all she knows of the connection between Hamilton and Reynolds." Clingman had been sent for by Hamilton and was about to be grilled by him. Clinton (or whoever the unnamed addresse might be) should use Clingman as an *"instrumentality"* but not tell or show him anything that might be compromising if Hamilton should worm it out of him; he should communicate only "thro' our common friend, Melancton Smith," a New York merchant and Anti-Federalist known to be one of Clinton's henchmen.

Hamilton would have liked nothing better than to worm out of Clingman proof that would link his intrigues to Jefferson, the master puppeteer in the loft manipulating all his persecutors. When Clingman went to Hamilton, Hamilton (according to Beckley) "used every artifice to make a friend of him, and asked many leading questions." On June 25, Hamilton cross-examined Clingman as follows (this is Clingman's report of it to Beckley):

H: Are you a friend of Mr. A. G. Fraunces of New York?

C: I know him.

H: Did you ever board at his house?

C: I never did.

H: Do you not frequently dine and sup with him?

C: Only once, at a stranger's house.

H: Do you not frequently visit Fraunces' office?

C: I have been there several times.

H: Do you not visit Mr. Beckley sometimes?

C: I know Mr. Beckley, I have seen him at Mr. Muhlenberg's.

H: [In disgust] Mr. Clingman, you do not put that confidence and trust in me that you ought. Every answer you give is as secretive as the grave.

Clingman did not tell Beckley his reply, which was probably smugly defiant silence.

H: Does not Beckley visit often at Mr. Muhlenberg's house? Who else visits there?

From Clingman, only silence. Hamilton gave up.

To "counterwork Hamilton" in "speculations and connection with Duer," Beckley set forth a plan of nine numbered points, which included obtaining from Fraunces the power of attorney for Glaubeck's pay with a correction in Hamilton's writing, obtaining Thomas Bazen's deposition concerning his part in the Glaubeck payment, Fraunces's first letter to Hamilton, Hamilton's friendly reply, copies of the two warrants, and receipts of Duer's. Clinton (or whoever) was also to find out more about the divorce Burr had obtained for Mrs. Reynolds and all she knew about Hamilton, and also obtain an affidavit from her and all other evidence he could find of Hamilton's speculating in public funds and collaborating with Duer. Clinton and others whose hands and strings remained invisible duly carried out much of this program.

After politely, but rashly, indicating he might approve payment to Fraunces, Hamilton's Treasury had refused to honor the two warrants. Fraunces then made threatening demands on Hamilton and also on George Washington and Attorney General Edmund Randolph, who referred his demands back to Hamilton for explanation and reply. Hamilton's friends in New York watched in alarm as the threats to him grew; newspapers aired the dispute several times during September, October, and November of 1793. Willcocks wrote Hamilton on August 25 that ''your enemies are at work upon Mr. Francis . . . he is to make affidavits, criminating you in the highest degree, as to some money matters etc.'' and again on September 5 that ''the idea was, that Mr. Francis can substantiate some official criminality against you, of a very serious nature. And yet no one pretends to any *precision*.'' Robert Affleck, a New York city merchant friend of Hamilton, also wrote him in alarm on September 7 that a ''lawyer from Philadelphia''—probably Beckley or possibly John M. Taylor, a close associate of Beckley—had been with Fraunces and had sought to make Thomas Bazen sign a 23-page affidavit implicating Hamilton in frauds. Bazen had refused—as he could neither read nor write. Affleck's purpose in writing Hamilton was ''to put you on your guard . . . to thwart the efforts of *Malice, envy* and *treachery,* which . . . are combined against uncommon abilities and worth.'' On August 25, Fraunces had published a long pamphlet attacking Hamilton, including copies of his correspondence with Hamilton and Washington. On December 18 he submitted his pamphlet to Frederick A. C. Muhlenberg, speaker of the House, by now a familiar figure in ''get-Hamilton'' intrigues, thus launching yet another Congressional investigation that would drag on through 1794 and 1795. After investigation, Congress eventually dismissed all charges against Hamilton and commended him for the vigilance with which he detected frauds and frame-ups like the one Fraunces and his puppetmasters were trying to pin on him.

Fending off such attempts to cut the throat of his political reputation in whispers took an incalculable physical and psychic toll on Hamilton that comes through the lines of his poignant plea to Catherine Greene for evidence from her to exonerate himself for trying to do her a favor.

> It is not uncommon thing for you women to bring us poor men into scrapes. It seems you have brought me into one . . . it is an affair of delicacy . . . it is not in one way only that I am the object of unprincipled persecution—but I console myself with these lines of the poet—
>
> > He needs must have of optics keen
> > Who sees what is not to be seen—

The lines fit Jefferson well, he thought.

Hamilton added, ''with this belief that in spite of Calumny the friends I love and esteem will continue to love and esteem me.''

Hamilton analyzed the persecution: "Fraunces, partly, I believe from its having been made *worth his while* by some political enemies of mine, endeavours to have it believed that this transaction was a speculation in which I was engaged; and in proof of it professes to have a draft of a power of attorney corrected by some interlineations in my handwriting."

Closing the exchanges with Fraunces in exasperation, Hamilton wrote him on October 1: "contemptible as you are, what answer could I give to your last letter?" He enclosed a copy of an advertisement to be published in the *Daily Advertiser* assuring the public that "Fraunces has been regularly and repeatedly called upon, to declare the grounds of [his charges]; he has repeatedly evaded the inquiry; he possesses no facts of the nature pretended; and he is a despicable calumniator."

Control of events more and more seemed to be slipping from Hamilton's grasp, though his eloquent efforts to engage popular support for his political views continued unabated in a series of broadsides over the names of *Americanus, Pacificus,* and *No Jacobin.* He may have heard it whispered that Monroe had now placed his original set of the Reynolds documents in the hands of a "respectable character in Virginia," his friend Thomas Jefferson.

On June 21, Hamilton wrote Washington that "considerations relative both to the public interest and my own delicacy, have brought me, after mature reflection, to a resolution to resign the office I hold, towards the close of the ensuing session of Congress." He was postponing "the final act" till then because "propositions necessary to the full develop-ment of my original plan" and "of consequence to my reputation" still remained to be submitted to Congress. Secondly, "I am desirous of giving an opportunity" while still in office for the "revival and more delicate prosecution of the inquiry into my conduct, which was instituted during the last session." His overly keen defensiveness about his public credit would not permit him to avoid making a dangerous situation worse by letting bad enough alone.

His friend Edward Carrington relentlessly abetted him in this folly, and goaded him on, writing on July 2, 1793, that "should your persecutors not come forward at the next session with an impeachment . . . you should explicitly call for one—it would ensure at once their destruction." Perhaps down there in Virginia, Carrington had not yet heard whispers of the covered up scandal. "Stand fast, and you cannot fail," he exhorted. "Resign, under the pressure of the present opposition and you fail irretrievably."

Hamilton's series *No Jacobin,* attacking France and neutrality, ends abruptly with No. IX on August 28. Hamilton had overcommitted his physical strength. His body crumpled under the stressful incursions made upon it by his public, private, and secret lives and by the plaguey Philadelphia summer. The plague, a form of yellow fever, raged in Philadelphia that summer. Hamilton and his Betsy both contracted it, although she caught a less severe case than his. It fastened on him in its most virulent form. Few who showed his symptoms survived, and for a time his life was despaired of. The epidemic lasted from mid-August till late November. More than 4,000 died of it. Loads of the dead were carted away out of the city every day. Not knowing what else to do, the Hamiltons attempted to flee the fevers by moving to a house two miles outside the city.

The usual method of treatment was the one prescribed by Dr. Benjamin Rush: purging and bleeding the victims.

But Dr. Edward Stevens, Hamilton's boyhood friend from St. Croix who was now a practicing physician in Philadelphia, disagreed with Dr. Rush. Called in to treat Hamilton,

Dr. Neddy Stevens ordered cold baths in constant succession and dosage with infusions of tanbark tea. A host of attendants was required to fill the baths, carry the gasping man in and out, and attend him in accordance with Dr. Stevens's orders. The five Hamilton children, the youngest now only a year old, were sent off to a neighbor's house and not even allowed to see their mother, except in the distance through the window. Later on, the children were sent still farther away to the Schuylers.

That both father and mother recovered was considered a miracle of science due to Dr. Stevens's treatment. "This is a strong confirmation," the *Federal Gazette* announced on September 13, 1793, "of goodness of the plan, pursued by Dr. Stevens, and ought to recommend it to the serious consideration of our Medical Gentlemen." A friend from nearby Burlington joined "with all ranks in the general joy . . . upon hearing of your safe recovery." Benjamin Walker wrote, "for God sake or rather for our sakes take care to avoid a relapse." Washington's secretary Tobias Lear, congratulating Hamilton on his recovery, had found in New England "unfeigned sorrow . . . on a report of your death and . . . marks of joy . . . when the report was known to be unfounded."

Congratulations on survival poured in to the Hamiltons from all directions.

But as Jefferson saw it, Hamilton could do nothing right, not even get well. He wrote Madison: "Hamilton is ill of the fever as is said. He had two physicians out at his house the night before last, his family think him in danger, & he puts himself so by his excessive alarm." Of the hero of the last redoubt at Yorktown, the deserter of Richmond added, "He had been miserable several days before from a firm persuasion he should catch it, a man as timid as he is on the water, as timid on horseback, as timid in sickness, would be a phaenomenon if the courage of which he has the reputation in military matters were genuine."

Now back in Philadelphia after a good rest with family and Schuyler in-laws at Albany and Schuylerville, Hamilton was sufficiently recovered to make an aggressively foolish misjudgment. On December 16 he wrote a formal letter to the House of Representatives, requesting "that a new inquiry may without delay be instituted in some mode, the most effectual for an accurate and thorough investigation; and I will add, that the more comprehensive it is, the more agreeable will it be for me."

He was reopening the whole cancerous subject that might otherwise have remained in remission, by himself calling for a new investigation of himself. To Hamilton, his reputation and his honor had to be proven to the public; it had to be "devised and play'd to spectators." Public credit was his watchword. Hamilton recklessly ignored Shakespeare's warning against asking for too much: "This is more than history can pattern."

Hamilton's request may not have been the rash example of his heroic inability to let sleeping dogs lie that it seemed on its face. Washington, having heard the whispers, may have been forcing his hand behind the scenes. In September, replying to complaints about Hamilton's policies from Edward Pendleton of Virginia, Washington had said that doubtless Hamilton would seek a further inquiry into his conduct at the coming session, adding that he devoutly wished all charges to be "probed to the bottom, be the result what it will."

But Hamilton was now blundering into a tactical mistake. If the form of the question presented called for an affirmative finding of Hamilton's innocence, all those whom Jefferson had called undecided, stupid, lazy, or ignorant for voting against Hamilton's censure or impeachment would be ranged against him. Who could affirmatively vote that, in all the complex mass of material on his operations before Congress, there was not some telltale clue to his misdeeds: Honor or dishonor all came down to the form in which the issue was presented.

If anything, Hamilton's near brush with death had whetted the desire of the Virginia junto to carry out Jefferson's orders now to "cut him to pieces." After some delay, a committee appointed to inquire into the Treasury Department focused on the hoary—and already much-investigated—issue of Hamilton's management of the two foreign loans of August 4 and 12, 1790. The committee demanded that Hamilton turn over every communication that he had ever made to Washington; Hamilton created one of the earliest precedents for the doctrine of executive privilege by retorting that he would yield only those he judged to be pertinent to the specific issue. The committee wished to know "by what authority any portion of the moneys borrowed abroad have been drawn to the United States?" He replied that he had received a general commission from the president and specific sanctions for each disposition, "always bottomed upon the representation of the Secretary, and always expressly or tacitly qualified with this *condition*—that whatever was to be done, was to be agreeable to the Laws."

Hamilton wrote Washington, asking him for a written endorsement of what he had done and reminding Washington that "the sanctions were [*sic*] verbal whenever the President was at the seat of Government. In a case of absence they were in writing." Washington endorsed a "certificate" for Hamilton in the form of a letter dated April 8, 1794, written on Hamilton's official report on the 1790 borrowings that was broad enough, but not one word broader than necessary, to give Hamilton what he needed for vindication in the inquiry:

> Sir,
>
> I cannot charge my memory with all the particulars, which have passed between us, relative to the disposition of the money borrowed. Your letters, however, and my answer, which you refer to in the foregoing statement, and lately reminded me of, speak for themselves, and stand in no need of explanation.
>
> As to verbal communications, I am satisfied, that many were made by you to me on this subject; and from my general recollection of the course of proceedings, I do not doubt, that it was substantially as you have stated it in the annexed paper, that I have approved of the measures, which you, from time to time, proposed to me for disposing of the Loans, upon the condition, that what was to be done by you, should be agreeable to the Laws.
>
> Go. Washington
>
> United States
> April 8, 1794

Hamilton went back to Washington the same day in great distress. Washington's letter was not a sufficient endorsement. His enemies would read into it an approval withheld. Enemies were too much on his mind to let him see that his chief had saved him by the surest way to be saved. Hamilton wrote:

> Under all that has happened Sir, I cannot help entertaining and frankly expressing to you my apprehension, that false and insidious men, whom you may one day understand, taking advantage of the want of recollection, which is natural, where the mind is habitually occupied with a variety of important objects, have found means by artful suggestions to infuse doubts and distrusts very injurious to me.

The pain of apprehension skewed his judgment: "Those who are disposed to construe everything to my disadvantage will affirm That the Declaration of the President has entirely waived the main point and does not even manifest an opinion that the Representation of the Secretary of the Treasury is well founded.''

Here is sad evidence of preoccupation with enemies blunting Hamilton's ability to make accurate judgments of the effect of political actions. Washington's reserved but complete ratification of all of Hamilton's official acts was worth more to defend him with Congress than a peck of predictable, praiseful, opinion, but Hamilton failed to see it that way.

His desperate, inward, personal need was not so much to be ''rescued'' from indesinent investigation by Congress—he could ride that out—but to obtain some signal from Washington that whispers of scandal had not cut away the only base on which Hamilton had erected ''my administration.'' Hamilton concluded that to what his enemies said ''would be added, that the reserve of the President is a proof that he does not think that representation true [that is, Hamilton's defense]—else his justice would have led him to rescue the officer concerned even from suspicion on the point.''

After he had observed Hamilton resolve hard questions over 15 years of service, Washington's overall conclusion was that Hamilton's judgment was ''intuitively great.'' Here it was wrong, and Washington's was right. Washington, having heard the whispers, could easily make and act on the correct judgment of Hamilton's situation, yet also sympathetically understand the pressures warping Hamilton's judgment into error. A lawyer who argues his own case has a fool for a client.

Hamilton was right to be apprehensive of the use his enemies would make of Washington's certificate, but wrong in his fear of the end result. On April 14, 1794, Madison wrote sycophantically to Jefferson: ''The letter from the P. is inexpressibly mortifying to his [H's] friends, and marks his situation to be precisely what you always described it to be.''

In an impeachment proceeding, unlike a court trial, the investigators have no responsibility to resolve ultimate questions of the truth or falsity of even the wildest charges. Of all the congressional investigations in American history, the Virginia junto's two-year investigation of Hamilton's Treasury Department operations proved to be one of the most resounding flops. The sacrosanct president's stiff and reserved but unimpeachable and unarguable blanket endorsement of all of Hamilton's operations served the secretary as a better security blanket than any fulsome testimonial.

The very length and persistence of the inquiry became in itself for his enemies evidence of Hamilton's guilt; for his friends, of his innocence. But it was he who had demanded reopening of the inquiry; so the time tilt sloped against him with the wide public who reach political conclusions on emotional, not legally admissible evidence.

The congressional committee's report of April 1794 approved Hamilton's Treasury administration. It found he had not used official influence with the banks to secure private favors. It concluded that ''no moneys of the United States, whether before or after they have passed to the credit of the Treasurer, have ever been, directly or indirectly, used for, or applied to any purposes, but those of the Government, except so far as all moneys deposited in a bank are concerned in the general operations thereof.'' The committee's report was unanimous.

Whether an impeachment proceeding or a congressional investigation succeeds or fails, either way it remains an impeachment. There is nothing like a jury's verdict of ''not guilty'' to end it. The pressures it put on Hamilton compounded his anxieties. He could take no comfort in what *The Federalist* had once known well but he now seemed to have forgotten: ''The decision will be regulated more by the comparative strength of the parties, than by the real demonstrations of innocence or guilt.''

27

Neutrality

My health which had suffered a severe shock by an attack of the malignant disease lately prevalent here is now almost completely restored. The last vestige of it has been a nervous derangement; but this has nearly yielded to Regimen, a certain degree of exercise and a resolution to overcome it.

—To Angelica Church, December 27, 1793

No issue except that of Hamilton's impeachment would give rise to fiercer battles in the war going on inside Washington's cabinet than the subject of American neutrality. Questions of Hamilton's handling of the proceeds of foreign loans were compounded with questions of recognition of foreign governments, particularly revolutionary foreign governments like those in France—and Saint-Domingue—and the departmental war between Jefferson and Hamilton. The French Revolution had changed from a movement for a limited monarchy to one for a republic. Amid the massacres of September 1792, it deposed and imprisoned King Louis XVI, who, when Hamilton was at Valley Forge, had been woebegone America's most "powerful friend among the princes of the earth." Now Hamilton had suspended American payments on the French debt. It mattered little to Hamilton that shortly after suspending the king, the Revolutionary National Assembly had named Hamilton—and Washington and Madison, but not Jefferson—honorary citizens of the revolutionary republic.

No doubt, Hamilton's activities in foreign affairs were more effective because his own personal reputation was not immediately involved in that sector. No doubt, Jefferson's were less so because his was. In foreign affairs, circumstances and character made it easier for

Hamilton to act selflessly and impossible for Jefferson to do so. It seems fair to say—rather surprisingly of a man who was not the president or the secretary of state—that when it came to formulating policy and devising actions, contacts, statements, and documents for carrying out the policy of American neutrality, no man did more in his time than Hamilton to keep America out of the great powers' wars.

On March 7, 1793, when only rumors of war were abroad, George Hammond wrote home that Hamilton "has assured me that *he* shall exert his influence to defeat the success of any proposition on the part of France, which, tempting as it might appear, might ultimately render it necessary for this government to depart from the observance of as strict a neutrality as is compatible with its present engagements, and which is so essential to its real interests." He attributed Hamilton's stand to "the knowledge that any event which might endanger the *external* tranquility of the United States, would be as fatal to the systems he has formed for the benefit of his country as to his present personal reputation and to his future projects of ambition."

On April 2, under the heading, *"Most Secret and Confidential,"* Hammond was able, on Hamilton's word, to assure his government that the United States would not permit its treaties with France to involve it "in any difficulties or disputes with other powers." All Hamilton's policies were directed toward the "continuance of peace."

On April 5, Hamilton wrote Washington of reports that "War had been declared by France against England, Russia and Holland. . . . There seems to be no room for Doubt of the Existence of War." He added by postscript that "English Papers in Town by way of St. Vincents mention that on the 8th of February the late Queen of France was also put to Death after a Trial and Condemnation."

Hamilton's report of the queen's death was premature. Although the revolutionary government of France had cut off the head of America's friend Louis XVI on January 21, 1793, it would not lop off Marie Antoinette's until October 16. The revolutionary government had indeed declared war on Britain and Holland on February 1, but not on Russia. This word from Hamilton was probably the first that George Washington received of these calamitous foreign events.

News of new war between the two greatest European powers created a sensation in America. On April 18, Washington submitted a series of 13 questions to the members of his cabinet "with a view to forming a general plan of conduct for the executive" in this grave emergency.

When Jefferson received Washington's questions, he saw in them Hamilton's hand, which was becoming an obsession with him. "It was palpable from the style," he confided to his *Anas,* and from "their ingenious tissue & suite that they were not the President's, that they were raised upon a prepared chain of argument, in short that the language was Hamilton's and the doubts his alone." Edmund Randolph, the attorney general, had confirmed his suspicions, he delcared.

The questions Washington had posed to his department heads ranged across all American involvement with the war. Should the United States issue a proclamation of neutrality? Should the United States consider the old treaties with France that had created the alliance during the American Revolution to be still in effect, or ought they to be renounced or suspended? Did they require America to join France and declare war on Britain? Ought the United States receive the new minister from the French revolutionary government, Edmond Genêt, now on his way, absolutely, or with qualifications, or refuse to receive him at all?

As Jefferson saw it, there was no occasion for "doubts" to be raised: According to the treaties, the United States and France were bound to each other as allies. Hamilton, of course, was prepared to answer the president's questions before they arrived; he sent on his views to John Jay with a request that Jay draft a proclamation of neutrality along the lines he suggested for Washington's review and signature. Jay obliged with a hasty draft of ideas for such a proclamation and Hamilton forwarded this useful material to Washington. Jefferson did nothing. No secretary of state could fail to smolder and fume with rage, or at least sulk, if the secretary of the treasury has preempted the making of foreign policy on the most important foreign policy issue to confront his administration.

According to the treaties with France, the United States was, in effect, the ally of France in any war with England in which England was the aggressor. By the treaty, the United States had also extended protection and favored status to French possessions in the West Indies. Answering Washington's 13 questions, Hamilton and Jefferson split to the maximum extent that it was possible to do for two men who were in basic agreement over policy. Both agreed with the view Washington had already laid down from Hamilton's draft: neutrality was the best policy. Neither would disagree with Washington or wished to drag the weak, unarmed United States into a war. But on details of neutrality and the complex questions in its train, there was no agreement and wide divergence. It was partly a question of which way the government's officially neutral stance would tilt.

The cabinet met at Washington's house in Philadelphia on April 18 to give their opinions on ''a general plan of conduct for the Executive.'' Hamilton argued for an immediate proclamation of neutrality. Jefferson opposed. Let us act neutrally without expressly saying so, he recommended. ''It would be better to hold back the declaration of neutrality,'' he suggested, ''as a thing worth something to the powers at war, that they would bid for it, & we might reasonably ask a price, the *broadest privileges* of neutral nations.'' He also argued that the president had no inherent or implied power under the Constitution to issue such a proclamation without the consent of Congress. To this, Hamilton retorted that Congress was not in session and that Washington had ample authority under the implied constitutional powers of the executive to act, at least until Congress convened.

Hamilton's minutes of the meeting next day show that ''it was determined by all that a proclamation shall issue.'' On this point Hamilton won. On April 22, Washington published the famous proclamation, which Edmund Randolph, the attorney general, had drafted for him. The fact of neutrality was proclaimed, but the word itself was avoided. It expressed a determination on the part of the United States to ''adopt and pursue a conduct friendly and impartial toward the belligerent powers'' and ''to exhort and warn the citizens of the United States carefully to avoid all acts and proceedings whatsoever, which may in any manner tend to contravene such disposition.''

This saved the good points Jefferson had made. At Hamilton's prodding, the thing was done, and for the record; Jefferson's reservations preserved the subtleties of his approach. The joint result is a good example of how both men, working against each other together in Washington's cabinet, could bring about a result better for the nation than either would have arrived at by himself. It is also an illustration of Washington's genius as president for coping patiently with two contentious rivals yoked together, and making the most of the peculiar contributions of each for the good of the nation.

A yet more subtle question was what to do about ''Citizen'' Edmond Charles Genêt, the new envoy now on his way from France to replace Ternant, the holdover minister from Louis XVI. Any French envoy would hold due bills against the United States. But acknowledging them now would contradict the terms of the neutrality proclamation and tie the country more closely to France in the war she had just declared against England. But to refuse to receive Citizen Genêt at all would not be "conduct friendly and impartial" toward a belligerent that the proclamation required of the country.

"The King has been decapitated," Hamilton had written Jay on April 9. If the European powers ranged against France should appoint a regent who, in turn, should appoint an ambassador to the United States, "Should we in such case receive both?" Further, at the moment it was uncertain which government of France was the *established* one: if the revolutionary government were not, then its demand for enforcement of the existing treaties need not be recognized. Moreover, the United States had no obligation to support France— she was the aggressor in a war she had declared; the American obligation was only to help defend her against aggression by others. Hamilton acknowledged the validity of the treaties themselves: "I doubt whether we could *bona fide* dispute the ultimate obligation of the treaties."

Jefferson opposed Hamilton's approach. It was the French people with whom the treaty had been made, regardless of the form supported by their governmental representatives, whether monarchy or republic.

No, not at all, Hamilton argued. To abandon Louis XVI now might be regarded by "mankind as not consistent with a decent regard to the relations which subsisted between them and Louis XVI." But the crux of the matter was that, in dealing with foreign governments, practical outcomes, not slogans or sentiments or old attachments, were what counted most.

Hamilton's minutes of the April 19 cabinet meeting show that it was finally agreed by all present that Genêt should be received. On the subordinate question of just how he should be received, Hamilton noted: "The Attorney General Randolph and Secretary of State are of opinion he should be received absolutely & without qualifications." As for the secretaries of the treasury and war, Hamilton recorded only a "?" and added, "This & the subsequent questions are postponed to another day."

Washington followed Jefferson's advice to receive Genêt without any qualifications. The practical difference was hardly perceptible. All awaited the arrival of the new French minister with strong emotions, strongly counterpoised along partisan lines.

Surprisingly contrary winds or else a design to make his first landfall in politically friendly Republican territory brought Citizen Genêt to the United States at Charleston, South Carolina. Like Robespierre, Saint-Just, and others of the Jacobins of the Mountain who had sent him, Genêt was egotistic, brash, full of self-importance, and convinced that his mission was to reexport revolution to the populace of the United States. With a tendency to ignore the constitutional government to which he had been accredited and to act as if only "the people" counted, he was the worst possible sort of minister that the revolutionists could have sent to cement official relations with France's old ally.

Instead of proceeding straightway to Philadelphia to present his credentials to Washington, Genêt lingered in the South to bask in adulation and arrange for the recruitment and outfitting of privateers to prey on British shipping. He distributed military commissions to American adventurers to serve in French incursions against Florida and Louisiana. He gave letters of marque or authority (he came with 300 of them) to American privateers "who may fit out and try their chance against the English, Dutch, Russians, Prussians and Austrians." The French consul condemned and sold the first prize ship brought in. All of this was illegal by the rules of international law.

Through the Southern towns Genêt traveled slowly northward through tableau after tableau of triumph. Federalists watched his triumphal progress with mounting alarm. Some saw in Genêt the imminent onset of the wildest excesses of the Reign of Terror.

With a keen sense of affronted dignity, Washington awaited Genêt's dawdling advent in Philadelphia.

Jefferson, by contrast, seemed thrilled at the approach of this live apostle of liberty, who spoke directly from "the people" to "the people," not to their governments. He described with obvious relish the enthusiasm of the "yeomanry" of the city at the sight of a French frigate victoriously bringing into port a beaten and captured British prize, portentously named the *Grange*, which had been seized inside American territorial waters. Randolph and Hamilton agreed that this violated international law; the cabinet, including Jefferson, concurred; Genêt eventually had to give orders to yield the prize.

Genêt finally arrived at the capital May 17, 1793, five and a half weeks after landing in Charleston. True Americans not exactly bowled over by his brand of the politics of joy included Washington and Hamilton. Washington received Genêt with frigid politeness, which Genêt ascribed to jealousy.

British Minister George Hammond strongly protested Genêt's commissioning of the many privateers that preyed on British shipping, as well as seizures of ships like the *Grange*. Hamilton agreed and gave Washington his opinion that for France to equip, man, and commission vessels of war within the United States to prey on British ships was "an injury and an affront of a very serious kind" under the law of nations.

Genêt demanded advances on payments of the debt to France; Washington refused. Genêt then refused to permit payments to American creditors for aid given by them earlier to the French in Saint-Domingue under the agreement made earlier with Ternant. Hammond reported that an angry Hamilton had told him that "Mr. Genêt's conduct was a direct violation of a formal compact, originally entered into with Ternant." Hamilton told Genêt that the American government would apply the next installments due on the French debt to paying these American creditors whose claims Genêt had disavowed.

Two new privateers were being armed in Baltimore, and Hammond renewed British protests. Washington disregarded Hamilton's advice that British prizes be returned, as Hammond demanded, only partly followed Jefferson's, and took a middle course: no privateers could be fitted out or supplied in American ports, but captured prizes could remain. The cabinet would merely "consider whether any practicable arrangement can be adopted to prevent the augmentation of the privateer force." This response to Hammond's remonstrance was much too feeble for Hamilton. Genêt simply ignored the feeble protest and went on arming privateers in American ports.

With few of his recommendations on neutrality being followed by Washington and with Jefferson's efforts to impeach him having continued after the defeat of Giles's resolutions, Hamilton submitted his resignation June 21, to take effect "toward the close of the ensuing session of the Congress." Since the night of December 15, the tides of politics and cabinet warfare had been running against him. His continued presence in the cabinet would only weaken the Union and the system he had done so much to build. It appeared that Jefferson had succeeded in forcing him out of office and outlasting him in power. But the secretary of state's word of reassurance to Hammond that he would "prevent the augmentation" of the privateer force, feeble as it was, would soon leave Jefferson open to charges of duplicity.

The *Little Sarah*, an English merchant vessel, had been captured sailing out of Philadelphia by a French frigate, *L'Ambuscade*, and brought back to port as a prize of war in May. Hamilton and Knox warned Jefferson pointedly in July of reports coming to them that the *Little Sarah*, renamed the *Petit Démocrate*, was being secretly outfitted as a French privateer with 14 iron cannons, six swivels, and a crew of 120 to prey on British shipping.

No kind of privateer would be more deceptive and effective to prey on the British than a former British merchant vessel like the *Petit Démocrate*.

Governor Thomas Mifflin of Pennsylvania sent the secretary of the Commonwealth, Alexander J. Dallas, to Genêt's house at midnight on July 6 to ask him to hold up departure of the new privateer.

Genêt "absolutely refused" to give any assurance, complained bitterly of his treatment by the authorities, and "declared that he would appeal from the President to the people." Any attempt to seize the *Petit Démocrate* would be resisted with force.

Governor Mifflin at once called up 100 infantry and 20 artillerymen with their cannon and gave orders that no pilot take the vessel out. Dallas told Jefferson of Genêt's flat and absolute refusal to cancel the orders for sailing. Jefferson hurried to Genêt's house Sunday morning, July 7, to request him to hold it back, at least until Washington, then at Mount Vernon, returned to Philadelphia. Genêt again refused. According to Jefferson, he merely indicated that the ship would not be ready to sail "for some time," but that she would drop down the river just a little way in order to continue her outfitting and preparations.

As Jefferson described his meeting with Genêt, whenever he tried to obtain Genêt's commitment to fix the departure to the president's return, Genêt, "gave the same answer, that she would not be ready for some time, but with the look and gesture, which showed he meant I should understand she would not be gone before that time." Jefferson failed to insist that Genêt direct the vessel not to sail; he failed to carry out the cabinet's policy expressed in the reassurance given to Hammond. Jefferson told Mifflin and Dallas that "though the vessel was to fall somewhere down the river, she would not sail." Mifflin countermanded his orders to arrest the privateer.

At the cabinet meeting on July 8, the day after Jefferson's meeting with Genêt, with Washington and Randolph absent, Jefferson reported the conversation. Hamilton, with Knox concurring, insisted that a battery of guns at once be placed in position on Mud Island, below Philadelphia, to fire on the ship if she should attempt to sneak out to sea. Jefferson strongly disagreed. He insisted that nothing be done to detain the vessel until Washington's return three days later. Dallas, the secretary of the Commonwealth of Pennsylvania, had reported that Genêt had told him *"that he would appeal from the President of the United States to the people."* Hamilton, supported by Knox, argued that Genêt's conduct must be interpreted as part of *"a regular plan to force the United States into the war."* Furthermore, Hamilton said, there was evidence of "a *regular system to endeavour to control the government itself, by creating, if possible, a schism between it and the people,* by enlisting them on the side of France."

Hamilton composed a 13-point written opinion to Washington giving the reasons for his stand. The cabinet was in an uproar. Factions in the country at large reflected the division in the cabinet. Washington sent a request to Genêt to detain the privateer in port until the legal questions involved could be referred to "persons learned in the laws," which Jefferson transmitted July 12.

Jefferson's dilatory and feeble execution of Washington's instructions had given Genêt all the time *Petit Démocrate* needed. She hauled anchor, hoisted sail, and escaped unscathed to the open sea, where she would soon seize at least four British vessels as prizes.

When the justices of the United States Supreme Court assembled in Philadelphia July 18, they had before them 29 questions, the first 22 drafted by Hamilton, the last seven by Jefferson and others, all agreed to, concerning the legal problems raised by privateering and related matters under the Proclamation of Neutrality. It was a very deliberate way of trying to deal with ultimate questions like war or peace. While the country waited on the judges, war fevers rose.

John Adams recalled the frightening scenes of the summer of 1793, when "ten thousand people in the streets of Philadelphia, day after day, threatened to drag Washington out of his house, and effect a revolution in the government, or compel it to declare war . . . against England." In New York anti-Hamilton leaders—James Nicholson, Melancton Smith, Brockholst Livingston, and others—held a meeting in The Fields to show their support for Genêt.

Under the pseudonym *Pacificus*, Hamilton had been defending the Proclamation of Neutrality against attacks of the Republicans in the press. His first paper of the series appeared on June 29, 1793, in Fenno's *Gazette of the United States;* and the seventh and last, on July 20. Hamilton pointed out that the treaties called for a defensive alliance only, and France had declared offensive war. The United States had no duty to go behind that declaration, he argued, to determine who had been first to injure whom. "Self-preservation is the first duty of a nation," he declared. "Good faith does not require that the United States should put in jeopardy their essential interests, perhaps their very existence, in one of the most unequal contests in which a nation could be engaged, to secure to France—what? Her West India islands and other less important possessions in America?"

Pacificus discounted the argument that gratitude for French aid during the Revolution required repayment by aid to her now. France had aided the United States then not from motives of altruism, he declared, but to seek revenge for former defeats at the hands of England. The revolutionary government that now sought to bring America into war "are not ashamed to brand Louis the XVI as a tyrant, Lafayette as a traitor." Such things "ought to teach us not to over-rate *foreign friendships*—to be on our guard against *foreign attachments.*"

Hamilton's *Pacificus* broadsides, white-hot from week to week, fanned Jefferson's hot ire. Never effective in direct debate, he called on Madison to do battle with mighty *Pacificus*. "Nobody answers him," he wrote urgently to Madison, "& his doctrines will therefore be taken for confessed. For God's sake, my dear Sir, take up your pen, select the most striking heresies and cut him to pieces in the face of the public. There is nobody else who can & will enter the lists with him."

With no one else to carry Jefferson's spear, Madison finally took up his pen under the mask of *Helvidius*. He branded *Pacificus'* arguments superficial, but there was little fire or conviction in his rebuttal, as Genêt's antics cut the ground from under his pleas for sympathy and gratitude toward France.

At a cabinet meeting on August 1, Hamilton moved to notify France that Genêt must be recalled. Too, Genêt had just been elected president of an American democratic political society, the Friends of Liberty and Equality. There was his outrageous declaration that he would appeal from the president to the people. Jefferson proposed that Genêt's abusive correspondence be communicated to France "with friendly observations." Washington remained silent while his cabinet heads debated.

Even Jefferson was becoming disenchanted with Genêt, whom he described as "Hotheaded, all imagination, no judgment, passionate, disrespectful and even indecent towards the President." He eventually came to believe, he said, that Genêt's appointment had been "calamitous" and that he would "sink the Republican interest if they do not abandon him."

Hamilton was for disclosing to the public all the Genêt papers; Jefferson insisted that they be kept secret. Tempers were short.

Next day according to Jefferson's notes, when the cabinet "met again, Hamilton spoke again ¾ of an hour." Jefferson still opposed publishing the Genêt papers but the president, like Hamilton, was "manifestly inclined to the appeal of the people." The question was not resolved.

The Supreme Court justices refused to ease matters for Washington and his irreparably cleft cabinet. They refused to give a ruling on the 29 questions on neutrality that Hamilton and Jefferson had submitted to them. Instead, they established an important new constitutional doctrine by holding that the court would refuse all requests to issue advisory opinions, only opinions in justiciable controversies. It firmly underscored the constitutional doctrines of separation of powers, checks and balances, and the independence of the executive branch. It followed the letter and spirit of Federalist doctrines laid down by Hamilton in *The Federalist*.

Jefferson was forced to draft the letter demanding Genêt's recall. Hamilton had an objection to a passage in it saying that it would be a shame if, through Genêt's tactics, America were drawn into war with France, as that would be "liberty warring on herself." Hamilton argued that this should be stricken because the United States should not affirm that the cause of France was ipso facto the cause of liberty. Jefferson reported that "Knox according to custom jumped plump into all his [Hamilton's] opinions." Jefferson argued that his allusion to French liberty would be an antidote to charges that America "in some of its parts was tainted with a hankering after monarchy." That was no way to win arguments with Hamilton and Washington. The offending clause was deleted.

Genêt was recalled in disgrace. Jefferson was widely criticized for having supported him. Genêt turned on Jefferson and charged him with having led him on to his downfall. Jefferson submitted his own resignation, to take effect on December 31, 1793. Hamilton stayed on.

Six months after Jefferson's letter demanding his recall, Genêt still lingered in the United States. His successor, Jean Antoine Fauchet, arrived and demanded that Genêt be arrested and sent back to be tried by the new set of Jacobins now in power. The United States declined to ship the former minister plenipotentiary back home for a last ride in the tumbrels in the name of *Liberté, Egalité,* and *Fraternité*. Citizen Genêt became an American citizen; certified his Republicanism by marrying Cornelia Clinton, the daughter of Governor George Clinton; and bought a 325-acre farm near Jamaica, Long Island, with her dowry and his savings, which he named "Cornelia's Farm." As he wrote Cornelia on February 24, 1794, his sole desire now was to settle in a country where virtue was honored and liberty respected and where a man who obeyed the law had nothing to fear from despots, aristocrats, or ambitious men.

As 1793 ended, confusion beset Hamilton's enemies. Neutrality tilting away from the French treaties prevailed. Genêt was in disgrace and blaming Jefferson for duplicity. Jefferson had cried out to Madison to cut *Pacificus* to pieces, but *Helvidius* had only feebly gone through the motions of doing so. Jefferson's impeachment resolutions had been discredited and backfired on their supporters. The follow-up congressional investigation that Hamilton had insisted upon to clear himself (of what he failed to realize was an ineradicable stain) was about to vote to clear him of misconduct in the Treasury. And Jefferson had resigned under a Genêt cloud.

There is no record of frank comment by Hamilton on Jefferson's resignation, but there is little doubt that he would have agreed with every word John Adams said on the subject:

> Jefferson's want of candor, his obstinate prejudices both of aversion and attachment; his real partiality in spite of all his pretensions, and his low notions about

many things have so nearly reconciled me to it that I will not weep. . . . Instead of being the ardent pursuer of science that some think him, he is indolent and his soul is poisoned with ambition. . . . He has talents I know, and integrity I believe; but his mind is now poisoned with passion, prejudice, and faction.

By his retirement, Adams wrote to his son John Quincy, on January 3, 1794, Jefferson

thinks by this step to get a reputation of an humble, modest, meek man, wholly without ambition or vanity. He may even have deceived himself into this belief. . . . Ambition is wonderfully adroit in concealing itself from its owner, I had almost said from itself. . . . But if a prospect opens, the world will see and he will feel that he is as ambitious as Oliver Cromwell though no soldier. . . . Numa was called from the forest to be King of Rome. And if Jefferson, after the death or resignation of the President, should be summoned from the familiar society of Egeria, to govern the country forty years in peace, so be it. . . . I am not sorry for his desertion on the whole, because . . . his temper [is] embittered against the constitution as I think.

A letter from Angelica Church, the only "foreign attachment" toward whom Hamilton would always be unneutral, written by her on August 15 would reach him with a stab of "happy" ironic rebuke as he was on the verge of dying of the plague and the other onslaughts of that awful Philadelphia summer:

Are you too happy to think of us? Ah *petit Fripon* you do not believe it: no I am not too happy, can I be so on this side of the Atlantic? Ask your heart and read my answer there.

My silence is caused by despair; for do not years, days and moments pass and still find me separated from these I love!

There was no respite for her either.

"Can a mind engaged by Glory taste of peace and ease?" She must have heard of his plans of resigning. "When will you come and receive the tears of joy and affection?"

Angelica's affectionate letters would revive the smoldering passion for her that he had resettled on Maria Reynolds after seeing Angelica off to England and sharing her tears after her autumn sojourn in the secret lodging they had shared in New York. The nightmarish scenes of his break-off with Maria, his frantic battles to fend off impeachment, his "dread" of "malicious intrigues" against him, and his brush with death of the plague had kept it sublimated, burning with more intensity the deeper he thrust it beneath the surface of his attention. Now he had outlasted Jefferson in the cabinet and ostensibly, for the moment at least, triumphed over all his enemies. But far from lifting his spirits his outlook from this pinnacle of the "jumble of events" only left him in greater "dread."

Hamilton's mental processes tended to confuse political opposition to "my administration" with a conspiracy of enemies that he saw as a personal threat. He discloses irrational fears in a fragment found among his unpublished papers: "On the Rise of a War Party."

His enemies "watch to defame and if possible to convulse the government," he writes. "No important measure can escape their malevolent vigilance . . . they endeavour to seduce the public . . . in paroxysms of their frenzy; they tear aside the veil of their own hypocrisy . . ." They are "incorrigible adversaries of national order." Virtuous men were made "the dupes of perpetual and implacable conspiracy against the general weal."

In such a mental state, no score of triumphs over real enemies in the objective world would be able to cancel out for Hamilton even a single such nightmarish delusion. He must have written the fragment while suffering from a nervous disorder. After recovering his senses sufficiently to see the touch of madness in what he had written, he put it aside. By December 27 he was well enough to write Angelica a letter to be delivered by his friend James Marshall, the brother of John Marshall, to tell her his health had ''suffered a severe shock by an attack of the malignant disease lately prevalent here,'' but was now ''almost'' completely restored. ''The last vestige of it has been a nervous derangement; but this has nearly yielded to Regimen, a certain degree of exercise and a resolution to overcome it.'' Writing her, he was enjoying a period of remission from morbid ''dread'' of ''malicious intrigues to stab me in the dark.''

But ''in this sublunary scene, I am just where I do not wish to be,'' he groaned. ''How long dear sister are the best friends to be separated?'' he asked, after confiding to her the secret of his nervous derangement. ''I know how I could be much happier,'' he sighed. ''I will break the spell. Nothing can prevent it at the opening of the spring, but the existence or the certainty of a war.'' A war would now be ''an event which I most sincerely deprecate but which reciprocal perverseness, in a degree, endangers.'' Worst of all, a war just now would keep him from the early spring rendezvous with Angelica in London that he was promising her and planning to fit into his political future.

Nearly, but not quite recovered, he told her that in his makeup ''a certain elasticity of constitution and temper reacts with a degree of vigour at least proportioned to the pressure.'' To one who loved him as well as Angelica, this was glum reassurance indeed. It made her still glummer that he found it necessary to add, as if still in doubt, ''I hope it will be so still.''

As a one-woman cultural exchange program during 1793 and 1794, Angelica Church would be sending on to America with letters of introduction to Alexander and Betsy Hamilton all sorts of distinguished French refugees from the turmoil and terror in Paris, including the statesman Charles Maurice de Talleyrand-Périgord, the jurist Bon-Albert Briois, the Chevalier de Beaumetz, as well as the British scientist and philosopher Joseph Priestley, who, like Hamilton, had been made an honorary citizen of revolutionary France.

Angelica recommended that all such friends of hers who had fled ''anarchy and cruelty'' in their own countries see the ''image of your domestic happiness and virtues for all that they have suffered in the cause of moderate liberty.'' Having followed up her introductions, Talleyrand and Beaumetz would ''write in raptures to all their friends of your kindness, and Colonel Hamilton's abilities and manners,'' she told Betsy on July 30, 1794. ''I receive innumerable compliments on his and your account—dear Alexander the amiable.''

The Constitution had given body to American nationality. But as Samuel Flagg Bemis summed up the matter on the first page of his authoritative treatise, *Jay's Treaty,* ''The administrative genius of Alexander Hamilton endowed the body with life and kept it functioning. Without commerce life would have been impossible, because the revenue which vitalized the nation came from the imposts.'' Some of the revenue came from interior excises, like the tax on whiskey, which would soon plunge Hamilton into trying to put down an insurrection, but, as Bemis notes, ''Most of the commerce in those years was with Great Britain. Therefore the life of the new nation depended on the tranquility of Anglo-American relations.''

Seven of the eight British fortified border posts were on the American side of the frontier. They served as the ''military guaranty of civilized nations'' over the immense domain claimed but not settled by America that stretched into the heart of the continent all the way to the Lake of the Woods in northern Minnesota at the headwaters of the Mississippi River.

Roaming this vast expanse were French habitants and priests; Canadian fur traders; British soldiers; and warlike Indian tribes, allied with the British and increasingly dependent on the lucrative fur trade. Unfortunately, there were few American settlers to bolster and ratify America's far-ranging continental claims.

Article II of the peace treaty of 1783 ending the Revolution had provided for the evacuation of American soil by British troops with "all convenient speed." But soon after, as the strategic importance of the posts for the protection of Canada, for the increasingly profitable fur trade, and for the profitable trade with the Indians became more obvious to Britain, "there was a settled policy to refuse delivery of the posts, notwithstanding the terms of the treaty." The fur trade at the time was the most profitable single industry in America, producing about £200,000 revenue annually.

To protect this rich trade, British and Canadian authorities naturally backed the Indian tribes against the occasional American military expeditions and attempts to establish permanent settlements in the Mohawk and Ohio River valleys. These expeditions often erupted in bloody frontier warfare and massacres. When various separate American states passed jingoistic laws putting obstacles in the way of collection of British debts guaranteed by the peace treaty and took to harassing former loyalists and Tories, it gave the British all the justification they needed for refusing to comply with the treaty obligations on their side to evacuate the posts. They would continue to hold them firmly until finally forced out when Jay's Treaty became effective in 1796.

As Hamilton was acutely aware, all but two of the British forts were in the upper reaches of New York State or on its Canadian border, at Oswego, Oswegatchie, Niagara, and Fort Erie. They controlled all navigation down the St. Lawrence River, Lake Ontario, and the eastern end of Lake Erie. Detroit and Michilimackinac, at the north end of the Michigan peninsula, controlled all waterborne commerce moving toward upper New York State from Lakes Michigan, Superior, and Huron. Dutchman's Point and Pointe-au-Fer secured the northern outlet of Lake Champlain and the old military corridor from Montreal to Albany.

No commercial treaty existed between the United States and Great Britain. To Britain, foreign commerce, then as always, was a matter of life or death; and for Britain, America was the single most important and profitable trading partner. To the United States, trade with Britain constituted more than 75 percent of all foreign commerce; over 50 percent of American trade was carried in British ships.

No American understood such economic, political, and emotional realities better than Hamilton. His domestic political opponents of the period—those whom he characterized in his black moods as his "enemies"—seemed to him to speak often from smug, but naïve domestic isolation unschooled by contact with realities of worldwide power politics.

After it became known that Genêt had turned against Jefferson, Hamilton's old friend Robert Troup wrote Rufus King on January 1, 1794: "What a pleasant thing it is to see Jefferson, Randolph and Genêt by the ears. All has ended well." American commerce was safe from seizure at sea, no matter what flag the ship carrying it might fly. Divided at home against themselves, Americans seemed to be stumbling heedlessly toward war with Great Britain.

By a series of orders-in-council, the British had forbidden all American trade with the French West Indies. They seized hundreds of American ships and cargoes that disobeyed those orders. Jefferson, as secretary of state, had protested these apparent breaches of American neutrality, but the British claimed legal justification, pointing to the United States' guarantee of the French West Indies contained in Article II of the 1778 treaty of alliance between the United States and France. By British reasoning, the United States was not a neutral. Therefore, American vessels and cargoes were not entitled to the immunities of neutrals. A principal reason Hamilton had labored so diligently to avoid re-recognition of the French treaty was to cut the ground from under just such later after-the-fact British justifications for refusing to grant American commerce the same immunities granted to true neutrals.

For domestic consumption, as *Pacificus III*, published in the *Gazette of the United States* on July 6, 1793, Hamilton had denounced the American commitment to the French West Indies and explained that the United States should not be bound by it: "Our guarantee does not respect France herself. It does not relate to her own immediate defence or preservation. It relates merely to the defence & Preservation of her American colonies; objects of which (though of considerable importance) she might be deprived and yet remain a great and powerful and a happy nation."

Pacificus warned domestic readers that "we are wholly destitute of naval force. France, with all the great maritime Powers united against her, is unable to supply this deficiency." He scouted the frontiers and flanks and found the United States dangerously vulnerable:

> With the possessions of Great Britain and Spain on both Flanks, the numerous Indian Tribes, under the influence and direction of those Powers, along our whole Interior frontier, with a long extended sea coast—with no maritime force of our own, and with the maritime force of all Europe against us, with no fortifications whatever and with a population not exceeding four Millions—it is impossible to imagine a more unequal contest, than that in which we should be involved in the case supposed; a contest from which, we are dissuaded by the most cogent motives of self preservation, as well as of Interest.

America's denunciation of the guarantee would not be a breach of the laws of nations, said *Pacificus*. "We may learn from Vattel" that "if a State which has promised succours finds itself unable to furnish them, its very inability is its exemption; and if the furnishing the succours would expose it to an evident danger this also is a lawful dispensation."

On December 19, 1793, two weeks before finally resigning from office, Jefferson submitted a report to Congress, emphasizing that British depredations against American commerce were much more extensive than French depredations, a strongly pro-French tilt. Any secretary of state was foolish to say, as Jefferson did, that British reprisals would, in effect, be "nothing."

On January 3, 1794, Madison followed up Jefferson's report by reintroducing in the House his resolutions of 1791, which called for retaliation against Britain by a levy of additional duties on all imports and shipping coming from countries like Britain, with whom the United States had no commercial treaty. Madison also called for extra tonnage duties on British vessels trading between the West Indies and the United States, trade from which American ships were excluded by the British Navigation Acts.

The increasing severity of the British orders-in-council tended in a warlike direction. France's declaration of war and the French treaty would provide Britain all the pretext it needed for new outrages. "To be in a position to defend ourselves and annoy any who may attack us will be the best method of securing our peace," Hamilton advised. Then "there will be much less temptation to attack us and much more hesitation to provoke us."

Furthermore, Hamilton counseled, modest as its effect on Britain might be compared with its momentous adverse effects at home, an embargo was the only really effective weapon in the whole American arsenal for waging big power politics.

Hamilton's measures were carefully defensive, but Madison's resolutions were offensively hostile. Such official actions would provide new grounds for a British declaration of war or still more devastating orders-in-council just short of a declaration of war.

But Republicans pressed for immediate adoption of Madison's resolutions while Hamilton's followers maneuvered for delay and sought to allay the popular frenzy. Hamilton's friend William Loughton Smith of South Carolina rose in the House to oppose Madison's resolutions with a powerful speech, whose arguments were the same ones Hamilton had used in his *Pacificus* and *Americanus* papers of January and February 1794, urging neutrality. Madison's resolutions, he charged, were "a covert design to embark the United States in the war" on the side of France.

Jefferson, from retirement at Monticello, wrote Madison: "I am at no loss to ascribe Smith's speech to its true father. Every tittle of it is Hamilton's except the introduction. . . ." Jefferson's "Scourge" Smith, according to Jefferson, was literally Hamilton's puppet.

Following Hamilton's advice, Washington declared a 30-day embargo on all vessels bound for British ports. Congress ratified it on March 26. Britain's limited war against America was escalating. The American embargo was extended another 30 days to May 25.

Hamilton left George Hammond in no doubt of the seriousness with which he and the country at large regarded escalating British seizures of American vessels. On April 14 and 15, 1794, Hammond wrote back to Lord Grenville that Hamilton, who had hitherto been "uniformly the most moderate of the American Ministers," now reflected the dangerous popular ferment and anger against Britain.

Hamilton wrote Washington to suggest cooling the tension by sending a special envoy to Britain, while at the same time preparing defenses for war. The envoy "should be a person, who will have the confidence of those who think peace still within our reach." More than a month earlier, on March 10, a coterie of influential Federalists had met in the rooms of Rufus King, senior senator from New York, to see what they could do to rescue the country from the disastrous war that they feared was coming. They were the best minds of Hamilton's party: King, George Cabot and Caleb Strong of Massachusetts, and Oliver Ellsworth of Connecticut.

Ellsworth was instructed to tell Washington that "unless a person possessing Talents of the first order, enjoying the Confidence of the friends of Peace, and of the Government, and whose character was unexceptionable in England was selected, it would be fruitless to make such an appointment." Who was such a man? Colonel Hamilton was such a man, they all agreed. Apart from all the reasons his friends could urge on Washington better than he could himself, Hamilton longed to see Angelica and find himself an honorable way out of the day-to-day calumnies and pressures of the Treasury. There was a world of difference between a resignation under fire and the public credit that would accrue to a graceful resignation to accept a mission to save the peace.

Ellsworth reported back on March 12 that the president had been "at first reserved," but finally much impressed. However, he was doubtful that Hamilton would be a proper envoy, because although Washington was sure of him, he "did not possess the general confidence of the country."

Washington himself was convinced of the necessity of sending an envoy. The only question was, who? Washington had thought of John Adams, Hamilton, Jay, or Jefferson as possibilities. Robert Morris objected to either Adams or Jefferson and expressed a decided preference for Hamilton. Jay agreed "in the propriety of Hamilton's appointment."

Meanwhile, the news leaked out that Hamilton would very likely be given the mission.

Federalists were delighted. Republicans were not. Monroe wrote a hasty hatchet man's protest to Washington that ''I should deem such a measure not only injurious to the publick interest, but,'' he added menacingly, ''also especially so to your own.'' That last he said he would gladly explain to Washington in private. It would be all he needed to say about the confrontations of December 15, 1792, even though his triumvirate had never released the accusing letter he had prepared for it to send on to Washington.

Furious at the impropriety of a senator's advance interference in an executive appointment of this kind, Washington wrote Monroe on April 9, ''If you are possessed of any facts or information, which would disqualify Col. Hamilton for the mission to which you refer . . . you would be so obliging as to communicate them to me in writing.'' He rebuked Monroe for interfering: ''I *alone* am responsible for a proper nomination, it certainly behooves me to name such a one as in my judgment combines the requisites for a mission so peculiarly interesting to the peace & happiness of this country.''

Jefferson joined the anti-Hamilton campaign with snide vigor, writing Monroe: ''. . . H. the missionary . . . besides the object of placing the aristocracy of this country under the patronage of that government,

> has in view that of withdrawing H. from the disgrace & the public execrations which sooner or later must fall on the man who partly by creating fictitious debt, partly by volunteering in the payment of the debts of others,. . . has alienated for ever all our ordinary & easy resources, & will oblige us hereafter to extraordinary ones for every little contingency out of the common line.

Hamilton had also, Jefferson said, ''brought the P. forward with manifestations that the business of the treasury had got beyond the limits of his comprehension.''

Randolph, who had been appointed secretary of state after Jefferson's resignation, discussed with the new French minister, Jean Antoine Fauchet, with whom he was becoming undiplomatically intimate, possible ways to kill Hamilton's appointment. Madison also worked to scuttle it.

By April 14, Hamilton could see that anxiously as he had hoped for the appointment, it would be a political impossibility. He advised Washington ''with decision'' to ''drop me from the consideration and fix upon another.'' He knew of Washington's ''byass'' in his favor, but he was also ''well aware of all the collateral obstacles which exist.'' Such ''collateral obstacles'' included, of course, what enemies like Monroe knew of the night of December 15 and his nervous derangement of the following year. ''Of the persons whom you would deem free from any constitutional objections,'' Hamilton went on, ''Mr. Jay is the only man in whose qualifications for success there would be a thorough confidence. . . . I think the business would have the best chance possible in his hands.'' On April 16 Washington sent Jay's name to the Senate. Monroe and Aaron Burr led bitter opposition to Jay on grounds of his being pro-British, but on April 18, the Senate approved Jay by a bare party-line, two-thirds vote of 18 to 8.

Twelve years older than Hamilton, John Jay seemed to have a character so fine and qualifications so perfect for every high office that everyone marveled at his lack of personal influence. No one could have had better qualifications for the mission Hamilton had created for himself but Hamilton himself. Active early as a patriot in the colonies, in the first and second Continental Congresses, Jay had drawn up important appeals to the people of Great Britain, Canada, Jamaica, and Ireland, as well as the resolutions that authorized the New York delegation to sign the Declaration of Independence. He chaired the committee that drafted the New York State constitution, served as first chief justice of the state, returned to the Continental Congress, and became its president. Sent to Spain in 1789 to seek an alliance similar to the French treaty—to guarantee Florida to Spain in case of Britain's defeat and to reserve to the United States free navigation of the Mississippi—he was still negotiating firmly when Cornwallis surrendered at Yorktown. Commissioned in 1781 along with Franklin, John Adams, Jefferson, and Henry Laurens to negotiate the peace treaty with Great Britain, Jay persuaded his fellow negotiators to treat independently with Great Britain for a treaty more favorable to the United States than Congress had dared to expect, so good it had been a rude shock to the courts of France and Spain. On his return to New York in July of 1784, he was awarded the freedom of the city. A delegate to the Continental Congress, he later resigned his seat to become secretary for foreign affairs under the Articles of Confederation. As *Publius,* he had written numbers 2, 3, 4, 5, and 64 of *The Federalist,* dealing primarily with foreign affairs. Under the new Constitution, he would serve as first chief justice from September 1789 to June 1795. In the most famous case to come before him, *Chisholm* v. *Georgia,* it was his opinion for the court that permitted a citizen of another state to sue the state of Georgia. Georgia had no ''sovereign immunity,'' he held, because in the United States sovereignty rested not in the states, but in the people alone.

At Washington's request on April 23, Hamilton submitted a set of instructions for Jay's mission that were specific, concise, and precise. Little scope was left to Jay's ''discretion.'' He should obtain: (1) indemnification for depredations on American commerce according to a rule to be settled by resort to the law of nations, (2) future guarantees of freedom from seizure of all cargoes except articles that were specifically contraband of war, and (3) prompt compliance by the British with the terms of the peace treaty of 1783 for indemnity for the slaves who had been carried away and surrender of the frontier forts still held, in return for which the United States would pay damages for obstructions the states had put in the way of the recovery of British debts, not exceeding a total to be specified in the treaty.

Hamilton allowed room for modification of these demands, but he laid down two inflexible rules: (1) no treaty was to be entered into that would affect unfavorably the existing treaty with France, and (2) American ships must be granted unrestricted entry into the West Indies.

Hamilton's instructions were concrete and specific, limited to the main points of dispute. By contrast, Secretary of State Edmund Randolph's instructions to Jay were more than five times as long, a hodgepodge of detailed exhortations and points left entirely within Jay's ''discretion.'' Jay was to present expressions of ''general irritation'' with ''vexations, spoliations,'' and so on. In content, they were nothing but a grab bag of complaints to be ''strenuously pressed.'' They seemed purposefully written more to exacerbate the breach with Britain than to heal it.

It would have been impossible for any diplomat to comply with such a farrago. No matter what the outcome of the negotiations might be, each topic head of Randolph's grab bag would open a sector of attack on Jay to any critic whose hindsight was disconnected from his foresight. Randolph, like Hamilton, also gave suggestions for a commercial treaty, listing more objects, but not indicating minimum terms. He did not expect that Jay would effect any treaty ''with so great a latitude of advantages.''

For better or worse, judging by the result, Jay followed Hamilton's instructions. The younger man was his political ally, and Jay often, but not always, sought Hamilton's advice. It is ridiculous to believe the charges made later and throughout American history that Jay was no match for his British counterparts in firmness and shrewdness negotiating what later came to be called, often pejoratively, Jay's Treaty. Probably no man in the United States at the time could have negotiated a better treaty in the circumstances except Hamilton himself.

Sending Jay on his way to the mission for which he had urged him on Washington in place of himself, Hamilton suddenly, indeed, rather surprisingly, surveyed the world scene from a new pinnacle of power in "my" administration. With Jefferson out of office, Hamilton now dominated the much weaker Randolph, who usually opposed him at first, but often would yield in the end. William Bradford, the new attorney general, was a congenial friend. Knox in the War Department was always his faithful follower. Washington listened with profound respect to Hamilton's advice and usually followed its broad thrust if sometimes differing in detail. Hammond, the British minister, treated almost wholly with Hamilton, exhibiting an insulting disregard for the titular secretary of state. The French minister, Fauchet, was only a little less confiding. Federalist leaders were devoted followers. Hamilton's unpopularity with Republicans was the natural tribute that reverses frequently suffered at his hands would pay to the skill of the elder statesman of the ruling party, still only 37 years old. Washington had stiffly discountenanced James Monroe's attempts to whisper firsthand reports of secret scandal into his ear. The select committee of the House had unanimously cleared him of all impeachable offenses.

To insure the success of Jay's mission and all it meant toward securing the removal of the British from the frontiers and his commercial system from the vicissitudes of foreign war, Hamilton would have to remain in office instead of going through with his resignation, now that he had been cleared by the House. On May 27, reminding Washington of his plan of a year earlier to resign, Hamilton noted that recent events "render the prospect of a continuation of our peace in a considerable degree precarious." He was "reluctantly obliged to defer the offer of the resignation."

Hamilton still feared whispers that might have come to Washington's ear or Washington's concern about his fever or nervous derangement might have undercut his support. Washington's impersonal confirmation of Hamilton's authority in dealing with the two foreign loans, but withholding a strong personal endorsement still rankled.

The inner Hamilton still yearned for some such endorsement: "If any circumstances should have taken place" since his resignation announcement, he wrote Washington, "or should otherwise exist which serve to render my continuance in office in any degree inconvenient or ineligible . . . I should yield to them."

Hamilton felt that even a "momentary stay" in office by him was opposed by "the strongest personal and family reasons and could only be produced by a sense of duty or Reputation." Washington responded that he was pleased to have the secretary remain "until the clouds over our affairs, which have come on so fast of late, shall be dispersed." It had taken a year and a half, but Hamilton had finally extracted from Washington this one line of affirmation he had to have to "leave him with the impression his suspicions had been removed."

Jay submitted a draft of a proposed treaty to Lord Grenville that contained, for the record at least, many of the maximum demands suggested by Randolph's instructions, but Grenville rejected its terms. Nonetheless, Jay wrote privately to Hamilton that "appearances continue to be singularly favourable, but appearances merit only a certain degree of circumspect reliance . . . I will endeavour to accommodate rather than dispute; and if this plan should fail, decent and firm representations must conclude the business of my mission." He had just dined with Lord Grenville as the only foreigner present, and next

Monday he was to dine with the lord chancellor, the first Baron Loughborough; on Friday he was dining with Prime Minister William Pitt himself.

Jay told Hamilton that these "favorable appearances" should best "remain unmentioned for the present and they make no part of my communications to Mr. Randolph or others." His old friend Hamilton would understand his businesslike reasons: "They may be misinterpreted, tho' not by you."

Of armed neutrality proposals and treaties involving Denmark, Sweden, and Russia, Hamilton told Hammond in private, "with great seriousness and with every demonstration of sincerity . . . that in the present conjuncture it was the settled policy of this government in every contingency, even in that of an open contest with Great Britain, to avoid entangling itself with European connexions." Such alliances, as the troublesome one with France demonstrated, might "commit it in a common cause with allies, from whom in the monent of danger it would derive no succour."

Hamilton's opponents and Jeffersonian historians, commenting on Hamilton's conversations with Hammond about the proposed treaty with Denmark and the like while Jay was negotiating in London, have described Hamilton as "standing behind Jay . . . holding a mirror, however unconsciously, which reflected the American negotiator's cards to the enlightenment of the suave and smiling Grenville."

It may indeed have been a mistake for Hamilton to have talked at all with Hammond while Jay was negotiating in London. In Hamilton's defense it may be said that the card of Jay he is supposed to have given away was a ludicrously weak one, face up in full view of all players, and anyway Jay had been given no Senate authority to play it.

What Hamilton was doing for Jay was ostentatiously throwing a weak card, at minimal cost to any significant American interest, but avoiding admission of real American weaknesses by preventing Jay from leading from such weakness. At the same time, Hamilton was establishing invincible credibility with Hammond and Grenville at considerable domestic political risk to himself to win the big hand: getting the British out of the forts on the frontiers without any credible American military strength to fight them out. Whatever else came of his mission, if Jay could succeed in this, it would have saved America many regiments, warships, casualties, and millions of dollars.

On November 19, 1794, after five months of intense give-and-take, Jay signed a treaty, which won the two points his instructions had indicated as minimum terms, but not much more. Britain committed itself to evacuate the forts still held by June 1, 1796. The Mississippi would be "entirely open to both parties." Britain yielded permission for vessels of 70 tons or less to enter the West Indies, with the counterproviso that American vessels were to be prohibited from exportation of molasses, sugar, coffee, cocoa, and cotton, the assumption being that those would have originated in the West Indies. British vessels were to be allowed unlimited trade between the islands and the United States. The United States agreed to pay for British vessels seized by Genêt's privateersmen. The United States would pay private debts of Americans to British subjects in cases where payment had been prevented by legal obstructions interposed by the states after the Revolution.

Britain was to pay for all American ships seized "under color" of right. Commissioners were to be appointed to establish the boundary line between Maine and New Brunswick and in the upper Mississippi Valley and Lake of the Woods areas. Jay had dutifully demanded indemnity for slaves lost, by Southerners mostly, during the Revolution. Jay, like Hamilton, had pressed Americans to free their own slaves and probably did not press the British, who had freed them, very hard for payment to American slave owners whose slaves had probably not resisted much being "carried away." Far from perfect, the treaty nonetheless helped to protect and enhance the free status of former slaves. It also went far to safeguard the small farmers, fur traders and trappers, artisans and settlers, pioneers and new frontiersmen who had sought to make new lives by moving west near the New York, Ohio, Michigan, Minnesota, and Mississippi frontiers. It tended to ease the threats to such people posed by the British, the Indians, the French, and Spain.

It did less for merchants, shipping interests, and traders, but its wide-ranging commercial provisions did provide some security within delineated limits of risk for them. The treaty did nothing for former slave owners whose chattels had fled to freedom.

It boldly advanced the interests of most of the people of America, at the cost of some money claims by the wealthy. It provided an accurate reflection of Hamilton's basic political concerns for the poor, the enterprising, and the unprotected and his unconcern for the interests of slave owners. It also assured the Federalists some peace without dishonor in their time for Hamilton's system to revive public credit and prove itself.

What Hamilton's emotions may have been as he read the confidential text of the treaty is unknown. For the benefit of the public, preparing for the battle over ratification, he put upon it the best political face he knew how: As in the battle for ratification of the Constitution, it was "better than nothing." Jay's Treaty finally liquidated the Revolutionary War a dozen years after the close of hostilities. Gaining possession of the military posts on the frontiers and fixing the disputed western boundaries opened the way to westward territorial expansion and the new frontier. Some of the differences that had divided the people were subdued, though others were heightened. The way was cleared for a period of economic and political consolidation of nationhood.

Jay's Treaty would govern American foreign policy far into the future until the eras of World Wars I and II. By the time Jefferson and his Republican party came to power in 1801, their earlier radical policies had become sufficiently tempered so that in important respects, notably in the purchase of the Louisiana territory, they perpetuated Hamilton's and Jay's westward-looking domestic and foreign policies. Jay's Treaty was peculiarly Hamilton's brain child. He had proposed it to Washington as a practical measure to avert war with Britain and preserve the chief source of American public revenue, import duties. He helped to choose Jay and draw up Jay's instructions. At every stage he was President Washington's principal adviser concerning it.

With Jay off negotiating neutrality in London and Betsy pregnant again off in Albany with the two youngest boys, James Alexander, age six, and ailing John Church, two, Hamilton remained in Philadelphia to look after the three oldest, Philip, now 12; Angelica, ten; and Alexander, eight. After seeing Betsy as far as New York City and then returning to Philadelphia, he wrote her on July 31,

"The precious little ones we left behind are well."

"I shall expect with infinite anxiety a letter from you and heaven grant that it may bring me good tidings of the health of yourself and the dear children with you." A dual purpose valediction would serve for both his Johnnies, Church and Jay: "Alas my beloved Johnny—what shall I hear of you! The question makes my heart sink. Adieu."

Among other health problems that John Jay's treaty would soon add to Hamilton's lengthening list was an insurrection of the interior of the country, and a bloody bruise on the temple from being stoned by a Wall Street mob.

28

The Whiskey Insurrection

You must not take my being here for proof that I continue a quixot.

—To Angelica Church, from 205 miles westward of Philadelphia,
October 23, 1794

School was out. It was vacation time. Betsy, Johnny, and James Alexander were off at Old Saratoga. Congress adjourned and scattered to the far reaches of the country. Chief Justice John Jay was negotiating in London, President Washington sojourned at Mount Vernon, Vice-President John Adams relaxed at Quincy, Secretary of State Edmund Randolph took his ease at Carter Hall in Virginia, Secretary of War Henry Knox packed up to leave for Boston and a tour of his property interests in Maine, and Thomas Jefferson was in retirement at Monticello. All that remained of the government of the United States at the capital were office staffs and Secretary of the Treasury Hamilton. But even with no one but Hamilton in town, no sense of slack was felt in the reins of the government.

Hamilton was sending daughter Angelica and son Alexander out to the country to stay with Mary Morris, the wife of Robert Morris, who had asked for them. So had Susan Bradford, wife of Hamilton's friend William Bradford, the new attorney general. There they would be beyond the immediate reach of the usual summer plague. With no one left at home in town but his eldest and favorite son, Philip, Hamilton could look forward to a quiet, restful August, free at last of the clandestine visits and harrowing blackmail threats of the summers of 1791 and 1792 and of the fevers and nervous derangements of 1793. But summer of 1794 was not to be one of domestic tranquility. Colonel Francis Mentges of the Pennsylvania militia brought word to Hamilton of an insurrection that had just erupted in the

405

four western counties of Pennsylvania and adjacent parts of western Virginia. It was the most dangerous threat yet to the unfolding progress of "his" administration. Back of the uprising he would see the hand of his enemies.

At a meeting held July 23, 1794, at the Mingo Creek Meeting House in Washington County, Pennsylvania, "consisting generally of the most respectable people of that County," it had been proposed that the people of the area work together until the excise tax on whiskey was repealed and an act of oblivion passed. But this lawful proposal, which envisaged working through the established structure of the constitutional government, had been voted down at the meeting. Instead, the Mingo Creek Meeting House Convention had proposed an extralegal rump caucus "to assemble by delegates in a Convention to be holden on the fourteenth of [August] in Mingo Creek at Parkinson's Ferry." The summons proposed to "take into consideration the situation of the Western Counties and adopt such measures as should appear suited to the exigency." The rebels had appropriated one of Hamilton's own favorite words—*exigency*—to rouse up a broad-based rebellion against all established federal authority.

On the Western frontiers where the borders shaded off into the conflicting and often encroaching claims of Britain, Spain, and the Indian tribes, suddenly there was civil disorder, defiance of national laws, and threats of disunion and secession. At a time when Jay in London was doing his utmost to remove the British from the frontier forts and all that their stand on American soil meant in terms of divisive threats to the nation, only open war could have been a more serious threat or come at a worse time than what came to be called, in a misleadingly derisory phrase, the Whiskey Insurrection.

The force of the rebellion fell directly upon the revenue collectors of Hamilton's department who had local responsibility for collecting the excise tax. Mentges reported that on July 17 armed men had "made repeated attacks upon the house of General John Neville, Inspector of the Revenue, for and on account of his holding and exercising the said office and to oblige him to relinquish the same." The United States marshal for the district, David Lenox, who had tried to serve process to collect the tax on whiskey and stills, had been seized by a mob of 700 armed men who had assembled and attacked Neville's house, with only Neville and Major Kirkpatrick and ten soldiers defending it.

General Neville rallied David Lenox, Isaac Craig, and two others. They led an attack to try to break through the besieging armed mob to bring ammunition to Major Kirkpatrick and raise the siege, but their rescue attempt failed. They were seized, made prisoners, disarmed, and confined. The brave Major Kirkpatrick surrendered. According to Craig, "The enemy set fire to the house, which is consumed to ashes with all the property it contained, not a single article saved."

At mass meetings Republican orators churned up the passions of whiskey producers and consumers alike. Liberty poles—reminiscent of the Revolution and of the world war between Britain and France raging around the globe—appeared on courthouse lawns and meetinghouse squares, flying flags with such inscriptions as: "An equal tax, and no excise" and "United we stand, divided we fall." Some bore the significant device of the Union as a writhing snake cut up into separate sections, which ranged in number from two to 13. Mass meetings broke out into riots. Rioting spread south into western Virginia and South Carolina. The United States mails were intercepted, seized, and trashed.

News of these disorders was good news to British Minister George Hammond, who cheerfully reported them to his chief, Lord Grenville, on August 3: "The avowed pretext for these discontents is a dislike of the excise law, but the real origin of them is unquestionably a rooted aversion to the federal constitution, and to all the measures emanating from it."

Hammond was briskly optimistic that the outlook was dark for the former colonies "in this emergency which is certainly the most serious and alarming that has yet arisen, since the establishment of the constitution." The British Foreign Office should not be misled by anything John Jay might say into thinking that he was negotiating his treaty from strength.

The specific grievance that had given rise to the general defiance of all federal law was the federal government's excise tax on whiskey. The tax had originally been imposed by Congress at Hamilton's urging in order to help fund—pay for—Hamilton's hardwon program for federal assumption of state debts. That the immediate provocation was the tax on whiskey was no more reason to make light of the matter than the fact that a tax on tea could be said to be the immediate provocation of the Revolution. The British might have had more success putting it down if they had thought to label it lightly the "tea rebellion." The parallels in the two situations probably hit Hamilton harder in his present unhealthy mood than the differences.

For frontiersmen on the Western fringes—western Pennsylvania, Virginia, and North and South Carolina—whiskey was, of course, a common article of consumption. But what was not consumed was also the best available medium of exchange, better than money. It cost too much to transport grain over the mountains eastward, but grain distilled into whiskey found a ready market in the East and brought Western distillers cash with which to purchase manufactured goods from the East. Eastern plantation owners like Jefferson grew their own grapes from slave-tended vines or drank mostly vintages imported from abroad, on which they paid import duties. It cost them nothing extra to proffer political sympathy to the rebels in the West, won them great political credit, and served their favorite purpose of discrediting the secretary of the treasury.

Furthermore, the states had always claimed internal revenue for themselves. Fear of federal encroachment on their tax base had been one of the most effective arguments state supremacists had raised against the Constitution. For Hamilton, the very existence of the tax on whiskey was proof positive that the national government had the right and power to impose internal taxes within a state. If Hamilton had deliberately sought to force the issue, he could not have found a more hated tax to impose on those who had to pay it.

Hamilton's pressure for it to cover the huge national debt taken on by assumption had forced Congress reluctantly by the act of March 3, 1791, to tax domestic spirits on a sliding scale ranging from nine to 25 cents a gallon. Even then, three years earlier, mobs had chased away tax collectors who had to flee empty-handed for their lives. Tax rates were reduced. Very little money trickled in.

Now, on August 5, 1794, Hamilton reminded Washington of these earlier threats of violence and mass meetings. Then, too, the rebellion had not been limited to specific taxpayer complaints. Meetings at Red Stone Old Fort and elsewhere in Washington County had resolved then that every federal officer who attempted to carry out the law "should be considered as inimical to the interests of the country." They had proclaimed that every citizen should treat federal officers "with contempt, and absolutely refuse all kind of communication . . . and withhold from them all aid, support or comfort."

Collections of import duties under the Tariff Act of 1790 were not sufficient to fund the state debts assumed by Hamilton's program. There was not much objection to import duties, but internal taxation of whiskey by the federal government was something else. No wonder Hamilton and his system were controversial; the wonder is that they were politically possible at all. The tax on whiskey fell directly on a not very numerous group of self-sufficient frontiersmen; it hardly touched the rich landed gentry; it probably fell hardest on small farmers, merchants, and artificers, the people among whom Hamilton found most of his support. Hamilton would also pick up some scattered approval from all who deplored strong drink on moral grounds.

In 1792 Congress had turned to the executive branch and asked for its recommendations on what to do. While James Reynolds's blackmailing letters were raining on him thick and fast, Hamilton had taken the political onus off Congress by submitting to it on March 6, 1792, his lengthy ''Report on the Difficulties in the Execution of the Act Laying Duties on Distilled Spirits.'' In it he noted that four main objections to the excise taxes had been made: their ''supposed tendency'' (1) ''to contravene the principles of liberty,'' (2) ''to injure morals,'' (3) ''to oppress by heavy and excessive penalties'' and (4) ''to injure industry and to interfere with the business of distilling.''

Hamilton's report discussed all such objections with minute particularity. He disposed of one principal objection in two sentences that exposed its speciousness: ''The argument, that they are obliged to convert their grain into spirits'' to transport it to distant markets, ''does not prove the point alleged. The duty on all they send to those markets will be paid by the purchasers. They will still pay only upon their own consumption.'' As a general rule, he observed, ''duties on articles of consumption are paid by consumers.''

Hamilton was sympathetic to complaints of imperfect justice in any tax structure, but firmly realistic on the subject of equality of bearing tax burdens. As to equality, ''It may safely be affirmed to be impracticable to devise a tax which shall operate with exact equality upon every part of the community. Local and other circumstances will inevitably create disparities more or less great.''

Hamilton had proposed a number of amendments to improve the law, including an increase in the compensation of collectors, which passed Congress and became law on May 8, 1792. But the success of another of his important reports with Congress did not end his problems in the Western counties. A reading of Hamilton's report, particularly his constructive suggestions for ameliorating grievances, tends to confirm his judgment that objections to the tax on whiskey were largely a cover or focal point for general rebellion against all federal authority.

On July 30, 1792, while urging Washington to stand once again for the presidency, Hamilton had called his attention to the fact that ''nonexecution of the law in certain scenes begins to produce discontent in neighboring ones, in which a perfect acquiescence had taken place.'' This was a natural and obvious result of failure to enforce the law vigorously and ''implies a danger of a serious nature.''

On September 1, Hamilton sent Washington a full report of that year's Western insurgency and spoke of the ''persevering and violent opposition to the law'' that ''seems to call for vigorous & decisive measures.'' He had ordered a survey of the rebellious districts; he had asked the attorney general for an opinion whether indictable offenses had been committed and whether legal redress was possible in the courts. To Washington, he added that ''it is indispensable, if competent evidence can be obtained, to exert the full force of the law against the offenders.'' After all, peaceful steps had proved ineffective and ''if the processes of the courts are resisted,'' but only then, it would be necessary ''to employ those means which in the last resort are put in the power of the executive.'' ''If this is not done,'' Hamilton added, ''the spirit of disobedience will naturally extend, and the authority of the government will be prostrated.'' It is important to note that Hamilton was specifically urging resort to prosecutions in the courts, not military action, when he added, ''Moderation enough has been shewn; 'tis time to assume a different tone.''

The old surveyor was in full agreement with his secretary of the treasury. He gave Hamilton express authority to institute court proceedings if the opinion received from the attorney general should warrant it. Hamilton drafted a proclamation for Washington to issue, warning the public against interfering with the collectors and proclaiming that "the laws will be strictly enforced against the offenders."

The draft had been sent off to Monticello for Secretary of State Jefferson to sign. He did so. It was returned to the capital and was published there on September 25, 1792. For two years past it had served to damp down the Western rebellion.

But now in 1794, Western defiance of the excise tax had erupted anew. Losses of import duties owing to French and British seizures of American ships and cargoes were cutting off the government's most important source of revenue. If America were ever going to be able to to muster regular troops and a naval force and build harbor fortifications to assume even the most limited posture of credible defense against British and French depredations, secure internal tax revenue was more desperately needed than ever.

Hamilton patiently listened to complaints and made administrative changes.

This long, troubled history of defiance of federal law in the Western counties and Hamilton's record of patience and moderation in devising measures to cope with it meant that there was a deep base under George Washington's ire when he called upon Edmund Randolph in August 1794 to advise him without delay of "all the means vested in the President for suppressing the progress of the mischief."

Why not simply call out the regular army to put down the rebellion? To Hamilton this was impossible both as a practical and as a political matter. When it had ventured north from the protection of its base at Fort Washington (Cincinnati) into Indian country under General Josiah Harmar in 1790, the U.S. Army—what little there was of it—had suffered a bloody defeat at Fort Jefferson before skulking back to safety; in 1791 a reorganized army under Arthur St. Clair had been all but wiped out by the Miami Indians when it dared approach their villages on the Maumee River in present northeastern Indiana. Now, in the summer of 1794, after three years of further reorganizing, under General Anthony Wayne, the army had just moved out on yet another armed—but apprehensive—sortie into Indian country. In the vast Northwest Territory it claimed, the United States had never yet established an effective military presence to protect settlers and establish the national government's authority. The British and their Indian allies still held sway throughout most of it from their forts at Detroit and Michilimackinac, on the Maumee, and from similar garrisons elsewhere. No help was to be expected from the little regular army that had not yet shown it could even secure itself.

On August 2, 1794, Washington called Randolph, Hamilton, Henry Knox, William Bradford, and the leading officials of Pennsylvania—Thomas Mifflin, the governor; Thomas McKean, the chief justice; Jared Ingersoll, the attorney general; and Alexander J. Dallas, the secretary of the Commonwealth—to an emergency conference on the insurrection.

The minutes of the "conference concerning the Insurrection in Western Pennsylvania" from the Pennsylvania archives show Washington's angry determination to act with force, in light of Mentges' report, even without the army, with Hamilton's full support. Washington declared to all present that "the circumstances . . . were such as to strike at the root of all law & order; that he was clearly of opinion that the most spirited & firm measures were necessary to rescue the State as well as the general government from the impending danger, for if such proceedings were tolerated there was an end to our Constitution & laws."

Washington vowed "to go every length that the Constitution and Laws would permit, but no further." He called for cooperation of the Pennsylvania state government and enquired whether the governor could not adopt some preliminary measures under the state laws, "as the measures of the General Government would be slow, and depended on the certificate of Judge Wilson."

Here Washington was referring to the fact that Randolph had referred Washington's earlier demand to be informed of the legal basis for federal action to Justice James Wilson of the Supreme Court for his opinion, but this had not yet been handed down.

When it came Hamilton's turn to speak, he began "by argument upon the general necessity of maintaining the Government in its regular authority," noting a number of other recent examples of serious local opposition to the Constitution and laws of the United States and citing the "Judiciary, excise, Mississippi navigation, erecting a new State, etc., etc." By opposition to "the Judiciary," Hamilton was referring to John Jay's decision in *Chisholm* v. *Georgia,* in which he struck down Georgia legislation declaring that the state would not be bound by the decision of the Supreme Court. By opposition to the "excise," Hamilton was, of course, referring to his own five-year history of coping with opposition to the tax on distilled spirits in the Western counties. By "Mississippi navigation," Hamilton meant the objections of citizens of Kentucky, embodied in the secessionist-leaning Kentucky Resolutions of May 24, 1794, to the government's negotiations with Spain for free navigation of the Mississippi River. And by "erecting a new State," Hamilton meant the efforts of Major General Elijah Clark and his followers to erect a new state on Georgia lands in defiance of action by the United States, which had reserved the same lands for the Creek Indians.

Finding in these striking recent examples of defiance of federal authority a trend toward national disunity, disintegration, and separatism only seven years after the Union had been forged at the cost of heroic effort, Hamilton insisted on an immediate show of military force. It would not be enough if the rioting were merely quieted down. Defiance of the laws of the United States had been expressed in a formal, explicit manner in the Mingo Creek resolutions, which had flung down the gage. The Government must show it could maintain itself. The exertion must be made not only to quell the rioters, but to protect the officers of the Union in executing their offices, to compel obedience to the laws, and to show George Hammond and John Jay in London that the Union was not about to dissolve.

The Pennsylvanians at the meeting disagreed with Hamilton. Dallas stated that Judge Addison, the presiding judge of the County Court of the Western District of Pennsylvania, had declared it as his opinion that the business should be left to the courts, the rioters prosecuted and punished there, and the matter peaceably terminated. A resort to military force would unite both the peaceable as well as the riotous opponents of the excise in resistance.

Hamilton retorted sharply that "Judge Addison was among those who had most promoted the opposition in an insidious manner." Here the minutes of the meeting abruptly terminate—with the conferees breaking into an uproar, and stalking away in hot anger.

Hamilton sent a formal opinion to Washington that amplified the argument he had made at the conference calling for immediate and vigorous measures. Let the national government issue a call for 12,000 militia, 9,000 foot, and 3,000 horse. They should rendezvous in Pennsylvania and Virginia on September 10. Hamilton, not alone, but joined by the other cabinet members, advised Washington to invoke a federal statute under which the president was empowered to call up the militia if he were "notified" by a member of the Supreme Court that military force was needed to enforce federal law or suppress disorder. Three days later, Hamilton followed this up with another and even more urgent report and drafted a new proclamation for the president to issue, calling on the insurgents to disperse.

On August 4, 1794, pursuant to the federal statute, Justice James Wilson of the Supreme

Court submitted his opinion that, in the counties of Washington and Allegheny, "laws of the United States are opposed, and the Execution thereof obstructed by Combinations too powerful to be suppressed by the Ordinary Course of judicial proceedings." With this judicial opinion for legal sanction, without awaiting further action by Pennsylvania, action bound to be politically distasteful for local elected officials, the federal government had all the authority it would need to step in.

On August 7, Washington issued a stern proclamation following Hamilton's outline calling out the state's militia under federal colors. It warned "all persons, being insurgents . . . on or before the 1st day of September next, to disperse and retire peaceably to their respective abodes. And I do moreover warn all persons whomsoever, against aiding, abetting, or comforting the perpetrators of the aforesaid treasonable acts. . . ."

Five thousand insurgents rose in defiance of Washington's proclamation and staged a riotous demonstration on Braddock's Field near Pittsburgh. Hugh Brackenridge wrote Tench Coxe on August 8, 1794, that "the United States cannot effect the operation of the law in this country. It is universally odious in the neighboring parts of all the neighboring states, and the militia under the law in the hands of the President cannot be called out to reduce an opposition. . . ." Brackenridge added that "the first measure . . . will be the Organization of a New Government" comprehending the Western counties. To Hamilton's assistant at the Treasury, he sent the further threat that "should an attempt be made to suppress these people, I am afraid the question will not be, whether you will march to Pittsburgh, but whether they will march to Philadelphia?"

Hugh Brackenridge was the most prominent rebel leader in the area. A member of the state assembly in 1786–1787; a founder of Pittsburgh's first newspaper, its first academy, and its first bookstore; and a lawyer and playwright as well, his warning to Tench Coxe could not be dismissed by Hamilton and Washington as but the perfervid product of a literary man's imagination.

Secretary of War Henry Knox chose August 8, the day after Washington's proclamation summoning up the militia and the rioting on Braddock's Field, to obtain a leave of absence as secretary of war to go up to Maine for a look at real estate interests there. Otherwise, Knox said, he was faced with "permanent pecuniary ruin or something very like it." Responsibility for administration of the War Department, as well as the Treasury, would have to be turned over to Hamilton, until Knox's return to Philadelphia.

Hamilton would now do openly what his enemies charged he had been doing secretly for a long time behind the stout figurehead of Henry Knox: administer the War Department. Hamilton's critics who tax him with overplaying his military role in the crisis ignore the fact that it was not Hamilton's militaristic aggressiveness, but Knox's real estate speculations in Maine that fobbed off the War Department's duties on Hamilton at the climax of the crisis.

At least one-sixtieth of the nation had accomplished a de facto secession from the Constitutional union and were threatening to seize Fort Fayette at Pittsburgh. Contemporary academics who are inclined to ridicule Washington's and Hamilton's resort to military measures even after three years of violence and under judicial authority, might consider what the response of a contemporary American president to formal and warlike secession on such a scale might be. It would probably include (without judicial authority) calling out the FBI, the CIA, the National Guard, the regular army and air force, and armed helicopter gunships laying down barrages of tear gas, merely as starters, to deafening popular applause, without a peep of criticism from a single college president.

On the same August 12 that Hamilton received alarming news of the continuing rioting at Braddock's Field, more alarming news came in from the North. From Albany, Eliza had written that their beloved Johnny was still ailing. Pregnant Eliza's own health remained in a precarious state. Johnny had lost strength and "was not so well as he had been."

"Would to heaven I were with you but alas 'tis impossible," Hamilton wrote Betsy. "My fervent prayers are not wanting that God will support you and rescue our loved child." Since late 1792 the religious bent that had marked Hamilton's earlier years had begun to be evident again.

Besides prayers, he also had practical advice to offer in lieu of his presence: "I am somewhat afraid of the relaxing effect of the laudanum. I think well of the lime water but I count most on exercise and nourishment." His concern is not for beloved Johnny alone. "Alas my Betsey how much I wish you with me," but she is better off out of feverish plaguey Philadelphia. "I really hope more from the climate you are in than from this . . . Receive my most tender and affectionate wishes for you both. They are all I can now offer." He closes with impulsive words that take force from their contrast with the usual stylistic regularity of even his most intimate correspondence: "hard, hard situation."

And by a postscript he adds, "I can advise you nothing better than to pursue the Doctor's advice."

Suffering rare second thoughts about his own earlier expert advice and the doctor's, he wrote her a second letter the same day full of more prescriptions. "My heart cannot cease to ache till I hear some more favorable account from you," he began. "If my darling child is better when this reaches you persevere in the plan which has made him so. If he is worse—abandon the laudanum and try the cold bath." But not at once. "Abandon the laudanum by degrees giving it overnight but not in the morning—then leaving it off altogether." As for the cold baths, let the water stand in the kitchen overnight, and then "let the child be dipped in it head foremost wrapping up his head well and taking him immediately out, put in flannel & rubbed dry with towels. Immediately upon his being taken out let him have two teaspoonsfull of brandy mixed with just enough water to prevent its taking away his breath."

> Observe well his lips. If a glow succeeds, continue the bath. If a chill takes place forbear it. If a glow . . . the quantity of brandy may be lessened.
> Try the bark at the same time in tincture about midday. . . .
> When you exercise him, if he can bear it, give him eight or ten miles at a time.
> May heaven direct and bless the means which shall be used. My love to all the family.

Because of, or in spite of, such a rugged regimen, two-year-old John Church Hamilton survived to become his anxious, loving father's adoring first biographer.

Henry Knox issued orders to the governors of New Jersey, Pennsylvania, Maryland, and Virginia to call out 12,950 militiamen and promptly set off for the Maine woods, dumping the War Department in Hamilton's lap. Writing Lord Grenville again on August 16, George Hammond had more good news, even better than two weeks earlier. Hammond thought the government's force of 15,000 "will be found inferior to that of the insurgents." In fact, he added, "the present general situation of this country is . . . extremely critical." The silver cloud that Hammond saw had a black lining for John Jay in London. He had just written Hamilton in cautious terms that he considered the "scale as capable of turning either way." He strongly advised "not to relax in military preparation."

Hamilton continued to do everything possible to avoid having to make combat use of the militia in the field. He sent three federal commissioners west to negotiate with the insurgents, but they reported back that they saw little hope for success and planned to return to the capital. Hamilton, Washington, and Randolph pressed them to stay and continue their efforts.

Pennsylvania authorities remained temporizing and difficult. Governor Mifflin had already fallen into the habits of heavy drinking which would totally disable him in later years, and the whiskey rebellion crisis made them worse. Hamilton's real opposition was Mifflin's alter ego, Secretary of the Commonwealth Dallas.

Hamilton, writing for Edmund Randolph, answered Dallas's doubts and evasions with the same arguments he had used before.

In all of these exchanges seeking local backing for exercise of national authority, Hamilton was meticulous, patient, and moderate. No doubt, he was mindful of his own experiences of a decade earlier when, as a member of Congress, threatened by mutinous revolutionary troops, he had sought but been unable to enlist protection from Pennsylvania militia and had found it necessary to adjourn Congress to Princeton for safety. On August 24 the proclamation for mobilizing the militia was formally issued. At the same time Hamilton was doing his best with his pen to keep people in the rest of the country in sympathy with his policy. Under the pseudonym of *Tully* in four essays issued between August 23 through September 2, 1794, addressed "To the People of the United States," he put the arguments for federal intervention directly in the form of questions: "Shall the majority govern or be governed? Shall the nation rule or be ruled? Shall the general will prevail, or the will of a faction? Shall there be government or no government?"

With pressures on him building in intensity, Hamilton fell into his now habitual summer illness, and it aroused Washington's concern. Pressure lifted a little when Hamilton received word that Johnny and Betsy were getting better and would soon be home. He wrote her on August 21 that her last to him "gave me inexpressible pleasure." His prescriptions had worked. "My precious boy was fast recovering." He would pick up his dear ones at Elisha Boudinot's.

He wrote out the orders to Henry Lee, governor of Virginia and field commander, on August 25: "The President anticipates, that it will be as painful to you to execute, as it is to him to direct, measures of coertion against fellow citizens however misled."

The commissioners hung on in the Western counties and kept trying to treat with the insurgents. As mobilization of militia proceeded, in Fayette County, a center of terrorism, under the guiding hand of Albert Gallatin, some committees hastily drafted a set of resolutions, which exhorted followers to employ only peaceful means when agitating for repeal of the tax and not to resist in anywise the military expedition set in motion against them. From the War Department on September 10, Hamilton, his health recovering, reassured the governors that their militia would no longer be in much danger of actual combat: "Although the restoration of order had gained powerful advocates and supporters; yet . . . there is a violent and numerous party which does not permit to count upon a submission to the laws without the intervention of force. . . . The final resolution has been taken by the president . . . to put the force which had been provisionally called for in motion."

An autumn outing across Pennsylvania might be a welcome change from Philadelphia for Hamilton. He wrote Washington on September 19 for permission to accompany the troops:

> It is advisable for me, on public grounds, considering the connection between the immediate ostensible cause of the insurrection in the western country and my

department, to go out upon the expedition against the insurgents. In a government like ours it cannot but have a good effect for the person who is understood to be the adviser or proposer of a measure, which involves danger to his fellow-citizens, to partake in that danger; while not to do it might have a bad effect. I therefore request your permission for the purpose.

Hamilton's spirits lifted. By September 28, he was writing last instructions for procurement of supplies to meet the militia on their march and directing that future correspondence be with his deputy, Tench Coxe. On September 29, Hamilton dashed off a last letter to his two sons Philip and Alexander, now after vacation back at school under William Fraser, rector of St. Michael's Church at Trenton. Like the rest of the family, his dear Alexander had been unwell, too, "but thank God he was better." Hamilton went on, "I expect to set out tomorrow for Carlisle. . . . There will be no fighting and of course no danger. It will only be an agreeable ride which will I hope do me good."

When Hamilton and the president arrived at Carlisle on October 4, they shared in a gala reception given by the governors of Pennsylvania and New Jersey. Hamilton here was occupied with every sort of expedition business. At camp he found 3,000 citizen soldiers as remarkable for the variety of their fortunes as for the uniformity of their loyalty. He was strict with looters. He insisted that those who came out to enforce the laws had a duty not to offend against them.

The show of federal force worked peaceable wonders.

With Gallatin's resolutions calling for nonviolent solutions in hand and with the commissioners still at work and the disturbances quiescent, the question arose whether earlier plans for marching on into the Western counties should be put into effect at all. Hamilton's opponents were ridiculing him for having called up an unnecessarily large force. The president refused to call off the march.

Findley felt he was expressing the common view when he said that Hamilton "gave the supreme direction to the measures that were pursued" in suppressing the disturbances. Much of his "paramount influence" was in seeing to efficient supply arrangements and the comfort of the men. Hamilton's critics were sure that the secretary went beyond his proper function in accusing and arresting suspects. At any rate, "while the President was with the different wings of the army, the secretary accompanied him, and appeared to act as his official secretary."

Hamilton swung south with the president from Carlisle to Williamsport and Cumberland, Maryland, to inspect the southern wing of the army and from there back to the northern wing at Bedford, Pennsylvania. From Bedford the president retired to Philadelphia to report to Congress, leaving the army to the command of Governor Henry Lee of Virginia and under Hamilton's civil supervision giving orders in Washington's name. As the militia marched on west to Pittsburgh and Washington beyond for four weeks through rugged, mountainous country, Hamilton kept Washington informed of all developments.

Personal observation while on the march confirmed Hamilton's earlier impression of the seriousness of the dissidence. He recommended that Congress authorize the raising of 500 infantry and 100 horse "to be stationed in the disaffected country. Without this, the expense incurred will be essentially fruitless." The ringleaders, the best objects of exemplary punishment, would doubtless flee. "They ought to be compelled by outlawry to abandon their property, homes, and the United States. This business must not be skinned over. The political putrefaction of Pennsylvania is greater than I had any idea of. Without rigor everywhere, our tranquillity is likely to be of very short duration, and the next storm will be infinitely worse than the present one."

The conversion of early critics like Mifflin and Dallas to Hamilton's view of the rebellion by direct observation in the field is the best answer to those who continued to charge from afar that Hamilton had unnecessarily improved the occasion to aggrandize the national government.

Still in the field with the army, Hamilton was full of concern for his family on October 20, when he wrote Elizabeth that he was "very sorry that some of my sweet angels have been again sick. You do not mention my precious John. . . . Have patience my love & think of me constantly as I do of you with the utmost tenderness. Kisses & blessings to you and my children."

Three days later, in a letter he datelined "Bedford, Pennsylvania, 205 miles westward of Philadelphia," he unburdened himself jokingly to Angelica Church of self-conscious concern that his westward foray made him look quixotic in the eyes of those who loved him, as well as his critics. In intimate moments, when at his best, Hamilton was never too sure he was right or afraid to reveal self-doubts to those he loved most and whose love meant most to him:

> I am thus far my dear Angelica on my way to attack and subdue the wicked insurgents of the West. But you are not to promise yourself that I have any trophies to lay at your feet. A large army has cooled the courage of these madmen & the only question seems now to be how to guard against the return of the phrenzy.

Hamilton knew as well as anyone that the easy, conventional wisdom of most political men would be to laugh off such an insurgency as a mere unpleasantness, avoid doing anything about it, and remain popular. He adds to Angelica, "You must not take my being here for proof that I continue a quixot."

Hamilton was not living an unself-examined life. He went on, "In popular governments 'tis useful that those who propose measures should partake in whatever dangers they may involve. 'Twas very important there should be no mistake in the management of the affair—and I *might* contribute to prevent one." He seemed to hold himself responsible as a national steward for the well-being of all the inmates of America, and of foreign visitors as well: "I wish to have every thing well settled for Mr. Church and you, that when you come, you may tread on safe ground. Assure him that the insurrection will do us a great deal of good and add to the solidity of every thing in this country. Say the same to Mr. Jay to whom I have not time to write & to Mr. Pinkney." He closed saying, "God bless You dear sister & make you as happy as I wish you. Love to Mr. Church."

Exemplary prosecutions were the most important, but, ipso facto, the most unpopular part of Hamilton's mission. The visible opposition having melted away before the advancing troops, the arrest of individuals in a now quiet district was easily represented as harsh and vindictive. Some of the principal offenders escaped. The most bellicose of the rebels, David Bradford, who had been the self-styled general at Braddock's Field, fled to Louisiana. Hugh Brackenridge, the most conspicuous leader of the rebellion, was early described by Hamilton as "the worst of all scoundrels," but he had cooperated with the commissioners and so purchased immunity. The more sophisticated of the insurgent leaders, like Brackenridge, would claim that although pretending to sympathize with the insurgents and attending their meetings, they had really been using their influence to prevent violence.

Hamilton wrote Washington: "I hope there will be found characters fit for examples, and who can be made so.'' Sheriff John Hamilton had surrendered himself, though it was not certain how much could be proved against him.

Alexander Hamilton declared that all possible means were being used to obtain evidence and that ''accomplices will be turned against the others.'' Hamilton personally questioned many suspects. Findley charged that the secretary used threats to browbeat some suspects and witnesses, but such stories were all secondhand. Brackenridge thought his own examination by Hamilton had been fair, but said that while he as a lawyer and literary man could protect his own rights, Hamilton's tactics might put the ignorant and fearful at a disadvantage. There was no direct evidence of Hamilton's having used any browbeating tactics beyond skillful cross-examination.

Hamilton had been busy with rounding up suspected insurgents when he wrote to the president from Washington, November 15, 1794, that 20 men were in confinement there, mentioning a half-dozen ''most conspicuous . . . . for character or crime.'' Two days later, when he arrived at Pittsburgh with the judiciary, the list of prisoners had increased to 150.

Hamilton had asked General Lee to map out homeward routes for the troops, so that their provisions and pay could be deposited to await them at Pittsburgh. He also felt, ''I would add . . . that it would scarcely appear advisable to leave any considerable number of Artillery in so disaffected a Country.'' On November 19, Hamilton notified President Washington by a hasty line from Pittsburgh that the army was in motion homeward and that he would himself set out for home in five minutes.

Edward Carrington of Virginia, who had been in the expedition, later wrote to Hamilton, ''Our returned troops pretty generally agree, that a less force than was called forth could have been opposed, and that a small army could have effected nothing but the establishment of a civil war.'' Recent years have retaught the lesson that national agony can arise from launching a military force against a civil insurrection if the force is not seen to be sufficiently overwhelming. To try to escalate the progovernment force inconspicuously only insures escalation of the insurrection. It is the show that makes a success of the force.

Hamilton, thought to have ordered all the arrests, feared assassination attempts on his return journey through the rugged rebel country. The secretary of the treasury, acting secretary of war, and ad hoc, de facto attorney general was therefore escorted by a protective guard cordon of six armed horsemen for a hundred miles through the hostile mountains and forests all the way from Pittsburgh to safe arrival back at Bedford. There awaited him news, transmitted at the president's express request, of a death in the family.

Henry Knox's letter of November 24 reported that Mrs. Hamilton ''has had, or been in danger of miscarriage, which has much alarmed her.'' Doctor Kuhn and Hamilton's boyhood friend Edward Stevens had been in close attendance and ''assure that she is in no danger to her.'' But ''she is extremely desirous of your presence to tranquilize her.'' She had indeed suffered a miscarriage. Her life had been in danger. They would not have another child for three more years. In Hamilton's absence, Eliza's father, Philip Schuyler, had done his best to console her. He assured her on December 2 that her husband would return safely and in health ''and as usual triumph over his ungenerous enemies.''

On December 1, 1794, immediately upon return from the field, Hamilton wrote to George Washington:

> I have the honor to inform you that I have fixed upon the last of January next as the day for resignation of my office of secretary of the treasury. I make the communication now, that there may be time to mature such an arrangement as shall appear to you proper to meet the vacancy when it occurs.

With perfect respect & the truest attachment I have the honor to be Sir Your very obedient servant.

On December 8 he wrote Angelica Church, ''My dear Eliza has been lately very ill. Thank God she is now quite recovered, except that she continues somewhat weak. My absence on a certain expedition was the cause. You will see, notwithstanding your disparagement of me, I am still of consequence to her.''

It was coldly quixotic of him (putting it most charitably) to write so lightly to Angelica of her sister's painful miscarriage, or thus pass off guilt he should but did not seem to feel for his neglect of his wife. Not to be numbered among triumphs over ungenerous enemies were illnesses and mortality within his own family for which he might have been expected to shoulder some responsibility. In the circumstances, the misguided callousness of his letter might have suggested to Angelica that he was suffering a recurrence of his nervous derangement of the previous winter. The best possible reason for his irreversible decision to resign the pressures of too many offices for reasons of health was unmentionable because of its roots in his mental derangement.

29

Public Credit

But what can I Direct who am (I Fear) insolvent?

> —To Robert Troup, named executor of Hamilton's last will and testament, July 25, 1795

Hamilton is really a colossus to the anti-republican party—without numbers, he is a host within himself.

> —Jefferson to Madison, September 21, 1795

Hamilton's "agreeable ride" through the "disaffected country" had successfully demonstrated to the Western insurgents that they could not get away with defying federal tax collectors or seceding from the Union. Eliza was recovering from her miscarriage. He was in a peculiarly lighthearted mood on December 8, 1794, when he wrote Angelica Church:

> You say I am a politician, and good for nothing. What will you say when you learn that after January next, I shall cease to be a politician at all? So is the fact. I have formally and definitely announced my intention to resign at that period, and have ordered a house to be taken for me at New York.

Despite his being out of office, Angelica should not fear for the country:

> Don't let Mr. Church be alarmed at my retreat—all is well with the public. Our insurrection is most happily terminated. Government has gained by it reputation and

strength, and our finances are in a most flourishing condition. *Having contributed to place those of the nation on a good footing, I go to take a little care of my own; which need my care not a little.*

After the miscarriage of her sixth pregnancy while Hamilton remained with the militia command in western Pennsylvania, Elizabeth badly needed some tender care. "Little" Philip, now 13, and the four younger children stairstepping down to John Church, two and a half and just beginning to mend, commanded his attention to parental office and financial preparation for many expensive educations. Without the more or less continual but surreptitious aid of Philip Schuyler, the Hamiltons would have been in even more serious financial straits than they were. But it is probable that only Hamilton's closest friends realized that when he quit his Treasury post he was a poor man. His elegant air and comfortable style of living and Schuyler connections would have persuaded most acquaintances and strangers as well that he was rich. It suited his enemies to let people think so to support their charges of corrupt financial dealings with William Duer, James Reynolds, A. G. Fraunces, and others during his tenure as secretary of the treasury.

Not only was Hamilton poor, he was continually involved in money difficulties. His $3,500 annual salary as secretary of the treasury had obliged him to exhaust "almost the whole of the small fortune he had acquired" before taking office, and he regularly overdrew his account.

From time to time he was forced to borrow petty sums of as little as $50 from friends. Ruefully, he told Tobias Lear and Major William Jackson, both of Washington's secretarial family: "I am not worth exceeding five hundred dollars in the world; my slender fortune and the best years of my life have been devoted to the service of my adopted country; a rising family hath its claims."

He found a small house at 56 Pine Street, which served for about a year as both living quarters and office. From there he and the family moved from one address to another, winding up at 24 Broadway, where they remained until 1802, when they finally moved to The Grange on Harlem Heights. As he resumed his law practice he was compelled to borrow some more money from his old friend and college classmate, Robert Troup, who had never quit the law to hold public office. Troup would help him out by bringing him into cases as co-counsel all during the rest of his life.

Troup also tried to bring him into a land speculation in Ontario County on which he was embarking with English and Dutch capitalists to buy several million acres. He hoped Hamilton and John Jay, too, would serve secretly in an advisory capacity. "Why should you object to making a little money in a way that cannot be reproachful?" Troup asked. But Hamilton rejected Troup's offer, writing him April 13, 1795, that "I am now in no situation that restrains me." However, "I think there is at present a great crisis in the affairs of [man]kind which may in its consequences involve this country. . . . The game to be played may be a most important one." Out of office, Hamilton continued to see himself as a public exemplar. With sad sarcasm, Hamilton noted that such deals were "very harmless in the *Saints,* who may never fatten themselves on the opportunities or if you please the spoils of the office" and "profit by every good thing that is going . . . [without] hazarding their popularity."

Hamilton had learned the hard way he was not one of thos lucky saints like Burr who could get away with anything: "Those who are not of the *regenerating* tribe may not do the most unexceptionable things without its being thundered in their ears—without being denounced as speculators, peculators British agents etc. etc." Still, as Hamilton saw it,

"There must be some *public fools*" like himself "who sacrifice private to public interest at the certainty of ingratitude and obloquy."

Troup thought Hamilton was foolish: "I sincerely hope . . . that you may by some fortunate & unexpected event acquire the means of perfect independence in spite of all your efforts to be poor," he replied. But Hamilton insisted, "My *vanity* whispers I ought to be one of those fools and ought to keep myself in a situation the best calculated to render service."

Troup answered, "I have often said that your friends would be obliged to bury you at their own expense." His grisly prophecy turned out to be grimly true.

Contrary to the idyllic picture Hamilton had jocularly sketched for Angelica's and John's benefit, the country was in turmoil. As the Republicans saw it, the insurrection had been brutally repressed. Congress was in an uproar. The opposition press, led by Benjamin Franklin Bache's *Aurora,* stormed with public criticism. Fenno's *Gazette of the United States* no longer functioned to publish Hamilton's rebuttal: it had failed the year before.

The proclamation Hamilton drafted for Washington to issue January 1, 1795, called attention to "the great degree of internal tranquility we have enjoyed." Such tranquility had recently been confirmed "by the suppression of an insurrection which so wantonly threatened it." Washington went on to "bow down before the majesty of the Almighty" and to set Thursday, February 19, "as a day of public Thanksgiving and prayer."

In Hamilton's words, it would be a day of grateful thanks for "the reasonable check which had been given to a spirit of disorder." The "kind author" of America's blessings was beseeched "to preserve us from the wantonness of prosperity." (Washington softened the hard word *wantonness* of Hamilton's draft to *arrogance,* but changed little else.) This would "render this country more and more a secure and propitious asylum for the unfortunate of other countries." Hamilton's view of what his enemies liked to dismiss as the "Whiskey Rebellion" thus became the specific occasion for Washington's first pro-clamation of the unique American holiday, Thanksgiving Day.

President Washington also commissioned from Hamilton a draft of the message he would present to the new session of Congress. The bustle of camp at Carlisle would not permit Washington to do more than edit paragraphs supplied to him, but he wanted to emphasize one topic: reproof of "these self created societies" which threatened to "destroy the government of this Country" like the one at Mingo Creek, whose members had stirred up the insurrection. Washington took much of his text from the report on the rebellion that Hamilton had prepared for him. Leaders of these societies would "destroy all confidence in the Administration, by arraigning all its acts. . . ." The parent society had been founded by Genêt in Philadelphia "for the express purpose of dissension," and the Western insurrection was the "first *ripe fruit* of the Democratic Societies."

Political parties were beginning to take form, and the issue of the insurrection was firming up ranks on both sides. The president's declaration of "public odium" upon the democratic societies in his message to Congress begat swift rebuttal from Republicans. The seeds of insurrection were planted, they said, not by the societies, but by Hamilton's excise tax law, which had been adopted long before the societies were established.

Thomas Scott, the representative from Washington County, at the very epicenter of the insurrection, rose to his feet in Congress at the same moment as Fisher Ames to put such misconceptions to rest. The quick-witted gentleman from Massachusetts instantly yielded the floor. Scott's knowledge of local conditions in western Pennsylvania would outweigh the most eloquent rhetoric. Scott "knew that . . . self-centered societies in that part of the country . . . had inflamed the insurrection; some of the leaders of those societies had likewise been the leaders of the riots." Scott avowed that he could not, with all his personal knowledge, give "a more candid and accurate account" of the rebellion "than the President and Hamilton had given." The deluded people of the Western region were "objects of real pity. They were . . . grossly ignorant, and they had been persuaded by . . . utmost diligence . . . that the American Government was . . . the very worst in the world . . . when people had got their length in absurdity, it was not difficult to make them fight against such a Government."

Uriah Tracy of Connecticut, fed up with Republican cant about "the people," the hackneyed, automatic, knee jerk response that served them in lieu of logical argument, shied a simile at McDowell of North Carolina that echoed through later speeches. ". . . if the President had not spoken of the matter," Tracy said, he "should have been willing to let it alone, because whenever a subject of that kind was touched . . . certain gentlemen . . . shook their backs, like a sore-backed horse, and cried out 'the Liberties of the People.' "

Votes on significant phrases of the president's message were evenly divided, and the result turned on the votes of only one or two members. In the end, to the surprise of the Federalists, it was John Nicholas of Virginia who came forward with the compromise that upheld the president's statement on the insurrection. Avoiding a verbal chastising of democratic clubs everywhere, it left standing his reproofs to those in the Western counties.

In the Senate a committee under Rufus King's chairmanship charged the societies with being "founded in political error, calculated if not intended to disorganize the government." Aaron Burr and Senator James Jackson of Georgia rose and spoke in rebuttal. The Federalist two-to-one majority in the Senate held. Madison's and Jefferson's private correspondence is full of chagrin at the military and political credit Hamilton won, first by crushing the insurrection in the field and then by defeating all political efforts to discredit suppression in Congress. To Jefferson, as to Hugh Brackenridge, the "infernal" excise would yet be "the instrument of dismembering the Union."

Fisher Ames took up the defense when Thomas Scott subsided. "The private history" was "that the faction in the House fomented the discontents without; that the clubs are everywhere the echoes of the faction in Congress." James Madison was an honorary member of one of the societies, and the Speaker, Frederick A. C. Muhlenberg, was a member of one, too, although he had taken pains when casting his vote to disclaim their influence.

As the date of his resignation approached, the attention of everyone in Congress, as well as of the public at large, remained riveted on Hamilton for other important reasons. His friend Edward Carrington wrote Hamilton, "Your notification to the House of Representatives is a necessary caveat against future slander, for had you remained till the last day of the session, and then resigned without such a precaution, a retreat from inquiry would have been charged against you."

Accordingly, on December 1, 1794, the same day he had submitted his resignation to be effective January 31, Hamilton requested of Speaker of the House Muhlenberg that the unfinished investigation of his stewardship of the Treasury be wound up. He wrote that "I make this communication in order that an opportunity may be given, previous to [resignation], to reinstitute any further proceeding which may be contemplated, if any there be, in consequence of the inquiry during the last session into the state of the department." None was reinstituted.

Hamilton's last days in office were among his most significant. On November 19, 1794,

George Washington in his sixth annual message to Congress had called for "a definitive plan for the redemption of the public debt," and two days later the House appointed a committee to report such a plan, naming as its committee chairman Hamilton's friend and spokesman William Loughton Smith of South Carolina. The Smith committee struggled with the problem for a while and proposed some statutory amendments to existing law, but, finally, as previous Congresses had done, it asked Hamilton to supply it with well-organized and definitive answers to many large questions. Hamilton obliged. If it were true that his department was involved in confusion, Hamilton would allow Congress to share it with him through the medium of his last great (and unaccountably neglected) public report, his "Report on a Plan for the Further Support of Public Credit," often called his Final (or Second) Report on the Public Credit. The tactics and timing of Hamilton's submission of this valedictory report on January 16 were as masterful as its text. The disgruntlement it caused Madison and Jefferson is an index of its significance. "Hamilton has made a long and arrogant valedictory Rept," Madison wrote Jefferson. "It is not yet printed, & I have not read it. It is said to contain a number of improper things. He got it in by informing the Speaker he had one ready . . . for the House whenever they shd please to receive it. Berdinot [Boudinot] the ready agent of all sycophantic jobs, had a motion cut & dry, just at the moment of the adjournment . . . which passed without opposition & almost without notice."

Hamilton's Final Report on the Public Credit, which runs to 103 pages in Volume XVIII of the Hamilton Papers, is divided into three separate but related sections, the first a history of the fiscal system of the United States during his almost five-and-a-half-year term as secretary of the treasury, the second, ten "propositions, which appear necessary . . . to complete our system," and the third a wide-ranging essay on the nature and meaning of public credit. The report is followed by a series of statistical tables designed to illustrate, illuminate, and document the points he makes.

"Credit public and private is of the greatest consequence to every country," Hamilton intones. ". . . it might be emphatically called the invigorating principle. . . . No well informed man can cast a retrospective eye over the progress of the United States, from their infancy to the present period, without being convinced that they owe, in a great degree, to the fostering influence of credit, their present mature growth."

"Credit," Hamilton insists, "is among the principal engines of useful enterprise and internal improvement. As a substitute for capital it is little less useful than gold or silver, in agriculture, in commerce, in the manufacturing and mechanic arts . . ."

Hamilton's enemies always charged that he wished to impose an everlasting debt structure upon the country, but the major emphasis in the report is on plans for extinguishing the public debt. Citing the statement in Washington's sixth annual message to Congress that "progressive accumulation of debt must ultimately endanger all governments," Hamilton warned that "a tendency to it is perhaps the NATURAL DISEASE of all governments. . . . There is a general propensity in those who administer the affairs of a government, founded in the constitution of man, to shift off the burden from the present to a future day; a propensity which may be expected to be strong in proportion as the form of a state is popular . . ." To Hamilton, it was a common "spectacle to see the same men clamoring for occasions of expense . . . declaiming against a public debt, and for the reduction of it as an *abstract thesis*; yet vehement against every plan of taxation which is proposed to discharge old debts, or to avoid new by defraying the expenses of exigencies as they emerge . . ."

Hamilton laid down as two fundamental principles for all public debt that (1) there be established at the time of contracting it, a sinking fund or retirement fund for the repayment of the principal and the interest on it within a determinate period, and (2) that it be made a part of the contract that the fund so established "shall be inviolably applied to the object."

Hamilton gave ten propositions for completion of the fiscal system he had established, which would, if followed, provide for every obligation, deferred and accruing, to be met out of revenue sources existing at the time of creation of the debt and without resort to new sources of revenue at later times. Tables appended to his report gave the figures down to the last penny. As of December 31, 1794, domestic debt of the United States was $64,825,538.70; foreign debt owed to France, 14,000,000 livres ($3 million); and foreign loans owed at Amsterdam and Antwerp (the guilder at 40 cents), $12,387,000. By Hamilton's proposals for management of the sinking fund, the whole of the existing debt, foreign and domestic, funded and unfunded, would be redeemed in 30 years or by the year 1826. The government was currently operating in the black. Current expenditure was $5,481,843.84, and the excess of revenues beyond expenditures was $1,070,456.90.

Hamilton warned Congress that without the kind of national self-discipline he had urged, "the public debt swells till its magnitude becomes enormous, and the burthens of the people gradually increase, till their weight becomes intolerable. Of such a state of things, disorders in the whole political economy, convulsions and revolutions of government, are a natural offspring." He cast imprecations on any who would divert the sinking fund, in whatever emergencies, to uses other than its original objects. He declared again that his purpose was to create public credit, not to accumulate debt; the two things were antithetical.

He rejected the proposal that the government was at liberty to tax its own bonds or to seize and sequester them in time of war. He protested, with logic and moral conviction, that to do either in any form would be to violate its commitment to the lender. "The true definition of public debt," he observed, "is a property subsisting in the faith of the Government. Its essence is promise." Once it contracts a debt, the government loses legislative power to change its terms and becomes, like an individual, a "moral agent" obligated to faithful compliance with them. This was "a principle . . . most sacred." Even war should not impair the claim of an enemy who was also a creditor. Any partial and temporary gain obtained from wronging a few creditors must produce vastly larger losses to the nation because "credit is an *intire thing*. Every part of it has the nicest sympathy with every other part; wound one limb, and the whole tree shrinks and decays. The security of each creditor is inseparable from the security of all creditors. . . ." He concluded by saying, "Twill be the truest policy in the United States to give all possible energy to public credit."

Hamilton's valedictory report unified, orchestrated, and dramatized the piecemeal resolutions of William Loughton Smith's committee with an almost poetic, Shakespearean intensity. It was spare language for a prospectus for U.S. government bonds, but the words seemed infused with an eloquence never since found in such a document. The Smith committee saw the debt as a problem; Hamilton approached it as a challenge. He offered a variety of solutions that added up to a comprehensive fiscal and monetary policy for the United States that would keep its public credit high for years, decades, and centuries to come.

Often before, Smith had been the Treasury's spokesman and champion in the House. Smith now complimented the president for promoting prosperity through keeping the country at peace and gave public credit to the retiring secretary, whose "assiduous labors had given energy and system to the complex machinery of an extensive and intricate Department." A large committee of the House had recently (after investigation) borne testimony to his "fidelity and services." Smith's resolutions went beyond providing for paying interest only; they looked to the complete redemption of all public debt. The Treasury supplied Smith with all necessary statistics and arguments to support his motions to continue temporary taxes, sell Western lands, and devote the surplus to the retirement of the principal.

Smith's bills embodying Hamilton's last great report passed both houses of Congress, carrying with them all of his objects except one; it omitted a proposal of Hamilton's for paying off "non subscribers"—persons who held debt certificates issued under the Confederation who had failed to exchange them for new debt certificates of the new government, some because they had applied too late, others because they believed the exchange terms offered were too low. Their numbers and claims were small in comparison with all classes of security holders affected, but Hamilton was intensely concerned that the government treat all smallholders fairly as a matter of sacred principle, regardless of the unimportance of the sums involved.

He was grieved and angry. Some weeks out of the Treasury and away from the Philadelphia scene, he entreated Sedgwick and King to retrieve the country's honor by keeping faith with all creditors, including poor nonsubscribers. He wrote Sedgwick on February 18 that he was "tortured" by the discrimination. On February 21 he wrote King, "The unnecessary capricious & abominable assassination of the national honor by the rejection of the propositions respecting the unsubscribed debt . . . haunts me every step I take, and afficts me more than I can express." At the moment of one of his greatest triumphs, he seemed to be suffering another anxiety attack when he asked his friend King, in a mixture of violence and pathos, this curious question: "Am I, then, more of an American than those who drew their first breath on American ground? Or what is it that thus torments me at a circumstance so calmly viewed by almost everybody else? Am I a fool—a romantic Quixote—or is there a constitutional defect in the American mind?" He called on King: "I conjure you, my friend, make a vigorous stand for the honor of your country! Rouse all the energies of your mind, and measure swords in the Senate with the great slayer of public faith—the hackneyed veteran in the violation of public engagements. Prevent him if possible from triumphing a second time over the prostrate credit and injured interests of his country. Unmask his false and horrid hypothesis."

Who was this "hackneyed veteran in the violation of public engagements"? Who had led the fight against his report in the Senate? The inimical "man of subtleties" Hamilton was describing in so hysterical a fashion was Aaron Burr. He implored King to "root out the distempered and noisome weed which is attempted to be planted in our political garden—to choke and wither in its infancy the fair plant of public credit."

Fisher Ames had fought hard on the floor of the House for the Treasury's bill and was well satisfied with the overall outcome. The bill as a whole was a famous victory for the Federalists and Hamilton, anything but the defeat Hamilton considered it to be. The shape of the bill "pins fast the funding system, converts the poison of faction into food for federalism; it puts out of the reach of future mobocrats" control of the funds. "It is therefore the finale, the crown of federal measures." Although the crown was a little tarnished by refusal to embrace the small unsubscribed debt, "prudence prevented many of us, who think as formerly, from pressing the right principle, which would have been in vain."

In this corons of public credit, Hamilton resigned office full of praise and honor from his friends—and "horrors" mostly of his own imagining linked with the name and person of Aaron Burr. To Hamilton, Burr's "despicable" actions now always seemed to bring on "horrors" and nervous derangements.

The Monday after his resignation became effective, Hamilton received one of the supreme testimonials of American history:

> Dear Sir,
> After so long an experience of your public services, I am naturally led, at the moment of your departure from office—which it has always been my wish to prevent—to review them.

George Washington wrote:

> In every relation which you have borne to me, I have found that my confidence in your talents, exertions, and integrity, has been well placed. I the more freely render this testimony of my approbation, because I speak from opportunities of information which cannot deceive me, and which furnish satisfactory proof of your title to public regard.
> My most earnest wishes for your happiness will attend you in your retirement, and you may assure yourself of the sincere esteem regard and friendship of
> Dear Sir Your Affectionate Go: Washington

On February 2 Hamilton gratefully acknowledged Washington's thank you note by saying, "As often as I may recall the vexations I have endured, your approbation will be a great and precious consolation."

He guarded the deep bond linking the two of them beneath a surface reserve and dignity of expression that were no less intense for matching Washington's. "I entreat you to be persuaded," Hamilton wrote "(not the less for my having been sparing in professions) that I shall never cease to render a just tribute to those eminent and excellent qualities which have been already productive of so many blessings to your country—that you will always have my fervent wishes for your public and personal felicity. . . ."

Another letter to lift Hamilton's spirits out of the "horrors" brought on by Aaron Burr's despicable tactics was Angelica Church's to Elizabeth of December 11, which his wife would receive about the time of his leaving office. "Do you believe there is hope of your going to New York to sit for life! . . . I confess I should not like to settle at Philadelphia (much more expensive . . . than in cities of the same size in England)." But if the Hamiltons came back to New York, Angelica would rush there to join them, without waiting for her husband: "If my brother resigns there will be no reason for my not going immediately to New York and be under his and your care till Mr. Church can leave this country."

Hamilton had not seen her since that late afternoon in November of 1789 just after first assuming the office he was now resigning, when he had stood on the Battery with Baron von Steuben and his little Philip and watched her ship sail down toward the Narrows and wept. On March 6, 1795, he wrote her from Albany, where he was sojourning with Eliza and the children,

> . . . here at your fathers house who is himself at New York attending the Legislature, we remain till June, when I become stationary at New York. . . . My dear sister, I tell you without regret . . . that I am poorer than when I went into office. I allot myself full five or six years of more work than will be pleasant though much less than I have had for the last five years. . . . You know how much we all love you. Tis impossible you can be so well loved where you are.

George Hammond, the British minister, commented to his home government that he thought Oliver Wolcott, Jr., the comptroller, would succeed Hamilton. Wolcott was ''a very candid and worthy man, and much in Hamilton's confidence. He is also said to possess very considerable talents. Yet . . . it is not probable that he will ever be able to acquire the influence which his predecessor possessed.''

On Hamilton's recommendation, Washington appointed Wolcott to succeed him as treasury secretary. Wolcott, as friendly to Hammond as his mentor had been, was soon furnishing Hammond with useful confidential news of the Senate's rejection of Article XII of Jay's Treaty.

Republican uproar over Hamilton's firm suppression of the Whiskey Insurrection helped Republicans win a majority of New York's congressional delegation in the elections of 1794. So when George Clinton announced that he would not run for governor again in 1795, members of both parties began looking to Aaron Burr as a possible successor. But if John Jay, now absent in London, should return to the United States with a treaty that removed the British from the posts on New York's frontiers and settled some of the rights and wrongs of British seizures of ships at sea, the Federalists might be able to snatch the ''peace and prosperity'' issue away from the Republicans, run John Jay for governor, and win the state for themselves.

One David Campbell wrote Hamilton offering his support and that of his friends to elect Hamilton governor. Suspicion of a tactic of Burr may have led Hamilton to scribble on the back of Campbell's letter: ''This letter was probably written with some ill design—I keep it without answer as a clue to future events.'' Philip Schuyler placed a notice in Noah Webster's paper of Hamilton's ''firm determination to serve in no public office whatever.'' Talk of Hamilton as a candidate for governor would divide support between himself and his friend John Jay and serve only the fell purposes of Aaron Burr.

Hamilton's friends hoped, and his enemies feared, that his withdrawal from the Treasury left him available for a call to run for higher office even than the governorship of New York, although at all times after the night of December 15, 1792, his reputation had been hostage to the gossip of insiders.

John Beckley kept busy digging up new shards of Hamilton scandal and sending them to Madison for his and Jefferson's and Monroe's files. On May 25, 1795, Beckley wrote Madison that ''about six or eight weeks ago, whilst Hamilton was in N. York Commodore James Nicholson in conversation with the friend of Hamilton's [Josiah Ogden Hoffman] stated that he had authentic information . . . that Hamilton had vested 100,000 sterling in the British funds, whilst he was Secretary of the Treasury, which sum was still held by a Banking house in London, to his use and interest.'' Back in 1788, Commodore Nicholson had been commander of the symbolic model ship *Alexander Hamilton,* which had served as the centerpiece of the parade celebrating New York's ratification of the Constitution. Now one of Hamilton's enemies, Nicholson told Beckley that ''if Hamilton's name is brought up as a candidate for any public office, he will instantly publish the circumstance.''

The dealings Hamilton had carried on over the years for his brother-in-law and principal client, John Barker Church, had a remarkable scope and dimension, from which a John Beckley could easily root out other shards of suspicion of scandal for his mentors' jottings. Hamilton had served as his agent most of the time he had been secretary of the treasury, and appointed William Seton of The Bank of New York as his subagent, with instructions to purchase or sell the funded debt and United States bank shares for Church as the occasion might require. Somewhat similar to the use of a ''blind trust'' by politicians in contemporary times, this served to insulate Hamilton from charges that he himself was making improper use of inside information for Church's benefit, but this was a refinement easily left unmentioned by a Beckley. In 1793, Church's orders to purchase national bank shares, relayed through Hamilton, were not backed up by cash. In alarm, Seton had written to Hamilton: "I think you will not blame me for making this further observation; Mr. Church's circumstances and responsibility I am totally ignorant of, £10,000 [sterling] is a very large sum to run the risk of even a 20 p Cent [damages?] upon. Now my dear Sir for you or under your absolute guarantee of course I would commit myself for any sum." Seton seemed under the illusion that Hamilton himself was affluent enough to make good Church's debts.

Retrieving his own private credit by going back into private law practice would mean much riding out of such excruciating conflicts of interest, and often serving profitable but embarrassingly unmeritorious causes like the ventures in which Church was usually involved.

From abroad Church lent out money, through Hamilton, as his attorney in fact, at substantial rates of interest. One of the borrowers was no less a personage than Robert Morris, whose reputation as the Financier of the Revolution and one of the richest men in the country kept Hamilton and Church from realizing until too late that he had overextended himself and was secretly bankrupt. To stave off a final crash like Duer's and debtors' prison, Morris asked repeatedly for extensions, which Hamilton granted.

Finally, Church demanded that Hamilton insist upon immediate payment. Hamilton was also rendering legal services to his erstwhile friend Morris, who had been his sponsor for appointment to the Treasury office. Their dealings continued until by 1797, another terrible year of pressure and nervous derangement for Hamilton, Morris owed legal fees to Hamilton of $12,088.33 and still had not been able to pay back Church. Under the pressure of Church's lash, Hamilton pressed Morris to pay up both accounts. This failed, and Hamilton, still under pressure from Church, finally felt compelled to issue an attachment against Morris's property.

Morris never recovered. His magnificent home outside of Philadelphia was seized by his creditors, and in 1798 the man who had managed the economy of the revolutionary states through the most perilous period of their history was thrown into the debtors' prison. Only after Gouverneur Morris, who had once been Robert Morris's junior partner, returned from Europe in 1799, was a plan worked out to set up a trust in the name of his wife, Mary, and settle the most pressing debts so that he could be released from jail. In this, Hamilton's services as counsel were instrumental in helping arrange his ultimate deliverance from debtors' prison.

The tension and pressure of his lawyer-client relationship with a brother-in-law like John Barker Church were a curious complement to the ties of affection that bound Hamilton to Angelica. Once when he wrote of the possibility that he might make "a short excursion to Europe," Angelica was suddenly thrilled. Months passed, the prospect faded, and she told her sister Eliza despairingly: "You and my dear Hamilton will never cross the Atlantic, I shall never leave this Island and as to meeting in heaven—there will be no pleasure in that."

Rarely did she mention her successful businessman husband; always it was Hamilton, his career, his prospects, her pride in his fame and achievements, her despair at his absence. To her sister she wrote recklessly of her "Amiable":

> . . . by my Amiable you know I mean your husband, for I love him very much and if you were as generous as the old Romans, you would lend him to me for a little while, but do not be jealous, my dear Eliza, since I am more solicitous to promote

his laudable ambition, than any person in the world, and there is no summit of true glory which I do not desire he may attain; provided always that he pleases to give me a little chit-chat, and sometimes to say, I wish our dear Angelica was here.

Having cast an unforgettable spell on American ministers in Europe like John Adams and Thomas Jefferson, Angelica Church had the same effect on Europeans heading for America. She passed on to the hospitality of the Hamiltons the duc de La Rochefoucauld-Liancourt, Talleyrand, Beaumetz, Chastellux, Moreau de Saint-Méry, and many others. They found in Hamilton a charming host full of sympathy for all they had suffered at the hands of the terror they had fled. His elegant manners, lively, warm, confiding personal style, and political point of view were something few had expected to find in what many thought of as the raw American wilderness. Arriving in Philadelphia while Hamilton was still secretary of the treasury, Saint-Méry was amazed by the Spartan simplicity of the office of a man whose power seemed to be that of a prime minister. Rochefoucauld-Liancourt thought Hamilton "one of the most interesting men in America," uniting dignity and feelings and much force and decision with delightful manners and great sweetness.

Charles Maurice de Talleyrand-Périgord became a close friend of Hamilton during the two years he was compelled to spend in exile in Philadelphia and New York. Hamilton considered Talleyrand "the greatest of modern statesmen, because he had so well known when it was necessary both to suffer wrong to be done and to do it." For his part, Talleyrand later was quoted as saying: "I consider Napoleon, Pitt and Hamilton as the three greatest men of our age, and if I had to choose between the three, I would unhesitatingly give the first place to Hamilton. He has divined Europe."

Late one evening during his stay in New York, Talleyrand passed Hamilton's law office on his way to a social engagement. Through the window he saw the spare figure of his friend bent over his desk, quill in hand, writing out a long legal document by yellow candlelight. When he arrived at the party, said to have been a glittering levee, bright with beautiful women in shimmering crinolines, brilliant conversation, and Mozartean divertimenti rippling through the salons, Talleyrand exclaimed, "I have just come from viewing a man who made the fortune of his country, but who is working all night in order to support his family." In France, Talleyrand and men like him became richer, not poorer, while holding high public office.

When Talleyrand sought to be officially received by the president, it was probably Hamilton who handed Lord Lansdowne's letter of recommendation to Washington. But Jefferson, as secretary of state, strongly opposed Washington's receiving him, and Washington followed Jefferson's advice. The résumé that Gouverneur Morris sent on about Talleyrand, the Bishop d'Autun, a bishop of the Catholic Church, had probably not helped open doors for him at Martha Washington's. Morris had said, "With respect to morals, none of them [Talleyrand, Narbonne, and Choiseul] is exemplary. The Bishop [Talleyrand] is particularly blamed on that score. Not so much for adultery, because that was common enough among the clergy of high rank, but for the variety and publicity of his amours, for gambling, and above all for stock jobbing during the Ministry of M. de Calonne. . . ." Talleyrand was a past master of the uses in diplomacy of nonrecognition and snub. For denying him the public credit of an official reception after Hamilton's introduction, Washington, Jefferson, and the United States would be chastised in kind with interest three years later by means of the nocuous affair of XY and Z and maybe W.

John Jay had finally returned from his mission to London on May 28, 1795, while the votes in his race against Robert Yates for governor of New York were still being canvassed, and on June 5 the chief justice of the United States was officially proclaimed the winner over Yates, the chief justice of New York. Jay resigned his chief-justiceship and took over from George Clinton, who was retiring undefeated. William Bradford of Pennsylvania, a friend and admirer of Hamilton, who had replaced Edmund Randolph as attorney general, needed Hamilton's advice when he wrote him on July 2, 1795. ''Your squabbles in New York have taken our Chief Justice from us,'' he noted; ''ought you not to find us another?'' In Brandford's mind and probably also in Washington's, Hamilton would be the ideal choice. They wanted him, but it was not a draft. Bradford added:

> I am afraid that department, as it related neither to War, finances nor negotiations, has no charms for you: and yet when one considers how immensely important it is, where [the justices] have the power of paralyzing the measures of the government by declaring a law unconstitutional, it is not to be trusted to men who are to be scared by popular clamor. . . . I wish to heaven you would permit me to name you: If not, what think you of Mr. Randolph?

No lawyer who was also a devoted friend of Hamilton could have made him a more persuasive argument for accepting the appointment. Who else but Hamilton would be more likely to interpret the Constitution in a way that would give reach and power to public credit, to the Federal government, and to the court itself? When would such interpretations be more necessary than in the immediate future? Appointment to the chief-justiceship of the United States Supreme Court for one of the most critical periods of American history was Hamilton's now for the asking.

The chief-justiceship was loftily above the political arena, far removed from the cross fire of partisan politics, where Hamilton, as Federalist party leader, remained the prime target of opportunity for Republican enemies like John Beckley, James Nicholson, Madison, Jefferson, Burr, and all their congressional and journalistic myrmidons. Its light, early case load and regular hours and terms would free Hamilton from the economic pressures of working late into the night to support his family and the political pressures of the attacks by his enemies that would bring on worse nervous derangements than any he had yet suffered.

Of all the sad things a sympathetic follower of Hamilton's career may say of it with perfect hindsight, one of the saddest is that he could have been the second chief justice of the United States Supreme Court beginning on or about July 2, 1795, but turned down the offer. If he had only wrapped himself in the nonpartisan armor and dignity of the chief justice's robes at 38, he would have been shielded from all the skeins of scandal with which Beckley and Callender and their masters soon would assail him. He would have escaped the eye of the political storm over Jay's Treaty that was about to break around his head. His innate style and sense of the dignity and propriety the role demanded would probably have restrained him from nervous and violent overreaction to enemies real and imagined that would mark and mar the rest of his life. Positioned above the political fray for three or four decades to come—longevity in this Valhalla of the law is real, not legendary—he would have brought to the fleshing out of a supreme Constitution for the Union a tone of strength and power to match or even surpass the achievement of his great friend and admirer John Marshall. He would have remained ready, waiting, and supremely eligible to accept a call to the presidency at any time it might come during the next decades and pass the robes of chief justice on to Marshall when it came. But Hamilton felt too much the need to make some money quickly in the private practice of law and restore his private credit to the level of the public credit he had left the nation as his legacy on leaving office. Yet no conceivable sum of lucrative fees ground out of a private law practice would compensate him for the loss of psychic dividends forgone with this last proffered office of public credit. He turned down Washington's and Bradford's offer of the chief-justiceship. He consented, however, to act as special counsel with the attorney general in the carriage tax case, a vital case necessary to secure Supreme Court confirmation of the national government's right to levy excise taxes. Seven weeks later, on August 23, William Bradford died. The other offer would never come his way again.

John Jay and Lord Grenville had signed Jay's Treaty in London on November 19, 1794, but the first copy of it did not reach Philadelphia until March 7, 1795. For the next two months George Washington and Secretary of State Edmund Randolph kept its contents secret before they submitted it to the special session of the Senate that convened on June 8, "under an injunction of secrecy." All the while, public suspicions smoldered. Just as if he had never resigned as the principal figure in Washington's administration, Hamilton wrote Oliver Wolcott, Jr., that "decorum requires" that the French minister be told of it "to satisfy him that there is nothing in it inimical to his country." He disapproved of the secrecy, was for full and prompt disclosure to the public, and believed the secrecy was political folly: "The nonpublication of the treaty is working as I expected, giving much scope to misrepresentation & misapprehension."

In the still secret Senate debates, Aaron Burr moved on June 22 to reject Jay's Treaty *in toto* and renegotiate it. Senator Henry Tazewell of Virginia moved on June 24 to vote it down on various grounds, one being that it "hath not secured satisfaction from the British government, for the removal of negroes, in violation of the treaty of 1783." The treaty also asserted "a power in the President and Senate, to control and even annihilate the constitutional right of the Congress . . . over their commercial intercourse with foreign nations." Complaints about noncompensation for slaves were to be expected from Virginians, but Tazewell also seemed to be raising the new constitutional point that the House of Representatives, as well as the Senate, must pass implementing laws before the treaty could take effect.

The most objectionable provision was Article XII, one of the commercial provisions, limited as to time, which granted America only restricted trading privileges in the West Indies. Hamilton foresaw that the Senate would not approve it, and on June 11 he had suggested a shrewd device to Rufus King that might yet save the worthwhile parts of the treaty. The United States should ratify the treaty as a whole, but declare that they take Article XII as being intended by Britain as a "privilege." Then the United States should declare that they forbear to exercise the "privilege" until a more acceptable modification is agreed on between the American minister and the British court. Final ratifications of the treaty would not be exchanged unless this qualification was accepted.

On June 24 the Senate approved the treaty, except for Article XII, by a vote of 20 to 10, a bare two-thirds Federalist majority, with not a single vote to spare. On Article XII it followed Hamilton's advice, suspending its effectiveness until the British should modify it. After rescinding the president's injunction of secrecy, but enjoining themselves "not to authorize or allow any copy of said communication," the Senate adjourned on the twenty-sixth. Several senators explained to Hamilton that the reason they had still not authorized publication of the text was because "they thought it the affair of the President to do as he thought fit."

Washington and Randolph agreed that the full text of the treaty should be published in *The Philadelphia Gazette* on July 1. But as is customary with secret Senate deliberations, a copy was leaked to the press. On June 29 an abstract of the treaty was published in Benjamin Franklin Bache's Philadelphia *Aurora*. The whole intensely curious nation pounced on it with cries of outrage.

Thomas Jefferson sounded off with characteristic extravagance, telling Madison in private that it was the boldest "party stroke ever struck." He imputed sedition to its supporters, calling it "an attempt to undermine the government." He wrote Edward Rutledge that it was "a treaty of alliance between England and the Anglomen of this country against the legislature and people of the United States." He wrote Mann Page that "a rogue of a pilot" had run the ship of state "into an enemy's port." He was still fulminating behind the scenes the following year when he wrote on March 27, 1796, that Washington was "the only honest man who has assented to" the treaty. He charged that through intrigue "a faction" had "entered into a conspiracy with the enemies of their country to chain down the legislature at the feet of both." Still later, after Washington had finally signed the treaty, Jefferson lamented to his friend and neighbor Philip Mazzei that Washington had been duped: "Men who were Samsons in the field and Solomons in the council . . . have had their head shorn by the harlot England." It was characteristic of Jefferson to attack the person and character of political opponents in terms of sleeping with harlots, and that he would later deny that his allusion to a Samson "shorn by the harlot England" had meant Washington.

Other Southern slave owners like John Rutledge and General Charles Cotesworth Pinckney of South Carolina, who were normally Federalist supporters, also opposed the treaty, although Rutledge later, upon sober reflection, let it be known that he regretted having spoken intemperately against it. At first, even in Boston the "merchants and steady men" joined the emotional opposition, although Massachusetts later swung round to support the treaty. In Philadelphia on July 3 a sullen mob turned out in response to handbills that urged attacks on a British vessel at Goldbury's Wharf in the harbor. The following night, only calling out the cavalry had prevented another mob from burning John Jay in effigy in front of Washington's house on Market Street. They burned the sober, upright envoy in the image of a straw man in the suburb of Kensington instead. The ten senators who had voted against ratification were toasted by Republicans for having "refused to sign the death warrant of American liberty," glasses were raised to "a perpetual Harvest to America—but clipped wings, lame legs, the pip and an empty crop to all Jays."

Opponents sneered that Jay had resigned from the Supreme Court to serve as governor of New York, just in time to escape being impeached. Washington nominated John Rutledge of South Carolina to succeed him, but Rutledge had been the bitterest foe of Jay's Treaty in his home state. The Federalist Senate rejected Rutledge, but the unpopularity of the treaty bearing Jay's name removed him as a future rival to Adams for the presidency—and also as a Federalist counterweight to Jefferson, who, as usual, absquatulated from the public fray.

Washington was appalled by the violence of the attacks. He complained to Hamilton that it was like "a paroxysm of the fever," a cry "like that against a mad dog," with "everyone, in a manner . . . engaged in running it down."

Washington had not yet signed the treaty. Before doing so, he pleaded for Hamilton's counsel. Sending him a copy of the treaty on July 3, Washington sought his opinion as a "dispassionate" man who had "knowledge of the subject, and abilities to judge of it." Hamilton, he said, had "given as much attention to" the entire subject "as most men," and "your late employment under the general government afforded you more opportunities of deriving Knowledge therein, than most of them who had not studied and practiced it scientifically, upon a large and comprehensive scale.'' He also asked Hamilton whether, if one assumed that Britain should agree to suspension of Article XII, as the Senate directed, it was necessary to have the treaty again ratified by the Senate.

Hamilton's reply of July 9–11, running to 43 pages in print, is characteristically scholarly, penetrating, and moderate in criticism and advocacy of the treaty in his best ''better than nothing'' vein.

As Hamilton explained, during the Revolution many slaves had gained freedom from their owners by joining the British army or by escaping during British occupation of their owners' plantations to one of the few states like Pennsylvania where the gradual abolition of slavery had been instituted by law. In other cases, the British had taken the slaves away from their owners.

The Treaty of Paris ending the war provided that restitution should be made to the former owners in the latter cases. But the question of whether the British—or the slaves' own human desire for freedom—had resulted in the loss to the owners was a vexed one in many cases. When the slave owners returned, they had demanded compensation in money from the British for loss of their cattle, slaves, and other chattels. Back in 1784, when Virginia had opened its courts to permit British nationals to sue to collect pre-Revolutionary War debts owing to them from large plantation owners like Thomas Jefferson, it was made a condition of suit that the British first pay compensation for loss of slaves. But under English common law, as laid down by Sir William Blackstone, following the law of nations generally, Hamilton explained, once a slave became free, he ''becomes a free man'' for all purposes forever afterward. Once the original contract of servitude between slave and master was broken, the relation of slave and master could not be resumed, ''that Right being now Extinct, which the victor by war obtained over his slave, natural liberty returns.'' Jay's Treaty omitted compensation to slave owners and breeders like Jefferson for slaves the British had permitted to become free. The British were being asked to pay compensation for slaves for which they had received no equivalent value, only nonmonetary credit for humaneness in freeing them.

Advising a Virginia slave owner like Washington, Hamilton dealt judiciously but humanely with the issue. Britain's action in ''seducing away our negroes'' during the war was infamous, he allowed, but, ''having done it, it would be still more infamous to surrender them to their masters.'' Though in the interpretation of treaties, ''the restoration of property is a favoured thing yet the surrender of persons to slavery is an odious thing speaking in the language of the laws of nations.''

The question of which nation had first broken the treaty of peace was a vexed one. Hamilton concluded that American obstructions to payment of private British creditors had occurred even prior to British taking of the Negroes. He heartily endorsed the promise not to sequester British property in American funds. Any taking of these would be disreputable to public credit.

Other objections to the treaty had more merit, he thought. It failed to deal with the impressment of American seamen by the British navy. A disarmed border between Canada and the United States had been one of Hamilton's cherished goals throughout his career; Jay's Treaty did provide that the British posts were to be evacuated by June 1, 1796, after which Indians living on either side of the border would be free to cross it to carry on normal trade without payment of fees or duties. This delay was objectionable to Hamilton even though under the treaty, ''citizens of both the United States and Canada would have access to inland waterways of both parties.'' The commercial articles of the treaty, which were to be binding for only 12 years, included guarantees against future tariff and tonnage discrimination and opened East Indies and West Indies trade to American vessels. But the West Indies were only partially opened—to American vessels of not more than 70 tons burden, and there was a specific prohibition against exportation of "molasses, sugar, coffee, cocoa, or cotton" in American vessels even from the United States, the assumption being that these items would have originated in the West Indies. This restriction was the notorious Article XII, on which Republican cries against the treaty came to focus. But this had already been rejected by the Senate before ratification. Hamilton told Washington he considered this article "exceptionable," "unprecedented," and "wrong." Hamilton gave Jay credit for his reasoning in accepting the article—that gaining even limited access to the British West Indian islands while Britain and France were at war was all-important—but Hamilton thought this was insufficient to warrant that limitation on American trade with other customers even for a limited period. By contrast, the article giving American ships admission to the ports of India was a clear gain, for which Britain had obtained no quid pro quo.

The worst article in the treaty after Article XII was XVIII. Jay's Treaty embodied the old rule of 1756 sanctioned by international law that an enemy's goods might be taken from a neutral's vessel. Under the "Armed Neutrality" doctrine, Americans had contended that "neutral ships made neutral goods" or "free ships made free goods." Many Americans had hoped to win that new rule because it would protect American ships carrying noncontraband goods to France. Opponents cried that Jay had given sanction to Britain's order-in-council of June, permitting the seizure of provisions as contraband if they had been paid for, which would cut off food shipments to France. Britain might abuse this clause, and France complain of it, but Hamilton did not think it alone was ground for rejecting the entire treaty.

The treaty expressly provided that it could not be repugnant to prior American commitments to France. True, it would stop Americans from permitting France to sell her prizes in American ports, but this was not a treaty commitment to Britain. It simply eliminated an unneutral concession to France, which should have been done away with in any event.

In general, Jay's Treaty finally clinched the peace with Britain and promised American immunity from "the dreadful war that is ruining Europe." America's prime need was for peace. We preserved our faith with other powers, particularly France, made no improper concessions, and gained "rather more" than we gave. It was better than nothing, Hamilton counseled, and should be signed by Washington. Hamilton's advice to Washington served as the Federalist brief for political defense of the treaty.

Jefferson later wrote that Hamilton himself, when discussing the treaty with Talleyrand, called it an "execrable" one and said that Jay was "an old woman for making it." Such typically open but indiscreet comments in private conversation were not inconsistent with Hamilton's advice to Washington. Having weighed the question carefully and reached his conclusion upon a preponderance of evidence that tipped the balance slightly in its favor, Hamilton set to work to make it a reality as if none of its defects had ever crossed his mind. He soon earned place beside Jay as the chief target of public and private Republican abuse.

Fisher Ames, a supporter of the treaty, wrote Thomas Dwight that a measure that had secured "peace abroad" had kindled "war at home." Oliver Wolcott, Jr., wrote Hamilton on July 28 that "attempts are made to stir up a flame & convulse the country." He suspected that the uproar was being orchestrated by the unseen hand of a master puppet master: "Though the actors hitherto are known to be a factious set of men & their followers generally a contemptible mob, yet from the systematical manner in which they have proceeded and some curious facts which have recently come to my knowledge, I cannot but suspect *foul play,* by persons not generally suspected."

Hamilton, too, suspected, as he told Wolcott, "that our Jacobins meditate serious mischief to certain individuals," including himself. The New York militia was not to be relied on for protection. Wolcott assured Hamilton that regular troops would remain in New York, as he wished, in case of mob violence, which came.

The plague broke out in New York that summer. Hamilton's family fled north to the Schuylers', but Hamilton, who by now had a lengthening medical history of serious illnesses and derangements each summer, stayed behind to perform what he saw as his duty.

Handbills and notices in newspapers, carefully timed and coordinated with similar ones in Philadelphia and Boston, summoned the citizens of New York City to meet at City Hall at high noon on Saturday, July 18, 1795, "to deliberate upon the proper mode of communicating to the President their disapprobation of the English Treaty."

To forestall the devastating threat of a seemingly unanimous mass public condemnation of the treaty like that contrived at Faneuil Hall, Hamilton and Rufus King hastily called a meeting of merchants and other supporters at the Tontine Coffee House for the Friday night before the Saturday meeting. James Watson served as the chairman. Impassioned speeches by Hamilton and King drawn from the texts of a series of pamphlets called "The Defence" by *Camillus,* which they were just then composing to publish beginning the following week, warmed the ardor of their supporters. They cried down the "spirit of precipitation" and "intemperance" that would prevent the "most considerate citizens from attending the meeting." If good citizens took their ease or fled to estates in the countryside for the July weekend, those who would attend would be "under the guidance of a set of men, who, with two or three exceptions, have been the uniform opposers of government."

Hamilton and King objected particularly that the Saturday meeting had been called not "to consider or discuss the merits of the treaty," but "to induce the citizens to surrender their reason to the empire of their passions" by inflammatory calls for its "disapprobation" without having read it.

Saturday morning the city was filled with a new set of handbills signed by James Watson, containing Hamilton's and King's condemnation of the tactics of the opposition. Their handbill declared that the treaty was not *quite* as bad as represented by its opponents and challenged opponents to debate it on its merits. They pressed fair-minded citizens to be critical of the arguments of its opponents. In a good, but not perfect, cause, the demand for a fair hearing is a better tactic than a head-on argument for the cause itself.

As a result of the handbills issued by both sides, a crowd of 5,000 to 6,000 people—some said 7,000—had collected by high noon Saturday in front of City Hall, filling up Broad Street for a block to the southward and west in Wall Street almost to Trinity Church at the corner of the Broad Way. Leaders of the opposition to the treaty standing on the steps of City Hall were preparing to call their followers to order as the bells in the Trinity church belfry tolled twelve. Suddenly Hamilton and two or three followers strode out of the surging mass of people jamming Broad Street. He leaped up on the stoop of an old Dutch frame house. His friends Josiah Ogden Hoffman, Senator Rufus King, and Richard Harison quickly closed ranks around him. He began to speak to the crowd in low-keyed words of intense ardor. Thousands of heads and eyes that had been focused on the opposition leaders whispering on the steps of City Hall swung round to stare at Hamilton and his supporters. He had hardly got beyond an innocuous disclaimer of having called the meeting himself, when hoots and calls from down in the crowd interrupted him. "Let us have a chairman," they yelled. Opponents called the crowd's attention back to their leaders on the steps of City Hall. When order was restored, Col. William S. Smith, Vice-President John Adams's son-in-law, was nominated chairman of the meeting. He climbed up onto the balcony where his father-in-law had first taken his oath of office as vice-president.

Peter R. Livingston then began to address the chairman. Hamilton resumed speaking again and interrupted him. Some voices from the crowd called out for order. Who should be allowed to speak first, Livingston or Hamilton? It was a vote on a parliamentary point, not critical to the substantive issue, but it would give some reading of the relative strength of the two factions all mixed up together in the crowd without risk to either of losing the vital vote itself. Chairman Smith put the question to the crowd, and a large noisy majority shouted Hamilton down. Motion carried in favor of Peter Livingston!

Livingston cried that the purpose of the meeting, as the announcements proclaimed, was the same as the Faneuil Hall meeting, to call on the president not to sign the treaty. But as he spoke, more shouts and catcalls rose on all sides to levels that drowned his words. Livingston angrily accused the friends of the treaty of disrupting the meeting, of trying to prevent discussion, and of staving off a vote on the provisions of the treaty itself. He moved "that those who disapproved of the treaty should go to the right, and those who approved of it to the left." This would send the part of the disorderly crowd that supported Hamilton over to the front of the stoop where he was standing and leave the treaty's enemies clustered around the steps of City Hall or filling up Wall Street all the way to Trinity. Pushing, shoving, shouting, confused, and hemmed in as it was by the buildings lining the streets, the crowd kept growing more noisy, rancorous, and disorderly. It turned into a mob. Believing that the die-hard enemies of the treaty had moved away, Hamilton resumed speaking above the hubbub, passionately urging upon his listeners temperate discussion before they jumped to, or voted on, misguided conclusions. Very little of what he said could be heard "on account of hissings, coughings and hootings, which entirely prevented his proceeding." Some of the mob's members began to turn to other modes of expression than words. They picked up stones and rocks and sticks, and some took aim and flung them toward the stoop where Hamilton stood.

John Jay's brother-in-law, another Livingston, Brockholst Livingston, took his turn trying to cry Hamilton down. He shouted that the treaty had been published for two weeks, that the people had already made up their minds about it, that the street was an improper place for discussion because the speakers could not be heard, that it was impossible to find a building large enough to hold the whole crowd, and that the purpose of the meeting would be defeated by procrastination. Word of ratification might arrive at any moment! If anyone had not already made up his mind against the treaty and would retire to Trinity Church, he would send someone there to discuss it with him, article by article, in opposition to Mr. Hamilton. Hamilton again tried to make himself heard. Opponents of the treaty found it impossible to silence him or draw off the friends of the treaty from the opposition. Unable to organize a unanimous vote of disapprobation, about 500 of the enemies of the treaty finally drew off themselves, marched three blocks down to the Battery, formed themselves in a circle, and "there BURNT *the treaty,* opposite the government house."

While the most militant members of the mob were off on this mindless mission, Hamilton introduced a resolution written by Rufus King and handed it up to Chairman Smith, who attempted to read it above the tumult. With the treaty burners off in the distance, the crowd quieted down a little and listened out of respect for the chairman and the resolutions' authors. Hamilton's and King's resolution "declared it unnecessary to give an opinion on the treaty" and reposed full confidence in the president.

But when the opponents in the crowd who had stayed to listen grasped the import of the resolution, according to the account contained in the following Monday's *Argus,* a Republican newspaper, it "roared, as with one voice: *We'll hear no more of it, tear it up, etc.*" A volley of rocks and stones punctuated the interval of quiet. The mob's most violent members returned in triumphant exaltation from the treaty-burning ceremony like the "mad dogs'' Washington had called them. They were now panting, yowling, and slavering for new targets of violent opportunity.

Shouts from the mob called for a vote on the question of appointing a committee of 15 to draft resolutions *"expressive of their disapprobation of the treaty,"* though there had not as yet been any discussion of the merits. Probably at about this time, one of the stones the mob had been shying toward the stoop struck Hamilton on the forehead. Seeing that he and his supporters could never carry any question against the angry passions of this mob or even get a hearing from them, Hamilton called out the question of approving his and Rufus King's resolution. His supporters, at least those standing within his hearing, loudly called *aye!* As if celebrating an overwhelmingly victorious vote on his and King's resolution, Hamilton then loudly called out to those who were "friends of order" to follow him. They separated themselves from the truculent, dangerous mob that filled the streets and moved away. Wiping the blood streaming from the stone bruise out of his eyes, Hamilton, according to his son John Church Hamilton, made a graceful bow to the mob and announced, "If you use such knock down arguments I must retire."

According to one eyewitness, Hamilton's retreat from the mob was less graceful than Hamilton's beloved son Johnny, too young at only three to have been an eyewitness to anything but the bloody wound, had reported. Grant Thorburn, a young Scotsman, later wrote that Hamilton's eloquence had "inflamed their plebeian souls." So "they cut short his speech, forced him from the stoop, and dragged him through the gutter."

With Hamilton gone, the question of appointment of the committee of 15 to draft the resolutions and report back on the following Monday was moved and seconded. But on the voice vote, Chairman Smith could not determine whether the majority was louder for than against it, any more than he could be certain which way the vote had gone on Hamilton's resolutions. Many in the crowd full of holiday high spirits or high jinks, as mobs often are, had yelled out approval or disapproval of both. To Adams's son-in-law, it seemed likely that the loudest shouters had the least idea of the issues the uproar was about.

With another tumultuous fight in prospect, Monday's crowd was even larger than Saturday's. Those hostile to the treaty now clearly controlled the meeting. They permitted no discussion of it before Brockholst Livingston read the hostile resolutions, which were rubber-stamped paragraph by paragraph and dispatched to the president. Filling four newspaper columns, they damned the treaty roundly. According to the *Argus*, all present had unanimously approved.

Hamilton and the other leading Federalists made no appearance at the Monday meeting. Next day at a full meeting of the Chamber of Commerce, the entire treaty was read and discussed. Then a vote was taken. A majority passed a set of resolutions reading like King's of the Saturday before, which expressed qualified approval. They deplored the passion that misled the popular mind and commended the treaty in general and in important particulars. Nevertheless, Monday's mass meeting added New York to other ports—Boston, Philadelphia, Baltimore, and Charleston—admonishing the president to reject the treaty.

Two days after this setback, on July 22, while Hamilton was still nursing the stone bruise on his forehead, there began to appear in Greenleaf's *Argus* or *New Daily Advertiser* the first of a series of papers mostly of his authorship entitled "The Defence" of the treaty and signed *Camillus,* which would continue to appear for the next five and a half months and eventually total 38 numbers in all.

The series is known to history as the *Camillus* papers. It is believed that of the 38, Hamilton wrote 28 himself and outlined, provided material for, and edited most of the remaining ten, which are attributed to Rufus King. Before the series ended on January 9, 1796, with Number 38, Hamilton had defended the treaty generally, provided a detailed analysis and defense of each of its articles, argued its constitutionality, and sought to refute the arguments brought against it by Republican pamphleteers like Brockholst Livingston.

The first numbers cited the malignant hostility of his enemies—the leaders of the mob that had stoned him—for reasons having nothing to do with the treaty: "There will always exist among us men irreconcilable to our present national constitution . . . such men will watch with Lynx's eyes, will display a hostile and malignant zeal . . . for opportunities of discrediting the government. . . ." To such men, men like Aaron Burr, for example, the advantages and weaknesses of the treaty itself were unimportant; it was important to them only as a handy tool to use for personal aggrandizement: "Every country, at all times, is cursed by the existence of men, who, activated by an irregular ambition, scruple nothing which they imagine will contribute to their own advancement." Such men trafficked in "weaknesses, vices, frailties or prejudices . . . more on the passions than on the reason of their fellow citizens."

On a higher level, Hamilton argued that, imperfect as the treaty might be, it was a means of staving off a war that might end in disaster. "If we can avoid a war for ten or twelve years more," he argued, "we shall then have acquired a maturity, which will make it no more than a common calamity, and will authorize us, in our national discussions, to take a higher and more imposing tone."

He played down its weak points and hammered on the strong.

Forcing the British out of the Western posts would clear the way for peaceful expansion of the American empire across the entire continent to the westward. Not incidentally, Marcus Furius Camillus was a Roman soldier and statesman of patrician descent, the censor in 403 B.C., who was honored with the title of second founder of Rome. Professor Mommsen summed up his place in history by calling him the man who "first opened up to his fellow countrymen the brilliant and perilous career of foreign conquest."

The *Camillus* papers were Hamilton's most masterful and effective essays in molding public opinion. While arguing for a particular action, the papers range wide, amounting to a survey of the political and economic situation of the Western world of the time. They are distinguished by an incisive style, richness of citation, and logical narrative flow. Without Hamilton and *Camillus,* popular clamor would probably have never allowed Jay's Treaty to go into effect.

After reading "The Defence, No. 1," Washington wrote Hamilton on July 29, 1795, with uncharacteristic warmth: "To judge of this work from the first number, which I have seen, I augur well of the performance; & I shall expect to see the subject handled in a clear, distinct and satisfactory manner."

The president urged Hamilton to disseminate the papers widely to counter the "poison" spreading in all directions from the opposition. He ended with the striking observation that "the difference of conduct between friends and foes of order & good government, is in nothing more striking than that the latter are always working like bees to distil their poison; whilst the former, depending oftentimes *too much* and *too long* upon the sense and good disposition of the people to work conviction, neglect the means of effecting it."

Jefferson's angry reaction to the *Camillus* series produced the strongest personal testimonial to Hamilton ever written. Here was Jefferson's master plan to discredit the Federalists on a burning national issue about to be thwarted by Hamilton, who seemed to stand alone in the van of the Federalists. From his retreat in Monticello on September 21, Jefferson wrote in alarm to Madison, his usual confidant in desperate situations, "Hamilton is really a colossus to the anti-republican party. Without numbers, he is a host within himself."

In the group of Hamilton's Federalist friends who had bravely mounted the stoop on

Broad Street with him to face the mob and defend the treaty was Josiah Ogden Hoffman, a young lawyer about ten years Hamilton's junior. It was his name John Beckley had passed along to Madison and Jefferson as Hamilton's friend with whom (Commodore James Nicholson had charged) Hamilton had vested £100,000 sterling in British funds in London while secretary of the treasury. Very likely Nicholson or someone else had shouted these charges at Hoffman during Saturday's hubbub in the street, perhaps just after Hamilton had shoved his way out or been dragged away, blood trickling down his forehead. The quarrel at first seemed to lie between Nicholson and Hoffman, standing in the street defending Hamilton against the shouted charges, but Hamilton had stepped in to take his own part, trying to calm both men down. Commodore Nicholson later admitted that Hamilton's first words were intended to apply equally to himself and Hoffman. But, according to Hamilton, "Mr. Nicholson replied very harshly . . . that he [Hamilton] was not the man to prevent his quarreling [,] called him an Abettor of Tories and used some other harsh expressions." According to Beckley, Nicholson also charged that in the Constitutional Convention, Hamilton had sought a government of kings, lords, and commons. Hamilton had told Nicholson that the city street was not a fit place for yet another fierce altercation. Nicholson retorted that Hamilton feared to pursue the affair because on a former occasion Hamilton had backed off from challenge to a duel.

Hoffman was forgotten. Furious at Nicholson's slur on his honor, Hamilton cried out that "no man can affirm that with truth!" Hamilton added, "I pledge myself to convince Mr. Nicholson of his mistake." Hamilton's mental balance, always hypersensitive to pressures from enemies, was near a breaking point. That afternoon he and Hoffman roamed the hot New York City streets, seeming to seek out new enemies everywhere to be confronted. At the door of Edward Livingston's house, Hoffman engaged Peter Livingston in another fierce argument that turned personal. Rufus King and Peter's brother, Edward, interposed, telling them that personal disputes should be settled somewhere else. As Edward Livingston wrote his mother two days later, Hamilton then thrust himself forward belligerently, like a mad dog, saying, "If these two are going to fight, I will fight the whole opposition party one by one." Edward Livingston moved toward him to try to calm him. Hamilton threw up his arms and repeated, "I am ready to fight your whole detestable faction one by one." Another brother, Maturin Livingston, arrived just then and said very coolly that he accepted Hamilton's challenge and would meet him in half an hour anywhere Hamilton pleased.

Hamilton replied that he had one such affair on his schedule already, with Nicholson. When that was settled, he would get back to Maturin Livingston. To their mother, Edward Livingston confided of Hamilton, "you may judge how much he must be mortified at his loss of influence [to] descend to language that would have become a street bully."

But as Hamilton saw it, still wiping blood from his brow, Nicholson had clearly given him "a violent offense without provocation." The following Monday, July 20, the day the mass meeting of treaty opponents reassembled, Hamilton sent his friend Colonel Nicholas Fish to Nicholson with a challenge written out in Fish's hand:

> Sir [:] The unprovoked rudeness and insult which I experienced from you on Saturday leaves me no option but that of meeting with you, the object of which you will readily understand. I propose to you for the purpose Paulus Hook as the place and Monday next eleven o'clock as the time. I should not fix so remote a day but that I am charged with trusts for other persons which will previously require attention on my part.

It was a vital part of the code duello, as well as to avoid being arrested for violating penal laws against dueling, to keep the intended meeting absolutely secret and outside of New

York. Until the day, both principals must appear normal in their most intimate relations—while giving close attention to transfers of trusts and other responsibilities for other persons for whom the duelist might be responsible.

Commodore Nicholson answered briskly. He declined the invitation of Mr. "Hambleton"; the "peremptory tenor" of the challenge precluded his "discussion of the merits of the controversy." Nicholson added that Fish's call had alarmed Nicholson's family. He feared interference from them.

Hamilton's wounds had healed a little. If Nicholson could explain his remark "on a certain very delicate point," Hamilton would not decline "an explanation if you see in the original transaction room for it." He hoped the Commodore could quiet the alarm of his family. More exchanges sped back and forth between the two men during the next few days.

Late the afternoon of July 21 the Nicholsons received a visit from a lady "of our (evidently mutual) Acquaintance," who tried to speak to Mrs. Nicholson alone in the garden. The commodore guessed her errand, interrupted her intended confidences, and ushered her home. He was left with "no doubt . . . she came to Alarm my family of what was likely to take place." He told Hamilton of the mysterious visit in a predawn note penned at half-past five of Wednesday morning.

Who was the mysterious lady? Mrs. Rufus King? Elizabeth Hamilton? Mrs. Josiah Ogden Hoffman? Most likely the last, who must have felt compunction that Hamilton's defense of her husband in his quarrel with Nicholson had drawn Hamilton into mortal danger. One woman at least was not willing to see two able men make fools of themselves if she could prevent it in the only way open to a lady.

Even though Hamilton knew as well as any man how to avoid a duel without sacrificing honor, he had not done so by July 25. Ominous exchanges with Nicholson were still passing back and forth as Hamilton made out his will. He wrote instructions to his old friend Robert Troup, whom he named as executor. There would be nothing left over for legatees: "I might have dispensed with the ceremony of making a will as to what I may myself leave, had I not wished that my little property may be applied . . . readily and . . . fairly . . . to the benevolence of others, if my course shall happen to be terminated here." He had quit the Treasury a poor man—"I hope what I leave may prove equal to my debts." His list of debts added up to about $30,000.

He wanted to give a preference to only one creditor, Nicholas Fish, one of his seconds in the impending duel with Nicholson. The amount was small, but Hamilton wished "to secure him in this mere act of friendship from the possibility of loss . . ." He was pained not to be able to make a preference for drafts drawn by his father, James Hamilton, for $700 "lest they should return upon him and increase his distress," but these were a "voluntary engagement," and he "doubted the justice" of putting them ahead of other commitments. His brother-in-law, John B. Church, was by much his largest creditor. Hamilton hoped that Church would accept any net loss from settlement of the estate. Uncharacteristically apologetic, Hamilton wrote that "I regret that his affairs as well as my own have suffered by my devotion to the public service. . . . they will not have been as profitable to him as they ought to have been & as they would have been if I could have paid more attention." There were special instructions for certain mysterious bundles he would leave marked *AA, AB,* and *D.* He felt he had been overpaid by retainers from some of his clients, "large fees for which the parties could not have had equivalents," at least if he died just then before finishing their cases. He named them, but added poignantly, "It would be just if there were means that they should be repaid." Unfortunately, there was no way because "what can I direct who am (I fear) insolvent?"

No mention was made of any £100,000 allegedly secreted in a London bank. The more than $1,100 of blackmail money he had paid to James Reynolds could hardly have been far out of mind as he wrote these painful self-reproaches for the fact of his own insolvency.

By way of postscript to this last testament before the impending duel, Hamilton pointed to one last mysterious bundle that was in the leather trunk:

> In my leather trunk where the bundles above mentioned are is also a bundle inscribed thus—J R *To be forwarded to Oliver Wolcott Junr. Esq.*
> I entreat that this may be early done by a careful hand.

Wolcott, of course, as well as the host of Hamilton's enemies—Beckley; his assistant, Bernard Webb; Madison; Monroe; Jefferson; and Burr—would easily identify the initials *J R* on this last little bundle of "interesting papers" as standing for the name of James Reynolds. Troup, like John Jay and other close friends, could also probably guess the secret by now, but from prior knowledge only Wolcott would be certain to know the contents of this last pathetic bundle.

Following Hamilton's entreaty to "careful hands," the last sentence of his testament reads: "This trunk contains all my interesting papers." Below this sentence, at some later date, five more words were written, probably after he was dead, in the firm regular script of Elizabeth Hamilton: "To be retained by myself."

In the continuing exchanges with Commodore Nicholson through their seconds, Hamilton denied he had prompted the unnamed lady to call on Nicholson's family. He sent back a reply by Nicholson's second, De Witt Clinton, the fiery young nephew of Governor George Clinton. Hamilton wrote, "Measures it is true toward an accommodation have been subsequently in train but I have had no other agency in the affair than that of meeting them . . . in a liberal & Gentlemanlike manner."

By the end of the week, after more exchanges, Rufus King joined Hamilton's seconds; and Brockholst Livingston, Nicholson's; and all joined good offices to ease the way to an understanding between the principals. Nicholson signed a written statement denying having said that Hamilton "had declined a former interview." He regretted the pain his insult had caused.

This episode shows that Hamilton knew as well as any man the etiquette of the dueling code and the graceful means available for settling such an affair without dishonor to either party, if he should be disposed to settle, without bloodshed. When such an episode reached the exchange of bullets, it did so because a principal insisted on no other way out.

By the end of August, Hamilton's early *Camillus* papers had helped convince Washington that the treaty should be signed and ratified. Earlier, Washington had understood that his attorney general, William Bradford, his secretary of state, Randolph, and the majority of the Senate were all of the opinion that if the British accepted the American revision of Article XII, the treaty need not go before the Senate a second time for its advice and consent. The president had been disturbed to learn that Hamilton was of the contrary opinion and had told his cabinet and attorney general to change their opinion to agree with Hamilton's.

Ratifications were exchanged in London, the president proclaimed the treaty in effect, and laid it before the House of Representatives on March 1, 1796. In the administration's view, the treaty was now in full force and effect; the role of the House was merely to vote the funds necessary to implement the treaty in various ways.

But the Republicans in the House did not see themselves confined to any such mere rubber stamp role.

Hamilton's secret instructions to Jay for the treaty negotiations had called for Jay to "insert a formal *stipulation*" in the treaty itself agreeing to pay for British vessels seized by American privateersmen commissioned by Citizen Genêt, instead of leaving it to implementing laws, so that "the Senate only will have to concur. If provision is to be made by law, *both Houses* must concur. The difference is easily seen." There would be trouble in the House.

Edward Livingston of New York now moved that the president furnish the House with Hamilton's secret instructions to Jay, and the motion carried.

Hamilton had forewarned Washington how to respond to such a resolution on March 7. "If the motion succeeds, it ought not to be complied with. In a matter of such a nature the production of the papers cannot fail to start a new and unpleasant game—it will be fatal to the negotiating power of the Government."

Hamilton gave Washington the language the president ought to use in denying the House demand. The right of the House to demand "communications respecting a negotiation with a foreign power cannot be admitted without danger. A Discretion in the Executive Department how far and where to comply in such cases is essential to the due conduct of foreign negotiations and is essential to preserve the limits between the Legislative and Executive Departments." The executive "cannot therefore without forming a very dangerous precedent comply." The narrower principle at stake was that the power to make and ratify a treaty was vested exclusively in the president and Senate, with the House having no part in the process. Washington followed Hamilton's advice and his text and refused the House demand. This advice of Hamilton created the earliest precedent for the broad doctrine that later came to be known as "executive privilege."

James Madison drafted a set of resolutions declaring that the House had the right to pass on portions of treaties involving matters that were its constitutional responsibility—such as voting appropriations—and that the president must make available all information that concerned the House's functions. Hamilton wrote out for Rufus King a plan for meeting this new flank attack on the treaty that reads like an order of battle: "To me our true plan appears to be the following: The President ought immediately after the House has taken the ground of refusal to send them a solemn protest." The Senate should "express strongly their approbation of this principle, assure him of their firm support and advise him to proceed in the execution of the Treaty."

Merchants should "meet in the cities . . . second the president and Senate . . . address their fellow citizens to cooperate. . . ." Petitions "should be handed throughout the United States . . ." The Senate should "hold fast and consent to no adjournment till the expiration of the term of service of the present House . . ."

A constitutional crisis was at hand, said Hamilton. "Great evils may result, unless good men play their card well and with promptitude and decision. . . . In all this business celerity, decision and an imposing attitude are indispensable. The Glory of the president, the safety of the constitution, the greatest interests depend upon it."

But no matter how important it might be to beat down the House's opposition, the end did not justify illegal or improper means. It would not be "eligible" for Federalists in the House to trade off execution of the Spanish and Algerine treaties, also pending, as a quid pro quo for Republican approval of Jay's Treaty: "The misconduct of the other party cannot justify in us an imitation of their principles. . . . Let us be *right,* because to do right is intrinsically proper, and I verily believe it is the best means of securing final success. Let our adversaries have the whole glory of sacrificing the interests of the nation. . . . We must seize and carry along with us the public opinion . . . in the confidence that . . . the virtue and good sense of the people, constitutionally exerted,. . . may still be the instrument of preserving the Constitution, the peace, and the honor of the nation.''

The great debate came to a climax on April 28, when Fisher Ames made a last famous appeal. He began by speaking of his own frail health. He closed by saying that ill as he was, his country would perish first if Jay's Treaty were not upheld. Between exordium and peroration, his mental vigor and emotional force belied his physical weakness. His speech was Hamilton's *Camillus* compressed. He ridiculed Anti-Federalists, as pretended champions of the people against a tyrannical government. They seemed more like a little group of willful men. The speech of the greatest of Federalist orators ''was attended to with a silence and interest never before known, and made an impression,'' according to John Adams, ''that terrified the hardiest'' of the Antis and ''will never be forgotten.''

Two days later, April 30, 1796, a motion to make the necessary appropriations narrowly carried, 51 to 48. Passions still ran so high that after casting a deciding vote in favor of the treaty, Frederick A. C. Muhlenberg, Speaker of the House, was stabbed by a fanatical Republican—who was also his brother-in-law.

In the closing paragraphs of his magisterial work, *Jay's Treaty,* Professor Samuel Flagg Bemis observes:

> the political and economic foundations of the American nation had been laid by the hands of genius, but those foundations in 1794 were by no means unshakeable. The power of the Federal Government to hold the union together under the Constitution depended on the financial system which Hamilton had created. . . . national credit which energized the government depended almost wholly on imports, which a war or even commercial hostility with Great Britain would have destroyed. . . . This danger is what Alexander Hamilton realized with the clear eye of the *realpolitiker.*

The treaty gave the United States time to develop in population and resources and in a consciousness of nationality that made resistance to Britain possible in 1812 that would have been impossible in 1794. As Hamilton had written Washington in 1794, disruption of commerce with Britain would ''bring the Treasury to an absolute stoppage of payment—an event which would *cut up credit by the roots.''* The last words of Bemis's treatise are the following:

> The terms of [Jay's] treaty were the result of the powerful influence of Alexander Hamilton to whom in the last analysis any praise or blame for the instrument must be given. . . . More aptly the Treaty might be called Hamilton's Treaty.
>
> As he ruefully fingered the scar of his stone bruise, put his duelling pistols back in their case, reflected on his insolvent estate and the three-vote margin in the House that had headed off the Constitutional crisis, the hot-tempered *realpolitiker* would hope his public credit stood higher than his private.

30

An Out-of-Town, Undercover Prime Minister

Aid me I pray you. . . .

—From George Washington, October 29, 1795

We are laboring hard to establish in this country principles more and more *national* and free from all foreign ingredients, so that we may be neither *Greeks* nor *Trojans*, but truly Americans.

—To Rufus King, December 16, 1796

In the summer of 1795, just after the popular uproar over Jay's Treaty had reached a crescendo with the stoning of Hamilton in Wall Street, Secretary of the Treasury Oliver Wolcott, Jr., had written Hamilton of the "curious facts" that had recently come to his knowledge that led him to "suspect *foul play*, by persons not generally suspected." Two days later, Wolcott wrote Hamilton again, still more alarmed, "I dare not *write* & hardly dare *think* of what I *know* & believe respecting a certain character; whose situation gives him a decided influence." The "certain character" to whom Wolcott referred was none other than that uncertain character, Secretary of State Edmund Randolph, now the highest ranking senior member of Washington's cabinet. Wolcott would take counsel with two of his Philadelphia colleagues, Timothy Pickering of Massachusetts, the new secretary of war and Attorney General William Bradford. But it would be well, he concluded, if Hamilton or Rufus King or John Jay "could be here some time next week—provided too much speculation would not be excited."

Wolcott, Pickering, and Bradford sent off a summons to Washington, calling him back from Mount Vernon. They adroitly arranged to have Randolph himself urge Hamilton to return, too, without Randolph's suspecting why he was being asked to do so.

On arrival at the president's house for a cabinet meeting, Randolph found Wolcott and Pickering already in consultation with the president. Without preface, in a towering rage, Washington thrust under Randolph's eyes a copy of a dispatch that the French minister, Jean Antoine Joseph Fauchet, had sent to his home government on October 31, 1794, coded "Dispatch no. 10." It had been intercepted by the British, passed to George Hammond, the British minister, and passed on to Wolcott who had, in turn, advised Hamilton, Washington, and Pickering.

Was it true, Wolcott demanded of the shamefaced Randolph, that Randolph had solicited money from Fauchet?

"No," replied Randolph. "Except on one occasion."

To the shocked questioners Randolph quibbled that he had not asked the French minister to give him money, he had merely asked Fauchet to pay for some spying for France. Wolcott warned Hamilton, who had not troubled to come down to Washington for the grim confrontation, that "attempts will be made to represent you as concerned in it." His involvement was in every page. Randolph wanted money from France to pay for evidence that Hamilton's suppression of the Whiskey Insurrection had been stirred up by British agents to discredit American supporters of France, particularly the Democratic societies.

Protesting weakly under fire only that he "never made an improper communication to Mr. Fauchet," Randolph resigned as secretary of state the same day and posted off to Newport to seek an explanation from Fauchet that would exonerate him, but Fauchet sailed off for home.

Washington exploded all over again when he read the pamphlet that Randolph published December 18, 1795, *A Vindication of Mr. Randolph's Resignation*. On December 22, he asked Hamilton what notice should be taken of it?

Hamilton replied promptly December 24 that he could not fail to note Randolph's wild tergiversations:

> I have read with care Mr. Randolph's pamphlet. It does not surprise me. I consider it as amounting to a confession of guilt and I am persuaded this will be the universal opinion. It appears to me that by you no notice can or ought to be taken of the publication. It contains its own antidote.

Jefferson came to much the same conclusion as Hamilton about what his fellow Virginian and erstwhile follower Randolph had done and washed his hands of poor Randolph in a memorable characterization to Madison: Randolph "has generally given his principles to the one party, & his practice to the other; the oyster to one, the shell to the other. Unfortunately the shell was generally the lot of his friends the French and republicans, & the oyster of their antagonists."

Without Hamilton at the capital to help dispose of such crises briskly one by one as they arose, Washington, Wolcott, and Pickering posted most major policy questions up to Hamilton in New York for his consideration, review, advice, and counsel. Washington told him, "Although you are not in the administration—a thing I sincerely regret—I must nevertheless (knowing how intimately acquainted you are with all the concerns of this country) request you to note down proper subjects for communication to Congress."

Attorney General William Bradford's death and Randolph's disgrace created two vacancies in the cabinet, but no one seemed to want to join an administration that now seemed to be under siege by smear of Madison and Jefferson and their followers and run by proxy from New York. On October 29, Washington passed on a number of names for Hamilton's consideration for the offices of secretary of state, secretary of war, and attorney general. But, he added, what with "the nonacceptance of some; the known dereliction of those who are most fit; the exceptionable drawbacks from others; and a wish (if it were practicable) to make a geographical distribution of the *great* officers of the administration, I find the selection of proper characters an arduous duty."

Washington also implored Hamilton for help in writing his seventh annual message to Congress both as to "the proper subjects for my communications to Congress . . . and the manner of treating them." This would include the prickly subject of Jay's Treaty, the proper manner of dealing with the actions of the House and Senate concerning it, the pending negotiations with Spain being handled by Thomas Pinckney, the problems of treaty negotiations with Algiers and Tunis, the treaties with the Indian tribes, the statement concerning the military establishment, and what to say about domestic fiscal matters and foreign loans. Washington pleaded for Hamilton's help: "Aid me I pray you with your sentiments on these points." If there were any other problems about which he had forgotten to ask Hamilton for advice, Hamilton should also aid him with "such others as may have occurred to you."

Still other vexing questions backed up on the national agenda. George Washington Motier Lafayette, the son of the Marquis de Lafayette, Washington's favorite of all his wartime aides, had arrived incognito in New York with his tutor, Felix Frestal, on October 1, expecting that the childless president would receive them warmly, acting the part of a surrogate grandfather. The Hamiltons had given them temporary hospitality in their already overcrowded household. Strong appeals to receive the lad officially showered in on Washington from Frestal, from George Cabot, and from Henry Knox.

The problem was that the marquis, his father, was now being held in prison in Austria under orders of the French Directory, and Washington had no wish to give offense to the official French government. Washington hesitated, about to be cut by one or the other of "two edges, neither of which can be avoided without falling on the other. On one side, I may be charged with countenancing those who have been denounced as the enemies of France; on the other, with not countenancing the son of a man who is dear to America."

Washington's first impulse was to have the young man and his tutor "proceed to him without delay . . . to take them at once into my family . . . unless some powerful reasons can be announced to the contrary." What did Hamilton think?

After Hamilton had turned down Bradford's offer of appointment to be chief justice of the Supreme Court, Washington had nominated John Rutledge, who now seemed to be suffering from physical and mental instability and decline. What did Hamilton think should be done about the nomination—withdraw it? Let him dangle? Or what?

Hamilton doggedly dealt with all. As for appointments to the vacant cabinet posts, he had asked Rufus King to take over State and been turned down. He canvassed the field to Washington on November 5 with corrosive wit and obsessed with enemies:

> Circumstances of the moment conspire with the disgust which a virtuous and independent mind feels at placing itself *in but* to the foul and venomous shafts of calumny which are continually shot by an odious confederation against virtue . . . for a secretary of state . . . [William Loughton] Smith, [Congressman from South Carolina] though not of full size is very respectable and . . . has more real talent than the last incumbent of the office. . . . He is popular with no description of men

from a certain *hardness of* character and more than most other men is considered as tinctured with prejudices toward the British. . . . Mr. [James] Innes I fear is too absolutely lazy for secretary of state. The objection would weigh less as to Attorney General. Judge Nathaniel Pendleton writes well, is of respectable abilities and a gentlemanlike smooth man. . . . But I fear he has been somewhat tainted by the prejudices of Mr. Jefferson and Mr. Madison and I have afflicting suspcions concerning these men. . . .

Having reviewed all the possibilities, Hamilton gave the following hardheaded advice: "A first rate character is not attainable. A second rate must be taken with good dispositions and barely decent qualifications. . . . Tis a sad omen for the government."

There was his old crony and Washington's former aide James McHenry of Maryland. "I mean the doctor," he reminded Washington. "You know he would give no strength to the administration but he would not disgrace the office—his views are good—perhaps his health, etc. would prevent his accepting."

Among others who might not turn down attorney generalship (where absolute laziness was no real objection) was Charles Lee, a former Treasury Department collector of revenue of Alexandria, Virginia.

After shifting Pickering from the War Department to secretary of state, Washington obediently to Hamilton's advice appointed Charles Lee attorney general on November 19, 1795, and James McHenry secretary of war on January 24, 1796.

For good measure, Washington also appointed Hamilton's friend and mentor Elias Boudinot as director of the Mint.

As for Rutledge's imminent appointment as chief justice, the subject was a perplexing one, as Hamilton wrote Senator Rufus King December 14: "If it be really true—that he is sottish or that his mind is otherwise deranged or that he has exposed himself by improper conduct in pecuniary transactions, the byass of my judgment would be negative."

This decision was more important than many others to Hamilton because "it is now, and in certain probable events will be still more, of infinite consequences that our judiciary should be well composed." King wrote Hamilton on December 16, "Rutledge was negatived yesterday by the Senate."

As for young George Washington Motier Lafayette, Hamilton advised that though his fondest wish would be for Washington to welcome him into his open arms immediately without more ado, it would be wise to delay the welcome awhile because "the factions might use it as a weapon to represent you as a favorer of the anti-revolutionists of France." Republicans, led by Edward Livingston, called for a Congressional investigation to embarrass Washington. Popular sympathy for the lad against his and his father's persecutors welled up, the Republicans overplayed their hand, and six months later Hamilton was able to dispatch young Lafayette to Washington for an official reception unspoiled by any Jeffersonian "aliment to their slanders."

The carriage tax, one of the key measures of Hamilton's program for the creation of public credit, was a crude form of graduated income tax because it was borne by the well-to-do, who bought carriages, and not by the less well-to-do, who did not. The carriage tax case was the first to come before the Supreme Court in which it would pass upon the constitutionality of an act of Congress.

Just as he was now denying the supremacy of treaties from the House floor, Madison was claiming that the carriage tax was unconstitutional because it was a "direct" tax, which would have to be apportioned state by state, according to state populations. This the federal carriage tax did not do.

Charles Lee, the new attorney general, called on Hamilton to argue the government's case for the carriage tax in the Supreme Court on February 24, 1796. Against them for the plaintiff were Alexander Campbell, attorney of the Virginia District, and Jared Ingersoll, attorney general of Pennsylvania.

Hamilton's argument to the Court, with a distinguished audience in attendance, filled three hours. He found no reliable distinction, legal or economic, between a "direct" and an "indirect" tax. It was enough if the tax were uniform like other duties, imposts, and excises under the Constitution.

Then as he often did, Hamilton enlarged his frame of reference to sound a national theme that went far beyond the narrow issue of the case: "No construction ought to prevail . . . to defeat the . . . necessary authority of the government . . . a duty on carriages . . . is as much within the authority of the government as a duty on lands or buildings."

Chief Justice Oliver Ellsworth, who had just been sworn in after Rutledge's rejection by the Senate, and Justice Cushing, who had been ill during the argument, took no part in the decision. Justice William Paterson, writing for the majority, joined by Samuel Chase and James Iredell, held with Hamilton that the carriage tax was a circuitous means "of reaching the revenue of individuals, who generally live according to their income." It was not a direct tax. It was properly an excise tax and, therefore, constitutional so long as it was uniform. It did not need to be proportioned to the populations of the several states. All agreed with Hamilton that the framers of the Constitution intended that Congress should have power "over every species of taxable property, except exports."

Hamilton's was the seminal Supreme Court tax case. Few any longer doubt the principle that the authority of Congress under the Constitution to levy taxes is sovereign, though many might wish with Madison that such were not the case.

Writing Hamilton from London on March 4, Gouverneur Morris summed up France's angry reaction to presidential and senatorial ratification of Jay's Treaty. Washington, as usual, asked Hamilton to advise him what to do, after discussing the matter with Jay. Hamilton replied calmly to Washington that he should not worry over much with speculation about French reactions until he should learn exactly what the Directory actually did. If the Directory should demand that the United States renounce Jay's Treaty, "the answer will naturally be that this . . . [is] too humiliating and injurious to us . . . a thing impossible . . . the sacrifice of our honor by an act of perfidy which would destroy the value of our friendship to any nation." Besides, Hamilton added, "The executive is not competent to it—it being the province of Congress by a declaration of war or otherwise in proper cases to annul the operation of treaties."

Senator Rufus King confided to Hamilton that he was "not a little tired" of his senatorial burdens; Thomas Pinckney was resigning as minister to England. Hamilton advised Washington that he should name his friend King "a remarkably well informed man—a man of address—a man of fortune and economy—a man of unimpeached probity where he is best known—a firm friend to the government—a supporter of the measures of the president—a man who has strong pretensions to confidence and trust," to the post. Washington hastened to appoint him.

The Directory on July 2, 1796, had ordered French privateers to stop and seize the cargoes of all neutral vessels bound to English ports, and as 1796 wore on, reports of new French attacks on American merchant vessels began to come in thick and fast. Far from protesting such outrages, James Monroe, the American minister in Paris, continued to minimize them and to exude friendly support for the Directory. A troubled Washington, of course, asked Hamilton to discuss the Monroe problem with Governor Jay and report back to him. In Hamilton's and Jay's opinion, Senate concurrence would indeed be necessary for the appointment of a new envoy extraordinary to France. In periods of derangement Hamilton would tend to see Monroe as his archenemy; "there are weighty reasons against removing Monroe," Hamilton responded, "But we think those for it preponderate." A new man "ought at the same time to be a friend to the government and understood to be *not unfriendly* to the French Revolution." General Charles Cotesworth Pinckney "is the only man we can think of who fully satisfies the idea." An even weightier matter loomed. Washington's second term was drawing to a close, and he was determined not to seek a third. Hamilton's counsel was the political wisdom of the best second term presidents: "It is not to be regretted that the declaration of your intention should be suspended as long as possible . . . you should *really hold the thing undecided to the last moment.*" Washington duly appointed Charles Cotesworth Pinckney as envoy extraordinary to Paris, and held off announcing his irrevocable decision to leave office until after he had released the *Farewell Address* that Hamilton had been helping him compose since May.

One of the greatest joys in prospect for Hamilton when his impending resignation would remove from his shoulders all the government's problems—or so he thought—was symbolized by the search he was making for a New York house for John and Angelica Church to live in when they returned to America. But concerns for the public's political welfare no longer served as a viable excuse for a lawyer in private practice to allow his attention to wander from the immediate concerns of his private clients.

By February 19, 1796, Angelica Church had received some letters from Hamilton, "but no plan of the lot, and no description of the house. How can I bring out the furniture when I do not know the number of rooms my house contains," she wrote him reproachfully.

To the petulant annoyance characteristic of a slightly neglected client with time on her hands, Angelica joined her own special barb, as if she were suffering an anxiety attack brought on by fear of rejection by her lover—or worse still, of being taken for granted. Nothing could have brought more anguish to Hamilton, nor have been calculated to do so:

> I am sensible how much trouble I give you, but . . . it proceeded from a persuasion that I was asking from one who promised me his love and attention if I returned to America . . . for what do I exchange ease and taste, by going to the new world, where politics excludes all society and agreeable intercourse, where all that is not given to fame seems to be regretted and forgotten . . . what an agreeable amiable fellow, has Jay's LITTLE treaty turned into a defender of what he never would himself have designed to submit to. Violà mon sentiment, changes le si vous veules.

Letting all other concerns slide, Hamilton arranged to pay $4,250 for the house and four lots on the east side of Broadway, near Robinson Street north of Marketfield, and finally sent off to Angelica some sketches of the house and lot, seeking forgiveness, pleading with her on June 25, "How do you manage to charm all that see you? Naughty tales are told to you of us, we hear nothing but of your kindness, amiableness, agreeableness etc."

But there was no mistaking that a welt remained from the lash of her February anxiety: "Why will you be so lavish of these qualities upon those who forget them in six weeks and withhold them from us who retain all the impressions you make, indelibly?" Hamilton and Eliza were "strangely agitated between fear and hope, anxiously wishing for your return. . . . We feast on your letters. . . . The only rivalship we have is in our attachment to you and we each contend for preeminence in this particular. To whom will you give the apple?''

Yes, ''Jacobins have made a violent effort against me,'' he told her, ''but a complete victory has been gained to their utter confusion.'' He closed: ''Yours as much as you desire. A. H.''

When Hamilton had been in Philadelphia in February to help Charles Lee argue the constitutionality of the carriage tax, Washington had asked him to *"re-dress* a certain paper'' that he had prepared sometime before. On May 15, Washington sent Hamilton the ''certain paper.'' It turned out to be nothing less than the first draft of his *Farewell Address*.

On May 15 the ''certain paper'' consisted of two separate papers, the first being a rough draft written by James Madison following conversations with Washington in May of 1792, headed ''Substance of a Conversation with the President.'' The second was a paper written by Washington very recently, intended to explain the ''considerable changes'' that had ''taken place both at home and abroad'' since 1792 during Washington's second term.

On May 12, Washington had invited Madison to a private dinner. The subject of the ''considerable changes'' in their relationship since 1792 was, no doubt, a principal topic of their conversation. When the dinner was over, Washington struck out all references to Madison and Jefferson and expunged Madison's name from the first page of Madison's draft.

When Washington and Hamilton had talked it over in February, they had considered two alternative ways to proceed, either by Hamilton's revising the earlier drafts or by preparing an entirely new address. All these observations of his, Washington said in his letter forwarding the earlier drafts to Hamilton, are confined ''to *my draft* of the valedictory address. If you form one anew it will, of course, assume such a shape as you may be disposed to give it, predicated upon the sentiments contained in the enclosed paper.''

He was sending Hamilton his only copy of the earlier draft; so ''even if you should think it best to throw the *whole* into a different form,'' Hamilton should send back Washington's old version together with the new, ''with such amendments and corrections, as to render it as perfect as the formation is susceptible of.'' He added, ''My wish is, that the whole may appear in a plain style; and be handed to the public in an honest, unaffected, simple garb.''

On July 30, Hamilton sent along his own completely rewritten ''Draft of Washington's Farewell Address,'' and on August 10 he returned Washington's draft with his own corrections entitled ''Draft on the Plan of Incorporating.'' Hamilton much preferred his own completely rewritten draft to Washington's. His own he had ''endeavoured to make as perfect as my time and engagements would permit . . . *importantly* and *lastingly* useful, and avoiding all just cause of present exception, to embrace such reflections and sentiments as will wear well, progress in approbation with time and redound to future reputation.''

As for Washington's own draft, he said frankly, ''There seems to be a certain awkwardness in the thing.'' ''Nonetheless,'' Hamilton added, ''when you have both before you you can better judge.'' Washington did, and his judgment was that Hamilton was right. Hamilton's draft, he thought, was ''more copious on material points, more dignified, with less egotism less exposed to criticism, better calculated to meet the eye of discerning readers.'' It comprehended most, if not all, of what was contained in the earlier draft, ''is better expressed,'' and ''goes as far as it might with respect to any personal mention of myself.''

He sent it back to Hamilton on August 25 for minor revisions in accordance with some marginal notes he made in pencil, but to be used only if Hamilton wished to accept such revisions. Any further revisions Hamilton made now should be "clearly interlined" so that the printer would make no mistake setting it in type. There would be no further reading or change by Washington.

Hamilton sent back his final corrected version of Washington's *Farewell Address* on September 5. On September 15, Washington submitted the text to the cabinet for its approval. His secretary, Tobias Lear, asked David Claypoole of the *American Daily Advertiser*—recommended by Hamilton—to come to see Washington. At the interview, they fixed on Monday, September 19, as the date for first publication. Lear brought the copy to Claypoole on Friday, and Claypoole brought back a proof and then a corrected proof to Washington, who made only a few corrections in punctuation. The *Farewell Address* was also printed on the same day in Fenno's *Gazette of the United States,* which after its period of insolvency was now back in print.

The exact authorship of the *Farewell Address* was disputed for more than a century. Hamilton's family insisted that Hamilton had been responsible for both content and phrasing. Madison's champions claimed the largest credit for him on grounds of priority. John Jay, in 1811, recalled that Hamilton had consulted him on this, as on so much else, and had gone over it with him "paragraph by paragraph, until the whole met with our mutual approbation." Washington's admirers tended to deny all such claims as a reflection on the hero. Comparison of the various drafts makes clear that although most of the general ideas were Washington's, the organization, elaboration, and phrasing of the text were Hamilton's.

As years and decades and a century and more rolled on, the words and phrases of the *Farewell Address* took on the authority of an American credo. The *Farewell Address* was and will always be one of the greatest documents of American history.

After Hamilton and Washington were both dead, Nathaniel Pendleton, one of Hamilton's executors, turned over all of Hamilton's papers relating to composition of the *Farewell Address* to Rufus King "to prevent their falling into the hands" of Hamilton's family because of Elizabeth Hamilton's "endeavour to show that General Hamilton, not General Washington, was the author and writer of the Farewell Address." After a suit in chancery court, the Hamilton family finally obtained the papers in 1826. In 1840, when Elizabeth Hamilton was 83 years old and still as passionately devoted to her husband, who had been dead for 36 years, as she had been when they were married 60 years before, made the following statement for posterity: "In the year 1796 General Hamilton suggested to him the idea of delivering a farewell address to the people on his withdrawal from public life, with which idea General Washington was well pleased." The address was written by Hamilton "principally at such times as his office was seldom frequented by his clients and visitors, and during the absence of his students to avoid interruptions." As Elizabeth fondly recalled, "He was in the habit of calling me to sit with him, that he might read to me as he wrote, in order, as he said, to discover how it sounded upon the ear." He was not thinking of illnesses when he remarked to her, "My dear Eliza you must be to me what Molière's old nurse was to him."

"The whole or nearly all the 'Address' was read to me by him as he wrote it," Elizabeth Hamilton reminisced, "and a greater part if not all was written by him in my presence." Washington approved of it all, she remembered, "with the exception of four or five lines, which if I mistake not was on the subject of public schools, which was stricken out. . . . Mr. Hamilton made the desired alteration, and it was afterward delivered and published in that form." She added, "The whole circumstances are at this moment, so perfectly in my remembrance, that I can call to mind his bringing General Washington's letter to me, which returned the 'Address' and remarking on the only alteration which he had requested to be made.''

The *Farewell Address,* in its final form, spoke to both future and past. Washington's matter of fact opening announcement declining to run for a third term set a precedent now embedded in the Constitution itself. ''The great rule of conduct for us in regard to foreign nations ought to be to have as little political connection with them as possible. . . . Inveterate antipathies against particular Nations, and passionate attachments for others, should be excluded,'' in favor of ''amicable feelings toward all.'' And: ''Cherish public credit as a means of strength and security. As one method of preserving it, use it as little as possible. Avoid occasions of expense by cultivating peace. Avoid the accumulation of debt . . . not ungenerously throwing upon posterity the burthen which we ought to bear ourselves.'' Its every paragraph seemed to call the attention of the nation and the world to America as a supreme example of the harmony and freedom that were possible under law for ''a people always guided by an exalted justice and benevolence.'' In the *Farewell Address,* Hamilton was groping toward a definitive statement of the grand theme of his own life work, but not yet quite expressing it in its perfect form: ''The name of American must always gratify and exalt just pride of patriotism. . . . you have slight shades of difference [but] the same religion, manners, habits and political-institutions and principles. . . . By your union you achieved them, by your union you will most effectually maintain them.'' But he did not complete the final formulation of the thought until four months later that same year, in the closing sentence of the letter he wrote to Rufus King in London on December 16, 1796: ''We are laboring hard to establish in this country principles more and more *national* and free from all *foreign ingredients,* so that we may be neither 'Greeks' nor 'Trojans' but truly Americans.''

The address was republished everywhere throughout the United States to great acclaim. As it first appeared, it began with the simple salutation ''To the People of the United States'' and closed with the signature ''G. Washington, United States, September 17, 1796.'' Only later reprintings carried the caption ''The Farewell Address.''

There were also the inevitable derisory yawns and yawps. James McHenry reported to Washington that ''the enemies of the government . . . discovered a silence and uneasiness, that marked chagreen and alarm, at the impression it was calculated to make on the public mind.''

Forty-four years later, Elizabeth Hamilton still remembered one fine day in New York City when ''shortly after the publication of the address, my husband and myself were walking in Broadway.'' And old soldier accosted the two of them and familiarly begged Hamilton, a former comrade-in-arms, to buy a reprint copy of General Washington's *Farewell Address* that he was peddling. Hamilton smilingly did so. Then he turned to Betsy and said, ''That man does not know he has asked me to purchase my own work.''

Thomas Pinckney, Rufus King's predecessor in London from 1792 to 1796, had also doubled as envoy extraordinary to Spain in 1794 and 1795 and, while there, successfully negotiated the Treaty of San Lorenzo el Real. By this important treaty fixing the boundaries of Florida and Louisiana, Spain had relinquished all other claims east of the Mississippi, and the United States had secured freedom of navigation of the river all the way down the delta. Thomas Pinckney was now returning home to become Hamilton's handpicked favorite to join John Adams on the Federalist presidential ticket for the election of 1796. As

King had written Hamilton on May 2, "to his former stock of popularity" Pinckney "will now add the good will of those who have been peculiarly gratified with the Spanish Treaty. . . . will he not receive as great, perhaps greater southern and western support as any other man?"

Hamilton wholeheartedly agreed with King about Thomas Pinckney. Like his beloved, long dead, but never-to-be-forgotten wartime friend John Laurens, Pinckney was a South Carolinian who had served with distinction during the Revolution until badly wounded at the Battle of Camden and captured by the British. He had presided over the South Carolina constitutional ratifying convention and served as governor of the state. Soon Hamilton would be dispatching his elder brother, Charles Cotesworth Pinckney, another fellow Cincinnatian, to be minister plenipotentiary to France. James Monroe's ambiguous behavior at and after the confrontations of the morning and night of December 15, 1792, and in Paris since, were never to be forgotten or forgiven. Nothing seemed more important to Hamilton now than a trustworthy Pinckney to replace Monroe in Paris.

Hamilton felt it essential to keep Jefferson from winning the presidential election of 1796 and, if possible, to deny him the vice-presidency as well. If Washington's farewell meant that Jefferson would be his successor, Hamilton saw his whole coherent system of government being plunged into chaos. It is "all-important to our country," Hamilton wrote, that Washington's "successor shall be a safe man. But it is far less important who of many men that may be named shall be the person, than that it shall not be Jefferson. . . . All personal and partial considerations must be discarded, and every thing must give way to the great object of excluding Jefferson."

Few good Federalists could contemplate Thomas Jefferson without a similar shudder. Remote in his cupolated château on its mount, served by platoons of slaves and his octoroon concubine Sally Hemings, he was thought of by most as one of the largest and richest property owners of America, yet a man who repudiated, on philosophic grounds, repayment of debts he owed and debts in general. To them his liberal protestations seemed merely a self-serving touching up of a self-created self-image as a Francophile, a Jacobin, a Deist, a physiocrat, a leveler, and a random radical—a random tandem radical! To most of the small handful of Federalists rich enough to qualify for membership in the propertied elite into which Jefferson had been born he was also a traitor to his class.

Even though Vice-President John Adams, now 60 years old, had been a prominent figure on the national scene for more than two decades, he remained something of an enigma, even, or especially, to those who knew him best. In his well-known political work "A Defence of the Constitution of . . . America," Adams had argued that in every society there is a constant conflict between rich and poor, each trying to despoil the other, and that the task of statesmanship is to set bounds and limits to the struggle. Adams had a strong, sometimes violent temper, a thin skin, a highly developed sense of his own importance, and an impulsiveness that many considered dangerous in a man a heartbeat away from the highest office. They agreed with Benjamin Franklin's remark that "Adams was an honest man, often a wise one, but sometimes wholly out of his senses." Enemies called him squeamish, cold, and unsocial. So did friends. One of them remarked that, unlike a Hamilton, for example, "He can't dance, drink, game, flatter, promise, dress, swear with gentlemen, and small talk and flirt with the ladies." Hamilton would, of course, privately agree with Adams's friend's appraisal.

To men who did not know both men well, to men who knew them only by report, Hamilton and Aaron Burr seemed to have more in common than any other pair of great antagonists of their time. But to those who knew Hamilton and John Adams well—in their rather humble backgrounds, frequent illnesses, paroxysms of obsession with enemies, formidable wives, and firm Federalist convictions forged in wide experience of the world and the creation of the nation—no two of the Founding Fathers were on a fundamental level more alike, except perhaps Hamilton and Washington. Such close affinities with Hamilton—Burr's on a superficial level, Adams's on a profound level—prepared Burr and Adams better by nature than any other two men of Hamilton's acquaintance to rank second to none but Jefferson as the deadliest of the extraordinary circle of enemies that Hamilton would summon up to test the meaning of his life and all his works.

If Adams himself did not quite share his own party's general abhorrence of Jefferson, this was due, in part, to his suspicion that many Federalists—including Hamilton—would have much preferred to see Thomas Pinckney—or Hamilton—elevated to the presidency in place of himself. But among most Federalists, Adams was generally acceptable as the candidate for president, as was Thomas Pinckney for the vice-presidency. However, Hamilton and others feared that New England might withhold some of its votes from Pinckney to ensure more votes for Adams than for Pinckney and Jefferson. This would mean that Jefferson might receive more votes than either one of the Federalists. The constitutional electoral system, by which the electors cast two votes, one for president and one for vice-president, without designating which man for which office, did not work at all well in the context of an unforeseen two-party system. This defect in the draftsmanship of the demigods—including Hamilton—would produce frantic intrigues and strange and fateful consequences for Hamilton in 1796 and 1800.

Fisher Ames said that Washington's *Farewell Address* was "a signal, like dropping a hat, for the party racers to start." Republicans, with John Beckley acting as campaign manager, began spreading reports that Federalist strength in the coming election would be divided among Adams, Pinckney, Hamilton, and Jay. The way for Republicans to win would thus be by concentrating all votes for either president or vice-president on Jefferson. As their vice-presidential candidate, a man from a middle state who would draw no presidential or vice-presidential votes away from Jefferson, the Republicans shrewdly selected Aaron Burr.

From the Federalist point of view, the difficulty was that Adams was weak in the South, and Pinckney was weak in the North. Jonathan Dayton of New Jersey thought Adams's chances of election were dim. What did Sedgwick think about having the Federalists support Burr?

Although no true Federalist would consider crossing over to vote for Jefferson, by no means all of them felt the same antipathy toward Burr. In policy he always stood somewhere near the middle of the political spectrum, he was personally on good terms with many staunch Federalists, and his suave, genial, yet aristocratic, bearing and his ready wit made him *persona grata* to many men who looked on Jefferson as the reclusive horned beast of anarchy. Without waiting for Sedgwick's reply, Dayton wrote him again, this time boldly urging what he had merely hinted at before: "Every moment's reflection serves only to impress me more with the importance of our fixing upon some plan of cooperation to defeat the designs of Mr. J[efferson]'s friends. If Mr. A[dams] cannot succeed, is it not desirable to have at the helm a man who is personally known to, as well as esteemed & respected by us both?" Burr was his man. The fact that a Federalist like Dayton was urging Burr upon his Federalist friends for vice-president instead of Pinckney or even Jay was a bitter blow to Hamilton.

Sedgwick volunteered a prophecy of how Jefferson and Beckley would deal with Burr that proved prophetic. "They court the aid of his character & talents," he declared, but they "have not the smallest confidence in his hearty union to their cause. Indeed it is my firm belief that their views and his are not only distinct but opposite."

On the back of Sedgwick's letter telling him of the plot, Hamilton wrote, "concerning Dayton's intrigue for Burr."

This effort of Dayton and others to wrest control of his own Federalist party away from him by obtaining Federalist votes for Burr would strike Hamilton as a more serious grievance than almost anything Jefferson might have done.

From the other side of the political lines, John Beckley was also busily sowing tares in Hamilton's path. He falsely put it about that Hamilton had "admitted . . . there may be a state of things in which it would be desirable that Mr. J should be elected without opposition. . . ." This was because "Mr. J's influence could alone preserve the Union, and produce a favorable termination of the breach . . ." with France. Beckley trotted out Hamilton's name as a stalking horse that would be of maximum horrific aspect to Republicans. "Hamilton himself industriously propagates that Adams and Pinckney are [the Federalists'] choice," but this was only a cover-up for himself. Hamilton's real plan was this: "Quere: May not Strong & Cabot design to become electors, and if a suitable election prevail thro' Massachusetts, to suddenly nominate & by their influence carry Hamilton in that State? Rh. Island, Vermont, Connecticut, New York, New Jersey, & Maryland, would all probably follow . . . unanimously. Some late indications seem to warrant the suspicion." Therefore, every Republican effort must be made to preserve all Virginia votes solid for both Republican candidates to keep out Hamilton.

Jefferson went along with Beckley's strategy, writing Madison on January 22, 1797, that "He [John Adams] is perhaps the only sure barrier against Hamilton's getting in." The threat of Hamilton, just turning 40, was not limited to the election of 1796, but would loom in future elections as well. On the Federalist side, John Adams found no difficulty in going along with Beckley's and Jefferson's theory that Hamilton was leading a conspiracy to slip himself into the presidency by scuttling Adams.

Years after Hamilton's death, Adams approved William Cobbett's appraisal that "all Parties affected to regret that loss of Washington, but none were truly Sorry." The fact was, said Adams, that "one party acquiesced in the resignation of Washington because they believed it a step towards the introduction of Mr. Jefferson, and the other because they thought it an Advance toward the election of Mr. Hamilton who was their ultimate Object."

None of the objective evidence lends credibility to Beckley's and Jefferson's and Adams's charges that Hamilton was seeking to intrigue his way into the presidency, and the weight of it indicates that such charges were false. Hamilton's role was that of the professional party leader. He and Jay formally withdrew their own names from consideration as candidates so that no votes would be wasted on them.

When all the votes were in, the official tally was Adams, 71; Jefferson, 68; Pinckney, 59; and Burr, 30, with the rest of the electoral votes thrown away among George Clinton and others.

It was about what Hamilton realistically had expected. It could have been much worse; he was not dissatisfied with the result. His calm acquiescence in it betrays no suggestion of disappointment that an intrigue he had planned had failed. But ominous for the future union of the nation was the sectional distribution of the votes: not a single vote for Jefferson came from any state north and east of the Delaware River. Northern Federalists had thrown away their votes rather than vote for Pinckney; Southern Republicans had thrown away theirs rather than vote for Burr.

It gave Hamilton some grim satisfaction that Jefferson's Virginians and other Southern

Republicans had held back so many votes from Burr. He wrote King, "The event will not a little mortify Burr. Virginia has given him only one vote."

Jefferson wrote a letter to Adams eagerly looking ahead to 1800, but pretending no personal interest in what might happen then. He elaborately disclaimed disappointment at not having won the top post—and sowed some Beckley-style tares: "Indeed it is possible that you may be cheated of your succession by a trick worthy the subtlety of your arch-friend of New York, who has been able to make of your real friends tools to defeat their & your just wishes. Most probably he will be disappointed as to you; & my inclinations place me out of his reach."

Jefferson sent this revealing letter to Madison for review and then forwarding to Adams. An embarrassed Madison wrote back that he was holding it up, dryly remarking that Adams was aware of Jefferson's warm feelings toward him and adding, "it deserves to be considered whether the idea of bettering it is not outweighed by the possibility of changing it for the worse. . . . There is perhaps a general air on the letter which betrays the difficulty of your situation in writing it." Madison reassured Jefferson that Adams was already aware of Hamilton's alleged machinations: "There may be danger of his suspecting in mementos on that subject, a wish to make his resentment an instrument for avenging that of others."

After all Hamilton's urgings to Federalists north and south to vote for Adams and the fact that he had won, the "resentment" they were trying to teach Adams to feel toward him seemed unfair, but it was real, and Adams made it manifest to all. After the votes were in and Adams's victory assured, Stephen Higginson wrote Hamilton on January 12 that instead of being satisfied with his being elected, Adams and his partisans are "alarmed at the danger he was of failing."

They placed Hamilton and Jay "at the head of this junto, as they call it," who were intriguing to exclude "Mr. A. from the chair." Believing this, "Adams may be cool & distant" toward men like Hamilton "whom he ought to be intimate with & consult upon important occasions." Adams would "adopt a line of conduct toward his former friends" that will divide and weaken the Federalist interest." He urged Hamilton to "think of some mode of preventing the inconveniences which I fear to result from Mr. Adams feelings." Here Higginson was accurately apprehending new disasters that the mistrust sown between the two men would bring. It would in the end, among other things, destroy the political fortunes of Hamilton, Adams, and the Federalist party; keep Adams from a second term; insure the succession of Jefferson, Madison, and Monroe; and threaten the secession of the New England states, New York, and New Jersey from the constitutional union.

In the congressional election of December 13–15, 1796, in New York City, the Republican candidate was the incumbent Edward Livingston, while the Federalists nominated John Watson, a merchant who had served as speaker of the assembly in 1794 and was now a member of the state senate.

A member of the great family of the colonial lords of Livingston Manor, Edward Livingston was a scion of inherited wealth; Watson was a self-made man. Hamilton felt the distinction keenly. "If Mr. Livingston has some outside showy talents," Hamilton wrote, "they are more than counterbalanced by the good sense, discretion, knowledge of business and commerce, maturity of years and experience of Mr. Watson." The Federalists' candidate was "a man of republican principles, *manners* and *habits*." Voters could "judge for themselves how this description" would apply to Watson's aristocratic young rival. As for Mr. Livingston, *"his democracy if genuine, is at least more at ease in a coach."*

Watson's campaign lagged badly, and Livingston was reelected by a margin of 550 votes in a total of 4,174.

To Hamilton, the problem of how any self-made man could afford to serve a republic in high office was one of painfully acute, personal perplexity. In his November draft of Washington's Eighth Annual Address to Congress, Hamilton had analyzed the problem of keeping in public office honest men who were poor in words wrung from the heart of his own bitter experience with calumnies of illicit speculation.

The compensation of high public offices must be raised, he warned. "The expense of the most frugal plan of living in our great cities" was prohibitive to men without private means. "It would be repugnate to the first principles of our government to exclude men from public trusts because their talents & virtues however conspicuous are unaccompanied by wealth. . . . The compensations which our government allows ought to be revised and materially increased. . . . The character & success of Republican government appear absolutely to depend on this policy. . . . If their own private wealth is to supply in candidates for public office the deficiency of public liberality then the sphere of those who can be candidates is much narrowed." "Those who have talents and are too virtuous to abuse their stations cannot accept offices to make a dishonest & improper use of them."

He went on, "The tendency is to transfer the management of public affairs to wealthy but incapable hands or to hands which if capable are as destitute of integrity as of wealth." The general lesson about men and governments to be drawn was that "no plan of governing is well founded which does not regard man as a compound of selfish and virtuous passions. To expect him to be wholly guided by the latter would be as great as error as to supppose him wholly destitute of them." For proof of such conclusions, Hamilton needed only to look deep within himself.

Also picked up in Hamilton's draft of Washington's Eighth Annual Address to Congress was Washington's plan for a national university. Here and elsewhere, Hamilton laid the basis for his claim to being the ancestor of the Departments of Commerce and Agriculture; the regular army, navy, and marines; and the service academies.

James Monroe, like his fellow influential Republicans Jefferson and Madison, had little sympathy with Jay's Treaty. Adams's son John Quincy Adams, American minister at The Hague, heard that the Directory had been told by Monroe that Jay had been taking bribes in London and that the House of Representatives had also been bribed to give its final three-vote margin of funding approval to the treaty. Most of the French anger over Jay's Treaty did not "proceed from themselves" according to John Quincy Adams, but was "inspired by Americans at Paris" like Monroe. "The greatest enemies of America in France," he said, "are Americans themselves."

For his part, Monroe, who was sharing lodgings in Paris with Thomas Paine, blamed Hamilton for the "evil" treaty that Secretary of State Pickering had charged him to defend. Monroe complained to Madison on September 1, 1796, that Pickering had written him like "an overseer on the farm to one of his gang." Pickering's explanation "corresponds so much" with Hamilton's *Camillus* that Monroe suspected both "were written by the same hand," that is, Hamilton's.

Oliver Wolcott, Jr., for whom the confrontation with Senator Monroe and the two congressmen the night of December 15, 1792, would be as unforgettable as it was for Hamilton, thought Monroe ought to be recalled to "stop the channels by which foreign poison is introduced into the country." Hamilton, too, sought Monroe's recall, writing to Secretary of War McHenry that he should "be superseded with a kind letter to him" because "we must not quarrel with France for *pins* and *needles*." After Hamilton had repeated the suggestion to Washington in June, saying that the United States should "have some faithful organ near the French government to explain their real views," Washington agreed and followed Hamilton's recommendation that Charles Cotesworth Pinckney replace Monroe.

By May of 1796, Washington was incensed by the rumors that France would declare war and launch an invasion. "We will not be dictated to by . . . any nation under heaven," he thundered. But French raids of all kinds on American seaborne commerce had been increasing. In a report to President Adams on French depredations of June 21, 1797, Timothy Pickering pointed out that as a result of the Directory's decree of July 2, 1796, the seas of the West Indies "swarm with privateers and gun boats called forth by the latitude allowed to depredations" by French agents at Guadaloupe and Saint-Domingue. The French had illegally seized 316 American vessels.

In the succession of French ministers to the United States, Genêt had been outrageous, Fauchet, although less obtrusively persistent, was privately more troublesome, and Fauchet's successor, Pierre Auguste Adet, was even more outspoken in circulating propaganda for France throughout America. Washington, Pickering, and Wolcott all sought Hamilton's advice and counsel on how to deal with Adet's outrages.

After consulting Jay, Hamilton advised Washington on November 4 that whether Adet had acted with or without authority, "he committed a disrespect towards our government which ought not to pass unnoticed. The manner of noticing it ought to be *negative* . . . that is, by the *personal conduct* of the President towards the minister."

Adet should be received by Washington "with a *dignified reserve,* holding an *exact medium* between an *offensive coldness* and *cordiality."* Hamilton added that "the point is a nice one to be hit, but no one will know better how to do it than the President." Few, if any, were on such intimate terms with him as to take note of the famous presidential reserve by even so mild a joke at his expense as this.

Overt insult to Adet was to be avoided. Indeed, Hamilton was "afraid of Mr. Pickering's *warmth"* toward Adet. He disapproved the caustic tone of Pickering's reproof. It was too "epigrammatical and *sharp."* The proper "card now to be played is perhaps the most delicate that has occurred in our administration." Hamilton's use here of the first person plural form—"our" administration—writing confidentially from New York, retains the old prime ministerial ring. "Nations, like individuals, sometimes get into squabbles from the manner more than the matter," he reminded the chief of state. Furthermore, it was "all-important . . . if possible to avoid rupture with France, and if that cannot be, to evince to the people that there has been an unequivocal disposition to avoid it." All discussions should be *"calm"* and *"smooth,"* in the "language of moderation, and, as long as it can be done, of friendship. . . ."

On November 15, making a careful distinction between Hamilton and Washington's government on the one hand and the American "people" on the other, for which France still professed the warmest friendship, Adet claimed that the government had betrayed its words, declared himself suspended from duty, and commenced to work actively for Beckley and Jefferson in the presidential election campaign.

Washington protested to Hamilton on January 12 against Adet's barefaced interference in a domestic election: It was "outrageous beyond conception." John Adams fumed at Adet's "most opprobrious and contumelious language." Federalist citizens of Philadelphia, fearful of war with France, would switch their votes to Jefferson's party because they believed that "the election of Mr. Jefferson was necessary to prevent a rupture with France."

On December 8 in *The Minerva* appeared a long piece written by Hamilton, entitled "The Answer," signed *Americanus.*

Americanus pointed out that here was a foreigner meddling in domestic affairs to persuade the timid, in the approaching election, to vote out the president and vice-president, whom he traduced. Recondite beyond the comprehension of much of the public, "The

Answer'' was an expert brief aimed at members of the new Congress, who had just assembled, and served as an unofficial white paper defending ''our'' administration's policy in relations with France.

As 1797 began, the *Americanus* who had written ''The Answer'' contracted his pen name slightly to an *American* to write a new, more partisan series of six broadsides dealing with the French imbroglio entitled ''The Warning.'' Numbers I through VI appeared on January 27, February 7, 21, and 27 and March 13 and 17, of 1797. Between ''The Answer'' in December and No. VI of ''The Warning'' late in March, Hamilton's tone waxed ever more ominously shrill and provocative, suggesting the kinds of pressures that on earlier occasions had signaled illness and nervous derangement. The machinations of France, through her envoys like Adet, now sought to keep the American government feeble and distracted, perpetually in quarrels with Britain, and the dupe of French designs. French aggression was more iniquitous than anything hitherto suffered at the hands of the British. ''The man who, after this mass of evidence,'' Hamilton wrote, working up to the sort of hysterical climax that was becoming all too typical of his style when he dealt with enemies, ''shall be the apologist of France, and the calumniator of his own government, is not an American. The choice for him lies between being deemed a fool, a madman or a traitor.'' Writing Pickering on March 22, Hamilton called for ''a day of humiliation and prayer. . . . it will be politically useful to impress our nation that there is a serious state of things—to strengthen religious ideas in a contest . . . against atheism, conquest and anarchy. . . . the war may call on us to defend our firesides and our altars.''

Adams had no friends among the leaders of the Federalist party who gave personal fealty to him in the same way so many gave close personal fealty to Hamilton. Lacking such support for himself, after his election Adams sought to draw it toward him by retaining without change Washington's cabinet and chief diplomatic appointees, all of whom had been handpicked for Washington by Hamilton. Adams seemed to be entirely ignorant of the strength and depth of their fealty toward their selector, leader, and master.

As vice-president, Adams had spent the long months when Congress was not in session at home with Abigail in Quincy far from day-to-day touch with the men who ran the government in Philadelphia. Few expected that election to the presidency would much change his ingrained habits. So as Washington looked toward retirement at Mount Vernon and Adams made his way to Philadelphia for his inauguration on March 4, 1797, the power of the lawyer in private practice up in New York to control the executive government through its department heads in Philadelphia and diplomatic representatives abroad did not diminish, but markedly increased. Three years more would pass before a thunderstruck and furious Adams would comprehend the full reach of the control Hamilton had exercised over his presidency's government.

Before leaving office, Washington had asked Hamilton for advice on sending a special envoy to France, as Jay had been sent to London in 1794 during a similar crisis with Britain over depredations against American shipping. On January 25, Hamilton replied that he favored a special mission to France ''under some shape or other.'' To France, ''Pinckney will be considered as a mere substitute in ordinary course to Monroe.'' An extraordinary mission, in addition, ''will in some degree soothe her pride.'' Besides if the mission should include a Republican and fail, ''the influence on party'' would be favorable. ''And it will to be to France a bridge over which she may more easily retreat.'' The best form would be three persons, called *''Commissioners* plenipotentiary and extraordinary.'' Two of the three should be Madison and Pinckney, and the third should be George Cabot of Massachusetts, ''the Nestor of the Federalists,'' to give geographical balance, but with any two empowered to act. Even two—Madison and Pinckney—without the third would be satisfactory, but "unless Mr. Madison will go there is scarcely another character that will afford advantages."

But Washington took leave of office without appointing the new commission.

Sedgwick had Adams's ear; so Hamilton told him, too, that the commission should consist of Madison, Pinckney, and Cabot. Adams rejected Hamilton's advice and asked Vice-President Jefferson to be his special emissary to France. Jefferson refused. Then Adams suggested Madison, Pinckney, and his friend Elbridge Gerry, a lukewarm Federalist with Republican leanings. Jefferson said he would use his good offices to see if Madison would accept. Adams's inaugural speech warned against foreign meddling in domestic politics: by such interference it would be foreign nations "who govern us, and not we, the people, who govern ourselves." He also expressed "personal esteem for the French nation," but promised to seek reparation for injuries to American commerce. Federalists like Ames thought his speech was weak, whereas Republicans praised Adams as a "friend of France, of peace, an admirer of Republicanism, the enemy of party." Next day at his first cabinet meeting, Adams proposed a three-man commission with Madison as a member. Then Jefferson reported back that Madison would not agree to serve in any event. After being led into this humiliating cul-de-sac, Adams ceased to consult Jefferson on the policies of his administration.

Timothy Pickering soon sent Hamilton word that the Directory had not only refused to receive Pinckney, a man whom many considered, "the first gentleman of America," but had driven him out of Paris like a despised, undesirable alien or common felon.

The Directory had also passed a harsh new edict on March 2 that allowed French warships to bring all neutral vessels carrying any British goods into French ports. The French would treat Americans on enemy ships as pirates and would seize as prizes all American ships not carrying a full list of crew and passengers, a *"rôle d'équipage,"* which American ships usually did not bother to carry. By this edict, the Directory had, in effect, launched a limited maritime war against the United States in complete violation of the commercial treaty of 1778.

To orthodox Federalists like Fisher Ames, but not to Hamilton, such a declaration justified a reciprocal American declaration of war.

In the mounting crisis, Adams turned to Pickering, Wolcott, and McHenry and asked them a series of questions. What preparations should we make for war with France? Should the government commission new frigates? Commission more privateers? Or try new negotiations? On March 25, 1797, he summoned Congress to a special session to convene on May 15. Jefferson and Republicans generally put it about that all of the Federalists were taking "the high ground of war."

Hamilton and his friends in Adams's cabinet exchanged many letters discussing the crisis. Pickering, Wolcott, and McHenry opposed the mission to France, but Hamilton still favored it because it would meet the Republicans "on their own ground and shut their mouths." Hamilton warned Wolcott "that a suspicion begins to *dawn* among the friends of government, that the *actual* administration is not much averse to war with France." By "actual" administration, he meant his three old friends who headed the Departments of State, Treasury, and War, not the figurehead Adams. "How very important to obviate this!" he insisted to them. Furthermore, they must agree to putting a prominent Republican like Madison or Jefferson on the commission. Hamilton told McHenry, "No *mortal*" must see "his letter or know its contents."

All three department heads dutifully swallowed their own opinions and adopted Hamilton's. They duly advised Adams as Hamilton had told them to do. He should send the commission, but at the same time arm merchant ships and create a naval force.

Thereafter, President John Adams's cabinet sought and followed Hamilton's advice on the most important issues that would come before it during the rest of the century. Adams remained largely unaware of Hamilton's role until the explosion near the very end. Out of office and ostensibly a busy New York lawyer immersed in private affairs, Hamilton remained, in fact, the guiding spirit, the hidden prime minister, of Adams's administration down in Philadelphia. Although Adams himself never called on Hamilton for suggestions or advice—nor did Hamilton attempt to proffer any to him directly by word of mouth or letter—Adams's official family turned to him on every significant occasion for aid, comfort, and revealed Federalist truth, as well as specific language in which to clothe answers to questions Adams would ask. Adams's discovery of the curious truth at last would produce the paroxysms of pigheadedness on all sides that wrecked the Federalists, assured loss of the election of 1800 to Jefferson, the demise of the party, and mortal enmity between the two men. The peculiar paradox of it all was that no important Federalist was more closely in agreement than Hamilton with Adams's basic policy of practical steps to preserve neutrality and peace. Through his department heads, Hamilton was spoonfeeding Adams the arguments that persuaded him of its rightness.

Adams turned to his department heads. What should he say in his special message to Congress? What should be his reaction to Pinckney's humiliation? What instructions should he give to emissaries? What should they demand of France? What defensive forces would be needed to protect the country from invasion? What would be the cost?

As before, Pickering, Wolcott, and McHenry severally passed Adams's questions back to Hamilton for answers. Hamilton was occupied in Albany with "court avocations" and the serious illness of his father-in-law, Philip Schuyler. But his dear old friend "Mac" McHenry needed Hamilton's "answer at length" because "you have all at your finger tips." Hamilton must not tell anyone of Mac's request or his reply. Hamilton turned back to his main avocation and replied promptly to McHenry with detailed advice covering virtually all aspects of governmental relations with France.

The United States had little to gain and much to lose from war with France, he warned. Indeed, they might be "left alone to contend with the Conquerors of Europe." Even a "considerable degree of humiliation may, without *ignominy* be encountered to avoid the possibility of much greater and train of incalculable evils." In this context, the word *honor* could be spoken at an unusually low level of intensity. McHenry copied Hamilton's letter in his own hand, added a few paragraphs, and handed it to Adams as his own program.

Wolcott's reply to Adams also incorporated Hamilton's advice, and Pickering laced Hamilton's advice to him into a 25-page report otherwise his own. Taken together, their three reports to President Adams provided a many-sided yet amazingly unified and cogent platform for policy toward France—not really so amazing because most of it flowed from Hamilton's pen. Adams was quite pleased by the cabinet's advice. He wove whole conciliatory sentences and phrases, combined with a verbally defiant attitude, all derived from Hamilton, into his own speech to Congress. Public passions rose, and the popularity of the Federalist stance with it.

At this time, it was still the custom for each house of Congress to give a ceremonial reply to the president's message. Congress's reply, as well as the government's preparedness program, embroiled Congress in debates of ever-mounting acrimony until it would finally adjourn July 8. On June 5, William Loughton Smith introduced, and Congress approved, ten resolutions that ostensibly embodied the president's program and were, in fact, Hamilton's, including appointment of the three commissioners. Adams called his cabinet together and proposed to appoint Pinckney, John Marshall of Virginia, and Elbridge Gerry of Massachusetts. The cabinet objected to Gerry and demanded a more reliable Federalist in his place. They refused to accept "a piebald commission." Adams yielded and substituted the name of Francis Dana of Massachusetts for Gerry's, and the Senate confirmed the three nominations. Dana then withdrew. Without consulting his cabinet again, Adams appointed Gerry to Dana's place. This suspicious sequence of events outraged the cabinet and most good Federalists—not so much the action itself, but Adams's quirky, secretive manner of doing it. Republicans were full of glee. Jefferson wrote Gerry that his appointment and confirmation brought "infinite joy to me."

In July the plague came on in Philadelphia. Congress adjourned without declaring war. Adams and his family left the capital for Quincy. John Marshall sailed for France from Philadelphia on July 20, and Gerry departed from Boston three days later, carrying with them toward Paris Hamilton's and Adams's fondest hopes for averting war. As Hamilton had calmly told Wolcott on June 6, "I like very well the course of Executive conduct in regard to the controversy with France."

Contributing greatly to Hamilton's serene mood in giving generous credit to Adams's policy, aside from the fact that it happened to be his own, was a momentous event that had occurred in Hamilton's private life two weeks earlier.

The previous summer, on August 20, 1796, Hamilton had packed off Rufus King, his handpicked minister plenipotentiary to Great Britain, with a glowing letter of introduction to Angelica. "To be sure of everybody's approbation he is instructed to do nothing but after a previous consultation with you." There would be no more entangling alliances—except with her. Would that "have no charm for your_____?" he asked, then filled in the flirtatious blank he had left: "But I had forgotten. You have none."

King's wife, the former Mary Alsop, was a fully fleshed out figure of a woman who looked not at all like the slender Angelica he would remember from his first glimpse of her 20 years earlier, at The Pastures, on one of the nights of his desperate mission to General Gates. Angelica would always pride herself on possessing the smallest waist in any company of elegant women, and her firmly boned and tightly laced corsets would cinch her slenderer still even now as he remembered her. On some long ago evening that she would remember well without more than his passing allusion to it Hamilton had complimented her on her unexceptionable figure, so he would not need to spell it all out writing her of Mary Alsop King, "She has not the proverb in her favor '*the nearer the bone, etc.*' " His "etc." for "the sweeter the meat" would recall for both of them unspoken but unforgotten intimacies of long ago. For Mary King, he had a gentlemanly afterthought: "But I daresay she is sweet enough."

For eight years past he had been repining for Angelica Church to return from London. He had obtained for her and her family as a permanent residence the governor's former private mansion house just off Broadway in Partition Street. "Our impatience increases as the prospect becomes more promising," he had written her earlier. But "expectations must be converted into realities," he added. "Life is too short to warrant procrastination on of [*sic*] the most favorite and precious objects." He had written both words—*on* and *of*—for his "precious objects." This was the secret code they sometimes playfully used with each other; or perhaps it was only a mistake. He added a heartfelt "we are anxiously wishing for your return." But by September his hopes had been dashed again: "Our apprehensions are realized and your coming is deferred. . . . life is too short to lose a winter in the passage from hope to enjoyment. . . . do really come in the spring . . . prithee do not let winter freeze the inclination . . . one cannot always live on hope. Tis thin diet at best.'' Thin indeed.

Winter had brought to her the frightening reports of arsonists' fires set in New York City. Then Hamilton had marched out on patrol and injured his leg. She implored him in January, in a contemporary way, to tell her that in moving to New York City, she and her four children would be safe ''from terrors of fevers and negro plots . . . the cause of your fires.''

She was not at all impressed with Rufus and Mary Alsop King. Yet she could not keep herself from re-arousing in him the old prurient desire for herself, as she delicately put both the Kings down: ''Mon très cher monsieur, my eyes have recovered all their former lustre, and have been ineffectually employed in searching for the grace and elegance of your friend, nor have I yet been able to discover that ease and je ne sais quoi by which Sterne observes *the gentleman* may be so readily ascertained. . . . As to his capacity for bargain making that I cannot deny. I really do believe that he took his *Carasposa* weight and measure.''

She closed her letter to him: ''It was not so in the days of chivalry, nor when you were young.''

Now, after all the years of repining on a thin diet of hope and growing older, winter had passed, and spring had come again, and with it from London on May 22 aboard Captain Dupleix's well-named ship, the *Fair American,* Angelica Church had at last come home to stay. But little more than a month would be left them before onslaughts of enemies and his preoccupation with honor—and a sore throat—would kill every tremor of his joy at having her back.

PART THREE

An Angel Daubed by Wizard Painters

31

The Threadbare Lawyer's Old Affair Laid Bare

[Those who] have long known you as our eminent and able statesman . . . will be highly gratified by seeing you exhibited in the novel character of a lover.

—From James Thomson Callender, July 10, 1797

William Hamilton, the brother of Hamilton's ne'er-do-well father, was now the laird of the Grange at Ayrshire, Scotland. The laird had a son, Robert W. Hamilton, who now besought the aid of his self-made cousin for advancement in life. Robert W. Hamilton of the Grange wished to become an officer in the new American navy Hamilton was so busily working to expand. Hamilton replied to his uncle William Hamilton on May 2, 1797, that "it will give me the greatest pleasure to receive your son Robert in New York and still more to be of use to him." As good as his word, Hamilton eventually wangled from President Adams an appointment for his cousin Robert W. Hamilton to be a lieutenant aboard the new warship, the *U.S.S. Constitution*.

Uncle William had written Hamilton an "extremely gratifying" account of all his Hamilton relations living in Scotland. Hamilton replied in a letter whose 12 paragraphs constitute a thumbnail autobiobraphy of Hamilton at his, and every man's, milestone age of 40. Hamilton's letter to the uncle he had never seen is precious for containing some of the only extant statements he ever made privately about himself, why he had done what he did, and how he had become the man he was. Unlike John Adams, Thomas Jefferson, and other American demigods, Hamilton kept no one-party diaries full of special pleading for the plaudits of posterity. So his letter to William Hamilton, like his *Reynolds Pamphlet* of the same year, are rare examples of Hamiltonian self-revelation.

He had, he told his Uncle William, "engaged in some interesting operations" at the siege of Yorktown. He had then settled in New York "in a very lucrative" law practice. But "the derangement of our public affairs . . . drew me again reluctantly into public life." Having taken part in the framing of the Constitution, "I conceived myself to be under an obligation to lend my aid towards putting the machine in some regular motion." As secretary of the treasury, "I met with many intrinsic difficulties, and many artifical ones, proceeding from passions, not very worthy, common to human nature."

He had succeeded in his object of "establishing public credit and introducing order into the finances." However, Hamilton went on sadly to his uncle, "public office in this country has few attractions." There is "inconsiderable emolument"; there is "pecuniary sacrifice"; there is "jealousy of power and the spirit of faction." These "diminish a virtuous man's power of doing good." In fact, "the prospect was even bad for gratifying in future the love of Fame, if that passion was to be the spring of action." This suggests that at only 40 Hamilton had already given up the idea of pressing on in future to try to reach the only assured fame in the American pantheon—the presidency.

Neither Jefferson, Burr, Adams, Monroe, Madison, or John Beckley would have believed Hamilton capable of etching a self-portrait in such muted half-tones. Had they believed him, what followed would have had to be overkill on their part, and self-destruction on his.

Having resigned himself now to private life, Hamilton went on, "It is impossible to be happier than I am in a wife. I have five children, four sons and a daughter, the eldest a son somewhat past fifteen, who all promise well, as far as their years permit and yield me much satisfaction. . . ."

Hamilton had "strongly pressed the Old Gentleman" his father, William's brother, now living on the island of St. Vincent in the West Indies, "to come to reside with me . . . to afford him every enjoyment . . . but he has declined . . . on the advice of physicians that the change of climate would be fatal to him." Hamilton would, of course, continue sending him all the money he could spare as his father needed it for support from time to time. On the whole, then, Hamilton felt, "my situation is extremely comfortable and leaves me nothing to wish but a continuance of health. With this blessing . . . other prospects . . . will render the eve of life easy and agreeable."

In this forecast of his future, by far the most personal of any Hamilton had made so far in life, he could not have been more horribly wrong. The plagues, passions, fevers, follies, and nervous derangements of the following months would render for him "the eve of life" unblessed, unhealthy, uncomfortable, disagreeable, anxious, bizarre, mad or half mad, tragic, painful, and short.

Unlike Angelica Church's New York homecoming, James Monroe's arrival in Philadelphia from France at the height of the war crisis on June 27 brought no joy to Hamilton. Republicans, of course, hailed Monroe's return as if he were some bringer of glad tidings of great joy in the nick of time. What lent more zest than anything else to their joy in Monroe's advent was the series of humiliating setbacks Republicans had been suffering at the hands of Hamilton's surrogates in the still pending session of Congress that Adams had called to push forward Hamilton's peace program as his own.

Summer came on, bringing the fever season to the capital and partisan political temperatures to a tired boil.

Typical of factional rancors was the case of William Blount, a former British soldier and Indian agent and also a Republican senator from Tennessee. Federalists gleefully implicated Blount in a British plot backed by Robert Liston, the British minister, to lead a proposed filibustering attack against the Spaniards in Florida and Louisiana. Wagging their fingers at Blount, Federalist orators charged that he was not the only Republican tainted with treason; Jeffersonians seized on the scandal as British interference in American affairs as bad as anything done by Genêt, Fauchet, or Adet.

Jefferson's protégé Tom Paine had written a letter to Washington, his former friend and benefactor, that said, "And, as to you, sir, treacherous in private friendship (or so you have been to me, and that in the day of danger) and a hypocrite in public life, the world will be puzzled to decide whether you are an apostate or imposter, whether you have abandoned good principles, or whether you ever had any." Bache's Republican *Aurora* published Paine's letter, piously professing pained outrage at its insult to Washington, thereby making sure, Beckley style, that no one could possibly miss it.

Jefferson had written his friend and neighbor Philip Mazzei that there were apostates "who were Samsons in the field & Solomons in the council, but who have had their heads shorn by the harlot England," calling Washington a pitiful, helpless giant. Federalists rumbled ominously in Congress and committees that Vice-President Jefferson should be impeached along with Blount.

Jefferson would confide to his secretary, William A. Burwell, that Hamilton had long known about his affair with Betsey Moore Walker, the wife of one of Jefferson's oldest friends, and that "about the time he was attacked for his connection with Mrs. Reynolds," Hamilton "had threatened him—with a public disclosure."

Federalists, led by Hamilton's spokesman William Loughton Smith, had managed to beat back John Beckley's bid for reelection as clerk of the House by a vote of 41 to 40, with 25 congressmen absent or not voting. Bache's *Aurora* denounced the Federalists' ouster of Beckley as "a specimen of party rancour."

To Federalists like Hamilton and Smith, John Beckley was nothing but a political hatchet man in the service of Jefferson, Madison, and Monroe. His ouster by Hamilton's men, reminiscent of his earlier defeat by them for the office of secretary of the Constitutional Convention a decade earlier, left Beckley a jobless, impecunious, angry man with a growing family to feed, and scores to settle with Hamilton.

Beckley became the partner in poverty of another man whom William Loughton Smith had also helped to remove from a congressional livelihood, the Anti-Federalist journalist James Thomson Callender, who had formerly been employed by the *Philadelphia Gazette* to report congressional news at a salary of $4,000 a year. Callender had dared to dub Smith, chairman of the powerful House Ways and Means Committee, the "British agent," adding that "Dr. Smith was far more rancorous than the other gentlemen collectively." Thomas Jefferson called Callender "a man of genius suffering under persecution."

Callender's book, *The Prospect Before Us,* had described the British Parliament as "a phalanx of mercenaries"; the English constitution was but "a conspiracy of the rich against the poor." Having been indicted in England in 1793 for sedition and radical views, Callender had fled to the United States with his wife and four young children. A pro-Jefferson study of Jefferson's relations with Callender published in 1896 would begin, "Of all the foreigners who were connected with journalism in the United States at the beginning of the century, James Thomson Callender was easily first in the worst qualities of mind and character." On the evidence of his writings, he was a well-educated man with a gift for caustic phrasemaking that was the equal of Beckley's.

Upon being fired from the *Philadelphia Gazette* through Smith's efforts, Callender appealed to James Madison to find him a new job. He was still looking when in June of

1797, according to Jefferson's notebooks, the vice-president paid a personal call upon him at the shop of Snowden & McCorkle, a newly established firm of job printers. There Jefferson paid $15.14 for 15 copies of a series of pamphlets of Callender's authorship that the printers were about to publish under the collective title of *The History of the United States for 1796*. The series was quickly forgotten for what it said about the United States or about 1796, but it will never be forgotten for what it said about Hamilton. It revealed to the public for the first time Hamilton's affair with Maria Reynolds in 1791 and 1792, which had remained covered up ever since. Carefully, characteristically, Jefferson later wrote that it was "probably not till 1798" that he first "saw" James Thomson Callender.

On October 23, 1795, Bache's *Aurora* had twitted Oliver Wolcott, Jr., about "a certain enquiry of a very suspicious aspect, respecting real mal-conduct on the part of his friend, patron and predecessor in office in the month of December 1792." *Aurora* had asked, "Why has the subject been so long and carefully smothered up?"

When Federalists turned toward the elections of 1800 and beyond, and the question of who might become their presidential candidate after John Adams, they naturally thought of their elder statesman Hamilton. Thus built up reciprocal pressure on Anti-Federalists to expose Hamilton's secret affair to the public's gaze. If all else failed, the news of it would serve to puncture Hamilton's swelling pretensions to the highest executive power.

During the presidential campaign of 1796, Noah Webster's *Minerva* had suggested that "Mr. Hamilton would be an advisable candidate" for president, but on seeing such a significant Hamilton-for-president trial balloon go up, "someone" in Philadelphia told "someone" in New York to tell Hamilton to tell Noah Webster that if the *Minerva* in future should dare "print a single paragraph" boosting Hamilton for president, all the Reynolds papers "were instantly to be laid before the world." Federalists had no doubt that John Beckley was the "somone" in Philadelphia who had contrived the threat. Beckley's friend and coadjutor Callender later sneered that "the message was delivered to Mr. Hamilton" with the result that "the *Minerva* became silent." Callender implied that only this threat, not Hamilton's self-abnegating concern to advance the 1796 Federalist ticket of Adams and Pinckney, was what had forced Hamilton to withdraw his own name from consideration for the presidency in 1796.

On June 24, three days before Monroe's arrival in Philadelphia, Hamilton's loyal old friend Senator Theodore Sedgwick of Massachusetts wrote Rufus King in London that Beckley's ouster from the clerkship was "resented not only by himself but the whole party [Republicans]. They were rendered furious by it." For revenge, "Beckley has been writing a pamphlet mentioned in the enclosed advertisement. The authentic papers there mentioned are those of which you perfectly know the history, formerly in the possession of Messrs. Monroe, Muhlenberg and Venable. This conduct is mean, base and infamous."

The very day before Monroe landed in Philadelphia under his own cloud of controversy, rightly suspecting Hamilton of a major role in his recall, Callender published issue Number V of his *History of the United States for 1796*, containing "some singular and authentic papers relative to Mr. Alexander Hamilton." Federalists at once traced the source to John Beckley. Even Abraham Venable, a Virginia Republican, admitted that Beckley, the man who had copied all the papers, "had been present during the whole investigation, both before and after my being called on." But Callender coyly denied that Beckley had "written a single sentence of it."

Callender's scandalous chronicle began with a pietistic preface. His *History*, he said, was only a response to scurrilous Federalist journalism like Hamilton's *Camillus* papers. Noah Webster's Connecticut was not the true center of Republicanism, Callender went on, because that honor belonged to the Old Dominion of his mentor, admirer, and charter subscriber, Thomas Jefferson, which was Virginia. The first four numbers of Callender's *History*, Numbers I through IV, replying to Hamilton's *Camillus* and *Phocion*, had taken him to task on such public issues as Hamiltonian finance, Jay's Treaty, and relations with France and England, but were relatively free of personal attacks. Number V, issued June 26, now took the offensive.

Callender's purpose, he declared, was only to reply in kind to the calumnies Federalists had heaped upon poor James Monroe as minister to France. Hamilton's affair with Mrs. James Reynolds had been known for a long time to many members of Congress. "If any republican character had been the hero of the story," Callender whined, "it would have been echoed from one end of the continent to the other." It was greatly to Monroe's credit, Callender toadied, that he had "observed profound silence. . . . Attacks on Mr. Monroe have been frequently repeated from the stockholding presses. They are cowardly because he is absent. They are unjust, because he displayed, on an occasion that will be mentioned immediately, the greatest lenity to Mr. Alexander Hamilton, the prime mover of the Federal Party."

There seemed no obvious reason why Callender should here ladle out fulsome praise for Jefferson, except to give Jefferson his money's worth. Jefferson too, he wrote, had nobly kept silent about Hamilton's scandal. Jefferson's *Notes on Virginia* were historically important because in them Jefferson "unites the sweetness of Zenophon with the force of Polybius, information without parade, and eloquence without effort," a happy contrast to Hamilton's disgraceful antics. With Jefferson gone out of Washington's cabinet, Callender felt, the government had sagged. By contrast to rich Jefferson, Hamilton, far from being the colossus of the anti-Republican party, was but "a threadbare lawyer, forgetting to earn daily subsistence for his family, that he may write 200 newspaper columns for nothing." Beckley's and Callender's public animadversions toward Hamilton closely tracked the private animadversions toward Hamilton that Jefferson had been writing in letters to Madison for a long time.

Unless Jefferson had ghostwritten Callender's preface for him, it was a stroke of genius for an unemployed hack journalist like Callender to have hit upon the epithet "threadbare lawyer" to describe Hamilton. For years the former secretary of the treasury had been charged in the press with vast, lucrative, illicit speculations and with being the crony of capitalists like William Bingham, Robert and Gouverneur Morris, John Barker Church, William Constable, William Duer, and Theophile Cazenove. He was a founder of the SUM and the Bank of New York and the son-in-law of patroon Philip Schuyler. He dressed with elegance and seemed to have plenty of money. How could a Callender have probed deeply enough beneath the surface of his public image to come up with the word *threadbare?* Who but a man with inherited wealth of his own and his late wife's and an incisive style like Thomas Jefferson could have perceived that behind his colossal facade, Hamilton was living high in hand-to-mouth, cash-short style. It was a secret Hamilton knew about himself. But only a rich patrician with the peculiar but pointed perceptions of a Thomas Jefferson would be able see him as he saw himself. A threadbare journalist like Callender, even if he were the genius Jefferson had said he was, would hardly see a Hamilton as being almost as threadbare as himself, without the aid of the insight of a Jefferson.

Callender's series was subsequently published as a book of eight chapters, *The History of the United States for 1796; Including a Variety of Interesting Particulars Relative to the Federal Government Previous to that Period.* But the way Callender first issued it section by section proved to be a trap for Hamilton. On July 3, Oliver Wolcott, Jr., from

Philadelphia sent Hamilton a copy of Pamphlet No. V, warning him that "the subject is but partially represented." Callender's design, he said, was to establish that Hamilton "was concerned in speculations in the public funds." Wolcott added that Venable "speaks of the publication as false and dishonorable." Wolcott had "good reason," probably firsthand from Venable, "to believe that Beckley is the real author, though it is attributed to Callender." It was certainly false "that Duer had any hand in the transaction." Wolcott had the Treasury lists in his own hands, he said. Simeon Reynolds, the faithless clerk who had leaked the lists, had been dismissed, and "his name has hitherto been concealed"—for the obvious reason that his surname, of all possible surnames in the world, was also Reynolds. Twice Wolcott cautioned Hamilton to "write nothing at least for the present. . . . the faction is organized. . . . public business is at a stand, and a crisis is approaching."

Most men of the world in their right minds would have followed Wolcott's advice and written nothing. But for years July for Hamilton had been a month of fevers, plagues, a stoning, and the onset of nervous derangements. So it was now.

Callender's "partial" account in Pamphlet No. 5 included only the four documents that Monroe, Muhlenberg, and Venable had been prepared to transmit to Washington with their accusatory letter the night of December 15, 1792: (1) Muhlenberg's account of his first visit to Hamilton to intercede for Jacob Clingman in the company of Aaron Burr representing James Reynolds, (2) Monroe's and Venable's statement of the charges that Reynolds and Clingman had made against Hamilton, (3) Monroe's and Muhlenberg's account of their interview with Mrs. Reynolds, during which she had given them the six notes Hamilton had written, and (4) part of Clingman's statement to them of December 13, but not his later statements.

Like a shrewd prosecutor, Callender had held back from No. V later statements of Clingman's to Monroe that Hamilton still would know nothing about. So the first angry rebuttals that he would fire off would contradict, or fail to explain away, the later statements of the witnesses that the prosecutor held back to impeach the first outraged, ill-thought-out reaction Hamilton would blurt out. His first hot, impetuous denials would inadvertently confirm or fill in gaps of worse revelations Callender still had up his sleeve.

Beckley's and Callender's tactics were masterfully "organized," as Wolcott had forewarned Hamilton they would be. The greatest Wall Street lawyer of the day took the bait. On July 5, 1797, Hamilton wrote Senator Monroe and the two congressmen, furious at their breach of confidence and demanding that each reconfirm the affirmation of Hamilton's innocence with which he had departed the unforgettable confrontation of four and a half years before:

> I shall rely upon your delicacy that the manner of doing it, will be such as one Gentleman has a right to expect from another—especially as you must be sensible that the present appearance of the papers is contrary to the course which was understood between us to be proper and includes a dishonourable infidelity somewhere.

With his letter, Hamilton enclosed what he alleged to be a copy of a memorandum of the "substance of your declaration made by me the morning after our interview."

The memorandum, which seemed suspiciously more apposite to 1797 than to 1792, read as follows:

> Memorandum of Substance of Declaration of Messrs. Monroe, Muhlenberg, and Venable concerning the Affair of J. Reynolds.

That they regretted the trouble and uneasiness which they had occasioned to me in consequence of the representations made to them, that they were perfectly satisfied with the explanation I had given, and that there was nothing in the transaction which ought to affect my character as a public officer or lessen the public confidence in my integrity.

Hamilton demanded that each send him "a declaration equivalent to that which was made at the time," a contradiction of Callender's comments, and "the favor of expedition in your reply."

A man of the world, even a rash one, ought to have cooled down enough by this time to let the matter end with these requests for private reassurance. But not Hamilton. The following day, July 6, he fired off a public reply to Callender for publication in Fenno's *Gazette of the United States*. By the very particularity of its denials, it for the first time publicly admitted the truth of the general substance of Callender's charges. Hamilton admitted that the four documents Callender published appeared to be authentic. His countercharge that the three congressmen's inquiry of 1792 had been politically motivated was hardly news. Through their intercessions, he wrote, two of "the most profligate of men" had sought escape from prison "by the favour of party spirit." Two of the three congressmen were his "known political opponents." But to the public, learning of it for the first time, the statements he offered as proof of his innocence would be seen as an admission of theretofore uncorroborated charges. "A full explanation took place between them and myself . . . in which by written documents I convinced them of the falsehood of the accusation," Hamilton said. "They declared themselves perfectly satisfied with the explanation and expressed their regret at the necessity which had been occasioned to me of making it."

Hamilton added a rash promise "to place the subject more precisely before the public," thus publicly burning behind him any bridge of silence that a sensible man's discretion might have left open for retreat.

Publication of No. VI of Callender's *History*, following publication of Hamilton's hasty retort in Fenno's *Gazette* on July 12, transmuted Callender's No. V from nothing more than a one-sided, one-day, scurrilous wonder to a credible public paper that could no longer be brushed aside as partisan poppycock. With the public's tongues wagging and heads shaking, Callender released pamphlet No. VI on July 4 or 5 with disclosures of juicy new details. Callender also gave a separate direct reply to what Hamilton had just published in Fenno's *Gazette*. Callender's reply was all the more devastating because, instead of being a wordy, adjectival, polemical broadside like Hamilton's, it took the form of an understated dialogue that cut the heart out of the credibility of Hamilton's denial in Fenno's *Gazette*, sentence by sentence, line by line, and phrase by phrase.

Hamilton had harshly said "the papers" were "the contrivance" of Clingman and Reynolds "to obtain *their* liberation from imprisonment, for a serious crime, by the FAVOUR OF PARTY spirit."

Not so, said Callender; Clingman had not been in jail during any of the time in question (he was out on bail). And Reynolds had been released by December 15—being last seen that day with Hamilton before vanishing. Reynolds had no part in "the contrivance" of the papers. Far from being motivated by party spirit, Muhlenberg and Venable had received no information until *after* Reynolds had been released from jail. Reynolds had refused to tell details until after his release: "He was afraid of speaking to them." On their face, the documents in Callender's Numbers V and VI tended to discredit Hamilton's defense in Fenno's *Gazette* and corroborate Callender. Lamely, Hamilton was forced to admit that his memory had been at fault in what he had first written to Fenno, thus badly damaging the credibility of all his defenses to come.

Callender's reply scoffed: the "written documents" by which Hamilton claimed he had "convinced them of the falsehood of the accusation" were nothing but "a series of letters pretended to be written relative to your alleged connection to Mrs. Reynolds. . . . they did not believe a single word." Callender derided him: "They must have found it hard to help laughing in each other's faces" "at your penitential tale of your depravity at The George. A more ridiculous scene cannot be conceived," Callender taunted him. When "you place the matter more precisely before the public," as you promised, your friend Wolcott and the others who "have long known you as an eminent and able statesman . . . will be highly gratified by seeing you exhibited in the novel character of a lover."

Callender goaded Hamilton to reprint "the whole original papers on which the suspicion is grounded . . . no extract . . . or general reference to them can be satisfactory." Little did Callender dream that the onset of nervous derangement under his onslaught would drive Hamilton to such an extremity of folly. But seeking a total cure for the sickness, he gulped down Callender's poisonous prescription.

The most important of the new documents never before seen by Hamilton now published in Number VI of Callender's *History* was Monroe's memorandum, dated December 16, 1792, written the day after the confrontation, that concluded with the fatefully ambiguous phrase "we left him under an impression our suspicions were removed." This was equivocal on the essential point. It would leave any percipient reader with a gnawing doubt that although they had placated Hamilton with the "impression," Monroe's, Muhlenberg's, and Venable's suspicions were far from entirely removed.

A second new revelation of Callender's Number VI was Monroe's memorandum of the conversation he had had with Jacob Clingman on January 2, 1793, two weeks after the confrontation, a date Hamilton had thought until now was one after which the matter had already been "smothered up" for more than a fortnight. According to Monroe's memorandum, Clingman said then that he had heard from Oliver Wolcott, Jr.—of all people—that the three congressmen, in an interview, had vindicated Hamilton of any guilt in his public capacity. Clingman "further observed to me," Monroe had written, "that he communicated the same to Mrs. Reynolds, who appeared much shocked at it, and wept immoderately." Clingman added that Maria denied that she had ever had an affair with Hamilton "and declared, that it had been a fabrication of Colonel Hamilton, and that her husband had joined in it."

Yet if it were true that Aaron Burr had obtained a New York divorce for James and Maria on adultery grounds—the only grounds—less than six months after the confrontation, Hamilton would have had to be the unnamed corespondent; or if not, her alleged affairs with other men concurrently with her intense involvements with Hamilton, Clingman, and James—not to mention James Wadsworth—imply such reckless, randy promiscuity that it discredits her testimony on this point and confirms Hamilton's.

According to Clingman and Maria, James Reynolds had written out the receipts and fabricated the letters at Hamilton's behest so as to give countenance to Hamilton's defense. Maria added that Reynolds had been "with colonel Hamilton, the day after he left the jail, when we supposed he was in Jersey." Clingman also said he believed Maria when she said she was entirely innocent of having had intercourse with Hamilton. What gentleman could contradict Clingman without compromising his own honor as a gentleman by compromising hers?

The thing that made this alleged statement of Clingman to Monroe of January 2 so damaging to Hamilton was that, as far as the public could tell, neither Clingman nor Maria would have had any way of knowing the nature of the defense Hamilton had pleaded to the "three gentlemen" the night of December 15. Therefore, it would appear that the tale that Clingman was telling to Monroe coincided with the truth. It would not occur to the public at large that Monroe (or Beckley or Callender or Aaron Burr) had told him. Why would Clingman be telling Monroe something Monroe had already known, and why would Monroe be ostentatiously listening and jotting it down? But to anyone who knew Oliver Wolcott, Jr., Clingman's tale that it was Wolcott who was the leak would be unbelievable on its face. A discreet, experienced public servant like Oliver Wolcott, Jr., who was also Hamilton's closest associate in the Treasury, personal friend, and confidant, as well as the official who had instituted the original prosecutions against Clingman and Reynolds, was the last (or next to the last after Hamilton) man in the world to have let the secret of Hamilton's defense slip out to a couple of ex-prosecutees. To Hamilton, anyone who, like Monroe, could have given enough credence to Clingman's charge to jot it down, let alone allow it to be published without further checking—could be no gentleman.

In the meantime, Muhlenberg and Venable, by letters written from Philadelphia on July 10, both reassured Hamilton that they had kept no copies of the papers, that they had given them all to Monroe, and that they did not know how they had come to be published. They were shocked that they had been. They had both been "perfectly satisfied with Hamilton's explanation." They had not sought to mislead Hamilton: the impression with which they left him coincided with their own true beliefs. Muhlenberg, a fellow Federalist, added some friendly counsel that Hamilton continued to ignore: "were I to undertake to contradict the many absurdities & falsehoods which I see published on a variety of subjects . . . it would require more time than I am willing to sacrifice."

On July 10, Hamilton demanded an interview with Monroe as soon as possible. Monroe was in New York collecting information to vindicate himself from charges like Hamilton's that had led to his recall from France under a cloud. He agreed to meet Hamilton Tuesday morning, July 11, at the house of Thomas Knox, a merchant, where Monroe was lodging. Monroe, himself a lawyer, brought with him another lawyer, David Gelston, the surrogate of New York County, an office awash with dispensable patronage, which only the sliest and shrewdest of lawyers ever comes to hold. Hamilton brought with him his brother-in-law, bluff businessman John Barker Church, only recently arrived from London. The outcome provides yet another illustration of an old saw Hamilton would never learn: that the lawyer who handles his own case has a fool for a client.

Gelston afterward wrote out a memorandum of the meeting on which the following account is based. Unfortunately, no transcript was made for Hamilton's side to compare with what Monroe's own lawyer wrote down to serve his client.

On entering the room, according to Gelston, Hamilton "appeared very much agitated." He announced that "the cause or motives of this meeting, I presume, are pretty well understood."

Then, Gelston said, "he went into a detail of circumstances" about the Philadelphia confrontation of December 15, 1792. "At considerable length."

"What's all that mean?" asked Monroe. "If you wish me to tell you anything relating to the business all this history is unnecessary. Get to the point."

"I shall come to the point directly," Hamilton snapped back.

Here Gelston notes that "some warmth appeared in both gentlemen."

They calmed down for a moment. Then "some explanation took place." Monroe explained that "it was merely accidental my knowing anything about the business at first. . . . I was told that one Reynolds *from Virginia* was in Gaol.'' Monroe did not say who had told him—whether it had been fellow Senator Aaron Burr or someone else.

In any event, ''I called merely to aid a man that might be in distress,'' Monroe went on, ''But I found it was a Reynolds from New York.''

After the December 15 confrontation, Monroe said, ''I sealed up my copies of all the papers and sent or delivered them to my friend in Virginia.'' He added, ''I had no intention of publishing them.''

Oddly enough, according to Gelston, upon this interesting revelation, no one found it necessary, or had the curiosity, or dared, to ask the name of Monroe's ''friend in Virginia.'' Probably it was because none was in any doubt that Monroe's ''friend in Virginia'' was Thomas Jefferson. If anyone present in the room did, in fact, say out loud the name of the powerful leader of Gelston's party, Gelston was too shrewd a politician to let it stand undeleted from his transcription.

''How then did these papers come to be published?'' Hamilton demanded to know.

''Upon my honor,'' Monroe vowed, avoiding a direct answer to Hamilton's question, ''I knew nothing of their publication until I arrived in Philadelphia from Europe. In fact,'' Monroe added, ''I was sorry to find they were published.'' It seemed obvious that he knew how, but refused to tell Hamilton.

''I've written to you,'' Hamilton said in anger, ''and Muhlenberg and Venable too, to find out how the papers came to be published. You haven't replied.''

''Calm down,'' said Monroe.

But Hamilton grew still more agitated. ''My own character and the peace and reputation of my family are deeply involved,'' he cried.

''If you'll be quiet for a moment,'' Monroe interrupted, ''and be a little temperate, I'll tell you candidly why I haven't answered.''

''Why?''

''I didn't receive your letter until ten o'clock at night and I had planned to leave for New York the next morning and did. Even so, I went to Venable's lodgings late that night, to look for him, but it was impossible for the three of us to get together then.''

Hamilton and John Church stared at Monroe in disbelief. Venable's letter to Hamilton of July 9 had made no mention of any such extraordinary late night visit by Monroe.

Church angrily pulled out of his pocket and brandished in Monroe's face copies of the two offending pamphlets, Numbers V and VI of Callender's *History*.

Monroe went on, ''Since all three of us were present then and all three signed the certificate then, I thought we should all meet and return a joint answer now. I still mean to do this on my return to Philadelphia.'' Monroe still artfully dodged answering the real question.

''Number V contains the statement signed by all three,'' Hamilton agreed. ''But number VI contains statements signed by you alone.''

''If you wish me to give the story of the facts and circumstances as they appear to me, individually,'' Monroe let go, ''I'll do it on my return to Philadelphia.''

''Do so,'' Hamilton snapped back.

''As I said before,'' Monroe began again, ''I still believe that the packet of papers that I had still remain sealed up with my friend in Virginia.''

''What you say is totally false!'' Hamilton shouted. The words Hamilton had shouted at Monroe may well have been, ''You're a liar.'' But Gelston would, no doubt, have transcribed it ''your representation is totally false,'' as, in fact, he did.

To these words, Gelston added, by way of a discreet escape hatch from hard words muted by euphemism, "(as nearly as I recollect the expression)."

Next, according to Gelston, "The gentlemen both instantly rose, Monroe rising first."

Monroe: "Do you say I represented falsely? You are a scoundrel."

Hamilton: "I will meet you like a gentleman."

Monroe: "I am ready. Get your pistols!"

Both: "We shall not or it will not be settled any other way."

Gelston and Church jumped to their feet "at the same moment. We put ourselves between them," Gelston wrote.

Church: "Gentlemen, gentlemen, gentlemen, be moderate."

After a few moments, Gelston went on, "we all sat down and the two gentlemen, Colo. M. and Colo. H soon got moderate."

Gelston noted "very clearly" that "Colo. H appeared extremely agitated & Colo. M. appeared soon to get quite cool."

Monroe then "repeated his entire ignorance of the publication and his surprise to find it published." Furthermore, he told Hamilton, if he would not be so "warm and intemperate" he "would explain everything he knew of the business."

But Hamilton, too agitated, and Church, no lawyer, let this sudden door opening for meaningful cross-examination of Monroe slip by.

For Monroe, Gelston quickly stepped in and slammed the door shut. Gelston "addressed myself to Colo. H.," saying he had a "proposition." Would Hamilton like to hear it?

"By all means," said Hamilton, taking the bait, distracted from the opening Monroe had left.

"As Colo. M. has satisfied you" on the question of the leaked publication and "as the other part was a transaction of the three gentlemen," Gelston proposed, "would it not be much the best way to let the whole affair rest until Colo. M. returned to Philadelphia." Then he could get together with the other two on a joint answer "as Colo. M. had proposed."

Hamilton and Church had pried nothing out of Monroe in the confrontation they themselves had demanded, and Monroe, by Gelston's quick thinking, had seemingly gained their acquiescence in Gelston's smooth confirmation of Monroe's total ignorance of the source of the leak.

"I observed a silence," wrote Gelston. Then "Colo H. made some answer in a word or two which I understood as not disapproving" the Gelston proposition. "But what Hamilton had actually responded," Gelston said, "I cannot recollect with precision." With Hamilton seemingly about to repudiate his formulation, Gelston quickly turned to Church, saying, "Perhaps my proposition would have been made with more propriety to you than to Colo. H." Church now took the lure, too.

Church asked Monroe when he would be going back to Philadelphia. Monroe said Friday (three days later) at the latest. Like the brusque businessman he was, weary of so much lawyers' talk about an unprofitable old affair and anxious to close, Church said briskly that he and Hamilton "would go on Saturday and as the business could be finished on Saturday he thought it would be much the best way."

Church rose and Gelston and Monroe eagerly jumped up, too.

Hamilton seem dissatisfied and unhappy.

Church tried to buck him up some by saying, "there will be an explanation by all three gentlemen."

He disassociated himself from Hamilton's white-hot chagrin at the outcome by adding, "any warmth or unguarded expressions that happened should be buried . . . considered as though it had never happened."

Monroe threw in bluntly, "I shall be governed by Hamilton's conduct." This and probably a hard stare from Church forced Hamilton to swallow his own mortification. "I think any intemperate expressions should be forgotten," he agreed meekly.

As Church hustled Hamilton out the door, Monroe said, "I agree."

Gelston closed his statement with the words "The interview continued about an hour or a little over." Skillful lawyer that he was, in order to insure that there would be no gap that might permit his account to be discredited later he added, "myself being present throughout the whole."

Obviously at odds with his brother-in-law and most important client on how much to make of the matter from this point on, Hamilton rushed off to Philadelphia the next day, Wednesday, instead of waiting till Saturday. Church begged off making the trip at all. For excuse, he said "My Angelica is not very well—she complains that her throat is a little sore." As for Hamilton's Eliza, Church wrote him, "she put into my hand the newspaper" with Callender's letter in it. "It makes not the least impression on her. . . . she considers the whole knot of them opposed to you to be scoundrels."

Church told Hamilton tactfully that "from what I observed yesterday," Monroe is "inclined to be very generous." He "is much embarrassed how to get out of the scrape in which he has involved himself. . . . from present appearances you will not be long detained at Philadelphia, but be able to return Sunday or Monday."

From his lonely Philadelphia lodgings, Hamilton wrote home to Elizabeth, with the weird lack of proportion that was typical of his periods of nervous derangement. How happy he would be "to return to her embrace and the company of our beloved Angelica. I am very anxious about you both, you for an obvious reason [Elizabeth was eight months along in at least her seventh pregnancy with their sixth child], and for Angelica because . . . Church mentioned she complained of a *sore throat*. Let me charge you and her to be well and happy, for you comprize all my felicity."

Hamilton's stay dragged on for almost two weeks as he busied himself with writing and documenting a public reply to his enemies. All who befriended him counseled him not to publish. But he seemed hell-bent on self-destruction. In Hamilton's unluckiest city during plague season when he now regularly suffered from nervous derangements, he shared the lodgings of his old friend William Loughton Smith, whom he had characterized to Washington as a man "of an uncomfortable temper . . . a certain hardness of character." The unfortunate impact of such an environment would be imprinted plainly on Hamilton's performance. From Philadelphia between mid-July and early August, he fired off a dozen challenging letters to Monroe. Monroe fired back replies in kind that did not much change the stands the two men had aired in the heat of the interview in New York recorded by David Gelston.

On July 17, Monroe and Muhlenberg sent Hamilton a joint statement that was all any man in Hamilton's position could have wished—if he had been in his right mind. They explained that Venable was away, but in agreement with them, "that we had no agency in or knowledge of the publication of these papers till they appeared" and that the original papers had been "deposited in the hands of a respectable character in Virginia where they are now." Also, "the impression which we left on your mind . . . was that which rested on our own." Hamilton's explanation of his connection with Reynolds "removed the suspicions we had before entertained of your being connected with him in speculation." To drive home this reassurance, they added that, as gentlemen of honor, "had this not been the case we should certainly not have left that impression on your mind." And had this not been the case, they would not "have desisted from the plan we had contemplated in the inquiry of laying the papers before the President of the United States."

As to Clingman's statement of January 2, taken down over Monroe's signature alone, which Hamilton charged made it appear that Clingman "had revived the suspicions which my explanation had removed," Monroe insisted that "I did not convey or mean to convey any opinion of my own, as to the faith which was due to it, but left it to stand on its own merits reserving to myself the right to judge of it, as of any fact afterwards communicated, according to its import and authenticity."

But in the hardness of mind that attacks of enemies always brought on, this joint statement was not good enough for Hamilton. Out of Hamilton's anxiety, Monroe's innocuous, legalistic, basically rather silly reservation extracted from Hamilton the black charge that Monroe now betrayed a disposition toward him that would "merit epithets the severest that I could apply" (on July 20, 1797) and, two days later, as the fever season heated up, that "you are actuated by motives toward me malignant and dishonorable." His mind now seemingly out of touch with any coordinate of objective reality to mark reasonably sane opinion, Hamilton added, "This will be the universal opinion when the publication of the whole affair which I am about to make shall be seen."

Monroe replied July 25, "Why you have adopted this style I know not," but he would not challenge Hamilton to a duel. On the other hand, he would not shrink from one if "called in a way which always for the illustration of truth, I wish to avoid, but which I am ever ready to meet."

Hamilton's customary iron sense of the formality appropriate to such affairs was so far askew by July 28 that he unguardedly, yet disarmingly, let slip in a letter to Monroe that "the subject is too disgusting to leave me any inclination to prolong this discussion of it."

Helping him in these harsh and pitiful exchanges as Hamilton's intermediary was William Jackson, Washington's longtime personal secretary, the same man Hamilton had helped start on his way to an important footnote in history by successfully backing him as secretary to the Constitutional Convention, while at the same time earning for himself unforgiving hatred from John Beckley for his defeat for the office.

Jackson's comments would probably reflect Washington's view of the whole sorry affair as well as his own. He wrote Hamilton on August 7 that though "injured you may be by his conduct . . . it by no means appears to me that you are the person injured by the correspondence. . . . there is not a word in *his correspondence* that calls for a direct challenge from you." Moreover, if Monroe were the kind of man "whose sense of injury is not to be awakened" by being told that his motives are "malignant and dishonorable," he was not a person Hamilton should challenge. Monroe was not really a gentleman, or he would have responded by a challenge to Hamilton. Or else there was some secret reason for his failure to respond. I "advise you to decline giving a direct challenge," Jackson advised, "and await the effect of your publication."

Hamilton's close friends like Jeremiah Wadsworth and James McHenry continued to implore him to forget about further publications and let the whole matter drop. Elizabeth gave birth to their sixth child, William Stephen Hamilton, on August 4. Hamilton apologized for being late in repaying $100 that McHenry had sent him, as well as a further sum to reimburse "some money paid for me by Lewis." But he forgot to enclose the check. McHenry's reply had a tactful P.S.: "There was no money in your letter."

Elizabeth pregnant and lying in with a new baby, Angelica complaining of a sore throat, and good-paying clients neglected to rehash an old affair for the sake of public credit left Hamilton no money to repay IOUs to friends.

In his exchanges with Hamilton and William Jackson, Monroe stuck rigidly to the same agonizingly equivocal stance, but in private he was meekly endorsing on his copy of one letter of Hamilton's "no occasion for a reply, as it may lead on and irritate." Monroe sent copies of the whole Hamilton correspondence to Aaron Burr in New York, saying, "I never meant to give him a challenge." Monroe was ready to accept one from him—but would not be ready for three months or so. "In case of accident I should leave Mrs. M. almost friendless in Virginia she being of New York," Monroe added. Burr should arrange all details for him with Hamilton. The place for the duel should be "somewhere near the Susquehanna," Monroe explained fearfully. "He is pushed on by party friends here [like Smith?] who to get rid of me would be very willing to hazard him." Burr's reaction to the correspondence was that "I wish it all burnt." Burr added that he himself believed and that Monroe, Muhlenberg and Venble must also believe that "H is innocent of the charge of any concern in speculation with Reynolds. You expressed to me the same idea when we were together." Burr added that "it will be an act of magnanimity and justice to say so in a joint certificate." To Burr, the amusing little badger game of a sex scandal that he may have helped his New York clients, the Reynoldses, set in motion was now threatening too many lives and wives and children. He duly wrote out a certificate for Monroe's signature, dated August 16, affirming "that it was not my intention to give any sanction to" Clingman's statement. This certificate probably never reached Hamilton or, if it did, came too late.

To leave no doubt about where he and Martha stood amid all the uproar, George Washington from Mount Vernon on August 21 sent Hamilton and Betsy

> Not for an intrinsic value the thing possesses, but as a token of my sincere regard and friendship for you, and as a remembrancer of me . . . a wine cooler for four bottles . . . one of four which I imported in the early part of my late adminsitration. . . . I pray you to present my best wishes, in which Mrs. Washington joins me, to Mrs. Hamilton & the family; and that you would be persuaded, that with every sentiment of the highest regard, I remain your sincere friend, and affectionate Hble Servant
>
> Geo. Washington

At just this time of desperately needed reassurance, it would mean much to Hamilton that with exquisite tact George and Martha's affectionate remembrancer did not make special mention of the family's new baby as the particular reason for the gift. It probably made it that much easier for Hamilton to brush aside sympathetic counsel of friends and besetting second thoughts of his own as he strode unswerving into the jaws of his next self-made disaster: the publication on August 25, 1797, of what came to be known as *The Reynolds Pamphlet*.

Rarely has a tract containing such violent political partisanship coupled with such intimate personal revelations borne a more innocuous title: *Observations on Certain Documents, Contained in No. V and VI of "The History of the United States for the Year 1796," in which the Charge of Speculation against Alexander Hamilton, late Secretary of the Treasury, is Fully Refuted. Written by himself.* In Volume XXI of the Hamilton Papers the printed version of *The Reynolds Pamphlet* runs to 29 pages and 52 separate documents are appended as exhibits. The blurb announced that the pamphlet "presents . . . a statement of the base means practiced by the Jacobins . . . to asperse . . . characters of those . . . considered as hostile to their disorganizing schemes. It also contains . . . correspondence . . . proving . . . that the connection between [Hamilton] and Reynolds, was the result of a daring conspiracy on the part of the latter and his associates to extort money.''

Hamilton begins his *Observations* with a tirade against his political enemies that approaches the line that marks off hysteria and incoherence from rationality. Only the ingrained elegance of Hamilton's habitual style and manner of writing keeps it from crossing the line that marks the edge of madness:

> THE spirit of Jacobinism, if not entirely a new spirit, has at least been clothed with a more gigantic body and armed with more powerful weapons than it ever before possessed. . . . it threatens more extensive and complicated mischiefs to the world than have hitherto flowed from the three great scourges of mankind, WAR, PESTILENCE and FAMINE. . . . its progress may be marked with calamities of which the dreadful incidents of the French revolution afford a very faint image. Incessantly busied in undermining all the props of public security and private happiness, it seems to threaten the political and moral world with a complete overthrow. . . .

It is necessary to keep firmly fixed in mind that what Hamilton is raving about here with such eloquence is a published charge that he had paid a prostitute's husband a little hush money five years or more earlier to keep him quiet. To treat such ancient trivia in such extravagant terms shows the seriousness of Hamilton's loss of touch with reality and sense of proportion, marking a serious onset of recurrent nervous derangement.

The gigantic forces he describes are targeted in and bearing down upon him. ''A principal engine is calumny. . . . men of upright principles shall at all events be destroyed.'' Their best efforts for public good are traduced, their motives misrepresented, their criminality hinted at. ''Direct falsehoods are invented and propagated with undaunted effrontery and unrelenting perseverance. Lies detected and refuted are revived and repeated . . . profligate men are encouraged, probably bribed . . . with patronage . . . money to become informers and accusers . . . corroding whispers wear away the reputations which they could not directly subvert. . . .'' There is ''a conspiracy of vice against virtue . . . odious insinuations . . . rancour and venom . . . any little foible or folly traced out . . . becomes in their hands a two edged sword . . . to wound the public character and stab the private felicity'' of the persecutee. ''With such men, nothing is sacred. Even the peace of an unoffending and amiable wife is a welcome repast to their insatiate fury against the husband.''

He is an innocent victim of his and all mankind's enemies:

> Relying upon this weakness of human nature, the Jacobin Scandal-Club, though often defeated, constantly return to the charge. Old calumnies are served up afresh, and every pretext is seized to add to the catalogue. The person whom they seek to blacken, by dint of repeated strokes of their brush, becomes a demon in their own eyes, though he might be pure and bright as an angel but for the daubing of those wizard painters.

The elegance of his usual mode of self-expression would not bend far enough to permit Hamilton simply to say, ''I am not a crook.'' Instead he says: ''no man ever carried into public life a more unblemished pecuniary reputation . . . a character marked by an indifference to the acquisition of property rather than an avidity for it.''

Going on and on in this frantic mode, he is far into his pamphlet before he states the real question at issue, as he should have done at the beginning:

> The charge against me is a connection with one James Reynolds for purposes of improper pecuniary speculation. My real crime is an amorous connection with his wife for a considerable time, with his privity and connivance, if not originally brought on by a combination between the husband and wife with the design to extort money from me.

The 52 documents attached as exhibits to his pamphlet included copies of the statements and correspondence of Muhlenberg, Venable, and Monroe, and all the letters from the Reynoldses. The most significant of these documents and his explanation for them have been quoted or paraphrased in earlier chapters of this book in the context of the time in 1791 and 1792, when they first came to be a part of the record of the affair in Hamilton's mind, and are not repeated here.

Hamilton also included a certificate of a Philadelphia boardinghouse keeper identifying Mrs. Reynolds's handwriting in her letters; he included as well Noah Webster's certificate denying Callender's charge that Hamilton had forced him to suppress stories sending up trial balloons for his now suddenly forever self-scuttled prospects for the presidency. He sideswiped Jefferson by quoting two friendly letters the vice-president had written to the discredited scandalmonger Andrew G. Fraunces. He decried Monroe's conduct throughout. Hamilton said that though he was ''not permitted to make a public use'' of an important statement by Richard Folwell, ''I am permitted to refer any gentleman'' who wanted to see it ''to the perusal of his letter in the hands of William Bingham, Esq., who is also so obliging as to permit me to deposit with him for similar inspection all the original papers which are contained in the appendix to this narrative.'' At the conclusion of the appendix to his pamphlet, Hamilton again referred to ''the gentleman'' with whom the papers are deposited, referring back to his old friend William Bingham.

Hamilton seemed to think his public confession would cause only a little mild embarrassment, instead of the sensation it did. He betrayed his miscalculation by tendering only a mild apologia for it:

> I owe perhaps to my friends an apology for condescending to give a public explanation. A just pride with reluctance stoops to a formal vindication against so despicable a contrivance, and is inclined rather to oppose to it the uniform evidence of an upright character.

The only reason he was breaking this wise rule on this occasion was that ''the tale'' seemed ''to derive a sanction from the names of three men of some weight and consequence in the society; a circumstance which I trust will excuse me for paying attention to a slander that, without this prop, would defeat itself by intrinsic circumstances of absurdity and malice.''

Hamilton's agonizing sense of injury seems to arise not so much from the words contained in Monroe's ''*correspondence*,'' as from his ''conduct'' toward him. By refusing to rise to Hamilton's challenge to a duel as a gentleman should, Monroe seemed to be denying to Hamilton his pretensions to being a fellow gentleman. While busy, bustling practical men of the world like Church might not be able to see much difference between

Monroe's telling Hamilton that the impression he had intended to leave with him coincided with his own, but refusing to add that Clingman's later testimony had not changed it, the refined insight of a genius like Jefferson would quickly descry the inestimable importance of such an affirmation to a Hamilton.

In the pamphlet Hamilton wrote, "This confession is not made without a blush. I cannot be the apologist of any vice because the ardor of passion may have made it mine. I can never cease to condemn myself for the pang which it may inflict in a bosom eminently entitled to all my gratitude, fidelity, and love." But public credit was of more importance to him—and her:

> That bosom will approve, that, even at so great an expense, I should effectually wipe away a more serious stain from a name which it cherishes with no less elevation than tenderness. The public, too, will, I trust, excuse the confession. The necessity of it to my defence against a more heinous charge could alone have extorted from me so painful an indecorum.

James Thomson Callender, with malicious glee in the sweet journalistic revenge he had visited upon the King of the Feds, wrote to Jefferson that Hamilton's *Observations* were "worth all that 50 of the best pens in America could have said against him. My sale has been repaid beyond all hope. In less than five weeks, 700 have gone off, and some commissioners and subscribers are yet unanswered." He was delighted that the Episcopal Bishop of Pennsylvania, William Whyte, the brother-in-law of Robert Morris, had declined at a public function to drink to the health of Hamilton, the self-confessed adulterer.

James Madison on October 20, 1797, piously called Jefferson's attention to Hamilton's "malignant insinuations" against him, adding "The publication is a curious specimen of the ingenious folly of its author. Next to the error of publishing at all is that of forgetting that simplicity and candor are the only dress which prudence would put on innocence." The malignant insinuation against you "is a masterpiece of folly, because its importance is in exact proportion to its venom."

Jefferson, privy to the whole affair since December 17, 1792, at latest, could surmise that Hamilton's glancing references to him in *The Reynolds Pamphlet* meant that Hamilton suspected him of being the hidden prime mover who had set the whole affair in motion a year and a half earlier than the date of his entry. Jefferson's air of distantly amused detachment belied his close, intense involvement with the intimate details of the affair from beginning to end as he disclosed to John Taylor of South Carolina,

> I understand that finding the strait between Scylla and Charybdis too narrow for his steerage, he had preferred running plumb on one of them. In truth, it seems to work very hard with him; and his willingness to plead guilty to adultery seems rather to have strengthened than weakened the suspicions that he was in truth guilty of speculations.

Other Anti-Federalists wallowed waggishly in Hamilton's political wake. *Zanga*, whose style was exactly like John Beckley's, writing in the *Aurora*, took Fenno to task for copyrighting Hamilton's pamphlet: ". . . this precious piece of property of yours is not a vindication of the Ex-Secretary, but . . . of . . . adultery . . ." Hamilton "holds himself out as trotting from one lodging in Philadelphia to another after . . . a prostitute!" His ambition was "to bring a . . . strumpet, to the level of his own personal infamy." Andrew G. Fraunces fired back at Hamilton's thrusts at him and Jefferson by a series of questions:

Did not Hamilton procure one of Fraunces's letters from Jefferson under false pretenses? "Have not you been the instrument of robbing me . . . of liberty, health, property, wife, and children?" He recalled another of Hamilton's amours: "I speak nothing of the Lady in Market Street" [the Reynoldses lived at Fifth and Vine]—"time will shape that!"

James Cheetham, another popular polemicist, reminded his readers that Hamilton had "rambled for 18 months in this scene of pollution, and squandered . . . above $1,200 to conceal the intrigue from his loving spouse." The *Chronicle* chortled over Mrs. Reynolds's "violent attack" on "the virtue of the immaculate secretary . . . in Mr. Hamilton's own house." He had fallen "as compleat a sacrifice to his passions, as ever an old soldier did to his funding system." Jefferson had at last found a writer worthy to take up the pen against "the colossus of the anti Republican party." The pen was Hamilton's own.

It was nonsense, all nonsense, Callender charged, to accept Hamilton's story of having had an affair with Maria Reynolds at all. His tale was nothing but a cover-up for a larger and more heinous scandal that involved embezzling money from the Treasury. No originals of the correspondence between Hamilton and Maria and James Reynolds had ever existed, or if they had, they had been forged by Reynolds and Hamilton, as Maria and Clingman had charged. Callender issued a direct challenge to Hamilton on October 29, 1797:

> The facts which you . . . bring forward, and the conclusions which you attempt to draw from them do not appear Satisfactory to me, I intend introducing a reply to them in a volume upon your administration that I am now engaged in writing. My object in this letter is, to request that you will give an order to a friend of mine and myself to inspect the papers lodged with Mr. Bingham, that I may judge what credit is due to them. . . . if they appear to be genuine, I shall be as ready to confess my conviction to the public, as I was to declare my former opinion.

Callender pointed out to Hamilton that he had made "a palpable mistake" in writing of "visiting her at Inskeeps" because it "never was a house of that sort." Hamilton would certainly have to publish a second pamphlet to correct such ridiculous mistakes as this.

Hamilton had specified that only "gentlemen" might apply to Bingham to see the papers. Callender was notoriously no gentleman. This was demonstrated, ipso facto, by his effrontery to apply to see the papers lodged with Bingham. On the back of Callender's letter, Hamilton wrote "impudent Experiment *NO NOTICE.*" He made no further reply. Callender kept digging and reporting. In his *Sketches of the History of America* published early in 1798, he claimed to find many other contradictions in Hamilton's story.

Clingman had married Maria Reynolds, and they were now living in Alexandria; Reynolds was living in New York. Aaron Burr had arranged their divorce.

"If the letters published by Mr. Hamilton in the name of Maria are genuine," Callender argued, "it would be very easy to obtain her attestation of the fact. A justice of the peace . . . could dispatch the business in half an hour. She could be directed to give a sample of her hand; and by comparing this with the letters, it would be ascertained whether or not they really came from her pen. But Camillus dares not meet this test."

Callender also called attention to textual incongruities in the Reynolds letters: "The construction of the periods disagrees with this apparent incapacity of spelling. . . . A few gross blunders are interspersed . . . but, when stript of such a veil, the body of the composition is pure and correct. In the literary world, fabrications of this nature have been frequent." Callender piously added: "He who acknowledged the reality of such epistles, could feel no scruple to forge them. The latter supposition is as favourable as the former to his good name.'' Callender's comment echoes the same doubts concerning the authenticity of the Reynolds letters Jefferson was confiding to his diary at about the same time. Callender then addresses Hamilton directly:

> The whole collection would not have required above an evening to write. . . . You speak as if it was impossible to invent a few letters. Yet, upon this very business, you wrote a feigned hand. And what is your molehill appendix, altogether, to the gigantic fabrications of Psalmanazar and of Chatterton? Send for the lady, and let us hear what she has to say. . . . Never pretend that you scorn to confront accusers. The world will believe that you dare not.

Of course, Maria and James Reynolds were as easily available to interrogation by a journalist like Callender as they were to Hamilton. Because they would on the face of it be witnesses friendly to Callender—he accepted their latest story—and hostile to Hamilton—a greater mystery than why Hamilton failed to question them is why Callender did not.

If a "hireling editor" like Callender were to be believed, Hamilton was not only a defalcating secretary of the treasury, a speculator, a peculator, and an adulterer, he was also a liar and a forger. According to Callender, he was the contriver of a vast cover-up scheme put out under the false guise of coming clean. He was not a seducer and an adulterer; he was a false confessor to nonexistent affairs. He was the traducer of the good reputation of a virtuous woman and a bumptious boaster wearing false hair on his chest.

Present-day Jefferson scholars who have studied these matters closely go farther than Callender. Without examining the original Reynolds letters, which have never been found, they agree with Callender that in addition to his other alleged crimes and shortcomings, Hamilton was also a perjurer and a forger.

Foremost among these learned scholars is Professor Julian P. Boyd, the editor of the definitive edition of *The Papers of Thomas Jefferson*. In an 80-page appendix to Volume 18, entitled "The First Conflict in the Cabinet," Professor Boyd writes (page 680):

> . . . the letters of James Reynolds and his wife as published by Hamilton present a character that is so immediately recognizable as to place their true nature beyond doubt . . . the conclusion is obvious. . . . They exhibit in their texts, in their substantive incongruities, and in their conflict with verifiable evidence overwhelming proofs of their own insufficiency. They are the palpably contrived documents of a brilliant and daring man who, writing under much stress in the two or three days available to him in 1792, tried to imitate what he conceived to be the style of less literate persons. The result was inexpert to the point of naïveté, but its character is beyond doubt. The purported letters of James and Maria Reynolds as published in Hamilton's *Observations* cannot be accepted as genuine.

It is a shocking charge. Professor Boyd's argument, following Callender, runs that Mrs. Reynolds's letters contain good grammatical construction and correct spelling of longer words like *tortured, happiness, disappointment, anguish, insupportable, language, affliction, inexorable, consolation, existence, complaining,* and *adieu,* but misspellings of easy words of one or two syllables like *se* for *see, rite* for *write, mutch* for *much, moast* for *most, pilliow* for *pillow,* and so on. This is suspicious. Also, she misspelled words in ways unusual even for unlettered persons of the day, such as *kneese* for *knees, youse* or *yuse* for *use, greateest* for *greatest, gleme* for *gleam, voed* for *void,* and so on, and also misspelled some words the same way her husband did. This is still more suspicious.

James Reynolds's letters and receipts, beginning with his discovery of the alleged amour, changing in tone from that of an outraged and threatening husband to one of an importunate, obsequious, and wheedling extortionist pimp, misspell simple words too: *fue* for *few*, *boath* for *both*, and *shush* for *such*, but he spells polysyllabic words without error, such as *distraction, imprudent, disagreeable,* and *calculation.* Also, like Maria, he spells the same word sometimes correctly and sometimes incorrectly, sometimes both ways in the same letter. Thus Maria could write *deer freend* and also *dear sir*, and James could write *exspess* as well as *express*. Such peculiarities give away Hamilton as an inexpert and naïve forger, Boyd argues.

Did Hamilton fabricate the Reynolds letters? Did he, with Reynolds's help, forge them during the day or two between Reynolds's release from jail and the confrontation with Monroe and the others in his office on the night of December 15? Was his affair with Maria Reynolds not merely one that he did not enjoy for very long, but one that he never had? Are Callender's revelations a fine example of the free press at its best laying bare without fear or favor a cover-up of moral rot and political corruption in high places? Or at its worst, with hireling editors printing an artful hatchet job of unsubstantiated innuendoes and false insinuations, guilts by association, and character assassination?

Hamilton's defense begins with his own special pleading in *The Reynolds Pamphlet* summed up in his rhetorical question:

''Is the preexistence of a speculating connection reconcilable with this mode of expression?''

The ''mode of expression,'' the twists and turns, the hesitations and reversals of the correspondence display comedic and dramatic invention that seem to range far beyond anything known about James Reynolds's literary talents—or Hamilton's. *Publius* could write in many modes—dignified state papers, crisp letters of advice, monumental great reports, proposed statutes, gravely ardent or playful love letters, and stilted imitation pastorals. But the mode of the Reynolds letters is one that on the evidence of all his other writing was beyond his powers of literary invention.

The pointless hesitations and the indecisiveness of Reynolds's Sign of the George letter, for example, seem as inconsistent with the direct, linear, forward thrust of Hamilton's usual style as they are consistent with Reynolds's acting upon advice from someone behind the scenes like Aaron Burr about what to do next. In its crude way, Reynolds's December 15 letter stated all the points for a good legal cause of action for a lawsuit against Hamilton for alienation of affections as only a sharp lawyer could.

That the printed version of the Reynolds documents differs in minor respects from the originals would not necessarily mean that the missing basic documents are forgeries. Variances in orthography and spelling between the original manuscripts and the printed version may have arisen from inaccurate transcription by Hamilton for the printer or inaccurate typesetting by the printer from Hamilton's copy or faulty proofreading by Fenno or some of all three. Evidence of white lies, self-serving recollections, forgetfulness, haste, and carelessness on Hamilton's part can be found in *The Reynolds Pamphlet* and its appendix. For example, Hamilton probably met or had prior acquaintance with James or Maria Reynolds well before the time he says Maria first came to his house in Philadelphia—Hamilton mentioned James Reynolds in his letter to Jeremiah Wadsworth of August 20, 1787. Yet to this writer Hamilton's account of the affair in *The Reynolds Pamphlet* in its main outline has the ring of truth.

Another important aspect of Hamilton's defense is the discrediting of the long series of impeachment inquiries brought against him in Congress that had grown out of Jefferson's and Giles's impeachment resolutions. "Finding no handle for their malice," they exonerated him of corruption in office. Congress's investigation of all Treasury operations failed to turn up any link to Reynolds. The charges of Andrew G. Fraunces against him relative to the Baron de Glaubeck's pension and Duer's warrants had also been extensively investigated by Congress and exposed as groundless. Furthermore, Hamilton pleaded, nothing in the evidence "ever specified the objects of the pretended connection in speculation between Reynolds and me." If the sums of $20 or $30 or $50 or a total of $1,100 that he had given Reynolds were all that was involved, "what a scale of speculation is this for the head of a public treasury" charged elsewhere with funding at $40 million a debt that ought to have been funded at $10 million or $15 million to enrich himself and his friends. Yes, Hamilton had written notes to Reynolds in a disguised or feigned hand. But this was so that Reynolds would not be able to use these notes as an "engine of false credit" with third persons. When confronted by his own accusers with these notes, Hamilton had admitted at once they were his.

Callender had snickered that Hamilton would not have paid hush money to Reynolds because Hamilton "had nothing to lose as to his reputation for chastity concerning which the world had fixed a previous opinion." A foul blow, Hamilton groaned. "No man not indelicately unprincipled with the state of manners of this country, would be willing to have a conjugal infidelity fixed upon him with positive certainty." On the contrary, he was "tender of the happiness" of his "excellent wife" and felt "extreme pain" at the affliction she would endure from the disclosure. "Those best acquainted with the interior of my domestic life will best appreciate the force of such a consideration," he agonized. He "dreaded extremely" a disclosure—and "was willing to make large sacrifices to avoid it."

Professor Harold C. Syrett, the editor of the *Hamilton Papers,* finds that "most historians" assume that the Reynolds documents are authentic and disagrees with Professor Julian Boyd.

But Hamilton's preoccupation with political "enemies" of the Jacobin scandal club, his outrage at the "gentleman" who shrank from rallying to his side to furnish him an unequivocal defense, and his old prurient preoccupation with Maria Reynolds herself, converge to make *The Reynolds Pamphlet* a far less persuasive brief for Hamilton's defense than it could have been.

Personal reflections on Maria distracted from the impact of his star defense witness's testimony when he introduced Richard Folwell, a solid and persuasive character, by saying, "The variety of shapes which this woman could assume was endless." In a conversation with

> a gentleman whom I am not a liberty publicly to name, she made a voluntary confession of her belief and even knowledge, that I was innocent of all that had been laid to my charge by *Reynolds* . . . spoke of me in exalted terms of esteem and respect, declared in the most solemn manner her extreme unhappiness lest I should suppose her accessory to the trouble which had been given me . . . and expressed her fear that the resentment of Mr. Reynolds on a *particular score* might have urged him to improper lengths of revenge.

Folwell's statement had also been deposited with William Bingham, Esquire, and shown to James Monroe.

Richard Folwell was a reputable journalist who in 1797 had published *A Short History of the Yellow Fever.* In 1801 he would issue the authorized Folwell edition of the *Journals of*

Congress, and from 1805 to 1813 he would publish a periodical called *The Spirit of the Press*, for which he solicited a subscription from Thomas Jefferson as "the principal Pillar of the public Will" and to which Jefferson subscribed for eight months. While Hamilton was in Philadelphia collecting the material for his *Reynolds Pamphlet*, Folwell wrote Hamilton's friend Edward Jones on August 12, 1797, that he had read Callender's charges against Hamilton in Nos. V and VI of his *History*, had been shocked and outraged, and wished "to see Right prevail, and Innocence protected." He had personal knowledge "that would render Improbably . . . the Imputations" that Callender had leveled at Hamilton.

According to Folwell, "a few days after Mrs. Reynolds' first appearance in Philadelphia," Folwell's mother was persuaded "to receive her for a few days into our house, as she was a stranger in the city, and had come here to endeavour to reclaim a prodigal husband, who had deserted her and his creditors in New York." Folwell's mother had taken her in because "her innocent countenance appeared to show an innocent heart." Maria soon found her husband "had been in gaol and was but just liberated." Maria and James had a meeting, she said, "but could not come to terms of pacification." In Maria, Folwell had noted the same emotional fireworks Hamilton had seen. They are on tumultuous display in Maria's letters appended to *The Reynolds Pamphlet*. "Almost at the same minute that she would declare her respect for her husband, cry and feel distressed, they would vanish, and levity succeed, with bitter execrations on her husband." Hamilton, too, had written allusively of "paroxisms" of love for a foreign mistress. Folwell at first ascribed the "inconsistency and folly" Maria displayed "to a troubled but innocent and harmless mind," until, "in one or other of these Paroxysms, she told me, so infamous was the Perfidy of Reynolds, that he had frequently . . . insisted that she should insinuate herself on certain . . . high and influential Characters . . . endeavour to make assignations with them, and actually prostitute herself to gull Money from them."

After five days of this, Folwell and his mother decided she had to leave. "She commanded commiseration," the Folwells thought, but "a character so infamous as her Husband should not enter our House."

So Maria and James Reynolds moved "to a reputable Quaker Lady's at No.——North Grant Street." There "they lived together; but . . . did not sleep together." Instead, she kept busy at night plying their trade.

"Letters were frequently found in the Entry inviting her Abroad;—and at Night she would fly off . . . to *answer* their Contents."

"Contents" of the letters or contentments of the writers? Both. So different from Hamilton's characteristic style, Folwell's sly, slightly old maidish sense of humor describing the harlot and her procurer plying their trade out of a respectable Quaker lady's boarding house rules out, for many readers at least, the possibility that Hamilton could have fabricated Folwell's testimony. His self-characterization as he also characterized the Reynoldses is too convincing to have been worked up that August in Philadelphia by a frantic, feverish, and deranged Hamilton. The respectable Quaker lady's "house eventually getting too got for them," Folwell went on, "they made their exit." Before their hasty exit, however, somebody proposed that money be paid to somebody else by a method confusingly described by Folwell as follows:

> She informed me she had proposed pecuniary aid should be rendered by her to her Husband in his Speculations, by her placing Money in a certain Gentleman's Hands, to buy of him whatever public Paper he had to sell, and that she would have that

which was purchased given to her,—and, if she could find Confidence in his future Prudence, she would eventually return him what he sold.

Later, Reynolds tried to get Folwell to "adventure with him" in Lancaster turnpike scrip. One of the Reynolds-Hamilton letters contained a similar reference to Reynold's investing in Lancaster turnpike scrip. Professor Boyd cites the above quoted passages from Folwell's statement as proof that Hamilton forged Folwell's statement as well as the Reynolds letters because, as he reasons by bootstrap, Folwell's statement ties in so neatly with Hamilton's other forgeries. This writer submits that it ties in more neatly with the disinterested character witness's testimony.

For a reader familiar with Hamilton's usual style of precisely recording—often with a true bookkeeper's mindless zeal—money transactions in his army paybook, his cash books, journals, ledgers, and Treasury Reports—even the expenses he laid out for a secret rendezvous with Angelica Church—these passages from Folwell prove the opposite of Professor Boyd's conclusion: it would be an impossibility for a man like Hamilton with such deeply ingrained habits of careful reporting of complex money transactions to describe such simple ones with such confusion.

"Some considerable Time after [if necessary, data can be procured]," Folwell testified, "they removed and lived in stile [*sic*] in a large House in Vine Street, next to the Corner of Fifth. Here I had an Invitation, and being disposed to see if possible how People supported Grandeur, without apparently Friends, Money or Industry, I accordingly called."

But at the point in time when Folwell paid his call to see this newfound "grandeur," Reynolds's latest fraudulent scheme had just been found out by Oliver Wolcott, Jr. Fallen again from his sudden grandeur, Reynolds languished in jail. Folwell sympathetically asked Maria, "In jail for what?" Out came her comical tale of Reynolds and Clingman applying for letters of administration on the supposedly deceased soldier's estate—and the solemn moment preceding by a beat the farcical denouement she describes, when "The soldier came to life." After which, Folwell concluded, "the curtain dropt from my view."

Later, Folwell received Maria's "very pathetic letter"—Hamilton well knew her pathetic mode. Folwell had mislaid it, but, as he recalled, "it would move almost anyone to serve her."

Checking himself in the nick of time as he was about to fall into this fatal Circe's circle of servitors, Folwell amended his recollection: not everyone would serve her—only someone who "was not perfectly acquainted with her character, confirmed by actual observation."

Folwell's statement said nothing of knowledge of Maria and Hamilton's affair or that Reynolds had blackmailed Hamilton, but this is not very surprising. Word of such affairs was generally forbidden to pass the lips of a proper gentleman like Folwell. Folwell's corroboration of Hamilton's own account of the Reynoldses' activities and proclivities remains a convincing piece of juridically inadmissible evidence for the defense, which Hamilton, writing his feverish public defense, all but threw away and mostly wasted.

The most important point of all about Folwell's willingness to testify for Hamilton is the fact of his having done so. Such an uninvolved man's willingness to testify for a man he did not know confirms better than any friendship-serving words could ever have done that he believed in the essential truth of Hamilton's defense and the falsity of Callender's charges. In this he agreed with the men and women of the time who knew most about the Reynolds affair and all the leading actors in it. Besides Fo!well there was his and Hamilton's helpful friend Edward Jones, Wadsworth, Wolcott, McHenry, William Jackson, and George Washington. Muhlenberg and Venable unequivocally believed his story, too. Aaron Burr told Monroe that he should believe it.

Monroe's refusal to give the same unequivocal public affirmation of his private belief in the truth of Hamilton's story, which his actions affirmed, coupled with Hamilton's deranged reaction to Monroe's cover-up of Beckley, the source of the leak, and Monroe's counterreaction to Hamilton's suspicion, deprived Hamilton of the strongest possible character witness to his public defense: James Monroe. Hamilton, not seeing this, was blinded by his obsession with his enemies.

Monroe was not directly responsible for the leak of the papers, but he, of course, had known the source of the leak all along. Hamilton knew Monroe would know. Who then was the source of the leak? And why did Monroe refuse to name him?

In his December 17, 1792, memorandum of the Reynolds affair, Thomas Jefferson had written: "Known to J[ames] M[adison], E[dmund] R[andolph] [John] Beckley and [Bernard] Webb." (The names in brackets were filled in by editors familiar with Jefferson's shorthand code.) Gentlemen with public reputations to be safeguarded by the use of such initials, like the first two men on Jefferson's list and like Monroe, could not afford to be involved in such a leak.

But a party hatchet man like John Beckley and an obscure hack like Bernard Webb had no future personal political hopes at risk—they were creatures available to do as told by principals—lack of scruples would be more or less expected of them in any event. One of the two of them was the leak.

Monroe's repeated statements that he had deposited the *originals* "in the hands of a respectable character in Virginia" was a meaningless red herring, but it shut off further inquiry that would have led straight to Beckley and Webb.

After the uproar had died down, Monroe rather casually owned up to having known all along the truth he had so evasively hidden from Hamilton. As a throwaway postscript to a letter to Aaron Burr dated December 1, 1797, Monroe wrote, "I presume that Beckley published the papers in question. By his clerk [Webb] they were copied for us."

Hamilton had been so rattled the night of December 15, 1792, that he had forgotten to ask for copies of the original documents in his hand for which his accusers had demanded his explanation; the next day he asked Monroe for copies. Monroe gave the originals to John Beckley, to be copied, and Beckley had given them to Webb. Webb had then "carried a copy to H." At H's, a second confrontation had occurred, which Beckley had told Monroe all about. Hamilton had asked Webb "('as B. says,')," "Is anyone else privy to the affair?"

Webb replied, "Beckley is."

Hamilton: "Tell Beckley I consider him bound not to disclose it."

Webb took this injunction back to Beckley.

Beckley "replied by the same clerk that he considered himself under no injunction whatever." Beckley added that "if Hamilton has anything to say to me it must be in writing."

In his December 1 letter to Burr, Monroe certified, "This from B."

To Burr, Monroe concluded with a resigned shrug and an implied grin, "After our interviews with H. I requested B. to say nothing about it."

By this extraordinary postscript Monroe was admitting to Burr that he had known all along what he had stubbornly refused to admit to Hamilton that he knew. Hamilton knew all along he was hiding it.

Monroe failed to copy this devastating postscript of self-revelation on his retained copy of his December 1 letter to Burr.

None doubted, though most averred, but not for the record, without naming Jefferson's name, that he was the highly placed "respectable character in Virginia" with whom Monroe's set of the original documents had been lodged. Only if Hamilton could succeed in goading Monroe into letting slip out the names of Beckley and Webb, would they become fair game to stalk to the lair of their lofty principal. Otherwise, no one, not even *Camillus*, though he might scatter oblique hints and insinuations and even Jefferson's name through his *Reynolds Pamphlet,* would dare to level against Jefferson the direct charge that he, the Republican empire builder, was indecently exposed as the sponsor of the leak.

It was probably awareness of this lack of forthcoming in Monroe's conduct toward him (although no one else knew of it) that caused Hamilton to fail to see that the certificate Monroe had already given him was by far the best evidence Hamilton could possibly have used to bolster the credibility of his defense: A prominent public man who was known to the public as a political enemy of Hamilton.

The threadbare lawyer who pleads his own case has a fool for a client. Hamilton's failure to present a better case in his own defense than he managed to do in *The Reynolds Pamphlet* was a self-inflicted wound. Weaknesses in his brief opened the door for James Thomson Callender and Professor Julian P. Boyd and others of their ilk to raise up new charges more serious than those he had sought to rebut by confessing to an old affair. Now his once bright prospects of being called by the Federalists to stand for the presidency were "smothered up" forever.

Upon Elizabeth, his children, Angelica, John Barker Church, and uncounted friends, clients, acquaintances, and admirers who loved him passionately, respected him deeply, liked him warmly, or admired him fervently, his public confession had inflicted incalculable pain, sorrow, regret, disappointment, and disillusionment.

Unworldly souls might call this Hamilton's finest hour—it is all but unheard of for a world statesman to indulge in such a public confession—but Talleyrand, back again in an office of power and glory, under the Directory in Paris, growing richer every day, would sadly wag his head. He might even reconsider his lofty ranking of his friend as the foremost among the three greatest statesmen of his world. In a period of remission from the spells of nervous derangement that had allowed him to fall on his sword, Hamilton would come to feel the depth of the wound *The Reynolds Pamphlet* had inflicted on him and all who loved him. He would see himself, as he saw so much else, as Talleyrand would see him, and suffer fatal disenchantment with himself.

32

My Own Opinion of My Own Pretensions: Quasi Commander of the Quasi War

[Washington] compelled me to promote . . . the most restless, impatient, artful, indefatigable, unprincipled intriguer in the United States, if not in the world, to be second in command under himself.

—John Adams

You can hardly conceive what a powerful interest is made for Hamilton. . . . That man would in my mind become a second Buonaparty if he was possessed of equal power.

—Abigail Adams to William S. Smith, July 7, 1798

War? War with France? The very thought of war with the ally of the Revolution, with the great senior partner in the Treaty of Paris of 1778, first announced at Valley Forge, was unthinkable. But in relations between nations it often is a process of no more than a year or two for the impossible to evolve into the unthinkable, the unthinkable into the unmentionable, the unmentionable into the debatable, and the debatable into a torrid political issue, until the unthinkable has become official policy. American ratification of Jay's Treaty with Britain had touched off a powder train that through 1797 and 1798 would result in the first of the nation's undeclared wars: The Quasi War with France of 1798–1800.

As disclosure of the Reynolds scandal was breaking, Hamilton received a letter from his old friend and protégé Rufus King, now American minister in London, written June 27,

1797, that added to the pressures on his mind. A copy of John Adams's (and Hamilton's) special message to Congress of May 16 had just reached London.

"It has arrived at a critical hour," King said ominously, adding, "These are days of wonder. The march already made by France has astonished, and confounded almost every beholder . . . All Italy will be overturned—Venice is no more; Genoa has been completely revolutionized; Portugal sees, but seems unable to escape her fate." Napoleon Bonaparte was installing puppet governments subservient to France all over the continent. But this was only the first stage of the threat Napoleonic France posed to the world. Neither Britain nor the United States nor the rest of the Western Hemisphere was safe. "She meditates and will attempt projects still more gigantic—which will operate a change in the whole face of Europe, and extend to every other quarter of the Globe," King warned.

French cruisers had captured 316 American ships as prizes in 1795. France had laid embargoes on American ships at Bordeaux, seized American goods for public use without paying for them, and condemned American ships and cargoes under laws that violated her commercial treaties with the United States. On Christmas Day of 1796 a French privateer had fired a broadside into the unresisting American ship *Commerce*, wounding four of the crewmen. In March 1797 a French armed brig had captured the *Cincinnatus* out of Baltimore and tortured the American captain with thumb screws to make him say that his cargo was English property so the French could then confiscate it legally. When he refused to blurt out a false confession, they robbed him and plundered his ship's provisions.

The French justified their plundering of American commerce as reprisals for America's allegedly abandoning the principle of "free ships, free goods." This meant that if a ship flew the flag of a neutral country, neither the vessel nor the cargo it carried, as long as it was not contraband such as guns or ammunition, was subject to capture. But now, the French claimed, the broad definition of contraband of war in Jay's Treaty gave the British excuse for seizing many new classes of goods, as well as the ships that carried them.

Secretary of State Timothy Pickering feared that France, by recovering Louisiana from Spain, intended "to renew the ancient plan of her monarch of *circumscribing* and encircling what now constitutes the Atlantic States."

The shrewdest and most effective avatar of France's old dream of accomplishing exactly what Pickering and John Quincy Adams feared most in Louisiana was none other than Hamilton's old friend and admirer Talleyrand. In July 1797, less than a week before John Marshall and Elbridge Gerry would set jail to join Charles Cotesworth Pinckney as American commissioners on the peace mission to France that Hamilton had urged on Adams, the Directory had restored Talleyrand to official favor by appointing him as its new minister of foreign affairs.

On October 8 the commissioners met with Talleyrand for the first time, but only informally, not officially, at his home. From then on, for more than six months, Talleyrand kept them dangling in Paris while Napoleon consolidated his mastery of Europe, and the Directory became more hostile and warlike toward America. In January, with the three Americans still cooling their heels in Paris, the Directory adopted a harsh new decree which would permit French ships to seize all American ships having any English goods of any kind aboard, whether such goods were contraband of war or not. It was insult direct to the already long-suffering commissioners.

The instructions the commissioners had brought with them were to carry out Hamilton's foreign policy of seeking to put an end to all French seizures, not to provoke more rigorous anti-American decrees like the new one just adopted. Talleyrand and the Directory refused to accord Marshall, Pinckney, and Gerry any official reception. Instead, while he kept them dangling, he sent various agents and emissaries to demand from them loans and bribes of various sorts. The main bribe demanded was one million two hundred thousand *livres*, or approximately a quarter of a million dollars, "for the purpose of making the customary distribution in diplomatic affairs" to Talleyrand himself, to the directors, and to various other officials, or so the American commissioners were told. In addition, the Americans must make them a "loan" by buying 32 million Dutch florins, paying their face value of $12.8 million, and thereby giving France a profit of more than 100 percent because the discounted current market value was only $6 million.

In great indignation, the commissioners refused.

Hottinguer threatened all-out war on America. The commissioners should beware of the "power and violence of France."

The commissioners replied that if war came, the United States would defend itself.

"You do not speak to the point," Hottinguer cried. "It is money, it is expected that you will offer money."

"We have already answered that demand," the commissioners retorted.

"No you have not," Hottinguer insisted. "What is your answer?"

Charles Cotesworth Pinckney told him again with scorn: "It is no, no; not a sixpence."

And back in America, "No, no, not a sixpence!" soon became one of two great political rallying cries for the Federalist faithful.

Alarming news was coming back from Britain that the Bank of England had stopped cash payments; that an alliance between France, Holland, and Spain was bringing together a battle fleet larger than Britain's; and that Napoleon was poised at Boulogne, gathering a force of veterans known as the *Armée d'Angleterre*, to launch an invasion across the channel. On January 24, 1798, Adams asked his department heads to furnish him with their recommendations for dealing with these mounting threats. What should he do if France continued to rebuff the commissioners? Should he declare war? Or an embargo? What if England fell, and with her the protection her command of the seas afforded America against Napoleonic encirclement by control of Louisiana and Florida? Should the United States seek an alliance with Britain? Would the conflict bewteen the two great powers lead to civil war between their partisans within the United States?

On January 26, 1798, McHenry, as usual, forwarded Adams's inquiries to Hamilton for answer, entreating him "will you assist me or rather your country with such suggestions and opinions as may occur to you. . . . I cannot do such justice to the subject as you can." Though heavily engaged in court in Albany, Hamilton replied within two weeks.

The first and most important point that should guide McHenry's thinking, he said, was the views of the American people. "There is a very general and strong aversion to war in the minds of the people of this country," Hamilton noted. "Next there is nothing to be gained by a formal war with France." This would "take all the chances of evil which can accrue from the vengeance of France stimulated by success." Therefore, his conclusion was that the course to be pursued was "a truly vigorous defensive plan, with the countenance of a readiness still to negotiate."

Outraged by the bribe demand, Marshall and Pinckney broke off negotiations with Talleyrand, quarreled with Gerry, and left Paris in April of 1798. Gerry remained there alone as a presence and symbol of nonwarlike American intentions toward France until August. In January, Hamilton had advised McHenry that, even if rebuffed, "if one or more of our commissioners remain in Europe it may be expedient to leave him there (say in Holland) to have the air of still being disposed to meet any opening to accommodation." An embargo against France, he added, "seems now to be out of place and ineligible."

As to England, it is "best in any event to avoid *alliance*. Mutual interest will command as much from her as Treaty." With a treaty "we take all the chances of her fall. Twill be best not to be entangled." For "a truly vigorous defensive plan," Hamilton urged that, in the event of failure of the negotiations, merchant vessels should arm for defense; that the three frigates whose construction had been delayed, the *Constitution,* the *United States*, and the *Constellation*, be completed as quickly as possible; that more be built in the event of open rupture; that a number of smaller sloops of war of 10 to 20 guns each be built or converted; that a regular army of 20,000 men, including 2,000 cavalry, be raised; and that an auxiliary provisional army of 30,000 also be organized.

To support these preparedness measures, all sources of revenue should be seized, and a loan raised. "By taking a *rank* hold from the commencement, we shall the better avoid an accumulation of debt. This object is all important," Hamilton exhorted. With all this, the "hope of accommodation without open rupture ought not to be abandoned while measures of self preservation ought not to be omitted or delayed." All should be done by Adams "with *manly* but *calm* and *sedate* firmness and without strut."

As far as they went, Hamilton's recommendations generally reflected Wolcott's and Pickering's views, as well as those of Attorney General Charles Lee, but Pickering and Lee now went farther than Hamilton. Like other extreme Federalists, but not Hamilton, both contemplated seizing Louisiana from Spain before France could reacquire it. Pickering wanted to form an alliance with England. Lee recommended recall of the three commissioners and an immediate declaration of war.

McHenry rewrote Hamilton's plan with a few changes in his own hand and sent it on to Adams as his own. As it turned out, Adams's policy in the ensuing crisis closely followed the guidelines Hamilton offered in this letter, except in one respect that to Hamilton was as important as anything else, the matter of style. Instead of carrying out Hamilton's policy steadily, in a manner that was "solemn and manly" and "grave and firm but without invective" and, in two words, "without strut," Adams in his manner seemed to oscillate back and forth between extremes of belligerency and pusillanimity. By so doing, as Hamilton saw it, he nullified the useful effects that consistent adherence to either one policy or the other might have produced. His vacillations exacerbated both provocative effects abroad, and divisive effects at home, the dangers inherent in both extremities.

When the dispatches describing Talleyrand's bribe demands and other insults to the commissioner arrived in Philadelphia on March 4, Adams's first reaction was a lunge toward all-out war. On March 13 he asked his department heads whether he should not recommend "an immediate declaration of war." Should he whip up public enthusiasm for war by making public the whole story of French insults to the commissioners, including the bribe demands and Pinckney's "No, no, not a sixpence"? Disregarding Hamilton's more moderate advice, Adams drafted a war message to Congress denouncing the Directory. In it he demanded from Congress "a state of declared war." He was full of empty "strut."

Mere arming of vessels would not be enough. It would be inefficient and dangerous to American lives, said Adams. "All men will think it more honorable and glorious to the national character when its existence as an independent nation is at stake," Adams wrote, "that hostilities should be avowed in a formal declaration of war."

Then, coming round to Hamilton's view, Adams rewrote his message, omitted from it his demand for a declaration of war, and called instead for limited hostilities. He recommended that Congress adopt most of the other measures of quasi war that Hamilton had called for. He followed the substantive program Hamilton had advised, but omitted steadiness of style.

Jefferson called his message "insane" or almost so in its truculence. Bache's *Aurora* of

Philadelphia charged that Adams had, in effect, declared war on the side of England without consulting Congress and the people. Republicans joined by some of the more extreme Federalists in Congress demanded for opposite reasons that all the deciphered dispatches from the three commissioners be laid before to the House.

On April 3, Adams complied, sending over all the dispatches, but substituting for the names of Hubbard, Beaumarchais, Hottinguer, Bellamy, and Hauteval the letters *W, X, Y,* and *Z.* Congress voted that copies of the dispatches be reprinted and distributed. Wide republication whipped up American public opinion to a frenzy of self-righteous outrage over the degrading bribe demand rebuffed that came to be known in infamy as the XYZ Affair.

To Hamilton Adams's policies seemed to be lurching toward war without foresight or plan or advice—other than his repeated calls for advice from aides so inept that Hamilton had to supply them with all the answers.

"The enlightened friend of America never saw greater occasion of disquietude than at the present juncture," was the way Hamilton began a public broadside entitled "The Stand No. I," signed *Titus Manlius,* which appeared in the *New York Commercial Advertiser* on March 30, 1798, the first of a series of six articles from *Titus Manlius* that would appear as the crisis continued to deepen that spring. The people's views were what counted, and they had to be brought around to backing the government if there were to be a war crisis. Hamilton denounced the current French Directory dominated by Napoleon as the most "flagitious, despotic and vindictive that ever disgraced the annals of mankind." It was "marching with hasty and colossal strides to universal empire in a hideous project wielding with absolute authority the whole physical force of the most powerful nation on earth." To protect the United States against its veteran French troops "drenched with blood and slaughter and led by a skillful and daring chief," Hamilton called for firm support of the "respectable" defensive measures he had earlier recommended to Adams through McHenry, Pickering, and Wolcott. In "The Stand No. II," Hamilton applied Alexander Pope's definition of "vice" to the revolutionary government of France. It was

> A MONSTER of such horrid mien,
> As to be *hated*, needs but to be *seen*.

The emotional tone of his broadsides was well calculated to bring members of the public still open to persuasion around to backing the government, but Hamilton's summons to action did not call for anything more than limited hostilities—quasi war.

Through the series runs an undercurrent of criticism of the style and manner of John Adams's government in dealing with the crisis: "How great is the cause to lament," *Titus Manlius* grieved, "how afflicting to every heart, alive to the honour and interest of the country, that distracted and inefficient councils, a palsied and unconscious state of the public mind afford too little assurance of measures adequate to the urgency of the evils or dangers."

Republicans took the line that France and the Directory had not caused the trouble, the villain was Talleyrand alone; Bache's *Aurora* of April 7 turned the knife of blame back on Hamilton: "M. Talleyrand is notoriously anti Republican; he was the intimate friend of Mr. Hamilton, Mr. King and other great federalists." Bache concluded "that it is probably owing to the determined hostility which Talleyrand discovered in them toward France, that the government of that country considers us only objects for plunder." Jefferson detected hopeful signs of open insurrection in Pennsylvania and "inquietude" in New Hampshire and New York.

Factious divisions within the country cut deeper. War hysteria rose. Samuel Sewall of Massachusetts introduced into Congress the defense program Hamilton had outlined to McHenry, including the Navy Department. President Adams set aside May 9 as the day for fasting and prayer that Hamilton had called for. There were anti-French sermons, and riots between pro-French Republican wearers of French tricolor cockades or all red Republican cockades and Federalist wearers of their recently adopted black cockade badge, like the cockades worn by soldiers in the American Revolution, "as the open and visible sign of Federalism."

From May to August, Adams stomped about the country making demagogic speeches that linked "foreign hostility with domestic treachery." He told a Vermont regiment that the Directory was trying to obtain control over the American government. "Rather than this I say with you let us have war!" he cried. He whipped up another crowd shouting, "The finger of destiny writes on the wall the word: war!"

Jonathan Dayton announced that troops Napoleon Bonaparte was massing in Boulogne and other French ports under the name of *Armée d'Angleterre* were, in fact, about to embark for an amphibious assault on the United States itself. Pickering told Robert Goodloe Harper of South Carolina that France was secretly fomenting a slave rebellion in the South and would support it with an invasion from the island colony on the western part of the island of Hispaniola, then called Saint-Domingue.

When John Marshall returned to Philadelphia on June 18 to a hero's homecoming banquet at Oeller's Hotel, the thirteenth of the 16 toasts was "Millions for defense, but not one cent for tribute!" It became a second Federalist rallying cry to match Pinckney's "No, no, not a sixpence!"

Adams and the Federalists rammed through Congress the Naturalization Act, the Alient Friends Act, and the Alien Enemy and Sedition Acts. The Naturalization Act extended the period of residence for an alien before he could become a citizen from five to 14 years. The Alien Friends Act gave Adams the power to deport any aliens deemed to be "dangerous to the peace and safety of the United States." The Alien Enemies Act, which would apply only in the event of declared war or invasion, gave the president power to restrain, arrest, or deport enemy aliens. The Sedition Law was intended as a gag on the hostile press. It prescribed punishment by fine and imprisonment for conspiracies or scandalous statements against the government; it was to expire on the last day of Adams's term of office.

Hamilton deplored these repressive laws. "Let us not be cruel or violent," he counseled Pickering on June 7. The Sedition Act was "highly exceptionable" and objectionable and "may endanger civil war." It should "not be hurried through. Let us not establish a tyranny. Energy is a very different thing from violence. If we push things to an extreme we shall then give to faction *body* and solidarity." When he complained to Pickering that, at the distance of New York City from the capital, his difficulty was that he "does not see all the cards," Pickering urged him to come to Philadelphia. "I wish you were in a situation not only 'to see all the cards' but to play them," he wrote. To a better player like Hamilton, Pickering would "give you my *hand* on the same side *to win the stakes.*"

Throughout the crisis, Hamilton's policy remained one of evenhanded dealing with both Britain and France. "The same measure to both of them," he insisted, "though it should ever furnish the extraordinary spectacle of a nation at war with two nations at war with each other. . . . It will evince that we are neither *Greeks* nor *Trojans*." When Governor John

Jay offered Hamilton an appointment to the United States Senate to fill the seat vacated by the appointment of John Sloss Hobart to a federal judgeship, Hamilton declined to join Pickering in Philadelphia to play the cards from the position of a mere senator. As such he would have less influence than he already had as the undercover Federalist prime minister in New York.

When Congress finally adjourned on June 19, the formal declaration of all-out war that Adams had at first thought called for and Hamilton had feared and opposed, remained unadopted, dead, at least until the next session. Hamilton's program of defensive preparedness, not Adams's push of policy toward war, remained the government's policy.

"To have a good army on foot will be the best of all precautions to prevent as well as repel invasion," Hamilton proclaimed as *Titus Manlius* in "The Stand No. VI" on April 19. But who would command such an army? In rather peremptory Dutch Uncle fashion on May 19, Hamilton wrote Washington, telling him he would have to assume command and how best to go about it. Washington should first make a ceremonial circuit through Virginia and North Carolina "which would throw the weight of your character into the scale of government." Then, "in the event of an open rupture the public voice will again call you to command the armies of your country . . . you will be compelled to make the sacrifice." Washington in command again would "give an additional spring to the public mind."

Washington groaned. Though he would have no choice but to return to public life if called, he would do so with "as much reluctance . . . as I should do to the tombs of my ancestors." He flatly refused to go out on the Southern junket. Hamilton replied on June 2, satisfied that at least he would not refuse to serve as commander in an "adequate emergency." As for himself, Hamilton added, "if I am invited *to a station in which the sacrifice I may render is proportioned to the sacrifice I am to make,* I shall be willing to go into the army. If you command," said Hamilton, his own place ought to be "Inspector General with a command in the line."

Here now was dealt a hand to be played for the highest command below Washington's own.

At the end of June, Hamilton journeyed to Philadelphia so he could not only "see all the cards" but play them. Shortly before he left New York, he had written to Betsy in Albany that "I continue to enjoy good health and my spirits are as good as they can be in absence of my love." He went on, "But I find as I grow older her presence becomes more necessary to me. In proportion as I discover the worthlessness of other pursuits, the value of my Eliza and of domestic happiness rises in my estimation." Nevertheless, his closing line to her was of other pursuits: "There is every prospect that we shall not put on the French yoke."

Under the urgings of Hamilton and others, Congress finally authorized the president to increase the regular army, in accordance with tables of organization largely laid out by Hamilton, by an "additional army" of 10,000 men and also to call up a "Provisional Army" of 50,000 more, including 12 infantry regiments of 700 men each and six troops of light dragoons, but only when and if full-scale war should begin or when the president decided that national security was threatened by invasion. Congress also authorized calling 80,000 militia to active duty if necessary. A formal declaration of war would thus automatically lead to the calling up of an army many times larger than any Washington had commanded at any time during the Revolution.

By July 4, Washington still had not received the word that Adams had appointed him lieutenant general and commander in chief of the new army. He wrote the secretary of war and the president to say that, if called to serve, he demanded a free hand in naming his principal subordinate officers whom he "considered as so many parts of the commander in chief.'' Adams looked to Washington for advice as to whether to rely on ''old generals . . . or appoint a young set?'' Washington said selections must be made ''without respect to grade.'' To McHenry, Washington insisted still more emphatically that he must have the choice of his own staff of officers. Some he had in mind, like Hamilton, he thought would not agree to serve under anyone but him. Writing Washington from Philadelphia on July 8, Hamilton was critical of Adams for having announced Washington's appointment publicly and having it ratified by the Senate all without having received Washington's prior consent to serve.

Another problem to Hamilton was that Adams ''has no relative ideas and his prepossessions on military subjects in reference to such a point are of the wrong sort.'' It was essential that all arrangements be ''such as you would approve.''

Washington approved.

Secretary of State Pickering urged upon Washington that Hamilton rank second only to him ''and Chief in your absence.'' All felt unspoken, or spoke of, concern for who might succeed to the supreme command should the aging and infirm Washington be disabled or die. President Adams was all for giving Hamilton a lower place.

But to Washington, Hamilton's services ''ought to be secured at almost any price.'' Almost. The difficulty was that any French invasion would strike at the southern coast below Maryland, the weakest, most partisan flank, closest to French possessions, full of sullen, rebellious slaves eager to be armed against their masters. This Southern strategy suggested that General Charles Cotesworth Pinckney of South Carolina should be first of the generals. He enjoyed high military and public reputation and influential family connections, was indispensable to Southern resistance, and, being senior in rank to Hamilton from the Revolution, would probably refuse to serve under him now. However, Pinckney was still over in France, and if he would not be returning soon, Hamilton might be preferred.

After spending five days with Washington at Mount Vernon, McHenry brought back to President Adams word of Washington's acceptance of command. Washington had ''love and esteem'' for Knox, but ranked him below both Pinckney and Hamilton. Washington's tentative list of general officers put Hamilton first, but he was fearful lest Pinckney, if made junior to Hamilton, would refuse to serve. Anyhow, President Adams must ''use his pleasure.'' When McHenry brought the list in to Adams while he was at breakfast with Abigail on July 17, Adams questioned McHenry sharply. McHenry insisted the order of names was the one Washington had insisted on, which also happened to be in alphabetical order. Adams wrote out the list for submission to the Senate with the names in Washington's order. To the list, which included a number of other names, Adams added that of his son-in-law, William S. Smith of New York, to be a brigadier general and adjutant general. Pickering and McHenry strongly objected to Smith, but Adams insisted.

Washington told Hamilton that he wanted his former aide as ''coadjutor and assistant'' (whatever his relative ranking might be), but the obvious problem was that if Hamilton were to be made senior major general, he would have to be leapfrogged over the heads of the other senior major generals, Knox and Pinckney, who had far outranked him at the end of the Revolution. Adams completely agreed. He held up issuing the commissions.

In Philadelphia, Pickering loyally reported to Hamilton all he had done to help his promotion along. Hamilton replied to Pickering by letter on July 17 that he was ''content to be second to Knox, if *thought indispensable. Pinckney,* if placed over me puts me a grade lower. . . . I am willing that the relative ranks may remain open to future settlement. . . . I am not satisfied with the principle that every officer of higher rank in the late army is to be above me . . . this will not accord with my own opinions of my own pretensions.'' Public opinion was of great importance: a rank below the highest would ''fall far short of public opinion.'' Few had made as many sacrifices as he. To few others ''would a military appointment be so injurious as to myself—if with this sacrifice, I am to be degraded below my just claim in public opinion—ought I to acquiesce?'' He would if he had to accept second, but not third place.

The Senate approved the list of appointees in the order presented, with Hamilton's name listed first. It rejected William S. Smith, and Adams would add that to his score of grievances against Hamilton. Adams went home to Quincy without having signed the generals' commissions. By July 29, Hamilton was becoming increasingly impatient and annoyed with what he saw as further proof of Adams's wavering, indecisiveness, incompetence, and personal hostility. He wrote Washington: ''With regard to the delicate subject of the relative rank of major generals, it is very natural for me to be a partial judge, and it is not very easy for me to speak upon it.'' But public opinion drove him to do so: ''In a case like this, am I not to take the opinion of others as my guide? It is a fact, there is a flood of evidence that a great majority of leading federal men were of opinion, that in the event of your declining command of the army, it ought to devolve upon me, and that in case of your acceptance, which everybody ardently desired, the place of second in command ought to be mine.''

There was another side to it, Hamilton added, that was ''of far greater moment'' than the relative rank of the general officers. That was ''that my friend McHenry, is wholly insufficient for his place, with additional misfortune of not having himself the least suspicion of the fact!''

True as it was—Hamilton had the evidence, in all of McHenry's appeals to him for help—it was a rather shocking thing for Hamilton to say about his loyal, old, admiring friend, McHenry. But by saying so here in his letter to Washington, he was leading from his strongest suit. All acknowledged Hamilton's abilities as an administrator, if not as a commanding general. ''You perhaps may not be aware of the whole extent of the insufficiency.'' He knew Washington knew McHenry well—''It is so great as to leave no probability that the business of the War Department can make any tolerable progress in his hands.'' This was particularly true in view of ''the large scale upon which he is now to act.''

Obviously, neither Knox nor Pinckney had the administrative skill to plug up such a large insufficiency in a crisis, in which ultimate blame for the results of any insufficiency would inevitably fall on Washington. Coming to Philadelphia, Hamilton now was playing his hand for all it was worth.

''My real friendship for McHenry concurring with my zeal for service predisposed me to aid him in all that he could properly throw upon me . . . the organization of the army . . . the conduct of the recruiting service,'' Hamilton wrote. But there remained much to do. ''The idea had been thus far very partially embraced.'' Without first place in formal rank and status, Hamilton could not be properly useful. The mere thought of trying to preside with credit over such a large new enterprise with no coadjutors but the inept McHenry, an aging limited Knox, and a remote Pinckney must have made the reluctant Washington shudder. It would be all aging chiefs and no young Indians: Hamilton knew the strength of the card he was leading. To bring matters to a head, he suggested that Washington summon the major generals to Philadelphia to begin contingency planning for the war. But Knox still insisted on clear rank over Hamilton and Pinckney. Adams, mindful of the political damage his rebuff to Knox would do in his own New England, finally made up his mind to issue the commissions. He made Knox the senior major general.

He thought he saw a clever way out of the impasse with Washington by declaring that the

Senate's order of nomination of the major generals meant nothing. What governed was "rank according to antecedent services." This way, Hamilton, of course, would have no rank above any other major general and no command in the line. Adams was "willing to settle all decisively" by dating the commissions in order of Knox first, Pinckney second, Hamilton third. Such power was in the president, and he was ready to exercise it. Learning from McHenry of Adams's final decision, Hamilton, perhaps recalling his earlier brinkmanship—resignation of his commission in protest had ultimately won him his command at Yorktown—wrote the secretary of war on September 8, "My mind is unalterably made up. I shall certainly not hold the commission on the plan proposed."

Letters crisscrossed; injunctions of senders to burn them lest embarrassment follow went unheeded. Washington learned from McHenry that Adams had reversed Washington's own order of ranking. But to hear it from him officially, Washington addressed an unusually long letter to Adams, reiterating his reasons for placing Hamilton's name first.

Washington had written stiffly, "I have addressed you, Sir, with openness and candor, and I hope with respect, requesting to be informed, whether your determination to reverse the order of the three Major-Generals is final. . . ." The implication was clear: Washington might resign himself.

Events shoved Adams unhappily toward one of the most distasteful self-reversals of a life of many.

To prideful President Adams it must have come as a shock that, like his party in Congress and his principal department heads, his commander in chief was also under the thumb of the upstart outsider in New York. Unlike Adams's descent from an ancient "virtuous and irreproachable race of people," in whom he took great pride, Hamilton, said Adams, was nothing but "a bastard brat of a Scotch Pedlar."

Cursing Hamilton, Adams caved in. He dated all three major generals' commissions the same day, explaining ingenuously to Washington that he had done so "in hopes, similar to yours, that an amicable adjustment, or acquiescence, might take place among the gentlemen themselves. But, if these hopes should be disappointed and controversies should arise, they will, of course, be submitted to you as Commander-in-Chief, and if, after all any one should be so obstinate as to appeal to me from the judgment of the Commander-in-Chief, I was determined to confirm that judgment."

This saved face all around and fudged the question of ultimate responsibility. Washington promptly made Hamilton second to himself in titular command, which meant first in actual command, at least until Congress should formally declare war. He would be the quasi commander of the Quasi War.

Henry Knox, fat and old and sick, struggling under intense personal pressures from creditors to pay debts, refused to serve under Hamilton. His plaint to McHenry could be read as another Hamilton testimonial: ". . . Mr. Hamilton's talents have been estimated upon a scale of comparison so transcendent, that all his seniors in rank and years of the late army, have been degraded by his elevation." Knox could not "act under a constant sense of public insult and injury."

It was Pickering who had made the surprise ploy that won his leader the appointment to the first place. "Altho', by the delay of the nominations one day," he wrote Hamilton, "I received your letter expressing your willingness to serve under Knox, yet I concealed it, in order that the arrangement of nominations . . . by Genl Washington . . . which I saw would govern, might leave you . . . in the first place."

"The sun begins to shine," McHenry wrote Hamilton on October 5, 1798: To which Hamilton responded: "I cannot but observe with satisfaction the conclusion of your letter as to the relative rank of the three major-generals.''

It was a characteristic understatement by Hamilton to express much satisfaction.

To burn away the miasmic clouds which *The Reynolds Pamphlet* had cast over his public credit, no brighter beams of sunlight could be imagined by Hamilton than those reflected from the brand-new major-general's stars pinned on his epaulets by Adams's palsied and reluctant hands, forced there by Washington's invisible hand, which had in turn been forced by Hamilton's invisible hand, with a last helpful lucky finesse from Pickering.

By way of clinching his comeback, Hamilton forced Adams's hand on yet another important issue. Adams had nominated Aaron Burr, for whom he had high regard, for the rank of brigadier general. Hamilton and his triumvirate reminded Washington that Burr was an ''intriguer.'' Washington vetoed Burr's name, on the ground that Burr was an intriguer.

Hamilton, through his cabinet and Washington, calling Burr an intriguer? Adams all but atomized in choleric bursts of outrage at such procacity. Years later he was still fulminating: ''How shall I describe to you my sensations and reflections at the moment?'' he spluttered splenetically. Washington ''compelled me to promote, over the heads of Lincoln, Gates, Clinton, and Knox and . . . Pinckney, one of his own triumvirate, the most restless, impatient, artful, indefatigable, unprincipled intriguer in the United States, if not in the world, to be second in command under himself.''

And now, in Aaron Burr, that ''bastard brat'' Hamilton ''dreaded an intriguer in a poor brigadier.''

All the same, Adams was not allowed to appoint Aaron Burr, the Reynoldses' lawyer, or even his own son-in-law, William S. Smith, to the rank of brigadier. Hamilton might have been wiser to let Adams and Burr and Smith win a few little throwaway hands like these.

He had played the cards he held for all they were worth and had a pinch of winner's luck besides. On July 9, the night before leaving Philadelphia for home, the quasi commander of the quasi war wrote Betsy a letter in a very commanding tone: ''I command you as you love me to take care of yourself, to keep up your spirits, and to remember always that my happiness is inseparable from yours.'' Like a small boy with a new toy, in the closing line he added that Decatur's capture of a 12-gun French privateer ''gives general satisfaction.'' Oh yes, and ''God bless my beloved. A. Hamilton.''

When Congress adjourned on July 19, 1798, with the war crisis and the political divisions within the country becoming more menacing, John and Abigail Adams set off northward as usual for Quincy. Testimonial receptions and dinners at towns along his and Abigail's northward route fed his vanity, and he responded with ripsnorting speeches that whipped up listeners' enthusiasm for a declaration of all-out war. But by time they reached Quincy Abigail was seriously ill, and the ''black cockade fever'' for war was receding.

While the Adamses remained in Quincy during the summer's dispute over Hamilton's appointment which was not finally resolved until October, Hamilton did not so much usurp power in the capital as simply lay hold on slack reins that Adams idly let slip through his fingers. Hamilton's subalterns Pickering, McHenry, and Wolcott, secretaries of state, war, and the treasury—and, to a lesser extent, Benjamin Stoddard, secretary of the navy, and Charles Lee, the attorney general—all sought out his views. So did so-called High Federalists in Congress like George Cabot, Stephen Higginson, Theodore Sedgwick, Fisher Ames, and Philip Schuyler and others.

Rufus King, minister in London, kept Hamilton informed of developments abroad. Hamilton was the leader of a strong Federalist party in his home city, state, and nation, a potential future presidential candidate, as well as the most visible target for all Republican abuse, which reinforced his high standing with his own party.

From the abstracted distance of Mount Vernon, Washington told Hamilton pointedly to "Give, without delay, your *full* aid to the Secretary of War." Hamilton set to work.

Without dissent, all military experts whose opinions Hamilton obtained recommended the establishment of a national army—despite the existence of the militia, despite the Confederation's slight financial resources—in order to protect the frontiers, to defend settlers and property there against the Indians, and to maintain internal order in extreme situations.

But would not the militia be enough for these functions?

No, von Steuben snorted, recommmending a horse guard to protect the government. "Congress and its followers should never be exposed to the Mad proceedings of a Mob." The country also needed the skeleton of a regular army in peacetime to serve as a model for expansion into wartime armies. Hamilton reported, "There are conclusive reasons in favor of federal in preference to state establishments." But the federal military establishment recommended by Hamilton's civilian congressional committee was less extensive than those recommended by Washington and the other experts. If Hamilton's motive in championing a peacetime military establishment had been to serve his own political aggrandizement, for patronage, or some other such unworthy purpose conventionally ascribed by scholars to him as their chief horrific exemplar of "American militarism," his recommendations would have sought a larger military establishment, one not less extensive than those the other military experts recommended.

At the Constitutional Convention there was not the slightest doubt among the majority that the new government had to be able to create a standing army and navy. When the "raise armies" clause was considered in August 1787, the convention changed the wording to "raise and support" to make the authority for peacetime national forces unmistakable. Gouverneur Morris wrote to Moss Kent on January 2, 1815, remembering that "those, who, during the Revolutionary storm, had confidential acquaintance with the conduct of affairs"—his friend Hamilton had more than any other member of his committee—"knew well that to rely on militia was to lean on a broken reed."

Hamilton's Numbers 8, 16, and 22 through 29 of *The Federalist* are largely devoted to the same subject. Hamilton characteristically began with first principles in No. 23:

> Whether there ought to be a Federal Government intrusted with the care of the common defence, is a question in the first instance open to discussion; but the moment it is decided in the affirmative, it will follow, that that government ought to be cloathed with all the powers requisite to the execution of its trust . . . if we are in earnest about giving the Union energy and duration, we must abandon the vain project of legislating upon the states in their collective capacities; we must extend the laws of the Federal Government to the individual citizens of America.

Hamilton sympathized with the traditional fear of militarism and standing armies. Such fear arose in England after the Norman Conquest, he explained in No. 26, when "the authority of the Monarch was almost unlimited," and his standing armies encroached on the liberties of the people. But after the "revolution in 1688, which elevated the Prince of Orange to the throne, the kingly prerogative was abolished, and it became an article of the Bill of Rights then framed that the raising or keeping a standing army within the kingdom in time of peace, *unless with consent of Parliament* was against law." The same restraint was created for the American people by the constitutional provisions restricting congressional military appropriations to two years, Hamilton pointed out. This obliges Congress "once at least in every two years, to deliberate upon the propriety of keeping a military force on foot; to come to a new resolution on the point; and to declare their sense of the matter, by a formal vote in the face of their constituents. They are not *at liberty* to vest in the executive department permanent funds for the support of an army." As if by prescript, in reply to the conventional cavils of critics, Hamilton adds dryly in No. 26, "The provision for the support of a military force will always be a favourable topic for declamation."

"The fabric of American Empire," he had counselled in No. 22, "ought to rest on the solid basis of THE CONSENT OF THE PEOPLE. The streams of national power ought to flow immediately from that pure original fountain of all legitimate authority." In No. 25, he adds that a prohibition against the

> . . . *raising* of armies in time of peace . . . would exhibit the most extraordinary spectacle, which the world has yet seen—that of a nation incapacitated by its constitution to prepare for defence, before it was actually invaded. . . . We must receive the blow before we could even prepare to return it. We must expose our property and liberty to the mercy of foreign invaders, and invite them, by our weakness, to seize the naked and defenceless as prey.

Hamilton's military peace establishment was to consist of only four regiments of infantry and one of artillery incorporated in the Corps of Engineers. Each infantry regiment would consist of two battalions, each battalion of four companies, each company of 64 rank and file, to be recruited up to 128 rank and file in time of war. His total force of 2,048 peacetime infantrymen would hardly be an awe-inspiring juggernaut. Yet its mission was to protect thousands of miles of frontiers and interior territories that extended from the farthest reaches of Maine, west beyond Fort Michilimackinac, to Lake of the Woods in Minnesota, down the Mississippi to Louisiana, east to Florida, and up all the continental coastal reaches northward back to Maine. Such a tiny army might easily get itself lost or massacred by Indians in so vast a sector of operations. Congress had approved a plan similar to Hamilton's recommendation in June 1794, and this led to creation of the Legion—the first real American peacetime military establishment.

Hamilton did his best to raise and outfit the Quasi War army from practically nothing in the face of public apathy and partisan hostility. In his own party, Adams, after his humiliation on the generalships, was bitterly hostile to Hamilton.

It was harder to recruit privates than generals for service in an undeclared war in what still appeared to be a time of peace. Much of the work was routine, or confined him to petty details that subordinates far down the line could as easily have dispatched, had there been such subordinates. Hamilton had only a single aide, his nephew, Angelica and John Church's son, Captain Philip Church, who took care of copying dispatches and as much of the other office detail work as he could manage. A secretary was later added to the staff, but a large proportion of the reports and other communications, many dealing with trivial matters, are written in Hamilton's own hand. James McHenry, the secretary of war, who had been at least nominally responsible for the prior neglect of preparedness, seemed incapable of managing a preparedness program on any new enlarged scale.

Washington agreed with Hamilton as to "the unfitness of a certain Gentleman for the office he holds." He told McHenry to permit Hamilton to take full charge of matters that would ordinarily belong to the War Department. General Gunn wrote Hamilton:

> I am persuaded it can be no part of your plan merely to execute the feeble arrangements of other men. The President has no Talent for War, and McHenry is an infant in detail, and, if I am correct, Genl. Washington is not to take the field, but in the event of the provisional army being called into Service—you are of course not only charged with the command of the army, but, in a great degree, the direction of the War Department. . . .

Hamilton forwarded to Wolcott in confidence a copy of the program he had submitted to McHenry earlier for providing and issuing military supplies: "Make the Secretary of War talk to you about it, without letting him know that I have sent it to you. And urge . . . some plan which will effectually organize this important branch. . . ." Wolcott urged Hamilton to come on at once, "with the expectation of being Secy of War in fact."

McHenry, acknowledging that his own talents were "unequal to great exertions or deep resources," at least by comparison with Hamilton's, was only too happy to depute most of the work of his department to Hamilton. "Permit me . . . to request," began a typical communication, "that laying aside other business you will occupy yourself on the two military bills only. . . . If possible, let me have the bills by Monday's mail or at furthest Tuesday's." These bills were the basis for the laws passed by Congress expanding the military establishment.

Hamilton's health was failing during this hectic period. Several times sickness slowed his work or confined him to his bed, but throughout the yellow fever epidemic that gripped New York and Philadelphia in 1798, he tried to remain on the job. The most painful thing about all these labors of Hamilton through sickness and health was that he was not billing or getting paid for any of them. He had acquiesced in President Adams's request that the generals receive no pay until called into actual service, and by the first of the new year 1799, he had forfeited most of the income from his law practice. What remained was fast melting away. "Were I rich," the inspector general wrote McHenry in desperation, "I should be proud to be silent on such a subject," but he was not. With a wife and six children to support, he would be obliged to reduce his sacrifices to the public unless his army pay, small at best, should immediately commence. McHenry's reply by return mail, fixed Hamilton's pay and emoluments; President Adams directed that he be considered formally on duty from November 1, 1798, at a salary, with allowances for subsistence and forage, of $268.35 a month, less than one-fourth of what he had recently been earning as a preeminent Wall Street lawyer.

McHenry wondered whether it might be advisable to withdraw troops from the Southern and Western frontiers to guard the seaboard. Hamilton thought not, counseling against doing so on December 13. But troop dispositions in the West and South required careful rethinking. Brigadier General James Wilkinson, the commander of the Western army, should be directed to return to Philadelphia for conferences on these matters.

A lifelong master of the art of serving more masters than one, Wilkinson's contacts with the Spanish authorities called for him to act as a diplomat as well as a commander. Hamilton distrusted him, but thought he could make use of his peculiar talents. He ordered Wilkinson's reports sent back open to the secretary of war for reforwarding to him and wrote McHenry's letter informing Wilkinson of this arrangement. Opening his official correspondence with the inspector general, Wilkinson replied with obsequious, ironic pomposity of "the high satisfaction I feel, at finding myself under orders of a Gentleman, able to instruct me in all things." It is not known whether Hamilton knew for certain at the time a fact which later shocked scholars, that Wilkinson was also in the pay of Spain.

On January 24, Hamilton told McHenry how the orders dividing up other commands between himself and Pinckney should read. Hamilton would command "all the troops and posts north of Maryland"; and General Pinckney, all to the south. All the separate commands on the Great Lakes, the Miami River, and in Tennessee and supreme command of the Western army should also "be placed under the superintendence of the Inspector General."

Scanning the American frontiers of the new world beyond his far-flung command from his New York offices as supreme quasi commander of the quasi war for opportunities as well as weak spots, Hamilton's gaze would pause to contemplate the military and political situation in the French colony of Saint-Domingue and the Spanish possessions of Louisiana and the Floridas.

Many American vessels being seized by France in the West Indies were brought into the French-held ports of Saint-Domingue as prizes. The colony itself would be a tempting prize for America in the event of open war with France. From as far back as 1791 and 1792, Hamilton had been deeply involved in American relations with the colony. Then he had counseled Washington on how to respond to appeals from France for funds and supplies to aid it in putting down slave revolts. He had warned Washington that "nothing can be done without risk to the United States" because it was unclear which government, French or slave, was of sufficient legitimacy to be entitled to recognition. Therefore, *"as little as possible ought to be done"* and "whatever may be done should be cautiously restricted to the single idea of preserving the colony from destruction by famine." This would "avoid the explicit recognition of any regular authority or person." On this basis, for purely humanitarian reasons, "succours ought to be granted."

The principal leader of the slave revolt was François Dominique Toussaint (usually called Toussaint L'Ouverture), the son of an African chieftain who had been sold into Negro slavery. By 1798, Toussaint had driven the British and French out of all but a few parts of the island, subdued a rival group of mulattoes under Benoit Joseph Rigaud, and turned to the United States to ask for recognition and foreign aid. But France had not acknowledged Toussaint's de facto control, and Saint-Domingue officially still remained a French colony.

Secretary of State Pickering and Secretary of the Treasury Wolcott called on Hamilton for advice on how to respond to Toussaint's plea. Adams thought the United States "should make some kind of agreement with the blacks" and open regular trade relations. But internationally, to do so might touch off a reprisal by France or open war. Domestically, to do so would certainly be politically divisive. Southerners like Jefferson were horrified at the idea of giving official recognition to a country of former Negro slaves who had successfully won a bloody revolution for freedom against their white masters. A free Saint-Domingue under Toussaint little more than a hundred miles off Florida would stand like a dangerous beacon of freedom or a tree of liberty, always beckoning Jefferson's own slaves to revolt.

Hamilton answered Pickering on February 16, 1799, that the law authorized opening relations with Toussaint's black government in Saint-Domingue, but that the United States "must not be committed to the independence of St. Domingo—nothing that can rise up in judgment." The United States would open trade if American vessels would be protected in his ports. This was the policy the government adopted.

The consul general who was picked to carry out this delicate mission of such intense interest to Hamilton was none other than his oldest boyhood friend, Dr. Edward Stevens of St. Croix. To Neddy Stevens before his departure, Hamilton furnished a suggested plan of government for Saint-Domingue that would not offend a Toussaint still battling pockets of resistance held by Rigaud and the French. "No regular system of liberty will at present suit

Saint Domingue,'' Hamilton advised. ''The government if independent must be military—partaking of the feudal. . . . A hereditary chief would be best but this I fear is impracticable.''

Hamilton's plan called for ''a single executive to hold his place for life,'' his successor to be either the officer next in rank or one chosen by a plurality of commanders of regiments. There would be a supreme court of 12 men chosen for life by the chief military officers, with trial by jury in criminal cases. The most important laws, those for raising revenue and for capital punishment, would be passed by the assembly of military commanders; other laws would be decreed by the executive. The executive would be advised by ministers of finance, war, and foreign affairs. This cautious suggestion, given ''for what it was worth'' to his old friend Neddy Stevens, was later twisted by Jefferson into the usual charge that Hamilton would help or recognize no free revolutionary government except one that was headed by a king.

Saint-Domingue was more a prize than a menace. The wide open, largely unpopulated, undefended, and almost limitless expanse of the Florida and Louisiana quadrants as Hamilton scanned them on the situation maps in his New York office were both a menace—and a prize—of incalculable size and scope.

In April of 1798, Pickering had asked him ''what ought we to do, in respect to Louisiana?'', when it had been suspected that France was on the point of forcing Spain to cede these territories to her, or compel Spain to do so at any time it might suit her plan for world dominion. Hamilton's reply made it plain that he stood ready at all times to give aid to any plan that would make Louisiana and the Floridas part of the United States short of entangling the United States in open war with France by doing so.

As far back as 1784, Hamilton had listened sympathetically in New York as Francisco de Miranda described his own dream of liberating all the Spanish possessions in the New World from the yoke of Spain. Recently Miranda had written Hamilton again, sure that the time was now ripe ''for the Exeuction of those grand and beneficial projects we had in Contemplation, when in our Conversation at New York the love of our Country exalted our minds with . . . Ideas, for the sake of unfortunate Columbia.''

Seven years older than Hamilton, Francisco de Miranda was a Venezuelan soldier of fortune who had served in the American Revolution and now came armed with a quiver of charm, eloquence, and a personality yeasty with the spirit of liberty. A refugee from his Spanish overlords when he had visited the United States in 1784, he had preserved a list of names of some 30 American officers he considered qualified for an ambitious campaign against Spanish possessions, written out in Hamilton's own hand. The names of Washington, Greene, Knox, Lafayette, von Steuben, and Arthur St. Clair headed the roster, which Hamilton must have written out still earlier and perhaps for another purpose, because it also included two of the brightest and best of Hamilton's friends, Colonels Francis Barber and John Laurens, who were both dead by 1784.

General Knox had copied out the names Hamilton supplied and added budgetary estimates of the expenses of raising, equipping, and supporting an army of 5,000 New Englanders for a year, including infantry, cavalry, and artillery, with all appropriate logistical support. To outfit such a force required funds, and Miranda had sailed off to England to obtain them. The British had given only vague words of encouragement then and no money. Discouraged, off to the Continent, into the French Revolution, promoted to a general, Miranda had become disillusioned with Napoleon as he turned imperial, had been arrested for treason, tried, acquitted, rearrested, and expelled from France. He looked on the American Federalist system as the perfect pattern for popular freedom under government everywhere. A visionary plotter and dreamer, a precursor of Martin and Bolivar as a liberator of Spanish America, he invented his own legend as he went along, and counted Hamilton as the greatest of all American revolutionaries and one of his best friends.

On February 7, 1798, he wrote Hamilton from London where he had seen Rufus King and taken him into his confidence. Would Hamilton be so good as to write King on the following subject? On the back of this letter, at some time after receiving it—how long after is the critical question—Hamilton wrote a cautious, slightly acrid, self-serving comment:

> Several years ago this man was in American much heated with the project of liberating South America from the Spanish Domination. I had frequent conversation with him on the subject, and I presume expressed ideas favourable to the object and perhaps gave an opinion that it was one to which the United States would look with interest—he went then to England upon it—Hence his present letter. I shall not answer because I consider him as an intriguing adventurer.

If Hamilton endorsed this negative endorsement on the back of the letter immediately upon receipt of it, then the events that followed immediately in train are most surprising. It is more likely that Hamilton wrote the endorsement several years later, when it seemed to be the part of wisdom to dissociate his name from Miranda's scheming and dreaming. In 1798, Hamilton probably responded warmly to Miranda's plan as it unfolded in rather impressive detail.

In June of 1798, Miranda had sent a fellow revolutionist, Pedro José de Caro, on from London carrying dispatches for President Adams and confidential messages for Hamilton. The moment of emancipation approached! Miranda proclaimed, "the establishment of liberty on the whole continent of the New World is . . . entrusted to us by providence." The British were to be drawn in to a suitable form of joint government for all the emancipated country. Hamilton must not refuse aid at this critical moment: "We should like to have you with us for this important object. Your Greek predecessor Solon would have done no less, I am sure!"

William Cobbett, as *Peter Porcupine,* summed up the strong appeal of Miranda's plan for all High Federalists: "A war with Spain is absolutely necessary to the salvation of this country, if a war with France takes place, or if the Spaniards have ceded Louisiana to France. They must both be driven into the Gulf of Mexico, or we shall never sleep in peace. Besides, a war with Spain would be so convenient!" To seize the gold and silver of Spain's mines "would be the cream of the war."

Hamilton delayed answering until August 22, 1798. Then he sent his reply to Miranda's plea via Rufus King, giving King the option after reading it to deliver it to Miranda or not as circumstances warranted. "With regard to the enterprise in question," Hamilton confided, "I wish it much to be undertaken, but I should be glad that the principal agency to be in the United States," which should furnish the whole land force, of which he expected soon to be named the field commander.

Although Hamilton favored Miranda's plan, he would do nothing without proper authority: "The Sentiments I entertain with regard to that object have been long since in your Knowledge. But I could personally have no participation in it unless patronized by the Government of this Country." It was frustrating that Adams had not yet issued his commission: "It was my wish that matters had been ripened for a Cooperation in the Course of this fall on the part of this Country. But this can now scarcely be the Case." If winter should bring progress, "I shall be happy in my official station to be an Instrument of so good a work."

Success of the expedition was conditioned on support of a British fleet, an American army, and a government for the liberated territory agreeable to the joint venturers. "To arrange the plan a Competent Authority from Great Britain to some person here is the best Expedient," Hamilton told King. "Your presence here will in this Case be extremely essential." As he sent off his letter to Miranda via King, Hamilton could not have known that the highest levels of the British government now saw Miranda's plan almost exactly as he did and took it seriously.

John Adams in Quincy, preoccupied with Abigail's illness and unused to carrying on presidential work in the summer months, had done nothing about the dispatches received from Miranda. Pickering was left with no instructions. William Pitt and Lord Grenville, interested in pursuing Miranda's plan, sent Robert Liston, the British minister in Philadelphia, journeying to Quincy in September to pursue with Adams the idea of an American alliance or joint venture with Britain. Liston reported back that on September 27 Adams had finally agreed that it would be in the United States' best interest, as well as Britain's, to join in a temporary alliance against France. That was why it seemed so inexplicable to anyone not familiar with what Hamilton called the "desultoriness" of Adams's mind that two weeks later Adams switched and turned down Miranda's plan.

The missing fact necessary to explain Adams's sudden switch is that it was during the span of those same two weeks that he had humbly but furiously caved in to Washington's insistence, reversed another earlier stand, and signed Hamilton's appointment as inspector general. Meanwhile, King, as eager for the joint offensive as Hamilton was, or rather more so, quickly passed on Hamilton's letter to Miranda, who answered with mounting excitement that all had progressed as Hamilton wished: ". . . we await only the fiat of your illustrious President to leave like lightening. . . . Let us save America from the frightful calamities that, in upsetting a large part of the world, threaten with destruction the parts which are still whole."

Unfortunately for the project, de Caro, the emissary Miranda had sent to Adams, detoured to South America without seeing him to buck up his resolve, and postponed a small and partial revolution that was about to break out until the United States and Britain could join him in a large complete one, to "save the whole world which totters on the brink of the abyss." King had prepared the way with the highest officials in Britain for "lightening action" the moment America was ready. Venezuela would be the ultimate objective, but along the way Louisiana and Florida would be plucked from Spain to add to the United States.

At the opening of the new year, 1799, King from London was still begging Hamilton for God's sake to attend to the subject of his recent ciphered dispatches to the secretary of state. The time had arrived to push ahead toward Miranda's main objective: "Providence seems to have prepared the way, and . . . pointed out the instruments of its will. Our children will reproach us if we neglect our duty. . . ." It was manifest destiny. It "will be the moment for us to settle . . . the extensive system of the American nation. Who can hinder us? One nation alone has the power; and she will cooperate in the accomplishment in South America of what has so well been done in North."

Hamilton's power was burgeoning in all directions following his appointment as inspector general, and his enthusiasm for ambitious offensives warmed to a degree that almost matched Miranda's and King's. Adams's enthusiasm reciprocally cooled and gradually receded toward the moderate policy line that Hamilton had advocated from the beginning of the war crisis: "leaving to France the option of seeking accommodation, or proceeding to open war."

Hamilton duly noted and gave full credit to Adams for his striking switch in backing away from his earlier fire-breathing stance, so that "the latter course prevailed." Hamilton gave him credit for this even while publicly attacking Adams a year and a half later on many other counts for alleged misfeasance in office: "Considering the prosperous state of French affairs" when Adams finally adopted Hamilton's cogent policy, Hamilton granted, "the conduct pursued bore sufficiently the marks of courage and elevation to raise the national character to an exalted height throughout Europe." Notwithstanding all the heady temptations toward aggrandizement that supreme command proffered, at no time did Hamilton suggest that any of his military projects be undertaken without proper authority from the president and Congress and with the backing of a fully informed public.

More than mere mistrust of Hamilton in command at the pinnacle of power had caused Adams's switch from aggressive belligerence of the summer and fall to the conciliatory tone he adopted in his message to the third session of the Fifth Congress assembled on December 8, 1798. The most virulent manifestations of the summer's "black cockade fever" were already subsiding. The popular passion for a declaration of all-out war against France that had been so strong when the second session adjourned in July had begun to fade at the very time when Hamilton, finally secure in his appointment to quasi supreme command, might have exploited the possibilities that such vast power opened up to his ambition for vindication of his public honor.

As Congress was seen adopting a strong posture of preparedness for war on land and sea and abrogating the French treaties of 1778 and 1788, the Directory under Talleyrand's silken hand repealed many of the obnoxious restrictions on American shipping and lifted the harsh embargo it had proclaimed only a short time before. The British navy under Admiral Horatio Nelson defeated the French fleet at Aboukir Bay. Newly launched American frigates on patrol in the West Indies were winning engagements with French armed raiders and privateers. American commerce and shipping were prospering as a result of more profitable voyages. Marine war risk insurance rates were coming down.

Talleyrand's invisible hand silkily steered the Directory onto a course that was almost a mirror image of Hamilton's American policy: each would leave to the other the option of seeking accommodations or proceeding to open war. Talleyrand also blandly let it be known that the *WXYZ* imbroglio had been caused, not by his government or himself, but by inept and bungling underlings.

Talleyrand, like Hamilton, understood the uses of influencing public opinion in a free country in support of the interests of an adversary. His policy of making use of contacts through underlings, while avoiding the wide open official channel of Secretary of State Pickering and Commissioners Pinckney and Marshall, strengthened the hands of American Republicans and weakened and angered High Federalists. He thus kept France's potential enemy divided against itself internally while committing the Directory to nothing and risking nothing at home.

Adams's second annual message to Congress, which like the first was full of Hamilton's policies secretly spoon fed to Adams through Wolcott and McHenry, held that a formal declaration of war was "inexpedient and ought not to be recommended." This threatened to cause a split between the moderate Federalists, and the hawkish High Federalist wing of the party.

Hamilton suggested a subtle compromise that might help avert the split. When Harrison Gray Otis, chairman of the House Committee on Defense, requested "instruction," Hamilton suggested that Congress pass a law empowering the president *at his discretion* "to declare that a state of war exists between the two countries if negotiations with France should fail." Although the Constitution reserved to Congress the power to declare war, the provision was not intended to deprive the president of full power to lead the country to the brink of war and thus make a declaration inescapable. Congress's formal power to declare war was meant only as a curb on a rash presidential declaration, for which popular opinion was unprepared. If there were to be a war the president should have the power to unite the country in support of it first. Hamilton's view tended to add responsibility, as well as power, to the office of the president and made it more important that any president be a strong one and this prodded Adams into irascible rage. He wrote to Otis of Hamilton: "This man is stark mad, or I am. He knows nothing of the character, the feelings, the opinion and the prejudices of this nation. If Congress should adopt this system, it would produce an instantaneous insurrection of the whole nation from Georgia to New Hampshire." Yet the authority Hamilton besought Congress to confer on the president to preclude his playing politics with the war issue presaged powers that modern presidents have assumed without such authority.

Hamilton had also suggested to Adams through Wolcott that he put something in his message to the effect that, if France should send a minister, "he would be received with due respect to his character and treated with in the frankness of a sincere desire of accommodation."

Adams blew up all over again! This was pussyfooting. "If France should send a minister tomorrow," he swore, "I would order him back the day after."

The three cabinet ministers waited patiently till Adams's pugnacious paroxysms passed, counseled him that such a threat would be a foolish and "imprudent idea," and not 48 hours later, according to Hamilton, "the mind of Mr. Adams underwent a total revolution." Adams suddenly decided to go far beyond what Hamilton had suggested. He would send a minister if France gave explicit assurances he would be received. This was a "pernicious" reversal, Hamilton and the others felt, because it would deprive France of the opportunity to bargain to get what should be the ultimate outcome: a new American mission to Paris. "Here some salve for her pride was necessary," Hamilton felt. In his message as finally delivered, Adams moved back to the middle ground and more or less echoed Hamilton.

To Rufus King's continual urging that Hamilton get on with the alliance with Britain and get Miranda's plan under way, Hamilton replied in January 1799 that he would leave the way open for accommodation, but if France attempted to take the Floridas and Louisiana from Spain, the United States should be prepared to fight. These regions were the key to the whole Western country and Hamilton had long considered their acquisition "essential to the permanency of the Union . . ."

Hamilton went further. If universal empire were the ambition of France, what could better counteract it "than to detach South America from Spain, which is only the channel through which the riches of Mexico and Peru are conveyed to France?"

On February 18, 1799, without prior consultation with the secretary of state or any of his other department heads, without seeking outside advice from other Federalist leaders, and without any formal assurances from France that his minister would be properly received, Adams impetuously sent the name of young William Vans Murray to the Senate asking for his confirmation as American minister plenipotentiary to the French Republic. Through informal channels, Murray's name had been suggested to Adams by Gerry, whom many Federalists now considered as more or less a traitor to party and country.

But not by any regular Federalist or friends of the government, as they often called themselves, who were thunderstruck. To Hamilton the "measure was wrong, both as to mode and substance. . . . Surely, Mr. Adams might have benefited by the advice of his ministers." Hamilton's further strictures on Adams's "mode" are worth noting: "The greatest genius, hurried away by the rapidity of its own conceptions, will occasionally overlook obstacles which ordinary and more phlegmatic men will discover, and which when presented to his consideration, will be thought by himself to be decisive objections to his plans.'' These words of Hamilton will describe his own folly in issuing *The Reynolds Pamphlet* and the worse folly he was about to commit by publishing his infamous attack on John Adams. He added, ''When, unhappily, an ordinary man dreams himself to be a Frederick and through vanity refrains from counselling with his constitutional advisers, he is very apt to fall into the hands of miserable intriguers, with whom his self love is more at ease, and who without difficulty slide into his confidence, and by flattery govern him.'' Here Hamilton's reobsession with ''miserable intriguers'' signals a recurrence of another spell of nervous derangement.

A committee of five leading Federalist senators stalked into Adams's office in anger and echoed Hamilton's demand that he withdraw Murray's appointment.

In high dudgeon, Adams refused. Never, he swore.

The senators would vote against the confirmation of Murray on the ground that he was unqualified, they replied.

Adams threatened to resign the presidency. Yes, the presidency itself.

And let in Jefferson? they cried.

Hamilton hastily suggested a face-saving way out of the impasse: appoint two trustworthy envoys to accompany Murray.

The Senate caucus urged appointment of George Cabot as one—and Hamilton as the other.

Adams exploded again all over the ceiling. Appoint Hamilton again? Never. Never. Never. ''I have upon mature reflection, made up my mind,'' he said when he came down, grimly trying to appear calm. ''I will neither withdraw nor modify my nomination.''

The Senators evenly told him they would reject it.

Adams caved in. He agreed to enlarge the commission to three. But he would be damned if Hamilton would be jammed down his throat again. Or Cabot either.

After further bickering, it was agreed that Chief Justice of the United States Oliver Ellsworth and William R. Davie, the Federalist governor of North Carolina, would join Murray as the commissioners.

What with one delay and another, more than a year would go by—and two more revolutions of the regime would roil France—before the three commissioners would sit down in Paris on April 2, 1800, to begin negotiations with their opposite number, the recently reappointed minister of foreign relations of First Consul Napoleon Bonaparte. Who? None other than that suave survivor the Bishop d'Autun, Charles Maurice de Talleyrand-Périgord. In French revolutions, *plus ça change plus c'est la même chose*.

Two things were a little changed from earlier unhappy American ministerial confabulations in Paris, which represented progress or at least sort of inching ahead. The chief justice and the governor added to the mission at Hamilton's suggestion would keep their young colleague Murray, whom Talleyrand had help handpick, on a shorter leash than Marshall and Pinckney had kept Gerry. This time Talleyrand, a quick learner from past miscalculations, would not send *X* or *Y* or *Z* or *W* around to collect for a pretalk bribe.

But Talleyrand would never cease to profess amazement that his *realpolitiker* counterpart across the water, while making the fortune of his country (and being vilified for friendship with Talleyrand, and Talleyrand-like peculations in the process), could have failed along way to learn from him how to secure a fortune of his own. But it was really no more amazing than the difference between young America and worldly old France.

33

The Evil Genius
of This Country

All sovereignty then existing in the nation was in the hands of Alexander Hamilton. I was as president a mere cipher.

—John Adams to Harrison Gray Otis, 1823

In times like these in which we live, it will not do to be over scrupulous. . . . It is easy to sacrifice the substantial interests of society by a strict adherence to ordinary rules.

—To John Jay, May 7, 1800

Believe me, I feel no despondency of any sort. As to the country, it is too young and vigorous to be quacked out of its political health—and as to myself, I feel that I stand on ground which, sooner or later, will ensure me a triumph over all my enemies.

—to Henry Lee, March 7, 1800

Now, at the turn of the century, at age 43, Hamilton was described by one who knew him well as "thin in person, but remarkably erect and dignified in his deportment." His hair was of fine texture, brown with a hint of red, now flecked with white. He wore it turned back from his forehead, usually powdered and collected in a club behind. His complexion was exceedingly fair, "varying from this only by the almost feminine rosiness of his cheeks." His eyes were dark blue and deep-set. His might be considered, as to configuration and color, an uncommonly handsome face. When at rest, it had a rather severe, thoughtful expression, "but when engaged in conversation it easily assumed an attractive smile."

William Sullivan in his *The Public Characters of the Revolution* recorded the moment in

December 1795 when Hamilton entered a room. It was apparent from their respectful attention that here was an uncommonly distinguished man. He was dressed in a blue coat with bright buttons. The skirts of his coat were unusually long, making him seem taller than his five feet seven inches. He wore a white waistcoat, black silk small clothes, and white silk stockings. The host introduced him to those of the company who were strangers to him. "To each he made a formal bow, bending very low, the ceremony of shaking hands not being observed . . . At dinner, whenever he engaged in the conversation, every one listened attentively." His mode of speaking was deliberate and serious; and his voice, engagingly pleasant. But when he joined the ladies, there was a distinct change of manner. "In the evening of the same day, he was in a mixed assembly of both sexes; and the tranquil reserve, noticed at the dinner table, had given place to a social and playful manner, as though in this he was alone ambitious to excel."

While Washington remained inactive at Mount Vernon, more seriously ailing than the public knew, Hamilton took on full responsibility for all aspects of raising, equipping, and drilling a brand-new American army, as well as full command of the dispositions of its forces in the field.

He had just won an important lawsuit for Louis Le Guen, who had paid him the largest single fee he would ever earn. He wound up his law practice and substituted Robert Troup as counsel for himself in continuing matters and in January 1799 he turned his full attention to the large duties and small emoluments of the inspector general's office.

Since the close of the Revolution, next to nothing had been done in the United States for the military establishment. Hamilton sought to make his army a model for future armies to be called up in future crises. He worked out regulations for exercise of troops in camp and battle and for the police of garrisons; he expanded the infantry drill manual prepared by von Steuben a dozen years before and included discipline and tactics for cavalry and artillery; he sent on the portions dealing with regimental maneuvers to General Charles Cotesworth Pinckney and others for criticism and comment.

There was virtually no facet of the military that did not concern him—from the design of the uniform and the length of the infantryman's marching step, to remonstrances against artillery uniform buttons being changed to white from yellow and complaints about a surgeon's mate. Hamilton meticulously wrote out the best answers he knew to all of them.

When Brigadier General James Wilkinson arrived in New York to discuss campaigns on the frontier, it was a welcome opportunity for Hamilton to lift his gaze from the frustrating details of "established forms" to the distant horizons of Louisiana and the Floridas. Hamilton's agenda for the meetings with Wilkinson included his ideas for preserving peace on the frontiers with Spain and organizing the forces necessary for "attacking the two Floridas."

Hamilton urged on both McHenry and Washington that Wilkinson now be promoted to major general.

Hamilton's reasons were full of odd qualifications. "I am aware," he wrote Washington, "that some doubts have been entertained of him, and that his character on certain sides, gives room for doubt . . . he will be apt to become disgusted, if neglected; and through disgust may be rendered really what he is now only suspected to be." Hamilton probably knew more than he wrote, but he may have thought that Wilkinson's promotion would cause the Spanish to mistrust him.

Washington, who had denied an unimportant commission to Burr on Hamilton's advice because of his "talents for intrigue," now agreed to promote Wilkinson on Hamilton's advice to command of all the vast Western territories, because of "talents for intrigue."

McHenry put his strong disapproval on record to Hamilton:

> Be assured, that until the commercial pursuits of this gentleman with and
> expectations from Spain are annihilated, he will not deserve the confidence of
> government. . . . avoid saying anything to him which would induce him to
> imagine government had in view any hostile project, however remote, or dependent
> on events, against any of the possessions of Spain.

This surprising letter shows that McHenry knew a thing of which Hamilton claimed to be
in doubt: that Wilkinson was, in fact, a spy and pensioner in the employ of Spain and that a
highly placed official in the American government—that is, Hamilton—unknown to
President Adams—was contemplating the use of the newly raised army not merely for
defensive purposes in case of war with France, but for offensive purposes against Spanish
possessions in America.

Hamilton's letter to McHenry of June 27, 1799, which crossed McHenry's to him in the
mail, confirmed McHenry's fears: "It is a pity, my dear sir, and a reproach," he wrote, that
Adams's administration had no general plan. "Certainly there ought to be one formed
without delay. If the chief is too desultory, his ministry ought to be more united and steady,
and well-settled in some reasonable system of measures. . . . Besides eventual security
against invasion, we ought certainly to look to the possession of the Floridas and Louisiana,
and we ought to squint at South America."

McHenry's letter is strong evidence that at this time the pressures on Hamilton were
causing his judgment to become warped and unbalanced—and that this dangerous condition
was beoming manifest to his oldest, closest and most sensible friends.

Many years later Edward Everett Hale asserted that he had seen an extensive correspondence between Wilkinson and Hamilton concerning a plan that was similar to, but on a more
grandiose scale, than the expedition Aaron Burr later actually led down the Ohio and
Mississippi rivers from Blennerhasset Island, near present-day Cincinnati, for which in
1807 Jefferson had Burr, his former vice-president, prosecuted for treason. The key piece
of evidence in the case against Burr was a letter to Jefferson in cipher, telling him of the
plan, from General James Wilkinson.

Many men who might have made fine soldiers refused to enlist because they opposed the
Quasi War on political grounds, taking their cue from Republican party leaders like
Jefferson and Madison who contended that it was a "phony" war, a crisis whipped up by
the Federalists to keep themselves in office. It was, they charged, only an excuse to ram
through the Alien and Sedition Laws, suppress domestic dissent, build up the standing
army, increase government expenditures, pass a new Stamp Act and a direct tax on land,
and put a large number of new revenue agents on the public payroll.

A Dedham, Massachusetts, Republican warned that the new house taxes and land taxes
caused great resentment. "Silent indignation hath not yet exploded—tho' hard threatened. I
fear civil war may be the result of government measures."

Jefferson saw that a Republican attack on the Alien and Sedition Laws would bring
together the fragmented opposition to the entire costly federal war preparedness and tax
programs. He dramatized the issue for maximum political effect by writing sets of resolutions that he arranged to have introduced into the Kentucky and Virginia legislatures and
signed into law as 1799 began, by which the sovereign commonwealths of Kentucky and
Virginia declared that the Federal Alien and Sedition Laws were unconstitutional and void.

They demanded repeal.

This meant that state laws remained supreme and that Virginia and Kentucky would not enforce federal laws within their borders. This, in turn, raised the vexed question that had plagued Hamilton at the time of the Whiskey Insurrection: would his new "Additional Army" troops from states like Virginia and Kentucky obey their officers or their political leaders, if the military commands of the former conflicted with the political dictates of the latter? Some extreme High Federalists went so far as to charge that Jefferson's resolutions were part of a French plot to detach Kentucky from the Union and annex it to Louisiana— which Talleyrand was now on the point of snatching back from Spain.

A *Virginian*, writing in Bache's pro-Republican *Aurora*, alleged that Hamilton's newly recruited "Additional Army" units were nothing but Federalist "Pretorian Bands" and instruments of "Party Persecution." Every member would be ready at command to "imbrue his hands in the blood of a fellow citizen, a neighbor or a brother, should the president or his Little Mars [Hamilton] think proper. . . ."

In the Whiskey Rebellion, Hamilton had "trembled every moment lest a great part of the Militia should take it into their heads to return home rather than go forward." With a professional army, he would have no hesitation in proceeding to "subdue a refractory and powerful State." In the present crisis, he suggested, let a force "be drawn towards Virginia for which there is an obvious pretext—& then let measures be taken to act upon the laws, & put Virginia to the Test of resistance." No such "pretext" was necessary; Pennsylvania rose again. When revenue agents came to assess the new direct tax on houses and land, they would count the windows. Housewives of Germanic origin in Bucks and Northampton Counties of Pennsylvania would pour scalding water out of upstairs windows on the heads of revenue agents counting down below. John Fries, 50 years old, father of ten children, gathered a band of more than 50 armed horsemen and galloped from house to house and village to village attacking the unfortunate revenue agents, some, no doubt, still nursing fresh hot water burns. Eighteen demonstrators were arrested and clapped into jail in Bethlehem on March 6, 1799. Next day, Fries and a band of about 140 rumbustious farmers, some armed with rifles and swords, some wearing tricolor cockades, some drunk, ramped uproariously into town and cowed the federal marshal into releasing all the prisoners. Not a shot was fired. The episode came to be known as the "hot water insurrection."

On March 12 Adams issued a stern proclamation denouncing Fries and his roughnecks. He begged bibulous Gvernor Thomas Mifflin to call out the state militia. Mifflin bucked Adams's call over to the state legislature, which refused to order any such politically unpopular mobilization.

Adams was finally reduced to going back to ask McHenry—and Hamilton—for help from the regular army. He then quickly scuttled off to Quincy leaving all responsibility in Hamilton's hands. Hamilton moved fast. He sent Captain John Henry to the rebellious townships next day with a detachment of 100 from Fort Jay, New York. He sent William Macpherson forward with 240 horsemen and two companies of artillery in support. There was talk that the insurgents were led by officers commissioned by Pennsylvania; so Judge Richard Peters of the United States District Court was sent along to be on hand when arrests were made, to hold prompt hearings, to discharge those wrongly accused, and to commit to prison any who might be found guilty of the treasonous offenses that Adams had publicly charged to Fries and his men.

Hamilton's troops marched briskly into Bucks County, captured Fries and a few other ringleaders, clapped them into jail, then marched them off to the capital to stand trial for treason. After two jury trials in federal court, the second lasting nine days, the jury found Fries guilty of treason as charged and condemned him to be hanged. While the trials were pending, Hamilton understood that Adams had made rash and improper comments that might tend to prejudice the jury; Adams "more than once imprudently threw out that the accused must found their hopes of escape either in their innocence or in the lenity of the juries; since from him, in case of conviction, they would have nothing to expect." Adams had also said the grants of clemency by Washington after the Whiskey Insurrection were what had helped bring on Fries's. Moreover, "he would take care that there should not be a third, by giving the laws their full course against the convicted offenders."

Adams asked his cabinet if he should pardon the rebels, and they said no. Almost a year later, on May 21, 1800, the day before the date set for Fries's hanging, Adams pardoned the rebels. "It is by temporizings like these," Hamilton railed at the time from the depths of a serious onslaught of nervous crisis, that men at the head of affairs, in time of fermentation and commotion, lose the respect of both friends and foes."

Few things were more frustrating to Hamilton than seeing the symbolism of his strong response to Adams's call for a show of force by the regular army against Fries's insurrection dissolve in Republican ridicule of the whole episode as another repressive overreaction. The Republican press gleefully twisted Pickering's suspicions of a secret French plot to foment a slave rebellion in the South into a charge that General Charles Cotesworth Pinckney, while on the peace mission to Paris, had sired an illegitimate mulatto bastard child, whose abandoned mother had pursued the general to Charleston. The "Tale of the Tubs" with false bottoms for them to hide in could not fail to rouse the public's memories of that sex scandal two years earlier in high Federalist places in which that other high Federalist general had been involved. Hamilton wrote Jonathan Dayton that there should be "laws for restraining and punishing incendiary and seditious practices." The reputations of federal officers, necessary to the discharge of their duties, should be taken under guardianship of the national judiciary and not be left to "the cold and reluctant protection of State courts always temporizing." It was an outrage: "Are laws of this kind passed merely to excite odium and remain a dead letter?" Executive vigor now conspicuous by its absence was called for: "If the President requires to be stimulated those who can approach him ought to do it." But Hamilton no longer was among those who could communicate with the absent president.

The Sedition Law punished by fines and imprisonment conspiracies or scandalous statements uttered against the government, Congress, and the president, but unfortunately for Hamilton's mental health, as a military chieftain, he did not come under the wide gag the law imposed on the Republican press. As the highest ranking, most conspicuous leader of the government's party, the visible symbol of its increasingly costly and unpopular war mobilization policy, without such protection Hamilton became the principal and only safe target of opportunity permitted by the press gag law.

Benjamin Franklin Bache's *Aurora* of Philadelphia, which his widow had continued to publish following his recent death, was still probably the most influential of all the lively Republican newspapers. In New York, Thomas Greenleaf's widow, Ann, continued to publish the *Argus*, or *Greenleaf's New Daily Advertiser*, which often was filled with little more than juicy scraps of Anti-Federalist scandal reprinted from the *Aurora*.

One such reprinted item was a spurious letter supposedly written by a man in New York to a doctor in Philadelphia that was exquisitely calibrated to sow divisive tares between High and moderate Federalists with a needling nicety worthy of John Beckley's and James T.

Callender's finest collaborations in the genre. The writer had found Hamilton "in a sweat" upon hearing that Adams would resign from office so that Jefferson, "that cool casuistic Frenchified fellow will be thrust in his place." Hamilton would run for president and win because Hamilton had said, "The dollars I have heap'd together whilst handling the government's cash will not be without their use." Another such story reprinted by the *Argus* was that Hamilton was at the bottom of a plot to suppress the *Aurora* by purchasing it from Bache's widow. Editorial commentary following the story wallowed in wonderment. How could Hamilton now command $15,000 or $20,000 when in 1792 he could not meet James Reynolds's demand for $1,000 except in two installment payments? Perhaps an illicit slush fund from the British secret service would be doled out to him by Robert Liston, the British minister. Why did Major General Hamilton not use a more economical method to suppress the *Aurora?* He could have marched out the same army troops that had put down poor John Fries to gibbet the *Aurora'*s editor and destroy its offices in half an hour.

Here was yet another tweaking of Hamilton's raw Reynolds case nerves. His angry reply letter, published in New York in *The Daily Advertiser* on November 9, 1799, raged at the *Argus*: "One principal Engine" for pulling down the pillars of society was "audacious falsehoods to destroy the confidence of the people in all those, who are in any degree conspicuous among the supporters of the government. . . ." He had at other times treated such "malignant calumnies" with contempt, but now it was his "duty to the community" to suppress them by the force of the laws.

He was conscious that such a linking of personal charges against himself with injury to the nation might seem to some a little vain, but he "must be content with the mortification." He concluded, "In no event, however, will any displeasure I may feel, be at war with the public interest. This in my eyes is sacred."

Hamilton demanded that his friend Josiah Ogden Hoffman, the New York state attorney general, commence an immediate prosecution against the *Argus*. Its scandalous stories were likely to have "very fatal consequences" for the American government, Hamilton insisted. "Such an attack demanded peculiar attention. A bolder calumny; one more absolutely destitute of foundation, was never propagated." Its "dangerous tendency," he said, needed no comment. He commented anyway; it was calculated "to inspire the belief that the independence and liberty of the press are endangered by the intrigues of ambitious citizens aided by foreign gold." His and Hoffman's criminal prosecution of the *Argus* could be brought under state, not federal law, for the printing of a private defamatory libel.

On November 7, Assistant New York State Attorney General Cadwallader D. Colden went to the *Argus*'s office and told Mrs. Greenleaf of Hamilton's intended prosecution. She disclaimed guilt under the Sedition Law—the article that offended Hamilton had been a reprint from the Boston *Telegraph* and plainly labeled as such. Her shop foreman, journeyman printer David Frothingham, looked at the article and gallantly took the rap for the widow, saying he supposed he was the one responsible for reprinting it, although he strenuously denied having had anything to do with writing or composing it. Because Mrs. Greenleaf was already under federal indictment under the Sedition Laws, and a conviction against the *Argus* might be easier to obtain under state libel law in Hamilton's case, Colden arrested Frothingham on November 9, took him into custody, and released him on bail pending the trial scheduled to begin on November 21.

With nothing to lose but its life in any event the *Argus* struck back. It charged Hamilton and Federalists generally with pursuing a cheaper method to gag hostile papers than buying them up: swamping them with lawyers bills to defend federal and state prosecutions which cost a complaining witness like Hamilton nothing. Hamilton was a hypocrite, cried the

Argus, trying to identify his personal resentment with the "social security and happiness" of America, when he himself was one of the worst offenders against "social security and happiness" by his own confessed unchastity.

The names of Frothingham's defense counsel, Brockholst and Edward Livingston, guaranteed that the harsh rigidity of the Federal sedition and state libel laws and Hamilton's own exposed position, would receive the widest possible public airing when they fought back against attorney generals Hoffman and Colden. It was a celebrated political trial in every sense.

Hamilton won the right to testify to what the *Argus*'s innuendoes meant. This led him into having to rehash all over again, under oath from the witness box at a well-publicized public trial, all his by now no doubt only too well-rehearsed reasons for having made payments to James Reynolds. In Frothingham's defense, Livingston sought to argue that he was not responsible—he was only an eight-dollar-a-week journeyman printer. But the court refused to admit any evidence of Frothingham's position at the *Argus* or any evidence to disprove the imputation of malice raised by Hamilton's testimony.

The article itself had not charged Hamilton with being anti-Republican; it was his own reaction that derived that insulting innuendo from it and found offense in the charge. Brockholst Livingston argued ingeniously that the word *Republican* as used in the article had been a party label. Everyone knew that there were now two political parties in the United States: one, the Federalists, who favored the administration; the other, the Republicans, who opposed it. If the *Argus* had called Hamilton anti-Republican, he should have taken it as praise, not blame; it was only another way of calling him a good Federalist.

Livingston also argued in Frothingham's defense that suppression of a newspaper by legal means such as buying it was a private, not a criminal matter; that if, as Hamilton claimed, the Baches' *Aurora* was subversive of the government, for Hamilton to suppress it by buying it out "would be a feather in his cap, and entitle him to the thanks," not the "ridicule and hatred of his fellow citizens." Therefore, Frothingham's reprint was praise of Hamilton, not a damaging innuendo as he claimed.

The only questions the court would permit the jury to decide was whether the article was designed to expose Hamilton to hatred and contempt and whether Frothingham had printed it. Acting on these instructions on the law, the jury returned after three hours with a verdict of guilty. They added a recommendation for clemency. Poor Frothingham's salary of eight dollars a week was the sole support of his wife and six children. Besides, he had only been trying to protect the widow Greenleaf.

Judge Radcliffe sternly sentenced him to four months in prison or until he paid a fine of $100, required him to post a bond of $2,000 before release and to give a guarantee of good behavior for two years.

The Federalist *Gazette of the United States* groaned that the sentence was much too lenient; the *Argus* called the trial a political one, in which the jury had been packed with Federalists. The costly pressures of both state and federal prosecutions succeeded in suppressing the *Argus.*

Hamilton's successful prosecution was a Pyrrhic victory that would help swell the Republican tide in May that swept Hamilton's old Federalist-dominated state legislature out of office and Aaron Burr's Republicans into power just in time to control New York's pivotal electoral vote in the national elections now coming up. New York was a swing state, and whoever won New York was likely to win the nation.

It may have been these attacks that made him suddenly "beg" McHenry to get back for him his set of the original Reynolds letters. In his *Reynolds Pamphlet*, Hamilton had written that "all the original papers" contained in his appendix had been deposited with William Bingham, Esq., for "perusal" by "any gentleman." No one but Callender, who was no gentleman, had applied to peruse them, and Callender had been rebuffed. McHenry's reply to Hamilton on November 18 must have come as an incredible shock:

> I recd two hours ago your letter of the 14th, begging me to call upon and send you certain papers you had lodged with Mr. Bingham. . . . I dispatched my servant with a note to which I have received the following answer enclosed: "I do not remember to have seen the papers alluded to."

By this last stunning sentence, McHenry spared Hamilton the entire text of Bingham's letter, which did not allow Hamilton to think Bingham had had a lapse of memory, as McHenry's did. Bingham flatly contradicted Hamilton in no uncertain terms, with some asperity, and in effect, called Hamilton a liar. Bingham's note to McHenry had said, "It surely must have escaped Genl Hamilton's recollection that the papers he alluded to, *never* were deposited with me." Bingham went on to add, "After reading the publication in which he mentioned this deposit being made, I was surprised at the omission in case I had been applied to for a view of them."

The apparently untrue statement Hamilton had published had greatly troubled Bingham. "I should certainly have reminded him," he told McHenry, but until now "under any other circumstances, it would not have been delicate to have addressed him on the subject."

Now, by his own "begging" appeal to McHenry, Hamilton had given not only Bingham, but McHenry too, men he had considered to be among his staunchest friends, grounds to believe that the defense he had made in *The Reynolds Pamphlet* had been a lie that he had published to the public.

But why had Hamilton suddenly "begged" McHenry and Bingham for the papers? Would he have done so if he had not himself absolutely believed that he had deposited them with Bingham? Could Callender or another of his enemies have stolen them? Had Bingham turned against him? Had his own mental processes failed him somewhere in the crisis? After the Reynolds affair had haunted him for years and he had agonizingly aired it, he had unwittingly conjured it up again in a way that impeached his own honor to himself more inexplicably than anything that had gone before.

When all votes were counted, Burr and the Republicans of New York City had elected their entire slate to the legislature over Hamilton's obedient ciphers. Gains upstate gave Republicans a large enough margin in the assembly, even though the senate remained in Federalist control, to give them a majority in the combined houses—of a single vote. But that one was enough to elect a solidly Republican slate of electors to cast New York's 12 votes for president and vice-president.

Stunned and shocked by his repudiation, Hamilton wrote Senator Theodore Sedgwick on May 4, before all tallies were in, that "to support *Adams* and *Pinckney* equally is the only thing that can possibly save us from the fangs of Jefferson." The Federalist congressional caucus just then in session to choose the presidential candidate "should not separate without coming to a distinct and solemn concert to pursue this course *bona fide.*" Uncoded, this meant that the Northern states must give all possible support to Charles Cotesworth Pinckney, not withholding a single vote as Massachusetts had done in 1796. The words *bona fide* would lend weight to suspicions of anyone as suspicious as Adams that Hamilton's promise of equal support for him and Pinckney meant equivocal support in 1796 and equally equivocal support in 1800.

Hamilton delivered his advice to the senator from Massachusetts like a general's command to a lowly aide, without accompanying social grace notes: "Pray attend to this, and let me speedily hear from you that it is done." The day before Hamilton's letter, the Federalist caucus in Philadelphia had duly chosen Adams and Pinckney as the Federalist candidates respectively for president and vice-president. One week later, a Republican caucus chose Jefferson for president and, largely on the strength of his sensational victory in the recent New York elections, Aaron Burr to be their candidate for vice-president.

Far from "triumphing over all his enemies," as he had confidently promised Henry Lee he would do only two months earlier, three of Hamilton's leading enemies now stood on the threshhold of an all but certain electoral triumph over him. In anger, disgust, and desperation, his pen in the tight grip of paranoia or, at least, of a manic defense, he wrote and sent a letter to Governor John Jay that contained what was probably the most shocking and unworthy political proposal he had ever made in his life. It was a "moral certainty," Hamilton wrote, that "there will be an antifederal majority in the ensuing Legislature." This "will bring *Jefferson*, an atheist in religion and a fanatic in politics into the chief magistracy." The Anti-Federal party "is a composition of very incongruous materials, all tending to mischief—some of them, to the OVERTHROW of the GOVERNMENT, others of them, to a REVOLUTION, after the manner of BONAPARTE." To Hamilton, these were not "conjectures or inferences," but "indubitable facts." Jefferson, Burr, and the Anti-Federalists must be kept "from getting possession of the helm of state" by the plan Hamilton was now about to propose. Call the existing lame duck legislature into special session. Have the old Federalist majority change the law to provide for "the *choosing of electors by the people in districts.*" This "will insure a majority of votes in the United States for a federal candidate."

Hamilton was proposing to Jay that he steal the election that Burr and the Republicans had just won by having the lame duck legislature take away from the newly elected legislature its right to select presidential electors, and give it to district conventions instead. Hamilton saw clearly enough that the opposition would condemn this. But, he insisted to Jay, "it is justified by the unequivocal reasons of PUBLIC SAFETY." "Think well," he commanded Jay, "appreciate the extreme danger of the crisis."

Hamilton's conscience nagged him a little, but he resolved all doubts in favor of quick action: summon the legislature! No time must be lost, he told Jay. He saw the issue as a conflict between absolutes of vice and virtue: "Popular governments must certainly be overturned, and while they endure prove engines of mischief, if one party will call to its aid all the resources which vice can give, and if the other (however pressing the emergency) confines itself within all the ordinary forms of delicacy and decorum."

His proposal was "*legal* and *constitutional*," he insisted. Pitifully out of touch now with political reality, to the old friend who had known him in his prime, he added, "the motive ought to be frankly avowed." Yes, he went on, "in times like these in which we live, it will not do to be over scrupulous." The right end, as he saw it, seemed to justify almost any wrong means. He even exalted this pernicious prescript into the form of a general maxim for societal management by underscoring it for Jay's benefit in case he had missed the point: "*It is easy to sacrifice the substantial interests of society by a strict adherence to ordinary rules.*" At best, this is a meaningless statement not worth the paper it is written on. At worst, as a political or social maxim, it is a shocking, lawless reversal, a ripping out of all the innumerable stitches Hamilton had contributed by words and actions of more than 20 years to the fabric of law-abiding, moderate, constitutional American government before his breakdown in the face of the threats of his enemies in 1800.

John Jay had won a gubernatorial election from George Clinton by a narrow margin in 1792, only to have Aaron Burr snatch victory from his grasp by ruling in favor of Clinton on the disputed ballots. But Jay would also know of Hamilton's proneness to nervous derangements. No prosy Jay could ever forget the haunting imagery of the letter Hamilton had written him three days after Monroe and the congressmen had confronted him the night of December 15, 1792, with evidence of what he called "malicious intrigues to stab me in the dark." Neither Hamilton's vehemence now, nor the chance for reprisal against Burr, caused Jay to swerve from majestic rectitude. He endorsed on Hamilton's appeal the following words: "Proposing a measure for party purposes which it would not become me to adopt."

He did not even deign to acknowledge Hamilton's letter. The pointed rebuke from Hamilton's oldest political ally and most intimate confidant in a time of deepest stress was yet another prick of persecution from an unexpected quarter.

As summer came on, word arrived of still another upheaval in France, the coup d'état of 30 Prairial, in which the legislature purged all members of the Directory including Talleyrand, who had just sent Adams assurances that the new set of commissioners would be honorably treated. Adams remained serenely confident that he could effectively preside over the country in this kaleidoscopic period of crisis by remote control from Quincy. His friend Uriah Tracy warned him that "your real friends wish you to be with your officers, because the impression is, the government will be better conducted." But Adams hotly insisted that "the Secretaries of State, Treasury, War, Navy and the Attorney General transmit to me daily by post all the business of consequence." He fatuously added, "nothing is done without my advice and direction." He, therefore, saw no need to return to Philadelphia, which he sneeringly called "the chief seat of the synagogue."

Hamilton in the meantime was urging the cabinet, in their "desultory" chief's absence, to "agree what precise force should be created, *naval* and *land*." Many other decisions needed to be made that were not being made. They should take policy decisions into their own hands. "If there was a disposition, without prejudice and nonsense, to concert a national plan," he proffered, "I would cheerfully come to Philadelphia and assist in it," adding, "Nor can I doubt that success may be insured."

He directed McHenry to "break this subject to Pickering. His views are sound and energetic. Bring the other gentlemen to a consultation. If there is everywhere a proper temper, and it is wished, send for me and I will come." It was a discreet suggestion for an interregnum regime with Hamilton as its brightly uniformed head.

No immediate summons came to Hamilton from McHenry. Finally, he decided to call the meeting himself, only to hold it at Trenton, a few miles away from the usual late summer plaguey fevers of Philadelphia. He summoned General Charles Cotesworth Pinckney down from Rhode Island, where he had been visiting, and brought General James Wilkinson with him from New York. They would meet with McHenry and Pickering at a Trenton summit meeting without the president to decide all the vexed questions that Adams's half year of absence in Quincy had left dangling. In recent months Adams had not even deigned to reply to many letters the triumvirate had written him suggesting that the mission to France be called off because of the upheavals in government there.

What Hamilton and General Wilkinson, who had been hatching plans together in New York for months, did not know when they arrived in Trenton early in October was that

Adams had finally bestirred himself and was on his way south from Quincy. After seven months away from the seat of government, Adams reached Trenton on October 10.

The vain, proud, touchy Adams was astounded and outraged at what and whom he found there: Hamilton already installed, with all Adams's heads of departments paying him court! Hamilton, the leader of both the High Federalist and moderate factions of Adams's own divided party, apparently was presiding as kingpin at a summit meeting—a meeting at which Adams should have been the pinnacle, to which he had not even been invited. Worse, it had been kept secret from him. He had stumbled onto it by accident. How long had this been going on?

He was shocked; he was furious. He was choleric. Fifteen years later he was still at self-discrediting pains to describe how incredibly equable his own demeanor had been when Hamilton came to call on him to try to make him delay the French mission.

"I received him with great civility, as I always had done from my first knowledge of him," Adams insisted, making it perfectly clear. "I was fortunately in a very happy temper, and very good humor." Hamilton spoke, Adams recalled, "in a style of dogmatical confidence" of the future. He predicted that the days of the "sans culotte Republic" were numbered. How ridiculous, said Adams. (Less than a month later, the coup d'état of 18 Brumaire would overthrow the Directory once and for all and bring Napoleon to supreme power as first consul of the consulate.) Hamilton argued that peace negotiations now with France might bring Britain into war against the United States. "Great Britain could not hurt us!" Adams cried out.

After years of calm reflection, Adams still said, "Never in my life did I hear a man talk more like a fool." Every time he heard a man talk of the imminent downfall of France, Adams was inclined to laugh in his face, he said. (Two French governments fell within the year.)

Adams claimed he had said that the French revolution would last seven years more (it ended within the year). He averred that it was more probable that Great Britain than France would sue for peace (Britain never sued for peace; it was bumbled into war with the United States by Jefferson and Madison; Napoleon as first consul within a month adopted an actively pro-American policy and in effect sued for peace).

Hamilton pointed out that if monarchy were restored in France, the peace mission would be useless. This set Adams off again.

"I should as soon expect the sun, moon, and stars will fall from their orbits, as events of that kind take place," he raged (Napoleon as first consul then held de facto imperial power and became de jure Emperor in 1804).

"No matter what happens in France," he fumed, "it cannot do any injury to our country to have envoys there."

"Yes, it will," Hamilton coolly insisted.

"But if she proves faithless," Adams cried, "if she will not receive our envoys, does the disgrace fall upon her or us?" He ranted on: "Only then will the people of our country be satisfied that every honorable method has been tried to accommodate our differences."

"It's not that simple," Hamilton explained. "The damage will have been done to us."

"No! Absurd! Nonsense!" Adams erupted.

"It will increase our internal differences," said Hamilton.

Writing his self-serving account of this tense Trenton confrontation later, with the benefit of 15 years of hindsight, with knowledge of his loss of the presidency in 1800, and the split that would soon destroy the Federalist party, Adams still seemed not to grasp the point that to Hamilton's foreknowledge was central: "It will increase our internal differences." By leaving domestic and Federalist interests out of his self-justifying memories of the Trenton summit conference, Adams naïvely exposed his own ignorance of the political fact that Hamilton understood: no president could carry on effective foreign policy without a solid domestic political base. Adams, by his dogmatic self-righteousness, was splintering his and Hamilton's party, and committing political suicide.

Adams's rage distracted him from seeing that conditions had changed greatly during the half year he had been away. But there could be no changing course and yielding to Hamilton's urgings now, even to save the Federalists from a fatal split. He had to prove his own potency as president; another switch from a previous firm stand would betray impotence and "desultoriness."

The following year Hamilton would coolly ascribe Adams's intractable choler at Trenton to his personal ire at finding him present there. His own unexpected presence, Hamilton wrote, "was considered as evidence of a combination between the heads of departments, the Chief Justice [Hamilton's friend Ellsworth who had arrived there a few days after Adams] and myself, to endeavor to influence or counteract him in the affair of the mission. . . ."

He had summoned Adams's ministers to meet there "at the fountain head of information," where at Hamilton's feet they "would obtain any lights or information which they might suppose. useful."

At Adams's insistence, the final wording of the instructions to the commissioners was hammered out in a late night session on October 15.

Next morning, without consulting anyone, Adams ordered the commissioners to embark on the frigate *United States*, then lying off Newport, Rhode Island, on November 1 "or sooner" if the ship were ready.

A shocked, incredulous Pickering told his fellow Federalists that "the great question of the mission to France has been finally decided by the *President alone*." Fisher Ames wrote Pickering on November 5, 1799, that the mission would "*make* dangers and nullify resources; to make the navy without object; the army an object of popular terror . . ." He added, "The government will be weakened by the friends it loses and betrayed by those it will gain. . . ." The effect of Adams's "miraculous caprice" would be "at home, to embroil and divide; abroad, to irritate and bring losses and disgraces." Adams's reckless act, to Ames and Pickering, had been nothing but a cheap bid for popularity with an opposition that would never become his allies; it would be "fatal to the peace and reputation" not only of Adams but the solidarity of the Federalist party as well. Never had a sudden diplomatic move seemed to have less inherent urgency about it, except to Adams's unpredictable mind. They also agreed that it would give vastly more strength to the Republican opposers of the government.

Hamilton, as inspector general, was not particuarly worried about the Ellsworth mission as such, apart from its domestic political effects. Ellsworth and Davie, at least, would be "safe persons to be intrusted with the execution of a bad measure." But to McHenry and other Federalists, whatever its merits apart from party politics might be, the mission "is become an apple of discord."

As summer came on, instead of filling up complement with recruits, army enlistments fell farther and farther behind. By August 19, Hamilton was complaining bitterly to McHenry that the business "drags on," supply "proceeds heavily and without order or punctuality, in a manner ill-adapted to economy on a large scale" or efficiency or contentment of the army. By September 21 things were still worse. "Symptoms bordering on mutiny for the want of pay have been reported to me . . ."

Hamilton wrote out a detailed plan for Secretary of War McHenry to submit to Congress and sent a copy to George Washington. "One [measure] which I have always thought of primary importance," Hamilton said, "is a Military Academy." Washington responded warmly to Hamilton on November 28, 1799: "The Establishment of an Institution of this kind, upon a respectable and extensive basis, has ever been considered by me as an object of primary importance to this Country." Although unable to comment on details, he hoped Congress would "place it upon a permanent . . . footing."

But Hamilton's unexceptionable paper work did not erase an earlier stinging criticism by Washington of Hamilton's failure of performance in organizing the "Additional Army":

> If the augmented force was not intended as an in terorem [sic] measure, the delay in recruiting it, is unaccountable, and baffles all conjecture. . . . The . . . en-thusiasm . . . excited by the Publication of the Dispatches of our Commissioners at Paris (which gave birth to the Law authorizing . . . the twelve Regiments &c) are evaporated. It is now no more, and if this dull season, when men are idle . . . and from that cause might be induced to enlist, is suffered to pass away also, we shall . . . set out as a forlorn hope, to execute this business.

A little later, Washington had acknowledged Hamilton's failure as a fact and did not speak of the army, but "more properly of the embryo one, for I do not perceive . . . that we are likely to move beyond this."

George Washington died at Mount Vernon on December 14, 1799. HIs letter complimenting Hamilton on his plan for a military academy proved to be the last he ever wrote. For Hamilton, it did not much salve the sting of the earlier rebukes. Washington's death dissolved the last symbolic cement that had yoked the High Federalists and the moderate Federalists together in one team as "friends of the government," as their powerful slogan had insisted all good Federalists were. Adams—and Hamilton—had lost the lasting remaining symbol of Federalist unity at the very time they needed it most.

To Hamilton, Washington's death was a stunning political loss. He reacted to it in largely political terms. He had always been able to count on Washington for support in moments of crisis; Washington had been his shield and protector against all enemies, and now the shield was gone. Washington's death ended Hamilton's ability to manage Adams. Of all the terrible blows that fell on Hamilton as his century drew to its close, Washington's death was probably the heaviest. Hamilton's notes of condolence betray his own unique blend of political concerns for his own and the country's future. "Perhaps no friend of his has more cause to lament on personal account than myself," Hamilton told Pinckney. "From a calamity which is common to a mourning nation," he wrote to Martha Washington, "who can expect to be exempt? Perhaps it is even a privilege to have a claim to a larger portion of it than others."

With singular infelicity, he added to the widow, "I may, without impropriety, allude to the numerous and distinguished marks of confidence and friendship of which you have yourself been a witness, but I cannot say in how many ways the continuance of that confidence and friendship was necessary to me in future relations." And to Tobias Lear, Washington's longtime personal secretary, he wrote, "Perhaps no man . . . has equal cause with myself to deplore the loss. I have been much indebted to the kindness of the General, and he was *an Aegis very essential to me.*"

Hamilton then added a metaphysical speculation that revealed his own concern for public credit. "If virtue can secure happiness in another world, he is happy. In this the seal is now set upon his glory. It is no longer in jeopardy from the fickleness of fortune.''

Summing up the era that ended with Adams's unexpectedly stumbling upon Hamilton's summit conference with his triumvirate at Trenton and Washington's death, Professor Samuel Eliot Morison, in his biography of *Harrison Gray Otis*, wrote: ''At no period in the history of the United States has one man possessed so potent an influence over the federal government as Alexander Hamilton exerted during Washington's second administration and the first half of his successor's. . . . All important steps in executive policy, during the first two years of Adams's administration, originated in Hamilton's brain.'' It was not until a quarter of a century later, when he was 87 years old, that Adams himself had simmered down enough to see himself as others saw him, writing to Otis—still a suave genial Hamiltonian Federalist—''That all the sovereignty then existing in the nation was in the hands of Alexander Hamilton.'' Indeed, after so many years, Adams could even force a grim smile: ''I cannot review that tragicomic farce, grave as it was to me, without laughing. I was as President a mere cipher, the government was in the hands of an oligarchy consisting of a triumvirate who governed every one of my five ministers; both houses of Congress were under their absolute direction.''

To Rufus King, still in England, Hamilton wondered out loud: ''Who is to be Commander-in-Chief? Not the next in command [Hamilton]. The appointment will probably be deferred.''

In this he was correct.

After Trenton and with Washington's passing, it did not take an especially acute sense of realism to know that Adams would never consider Hamilton for any office of public credit again. Nevertheless, Hamilton automatically became the acting commander in chief. So Hamilton saw it as a humiliation that official recognition of his rank by automatic elevation to Washington's rank of lieutenant general would be denied him, along with the unqualified right to wear the commanding general's white plume.

Pickering again did his utmost. He announced to John Quincy Adams that ''the command of the army devolves of course on General Hamilton.'' Wilkinson, recognizing in himself the same kind of forlorn secret hope of promotion that plagued Hamilton's own mind, hastened to write him to say that ''it must be a consolation to the military to find the chief command in hands so able to administer the functions of the station. . . . I cannot more safely consign my own interests than to the sensibilities of your bosom—20 years a brigadier, a *patient* one too, I pant for promotion.''

Hamilton advised his aide George Izard on February 27, 1800, that he should quit the army; ''the military career in this country offers too few inducements.'' Hamilton no longer saw himself as an aegis under whom such a young man might rise. ''It is equally certain that my *present* station in the army *cannot* very long continue under the plan which seems to govern.'' He also was beginning to doubt even his own usefulness to the Federalists' cause. He inquired anxiously of Senator Sedgwick the same day he wrote young Izard, ''Will my presence be requisite as to this—or any other—purpose, and when?'' He seemed to assume that the sudden decline in future prospects for American greatness were coincident with, or a result, even, of his own (unmistakable to himself) decline. ''By the jealousy and envy of some, the miserliness of others, and the concurring influence of *all foreign powers*, America, if she attains to greatness, must *creep* to it. Will it be so?'' He claimed, unconvincingly, to be reconciled to impotence. He cited a maxim that was completely at odds with all the lessons of his life till now: ''Slow and sure is no bad maxim. Snails are a wise generation.''

Henry Lee wrote to Hamilton, at pains to disavow suggestions currently appearing in Republican newspapers that President Adams should leapfrog Lee over Hamilton's head to succeed Washington as the titular commander, just as Hamilton had been leapfrogged over Knox, Pinckney, and many others. Hamilton's reply to Lee on March 7, 1800, was at too great pains to deny hard truths that were becoming more and more evident to everyone but him: ''The truth is, that I pay very little attention to such newspaper ebullitions . . . You have mistaken a little observation in my last. Believe me, I feel no despondency of any sort.'' He went on despondently, ''I am not wholly insensible of the injustice which I from time to time experience, and of which, in my opinion, I am at this moment the victim.'' Malicious miscreants were seeking to impair his and Lee's friendship. ''Join me in looking with indifference upon their malicious efforts,'' he begged. ''As to the country, it is too young and vigorous to be quacked out of its political health; and as to myself, I feel that I stand on ground which, sooner or later, will assure me a triumph over all my enemies.''

Hamilton's anxiety and depression were patent to Lee, yet here was Hamilton vehemently denying ''despondency of any sort.'' With all hope of future promotion denied him, his policies toward France discarded, his cabinet triumvirate discredited, his party hopelessly splintered, and Washington dead, his lonely claim that he stood on ground that would assure him ''a triumph over all my enemies'' could hardly have been more tinny with false bravado.

Adams had won New York's electors in 1796. He ladled out a large share of the blame for having lost control of the New York legislature for 1800 to Hamilton's inept leadership, his suit against the *Argus,* and intrigues with Sedgwick and other high Federalists to slip Charles Cotesworth Pinckney into the presidency ahead of himself. In 1800, as he prepared to leave the capital as usual for Quincy, Adams suddenly decided to fire the cabinet inherited from Washington that had originally been handpicked by Hamilton.

On May 5 he summoned McHenry from a dinner party to confer on a routine matter. Seeing the Secretary standing before him full of what he suspected was a fawning, false deference, Adams lost his temper. He had heard that McHenry wished to hold on to his office after the coming presidential election. McHenry replied evasively. Adams exploded.

''Hamilton has been opposing the administration in New York,'' Adams charged furiously.

McHenry was not aware of it.

''No head of a department shall be permitted to oppose me,'' Adams cried, his face flushed with anger.

''I have heard no such conduct ascribed to General Hamilton and cannot think it to be the case,'' McHenry answered deferentially, but firmly.

''I know it, sir, to be so,'' Adams stormed, in effect calling his secretary of war a liar. ''You are subservient to him!'' he raged on. If Adams's matter had the ring of truth, his manner had a manic ring.

''Hamilton ruled Washington, and would still rule if he could.''

McHenry demurred.

''It was you who biased General Washington's mind.''

Nothing McHenry could do could stop Adams's torrent of abuse.

''You induced Washington to place Hamilton on the list of major generals, ahead of Knox and Pinckney.''

When this humiliation crossed Adams's mind, as McHenry recalled, Adams completely lost control of himself and began to rant. Hamilton was "an intriguant, the greatest intriguant in the world ." He was a man "devoid of every moral principle!" Hamilton was "a bastard," "a Creole bastard," and "as much a foreigner as Gallatin." As for Adams, he would rather serve under Jefferson as vice-president or even as resident minister at The Hague than to be indebted "to such a being as Hamilton for the presidency." To Adams, it was not to be borne that Washington had saddled him with three cabinet ministers who were babes in the woods of foreign policy. Wolcott was no use when it came to international diplomacy. "How could such men," he all but screamed, now entirely out of control, "dictate to me on such matters, or dare to recommend a suspension of the mission to France!"

He loosed a flood of suspicion, resentment, hatred, frustration, vexation, and uncontrolled fury on McHenry. When the crazy outburst finally subsided, McHenry, near tears, answered, "I shall, of course, resign at once."

Adams accepted. "Very well, sir," he said.

Then he began to cool off—indeed, feel shame. "For myself, I have always, I will acknowledge, considered you as a man of understanding and of the strictest integrity."

Poor McHenry slunk out of the room. The next day he submitted his resignation in writing, and Adams accepted it.

By this time Adams had probably got word that Pickering (as he had written Fisher Ames and William Bingham on October 24 and 29, 1799) was saying that Adams's sending off Ellsworth and Davie on the peace mission "will subvert the present administration and with it the government itself" and that only by refusing to seek a second term could Adams "unite the Federalists and save our country."

Four days later by a curt note Adams demanded Pickering's resignation. Two days later, Pickering replied to Adams that he could not afford to resign. He needed the salary and had counted on drawing it until the following March, when Jefferson would become president. Until then, Pickering said, "I do not feel it my duty to resign."

This was not only insulting to Adams, but witheringly defeatist. Adams exploded again. He fired a second note back to Pickering, telling him simply, "You are hereby discharged from any further service as Secretary of State."

To Hamilton, writing his attack on John Adams six months later, these dismissals confirmed his worst fears of Adams's "ungovernable temper" and "paroxysms of anger, which deprive him of self command, and produce very outrageous behaviour to those who approach him." Distinguished members of Congress, Hamilton added, not to speak of his own cabinet ministers, "have been humiliated by the effects of these gusts of passion."

Hamilton charged sarcastically that Adams's "little consideration for his ministers" in declining to consult them "had occasioned great dryness" between them. Hamilton was acutely conscious that he himself had been the cause of the firings. "It fell to my lot," he had been told, "to be distinguished by a torrent of gross personal abuse." Besides calling him a "Creole bastard," Adams had accused him of having caused the loss of the New York election out of ill will.

The confrontation between Adams and poor, gentle, inept McHenry "was of a nature to excite alternately pain and laughter," Hamilton sighed, pain for Adams's "weak and excessive indiscretions" and "laughter at the ludicrous topics which constituted charges." One such charge was that McHenry in a report to the House had "*eulogized* General Washington, and had attempted to eulogize General Hamilton." This was "Wonderful! passing wonderful!" Hamilton chortled. "That a eulogy of the dead patriot and hero should be in any shape, irksome to the ears of his successor!" The crowning folly of Adams's manic defense was his denying praise to Hamilton. It was "singular, that an encomium on the officer, first in rank of the armies of the United States, appointed and continued by Mr. Adams, should in his eyes have been a crime in the head of the War Department and that it should be necessary in order to avert his displeasure, to obliterate a compliment to that officer from an official report" to the House of Representatives.

Adams immediately appointed Samuel Dexter, a Massachusetts senator, whose Federalism was so moderate that his friends called him "Ambi" Dexter, to be secretary of war and John Marshall as secretary of state. The Senate confirmed. Although Wolcott had served Hamilton longer and more intimately than, and as faithfully as the others. Adams left him to dangle in cabinet office. Wolcott observed that Adams "considers Col. Pickering., McHenry and myself as his enemies. His resentments against General Hamilton are excessive; he declares his belief of the existence of a British faction in the United States."

Before adjourning on May 14, Congress dismantled Hamilton's provisional army, suspended further enlistments, passed a law authorizing early discharges for officers and men, and cut the military budget from over four million to about three million, mostly by postponing construction of heavy frigates and ending army enlistments. Jefferson contentedly purred that "on the whole the federalists have not been able to carry a single strong measure in the lower house the whole session."

High Federalists saw these dovish measures of Congress as an electioneering effort of Adams to gain quick popular favor with Republicans, if not outright treachery to Federalist principles. Pickering charged that Adams had made a "corrupt bargain with the Democrats [Republicans] to secure his second election." When Adams denied such a deal, Pickering fired back, "I will only say that the President is not always consistent or accurate in his rememberance."

After an absence in Albany on private legal affairs for a month in January and February, leaving Adjutant General William North in charge of the dispirited army, Hamilton returned to duty with much brisk spirit. He visited the encampment at Scotch Plains, New Jersey, directed that old regiments be filled out by new recruits from those to be dissolved, and made sure that all soldiers, when discharged, were paid in full, including three months' dismissal pay. In June he took a swing through Massachusetts, New Hampshire, and Rhode Island, ostensibly to inspect troop encampments, but secretly to canvass federal electors in those states to find out how firmly they would hold their votes to Pinckney for second place after Adams. Hamilton thanked the departing troops for the president and himself and hoped their patriotism would lean them to a just construction of the motives of the government.

On July 1, 1800, Hamilton quit his headquarters in New York and next day notified the secretary of war that he considered his military service ended. He submitted his accounts and put his uniform away. On the same day he began to busy himself with his plan to install Pinckney as president.

With the next election still four months away, Federalist chances were by no means hopeless. New England's electors remained solidly behind Adams for president. Canvassing all the states in August, George Cabot forecast 67 votes for Pinckney, 65 for Jefferson, and 59 for Adams. Much depended on still uncertain electors in middle states like Pennsylvania, Delaware, and Maryland and on Adams's friends holding firm and voting for Pinckney too.

In his 1800 campaign for Charles Cotesworth Pinckney, Hamilton wrote Wolcott "his tour had shown him there were solid federal electors in all the New England states," but that "there is considerable doubt of a perfect union in favor of Pinckney." Therefore, he concluded, "it is essential to inform the most discreet of this description of the facts which

denote unfitness in Mr. Adams. I have promised confidential friends a correct statement.''
This was more of a threat than a promise.

Hamilton corresponded with leaders of Federalism throughout the country in similar
vein: Jefferson must be defeated, but it was just as essential that Adams be replaced by
Pinckney. But Harper of South Carolina sensibly warned ''that no direct attempt can safely
be made to drop or supersede Mr. Adams. It would create uncertainty, division and defeat.
Let both men be held up till the Electors come to vote; and then let those who think Mr.
Adams unfit to be President drop him silently.''

Hamilton was determined on a surer way to triumph over all his enemies. It was August,
his family was in Albany, and New York City's usual summer fevers gripped his brain. As
in other feverish summers of the past, he wrote another awful pamphlet better left unwritten.

Writing at speed, he produced the extraordinary document entitled ''The Public Conduct
and Character of John Adams, Esq., President of the United States.'' In the form of a letter,
it is addressed to an unnamed ''Sir.'' It is full of Hamilton himself in the first person singular
and Mr. Adams in the third person. It reads as if it is really addressed to all and sundry of the
enemies Hamilton's paranoia now senses to be crowding in on him; enemies all but crowd
Mr. Adams out of the opening paragraphs. Here would be the final ''triumph over all my
enemies'' Hamilton had promised Henry Lee in March.

''Warm personal friends of Mr. Adams are taking unwearied pains to disparage the
motives of those Federalists who advocate the equal support of General Pinckney at the
approaching election of President and Vice President,'' Hamilton begins his attack.
Adams's friends had exhibited Hamilton in all manner of ''derogatory aspects''; they were
''versatile factious spirits''; they were ''ambitious spirits''; they were ''intriguing partisans
of Great Britain.'' There had been ''a full share of obloquy'' vented against Hamilton and
others, but there were besides, he said, ''peculiar accusations devised to swell the catalogue
of my demerits.'' Therefore, defending his own manic defense more than attacking Adams,
he wrote, ''It is necessary, for the public cause, to repel these slanders, by stating the real
views of the persons who are calumniated, and the reasons of their conduct.'' President
Adams ''is a man of imagination sublimated and eccentric; propitious neither to the regular
display of sound judgement, nor to steady perseverance in a systematic plan of conduct.''
Worse, ''to this defect are added the unfortunate foibles of a vanity without bounds, and a
jealousy capable of discoloring every object.'' From the very beginning, Adams had been
guilty of ''disgusting egotism, distempered jealousy, and ungovernable indiscretion.''
These were the same defects Hamilton's warmest, fondest, and closest friends like Gouverneur Morris found in him. In support of this indictment, Hamilton described Adams's
explosions at Trenton with McHenry and Pickering.

It was inexcusable, as Hamilton saw it, that Adams raged against Mr. Hamilton and
overwhelmed him with ''a torrent of gross personal abuse.'' Adams had dismissed his
secretaries of state and war contemptuously from office, taken contradictory and equally
atrocious stands on both the hawkish and dovish sides of the issue of war with France, had
sunk the tone of the public mind, sowed the seeds of discord at home, and lowered the
reputation of the government abroad. He had tried to prevent the appointment of Mr.
Hamilton as inspector general and ''stigmatized'' him ''as the leader of a British faction.''

During the summer Hamilton had written at least two letters to Adams demanding to
know if Adams had ever called him the leader of the British faction, but Adams had never
deigned to respond. The specific examples Hamilton cited in support of such monstrous
charges fell pathetically short of carrying the weight of proof he assigned to them. Hamilton
gives an example of Adams's fatuous vanity: ''Being among the guests invited to dine with

the Count Vergennes, Minister for Foreign Affairs, Mr. Adams thought fit to give a specimen of American politeness by conducting Madame de Vergennes to dinner; on the way, she was pleased to make retribution in the current coin of French politeness—by saying to him 'Monsieur Adams, vous êtes le Washington de negociation.' '' Adams, noting down the incident, had made the following self-satisfied comment upon it: ''These people have a very pretty knack of paying compliments.'' Hamilton made the following supercilious comment on Adams's reaction: ''He might have added, they also have a very dexterous knack of disguising a sarcasm.''

His belaboring of Adams with this feeble anecdote betrays the rather trivial and personal nature of the grievances that to Hamilton's mind now seemed to undermine the security of the state. Hamilton's conclusion was that Mr. Adams ''does not possess the talents adapted to the administration of government, and there are great and intrinsic defects in his character, which unfit him for the office of chief magistrate.'' Here was absolute disqualification of Adams to hold the office that he had already held for almost four years.

But this was not Hamilton's conclusion. Here was his ludicrous *non sequitur:* ''Yet with this opinion of Mr. Adams, I have finally resolved not to advise the withholding from him a single vote.'' Why not? ''The body of Federalists for want of sufficient knowledge of facts, are not convinced of the expediency of relinquishing him. It is even apparent, that a large proportion still retain the attachment which was once a common sentiment.''

In the conclusion to his attack on John Adams, Hamilton exposes himself as a logical lunatic. He even insisted on signing his name to this double-talk—though men like Cabot and Wolcott had advised him against doing so. He rushed it to the printer.

Never in their most irresponsible heyday had the *Aurora* or the *Argus* published a more libelous, boldly malicious attack on a government official. Hamilton had set himself above the law.

In the text of the pamphlet itself, Hamilton admitted to being ''sensible of the inconveniences of giving publicity'' to such an unfortunate ''development'' in ''the character of the Chief Magistrate of our country.'' He lamented the necessity of taking the step he was taking. But, triumphing over enemies was of overriding importance. ''It would not do to be over scrupulous,'' he wrote. ''To suppress truths, the disclosure of which is as interesting to the public welfare as well as to my friends and myself, did not appear to me justifiable.''

He so far heeded the cooler heads among his friends that he caused the printing to be done with secrecy and arranged for the pamphlet to be sent out only to ''the leaders of the first class.'' But if Adams were really to be supported, ''bona fide,'' any fool could see that the pamphlet had better never been written. Perhaps Hamilton thought that the final statement could be used as a means of placating ''the leaders of the second class,'' to whom it might conceivably be shown, while the rest of the text would plant in their minds enough seeds of doubt so that they would switch to Pinckney as first choice at the last minute. To rational minds, such reasoning would expose its author as a contemptible hypocrite or a sick man.

Aaron Burr ripped aside all feverish subtleties and sophistries. He had always commanded the best political intelligence. Tammany included many artisan members who worked in printers' shops. Burr managed to purloin a copy of the pamphlet in proof or fresh off the press while it was still classified as a secret Federalist paper. Recognizing it for the political bombshell it was, Burr reprinted it in Republican newspapers before the originals had reached the hands of the Federalist inner circle, for whose eyes it had been intended.

Waves of laughter rippled through Republican ranks. Rank and file Federalists were aghast at the sorry secret story of the mess in Philadelphia within the highest circles of their own self-righteous paladins.

Federalist publicists rushed to attack Hamilton for what he had done to their party and president. Hamilton defiantly announced to intimates that he planned to issue a second pamphlet to explain the first. Of this, he was, for once, dissuaded. Cabot, whose warnings Hamilton had ignored, clenched his teeth and reported that many Federalists, even those who "approved the sentiments, thought the avowal of them imprudent, and the publication of them untimely." Other men whose opinions Hamilton had to respect accused him of exhibiting the same or worse vanity as that with which he charged Adams.

To Adams, Hamilton's "exuberant vanity and insatiable egotism prompt him to be ever restless and busy meddling with things far above his capacity, and inflame him with an absolute rage to arrogate to himself the honor of suggesting every measure of government." That was not all. "He is no more fit for a prompter than Phaeton to drive the chariot of the sun. If his projects had been followed they would absolutely have burnt up the world."

James Cheetham, a prime Republican pamphleteer and "disorganizer" of Federalists, sneered that President Adams had "too much judgment and independence to submit to the leading strings of the ex-secretary. Here was disappointed ambition; . . . a clue to that mysterious character, whose power, if equal to his will, would bestride the world."

Cheetham praised Adams for his policy of peace, for pardoning Fries, and for smoothing differences with France. But his principal praises were for Jefferson. By way of unhappy contrast with that virtuous Virginian, Cheetham pejorated Hamilton's *Reynolds Pamphlet* and deplored his lapses from personal chastity.

Another pamphleteer would "discover the black blood that eddies round [Hamilton's] heart." If the Jeffersonians won the election, all blame must be laid to Hamilton's "malice of disappointed ambition, animated with the hope of speedy resuscitation" if Charles Cotesworth Pinckney should slip in. Hamilton's army was useless; Adams's naval defense program was better liked by the people. Hamilton's sensitivites were badly deranged if he took umbrage at being called pro-British, while "this same tender mind could bear the reproach of breaking one of the most solemn ordinances . . . of God and man. . . ."

In 1800 the Republicans had similar but less intense blood feuds smoldering within their ranks, but managed to paper them over better, at least until they came to power. Jefferson was the unanimous choice for standard-bearer. Aaron Burr cashed a due bill claiming that in secret caucus four years earlier John Beckley had promised him Jefferson's support in 1800 if he would withdraw in 1796 to avoid taking votes from Jefferson. It was reluctantly honored. Aaron Burr was agreed on for vice-president over elderly George Clinton even though Burr's rising political star would be a long-term threat to the party's dominant Virginia junto. The junto could fix Burr later.

Burr's rise past him to the next-to-top rung of the ladder alarmed and enraged Hamilton as much as, if not more than, Adams's candidacy. On August 6, Hamilton wrote to Bayard that "there seems to be too much probability that Jefferson or Burr will be President." If, by some chance, it should be Burr, he "will certainly attempt to reform the government *a la Bonaparte*. He is as unprincipled and dangerous a man as any country can boast—as true a Cataline as ever met in midnight conclave."

By now, Hamilton had reached the point—unthinkable for a good Federalist—of openly preferring Jefferson to Adams. "General Hamilton makes no secret of his opinion that Jefferson should be preferred to Adams," wrote Troup. It had become a case of anyone but Adams—anyone, that is, anyone except Burr. Hamilton still had hopes for Pinckney. The "leaders of the first class" were now heartily with him on that point.

But Dr. James McHenry put his finger on the trouble with all this letter-writing among the "leaders of the first class." With some asperity, he wrote: "Have our party shown that they possess the necessary skill and courage to deserve to be continued to govern? What have they done? . . . They write private letters. To whom? To each other. But they do nothing to give a proper direction to the public mind.''

Federalists were split wide open, and Republicans were triumphantly united. Burr's skillful tactics in New York had snatched that pivotal state from Hamilton. South Carolina cast its electoral votes unanimously for Jefferson and Burr. When the smoke cleared, the Republicans had won. Jefferson and Burr had each received 73 electoral votes; Adams, 65; and Pinckney, 64; there was a solitary independent vote for Jay. The reign of the Federalists was over. The Second American Revolution had come.

But who had won, Jefferson or Burr? The fascinating "might have been" is that if Hamilton had never written his pamphlet, either Adams or Pinckney might have come out ahead of Jefferson and Burr. Cabot's earlier canvass of 67 for Pinckney, 65 for Jefferson, and 59 for Adams might have held up. Hamilton's man Pinckney would have been president, and Hamilton would, in truth, have been the King of the Feds. Or if Hamilton had held control of the New York legislature—instead of losing by a one-vote upset to Burr—his loyal henchmen there would have insured that Pinckney finished first and Jefferson second. At 43, Hamilton would have had many years remaining to move on into the presidency himself.

Nothing in the system guarantees that a man with the drive of a Hamilton cannot mount to the first office even after suffering one or more such secret psychic crises and more than one unexpected rejection in elections that should have been won. At least one other surmounted worse obstacles and won the presidency at last by an overwhelming margin, en route to a still more devastating downfall, similarly self-indicted by his own words.

The *Aurora* on November 6 published as an "advertisement" "PRO BONO PUBLICO, Hamilton's Last Letter and His Amorous Vindication Just Published. Price Fifty Cents." John Beckley wrote Ephraim Kirby on October 25, 1800, that "in a labored effort to belittle the character of the president" Hamilton had "belittled his own." Hamilton's "career of ambition is passed, and neither honor or empire will ever be his. As a political nullity, he has inflicted upon himself the sentence 'Aut Caesar, aut Nullus.' ''

But it was Noah Webster, the great lexicographer, a hardy son of the Northern states, an able, moderate Federalist long loyal to Hamilton's principles, writing under the pseudonym of Aristides, a *Federalist,* who struck the cruelest blow of all at the original *Mr. Federalist.* The policies that Hamilton reproached were recent. In the government and after his resignation, Hamilton had filled the office of prime minister with skill. But President Adams had restrained his influence "and called into *open* opposition, the *secret* enmity which . . . long rankled'' in Hamilton's breast. Hamilton's criticisms of Adams were of a private, trifling nature. It was Hamilton's fault that his party had been divided and defeated. The ill success of Hamilton's attempt to raise an army and the success of the president's mission to France, which removed every pretext for a permanent armed force, were what had produced "the deep chagrin and disappointment of a military character."

Hamilton's talents and confidence in his influence were so great that he disdained public opinion; he had overleaped and ignored ordinary scruples and rules. Webster was reminded of the mad times when Hamilton had invited the mob's attack defending Jay's Treaty in Wall Street. And the shock of his public avowal of his intrigue with Mrs. Reynolds'! But most reckless and lawless of all was his present attempt to split the Federalists "and . . . compleat our overthrow and ruin!''

By contrast to Hamilton, Adams was a man "of pure morals, inflexible patriotism, and the best read statesman'' of the Revolutionary period. Set beside these qualifications, his "occasional ill-humor at unreasonable opposition and hasty expressions . . . are of little weight." On the other hand, Webster charged Hamilton, "Your conduct on this occasion will be deemed little short of insanity." In sum, Hamilton's "ambition, pride, and overbearing temper" had marked him as "the evil genius of this country."

Noah Webster had a knack of coming up with pointed words that defined things.

When a mysterious-looking package arrived one day at the Hamiltons' it was much too late for William Bingham to repair the psychic damage he had inflicted on his friend by denying to McHenry that Hamilton had ever lodged the Reynolds papers with him. Bingham wrote Hamilton on July 21, 1801: "Having a packet of papers which by your desire were deposited with me, and which have long lain dormant in my possession and being about embarking in a short time for Europe, permit me to return them to you."

It seems certain that the packet he so offhandedly shipped back to Hamilton was indeed Hamilton's set of the Reynolds papers. Hamilton might brush aside the "ebullitions" of enemies, but this token to remind him of two years of self-exposure as a public liar to two of his closest friends must have been one more wrench of a ratchet in his mind toward madness. Bingham's earlier insistence that Hamilton had never deposited the Reynolds papers with him should probably be ascribed to a typical rich man's forgetfulness, heedlessness, annoyance earlier at the bother of looking for them, or unwillingness to become further entangled in an alliance that brought such scandalous notoriety with it, even for a friend.

There is no evidence of what became of the papers after Hamilton received them back. They have never been found. For what it is worth, *Bibliotheca Americana: A Dictionary of Books Relating to America, from its Discovery to the Present Time*, VIII, 28, says that Hamilton's edition of *The Reynolds Pamphlet* was bought up and destroyed by Hamilton's family. But his family was much too late. Nothing they could do would keep the apparition from reappearing to haunt him year after year all the way to the end of his course toward the certain security of self-destruction. In another world, the seal set upon glory would no longer be in jeopardy of such fickleness of fortune.

34

His Countenance Is Strongly Stamped with Grief

[Jefferson is] tinctured with fanaticism . . . crafty . . . not scrupulous . . . nor very mindful of the truth . . . and . . . a contemptible hypocrite.

[Burr is] one of the most unprincipled men in the United States . . . a voluptuary by system . . . far more cunning than wise.

—To James A. Bayard of Delaware, January 16, 1801

Jefferson or Burr? The former without all doubt.

—To Gouverneur Morris, December 24, 1800

The presidential electors chosen by the states in October 1800 would meet in each state on December 4 to cast their ballots for president and vice-president. During this tense period of uncertainty, congressmen and other government officials were gathering for the first time in the raw new capital at Washington to be there for the convening of the second session of the sixth Congress on November 21.

The records of the War and Treasury departments arrived from Philadelphia at half-finished new offices in Washington. A few days later, a fire broke out, which burned up most of the Treasury's records. Its timing and circumstances reminded the *Aurora's* new editor, William Duane, of the old charges of a cover-up at the Treasury under Alexander Hamilton, and, before him, William Duer. On November 19 he reported in a style worthy of Beckley that "The *federal fireworks* at Washington will be found to have made a very rueful chasm in our *war history;* Alexander Hamilton's projects and Timothy Pickering's transactions, while secretary will have had a *partial sweep*, to avoid the scrutinizing of a Jeffersonian administration."

533

Hamilton's friend James McHenry saw the same fireworks as a terrible misfortune for Hamilton and Wolcott: "What will it not enable the calumniator to say and insinuate, and how shall the innocent man find his justification?"

The first fire had been only a "partial sweep." When an even more suspicious second fire broke out January 20 in the building where the Treasury stored the records that had survived the first, Oliver Wolcott, Jr., escaping from the flames, was able to retrieve only two chests and a trunk. Notwithstanding Wolcott's rescue efforts, Republican newspapers charged him with a second political arson: "The friends of Hamilton begin to speak more boldly of his fame, since the Federal fireworks at Washington have rendered it impossible ever fairly to investigate the treasury accounts." Hamilton must have wondered apprehensively whether the two chests and the trunk retrieved by Wolcott contained the missing packet of Reynolds papers which William Bingham, Esq. had denied having in his possession until he returned them. It would torture Hamilton that records by which he corroborated his protestations of innocence of the calumnies of his enemies had all gone up in smoke, of suspicious origin. To Hamilton it would seem as Christopher Marlowe had written, that "Hell hath no limits," nor is it "circumscribed in one self-place." Despite everything that Hamilton had contributed to the Federalists' defeat in the presidential election—as both enemies and friends never ceased to remind him—the margin of defeat had been so narrow that the recriminations and might-have-beens were more painful than would have been the case in a loss by a landslide: his attack on John Adams might just have made the difference.

What with unpopular taxes, a Republican swing in Pennsylvania, fears of a standing army and its cost, hostility to Great Britain, the skill and enterprise of Beckley, Burr, and Jefferson, Hamilton's attack, the firing of the secretaries, the Alien and Sedition acts—the real wonder was that Adams had lost by the narrow margin of only 73 to 65. Abigail Adams put her finger on the single most significant cause of the disaster: "The defection of New York has been the source," she wrote her son Thomas on November 13, 1800. "That defection was produced by the intrigues of two men [Hamilton and Burr]—one of them sowed the seeds of discontent and division amongst the Federalists, and the other seized the lucky moment of mounting into power upon the shoulders of Jefferson."

The switch of a few dozen or hundred votes in Hamilton's own New York City would have given him enough votes in the legislature to elect his own docile electors to cast New York's 12 votes for Pinckney, with two (or more) dutifully throwing their vice-presidential ballots away from Adams to Jay. The result would have been Jefferson 61, Burr 61, Pinckney 76, Adams 75, and Jay 3. Or if South Carolina's electors had supported her native son, Pinckney, for only one of the two places on the ticket, instead of the relatively unknown Burr, and two or more had thrown away their Jefferson votes on someone else, Hamilton's man Pinckney could have won that way too, even without New York. At the same time, Adams would have been finished for good and all.

To many Federalist insiders, particularly High Federalists, the actual outcome demonstrated the absolute correctness of Hamilton's preelection strategy and tactics. A successful party leader would rather lose an election and survive in power for the next one than win if it means losing his preeminence in power to the winner of his own party. In this sense, Hamilton had snatched a personal victory from a disaster. With Adams and Pinckney finished politically, Hamilton was left as the sole surviving leader and rallying point for the Federalist faithful. A president of the same party in the White House would no longer threaten his preeminence—but a new one from his own home town would.

The tactic of an "equal vote" for president and vice-president that Hamilton had urged on Federalists had failed them, but it worked perfectly or, rather, too well, for their opponents.

With the 73-to-73 tie between Jefferson and Burr, the election would now have to be decided in the House of Representatives. As the only undiscredited major leader among the Federalists, Hamilton with his influence on the votes of Federalist congressmen would hold the balance of power. He busied himself exercising it by writing Oliver Wolcott, Jr., on December 16, taking note that many Federalists in Congress much preferred Burr to Jefferson: "I trust New England at least will not so far lose its head as to fall into this snare." Snare? A moderate like Burr? Yes, Hamilton explained, because "upon every virtuous and prudent calculation, Jefferson is to be preferred. He is by far not so dangerous a man and he has pretensions to character." Wolcott and others must take "early measures to fix on this point the opinions of the Federalists." Otherwise, "among them, from different motives, Burr will find partisans."

To rank and file Federalists, Thomas Jefferson remained Mr. Random Radical himself, a superrich slave master, a wealthy self-promoter by paid-off pamphleteers, a traitor to his class, the embodiment of all that was abhorrent to the wise and good. With Burr, on the other hand, most Federalists were personally on good terms. He seemed moderate, he was something of an aristocrat by temperament and socially acceptable, and though his political and financial ideas would bear no more careful scrutiny than Jefferson's, his ostentatious devotion to ailing Theodosia at Richmond Hill and gentlemanly promiscuity in Philadelphia and Washington seemed less decadently repellent than Jefferson's rumored concubinage at mysterious, many-cupolaed Monticello.

Pickering noted that Burr was "actuated by ordinary ambition, Jefferson by that and Jacobinic philosophy." Burr might "be satisfied by power and property. [Jefferson] must see the roots of our society pulled up. . . ." Pickering added that "the devoted friends of [Jefferson] are alarmed lest the federalists should prefer [Burr]. . . . the federal interest will not be so systematically opposed under Mr. B as under Mr. J."

Worst of all from Hamilton's point of view was that Burr, with Federal support, would be a threat to his own newly emergent leadership of the Federal Republican party in his home state, in a way that Jefferson would never be.

It was painful to Hamilton that one of his oldest and closest friends, Robert Troup, who was also a friend of Burr's, was warning other friends that "The influence . . . of this letter [Hamilton's attack on Adams] upon Hamilton's character is extremely unfortunate. An opinion has grown out of it, which at present obtains almost universally, that his character *is radically deficient in discretion*, and therefore the federalists ask, what avail the most pre-eminent talents—the most distinguished patriotism—without the all important quality of discretion? Hence he is considered an unfit head of the party—and we are in fact without a rallying point."

To head off the possibility that Burr would become such a rallying point, Hamilton wrote to leaders far and wide indicting Burr. To Senator Gouverneur Morris the day before Christmas 1800, Hamilton put the case crisply: "*Jefferson or Burr?*—the former without all doubt. The latter . . . has no principle, public or private—could be bound by no agreement—will listen to no monitor but his ambition; and for this purpose will use the *worst* part of the community as a ladder to permanent power, & an instrument to crush the better part. He is bankrupt beyond redemption except by the resources that grow out of war and disorder or by a sale to a foreign power or by great speculation." An immediate war with Great Britain would be, for Burr, an instrument of redemption. Burr, like Jefferson, owed staggering debts to British creditors. Burr would never be won to Federal views, would be "restrained by no moral scruple," would call to his side "rogues of all parties to overrule good men of all parties. . . ." Hamilton concluded, "He is sanguine enough to hope every thing, daring enough to attempt every thing, wicked enough to scruple nothing. From the elevation of such a man may heaven preserve the country!''

To Wolcott, Hamilton wrote on December 16 that Burr's ''private character is not defended by his most partial friends. He is bankrupt beyond redemption, except by the plunder of his country. . . . He is truly the Catiline of America.''

Hamilton sent Wolcott another letter the next day suggesting a deal with Jefferson: obtain his definite assurances, in exchange for Federal votes, on (1) preservation of the present fiscal system, (2) adherence to neutrality in Europe, (3) the continuance of federalists in sub-cabinet offices, with the president installing only the heads of cabinet departments, and (4) preservation of the navy and defense establishment.

As the time approached for the House to convene and ballot on February 11, Hamilton's animadversions against Burr became hysterical: To Sedgwick he railed:

> The appointment of Burr as President would disgrace our country abroad. No agreement with him could be relied upon. His private circumstances render disorder a necessary resource. His public principles offer no obstacle. His ambition aims at nothing short of permanent power and wealth in his own person. For heaven's sake, let not the federal party be responsible for the elevation of this man!

Troup wrote mournfully to Rufus King on February 12, ''Hamilton is profoundly chagrined with the prospect! He has taken infinite pains to defeat Burr's election, but he believes in vain. . . . Hamilton at our club on Saturday last declared that his influence with the federal party was wholly gone—and that he could be no longer useful.''

Hamilton's solitary fight against Burr seemed to his closest friends to be a reckless, irrational fight in which some unfathomable idea of personal honor was at stake. What they took to be Hamilton's paranoid anxiety on the subject of Burr was probably the outward manifestation of Hamilton's knowing a despicable secret about Burr's badger game that could be spoken of among gentlemen in no more explicit way.

The balloting to break the tie was done by states, one vote for each state, with each state deciding which way to vote by a majority of the members of its House delegation. A majority of the states—nine in number—was necessary to elect. Under this system, James A. Bayard's vote as Delaware's only congressman counted for as much as all the congressmen from Virginia. On the first ballot, Jefferson had eight states and Burr six; two states had tied within their delegations, and their votes were marked as blanks. A count of the votes of all the individual congressmen in all the delegations would have given Burr 55 to Jefferson's 51. Only a few Federalists, influenced by Hamilton, split away from the party caucus to vote for Jefferson. If Federalists in the state delegations had been unanimous for Burr, Burr would have been elected the third president of the United States. Had Hamilton done nothing and followed the advice of his closest friends, Burr would have won with undivided Federalist support. But Hamilton waged one of the hardest fights of his life to win the presidency for his mute and absent enemy Jefferson. It also, incidentally, helped to produce the result that would carry out the will of the voters of the country.

The deadlock continued as the House balloted 34 times over six hectic days. Outside the halls of Congress anger mounted in the country over the grim prospect that manifest popular will would be frustrated by a deal for Federalist votes.

There were threatening secessional rumbles from Southerners who saw the Federalists of the New England states about to frustrate their own electors, and from New England states fearful of Democratic domination by the South.

Most Federalists were still determined to elect Burr. They had all along assumed that he would be willing to take the presidency as their gift and make the same deal that Hamilton and others had demanded of Jefferson. They sent an emissary to him in New York, where he was busy with plans for the marriage of his famously attractive daughter, Theodosia. The emissary returned with the astonishing news that Burr would make no deal; he would make no commitments to them of any kind.

James A. Bayard was the key. Hamilton wrote him on January 16 pulling out all stops. He would not be Jefferson's apologist, for "his politics are tinctured with fanaticism; . . . he is too much in earnest in his democracy; . . . he has been a mischievous enemy to the principal measures of our past administration; . . . he is crafty . . . not scrupulous about the means of success, nor very mindful of truth, and . . . he is a contemptible hypocrite."

So much said, Bayard should remember that Jefferson was no sworn enemy to scope for the executive. Hungry for popularity, Jefferson would be slow to overturn what was established. He would be temporizing rather than violent. As favor for France cooled in America, so would Jefferson's zeal for the Jacobin delirium. Nor was he "capable of being corrupted." By contrast with Jefferson, Burr was "one of the most unprincipled men in the United States," "cares only for himself, and nothing for his country or glory." He was "a voluptuary by system," and he was "far more cunning than wise . . . more dexterous than able."

Bayard yielded to Hamilton, grumbling that "the means existed of electing Burr" if Burr had only cooperated. According to his own account, he determined to break the deadlock. He sought from Jefferson the assurances that Hamilton had declared to be requisite. Jefferson, he said, gave him the assurances. On February 17, on the thirty-fifth ballot, Federalist members of three delegations cast blank ballots, and on the thirty-sixth Jefferson was elected president by ten states to four, with two not voting.

Jefferson afterward denied that he had made the commitments to the Federalists that Bayard said had caused him to change his vote, but Jefferson's moderate actions afterward belied his words. Bayard afterward told Hamilton that he would have switched to Burr if Burr had been willing to make the same deal with the Federalists that Jefferson had agreed to make, but Burr had been "determined not to shackle himself with federal principles."

It would not have escaped Burr's notice—his sources of political intelligence were better than those of any of his contemporaries except Jefferson—that the frantic efforts of Hamilton, more than anyone else, were all that had prevented him from becoming the third president. Nor would Jefferson be likely to forget the compromise of his preferred stance above the fray and the unacknowledged debt to Hamilton his close victory had cost him.

So Aaron Burr became vice-president of the United States. He remains all but unique in the spotty annals of that peculiar office because he gained it by refusing to make a deal.

To Federal Republicans, the French Revolution had taken place in America. Some waited for the earth to heave and rumble, the heavens to fall, the tumbrels to roll, and the fabric of society to disintegrate. The lame duck Federalist House appointed the usual investigating committee to investigate whether or not Wolcott had set the suspicious fires; it found no Federalist wrongdoing. The outgoing Adams appointed John Marshall as chief justice and many other midnight jurists on January 31, the night of his leaving office.

On March 4, Jefferson made a conciliatory inaugural address. "We are all republicans; we are all federalists!" he announced. George Cabot mocked him sourly: "We are all tranquil as they say at Paris after a revolution." But he noted, with well-mixed emotions, that "Mr. Jefferson's conciliatory speech is better liked by our party than his own."

As he explained to John Dickinson on July 23, 1801, Jefferson was seeking to win over the mass of the Federalists. He wrote:

> The greatest good we can do our country is to heal its party divisions & make them one people. I do not speak of their leaders who are incurable, but of the honest and well-intentioned body of the people. . . . both sects are republican, entitled to the confidence of their fellow-citizens. Not so their quondam leaders, covering under the mask of federalism hearts devoted to monarchy. The Hamiltonians, the Essex-men, the revolutionary tories &c. They have a right to tolerance, but neither to confidence nor power.

Jefferson acknowledged no debt to Hamilton, and it galled Hamilton that Jefferson's soft words stole the hearts of many Federalists, especially those of the "2nd class leaders."

There remained to Hamilton but one more political hurrah. Following Jefferson's inauguration in the spring of 1801, New York would ballot for governor. The hardy perennial, old George Clinton, was again a candidate, this time to succeed John Jay, who was retiring. It was age versus youth when the disorganized Federalists nominated Lieutenant Governor Stephen Van Rensselaer, and Hamilton turned toward making a supreme effort to elect his brother-in-law, husband of Elizabeth's younger sister, Margarita "Peggy" Schuyler. If he could hold New York in the Federalist party column, Hamilton might be in a position later, when the "general convulsion" actually came, to lead the bemused nation out of the slough of Jacobinism into the clear air of true Americanism.

Hamilton mustered out the New York City party, issued addresses to the electorate, joined issue with Clinton's supporters, and argued the importance of the state contest to the politics of the nation. Without bitterness toward opponents, he rehearsed Federalist accomplishments during the decade just past that had brought the Republic, in the words of Jefferson's own inaugural address, to "the full tide of successful experiment." He pointed out that "success in the *experiment* of a government is success in the *practice* of it, and this is but another phrase for an administration, in the main, wise and good."

He castigated French revolutionaries for "the subversion of the throne of the *Bourbons*, to make way for the throne of the *Bonapartes*." He praised Jefferson for deserting his former allies, who would have had Americans follow the French example. He warmed to Jefferson's inaugural speech with "approbation of its contents."

He went on to say, "We view it as virtually a candid retraction of past misapprehensions, and a pledge to the community that the new President will not lend himself to dangerous innovations, but in essential points will tread in the steps of his predecessors." He contrasted Jefferson's recently proclaimed "moderate views" with "the violent projects of the men who have addressed you in favor of Mr. Clinton. . . ." Jefferson's switch, consistent with the deal Bayard said he had made, might well cost him the support of many who had elevated him, but "in the talents, the patriotism, and the firmness of the Federalists, he will find more than an equivalent for all that he shall lose."

As in campaigns of much earlier days, Hamilton's speeches now rang with eloquence and brilliance. For this period of Hamilton's life, they were remarkable for their moderation. But it was all in vain. The magic, the cutting edge was gone. He was going through the old motions, but something—his emphasis or his timing perhaps—was a shade of a fraction off, like that of someone in nervous convalescence after a nervous breakdown or enjoying a period of remission.

The populace even jeered the erstwhile great man. They shouted epithets at him—thief, rascal, villain, scoundrel! John Adams was calling him a "caitiff." Worse still, the so-called respectable citizens, the freeholders of the city, who had always before been the bulwark of the Federalist party, gave a majority to Clinton. "An event that had never happened before at any of our elections!" cried Robert Troup, appalled and shocked. If the violent style of Hamilton's attack on Adams had not worked, his moderation and praise of Jefferson had failed yet more wretchedly.

"Hamilton is supremely disgusted with the state of our political affairs," his faithful friend Troup wrote Rufus King on May 27. He predicts that Jefferson and his party will finally ruin our affairs, but "nothing short of a general convulsion will again call him into public life."

As Hamilton described his own feelings: "To men who have been so much harassed in the base world as myself, it is natural to look forward to complete retirement, in the circle of life as a perfect desideratum." But he was not a man to repine in melancholy: "This desire I have felt in the strongest manner, and to prepare for it latterly has been a favorite object." He added: "I might not only expect to accomplish the object, but might reasonably aim at it and pursue the preparatory measures." He had been engaged for almost two years in planning and building a permanent home for his family on Harlem Heights.

Back in the summer of 1798, Hamilton and Elizabeth and her sister and brother-in-law, Angelica and John, had shared a rented country house in Harlem Heights, for which Hamilton's half share of the rental came to $37.50. Harlem's wooded draws and barren rocky outcroppings must have been much on his mind when that November, as inspector general of the army, he sat down at his mahogany traveling desk in a boardinghouse room in Philadelphia and wrote a riddling rhyme to his Eliza back in New York. He hinted at a "sweet project" that he did not doubt would please her.

> I am always very happy my dear Eliza, when I can steal a few moments to sit down and write to you. You are my good genius; of that kind which the ancient philosophers called a *familiar*—. I have formed a sweet project, of which I will make you my confidant, when I come to New York, and in which I rely that you will cooperate with me cheerfully.

> You may guess and guess and guess again,
> Your guessing will still be in vain.
> But you will not be the less pleased when you
> come to understand and realize the scheme.

After 18 years of marriage, he closed this letter to his "familiar" of perhaps 22 years:

> Adieu, best of wives and best of mothers,
> Heaven ever bless you and me in you.
>
> A.H.

During the feverish heat of the August of 1800, Hamilton had taken time out from the presidential battle and scribbling down his attacks on President Adams to buy a strip of about 15 acres in Harlem Heights. The tract lay inland on the ridge to the east of the Bloomingdale Road and stretched on eastward almost to the Kingsbridge Road, as well as another triangular parcel of about 16 acres that adjoined it to the north. It was purchased from Jacob Scheiffelin, designated in the deed as a ''druggist,'' for a price of £30 an acre.

The rocky outcropping at the top of the rise commanded a spectacular view to the west and southward over the Hudson, the Palisades, the Heights of Weehawken, and the continent lying beyond. There was an even better view easterly over the Harlem River valley toward Westchester and New England. And to the south down the length of Manhattan Island lay Wall Street, the Bowling Green, and the Battery and the forest of ships' masts in the busy harbor and the ocean beyond the Narrows. On this rise Hamilton planned to build his ''sweet project.''

When he tramped over the property, in his mind's eye was the memory of himself as the 19-year-old captain commanding New York's crack Provincial Company of Artillery as it dug in on these same rocky heights in September 1776, the night he had first caught General George Washington's eye, just before the Battle of Harlem Heights.

John McComb, whom Hamilton selected to design his new house, was New York's leading architect, the designer of that gem of Federal architecture the City Hall, of Castle Clinton on the Battery, and the old Queens building of Rutgers University. McComb's plan called for a dignified but not pretentious Federal style clapboard house with a high basement, first and second floors, and four large brick chimneys, one at each of the four corners. Two of them would be real and two false to preserve the characteristic symmetry of his design. There would be a low balustrade surmounting the cornice, a front porch and back porch, a piazza on either side, and a flight of steps leading up toward a large entrance vestibule, reminiscent of the always hospitable front doorway of the Philip Schuyler family mansion at Albany.

The upper floor would contain eight fireplaces, designed according to plans that Hamilton sketched himself, following the newly discovered scientific principles announced by Count Rumford, so as not to smoke. Here also would be family and guest bedrooms, and a family living room, extending entirely across the northern or rear elevation of the house.

Three triple-hung, ceiling-high bay windows in each of the octagonal rooms on the ground floor would outline magnificent Arcadian views of the Hudson and Harlem River valleys and frame each scene with the columns on piazzas west and east. Full-length mirrors on the inner walls, except where the fireplaces opened, would enhance the effect of complete openness to the natural setting. These two octagonal rooms for public entertaining on an ambitious scale were as important a reason for building the house as any other. He would call it The Grange after the plantation estate of his once rich Lytton cousins on St. Croix and the family manor at Ayrshire, Scotland, where his uncles reigned as lairds.

Although the exterior dimensions of Hamilton's Grange are only about 50 feet by 50, the symmetrical purity, simplicity, and power of McComb's design give it a look that even today remains modestly monumental. Though such a house, like the Schuylers', in those days would usually be called a mansion, it did not take the net worth of a rich man to let out a contract to build one—particularly if the contractor happened to be Ezra Weeks, the brother of a grateful client of Hamilton like Levi Weeks. Hamilton had just gotten a jury to acquit Levi of first degree murder in the sensational Manhattan Well murder case.

A precious feature of family gatherings at The Grange would be daughter Angelica's playing on her harp or on the pianoforte that her Aunt Angelica had sent her from London. Seventeen-year-old Angelica Hamilton loved to accompany her father when he sang. In his rich, true voice, sometimes with harmony intoned by his older sons Philip, Alexander, Jr., and James, with John Church, eight, just humming along, Hamilton liked to entertain the family and their guests singing the popular songs of the day or, better still, the old songs of Revolutionary days that he had sung to Angelica's mother while courting her (or occasion-

ally to her Aunt Angelica in private while courting her). Songs like ''The Jolly Beggars'' or
''A Successful Campaign'' or an old soldiers' favorite like ''The Drum.'' To that one he
and his light infantrymen had marched to Yorktown, and he would sing it again at the
meeting of the Society of the Cincinnati a few nights before the last duel. The final verse
may have echoed in his soul with peculiar eloquence that is lacking in the unaccompanied
printed lines.

> Twas in the merry month of May
> When bees from flower to flower did hum.
> We're going to war, and when we die
> We'll want a man of God nearby,
> So bring your Bible and follow the drum.

Of the seven children, Hamilton placed his fondest hopes on Philip, now 19. Hamilton
expected Philip to join him soon in the practice of law and one day perhaps become his
junior partner.

His father was certain of ''his future greatness,'' Robert Troup wrote afterward. The
young man was indeed talented, Troup agreed, but, said Troup, Philip ''was however a sad
rake & I have serious doubts whether he ever would have been an honor to his family or his
country!''

When Philip had been barely one month old, Hamilton had written his friend and fellow
former aide Richard Kidder Meade that Betsy proposed a match between Philip and the
Meades' new daughter ''provided you will engage to make the latter as amiable as her
mother.'' And his aunt, Angelica Church, had written her sister from London, responding
to a long letter of Betsy telling her of him, that ''Philip inherits his father's talents. What
flattering prospects for a mother! You are, my dear sister, very happy with such a Husband
and such promise in a son.''

On Friday evening, November 20, 1801, 19-year-old Philip and a friend named Stephen
Price went out to the theater to see Mr. Hallam and Mrs. Jefferson in the comedy *The West
Indian,* ''a Grand Pantomimical Drama . . . Founded on a fact, which occurred . . . in the
island of Jamaica,'' boasting a cast of planters, slaves, soldiers, and Negro robbers. In the
box next to Hamilton and Price sat Captain George I. Eacker.

The previous Fourth of July—1801—had been a Republican field day in New York City.
The double Republican victory of Jefferson and Burr over Pinckney and Adams (and
Hamilton) and of Clinton over Stephen Van Rensselaer (and Hamilton) were triumphs to be
recelebrated all over again. James Cheetham's Republican *American Citizen and General
Advertiser* on July 6 had reported that ''we do not remember ever to have seen assembled so
vast a concourse of people on the occasion celebrating . . . the restoration of our *mangled*
Constitution.' '' Flags waved, bands played, and firecrackers exploded left, right, and
center.

In his fiery Fourth of July oration at the Brick Church, Captain Eacker, a prominent
Republican lawyer, had assailed Britain and all her American supporters who were seeking
to embroil America in war with France. Under the hated Alien and Sedition Laws, there had
been ''. . . persecution, for political opinions'' by those who ''stalked forth with . . .
erected crest''—so reminiscent of the blue inspector general plume Hamilton had worn
when campaigning. ''To suppress all opposition by fear,'' Eacker cried, ''a military
establishment was created, under pretended apprehension of a foreign invasion.'' He was
accusatory. ''This measure . . . the most hostile to liberty, was adopted under the

favorable crisis of public panic.'' Only now at last, in 1801, concluded Eacker, had the dangers of moneyed aristocracy been banished. ''The election of 'The Man of the People' . . . Jefferson . . . has completed the termination of the blind infatuation.''

If Philip had not been an unnoticed discomfited countenance at these otherwise happy scenes or even if he had, he would have read in Cheetham's paper of Eacker's execrations on everything for which his adored father had lived his life and which Philip had done his best to emulate.

In their box in the theater at *The West Indian*, Philip Hamilton and Price, who had probably stopped off for a few drinks on the way to fortify themselves for the rigors of blood-and-thunder melodrama, began to make loud, rude comments about Eacker and his Fourth of July speech. They pushed into Eacker's box and cast ''pointed ridicule on [the] oration.'' At first, Eacker pretended to ignore the remarks, but at the intermission, he asked Philip and Price out into the lobby. Eacker exclaimed, ''I will not be insulted by a set of rascals.'' Some say he called the boys ''damned rascals.''

Philip and Price demanded to know just who he meant by ''damned rascals.'' Eacker snapped back that he meant the two of them.

By this time, the hubbub was attracting a good deal of attention; so Eacker suggested they adjourn to a nearby tavern. Philip and Price continued to demand just whom he had meant by ''damned rascals.'' Eacker continued to say that he meant the two of them.

Enraged, all three stamped back after the interval to more tumult and shouting at the play. Eacker told them he lived at 50 Wall Street and would expect to hear from them forthwith. Price sent Eacker a challenge to a duel the same night. Sunday morning he and Eacker met at Paulus Hook, now off Elizabethtown, New Jersey, a state where killing another in a duel was not yet defined as murder under the penal law. They blazed away. Three or four shots were exchanged, but none of either's hit the other. The seconds then intervened to halt the waste of good powder and ball in such spectacular but aimless fireworks.

Philip consulted his friend, David S. Jones, and his cousin, Philip Church. Jonathan H. Lawrence, Eacker's second, who also was a good friend of the Hamiltons, urged Eacker to take back the words ''damned rascals,'' if Philip would apologize for his rudeness at the theater. Eacker refused to retract; Philip refused to apologize. Philip sent Eacker a challenge Sunday afternoon. He may have been emboldened by the evidence of Eacker's poor aim in the news of his inability to hit Price in the course of the morning's futile fusillade at Paulus Hook.

Philip's father had heard of the scheduled interview ahead of time, but took no action to prevent it. He ''commanded his son, when on the ground, to reserve his *fire* 'till after Mr. E. had shot and then to discharge his pistol in the air.'' But when Dr. David Hosack told Hamilton that his son had told him he might be needed, and gone on to the dueling ground, Hamilton fainted in his office. Early Monday morning below the Heights of Weehawken on the Jersey Shore, Philip met Eacker for the last time. Obedient to his father's command, Philip went to the field ''with a full determination to preserve'' Eacker's life. With him he brought the hair-trigger dueling pistols his Uncle John Barker Church had used in his duel with Aaron Burr and in many another such interview. Philip would let Eacker fire first, throw away his own shot, and let his antagonist decide whether to resume. He so informed David Jones, his second. On the ground each waited a minute or more for the other to make a move. If Philip had then fired his pistol at the ground, probably all would have been well. But as it was, both drew up their weapons to take aim at the same instant.

This time there was no futile exchange of shots. On first fire, Eacker's bullet penetrated

Philip's side above the hip, ripped through bone and flesh and stopped in his left arm. Under the shock of Eacker's bullet, Philip's pistol fired back, but his ball whistled through the air without hitting anything human. Philip fell, mortally wounded. He bore his pain in full consciousness, was carried away to die, and after a day and night of suffering, died early the next morning.

A Columbia classmate of Phil's reported that "On a bed without curtains lay poor Phil, pale and languid, his rolling distorted eyeballs darting forth the flashes of delirium—On one side of him on the same bed lay his agonized father, on the other his distracted mother, around him . . . relatives and friends weeping." At the funeral "His poor father was with difficulty supported to the grave of his hopes."

"Never did I see a man so completely overwhelmed with grief as Hamilton has been," recalled Troup. "The scene I was present at when Mrs. Hamilton came to see her son on his deathbed (he died about a mile out of the city) and when she met her husband & son in one room beggars all description!" Mother and father watched him writhe in agony for more than 20 hours before he died.

Angelica Church wrote grimly to her younger brother in Albany that Hamilton's "conduct was extraordinary during this trial. I cannot reach particulars now, my sister is a little composed, and the corpse will be removed from my house within an hour."

The family's distress was the more acute because Elizabeth Hamilton was three months pregnant. The shock and anguish of Phil's death threatened another miscarriage. She could not be comforted. Neither could Hamilton. Hamilton had done everything for the boy his own father had never done for him. Neither of Philip's parents ever really got over his death.

Troup must have been wrong about Philip's character. Only the rarest, most brilliant, and Apollonian of model 19-year-old sons would champion his father's politics, assail his father's traducers, and die at the hands of enemies raised up largely by his father's success and failure, while carrying out both of his father's pious but risky prescripts: not to shun the duel, and not to fire first.

After a while, Hamilton was able to compose himself and look to business, "but," Troup reported, "his countenance is strongly stamped with grief." For a long time, Elizabeth, too, remained but little composed.

Word of the tragedy did not reach Philip Schuyler, Phil's grandfather and namesake, in Albany until after Phil's funeral. Two weeks later he wrote his pregnant daughter, "I trust that resignation to the divine will has so far tranquillised your mind as to mitigate the severety [sic] of the Anguish which has been inflicted on you and all of us." It should afford Betsy consolation that her dear departed child had showed such aversion to shedding blood and "pursued every measure which propriety and prudence could dictate to avoid it." She had reason to trust that "his Spirit is in the realms of Eternal bliss."

Philip Hamilton's sister Angelica, next oldest to him, a beauty of whom all remarked how she strikingly resembled the beauteous aunt, her namesake, had passionately adored her elder brother. The shock of his agonizing death caused her to become incurably deranged. She remained insane the rest of a long life until death at 73. To the end, she would always speak of her dear brother Phil as if he were still alive. On her pianoforte she would play only the same old-fashioned songs and minuets she and Phil and her father had played and sung together when she was 17. She never afterward could learn any pieces that she had not known before that November when Phil was shot. Years of tender care at home by her mother did no good.

In February 1802, Philip Schuyler again wrote to try to assuage Elizabeth's seemingly inconsolable grief. He was glad to know that Philip had died "with a full determination to preserve'' his antagonist's life. He begged for her ''such . . . calmness in your mind, as that your health may not be injured and Ultimately . . . restore you to peace.'' He also advised:

> You have the Most . . . important duties to perform as the consort of that best of men, whose happiness depends on your weal. . . . Exert therefore . . . that energy, which was so conspicuous in you [,] ride out frequently, and collect . . . friends about you, that your thoughts may be diverted from painful reflection.

As always, as her ninth lying-in approached, Elizabeth's father could not have been more kind and solicitous, even as he suffered from the old war wound in his side and his gout. He was happy and relieved when he could congratulate Hamilton that she and their new child were both in good health. Their grief could never be composed. But perhaps it might be covered over a little. They named their new son Philip, too. Throughout his life he would always be known as ''little Phil.''

After recovering from her lying-in and weaning of little Phil and after a suitable or, rather, longer than usual period of mourning, Elizabeth composed herself a little. She returned to the rounds of public entertaining the Grange had been built for and the efficient performance of all the other important duties that were expected of her as the wife of a public leader and lawyer of Hamilton's stature. Her father's intense anxiety for her health during the year following her first Phil's death is the principal evidence of her grief that comes down to us from the two years through which she had been living next to nervous derangement, manic defense, and madness. Other than her father's letters to her, there is no evidence that a cry of anguish could, possibly, have been wrung out of her indomitable soul. There would be no more children.

35

Getting Religion/ Angelica's Garter

Though not yet in the field of Mars [Hamilton] maintains an unequalled reputation for gallantry. . . .

—Robert Troup to Rufus King, 1798

Hamilton's countenance was strongly stamped with grief. Letters of condolence for poor Philip poured in. Rufus King wrote on January 12, 1802, from London, wishing Hamilton "consolation . . . among the treasures of your own mind, which nature has so eminently endowed." A letter of December 5 from Washington's grandnephew, G. W. P. Custis, who had been a friend of Philip at Columbia, praised him for having "fallen in the field of honour." He wished Hamilton "Happiness and prosperity" and "May the shafts of faction fall harmless upon the shield of your integrity." Dr. Benjamin Rush, a close friend of Jefferson and a political opponent of Hamilton, told how much he and his family had enjoyed Philip's visits to the Rushes' Philadelphia home. James McHenry's understanding of Hamilton's grief went deep because he too had suffered the loss of an eldest child. "Is there ought in this world can console for such losses?"

Mixed in with the first letters of condolence arrived a letter of stinging rebuke from Washington's nephew and executor, Bushrod Washington, written November 21, 1801, two days before Philip's death. Hamilton had written him earlier asking for copies of letters from Washington's files that he might use to buttress a new series of attacks on Jefferson that he was planning to publish in the *New York Evening Post*, the newspaper he had founded a few months earlier; Bushrod Washington had turned him down.

The years when Jefferson had called Hamilton "a colossus to the anti-Republican party, without numbers . . . a host within himself'' were over. Yet Hamilton chose to blot out his griefs by furiously pressing on with writing a long broadside attack on Jefferson and all Jefferson's policies under the title *Examination of Jefferson's Message to Congress of December 7, 1801*. He signed it *Lucius Crassus* and published it in 18 installments in the *New York Evening Post*, beginning December 17, 1801, and ending April 8, 1802. The writing had a frantic, impassioned, personal, and largely retrospective tone that did not at all suit the rather narrow nature of his differences on most matters of future national policy, with which Jefferson's message to Congress had dealt in broad and unemphatic brush strokes. Hamilton wrote as if he saw himself as the sole remaining prop of the frail fabric of the Constitution. He attacked Jefferson and his policies as if striking out in revenge—or as if taking a reprisal against him for the death of his eldest son.

Jefferson had sent a "message" to Congress at the opening of the session instead of delivering a "speech" as his predecessors had always done. It was a "mark of consistency" in him to differ from his predecessors "in matters of form." "Whoever considers the temper of the day," Hamilton sighed, "must be satisfied that this message is likely to add much to the popularity of our Chief Magistrate."

Whereas "those whose patriotism is of the OLD SCHOOL . . . would rather risk incurring the displeasure of the people by speaking unpalatable truths than betray their interest by fostering their prejudices," Jefferson's "bewitching tenets" promised "emancipation from the burdens and restraints of government" and "a foretaste of that pure felicity which the apostles" of Jefferson's "illuminated doctrine have predicted." Even if such happy predictions proved wrong and "the viands they offer prove baneful poisons instead of wholesome ailments, the justification is both plain and easy—*Good patriots must, at all events, please the People.*"

Among specifics, *Lucius Crassus* attacked Jefferson's proposal to abolish internal revenue, but at the same time preserve "PUBLIC FAITH." Such promises were "merely to amuse with agreeable but deceptive sounds," Hamilton declaimed. "Alas! How deplorable it will be, should it ever become proverbial, that a President of the United States like the *Weird sisters* in Macbeth, *keeps his promise to our ear, but breaks it to* The sense!''

Hamilton is mistaken, for the lines are said by Macbeth to Macduff and should read:

> Accursed be that tongue that tells me so,
> For it hath cow'd my better part of man.

The "lame duck" Federalist Congress of the year before, as one of its last actions, had passed the Judiciary Act, which expanded and elaborated the federal court system, thereby giving Adams the opportunity to make "midnight appointments" of many Federalists to the bench before Federalism was swept out of power forever. Jefferson proposed to get rid of them by simply repealing the act, or, as his message had euphemistically put it, "the judiciary system will, *of course*, present itself to the contemplation of Congress."

Hamilton urged some of his closest friends to oppose repeal of the Judiciary Act but in a temperate, dignified manner. This infuriated them and showed he was out of touch with most of his own party. Gouverneur Morris had sought to have the New York bar petition Congress against repeal, but Hamilton had opposed this tactic. Morris wrote Hamilton a gentle remonstrance on February 22, 1802: "You must pardon me for telling you I am sorry you opposed sending a petition to Congress. . . . It will stop . . . petitions which might have come on from the eastward, and . . . leave our enemies to conclude against us from the silence of our friends.''

Not used to rebuke from so close a friend as Morris, Hamilton bridled in his reply of February 29, 1802: "I should be a very unhappy man, if I left my tranquility at the mercy of the misrepresentations which friends as well as foes are fond of giving to my conduct." If his dear, perceptive, witty old friend Morris could not fathom him, no one could. He opened up a little to give a rare look inward at himself at 45:

> Mine is an odd destiny. Perhaps no man in the U States has sacrificed or done more for the present Constitution than myself—and contrary to all my anticipations of its fate, as you know from the very beginning, I am still labouring to prop the frail and worthless fabric. Yet I have the murmurs of its friends no less than the curses of its foes for my reward. What can I do better than withdraw from the Scene? Every day proves to me more and more, that this American world was not made for me.

What Morris failed to see was that his own position was more like Hamilton's than he realized. Hamilton projected on, and saw reflected from Morris, his own exotic image of himself:" You, friend Morris, are by *birth* a native of this country, but by *genius* an exotic. You mistake if you fancy that you are more of a favourite than myself, or that you are in any sort upon a theater suited to you."

By the eighteenth number of his *Examination of Jefferson's Message,* published April 8, 1802, the whole array of Hamilton's criticism had become more extraordinary for its tone of personal pique, pettifogging, and nitpicking than for worthwhile substance. He had branded Jefferson a "philosophic *projector*" and ridiculed Jefferson's inflation of unimportant matters. Of them, if kept in proper proportion, it would be said, said Hamilton (as it might with more justice be said of Hamilton's *Examination*):

> Commas and points he sets exactly right
> And 'twere a sin to rob him of his mite.

Hamilton concludes this series, which can only be excused as occupational therapy for a mind whose grief over Philip had overwhelmed it, with a final bit of wishful thinking about the old rival he would not admit had finally overmastered him: "The credit of great abilities was allowed [Jefferson] by a considerable portion of those who disapproved his principles; but the short space of nine months has been amply sufficient to dispel that illusion." Some of "his most partial votaries begin to suspect that they have been mistaken in the OBJECT OF THEIR IDOLATRY." Yet in the country at large, belying his close election victory, Jefferson's popularity had never seemed greater, and it continued to grow.

It was not until March 29, 1802, more than four months after Philip's death, that Hamilton was able to refocus his mind on the immediate present and force it to admit that Philip was indeed dead, by finally acknowledging the many letters of condolence, as he did to Dr. Benjamin Rush.

He "felt all the weight of the obligation" he owed Rush and his family "for the tender concern they manifested," he said, "but I was obliged to wait for a moment of greater calm to express my sense of their kindness." Philip's death had been to him "an event beyond comparison the most afflicting of my life. . . . My loss is indeed great. The brightest as well as the eldest hope of my family has been taken from me. . . . He was a fine youth."

Dr. Rush, the leading medical man of America, a pioneer in the study of mental illness, had been observing Hamilton acutely and usually critically for more than a quarter of a century, ever since he had seen the 21-year-old aide at Germantown in 1778 and recorded that General Washington, the "Idol of America," was "governed by one of his aides."

In Hamilton's performances over the years, the most recent, if forgivable, being his long delay in acknowledging Dr. Rush's condolences while he "examined" Jefferson's message as *Lucius Crassus,* Dr. Rush might have noted in Hamilton the progression of a mental malady. It had begun, perhaps, with a peccadillo, a gentleman's old affair magnified by too keen a concern for public credit into *The Reynolds Pamphlet.* More serious was the dubious underhanded morality as well as logical lunacy of the attack on John Adams. On the evidence of the unbalanced confusions of morality, policy, and personality in Hamilton's recent *Examination* of Dr. Rush's old friend Thomas Jefferson, the progress of the malady would appear to be still unstabilized.

At the very least, Hamilton's was a classic case of political suicide propagated by means of newspapers and pamphlets. But more than that, to Dr. Rush, would be the dangerously weakened condition of both Hamilton's moral and judgmental faculty, as well as his recent physical debilitude. He was a prime risk for the new disease Dr. Rush believed he had identified called *micronomia*, "the partial or weakened action of the moral faculty." The missing fact that Dr. Rush would not know was that Philip's death in the duel holding his first fire on his father's advice had provided Hamilton himself with the closest possible exposure to the risk of imitative suicide. However, Dr. Rush would not fail to catch the new, strangely religious, even mystical turn Hamilton's thought had taken after Philip's death, a turn that seemed at odds with all that Dr. Rush knew about Hamilton as a public man. Hamilton's letter to him went on, "But why should I repine? It was the will of heaven, and he is now out of the reach of the seductions and calamities of a world full of folly, full of vice, full of danger—of least value in proportion as it is best known." The more Hamilton had come to know of life, the less he valued it. "I firmly trust, also, that he has safely reached the haven of eternal repose and felicity." Dr. Rush had mentioned a letter that Philip had written to his son. "Every memorial of the goodness of his heart is precious to me," Hamilton went on. "If no special reasons forbid it, I should be very glad to have a copy of that letter."

Elizabeth too "has drunk deeply of the cup of sorrow," and she joined him in affectionate thanks to the Rushes. "Our wishes for your happiness will be unceasing."

Hamilton had never been a member of any church so the deeply religious tone in these passages would be rather surprising to Dr. Rush because all he knew about Hamilton's religiosity were his professed abhorrence of the Deism and atheism he ascribed to Jefferson's French-leaning politics, and two widely retold wisecracks from the time of the Constitutional Convention. When Benjamin Franklin had moved that each session be opened with a prayer, Hamilton was supposed to have snapped that he saw no need for calling in "foreign aid." And when Hamilton returned to New York and his old friend Dr. John Rodgers of the Wall Street Presbyterian Church asked him why God had not been suitably recognized in the Constitution, Hamilton is supposed to have replied, "Indeed, Doctor, we forgot it."

Hamilton as a young man off the boat in New York to seek his fortune and presenting his first letters of introduction from the Reverend Hugh Knox of St. Croix to the Reverends John Rodgers and John Mason of New York was then remarkable for his conventional religious observances. Robert Troup, his roommate at strongly Anglican King's College, bore witness that Hamilton "had read most of the polemical writers on religious subjects; and he was a zealous believer in the fundamental doctrines of Christianity; and, I confess, that the arguments with which he was accustomed to justify his belief, have tended, in no small degree, to confirm my own faith in revealed religion."

In the household of Elias Boudinot, the devout Presbyterian layman with whom Hamilton stayed at Elizabethtown during his first year in America, "No one could have lived for a year without kneeling regularly in prayer, or becoming a confirmed atheist." It may have been this pull of competing sectarian loyalties between the Presbyterian and Episcopalian—which became closely identified with the opposing patriot and loyalist political sides of the Revolution—that made Hamilton hesitate and then fail to make any firm choice of church membership during his life.

Until Philip's death, Hamilton's religious expressions were so intimately woven into his political purposes and ideas of personal honor as to be practically meaningless as testaments of personal belief. Forty-four years afterward, Chancellor James Kent still remembered vividly that Hamilton, at the New York Constitutional Convention of 1788, had opened his first great speech by equating the need for a Union of the states and a government with powers adequate to uphold and preserve that Union with the doctrine of the immortality of the soul: there were modern doubts on the subject, he admitted, but "to convince men that they have within them immortal spirits is going very far to prepare their minds for the ready reception of Christian truth." The Union of the states required the same willing suspension of disbelief.

The depth of Hamilton's faith in the Christian religion as the cement of the Union also burns through his letter to William Loughton Smith of April 10, 1797, proposing that Congress include among "vigorous preparation for war" the mobilizing of "the religious ideas of Americans." Hamilton argues that a politician should consider "some religious solemnity to impress seriously the minds of the people. . . ." Religion is "an important means of influencing opinion." It would be a "valuable resource in a contest with France" to set the religious ideas of Americans "in active competition with the atheistical tenets of their enemies. . . . a day of humiliation and prayer, beside being very proper, would be extremely useful."

Atheism and the absence of religion in public polity filled Hamilton with unfeigned horror. He castigated it in his most passionately corrosive manner in broadsides like *The Stand*, No. III, published April 7, 1798: "The disgusting spectacle . . . profligacy . . . consummate infamy . . . terrible design" of the "unprincipled reformers" of France "to destroy all religious opinion, and to pervert a whole people to Atheism . . . betrays a plan to undermine the venerable pillars that support the edifice of civilized society, to "disorganize the human mind itself."

His sense of a religious duty to keep up his efforts to prop the "frail and worthless fabric" of the Constitution against "unprincipled reformers" was perhaps as much as anything else what served in the end to pull Hamilton out of the slough of grief into which Philip's death had plunged him and back into the bear pit of New York politics, only to be confronted there with an appalling new apparition. At the Federal Republicans' and Cincinnatians' annual Washington's birthday collation in the capital at Washington, who should push in but the Republican vice-president of the United States, Aaron Burr. Thinking of it, Hamilton's mind's eye must have recalled Macbeth's shocked incoherence at seeing Banquo's ghost at just such a banquet: "Blood hath been shed ere now . . . This is more strange than such a murder is . . . I have a strange infirmity . . . give me some wine; fill full. I drink to the general joy of the whole table. . . . Avaunt! and quit my sight! let the earth hide thee!"

But Burr, the man who had helped smash the hopes of Pinckney, Adams, and Hamilton and put many of their party colleagues out of good government jobs, did not fade silently in and out of the hall. He took center stage and cried out a cryptic toast: "To the union of all honest men."

"Union" and "honest men" were code words that carried magical connotations to good old boys of the Federalist rank and file.

"What meant the apparition and the toast which made part of the after-piece of the birthday festival?" Hamilton demanded of Gouverneur Morris on April 6, 1802. "Is it possible that some new intrigue is about to link the Federalists with a man who can never be anything else than the bane of a good cause? I dread more from this than from all the contrivances of the bloated and senseless junto of Virginia."

Ever since the election, Jefferson had been conspicuously widening the distance between himself and his "crooked gun" of a vice-president. He let it be put about that Burr had intrigued to snatch the presidency from him, deliberately passed over Burr in the distribution of patronage, omitted him from his councils, and did not invite him to dinners.

When Burr and Jefferson tied, Hamilton had happily written James A. Bayard that "Burr is solicitous to keep upon anti-federal ground, to avoid compromitting himself by any engagements, with the Federalists. . . . Ambition without principle never was long under the guidance of good sense." It deranged all of Hamilton's plans now to think that Burr, returned from the dead like Banquo's ghost, might seek to snatch away control of the Federalist party two years hence, turn out Hamilton and Gouverneur Morris and other leaders, and make it over into his own moderate instrument for seizing the presidency.

On second thought, Hamilton reflected, Burr's crookedness might be made use of, much as General James Wilkinson's had been, with knowledge that he was a double agent. Burr's situation could be rendered so "absolutely hopeless with his old friends," he would break from them and form a third party. "Then, if we think it worth the while, we can purchase him with his flying squadron," said Hamilton. In a third-party role, Burr would not threaten Hamilton's own titular leadership of the Federalists.

Bayard told Hamilton not to be alarmed: Burr's toast was "extremely well calculated to answer our views." What did Bayard mean by that?

Hamilton was not greatly relieved that redoubtable Federalists like Bayard and Morris claimed to be "using" Burr, even though only as "a tool." It should go no further, Hamilton warned, "as a chief, he will disgrace and destroy the party." He feared Burr's "irregular courtship." Eager to regain the reins, they might turn to anyone, even Burr. "I know of no important character, who has a less founded interest," insisted Hamilton. "His talents may do well enough for a particular plot, but they are ill-suited to a great and wise drama."

Federalists, Hamilton went on, had "erred in relying so much on the rectitude and utility of their measures, as to have neglected the cultivation of popular favor, by fair and justifiable expedients." Yet unless we "can contrive to take hold of, and carry along with us some strong feelings of the mind, we shall in vain calculate upon any substantial or durable results"—even though, he added ominously, there be "some deviations from what, on other occasions, we have maintained to be right." Hamilton drew a nice distinction: he discountenanced "the imitation of things intrinsically unworthy." But courtship that was "irregular" would be permissible on the hard road toward "a sound & stable order of things." "The present Constitution is the standard to which we are to cling," he vowed. "Under its banners, *bona fide*, must we combat our political foes, rejecting all changes but through the channel itself provided for amendments."

Hamilton wrote Morris on March 4, 1802, that he was "thoroughly confirmed . . . that it is true federal policy to promote the adoption" of amendments whereby electors would be chosen directly by the people, instead of the state legislatures, and would vote separately for president and vice-president.

"The people should know whom they are choosing." The existing mode of casting the die gave scope to intrigue and endangered public tranquillity, as the recent contest between Jefferson and Burr had shown. Choice of electors by the people in districts "removes thus far the intervention of the State governments . . . strengthens the connection between the federal head and the people, and . . . diminishes the means of party combination'' which had invited Burr's intrigues. To sum up, said Hamilton, ''it has ever appeared to me as sound principle to let the federal government rest, as much as possible, *on the shoulders of the people,* and as little as possible on . . . the state legislatures.'' New York, the state of all the states whose politics seemed most sensitive to the shifting tides of public opinion, adopted laws that enacted what he had urged.

Hamilton's preoccupation with both politics and religion during his slow swing back from the depths of his grief over Philip's death finally merged the two disciplines into what he hoped would create a moral majority. His letter to Bayard of April 16–21, 1802, presented a carefully thought-out plan for what he called *The Christian Constitutional Society.* He gave Bayard all the reasons why such an organization would help the Federalists ''to carry along with us some strong feelings of the mind.'' Its objects were ''1st the Support of the Christian Religion, 2nd the support of the Constitution of the United States.'' In organizational structure it was to be patterned roughly on the Society of the Cincinnati, with a national ''directing council,'' a ''sub-directing council'' in each state, and local societies under the subdirecting councils. Dues would be five dollars annually for eight years ''to be contributed by each member who can really afford it.''

Bayard replied reproachfully that such ''clubs'' would only ''revive a thousand jealousies and suspicions which now begin to slumber.'' Federalists must let the Democratic Republicans defeat themselves, he felt.

Another telling political objection to Hamilton's plan was that it was preaching only to those already saved. In many areas—particularly in New England—the churches were the bulwarks of Federalism. Nothing Hamilton did seemed to work very well against Jefferson's smooth and successful ''northern strategy.''

Writing to Rufus King, June 3, 1802, Hamilton reported that ''I as yet discover no satisfactory symptoms of a revolution of opinion in the *mass,* ''informe ingens cui lumen ademptum.'' The quotation from Vergil's *Aeneid,* Third Book, line 659, begins with the phrase, ''monstrum horrendum.'' It is the description Hamilton's favorite classical poet gives of the Cyclops Polyphemus after Ulysses had blinded his only eye. The allusion probably should be translated ''a horrible monster unnatural and without form, whose vision has been taken away'' by Jefferson's rhetoric. From that day to this, Hamilton's detractors have never ceased to translate his erudite, smoothly jocular sally to his old friend into the irrebuttable damnation of the charge that Hamilton said that ''the people, sir, is a great beast.'' Indeed, this mistranslation is the only thing many people remember about Hamilton at all.

Hamilton urged King to come home from his ministry in London. He could do greater good at home. Out of office, he reminded King, the Federalists' long-range purpose must be to reclaim the government they had built and lost by restoring the people's vision once more. The tide would turn. ''Vibrations of power,'' he wrote, ''are the genius of our government.''

But New York Federalists turned down pleas for campaign contributions. Troup complained bitterly that besides himself and Hamilton, only a few remained who were willing to dig down into their pockets. At the Federalist club the conversation grew strained. Troup wrote gloomily that ''Hamilton & I have determined to trouble ourselves no more about the public weal; but to let things take their course.''

''A disappointed politician you know,'' Hamilton wrote to Richard Peters on December 29, 1802, ''is very apt to take refuge in a Garden. . . . In this new situation, for which I am as little fitted as Jefferson to guide the helm of the U. States, I come to you as an Adept in rural science for instruction.'' He intended to devote his fields around The Grange to grasses and inquired after the best sorts; he commissioned Peters to send him a couple of bushels of seed of a special red clover, a kind he had not been able to find in the neighborhood.

Peters, wanting to be helpful, replied: "I *marvel* that you should be a disappointed Politician. I am a mortified but not disappointed one. You must have foreseen the Catastrophe that has befallen us. . . . I am glad you have this little Syren to seduce you from public Anxieties. But take Care,'' he warned sagely, "that the meretscious charms of this new Flame do not make too great Drafts on your Purse.''

On the same day, Hamilton wrote to solicit melon seeds from Charles Cotesworth Pinckney in South Carolina. Hamilton would also be grateful to Pinckney for parrakeets for his beloved daughter Angelica, he wrote, but he could not forbear ruefully looking back on the Federalist debacle and asking ''Amidst the triumphant reign of democracy, do you retain sufficient interest in public affairs to feel any curiosity about what is going on? In my opinion, the follies and vices of the administration have as yet made no material impression as to their disadvantages.''

Records are sketchy, but from what there are it appears that in the years before they finally moved into The Grange, the Hamiltons had lived at seven or eight different addresses in the Wall Street area of lower Manhattan, including 57 Wall Street, 26 Broadway, 107 Liberty Street, 58 Partition Street (now part of Fulton Street), 12 Garden Street, somewhere on Pine Street, and in what Meyer Berger of *The New York Times* in 1940 described as ''the ancient brick structure at 173 Cherry Street which stands under Manhattan Bridge among blackened tenements,'' where now tugboats and other ''deep-throated harbor craft bellow right into the backyard.'' While The Grange was still a-building, the Hamilton family stayed for various periods, beginning in 1800, in a small farmhouse on nearby Scheiffelin land known as the ''north cottage.''

As construction progressed on The Grange itself, but before it was finished, the Hamilton family started moving in and occupied some of the rooms. When all was done, John McComb's bill, as architect and contractor, came to $2,495.20. The bill of the general contractor, Ezra Weeks, of $9,324.85, might have been much higher if Hamilton, in association with Aaron Burr, had not been successful in defending Ezra's brother, Levi, in the celebrated criminal case of *People v. Levi Weeks*. With all these bills to pay and also the debt to Scheiffelin for the land, the judgment Hamilton had just won for his and Aaron Burr's client Louis Le Guen in the series of cases that went by the name of *Le Guen v. Gouverneur & Kemble,* including a judgment for $119,915.43, could hardly have come at a better time.

Moving into their new home when it was finally finished late in 1802 was a major event in all the Hamiltons' lives. All through the years of what she called her exile in London and Paris, the exquisite Angelica Church had pined for Hamilton's letters, read them over and over, and followed his public career with sometimes eager and sometimes fretfully jealous attention, concern, and adoration. After years of captivating European society, Angelica and John Church had returned to the United States in May of 1797. London and Paris were all right in their way, but desolate in their way, too, for Angelica because Hamilton was not there. The summer of 1798 the Hamiltons and Churches had lived together in the rented house on Harlem Heights. Now Betsy and the children would spend most of their time at The Grange, while Hamilton remained in their house in town, commuting the nine miles from Wall Street mostly on weekends.

Now the Churches were back in New York, installed in their sumptuous house in

Robinson Street, which Hamilton had picked out for them. Somehow Angelica's now being able to see him quite often, to blush to his sallies, to bask in his glow, to yield to his sometimes quicksilver, sometimes saturnine changes of mood and temper, never seemed to wither his charm for her. Nor could anything she did or failed to do slake or stale her hold on him.

The elegant Federalist Congressman Harrison Gray Otis of Massachusetts was a splendid raconteur who loved to retell a tale about Hamilton and Angelica that dated back to the winter of 1799 during the last wild fling of the Federal Republican court in Philadelphia before its displacement to Washington by Jefferson. It did not tend to stale because their intimate situation remained essentially the same as the years went by and more and more of a public scandal.

Anne and William Bingham's Mansion House remained the epicenter of glittering Philadelphia society having its last brilliant fling at the capital before exile to the boondocks on the Potomac. The Samuel Brecks, too, gave "truly *select*" parties at their mansion known as Greenbrier. Hamilton was in Philadelphia on inspector general's business when Otis dined there with him and Angelica Church, their spouses being absent, and a sparkling group of other guests on Christmas Eve of 1799. Only the sensationally beautiful and glamorous Anne Bingham missed the party because, Otis said, "she burst the gown she had prepared for the occasion Saturday." George Washington had died less than two weeks earlier, and there had been much funerary activity since, but neither this sad event nor the absence of Anne Bingham's profane wit could spoil the evening's smatch. A pretty, new Miss Schuyler, Angelica's and Elizabeth's teen-age youngest sister, Catharine, the god-daughter of Washington, helped greatly to rescue it. It enhances the charm of Otis's stories to know that when he repeats his best ones in letters to his wife, he tends to tone things down for home consumption back in Boston by bowdlerizing the best parts. Here is what he told her:

"Tuesday Dined at Breck's, with Mrs. Church, Miss Schuyler, Genl. Hamilton, Champlin &c. &c," Otis wrote. "Mrs. C[hurch] the mirror of affectation, but as she affects to be extremely affable and free from ceremony, this foible is rather amusing than offensive. Miss Schuyler a young wild flirt from Albany, full of glee & apparently desirous of matrimony. After Dinner Mrs. C[hurch] dropped her shoe bow [read garter?], Miss S— picked it up and put it in Hamilton's buttonhole saying 'there brother I have made you a Knight.'

" 'But of what order' (says Madam C) 'he can't be a Knight of the garter in this country.'

" 'True sister' replied Miss S— 'but *he would be if you would let him.' "

Otis also mentioned a conversation he had had with Christopher G. Champlin at the same party. Champlin, a member of Congress from Rhode Island, strongly resented Hamilton's casting what he called "some liquorish looks at his cara sposa." He complained to Otis that Hamilton "appears to him very trifling in his conversation with ladies." Champlin said his wife hastened to reassure him that "she did not really" like the caster of the "liquorish looks" at all. Otis sardonically noted in disbelief that Champlin, at least, "was evidently *satisfied* with this intimation." A reassurance of a kind that nobody but a husband, certainly not Otis, could be expected to believe. It all only served to thicken the cloud of scandal that was enveloping Hamilton and Angelica Church.

It seems to be of the nature of love that neither a man's imperceptible aureole of undercover amours, nor his enemies' awe or hatred, nor his air of command beneath a surface of urbane geniality that yet suffers not fools, not his antic squint toward ''libera-tion'' of romantic Antillean isles of origin, nor mad canicular fevers of brain and blood, disqualifies him for the passionate love of the most desirable of women. Such vincibilities seem to compel it, even through long separations. To such general rules Angelica Church's affection for Hamilton was no exception. What her husband, John Barker Church, privately thought or knew of it is unknown. From all that is known, he also liked Hamilton, but not all that well. He was a rich, practical businessman who could indulge his wife her social and aesthetic independences. He had returned to America because it seemed to be a good place for profitable investments. During his long absence, Hamilton had managed them for him, but Church was not at all sure that the former secretary of the treasury had handled them efficiently. He wrote to Jeremiah Wadsworth about a mortgage held jointly by the two of them: ''I will thank you as soon as you can to send me our Account Current, for our Friend Hamilton not being very accurate in his Accounts is not clear that he has not made some Mistakes respecting the Monies you have Paid him on my Account.''

Church, practical businessman though he was, would exchange fire in a duel with Aaron Burr, merely grazing him, over a matter that was primarily Hamilton's problem—the Holland Land Company fiasco. Church, of course, had served as Hamilton's second at the time of Hamilton's threatened duel with James Monroe. But the re-airing of the squalid Reynolds affair seemed in no way to affect Hamilton's relations with his own wife, Eliza, or with the Churches, except to make them all draw closer together, if possible, in the face of the storm of public scandal. Angelica still seemed to cherish his every word and gesture with no slight trace of disillusionment. Eliza was—as always—Eliza, for whom her husband could do no wrong. But now she spent much time at their country house or at the Schuyler's home in Albany or at Old Saratoga. Most of Hamilton's letters to her are suffused with affection and gratitude, some are perfunctory. Few husbands over so many years manage to maintain so consistent a pitch of epistolary affection as Hamilton did for Eliza; yet in them he rarely omitted Angelica's name from the ambit of his love.

His real affection for Eliza did not seem to keep him from pleasures of a more intense kind with Angelica and perhaps other ladies like Mrs. Champlin as well, but as might be expected no documentation for such involvements is known to exist.

Angelica took center stage as a leader of New York society. Her balls were the most brilliant and lavish seen in the city. When Hamilton was deeply engrossed in his frustrating duties as inspector general of the army, he still found plenty of time to dance attendance on Angelica. So much that Robert Troup commented sourly: ''Though not yet in the field of Mars he maintains an unequalled reputation for gallantry—such at least is the opinion entertained of him by the ladies. When I have more leisure,'' Troup told Rufus King in England, ''I will give you the history of the Ghost of Baron [Ciominie?] & Mrs. Church as published by our Gallant General.''

Whether the rumors of the affair between Alexander and Angelica were true or not, everyone in society believed they were, as such tales are always believed. They were damaging to Hamilton's reputation, and Troup believed them. He disliked Angelica, and he had nothing but contempt for her husband.

By 1801, Troup was writing King of the thickening clouds of scandal hanging over the Church and Hamilton families, particularly because Church no longer went home much in the evenings, and Hamilton went up to The Grange only on weekends:

> Mr. Church is working hard at cards—underwriting—and examining bankrupts.
> How his constitution stands it is a matter of amazement to us all! He has at least four

regular card clubs to attend every week & sometimes they do not break up till the morning. . . . He is famous for litigation on his policies; and yet he is said to do a great deal of business. . . . There is as little respectability attached to him as to any man amongst us; and unfortunately the whole family are enveloped in such a cloud that they enjoy nothing of esteem. The oldest daughter of Mr. Church is a most amiable girl and she is supposed to have a very cultivated mind & yet her family labor under such disadvantages that she has little prospect of marrying in a suitable manner!

None of this would have mattered so much to Troup if his best friend, Hamilton, were not so seriously sullied by the same Church "cloud":

> I believe I wrote you some time ago [he continued significantly] that I had ventured, at every risk, to communicate with a certain friend of ours on a certain subject. I fear notwithstanding that things continue in the same course. You can hardly [word illegible] how ruinous are the consequences of the general belief.

Still, when he did manage to get home to see the children, Hamilton seemed to be a model father. His son John Church Hamilton recalled how his father now "sought and found relief from the painful reflections which the growing delusion of the country forced upon him, in the duties of religion, in the circle of domestic joys, and in the embellishment of his rural retreat."

As Hamilton cultivated his garden, his new interest in horticulture and landscaping intensified his new interest in the Creator:

> His religious feeling grew with his growing intimacy with the marvellous works of nature [said his son], all pointing in the processes and their results to a great pervading, ever active Cause. Thus his mind rose from the visible to the invisible; and he found intensest pleasure in studies higher and deeper than all speculation. His Bible exhibits on its margin the care with which he perused it. Among his autographs is an abstract of the Apocalypse—and notes in his hand were seen in the margin of "Paley's Evidences." With these readings he now united the habit of daily prayer, in which exercise of faith and love, the Lord's Prayer was always a part. The renewing influences of early pious instruction and habit appear to have returned in all their force on his truest sensibilities.

His psychic transformation seemed to make his family, defined loosely to include Angelica, the new focus of his life. His children always afterward remembered him in this period as the ideal father, proud of all their accomplishments, patient as an instructor, and joyful as a companion in play and sport. John Church and James Alexander and all his other surviving children worshiped him.

Hamilton wrote Betsy, "My health and comfort both require that I should be at home—at that home where I am always sure to find a sweet asylum from care and pain." A change had taken place in his character. "While all other passions decline in me, those of love and friendship gain new strength. It will be more and more my endeavour to abstract myself from all pursuits which interfere with those of affection."

Only in his *Reynolds Pamplet* and in his private letter to James A. Bayard does Hamilton make mention of any sector of his affections that resembled an "irregular courtship." But Dr. Benjamin Rush's medical and psychological file on Hamilton would not be complete until receipt of a letter from John Adams written in September 1807. In it Adams brought

Dr. Rush up to date on his late critic, especially ''the profligacy of his life; his fornications, adulteries, and his incests.''

Yes, doctor, said Adams, his incests.

The patient did seem to be getting back some of his old pep.

36

Fifteen Years
of Competition

Before I Have done I Shall Make my learned friend cry out,
"Help me, Cassius, or I Sink!"

> —Gouverneur Morris, pointing first toward Hamilton and then toward Aaron Burr, during the final argument to the Court of Errors, in
> *Le Guen* v. *Gouverneur & Kemble,* February 12, 1800

As Hamilton traveled back and forth from New York City to the upstate county seats on the circuit where his legal cases took him, The Grange was always on his mind. About halfway between Wall Street and The Grange along his customary route up Broadway, near where Rockefeller Center now stands, Hamilton's physician friend Dr. David Hosack had laid out an extensive botanical garden which probably inspired Hamilton with ideas for overly ambitious and extravagant landscaping schemes. He wrote out directions to Elizabeth for a circular bulb bed 18 feet in diameter, containing nine separate sections, with beds of tulips, lilies, and hyacinths alternating by threes. He drew a plan to illustrate. A lovely touch were "wild roses around the outside of the flower garden with laurel at foot." Borders of shrubbery around the grove should be brightened with laurel, too, and sweet briars and dogwood.

The workmen should be kept busy at all times, even when the weather was bad: "When it is too cold to go on with grubbing, our men may be employed in cutting and clearing away the underbrush in the Grove and the other woods." But part of the land should be kept in its natural state: "Let the centre of the principal wood in the line of the different rocks remain rough and wild."

From a two-day stay at Peekskill, Hamilton wrote back to Elizabeth: "It has always appeared to me that the ground on which our orchard stands is much too moist. To cure this, a ditch round it would be useful . . . three feet deep by three feet wide at the bottom. The clay that comes out of the ditch will be useful to give firmness to our roads. . . ."

They kept some domestic fowl, and these needed gravel in the gizzard, he reminded Elizabeth: "Country people all agree that to fat fowls, it is essential to keep them well supplied with gravel . . . seashore gravel, not too large, is particularly good. . . . The coops must be cleaned out every two or three days." And "after the Fowls have had a sufficient opportunity of drinking, the remaining water must be removed."

No detail of husbandry escaped his close attention. Out of the scraps of lumber, the carpenters should knock together some birdhouses as "additional accommodations for the pidgeons."

After such a typically exhaustive catalogue of things for her to do, it was, of course, rather tiresomely supererogatory of Hamilton to add warmly to Elizabeth, "You see, I do forget The Grange. No that I do not; nor any one that inhabits it. Accept yourself my tenderest affection."

As the great project was nearing completion during the summer of 1802, the Hamiltons held a happy field day of their own—a veritable *fête champêtre*—on the grounds beside the "grove." There Hamilton had planted 13 sapling gum trees to symbolize the original 13 states. There were no fireworks, but the saplings were solemnized by prayer, speechmaking, and according to one account, "all the festivities peculiar to the olden times." The bill for the wine alone came to $150. The assembled guests must have included as many as possible of Hamilton family familiars—John and Angelica Church, the Robert Troups and the John Jays and Gouverneur Morris, Dr. Hosack, Nicholas Fish, Egbert Benson, Richard Harison, John Laurance, Richard Varick, Oliver Wolcott, Jr., William Seton, Charles Wilkes, Matthew Clarkson, Elias Boudinot, Thomas Cooper, Caleb Gibbs, William Bayard, and Chancellor James Kent—all with wives and ladies. It is a matter of dispute whether Aaron Burr was ever invited to join the Hamiltons and their friends at any of these elegant social gatherings at The Grange.

The Hamiltons would proudly serve the wine to all from the handsome silverplated, four-bottle wine cooler that George and Martha Washington had presented to them in 1797 at the time when public uproar over the Reynolds affair was reaching a crescendo.

Most of the Hamiltons' friends were much relieved that his preoccupations with The Grange had led him to confine his politicking these days to sniping from the sidelines. His comment to Pinckney of December 29, 1802, was typical. The "follies and vices" of Jefferson's administration, he noted, far from losing it favor, were only making it more popular all the time.

"The malady is rather progressive than on the decline in our Northern Quarter," he wrote. "The last *lullaby* message [to Congress], instead of inspiring contempt, attracts praise. Mankind are forever destined to be the dupes of bold & cunning imposture."

"Hamilton is closely pursuing the law," Robert Troup wrote Rufus King, "and I have at length succeeded in making him somewhat mercenary. I have known him latterly to dun his clients for money, and in settling an account with me the other day, he reminded me that I had received a fee for him in settling a question referred to him and me jointly. These indications of regard to property give me hopes that we shall not be obliged to raise a subscription to pay his funeral."

Hamilton had to mortgage his whole estate to raise the money to pay some of the expenses he had bound himself to pay to build it. Apparently, he could not obtain a construction loan from a bank; so in July 1801 he gave a one-year mortgage on the entire 34 acres to his client Louis Le Guen, at lawful interest, to secure his note for $5,000. Hamilton kept up the interest and was able to repay part of the principal, it was extended from year to year, but $3,000 of it was still owing at his death as a first lien on the property. Hamilton's old friend Oliver Wolcott, Jr., president of the Merchants Bank, looked over his application for a bank loan of $4,000 the next year, perhaps for a takeout of Le Guen's construction loan or perhaps a second mortgage, but informally turned Hamilton down, no doubt in a friendly way. Hamilton had told Wolcott that he did not even want to present his loan application "if there was even a prospect of hesitation." It is not clear that any loan was made, although Hamilton owed debts to several banks at his death. Obviously, if anything should happen to Hamilton any time soon, Troup's hopes that his friends would not have "to raise a subscription to pay his funeral" would be dashed.

Replying to the letter from Aaron Burr of April 18, 1804, which opened the exchanges that ended in the duel, Hamilton refused to allow himself to be interrogated about "whatever I may have said of a political opponent in the course of a fifteen years competition." Though Hamilton's phrase made it sound as if the lists where he and Burr had done battle were narrowly political contests, the truth was that both men had also been in fierce competition in private life and frequent adversaries in the practice of law, even though they sometimes also served as cocounsel on the same side of important cases.

Between lawyers who act as cocounsel on the same side of a case hidden clashes can be more bitter than the open clashes between adversary counsel for opposing parties. In their professional and personal lives, as well as in their politics, Hamilton and Burr clashed in a kaleidescopic variety of ways during their 15 years of competition.

Hamilton had invited Burr to be associated with him as cocounsel in the famous *Le Guen* case, but Burr had wound up taking the lion's share of the fee. Their joint client then handed Hamilton the awkward assignment of dunning his cocounsel Burr, not only to reduce his fee, but also to get him to pay another unrelated debt that Burr owed to Le Guen. On May 1, 1800, Le Guen wrote Hamilton that he was "still deeply moved by your generous proceedings, and full of gratitude." He found himself "obliged to do what you yesterday forbade me to," and sent Hamilton $1,500 for his fee.

With the same pleasant letter to Hamilton, however, Le Guen told him he was letting Burr have $4,636.66, $2,900 on account of his fee bill, and various additional sums as advances to him on other accounts. Burr's bill to Le Guen was much higher than Le Guen was paying him. On an unrelated debt of $13,200 that Burr owed to him, Le Guen relayed to Hamilton the unlikely story that Burr "has promised to settle up with me tomorrow morning." Le Guen charged Hamilton, "I beg you to kindly settle this bill with him," airily adding, "so that he will be satisfied."

Le Guen had blithely laid on poor Hamilton an intrinsically impossible task the same month that Hamilton was giving up the inherently impossible assignment of building up the quasi-war army, resigning as inspector general, and discharging all the bile built up by his sense of failure by beginning to compose his attack on President John Adams.

No position is more distasteful for a lawyer than to be charged by an important client to beat down another lawyer's bill, unless it is to be the lawyer whose bill is beaten down. Nor could it have added anything to Burr's regard for Hamilton that Hamilton had been assigned by Le Guen to beat him down. Knowledge of Burr's huge debts no doubt qualified Hamilton well for the role of beating Burr down.

In a statement enclosed in a letter to John Rutledge on January 4, 1801, Hamilton wrote that Burr "is without doubt insolvent for a large *deficit*. All his visible property is deeply mortgaged, and he is known to owe other large debts, for which there is no specific security. Of the number of these there is a judgment in favor of Mr. Angerstein for a sum which with interest amounts to about $80,000.'' Hamilton knew because he had represented Angerstein suing Burr in the case of *Aaron Burr v. John Julius Angerstein* in the New York Court of Chancery, 1801–1804. Hamilton had won the case for his client, Angerstein, but with the judgment against Burr still unsatisfied, so was Hamilton's client. It was not much consolation to Hamilton to know that financially he himself was only a little less deeply under water than Burr.

Chancellor James Kent, seven years younger than Hamilton, remembered that at the New York bar of the period Burr and Hamilton stood out as the preeminent lawyers among a distinguished group of colleagues. More than 30 years later he would write, ''though the New York Bar could at that time boast of the clear intellect, the candor, the simplicity, and black-letter learning of the elder Jones, the profound and richly varied learning of Harrison, the classical taste and elegant accomplishments of Brockholst Livingston, the solid and accurate, but unpretending common-law learning of Troup, the chivalrous feelings and dignified address of Pendleton,'' yet, said Kent, ''the mighty mind of Hamilton would at times bear down all opposition by its comprehensive grasp and the strength of his reasoning powers.''

''Colonel Burr,'' by contrast, Kent recalled, was ''acute, quick, terse, polished, sententious, and sometimes sarcastic in his forensic discussions.'' Kent noted that Burr, as he had from the beginning of his career, ''seemed to disdain illustration and expansion, and confined himself with stringency to the point in debate.''

Alexander McComb, a rich merchant and speculator, whom Burr represented in one case, with Richard Harison and Robert Troup as cocounsel, wrote William Constable in 1794 that all three were ''good and capable men, but Burr is too much of a politician to give the necessary application to his profession.''

In Judge Kent's considered opinion, ''among all his brethren,'' Hamilton was ''indisputably preeminent.'' Indeed, ''this was universally conceded.'' After his resignation as secretary of the treasury and return to New York, during the years ''between 1795 and 1798,'' Hamilton ''took his station as the leading counsel at the Bar. He was employed in every important and especially in every commercial case. He was a very great favorite with the merchants of New York, and he most justly deserved to be, for he had uniformly shown himself to be one of the most enlightened, intrepid, and persevering friends to the commercial prosperity of this country.''

Then, as now, ''insurance questions, both upon the law and the fact, constituted a large portion of the litigated business in the courts.'' As Kent pointed out, ''the business of insurance was carried on principally by private underwriters, and the law had not been defined and settled in this country by a course of judicial decisions. . . .; the litigation of that kind was immense. Mr. Hamilton had an overwhelming share of it.''

Hamilton's special excellence was his breadth and depth. As Kent found:

> He taught us all how to probe deeply into the hidden recesses of the science, or to follow up principles to their far distant sources. He was not content with the modern reports, abridgments, or translations. He ransacked cases and precedents to their very foundations; and we learned from him to carry our inquiries into the commercial codes of the nations of the European continent, and in a special manner to illustrate the law of insurance by the severe judgment of Emerigon and the luminous commentaries of Valin.

At least when an overload of personal exigencies did not bear in too heavily upon him, Hamilton displayed to Kent "the habit of thorough, precise, and authentic research which accompanied all his investigations. He was not content, for instance, with examining Grotius, and taking him as an authority, in any other than the original Latin language in which the work was composed."

For the other side, Burr's sympathetic biographers Samuel B. Wandell and Meade Minnigerode contrasted Burr with Hamilton in the following terms: "Hamilton was perhaps the more profound, the more erudite, the more long-winded; Burr the more superficial, the more concise, and the more successful. . . . Burr could say as much in half an hour as it took Hamilton two hours to establish."

Of the law in the abstract, Burr was fond of saying that "law is anything which is boldly asserted and plausibly maintained."

Wandell and Minnigerode accepted the appraisal written by Major William Pierce after observing Hamilton in action in 1787: "To a clear and strong judgment he unites the ornaments of fancy, and whilst he is able, convincing and engaging in his eloquence The Heart and Head sympathize in approving him." What Burr would call his long-windedness Pierce saw as Hamilton's profundity: "There is no skimming over the surface of a subject with him, he must sink to the bottom to see what foundation it rests on."

Beneath the urbane surface of professional affability that Burr and Hamilton each made a point of exhibiting toward the other, there were enough obvious differences in each man's personal style to provide him with an inexhaustible stock of reasons for loathing and hating the other.

For men of both such kinds of intellects and talents, the general run of civil cases that both handled, involving marine insurance claims, maritime liens, civil salvage, bottomry bonds, prizes, laws of impost, contracts, bills and notes, creditors' rights, trespass, debt and ejectment, and so forth, were not inherently fascinating or demanding of an exalted level of professional skill after the first dozen or two of each kind. But such cases were the bread and butter of most prosperous lawyers' practices. In Volume I of the Hamilton Legal Papers are discussed or calendared more than 100 such cases in which Hamilton was counsel, in Volume II there are about 310, and in Volume III several hundred more. Hamilton was undoubtedly involved in hundreds of legal matters other than these—wills, trusts, incorporation papers, and prospectuses—which did not reach the stage of recorded litigation or which were unimportant or of which all records have disappeared.

Between or concurrently with stretches of political activity, the greatest of lawyers, like Hamilton and Burr, of necessity turned to such uninspiring private legal practice to repair their fortunes: for example, to keep up payments on the debts they both owed to Louis Le Guen. Both men had helped make it possible for Le Guen to win the money that put them in his debt by helping him win a final judgment of $119,915.43.

According to Chancellor Kent, Le Guen had originally commenced the case at law on Hamilton's advice. It was one of Hamilton's two great cases in which, Kent said, "his reasoning powers, the sagacity with which he pursued his investigations, his piercing criticism, his masterly analysis, and the energy and fervor of his appeals to the judgment and conscience of the tribunal"—were "most strikingly displayed." Hamilton's passions, he added, were never "so warmly engaged in any cause."

Hamilton's grandson Allan McLane Hamilton recalled that the defendant, Isaac Gouverneur, had originally sought to retain Hamilton for his side of the case, but Hamilton had declined because of Gouverneur's indelicate comments that attorneys fees tended to be too high.

Le Guen's case was a cause célèbre in its own time because of the huge amount of money claimed and won, the financial ruin inflicted on Gouverneur and the other losers, the importance of the parties and lawyers involved, and the unprecedented publicity and bitterness it generated. The case gained nationwide importance, became a procedural precedent throughout the country, and has been cited more than a hundred times. Many states adopted its doctrine of the binding force of a judgment of a court of competent jurisdiction to preclude further litigation, both as to issues actually decided as well as those that could have been raised but were not, and of the power of appellate courts to review decisions of lower courts on factual issues.

Where the client's case is a weak one on the merits, winning a procedural point may be the only way there is to win it. This was how Hamilton finally won for Louis Le Guen. Because it is full of "lawyers' law," an accurate account of it would be too "dry and technical," as Kent said long ago, to attempt here, but a summary gives a sense of the magnitude of Hamilton's technical accomplishment in winning it.

Louis Le Guen was a French citizen who had come to New York in 1794 bringing with him a cargo of cotton and indigo, which he consigned to Isaac Gouverneur and Peter Kemble, merchants and factors, to sell for him. By March 1795, the cargo had still found no buyer, so Le Guen persuaded Gouverneur and Kemble to send it to Europe to sell for his account there, and they chartered the ship *White Fox* to transport it there. Just then three Spanish Jews, Isaac Gomez, Jr., Moses Lopez, and Abraham Rods Rivera agreed to take over from Gouverneur and Kemble the charter of the *White Fox* and the whole cargo for £48,966/6, payable in 12 months, with 10 months' interest at 6% per annum, represented by promissory notes, which could be paid out of the proceeds of sale of the cargo. As things turned out, the cargo could not be sold, Gomez et al. claimed they had been defrauded because the cargo was of inferior quality, and without paying for it, they finally turned it back to Gouverneur and Kemble's agents in London, who sold it for practically nothing.

Le Guen claimed that he was entitled to recover from Gouverneur and Kemble the entire sum that Gomez et al. had contracted to pay them, notwithstanding that they had lost a fortune carrying and shipping the cargo back to Europe.

Before the case was over, out of these facts grew eight separate actions and suits in the Supreme Court of Judicature, the Court of Chancery, and the Court for the Trial of Impeachments and the Correction of Errors during the period from 1796 to early 1800. Yet what seemed to be the heart of the matter was never reached: the question of whether or not Gomez, Lopez, and Rivera had been defrauded.

At the first Le Guen trial in the New York Circuit before Justice Morgan Lewis, Hamilton with Burr and Harison selected a "struck" jury, half of the members of which are listed in Hamilton's cash book of the period, indicating that they were fee paying clients of his. They awarded Le Guen only £39 6s. in damages and 6d. costs, but Hamilton obtained a new trial with a second jury which, like the first, was made up of merchants about half of whom were his clients. It awarded LeGuen $119,302.47 and six cents costs. To a skillful lawyer, nothing can be more important than the careful selection of a jury, as Hamilton, in his practice manual, *Practical Proceedings*, had been one of the first to point out. Apparently, in selecting the second jury, Brockholst Livingston had failed to make as effective use of Hamilton's precepts—and the challenges which permitted him to strike unwelcome names off the list—and his own mercantile clients—as Hamilton had done. From this point on it became Hamilton's role to defend the judgment in Le Guen's favor from "collateral attack"—the charge by Gomez et al. that they had been defrauded.

Le Guen retained three of the most prominent members of the New York bar, Hamilton,

Richard Harison, and Aaron Burr.

About the facts of the case, the most significant point, as Kent noted, was that Le Guen's claim "was in opposition to the mercantile sense of its justice." After "expensive trials and the most persevering and irritating litigation, pursued into the court of the last resort," Kent wrote, Le Guen "recovered upon technical rules of law strictly and severely applied." Chancellor Kent made it sound as if he would have decided the case the other way had it come before him.

Opposing counsel in the case, Brockholst Livingston, later joined by Peter Van Schaack, Gouverneur Morris, and Robert Troup as counsel for Gouverneur and Kemble, argued in outrage against the injustice of the result. Hamilton's position, Brockholst Livingston cried, "is an attempt to charge a factor with the loss of near $120,000; not for appropriating to his own use the funds of his principal—not for a palpable deviation from instruction—not for a gross violation of trust,—not for any known and established breach of duty—but for an imaginary default, and that in a point, on which two honest men might easily differ without an unfair imputation to either. It is an attempt to recover this immense sum, without proof, or even pretense, that the plaintiff [Le Guen] has received the smallest injury."

Gouverneur appealed the jury's verdict.

Le Guen wrote Hamilton on April 24 that he had no confidence in Burr "de vous seconder dans mon affaire." Nevertheless, with "Vos talents, voter Zelle," Monsieur Hamilton, directed by "Vos sages Conseils," I have not the least doubt that your efforts "me feront obtenir un Jugement favorable."

After the second jury had rendered the six-figure verdict against Gouverneur and Kemble, Gouverneur wrote Hamilton that Hamilton's "mistaken opinion . . . acts as a spur to make individuals less obstinate afterwards." Also, "it would be more becoming, to be less abusive." Furthermore, Gouverneur taxed Hamilton, "to move the feelings of the jury . . . you finally compared me to the odious character of 'Shylock in the Play.' I felt extremely hurt upon this observation, my dear Colonel, because I thot you was wounding yourself, as I am not without regard for you." He probably was not aware that Hamilton's own mother was named Lavien.

In New York's court of last resort argument began Februrary 4, 1800, before the state senate in Albany, sitting in its other capacity as the Court of Errors.

The time attorneys took in even routine cases for argument—as distinguished from examination of witnesses and introduction of evidence—seems incredible today, for both the intellectual energy and physical stamina that must have been required. In one case, Josiah Ogden Hoffman, summing up for the defendant on July 12, 1803, spoke from 10:15 A.M. to 4:54 P.M.; Egbert Benson, from 5:00 P.M. to 6:25 P.M. Then on the following day, Hamilton for the plaintiff spoke from 10:35 A.M. to 4:25 P.M., and Harison from 4:25 P.M. to 6:02 P.M.

Troup wrote Low on February 7, 1800, with a wry dig at Hamilton's prolixity:

> Hamilton devoted near two days to his arguments. He is the only person who has argued on the part of Le Guen. I followed him on the part of Gouverneur & Kemble & spoke near two hours—which I believe is more than an hour after a man has spoken what may be called common sense in any case. . . .

Troup was particularly struck by Hamilton's passionate involvement in the case:

> Between us, Hamilton has pushed this cause to the utmost extremity, and in my opinion with the utmost animosity & cruelty against Gouverneur & Kemble. I never

knew him on any occasion so heated and wound up with passion. He has attacked the whole body of witnesses on the part of Gouverneur & Kemble & he has even attempted to weaken the credit of my testimony on a fact which came to my knowledge about Lopez, one of the partners of young Gomez long before I was ever employed by Mr. Gouverneur. The manner of his treating the witnesses & persecuting poor Gouverneur has done his cause no good and I think we have grounds for expecting success on our part.

For this critically important appeal, Brockholst Livingston had recruited Gouverneur Morris for his team of cocounsel. Though it was Morris's first court appearance in many years, he was Gouverneur's kinsman, and he was a redoubtable orator. Morris recorded in his diary: "Mr. Hamilton opens. Thursday 6 Feb. Hamilton concludes forcibly—Harison opens the law and so does Burr." Morris adds, "I follow him. Find some impression is made." On Monday he finished his own argument, "which as I observe produced considerable effect." On Tuesday Morris noted that "Hamilton is desirous of being witty but goes beyond the bounds and is open to a severe dressing." On Wednesday, the twelfth of February, Morris snorted that "Colonel Burr is very able & has I see made considerable impression . . . I had an opportunity to retort to Hamilton which I did not use and am on the whole well pleased that I did not."

Hamilton's son James A. Hamilton, in his *Reiminiscences,* recalled Morris's reaction differently. Morris had initiated the sparring in the courtroom. After giving perfunctory praise to Hamilton's just concluded argument, Morris had said, "Before I Have done I Shall Make my learned friend cry out, 'Help me, Cassius' "—at this dramatic moment Morris pointed at Hamilton and then swung his arm around to point to his cocounsel Burr," 'or I sink.' "

Hamilton's son James says that Hamilton "alluded to the boast of his friend in a strain of irony that turned the laughter of the court and audience against him." Not surprisingly, General Schuyler also thought Hamilton had bested Morris, the most renowned of wits, in the courtroom exchange. Hamilton's riposte "afforded general pleasure to the Court and audience," said Schuyler. And "Mr. Morris felt so sensibly. I hope he will profit by it."

It would rankle with Hamilton that to the 34 judges and senators and all the spectators and reporters in the Albany courtroom, his friend Morris, the tall, spellbinding aristocrat only a little lamed by his wooden leg—the "exotic" whom he admired as much as any man alive—had made him out to be a tired Julius Caesar, who needed his false friend Cassius—Aaron Burr—to save him.

That night at a dinner at Stephen and Margarita van Rensselaer's, Hamilton walked up to Morris with an amiable smile and said, "By Cassius' help I meet you here with our friends at dinner."

The decision of the Court of Errors was 28 to 6 in favor of Hamilton's client.

Hamilton and his cocounsel had won by upholding a judgment of $119,915.43 for their client Le Guen on technical grounds without at any point having permitted the issue of fraud to come directly before any tribunal for consideration and adjudication. Wall, Franklin, Chestnut, and La Salle Street lawyers of today are proudest of the kind of victories won the same way. But they would not make the silly mistake that Hamilton did and Burr did not by underbilling Le Guen for his final fee.

On February 28, 1800, four days after the Court of Errors had handed down its ruinous reversal against him, Isaac Gouverneur died suddenly at the home of Attorney General Hoffman. On Hamilton's conscience his death must have fallen as an awful rebuke for racist slurs. Hearing of their popular fellow merchant's death, the merchants and masters of the vessels in New York harbor half-masted their colors. The *New York Gazette and Daily Advertiser* of March 6 called it "a singular, though pleasing token of respect to a gentleman not in public office."

Twelve days after coming home from the trial, the usually even-tempered Troup had barely calmed down enough from the tensions it had generated to give evenhanded credit to his old friend Hamilton's efforts in a letter to Rufus King of March 9, 1800:

> General Hamilton and Mr. Morris made great display of talent & eloquence. Hamilton is more solid, more logical, and more equal. Morris at times astonished us with bursts of sublime eloquence—at other times he was flat and uninteresting— Our friend Hamilton never appeared to have his passions so warmly engaged in any cause. He was full of acrimony against Gouverneur and Kemble, and was not without asperity towards their counsel. I think he was guilty of an indelicacy toward me which my hearts tells me I ought to forgive but which my friends will not permit me as yet to bury in oblivion.

English and Dutch capitalists, as well as wealthy Americans, dreamed of making quick fortunes from the limitless American back country slowly filling up with settlers. The Dutch capitalists who had combined to form the Holland Land Company appointed Theophile Cazenove as their American agent who arranged to purchase vast tracts of land in western New York and Pennsylvania. But according to New York state law, aliens could not become unrestricted owners of New York real estate. Cazenove retained Hamilton as counsel to push for removal of the prohibition, but Hamilton was only partly successful: he managed to obtain passage of a law permitting aliens to hold land for a period of seven years, long enough at least to permit them to make a profit from a quick turnover. But Cazenove was not satisfied and urged Hamilton to try for a still better law without any time limitations on alien ownership at all, and Hamilton pushed through a new law lengthening the term of alien holdings to 20 years. Cazenove claimed not to be satisfied with even the 20-year limitation. He would still like to see all restrictions on alien land ownership removed.

Hamilton replied by a cautiously worded letter painting a dark picture of the company's future prospects if it refused to accept the 20-year limitation. The story of the Reynolds affair was just now being publicly exposed for the first time and Cazenove turned to Aaron Burr and found him agreeably ready, willing, and able to help out the Holland Land Company.

Burr, with some of his own investment at stake and with a douceur of bribes for susceptible state legislators, managed to put through a superseding law granting aliens a wholly unrestricted tenure. John Barker Church, whose many insurance and banking interests Hamilton also represented, was heard to pass disparaging comments about Burr's role. Burr challenged him to a duel. On September 2, 1799, on the usual ledge at Weehawken, Burr and Church exchanged shots from Church's elegant, hair-trigger dueling pistols. No harm was done to either duelist except for the bullet hole that Church's bullet put in Burr's sleeve. On the same ground less than five years later Burr would demonstrate that practice had improved his aim.

If Levi Weeks had not been the brother of Ezra Weeks, the contractor who was building Hamilton's Grange, Hamilton might not have taken the case or, having done so, might not have waived his usual modest fee, as he did. Levi was charged with first-degree murder for allegedly killing pregnant Gulielma Sands and throwing her badly bruised body down one of the wells of the Manhattan Company in Lispenard's Meadow on the snowy night of December 22, 1799. Gulielma, about 20 years old, a very beautiful girl who was also very promiscuous, lived in a boardinghouse kept by her Quaker cousin, Catherine Ring, and Catherine's husband, Elias, in upper Greenwich Street, where Levi was also a boarder. Gulielma had gone out the night of December 22, allegedly to be married to Levi, but was never seen alive again.

It was said in the Ring household that she had departed with Levi. But later that night he came back to the house alone, asking if she had gone to bed. He was disappointed when a suspicious Catherine Ring told him that she had gone out. Levi expressed anxiety that she should have gone out alone so late at night in a dangerous place like Manhattan. Two days later, the day before Christmas, a young boy found a muff that Gulielma had borrowed from a friend—in the Manhattan Well. It was uncertain how soon afterward the Rings learned of this find, but one witness testified that Elias Ring had known of it no later than December 29. This seemed odd because on that same day, the twenty-ninth, Ring, who was quite familiar with the terrain around the Manhattan Well, had arranged to have the waters of the North River around Rhinelander's dock dragged for her body. The dock was many blocks away from the well where her muff had been found. When the well was finally looked into on January 2, it yielded her fully clad corpse. Levi Weeks was seized, brought to the *locus delicti*, and, after the coroner's inquest, charged with willful murder and committed to the Bridewell jail for trial. It was in Weeks's favor that the coroner ruled that Gulielma had not been pregnant.

Public mystification, curiosity, excitement, and indignation were intense. Hamilton's cocounsel for the defense of Levi Weeks were Aaron Burr and Brockholst Livingston. Both men were aligned against him in the impending spring election campaign for control of the New York legislature, on which the outcome of the crucial presidential election of 1800 would ultimately pivot.

On March 25, 1800, the morning of the trial in the old City Hall, at the corner of Wall, Broad, and Nassau Streets, "the concourse of people was so great, as was never before witnessed on a similar occasion." The public was "gaping with eager anxiety." The press of the huge crowd to get into the small courtroom was unbearable. The judges, Chief Justice John Lansing, Mayor Richard Varick, and the recorder, Richard Harison, ordered the constables to clear the room of "superfluous spectators." The best of many accounts of the trial was by Hamilton's friend William Coleman, later the editor of the *New York Evening Post*, but even it does not clearly tell which of the great lawyers did what. The prosecution brought on 24 witnesses, and the defense still more, for a total of 75 witnesses in all. Most spectators and jurors looked on Levi Weeks and his counsel "with a dark and sullen animosity." Popular feeling ran high against him. His defense demanded all the skill his three famous lawyers could bring to it.

Twenty-seven-year-old Catherine Ring and her husband, Elias, were the prosecution's chief witnesses. Catherine in particular colored all her testimony with glints of deep animosity toward Levi, although it came out, under cross-examination, that she had earlier thought of him as a wonderful young man. But the evidence she could give against him was only circumstantial. When Elma had first disappeared, before her body was discovered, Levi had told his Caty, as she spoke of herself when with him, except when testifying against him, "Mrs. Ring, it's my firm belief she's now in eternity."

Candlelit court sessions lasted late into the evening. Hamilton was particularly suspicious of one prosecution witness named Richard David Croucher.

William Coleman's report of Hamilton's cross-examination of Croucher confirms the expertness of the cross-examiner's technique. Hamilton could inculpate Croucher and exculpate Levi Weeks only if he could show (1) that Croucher had been near the Manhattan Well the night of the murder, but falsely denied he had; (2) that he had had a quarrel with Levi over Gulielma, but concealed it; (3) that Gulielma knew him, feared him, and had jilted him for Levi; (4) that he remembered vividly what it was like the night of the murder, but pretended he had forgotten; and (5) that he was a congenital liar, with a bad memory, and knew it.

But there was no way any such evidence could be admitted into the record, unless extracted unwittingly, or blurted out of Croucher's own mouth under the pressure of cross-examination. Here is how Hamilton got it all in:

Q: Do you know where the Manhattan well is?
A: I do.
Q: Did you pass by it that evening?
A: I did not—I wish I had—I might, perhaps, have saved the life of the deceased.
Q: Have you not said you did?
A: No.

A good liar must have a good memory of prior statements and confidence in it, which Croucher lacked. To cover, he volunteered: "I might have said I wished I did."

Q: Have you ever had a quarrel with the prisoner at the bar?
A: I bear him no malice.
Q: But have you never had any words with him?
A: Once I had—the reason was this, if you wish me to tell it:—Going hastily upstairs, I suddenly came upon Elma, who stood at the door—she cried out Ah! and fainted away. On hearing this the prisoner came down from his room and said it was not the first time I had insulted her. I told him he was an impertinent puppy. Afterward, being sensible of his error, he begged my pardon.
Q: And you say you bear him no ill will?
A: I bear him no malice, but I despise every man who does not behave in character.
Q: How near the Manhattan well do you think you passed that night?
A: I believe I might have passed the Glue manufactory.
Q: Do you not know what route you took?
A: I do not; I cannot certainly say; I might have passed by one route or another; I sometimes go by the road, sometimes across the field.
Q: Was it dark?
A: I believe there was a little moonlight—the going was very bad.

At this point in the cross-examination, to save his floundering and totally discredited witness and give him time to recover, Assistant Attorney General Colden derailed Hamilton's probing by asking a completely unrelated question.
Then,

Q: Were you ever upon other than friendly terms with Elma?
A: After I offended the prisoner at the bar, who thought she was an adonis, I never spoke to her again.

He had got in the evidence on all five of his points, effectively destroyed the witness, and converted him into a prime suspect.

Hamilton's case for the defense was soundly constructed. He began with establishing a good character for Levi Weeks and a solid alibi to account for his whereabouts for all but a few minutes of the night of December 22. He cast suspicion not only on Croucher, but also on Elias Ring whose possibly betrayed wife, Catherine, stood loyally by him. The testimony of Captain Rutgers brought out Ring's curious behavior in dragging the river after being told where Gulielma's muff had been found. The testimony of Joseph and Elizabeth Watkins, who lived next door to the Rings, tended to show that Ring had been carrying on an affair with Gulielma, while Catherine was away in the country.

Q: **[to Joseph Watkins]:** Do you remember anything in the conduct of Mr. Ring that led you to suspicions of improper conduct between him and Elma?

A: About the middle of September, Mrs. Ring being in the country, I imagined one night I heard a shaking of a bed and considerable noise there, in the second story, where Elias's bed stood within four inches of the partition. I heard a man's voice and a woman's.

Q: **[by one of the jury]:** Could you hear through the partition?

A: Pretty distinctly.

Q: Did the noise of the bed continue for any time?

A: It continued some time and it must have been very loud to have awakened us. I heard a man's voice pretty loud and lively, and joking; the voice was loud and unguarded. I said to my wife, it is Ring's voice, and I told my wife that girl will be ruined next.

By this kind of testimony, Hamilton and his cocounsel for the defense created good grounds for reasonable doubt of Levi's guilt. Catherine Ring or Croucher must have done her in, not Levi. Now came the prosecution's turn to try to save its case. Assistant Attorney General Cadwallader Colden tried to break down Watkins's credibility as a witness by probing to show that he simply did not know what he was testifying about or that perhaps his damaging testimony had been falsified.

Q: What kind of a partition is it which divides the houses?

A: A plank partition, lathed and plaistered on both sides.

So far so good. Colden might later be able to argue that it would be too thick for Watkins to have heard through, unlike more recent, flimsy Manhattan apartment construction.

But then Watkins, unasked but irrepressible, blurted out four words that wrecked all of Colden's hopes: "I made it myself."

Cross-examination by an expert lawyer can serve as the supreme lie detector in a courtroom. But expert cross-examiners are able to sense the times when it is wiser to waive the cross-examination of certain witnesses or rest before asking one question too many. Not Colden. Not being in the experts' league, Colden ploughed ahead asking Watkins the same list of prepared questions he had asked all the other witnesses who lived in houses on either side of the Rings'. He thereby permitted Watkins to help him demonstrate how maladroit cross-examination can also serve as the courtroom's supreme truth extractor—for the other side's benefit.

As derisory smiles and whispers at defense counsels' table subsided, Colden resumed:

Q: How could you distinguish between the voice of Mr. Ring and Mr. Weeks?

A: Ring's is a high sounding voice, Weeks' a low soft voice.

Q: How often have you heard this noise of the bed?

A: From eight to fourteen times.

Q (by prisoner's counsel, Hamilton perhaps):   Did you ever hear this noise after Mrs. Ring came back from the country?

A: I never did.

The celebrated Dr. David Hosack testified that, contrary to popular supicion and rumor, there had been no marks of violence on the cadaver, other than what might be inflicted by falling or being pushed down the well.

Her jealously envenomed charges against Levi now discredited, exposed as a betrayed wife jilted by her former paramour for the same younger and more beautiful woman who had also captured her husband, Mrs. Catherine Ring began to squirm. She found herself becoming the focal point of more and more accusatory stares from the packed galleries in the courtroom as the night wore on—she and her well-motivated, lying accomplice, Richard Croucher.

All the evidence was in by 2:35 A.M. The assistant attorney general, confessing that he was "sinking under fatigue," moved for an adjournment.

Hamilton jumped up. He moved for a verdict at once. The case was too plain to require any "laboured elucidation." He was so confident of acquittal that he was even willing to waive his own speech of summation to the jury—he was full of surprises that night. He would rest the defense on Judge Lansing's charge.

Not displeased with Hamilton's motion, the court denied the prosecution's request for adjournment. It did not wish to detain the jurors for a second night without the "conveniences necessary for repose." One is always left in suspense about 18th-century toilet facilities, or "necessaries." Justice Lansing's charge was virtually a direction to acquit. The jury then filed out, was out five minutes, filed back, and solemnly intoned its verdict—NOT GUILTY!

Before Hamilton could clap his grateful client, Levi Weeks, gleefully on the back and be happily hugged by Levi in return, Mrs. Catherine Ring gave a cry and jumped to her feet! Trembling as the flickering candles guttered out in the blackness, she swung her outstretched arm around the courtroom past Judge Lansing and the jurors, stopped at Hamilton, thrust a trembling fist and crooked forefinger into his face, and screamed in fury: "If thee dies a natural death, I shall think there is no justice in heaven!"

Fifteen years of Hamilton's kind of competition is too much for anyone, even, or especially, Hamilton in 1800.

The distinguished physician, alienist, and generally responsible biographer, Dr. Allan McLane Hamilton, relates the story of the awful witching hour curse that Mrs. Catherine Ring laid on his grandfather without expressing any doubts of its having been uttered. Other authorities at a greater distance, lacking other documentation, are not so sure.

Subsequent events did nothing to disprove its efficacy. On the contrary, they proved its power. Chief Justice Lansing left his hotel room one day in 1829 to take the riverboat up to Albany, but was never heard from again. His body was never found. He had managed to stave off unnatural death a quarter century longer than Hamilton. Cocounsel Aaron Burr suffered political death when Hamilton died, but physical death spared him until the age of 80, when he was in bed. Told by Dr. David Hosack that Burr was dying, the Reverend Mr. Van Pelt rushed to his bedside slavering for the parochial credit that would accrue to any divine administering last rites to a man with such a satanic reputation. He asked Burr whether he had "good hope, through grace, that all your sins will be pardoned . . . for the sake of . . . our Lord Jesus Christ?"

Burr's last words, as he expired unrepentant on September 14, 1836, were: "On that subject I am coy."

37

Dr. Cooper Heard Something Despicable

I could detail to you a still more despicable opinion which General Hamilton had expressed of Mr. Burr.

—Dr. Charles D. Cooper to Philip Schuyler, April 23, 1804

Less than ten months after Mrs. Catherine Ring laid her witching hour curse on Hamilton—"If thee dies a natural death, I shall think there is no justice in heaven"—Noah Webster, writing as *The Federalist*—of all names—had anathematized Hamilton in the press in November 1800 by his *Letter to General Hamilton occasioned by his Letter to President Adams*: Hamilton was a man of "ambition, pride and overbearing temper . . .," "the evil genius of this country," and the villain who would "compleat our ruin."

Both maledictions fell on him during a psychic crisis when his mood had never been blacker or more unforgiving. There may come a time, R. D. Laing has suggested, when a man needs to go mad. It is the time when unseen enemies' threats of throat cuttings, whispers and stabbings in the dark rising on all sides, disorient and imprison the victim's mind in multiple bonds. He seeks by opposing to end his troubles and fails, and can no longer think clearly or see any way out. For such a person, madness may be the first stage in the natural healing process of a too-acute mind, by which it begins to break down, to soften, to feel with less unbearable intensity, the logically unbearable contradictions of experience. If this analysis is correct, Hamilton may by now have already taken the first step on the path to recovery and eventually to normalcy. But recovery would not come all at once.

Hamilton attributed much of Jefferson's growing popularity, as well as the venerable George Clinton's recent comeback victory over young Stephen Van Rensselaer in New

571

York, to the lack of a really reliable party-lining Federal newspaper in New York City. Nationally, Freneau's *National Gazette*, Cheetham's *American Citizen*, and the Baches' and Duane's *Aurora*, all liberal Democratic-Republican journals, flourished, spreading Republican doctrine across the land. Hamilton considered Noah Webster's *Commercial Advertiser* and other local Federalist papers as weak and misguided even when they did not go so far as to brand the leader of the Federal party "the evil genius of this country."

After due consideration, Hamilton, Troup, and Wolcott picked William Coleman, the 35-year-old lawyer-journalist who had written the best published accounts of the trial of *People* v. *Levi Weeks*, to be editor and publisher of a New York City newspaper they and other true friends of Federalism planned to finance, write for, subscribe to, and read. Coleman was a kindly, easygoing man with some literary pretensions, not a typical hard-hitting polemicist like Cheetham or Callender who flourished in that day when newspapers and pamphlets were the preeminent medium for communicating all messages to a public of avid readers. Some years before, Coleman had worked as a law partner of Aaron Burr. He had all sorts of leads, contacts, spies, informers, and other news sources barred or unknown to Hamilton. Hamilton contributed about $1,000, which he could not afford, to help launch the *Evening Post*. Other backers also helped out, with reimbursement to be paid out of future profits of the paper, if any.

"We have set [Coleman] up . . . as a printer," Troup wrote. "His first paper will make its appearance in October next. . . . All our friends have Mr. Coleman's paper much at heart. We have not a paper in the City on the federal side that is worth reading."

The prospectus of the New York *Evening Post*, published in the first edition on November 16, 1801, announced that the paper "must derive its principal support from the Merchants of our City." Therefore "particular attention will be bestowed on whatever relates to that large and respectable class. . . . The design . . . is to diffuse among the people correct information . . ." and "to inculcate just principles of religion, morals and politics. . . ." The tone of the prospectus was surprisingly moderate and less dogmatic than most had expected from a paper with sponsors named Hamilton, Troup, Varick, Gracie, and the like: "Though we openly profess our attachment to that system of politics denominated Federal, because we think it most conducive to the welfare of the community . . . yet we disapprove of that spirit of dogmatism which lays exclusive claim to infallibility; and . . . believe that honest and virtuous men are to be found in each party."

The *Evening Post*'s prospectus also declared that the people wanted proper information "to enable them to judge of what is really best." It would cleave to a "line of temperate discussion and impartial regard to truth!" The date of that first edition, November 16, 1801, makes the New York *Evening Post*, published continually ever since, the oldest daily newspaper in the communications capital in the United States.

The leading editorial in the first edition urged harmony in party ranks because "the cause of Federalism has received as much injury from the indiscreet contentions . . . among those who profess to be its friends, as from the open assaults of its enemies." The *Post*'s jibe was directed at Noah Webster's paper, but it would remind many that the cause of Federalism had received more serious injury from the "indiscreet contentions" of its own founder than from anything Noah Webster had ever written.

The *Evening Post* owed its influence among orthodox Federalists not so much to Coleman's editing as to Hamilton's constant support, intervention, and publications. Such unity as the party continued to have after its crushing defeat by Jefferson and Burr came largely from the *Evening Post* and its weekly edition, called the *Herald*, which was sent to subscribers all over the United States. The *Herald*, with a larger circulation than the

Evening Post itself, kept alive Federalist pretensions to being a national party, not just a sectional party of the Northeast.

But harmony among Federalists seemed always fated to be rare and shortlived, and between Hamilton and Coleman it lasted less than a year. Burr was the immediate cause of the split; Jefferson, above the fray, was an unseen presence manipulating with invisible hands unseen strings tied to James Thomson Callender.

After Jefferson's election, Callender had importuned him for a job as a reward for helpful preelection pamphleteering of Hamilton's affair with Mrs. Reynolds. By the time of his election as president, Jefferson had paid Callender $150 or more for various anti-Federal publications, and after his election he had paid him several hundred dollars more. Jefferson helped raise contributions to pay for Callender's defense when he was put on trial by the Federalists for seditious libel, and helped him out with getting his fine paid. But he did not come through with payment of the whole fine himself, or give him a government job.

Jefferson made all these payments to Callender as secretively as possible to cover up his own role, sometimes using James Monroe as his go-between. It was unfortunate, Jefferson wrote Monroe on May 29, 1801, that Callender now considered all the money Jefferson had paid him to be "hush money." Monroe should pay him no more. "Such a misconstruction of my charities puts an end to them forever," Jefferson said he piously told his most confidential bagman. Monroe and other go-betweens of Jefferson scuttled nervously back to Callender one last time to try to get back all the letters Jefferson had ever sent him. Callender saw Jefferson's conduct as welshing on their own private "hush money" deal once he had reaped the benefits of Callender's help, and refused to give up Jefferson's letters.

Finally out of jail, in the summer of 1801, Callender began publicly charging in the Richmond *Recorder* that Jefferson had reneged on his promise to reimburse him for the whole fine. This and many of Callender's later charges against Jefferson were picked up and reprinted by Hamilton and William Coleman in the *Evening Post,* as well as in most other Federalist-leaning papers around the country.

Another excuse that Callender offered the public for his vicious attacks on Jefferson was that he was only trying to give evenhanded, objective press treatment to Jefferson to balance the attacks he had previously published on Hamilton. Four years earlier, Callender pointed out, the Democrats had reaped great political profits out of his account of Hamilton's affair with another man's wife. It was appropriate now to do the same for Jefferson by publishing the story of his affair with the wife of his old friend John Walker. According to John Walker's unpublished statement to Hamilton's old friend Henry Lee, Jefferson began his "improper conduct" toward Walker's wife, Betsy, back in 1768 while still a bachelor, "renewed his caresses" in 1769 or 1770, and kept them up for years even after he was married. Unlike Hamilton, Jefferson made no public reply to Callender's charges. Walker's written account, together with Jefferson's admission, were deposited with the distinguished South Carolina Federalist Thomas Pinckney as "security from calumny." This did not prevent Jefferson's old affair from being rehashed once again in later debate in the House of Representatives.

Another story published by Callender's *Recorder* was that the man "whom it delighteth the people to honor" was secretly keeping Sally Hemings—"Dusky Sally," the "African Venus"—as his concubine in the château at Monticello. After beginning their liaison in France, she had borne him five mahogany-colored babies, Callender reported, one of whom, Tom, "Yellow Tom," so strikingly resembled his father, the head of the "mulatto party," as to provoke pleased nods of recognition from guests when he served his own father-owner at table there.

The *Evening Post*'s recycling of such juicy tidbits about Jefferson's illicit sex life from Callender's *Recorder* did nothing to help avid readers forget about Hamilton's. Gossip about him and Angelica Church going the rounds in New York, and becoming spicier all the time, gave no one cause to believe that either man's affairs had ended with male menopause.

In September of 1802, Hamilton found it necessary to rebuke Coleman for rehashing so many old scandals of Callender's in the *Evening Post*. He also published a notice in the *Post* that he had not been consulted before the publication of the offensive reprints about Jefferson. He added that he was averse to airing in the press "all personalities, not immediately connected with public considerations."

Bayard wrote Hamilton on April 12, 1802, to clear up a mystery that had been troubling him. The "strange apparition"—Democratic Vice-President Aaron Burr's surprise invasion of the Federalists' Washington's Birthday banquet of 1802, leading to his toast "to the Union of all honest men!"—had been a carefully laid Federalist trap: Bayard and a few of the top leaders had secretly invited Burr without letting the rank and file in on the secret, so that Burr's barging in apparently uninvited would appear to them to be for some fell purpose of his own. It would be a still greater shock to the Democrats when they were told of it. "We knew," Bayard wrote Hamilton, "the impression which the coincidence of circumstances would make on a certain great personage; how readily that impression would be communicated to the proud and aspiring lords of the Ancient Dominion; and we have not been mistaken as to the jealousy we expected it would excite through the party."

Now that Burr had served to deliver the crucial electoral votes of New York State to Jefferson in the election of 1800, Vice-President Burr's usefulness to Jefferson was at an end. He lost no time putting the widest possible distance between himself and the man he called "a crooked gun." He ignored Burr's pleas for the crumb of a patronage appointment for Burr's closest friend Matthew L. Davis. He undercut Burr's political base in New York by sending a list of names of Burr's proposed patronage appointments, including Davis, to Governor George Clinton to be cleared by him, making Burr hostage to his local political rivals, the Clinton and Livingston factions of the New York Democratic party.

Jefferson's political genius saw that the way to dump Burr was to form a new alliance with George Clinton and his nephew, De Witt Clinton, and Burr's onetime allies, the Livingstons. He appointed Chancellor Robert R. Livingston minister to France and saw that the Clintonians gave Edward Livingston the offices of mayor of New York and also district attorney. Burr's man Matthew L. Davis got not a crumb.

Burr's creditors now hounded him more aggressively. He was forced to sell out his stock in the Manhattan Company. Soon he was purged from its board of directors, along with John Swartwout and others of his allies. A deal to sell a sizable part of Richmond Hill at a good price just then mysteriously fell through; someone "either utterly ignorant of the value or . . . from improper motives" put about rumors that it was not worth the price, Burr wrote William Edgar angrily on November 18, 1801. Jefferson's ally Brockholst Livingston suddenly pulled out of a deal of Burr's he had earlier promised to help finance.

Under fierce pressure from the enemies seen and unseen ringed around him, Burr made some political mistakes of his own that were characteristic of him; he remained too much in the middle, not making it clear which side he was on, being seen to swing from one side to the other, thus losing the trust of large segments of both. When two Senate votes on repeal of the Judiciary Act were taken on successive days, January 26 and 27, 1802, Burr, presiding as vice-president, had cast two tie-breaking votes. On the first, to permit a third reading of the bill, he voted with the Democrats; but on the second, to refer it to a select committee, he voted with the Federalists. As Gouverneur Morris saw it, Burr's fate pivoted on these two "yea" votes from one day to the next. On August 21, 1802, he remarked on Cassius's mistake to Robert Livingston in his familiar Shakespearean mode:

> There was a moment when the vice president might have arrested the measure by his vote, and that vote would, I believe, have made him President at the next election but there is a tide in the affairs of men which he suffered to go by.

Much as he had failed to make the same deal with the Federalists that Jefferson had been willing to make to snatch the presidency from him, Aaron Burr, always in the middle, had shrunk back from standing firmly on one side or the other when it was crucial to do so.

Ward and Barlas, New York publishers, advertised for sale 1,250 copies of a new pamphlet entitled *A History of the Administration of John Adams,* compiled mostly from material furnished to John Wood by William Duane, editor of the Republican *Aurora,* which, since Callender's defection, Jefferson had recently been subsidizing. The pamphlet balanced vicious libels and slanders against John Adams with captatious eulogies of Jefferson—and Burr himself. Burr took it upon himself to suppress the entire press run by buying up all copies, first agreeing to pay $1,250, but actually paying only $1,000 he could ill afford, thereby making an enemy of Wood. Burr's admiring biographer, the same Matthew L. Davis whom Jefferson ignored, said Burr did this to suppress tasteless eulogies, as well as to avoid possible libel. Burr's money was wasted. A new edition, allegedly printed from a purloined copy, was printed and offered for sale on June 2, 1802.

Earlier, Burr had helped James Cheetham set up a new Republican newspaper in New York, the *American Citizen,* with the secret financial backing of George Clinton's rising nephew, Senator De Witt Clinton. But Jefferson had now driven a wedge between Burr and the Clintons, so Cheetham began a vicious attack on his former patron in the columns of the *American Citizen* and in a pamphlet entitled "The Narrative of the Suppression by Col. Burr of the History of the Administration of John Adams." He followed it with "An Antidote to John Wood's Poison." The private views of Aaron Burr publicly exposed in Cheetham's pamphlets would win him enemies in all quarters: Burr had allegedly complained to John Wood on December 5 or 6, 1801, that "the character of Mr. Hamilton was *misrepresented,* meaning where encomium was bestowed upon him it was unmerited"; Burr liked Wood's "character" of Mr. Adams—"it was a bad one, and he thought it representative of the ex-president"; and Burr had said that "Jefferson was not a man of *genius,* he was a *plodding, mechanical* person, of little activity of mind, possessed of a judgment not very discriminative. . . . he courted and was fond of popularity." Furthermore, Cheetham's "Antidote" went on, the "Federal prints acknowledge that Mr. Burr cannot forgive General Hamilton for using his influence to effect the election of Mr. Jefferson in preference to himself"; Hamilton had said he "preferred, according to his toast, a 'dreamer' to a 'Catiline.' " Cheetham's "Antidote" also found occasion to rehash the whole story of Hamilton's affair with Maria Reynolds, recalling that Hamilton "avowed himself to the whole world to have been the seducer of an amiable though unfortunate woman."

The point of Cheetham's attack was that Burr had brought up John Wood's "Adams" chronicle to ingratiate himself with Federalists. Jefferson's mouthpiece William Duane reprinted this anti-Burr material in the *Aurora* and thereby opened an umbrella of quasi-presidential sanction over all hack journalistic hatchet men who wished to help cut up Burr.

They did. The "political perfidiousness" of "this Cataline" was matched by "his abandoned profligacy," according to one handbill, though "the numerous unhappy wretches who have fallen victims to this accomplished debaucher" would be known only to those familiar with the haunts of female prostitution. There followed a listing of the initials of courtesans whom he had ruined and thrown on the town to become "the prey of disease, of infamy and wretchedness." He had seduced the daughter of a Washington tradesman by bringing her to New York and maintaining her in Partition Street. He was "the disgraceful debaucher who permitted an infamous prostitute to insult and embitter the dying moments of his injured wife." Who would doubt that such leaks were plants by the higher-up principals of the power struggle using fearless reporters like Wood, Callender, and Cheetham as poor hack mercenary acolytes.

In their articles, these investigative reporters associated Aaron Burr with Hamilton and the Reynolds affair, without spelling out in so many words (that might have exposed them to libel suits by a skillful lawyer) exactly what Burr's role had been.

It would give wry satisfaction to Hamilton that John Wood in his rebuttal pamphlet entitled "A Correct Statement of the Various Sources . . ." from which he had compiled his earlier "Adams" pamphlet—written for but suppressed by Burr—now switched from censure of Hamilton to sympathy with him for his role in the Reynolds affair. In his earlier pamphlet, Wood had dated Maria Reynolds's first visit to Hamilton's Philadelphia home in the summer of 1790, not 1791, as Hamilton had done (Hamilton had not moved to Philadelphia until late in 1790). Wood sheepishly confessed that "following the misstatement of Callender," he had earlier erroneously represented Maria as an "amiable and virtuous wife, seduced from the affections of her husband by artifice and intrigue." Further investigation "even of her own acquaintances" had proved how wrong he had been. She was, in fact, "one of those unfortunates, who, destitute of every regard for virtue of honour, traffic with the follies of youth," like Burr's mistresses. They "lay [sic] their snares to entrap the feeling heart and benevolent mind; such was her acquaintance with Mr. Hamilton, whose unsuspecting generosity became the victim of her art and duplicity." Having found our Burr's and Maria's capacity for duplicity, Wood here hints broadly that he knows the despicable story of the badger game with which they had entrapped poor Hamilton.

Cheetham sent drafts of his articles against Burr to Jefferson, and on April 23, 1803, Jefferson wrote Cheetham, just as his press campaign against Burr was about to begin, "I shall be glad hereafter to receive your daily paper by post, as usual. . . . I shall not frank this to avoid post office curiosity, but pray you to add the postage to your bill."

All these attacks by low road and high on his former law partner caused William Coleman to break with Hamilton, defend Burr, and criticize Cheetham's and Duane's alleged libels against him. Callender in Richmond pitched in on Burr's side with a spirited attack on Cheetham. Duane hit back at Callender. By September 15, 1802, Callender was becoming incoherent and hysterical, saying, among other things, that Jefferson's reputation would have been better if his head had been cut off five minutes before he began his inaugural speech.

On November 25, after six months of newspaper abuse of Burr had gone largely unanswered except by desultory responses from Callender and Hamilton's maverick editor, Coleman, Burr set up his own paper, the *Chronicle-Express,* to hit back. However, the editor he chose, Dr. Peter Irving, brother of Washington Irving, lacked the killer instinct of his rival editors. His kindly, genial, cultivated literary style bored new readers, who turned back to the sensational scandals being printed and reprinted in Callender's Richmond *Recorder*, Duane's Philadelphia *Aurora*, Cheetham's *American Citizen*, Hamilton's *Evening Post*, and, in the little town of Hudson, New York, in Columbia County, 25 miles below Albany, Harry Croswell's *The Wasp*.

The junior editor of *The Balance and Columbian Repository*, of Hudson, Harry Croswell, had set up *The Wasp* in July 1802 "in the Garret of *The Balance*" under the editorship of one *Robert Rusticoat*, his pseudonym. *The Wasp*'s purpose, Croswell announced, was to cross stingers with *The Bee*, a new Democratic paper that Charles Holt was moving to Hudson from New London, Connecticut, where it had formerly made a loud buzz.

The reason *The Bee* had flown to Hudson was that in April 1800 its publisher, Holt, had been convicted under the Sedition Law by Judge Bushrod Washington and sentenced to a $200 fine and three months in prison for recirculating, among other things, scandalous stories about Alexander Hamilton's "amours"—stories of the Reynolds affair that even the Federal prosecuting attorney at the trial had conceded to be true.

Like many small-town editors, Harry Croswell cut corners on costs by filling out the local news in his four-page Federalist gadfly with juicy tidbits reprinted from big city papers whose views he shared, like Hamilton's *Evening Post*.

On September 9, 1802, in issue No. 7, *The Wasp* reprinted from the *Evening Post* an anti-Jefferson barb that on its face seemed no more pointed than many others:

"Holt says, the burden of the Federal song is, that Mr. Jefferson paid Callender for writing against the late administration." But "this is wholly false," said Croswell, because it so wickedly understates Jefferson's offense. The true charge, Croswell explained, "is explicitly this:—Jefferson paid Callender for calling Washington a traitor, a robber, and a perjurer—For calling Adams, a hoary-headed incendiary; and for most grossly slandering the private characters of men, who, he well knew, were virtuous. These charges, not a democratic editor yet has dared, or ever will dare to meet in an open [and] manly discussion."

A month earlier, in No. 4, under the title "A Few Squally Facts," *The Wasp* had excoriated both Jefferson's record before his election and his acts allegedly destructive of the Constitution after his election: "It would be an endless task to enumerate the many acts, in direct hostility to common sense and the constitution, of which the '*man of the people*' has been guilty—Do you not in all this plainly perceive the little arts—the very little arts, of a very little mind—Alas! what will the world think of the fold if such is the shepherd." To a poor hardworking small-town newspaperman like Harry Croswell, for Jefferson of many-cupolaed Monticello to play at being a "man of the people" was like Marie Antoinette and Louis XVI playing at being shepherds and shepherdesses at the Palace of Versailles. It was infuriating that so many of his fellow Americans—more all the time—seemed to enjoy being fooled by his playacting instead of dealing with him as the French had done with their voluptuary feudal monarchs.

Once safely installed in the highest office, Jefferson had done all he could behind the scenes to muzzle the hostile Federalist press by selective enforcement of the Sedition Laws that his Democrats had attacked so successfully in their campaign to win it for him. On February 19, 1803, Jefferson wrote Governor Thomas McKean of Pennsylvania:

> The federalists having failed in destroying the freedom of the press by their gag-law, seem to have attacked it in an opposite form, that is by pushing its licentiousness & its lying to such a degree of prostitution as to deprive it of all credit . . . I have therefore long thought that a few prosecutions of the most prominent offenders would have a wholesome effect in restoring the integrity of the presses. Not a general prosecution, for that would look like persecution, but a selected one. . . . .

Leonard Levy (in his *Legacy of Suppression: Freedom of Speech and Press in Early*

American History) says it would not be surprising if a letter from Jefferson to Clinton recommending the same sort of selective prosecution of Harry Croswell's *Wasp* should be discovered. Jefferson's sympathetic biographer, Dumas Malone, in *Jefferson the President, First Term 1801–1804,* snorts at Levy's speculation: "This is a presumptuous statement, though of course there is the *possibility* of such a discovery."

In any event, as Jefferson had suggested to Governer McKean, a prosecution was duly begun in Pennsylvania, and another in George Clinton's New York. In the person of Ambrose Spencer, the state's attorney general, all the legal power that the state of New York could bring to bear was trained on Harry Croswell's freshly hatched *Wasp* in an out-of-the-way town where the political killing of a newspaper by Jeffersonians could easily be ignored by liberal Democrats. On January 10, 1803, Attorney General Spencer obtained two indictments against Harry Croswell for seditious libel, for deceitfully, wickedly, maliciously, and willfully traducing, scandalizing, and vilifying President Thomas Jefferson and representing him to be unworthy of the "confidence, respect and attachment of the people of the United States." Croswell was arrested on a bench warrant and brought before the Court of General Sessions at Claverack, the county seat, four miles away from Hudson; the long indictments were read to him; his attorneys asked for copies of the indictments; the allegedly all-Republican bench of judges denied their motion, and Croswell then pleaded "not guilty" to both unread indictments.

Out of this state of the record arose *People* v. *Croswell,* the other of the two great cases in which, according to Chancellor Kent, who sat as one of the judges before whom Hamilton argued his last, never-to-be-forgotten appeal, Hamilton's "varied powers were most strikingly displayed." The case, Kent pointed out, "involved the discussion of legal principles of the greatest consequence." In it "General Hamilton's argument" was "the greatest forensic effort that he ever made."

The prosecutor, Ambrose Spencer, was a former Federalist who had switched to the New York Jeffersonian Republican party in 1798 to help Clinton win back the state after Jay's interregnum. He quickly became a political power when Clinton won. Claverack was conveniently near Albany, but sufficiently small and out of the way so that although the case might escape major press coverage, it would create a legal precedent on the books, one that later could be used for attacking big city papers like Hamilton's *Evening Post*. The *Post*, after all, had first printed the story for which Croswell was now being persecuted but had not been prosecuted for it.

People v. *Croswell* was a political trial if there ever was one.

Prominent New York legal talent quickly stepped to Croswell's side to defend him on a *pro bono* basis: the able William W. Van Ness, Burr's associate, close friend, and apologist, and Elisha Williams and Jacob Rutsen Van Rensselaer. After losing the motion to obtain written copies of the indictment, this great team of legal talent tried another technical tactic: delay—until the next session of the Circuit Court—the sort of dilatory motion lawyers hardly ever lose. They lost again. They then moved to delay the trial until the next session of the General Sessions Court.

Spencer opposed. No delay was necessary. Under New York law, proof of the truth of the story was irrelevant and unnecessary, and such evidence could not even be submitted to the jury for its consideration. The only question left for the jury to decide was whether Croswell had printed the story.

Van Ness and the other defense counsel disputed Spencer's dogmatic statement that New York law forbade introducing the truth into evidence; they insisted it did permit proof of truth. This was a question of law that might eventually be decided in Croswell's favor. Then they would bring in a star witness to prove the truth of the story. The name of their missing witness, not incidentally, was James Thomson Callender.

In the meantime, Spencer demanded that Croswell post an unusually high bond of $2,000 for "good behaviour." Elisha Williams and Van Ness argued that this would place a prior restraint on the freedom of his press. Indeed, it would put it out of business. No, Spencer insisted, it would only curb his licentiousness. "The torrents of slander which pour from the press opposed to government must be checked," said this zealous new convert of Jefferson, "or all that is dear to man would not be worth preserving." The court granted Spencer's demand for the high bond from Croswell and further conditioned it on his "good behaviour." This effectively silenced *The Wasp* forever.

Croswell's *pro bono* team of legal mights had lost a fifth consecutive round.

After this string of legal reverses, Schuyler wrote in desperation to his daughter Eliza, requesting her to plead Croswell's case with Hamilton to get him to take over Croswell's defense. But Hamilton was overwhelmed with business and could find no time to go to Claverack for the first trial on July 11, 1803, before Chief Justice Morgan Lewis, an active Republican politician, here sitting as an ordinary trial judge with a jury.

Two new reputed legal wizards, James Scott Smith of New York and Abraham van Vechten of Albany—at least they sported typical triple-threat trial lawyer names—joined the defense staff, making five, so that no single one could really be held responsible for further *pro bono* bungling. Ambrose Spencer brought in District Attorney Ebenezer Foote to help balance the ranks on his side of the counsel table.

At the close of argument, Judge Lewis charged the jury with deciding two narrow questions: (1) did Croswell print and publish the offending story? and (2) did it contain malicious innuendoes against Jefferson? If the jury came back with a "yes" answer to these two questions, it was for Judge Lewis, not the jury, to pronounce that his fellow Republican Jefferson had indeed been libeled by the story. After being out all night to gnaw on two questions that a child of ten could probably have answered in a minute, the jury came back with the verdict that Croswell had indeed done the printing and that the words printed indeed insulted Jefferson. It made no difference that they were true and, in fact, understated the extent to which he had subsidized Callender's attacks on his enemies. Judge Lewis held Croswell guilty of libel. The five great legal brains for the defense showed that they could lose as consistently as the earlier three.

Defense counsel next went before the full bench of the court, consisting of Lewis and two other judges, and moved for a new trial on the ground that Judge Lewis had misstated the applicable New York law in the charge he had given to the jury. The other two judges on the full bench, James Kent and Smith Thompson, were Federalists. This was Croswell's last chance, the round he had to win. Unsurprisingly, because this was a political trial, the two Federalists reversed their Republican brother Lewis and granted Croswell a new trial. This was calendared to be held at Albany in the Supreme Court on February 13 and 14, 1804.

Hamilton now agreed to take charge of Croswell's defense. Although Hamilton's name had not appeared in the record during the 1803 proceedings in the case, Croswell's defense counsel had probably been consulting him behind the scenes from almost the beginning. On June 26, 1803, Hamilton had written his friend William Rawle in Philadelphia to obtain information about the procedure used in a Sedition Act case Rawle had handled for obtaining the testimony of an absent witness upon deposition in another city: this would be used by Hamilton in examining the missing witness James Thomson Callender under oath in Richmond if he could not be compelled to come to Claverack.

It came as a stunning blow to Hamilton and other defense counsel that just after the three-judge panel reversed Lewis and granted Croswell's motion for a new trial, the missing star witness was murdered, accidentally died, or committed suicide, in circumstances similar to present-day gangland rub-outs.

A hastily impaneled coroner's jury found that James Thomson Callender had drowned himself—in water three feet deep. His many enemies did not mind saying that the corpse was found face down "in congenial mud." They added that it had been drunk. It was buried the same day in Richmond Churchyard, though if any burial record were made, it has disappeared. Richmond was full of rumors of foul play; the incident went all but unmentioned in the press except locally. No one in town seemed to give much credence to the coroner's verdict of accidental death by drowning. Most seemed to take it for granted that Callender's sudden demise had been hastily arranged and hushed up as part of some kind of a cover-up.

It is a criticism of the system that when a high personage fears that a witness about to be called to testify in a sensational trial may talk too much, such witness is occasionally found shortly before the hearing taken dead of a bullet through the mouth or a mouthful of mud. No sensible newspaper editor would dare risk another selective prosecution under the sedition laws, like the one that had now silenced poor Harry Croswell's *Wasp* and may have led to Callender's silencing, by daring to print the name of the high personage that was on every tongue, whose unsurrendered letters were now part of the late Mr. Callender's estate.

Hamilton discarded Croswell's former team of defense counsel preparing for the new trial as 1804 began, retaining only Aaron Burr's friend and apologist William W. Van Ness, and adding his able friend, the scholarly Richard Harison.

The argument began on Monday, February 12, before the Supreme Court in Albany and ran on for the next two full days and into the third morning. The public, journalists, and politicians crowded the courtroom. The argument almost emptied the chambers of the senate and assembly of their usual quorum of solons, because pending in the legislature was a bill to change New York law to permit truth to be admitted in evidence as a defense against a charge of libel.

To the earlier full bench of Chief Justice Morgan Lewis, a Democrat, and James Kent and Smith Thompson, Federalists, the Clintonians had managed to add another respectable Republican, Brockholst Livingston. He had fought at Hamilton's side for Levi Weeks, but against him in the *Argus* and *Le Guen* cases. A two-to-two vote of the four-judge bench would leave in force Croswell's earlier conviction. Livingston was not a man likely to desert his and Lewis's Republican politics to yield to Hamilton's eloquence the single vote he would need to overturn Croswell's conviction. Still he was the only one of the four who by any stretch of the imagination could be called a "swing" man. Thompson would follow Kent, and no one imputed independence of Hamilton's powerful spell to Judge Kent.

Van Ness opened the argument for Croswell, the appellant, followed by Harison, and Hamilton finished up by weaving the points each had propounded into 15-point argument that lasted more than six hours. Ambrose Spencer and George Caines argued in rebuttal against overturning the earlier decision of Judge Lewis and the jury. No transcript exists. What follows is a summary of the course of the arguments derived from the report contained in *The Speeches at Full Length*, published by G. & R. Waite, reproduced by Caines himself, which does not reproduce the speeches at full length, but is long enough. Material from James Kent's summary of Hamilton's speech and Hamilton's own 15-point outline for his argument, entitled *15 Propositions on the Law of Libel,* are also included.

What, then, is libel? How do you define it? asked Hamilton. He answered his own question. It is "a slanderous or ridiculous writing, picture or sign, with a malicious or mischievous design or intent, towards government, magistrates, or individuals.''

Not so. Hamilton is wrong, argued George Caines: ''Intent is immaterial.'' And so is the truth or falsity of what is said. Ambrose Spencer backed Caines up. The law, as laid down by Blackstone and other unimpeachable authority, defined libel as any scandalous publication that has a tendency to breach of the peace. Breaches of the peace might be caused by printing the story, even if it be true. ''You cannot do an unlawful act and say you did not mean to offend.'' Any insult published against the ruler, if the judge finds it to be insulting or likely to stir up objection, is libelous.

That cannot be the law, Hamilton retorted. ''We will trace the law up to its source.'' All eyes focused on him as he focused on the eternal political point: ''The liberty of the press consists, in my idea, in publishing the truth, from good motives and for justifiable ends, though it reflects on government, on magistrates, or individuals.''

It was nonsense to say the press might criticize measures without being able to criticize men by name. It is ''essential to say, not only that the measure is bad and deleterious,'' but to ''hold up to the people the author, that, in this our free and elective government, he may be removed from the seat of power.''

The legal doctrine that Jefferson and Spencer were urging, Hamilton pointed out, arose from English cases like *De Libellis Famosis* (5 Co. Rep. 125), decided by Sir Edward Coke when sitting as a member of the infamous court of the Star Chamber. But unlike the Star Chamber, earlier British statutes and courts had held that truth could not be a libel. Unfortunately, New York engrafted the Star Chamber's recent and false doctrine on its own common law. It ''originated in one of the most oppressive institutions that ever existed,'' the court of the Star Chamber, cried Hamilton, ''where oppressions roused the people to demand its abolition.'' It was ''cruel . . . tyrannical . . .'' and its ''horrid judgments cannot be read without freezing the blood in one's veins.'' Furthermore, the Star Chamber was abolished because it ''inflicted the most sanguinary punishments'' and it bore down the ''liberties of the people.'' Remembering Lord Coke's early battles for liberty, but later participation in Star Chamber oppression, it was sad, but true, Hamilton warned, that ''It is frequent for me to forget sound principles, and condemn the points for which they have contended.'' Why so? ''At all times men are disposed to forward principles to support themselves.''

Once let a political party get into power, ''they may go from step to step, and, in *spite* of canvassing their measures, fix themselves firmly in their seats,'' if ''they are never to be reproached [by name] for what they have done.''

No, said Hamilton, ''a libel is a complicated matter of fact and law. . . . The tendency to provoke is its constituent . . . must everyone who does not panegyrise be said to be a libeller?'' How absurd. But unless the court are disposed to go that extreme length, ''it is necessary that malice and intent be proved. . . .'' The threat to breach of the peace is not the sole, but only one of, the qualities of a libel. Others are ''time, manner and circumstances, which must ever be matters of fact for jury determination.''

But Chief Justice Lewis had charged the jury that intent was not its province. Here was an ''inroad of tyranny,'' Hamilton cried out, because in English jurisprudence the trial by jury has been considered ''as the palladium of public and private liberty, the barrier to secure the subjects from oppression.'' Indeed, ''the power of the jury to extricate the people, for the salvation of the nation, from the tyranny with which they were then oppressed . . . is a landmark to our liberties, a pillar which points out to us on what the principles of our liberty ought to rest.''

Dueling was much on Hamilton's mind. ''In duelling, the malice is supposed from the deliberate acts of reflecting, sending a challenge, and appointing the time and place of meeting.'' Therefore, in the case of libel, ''let the jury determine, as they have the right to do, in all other [criminal] cases, on the complicated circumstances of act and intent.''

Only the jury could be relied on to preserve to little men like Croswell ''the right of publishing the truth, from good motives and justifiable ends, though it reflects on government, on magistrates, or individuals.''

Hamilton himself had suffered as much as any man from the licentiousness of the press. ''I do not say there ought to be an unbridled license . . . the best of men are not exempt from the attacks of slander.'' Lord Loughborough had observed ''that passages from holy writ may be turned into libels.''

Ambrose Spencer argued that ''as no man rises at once into high office, every opportunity of canvassing his qualities and qualifications is afforded, without recourse to the press; his first election ought to stamp the seal of merit on his name.'' But the reverse is just as often true, said Hamilton. ''The hypocrite goes from stage to stage of public fame, under false array''—and ''how often when men obtain the last object of their wishes, they changed from that which they seemed to be. That, men the most zealous reverers of the people's rights, have, when placed on the highest seat of power, become their most deadly oppressors.'' The greatest danger comes not from ''a few provisional armies [a manifest shaft at his own quasi-war critics], but from dependent Judges—from selected Juries, from stifling the Press & the voice of leaders & Patriots. We ought to resist—resist—resist till we hurl the demagogues & Tyrants from their imagined Thrones.''

There was a final point, as Judge Kent wrote: Hamilton ''was as strenuous for the qualification of the rule allowing the truth'' as a defense, ''as he was for the rule itself.''

But is not such a qualification a prior restraint? Should not the press be free to print anything at all?

No, said Hamilton. As Kent explained it, ''While he regarded the liberty of the press as essential to free government, he considered that a press wholly unchecked, with a right to publish anything at pleasure, regardless of truth or decency, would be, in the hands of unprincipled men, a terrible engine of mischief, and would be liable to be diverted to the most seditious and wicked purposes, and for the gratification of private malice or revenge.''

For example, a rich man like Jefferson could pay a Callender to call a Washington ''a traitor, a robber and a perjurer,'' as Croswell and the *Evening Post* reported he had done. Being in power, such a man could destroy a newspaper that dared expose the ultimate truth: that it was he who was paying the press to publish false stories. ''Such a free press,'' said Kent, free of all limitation on selling itself out to publish whatever the highest bidder demanded, ''would destroy public and private confidence, and would overawe and corrupt the impartial administration of justice.''

If a free press were the most vital underwriter of free constitutional government, then as a corollary a bought press paid off by the ruler was the most deadly threat to such a form of government. ''It ought to be distinctly known,'' Hamilton thundered, ''whether Mr. Jefferson be guilty or not of so foul an act as the one charged.'' Such falsehoods, eternally repeated, would have affected even Washington's good name. ''Drops of water, in long and continued succession, will wear out adamant.'' Kent thought Hamilton's eulogy of Washington at this point was ''never surpassed—never equalled.''

As Hamilton concluded his long argument on the third day of the trial, Kent remembered that he displayed ''an unusual solemnity and earnestness . . . at times highly impassioned and pathetic. His whole soul was enlisted in the cause. . . . In contending for the rights of the jury and the free press, he considered that he was establishing the finest refuge against oppression.''

He closed with a noble warning: ''Never can tyranny be introduced into this country by arms; these can never get rid of a popular spirit of enquiry; the only way to crush it down is by a servile tribunal. It is only by the abuse of the forms of justice that we can be enslaved. An army can never do it. For ages it can never be attempted.'' No, ''it is not thus that the liberty of this country is to be destroyed. It is to be subverted only by a pretence of adhering to all the forms of law, and yet by breaking down the substance of our liberties. By devoting a wretched but honest man as the victim of a nominal trial.''

Appellant Harry Croswell's counsel rested his case. Judge Kent summarized Hamilton's performance by saying that ''he was persuaded that if he should be able to overthrow the hightoned doctrine'' contained in Lewis's charge, ''it would be great gain to the liberties of his country.''

After Hamilton's death, Ambrose Spencer wrote, ''In power of reasoning, Hamilton was the equal of Webster; and more than this can be said of no man. In creative power Hamilton was infinitely Webster's superior.''

Certainly, in defending Croswell, Hamilton had atoned for the part he had played four years earlier in the prosecution of David Frothingham and the *Argus*.

Hamilton exchanged whispers with Croswell and his fellow counsel, picked up his notes and briefs from the counsel table, and moved out of the courtroom through handshakes and backslaps and salutations from admirers in the crowd, including many a Schuyler and Van Rensselaer.

Hamilton failed to win the appeal. The judgment below was affirmed by a two to two vote that followed the judges' political party lines. But it was more than three months until the decision day when he would learn of his loss, and then he had little more than a month still left to live.

Nothing he said had changed the final vote of a single judge. Croswell remained at large and unpunished the same as if he had won. Ambrose Spencer took his place on the bench in the judgeship with which he had been rewarded after the first trial. Jefferson duly rewarded Brockholst Livingston for remembering which side he was on notwithstanding Hamilton's eloquence with an appointment to the United States Supreme Court. Clinton rewarded Chief Justice Morgan Lewis for his unwavering adherence to the party line by nominating him to replace Lansing as the party's regular candidate to run against Aaron Burr for governor in the April elections.

But aroused public sympathy for Croswell and Hamilton's side helped push through the legislature the bill to correct the outworn dictum that the truth could not be introduced as a defense to a charge of libel. It became law in 1805, after which the court unanimously awarded Croswell a new trial.

Such a new trial would now necessarily bring on testimony about the money Jefferson had paid to the late Mr. Callender and others to encourage them to libel Federalists. Croswell was troubled no more. Jefferson never instigated another such prosecution. In memory of Harry Croswell and Hamilton, Article 7, Section 8 of the New York State Constitution adopted in 1821 provided that ''every citizen may freely speak, write, and publish his sentiments on all subjects, being responsible for the abuse of that right; and no law shall be passed to abridge or restrain the liberty of speech, or of the press.'' It continued that ''in all criminal prosecutions or indictments for libels, the truth may be given in evidence to the jury; . . . and the jury shall have the right to determine the law and the fact.''

Other states adopted similar constitutional provisions and laws. Hamilton's position became the settled law of libel in the United States. His defense of the obscure "village printer" became part of the long struggle of English-speaking peoples for freedom of speech. "If his right [of criticizing those in office] was not permitted to exist in vigor and exercise," Hamilton held, "good men would become silent, corruption and tyranny would go on, step by step to usurpation, until, at last, nothing that was worth speaking, or writing, or acting for, would be left in our country."

According to Professor Clinton Rossiter, it was during the previous summer of 1803, when Hamilton, out of the public eye, was preoccupied with his private law practice, making inquiries behind the scenes concerning Callender's "suicide" or simply enjoying family life at The Grange, "that Hamilton's career as a constitutionalist reached its zenith in two events in which he played no active part."

One of these was Chief Justice John Marshall's assertion in *Marbury* v. *Madison* (1 Cranch 168) of the doctrine of judicial review of acts of Congress. In that landmark case, Marshall found that a congressional grant of authority to his court to issue a mandamus directing the executive to deliver a commission to William Marbury as justice of the peace was an unconstitutional legislative action. At the very end of his opinion, the chief justice announced "that a law repugnant to the constitution is void, and that courts, as well as other departments, are bound by that instrument." It was Hamilton who had provided Marshall with the best precedents he had for this sweeping assertion. In *Rutgers* v. *Waddington* in 1784, Hamilton had argued that a court had the power to set aside an act of a legislature if it conflicted with a higher law under which both court and legislature were supposed to function. Again in 1788 as *Publius* in *The Federalist* No. 78, Hamilton had announced to the American public for the first time that under the Constitution it would be the duty "of courts to exercise the almost unprecedented power" to declare all acts contrary to the manifest tenor of the Constitution void. "Without this," averred Hamilton, "all the reservations of particular rights or privileges would amount to nothing." His reasoning in *The Federalist* No. 78 was subtle, but strong enough to support the vast superstructure of judicial exegesis constructed upon it by Marshall and decisions of the Supreme Court ever since.

The doctrine of judicial review also involved the creation of vast power in the courts. "Though individual oppression may now and then proceed from courts of justice," particularly if they were being used by presidents for persecutions of the likes of Croswell, "the general liberty of the people can never be endangered from that quarter" alone, as it might be by the president or Congress. Hamilton went on to explain that "the power of the people is superior to both" judicial and legislative power. "Where the will of the legislature declared in its statutes, stands in opposition to that of the people, delcared in the constitution, the judges ought to be governed by the latter, rather than the former." Other antecedents and precedents for the doctrine of judicial review as John Marshall announced it in *Marbury* v. *Madison* were few.

Hamilton had once declined appointment to be Chief Justice; so it was a stunning triumph for him that in *Marbury* v. *Madison* his Virginia Federalist colleague had announced without citation that the precedent authority he had created in *Rutgers* v. *Waddington* and *The Federalist* No. 78 were now the supreme constitutional law of the land.

The second event of 1803 that marked Hamilton's zenith as a constitutionalist was the Louisiana Purchase. In approving the purchase of the Louisiana Territory from France for $15 million without proposing an amendment to the Constitution, Hamilton's archenemy Thomas Jefferson, the most adamant of strict constructionists, was forced to stretch the letter and spirit of the Constitution almost to the breaking point to find more implied powers in it than Hamilton had ever claimed existed and to give to the Constitution the last great Hamiltonian gloss that Hamilton would see in his lifetime.

Hamilton had always encouraged the westward growth of the nation. He had reminded Charles Cotesworth Pinckney on December 29, 1802, that he "always held that the *unity of our empire* and the best interests of our nation require that we shall annex to the United States all territory east of the Mississippi, New Orleans included." If, as he believed, Jefferson also sought to gain possession of the region, his "pretty scheme of substituting economy to taxation will not do here." Hamilton had stressed the importance of the region in his first pamphlet, his 1774 reply to the *Westchester Farmer* in *A Full Vindication*; during his terms in the Continental Congress; in *The Federalist* No. 11 of 1787; and again and again in advice and counsel to Washington and Adams, as well as in his contingency military planning with Rufus King, Miranda, and Wilkinson. Jefferson had not expected success in the Paris negotiations. As *Pericles* in the *Evening Post*, Hamilton had written with unusual obtuseness that "the attempt to purchase will certainly fail." So when Robert R. Livingston and James Monroe reported back from the negotiations with Napoleon Bonaparte and Talleyrand in Paris that they had bought the whole thing, Hamilton was as surprised as Jefferson, but he did not suffer from the same strict constructionist embarrassments Jefferson did. Jefferson wrote to his attorney general, Levi Lincoln, on August 30, 1803, "the less that is said about any constitutional difficulty, the better. . . . it will be desirable for Congress to do what is necessary, *in silence*."

Jefferson, privately assuming his own action to be unconstitutional, yet appealing to Congress and the nation to support it without any constitutional authority except possibly under some vaguely defined imperial powers of the president, in his way of handling the purchase probably did greater disservice to the cause of limited constitutional government than anything Hamilton had ever suggested or done.

While criticizing the way the deal had been handled and presented to the country, Hamilton approved the fact and the necessity of the purchase. Nothing did more than this stand to estrange Hamilton further from his fellow Federalists and to drive them toward the inviting candidacy of Aaron Burr in New York's gubernatorial election of 1804. Hamilton still believed, as he had written in 1787 in *The Federalist* No. 11, that "the importance of the Union, in a commercial light, is one of those points about which there is the least room to entertain a difference of opinion." But now among many New England Federalists smoldered all but irreconcilable differences that belied *Publius'* confident assumption that unity was inevitable and forever. They were for a separation from the rest of the nation. Jefferson's remarkable popularity, enhanced by the acquisition of Louisiana, contributed much to the feelings of impotent ire of men like Hamilton's old friend, former Secretary of State Timothy Pickering, as he wrote to their mutual friend Rufus King on March 4, 1804: "The coward wretch at the head, while, like a Parisian revolutionary monster, prating about humanity, could feel an infernal pleasure in the utter destruction of his opponents." Pickering railed, "We have too long witnessed his general turpitude—his cruel removals of faithful officers, and the substitution of corruption and baseness for integrity and worth."

Now Louisiana threatened to expand the ascendancy of the slave-owning South and West in the nation's government. Southern whites had the advantage of doing all the voting for their slaves, who still counted for purposes of representation as three-fifths of one white. George Cabot called Jefferson's government "the government of the worst," writing to Pickering February 14, 1804. John Adams likened him to a rake, full of fair promises, who had seduced a trustful maid.

The prime movers in the unfolding 1804 plan for separating the Northern states from the Union included Roger Griswold and Uriah Tracy of Connecticut, Senators Samuel Hart and William Plumer of New Hampshire, and other influential men. New York and New Jersey were expected to join it. But Hamilton refused to go along or even to accommodate his friends by remaining silent or acting the part of an accommodating trimmer for them. Not so Aaron Burr. He was the key to the plot, as Pickering wrote King, because he could break the "Democratic phalanx" in New York.

William Van Ness's public defense of Aaron Burr in the pamphlet entitled "An Examination of the Various Charges Exhibited Against Aaron Burr," reported that Clinton, now in "the imbecility of his age," had loudly and publicly called Jefferson an "accommodating trimmer," thus ending any remaining faint hope of favor Burr might expect from either of them.

Jefferson quickly enlisted Clinton in his service, writing him cordially on December 31 that Van Ness's *Aristides* pamphlet was libellous" and "lies," that "little squibs in certain papers had long ago apprized me of a design to sow tares between particular republican characters. But to divide those by lying tales whom truth cannot divide, is the hackneyed policy of the gossips of every society." In February 1804 a caucus of Republican congressmen unanimously renominated Jefferson for president and Clinton (who had just announced that he could not run again for governor of New York because of old age and ill health) was deemed well qualified for vice-president, not being dead yet. He was nominated with about two-thirds of the votes on the first ballot, while incumbent Vice-President Aaron Burr was dumped from the ticket without receiving a single vote.

This left as Burr's only hope for clinging to a political life his winning election to the governorship of New York State being vacated by Clinton. For this, a still loyal and strong splinter group of New York Republicans strongly backed him. The badly divided and discouraged Federalists had no strong candidate of their own, and many who were disillusioned with Hamilton's leadership considered Burr as one of themselves. So it appeared that Burr would win the nomination quite easily over the regular Republican candidate, John Lansing, Jr.

Pickering pressed the plot for Northern secession from the Union: "Were New York detached (as under his [Burr's] administration it would be) from the Virginia influence, the whole union would be benefited. Jefferson would then be forced to observe some caution and forbearance in his measures." This would be but the minimum benefit from backing Burr. The maximum would be a separation, splitting up the Union. "If a *separation* should be deemed proper, the five New England states, New York and New Jersey would naturally be united." This was a federation that would make a viable new nation. "Among those seven states there is a sufficient congeniality of character to authorize the expectation of practicable harmony and a permanent union; New York the centre." There would be great future benefits. But "Without a separation, can those states ever rid themselves of negro presidents and negro congresses, and regain their just weight in the political balance . . . ?"

The idea of Burr's becoming governor of New York, beholden for the votes that tipped the election his way to Federalists like Pickering who would demand that he lead a split-up of the Union, was too much for Hamilton to bear. He knew that nothing would please Burr more than being president of half a nation removed from Jefferson's control.

"Very, very confidential," Hamilton had written Bayard. "Burr is inferior in real ability to Jefferson." But more important,

". . . he has blamed me for not having improved the situation I once was in to change the government. When [I] answered that this could not have been done without guilt, he replied "Les grandes âmes se soucient peu des petits moraux." When told the thing was never practicable from the genius and situation of the country, he answered, "That depends on the estimate we form of the human passions, and of the means of influencing them."

Then Hamilton had understood Burr to be making a traitorous proposal to him like the one Pickering now was urging on him. Despite Hamilton's "very, very confidential" cautions to his correspondents, the fact that for years Hamilton had been circulating libelous stories about him among their friends and acquaintances would be well known to Burr, who had the best intelligence-gathering apparatus of any public figure except Jefferson himself.

Both Burr and Hamilton were successful lawyers, soldiers, lovers, family men, and politicians. Both were handsome, charming, quick-witted, brilliant, and ambitious. For 15 years and more, each had always seemed to stand athwart the path of the other's ambition. They were superficially alike, yet essentially very different, and so men perceived them. Burr's watchword, "Great souls concern themselves little with petty morals," offers a key to the difference. Unlike Burr, Hamilton seemed to follow a lodestar somewhere out beyond the obvious course toward his own public advancement. This lodestar was the Union of the states under the Constitution, the emancipation of slaves, the rights of the people, public credit, and liberty under law.

To these he had sacrificed the comfort of his family; all other private, public, and political concerns; his health, energy, personal safety, economic security, a son, and a daughter's sanity. What seemed to be monumental errors of discretion and judgment during his two years of nervous derangement around 1800 had not destroyed the regard in which discerning men of his time held him, or impaired the intense affection, admiration, and love his friends felt for him, or the respect and awe his enemies had for his abilities. With all his faults, Hamilton was and was seen by most who knew him as a man of integrity. Burr, for all his great intelligence, charm, wit, and grace, was not.

Pickering and others of the New England separatists had sounded out Burr, and though Burr's answers were equivocal, they read into his evasions, from their own knowledge of his politically chimerical character, a later acquiescence. They would support him in his race for the governorship of New York, even over Hamilton's opposition. Burr's election would provide a rallying point for all New England, New York, and New Jersey separatists who felt as Pickering did. The cumulative and reflexive influence of such a success might easily propel Burr, supported by Pickering and their followers, far toward the office of chief executive of a separate northern American confederacy. The threat seemed more real and painful to Hamilton than it did to those who did not know Burr as well as he did.

In the days immediately following the close of Croswell's trial John Lansing, Jr., suddenly and inexplicably withdrew as the Democratic candidate for governor, some said because Burr appeared to be unbeatable. The rival political factions scheduled caucuses in rapid succession: on February 20 Clinton's regular Democratic organization, consisting of party members of the legislature and other delegates, would meet; on February 18 Democrats and Federalists who backed Aaron Burr would convene; and on February 16 Hamilton and the Federalist party regulars would meet. With Lansing out of the running, Vice-President Burr's chances of winning the regular Democratic nomination at the February 20 caucus looked strong. Because the Federalists had no candidate of their own, his chances of winning major Federalist support on Februrary 16 were better than anyone else's. In a mixed political metaphor, it was predictable that from the sixteenth through the twentieth politicians from all parties jumping on the Burr bandwagon might be expected to snowball his candidacy into an unbeatable juggernaut.

Only Hamilton on the sixteenth stood in his way, all but alone.

Although proceedings at the Federalist caucus at Lewis's City Tavern on the sixteenth were supposed to be secret, Burr's political espionage system, in good working order as usual, posted two of his agents in a bedroom adjoining the dining chamber and noted down all the speeches. Dr. Charles D. Cooper said "General Hamilton's harangue at the city-tavern" against Burr that night was delivered with much of the same passion and fire that Kent had noted in Hamilton's argument for Croswell and freedom of the press in court the day before. The *Morning Chronicle* published a report of the proceedings within a few days.

"The Federalists are prostrate, and their enemies are predominant," Hamilton announced to the old guard of the faithful. "Burr has steadily pursued the track of democratic politics . . . either from *principle* or from *calculation*." Either way, he "will certainly not at this time relinquish the ladder of his ambition, and espouse the cause or views of the weaker party." In New England, "the only part of our country which still remains sound," the very issues that made the Federalists strong—the ill opinion of Jefferson and jealousy of the ambition of Virginia—"are leading to an opinion, that a dismemberment of the Union is expedient." Burr would promote this result "to be chief of the Northern portion. Placed at the head of the state of New York, no man would be more likely to succeed."

Burr was a man of "talents, intrigue and address . . . a man of irregular and insatiable ambition . . . Jacobinic principles . . .," given to "usurpation," a "despotic chief . . . whose temper would permit him to bottom his aggrandizement on popular prejudices and vices."

The Federalists must not support Burr. They should back Lansing or, indeed, whoever Clinton's candidate might be. Here for the first time in his life Hamilton was affirmatively backing a Democratic candidate, switching political sides, a thing he had anathematized John Adams and Burr for doing or seeming to do, something he himself had never done before in his life; such a switch well along in a notable political life usually has fateful consequences. A search of the text of Hamilton's address for a single motivation for his momentous switch produces only a tripartite, exquisitely balanced ambiguity: it was to preserve the Union; it was to save the Federal party; it was because of personal animosity toward Burr.

Writing to Robert Goodloe Harper, Hamilton said: "he will be the most dangerous chief that Jacobinism can have; . . . a dismemberment of the Union is likely to be one of the first fruits of his elevation. . . . I had rather see Lansing Governor and the party broken to pieces." Here, Hamilton, in a phrase of Henry Adams, literally "was joining hands with his own bitterest enemies to complete the ring" around Burr.

At Burr's caucus two days later a strong group of Democrats and anti-Hamilton Federalists cheered Burr to the rafters and gave him the Federalist nomination, thus breaking Hamilton's party to pieces. Clinton rewarded Chief Justice Morgan Lewis for steadfastly blocking Hamilton's efforts to let the Croswell jury hear anything discreditable to Jefferson by putting forward his name as the regular Democratic candidate, and he was duly nominated by the well-bossed Democratic caucus on the twentieth.

Still another blow for Hamilton was the defection of the New York *Evening Post*. William Coleman declared editorially on March 23 that Hamilton "will take no part in support of either of the present candidates." It was an open secret that Hamilton was working behind the scenes against Burr and for Lewis, but Coleman himself showed decided leanings toward Burr. Toward the end of the campaign he all but endorsed Burr's election.

In the spring campaign between Burr and Morgan Lewis leading up to the election on April 25, Cheetham charged that "your jealousy of General Hamilton afterward ripened into implacable hatred."

Van Ness defended Burr all along the line, citing Burr's explicit denial that he had "proposed or agreed to any terms with the federal party" in hopes of overtopping Jefferson in 1800. While praising Burr, Van Ness as *Aristides* missed no opportunity for flank attacks on Jefferson as an unfortunate disappointment in high office.

Jefferson announced that this "little band" of Republicans who had defected to Burr were discountenanced. Lewis Republicans took this cue from their demigod Jefferson to leave no congenial mud unslung in Burr's direction.

The writer of one handbill was revolted "at the terrible situation in which we should be placed, should this UNPRINCIPLED MAN [in capitals] succeed in his wicked purposes." Practiced in "vile plots," Burr was "dishonest and fraudulent." Another warned the electors of New York, "if you . . . love the fair name of your country, guard her from the fangs of such an unprincipled being—such a hydra in human form." Burr was also charged with embezzling money from a trust fund to pay off a personal note.

As a regular Federalist and party leader, Hamilton took no public position against the nominal Federalist ticket's standard-bearer, Burr. But in private conversations he showed no similar restraint.

One night in Albany at a dinner party at Judge John Tayler's house, not long after Croswell's trial, one of the guests had been Dr. Charles D. Cooper, Judge Tayler's son-in-law. He listened in fascination while Hamilton and Judge Kent and others were saying some devastating things about Aaron Burr that Cooper hardly knew how to characterize. No one knows exactly what Hamilton or the others actually said, but no doubt Hamilton repeated much of what he had said in his speech at Lewis's City Tavern—and probably also some specifications of such generalities besides.

More than a month after Judge Tayler's dinner party, Hamilton's and Kent's conversation was still on Dr. Cooper's mind when he wrote a letter to Andrew Brown of Bern, New York, on April 12, 1804, enclosing some anti-Burr election circulars. Dr. Cooper also passed along some inside information that would be valuable to lesser Federalists still willing to be led. "Gen. Hamilton . . . has come out decidedly against Burr; indeed when he was here he spoke of him as a dangerous man and ought not to be trusted." Dr. Cooper indicated that Judge Kent, John Barker Church, Stephen Van Rensselaer, and Nathaniel Pendleton all felt the same way. Cooper's letter, full of political dynamite if it fell into the wrong hands, fell into them. It was "embezzled and broken" open, published in the *Albany Register*, and reprinted in other newspapers and pamphlets, just in time for the opinions of all these distinguished Federal Republicans who had not so far been heard from to have maximum impact on the outcome of the election.

After a weekend visit at The Grange on April 21 and 22, Judge Kent wrote to his wife on April 26 that with the election nearly over, "the Burrites are sanguine and appear flushed with the laurels of victory. They claim a decided majority in this city." They had gotten out the Federalist vote. "The cold reserve and indignant reproaches of Hamilton may have controlled a few, but they are few."

Almost 30 years later, reminiscing to Hamilton's widow about this last visit, Kent recalled that his host's "mind had a cast usually melancholy." Among other things, "the impending election exceedingly disturbed him. He viewed the temper, disposition, and passions of the times as portentous of evil and to the sway of artful and ambitious demagogues."

Without Kent's necessarily even having to murmur a single injudicious word on the still secret subject, the inkling that the decision in Croswell's case would soon be handed down and go against him must have added to Hamilton's deep gloom.

Only the week before Kent's visit, on April 13, Hamilton had responded to an unhappy friend who was looking for a job with some brutally fatalistic advice that recalled Cassius' advice to Brutus from the same act 1, scene 2 of *Julius Caesar* that he seemed to keep soliloquizing in his mind:

"Arraign not the dispensations of Providence," Hamilton wrote, "they must be founded in wisdom and goodness; and when they do not suit us, it must be because there is some fault in ourselves which deserves chastisement; or because there is a kind intent, to correct in us some vice or failing, of which, perhaps, we may not be conscious; or because the general plan requires that we should suffer partial ill."

Cassius had put the idea more concisely:

CASSIUS: The fault, dear Brutus, is not in our stars, But in ourselves, that we are underlings.

But Cassius had discovered an easier way out for Brutus: kill Caesar.

Hamilton could think of nothing so easy. "In this situation it is our duty to cultivate resignation, and even humility, bearing in mind, in the language of the poet, 'That it is pride which lost the blest abodes.' "

The ring he had closed around Burr was a trap for Hamilton, too. Pride, and honor, of course, were bone, marrow, and nerve organic to his being alive.

To his son James A. Hamilton, just turning 16 on April 14, Hamilton wrote:

My dear James: I have prepared for you a Thesis on Discretion. You may need it.

Your affectionate father.

Dr. Cooper's letter to Andrew Brown might have passed unnoticed in the euphoria of a Burr election victory. But Burr unexpectedly lost. The opinions of the important Federalists Dr. Cooper's letter contained contributed to the margin of defeat in an election Burr had strong hopes of winning as late as election day. As is often the case in New York elections, a narrow margin in the city failed to overcome the late upstate returns. Morgan Lewis won in a sweep statewide by 30,829 to Burr's 22,139.

Burr might have let Dr. Cooper's first letter, the one to Andrew Brown, pass without making an issue of it if Philip Schuyler had not tried to protect Hamilton from the fateful consequences of its unauthorized disclosure and publication. Schuyler attempted a small, clumsy cover-up by contradicting Dr. Cooper. He wrote Dr. Samuel Stringer, chairman of the Federal Republican Committee, on April 21, denying what Cooper said had been said at Judge Tayler's about Burr by Hamilton, Kent, and Van Rensselaer. Published in the *Albany Register* on April 21, too late to change the election outcome, Schuyler's letter would set the record straight and protect the prominent men whose conversation at a private dinner had been embarrassingly—and mysteriously—exposed by theft and publication of Cooper's letter. In professional party politics, as under the code duello, remarks made in private conversations are supposed to be privileged, not properly the subject of public attention and challenges.

Having been, in effect, called a liar by Schuyler's letter, which came to him "annexed . . . to an anonymous handbill," Dr. Cooper, in anger, had no choice but to rise to defend his honor. He wrote a second letter, this one to Schuyler, on April 23, 1804. What he had written in his first letter was "substantially true," he insisted. He could prove it "by the most unquestionable testimony." He repeated, "I assert, that General Hamilton and Judge Kent have declared . . . that they look upon Mr. Burr to be a dangerous man, and one who ought not to be trusted with the reins of government." Schuyler ought to know perfectly well that Cooper was not lying. He went on. Hamilton had said much the same thing in his harangue to the Federalist caucus at the City Tavern. If Schuyler had been there when "General Hamilton made a speech on the pending election, I might appeal to you for the truth of so much of this assertion as relates to him." That was still not all, there was more, Dr. Cooper insisted. "For really sir, I could detail to you a still more despicable opinion which General Hamilton has expressed of Mr. Burr."

The *Albany Register,* making the most of newly won freedom of the press, published this letter the very next day. Excerpts from the whole correspondence made the rounds of reprints in pamphlets and other newspapers. The embezzlement, breaking open, and publication of the first letter, which had been intended for loyal Federalist eyes only, is reminiscent of the manner in which Burr's supporters had quickly obtained, circulated, and published copies of Hamilton's attack on John Adams and of his anti-Burr speech at the City Tavern caucus. The true facts of *how* the leak occurred remain a mystery.

Schuyler and Hamilton were in-laws closer than most fathers are to most sons. In any event, in the Hamilton family, another loving father had just inadvertently consigned another beloved son with a keen sense of honor to yet another interview at Weehawken.

38

The Duel

"To those, who with me abhorring the practice of Duelling may think that I ought on no account to have added to the number of bad examples—I answer that my *relative* situation, as well in public as private aspects, enforcing all the considerations which constitute what men of the world denominate honour, impressed on me (as I thought) a peculiar necessity not to decline the call.

> —Document written June 28—July 10, 1804, left with Nathaniel Pendleton, to be opened only in the event of his death in the duel

Aaron Burr "was determined to call out the first man of any respectability concerned in the infamous publications . . ."

> —Aaron Burr to Charles Biddle on the Washington to New York stagecoach

Vice-President Aaron Burr, hastening home on the stage from Washington where he had been presiding over the Senate to press his lagging campaign for the governorship of New York, confided the following secret to his fellow passenger Charles Biddle: "He was determined to call out the first man of any respectability concerned in the infamous publications concerning him."

Biddle "never knew Colonel Burr to speak ill of any man," so he could never forget the predetermined hostility of Burr's whispered threat "to call out the first man." Biddle carefully jotted it down in his *Autobiography*.

June 18, 1804, the day before the Hamiltons' party for Jerome and Elizabeth Patterson Bonaparte, William Van Ness stood waiting silently at Hamilton's elbow as he read and reread Aaron Burr's challenge letter:

> Sir,
>
> I send for your perusal a letter signed Ch. D. Cooper which, though apparently published some time ago, has but very recently come to my knowledge. Mr. Van Ness who does me the favor to deliver this, will point out to you that Clause of the letter to which I particularly request your attention.
>
> You might perceive, Sir, the necessity of a prompt and unqualified acknowledgement or denial of the use of any expressions which could warrant the assertions of Dr. Cooper.
>
> I have the honor to be
>
> > Your Obt Svt
> >
> > A. Burr

Van Ness pointed to the offensive sentences in the newspaper clippings, "Gen. Hamilton and Judge Kent have declared, in substance, that they looked upon Mr. Burr to be a dangerous man, and one who ought not to be trusted with the reins of government."

What was worse was everything unwritten that might be subsumed under Dr. Cooper's concluding words: "I have been unusually cautious—for really sir, I could detail to you a still more despicable opinion which General Hamilton has expressed of Mr. Burr."

Hamilton equivocated. No one knew better than he that what Dr. Cooper said in his letter was mild compared to the things Hamilton had been saying about Burr in private conversations and letters to friends for years. Neither Hamilton nor his friends had any reason to doubt that Burr already knew much of what Hamilton had been saying about him. They had many mutual friends like Robert Troup who enjoyed passing around political gossip. Burr's letter was a foreseeable consequence.

Hamilton found exasperating ambiguity in Cooper's use of the adjective *despicable*. Who or what or whose opinion of whom was despicable? Who was the despiser? Who the despisee? The only clear thing about the statement was Dr. Cooper's despicable syntax.

Burr had demanded "a prompt and unqualified acknowledgement or denial." An "acknowledgement" would bring on a prompt challenge to duel from Burr. A denial would brand Dr. Cooper a liar, which their friends knew he was not. It would be a dishonorable thing to do, and Cooper was not a man to let a false contradiction pass, as his second letter had demonstrated to Schuyler. It would expose Hamilton to the charge of personal cowardice; it would help kill such remaining influence as Hamilton might still possess in his party. Burr's words drove him into an impasse of honor and pride with few—or no—escape routes.

Hamilton had often dealt with the deadly game of the code duello, and had many close brushes with duels, but he had never issued or accepted a direct challenge. He had skillfully finessed dangerous challenges from Aedanus Burke and John Mercer and others. Acting as second for the dearest friend of his life, John Laurens, when Charles Lee had spoken disrespectfully of Washington after Monmouth, Hamilton had initiated peace overtures after the first exchange of shots. His epistolary exchanges with James Nicholson and James Monroe had reached the brink, but in each case Hamilton had demonstrated sure knowledge of how, with adroitness, discretion, and time, to finesse the challenge without dishonor to either principal. He abhorred the idea of dueling all the more passionately since the horror of Philip's death less than three years earlier. He had never actually fought a duel in his life.

To Dr. William Gordon, Hamilton had written in 1779 that "The good sense of the present times has happily found out, that to prove your own innocence, or the malice of an accuser, the worst method you can take is to run him through the body or shoot him through the head." In composing a quarrel between William Pierce and John Auldjo, he had remarked, "I can never consent to take up the character of a second in a duel till I have in vain tried that of mediator. Be content with enough, for more ought not to be expected." His marksmanship might be rusty, but Hamilton was anything but a naïf when it came to playing the deadly game of the code duello.

Even in Hamilton's day, even among men of his social circle, dueling was an exceptional rather than common response to real or imagined wrongs, and it was condemned by most of Hamilton's contemporaries. In volume XXVI of the Hamilton Papers, Professor Syrett speculates that Hamilton, "having risen from insular obscurity and bastardy to the upper reaches of society in Federal America, was more likely than other more socially secure individuals to abide by the code duello." Or, Professor Syrett asks, "Did he indeed have a death wish?"

Hamilton's reply to Burr on June 20, two days after Van Ness's visit, was long-winded, rambling, repetitious, and evasive: "I have maturely reflected on the subject of your letter . . . and the more I have reflected the more I have become convinced, that I could not, without manifest impropriety, make the avowal or disavowal which you seem to think necessary."

Dr. Cooper "plainly implies, that he considered this opinion of you, which he attributes to me, as a *despicable* one" but Dr. Cooper had failed to say "to whom, when or where" . . . "There had been others *'still more despicable,'* . . . the phrase admits of infinite shades, from very light to very dark."

In fact, "Between Gentlemen, *despicable* and *more despicable* are not worth the pains of distinction." It was "inadmissible, on principle to consent to be interrogated as to the justness of the *inferences*, which may be drawn by *others*, from whatever I may have said of a political opponent in the course of a fifteen years' competition . . ." Burr had mentioned no specific offending phrase of his. "I stand ready," Hamilton said, "to avow or disavow promptly and explicitly any precise or definite opinion, which I may be charged with having declared of any Gentleman."

Hamilton knew he could shut off further such contumelious summonses from Burr short of direct challenge by firmly denying that he had used an expression that Dr. Cooper could properly assert to be "despicable." It would have been a denial that conformed precisely to Burr's specifications, but less than the whole truth. It probably would have done no good.

Hamilton refused, or could not bring himself to take, or in haste under pressure overlooked this possible way out. He knew exactly what the guests at Judge Tayler's had heard him say and was quite sure Burr did too. His final sentence to Burr closed off any possible future use of a qualified denial. It would force Burr toward a challenge. If Burr would not come forward to specify the particular words he found objectionable, said Hamilton, "I can only regret the circumstance, and must abide the consequence."

In a lifetime of experience dealing with such epistolary challenges and responses, here was apparently the first time Hamilton invited a challenge by such a "take it or leave it" response.

Burr's fast answer next day by Van Ness ripped through all equivocations. He would not take Hamilton up on any of his proffered ways out. In fact, "I regret to find in it nothing of that sincerity and delicacy which you profess to Value," Burr sneered. "Political opposition," Burr purred, "can never absolve Gentlemen from the necessity of a rigid adherence to the laws of honour and the rules of decorum: I neither claim such privilege nor indulge it in others." As for Hamilton's labored attempts to parse and construe the reference of the word *despicable*, "the Common sense of Mankind affixes to the epithet adopted by Dr. Cooper the idea of dishonor: it has been publicly applied to me under the Sanction of your name."

Always elsewhere the precise wordsmith, here Burr betrays premeditated hostility. His assertion that "the common sense of mankind" affixed "the idea of dishonor" to the word *despicable* in Dr. Cooper's context is nonsense. Although the word *despicable* tells much about the attitude of the despiser, it says nothing very meaningful about the "honor" of the despisee or, in Dr. Cooper's usage, whether the despisee was Hamilton or Burr. The only satisfactory explanation for Burr's lapse here from the habitual verbal precision of a lifetime is that he had been told exactly what Hamilton had said at Judge Tayler's dinner and of necessity read all of it into the ambiguous word *despicable*. As Charles Biddle understood, no particular word would make any difference: Burr's determination to kill Hamilton was implacable. Burr's now twisting the issue into "the idea of dishonor" closed any possible way out for Hamilton that may have lain in Dr. Cooper's ambiguous use of "despicable." As in ancient Rome, as in Plutarch, as in Elizabethan tragedy, the issue between two great protagonists was always the idea of dishonor, and Burr had now arbitrarily read it into Dr. Cooper's usage of "despicable." Burr said:

"The question is not, whether he has understood the meaning of the word, or has used it according to Syntax and with grammatical accuracy but whether you have authorized this application either directly or by uttering expressions or opinions derogatory to my honor."

But both men knew that Dr. Cooper's syntax was not the real issue at all. The real issue was something that had long been a secret between the two men, the same secret that had caused Hamilton to vilify Burr in "religious," irrational terms to so many rational men over most of fifteen years of competition.

Burr went on evenly: "The time 'when' is in your own knowledge, but no way material to me, as the calumny has now first been disclosed so as to become the Subject of my Notice, and the effect is present and palpable." Burr closed: "Your letter has furnished me with new reasons for requiring a definite reply."

Hamilton had circulated numberless calumnies against Burr both in private and in public. They had left no aspect of Burr's personal, professional, political, and public life unbesmirched—Hamilton's speech at the Albany City Tavern had been only one of his most recent rundowns of Burr. Any of such rundowns might have provoked a challenge from Burr but none had done so—until this new calumny "now first disclosed." One new calumny of Burr that Hamilton had never publicly aired would be fresh titillating news to a party of politically sophisticated intimates of Hamilton who thought they had already heard everything despicable he had to say about Burr: Hamilton's tale of Burr's relationship with James and Maria Reynolds, and specifically his role in arranging for Maria Reynolds to "lay snares to entrap his feeling heart" (as John Wood put it) in the badger game Burr played on Hamilton by paying her call on him in Philadelphia the summer of 1791, ostensibly to beg money from him to pay her coach fare back to New York.

On June 22, Van Ness delivered Burr's reply to Hamilton, waited while Hamilton read it, and made a record of how Hamilton reacted. Hamilton's mounting horror seems to sweat out from between Van Ness's short-breathed lines: Hamilton "said it was such a letter as he had hoped not to have received—that it contained several offensive expressions & seemed to close the door to all further reply—that he had hoped the answer he had returned to Col. Burr's first letter would have given a different direction to the controversy—that he thought Burr . . .'' and so on. If Colonel Burr should be disposed, he ''was willing to consider the last letter not delivered.'' But if Burr would not withdraw it, Burr ''must pursue such course as he should deem most proper.''

For Hamilton, now entrapped by his own definition of honor, that equated it with public credit, to disavow ''uttering expressions or opinions derogatory'' to Burr, when, of course, he had been doing exactly that for years, and had done so at Judge Tayler's, would be an impossibility. Burr knew it. Hamilton knew Burr knew it, and Burr knew Hamilton knew he knew it.

The same evening Hamilton for the first time consulted his friend Nathaniel Pendleton, telling him that he had told Van Ness that Burr's latest letter, that of the twenty-second, was ''rude and offensive.'' Van Ness had requested him ''to take time to deliberate'' and possibly return a different answer. No, said Hamilton, it was ''not possible for him to give any other answer,'' unless Burr ''would take back his last letter and write one that would admit of a different reply.'' Hamilton gave Pendleton his quick reply note to Burr, also dated June 22. He called Burr's first letter ''too peremptory.'' Burr had made an ''unprecedented and unwarrantable'' demand. It had contained ''rude and improper'' expressions. These ''increased the difficulties to explanation, intrinsically incident to the nature of your application.'' On Pendleton's advice, he had crossed out ''rude'' and written in ''indecorous.''

Pendleton held this unfortunate letter undelivered for three days while he desperately tried to work out some sort of honorable compromise with Van Ness. Both agreed that Hamilton should make an entirely different reply to Burr, one that would amount to an affirmation of Burr's honor that ought to have been acceptable to him or any man within the normal rules of the code of duels. Pendleton wrote out the following statement for Hamilton to make to Burr, admitting reference to ''political topics,'' but denying anything relating to Burr's ''private character.''

> The conversation to which Dr. Cooper alluded, turned wholly on political topics, and did not attribute to Col. Burr any instance of dishonourable conduct, nor relate to his private character; and in relation to any other language or conversation of General Hamilton which Col. Burr will specify, a prompt and frank avowal or denial will be given.

But Van Ness demanded a very different disclaimer from Hamilton: he must disclaim expressions ''impeaching the honor'' and affecting the *''private reputation''* of Burr.
Hamilton accepted Pendleton's formulations and rejected Van Ness's.

If Hamilton had given Pendleton's compromise statement as his first reply to Burr's first letter instead of opening the door for Burr to introduce explicitly the issue of his ''private reputation,'' or if Hamilton had never written his letter of the 22nd, or if Pendleton had let it remain undelivered, Burr might have been required by strict adherence to the rules of the code to let the dispute end there (unless of course his implacable determination to ''call out'' Hamilton makes all such speculation futile). Now it was too late. On the twenty-fifth, Van Ness presented Hamilton's two statements to Burr: one, the compromise statement of the twenty-fifth, which he and Pendleton had worked out and which offered Burr an easy way to let the matter end with his honor affirmed; the other, Hamilton's uncompromising, belligerent reply of the twenty-second, which did not.

On the twenty-sixth, through Van Ness, Burr chose to reply to Hamilton's letter of the twenty-second. He brushed aside Pendleton's later compromise statement. Burr, often anathematized as a compromiser, a man widely mistrusted for seeming to be always in the middle, in this second crisis, as in the first of the two greatest crises of his life, rigidly rejected the reasonable compromise suggested by the rival who had so often been anathematized for his rigidity.

Burr stood on his own letter of the twenty-first. Hamilton's letter, he said, evinced "no disposition to come to a satisfactory accommodation." Therefore, said Burr, "No denial or declaration will be satisfactory unless it be general, so as to wholly exclude the idea that rumors derogatory to Col. Burr's honor have originated with Genl Hamilton, as have been *fairly* inferred from anything he has said."

Could anyone who had known Burr only casually or even a total stranger who had discussed the rumors, truthfully make such a denial, let alone a Hamilton? Burr knew it was not possible for Hamilton to do so.

Burr denied that his communications to Hamilton meant that he had issued the challenge to Hamilton; he disingenuously claimed Hamilton had challenged him. Burr turned Hamilton's letter to him of the twenty-second back on Hamilton. It had been a "communication demanding a personal interview" of Burr.

Pendleton replied to Van Ness on the twenty-sixth: Burr had "greatly extended the original ground of inquiry." He seemed "to aim at nothing less than an inquisition into his most confidential conversations, as well as others, through the whole period of his acquaintance with Col. Burr." To Hamilton, Burr's "indefinite ground" revealed "nothing short of predetermined hostility." Nevertheless, Hamilton "disavows an unwillingness to come to a satisfactory, provided it be an honourable, accommodation."

Hamilton's conciliatory reply to Burr of the twenty-sixth by way of Pendleton also contained, within an insult, one singular, extraordinary aside:

> Though he is not conscious that any charges that are in circulation to the prejudice of Col. Burr have Originated with him, *except one which may have been so considered, and which has been long since explained between Col. Burr and himself;* yet he cannot consent to be questioned generally as to any *rumours* which may be afloat derogatory to the character of Col. Burr, without specification of the particular rumours, many of them probably unknown to him. [Emphasis supplied by author.]

What single "charge" against Burr, not relating to a political topic, could have "originated" solely with Hamilton, but no one else? What old "charge" would have been "explained" between them "long since," but only by an explanation that, if repeated to others by Hamilton, Burr might still characterize, as he had to Van Ness on June 22, as "base slanders," "settled and implacable malevolence," "secret depredations on his fame and character?" Had Hamilton at Judge Tayler's let slip a secret (as Monroe had done) he had once pledged another gentleman to keep?

"Despicable" was an odd sort of word for an educated man like Dr. Cooper to have emphasized in conveying to Philip Schuyler something said in a conversation of a group of worldly men at Judge Tayler's dinner—if all he had meant to refer to was Hamilton's political attacks on Burr or one or another of the widely known and reported scandals involving women or money that Burr had lived with for so long. It was a word Hamilton almost never used. Yet "despicable" would have been the word Hamilton would apply to

Burr if castigating him for his badger game without revealing the whole secret. Such men would have used the same word to repeat precisely what Hamilton had said, or to describe the nature of the secret if he had revealed it, whether or not he had made a commitment to Burr not to do so.

That spring 13 years earlier, Robert Troup, who was almost as old and as close a friend of Burr as he was of Hamilton, had written Hamilton in alarm of the "passionate courtship" going on in New York involving Jefferson, Madison, Beckley, Burr, Clinton, and the Livingstons. What would this "passionate courtship"—an odd phrase for a man like Troup to use of such men—mean for Hamilton? The solid, steady, sensible, equable, down-to-earth Troup had twice warned Hamilton of its threat to him in apocalyptic terms that were starkly out of character for Troup: " 'Delenda est Carthago' is the maxim applied with respect to you." Even to a former roommate like Hamilton, a gentleman born like Troup would give away no more of the secret with which Burr had entrusted him than to sound for him Cato's Klaxon tocsin twice—and the broad hint of a sex scandal to come—with Burr in the role of a procurer.

No evidence for the above hypothesis that the particular word or words Hamilton spoke about Burr at Judge Tayler's dinner related to his and the Reynoldses' badger game has been found, except the circumstantial evidence in this book that points to that conclusion.

Wednesday morning, June 27, Burr sent Hamilton, by way of Van Ness, his formal challenge to the duel. In the language of the dueling code, this was "a message . . . such as was to be expected, containing an invitation which was accepted" on Hamilton's behalf by Pendleton. With the formal challenge Van Ness also delivered a long, expertly self-serving statement in Burr's behalf. With bootstrap reasoning it purported to shift responsibility for the challenge to Hamilton and on the broadest possible grounds.

Burr disavowed all motives of "pre-determined hostility, a charge [of Hamilton] which he thinks [is] insult added to injury." He felt "as a gentleman should feel when his honour is impeached or assailed . . . without sensations of hostility or wishes of revenge . . . determined to vindicate that honour."

Burr's ground? "Secret whispers traducing his fame, and impeaching his honour." They were "at least, equally injurious with slanders publicly uttered." Hamilton "at no time, and in no place" had a right "to use any such injurious expressions." To Burr, "the partial negative" Hamilton was "disposed to give, with the reservations he wishes to make, are proofs that he has done the injury specified."

Clearly it was not public charges such as Hamilton had made at the City Tavern—calumnious though they were—by which Burr was aggrieved. It was "secret whispers".

Pendleton discussed the statement and the challenge with Hamilton in "a very short conversation that night." Hamilton gave Pendleton "a paper of remarks in his own handwriting" to be handed to Van Ness "if the state of the affair rendered it proper," but Van Ness refused to take it from Pendleton's hand. The correspondence had been closed by Burr's challenge received and accepted. Pendleton insisted on telling Van Ness what was in Hamilton's letter of June 27 anyway: "There has been no intention to evade, defy, or insult, but a sincere disposition to avoid extremities, if it could be done with propriety." The "slanders said to be in circulation" against Burr, "whether openly or in whispers, have a form and shape, and might be specified."

If the secret whispers were indeed about Burr's role in the Reynoldses' badger game, Hamilton knew that Burr could never come forward to speak out about them without dishonoring himself—and Hamilton too, for revealing the secret.

If the duel were to take place, Hamilton wished a short delay, because, "I should not think it right in the midst of a Circuit Court to withdraw my services from those who may have confided important interests to me and expose them to the embarrassment of seeking other counsel, who may not have time to be sufficiently instructed in their case. I shall also want a little time to make some arrangements respecting my own affairs."

Van Ness and Pendleton finally set the time and place for the usual ledge at Weahawk, now Weehawken, on the Jersey Shore, at 7:00 A.M. on Monday, July 9.

Hamilton quietly made discreet arrangements for postponements, continuances, or substitution of other attorneys for himself in pending law cases. He made a new will. He wrote out a list of his liabilities for his executors. He wrote farewell letters to his wife, a grateful note for his friend Pendleton, and drew up an explanation of his conduct and motives in meeting Burr.

Not a word leaked out about the scheduled interview of two of the leading figures of the country, the vice-president of the United States and the former "prime minister" of Washington's and Adams's administrations, the man who remained the best hope of the Federal Republicans to win back the "good government" they had lost to Jefferson. Burr, it seems, told no one but Van Ness; Hamilton told only Pendleton and Rufus King, and King told Egbert Benson and John Jay, but they remained silent.

King strenuously tried to argue Hamilton out of his decision. Hamilton wrote out a lawyerlike summary of points for his arguments for and against backing out of the duel.

Hamilton's "religious and moral principles strongly opposed the practice of duelling." It would give him "pain to shed the blood of a fellow in a private combat forbidden by the laws."

"My wife and children are extremely dear to me, and my life is of the utmost importance to them . . . my creditors, in case of accident to me . . . may be in some degree sufferers. . . ." He had no life insurance. For the posthumous record, at least, he claimed that "I am conscious of no *ill will* to Col. Burr, distinct from political opposition."

But there were *"intrinsick"* difficulties in backing out. They made the duel impossible for him to avoid because "it is not to be denied, that my animadversions on the political principles, character and views of Col. Burr have been extremely severe." Moreover, "on different occasions I, in common with many others, have made very unfavourable criticisms on *particular instances* of the private conduct of this Gentleman [emphasis added by author]." The general disavowal that Burr required "was out of my power." Burr "doubtless has heard of animadversions of mine which bore very hard on him, and it is probable that as usual they were accompanied with some falsehoods. He may have supposed himself under a necessity of acting as he has done."

Burr was menacing, but Hamilton would absolve him from odium in the conduct of the challenge:

> Col. Burr appeared to me to assume, in the first instance, a tone unnecessarily peremptory and menacing, and, in the second, positively offensive. Yet I wished, as far as might be practicable, to leave a door open to accommodation. . . . I am not sure whether, under all the circumstances, I did not go further in the attempt to accommodate than a punctilious delicacy will justify.

If the unstated root reason for the duel was Burr's despicable secret role in the badger game and what Hamilton had let slip about it in conversation at Judge Tayler's, Hamilton's next argument gains special force from singularity that it would otherwise lack. "I trust, at the same time,'' Hamilton continued, ''that the world will do me the justice to believe that I have not censured him on light grounds, nor from unworthy inducements.'' The public did not know, and he would not reveal, all his secret reasons. ''I certainly have strong reasons for what I may have said, though it is possible that in some particulars, I may have been influenced by misconstruction or misinformation.''

Hamilton saw himself as a man accountable to the nation who would set it a bad example by the duel, but that could not be helped:

> To those, who with abhorring the practice of duelling, may think that I ought on no account to have added to the number of bad examples, I answer that my *relative* situation, as well in public as private appeals, enforcing all the considerations which constitute what men of the world denominate honour, impressed on me (as I thought) a peculiar necessity not to decline the call.

What did he mean by this curious reference to his *relative* situation? To his ''peculiar necessity'' not to decline the call? Two things, one inward. Men whom John Adams could never call the ''bastard brat of Scotch pedlar''; men whom no Monroe could refuse to deal with as a fellow gentleman; men who had not struggled all their lives to earn legitimacy, stature, and public credit for a name that technically ought to have been Levine but was not; men with regular birth certificates; men like Rufus King who seemed born to rule—such men might sense, but never consciously know, the Shakespearean quiver of constituents that Hamilton read into the idea of ''what men of the world denominate honour.''

The second, dependent on the first, was outward. Hamilton believed it was his own ''ability to be in future useful, whether in resisting mischief or effecting good, in those crises of our public affairs, which seem likely to happen, [which] would probably be inseparable from a conformity with public prejudice in this particular.'' Without preserving a high stock of personal public credit, he thought, his usefulness, to prevent New England secession from the Union, for example, would be at an end. The American most often pilloried by political enemies for alleged scorn of popular opinion was the one who would risk death and submerge other deeply held principles as well as the interests of his family, friends, clients, and creditors, to the dictates of the people's opinion. For them the bastard brat would sacrifice an exigent life to keep their and his own public credit.

Rufus King pleaded with Hamilton that these last arguments of his were false and specious and that he should refuse to go to Weehawken. King later wrote that ''Hamilton, with a mind the most capacious and discriminating that I ever knew . . . had laid down for the government of himself certain rules upon the subject of Duels, the fallacy of which could not fail to be seen by any man of ordinary understanding.'' Even so, King added, as if in on the secret Hamilton had let slip, ''it is my deliberate opinion that he could not have avoided a meeting with Col. Burr, had he even declined the first challenge.''

William Coleman and others agreed with King that because Burr's challenge issued from ''predetermined hostility,'' nothing Hamilton might have said would have caused Burr to withdraw it. Coleman asked a question that seems unanswerable if ''despicable'' did not refer to the badger game: ''Had a jealous care of his reputation been [Burr's] sole motive, why should . . . all the Clintons and the Livingstons, who have most *openly* reprobated him . . . have escaped his rage?'' (Emphasis added.)

Hamilton was a little troubled by the possibility that he was in the wrong in letting slip the ''despicable'' secret of Burr's role as a procurer. When he had discussed the topic of political disputation with Judge Richard Peters of Pennsylvania a little earlier, he had remarked that in New York, unlike Pennsylvania, ''they never carried party matters so far as to let it interfere with their social parties, and mentioned himself and Colonel Burr, who always behaved with courtesy to each other.''

A remarkable feature of this and other duels of the age was the concentration with which the principals were able to go about their daily business with the likely prospect of their own death, or the premeditated killing of the other, set for a fixed time and place at a near at hand terminal point of a crowded calendar of engagements. A week before the date, Hamilton called on William Short (who had been agent of the Treasury in negotiating the Dutch loans a decade before) ''to request the pleasure of his company at a Family Dinner in the Country, on Saturday next three oClock.''

Hamilton had succeeded Washington as president general of the Society of the Cincinnati, and for him there was no missing its annual 1804 Fourth of July celebration—if the duel were to be kept a secret. Burr turned out for it, too. Many of the veterans who had been there later recalled a strange singularity in the demeanor of their two most famous members. Hamilton, animated even beyond his wont, had raised his wineglass, sung with gusto, and leaped upon a table to sing out the stanzas of his favorite old song, ''The Drum.'' Later, severe disagreement broke out among the old soldiers about whether it was ''The Drum'' he had sung, or another old favorite, ''How Stands the Glass Around.'' That was the song General Wolfe had written the night before his death on the Plains of Abraham, where Burr had later had his first brush with glory. In any event, most agreed that there was something almost feverish about Hamilton's behavior.

They also recalled that Burr, by contrast, who at other times could be urbane, affable, smiling, and politely witty, had surveyed the festive sodality in impenetrable silence, staring at Hamilton with a saturnine expression like Banquo's apparition at Lady Macbeth's triumphal banquet.

Hamilton's son James Alexander, a 16-year-old student at Columbia, would recall that ''a few days before the fatal duel'' he had requested of his father a speech to deliver at one of the exhibitions. ''With his usual kindness,'' his father had complied, delivering it to him with a note:

''I have prepared for you a Thesis on Discretion. *You may need it.* God bless you. Your affectionate father.'' In the text Hamilton had written, ''The celebrated DEAN SWIFT calls discretion an Aldermanly virtue. With all his great and estimable qualities he possessed very little of it himself; and thus was disposed to turn it into derision. But his own experience should have taught him, that if not a splendid it is at least a very useful virtue, and ought on that account to be cultivated and cherished.'' James's father included, ''The want of discretion is apt to be considered as an indication of folly. The greatest abilities are sometimes thrown into the shade by this defect or are prevented from obtaining the success to which they are intitled. The person on whom it is chargeable is also apt to make and have numerous enemies and is occasionally involved by it, in the most difficulties and dangers.''

On the last Sunday, at home at The Granage, Hamilton led his family in the Episcopal family service of worship. Surrounded by all the children, he said aloud the noble prayer, ''O God, who knowest the weakness and corruption of our nature, and the manifold temptations we daily meet with . . . have compassion on our infirmities . . . that we may be effectually restrained from sin, and excited to duty.''

That night, as 13-year-old John Church Hamilton later recalled,

> I was sitting in a room at The Grange when at a slight noise I turned and saw my father in the doorway standing silently looking at me with a most sweet and beautiful

expression of countenance, full of tenderness, and without any of the preoccupations of business he sometimes had.

" 'John,' said he, 'won't you come and sleep with me tonight,' and his voice was frank as if it had been my brother's instead of my father's. That night I went to his bed. In the morning very early he awakened me. Taking my hands in his palms, all four hands extended, he told me to repeat The Lord's Prayer." There, all hands, together, they recited in unison.

During the week, Elizabeth regularly remained at The Grange with the younger children while Hamilton stayed at their house in town at 54 Cedar Street with the older boys. On Monday he went back to town. He called at Egbert Benson's office, where Benson's nephew and law clerk, Robert Benson, Jr., told him his uncle and Rufus King had gone to Massachusetts for a few days. As they talked, between the pages of a book he casually took from Benson's shelves, Hamilton placed a scrap of paper. On later examination, the book was *The Federalist Papers* and the scrap of paper proved to be a listing in Hamilton's hand of the numbers of *The Federalist* papers of his authorship. It was a somewhat inaccurate list.

The will he made the next day thrust unusual interpolations into the functional, impersonal, dispositive prose of the Wall Street lawyer's usual will form. He was "conscious that he had too far sacrificed the interests of my family to public avocations." To find the necessary witnesses before whom to execute it in compliance with the Statute of Wills, he went Monday evening to Oliver Wolcott, Jr.'s house, where his host and Joseph Hopkinson of Philadelphia and others of the Wolcotts' guests observed later that he had been "uncommonly cheerful and gay," though "the duel had been determined on for ten days." It was postponed from Monday to Tuesday and then to Wednesday, when it "finally took effect."

That same day or night he wrote a last letter, one of apology, to Theodore Sedgwick concerning one of his life's two major themes, the preservation of the Union against secessionists. He had planned a much longer letter, he said, "explaining my view of the course and tendency of our politics," but "my plan embraced so large a range that, owing to much avocation, some indifferent health, and growing distaste for politics," the long letter remained unfinished. Nevertheless, "I will here express but one sentiment, which is, that dismemberment of our empire will be a clear sacrifice of great positive advantages without any counter-balancing good, administering no relief to our real disease, which is *democracy*, the poison of which, by a subdivision, will only be the more concentrated in each part, and consequently the more virulent. King is on his way for Boston. . . . God bless you."

Hamilton "left town" for the dueling ground "about five o'clock" Wednesday morning. Weahawk, or Weehawken, is on the west bank of the Hudson directly across the river from the west end of what is now Forty-Second Street in Manhattan. The dawn was misty and pink, and the wind was fair. Hamilton traveled in a small sailboat with his second, Nathaniel Pendleton, and Dr. David Hosack, the celebrated surgeon who had been selected by both men's seconds to attend. They probably set sail from the foot of Horatio Street in what is now Greenwich Village.

Hamilton told Pendleton that "he had made up his mind not to fire at Colonel Burr the first time, but to receive his fire, and fire in the air." Pendleton remonstrated, but Hamilton insisted, "It is the effect of a religious scruple, and does not admit of reasoning. It is useless to say more on the subject, as my purpose is definitely fixed."

The passage was nearly three miles, the morning breeze was still fair, and they landed shortly before seven o'clock. Burr and Van Ness had already cleared away some branches and underbrush "so as to make a fair opening." The usual dueling spot was a shelf or ledge under the heights or southern extremity of the Palisades, some 20 feet above the water, a dozen paces long, and only about six feet wide.

According to the account agreed on by the seconds, when Hamilton came up, "the parties exchanged salutations." The seconds then measured off ten full paces and inspected the pistols to see that their barrels did not exceed eleven inches. They did not. The Wogden pistols, used in many duels, were of English make, had been purchased by Church in London in 1795 or 1796, were of high-quality workmanship, and of heavy .544 caliber, with barrels nine inches long. Set to discharge on their regular triggers, they required a pressure of ten pounds or so; set on the hair triggers, they would fire on a slight squeeze. The seconds cast lots for choice of position and the second by whom the commands should be given. Hamilton won both, a favorable beginning. The seconds loaded the pistols in each other's presence. When Hamilton received his, Pendleton asked if he would have the hairspring set. He answered, "Not this time." When Hamilton and Burr had taken their stations, Pendleton explained to them the rules that were to govern them in firing. He would "loudly and distinctly give the command 'present!' " "Pre-*sent*," as used in duels, means to elevate the arm, point, and aim, preparatory to firing. "After this," Pendleton directed, "the parties shall present and fire *when they please*. . . . if one fires before the other, the opposite second shall say one, two, three, fire . . . and he shall then fire or lose his shot. A snap or a flash is a fire."

According to Van Ness's account, while Pendleton was explaining these rules, "Genl Hamilton raised & levelled his pistol, as if to try his position, and lowering it, said, 'I beg pardon for delaying you but the direction of the light sometimes renders glasses necessary.' He then drew from his pocket a pair of spectacles & having put them on, observed that he was ready to proceed. . . ."

Pendleton then asked if they were prepared. Being told that they were, Pendleton cried "Present!"

According to the official report of the two seconds, "Both parties presented and fired in succession—the intervening time is not expressed, as the seconds do not precisely agree on that point."

According to the seconds' joint statement,

> The fire of Colonel Burr took effect, and General Hamilton almost instantly fell. Col. Burr then advanced toward General Hamilton, with a manner and gesture that appeared to General Hamilton's friend to be expressive of regret, but without speaking turned about and withdrew, being urged from the field by his friend . . . with a view to prevent his being recognized by the surgeon and bargemen, who were then approaching. No further communication took place between the principals, and the barge that carried Col. Burr immediately returned to the City. We conceive it proper to add that the conduct of the parties in this interview was perfectly proper as suited the occasion.

William Coleman, the editor of *The Evening Post*, added some particulars. After Pendleton had cried, "Present!" "Mr. Burr raised his arm slowly, deliberately took his aim, and fired. His ball entered General Hamilton's right side." As soon as the bullet struck, Hamilton raised himself involuntarily on his toes, turned a little to the left (at which moment his pistol went off), and fell upon his face. "Pendleton immediately called out for Dr. Hosack, who, in running to the spot, had to pass Mr. Van Ness and Col. Burr; but Van Ness had the cool precaution to cover his principal with an umbrella, so that Dr. Hosack should not be able to swear that he saw him on the field.''

Both seconds agreed that Hamilton's pistol had fired. But Van Ness always afterward insisted Hamilton had taken aim at Burr and fired first. Pendleton completely disagreed, and Coleman published his version. Burr had fired first. Hamilton had not fired until Burr's bullet struck his body, and then his pistol discharged accidentally as he fell.

The vexed questions of which man fired first, whether Hamilton took aim at Burr or not, whether he intended to throw away his fire or not, and whether his pistol discharged voluntarily or involuntarily will probably never be conclusively resolved. That in the event Hamilton fell and Burr survived would seem to place the burden of proof on those who dispute Pendleton's version. This writer accepts it.

Pendleton revisited the dueling ground the day after Hamilton died, found the mark made by Hamilton's ball, and thought it had clipped a branch off a cedar tree in its flight some twelve and a half feet above the ground and four feet to the right of where Hamilton had stood. He brought back the severed branch to prove it. No one's conscious marksmanship could be that rusty.

But the circumstances of Hamilton's dying, like his birth and the rest of his life, remain subject to fierce controversion, especially among Virginians. For example, in a 1976 article in *New York Magazine*, no less a Virginia gentleman than Virginius Dabney, chairman of the U.S. Bicentennial Society, suggests that Hamilton's knowledge and Burr's ignorance of the ''hidden'' hair triggers in Church's dueling pistols permitted Hamilton to take secret advantage of Burr in the duel. This despite the fact that Hamilton died, and Burr survived. To this writer, such innuendos are unjustified. That Church's dueling pistols, like many of the best of the time, contained a hairspring mechanism inside has always been known; to call it ''hidden'' or ''newly discovered'' bespeaks twentieth-century naïveté—in service of conventional Virginia wisdom concerning Hamilton—misunderstanding more complex eighteenth-century arms and men. Burr had used the same pistols earlier in his duel with Church; so far as is known Hamilton had never used them before in a duel. On the narrow ledge at Weehawken, both principals and their seconds would have heard Pendleton mention the hairspring to Hamilton in any event. If Hamilton could change the seconds' setting, so could Burr. The readying of the weapons—inspecting, testing, setting triggers, and loading—would, of course, be handled by the seconds, not the principals. All four men were friends of one another, had innumerable mutual friends, and were all, for the public record, at least, accounted by all to be gentlemen of honor. Disenchanted as he was with himself, never able to rid himself of his sense of public accountability, if Hamilton had wished to survive at all—a question ultimately unanswerable—the unlikeliest way he could have found to do so was by a secret trick that all four men and all their friends, whatever their other differences, would agree was dishonorable. Worse than dishonorable. Despicable. Honor was the subject of the morning's exercise.

In response to Coleman's request, Dr. Hosack described subsequent events: ''When called to him . . . I found him half sitting on the ground, supported in the arms of Mr. Pendleton. His countenance of death I shall never forget—He had at that instant just strength to say, 'This is a mortal wound, Doctor,' when he sunk away, and became to all appearance lifeless. . . . I immediately stripped up his clothes, and soon, alas! ascertained that the direction of the ball must have been through some vital part.'' Later Dr. Hosack's autopsy disclosed that the ball ''struck the second or third false rib, and fractured it about the middle; it then passed through the liver and diaphragm, and . . . lodged in the first or second lumbar vertebra . . . which was considerably splintered. . . . About a pint of clotted blood was found in the cavity of the belly, which had probably been effused from the divided vessels of the liver.''

As he slumped on the ground, according to Dr. Hosack, Hamilton's ''pulses were not to be felt; his respiration was entirely suspended; and upon laying my hand on his heart, and perceiving no motion there, I considered him as irrecoverably gone.''

With the help of the boatman, Hamilton's lifeless body was carried down the steep path, put aboard the barge, and rowed swiftly across the river. Once on the water, Dr. Hosack noticed that the freshening air and a liberal application of spirits of hartshorn rubbed on Hamilton's face, lips, and temples brought back a little consciousness. About 50 yards from shore, Hamilton made some ''imperfect efforts to breathe, sighed, and spoke the words, 'My vision is indistinct.' '' His sight returned. But my ''slightly pressing his side gave him pain.'' Then, ''soon after recovering his sight, he happened to cast his eye upon the case of pistols, and observing the one that he had had in his hand lying on the outside, he said, 'Take care of that pistol; it is undischarged, and still cocked; it may go off and do harm; Pendleton knows (attempting to turn his head toward him) that I did not intend to fire at him.' ''

''Yes,'' said Pendleton, ''I have already made Dr. Hosack acquainted with your determination as to that.''

Hamilton then fell silent, except to say to Dr. Hosack that he had lost all feeling in his legs, ''manifesting to me that he entertained no hopes that he should long survive.'' Approaching the shore, he said, ''Let Mrs. Hamilton be immediately sent for; let the event be broken to her; but give her hopes.''

On the wharf at the foot of Horatio Street, Hamilton's friend William Bayard, whose house at 80–82 Jane Street was nearby, stood in dreadful apprehension. One of his servants had seen Hamilton, Pendleton, and Dr. Hosack set sail for Weehawken; Bayard could hardly mistake their purpose. At seeing only Pendleton and Hosack returning erect in the stern sheets, he clasped his hands in violent apprehension; and when he saw ''his poor friend lying in the bottom of the boat, he threw up his eyes and burst into a flood of tears.'' Bayard and his family were so distressed they could scarcely move to obey the doctor's orders to get a bed ready. As Hamilton was carried from the wharf to Bayard's house, ''Hamilton alone appeared tranquil and composed,'' but obviously in terrible pain. Dr. Hosack observed that ''we then conveyed him as gently as possible up to the house,'' where he was put to bed in a large square room on the second floor.

Dr. Hosack ''gave him a little wine and water.'' Hamilton complained of the pain in his back. Dr. Hosack undressed him, darkened the room, gave him ''a large anodyne, frequently repeated'' and upwards of an ounce of laudanum the first day. Dr. Hosack noted that ''his habit was delicate and had been lately rendered more feeble by ill health, particularly by a disorder of the stomach and bowels.'' His sufferings during the whole day, Dr. Hosack said, were ''almost intolerable.'' During the night he had ''some imperfect sleep,'' and next morning ''his symptoms were aggravated, attended however with a diminution of pain. His mind retained all its usual strength and composure.''

After seeing off the messenger to fetch Elizabeth, Hamilton, still in terrible pain, begged that another be sent to summon his friend, Bishop Benjamin Moore, rector of Trinity Episcopal Church and bishop of New York, to come to his bedside at once. Although Hamilton attended church fairly regularly and as Troup testified ''was a zealous believer in the fundamental doctrines of Christianity,'' there is no evidence that he had at any time been confirmed at Trinity Church or joined any other.

When the bishop arrived, according to the bishop's account, Hamilton in agony managed the following speech: ''It is my desire to receive the Communion at your hands. I hope you will not conceive there is any impropriety in my request. It has for some time past been the wish of my heart, and it was my intention to take an early opportunity of uniting myself to the church, by reception of that holy ordinance.'' As reported, it was a remarkable speech for a man in his condition.

The bishop turned him down. His priestly office and Christian beliefs made it incumbent on him to condemn dueling, he said. Moreover, although welcoming sincere deathbed conversions, his church held it to be its duty to take especial care that such conversions did indeed represent a spiritual rebirth. Therefore, the bishop, conceiving it ''right and proper to avoid every appearance of precipitancy in performing one of the most solemn offices of our religion,'' duly refused communion to Hamilton. He comforted him in other ways as best he could, however, and took his leave.

Despite the intolerable pain, the dying man did not give up the ghost. Another messenger was rushed to another clerical friend, the Reverend Dr. John M. Mason, a Presbyterian. Again the desperate plea for the sacrament was turned down, Mason explaining that it was strictly forbidden to Presbyterians ''to administer the Lord's Supper privately to any person under any circumstances.'' Mason did what he could to comfort him with prayers and texts from the Scriptures, reminding him that Communion is merely ''an exhibition and pledge of the mercies'' of Christ. Sincere faith made this mercy accessible without the pledge. ''I am aware of that,'' Hamilton told Mason. ''It is only as a sign that I wanted it.'' But there was nothing else Mason could do. After a time he also left.

Taking note of strictures on the sin of dueling, Hamilton had declared to him, according to Mason, ''his abhorrence of the whole transaction.'' The dying man had even sermonized, '' 'It was always against my principles. I used every expedient to avoid the interview; but I have found for some time past, that my life must be exposed to that man. I went to the field determined not to take his life.' '' Most of Hamilton's deathbed responses were characteristically direct, but his final declaration according to Mason—often quoted afterward—is so liturgical for a man in his extremity it would be unbelievable, except upon the oath of a reverend. Clasping his hands toward heaven, Hamilton allegedly spoke with emphasis, ''I have a tender reliance on the mercy of the Almighty, through the mercy of the Lord Jesus Christ.''

Oliver Wolcott, Jr., leaving for a moment the scene of his friend's agony that morning, wrote to his own wife that Hamilton ''suffers great pain—which he endures like a Hero.'' He ''has, of late years experienced his conviction of the truths of the Christian Religion, and has desired to receive the Sacrament—but no one of the Clergy who have yet been consulted will administer it.''

Elizabeth Hamilton, unknowing, arrived from The Grange and reached his bedside at noon. To soften her first shock, Wolcott told her ''the cause of his illness . . . to be spasms''—because ''no one dare tell her the truth—it is feared she would become frantic.'' Elizabeth's sister Angelica knew at once that he was dying. But she hid her own anguish at this hideous end to a lifetime of stifled passion. She wrote her brother Philip in Albany: ''Gen. Hamilton was this morning wounded by that wretch Burr, but we have every reason to hope he will recover.'' Philip must notify their father, General Schuyler, now a sad widower since the death of their mother the year before. He might wish to come down to help them. ''My sister bears with saintlike fortitude this affliction. The town is in consternation, and there exists only the expression of grief and indignation.''

Making no mention of the disappointing doubts of the divines, Dr. Hosack noted that ''the great source of his anxiety seemed to be in his sympathy with his half-distracted wife and children. He spoke to me frequently of them—'My beloved wife and children' were always his expressions. . . . Once, indeed, at the sight of his children brought to the bedside together, seven in number," seeing him in his dreadful situation, "his utterance forsook him." Then "he opened his eyes, gave them one look, and closed them again, till they were taken away." In "a pathetic and impressive manner" but "with a firm voice, he alone could comfort the frantic grief of their mother" by saying to her, *"Remember, my Eliza, you are a Christian."* These must be regarded as Hamilton's last verifiable rational words, his later responses to clergymen's catechizing not being in the same category.

When Gouverneur Morris paid a last compassionate visit to his only friend who was as exotic as himself, he found Hamilton without speech and in agony, Eliza hysterical with grief, the children sobbing, Angelica Church weeping her poor heart out, friends in consternation, and all of New York City outside in an uproar. He agreed with Wolcott: "No person who witnessed [Hamilton's family's] distress will ever be induced to fight a duel."

Bishop Moore returned early in the afternoon of Thursday, the twelfth, in answer to a second summons. He again demurred. Finally, after catechizing the stricken man, to make him assure him that he had met Colonel Burr "with a fixed resolution to do him no harm," that he bore Burr no ill will, and that he received the consolations of the Gospel with a "humble and contrite heart," the bishop administered the Communion for the sick:

> Almighty, everliving God, Maker of mankind, who dost correct those whom thou dost love, and chastise everyone whom thou dost receive; grant that thy servant recover his bodily health, if it be thy gracious will; and that whensoever his soul shall depart from the body, it may be without spot; through Jesus Christ our Lord. Amen.

The bishop averred that Hamilton received it "with great devotion." According to the bishop, after surviving these rigors, "his heart afterwards appeared to be perfectly at rest." At about 2:00 P.M. on Thursday, July 12, with Elizabeth, all seven children (from simple Angelica to little Phil, only two), Angelica and John Church, Wolcott, Dr. Hosack, and Bishop Moore at his bedside, Hamilton "expired without a struggle, and—almost—without a groan."

The corpse was transported from Bayard's house on Jane Street to await the funeral procession at Angelica Church's house on Robinson Street. The Church house had served as a similar temporary resting place three years earlier for the corpse of the first Philip Hamilton.

Burr's barge had landed him and Van Ness at Canal Street, whence Burr had hastened to Richmond Hill to remain in seclusion. Bulletins on Hamilton's condition informed and outraged the public, and rumors and then news of his death plunged it into grief. Burr and Van Ness sensed that public indignation was mounting into serious menace toward them.

The morning of the twelfth, Burr in the third person sent out to request "Dr. Hosack to inform him of the present state of Gen. H. and of the hopes which are entertained of his recovery. . . . He would take it very kind if the Dr would take the trouble of calling on him as he returns from Mr Bayard's."

Van Ness made similar inquiry of Pendleton, hoping the wound had not been pronounced mortal, as he had heard it had been. His fears for Hamilton were mixed with fears for Burr's and his own safety, and he cautioned Pendleton not to publish any particulars out of agitation and solicitude until they had consulted.

Pendleton, pressed by Hamilton's friends, was eager to clear up the mystery, publish the correspondence that had preceded the duel, and the precise facts that would explain the interview at Weehawken. Van Ness was for delay and insisted that nothing appear in the newspapers unless he and Burr consented to it on every point. But conferences between Van Ness and Pendleton were difficult because Van Ness was fearful of mob violence if he should dare enter the city.

At Dr. Hosack's on Friday the thirteenth, Pendleton read Van Ness a statement he had prepared, but Van Ness objected to certain features of it and went away to consult his own notes, and the seconds did not meet again before the New York *Morning Chronicle* published Pendleton's account on July 17, the Tuesday following the Thursday Hamilton had died. Pendleton had waited for Van Ness until the printer demanded the copy, then had supplied the printer with wording that he hoped Van Ness would find to be accurate. Van Ness had failed to keep the appointment because "apprehensive that my visit to the City would be attended with danger I have stopt at Col. Burr's whose house is unoccupied and where I should be happy to see you." Pendleton accepted the changes Van Ness demanded; so instead of saying that Burr "took aim," he substituted "both parties presented." He did not quarrel with Van Ness's reason for not passing Hamilton's last letter on to Burr: Van Ness had considered the correspondence closed by what he took to be Pendleton's unqualified and final acceptance, for Hamilton, of Burr's challenge of the day before.

Eliza tore open and read the two letters Hamilton had written her, one on July 4 and the other the night before the duel, to be opened only in case of his death.

> . . . If it had been possible for me to have avoided the interview, my love for you and my precious children would have been alone a decisive motive. But it was not possible, without sacrifices which would have rendered me unworthy of your esteem.

So much for reasons of state and religion.

His anguish at the thought of death taking him from her found moving penultimate phrases:

> I need not tell you of the pangs I feel, from the idea of quitting you and exposing you to the anguish I know you would feel. Nor could I dwell on the topic lest it should unman me . . . with my last idea; I shall cherish the sweet hope of meeting you in a better world.
>
> Adieu best of wives and best of Women. Embrace all my darling Children for me. Ever yours
>
> AH

> July 4, 1804
> Mrs. Hamilton

And in a second letter, written July 10, the night before, a kind of afterthought, at the very end, he thought of his beginnings—and of accountability—to his cousin Ann Lytton Mitchell, who had given him some money to come to America—and of duty: "I have not hitherto done my duty to her . . . [The end of life did not mean an end of accountability.] I . . . intend, if it shall be in my power, to render the Evening of her days comfortable.

But if it shall please God to put this out of my power and to inable you hereafter to be of service to her, I . . . entreat you to do it, and to treat her with the tenderness of a Sister."

In his ultimate lines is a sense of fitness, of inevitability, of an eloquent melancholy, of work unfinished, of mystery, and of a fate not undeserved. The same mood hovers over the lines of Vergil's First Eclogue. He had become disenchanted with himself:

> . . . The scruples of a Christian have determined me to expose my own life to any extent rather than subject myself to the guilt of taking the life of another. This must increase my hazards, & redoubles my pangs for you. But you had rather I should die innocent than live guilty. Heaven can preserve me and I humbly hope will but in the contrary event, I charge you to remember that you are a Christian. God's Will be done. The will of a merciful God must be good.
>   Once more Adieu, my Darling, darling Wife.
>
> AH
Tuesday Evening 10 oClock

General Schuyler, in bed in Albany suffering agonizing pangs of gout, again did his best to console his daughter: "My Dear, Dearly Beloved and Affectionate Child . . . If aught under heaven could aggravate the affliction I experience, it is that incapable of moving or being removed I cannot fly to you. . . ." He opened his heart to her: "Should it please God so far to restore my strength as to enable me to go to you, I shall embrace the first moment to do it, but should it be otherwise, I entreat you my beloved Child to come home as soon as you possibly can, with my dear Grand-children." Next day he begged desolated Angelica to comfort Eliza for him: He forbore to write her directly "lest it should create a fresh paroxysm of grief." Fearing his own death, he trusted "that the Supreme being may prolong my life that I may discharge the duties of a father to my dear child and her dear children. . . . She knows how tenderly I loved My Dear Hamilton. . . . Much I feel all the duties which are devolved on me. The evening of my days will be passed in the pleasing occupation of administering . . . to a Child and Grand-Children so highly entitled to my best exertions." Schuyler was sending his son Philip to New York at once to help her look after her family.

Schuyler's wish to be a father to his grandchildren was unfulfilled. To his grief from the fall of his namesake, the first Philip Hamilton; the loss of granddaughter Angelica's mind; and the passing of his good wife, Catherine, was now added the pang of his son-in-law's death—as the apparent result of a chain of circumstances beginning with the few words Schuyler had forced Dr. Cooper to write him of the infamous embezzled letter.

Dr. Stringer lanced the ulcer in Philip Schuyler's foot. Much infected matter was discharged to relieve his pain, but he must remain in bed ten or twelve days more. "Pray let me know if you have as yet obtained a . . . convenient house[.]" He wrote Elizabeth: "Procure one if possible sufficiently large that you may not be in the least crowded, for remember, that it is my intention that you should be well accommodated,—and make every want immediately known to me that I may have the pleasure of obviating it."

One of her father's last letters told her he could not walk, but still hoped to visit her that winter in the city if there should be sledding. He wanted her table to be well supplied. As soon as his winter's store of fat cattle and hogs arrived, "everything will be prepared for you," including butter and "Pig's feet souse."

But the fond, tender promises of the bereft old paterfamilias remained unfulfilled when he died three months and four days after his son-in-law on November 18, 1804. The last letter Elizabeth Hamilton received from him was, "What your afflictions my dearly beloved child have added to mine, was the natural result of a parent's tenderness for a dutiful and affectionate child, as he invariably experienced from you."

Just before Schuyler's death, James McHenry had complained to Oliver Wolcott, Jr., that collections lagged for the fund they had set up to pay off the creditors of Hamilton's deeply insolvent estate and save The Grange. Friends saw no need because of ''the real or presumed great wealth of General Schuyler.'' Wolcott, the president of the Merchants Bank, replied: Schuyler ''owes money and has no funds at command.''

39

Elizabeth Hamilton
Survives

Mr. Monroe, if you have come to tell me that you repent . . . I understand it. But, otherwise, no lapse of time, no nearness to the grave, makes any difference.

—Elizabeth Hamilton to James Monroe, 1830

After Hamilton's death a note was found written to Nathaniel Pendleton the evening before the interview "thanking him with tenderness for his friendship to him" and informing him where the keys to certain drawers of his desk would be found. In the drawers Hamilton had deposited such papers as he thought proper to leave behind him, together with his last will. The papers included the statement setting forth his points on dueling, his own situation, and Burr, as well as the two last letters addressed to Elizabeth Hamilton.

His will, dated July 9, superseded the earlier will he had made July 25, 1795, just before his scheduled duel with Commodore James Nicholson the week after being stoned by the Wall Street mob for defending Jay's Treaty. It appointed John Barker Church, Nicholas Fish, and Pendleton as his executors and gave and devised his estate to them, with instructions to pay his debts if the fund were sufficient or, if it was not, pro rata in proportion to size of claims. The residue, if any, should go to Elizabeth, his wife. He imposed a highly unusual obligation on his family, yet one entirely consistent with his firmly fixed ideas on the subject of public credit: If there was not enough money to pay off his creditors, he entreated his children to pay up the deficiency, if they ever should be able to do so. "Though conscious that I have too far sacrificed the Interests of my family to public avocations & on this account have the less claim to burthen my Children, yet I trust in their magnanimity to appreciate as they ought this my request." In an "unfavourable . . . event of things" their

611

most sacred duty was "the support of their dear mother, with the most respectful and tender attention." The children were charged to bear in mind "that to them she has been the most devoted and best of mothers." A striking change in his new will from the old one of 1795 was that gone now was any mention of the "bundle inscribed thus—*JR To be forwarded to Oliver Wolcott Junr. Esq.*" Certainty of probate makes a will a public record. To have let this stand would have whetted up his enemies' hullabaloo about the old scandal all over again and by his own hand.

In a drawer was an estate-planning memorandum headed, "State of my property and Debts July 1, 1804." His assets were mainly Western lands, some 31,000 acres, which "stood him" $48,000. The Grange stood him $25,000. Total real estate was put down at $74,150; personal estate totaled $3,850 (furniture and library $3,000, horses and carriages $600, loan $250); there was due him for professional services about $2,500, making total assets of $80,500. His debts were principally $20,000 owing to several banks in New York and smaller sums borrowed from clients and friends, such as Louis Le Guen, $3,000; Herman Le Roy, $4,280; John B. Church, $2,610; Fish, $1,500; and Victor Du Pont, whom he had befriended in the past, $1,800. Adding other debts, mostly smaller, and deducting $54,722 liabilities from $80,500 assets, he had struck a balance in his favor of $25,778. He wanted a preference given to certain creditors, including those who had supplied labor and materials for The Grange. The bundle inscribed *JR* was nowhere on the list of assets—or liabilities. It was not found. It has never been found. The secrets it contained remain one of the profound mysteries of American history.

Of all the men in American history who have occupied the office of secretary of the treasury, Hamilton, the greatest, was probably the least affluent. He had set much too high a value on his Western lands, judging by their current selling prices, and on continuance of earnings from his law practice, from $12,000 to $14,000 a year. For some time he had been in poor health, as Dr. Hosack's bill for almost continual ministrations showed. Building The Grange had cost him much more than prudence dictated, though now it was the focus of the whole family's affections.

Sadly, Hamilton felt it necessary "to explain why I have made so considerable an establishment in the country." He had thought to prepare a place of retirement from the harassments of life. Within a reasonable period, he thought, his earnings would maintain his family and gradually discharge his debts. Construction costs for The Grange had all been incurred; nothing further would be spent for the present. He planned to reduce expenses of every kind to $4,000 a year exclusive of interest on the place, even if The Grange must be leased for a few years. In the meantime, his Western lands were increasing in value and in the end should leave him "a handsome clear property." His chief apology was to friends who from kindness had endorsed notes for him at the banks. He felt justified in securing them in preference to other creditors and entreated the indulgence of the banks toward them. He added wryly that if this statement of his net worth should come to public notice, it would at least be proof that his financial integrity in public office was beyond "even the shadow of a question."

He had forsworn the ordinary advantages of his military service. Being a member of Congress when the question of commuting the half pay owed to the army for a lump sum was in debate, he had relinquished his own claims so that his advocacy would not be suspect on grounds of self-interest. Nor had he applied for the bounty lands allowed by the United States and New York.

Although he had not seen his cousin Ann Lytton Mitchell in all the years since his youth, she had given him money to come from St. Croix to the mainland and to help pay for his education beyond the level of a clerk bookkeeper. In the packet committed to Pendleton was a sealed letter for her enclosing, ''as was mentioned on the outside,'' $400.

Dr. Hosack submitted his bill for $87.50 and closed his file on Hamilton with the following lines from Horace's Ode on the death of Quintilius Varus of Cremona: ''Incorrupta fides—nudaque veritas Quando ullum invenient parem? Multis ille quidem flebilis occidit.''

The merchants and other respectable citizens of the city met at the Tontine Coffee House on July 13 and voted to shut up their shops and stores and suspend all business the following day, Saturday, July 14, to march in the funeral procession. Owners and masters of vessels in the harbor would hoist their colors half-mast. The arrangements committee requested all fellow citizens ''to wear crape on the left arm for thirty days, as a testimony of their respect for the Integrity, Virtues, Talents and Patriotism of General Alexander Hamilton, deceased.''

The Common Council of New York City proclaimed that the funeral should be public, at the expense of the municipality, and ''that the usual business of the day be dispensed with by all classes of inhabitants.'' The ordinance prohibiting bell ringing at funerals was suspended. Muffled bells could be tolled morning, noon, and evening the day of his interment. Six weeks of mourning were proclaimed.

The Bar Association met at Lovett's Hotel, and ''all party distinction was lost in the general sentiment of love and respect for the illustrious deceased.'' Richard Harison spoke ''with a faltering tongue and a feeling heart.'' The gentlemen of the bar adopted a resolution expressing ''universal confidence and veneration'' for ''Alexander Hamilton, the brightest ornament of their profession.'' They lamented his loss as ''a severe private affliction''; they deplored it as a great public calamity. For their deceased brother they would wear crape for six weeks. Similar convocations were called by the Law Student Association, at the office of Josiah Ogden Hoffman; by the students and graduates of Columbia College on the college green; by the Brigade Company of Artillery, the Sixth Regiment, and other regiments at Mechanic Hall and in City Hall Park; by the Saint Andrews Society at the Masonic Hall; and by the members of the Tammanial Society ''in the great Wigwam, precisely at the setting of the sun,'' in ''the Season of Fruit, in the year of discovery 312, by order of the Grand Sachem, James D. Bisset,'' secretary.

On Saturday morning Colonel Morton's Corps began close order drill and desultory parading in City Hall Park at 10 o'clock, with six artillery pieces also on hand. Other marchers assembled in Robinson Street, now Park Place, west of Broadway, on the south side facing the house of John and Angelica Church, where the corpse had been brought to lie. The Sixth Regiment, ranks rested on reversed arms with musket butts up, muzzles down, facing the front stoop and entrance, while the colors and music of the several corps paraded back and forth in the street.

For this sad day the standard of the Society of the Cincinnati, carried at the immediate left of the national color, was shrouded in the blackest crape of all. At noon, precisely, on the command, ''Order, COLORS,'' the Color Guard aligned its formation. The color bearers grasped the pikes of their flags and drew them upright with each ferrule resting on the street against its bearer's foot. On the command, ''Carry, COLORS,'' each lifted his pike and inserted its heel in the socket of his carrying sling, and grasped his pike at shoulder height with his elbow crooked parallel to the ground so that his pike inclined forward at only a slight angle from the vertical.

On the command, ''Cincinnati, present, COLORS!'' its standard bearer alone slid his right hand up the pike staff to the height of his eye, straightened his elbow, and then flexed and straightened it again, causing the proud crape-shrouded standard to wave downward and then upward and then decline at a 45-degree angle toward the front entrance of the Churches' house.

The dip of the Cincinnatian standard was the signal for the Sixth Regiment to execute a brisk "present, ARMS." There followed in cadence the snap-slap-slap of hard palms on leather slings and musket butts and the rattle of frizzles on flints. Officers' flat hands and right forearms sprang into vibrant hand salutes. The "large and elegant" band struck up the melancholy dead march.

The front door of John and Angelica Church's house swung open. From within emerged Hamilton's corpse in its coffin on its pall-draped bier, borne by seven of his good friends: Oliver Wolcott, Jr., Richard Harison, William Bayard, Josiah Ogden Hoffman, Richard Varick, General Matthew Clarkson, and Judge John Lawrence. The colors and music rested for a moment. All joined in silent salute to the corpse. A signal trumpet sounded. On muffled drums the drummer boys beat out an open roll in the colonial manner—individual strokes slightly separated, giving the effect not so much of a merged rumble as of a sustained rattle. Colonel Morton's troops, which had been parading in the park, fell into columns and occupied Broadway.

On the second trumpet call, the Sixth Regiment shouldered arms, wheeled to the right by platoons, and occupied Robinson Street in front of the corpse. On the third trumpet call, the whole column stepped off, the band still playing the dead march in a slow, slow cadence to the rattle of the muffled drums. The flanks of the corpse on its bier were covered by two companies in single file with arms at trail. Behind walked the general's gray horse, caparisoned in deep mourning, led by two blacks dressed in white, wearing white turbans trimmed in black. The general's boots and spurs lay reversed on the gray's back across his empty saddle.

Following directly behind in deep mourning came Elizabeth Hamilton and the four eldest sons, Alexander, James Alexander, John Church, and William Stephen; Angelica, Eliza, little Philip II, and the Antil orphan were spared the two-mile march. John and Angelica Church and their children followed, supported by an ambience of Schuyler brothers and nephews and nieces. Gouverneur Morris, the appointed funeral orator, followed in his carriage. Then came the gentlemen of the bar, the lieutenant governor, the resident agents of foreign powers, "the various officers of the respective banks," the "chamber of commerce and merchants," and the president, professors, and students of Columbia College, all in mourning gowns. There followed the Saint Andrews Society, the Tammany Society, the Mechanic Society, and, finally the "citizens in general."

It was the greatest procession New York had ever seen since the one 16 years earlier in honor of Hamilton's efforts to obtain New York's ratification of the Constitution. He had not been present, except in spirit, to enjoy the public credit of that one, either.

As the ranks moved out of Robinson Street and curved around City Hall Park toward Pearl, they were augmented by Colonel Morton's troops from Broadway as they wheeled rank by rank into their places in the column ahead of the bier. The matrosses of two artillery pieces, which had been left behind in the Park, with priming and powder charges piled high beside their carriage, began firing off minute guns that would continue for the more than two hours it would take for the whole cortege to wind its way around the city through Pearl Street down to Whitehall and back up Broadway to Trinity Church.

Ever since 10 o'clock in the morning, the guns of His Britannic Majesty's ship of war *Boston*, anchored inside the Hook, and His Majesty's packet *Lord Charles Spencer,* with yard arms peaked and ensigns at half-mast in mourning, had been firing off minute gun salutes that reverberated gloomily across the island. As the artillery in the park took up the cannonade, the French frigates *Cybelle* and *Didion*, also with their colors half-hoisted and their yards peaked in mourning, now added the boom of their own minute guns to the concatenation of cannon fire that accompanied the dead march. So did the cannon of all the forts around the harbor.

In its more than three and a half centuries of history, New York City has been rocked by many a noisy celebration. But probably never before or since has it heard such thumps of doleful thunder as marked the passing of the greatest man who ever lived there and called himself a New Yorker. The streets were lined with people, and doors and windows were filled "principally with weeping females," William Coleman reported. Indeed, "even the housetops were covered with spectators, who came from all parts to behold the melancholy procession."

When the military advance guard reached Trinity Church, the whole column wheeled by platoons, flank by flank, formed a lane, and came to a halt. They slapped their muskets once again, on command, to reversed order, butts up. Through the avenue thus formed, while the band with muffled drums played "a pensive solemn air," the corpse, preceded and followed by the funeral party, advanced into the church between the ranks of the soldiers. In the customary attitude of grief, each one crooked his neck and rested his cheek on the butt of his piece.

From a stage erected in the portico of the church, Gouverneur Morris then rose and, with Hamilton's four sons seated beside him, "slowly and impressively delivered to the immense concourse in front an extemporary oration." Coleman committed it to memory and afterward quickly committed it to paper.

"Instead of the language of a public speaker," Morris began his exordium, "you will hear only the lamentations of a bewailing friend. But I will struggle with my bursting heart, to portray that Heroic Spirit. . . ."

To his diary the night before, musing on his assignment to deliver Hamilton's funeral oration next day, Morris had confided, "He was a Stranger of illegitimate Birth. Some mode must be contrived to pass over this handsomely."

"When the first sound of the American war called Hamilton to the field," proclaimed Morris, he was "a young and unprotected volunteer." Then, being selected by Washington as an aide, he was "a principal actor in the most important scenes of our Revolution." At Yorktown, "he stormed the redoubt . . . his gallant troops, emulating the heroism of their chief, checked the uplifted arm, and spared a foe no longer resisting." Not one perished.

In his diary, Morris had written the night before, "He was indiscreet, vain and opinionated. . . . He was on Principle opposed to republican and attached to monarchical government. His share in forming our Constitution must be mentioned and his unfavorable Opinion cannot therefore be concealed."

From the portico of Trinity church next day Morris, jealously proud of his own important role in creating the Constitution, particularly as chairman of the Committee on Style, acknowledged that Hamilton "assisted informing that constitution which is now the bond of our union, the shield of our defense, and the source of our prosperity."

Hamilton had indeed expressed apprehension that the Constitution "did not contain sufficient means of strength for its own preservation"; like other republics, notably France, he feared it might pass through anarchy and "shoot into" despotism. But like Morris himself, he "hoped better things. We confided in the good sense of the American people; and above all we trusted in the protecting Providence of the Almighty." By his enemies,

Morris pointed out, Hamilton's "speculative opinions were treated as deliberate designs." He was a man who "disdained concealment. Knowing the purity of his heart, he bore it as it were in his hand, exposing to every passenger its inmost recesses." Hamilton's "generous indiscretion subjected him to censure from misrepresentation." "You know"—"You all know," Morris sentiently prolated, "how strenuous, how unremitting were his efforts to establish and to preserve the constitution. If then his opinion was wrong, pardon, oh! pardon that single error in a life devoted to your service."

In his diary Morris had written "The most important part of his life was his administration of the finances. The system he proposed was in one respect radically wrong. . . ."

To the assembled mourners Morris proclaimed that Washington had sought out Hamilton as his secretary of the treasury for his "splendid talents, extensive information and incorruptible integrity." His system was widely criticized; it had its faults—"let it be remembered that nothing human is perfect"—but Hamilton, as the minister of a republic, must and did "bend to the will of the people." The result? "A rapid advance in power and prosperity, of which there is no example in any other age or nation. The part which Hamilton bore is universally known."

What should be said of the haunting Reynolds affair? To his diary Morris noted "He has long since foolishly published the avowal of conjugal infidelity. Something, however must be said to excite public pity for his family which he has left in indigent circumstances."

To the bereaved, Morris noted that Hamilton's openness, "his unsuspecting confidence in professions of others which he believed to be sincere, led him to trust too much" in people he should not have trusted. "This exposed him to misrepresentation." He felt obliged to resign. "But though he was compelled to abandon public life never, no never for a moment did he abandon the public service." In recent years he had probably been more open, frank, and confidential with Morris than with anyone else. Now, Morris swore, "I declare before God . . . that in his most private and confidential conversations, the single objects of discussion and consideration were your freedom and happiness. He never lost sight of your interests."

Hamilton had been charged with ambition and was wounded by the imputation.

"Oh! my fellow citizens," Morris cried in Mark Antonian tones, "remember this solemn testimonial, that he was not ambitious." When Washington was called forth from his retreat to lead your armies, "he asked for Hamilton to be his second in command. . . ." Washington knew that "the hand of time pinching life at its source" would soon remove him from the scene and that Hamilton would succeed him. Yet "he thought the sword of America might safely be confided to the hand which now lies cold in that coffin."

Hamilton was "indignant at the charge that he sought place or power" for his own aggrandizement. "He was ambitious only of glory, but he was deeply solicitous for you. For himself he feared nothing, but that bad men might, by false professions, acquire your confidence, and abuse it to your ruin." Turning to his brethren of the Cincinnati, Morris reminded them, "Oh! he was mild and gentle. In him there was no offence; no guile—his generous hand and heart were open to all."

Turning to the gentlemen of the bar, Morris enjoined them to "cherish and imitate his example," while, like him, "with laudable zeal, you pursue the interests of your clients, remember, like him, the eternal principles of justice."

Turning to his fellow citizens and for the benefit of American posterity, Morris recalled that "you have seen him contending against you and saving your dearest interests, as it were, in spite of yourselves. . . . you now feel and enjoy the benefit resulting from the firm energy of his conduct. Bear this testimony to the memory of my departed friend. I

CHARGE YOU TO PROTECT HIS FAME.'' Be not misled by all the rich panoply of the funeral, Hamilton had left his family almost destitute. His fame ''is all he has left—all that these poor orphan children will inherit from their father.''

A wave of emotion surged across the immense throng as people craned their necks and stood on tiptoe to stare at the impoverished Hamilton sons there on the stage beside the orator. Morris's towering frame, massive head, imperious glance, and Shakespearean cadences compelled a breathless silence as he paused a moment before rising to his peroration:

> My countrymen, that Fame may be a rich treasure to you also. Let it be the test by which to examine those who solicit your favour. Disregarding professions, view their conduct, and on a doubtful occasion, ask, *Would Hamilton have done this thing?*

He closed:

> You all know how he perished. On this last scene, I cannot, I must not dwell. It might excite emotions too strong for better judgment. Suffer not your indignation to lead to any act which might again offend the insulted majesty of the law; on his part, or from his lips, though with my voice—for his voice you will hear no more—let me entreat you to respect yourself.

Even so, Morris meditated to his diary that night, ''How easy it would have been to make them, for a moment, absolutely mad!'' But it had been his duty, he told himself, to allay mob passions, not to unleash them against Burr in an orgy of revenge.

The weeping subsided. The troops in the churchyard formed an extensive hollow square. The corpse was carried to the grave for the usual funeral services. Bishop Moore intoned the same words from the Book of Common Prayer that the Reverend Cecil Wray Goodchild had spoken over Rachel's grave in St. Croix:

> I am the resurrection and the life, saith the Lord; he that believeth in me, though he were dead, yet shall he live; and whosoever liveth and believeth in me, shall never die. . . . We brought nothing into this world, and it is certain we can carry nothing out. The Lord gave, and the Lord hath taken away; blessed be the name of the Lord.

The troops terminated the solemnities by firing blank musket volleys into clouds of smoky air above the grave.

The coroner of the City and County of New York began an inquisition and after several delays, upon the testimony of Dr. Hosack and the two clergymen, returned with a coroner's verdict of murder, implicating Burr, Van Ness, and Pendleton. In New Jersey, the 15-man Bergen County coroner's jury also charged Burr with murder. Burr feared he would be indicted as a result of one or another coroner's inquest for the nonbailable offense.

Burr's first significant postduel act was to become a fugitive from justice. When he was indicted for murder by the grand jury, he fled. John Swartwout brought a boat to the foot of the yard below Richmond Hill at ten o'clock on the night of July 21, rowed him downriver, and put him ashore in the morning at Perth Amboy, New Jersey. But the Bergen County indictment made it dangerous for him to dally in that state, and Burr was restless to press on. On Monday, Commodore Thomas Truxtun took his nervous guest by carriage as far as

Cranbury, where Burr hired a spring wagon, crossed the Delaware at Bristol to Pennsylvania, and continued by back roads to Philadelphia, where he took temporary refuge in the hospitality of his friend Alexander Dallas.

One Maryland newspaper, quoting Hamilton's favorite eighteenth-century poet, Alexander Pope, wrote that Burr was *"Damned* to everlasting fame." Far from wallowing in the tragedy, Burr displayed characteristic nonchalance: "Burr parades our streets with unparalleled effrontery," reported Hamilton's friend Joseph Hopkinson, "courting the attention of everybody with whom he has the slightest acquaintance. Our Governor has visited him. . . ." Burr also resumed the courtship of one Celeste, whom he had known earlier in the Biblical sense. Burr feared the genteel governor of Pennsylvania might feel obliged to extradite him back to New York for murder; so, incognito, he moved on southward. He harbored with Pierce Butler on St. Simons Island, Georgia, for a few days, and scouted that state and Spanish Florida for future adventures. Finally, after days in an open boat, the vice-president of the United States, as a fugitive from justice, reached the out-of-the-way home of his daughter, Theodosia, and her husband, Joseph Alston, at Statesburg, South Carolina.

When Congress reconvened, the vice-president, still under indictment for murder, returned to Washington and acted as presiding officer at the impeachment trial of Judge Samuel Chase. Many Jeffersonians, though not Jefferson, now became his partisans. Senator Giles arranged for a round robin of Republican senators to plead with Governor Bloomfield of New Jersey to quash his murder indictment there, and, after some demurrals, this was accomplished. The New York grand jury reduced the charge against him to the mere misdemeanor of sending a challenge to a duel. Burr was homeless in New York, however, for while he was in flight, Richmond Hill had been auctioned off for $25,000 to pay off his debts; and even after the sale, unsatisfied claims of creditors of at least $8,000 remained due.

The rest of the nation joined New York City in mourning. Newspapers everywhere rivaled each other in expressions of sorrow. The clergy composed heartrending sermons with the duel as their text. Mass memorial meetings were held in New York, Philadelphia, Boston, and Albany. Ordinances were suspended. Muffled church bells tolled throughout the nation.

Editorials, resolutions, and addresses in communities large and small throughout the 15 states pronounced encomiums on Hamilton. In these eulogies his name was often coupled with Washington's and great men of classical ages. Many editors who had been political opponents generously united in praise. James Cheetham, of the New York *American Citizen*, who had tried as hard as anyone to destroy him in print, was foremost in atonement and attempts at resurrection.

Some of the most perceptive comments came from Fisher Ames in an estimate read to friends and published unsigned in the *Boston Repository*. Ames observed that "the uncommonly profound public sorrow for the death of Alexander Hamilton, sufficiently explains and vindicates itself." This was because Hamilton "had not made himself dear to the passions of the multitude by condescending . . . to become their instrument . . . it was by . . . loving his country better than himself, preferring its interest to its favor, and serving it, when it was unwilling and unthankful, in a manner that nobody else could, that he rose, and the true popularity, the homage that is paid to virtue, followed him." On the same theme, Ames added, "No man ever more disdained duplicity, or carried *frankness* further than he. This gave to his political opponents some temporary advantages. . . ."

Although Hamilton had been withdrawn from public office to the bar for some years, yet "there was nevertheless a splendor in his character that could not be contracted within the ordinary sphere of his employments." Ames did not believe "that he had left any worthy man his foe who had ever been his friend." Ames acknowledged that it is difficult for such a greatly superior man to preserve the friendship of his associates without abatement: "Yet though Hamilton could not possibly conceal his superiority, he was so little inclined to display it, he was so much at ease in its possession, that no jealousy or envy chilled his bosom when his friends obtained praise." He was "magnanimous . . . frank . . . ardent, yet so little overbearing, so much trusted, admired, beloved, almost adored, that his power over [his friends'] affections was entire and lasted through his life."

Said Ames, "I could weep for my country, which mournful as it is, does not know the half of its loss. It deeply laments, when it turns its eyes back, and sees what Hamilton *was*; but my soul stiffens with despair when I think what Hamilton *would have been*." Words all but failed the ever articulate Ames. "But who alive can exhibit this portrait?" None had the skill. "If our age, on that supposition more fruitful than any other, had produced two Hamiltons, one of them might then have depicted the other."

A less polished but no less heartfelt tribute came to Elizabeth Hamilton from Harry Croswell, the village editor whose appeal Hamilton had argued so forcefully—and lost— less than five months earlier. "To me he . . . rendered unequalled service," said Croswell. "In my defense, and that of the American press . . . this greatest of men made his mightiest effort."

The usually articulate Jefferson made only two known mentions of the most sensational tragedy that had wracked the nation since its beginnings. One was the following meaning-less postscript to a letter to his daughter Martha, July 17, 1804: "I presume Mr. Randolph's newspapers will inform of the death of Colo. Hamilton, which took place on the 12th." The other, in a letter the following day to Philip Mazzei in Europe, coldly included Hamilton's name as one of several on a list headed "remarkable deaths lately."

Jefferson had made no recorded comment on James Thomson Callender's mysterious demise the summer before either. But now, by a single bullet, Burr had removed the only two of the younger men on the American scene who posed a threat to Jefferson's control of the presidential succession by the Virginia junto—James Madison and James Monroe—as far into the future as anyone alive could be expected to peer. Such extreme laconism about the dramatic simultaneous self-destruction of two rivals of the man who could descant by the quire on gossip Beckley brought him, suggests that Jefferson wished to keep the door tightly closed on the question of all else he knew about the secret meaning of the word *despicable*.

But Jefferson's creature John Beckley was as voluble about Hamilton's fall as his master was tight-lipped when he wrote to John Brown on August 8, 1804: "Federalism has monumented and sainted *their* leader up to the highest heavens, whilst the presses are made to groan under the weight of Orations, Eulogies, and mournings, and Burr is pursued with vindictive and unrelenting fury." Ever the faithful instrument of his master Jefferson's will, Beckley did not venture out with his own opinion. "But one opinion prevails here," he said. Burr was correct. Brown should read the correspondence. It justifies Burr's proce-dure. "Nothing but the want of *equal intelligence* and *equal* nerve, would prevent any man pursuing the same course."

Beckley's reference to Burr's "equal intelligence" gives ground to suspect that Beckley knew that the secret root of the duel lay in the special reference of the word *despicable* to the badger game that Beckley and Burr had played. Beckley had not admitted knowing this much when he had written William Eustis three weeks earlier, disclaiming all knowledge of the causes of the duel. He would "drop a tear at [Hamilton's] untimely fate" and admire his talents, virtues, and "useful public services."

Horace's injunction, *de mortuis nil nisi bonum*, did not temper John Adams's opinions of the departed; if anything, time seemed to heat up and concentrate Adams's desultory rage. He fumed that Federalist newspaper stories called Hamilton "the soul and Washington the body—Washington the painted wooden head of the ship and Hamilton the pilot and steersman." They reported that Hamilton had planned a history that would reveal the secret that Washington had been his puppet. To Benjamin Rush, Adams snorted that "I lose all patience when I think of a bastard bratt of a Scotch peddler daring to threaten to undeceive the world in their judgment of Washington, by writing a history of his battles and campaigns." Adams went on, "This creature was in a delirium of ambition; he had been blown up with vanity by the Tories, had fixed his eye on the highest station in America, and he hated every man young or old who stood in his way." Moreover, Adams wrote Mercy Warren on July 20, 1807, with like distemper, "in this dark and insidious manner did this intriguer lay schemes in secret against me, and like the worm at the root of the peach did he labor for twelve years underground and in darkness girdle the root while the axes of the Anti-Federalists, Democrats, Jacobins, Virginia debtors to English merchants, and French hirelings, chopping as they were for the whole time at the trunk, could not fell the tree."

Hamilton's New York friends organized themselves to try to mend the destitution in which he had left his family. Oliver Wolcott, Jr., president of the Merchants Bank, took the lead; Gouverneur Morris, Matthew Clarkson, Archibald Gracie, and William Bayard also helped, all with the approval of Church, Pendleton, and Fish, Hamilton's executors. Wolcott wrote to Hamilton's wealthy admirers in Philadlephia, Boston, and Baltimore, men who had benefited from his fiscal policies, and proposed a subscription of $100,000 to pay his debts and provide for his family. An application for a grant by the national or state government or a general subscription had been considered, but rejected in favor of private contributions by "a number of Gentlemen of easy fortunes." Thomas Willing of Philadelphia, president of the Bank of North America, responded with ardor and started a subscription among "our most respectable and monied Citizens, known for their warm and decided attachment to the character and principles of the General." When pressed further—as by McHenry, who complained that subscriptions in Baltimore lagged because "the real or presumed great wealth of Gen. Schuyler is in everybody's mouth"—Wolcott repeated that Schuyler had left no funds at command.

About $80,000 altogether was subscribed to pay Hamilton's debts. The Grange was sold for reimbursement of the contributors, purchased in at the sale for $30,000 and then surrendered by a select inner group of 29 friends back to Mrs. Hamilton for $15,000, thus saving The Grange for her to live in for a while. Thanks to them, Elizabeth Hamilton and the children were able to remain there until 1813. But the place was expensive to maintain, and she finally sold it and moved south to the city. From her father's estate she received some scattered lands near Albany and elsewhere in northern New York State. She would sell these off from time to time to meet her needs and permit her to contribute to the charitable causes in which she remained quite active. A year and a half after Hamilton's death, all his real estate other than The Grange, mostly shares in the Ohio Company and other interests he held in clients' properties, were advertised and sold at auction. It was a mortifying sort of bankruptcy.

The tribute that would probably have meant most to Hamilton himself did not come until almost a quarter of a century after his death, when the surge of emotion that had accompanied his funeral had long since subsided. John Quincy Adams, whose father had sustained politically mortal wounds from Hamilton's pen, was writing about the scheme of Northern secession, disunion, separation, and confederacy that had been hatched among Pickering, Senator William Plumer, other High Federalists, and Burr, in 1804, to withdraw from the Union "peaceably if they could . . . but violently if they must."

John Quincy Adams wrote "that the proposal had been made to General Hamilton, to be the Joshua of the chosen people; and I was told that he disapproved the plan, *but it cost him his life.*"

What Adams meant was that if Hamilton had gone along with most of his fellow Federalists in favoring secession of the Northern states as a protest against the Louisiana Purchase and for various other reasons, he would have escaped Burr's bullet. Adams believed that if Hamilton had gone along with his fellow Federalists, he would not have supported Morgan Lewis against Burr, Burr would have won the gubernatorial election, and no matter what Hamilton had said that night at Judge Tayler's, Burr would not have had occasion to vent his "predetermined hostility" on Hamilton by issuing the challenge direct. To Adams, Hamilton's stand in favor of preserving the Union was his "reason for going out to meet Colonel Burr, even to the stifling of the cry of his conscience, against the practice of dueling." Adams cited the fact that Hamilton had "closed the paper [giving his reasons for the duel] with these memorable words[,] 'The ability to be in future useful, whether in resisting mischiefs or effecting good, *in those crises of our public affairs, which seem likely to happen* [italics by Adams], would probably be inseparable, from a conformity with public prejudice in this particular.'" Here was the meaning of Hamilton's cryptic phrase, Adams concluded: "This paper was wholly unintelligible to those who did not know that a civil War and the command of an army had been for years sporting with Hamilton's ambition. . . . It was indistinctly understood by those, who knowing this were yet not apprized of the distinct proposal which had been made to him the preceding spring. To me who had been made acquainted with both there was nothing mysterious in the paper." Only with his honor intact, only by accepting Burr's challenge, Hamilton thought, could he retain whatever influence he had with his High Federalist friends to keep them from going too far with their secessionist folly.

Madison agreed with John Quincy Adams about Hamilton's lonely stand. He thought that a letter of Senator Plumer, associating Hamilton's name with a meeting in 1804 to discuss the plan for New England secession, was mistaken as to Hamilton. Of course, any men planning such a secession would covet the "leading agency of such a man" from New York, just as they had sought out Burr. But Hamilton would not join them, or if he appeared at the meeting at all, he would have done so "only to dissuade . . . from a conspiracy as rash and wicked, and as ruinous to the party itself as to the country."

Of the eight Hamilton children, Philip, who was 19 when he fell in his duel with Eacker in 1801, had been the most promising. Daughter Angelica's playing of the piano sent to her from London by her Aunt Angelica Church and still at The Grange was a special pleasure to her father, but after Philip's tragedy, when she was 17, she lost her mind and lived on to 73. Of the others, five sons and a daughter, four of the boys entered the law, the three eldest after graduating from Columbia College. All served in Mr. Madison's War of 1812–1814.

James Alexander had an active political career, first as a Whig, then as a Democrat, and, on President Andrew Jackson's appointment, served as acting secretary of state in 1829. John Church is remembered as his father's biographer and editor of his papers, and his work is far more extensive and thorough and full of emotional insight than is usual in such filial undertakings, but not less partisan. William Stephen, next in line, early went west and was visited by his mother in Wisconsin when she was 80. Eliza became Mrs. Sidney A. Holly, seemed to inherit her mother's faculty for good management, and was her dependence in old age. Little Phil, the youngest, the replacement for his brilliant brother, a baby at his father's death, had less formal education than the others; his special kindliness earned him a reputation and many grateful, nonpaying clients as a poor man's lawyer. The children of Alexander and Elizabeth Hamilton had respectable lives that did them and their parents credit, but none showed much evidence of the unique quality of their father and mother.

For a long time after Hamilton's death, Elizabeth's despair at his loss, weariness of "this world of disastrous event," lack of money, and the overwhelming responsibility for educating seven children made her wish for death that would reunite her with him. On February 9, 1805, she wrote that "my wounded heart is scarcely equal to" the demands upon it. "Permit me to fly to my blessed redeemer . . . that I may be permitted to remain in his blest abode and there view my Hamilton." A Christian's faith, however, would see her through: "But I must resign me to the will of my just God and long or short the remainder of my life I must devote it with resignation to his decree." It would be long. But she would survive it. For more than 50 years.

"Ah may it be to his [sic, not His] satisfaction," she closed. "Then all will be well."

In her last years Elizabeth Hamilton left New York to live with her widowed daughter, Eliza Holly, on H Street in Washington, D.C. Until the last, she went about alone, talked with animation, and received friends with grace.

One day when she was 92, Julia F. Miller paid her a call, and Anne Hollingsworth Wharton retold the story in her book *Social Life in the Early Republic*. Mrs. Hamilton was: ". . . a tiny little woman, most active and interesting, although she could never have been pretty in her life. She kept me by her side, holding me by the hand, telling me of the things most interesting to me." She spoke of Washington (with whom she had been a great favorite) and Lafayette, who was "a most interesting young man." "When she was young," she recalled, she "was free of the Washington residence, and if there was company Mrs. Washington would dress her up in something pretty and make her stay to dinner, even if she came uninvited, so that she was presentable at table." Mrs. Hamilton showed her guest the Stuart portrait of Washington, "painted for her," she said, "and for which he sat." There were the old Schuyler chairs and tiny mirrors ("most interesting to me," said Julia Miller). She added, "This tiny dot of a woman of such great age, happened to think of something in her room that she wanted to show Abbie, her granddaughter. Abbie offered to get it for her. "Sit down, child, don't you think I can get it myself?' and up she went and got it, whatever it was."

Her son, James A. Hamilton, in his *Reminiscences,* recalled the magnificent Stuart portrait as almost covering the side wall near the entrance. The wine cooler—which had arrived as a gift from the Washingtons when the uproar over the Reynolds' affair had been at its height—reposed "under a large, handsome centre table in the front parlor." And, he added, "I remember nothing more distinctly than a sofa and chairs with spindle legs, upholstered black broadcloth, embroidered in flowery wreaths by Mrs. Hamilton herself." And there was also, of course, Ceracchi's "marble bust of Hamilton standing on its pedestal

. . . That bust I can never forget, for the old lady always paused before it in her tour of the rooms, and, leaning on her cane, gazed and gazed, as if she could never be satisfied.''

Another thing she could never forget across the half century she survived the duel was what James Monroe had done to them. About 1830, when she was 93, former President Monroe, full of years and honors, came to visit her. One of her nephews, who was then 15, described Monroe's last Hamilton confrontation to Dr. Allan McLane Hamilton:

> I had been sent to call upon my Aunt Hamilton one afternoon. I found her in her garden and was there with her talking, when her maidservant came from the house with a card. It was the card of James Monroe. She read the card, much perturbed. Her voice sank, and she spoke very low, as she always did when she was angry. The words ''What has that man come to see me for?'' escaped from her. ''Why, Aunt Hamilton,'' said I, ''don't you know, it's Mr. Monroe, and he's been President, and he is visiting here now in the neighborhood, and has been very much made of, and invited everywhere, and so—I supposed he has come to call and pay his respects to you.'' After a moment's hesitation she said, ''I will see him.''
>
> The maid went back to the house. My aunt followed, walking rapidly, I after her.
>
> She entered the parlor. Monroe rose to his feet. She stood in the middle of the room facing him. She did not ask him to sit down. He bowed, and addressing her formally, made her what seemed to be a carefully set speech—That it was many years since they had met, that the lapse of time brought its softening influences, that they both were nearing the grave, a time when past differences could be forgiven and forgotten—in short, from his point of view, a very nice, conciliatory, well-turned little speech.
>
> She answered, still standing, and looking at him, ''Mr. Monroe, if you have come to tell me that you repent, that you are sorry, *very* sorry, for the misrepresentations and the slanders, and the stories you circulated against my dear husband, if you have come to say this, I understand it. But, otherwise, no lapse of time, no nearness to the grave, makes any difference.''
>
> She stopped speaking. Monroe turned, took up his hat and left the room.

She had not left him under an impression her suspicions were removed.

Not long before her death, a friend paid a call on this solitary survivor from the heroic age, whose memories went all the way back to Indian raids on the old Schuyler house in Albany—and to the time her father's other house at Old Saratoga had been burned to the ground by ''Gentleman Johnny'' Burgoyne. The friend wrote:

> The widow of Alexander Hamilton has reached the age of 95 and retains in an astonishing degree her faculties and converses with much of that ease and brilliancy which lent so peculiar a charm to her younger days. And then, after passing the compliments and congratulations of the day, she insists upon her visitors taking a merry glass from George Washington's punch bowl, which, with other portions of his table set, remains in her possession.

Her last illness was a short one. She died on November 9, 1854, at the age of 97, just as the ''bleeding Kansas'' uproar of Franklin Pierce's administration was widening the final split toward breakup of the Union, having survived her late husband by more than half a century. She was interred beside him in the sarcophagus on the Rector Street side of the graveyard of Trinity Church. She was a constant wife if there ever was one. Her silence, endurance, courage through suffering, and seemingly unwavering affection for the man who had been so publicly unfaithful to her showed he had probably not misjudged her character when he had written in his last letter to her, "But you had rather I should die innocent than live guilty."

She was Hamilton's champion in every arena of his life and after his death. Without her knowledge of and zeal in preserving the proofs of his greatness, his reputation would be the less.

And so would hers.

THE END

Finis coronat opus.

—from John Jay, November 19, 1794

HAMILTON CHRONOLOGY 1757-1804 HAMILTON'S TIMES

1755

Jan. 11   H born, according to some authorities.

?   James Hamilton, Jr., H's brother, who was two years older than H, born [or in 1753].

1756

May 4   Mary Uppington Fawcett, H's maternal grandmother, deeds three slaves to Archibald Hamm for life, then to Rachel Fawcett; dies on St. Eustatius shortly after.

Aug. 29   Seven Years' War begins, pitting Britain and Prussia against France, Austria, Sweden, and Saxony and leading to founding of British Empire and modern Germany.

1757

Jan. 11   H born, Charlestown, Nevis, British West Indies; mother: Rachel Fawcett Lavien, daughter of Dr. John Fawcett and Mary Uppington Fawcett, his wife; father: James Hamilton, son of Alexander Hamilton, laird of The Grange, Ayrshire, Scotland, and Elizabeth Pollock Hamilton, his wife.

1758

Oct. 1   Rachel Fawcett Lavien and James Hamilton on St. Eustatius as godparents to Alexander Fraser, son of Alexander Fraser and Elizabeth Thornton.

1759

Feb. 26   H's mother, Rachel Fawcett Lavien, sued by John Michael Lavien for absolute divorce in Temperret, or divorce court, Christiansted, St. Croix.

1760

H, age three, taken by James Hamilton and Rachel Fawcett Lavien with James, Jr., age five, from Nevis to St. Kitts about this year.

Oct. 25   King George III becomes king of England, succeeding George II.

1761

Oct.   William Pitt the Elder resigns as British prime minister.

1763

Feb. 15   Seven Years' War ends by Treaty of Hubertusberg.

1765

April   H, age eight, taken by father, James Hamilton and mother, Rachel, with brother James, Jr., from St. Kitts to St. Croix.

July   Stamp Act Congress, New York City, first major organized protest against British.

Aug.   H with mother, Rachel Fawcett Lavien, lives in house and shop at 34 Company's Lane, Christiansted, St. Croix, where H clerks for her.

1766

Jan. 8   H, Rachel, and James, Jr., left by James Hamilton after he collects judgment on St. Croix for employer, Archibald Ingram, and returns to St. Kitts.

March   British repeal the Stamp Act.

1767

H age ten, clerks in Rachel's store, 34 Company's Lane, Christiansted; perhaps works also at Beekman and Cruger's, 7 and 8 King's Street, Christiansted.

1768

H clerks in Rachel's store, perhaps also at Beekman and Cruger's.

Feb. 19   H's mother, Rachel Fawcett Lavien, dies, Christiansted.

H clerks at Beekman and Cruger's.

1769

July   H's uncle James Lytton, of The Grange, St. Croix, and cousin Peter Lytton, his closest relatives on St. Croix, die.

Nov. 11	H writes his first extant letter, to Edward Stevens: "I contemn the groveling condition of a clerk . . . and would willingly risk my life, though not my character, to exalt my station."

1770

	Britain removes American import duties, except for the tax on tea.
March 5	Boston Massacre.

1771

April 6	H verses "In Yonder Mead My Love I Found" and "Coelia's an Artful Little Slut" published in *The Royal Danish American Gazette*, Christiansted, St. Croix.
April 10	"Rules for Statesmen," attritubed to H, published in *The Royal Danish American Gazette*.
Oct. 15	H left in charge of Cruger's business while Nicholas Cruger is in New York City.

1772

Jan. 1	H manages Nicholas Cruger's business until Cruger returns March 15.
May 16	H gives receipt to cousin Ann Lytton Venton for remittances.
	H meets Reverend Hugh Knox, who begins Presbyterian ministry on St. Croix.
Aug. 31	Devastating hurricane strikes St. Croix.
Sept. 6	H writes so-called Hurricane Letter to his father, James Hamilton, on St. Kitts.
Oct. 3	H's Hurricane Letter published in *The Royal Danish American Gazette*.
Oct. 17	H's poem "The Soul Ascending into Bliss, In Humble Imitation of Popes Dying Christian to His Soul," published in *The Royal Danish American Gazette*.
Oct.	H sails from St. Croix to Boston about this date.
Nov.	H reaches New York City about this time.
	Samuel Adams organizes new committees of correspondence.

1773

Jan.	H boards with William Livinston's family at Liberty Hall, Elizabethtown, New Jersey, while attending Francis Barber's grammar school. Becomes acquainted with Elias Boudinot's family.
May	H gives cousin Ann Lytton Venton recepts for remittances, including one for proceeds of sale of 15 hogsheads of sugar, indicating that she helped pay for his board and schooling at Elizabethtown.
June	H writes out quotations and paraphrases from Book of Genesis, Book of

Revelation, translations from Homer's *Illiad,* notes on geography of the eastern Mediterranean, and a numbered list of 27 books on ancient and medieval history and philosophy at about this time, probably as part of his school exercises.

Oct.	H's application for admission to Princeton turned down. H matriculates at King's College, now Columbia University, New York City.
Dec. 16	Boston Tea Party destroys 340 chests of tea.

1774

May	Boston Port Act closes port of Boston.
July 6	H makes "Speech in the Fields" in New York City.
Sept. 4	H writes "Poem on the Death of Elias Boudinot's Child."
Dec. 15	H publishes first pamphlet *A Full Vindication of the Measures of the Continental Congress* in reply to "Free Thoughts on Congress" by A. W. Farmer (Samuel Seabury).
Dec.	H begins drilling with militia company (Corsicans or Hearts of Oak) in St. George's Churchyard.

1775

Feb. 23	H publishes pamphlet *The Farmer Refuted* as a reply to Seabury's "A View of the Controversy."
April 19	Battles of Lexington and Concord.
May 10	H and Robert Troup stand off riotous mob at King's College gates.
June 15	H publishes "Remarks on the Quebec Bill, Parts One and Two" in Rivington's New York *Gazetteer.*
June 17	Battle of Breed's Hill and Bunker Hill in Boston.
Aug. 23	H with Hearts of Oak militia removes cannon from fort at Battery under bombardment from the battleship *Asia*'s guns.
Nov. 23	H stands against Isaac Sears's raiders when they seek to destroy Rivington's printshop and press.
Nov. 26	H writes John Jay in Congress to take measures to prevent raids like that of Sears.

1776

March 14	H commissioned as captain of New York provincial artillery company by Alexander McDougall.
June 29	British begin invasion of New York.
July 4	Declaration of Independence signed in Philadelphia.
Aug. 29	H offers Washington plan for evacuation after Battle of Long Island.
Sept. 16	H's encampment at Harlem Heights; H first comes under Washington's eye and meets him.

Oct. 28	H's artillery at Battle of White Plains helps to hold off Hessian battalion.
Nov. 29	H's artillery covers Washington's Raritan crossing at Brunswick.
Dec. 25	H crosses Delaware with Washington and attacks Trenton.
Dec. 25	Adam Smith's *The Wealth of Nations* published.

1777

Jan. 3	H at Princeton fires round from battery of two fourpounders into Nassau Hall.
March 1	H appointed aide-de-camp to Washington; promoted to rank of lieutenant colonel.
April 20	H begins corresponding with Gouverneur Morris, George Clinton, Robert R. Livingston, and others of New York Committee of Correspondence.
Sept. 11	H at Battle of Brandywine.
Sept. 18	After Daverser's Ferry H warns Congress to leave Philadelphia.
Sept. 26	Cornwallis's army occupies Philadelphia.
Oct. 3	H at Battle of Germantown.
Oct. 17	Burgoyne surrenders to Horatio Gates at Saratoga.
Oct. 30	H sets out on mission to obtain reinforcements from Gates for Washington.
Nov. 5	H arrives in Albany to see Gates, Troup, perhaps General Philip Schuyler.
Nov. 12	H, returning from Albany, falls ill at New Windsor.
Nov.	Congress adopts draft of Articles of Confederation and recommends it to states for adoption.

1778

Jan. 17	H and Captain Caleb Gibbs return to Valley Forge from mission to Gates.
Jan. 29	H submits "Report on Army" to Congressional Committee to Supervise Army.
	H assists von Steuben with professional training of army and writing *Rules for the Order and Discipline of the Troops*.
May 5	Alliance with France announced at Valley Forge.
May 12	H swears congressional oath abjuring allegiance to King George III and promising to defend United States against him.
June 28	H issues and delivers orders to field commanders at Battle of Monmouth in Washington's name. On battlefield H tells Major General Charles Lee, "Let us all die here, rather than retreat."
July 4	At Brunswick court-martial of Major General Charles Lee, H begins testimony as witness for the prosecution.
July 13	H continues testimony against Lee and is cross-examined by Lee, who charges H with "a frenzy of valor."

July 19	H meets Comte d'Estaing to plan joint American-French operation against Newport.
Oct. 19	H's Publius letter No. I attacks Congressman Samuel Chase for profiteering from secret information about grain purchases. Publius II on October 26 and Publius III on November 16 continue attacks.
Dec. 22	H serves as second for John Laurens in his duel with Charles Lee.

1779

Feb.	H with Washington in Philadelphia confers with congressmen, including Robert Morris and others.
March 14	H writes John Jay to urge on Congress raising battalions of Negro troops ''to give them their freedom with their muskets.''
July 4	H receives word from Lieutenant Colonel John Brooks of charge that H had said it was ''high time for the people to rise, join General Washington, and turn Congress out of doors.''
Oct. 7	H goes to Lewes, Delaware, and Great Egg Harbor, New Jersey, to meet d'Estaing and and give orders for joint operation against New York.
Oct. 9	French-American amphibious expedition to retake Savannah fails.
Dec.	H writes long letter to member of Congress, probably Robert Morris, calling for plan to strengthen currency, enlist ''moneyed men'' in support of government, and establish a national bank.
Aug.	Spain declares war on Britain.
Aug.	Iroquois confederacy subdued by John Sullivan's expedition.
	John Paul Jones wins naval victory.
Nov.	British evacuate Newport; bring garrison back to New york.

1780

May	John Paul Jones drives British frigates to take cover.
May	British under Henry Clinton capture Charleston, South Carolina.
July 10	French under Comte de Rochambeau arrive at Newport.
Aug. 16	Cornwallis routs Gates at Battle at Camden, South Carolina.
Sept. 3	H writes long letter from Liberty Pole, New Jersey, to James Duane: ''The fundamental defect is a want of power in Congress . . . another defect is want of method and energy in the administration . . a convention would revive the hopes of the people.''
Sept. 22	H at Hartford conference with Washington, Comte de Rochambeau, Chevalier de Ternay, Chevalier de Chastellux.
Sept. 25	H with Washington discovers Benedict Arnold's ''treason of the deepest dye . . . to sacrifice West Point'' and pursues Arnold. Peggy Shippen Arnold accuses Washington of a plot to murder her child.

Oct. 2	Major John André hanged at Washington's insistence against André's and H's protest that he should be shot instead.
Nov. 15	H with Washington and army in winter quarters at New Windsor.
Oct.–Dec.	H rebuffed in several efforts to obtain transfer to a field command.
Dec. 14	H marries Elizabeth, daughter of General Philip Schuyler, in elaborate ceremony at The Pastures, Albany, New York.

1781

Feb. 6	H writes letter for Washington to Governor Thomas Jefferson of Virginia responding to report of British incursions; requests Virginia to help reinforce southern army.
Feb. 16	H breaks with Washington.
Feb. 18	H writes Schuyler from New Windsor describing circumstances of break with Washington.
March 1	H goes to Newport with Washington.
April 30	H resigns officially as aide-de-camp to Washington.
April 30	H writes long letter to Robert Morris urging an "executive ministry," financial reforms, plan for a national bank.
	Articles of Confederation ratified; executive departments created.
July 12	H publishes first "Continentalist" essay in *The New York Packet and the American Advertiser*, Fishkill, N.Y. Five more issues of "The Continentalist" follow on July 19, August 9, and August 30, 1780, and on April 18 and July 4, 1782.
July 31	At Dobbs Ferry, H is given command of New York and Connecticut light infantry battalion for Yorktown campaign.
Aug. 7	Tories and Indians raid The Pastures, leaving tomahawk scar on stairway bannister.
Oct. 14	H at Yorktown commands and leads bayonet assault on British Redoubt No. 10.
Oct. 19	H, as officer of the day, helps arrange British surrender ceremony at Yorktown.
Dec.	H returns to The Pastures; suffers spells of illness.

1782

Jan. 22	Philip Hamilton, H's eldest son, born.
May 2	H appointed Continental receiver of taxes for New York.
Jan.–July	H studies law in Albany; writes practice manual *Practical Proceedings in the Supreme Court of the State of New York*.
July 21	H urges New York legislature to pass a resolution calling for a general convention of the states to amend the Articles of Confederation.

July 22	H appointed delegate to Continental Congress from New York.
Oct. 30	H resigns as Continental receiver of taxes for New York.
Nov. 25	H takes seat in Continental Congress.
Nov. 30	Preliminary articles of peace treaty signed in Paris.

1783

Jan.–March	H participates in congressional debates for strengthening finances of the Confederation.
Feb. 13	H advises Washington of dangers of troop mutiny and suggests measures to forfend it: "The claims of the army urged with moderation, but with firmness may operate on those weak minds."
March 11	Washington addresses officers and men at Newburgh and regains influence over disaffected members.
June 17	Units of Anthony Wayne's troops mutiny at Lancaster and march on Congress in Philadelphia.
June 19–22	H heads committees of Congress dealing with mutineers and Pennsylvania Executive Council. H recommends removal of Congress to Princeton June 26.
July 16	H leaves Congress in Princeton and returns to The Pastures at Albany to rejoin family.
Nov. 25	British evacuate New York City, and Americans make triumphal entry.
	H takes house at 57 Wall Street and opens law office at No. 56.
Dec. 4	H attends Washington's farewell to his officers in Fraunces Tavern.

1784

Jan. 1	H writes pamphlet "Letter from Phocion to the Considerate Citizens of New York" criticizing the legislature's violation of Articles IV, V, and VI of the peace treaty by refusing to restore confiscated loyalist property and ignoring provision against further confiscations.
Jan. 14	Definitive treaty of peace signed in Paris.
Feb. 24	H attends Bank of New York founders' meeting and draws constitution, charter, and incorporation papers for New York's first bank.
April	"Phocion II" appears.
June 29	H argues case of *Rutgers* v. *Waddington,* raising question of judicial supremacy of United States law and treaties over state law provisions.
Sept. 25	H's second child, Angelica, born.
	Congress makes New York City temporary capital of United States.

1785

Feb. 4	H is founding member of Society for Promoting the Manumission of Slaves, and chairman of a committee to recommend to the society the "line of

conduct'' to be followed by members in respect of their own slaves. Also, he is to make a register for those who manumit slaves to record the names and identification of manumitted slaves that ''the society be the better enabled to detect attempts to deprive such manumitted persons of their liberty.''

1786

March	H is elected to New York Assembly.
March 13	H joins petition to New York legislature urging the end of the slave trade, ''a commerce so repugnant to humanity, and so inconsistent with the liberality and justice which should distinguish a free and enlightened people.''
March 16	H after legislative struggle is named one of six commissioners to meet at Annapolis for the ostensible purpose of framing trade regulations in the general interest.
May 16	Son, Alexander Hamilton, Jr., born.
Sept. 14	H as New York delegate to Annapolis Convention drafts resolution calling for a general convention to enlarge the powers of the federal government.
Nov.	Shays' Rebellion erupts in Western Massachusetts.

1787

Jan. 12	H takes seat in New York State Assembly.
May 25–June 29	H at Constitutional Convention in Philadelphia.
June 18	H holds floor all day prior to vote on Virginia and New Jersey plans in the longest speech delivered at the convention.
Aug. 6	H at Constitutional Convention after a visit to New York.
Sept. 17	Constitution adopted; convention adjourns.
Oct. 27	Publication of H's *The Federalist,* No. 1

1788

Jan. 22	H reappointed a New York delegate to the Continental Congress.
April 14	Son, James Alexander Hamilton, born.
June 17–July 26	H leads fight for ratification of the Constitution in New York at convention, Poughkeepsie, New York.
July 23	Parade in New York City in support of Constitution with the federal ship *Hamilton* as centerpiece.
July 27	Constitution ratified by New York State.

1789

April 30	George Washington elected president; government organized at New York City, the first capital.

Sept. 11   H appointed secretary of the treasury.

Nov. 5   H with son Philip and Baron von Steuben sees Angelica Church off to England after her summer in New York and weeps.

1790

Jan. 14   H sends first "Report on the Public Credit" to Congress.

Feb. 14   Thomas Jefferson accepts appointment as secretary of state.

April 12   H's assumption legislation defeated in the House.

June 20   H, Jefferson, and James Madison make "a deal by candlelight" for assumption and location of national capital; assumption measures pass Congress.

Sept.   H moves to Philadelphia with wife and four children.

Dec. 13   H submits "Second Report on the Public Credit"; leads campaign for assumption measures.

1791

Jan. 28   H submits "Report on the Mint."

Feb. 23   H gives Washington opinion upholding constitutionality of national bank under "implied powers."

May 17–   Jefferson and Madison make trip to New York and New England to
August 25   hunt the Hessian fly.

July   H begins affair with Maria Reynolds about this time.

Nov. 5   H submits "Report on Manufactures" to House.

1792

March 9   William Duer defaults on payments and is arrested in time of financial panic.

July 25   H writes defense of his policies in newspapers; attacks on Jefferson and Philip Freneau.

Aug. 3   Jefferson writes 21 objections to Hamilton's "system," and Washington refers them to H for reply.

Aug. 10   Suspension of French king.

Aug. 22   Son, John Church Hamilton, born.

Sept. 15   H publishes first "Catullus" paper.

Sept. 21-25   Creation of the French Republic; National Convention replaces legislative assembly; onset of war of the First Coalition of European powers against France.

Dec. 15   James Monroe, Frederick A. C. Muhlenberg, and Abraham Venable confront H with evidence of his affairs with Maria and James Reynolds.

Dec. 27   Congress adopts resolutions to inquire into H's administration of the Treasury.

1793

Jan. 4	H submits report on loans.
Jan. 21	King Louis XVI is executed, a fact that does not become generally known in U.S. until March.
Jan. 23	H is impeached by Giles Resolutions introduced into House.
Feb. 27	Second set of Giles Resolutions is introduced.
March 2	Giles Resolutions defeated.
March 4	Second inauguration of Washington and Adams.
April 7	French declaration of war on Britain, Holland, and Spain becomes known in U.S.
April 8	Citizen Genêt lands at Charleston.
April 22	H advises Washington on Proclamation of Neutrality.
June 21	H tells Washington of intention to resign.
June 29	H publishes first "Pacificus" letter.
July 10	H advises cabinet in crisis of the *Little Democrat*.
July 31	H publishes "No Jacobin" letter revealing Genêt's threat to appeal over the head of the president directly to the people.
August	H and wife, Elizabeth, stricken in yellow fever epidemic in Philadelphia.
Nov.	H helps to raise fund to keep Fenno's *Gazette of the United States* alive.
Dec. 31	Jefferson officially resigns as secretary of state.

1794

Jan. 6–13	H drafts presidental message on Genêt's diplomatic status.
Jan. 14	H advises Washington on request to king of Prussia for release of Marquis de Lafayette from prison.
Jan. 31	H publishes "Americanus," No. 1, urging neutrality in dealings with France.
March 8	H recommends that Washington fortify ports and raise troops in preparation for hostilities with Britain.
March 18	H submits report to House on all receipts and expenditures from commencement of government through 1793.
April 23	After withdrawing his own name from consideration for appointment, H urges John Jay for special mission to Britain and writes detailed instructions for Jay.

1795

Jan. 31	H resigns as secretary of the treasury; returns to New York law practice.
March	After this time H works on complicated law cases involving debts of Robert

	Morris to H, to John B. Church, to William Pulteney, William Hornby, and others.
April 13	H writes Robert Troup, "It has been the rule of my life to do nothing for my own emolument *under cover* . . . it is pride. But this pride makes it part of my plan to *appear truly what I am.*"
June 24	Jay's Treaty approved by U.S. Senate.
July 18	H is stoned by a Wall Street mob.
July 22	H publishes first of 38 articles entitled "The Defense" and signed Camillus in defense of Jay's Treaty.
July 25	H writes Robert Troup concerning his will.
July 27	H publishes "Philo Camillus," No. I.
July 30	H writes essay "Defense of the Funding System."
July	H publishes "Horatius II" essay in defense of Jay's Treaty.
August	Edmund Randolph is forced to resign as secretary of state after suspicious financial dealings with French minister.
Oct. 16	H advises Washington concerning treatment to be given to Lafayette's son in U.S.
Oct. 26	H defends Washington against newspaper charges that he has overdrawn his pay and allowances.
Nov. 28	H drafts Washington's Seventh Annual Address to Congress.
Dec.	H writes essay attacking "American Jacobins."

1796

Feb. 24	H argues in support of carriage tax in U.S. Supreme Court.
March 3	Thomas Pinckney's Spanish Treaty approved by Senate.
April 30	House votes provisions necessary to carry Jay's Treaty into effect.
May 15–August 25	H drafts Washington's Farewell Address, delivered September 19, followed by active presidential campaign.
Nov. 10	H drafts Washington's Eighth Annual Message to Congress, calling for a national university, a military academy, and a board of agriculture.
Dec. 5	Electors meet and elect Adams president, Jefferson vice-president.
Dec. 8	H publishes "The Answer," signed Americanus, to rebut Adet's criticisms of American policy toward France.

1797

Jan. 27	H publishes "The Warning," signed Americanus, first of six essays setting forth his view of Franco-American relations.
March 4	Adams and Jefferson inaugurated.
June 20	Adams appoints Elbridge Gerry to serve with Charles C. Pinckney and John Marshall on mission to France.

July 5	H discloses his 1791–1792 liaison with Mrs. James Reynolds and begins quarrel with Monroe.
July	H buys house at No. 58 Partition Street, New York, N.Y.
August 4	Son, William Stephen Hamilton, born.
August 25	H publishes *Reynolds Pamphlet*.

1798

March 30	H publishes "The Stand," signed Titus Manlius, attacking the Paris Directory.
April 3	Adams reports XYZ Affair to House.
June 25–July 14	Alien and Sedition Acts approved. H is critical of them.
July 25	H appointed inspector general of the army with rank of major general.
July	Quasi war with France has been going on for some time.

1799

March 16	H gives orders for suppression of Fries's rebellion.
June 3	Death of H's father, James Hamilton, on St. Vincent, British West Indies.
Oct.	Adams, overriding cabinet recommendations, orders commissioners to France.
Oct. 1	Francisco Miranda letter proposes expedition for liberation of Spanish colonies.
Nov. 9	Napoleon overthrows Directory in coup and installs Consulate with himself as first consul.
Nov. 20	Daughter, Eliza Hamilton, born.
Dec. 19	George Washington dies at Mount Vernon.

1800

May 6	Adams discovers H's influence on his cabinet and demands McHenry's resignation.
May 7	H requests Jay to revise method of choosing electors to reverse Federalist New York election defeat by Republicans.
July 1	H resigns as inspector general after disbanding troops.
Oct. 3	Treaty of Mortefontaine ends Quasi war with France.
Oct. 22	H publishes attack on John Adams in Bache's *Aurora* and elsewhere.
Nov.	H supports Federalists John Adams and Charles C. Pinckney in election campaign against Jefferson and Burr.
Dec. 16	H supports Jefferson over Burr after electoral tie.
December	Capital moved to District of Columbia.

1801

Jan. 15   Federalists in caucus decide to support Burr over Jefferson.

Jan. 16   H writes Bayard, characterizing Jefferson.

Jan. 24   Senate approves nomination of John Marshall as chief justice.

Feb. 17   H is instrumental in Jefferson's election over Burr on thirty-sixth tie-breaking ballot in House.

July 1   H plans house for Grange.

Nov. 16   H founds the New York *Evening Post*.

Nov. 23   H's eldest son, Philip, mortally wounded in duel with George Eacker, a supporter of Aaron Burr.

Dec. 17   H publishes first of 18 installments of ''The Examination,'' attacking Jefferson's program, as ''a performance which . . . makes a prodigal sacrifice of constitutional energy, of sound principle, and of public interest to the popularity of one man.''

Dec. 19   Senate approves treaty with France.

1802

Feb. 27   H writes Gouverneur Morris ''Mine is an odd destiny'' letter.

April 16–18 H advises Federalists to adopt Republican methods to achieve goals, including establishment of the Christian Constitutional Society.

Dec. 29   Hamiltons move into Grange and H writes Charles C. Pinckney ''A garden, you know, is a very usual refuge of a disappointed politician.''

1803

Feb. 24   Supreme Court issues decision in *Marbury v. Madison*.

April 30   Treaty ceding Louisiana to United States signed in Paris.

1804

Feb. 13   H argues in defense of freedom of the press in *People v. Croswell*.

April   H opposes separatist movement threatened by New England.

April 25   Burr defeated in New York gubernatorial election.

July 11   H mortally wounded in duel with Burr at Weehawken.

July 12   H dies at house of William Bayard, New York City.

July 14   H buried in Trinity Churchyard, New York City, with full military honors.

A NOTE ABOUT SOURCES AND QUOTATIONS

This book is based on my two volume biography of Alexander Hamilton *Hamilton I 1757–1789,* and *Hamilton II 1789–1804* published in 1976 by Mason/Charter Publishers, New York. The principal source for this and the two earlier Hamilton books not available to earlier Hamilton biographers is *The Papers of Alexander Hamilton,* volumes I through XXVI, with Harold C. Syrett as editor and Jacob E. Cooke and others as associate editors, published by Columbia University Press. These volumes are referred to as the Hamilton Papers. The other important, newly available source is *The Law Practice of Alexander Hamilton,* volumes I and II, edited by Julius Goebel, Jr., and published by Columbia University Press, volume I in 1964 and volume II in 1969, here referred to as the Hamilton Law Papers.

All significant letters and other documents written by Hamilton, all significant letters and other documents written by others to him, and all other significant documents that directly concern him (commissions, certificates, and so on) are printed in chronological order in the Hamilton Papers. Other sources have been *The Works of Alexander Hamilton,* edited by Henry Cabot Lodge, 12 volumes (New York and London: Putnam Federal Edition, 1904); *The Works of Alexander Hamilton,* edited by John C. Hamilton, 7 volumes (New York: J. F. Throw, 1850–1851); John C. Hamilton's *History of the Republic of the United States . . . As Traced in the Writings of Alexander Hamilton,* 7 volumes (New York: Appleton, 1857–1864); Allan McLane Hamilton's *The Intimate Life of Alexander Hamilton* (New York: Scribner's, (1910); *The Writings of George Washington,* edited by John C. Fitzpatrick (Washington, D.C.: 1931–1944); *Memoirs of the Administrations of Washington and John Adams: Edited from the papers of Oliver Wolcott, Secretary of the Treasury* by George Gibbs (New York: 1846); *The Works of Fisher Ames, with a Selection from His Speeches and Correspondence,* edited by Seth Ames, 2 volumes (Boston: 1854); *The Life and Correspondence of Rufus King* by Charles R. King (New York: 1894–1900); Broadus Mitchell's *Alexander Hamilton, Youth to Maturity, 1755–1788* (New York: Macmillan 1957), *Alexander Hamilton, The National Adventure, 1788–1804* (New York: Macmillan, 1962), and John C. Miller's *Alexander Hamilton, A Portrait in Paradox* (New York: Harper, 1959) and other books listed in the bibliography of *Hamilton I* and *Hamilton II.*

Annotations in the Hamilton Papers and the Hamilton Law Papers tell whether the paper in question is an autograph document; whether it is signed or a draft of a letter book copy or taken from a printed source, and so on; identify Hamilton's correspondent and the individuals mentioned in the text; explain events and ideas referred to in the text; cross-reference to related documents and events; point out textual variations and mistakes; inform whether the original is cropped or has been mutilated or bowdlerized in an earlier collection and the significance, if any, of such alteration; and supply historical and biographical background material. In the case of some important documents, such as Hamilton's "Report on a National Bank," both his first draft and final version are reproduced; they provide fascinating glimpses of his mental processes and the refinement of his thinking over time.

Routine letters and documents by Hamilton, routine letters to Hamilton, most letters and documents written by Hamilton for someone else (such as letters written for George Washington), letters and documents that have not been found, but that are known from references elsewhere to have existed, letters and documents such as polemical broadsides erroneously attributed to Hamilton, and letters that deal exclusively with his legal practice are chronologically calendared in the Hamilton Papers. Calendared references to events in Hamilton's law practice contained in the Hamilton Papers are dealt with in full in the Hamilton Law Papers. The list of "Short Titles and Abbreviations" found in the front matter of each volume of the Hamilton Papers also serves as a useful bibliography of source material for the time period covered by the volume. Each volume of the Hamilton Papers and the Hamilton Law Papers also contains an exhaustive index to names of persons, places, events, and other things dealt with in the volume which is invaluable to any scholar wishing to pursue research concerning matters mentioned in the Hamilton Papers or the Hamilton Law Papers or this book.

In this book nothing is presented as fact which I have invented or which lacks a basis in written authority. All material in quotations is from printed sources and not invented by me. Where documentary evidence is conflicting or admits of more than one interpretation, I have usually resolved doubts by deciding the question as I believe Hamilton would have done or from Hamilton's point of view, consistent with my own view of him as a flawed hero. Some such conclusions are based on evidence that can only be characterized as dubious or circumstantial. In the few instances where a surmise or supposition as to a matter of fact is presented—for example, in chapter 37, as to the story Dr. Cooper heard that he characterized as "despicable"—it is described as such in the context of the circumstantial evidence leading to my conclusion. For unconvincing inferences, implications, insights, conclusions, and opinions, I assume full responsibility.

Other books about Hamilton will be written, and new evidence will crop up from time to time, but the Hamilton Papers and the Hamilton Law Papers are comprehensive, authoritative, definitive, and of a scholarly quality that is not likely ever to be surpassed. To include an elaborate apparatus of footnotes, source notes, citations, bibliography, index, and so forth in this book would increase its bulk, weight, and cost for the nonspecialist reader and needlessly impede the stride of Hamilton's story, yet provide the specialist with little that is not readily available to him in more complete and exhaustive form in the Hamilton Papers or Law Papers or one or another of the books and articles listed in the Bibliography of *Hamilton I* and *Hamilton II*. Accordingly, in lieu of such apparatus in the text, I have simply included in the text the dates of documents, events, and actions with more frequency than is usual in books of this kind. These will provide the reader who wishes to pursue particular avenues of inquiry further an appropriate introduction to such material. The period and subject matter are all but inexhaustible.

INDEX